Contents

10.95

ESSENTIAL
GOVERNMENT & POLITICS

Jim Cordell

CollinsEducational

An imprint of HarperCollins*Publishers*

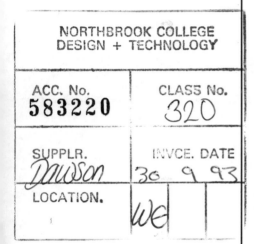
Also in the HarperCollins Essential Series

Essential Psychology
G.C. Davenport

Forthcoming titles

Essential Accountancy and Finance
Bijon Kar

Essential Business Studies
Stephen Barnes

Essential Marketing
Tony Proctor

Series Editor Roger Gomm

© J. Cordell and Collins Educational Ltd 1992
This book is copyright under the Berne Convention.
No reproduction without permission. All rights reserved.

The author asserts the moral right to be
identified as the author of this work.

Published by
Collins Educational Ltd
77–85 Fulham Palace Road
Hammersmith
London W6 8JB

First published in 1992

British Library Cataloguing in Publication Data

Cordell, Jim
Essential government and politics
1. Politics
I. Title
320

ISBN 0–00–322265–9

Typeset by Ellis Associates
and printed in Great Britain by Cambridge University Press, Cambridge.

Cover design by Ridgeway Associates.

Acknowledgements

The author and publisher would like to thank the following for permission to use material reproduced in this work: the *Independent* for permission to reproduce extracts from 'Unionists heckle their alternative tendency' by David McKittrick, originally published 29 October 1990; 'Muffled voices from deep in the sand' by Isabel Hilton, originally published 31 July 1990; 'Cases will show judges their powers' by Patricia Wynn Davies, originally published 30 May 1990; 'Tempers fray in textile town as Asians switch allegiances' by Alex Renton, originally published 27 April 1990; 'Ministers warn over the perils of being Thatcher "Yes Men"' by Colin Brown, originally published 29 June 1990; 'Hattersley rejects call for Labour to back PR' by Colin Brown, originally published May 1990; 'Violence as an effective form of collective bargaining' by John Williams, and 'When the mob rule betrays the principals of democracy' by Graham Riddick, originally published 7 April 1990; the *Economist* for permission to reprint 'With one bound he was ...' originally published 27 April 1991; the *Sunday Correspondent* for permission to reproduce extracts from 'Democratic surgery to cure a bad case of inertia' by David Blake, originally published 10 June 1990; 'Whitehall turning a paler shade of green' by Andrew Morgan, 22 April 1990; 'Kinnock seeks Labour overhaul' by Donald McIntyre, originally published 22 April 1990. Charter 88 reproduced with the permission of the organizers and *New Statesman and Society*.

Foreword

Every book in the Essential Series is designed carefully to put you in control of your own learning.

When you use this book, you will not only cover the core elements of your course but you will also benefit from the author's use of modern teaching and learning techniques, with the result that you will make the best possible use of your time.

This book has:

• an introductory section at the beginning of each chapter, which focuses your attention on its contents and which tells you exactly what you will have learned by the end of the chapter. These are your 'learning objectives'

• periodic summaries and reviews which regularly remind you of the content you are covering and so reinforce your learning

• notes in the margin of the text, where the author takes the role of a tutor: picking out key facts, highlighting and explaining difficult concepts and guiding you to a better understanding of the main text

• a guide to making notes as you work through the book

• essay questions and other assignments which will give you exam practice and help you to develop your skills in presenting written work

• suggestions for further reading that you can fit in which will help you to develop a broader understanding of your subject. This is always worth extra marks in the exam, as well as being more satisfying

• advice on study skills which gives valuable suggestions for making the best use of your study time and improving your learning. When you have developed these basic skills you will be much better equipped to direct and control your own learning.

Learning is not easy: nobody learns without effort. However, if you use this book effectively you will not only succeed in your course and in your exam but you will also enjoy the experience of learning.

Author's preface

In writing this book I constantly reminded myself of the series title 'ESSENTIAL' – that which is of the essence.

It seemed to me that three things were needed to provide a substantial basis for the student:–
• an understanding of the concepts used to make sense of the political world,
• practice in the skills necessary to analyse and form critical judgements on political issues and institutions,
• and information and examples from which to work.
As well as dealing with skills and concepts in the first three chapters, I have emphasized the conceptual framework throughout the book. To develop skills each of the subsequent chapters contains an exercise in discussion, a note making guide, an assignment requiring students to gather information for themselves and a stimulus passage – usually a newspaper article, with open ended questions.

I encountered the usual problem with factual material and historical events – what to put in and what to omit. I have based my decisions upon the 'core' content of three major A level syllabuses – London, JMB and AEB. Some of it however, should prove useful with the 'Option' papers. Because the book covers a broad range of topics it should also prove valuable for students taking appropriate BTEC and GCSE courses and for students entering Higher Education courses with a politics content. Issues and recent controversies have been used as examples to illuminate the nature of the British political system, but, except in the case of Ireland, I have avoided separate issue-based sections, since these rapidly become out of date. Reading newspapers, the publication *Talking Politics* and the *Developments in British Politics* series will provide a means of keeping up-to-date once the essentials have been grasped. I make suggestions for further reading at the end of each chapter. Supplementary material, comments, and remarks are included in the marginal notes which are optional and supplementary.

British politics is an intriguing, sometimes infuriating, but never boring labyrinth. I hope this book helps students to find their way through it.

I have had a lot of help. While making it clear that they are not responsible for the shortcomings of the final product, I should like to thank Patrick McNeill, Rosie Ward and Roger Gomm for editorial cool and patience, Chris Pugh for hard work at the keyboard, David Pugh for the cartoons, Sue Webb for the bibliographical help, Kevin Harrison and Hendrina Ellis for detailed criticisms, nearly all of which were gratefully accepted as improvements, and Angela McConnell for being there.

1 The skills you need

> ## Chapter objectives
> By the end of this chapter you should:
> ▌have organized yourself for study
>
> ▌be able to discriminate:
> - facts from value judgements
> - political myths from political realities
> - conclusions which follow from premises from those which do not.
>
> ▌be able to read:
> - widely and selectively to gain a variety of ideas related to a theme
> - intensively to deal with a particular question or topic.
>
> ▌be able to discuss the merits of different arguments
>
> ▌be able to bring an argument to a conclusion using supporting evidence.

 You will see this sign where I have indicated that it would be useful for you to make notes. Always give your notes a heading.

(ACT) You will see this sign where I have suggested an activity for you to carry out. Sometimes it will be an investigation, sometimes an essay, sometimes something else.

Introduction

The purpose of this chapter is twofold. On the one hand it provides general advice on how to study and how to organize yourself for study, and on the other hand it introduces you to some of the skills which are especially important in studying government and politics. Both kinds of advice will be important in helping you to use this book to the full.

SKILLS FOR GOVERNMENT AND POLITICS

To tackle Government and Politics at this level you need to acquire *skills* as well as knowledge and theoretical perspectives.

One leading Examining Board puts the case for skills like this:

> *Weighting of abilities*
> *The marks in the Examination will be divided as far as possible as follows:*
>
> | | |
> |---|---|
> | *Knowledge* | 30% |
> | *Understanding* | 20% |
> | *Application* | 20% |
> | *Evaluation and synthesis* | 30% |

GETTING ORGANIZED

INFORMATION

Find out, at the start of your course:

- how long it is, in hours per week and in total, and when the final examinations are. If you are directing your own studies without attending a course then at least find out when the examination is.

- what home work and course work you will have to do.

- which examination board sets your examination? What is the content of the syllabus? How will you be assessed? Your college library will have a copy of the syllabus and the assessment. Obtain your own photocopy.

PLACE

Identify a location in your home which is your study place and nothing else. Just a table will do. With practice you will reach a point where the act of sitting in that chair, at that table, triggers the 'work response' in you. This will not happen if you choose your bed or the armchair in front of the TV as your study place.

TIME

- how you will fit study into your other commitments?

You cannot simply add a course onto an already full life. You will have to reorganize your life to make time for study and make better use of any time you now fritter away.

- at which time of day do you work most effectively? (not 'prefer to work' but 'work effectively': there's a difference).

- for how long can you study EFFECTIVELY at a stretch, once you are in the habit of study? Practise, and test your own learning, until you know the answer to this question. For most people the answer is 'about an hour'. Then they need a short break.

- Private study for two hours every day is much more effective than a ten-hour stretch on Sunday.

- For each period of study, set yourself realistic objectives. In this book every chapter starts with a set of targets or 'objectives'. Most should take an hour or less to achieve. Use the chapter objectives to phase your study. Sometimes you will need to set objectives for yourself (e.g. 'I will have made a plan for this essay' or 'I will have revised the following concepts'). Don't stop until you have achieved your objective, but then DO stop, and reward yourself. Phone someone, eat a chocolate biscuit: watch the news.

This is amplified elsewhere in the syllabus like this:

Abilities to be tested
The candidate's ability to:
  i *Select and organize factual material from a variety of appropriate sources in answer to specific questions.*
  ii *Discuss issues, express and support views.*
  iii *Distinguish political realities from myths and formal arrangements.*
  iv *Construct arguments by selecting, organizing and presenting facts and ideas from authoritative sources in logical form and in good English.*

Don't be put off by this formidable list, or the percentages! The essential point is that a large part of your course will consist of doing and not just knowing.

The good news is that you've probably been practising these skills in one way or another since early childhood. For example, deciding upon a holiday might involve:

1 Knowing how much money you can spend.

2 Consulting brochures, looking at costs, travel times and fares.

3 Reading about various places, and discussing them with friends.

Up to this point you've been acquiring *knowledge* and *understanding*. Your next step is *application*, that is:

4 Computing the cost of various holidays and comparing them with what you can afford.

and *synthesis*:

5 Rejecting some alternatives as impractical and deciding on a 'short list' of possibles.

followed by *evaluation*:

6 Assessing alternatives, taking into account their main pros and cons and what you most want from a holiday.

Like the character in Molière's *Le Bourgeois Gentilhomme* who found he'd been 'talking prose all his life without knowing it', most of us have been applying, evaluating and synthesizing without knowing it.

Facts

Let's start with *empirical facts*. An empirical fact is one the truth or falsehood of which can be verified by appeal to *observation* and *experience* through one, several or all of the five senses.

The statement:
  'The Conservatives won a majority of seats at the 1983 Election'
is verifiable by evidence; it is an empirical fact, but
  'This represents a personal triumph for Mrs Thatcher and a massive vote of confidence in her leadership, by the British people'
is not! At least not on the evidence of the seats gained in Parliament. They were as follows:

Conservative	376
Labour	229
Alliance	22
SNP	3
Plaid Cymru	3
Unionists	13
Republicans	4

The Conservatives had a majority of 102.

Can you spot the weaknesses in the second statement when it is put forward as a fact supported by the election figures quoted? Think about it! Here are some suggestions:

The statement is problematic because:

1 *Most of the voters did not vote Conservative.* If by the 'British people' the statement meant all or even a majority of the British people, it is not supported by the evidence.

2 *There is no evidence in these figures to tell us what proportion of voters who voted Conservative did so because they admired Mrs Thatcher as a leader* (although there is opinion-poll evidence available on the standing of the party leaders). Many may indeed have voted as they did for this reason. With others it may have been a *contributory factor*, but not a *determining factor*. Others may have voted Conservative because they identified the party with certain values which they cherished, while others may have supported the Conservatives because they felt that a Conservative Government might be more likely to deliver certain valued policy objectives like 'greater prosperity' or a 'stable price level'. Some voters may have had mainly *negative* motives. They may have voted Conservative in order to keep out Labour or the Alliance.

On the evidence available, we just don't know!

(ACT) Select a newspaper article on a political theme. Distinguish statements in the article which are supported by evidence, or seem supportable by evidence, from those which are not.

However, this is not to say that the 'personal triumph' label is completely wide of the mark. It might be valid *to some extent*. One feature of the study of politics which you may find fascinating or infuriating (or both) is that, often, statements can be supported by *some* evidence, but cannot be demonstrated as absolutely true or untrue. Since they have some evidence in their favour they may be partially accurate. You need to cultivate the skill of weighing up the extent to which statements put forward as facts can be said to be true.

It would, for example, be possible to conduct a survey of Conservative voters designed to assess to what extent voters were influenced by their admiration for Mrs Thatcher, which would enable us to assess to what extent the 'personal triumph' label was valid. The sample population for such a survey would need to be carefully chosen, as would the questions, but it could be done.

TIME (continued)

- Plan your study sessions and their objectives a week in advance. An assignment is much less daunting when you have broken it down into specific tasks with specific objectives. This also makes it easier to use short study periods effectively. Things may not go exactly according to your week's plan, but at least you will know what you have to do to make up for lost time.

- Since this is a Government & Politics course you will need to make time to keep up-to-date with current political affairs. You can read newspapers at any time but you will need to plan carefully to catch TV and radio programmes.

- Keep lists of things to be done. These should be specific (e.g. 'take notes on the concept of the rule of law').

Give a realistic deadline to each and cross off items as you complete them.

Now go through all the 'Getting Organized' sections and make a list of the things you should be doing and when you are going to do them.

EQUIPMENT

The minimum you will need is

- A4 size paper, bought in a pad with holes ready punched

- A4 ring-binder files, so you can store your notes properly. File dividers are useful but you can make these yourself from cereal packets

- card index cards – you can find or make a cardboard box to keep them in

- a scrapbook for storing newspaper cuttings relevant to the course

- a pen you find it easy to write with

- pencil and rubber

- your textbook(s)

EQUIPMENT (continued)

Other materials, such as highlight pens, wallet folders, a stapler and so on are optional. Don't spend more than you can afford, but don't skimp on the essentials.

▶ *Tautology*
saying of the same thing twice over using different words: a truism.

▶ *Theory*
system of ideas explaining something, esp. one based on general principles independent of the facts, phenomena, etc., to be explained.

▶ That something is a matter of opinion doesn't mean that one opinion is worth as much as another. An opinion of a film which is backed up by detailed assessment of the quality of the acting, the subtlety of the characterization, the use of the camera, etc., is worth more than one that says 'Well, I liked it!'

 Design a question for a questionnaire, intended to establish the extent to which personal admiration for Mrs Thatcher was a factor in the Conservative victory of 1987.

Tautologies and theories

A *tautological* statement is one in which the conclusion *must* follow from the premise because it is repeating what the premise said. For example, look at the statement:

2 + 2 = 4

4 is another way of putting 2 + 2.

A tautology is in effect saying the same thing twice over in different words. Then why bother with it? You may need to distinguish tautologically obvious statements from those that are not.

'34 per cent of the electorate voted Conservative, therefore 66 per cent of the electorate either voted for another party or abstained' is obvious and is a tautology.

'34 per cent of the electorate voted Conservative, therefore 66 per cent rejected Mrs Thatcher's leadership' is not a tautology. The second half of the sentence does not 'therefore' follow from the first. Nor is it a statement of empirical fact since there are many different reasons why those who voted for parties other than the Conservatives might have voted apart from 'rejecting' Mrs Thatcher.

A *theory* is a set of general statements claiming to explain reality. In assessing the validity of a theory you need to assess

- its internal logical consistency
  ('Does x necessarily follow from y?')
- its tautological consistency
- its consistency with empirical evidence.

The acid test of a theory is its ability to predict what happens. Note however that this does not necessarily mean predicting events in the future. For example you could test a theory on voting behaviour by seeing how well it would predict the results of the 1964 election.

Value judgements

We all make value judgements in our daily lives. If you discuss with a friend a movie or TV show you've seen, a book you've read, or a song you've heard, the odds are that you will produce a value judgement. The value judgement is made when you pronounce on the merits of the film, TV show or song.

Unlike an empirical or a tautological fact, a value judgement depends on the *subjective* factor of what the person making the judgement *values*.

This cannot in the end be proved or disproved, in the sense that a fact can. It can be supported or attacked by appeal to facts, and people may alter their values as the result of acquiring information or new ideas, but there is an irreducible element of value involved. This may

Media Watch

For a Government and Politics course you need good up-to-date examples. This means following the political news in a serious newspaper and on radio and television. There are a great many relevant broadcast documentaries and while parliament is in session there is a large number of regular programmes on parliamentary affairs. At the time of writing these were the most important regular programmes.

TELEVISION
A Week in Politics
Around Westminster
Members Only
Westminster/Yesterday in Parliament
Parliament/Yesterday in Parliament
Westminster Live
Newsnight
Scrutiny

RADIO
Week in Westminster
In Committee
Today in Parliament
Yesterday in Parliament

I suggest you check the programme schedules in the *Radio Times* or *TV Times* and work out how you are going to fit viewing or listening into your own study programme.

prejudice, literally *pre-judge*, the issue as far as the holder of the value is concerned. Some evidence may be eagerly seized upon and given weight out of proportion to its seriousness, while contrary evidence may be ignored or given too little weight.

 Read 'A Green debate' (inset on page 6). What values dominate the judgement of A and B respectively?

Evaluation

Evaluation means deciding what an approach is worth. For example, to evaluate arguments in the Green dialogue you need to:
• Detect the prejudices of A and of B and bear them in mind.
• Establish which statements in A's and B's cases seem soundly based on evidence, and where the evidence seems 'stretched' to reach the conclusion, or where evidence seems non-existent. In particular look for statements so general in nature that they are almost incapable of proof.
• Identify evidence which A or B may have ignored because it didn't suit their case or through ignorance.

A Green debate

A   'I'm going to vote for the party that really does intend to do something about the environment. It's an absolute priority. The food we eat is being so tarted up with additives it's lethal, and the food chain is being distorted and broken by modern methods of agriculture. Aerosols are destroying the ozone layer. The senseless growth of the number of cars on the roads is killing some people fast through accidents and even more people slowly through pollution. In the pursuit of profit, big industrial outfits are using technology to eat the planet's resources faster than we can replace them, and turning away from low-impact technology because it doesn't make a quick buck. Any party that doesn't address these issues as a first priority doesn't get my vote.'

B   'You Greenies always overstate your case. You want us to turn the clock back. If your lot had their way, we'd all be riding bikes, dressed in broadcloth smocks, and living on a diet of lentils. Our only entertainment would be dancing round the maypole. Mind you, we'd need to do that to keep warm, since we wouldn't be allowed a proper heating system.'

A   'You just don't want to face awkward facts. We're not killjoys, and we're not against progress. We're against 'progress at any price', and creating false needs to fuel more production of things people would never have dreamt of if they hadn't been told that they needed them. The Friends of the Earth's literature deals in hard facts, confirmed by scientists with no axe to grind. They show that E factors in food *are* harmful, as is lead in petrol; that the Earth's resources *are* being depleted faster than we can replace them, and that there are environmentally friendly alternatives. You can't get away from facts, mate.'

B   'Highly selective facts! You don't hear much about *how much* of these E factors you need to do any real harm, and how this compares with the quantities in a typical pack of food. Also we don't hear about the positive side of economic progress. People are better fed, bigger and healthier than they ever were. Infant mortality which used to be appalling, is now very low. Most of the epidemic and endemic diseases that used to kill people off like flies have been conquered. We have choices of food, clothes and machines which cut out drudgery and make life pleasant; choices that our grandfathers would never have dreamt of. I support technology and progress. It's improved the quality of our lives and will go on doing so – if we let it.'

► Notice that A and B appeal to empirical facts to support their respective positions, and could probably produce statistical material if pushed, but they do so *selectively*.

► B is using an old trick used by politicians in debate: make your opponent's case sound ridiculous by expanding some of his/her ideas to grotesque proportions. See if you can spot this technique in a report of a Parliamentary debate.

Synthesis

This means bringing the different perspectives together into one of your own. It does not necessarily mean opting solidly for one perspective or the other, but you can't get out of it by setting out the different perspectives on a question and leaving your audience to choose the best one!

In the synthesizing process there must be a contribution of your own. Deciding that 'they've all got a point' isn't good enough. You need to come to a conclusion of your own, based on the strengths and weaknesses of each case. This will involve your own value judgements – make sure they are supported!

Political myths

In the Green argument over the environment, A would be quite justified in accusing B of perpetuating a *myth* about the supporters of the Green Party. They do not want us all to live on lentils and wear peasant gear. As you study the history of the British or any other political system, you will become increasingly aware of the impor-

▶ There is a sense in which myths, if they are powerful and generally accepted, acquire a *political* reality of their own, even though they may have little or no basis in *empirical* reality. 'The Nation', 'The Race', 'The Blood', 'The People' are examples.

The 'betrayal' of Germany

The end of the 1914–18 war between the major European powers came in two stages – the Armistice, then the Versailles Treaty in 1919, in which the victorious allies put their terms for the end of hostilities.

The German Government of the day agreed to what were seen afterwards as humiliating terms, including the concession of large and rich areas of territory, a ban on rearmament and crippling 'reparation' payments in cash and kind.

The politicians who accepted the deal were later reviled as the 'traitors' of Versailles by senior army officers in Germany, most conservatives, Hitler and the National Socialists, and the Prussian Junkers class. Opposition to the Weimar Republic (1919–1933), which was the basis of the German constitution after it was established in 1919, was rooted in the idea that Germany's parlous state in the early 1920s and between 1929 and 1933 was down to these cowardly politicians who had 'stabbed Germany in the back' and sacrificed the honour of its brave soldiers. The creation of unofficial armies, an armed *putsch* (unsuccessful) and support for illegal, unconstitutional and violent action on the streets were all justified by the 'stab in the back' by Weimar politicians.

Millions of German voters and many senior army officers and industrialists came round to supporting Hitler, who had made the 'betrayal' one of the foundations of his programme, outlined in *Mein Kampf* (My struggle).

It was a myth. The 'betrayal' didn't happen like that. As William Shirer demonstrates (in *The Rise and Fall of the Third Reich*) the politicians had no option. The very generals who perpetrated the idea of 'betrayal' were the men who told the politicians that they were in no position to resume hostilities after the Armistice and that they must accept whatever terms they could obtain. Germany was not betrayed; the German army was defeated.

tance of myths.

You need to be able to distinguish myth from reality and at the same time understand the peculiar power that political myths often possess, so that they are a form of political reality.

The characteristics of a political myth are:

- Its relationship to the relevant evidence and to facts generally is often tenuous or non-existent. Where evidence is available to support a myth it may be used, but evidence disproving the myth is ignored or rejected. Often evidence is invented and history rewritten to support the myth.

- Unlike ordinary generalizations, a myth is both *pervasive* – widely believed and often passed from one generation to another – and *powerful* – a myth may capture the imagination of those who respond to it, sometimes to the extent that they will die for it.

- It is a basis for political action. Myths may be used to justify a political line and political action.

(ACT) Which myths have been influential in British political life in the twentieth century? How do they differ from reality?

▶ The power of political myth can be exemplified by a myth that dominated Germany between 1919 and 1945, and was to have profound and disastrous consequences for Germany and Europe: that of the 'betrayal' of 1919.

READING AND MAKING NOTES

Reading and selection
General reading

There are several good reasons for reading widely and generally, without taking detailed notes, but to gain general understanding.

First, to obtain different perspectives. The more points of view and perspectives you know about, the better equipped you are to deal with any question with which you may be faced. Second, to keep in touch with current and recent events, and views on them. An essay is enriched by relevant examples from the recent past; these do not all appear in textbooks. You will get them from the more serious newspapers (*Independent, Guardian, Times, Daily Telegraph, Sunday Times, Observer, Sunday Independent* and *Sunday Telegraph*) and political weeklies (*Economist, New Statesman & Society*) and from the political programmes on radio and television.

Your general reading should not be superficial. While you may not need to remember every figure, date and detail, you should ask yourself after you have read a passage what the main points made in the passage were.

 Read the editorials of three serious newspapers and without referring back to them, summarize the main points of each. After this compare what you remember with the editorials themselves.

Then identify the ways in which the editorials distort the facts in line with the values of the newspaper. Don't fall into the trap of thinking that one newspaper is more factual than another because you share its values.

▶ **Scrapbook**
You will find it helpful to keep a scrapbook of news cuttings and notes from television and radio programmes. Some of the later chapters contain suggestions for the kinds of material you could collect.

Intensive reading

This should be done with some definite purpose in mind. Ask yourself before reading something intensively 'What is my purpose? What do I want to find out?' Find the relevant section of the book in question, and concentrate on the parts of it which answer your question or serve your purpose. Try to avoid straying into other material which is not immediately relevant.

Making Notes

The main purpose of making notes is that it helps you to record what you read or hear, which helps you to retain it in your memory, so that you can retrieve it later. That adds up to learning.

► Recording + memorizing + retrieving = learning

Making notes doesn't mean copying out large sections of a textbook. Don't write full sentences, but words and phrases. Leave lots of white space around your notes. You may find it helpful to use plain rather than lined paper, especially if you develop the skills of making pattern notes rather than linear ones. For pattern notes you jot down key words and phrases and link them together, using circles and arrows to show how an argument hangs together. If you have never used this technique ask your librarian for a study skills book which explains it in more detail. I am going to suggest you make two kinds of notes in using this book.

Firstly, to make good notes you need to know why you are making them. Think of note-making as asking questions of the text, and the notes as answers to your questions. In this book I have made things easy for you. Every now and then I will ask you a question or give you an instruction to guide you in note-making. Between them the notes you write in answer to these questions will build up into a fairly comprehensive set, but of course you will need to add to them from other books and from sources of information on current affairs.

A second kind of note-making which I recommend involves using card index cards. These are ideal for storing the definitions of important terms and concepts and examples of them. When an important new term is introduced in the book it will appear in *italics*. This should be a signal to you to make out a new index card. That's not the end of the matter however, since you will gain more knowledge about important concepts as your studies proceed and should add this to your cards.

(ACT) So far in this chapter the following important concepts have appeared:

Facts (empirical and tautological)

Theories

Myths

Value Judgements.

I suggest you make out index cards for these four ideas, giving definitions and examples, to start your card index.

The acid test of good notes is whether you can make sense of them six

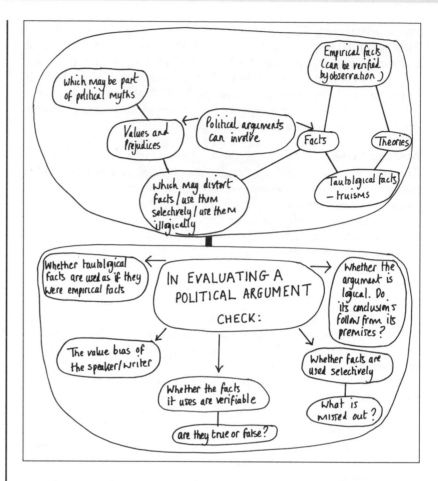

► You may find that you learn more from making pattern notes than from making notes in linear form. This is because in making pattern notes you have to organize ideas rather than simply copy them down without thinking much about them. Once you have the pattern you have an 'at a glance' picture of the way in which ideas hang together.

► This example shows how various ideas in this chapter relate together.

months or a year later when revision time comes round. This means storing and referencing your notes properly. A card index almost references itself, but other notes are more difficult to keep in order. Always head your notes to say what they are about: the chapter headings and sub-headings in this book provide you with one convenient way of dividing your notes into sections. If your notes are answers to questions always make the notes in such a way that it is obvious what the question was.

If you are following a college course don't carry all your notes backwards and forwards to college each time you go. Keep a file specially for your current notes and then transfer them to storage files when you get home. Not only does this mean that you review your notes as you transfer them, it also means that you avoid the possibility of leaving all of your notes on the bus or dropping them all in a puddle!

While you are developing your note-making skills, test yourself by using your notes as the basis of an explanation to a friend – or if you haven't got a friend, a tape-recorder. This will reinforce your learning, and it will show you what you know and what you don't know.

ANSWERING QUESTIONS

Consider the following examination question:

'British Prime Ministers and Leaders of the Opposition have enjoyed almost unquestioned dominance over their parties in recent years' – do you agree? Give examples to support your answer.

Don't worry at this time if you don't have the knowledge to answer the question. We are here concerned with the *method* of approaching and dealing with it.

In approaching this question you should note the following:

• *The words 'in recent years'*. However much you may know about Gladstone and Disraeli, resist the temptation to go back too far. Try to take your examples from the last decade and don't go any further back than twenty years.

• *You are being asked about the Prime Minister AND the Leader of the Opposition*. It is surprising how often, when asked to consider two or more areas, students only consider one, or give a disproportionate amount of attention to one.

• *Be sure of the proposition with which you are being asked to agree or disagree.* Note the words 'almost unquestioned'. You are not just being asked whether British leaders are dominant but whether they enjoy *almost unquestioned* dominance.

The steps in answering a question

1 *Read and understand the question.* Break it down into its component parts.

• *The question asks you to use recent examples.* You should do this anyway as a way of backing up your conclusion. You should also mention authoritative commentators you have read, and their views on the question. Try to give as many perspectives as possible. Don't leave the reader to guess their relevance. Link them to your conclusions.

• *You are being asked to agree or disagree with the proposition.* Don't duck out of this! Ensure that your agreement or disagreement is sup ported by relevant examples and that the link between the material and your conclusion is pointed out.

2 *Select relevant examples*, authorities and theories and concepts; resist the temptation to 'waffle'.

3 *Make your material work towards your conclusion* and point out the connection. Do not come to a conclusion not justified by your material or fail to link your material to your conclusion.

4 *Try to develop your answer* by bringing different perspectives to bear on it.

5 *Where you are asked to 'discuss' a proposition, do just that.* Examine the cases for and against it, weigh them up and come to some conclusion.

6 *Don't be tempted to include material which is suitable for the answer to*

a question different from the question set. Before you include anything, ask yourself 'How does this contribute to the answer to the question set?'

 Take one of the essay questions in succeeding chapters, break it down into its component parts and say how you would deal with it.

Revision

The time to start revising is at the beginning of a course. When you reach the end of a chapter you should look back at the objectives at the beginning and make sure that you have achieved them. At the end of this book you will find an appendix on the revision you should do at the end of the course.

Now that you have reached the end of the chapter, turn back to the objectives and make sure you have achieved each of them.

Chapter objectives

By the end of this chapter you should be able to:
■ define and use the following basic concepts and apply them to actual political situations
politics, power, authority, sovereignty, state, nation, nation-state, constitution. If you are making a card index, you should make a card for each of these terms.

Introduction

In this chapter you will not have the whole barrage of political concepts thrown at you! Most of them will appear as part of the chapters dealing with particular institutions, e.g. 'representation' is discussed in the context of the British electoral system.

A few, however, are so basic that you need to be at least on nodding terms with them before you proceed.

WHAT ARE CONCEPTS?

For our purpose concepts may be defined as *general ideas used to describe and characterize a whole class of phenomena, institutions or set of relationships*. We use concepts to try to understand complex and diverse phenomena. For example, 'sovereignty' may be used to describe a certain kind of power. The concept may then be applied to any exercise of power. We use concepts also to *evaluate*, e.g. 'Is this system a democracy?', with the implication that, to the extent that it is, it is a good system.

► It might be interesting to ask friends, colleagues or parents what they understand by 'democracy' and compare it with formal definitions – including that in Chapter 4 of this book.

Why do we need concepts?

We need concepts because they are part of the basic grammar of our subject. We conceptualize in order to understand. Since the word for a concept may mean different things to different people, we need to be able to understand the different uses of conceptual terms, and assess whether they are appropriate to what they describe. The problem can be illustrated by the fact that most countries represented at the United Nations describe themselves as 'democracies', including those that to others may look like dictatorships and one-party states, as well as multi-party parliamentary systems!

For examination students, there is a practical reason. The London University A level syllabus,

> 'seeks to encourage teachers and candidates to see that, in a sense, institutions are themselves concepts ... and that all institutions embody ideas, and all ideas seek institutional forms'.

► Ideas shape institutions, and vice versa.

It also emphasizes the centrality of concepts.

'Candidates are expected to show how different usages of certain basic concepts may affect the above differing characterizations of the systems. In particular, three groups of basic concepts will be examined:

- those associated with citizenship or being a subject such as natural and civil rights, individualism, freedom, equality and welfare;
- those which concern relationships between the individual and the State, such as law, justice, toleration, political influence and pressure;
- those associated with governing, such as power, authority, sovereignty, order and disorder.'

The same syllabus' 'Short question' section contains many questions which require you to sum up concepts, e.g.

i   'What is meant by Sovereignty?
ii   Distinguish between the concept of power and that of authority.'
(London A level, Paper I 1985)

The Joint Matriculation Board and the Associated Examining Board also stress the importance of concepts.

 Make notes to explain why concepts are important in politics.

POLITICS

▶ Politics is concerned with collective conflicts and attempts to resolve them.

Politics is concerned with *collective conflicts and attempts to resolve them*. It arises from some inescapable features of human life:

▶ If you are studying Economics as well, you may see an overlap – Economics looks also at the consequences of scarcity in the face of competing demands on resources.

- *Scarcity*. In order to live, people convert resources into the things they need and want. But the needs and wants, usually, far exceed the ability of the resources to cope with them. In addition, the needs and wants of one set of people may be fundamentally opposed to those of another set of people; so for example, even if there was no problem of resources, the aims of those who campaign against smoking would be fundamentally opposed to the needs of those who want to smoke and the aims of the tobacco industry.

This last example brings us neatly on to another feature of human life that creates the need for politics.

▶ In an argument like this, the protagonists often switch from values to facts and back again! A pro-smoker might appeal to the value of 'freedom to choose' and then pour scorn on the evidence for a link between residual tobacco inhalation and cancer. Sometimes the two lines of argument get confused.

- *Values and ideas*. Our smokers may express their desire to carry on indulging their habit in the name of 'freedom to choose' and accuse the anti-smoking groups of 'health fascism' (the term is in current usage), while our anti-smokers may emphasize the value of the health of present and future generations, the cost of treating smoking-related illness and the rights of non-smokers to be free from the danger of 'residual' effects of tobacco. Conflict is not just about material things. Difference of perspective, value, religion, ethnic or cultural identity can lead to bitter and sometimes fatal conflict.

So, it seems that an unavoidable feature of human life is:

- *Potential and actual conflict*. Controversy in recent years, still current, about the funding and organization of the National Health Service is about resources – what proportion of the country's labour, land and equipment should be used for the benefit of those who may use the NHS? It is also about values and ideas. Should more people be encouraged to seek private health care through the market-place, or should the NHS be completely publicly controlled and available to all without charge?

However, since communities do get on for a lot of the time without open and violent conflict, an important aspect of politics is:

• *Conflict resolution.* This arises out of the search for a decision from these conflicts. Since people live and work collectively in more or less organized groups, attempts are usually made to resolve conflict collectively.

We create formal and informal arrangements for conciliation and resolution. Much of the study of politics is concerned with these arrangements. A court of law is an example of a formal arrangement, meetings between trade union shop stewards and management to discuss issues at work is an example of an informal method.

It may be that a conflict is not resolved by the generally agreed method, or there may be no generally agreed method of resolution. In this case it may be resolved outside the agreed arrangements, by force (war or revolution). One side to a conflict may use the conventional arrangements, while the other may not accept them. Trade unionists may defy the Government's laws on striking and picketing, not on the grounds that they reject the whole system of making and enforcing laws, but on the grounds that these laws are a misuse of the powers given to the Government.

• *How the state should be run.* Politics is also about conflict at a much more general level than has been discussed so far. As well as quarrelling about whose ideas and values should prevail within the system or who should get the lion's share of the 'cake' of scarce resources, people argue about by whom, and according to what principles, the cake should be shared out. The whole business of who governs, and according to what principles and arrangements, is part of political discourse. This kind of discourse was dramatically exemplified in Poland, Czechoslovakia, the German Democratic Republic and Romania in the debate about the future of those systems, after the 'leading role' of the Soviet Union and the ban on opposition parties had been removed in 1989.

 Make notes to show how scarcities, values, ideas, conflict and conflict resolution feature in any example of a political situation you care to choose.

Consensus

Consensus (general agreement) or lack of it, is an important factor affecting the outcome of a political situation. Indeed, some commentators almost define politics in terms of the degree of consensus present. Thus there has been much discussion of a 'political solution' to the conflict in Ireland – defining by implication negotiation as

► Note that systems of conflict resolution are not always about reasoned argument and mutual acceptance of the result. Behind the courts of law as a conflict-resolving mechanism lie the police and the prison system.

► Political culture
The term 'political culture' is one you may come across in your reading. *Culture* is a very broad term referring to the way of life of a society. Thus a society's political culture refers to everything about that society which is relevant to the creation and resolution of conflict, the legitimation of power, the reasons why people support some policies and not others, and any other aspect of political life. Many factors in political culture contribute to the balance between cleavage and consensus.

politics and armed conflict as somehow 'outside politics'. Professor Crick defined a political solution as:

> that solution to the problem of order which chooses conciliation rather than violence, and chooses it as an effective way by which varying interests can discover the level of compromise best suited to their common interest in survival.

► Crick (1982) *In Defence of Politics.*

This seems an unnecessarily restricted view of politics. To restrict the study of politics to those areas where sweet reason prevails denies that force and the use of power are one very common way of attempting to solve a political problem. Nevertheless it emphasizes that, in the interest of common survival, the search for 'common ground' is a feature of most political situations.

 From newspapers, TV or radio choose two current issues, one where an agreed compromise seems likely, and another where such a compromise seems less likely.

1 Identify the groups involved, and their differing claims and values.

2 Identify the most important point(s) of difference.

3 State by what means resolution is being sought.

► Northern Ireland is an example of a province where the basic consensus needed for the smooth running of a democratic system is absent (see Chapter 13). Nevertheless, politics abounds, and the paramilitary groups have political parties attached to them. Provisional Sinn Fein, the political party linked to the Provisional IRA, has entered candidates for local and Westminster elections.

POWER, AUTHORITY, SOVEREIGNTY

Power and authority

The difference between power and authority can be illustrated by the two scenarios that follow:

1 *I am standing at a bar, having had several drinks. A large young man comes to the bar and buys a pint of beer which I, clumsily, knock over. He points out my clumsiness in no uncertain terms and demands an apology and a fresh pint, to be paid for by me. I hesitate. He threatens to 'sort me out'. Because he is bigger, fitter, and more sober than I am, I apologize and buy him another pint.*

2 *Standing at the same bar, in the same condition, I knock over a drink just purchased by a smartly dressed young woman. When she points out that I am drunk, I deny it noisily, leer at her and place my arm round her shoulder. She removes my arm from her shoulder, produces a warrant card identifying herself as Woman Detective Constable Green, and tells me that I am charged with being drunk and disorderly and in breach of the peace and that I am to accompany her to the Police Station after she has secured an escort using her two-way radio. I go quietly.*

> **Review – politics**
> Politics is about conflict between human groups, arising from differing material claims in the face of scarcity, and conflicting values, ideas and aims. It is the study of these, and the arrangements for reconciling them. It takes place within the context of conflicting views of how, and according to what principles, a political system should be run.

The young man was exercising *power* over me. This was given by his greater physical strength and his obvious determination to 'sort me out'. But he had no *authority* to issue the threat, or to carry it out. On the contrary, had he done so he might have fallen foul of one of WDC Green's colleagues!

The question of whether WDC Green had the power to arrest me against my will or 'sort me out' never really arose, since I *accepted* the authority of the warrant-card, the authority being that of the law of which WDC Green was an agent. It may be noted that I might have mixed motives in accepting WDC Green's instruction. I might accept because I am a good citizen who believes in accepting the law. Or I might be moved by the knowledge that she could summon several burly colleagues with more than enough power to sort me out.

WDC Green was claiming the law as the source of her authority. This is accepted, at least passively, and sometimes grudgingly, by most people most of the time. The notion of *consensus* comes in again here. Power (e.g. the Police, the Army) can be used to back up authority, but breakdown of consensus may lead to a situation where failure to accept authority means that power is insufficient to support it and authority begins to break down.

As well as the ability to make things happen, power may sometimes show itself as the ability to *prevent* things from happening. Some groups within the political community may operate principally as *veto* groups, limiting the freedom of action of others.

Why is the distinction important?

Much of the controversy that surrounds the actions of governments revolves around the question of whether they have the *authority* to do what they do, rather than whether they have the power to do so. Often the argument uses the idea of *moral* or *political* authority, rather than *formal* authority; that is, although a government has followed the accepted procedure, it may be claimed that it has misused its authority.

Since 1979, under the authority of a series of laws properly passed by the British Parliament, central government has given itself more and more control over local authorities, which run services in our towns and counties, to raise and spend money. In addition, central government has passed a law compelling local authorities to put many of their services out to tender (meaning, to allow private contractors to make bids to run them) and award the service to the most 'economic' tender.

A group of Labour local authorities, although they didn't deny that the Government had by law the *formal* authority to control local authorities in these areas, denied that they had the constitutional or political authority to do so.

They denied this on the ground that it 'destroyed local democracy' by rendering local councils unable to meet the needs of local people who democratically elected them for that purpose. The Government, of course, had an answer (see the Midfield TV script at the end of this chapter).

NM Make notes to distinguish between power and authority.

► *Power* is the ability to make things happen, and to make people do things whether or not they agree to do them.

► *Authority* is a *right*, claimed and generally accepted, to cause others to follow instructions.

► The Protestant Workers of Northern Ireland were able to use their power to veto power sharing – see Chapter 13.

► The terms power and authority are often used loosely. Sometimes they are used interchangeably. For example, if we talk about the 'powers of local authorities' we actually mean the 'authority of local authorities' – their rights to do what they are allowed to do by law. You should try to use the terms precisely.

► See Chapter 13 for further details of the Sunningdale constitution.

► We are here discussing a *constitutional concept*. The extent to which Parliament actually exercises sovereignty is a matter of furious debate, more fully discussed in Chapter 8.

Authority without power?

It is sometimes claimed that governments exercise power without authority, but there also exist occasions when they seem to attempt to exercise authority without the power to back it up. In 1973 an attempt was made to introduce a 'power-sharing constitution' for the six counties of Northern Ireland. The constitution would have given Catholics certain guaranteed rights, and a guaranteed share of government. After a strike by Protestant workers in 1974 which brought the province to a virtual standstill, the constitution was withdrawn. While there was no doubt about the British Government's authority to introduce such a constitution, after such a massive show of opposition it was doubtful that the necessary measure of consensus existed to make it work.

 Make notes giving an example of power without authority, and an example of authority without power. (Since authority is something which people grant each other, and people do not all necessarily agree with each other, your choice of examples will inevitably depend on opinion to some degree.)

 Essay questions

1 'Power tends to corrupt: absolute power tends to corrupt absolutely.' (Lord Acton, 1887)

   Discuss this proposition, using recent world events to illustrate your view.

2 Are citizens of the United Kingdom (England, Wales, Scotland and Northern Ireland) ever justified in breaking the law? If not, why not? If so, under what circumstances?

Page 11 gives a step by step guide to answering questions.

Sovereignty

Harry Truman, elected President of the United States in 1948, is supposed to have had a notice on his desk which said 'The buck stops here' to remind him that, when he had to make a decision, there was no one higher up to whom he could refer. The President's action gives us a clue to the meaning of *sovereignty*. Sovereignty is the right to exercise *ultimate* power. It is where the buck stops.

Sovereignty lies at the end of the chain of authority. If I don't fill in my Poll Tax (Community Charge) form, the Poll Tax Officer, under the authority of his or her employer, the local authority, can cause me to be fined. If I don't pay the tax, the local authority can, eventually, enforce payment with the authority of a court, by selling my possessions or deducting payments from my salary.

But where does the local authority's authority come from?

From central government.

Where does central government get its authority from?

From the law – the Community Charge Act.

On whose authority did the Government create the law?

The authority of Parliament – it passed through both Houses of Parliament and received the Royal Assent.

and that is the end of the chain. In Britain we speak of Parliamentary Sovereignty, since it is in Parliament, as the ultimate source of authority, that sovereignty lies.

THE STATE AND THE NATION

The state

Characteristic of the term *state* is its comprehensiveness. The word is used to denote the whole of the *organized political community*. In addition, it is often used to mean the territory it covers, which is not the same as the nation, although it may or may not cover the same area. The characteristics of the 'state' are:

• It refers to the claim to the right to exercise political power over everyone within a given territory.

• It refers also to the political community, to which all communities belong, whether they like it or not. Thus the State of Israel is a legal and political entity, in the sense that its government claims the right to exercise power over all those within the territory it claims is Israel.

You may find that the word is used in both a narrow and a wide context. It is sometimes used to describe the machinery or apparatus through which power is exercised by government: so, for example, you may read of 'state-owned' industries, like British Rail. The state here is the body set up by law to run the railways. Or you may read of 'The State of Israel' meaning the territory, its government and everyone who lives there. The crucial point is that when you refer to a 'state' you are referring to an entity defined by the claim to the right to exercise comprehensive power, not by language, ethnic identity or culture. Thus, the term means something different from 'nation'.

The nation

Britain has three nations – England, Scotland and Wales. These are recognized politically and legally, but they are not separate states; they are part of the British state. Between 1949 and 1990, Germans may have thought of themselves as belonging to one nation, but there were within the boundaries two states, those of Federal Germany and the German Democratic Republic, commonly referred to as West and East Germany. There were two constitutions, two governments, and two sets of people speaking the same language but living in different power systems.

The *nation*, then, is a group of people, who conceive of themselves as belonging to a nation, defined by all, some, or any of the following factors:

Culture   History
Language   Religion
Ethnic groupings

Power is the ability to cause things to happen and to make people to do things, even against their will.

Authority is the right, claimed and generally accepted, to order things to happen and people to do things.

Sovereignty is the ultimate source of authority in a political system.

Review

State indicates a complete *political* community, membership of which is not optional, defined by the claim to the totality of political power.

Nation is a group which identifies itself as a nation by reason of common cultural, linguistic, historical, religious or ethnic characteristics, or some combination of any or all of them.

► We are discussing here the political, psychological and historical idea of 'nation', not the legal concept of 'nationality'. England, Scotland and Wales are 'nations' but the people of those nations have British 'nationality'.

This territory and these people may or may not be coterminous with (having the same boundaries as) a state.

The nation-state

This is a state which covers, or claims to cover, a nation. Politically, the relevance of the concept lies in the fact that 'national identity' is often the basis for claims supporting the setting up of states to be coterminous with the nation. For examples of this we can look to Britain and Ireland, and to the 'nations' within the former USSR which are calling for autonomy (self rule) and in some cases have achieved this as independent republics wthin the new Commonwealth.

There is not necessarily agreement as to what constitutes a nation. Thus Scottish and Welsh Nationalists would like to see nation states established for the Welsh and Scottish 'nations' respectively. Their opponents however might claim that Britain is a nation-state because it coincides with a population with a common British culture and history. In this context the Welsh and the Scots are seen as kinds of Britons and part of a British nation.

 Make notes to explain the difference between 'a nation' and a 'state'. Give examples of political problems arising when groups of people claim that the state and the nation should coincide but do not.

GOVERNMENT AND THE CONSTITUTION

The Government

What do we mean when we talk about, for example, the 'Major Government'? – usually the group of Ministers of which Mr Major, when Prime Minister, is the Leader. Like 'state' the term 'government' is sometimes used loosely to mean anything to do with public life. For our purposes, however, government refers to *the people and organizations which make fundamental decisions and exercise power in the day-to-day running of the state.* For most practical purposes in Britain it means the Ministers responsible to Parliament for the running of the state.

The constitution

In the next chapter we will look at the peculiarities of the British constitution. Before we do that, however, let's try to clarify what we mean by a *constitution*.

The characteristic of a constitution, as opposed to an ordinary body of rules, is that it is *fundamental* to the exercise of power and the running of the organization. *It is the body of rules by which the ordinary rules are made and power is exercised.* As it is for a club, so for a state. A constitution is likely to have in it somewhere, the following:
• *The type of state it is.* The French constitution of 1958, for example, states that France is a republic.

- *The principles on which the State is to operate* (such as 'Democracy', 'Socialist', 'Marxist-Leninist', 'Liberty, Fraternity, Equality'.)
- *An attempt to define the rights of citizens* with respect to the powers of the State.
- *Identification of the institutions* where power and sovereignty are to lie, and drawing of boundary lines between the various institutions.
- *Arrangements for change.* Some constitutions (e.g. the United States) have written into them clauses to entrench the constitution, making it more difficult to change a constitutional law than it is to change an ordinary law. For example, to change the US Constitution requires a two thirds rather than a simple majority of the National Parliament, and the agreement of 75 per cent of 'second tier' parliaments within a federal system.

Constitutions vary enormously. They range from the copious, running to hundreds of clauses and sub-clauses, to the simple, a short statement of principles and structure. While many constitutions are written in documents labelled 'Constitution' which you can buy in bookshops, the British constitution has no special status and is contained in no document – you have to look for it among ordinary laws and practices.

The role of conventions

An American professor of politics used to forbid his first-year students to read the Constitution of the United States, on the grounds that it would give them a confusing idea of how the system worked! While this was probably delivered tongue in cheek, it was intended to make the point that important *informal* rules develop as the result of events and circumstances, which, while they are not part of written law, are followed almost as though they were part of written law.

Constitutions are not 'tablets of stone', however much those who write them would like them to be. No written document can second-guess all future changes, so conventions develop as a way of coping with change and pressure for change. For example, theoretically the Prime Minister and all the ministers are appointed by the Queen – she makes the choice. In practice, and according to a firmly entrenched convention, she has no choice. She chooses the leader of the party which can command a majority in the Commons, and accepts her Prime Ministers's 'advice' on which individuals to choose for which ministerial jobs. This convention developed with the increasing political strength of the elected House of Commons, and the rise of big political parties aiming to win majorities in the Commons. To appoint anyone other than the person who can command a majority would make no political sense, since normally no one else has the confidence of Parliament. Thus, again, the convention is firmly based in political reality. This is part of a group of conventions which enjoin that the Queen, as Head of State and the focus of people's loyalty irrespective of their politics, must not be identified with party political choice.

But what if there were no leader with a clear majority in the Commons, and more than one leader were to put himself/herself forward as being able to form a Government? Then, perhaps, the

▶ You may belong to an organization with a constitution such as a youth club, a football club or hockey club. The constitution is a body of rules and procedures which deals with things like membership, finance, who is to run the club, how and when they are to be elected or appointed, disciplinary matters (procedures for throwing people out), etc.. It is to this that club members are likely to refer if they want to know their rights as members and, if they so desire, how they can change the rules and how they can change the club's officers.

▶ The Constitution of the United States (1789), carefully separates and spells out the powers and limitations of Congress (Parliament), the President and the Supreme Court, and the respective powers of the individual States and the Federal Government.

▶ The British Labour Government of 1974–9 resigned when a motion of 'No confidence' in the Government was passed by the House of Commons. *Constitutional convention* obliged it to do so. There is no law that says that it could not carry on. It followed a convention, rooted in the political reality that a Government which carried on in such circumstances would have little power and no credibility.

Review – The constitution

A *constitution* is a body of rules, procedures and principles which attempts to lay down how, and according to what principles, the state is to be run. It is supplemented by *conventions* which are informal, but important in the operation of the constitution.

convention of non-involvement might be modified. The Queen might have to make a choice.

Conventions are rules, procedures and precedents which, while they do not form part of the formal *written* constitution, form an important part of the constitution because they are followed as though they were part of the formal rules.

 Make notes to explain why constitutions have numerous conventions supplementing the written laws? Include some examples of constitutional conventions in your notes.

CHAPTER SUMMARY

1 *Concepts* are general ideas used to describe and characterize as well as to evaluate a whole class of phenomena, institutions or set of relationships. The application of them varies from time to time and person to person.

2 *Politics* is about conflict between human groups, arising from differing material claims in the face of scarcity, and conflicting values, ideas and aims. It is the study of these and the arrangements for reconciling them. It takes place in the context of conflicting views of how, and according to what principles, a political system should run.

3 *Power* is the ability to make things happen, and to make people do things whether or not they agree to them.

4 *Authority* is the right claimed, and generally accepted, to exercise power over and give instructions to others.

5 *Sovereignty* is the right to exercise ultimate power.

6 *State* refers to the organized political community and the body claiming the totality of political power.

7 *Government* is the people and organizations which make fundamental decisions, and have the right to exercise power in the running of the state.

8 A *nation* is a group who define themselves as such, influenced by all or any of the following factors – culture, history, language, religion, ethnic identity.

9 A *nation-state* is a state which rules over, or claims to rule over, a nation.

10 A *constitution* is a body of rules, procedures and principles which attempts to lay down how, and according to what principles, the State is to be run. It is supplemented by conventions which are informal, but important in the operation of the constitution.

STIMULUS MATERIAL – THE MIDFIELD BATTLE

Read the following fictional account of a TV debate (written by me), and then answer the following questions:

1 How do the views of the two proponents on the distribution of resources differ?

2 Say what you think 'elective dictatorship' might mean, and why British opposition parties might accuse Governments of wielding it.

3 How do you think Councillor Fairfield might counter the Minister's view that the Government cannot be abusing its power because it has been properly elected, with a majority in Parliament?

4 Describe some differences in the basic values and aims of the two speakers, implied in what they say in the script.

Script: The Midfield battle

TV Link Man

Good evening; in tonight's edition of Viewpoint we are concerned with the question of the changing relationship between central and local government in Britain, and the increasingly bitter war of words between some of Britain's big urban local authorities and the Government. Here tonight to represent the local authority argument is Ken Fairfield, Labour leader of Midfield City Council. Midfield is famous for having attempted to set an 'illegal' budget, in defiance of the Conservative Government's expenditure limits, and for having come into conflict with the Department of the Environment for allegedly trying to circumvent the law requiring local authorities to offer council houses for sale to their tenants.

The Government is represented by the Minister for Local Government, the Right Honourable Jim Dawson MP, who has frequently used phrases like 'loony left', 'petty tyrants' and 'wreckers' to describe the politics and actions of local politicians like Mr Fairfield.

Councillor Fairfield, you are on record as accusing the Government of being 'hell-bent' on destroying local democracy and 'exhibiting the hall-mark of tyranny – a determination to crush any view of the situation but one's own'. Were these just rhetorical flourishes or do you hold to such accusations?

Councillor Fairfield

They certainly were not empty rhetoric. Not only do I hold to them, they are demonstrably true for anyone who cares to look at the record. We were elected by the people of Midfield. We told them, before they voted for us, that we wanted to maintain jobs in the Town Hall, and pursue a policy of no redundancies. We told them that we aimed to improve the quality of services – social services for the care of the elderly, homeless and handicapped, housing, education and a host of others. We also made it clear that we believed in equal opportunities and no discrimination on grounds of race, gender or sexual preference. The voters of Midfield are not fools – they chose us in full knowledge of what we intended, and knowing that it might involve spending more money. What have Mr Dawson and his fellow Tories done? They've tried to stop us at every turn. They've fiddled the level of grant from central government, then rate-capped us so that we can't raise the money on the rates. They've made us sell off our stock of council houses. They've effectively taken control of schools and colleges from us, allowing some to 'opt out' of our control altogether. Now they want to make us sell off our catering, transport and environmental service to any private cowboy who can put in the cheapest bid to run them. This Government is abusing its power in an attempt to demolish local government.

TV Link man
Minister? What have you to say to that?

Minister
All good knockabout stuff; I've no doubt that it goes down a storm with Councillor Fairfield's comrades when they meet in their smoke-filled rooms, but it really won't do for a programme which tries to make a sensible appraisal for ordinary sensible viewers. Firstly, the question of money: since Councillor Fairfield is so fond of invoking the voters, may I remind him that around ten million voters put the present Government into office, and one of the things they wanted us to do was to cut wasteful public expenditure. To court political popularity among those who gain from their policies, Councillor Fairfield and his comrades deal with every problem by throwing money at it – usually someone else's money, someone who doesn't benefit from the expenditure. We were elected to stop that, and stop it we will. The 'tyranny' accusation is just silly. The Government acts on the authority of laws – Acts of Parliament. Councillor Fairfield knows as well as I do that all the policies he is complaining about have as the source of their authority laws which have been discussed and voted on several times by democratically elected MPs.

Councillor Fairfield
It was one of your lot who came up with the idea of 'elective dictatorship' when there was a Labour Government in office – haven't heard much of it lately, have we?

Minister
Can I finish what I'm saying? I didn't interrupt him.

TV Link man
Please do.

Minister
Thank you. We are not, of course, trying to destroy local government, far from it. We are trying to give it back to the people, by making it

responsible for the way it spends their money, and by giving people a choice in housing and education. Councillor Fairfield can bid for council services against outside contractors, as he well knows. The trouble is, he's afraid of the efficiency that competition and the forces of a healthy market situation will force upon his council.

Further reading: Chapter 2

Crick B. 1982. *In Defence of Politics* (2nd edition). Harmondsworth: Penguin. A classic on the liberal democratic definition of politics.

Renwick A. and Swinburn I. 1987. *Political Concepts*. London: Hutchinson. A guide to political concepts aimed at A level students.

Weldon T.D. 1960. *The Vocabulary of Politics*. Harmondsworth: Penguin. An examination of political vocabulary from the view of a linguistic philosopher.

For a useful selection on political culture see
Burch M. & Moran M. 1987. *Modern British Politics*. Manchester: Manchster University Press.

Now that you have completed this chapter look back at the objectives and check that you have achieved each of them.

3 The British Constitution

WHAT IS THE BRITISH CONSTITUTION?

A unitary state

► Parliament has *sovereignty*, but it doesn't necessarily translate that sovereignty into power. A frequent criticism of Parliament is that MPs render it impotent by following the party line and obeying the orders of the party whips too readily.

The British constitution strongly reflects the history of the three nations of Scotland, Wales and England, in which England came to dominate the other two. Sovereignty is concentrated in *one place* – Parliament in London. This is the source of authority for the central government. The notion of one location for sovereignty gives us a clue as to the nature of a unitary state. It is a state in which sovereignty is *exclusively held by one central institution*. Note the word 'exclusively', meaning that sovereignty is not shared with any other area within the state, as it is in a *federal system*, and no area has the right to 'opt out' and govern itself as it has in a *confederal system*.

Note also that 'no sharing of sovereignty' does not mean that central government cannot share power and authority. In Britain, the central government does share these with, for example, local authorities. However the crucial point is that *it can always take powers back, or alter them*. Since Parliament is sovereign, Parliament can alter the relationship by passing a new law.

Until 1984, local authorities had the authority to raise money by a local tax on real property – the rates. They had wide discretion to set a rate which would raise the money they needed. In an effort to curb the spending of some local authorities central government passed a law through Parliament which gave the Government the power to direct some local authorities not to raise their rates above a certain level. Such directives had the force of law. This was popularly known as the 'rate-capping' power.

Remember that sovereignty lies with Parliament, not the Government which is bound by laws passed by Parliament. Central government can sometimes find itself constrained by the law. In 1976, Tameside Metropolitan Borough Council scrapped the comprehensive education system planned for the new school year and informed the children due to transfer to secondary schools that they would be going to different schools from those previously notified, based on grading by headmasters' reports.

The Minister of Education at the time issued a directive which the Government thought was legal under the 1944 Education Act, telling Tameside to revert to the previous scheme. Tameside refused to do so. The courts finally decided, however, that the Government's directive did not fall within its powers under the Act. Tameside proceeded with its scheme. Significantly, the Government passed an Education Act soon after, to try to ensure that no other authorities would 'do a Tameside'.

► A good example of the way in which parliament can grant powers and take them back is the Northern Ireland Parliament of Stormont. As a devolved Parliament, its powers came from Westminster in 1921 and were withdrawn with the imposition of direct rule in 1972. See Chapter 13.

In what way is a federal system different?

In a federal system, by contrast, governments other than the central government have *rights and functions guaranteed to them by the constitution*. For example, in the United States law and order, education, transport within an individual state and a host of other intra-state functions are the business of the individual state parliaments and governments, and not subject to any interference by the federal (central) government in Washington, unless there is overlap with a federal function or violation of the constitution.

 What is the main difference between a unitary state and a federal state?

► In a federal system constitutional wrangles over which powers belong to central government and which to state governments still surface. A US national police force (the FBI) seemed to be contrary to the constitution, since law and order were state matters. It was justified on the grounds that organized crime crossed state boundaries and therefore came under the heading of inter-state matters, for which the central government could be held responsible.

> #### Review – The unitary state
> Britain is a *unitary state*. This means that sovereignty is concentrated in one place, the British Parliament, and not shared with any other centres of power. Power and authority may be 'devolved' (handed down), but since sovereignty is in one centre they can always be taken back.

► At the time of writing, *Federalism* – the 'F-word' – is a hot political issue in Britain's relationship with the European Community.

The rule of law

In the examples quoted above, the law figured prominently. Even the central government, in the Tameside case, backed down when it was adjudged to be outside the law.

The idea behind the concept of the rule of law is that *the ultimate source of authority is the law*. Governments have always sought to legitimize (make respectable or acceptable) their actions by reference to some theory of sovereignty. For example, prior to 1660 there was much constitutional conflict around the issue of whether the monarch was sovereign and above the law passed by Parliament, or whether Parliament was sovereign and able to pass laws which were binding on the king. Charles I claimed the 'divine right' of kings to rule and attempted to dispense with the law when it didn't suit his purposes. This led to conflict with those who saw Parliament as sovereign and believed that the king should be subject to its laws. After the resulting Civil War, Charles I was executed. When the Monarchy was restored in 1660, Parliament made Charles II swear to rule 'According to the Laws in Parliament Agreed on' rather than the old wording 'According to God and My Conscience'. When James II succeeded Charles, he attempted to claw back some of the power lost but failed and was forced into exile. Since that time, the ultimate source of authority in the British constitution has been the law passed by Parliament. The term 'rule of law' indicates that there are no authorities, including governments, which are not bound by the law.

This is not the situation everywhere. In one-party states (such as China) the party and its principles may be regarded as standing above the law. In other systems (as in Nazi Germany) a leader may have sovereignty on the grounds that he embodies the spirit of the race or nation, and in yet others sovereignty may derive from the interpretations that religious leaders make of sacred books – as in some Islamic states.

What is meant by the 'rule of law'?

- *There is no higher authority than the law* – as we have seen.
- *Power must be exercised by the process of law.* In Chapter 2 we read of my arrest by WDC Green. In such a situation, not only would she need the authority of the law to arrest me, she should have followed certain procedures in doing so. She should not, for example, have arrested me or detained me without specifying a charge against me that my conduct had infringed a law. Once arrested, I should not have been detained for long without being brought before a magistrate.
- *The government's power is limited by the law.* Given that there is no higher authority than the law, it follows that governments which exercise power from day to day are, theoretically, as bound by the terms and conditions of the law as anyone else. In Britain, the government has power given to it by various Acts of Parliament, such as the laws passed by Parliament to compulsorily purchase land. In such a purchase, it is bound to follow the procedures laid down by law, for example, giving proper notice of its intention and consulting various people.
- *Where the law is silent, no offence can be punished.* In practise, the law is often so vaguely or generally worded that a whole variety of powers that no one had thought of may be exercised, and actions that had not been considered illegal may become so. In an ideal 'rule of law' state, however, the law would be unambiguous and anything not included in it would not be the basis for the exercise of power or the prosecution of an individual. In the ideal 'rule of law' system, governments are not supposed to 'make up' offences.

The rule of law is the idea that the law is the source of authority, above

---

Review – The rule of law

The characteristics of an ideal 'rule of law' state are:

- No authority outside or above the law.
- Power to be exercised by the process of law.
- Governmental power limited by the law.
- Where the law is silent, no power or offence exists.

the authority of any individual, group or theory.

 1 Find the constitution and rules of a club, trade union branch or other organization you know, and consider where, in that organization, authority lies.

2 You are a member of a group which wants to set up a youth club for young people aged 11–18 in an ethnically diverse inner-city area. You have agreed to take on the job of preparing a short discussion paper on the major areas to be covered by the club's constitution and rules, identifying any major problems framing them might pose. Draft the discussion document.

Sources of law

Statute law

As explained earlier, Parliament is the sovereign power in the British constitution. This does not mean that it is the only source of law, but it does mean that law passed by Parliament – *statute law* – should overrule any other law made in the United Kingdom if it conflicts with it. Since no statute can foresee every situation, the workings of statute law in practice are shaped by *case law*, especially decisions in the Court of Appeal and the House of Lords, since decisions in these courts are a binding precedent on future interpretations.

► See Chapter 14 for more details on the role of the judiciary.

Common law

A good deal of British Law is *common law* – law developed through precedents which are the result of decisions by courts in the past. Some very important areas of law are covered by common law, including the Royal Prerogative – the discretionary powers of Government ministers. However, much of what was formerly common law has been incorporated into Acts of Parliament, and where statute (Parliament-made law) and common law clash, it is the statute which prevails.

► If Royal Prerogative and statute clash, statute prevails (Rex versus Dekeysers Royal Hotels 1918).

Statutory Instruments

A *statutory instrument* ('delegated legislation') is law made by government departments or other bodies, *under the authority of an Act of Parliament*. For example, under the 1988 Education Reform Act, the Minister of Education has power to make rules for the delivery of the National Curriculum in schools, the type of examinations to be used to test students, and a multitude of other matters to do with the running of schools. These orders and regulations have the force of law, so long as:

• They are within the powers granted by the 'parent' act.

• The procedure laid down in the Act is followed. This procedure may require Parliament to pass a resolution before the instrument becomes law, or it may require the instrument to 'be laid' before Parliament for a certain time, in which case it becomes law if no-one successfully opposes it. For some routine matters, there is no requirement for Parliament to see the instrument.

► So far the sovereignty of Parliament has been useful as a concept to explain sovereignty in Britain, despite membership of the EEC. It might become much more problematic if Britain moves along the road of 'Federalism' and 'Political Unity' favoured by the EEC Commission and some other EEC Governments.

European Community Law

The implications of Britain's membership of the European Community (the Common Market) will be more fully discussed in Chapter 12, but it is relevant here to note one consequence. Many forms of law issued by the European Commission such as decisions, directives, regulations are supposed to be incorporated into British law by statute. Others are supposed to be followed by British citizens and the Government. Since European law is supposed to prevail over domestic law (according to the Treaty of Rome and case law developed in the European Court), membership of the European Community raises interesting questions about the sovereignty of Parliament which we'll discuss later in the chapter.

 List the sources and kinds of law in Britain. Note which is the superior source of law. What is meant by the 'rule of law'?

Why is 'sovereignty of Parliament' important?

There is no higher authority than Parliament

Leaving aside the thorny question of super-national bodies like the European Commission, the British system does not have a body with the power to set aside or overrule Parliament. In some systems this may be done by the courts (e.g. in the United States) on the ground that the parliament and/or the President has exceeded its authority under the constitution. The courts in Britain carry out and interpret the law made by Parliament. They may not set it aside or declare it invalid.

The Government's need for Parliamentary support

► The French Fourth Republic had collapsed in the face of opposition from sections of the Army, Navy, Air Force, police force and the white French residents in the French colony of Algeria, to any idea of independence for the colony. De Gaulle, in retirement since 1947, was able to come back as 'strong president' in a new constitution, on his own terms. Ironically, De Gaulle eventually gave Algeria its independence.

In the original constitution of the Fifth French Republic (1958) the President had the power, under certain circumstances, to overrule Parliament or to 'send it on holiday' – suspend it and rule by decree. Certain areas of decision making were reserved for the President. There is no such provision in the British system. The effective head of the Government, the Prime Minister, is not separately elected by all of us, as he/she would be in France or the United States. The Prime Minister's authority derives from an ability to command a majority in the House of Commons, and without it the Prime Minister is lost. The Prime Minister, the Foreign Secretary and the Home Secretary do have important discretionary powers under the Royal Prerogative, but even these could be removed by Parliament. In practice, of course, the Prime Minister and the Government usually command a majority in the House of Commons and are in no danger of removal.

No Parliament can bind another Parliament

Thus there is no theoretical limit to one Parliament's sovereignty. Since all laws passed by Parliament are constitutionally a source of ultimate authority, no law is 'stronger' than another.

This means that no Parliament need be constrained by the laws passed by a previous Parliament.

In case you might think this is all highly theoretical, here are some examples of what Governments have done in Britain, with the support of Parliament.

- Passed, in 48 hours, a law making it an offence to divulge *any* government information unless it was cleared for release (Official Secrets Act 1911).
- Abolished a whole layer of local government in Greater Manchester, Merseyside, Tyne and Wear, South Yorkshire, West Yorkshire and the West Midlands (Local Government Act 1985).
- When faced with a huge claim for damage to an oil company's installations by British forces during the 1939–45 war, altered the existing law, under which the compensation was payable, so that the Government paid a much smaller sum.
- Passed, in 48 hours, a law preventing Asian Commonwealth citizens living in Kenya from using their valid British passports to enter Britain (Commonwealth Immigrants Act 1968).
- Passed laws abolishing trial by jury in public courts in Northern Ireland, allowing detention without charge, banning membership of some organizations, and requiring others only to be indirectly reported on TV (Prevention of Terrorism Act 1974).

Whether these laws are good or bad is not directly relevant to the point being made here. There were and are strong arguments for and against them. The point is that, because of the sovereignty of Parliament, the British Government was able quickly to authorize drastic changes in its powers.

In many constitutions where sovereignty is not so concentrated and unfettered, governments would have found it extremely difficult or impossible to make such changes.

The division of power and 'checks and balances'

The constitution of the United States is based on the idea that power should be divided between the *Legislature* (the body which makes the law), the *Executive* (the body which carries out the running of the country) and the *Judiciary* (the body which applies and interprets the law).

In order to ensure division of power, the US Constitution specifies that the President (Executive), Congress (Legislature) and Supreme Court (Judiciary) may in certain circumstances 'block' an action of the other, and in the case of Congress and the President, each is often dependent upon the agreement of the other, failing which elaborate steps have to be taken to overrule the other. There is also a defined relationship between the Federal (central) Government and the State (regional) Government.

There is no such tight system of checks and balances in the British system. True, the judiciary – the corps of judges and magistrates – are separate from Parliament and Government. However, while they may interpret the law, they may not set it aside or declare it 'unconstitutional'. The Executive (Prime Minister and Government) are

---

The Royal Prerogative

The *Royal Prerogative* is the power of the Crown to make decisions without the prior approval of Parliament or Parliamentary (statute) law. It is recognized by the common law and therefore by the court. In practice the power is exercised by ministers in the name of the monarch. It operates mainly in the traditional areas of government such as defence, foreign policy, law and order, immigration and the summoning and dissolution of Parliament.

Examples of its use are:
- decisions to use troops abroad (the British Government has been involved in over 90 military activities overseas since 1945 with no formal declaration of war)
- the pardoning of convicted criminals
- treaties with foreign countries
- the deportation of undesirable aliens or their exclusion from the United Kingdom.

► See Chapter 4.

intimately tied up with and dependent upon Parliament, as we have seen.

 What are the checks and balances in the American system? What checks and balances exist in the British system?

The importance of conventions

You may find some accounts of the British constitution which label it 'unwritten'. This is not strictly accurate, since much of the constitution is contained in written statutes. But an important part of the constitution lies in the area of *conventions* – unwritten agreements to which everybody conforms.

Compared with many other systems, conventions play a fundamental part. There is no law which says how the Prime Minister is to be appointed, no law that defines the powers and functions of the Prime Minister. This very important office is governed by conventions. Although the Monarch theoretically appoints whom she pleases as her first minister, she invariably appoints the leader of the Party with a majority in the Commons, where such a single party exists, or the leader who is most likely to keep a majority together where it does not.

The constitution of the senior committee of the Government (the Cabinet) and its sub-committees is similarly derived from, and operates according to, unwritten conventions.

 Add to your notes from Chapter 2 on constitutional conventions.

Where are the written parts of the constitution?
Even the written parts of the British constitution are not brought together into one document or code – they are *uncodified*. They are scattered among the 'ordinary' laws of the land.

This doesn't mean that they are not important individually, but reflects the fact that there has never been a time when the whole constitution has been scrapped and rewritten, as might happen in the aftermath of revolution, civil war or foreign occupation.

The constitutional upheavals of the seventeenth century leading to the Settlement of 1688 are the closest Britain ever came to a revolution, but even here the Monarch was retained as head of Government so long as Parliament's laws were sovereign. The transformation of the system of electing the Commons took place between 1832 and 1928, but piecemeal by Acts passed in 1832, 1867, 1872, 1884, 1919 and 1928.

The expansion of the state's range of activity and power after 1945 again took place piecemeal and on the basis established during the Second World War, in a series of statutes, one passed by the wartime Coalition Government and the rest by the Labour Governments of 1945–51 . Note also the 1969 Representation of the People Act which lowered the voting age to eighteen.

▶ Most constitutional conventions are based on common sense. To appoint anyone other than the leader of the party with a majority in the Commons would be crazy. When there is no party with a clear majority the situation becomes more problematic.

No guaranteed rights

This piecemeal development is perhaps at the root of the reluctance of British Governments so far to adopt a body of rights as the basis for our constitution. Rights are implied by the existing laws rather than stated as the basis of them.

If you want to know what your rights are under the British system, you look at the particular law relating to your particular case and ask yourself questions like 'Can they do this to me?' or 'Have I done anything which contravenes any law?', not 'What are my guaranteed rights?'.

Britain, unlike other countries who are signatories to the European Convention of Human Rights, has not written the Convention into its own law. The issue of rights and a written constitution will be looked at later in this chapter and in Chapter 14.

 'Every citizen should have his/her rights clearly stated in the constitution and these should be inviolable, then we'd know where we stood *vis-à-vis* the State.'

Jot down your thoughts on this proposal. Later in the chapter I will provide you with more material on this topic and ask you to write a more complete answer.

> ### Review – The British constitution
> The outstanding characteristics of the British constitution are:
> 1   The unitary structure of the state.
> 2   The sovereignty of Parliament.
> 3   The absence of any strong division of power between Executive, Legislature and Judiciary, with corresponding 'checks and balances'.
> 4   The uncodified nature of the constitution, and the importance of conventions.
> 5   The absence of a 'bill of rights'.

Pressures and arguments

Like all systems which allocate and legitimize power, the British constitution has come in for its share of criticism. Since the late 1960s, however, the body of critics of the constitution has become larger, more articulate and more insistent. Furthermore there has been an increase in the number and intensity of the pressures on the consensus view that the constitution, while having its funny little ways, is basically 'all right'. In the next sections we will look at some of the pressures and the arguments to which they have given rise.

Pressures on the unitary state

Some factors in British society and its political culture subject the unitary state to strain: examples are

Ireland

The six counties of Northern Ireland, part of the United Kingdom,

▶ Britain has no Bill of Rights codifying all the rights of its citizens. Individual rights and obligations are scattered through thousands of different laws.

▶ The problem of knowing your rights is compounded by the fact that you have to look not just at the law, but at how the law is likely to be interpreted by the courts, based on previous judgments.

intermittently presented some problems for the Government in London from the creation of the province in 1921, until 1968. During that period, the seriousness with which the British Government regarded the problem can be gauged by the fact that Northern Irish affairs were regulated from London by a small group of administrators in the Home Office who also administered the licensing of London taxi cabs. The rest was left to the Stormont (the local Parliament) and the province's civil service.

Since 1972 and the imposition of Direct Rule, the Government has had a Minister for Northern Ireland, exceptional laws applying to the province, and a large military presence which looks like staying for the foreseeable future.

A province which once sent a solid phalanx of Ulster Unionist MPs to Parliament in London now presents MPs from four parties, two Loyalist parties, a Social Democratic Labour Party and Provisional Sinn Fein.

► Ulster Unionists were affiliated to the Tory party until 1974. They were *not* Conservative MPs. They saw themselves as a distinct political party.

Scotland and Wales

Between 1974 and 1976 the Labour Government had a tiny majority. After 1976 they depended on the Lib-Lab pact and when that folded they depended on support by nationalists. The Labour Government held referenda (a 'yes or no' vote) in 1979 on proposals for devolution of some power to a Parliament in Wales and to a Parliament and an executive in Scotland. The 'yes' vote in Wales was small (about 12 per cent) but in Scotland one third of those qualified to vote voted for devolution – about half of those voting.

In the end nothing came of the referenda, but it is significant that in the face of small but significant nationalist representation in the Commons a government came near to relaxing the grip of the central state.

Significant also is the fact that two parties – the Liberal Democrats and the Green Party – advocate greater devolution of power to the regions as part of their programmes.

► The electoral strength of the Scottish Nationalist Party and Plaid Cymru seems to have waned over the last ten years, but the suspicion of London-dominated government remains, especially in Scotland.

Local government

Since 1979 the Government has passed through Parliament more than fifty measures dealing with the powers of local authorities, nearly all of them in the direction of reducing the power and discretion of the local authorities. A number of local authorities, mainly but not entirely Labour controlled, have fought back by finding ways to observe the letter of the law while trying to defeat its spirit. In one case, Liverpool deliberately set an unbalanced and illegal budget to try to force the Government to increase its grant to the city.

The battle of words and legislation has been bitter, with local leaders accusing the Government of wishing to destroy democratically elected local government, and central Government accusing 'loony-left' (the *Sun*'s term) local authorities of wasting public money on extremist policies, and refusing to stay within the policy guidelines laid down by the democratically elected Government. Central Government's reply to local attempts to 'get round' legislation has been to pass more and more legislation in an effort to close loopholes.

► See Chapter 11 for a fuller discussion of the relations between central and local government.

Problems of the unitary state

With the exception of Northern Ireland, none of this has so far constituted a serious challenge to the survival of the unitary state in Britain, but the events described above do illustrate the problems of maintaining the consensus necessary to support a trouble-free unitary state. The acceptance by people that the unitary state is legitimate depends on their belief that a government in a parliament in London adequately represents their interests. Many people from Wales, Scotland, Northern Ireland, from the poorer areas of the North, from ethnic minorities, and from local authorities in opposition to central government contest this and propose alternatives to the strongly centralized pattern of power in Britain.

Some of the factors involved may be summarized as follows:

1 Physical distance
Many people resent the fact that decisions affecting a local community are being made by a small group of people two or three hundred miles away in London.

2 Cultural factors
Britain is physically a small country, but has a comparatively large population. There are culturally unifying factors. Most people speak English. Most of us read newspapers and watch television largely produced in London and watched and read all over the country. Most of us live in and around a few big cities, cheek-by-jowl, and shop in national and internationally owned supermarkets with branches in every town.

But there are sources of diversity. For example:
- *Language*. The Welsh language still thrives and is encouraged, and in parts of Scotland Gaelic survives. Asian and other languages are common in many cities.
- *Self identity*. Many local communities and community leaders reject the 'standard English' metropolitan image, and seek a regional identity in local accents, customs and history and, in the cases of Ireland, Scotland and Wales, foster a separate sense of national identity. This may vary from a demand for Home Rule, to devolution of more discretion to local authorities. Even the vaguely defined but often apparent suspicion of 'Southerners' by those who live North of a line from the Severn to the Wash may be counted as a factor.
- *Religion*. Although the majority of Britons are not active churchgoers, the strength of the Kirk in Scotland and Chapel in Wales, both institutions founded on religions which dissented from the established Church of England, may still be powerful influences on people's attitudes. In Northern Ireland, religion is a clearer and more bitter source of conflict. Another development has been the existence of a strong Islamic culture in some of Britain's cities, exemplified by the decision of Bolton imams (Islamic religious leaders) to run Islamic candidates for the local council, possibly splitting the Labour vote.

3 Economic factors
The South and South East of England are often characterized by

▶ The British state has survived intact in Northern Ireland since the 'troubles' began in 1968, but only by military intervention, the imposition of direct rule from London and the 'bending' of the normal principles of the rule of law – see Chapter 13 for a fuller discussion.

▶ In 1991 some British Muslims established their own 'Parliament'. Although only a 'talking shop', this indicated their dissatisfaction with the way in which Muslim affairs are dealt with at Westminster.

► The 'rip-off' accusation directed at the 'English' government by Scottish and Welsh Nationalists goes further than mere accusations of inequality. It argues that Scottish offshore oil (and in the past land clearances for sheep farming and stag hunting), and Welsh water (and in the past coal), have been exploited by the English and not paid for.

regional politicians as having more than their fair share of the 'cake' of wealth, income, capital investment and opportunities for employment.

As often with large generalizations this view glosses over the fact that there is also poverty in the South and South East and affluence in the North, Northern Ireland, Scotland and Wales. It concentrates on crude economic indicators and ignores the 'quality of life' assessment. However, the view is supported by statistics on unemployment, wealth, income, and level of consumer spending.

What is important here is the extent to which people *perceive* the metropolitan area as having more than its fair share.

All these factors and others put strain on the consensus needed to support a strong unitary state. Response to such factors may vary from defending the unitary status quo, through devolution without any surrender of sovereignty, to home rule, federation or confederation.

So far, with the exception of Ireland, the British state has proved resilient in the face of attempts to loosen the grip of the centre. Whether it will continue to be so successful lies in the realm of speculation.

(NM) What factors put a strain on the British unitary state?

What arguments do some British local authorities use to attack the central government's restrictions on their raising and spending money? What arguments do central governments use to defend such restrictions?

The sovereignty of Parliament – or 'elective dictatorship'?

Elective dictatorship is the situation where a government voted for by a minority of the population (as low as 30 per cent) has the power to make sweeping and radical changes because of its control of Parliament. Further it expresses the fear that a group of 'extremists' might overthrow the pillars of the constitution – the Monarchy, the House of Lords, free elections – without a consensus of public opinion behind them. This description of the British system was popularized by Lord Hailsham in his Guildhall Lecture in 1976.

► Lord Hailsham's critics have pointed out that he did not press his proposed alternatives to the constitution on the Conservative Government, elected in 1979, of which, as Lord Chancellor, he was a member.

Lord Hailsham popularized the notion of elective dictatorship at a time when Labour held office with a thin to non-existent majority, after an election in which only about 29 per cent of the population qualified to vote voted Labour. The party had what Lord Hailsham would regard as a radical programme, and some of its more militant politicians were making even more radical noises.

The elective dictatorship hypothesis is usually supported by the following observations:

• The fact, already observed, that there is no local authority that can check or balance Parliament if it is determined to go ahead with something.

• The fact that, at every general election in Britain since 1945 (including the election of that year), a government has been returned whose supporting party has received less than 50 per cent of the votes of those who voted and considerably less than 50 per cent of those entitled to vote. In only one case (February 1974) did the election not produce an overall majority for one party in the House of Commons.

• Some commentators (Roy Jenkins and Shirley Williams, for example) have claimed that there was consensus politics in the 1950s and 1960s, when the leadership of both major parties had policy aims which were broadly similar in the general principles if not in detail. This has been replaced by polarized Labour and Conservative parties, supposedly 'in hock' to the unions on one side and 'big business' on the other.

These critics claim that a body of voters in the centre who do not wish to vote either Labour or Conservative is growing, but is virtually unrepresented in Parliament and Government.

• British Parliamentary parties are highly disciplined organizations, in which MPs are expected to support the policies of their leadership. When that leadership forms the Government, the pressure is greater, and Governments usually get their way despite occasional rebellions.

This means, say the critics, that the awesome power conferred by the sovereignty of Parliament is in practice exercised by the more influential party leaders in the Government.

Lord Hailsham puts it thus:

> ... the sovereignty of Parliament has increasingly become, in practice, the sovereignty of the Commons, and the sovereignty of the Commons has increasingly become the sovereignty of the Government which, in addition to its influence in Parliament, controls the party whips, the party machine, and the Civil Service. This means that what has always been an elective dictatorship in theory, but one in which the component parts operated in practice to control one another, has become a machine in which one of those parts has come to exercise a predominant influence over the rest.

Predictably, not everyone agrees with Lord Hailsham. Two areas of contention are:

1 British Governments are not, in fact, dictatorial. The structure of the constitution – Parliament in two houses, the Monarchy, local government – remains. The cataclysm feared by Lord Hailsham does not seem to have arrived. Fred Sylvester MP, speaking in the Commons in 1987, said:

> It is a curious argument that we should make a radical change in our constitution on the hypothesis that evil may come, but without any evidence that it has. The elective dictatorship could only come about if all existing institutions that preserve our freedoms suddenly collapsed about us. However, I see no evidence of that.

2 Parliament may not be the supine and obedient body that the elective-dictatorship hypothesis labels it. A Government was removed from office in 1979, and since then policies and legislation have been modified in the face of Parliamentary opposition, often from the Government's own supporters.

► Some critics (the Charter 88 movement, for example) claim that the 'evil' denied by Mr Sylvester has arrived and that governments have misused the power given to them by their Parliamentary majorities (see Chapter 14).

► See Chapter 10 for further discussion of the relationship between ministers and the civil service.

This does not take into account the number of times that Governments have dropped or modified policies *before* introducing them, because of anticipated opposition.

• Some former ministers (e.g. Richard Crossman, Barbara Castle, Tony Benn) would not agree with the proposition that they 'controlled the Civil Service' since in their memoirs they accused civil servants of controlling and manipulating them!

 Make notes to explain the meaning of the idea of an 'elected dictatorship' and proposals to prevent it.

What arguments do some British local authorities use to attach the central government's restrictions on their raising and spending money? What arguments do central governments use to defend such restrictions?

How fair is the rule of law in practice?

The rule of law, it is argued, can only work as a guarantee of fairness and even-handedness if the laws themselves are clear, unambiguous and fairly applied. Some critics of the British state say that this is not always so.

The law relating to conspiracy is so vague that its opponents claim it can be used to 'pull in' and convict individuals in circumstances where they have neither committed nor encouraged a crime, or where no crime was ever committed. Community leaders, particularly in inner-city areas, persistently attacked the 'Sus' (suspicious person) law, claiming that the police used it as a basis for arresting and harassing Black youths who had committed no crime.

The Prevention of Terrorism Act (1974), and the 1984 and 1989 Trade Union Acts, are examples of laws which their critics claim are used by the Government to discriminate against certain groups by taking away from them the freedoms enjoyed by others.

 What criticisms have been made of the British system in term of the departure from the principle of rule of law?

Review – Criticisms of the constitution

The bases of the British constitution have come in for criticism, particularly over the last twenty years. Examples are:

1 *The unitary state* – under pressure from nationalist, regional and local demands.

2 *Parliamentary sovereignty* – criticized by Lord Hailsham and others as leading to 'elective dictatorship'.

3 *The rule of law* – criticized as having been violated in spirit, at least, by laws which are vague and so give too much discretion to the police, or are directed exclusively against certain groups within society.

However, these remain the criticisms of the minority, and the unitary state and the constitution remain intact.

POSSIBLE CHANGES TO THE CONSTITUTION

Devolution of power

As well as being supported by Scottish and Welsh nationalists, devolution of power is now part of the programme of the Liberal Democrats, the Labour Party and the Green Party.

The devolution of power is seen as more democratic, allowing people to express their regional identity and to shape their own regions in terms of the local environment, local investment and industrial development, education and social services. It is argued that some guarantee of even partial sovereignty would act as a check on, and a balance to, the over-mighty central state.

Opponents of the devolution of power argue that in addition to practical difficulties there are fundamental objections. Britain is a society in which the sources of unity are much more numerous and stronger than the sources of diversity and conflict. It is not a country which has developed by the coming together of previously autonomous states in recent history.

In any case, why should strong regional governments be a guarantee against the misuse of power? Some of the States which make up the United States of America do not have a particularly good reputation among champions of liberalism. Indeed, the central government has often been the liberalizing influence. Nationalist parties are discussed further in Chapter 5.

Reform of the electoral system

One reason for a reformed voting system is to ensure that a government supported by more than one party results from a General Election, or that if it is a single-party Government, that party has the support of the majority of voters. This would remove the criticism which forms part of the 'elective-dictatorship' hypothesis – that strong British governments never have the support of the majority. A system which produced seats in the Commons in proportion to support for the parties nationally would be likely to produce Parliaments in which no one party had a majority. This is claimed as a virtue, since it would result in coalition governments which would pursue 'moderate' policies. The argument surrounding this idea is examined in Chapter 4.

A written constitution

A written constitution could incorporate a bill of rights, or a bill of rights could be incorporated into the law. The idea that some elements of the constitution should be codified and 'entrenched' (given some special status that will make it difficult for future governments to remove them) has received much publicity in the recent past. The pressure group Charter 88 and Lords Hailsham and Scarman (*ex* Lord Chief Justice) have supported it; as have individual politicians from Labour, Conservative, SLD and SDP. The House of Lords has debated proposals to incorporate the European Convention on Human Rights into the British constitution.

The arguments *for* a written constitution have been highlighted in the discussion of elective dictatorship, plus the arguments touched upon in the discussion of the rule of law. They are that first, the Government has too much potential power; second, that individuals do not have guaranteed rights; and third, that those that they may have are not sufficiently protected by the existing system. A written constitution would guarantee rights, and provide counter-balancing powers and checks on the central government.

The arguments *against* a written constitution are as follows. First, the existing system is not tyrannical. Britain, this argument runs, is a *pluralist* society – one in which a rich variety of pressure groups flourish. They can and do make their voices heard. Many of them are as well-organized, staffed and informed as the Government.

An open society, it is argued, with a pluralistic system of pressure

A copy of the 'British Constitution' – is this some sort of joke?"

► Pressure groups are a check against government power.

For example, the 1966–70 Labour Government climbed down over its proposal to 'phase out' pay beds in NHS hospitals in the face of opposition from the British Medical Association (BMA). The Heath Conservative Government of 1970–4 failed to regulate wage rises by law in the face of opposition from the National Union of Miners (NUM), and lost the election declared over the issue. Mrs Thatcher's determination to introduce the compulsory football club membership identity cards for admission to matches was well known, and legislation was passed through Parliament in the face of tough opposition. However, after a chorus of disapproval culminating in the Taylor report on the Hillsborough football ground disaster (1989), the scheme was dropped.

► The European Convention on Human Rights is an agreed convention between governments about certain basic rights. Agreement to the Convention includes acceptance of the role and jurisdiction of the European Court of Human Rights, to which citizens may have access if action in domestic courts fails to give satisfaction.

Britain has been taken to the Court more often than any other signatory country, notably on corporal punishment in schools, birching as a punishment on the Isle of Man, the treatment of detainees interned for terrorism in Northern Ireland, the working of the Prevention of Terrorism Act, and the facilities afforded to prisoners who want to make complaints or take legal action against the authorities. In all of these, the verdict went against the British authorities.

groups is better protection than a legal 'right'.

Second, flexibility works both ways. Governments with the support of Parliament can, as we have seen, make drastic changes quickly. But this can be used to *increase* the rights of individuals and groups. Legislation outlawing racist words and acts of discrimination, giving women more rights in many areas, and increasing the obligation to provide facilities for handicapped persons, have all passed with comparative ease.

Whether these laws have been effective is the subject of bitter argument. The relevant point here is that in a system with a rigid or entrenched constitution, they might have run up against the constitution.

Further, the sovereignty of each Parliament means that it can change what it or any previous Parliament did, quickly and effectively. The public can therefore put pressure on Government, and the Government cannot plead the constitution as an excuse for failing to change things.

How do you define 'rights'?
In October 1988 the New York Transit Authority made new rules which included a ban on begging on the New York subway. In January 1989 a federal judge invalidated the rules on the grounds that begging is a 'free speech' right under the First Amendment to the Constitution which gives the right of free speech. He went on to say 'while often alarming and sometimes disturbingly graphic, begging is unmistakably informative and persuasive speech' which is protected by the First Amendment.

This illustrates the difficulty of defining rights. What about the rights of those who are accosted and roundly abused if they don't pay up?

How do you define a right so that it works fairly in all cases? The right to work may come up against the right to withhold labour in peaceful pursuit of an industrial dispute.

The European Convention on Human Rights, which has often been cited as a model for a British Bill of Rights, has also been criticized for being unhelpfully vague and general in its definition of rights.

Here is a problem. If you define rights very generally you promote endless arguments about what they mean and definition is, in practice, left to the lawyers. If you go for a 'tight' definition you are likely to exclude deserving cases because they do not fall within the definition.

Should judges be the final arbiters?
One group of critics (e.g. Professor J.A.G. Griffiths, Lord Lloyd of Hampstead, Sir Patrick Mayhew QC MP) object to the idea that judges should be the final arbiters of the constitution or of human rights.

Judges are not elected. Why then should they be empowered to overturn laws passed by an elected assembly of 650 MPs? It is further argued that they are not answerable to the public for the consequences of their actions as are elected politicians. Judges are drawn from a narrow, unrepresentative section of society – mainly white upper middle-class males – and are by training cautious. Many radically-inclined politicians believe, that judges would frustrate radical change even if it had widespread public support.

Lord Hailsham, however, defends judges in this role, because of their legal training which causes them to take a detached view and their freedom from the political battle.

► 'It is as bad to be judged by judges as it is to be judged by politicians.' Jackson.

The difficulty of entrenchment

Because Britain has sovereignty of Parliament, it seems to some to be stuck with it. Since there is no provision in the constitution for making a change in the constitution which could not be legislated away in 48 hours by a subsequent Parliament, how can the sovereignty of Parliament be removed?

Defenders of a written constitution argue that this difficulty is exaggerated. A basic constitution would acquire the status of a special law over time, and, if it was accepted by the Community, would be difficult to remove. Parliament in any case surrendered much of its sovereignty in passing the 1972 European Communities Act, which lays down that European Community Law (except for Treaty Amendments) prevails over laws passed by Parliament. True, Parliament could repeal the European Act, but as time goes on, this seems less likely.

 Use the notes you made for the activity on page 33 to plan and then write an essay on the desirability of a bill of rights for British citizens. Begin your planning by drawing up a table with two columns: one of points in favour of a bill of rights and the other of points against.

CHAPTER SUMMARY

1 The outstanding characteristics of the British constitution are:
   * The strong unitary state
   * The sovereignty of Parliament
   * The rule of law
   * The absence of entrenchment or codification
   * The importance of conventions which are not part of formal law.

2 Critics of the constitution have focused on:
   * The central government's domination of nations, regions and local authorities
   * The close link between party leadership, Government and majority in Parliament, which with the sovereignty of Parliament could lead to 'elective dictatorship'
   * The fact that the 'rule of law' is often violated in spirit, if not in letter, by vague laws giving wide discretionary powers, or draconian measures directed against particular sections of society.

3 Critics who believe the above have advocated:
- Devolution of power to national and regional assemblies and governments
- A reformed electoral system, giving more proportional results
- A written constitution with built-in 'checks and balances'
- A 'bill of rights' as part of the constitution.

4 But the constitution has its defenders, who point to:
- The constitution's flexibility, and the ease with which it responds to change
- The pluralist nature of the British system which responds to pressure from groups within society
- Suspicion of judges as arbiters of whether governments should or should not pass certain laws
- The difficulty of defining 'rights' so that they don't discriminate in favour of some and against others.

 In this chapter various examples have been cited. Check back and remind yourself which key issue raised by this chapter was illustrated by each of the following examples. Where appropriate add the examples to your notes.

> The imposition of direct rule over Northern Ireland in 1972
>
> The Tameside affair
>
> The establishment of the FBI in the USA in the 1930s
>
> The change in the coronation oath in 1660
>
> The judgment in the USA that 'begging' is a form of 'free speech' under the First Amendment of the American Constitution
>
> Rate-Capping (or Poll-Tax capping)
>
> The implementation of the National Curriculum in English Schools
>
> The passing of the Official Secrets Act 1911
>
> The 'sus' laws
>
> The 'pay-bed' conflict between the 1966–70 Labour Government and the BMA.

STIMULUS MATERIAL

The article below was placed in the *Weekend Guardian* (and other papers) by a group of constitutional reformists calling themselves 'Charter 88' in May 1990. Read the article and answer the questions which follow.

1 In paragraph seven it is suggested that a post-war consensus has broken down. What is (or was) the post-war consensus, and how and why has it broken down?

2 What pieces of legislation, policies and government actions might the Charter be referring to, when it lists a number of freedoms which governments since 1979 have eroded?

3 Why do you think that Charter 88 has developed and secured so much support?

4 Discuss the last paragraph, and particularly the justification for the Charter put forward in the last sentence.

5 Take three of the ten reforms suggested in paragraph eleven and assess the likelihood of each reform bringing about the improvements sought by the Charter.

CHARTER 88

1 We have been brought up in Britain to believe that we are free: that our Parliament is the mother of democracy; that our liberty is the envy of the world; that our system of justice is always fair; that the guardians of our safety, the police and security services, are subject to democratic, legal control; that our civil service is impartial; that our cities and communities maintain a proud identity; that our press is brave and honest.

2 Today such beliefs are increasingly implausible. The gap between reality and the received ideas of Britain's 'unwritten constitution' has widened to a degree that many find hard to endure. Yet this year we are invited to celebrate the third centenary of the Glorious Revolution of 1688, which established what was to become the United Kingdom's sovereign formula. In the name of freedom, our political, human and social rights are being curtailed while the powers of the executive have increased, are increasing and ought to be diminished.

3 A process is underway which endangers many of the freedoms we have had. Only in part deliberate, it began before 1979 and is now gathering momentum. Scotland is governed like a province from Whitehall. More generally, the government has eroded a number of important civil freedoms: for example, the universal rights to habeas corpus, to peaceful assembly, to freedom of information, to freedom of expression, to membership of a trade union, to local government, to freedom of movement, even to the birth-right itself. By taking these rights from some, the government puts them at risk for all.

4 A traditional British belief in the benign nature of the country's institutions encourages an unsystematic perception of these grave matters; each becomes an 'issue' considered in isolation from the rest. Being unwritten the constitution also encourages a piecemeal approach to politics; an approach that gives little protection against a determined, authoritarian state. For the events of 1688 only shifted the absolute power of the monarch into the hands of the parliamentary oligarchy.

5 The current administration is not an un-English interruption in the country's way of life. But while the government calls upon aspirations for liberty, it also exploits the dark side of a constitutional settlement which was always deficient in democracy.

6 The 1688 settlement had a positive side. In its time the Glorious Revolution was a historic victory over Royal tyranny. Britain was spared the rigours of dictatorship. A working compromise between many different interests was made possible at home, even if, from Ireland to India, quite different standards were imposed by Empire abroad. No criticism of contemporary developments in Britain should deny the significance of past democratic achievements, most dramatically illuminated in May 1940 when Britain defied the fascist domination of Europe.

7 But the eventual victory that liberated Western Europe preserved the paternalistic attitudes and institutions of the United Kingdom. These incorporated the popular desire for work and welfare into a post-war national consensus. Now this has broken down. So, too, have its conventions of compromise and tolerance: essential components of a free society. Instead, the inbuilt powers of the 1688 settlement have enabled the government to discipline British society to its ends: to impose its

values on the civil service; to menace the independence of broadcasting; to threaten academic freedom in universities and schools; to tolerate abuses committed in the name of national security. The break with the immediate past shows how vulnerable Britain has always been to elective dictatorship. The consequence is that today the British have fewer legal rights and less democracy than many other West Europeans.

8 The intensification of authoritarian rule in the United Kingdom has only recently begun. The time to reverse the process is now, but it cannot be reversed by an appeal to the past. Three hundred years of unwritten rule from above are enough. Britain needs a democratic programme that will end unfettered control by the executive of the day. It needs to reform a Parliament in which domination of the lower house can be decided by fewer than 40 per cent of the population; a Parliament in which a majority of the upper house is still determined by inheritance.

9 We have had less freedom than we believed. That which we have enjoyed has been too dependent on the benevolence of our rulers. Our freedoms have remained their possession, rationed out to us as subjects rather than being our own inalienable possession as citizens. To make real the freedoms we once took for granted means for the first time to take them for ourselves.

10 The time has come to demand political, civil and human rights in the United Kingdom. The first step is to establish them in constitutional form, so that they are no longer subject to the arbitrary diktat of Westminster and Whitehall.

We call, therefore, for a new constitutional settlement which would:

11
1. Enshrine, by means of a Bill of Rights, such civil liberties as the right to peaceful assembly, to freedom of association, to freedom from discrimination, to freedom from detention without trial, to trial by jury, to privacy and to freedom of expression.
2. Subject executive powers and prerogatives, by whomsoever exercised, to the rule of law.
3. Establish freedom of information and open government.
4. Create a fair electoral system of proportional representation.
5. Reform the upper house to establish a democratic, non-hereditary second chamber.
6. Place the executive under the power of a democratically renewed parliament and all agencies of the state under the rule of law.
7. Ensure the independence of a reformed judiciary.
8. Provide legal remedies for all abuses of power by the state and the officials of central and local government.
9. Guarantee an equitable distribution of power between local, regional and national government.
10. Draw up a written constitution, anchored in the idea of universal citizenship, that incorporates these reforms.

Our central concern is the law. No country can be considered free in which the government is above the law. No democracy can be considered safe whose freedoms are not encoded in a basic constitution. We, the undersigned, have called this document Charter 88. First, to mark our rejection of the complacency with which the tercentenary of the Revolution of 1688 has been celebrated. Second, to reassert a tradition of demands for constitutional rights in Britain, which stretches from the barons who forced the Magna Carta on King John, to the working men who drew up the People's Charter in 1838, to the women at the beginning of this century who demanded universal suffrage. Third, to salute the courage of those in Eastern Europe who still fight for their fundamental freedoms.

12 Like the Czech and Slovak signatories of Charter 77, we are an informal, open community of people of different opinions, faiths and professions, united by the will to strive, individually and collectively, for the respect of civil and human rights in our own country and throughout the world. Charter 77 welcomed the ratification by Czechoslovakia of the UN International Covenant on Political and Civil Rights, but noted that it 'serves as a reminder of the extent to which basic human rights in our country exist, regrettably, on paper only'.

13 Conditions here are so much better than in Eastern Europe as to bear no comparison. But our rights in the United Kingdom remain unformulated, conditional upon the goodwill of the government and

the compassion of bureaucrats. To create a democratic constitution at the end of the twentieth century, however, may extend the concept of liberty, especially with respect to the rights of women and the place of minorities. It will not be a simple matter: part of British sovereignty is shared with Europe; and the extension of social rights in a modern economy is a matter of debate everywhere. We cannot foretell the choices a free people may make. We are united in one opinion only, that British society stands in need of a constitution which protects individual rights and of the institutions of a modern and pluralist democracy.

14   The inscription of laws does not guarantee their realisation. Only people themselves can ensure freedom, democracy and equality before the law. Nonetheless, such ends can be far better demanded, and more effectively obtained and guarded, once they belong to everyone by inalienable right.

15   'This is the original Charter 88, now signed by 18,000 of us. Add your name to ours here and together we can make it happen.' Lord Scarman

Weekend Guardian
26 May 1990.

Essay question

'Britain is in more urgent need of a written constitution than ever before'

Discuss this with reference to the proposals of the Charter 88 group.

There is a step-by-step guide to writing essays on page 11.

Further reading: Chapter 3

Brazier R. and Street H. 1984. *De Smith's Constitutional and Administrative Law* (4th edition). Harmondsworth: Penguin. Useful as a reference book.

Jowell J. and Oliver D. 1986. *The Changing Constitution*. Oxford: Clarendon Press. Gives a good account of the forces for change in the constitution.

The following summarize the arguments for and against a written constitution:

Norton P. 1988. 'Should Britain have a written constitution?' *Talking Politics*, Vol. 1, No. 1.

Peele G. 1978. 'Britain's developing constitution' in Drucker H.M. et al. *Developments in British Politics*. London: Macmillan.

Now you have completed this chapter, look back to the objectives at the beginning and check that you have accomplished each of them.

4   *Democracy and the electoral system*

Media Watch

For this chapter look out for articles and programmes on electoral systems and electoral reform

Chapter objectives

By the end of this chapter you should
- be able to name the various kinds of democracy and discuss the differences between them

- be able to describe the features of 'liberal democracy'

- be able to deploy and assess the arguments surrounding the British electoral system, in the light of notions of liberal democracy

- be able to assess the case for changing the British electoral system, describing and evaluating alternatives

- know the meaning of and be able to use the following terms: direct democracy, representative democracy, liberal democracy, referendum (plural, referenda) or plebiscite, constituency, representative, delegate, majority/plurality, hung parliament, coalition government, proportional representation (list system, single transferable vote, list/constituency (or additional member) system).

Introduction

In this chapter we will consider what 'democracy' means, and in particular what 'liberal democracy' and 'representative democracy' mean. We will then look at the British electoral system in the light of these concepts, and consider some of the alternatives to the British system.

WHAT IS DEMOCRACY?

Democracy is a much used (and abused!) word. It is from the Greek word *demos*, meaning the people, and *kratia* meaning power. So in its literal meaning the concept is simple – it means *rule by the people*. But like most simple ideas, it becomes alarmingly complex when you try to put it into practice.

Direct democracy

Direct democracy is a system where everyone is entitled to take a direct part in law and decision-making. It arose from the system developed in the ancient Greek city-state of Athens around 500 BC. All free men of the city (about the size of modern Bristol) were entitled to attend forum meetings at which policies were approved or rejected. During this period the major offices of state were allocated by lot (rather like our present system of selection for jury service). Other

► The democracy of ancient Athens is often regarded as a good example of democratic practice but it did not permit participation by everyone. Women were excluded, as were slaves (who were often quite wealthy individuals) and people who were born outside Athens. This represented a large number of people who lived in Athens but did not have the vote.

examples of direct democracy are some of the Cantons of Switzerland where, until recently, periodic meetings of electors took place at which policy proposals were put to the meeting; and some small British villages which have parish meetings to which all electors can go, rather than elected parish councils.

The use of the *referendum* (or *plebiscite*) can be considered as a form of occasional direct democracy. This is an arrangement by which Government puts a proposition to the voters who make a choice, or vote 'yes' or 'no'.

There are certain problems with direct democracy:

• *The numbers involved.*

It is difficult to imagine operating day-to-day or week-to-week consultation with everyone in any but a very small unit. Even in Athenian democracy at its height the numbers involved were only a small proportion of the population, as foreigners, women and slaves were not allowed to participate. In contemporary Britain, regular consultation of forty million adults might prove difficult (though not perhaps impossible with modern information technology).

• *Where does the power lie?*

Mere *consultation* with a demand for a 'yes' or 'no' answer is hardly *full participation*, since the agenda of policies has been set by whoever is in power, as has the framing of the question. Referenda have been criticized on these grounds as 'pseudo-democracy' – a means of giving credibility to those in power. The referenda held by the 1975–9 Government were seen, by some critics as a means of silencing anti-Common Market Labour MPs in one case, and in the other, as appeasing nationalist parties whose support in Parliament the Government sought, rather than as genuine attempts at 'direct democracy'.

• *Complexity and expertise.*

Advanced industrial economies and the social and political systems that go with them work on a high degree of specialization and division of labour. Except on simply-stated broad issues, it is doubtful whether the majority of the population have an informed view.

Despite these reservations about direct democracy, the *ideal* of democracy is widely held in the modern world. It has been the rallying cry of the opposition to Party and Government in the upheavals in Eastern Europe in 1989–91. This ideal of democracy falls short of complete rule by the people, but encompasses the idea of the exercise of power by professional politicians owing the power to the people in consultation with the people.

Two notions allied to this version of democracy are 'representative democracy' and 'liberal democracy'.

(NM) Make a list of the reasons why direct democracy would be difficult to organize in a country like Britain.

Representative democracy

Where the majority of people are unable or unwilling to exercise power, they may elect people to *represent* them, either in Government,

► Referenda were used twice by the Labour Government in Britain, in 1975 and 1979, once to test opinion on whether Britain should remain in the European Community (the Common Market) and once to test opinion in Wales and Scotland on devolution.

► Leaders who have based their authority on their personal popularity have sometimes used referenda as a means of silencing opposition from party, army or Parliament. President de Gaulle of France, in his referendum on giving independence to Algeria in 1962, made it clear in his TV speech to the people of France that he was appealing to them over the heads of the French establishment. The broadcast ended with the imposing figure of the President stretching his arms in supplication and saying, 'Men and women of France, help me'. It was an impressive performance. Critics of referenda sometimes claim that they are used to support 'demagoguery'. In Autumn 1991, Mrs Thatcher who opposed the 1975 referendum when Leader of the Opposition, was calling for a referendum on the issue of a single European currency.

and/or in an assembly from which the Government is chosen and to which it is responsible.

The concept of representation

'Representation' may mean different things, for example:

• *Acting on the instructions of someone.*

Acting on the instructions of someone such as an estate agent acting for me in selling my house, or a barrister in pleading for me in court.

• *Interpreting and defending someone's interests.*

This broader definition leaves the representative with discretion as to what is the best course to pursue. This has often been a point at issue between electors and their representatives. Edmund Burke, the eighteenth century MP and politician, provided the classic reply of a representative to his constituency on an occasion when he had not voted the way they wanted on a revenue issue. He defended the right of a representative to exercise his own judgement, in the light of all the relevant facts and arguments, and made a distinction between a *delegate* who merely follows an order from those who have elected him, and a *representative* who exercises his own judgement. Arguments abound about the extent to which an MP should act according to the wishes of groups of electors, and especially the local constituency party.

• *Acting as a small 'mirror image' of the wider body of electors.*

A painting or a sculpture is a 'representation' of reality. In this view of representation, the elected assembly should be a microcosm (model in miniature) of the society it represents. You may hear complaints that women, Black people, manual workers, etc. are 'under-represented' in the British Parliament. In the sense that MPs who are Black, female, or ex-manual workers form a much smaller proportion of the membership of the House of Commons than they form of British society, this is true. It leads on to the question of whether an assembly like the Commons should represent the major groups within society in rough proportion to their distribution in the population. It also raises the question of whether a middle-class white male can properly represent Black people, women and manual workers.

British MPs and representation

Each of the 650 British MPs is elected as the sole representative of a geographical area – called a *constituency*. He or she is the person in the election who received more votes than any other candidate, but not necessarily a majority of the votes.

Nearly all MPs, however, are sponsored, financed and stand in the name of a national political party, e.g. Labour, Conservative, Liberal Democrat. If elected as *party* MPs they will be expected, in general, to follow the line laid down by the party leadership.

The *party* role may thus clash with the *constituency* role. An MP representing a constituency centred on a fishing port, for example, may find his or her constituents urging opposition to an extension of catch quotas for European Community fishing in British waters, while the leadership expects support for the measure.

▶ Edmund Burke's speech to the electors of Bristol is regarded as one classic statement of the way in which MPs should *represent* their constituents.

'Your representative owes you, not his industry only, but his judgement; and he betrays instead of serving you, if he sacrifices it to your opinion.

...Parliament is not a congress of ambassadors from different and hostile interests; which interests each must maintain, as an agent and advocate against other agents and advocates; but Parliament is a deliberative assembly of one nation, with one interest, that of the whole; where not local purpose, not local prejudices ought to guide, but the general good, resulting from the general reason of the whole. You choose a member indeed; but when you have chosen him, he is not a member of Bristol, but he is a member of Parliament.'

At constituency level, an MP is seldom faced with unanimity about what the people want. It is likely that numerous groups and individuals will press him or her to go this way or that.

This is not to say that MPs don't represent anyone, but that the opportunities for representation are numerous and sometimes contradictory, and the choice rests with the individual MP.

Responsibility
Closely allied to the notion of representative democracy is that of *responsibility* or accountability. Without some mechanism or procedure by which representatives are made answerable to those who elected them, the idea of representation would not mean much in reality, since voters would have no way of putting pressure on those who represented them.

One method of trying to ensure responsibility is to provide for periodic election. Between elections, communication with and access to MPs by voters is the key issue.

 Make notes on the variety of meanings given to 'representative'. In terms of the different meanings how far is the British political system a representative one.

Liberal democracy
The features of representative democracy combined with certain others listed below form a model by which about forty of the states represented at the UN, including Britain, the United States, and most of the non-communist states of Western Europe, like to characterize themselves – the model of *liberal democracy.*

An ideal liberal democracy would exhibit the following features:

Free, fair and regular elections
- Elections should be free from corruption and private influence.
- The franchise (the right to vote) should be widespread – everyone should have the right to vote (unless under age, unable because of mental handicap, etc.).
- Voting strength should be equal – each elector to have the same number of votes.
- There should be fair allocation of seats. Constituency boundaries should not be 'gerrymandered'– organized in such a way that they are likely to produce a pre-determined result.

Freedom of expression and organization
This is the 'liberal' part of liberal democracy, by which liberal democratic regimes liked to distinguish themselves from the former 'people's democracies' of Eastern Europe (e.g. the German Democratic Republic).

In a people's democracy one party plays a leading role and there is usually strict control of the media, the arts and public meetings. The formation of groups other than the institutions of state and the leading party is also controlled.

In the model liberal democracy, by contrast, people may say what they like, write what they like, paint, sculpt and compose what they

---

The social composition of the House of Commons

After the 1987 election, out of a total number of seats of 650, 41 women were elected to the Commons. 243 female candidates had been put up by the main parties. Twenty eight candidates from ethnic minorities were fielded by the main parties and four were elected: three Black and one Asian – the first Asian MP since 1929 and the first Afro-Caribbean ever.

In the House of Commons Black and Asian people are under-represented and women are grossly under-represented by comparison with the composition of the electorate.

▶ A German friend of mine, who lived in the German Democratic Republic (the former communist part of Germany) and owned a cage bird, claims that both the bird and the fanciers' society to which he belonged were registered with the State.

like, and organize into as many political groups and parties as they like, within a system of law which sets very wide limits.

Freedom of assembly and movement
This means that groups should be able to meet where and when they like in any number they like, to discuss what they like, provided they do not break the law in other respects, e.g. impeding the traffic or inciting a riot. It also means that restrictions on movement about the country – internal passports, travel restrictions of various sorts – should be absent.

An elected assembly
There is an elected assembly which effectively controls the government and represents those who elected it. In our model democracy between elections, those who exercise power and make day-to-day decisions do so under the effective scrutiny and under the authority of an elected assembly.

 Contact someone who acts in a representative capacity as local councillor, MP, trade union representative, or representative in another organization. Interview him or her, and find out what they understand by being a representative and the difficulties they encounter in playing a representative role.

 Make a list of the characteristics of a model liberal democracy. For each of the characteristics give examples of British political institutions which coincide with the model. For each of the characteristics give examples of ways in which it might be said that Britain departs from the model liberal democracy.

Consensus, cleavages and representation
Britain like most societies has some characteristics which make for consensus and some which make for cleavage. Producing a workable government in a liberal democracy involves a nice balance of the two factors. Too much emphasis on differences and conflicts is likely to make the society ungovernable. Too much emphasis on consensus may involve stifling the voices of dissenting groups the expression of which is supposed to be one of the aims of a liberal democracy.

 From your own knowledge of British society make a list of the kinds of factors which divide people into groups with different political interests which make for cleavage in British society.

THE BRITISH ELECTORAL SYSTEM

The British electoral system fulfils many of the criteria of a free and representative system, yet it has come in for a great deal of criticism in recent years. Two parties – the Liberal Democrats and the Greens – are pledged to reform it, and substantial reform groups exist within the Labour and Conservative Parties.

The characteristics of the British system are:

Universal suffrage (or universal franchise)
With very few exceptions, everyone over the age of 18 who is a British citizen has the right to vote.

One person one vote
The last vestiges of plural voting (some voters having more than one vote) disappeared in 1949 with the abolition of the university constituencies (which gave university graduates a vote in the university constituency and a vote in their area of residence) and the multiple vote for those owning business premises in one constituency and living in another. Now each of us has one vote only.

The secret ballot
We vote in secret, and our ballot paper is subsequently kept a secret. This was introduced in 1872 to prevent 'undue influence' being exerted on voters.

► The 'secret ballot' proposal was opposed by many established politicians at the time, including Gladstone, on the grounds that it would exclude 'proper influence' – advice to working men from their betters as to the 'responsible' way to vote.

Regular elections
Since 1911 the law has required that Parliament should be dissolved at least once every five years. A general election is then held, in which we re-elect all 650 members of the House of Commons.

Technically the Monarch dissolves Parliament; in practice, she or he does so on the advice of the head of Government – the Prime Minister.

Note that neither the date nor the frequency of elections is fixed. The only requirement is that one election should be held in each five-year term.

In 1974 there were two general elections (February and October) because the first produced no majority for any one party. In 1979 an election was forced upon the Labour Government after a defeat in the Commons on a motion of 'No confidence'. When an election is not forced upon the Government, the Prime Minister decides within the time limit set by the law.

The power of the Prime Minister to bring about an election when he or she wants it has been criticized, since the election can be timed when the Government is most popular due frequently to the pursuit of popular policies in the period just before the election.

The four characteristics above tie in well with the criteria for an electoral system appropriate to a representative democracy; this next, however, is more problematic.

► There are no examples of the Monarch having refused a dissolution in Britain in this or the last century, although her representative, the Governor General, has done so in Canada and South Africa, and in Australia the Governor General has dissolved Parliament without the advice of the Prime Minister.

Single-member constituencies
Each constituency (geographical area) elects one member to the House of Commons. The winner of the election is the candidate who receives more votes than any other single candidate, *not necessarily a majority*.

Consider the following hypothetical example.

Smith	23,000 votes
Jones	18,000 votes
Brown	12,000 votes

Under the British system Smith wins, though she does not have a

► No-hopers

The arguments for putting up candidates and asking people to vote for your party where it stands no hope of success are:

1 Significant swings away from the dominant party in a constituency, even if it still wins comfortably, can be used as propaganda against that party nationally.

2 'Hopeless' constituencies provide a training and proving ground for new candidates, who may be offered something winnable next time.

3 It keeps party workers of the dominant party in the constituency at election time, which means they are not available to 'beef up' the campaign in marginal constituencies.

4 You never know – the electors of Bournemouth might change their minds *en masse*.

► Deposits

Candidates in general elections are required to pay a deposit of £1500 which is forfeit if the candidate secures less than 12.5 per cent of the votes cast. However, the Monster Raving Loony Party, headed by Screaming Lord Sutch and The Corrective Party, headed by the former madam of a brothel, continue to enliven British elections.

majority. Some critics would argue that the majority of voters have voted against Smith (although this raises the question of whether a vote for Jones or Brown is a vote against Smith). Smith has won on a *plurality*, not a majority.

Furthermore if I have voted for Jones or Brown, I have no second chance when I realize that they are no-hopers. The British elector's vote is *non-transferable*. My vote says 'I vote for Brown (or whoever) and nobody else' not 'I vote for Brown but if he doesn't win, or if he has more votes than he needs, I would like my vote to go to ...'!

The consequence of this is that, in terms of influencing the outcome of the election, many votes are 'wasted'. This becomes important if electors are voting mainly with party rather than person in mind, as most British electors do. I may vote Labour because I wish to see a Labour Government, or as an expression of general support for the Party, rather than because I favour the individual candidate as a representative for my area.

If I live in Bournemouth the act of voting Labour may be personally important to me, but it is not of practical value (without a major psychological or social upheaval) since the election of a Labour member in Bournemouth is a remote possibility. If I vote Labour in the Rhondda Valley, my vote may be of more practical use than it would have been in Bournemouth, but not much, since the Rhondda regularly returns a Labour member, with a massive majority. If I vote in the afternoon or evening I'll probably be giving my vote to a candidate who already has more than enough to win!

 List the main characteristics of the British electoral system.

THE DEBATE ON THE BRITISH ELECTORAL SYSTEM

Deliberating on the pros and cons of the British electoral system is not just an academic exercise. It is a live political issue within the Labour and Conservative Parties who, though they do not officially endorse electoral reform, have strong groups within them that do. The centre parties (all Liberal Democrats and Greens) champion the cause of electoral reform, and would probably demand it as a condition of support for an agreement with Labour or Conservative should the question arise in a future 'hung' Parliament (one in which no one party has an overall majority).

Some of the factors in bringing this debate to the foreground of British politics are:

Increased support for parties other than Labour and Conservative

In the elections from 1950 to 1970, the total percentage of those voting who voted for one of the two *'big' parties* (Labour or Conservative) was as follows:

Year	Percentage voting for the 'big' parties
1950	89.6
1951	96.8
1955	96.1
1959	93.2
1964	87.5
1966	90.0
1970	89.5

From 1974 to 1987, the picture was as follows:

1974 (Feb.)	75.1
1974 (Oct.)	75.0
1979	80.9
1983	70.0
1987	73.0

Critics of the British electoral system, especially those in the centre parties, claim that the shift away from the two main parties in the last two decades means that an electoral system which tends to favour those two parties cannot be justified. They see the increased support for the centre (shown in the table below) as evidence of support for centre politics and coalition (mixed party) government.

19.3% for the Liberals in February 1974
18.3% for the Liberals in October 1974
13.8% for the Liberals in 1979
25.4% for the Lib/SDP Alliance in 1983
23.0% for the Lib/SDP Alliance in 1987

Heath *et al.* give some academic support to this view.

> The Alliance vote is not, as previous interpretations have suggested, a protest vote drawn evenly from different social classes. Its base, though small, is an expanding one and thus its shared vote might be expected to have an underlying upward trend.

Heath, Jowell and Curtice (1985) *How Britain Votes.*

But the results in terms of seats won do not reflect the support given in terms of the votes cast.

A second criticism of the British system is its lack of choice. Political parties in Britain are 'broad churches'. They include a wide range of views and personalities. I may wish to vote Labour, but 'moderate' Labour rather than left-wing Labour. I may wish to vote for a Labour woman or a Labour Black candidate, because I feel that they are under-represented.

In practice, because of the single-member constituency system, the party I wish to support presents me with one candidate chosen by a small caucus, and I must like it or lump it.

► British political parties will be examined in more detail in the next chapter.

► Class and voting will be examined in more detail in Chapter 6.

► See Chapter 3 for more discussion of the concept of 'elective dictatorship'.

► *Coalitions*
Much of the argument about the reform of the electoral system revolves around the notion of coalition government. This is a government in which more than one party agrees to take part, their members sharing ministerial office and taking responsibility for the policies and actions of the government.

The changing class base of British politics

It is claimed that the traditional class boundaries which provided loyal support for the two big parties have been eroded, creating a large, but largely unrepresented group of voters. To quote Heath *et al.* again:

> The working class has contracted, reducing Labour's electoral base. The salariat has expanded, in particular its Liberal wing of educated, public-sector professionals who are out of tune both with the free enterprise ideology of the entrepreneur and with the interventionist ideology of the working class.

This group provides fertile soil for the centre parties.

The dangers of 'elective dictatorship'
Critics of the electoral system claim that elective dictatorship is more likely where there is a tendency of the system towards single-party government, based on a minority of votes.

The defence of the British system

Some anti-reform arguments are as follows:

The British system helps to produce stable, single-party governments
Apart from two war-time coalitions which were widely accepted as necessary, most British Governments have been made up from a single party, usually supported by a Parliamentary majority.

Labour did not have a majority in the brief Government of 1924, in 1929–1931, and October to November 1974. Its majority during the 1974–1979 Government varied from tiny to non-existent, but it survived as a single-party Government. The National Governments of 1919–22 and 1931–35 were technically-speaking coalitions, but were effectively dominated by the Conservative Party.

More often than not Britain has had one party in power, supported by a Parliamentary majority of that party's supporters. This, say the defenders of the existing system, is a good thing because:

• It is democratic. A large proportion of the voters get what they voted for – a Government elected on a programme of policies outlined in the party manifesto. By contrast a system which produces 'hung' Parliaments encourages parties to 'horse-trade' with one another to produce coalition governments and programmes of policies which nobody actually voted for. Furthermore the smallest party, if it held the balance, might be able to exercise an influence on policy out of all proportion to the number of its MPs, by threatening to walk out on the coalition unless it got its way.

• It is stable. Single-party Governments, their advocates claim, are inherently more stable. Loyalty and ideology form a common focus, making for discipline and unity. The coalitions which would probably result from a more proportional voting system would be 'marriages of convenience', likely to break up in the face of a crisis, continually searching for the compromise rather than the right solution.

Give the main arguments for and against coalition governments.

The British system is straightforward and simple

Voters need only put one cross against one name. There is no formidable list with eight to ten choices to be made, or the requirement to put several candidates in order of preference. Each constituency is relatively small (average electorate 60,000) and has one representative.

Critics of the system are not daunted by these kinds of argument. Coalitions, far from being an aberration, are to them a stronger and more democratic form of Government. A coalition is more likely to reach sensible conclusions because of the need to compromise, and more likely to listen to representatives in Parliament, rather than trying to 'whip' them into line by the use of party discipline.

Such critics point to stable coalitions in Western Europe (West Germany, Austria) which have provided successful Governments, and the apparent internal turmoil of British Governments with huge

---

Review – the British electoral system

1 *It has the following characteristics:*
   - Universal franchise – one person one vote.
   - Secret ballot.
   - Single-member constituencies: election on a plurality, vote non-transferable.
   - One election at least every five years, or more frequently on dissolution of Parliament.

2 *Its critics attack it on the following grounds:*
   - It produces Parliaments which in their political composition do not reflect the way people voted.
   - It discriminates against smaller parties.
   - It leaves the very large minority of those who wish to vote for centre parties almost unrepresented.
   - It leaves Scottish Conservatives and southern and south eastern Labour supporters almost unrepresented.
   - It may produce an elective dictatorship.
   - It restricts choice.

3 *Its defenders emphasize:*
   - The fact that more often than not, it has produced stable single-party governments with a working majority in Parliament.
   - The transient and shaky nature of coalitions which would probably result from a system of proportional representation.
   - The undemocratic nature of coalitions arrived at by 'horse-trading' between party leaders.
   - The simplicity and clarity of one non-transferable vote, and one representative per constituency.

single-party majorities like the 1945–50 Labour Government, and the 1979 onwards Conservative Governments, with frequent ministerial resignations and sackings and continual re-shuffles.

 Look at the review panel on page 55. Take each of the criticisms of the British electoral system listed and note down the responses defenders of the British system might make. Then take each of the defences and note down the responses which might be made by the critics.

ALTERNATIVES TO THE BRITISH SYSTEM

Three systems are proposed as alternatives to the British electoral system. Each aims to provide better proportional representation.
  They are:
- The list system (there are several variants).
- The single transferable-vote system (STV).
- The list-constituency system.

The list system

The basic idea behind the list system is simple. Each party puts forward a list of candidates, and the voter chooses a party list. A proportion of each party's list, corresponding to the proportion of votes received for each party, is elected. Thus, if a party receives 40 per cent of the votes, in a list system it should receive 40 per cent of the seats in Parliament.

  In effect, under the list system the voter says:

  'I support ... party list.'

  To obtain such exact proportionality, however, would mean having national lists, with the whole country as a single constituency. This is the situation which prevails in Israel, in the elections for the Knesset.

  Most list systems, however, operate on large multi-member constituencies electing eight to ten members. Seats are allocated to each list according to a quota, obtained by dividing the number of seats into the number of votes, with seats going to the party with the largest remainder when no party has enough votes left to fulfil the quota.

  An alternative method is the 'highest average' method in which remaining seats are allocated successively to the party with the highest average, when its votes are divided by the number of seats left.

The supporters of the list system
Supporters see it as the only truly representative system, which gives each vote equal weight and ensures that all parties get a fair chance.

The opponents of the list system
Opponents emphasize the large unwieldy constituencies, in which there is little incentive for MPs to cultivate their electors, since the list is drawn up by the party.

  They say that because the list system encourages the representation of small parties, it might produce an unrepresentative Parliament. It is more likely to produce a government which is a coalition depending for its continued existence on the support of small parties. Such a government, this view emphasizes, would be inherently unstable. Members from the small party are likely to resign when they don't get their way since they have no great share in government and no urgent reason to remain. This, it is argued, will cause continual reformations and re-alignments or lead to a situation in which the small parties exercise influence out of all proportion to their representation. Moreover they argue that by giving a fair chance to every party, no matter how small, a list system will generate dissension at the expense of consensus.

The single transferable-vote system (STV)

This system looks dauntingly complicated when you examine it in detail, but don't despair! You don't need to be able to do the arithmetic, and the basic idea behind it is fairly straightforward. It is this:

STV tries to avoid 'wasted' votes by giving the voter the option of transferring his or her votes to another candidate, should the first-choice candidate either stand no chance of gaining a seat, or receive a surplus of votes over the minimum number necessary to be elected.

In effect, under STV the voter can say,

'Here is my first choice.

If he/she doesn't get elected I want my vote to go to ...

If my first choice gets more than enough votes to win, I want the proportion of my vote by which his/her support exceeds the minimum necessary to go to ...'

STV has the following characteristics:

• *Multi-member constituencies*

Each constituency elects more than one MP. You cast your vote in order of preference

For example,

Black	1st choice
Green	2nd choice
White	3rd choice
Brown	4th choice

Note that the voter does not have four votes. He or she has one vote and expresses a preferred order of candidates.

• *There is a quota of votes*

The minimum number of votes necessary to be elected is arrived at by the formula:

$$\frac{\text{Number of voters}}{\text{Number of seats} + 1} + 1$$

Thus if the constituency has 250,000 voters and elects four MPs the quota would be:

$$\frac{250,000}{4 + 1} + 1 = 50,001$$

If four candidates have 50,001 votes each, they have enough to be elected, since there are only 49,996 votes left. But 50,000 each would be too few.

▶ It is sometimes claimed for STV that it would give a more representative (in the sense of mirroring society) Parliament. Black Labour voters would still be able to vote Labour, but could give priority to a Black candidate. Feminists could give priority to women.

- *The surplus votes are redistributed*

In the first round of counting, all the first preference votes are counted. If no candidate gets enough votes to pass the quota the candidate with the fewest votes is eliminated and his/her votes are redistributed on the second preference. If a candidate gets more votes than the quota, his/her excess votes need to be redistributed. For example, if the quota is 1001 and a particular candidate has 1200 votes, 199 votes need to be redistributed. Each of these excess votes is given the value 199/1200th of a vote. Counting continues in this manner, redistributing votes from elected or eliminated candidates until all the seats are taken.

The supporters of STV argue:

- *STV retains the constituency link without wasting votes.*

A frequent criticism of the present British system is that it wastes votes. Yet one virtue often claimed for it is the constituency link, in which each area has an MP to represent it, who has a vested interest in looking after it. STV, by giving the voter a transferable vote, seeks to avoid wasted votes. But the constituency link is maintained as prospective MPs are not automatically going to receive the party vote, but must compete with other candidates of the same party for first-choice votes.

- *The elector chooses the person as well as the party.*

If I am a Labour or Conservative supporter, I can vote for my party but exercise some influence over which person or political group within that party is successful, since I am faced with several candidates from the party whom I can place in order of preference. If I am not into party politics I can cast my votes in different ways – say to candidates with strong local connections, or particular views on the environment.

- *STV makes stable coalitions more likely.*

Austria uses the STV system, and it has been governed since 1948 by a series of stable centre-based coalitions. It is argued that STV would produce this kind of government. This is seen as a virtue by those who consider centre-based coalitions as the ideal form of government.

The critics of STV make these points:

- *The system is complicated and sophisticated.*

It is of the essence of a democracy that people understand the system of voting. Critics of STV claim that it is too complicated for the person-in-the-street. They also claim that the choices to be exercised – putting a number of candidates in order – requires a degree of knowledge of the various candidates that most voters would not bother to acquire.

- *Candidates may be elected on second and third choices.*

Under STV candidates who few electors are actually opposed to, rather than those who they positively support, tend to gain a large number of second-choice votes. Results may therefore favour those to whom nobody has a strong objection rather than reflect the strength of support for candidates.

- *STV discriminates against small parties.*

This can be seen as a virtue or a vice, depending on what you think of

small parties.
- *STV is not truly proportional.*

Again, this depends on what you think of exact proportionality as a goal.
- *It is divisive of party unity.*

Another in the 'could be good or bad' category. In vying for first choice in a multi-member constituency system, members of the same party might campaign against one another.

 Without describing the system draw up a table summarizing the pros and cons of the single transferrable-vote system of election.

The list-constituency (or additional member) system

The model for this system is that used in Germany. It is an attempt to combine the virtues of the British type of single-member constituency system with those of the national list, while avoiding their vices. It works like this:
- *50 per cent of seats allocated to British-style constituencies, 50 per cent to a national list.*

For the constituency seats, candidates stand and are elected on the same basis as that obtaining in Britain, i.e. one member, one vote. For the national-list seats, candidates are elected proportionally to the national votes for each party.

Each elector votes for a constituency MP and a national-list MP.
- *Parties need a qualifying minimum percentage of the national vote.*

To qualify for seats in the Parliament, even though it may have won constituency seats, a party must obtain a certain percentage of the national vote.
- *Constituency seats are 'topped up' with national-list seats.*

Each party has the constituency seats that it has gained topped up, to a number proportional to its national vote, with national list seats.

Supporters of the list-constituency system argue that:
- *Adaptability*

It would easily adapt to the existing British system.
- *It combines the virtues of constituency representation with those of proportional representation.*
- *The minimum quota would exclude small or purely local parties.*

Critics of the list-constituency system argue:
- *Overstretching MPs.*

Halving the number of constituencies would mean doubling their size, thus over-stretching the MPs who had to represent them.
- *It would create two classes of MP*

Those on the top of the national list, without serious constituency responsibilities, as the potential ministers – 'high-flyers' – and those who represented constituents.

List constituency system

Suppose a 650-member Parliament has 325 MPs elected for constituencies and 325 on the national list.

Suppose Labour receive 36 per cent of the total vote: they are entitled to 234 seats (36 per cent of 650 seats).

Now suppose that Labour have won 150 constituency seats, many of them in strongly Labour constituencies: they will receive 84 additional national seats to bring them to their representational strength of 36 per cent.

Let us now consider the rather different situation of the Liberal Democrats. Suppose that they obtain 20 per cent of the national vote. They are entitled to 130 seats (20 per cent of 650 seats). Due to the geographic dispersal of Liberal Democrat voters, however, they only win 40 constituency seats. They will therefore receive 90 national seats (more than the Labour party).

Has the time now come for Britain to change its electoral system to one which produces proportional representation? If so, which system should Britain adopt, and why? If not, why not?

Electoral systems and elections in perspective

You may by now have seen the connection between support for various electoral systems and the results which they are supposed to produce. Support for proportional representation in Britain is often tied up with support for centre-based coalitions. It may reflect a liking for consensus rather than confrontational politics. A liking for STV may spring from a desire to see more real personal choice for the voter, while support for the list system may reflect the belief that small parties should be represented. Support for the two-party status quo in Parliament goes with opposition to reform.

It would, however, be a mistake to attach too much importance to electoral systems as guarantees of certain outcomes. For a long time Britain's two-party Parliament was a reflection not just of its electoral system, but of the fact that nearly all of its voters voted for one of the two big parties. The system reinforced, but did not create, a political culture.

In the context of liberal democracy elections are important, but they do not define liberal democracy. They are only one element. A general election, after all, only tells us how the voters felt on one day every few years. The responsiveness of a government to Parliament and to the people, and the opportunities for participation, are very important. The quality of the dialogue between government and governed between elections is at least as important as the electoral system.

Different kinds of electoral system allow for different patterns of interest to be represented. In most constituencies British electors have to vote for one or other of the major parties if they are not to waste their votes. By contrast the various systems of proportional representation discussed in this chapter offer opportunities for election to a wider range of smaller parties representing smaller interest groups.

► The German Weimar Republic (1919–33) and the Fourth French Republic (1947–58) both had multi-party Parliaments, and frequent changes of government. These were not the result of proportional representation, since neither of those states had such a system. They were the product of deep and bitter differences within those societies.

 The activity on page 50 asked you to make a list of the cleavages in British society. Systems of proportional representation would allow political parties to crystallize around these differences of interest which would have some chance of being the foundation of electoral success. Which of these cleavages do you think might become important electorally if Britain changed to a system of proportional representation? For example do you think a 'Women's Party' might have a future?

CHAPTER SUMMARY

1 Democracy means 'rule by the people'.

2 In systems like Britain's, representative democracy with power held by an elected assembly on behalf of the people is the prevailing pattern.

3 The characteristics of a model liberal democracy are:
   - Free regular elections
   - Government responsible to an elected assembly
   - Maximum opportunities for citizens to participate in the political life of the country
   - Freedom of expression, movement and action within wide limits

4 The British electoral system has free, regular and open elections, with election of a 650-member Parliament on the basis of one member per constituency elected on a plurality of votes.

5 This system has come in for much criticism over the last twenty years. The under-representation of centre parties is, its critics claim, a serious problem now that British voters are less tied to a 'two class' voting loyalty.

6 Alternatives to the British system are the list, single transferable-vote (STV) and list-constituency (alternative member) systems. Each tends to produce different sorts of results.

7 Electoral systems may reinforce political cultures, but they cannot alter them.

STIMULUS MATERIAL

Read the press cutting (page 62) from the *Independent* and the commentary, and answer the following questions.

1 Reply to paragraphs four and five of the press cutting from the point of view of one who supports PR.

2 Apart from those reasons given by Mr Hattersley in the cutting, for what other reasons might a Labour supporter oppose PR?

3 Which 'section' or 'wing' of the Labour party is an opponent of PR likely to come from? Explain why.

4 Critically examine points 1 and 2 in the third paragraph of the commentary.

5 When the commentary refers to Centrism as an ideology, what is it referring to? Is the criticism in the last part of the commentary justified?

HATTERSLEY REJECTS CALL FOR LABOUR TO BACK PR

1   A call for Labour to support electoral reform was rejected yesterday by Roy Hattersley, the deputy leader of the party and the Shadow Home Secretary, *writes Colin Brown.*

2   Mr Hattersley, an implacable opponent of proportional representation for the Commons, said Labour would not set up a working party on electoral reform for the Commons. A working party was set up by the party's national executive to look at PR for other institutions, including a new upper chamber to replace the House of Lords.

3   'The party six months ago [at the annual conference] defeated the notion of Westminster PR by four to one. It would be a waste of time' Mr Hattersley said in the BBC 1 programme *On the Record*

4   'The democratic objection to PR is, it produces coalition governments. It produces the domination of coalition governments by small centre parties that cannot produce votes of their own.

5   It is no coincidence that Dr Owen wants PR, because it gives parties like his a status which they don't deserve and that is not democratic.'

6   The call for Labour to accept PR for Commons elections was made by Jeff Rooker, chairman of the Labour campaign for electoral reform. He told a meeting in Worthing, West Sussex, that Labour was on an unstoppable journey towards electoral reform. 'Slowly but surely, Labour is serving notice of an end to our bipartisan support with the Tories defending the first-past-the-post, winner-takes-all system', Mr Rooker said. 'Outside a small section of Labour Party membership it is now difficult to find anyone wanting a change of government willing to justify the present electoral system.'

The Independent
June 1990
Colin Brown, Political Correspondent

► In 1991 public opinion polls were showing 78 per cent of the electorate in favour of PR.

Commentary

Thank goodness one senior politician has dealt with this nonsense of PR. The whole PR argument is based on a fallacy – the fallacy that if you have a *Parliament* that mirrors the way people have voted you'll get a *Government* that is democratic, responsive, and all-round wonderful.

As Mr Hattersley rightly points out, what you'll get is a hung Parliament and Governments formed as the result of back-stair deals, with the tail wagging the dog – the smallest party in the coalition dictating to the largest.

As well as being undemocratic, coalitions are weak in two respects:

1 They go for weak solutions – when you've got people with strong opposing views on a number of topics, they will, in order to keep the coalition together, go for the one that no one cares passionately about, but no one violently objects to – a fudge!
2 People are loyal to parties – they grew up with them, worked with them. Loyalty to a coalition which has no historical, ideological or cultural unity will vanish at the first whiff of grapeshot – a crisis, or a difficult decision to be made.

Centre politicians who want PR condemn the ideology of Right and Left. But they have their own ideology – the ideology of Centrism. If we had PR, the Centre would tend to prevail in coalitions, and we'd be condemned to a succession of SLD'ish' Governments with a Centrist ideology – what's democratic about that?

Further reading: Chapter 4

Batchelor A. 1990. 'The Referendum – out-of-date device or useful instrument of Government?' *Talking Politics* Vol.3, No.1. A summary of the arguments about referenda.

Birch A.M. 1972. *Representation*. London: Macmillan. Useful for the discussion of the different meanings of political representation.

The following give the case for electoral reform in more detail.

Finer W.C. 1980. *Adversarial Politics and Electoral Reform*. London: Anthony Wigram.

Lakeman E. 1982. *Power to Elect: the Case for Proportional Representation*. London: Heinemann.

The following are good up-dates on the question of electoral reform.

Drucker H. *et al* (eds). 1986. *Developments in British Politics 2*, Chapter 3, pp 78–82. London: Macmillan.

Dunleavy P. *et al* (eds). 1990. *Developments in British Politics 3*, Chapter 3. London: Macmillan.

For a useful selection on political culture see

Burch M. & Moran M. 1987. *Modern British Politics*. Manchester: Manchester University Press.

Now you have reached the end of this chapter, turn back to the beginning, look at the objectives and make sure that you have achieved each of them.

(5) *British political parties*

Media Watch
For this chapter you should look out for news coverage of the major events in the party political calendars, especially party conferences, and for stories about conflicts and struggles within the parties.

Chapter objectives

By the end of this chapter you should
■ be able to describe the nature and role of political parties in a liberal democracy

■ be conversant with the main events in the history and development of the Labour, Conservative, Liberal, Social Democratic and Liberal Democratic Parties, and how these events have shaped modern parties

■ be able to describe the ideologies of the parties and their internal ideological divisions

■ be able to discuss the structural features affecting policy making, decision making, and management in the Labour and Conservative Parties

■ be able to describe the policies and aims of the Scottish and Welsh nationalist parties, and the smaller parties on the extreme left and right of politics in England, Scotland and Wales.

■ be able to define and use the following terms: political party, constituency party, party agent, aggregation, manifesto, ideology, beliefs, values, policies, affiliation, de-selection, entryism.

► Pressure groups, e.g. CND, have on occasion put up candidates in parliamentary elections. However, this was intended to take advantage of the electoral campaign to make propaganda rather than to take over power.

Pressure groups are dealt with in Chapter 7.

(Political parties in Northern Ireland are dealt with in Chapter 13).

WHAT ARE POLITICAL PARTIES?

A political party may be defined as *an organized and recognizable group which puts itself forward as a unity and seeks support in order to gain power to govern the society in which it operates.*

There are two main kinds of group organized to exert political influence: *pressure groups* and *political parties*. Political parties differ from pressure groups in that, first, they seek to take over government rather than to influence it. Second, their aims are *general*, purporting to cover the whole range of political life, rather than one aspect of it. They offer to take on responsibility for law and order, policy, economic policy and social policy. In a liberal democracy, this means organizing to win mass support and attempting to win elections by securing people's votes.

There may be parties (fascist or revolutionary socialist) which, paradoxically, reject the liberal democratic system, but operate within it to pursue their aims. For example, the National Socialist Party in Germany in the 1930s secured power through the liberal democratic system and soon abolished liberal democracy in Germany.

The need to organize in order to secure masses of votes has helped to determine the structure of modern political parties. The history of the British Conservative Party is a good example of this. Until 1832, when the electoral system was first changed nationally, the Party's predecessor, the Tory Party, was a loosely constituted network of like-minded politicians connected by family, common beliefs or financial links, and their supporters. Loosely centred on the Junior Carlton Club in London, it had almost no formal organization.

After 1832 Registration Societies linked to the Junior Carlton Club were set up to insure that sympathetic voters got on to the new register of electors. The Reform Act of 1867 gave the vote to some

---

The landmarks in franchise reform were:

1832 Reform Act: passed after much demonstration and many clashes between demonstrators and the authorities. The Act:
  i standardized the criteria for voting in all areas with a property qualification which excluded all but the fairly well-off and excluded all women.
  ii gave large industrial cities such as Manchester and Birmingham representation in Parliament.
  iii abolished most of the very small ('pocket') and corrupt ('rotten') boroughs with only a handful of electors which had helped political leaders secure their own candidates as MPs.
  iv introduced a register of electors. This led to the formation of Tory 'Registration Societies' in local constituencies – the fore-runners of today's constituency parties.

1867 Reform Act: passed by a Tory government: extended the franchise qualification so that large numbers of urban working-class men who were tenants or owners of houses gained the vote.
After losing the subsequent election the Tories renamed themselves 'Conservatives' and re-organized themselves into an efficient electioneering machine. The Whigs followed suit, renaming themselves 'Liberals'.

1872 Secret Ballot Act: introduced voting in secret. This was previously opposed by the Liberal Leader Gladstone on the grounds that it would prevent 'proper influence' from being brought to bear on voters. Once people could vote in secret it became much more important for parties to woo support through electioneering – rather than through threats and bribery.

1884 Reform Act: result of a deal (the Arlington House Compact) between the parties. This extended the vote to male working-class householders in the countryside in exchange for a re-distribution of seats which benefited the Liberals.
The electorate was still only about 4 million strong.

1918 Representation of the People Act: for the first time virtually all men over 21 were given the right to vote, and (after a long and sometimes bitter campaign by two pressure groups) women over 30 obtained the vote.
A redistribution of seats removed a strong southern bias from the system. MPs were paid a salary, helping the Labour Party. The huge increase in the working-class vote made it possible for the Labour Party to become a major political force. While the Liberals seemed to retain support from older working-class voters, many of the new voters turned to the Labour Party.

1927: Voting age for women reduced to 21 years.

1948: Established the Boundary Commission; a machinery for keeping the relationship between constituency boundaries and the number of voters under review, and for adjusting boundaries to create constituencies of roughly equal size every ten years.

1968: Voting age reduced to 18.

▶ Universal franchise and main political parties
The development of the Conservative Party is a good example of the way in which political parties have developed in response to changes in the franchise.

Review –
Political parties

1 A political party is a collective organization aiming to take general power.

2 British mass parties which have developed since 1867 have common characteristics:

- A strong leadership
- A central bureaucracy which 'runs' the party.
- Ward and constituency organizations whose most important function is the selection of candidates for election.
- A parliamentary organization – the 'whips' – designed to maintain disciplined adherence to the leadership's line.
- A system of 'agents' providing links between centre and constituencies.
- An annual conference and other means by which the 'lay' membership have their say.

sections of the male working class in big cities. The Tories were defeated at the subsequent election and under Disraeli they set about organizing the challenge of mass voting. They renamed themselves the Conservative Party and set up a strong central office to run the Party machine under the control of the leader, and a system of paid political agents to encourage the development of constituency associations within a National Union of Conservative Associations. This was designed to encourage participation, but leave power and policy making in the hands of the leadership.

Political parties and franchise reform

The history of political parties has to be understood in terms of the development of the mass electorate. Early political parties were simply cliques of people who knew each other and could raise support by speaking or writing to the handful of people who had the vote. As the vote was given to a larger and larger proportion of the population so it became necessary for parties to develop efficient ways of involving large numbers of activists, and of marketing their policies.

 Make notes to explain how the development of modern political parties relates to the growth in the franchise.

The organization of British parties

The larger British parties are organized to take power by forming a government. This means winning majorities in 326 or more of the 650 constituencies.

The need to do this leads to common structural characteristics:

Strong leadership
A strong leader is put forward as a potential Prime Minister, who will pick his/her Government from amongst elected MPs with the party label.

A central bureaucracy
An office staffed with full-time employees who run the party's finances and administer it from day-to-day, and exercise control over the constituency parties.

Constituency organization

At local level, ward parties based on local council constituencies send representatives to constituency parties, based on the area for which the MP is elected. Run mainly by 'amateur' lay members, the local organization carries out the following important functions:

- The selection of candidates for local and parliamentary elections
- The recruitment of supporters
- Raising funds
- Providing a means of party participation at local level for activists
- Maintaining a continuous presence locally.

Most British parties at local level are subject to strong central control. Although selected at local level, candidates have to receive the approval of the centre, in the form of the Leader in the Conservative Party and the National Executive Committee in the Labour Party.

Organizations enabling lay members to participate at national level

All the major parties have annual conferences, though as we shall see their powers and functions differ from party to party. The Conservative Party has the national union of lay members. Each party has lay organizations at regional level.

A Parliamentary organization

The larger political parties have a disciplined parliamentary organization, where the emphasis is on the leadership. MPs, though constitutionally independent, usually accept (sometimes grudgingly) the 'party whip' – the name given to party officials who try to ensure attendance and adherence to a common line. Especially important is the job of turning out a near unanimous body of support for the leadership's line at Parliamentary *divisions* (votes). The purpose of the exercise is to present to the public a single, disciplined Government party or 'alternative' government.

Links between national and local parties

These are in the form of agents of the central body, 'looking after' the constituency party.

THE ROLE OF MASS PARTIES IN A LIBERAL DEMOCRACY

It is said that political parties perform a function of *aggregation*. They do this in five main ways.

First, they provide a *national team* for which the voter can express his/her preference. Supported by a party machine and a sufficient number of MPs, this team can offer itself as a potential Government, with its leader as Prime Minister and about a hundred of its MPs as Ministers in charge of the various aspects of Government.

Second, they provide a *focus of support* for values and ideas and loyalty. While Conservative, Socialist, and centrist values may sometimes seem obscured by the actions and statements of party leaders, they are there.

As we shall see in the next chapter, political parties provide for some voters not just an 'instrumental' means of achieving certain objectives, but a means of expressing a more general loyalty to social class, neighbourhood and family.

Third, they provide a *programme of policies*. The term usually used for this is a *manifesto* – a statement, in advance of an election, of what changes the party intends to make and what values and policies it would pursue if it took over government. The doctrine of the 'mandate' – the idea that parties establish authority for the realization of their programme by winning general elections – is, as we shall see, subject to many doubts and qualifications. However, party manifestos have been a feature of British general elections since the

► Political parties *aggregate* by:
- providing a national team
- providing a focus of support and loyalty for those who subscribe to particular ideals or values
- providing a programme of policies
- providing opportunities for individuals to participate in the political process
- providing political socialization.

You can see the value of *aggregation* by imagining what things would be like in its absence. Under our single-member constituency system, you would be voting for an individual, to represent your geographical constituency – one MP out of 650. How would you decide how to vote without a party label? On the basis of personality perhaps, or electoral promises, or a mixture of both. But since your representative would be one isolated individual amongst 650, how much would the promises or the personality count?

Tamworth manifesto of 1834, in which Peel committed the Tory Party to acceptance of the 1832 Reform Act, even though the Tories had opposed its passage in 1832.

Recent research suggests that issues and the position of the parties on them are increasingly the most important factor in determining the choice of party for many voters.

Last, they provide a means of *participation* and *political socialization*. Almost anyone can join one of the larger political parties at constituency level, and involve himself/herself to various degrees and levels, from merely paying dues through occasional help at election time to seeking candidature for election to Parliament.

Socialization is a process of learning about socially acceptable values and behaviour. It starts in infancy. Political socialization, or learning about the political world, is inevitably affected by the existence of national parties which seek to influence the way people think about politics. (It will also be affected by the attitudes of family and friends, the media and by direct personal experience).

 Make notes on the major functions played by political parties in a liberal democracy.

(ACT) Consider one of the Conservative Party's manifestos since 1979. (*Keesing's Diary of Contemporary Events* provides a summary.)

1 What basic values does it emphasize?

2 What specific commitments to action does it make in major areas of policy?

3 How far has the Conservative Government, following the election for which you have considered the manifesto, realized parts (1) and (2) above?

You will find a copy of *Keesing's* in any large public library.

Ideology and policy

Ideology

One of the *Oxford Dictionary*'s definitions of ideology provides us with a useful clue to this concept: 'Ideas at the basis of some economic or political theory or system'. The important word for our purposes is 'basis'. At the base certain values and beliefs differentiate and define British political parties.

These may not always be obvious from the actions and policies of the parties when in office or opposition, which may take all manner of twists and turns, but they form the basis of many policies, and serve to give a sense of common identity to party members. Thus the intention announced in the Conservative Party's manifesto in 1979 of 'rolling back the frontiers of the state' expressed a fundamental belief in market forces and individual choice as the basis of economic and social policy.

► In descending order of generality one could arrange *beliefs*, fundamental faiths, or things that one believes to be true; *values*, things that one considers important as a consequence of one's beliefs; and *policies*, commitments to specific aims and objectives arising from beliefs and values. Thus a policy of giving the British police forces more powers, equipment and personnel might proceed from a high value set on law and order which in turn might flow from a belief in original sin and the fundamental wickedness of people not subject to control.

Policy

Policy is more specific. It has been described as 'the authoritative allocation of values' (Eastwood) – the use of political power to translate value into action. Policy is usually expressed as a set of aims and objectives. This definition emphasizes that policies usually have values behind them. Many of the policies of the Thatcher Governments were attempts to express the values of private ownership and the free market. Examples of such values being authoritatively translated into action were the policy obliging local authorities to offer council tenants the choice of buying their houses, and the policy allowing groups of council tenants to vote for their estates to pass into the hands of private landlords or trusts.

THE CONSERVATIVE PARTY

Conservative ideology

To define 'Conservatism' is no easy task, since many Conservatives would define themselves as free of the shackles of 'grand theory' and ideology and able to respond to the twists and turns of history in the most practical manner, without trying to push history in a preconceived direction. That way, many Conservatives would claim, lies the kind of totalitarian system exemplified by the Soviet Union under Stalin. A leading Conservative academic (Michael Oakeshott) claimed that 'In political life, then, men sail a boundless sea; there is neither harbour for shelter nor floor for anchorage, neither starting place nor appointed destination. The enterprise is to keep afloat on an even keel.'

Conservative leaderships have exhibited this pragmatism in the past 150 years in what look like confusing twists and turns of policy. Initially opposed to the free market individualism of the Liberals in the nineteenth century, they seem lately to be its advocates. Although opposed to the 'welfare-state' and public-ownership measures of the Labour Government (1945–50), they preserved most of them during their continuous period of office from 1951 to 1964. Known as the party which most vigorously supported the British Empire, it was nevertheless Conservative Prime Ministers who did most to give independent rule to former colonies, and bring about its disintegration. Behind this pragmatism, however, some consistant elements can be detected.

The imperfectibility of humanity

Behind much of the optimism of Liberals and Socialists lies the assumption that humankind is perfectible, or at least capable of being substantially improved by the right sort of society and the right sort of political system. Scratch a Conservative and below the surface you are likely to encounter a good deal of scepticism about this notion, and alarm at the possible consequences of pursuing it. As one leading Conservative has put it, Conservatives 'believe in original sin'.

► Michael Oakeshott (1901–1990), was professor at the London School of Economics from 1951–69. The 'boundless sea' analogy was used in his inaugural lecture in 1951. Oakeshott was profoundly suspicious of rational blueprints for changing society, believing them to be a distortion or abbreviation of a tradition. In his view a society's history and tradition was the only proper starting point for the understanding of how it worked, and how it should change. Many contemporary Conservatives would agree with him.

► Burke attacked the French Revolutionaries for wanting to destroy the old 'body politick' and replace it with one of their own making. He claimed instead that if the body politick was ailing it should be approached as one would approach the body of a sick loved one; with a desire to preserve the body by healing the illness, rather than a desire to destroy its life.

Emphasis on order

In its opposition to nineteenth-century Liberalism, the Conservative Party emphasized the dire consequences of the doctrine of 'individual liberty' for the cohesion of society. To this day Conservative manifestos place a stronger emphasis on 'law and order', with greater spending on police and armed forces, thansocialist manifestos.

Suspicion of radical change

The record of British Conservative Governments would not lead you to the conclusion that Conservatives are against change. They have been responsible for many quite sweeping changes. This, however, would be seen by most Conservatives as change in order to preserve what is good in the existing order. You may wonder how this suspicion of change, and inclination to preserve the status quo, applied to Mrs Thatcher's Governments (1979–90). She was described as a 'radical' Prime Minister, and did not reject the label. From her statements on the subject, it would seem that she saw the period 1945 to 1979 as an abnormal period, in which 'consensus' policies brought about inflation and stagnation. Her programme, therefore, was needed to restore Britain to a healthy capitalist economy, and a strong and free policy. Interestingly, there are those among Conservatives who feel that she is not really a Conservative at all, but a nineteenth-century laissez-faire Liberal!

Acceptance of hierarchy

While Conservatives might approve of *equality of opportunity*, few would accept the idea that all people are equal, or are entitled to equal treatment. Some people are brighter, luckier, more able or more hard-working than others. That the more able should constitute an élite within society, and should be recognized and rewarded, is appropriate and necessary to make the best of their talents.

The party of economic freedom?

The Conservative Party receives much of its financial backing through donation from private firms. It receives the support of most of the business community, including small, sole proprietors. In the last decade, the leadership has emphasized the value of the free market, private property and enterprise.

Internally the Conservative Party is divided on how much control the state should exert over the economy. In the past Conservative governments have put reigns on the free market when unrestrained market forces seemed likely to create large divisions of wealth and poverty, or have damaging environmental effects. Today the so-called 'Wet' members of the Party continue to support policies which limit the freedom of companies. However the ruling group within the Party, associated first with Mrs Thatcher and now with John Major are very reluctant to interfere with private enterprise.

► 'Interventionist' economic policies are those which involve the Government in using taxation and spending not just to raise money and spend it but, by influencing the level of effective demand in the economy, to steer it towards certain goals – e.g. full employment. This type of policy also supports the idea of more direct government intervention – e.g. fixing minimum wages, giving grants to 'inner-city' projects in order to revive the economies of those areas. Opponents from the right would rather let the free market take care of these matters.

The organization of the Conservative Party

The ideology and the history of the Conservative Party place a strong emphasis on leadership, and this is reflected in the power structure of the party.

The Leader

Since 1965 the Leader has been elected by Conservative MPs. Before then the Leader 'emerged' as the result of consultations behind closed doors between the Party elders.

The present system is as follows. To be elected on the first ballot, a candidate must receive not just a majority of votes but a 15 per cent lead. In the second ballot, previous candidates may drop out, and new candidates may enter the list. At the second ballot a simple majority will suffice: if this is not forthcoming all but the top three drop out, and the alternative-vote system is used. In this voters place candidates in order of preference, and, if no-one has a majority of first-choice votes, the candidate with the least first-choice votes is eliminated and his or her votes go to the second choice on those papers.

Once in office, Conservative leaders, whether as Prime Minister or as Leader of the Opposition, enjoy considerable power and, usually, strong loyalty. Such loyalty, however, may be tempered by the expectation that the Leader should be an electoral asset. Conservatives do not easily forgive losers. It is almost certain that Eden would have been ousted after the failure of the Suez operation in 1956 had he not retired on the grounds of ill health. The recently appointed Lord Home went quickly after the narrow election defeat of 1964, and Edward Heath was despatched after the defeat of 1974. There were strong indications that Mrs Thatcher might have faced pressure to go in 1981 had her popularity not received the boost of the successful Falklands operation.

► See page 73 for further discussion on divisions within the Conservative Party.

► Although since 1975 Conservative leaders have been liable to annual re-election, Mrs Thatcher faced no challenge until 1989 when a back-bencher, Sir Anthony Meyer, put himself forward as a 'stalking-horse' candidate – a candidate who will not win but may on the first round receive enough votes to precipitate a second round, at which more serious candidates will enter the ring. He failed to secure enough votes. In November 1990 Michael Heseltine made a more serious challenge, which resulted in the election of John Major as leader after a second-round election from which Mrs Thatcher was persuaded to withdraw.

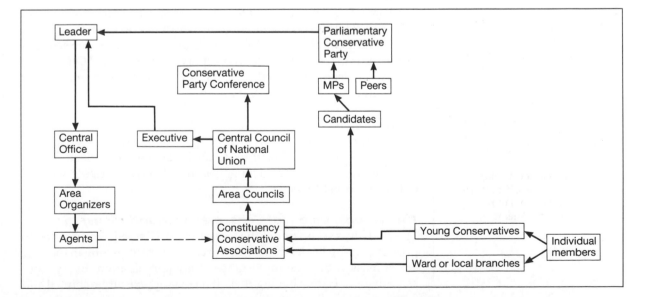

The Conservative Leader has considerable powers, in particular:

- *The Leader is responsible for policy*. In consultation with colleagues, he or she draws up the manifesto. Whether in office or opposition, the Conservative policy is the Leader's policy.
- *The Leader appoints the Party Chair*. Central Office, the organization of full-time workers who 'run' the Party, has at its head the Party Chairperson and a Vice Chair who attends to day-to-day matters. Both are directly responsible to the Leader.
- *The Leader appoints shadow spokespersons*. As Prime Minister, both Labour and Conservative Leaders appoint their Ministers. The Conservative Leader, however, also appoints 'shadow' ministers when the party is in opposition.

The Leaders of both big parties exercise great power when in office, since they gain the powers attached to the office of Prime Minister. However, the Conservative Leader is freer from constraints than the Labour Leader when in opposition, and to some extent, when in office. For instance:

- *The Leader may exercise direct control over the party bureaucracy*. The Conservative leader appoints the head of Central Office, whereas its equivalent in the Labour Party, the National Executive Committee, is elected by Annual Conference.
- *The Leader appoints Shadow Ministers in Opposition*. The Labour Leader must draw from a Parliamentary Committee elected by the Parliamentary Party.
- *The Leader makes policy*. So to some extent do Labour leaders, but when in opposition they have to pay far more attention to Conference policies, and consult the National Executive Committee.
- *The Leader is elected by the Parliamentary Party*. (The Labour Leader is elected by an electoral college which includes affiliated trade unions and constituency parties, as well as MPs. See page 80.)

Central Office

The Party bureaucracy looks after organization, finance, research and publicity. It trains and finances agents who liaise between the constituency and Central Office. While candidates for election are selected locally, this takes place under the supervision of Central Office who maintain a list of approved candidates (though constituencies may adopt others, subject to central approval).

Area councils

Each area council covers an area of approximately fifty constituencies. They have a paid staff and consist of members elected from constituency associations acting as a middle layer between Central Office and constituency.

The National Union (of Conservative Associations)

This body was set up under the leadership of Disraeli, who wanted to preserve strong leadership of the Party, while recognizing in the new era of mass voting the importance of lay participation. Every Conservative association belongs to it. It has a large executive council and

▶ Party Agents. Agents are the official minders of the constituencies on behalf of the central organization. They advise and help the constituency party on matters of finance, administration interpretation of party rules and running election campaigns. They are the liaison lines between the central and local organizations. All Conservative and most Labour agents are full-time officials. The Conservative Party maintains a training school for agents.

an executive committee, with sub-committees on particular policy areas.

Annual Conference

At Conference representatives of the constituency associations, the Young Conservative Organization, the Conservative Trade Unionists and the women's organizations meet the 'professionals' – Central Office officials, MPs, and above all the Leader.

The Conservative Party conference is just that – a conference. It does not act as a policy-making body. The Leader is under no constitutional obligation to take any notice of its deliberations (until fairly recently, the Leader did not even attend the formal conference, but addressed a 'rally'. Members do not see themselves as mandated delegates, the debates are heavily 'stage managed' and motions are usually framed so that nearly everybody can support them.

But the Conservative Party conference is not just the mutual admiration society which some critics have labelled it. It is an important media event, in which the Leader's popularity with the party activists is assessed. It gives activists a chance to meet their Leader and express themselves. From the leadership's point of view, conference is a valuable opportunity to assess the feelings of those upon whom the Party depends for the unpaid, unglamourous, but necessary work in the country.

Constituency associations

The constituency associations are controlled by an executive council, elected from ward and district parties. The selection of candidates for Parliamentary and local government election is from a short list drawn up by a sub-committee of the executive council, at a selection conference of the executive council. A meeting of the association membership ratifies the decision. Finally the decision must be ratified by Central Office, if the candidate is not from Central Office's list.

Groups within the Conservative Party

The Conservative Party is not riven with internal quarrelling, at least not publicly, to the extent that the Labour Party often is, but as you would expect of any large party, it has its sub-groups. Some of them which have a degree of formal organization represent the 'right' of the Party – advocating free market economics, strong law and order policies, more privatization, including the encouragement of private health and education, and suspicion of Liberal ideas like that of a multi-racial society.

Others incline to the 'left' of the Party – One-Nation Tories, in the Disraelian tradition. They advocate some government intervention in the free market, a welfare policy which provides adequate social security for the old, sick and unemployed, and a tendency to 'interventionist' rather than free-market economics.

On the right are the Monday Club, which is well known for its opposition to new commonwealth immigration, and its dislike of equal opportunities legislation, and the Selsdon Group which is for

One-Nation Toryism

The term One-Nation Toryism is derived from a phrase used by Benjamin Disraeli. Disraeli (1804–81) took over the leadership of the Tory Party from Peel when it was badly split over the Corn Laws. His great contribution was to re-unite and rebuild the Party, laying the basis of its modern organization. He also persuaded the party to accept the 1867 Reform Bill which gave the vote to many urban working-class men. Disraeli was a novelist. In his novel *Sybil*, a character is given a Disraeli-like speech in which he refers to Britain as 'Two Nations': the rich and the poor. Disraeli believed that the Conservative Party should combine respect for tradition with policies that would unite the nation, rich and poor alike (and hence gain the trust and the votes of the poor). He favoured policies which would look after the welfare of the poor.

Review – The Conservative Party

- The Conservative Party is the oldest party. It streamlined its organization after 1867, when the franchise was greatly expanded, to cope with the demands of mass politics.

- Conservative ideology is difficult to define, since Conservatives tend to eschew ideology and show a suspicion for 'blueprints' for the future. They claim to respect what exists and is working, but are highly selective as to which British traditions they seek to preserve. Though it has not always done what private enterprise wants, it is regarded as the Party of business and is supported financially by industrial and commercial firms.

- Conservative Party structure is oriented towards the Leader who is elected by Conservative MPs. The Conference is an occasion for activists to express their views, and a 'media event', but not a policy-making body.

- The body responsible for running the Party outside Parliament is Central Office. The Chair of the Party (the head of the extra-Parliamentary party) is appointed by the Leader.

- The National Union is the body representing the constituency activists at national level. It has a consultative, not a policy making, role.

- The Conservative Party has groups within it representing different brands of Conservatism, but they are seldom as troublesome to the Leadership as their Labour counterparts.

---

the free market and low taxation. Additionally, there are a number of 'research' groups committed to developing policies which will promote free-market economics. These include the Centre for Policy Studies, the Institute for Economic Affairs and the Adam Smith Institute.

On the left, the One-Nation Tories (christened 'Wets' by Mrs Thatcher – the name has stuck) are represented by the Tory Reform Group, and to some extent the Bow Group, although this claims to be open to all views.

 Take any three important features of Conservative ideology, and match them with examples of the policies pursued by the Thatcher/Major governments.

Identify four groups within the Conservative Party and what makes them distinctive.

THE LABOUR PARTY

In considering the ideology and the structure of the Labour Party, it is helpful to look at its origins at the beginning of this century, since many of the events of its early years have left their mark.

Whereas the Conservative Party already existed as a parliamentary and extra-parliamentary group when the franchise was progressively widened (in the last quarter of the nineteenth century and the first quarter of the twentieth) and adapted itself to this change, the Labour Party was the *product* of the change. Activists in the working-class and trade-union movement were concerned that working-class voters should be represented by working-class MPs. The barriers to this were, first, the belief by many voters and Liberal Party members that working men were not fitted for such a role; second, the fact that MPs in those days received no salary and a working-class MP would have to give up his job. And third, the fact that large sections of the urban working-class voters were loyal to the Liberal Party, and many of their community leaders were Liberals, but the active section of the Liberal Party was mainly middle class.

Money to sponsor MPs came from the trade unions who were concerned that the proprietors' interests were well represented in Parliament whereas theirs were not. The first working men to become MPs were sponsored by the National Union of Miners (NUM). Initially these 'Lib-Labs' were adopted by constituency Liberal parties. It was partly from the problems to which this arrangement gave rise that the impetus to create the Labour Party arose.

Some leading working-class politicians failed to get selected by local Liberal parties. There was, in any case, doubt about the extent to which a middle-class party committed to the doctrine of free trade would serve the interests of the working class. While the NUM was relatively happy with the 'Lib-Lab' arrangement since it served them reasonably well, other unions, especially the newer unions of unskilled workers, got nothing from the union link, and were prepared to support a new party. A break-through came in 1892 when Keir Hardie stood as working-class candidate for West Ham, not sponsored by the Liberal Party, and was elected.

While the trade union movement provided the potential funds and mass support, a number of relatively small political groups were to co-provide the ideology and policies.

These small groups were:

The Independent Labour Party, founded in 1893, based upon Bradford and publishing a lively and influential newspaper, *The Clarion*.

The Social Democratic Federation, founded in 1881 – a small but active Marxist group, and

The Fabians, founded in 1884, a group of middle-class intellectuals and writers, including Sydney and Beatrice Webb and George Bernard Shaw, who believed that a socialist society could be achieved by radical but peaceful and piecemeal reform.

As the result of all these pressures, a special TUC conference in 1899

► Significantly, some of those who subsequently became leaders or leading members of the Labour Party, tried and failed to secure adoption as 'Lib-Labs' voted (quite narrowly) in favour of a further conference of interested unions and political groups to set up what became the basis of the modern Labour Party. The result was the *Labour Representation Committee*, founded in 1900, answerable to an annual Conference for the selection and promotion of independent Labour candidates for election to Parliament.

At this point it should be noted:

- That the Labour Party started as a conference of diverse groups. Conference still, in theory at least, occupies a sovereign position within the Party.
- That the trade union movement provided the money and most of the membership of the original Party. This is still reflected in the Party's power structure.
- That from the beginning the Party was a mixture of pragmatists, seeing the Party as a means of obtaining representation of union interests in Parliament, and ideologists, seeing it as a means of achieving a socialist society. The tension between adherents of the two approaches continues to characterize the Party's internal debate.

The 1918 constitution

Due largely to an electoral 'deal' with the Liberals in 1906, the Labour Party secured 26 MPs. It did not significantly increase its representation until after 1919. A large proportion of the working-class electorate remained loyal to the Liberal Party. Until then the Party was made up of affiliated groups. In order to attract the support of a new and expanded working-class electorate a new constitution was devised providing for individual as well as affiliated membership. This constitution also provided a statement of the party's ideological aims.

Clause IV of the constitution states as an aim:

'To secure for workers by hand and brain the fruits of their labour by the Common Ownership of the Means of Production and Distribution'

('and Exchange' was added later.)

This clause has remained in the Party's constitution, despite attempts in the 1950s by Gaitskell, the Leader of the Party, to have it removed. We could argue at length about the meaning of 'Common Ownership' – it does not necessarily mean ownership of industry by monolithic state corporations. However, whatever our definition, Clause IV represents a commitment to socialism, that is the socialization of the means of production, distribution and exchange, rather than its control by private ownership for profit, and production for social goals rather than for the private market. It represents one strand of thought and commitment within the British Labour Party – that of the pursuit of socialism, which has frequently clashed with the other short-term aims.

► A prophetic *Punch* cartoon of the time showed a small horse and buggy labelled 'Liberal Party' giving a lift to a figure labelled 'Labour' which is so huge that it threatens to crush or tip over the buggy. The weedy driver is saying 'Welcome aboard'.

Labour Party ideology

Socialism

Marxism, with its prediction that capitalism should and will be overthrown by a working-class revolution has had some influence on the British Labour Party, but not much. The peaceful achievement of socialism through the ballot box and piecemeal reform, or 'gradualism' has been much more influential in the British Labour Party. Figures such as Robert Owen and William Morris had great hopes for the transformation of society through the voluntary formation of cooperative ways of producing and distributing goods.

Equality

The 1979 manifesto of the Party spoke of the need for a 'permanent and irreversible shift' of wealth and power away from the rich and powerful towards the poorer, less privileged, members of society. Municipal socialism in the 1980s in some inner London Boroughs, Manchester, Liverpool and Sheffield, emphasizes the promotion of more equality through more opportunities for the exploited and underprivileged. A powerful belief in the promotion of greater social justice by shifting resources and life chances to the less privileged remains a characteristic of the British Labour Party.

Social welfare

One of the abiding achievements of the Labour Government of 1945–1950 was the creation of the world's first completely free and universally available state health service. This, and the Party's policies on education, social services and state benefits, reflects a belief that the state should, by providing benefits, ensure that at least no-one falls below a certain level as far as basic requirements for health and welfare are concerned, and at best welfare measures can be used to promote greater equality.

The Labour Party do not have a monopoly on this idea. The first welfare-state measures were introduced by the Liberal Government of 1906–1914, and the author of the report that led to many of the post–1945 reforms was a Liberal (Beveridge). Until 1979 post-war Conservative governments and Labour governments alike were favourably disposed towards the welfare state and even after 1979 One-Nation Tories remain broadly in favour. Nonetheless, the Labour Party has been the strongest advocate of state provided welfare.

Trade unionism

The relationship between the trade union part of the movement and the Parliamentary Party has not always been completely harmonious. However, as a Party to which most of the big unions are affiliated, it has done most to acknowledge and promote trade union rights.

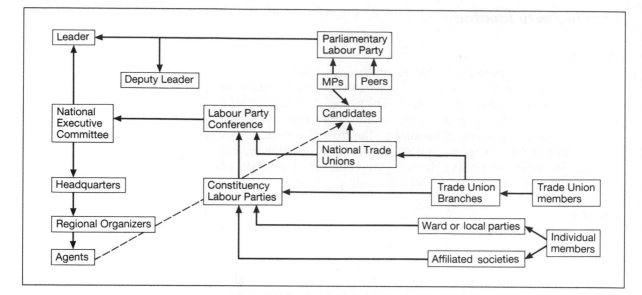

The structure of the Labour Party

Conference
'Conference' is made up of delegates from:
- Affiliated trade unions
- Constituency Labour Parties
- Other affiliated organizations (co-ops, socialist societies)
- MPs

Voting is on the 'card-vote' system, in which delegates vote according to the number of affiliated members in the organization which they represent. Because the number of members through trade union affiliation vastly exceeds the number of members in constituency parties and other organizations, trade union votes constitute about five-sixths of the votes cast. The five biggest unions have between them a majority of Conference votes. Different delegations representing a single large trade union usually cast their votes as a block – that is, all vote one way. Unions, however do not vote identically with one another. The differing blocks of two big unions may cancel one another out.

Of late, there has been discussion between the Party Leadership and leaders of some of the unions about reducing the influence of the 'union block vote', but no conclusion has been reached. Since the five-sixths of the vote reflects the fact that the Labour Party, always up against it financially, receives five-sixth of its income from trade union affiliation fees, this is a delicate question!

The functions of Conference

1 *Guardian of the Party constitution.*
As the sovereign body of the Party, Conference is the body which controls the Party's rules. A two-thirds majority of Conference votes is needed to change the constitution. On two occasions since 1945,

Conference has been the scene of a titanic struggle over rules. On both occasions the argument about the Party's constitution was a focus for essentially ideological arguments between opposing wings of the Party.

In 1955, the Leader Hugh Gaitskell and his 'moderate' supporters attempted to remove Clause IV from the constitution, claiming that it was no longer relevant to Labour's policies and spoilt its 'image' with voters. After a bitter battle between revisionists (who would dispense with clause IV) and fundamentalists (who would not), Gaitskell failed to secure the necessary majority.

In 1980–81, in the aftermath of defeat in the 1979 election a number of left-wing groups within the Party, under the umbrella of the Labour Co-ordinating Committee, sought to change the Party's constitution. They wanted to make the Parliamentary Leadership, the Parliamentary Party and a future Labour Government more responsible to Conference and constituency parties. They proposed that:

- The Leader should be elected by an electoral college at Conference, made of trade union votes, constituency party votes and MPs, rather than the current practice of election of the Leader by Labour MPs.
- There should be mandatory re-selection of Labour candidates for Parliamentary election. This means that Labour MPs have to submit themselves for approval by their constituency parties, rather than carrying on until they are opposed.
- The National Executive Committee (NEC), which is elected by Conference, should have the final say as to what goes into the Party's manifesto for a general election, rather than the Parliamentary Leadership.

At the specially convened 'Wembley' Conference in 1981 the Left got two out of three of the changes it sought – the electoral college and mandatory re-selection.

1981 was a significant year for several reasons. First, four ex-ministers in Labour governments, Shirley Williams, David Owen, Roy Jenkins and Bill Rodgers announced that, because trade union voters had 40 per cent of the electoral college vote for the Leadership, the Party had been delivered into the hands of the trade unions.

Next, it brought to a head a quarrel that had been rumbling along since the party had been created – the relationship between the wider movement of activists in the country and the Parliamentary Party, particularly when that Party was in office.

Finally, while internal divisions were not the only reason why Labour lost votes in subsequent by-elections, and disastrously in the 1983 general election, it was a factor in these defeats.

2 *Conference as maker of policy resolutions.*
The Labour Party Conference, unlike its Conservative counterpart, considers motions submitted from affiliated bodies, usually 'composited' (groups of motions put together) and amendments to those motions, with a view to changing policy.

To what extent such resolutions commit the Parliamentary Party, or

► Under Clause V of the Labour Party's constitution, Conference can by a two-thirds majority insist that a policy resolution become part of a future manifesto, but not when it should be included.

▶ It is acknowledged by supporters and even, grudgingly, by opponents within the Party, that Kinnock has 'turned the Party round' in many areas, while consolidating his position as Leader. In particular, he persuaded the Party to abandon unilateral nuclear disarmament, which was regarded as an election loser, to become more pro-European Community, to avoid commitments to nationalization and retain some of the current controls on trade unions. He made a determined and partially successful attempt to purge 'Militant' supporters from positions of authority in the Party. This has drawn the accusation of unprincipled opportunism from some left-wingers.

even more crucially a future Labour Government, is part of the continuous argument that has gone on in the party since its early years. In Labour Party constitutional theory, Conference would seem to be the boss. The constitution gives no power to a 'Leader'.

In political practice, however, and in British constitutional theory, the Prime Minister leads the Government and the Leader of the Opposition leads the opposition. On a number of issues, including unilateral nuclear disarmament, Britain's continued membership of the European Community, Britain's attitude to the United States' forces' presence in Vietnam in the 1960s, the extension of public ownership, Conferences have had one policy, and Labour Governments another.

3 Conference and the election of the NEC.

The body that runs the Labour Party outside Parliament – performing functions similar to those of Conservative Central Office – is the National Executive Committee (NEC). It has members elected by the various groups within Conference, and is elected by Conference delegates, as follows:

    12 members elected by trade union delegates
    7 members elected by constituency parties
    1 member elected by other affiliated organizations
    5 women elected by Conference as a whole
    The Party Treasurer elected by Conference as a whole
    Leader and Deputy elected by electoral college

Since 1981, the Leader and Deputy Leader of the Party have been elected by an electoral college in which the weighting of votes is:

Trade unions	40%
Constituency parties and other organizations	30%
MPs	30%

    The Leader and the Parliamentary Party

The leader of any British party which is likely to be in a position to form a Government is in a powerful position. He or she is a potential Prime Minister. When in office as Prime Minister, a Labour Party Leader has followed the conventions attached to the office and appointed whosoever he chose, from MPs and peers, to ministerial office. When in opposition he must choose from the Parliamentary committee elected by the Parliamentary party.

As far as policy goes, the Labour Leader has a more ambiguous role than his Conservative counterpart. Election manifestos are theoretically drawn up by the Leadership in consultation with the NEC. It was as a reaction to what was seen as Callaghan's 'heavy handed' role in the 1979 election manifesto that some left-wing groups within the Party and the unions sought to give the NEC the final word. When the Party is in opposition, the NEC and its various committees are likely to have considerably influence over policy, with the Leader seeking their approval for policy documents. This task is often made easier by the presence of MPs friendly to the Leader, often elected to the NEC by trade union leaders of the bigger trade unions are not usually keen to stand for membership of the NEC of the Labour Party, since this debars them from standing for the more prestigious and powerful TUC General Council.

Thus the Leader may 'steer' the NEC and Conference round to his approach rather than dividing from them. In office, a Labour Leader has the weight and gravity attached to the office of Prime Minister – the patronage power of appointing about 100 ministers and junior ministers, the backing of the civil service and the argument that the practicalities of running the country make certain unpopular decisions necessary.

The Labour Leader has, on the face of it, more problems than his Conservative counterpart. He does not directly control the body that runs the Party outside Parliament and influences policy and the manifesto. He owes his position not entirely to the Parliamentary votes, but to trade unions and constituency parties. His party's Conference sees itself as a policy-making body rather than a supportive rally, and has some power to back the claim. His Parliamentary Party has a tradition of being more abrasive and oppositional than their Conservative counterparts.

All of this influences the position of the Labour Leader in Opposition. When in office, however, as Robert McKenzie claims in *British Political Parties*, a Labour Prime Minister disposes power in much the same way as any other British Prime Minister and usually gets away with it. It might be objected that Harold Wilson 'backed down' on issues like legislation to outlaw certain forms of strike and require 'cooling off' periods for other disputes, the devolution referendum requirements, and involvement in the Six Day War in the Middle East. Such tactical withdrawals, however, were not unknown in the three Thatcher Governments, and are the exception rather than the rule.

 Compare and contrast the role of Conference in the Conservative and the Labour Parties.

Compare and contrast the difference in powers of the Leader of the Labour Party, and the Leader of the Conservative Party.

Constituency organization

Constituency Labour Parties are made up of delegates from ward parties, and from locally affiliated trade union branches and other organizations. As affiliates, they may be disaffiliated (e.g. Pembroke Labour Party in 1968). The functions and structures of a constituency Labour Party are broadly similar to those of its Conservative counterpart.

Candidate selection

In choosing a Parliamentary candidate the selection meeting of a constituency Labour Party may, and sometimes does, add its own candidate to the short list: Tony Benn was such an addition in the Chesterfield by-election selection in 1984.

Sponsorship of candidates

A major difference between the Labour and Conservative Parties lies in the fact that in the Labour Party candidates may be 'sponsored' (financed) by affiliated organizations – usually trade unions. The central headquarters of the Party, presided over by the General Secretary – a full-time employee of the NEC – maintains two lists of candidates, sponsored and non-sponsored.

Another difference is that nominees for candidature are not nominated by individuals, but by locally affiliated organizations, on invitation from the local executive committee of the general management committee of the constituency.

'De-selection' controversies

NEC approval is required for the final candidature, and is usually given. There have, however, been conflicts over the 'de-selection' of sitting MPs. Prior to the 1974 general election, a number of MPs perceived by their constituency party activists to be 'right wing' were de-selected. One of them, Reg Prentice, former MP for Newham, took an appeal to the NEC, and then to Conference. He was unsuccessful in his appeal, but the public quarrel brought many old animosities into the open. 'Moderate' Labour supporters spoke of 'Bed-sit Trotskyites' moving into the area and taking over the leadership of the local Party, and counter-accusations were made by local activists about 'time-servers' who refused to follow Party policy, as laid down by Conference.

De-selection was made easier by the rule change at the Wembley Conference of 1981 which meant that all Labour MPs had to be re-selected within three years of the previous general election. In 1989 the de-selection of Frank Field, MP for Birkenhead, led to a similar row, with claims of irregularities in the selection process and calls for investigation into the internal affairs of the local Party.

Organizations within the Labour Party

As might be expected in a Party whose origins lie in the coming together of a number of different organizations, the Labour Party has many groups within it. Whether you see this as evidence of a 'broad, democratic church' or a Party 'beset by faction' depends on where you are standing at the time! These groups have been given, a variety of ideological labels:

• *Right.* Tending to favour a pragmatic and gradualist approach to policy; against wholesale public ownership, supporting a strong private sector, suspicious of trade union power inside and outside the Party; supporting membership of the EC and NATO and also an independent British nuclear deterrent. Most right-wingers within the Labour Party would have opposed the changes brought about by the Wembley Conference, and would wish to go back to selection of the leader by the Parliamentary Party, 'one member one vote' for the selection of candidates, and a reduction of trade union power over Conference.

▶ Right/Left labels act as a convenient shorthand but should not be used to obscure reality by over-simplification. Many politicians turn out to be 'left' on some issues, 'right' on others and confused on others. You may come across further divisions such as 'centre right' or 'centre left' or even 'the centre left of the Tory party' – journalists sometimes get a bit carried away with these labels.

The Labour Party Wembley Conference of 1981 and the SDP.

At the Labour Party annual party conference in 1981 most of the left-wing groups within the Party had united around a programme for the constitutional reform of the Party. Their proposed reforms would have weakened the position of any Labour Prime Minister. The reformers hoped that this would prevent a repeat of what they saw as a 'sell-out' to capitalism by Prime Minister Callaghan. The special 1981 Wembley Conference was convened to discuss these reforms.

The leadership proposed that the major say in electing a Labour Party Leader should be by the Labour MPs (the Parliamentary Party). This was rejected by Conference in favour of a solution which gave the trade union delegates the biggest (but not the majority) say in the leadership election. The agreed *electoral college* was made up of:

Trade union votes	40%
Parliamentary Party	30%
Constituency Parties and other groups	30%

This gave a group of senior right-wing Labour politicians the excuse they needed to do what they had been planning – to leave the Labour Party and form their own party. Thus the 'Gang of Four': Roy Jenkins, Shirley Williams, Bill Rodgers and David Owen, founded the Social Democratic Party. In his book, *Breaking the Mould* (1981) Bradley comments, 'Paradoxically, for the Gang and their supporters the result [of the Wembley Conference] proved an unexpected bonus. They could now leave the Labour Party on the popular issue of opposition to the power of the trade union block vote and not on the unpopular issue of support for Britain's continued membership of the EEC'.

► Dick Taverne, Labour MP for Lincoln, was the subject of a 'de-selection' resolution from his constituency over his support for Britain's membership of the European Community. He promptly resigned as an MP, thus creating a by-election. He stood as an independent, and won. However, he lost in the subsequent general election.

Prentice was de-selected in 1976. He later joined the Conservative Party and became a Minister in a Conservative Government.

What happened at the Wembley Conference in 1981? How does it illustrate the tensions and divisions within the Labour Party?

'Solidarity' would be classified under this heading. It was formed to oppose the 1981 Wembley Conferences changes, as would the 'Manifesto Group', formed as a reaction to what they saw as a threat of a left-wing take-over of the Party.

• *Soft left*. Aiming for a broadly socialist society, on the lines of Clause IV, but to be achieved gradually through consensus and by legal, mainly Parliamentary means; suspicious of the EC and unilateralist in defence policy.

You might put under this heading the Tribune Group which has existed since 1937, grouped around the weekly newspaper *Tribune*. Two Labour leaders, Michael Foot and Neil Kinnock, have been members of the Group.

Also included would be the 'Labour Co-ordinating Committee'

(LCC) formed to reflect the disillusionment felt with the Wilson/ Callaghan Governments of 1974 to 1979 and their failure to follow Conference policies. They were influential in securing the Wembley Conference changes in the Party's constitution.

- *Hard left*. This differs from the soft left principally in its insistence upon the achievement of certain socialist objectives now, rather than eventually, and on its readiness to consider a variety of ways to achieve them, including extra-Parliamentary means, and methods that might be against the law. Thus the hard left would be much more likely than the soft left to condone non-payment as a means of opposing the Poll Tax (Community Charge), or illegal strikes as a means of furthering an industrial dispute.

The 'Campaign for Labour Party Democracy' was formed, like the Labour Co-ordinating Committee, as a reaction to the disappointments of the left with the Governments of 1974 to 1979. It has remained part of the hard left, while the LCC has accepted Neil Kinnock's Leadership and his gradualist approach to socialism

The 'Campaign Group', with Tony Benn as a leading member, seeks further changes in the Party's rules to ensure that future Labour Governments do not depart from the policies of the wider movement, such as the election of the Labour Cabinet by electoral college; and back-bench policy advisers, responsible to the Party, to advise future Labour Ministers, as a counterweight to the influence of the civil service. It also supports changes in the British constitution such as the abolition of the House of Lords and the Crown prerogative enabling Ministers to make decisions without prior consultation of Parliament.

The 'Militant Tendency' denies that it is an organization within the Party, and claims not to be a membership organization but a group of supporters of the newspaper *Militant*. Its slogan is 'Labour to power on a Socialist Programme' and it has a number of specific policy objectives such as a minimum wage of £150 per week, unilateral disarmament, widespread public ownership and massive public investment. Its real nature, its critics and opponents claim, is that of an *entryist* revolutionary socialist group who (following one of the ideas of Trotsky) seek to infiltrate the Labour Party to get a Labour Government elected with a programme that it will be unable to carry out, then take over from there.

▶ The *entryism* referred to is the tactic of joining liberal democratic parties with the aim of converting active members to revolutionary politics.

Militant councillors are held to be behind Liverpool Council's defiance of Government spending limits in 1985, to the point of setting an illegal budget. Neil Kinnock then declared that 'there is no room for them in this party' and set about trying to expel them. After numerous hearings and legal wrangling ten of the 'Liverpool 16' were expelled. However, one-third of Liverpool Labour councillors are Militant supporters, and Militant claims a thousand activists and wide-spread community sympathy on Merseyside. In the Parliament elected in 1987, Militant had four Labour MPs who were overt supporters. Two were subsequently suspended from Party membership.

In 1990 Militant emerged as the leadership group in the anti-Poll Tax protests. The Conservative Government gratefully seized on this as a means of attacking Labour for being unable to control its extremists while Mr Kinnock condemned the non-payment campaign, the scuffles with the police, and Militant whom he described as 'Toytown Revolutionaries'. The leader of the anti-Poll Tax union pointed that most of their members and supporters were not Militant supporters. Small but not minuscule, well financed and well organized, it seems unlikely that Militant will go away in the near future.

 Identify four main groups within the Labour Party and their distinctive characteristics.

Review – The Labour Party

1 The origins of the Labour Party at the beginning of the century involved the coming together of diverse groups who sought working-class representation in Parliament independently of the Liberals.

2 This diversity is reflected in the constitution and role of Conference.

3 Conference:
   - Debates and passes policy motions.
   - Elects the National Executive Committee, which runs the Party outside Parliament.
   - Makes and changes the rules of the Party.
   - Is, in theory, the sovereign body of the Party.
   - Contributes to the drawing-up of the election manifesto.
   - Elects the Leader and Deputy Leader.

4 The constitutional changes of 1980, brought about by the left of the Party, led four leading Labour Party members, to leave the Party and form the SDP.

5 In opposition the Labour Leader is likely to encounter more dissent than his/her Conservative counterpart.

6 Labour has a number of groups within the Party, moderate, 'soft left' and 'hard left'.

(ACT) Select any major area of policy (e.g., education, defence, health). Using Keesing's Contemporary Archive or any other sources, draw up a table of contrasts between Labour Party and Conservative Party policy in this area. Then explain how their policy differences derive from the fundamental ideological differences between the Parties.

► The *Radicals* in the English Liberal Party, around the turn of the century – Joseph Chamberlain, followed by Winston Churchill and David Lloyd-George – developed 'caring' policies to meet the criticism that classic liberalism did nothing to help the poor, and also to retain the support of working-class voters. Thus, it was a centre party, the Liberals, in their Government of 1906 to 1911, who introduced pensions, unemployment benefit and sickness benefit, to be paid for by taxes which took proportionately more from the rich. The ideas and policies of the British centre have since then reflected liberalism tempered with social justice.

► William Henry Beveridge (born in 1879) was a Liberal concerned at the beginning of his career with social work at Toynbee Hall. He joined the civil service in 1908 and was involved in the social reforms of the Liberal Government of that era. Later, he was called to chair the committee co-ordinating the social services which produced the report named after him in 1942. It was one of a group of influential documents which became the basis of post-war reconstruction.
Beveridge took Rowntree's concept of a minimum standard of living below which no-one should be allowed to fall. He argued that poverty could be abolished by a universal contributory and free system of social benefit. He pressed for economic policies which would avoid mass unemployment, a comprehensive health service and family allowances.
He lost his seat as Liberal MP for Berwick in 1945, was made a baron and died in 1963.

THE CENTRE PARTIES

Centrist ideology

Centre parties, as their title would imply, lie somewhere on the ideological spectrum between right (Conservative) and left (socialist). Ideally they would hope to incorporate what they see as the good things about both extremes, whilst avoiding the nasty bits. Thus they would support the free market for its incentives to efficiency and for the choice and sovereignty it gives to the buyer, whilst seeking to avoid some of its darker consequences – unemployment, inequality and the failure to provide basic social benefits for less well-off people. Conversely, whilst supporting the idea that the state should provide social benefits where needed, and 'steer' the economy using public investment, they would shrink from the socialist advocation of an all-powerful state as being a threat to individual liberty. Some abiding elements of centrist ideology are as follows:

Liberalism tempered with social conscience

Classic nineteenth-century liberalism is based on the ideal of the sovereign individual. Thus the state should ensure that each individual has as much freedom, including the freedom to own and enjoy property, as possible, consistent with the freedom of every other individual. The state, through the law, should protect private property, and the rights of individuals from abusing their freedom to curtail the freedom of others. In the nineteenth century the doctrine was associated with free trade, freedom of religion and belief, and freedom for colonial countries to rule themselves.

Critics have always pointed to the *negative* nature of the 'freedom from' concept – government control, heavy taxation, oppressive laws. This kind of freedom is all very well if you have the money and the security to enjoy it. It is not much use to the poor, the unemployed, the sick who cannot afford medical help, the aged with no pension, or the illiterate who cannot afford education. Liberals have attempted to develop the idea of 'freedom to' as well as 'freedom from' by supporting policies to ensure that no individual is so powerless that he or she is precluded from participation in civil society.

Consensus and compromise

Centrist ideology emphasizes that the best policies are likely to be those upon which most people agree, that is, *consensus policies*. Consensus policies are to be supported from the practical point of view – they are more likely to work if most people support them – and from the democratic point of view – it is undemocratic to force the view of a minority on a majority.

The Liberals, now called the Liberal Democrats, support proportional representation (PR) for British Parliamentary elections (see Chapter 4). In answer to the suggestion that PR produces a succession of 'hung' Parliaments in which no single party would have a majority, leading to coalition governments, they argue that this would represent a wider spectrum of views, would mean parties reaching compromises on policy, and would ensure that Parliament was not be dominated by one narrow ideology. They deplore what they see as the politics of class conflict, and support politics that identify and work on areas of agreement.

The mixed economy

The centrist ideal is based neither on an economy with 'tooth and claw' free-market competition, nor on a state-controlled 'command' economy, but one with elements of both. The economics of John Maynard Keynes, in which the state steers the economy to ensure full employment, economic growth, and fair distribution informs the economic ideas of the centre. Governments may use public money to invest in or support basic industries, and have taxation and spending policies to influence price, growth and employment levels. A large private market sector, however, should remain the motor of the economy.

Keynesianism and monetarism

John Maynard Keynes sought in *The general theory of prices, interest and money* (1936) to provide a theoretical framework in which the persistently high levels of unemployment in Britain from 1925 to 1939 could be explained. What Keynes called 'classical' economic theory posited that the economy would move back to a full employment equilibrium.

Keynes argued that the economy could be in equilibrium with unemployment as a permanent feature if the level of effective demand was not sufficient to maintain a full employment level of national income.

His remedy was government intervention – the government should use its spending and money to create powers to bring the economy to near full employment.

To some extent all governments of developed capitalist economies have followed Keynsian policies since 1945. According to Milton Friedman (a monetarist and professor of economics at the University of Chicago) it has been the misuse of Keynes' ideas that has led to inflation and 'over-employment'. Friedman claims that Western governments have courted electoral popularity by pursuing policies designed to ensure full-employment by high levels of government spending, especially on welfare measures. They have spent more than they have raised through taxation and the difference has been covered by 'printing money' – an increase in the money supply, causing inflation.

Monetarists are also against high levels of taxation, seeing them as undermining incentives to work and to invest, and seeing governments as incompetent in spending the money they raise through taxation.

The monetarist answer is to stop the steady increase in the money supply by cutting public expenditure, and by controlling credit. Governments should cut taxation and should not create jobs by printing extra money to pay the wages, and trade unions should not be allowed the power to bid up wages.

Monetarism, (or 'supply side economics') had a great influence on the Thatcher Government in its earlier years. However, in overall terms, the Thatcher Government did not reduce government expenditure nor the money supply, nor the percentage of the national income taken in taxation. Inflation fell but in response to rising unemployment and rising interest rates. Monetarism was followed more in rhetoric than in reality.

The word 'liberal'

My editor points out that the word 'liberal' means different things in different sections of this book. Since you are likely to encounter this problem elsewhere it would be useful to familiarize yourself with the different common meanings:

- In economic policy 'liberal' is associated with 'freeing' or liberalizing trade, the free market, and competition unhindered by State interference. This approach is now often associated with the right wing of the Conservative Party. In the nineteenth century it was the Liberal Party which championed economic liberalism.

- In policies on law, order and morality 'liberal' usually refers to tolerant attitudes towards minorities or deviant groups. Liberal policies here would be for abortion on demand, gay rights, or the legalization of 'soft' drugs. Conservatives who champion economic liberalism may be far from liberal on these issues.

- Since it was the Liberal Party in Britain who introduced state pensions, state subsidized medicine and unemployment benefit between 1906 and 1913, advocates of the Welfare State are sometimes called 'liberals'.

- As part of the label 'liberal-democratic' the term 'liberal' is used to designate systems with free elections, uncensored media, free rights of assembly, etc. In this sense all the main parties in Britain are liberal-democratic.

▶ For all practical purposes the SLD is now known as the Liberal Democratic Party. The 'social' referred to the partial merger with the Social Democrats in 1988.

The evolution of the Liberal Democratic Party

The Liberal Democratic Party has emerged (1990) from the conflicts and compromises of the centre parties since 1981 when the SDP was formed. The elements of this fusion were at various times the SDP, the SLD and the Liberal Party.

The Social Liberal Democrats was formed as a party in 1988, in the wake of the Alliance's disappointing result of the 1987 general election. The assemblies of both these centre parties (the Liberal Party and the Social Democratic Party) endorsed the decision to merge by an overwhelming majority. The argument put forward was that a merger was the only means by which the centre was going to become a credible electoral force. It was argued that voters had been deterred from supporting the Alliance by barely patched-up internal quarrels over which party should have which constituency, disagreement over policy, particularly on nuclear disarmament, and uncertainty as to who would lead the Alliance in Parliament and whether it sought to gain total power or hold the balance between the other two.

Nevertheless, David Owen, leader of the SDP, did not accept the merger and pledged himself to lead a separate party, while a small group of Liberals led by Michael Meadowcroft set up a separate Liberal Movement. The SDP ended its existence in 1990.

The history of the Liberal Party

Like the Conservatives, the Liberals developed from a group that existed before the popular franchise arrived – the Whigs. This group stood for religious tolerance and the limiting of royal power by Parliament.

In the last quarter of the nineteenth century the Party had the support of large numbers of urban working-class voters, which inclined some of its leaders (notably Joseph Chamberlain) towards state intervention to ameliorate the conditions of that class. Unfortunately this approach clashed with the traditional Whig and Liberal dedication to the freedom of the individual from state interference, and to free trade. Nevertheless the Liberal Government of 1906–11 pioneered many of the measures associated with the welfare state (pensions, unemployment benefit, assisted medical treatment, etc.). By the 1880s, the Party, always the champion of small nations' right to self-determination, had committed itself to Home Rule for Ireland.

Due partly to a split in the Leadership between Lloyd George and Asquith in 1916, and partly to the capture of 'new' working-class voters by the Labour Party, the Liberal Party's fortunes declined to that of third-party also-ran after 1923. After 1945 the Party remained in the doldrums, its seats in Parliament reaching double figures only twice, until a marked revival in February 1974, when it polled 19.3 per cent of the votes. There was a dip in its support in 1979 but support has since remained about twice the 1945–70 level.

Political reasons for the revival of the centre are discussed elsewhere. However, the Liberals' improving performance may have owed much to its strong local organization, driven by the Young Liberals and the Association of Liberal Councillors who, with their emphasis on community politics and good local organization, strengthened the Party on the ground.

The Lib-Lab pact
The Labour Government of 1974 to 1979, having seen its paper-thin majority in the Commons whittled away by election defeats, formed a pact with the Liberals in 1977 which fell short of a coalition, but gave the Liberals a say in Government policy and the air of being a serious party once again. The withdrawal of support by Liberal MPs helped to bring down the Labour Government on a vote of no confidence in 1979, although the Lib-Lab pact actually ended in 1978.

In 1976, the Liberal Party introduced a system by which ordinary members participated in the election of the Leader, and in 1981 a system of 'one member one vote' was introduced.

The Alliance
David Steel, elected Liberal Leader in 1976, took the crucial decision to form an electoral alliance with the newly-formed Social Democratic Party in 1981. It was emphasized at that time that it was an electoral alliance only, lasting only until the election, after which both Parties might take their separate paths, or cooperate. But in any case, both parties were at pains to insist on their separate identities, and policies.

At this stage the Alliance strategy was limited to ensuring that the two centre Parties did not split their vote in the constituencies. Should this strategy give the two Parties, or the two Parties and any others who wished to support them, the balance of power between the larger Parties, they would be able to insist on the introduction of proportional representation by any government seeking their support, and would ensure that the centre would be come a force to be reckoned with for the foreseeable future.

► Joseph Chamberlain was almost a socialist in his attitude to domestic politics, but he was also a convinced imperialist. It was his imperialism that caused the break with the Liberals. Had he stayed in the Liberal Party and become its leader, it might have pursued more pro-working class policies, and welcomed more working-class activists into its ranks. Perhaps, then, the Labour Party would never have got off the ground.

► As an electoral alliance the Alliance had a lot going for it. The SDP had famous names with experience of high office, the Liberal Party had the organization in the constituencies. Its failure to agree upon what it was to do after the election, however, was to prove a serious and ultimately fatal weakness.

The Social Democratic Party (SDP)

As has already been noted (page 83), the SDP was founded in 1981 by 'moderate' members occupying leadership positions in the Labour Party – the Gang of Four, as they were immediately dubbed by the media. Although the immediate trigger to the formation of the new Party was the rule changes brought about by Labour's Wembley Conference, the roots of the SDP go back further. The heirs to Gaitskell's 'revisionist' approach to the Labour Party, which was responsible for the attempt to remove Clause IV from the Party's constitution, remained a more or less organized and distinct group after Gaitskell died and Wilson, (regarded then as a left-winger) took over. As the Campaign for Social Democracy, they expressed alarm at the leftward trend of the Party from 1974 onward, in particular the anti-European Community motions passed by Conference and its commitment to unilateral nuclear disarmament and widespread public ownership. Several moderate Labour MPs were de-selected by their left-wing constituency general management committees. Prentice took his appeal against de-selection by Newham as far as Conference, while Dick Taverne in Lincoln precipitated a by-election by resigning, then stood as a Social Democratic candidate in that election, and won. He was, however defeated in the subsequent general election.

Roy Jenkins, a former Labour Home Secretary, Chancellor of the Exchequer and Deputy Prime Minister, returned from his term of office as President of the European Commission to deliver a public lecture in which he argued for the establishment of a third party in British politics, and that the Liberal Party would not fulfil that role. In 1980 discussions and negotiations were already going on to form the basis of such a party.

Roy Jenkins, Shirley Williams, David Owen and Bill Rodgers made up the Gang of Four. All were experienced politicians with high media profiles and they had their differences. What they had in common was:

- A belief in the European Economic Community (the Common Market) and the need for Britain to join it.
- A belief that the Labour and Conservative Parties had become in thrall to trade union barons and big business respectively.
- The view that, with the change in Britain's economic and social structure associated with post-industrial society, there was a growing number of voters whose aspirations were represented by the programmes of neither of the big parties.
- A broadly centrist ideology which accepted the mixed economy and the welfare state, but insisted on a thriving private sector and pluralistic political system.

▶ Shirley Williams, in particular, expounded the view that the traditional class/party alliances – manual workers/Labour and middle-class/Conservative – were no longer very useful as descriptions of the British electorate.

The Party's early months were auspicious. It recruited 70,000 members, and built up a reasonably substantial financial base. The collective leadership received good coverage in the media. A democratic structure with a president and leader elected by a postal ballot of the whole membership and a council for social democracy elected by area groups, was established. Two spectacular by-election wins followed (Crosby and Glasgow Hillhead) together with successes in local government elections. As part of the Alliance their popularity increased until, at one point at the end of 1981 Alliance looked like a credible alternative to either of the big parties with a good chance of holding the balance in a future Parliament, if the opinion polls were to be believed.

 Who were the Gang of Four and what did they do?

By 1983, Mrs Thatcher and her Conservative Party had recovered their former level of support and the Alliance's popularity fell back to a still creditable 25 per cent but was not enough to make a major impact upon a future Parliament. The distribution of the Alliance's 23 seats in the 1983 Parliament gave the SDP cause for concern. They won only six seats, while Liberal representation increased by five. This reflected, claimed the SDP leadership, not the relative support for the two parties, but the fact the Liberals had got more than their fair share of winnable constituencies in the arrangement by which constituencies were divided between the two parties. After 1983 the two parties agreed to a new arrangement for the allocation of constituencies. The two parties also agreed on some policies – electoral and House of Lords reform and a Bill of Rights, for example.

Nevertheless, the SDP-Liberal relationship remained tense and uncertain. Sources of this tension and uncertainty were:

• *The differences over candidate selection* already noted.

• *Policy differences*. The Young Liberal movement within the Liberal Party had tinged the Party's defence policy with nuclear unilateralism. The SDP firmly supported the deployment of the American Cruise missiles. Eventually a compromise was reached (keep the existing missiles, but introduce no more) but it was an uneasy compromise. The SDP approach to devolution was not as federalist (see Chapter 3) as that of the Liberal Party.

• *Leadership*. The leaders of the two parties – David Steel and David Owen – did not reach agreement about who was to lead the Alliance, should it have been successful. The relationship between the two leaders certainly does not seem to have accorded with the TV programme *Spitting Image's* view of Owen as the bullying master and Steel as the sycophantic wimp!

• *Attitude to merger*. While David Steel proposed merger between the two parties after the defeat of 1987, Owen always set his face against such a policy, and took himself and the 'rump' of the SDP to continue as a separate party after the formation of the SLD.

 Select any three important features of 'centrism' as a political ideology, and match these with policies advocated by British centre parties.

► Since I wrote this, cause for
cautious optimism on the part of
the Liberal Democrats has
appeared in the shape of their
success in the Eastbourne and
Bradford by-elections (1990).

► At its 1990 conference the
Green Party faced the problem of
whether to streamline its
organization and give more
power to a 'leadership' committee
and officers. This was resisted by
many members who wanted
power to remain with the grass
roots.

Has the centre a future in Britain?

As is explained in the next chapter, the pattern of party loyalty among
British voters has changed over the past 25 years. There is much
greater willingness to vote for a third party, and to change allegiance
between elections.

While this augurs well for a credible 'third force', the fortunes of the
heirs to the Alliance since 1987 have waned. Opinion polls have
consistently shown the SLD in single figures, with the SDP behind
them. In the elections for the European Parliament in 1988 the Green
Party received more votes than the SLD. In the mid-Staffordshire by-
election in 1990, support for the SLD (11 per cent), SDP (2.5 per cent)
and Greens (2 per cent) combined was only 15.5 per cent compared
with 23 per cent for the Alliance in that constituency at the general
election of 1987.

The SDP ceased to exist as a national party, then ceased altogether
when Dr Owen announced his decision to leave politics in 1990.

It is probably too soon to say whether this decline of support for
centre parties is terminal. The Labour Party may have re-established
its credibility amongst potential centre voters, having apparently
sorted out its internal quarrels and dropped some of its more unpopular policies. The partners to the Alliance probably left their merger
too late, having failed to capitalize on the surge of support for the
Alliance in the early 1980s. The Green Party may yet replace the
Democrats as the main centre party.

Whatever the future holds in terms of electoral fortunes, the best
hope for a centre party seems still to lie in getting 30 per cent or more
of the voters behind it, holding the balance between the two big
parties in a 'hung' Parliament, and demanding the introduction of
proportional representation as the price of joining a coalition.

The Green Party

The Green Party's forerunner was the Ecology Party which in turn
grew from the fusion of a number of pressure groups concerned at
what they saw as the destruction of the environment.

The Greens put forward 133 candidates at the 1987 election, and
gained around 90,000 votes. It has also made some progress in local
elections. In the elections for the European Parliament of 1989 it did
surprisingly well, polling 15 per cent compared with 0.6 per cent in
1984.

Green ideology

This encompasses:
- *Conservation.* The idea that the resources of the planet should be
  protected against destruction resulting from the pursuit of short-
  term gain in the production and consumption of goods and services.
  To this end, a policy of low-impact ('wind and water') technology is
  advocated.
- *Anti-pollution.* As well as destroying the resources of the planet, we
  are, according to the Green view, polluting the atmosphere, the rivers

and oceans, and the stratosphere. Government policies should concentrate on outlawing various processes that cause pollution, and making polluters pay penalties, or discouraging them.

• *The balance of nature*. Mass consumption and production, by wiping out some animals and organisms in the food chain and over-developing others, is interfering with the balance of nature to the eventual detriment of the whole planet. There is also concern for the preservation of species for their own sake – here the movement shades into the animal rights movement.

• *Suspicion of the pursuit of growth*. The pursuit of economic growth – more goods and services produced and consumed every year – for its own sake, is at the bottom of our environmental problems. Policies aimed at restraining growth for its own sake, and no growth policies which concentrate on economical use of resources, are the answer.

Though sometimes derided by right and left, Green policies are being taken seriously by both the big parties who have incorporated Green ideas into their policy documents. Industry, too, is taking the Green consumer seriously, by proclaiming the environmental friendliness of many of its products in its advertising. This reaction reflects the popularity of Green ideas.

It remains to be seen whether the big parties will steal the clothes of the Greens. Many of the measures advocated by members of the Green movement seem revolutionary in their implications, yet the Green Party is resolutely Liberal-Democratic, eschewing autocratic means of achieving its aims. Their task is therefore a difficult one – to persuade a society used to regular economic growth, the benefits of mass production and a consumerist ideology to change many of its fundamental attitudes.

POLITICAL PARTIES OF THE EXTREME LEFT AND RIGHT

The Marxist left

As noted in the discussion of the Labour Party, Marxist socialism has never been the basis of any mass political party in Britain. It has persisted within and outside the Labour Party, but as a minority pursuit. Nevertheless, small but well organized and often influential (influence is not always proportionate to size) Marxist groups exist in Britain.

Marxist parties divide roughly according to whether they see themselves as the true heirs to the ideas and policies of various great revolutionary leaders and theorists – Lenin, Trotsky, Stalin, Gramsci, Mao – and on their attitude to the former Soviet Union. There is also division on the appropriate tactics for a Marxist party in contemporary Britain.

The Communist Party of Great Britain and its heirs

Since the early 1960s, with the publication of *The British Road to Socialism*, the Communist Party of Great Britain has moved further

► *Karl Marx* (1818–83) With Frederick Engels the founder of the international communism. In *Das Kapital* he argues that capitalist economies depend on surplus labour – the difference between the cost of subsistence wage paid to labour, and the considerably greater value produced by it. Capitalist competition has inherent contradictions within it. Competition leads to shrinking profit margins, and attempts by capitalists to drive down wages. The working class (proletariat) reacts by revolution leading to a classless society – a dictatorship of the proletariat. The role of the Communist Party is to show the proletariat its historical role, demystifying the way in which they are being misled by the bourgeoise ideology of religion, the political system, the mass media, the law, etc.

► *Eurocommunism* refers to the idea of achieving a Socialist society without revolution. It is characteristic of most of the major communist parties of Western Europe.

► The Communist Party of Britain is (in 1991) engaged in deciding its future title and ideology in the light of recent events in Eastern Europe.

► *Vanguard party*
Lenin (the main architect of the communist revolution in Russia) believed that the working class needed the leadership of a small well-disciplined party to make a successful revolution. There is no place in such a vanguard party for endless dissent and public squabbling about policy.

► *Trotsky* was exiled from the Soviet Union and then assassinated because of his opposition to Stalin. In his view Stalin subverted the revolution by turning away from world revolution and by concentrating power into his own hands through using a rigid bureaucracy. Trotskyite parties are dedicated to international communism and to permanent revolution.

and further away from the idea of revolution. It has been especially influenced by the ideas of the Italian Marxist, Gramsci, who was a founder member and leader of the Italian Communist Party in the 1920s. He believed that communism could be achieved without revolution, using the democratic process. This belief in non-revolutionary communism is the basis for most of the major communist parties in Western Europe: so-called *Eurocommunism*.

The official leadership of the Party, through its publications *Marxism Today* and *Seven Days* presses support for the moderate wing of the Labour Party, and emphasizes the importance of working with cross-class groups who oppose established hierarchies, such as gay rights groups, Black community and political groups, and the women's movement. This cuts across the notion of class, and repudiates the traditional Marxist-Leninist idea of class struggle as the road to working-class victory and socialism. The Communist Party remains the largest Marxist party in Britain.

Some of those who saw the above move as a betrayal of Marxist-Leninist principles left the Party and formed break-away groups or parties. These include:

• *The Communist Party of Great Britain (Marxist/Leninist)*. This was formed by Reg Birch, former Vice President of the AUEW in 1968. Drawing its inspiration from Maoist notions of guerrilla political tactics, it emphasizes the role of a vanguard party and the centrality of class struggle and the replacement of the capitalist system by socialism.

It publishes a weekly newspaper *The Worker* and although small, it has supporters amongst activists in some industrial and 'white collar' unions.

• *The New Communist Party* was formed as a reaction to the anti-Soviet attitude of the Communist Party of Great Britain. It pursues a pro-Soviet policy. It publishes a paper *The New Communist*.

• *The Communist Party of Britain* resulted from an internal quarrel within the Communist Party of Great Britain over editorial policy and control of the daily newspaper, the *Morning Star*, formerly the *Daily Worker*. Although regarded as the newspaper of the Party, it was controlled and owned by a group which quarrelled with the official Party when they tried to secure control of the paper to change its outlook to one more sympathetic to the Eurocommunist outlook of the official Party.

The supporters of the paper in its original form formed first the Communist Campaign Group, to further a more left-wing, class-based policy within the Party, and then their own party.

The Fourth International, formed by Trotsky in 1938, propagated the idea of international socialism as opposed to Stalin's 'Socialism in one country', the need for permanent revolution to prevent the ossification of revolutionary ideas, and genuine democratic centralism as opposed to the 'bureaucratic dictatorship' of Stalin's Soviet Union.

These ideas have given rise to many parties and groups in Britain. The Militant Tendency (or Militant), one of the most successful in terms of publicity and membership has already been mentioned in the context of the Labour Party. Others are:

• *The Socialist Workers' Party* formed out of the International Socialists ('Neither Washington nor Moscow, but International Socialism') in 1976. The SWP has about 5000 members, and publishes a weekly paper the *Socialist Worker*. It has a network of activists in trade unions, and has organized a number of broad 'campaign' groups, such as the Right to Work Campaign and the Anti-Nazi League, which have been well supported and organized.

• *The Workers' Revolutionary Party* saw itself as the 'true' heir to Trotsky, and saw other groups as revisionist. The Party had industrial contacts, working through the All Trade Union Alliance. Attacks on the conduct of its leader, Gerry Healey, led to a series of splits, so that at the last count there were four groups claiming to be the true party.

• *The Socialist League* grew out of the International Marxist Guild which was linked to the Fourth International.

• *The Revolutionary Communist Party* publishes a monthly glossy magazine *Living Marxism* which aims at a more lively style of article, combining politics with general interest and the arts.

• *The Revolutionary Communist Group* concentrates in its paper *The Next Step* on the fight against imperialism, supporting the IRA and all 'anti-imperialist' groups.

 What are the main ways in which the parties of the far left differ from each other?

► All the parties of the far left are reviewing their position and policies in the light of events in Eastern Europe and the Soviet Union. The Communist Party of Britain is likely to change its name to Democratic Left.

The extreme right

The ideology of the extreme right, fascist and quasi-fascist groups, is difficult to pin down, since it is based to some extent on emotive concepts which are difficult to define ('The Blood', 'The Race', 'Honour', etc.).

Some features of extreme-right ideology are:

• *Race as a political factor*. The identification and preservation of one's race.

• *Discipline and order*. An emphasis on the military virtues of physical courage and discipline and obedience.

• *Rejection of liberal democracy*. In common with some supporters of the extreme left, fascists despise liberal-democratic values, seeing them either as a recipe for vacillation and weakness, or as a con trick designed to fool ordinary people into believing that they are responsible for their own destiny.

• *Extreme nationalism*. For some fascists, 'The Nation' along with 'The Blood' and 'The Race' is an entity to be defended with one's life. These collective entities have a power and value which are not rationally definable, but which are nevertheless real to fascists, and worth more than the lives of the individuals who make them up.

There are a number of British far-right parties. The National Front was first formed in 1966 by the merging of the British National Party

► Emphasis upon the organic nature of a nation or people and the need to pursue organic unity is a recurrent theme in fascist polemic. For example, 'The Italian nation as an organism has ends, life and means of action superior to those of the separate individuals or groups of individuals which compose it'. (Mussolini, Italian fascist leader, in the *Italian Labour Charter* 1927)

► 'We, as Aryans, are therefore able to imagine a state only to be the living organism of a nationality which not only safeguards the preservation of that nationality, but which, by further training of its spiritual and ideal abilities, leads to the highest Freedom' (Adolf Hitler *Mein Kampf*)

(essentially a National Socialist party) and the League of Empire Loyalists (an ultra-conservative organization) and several smaller groups.

Between 1966 it went through a number of power struggles and ideological splits, notably that between the pro-Hitler Nazis and the more 'socialist'-minded Strasserites, named after the Strasser brothers who ran a wing of Hitler's movement in Germany which attracted much working-class support until Hitler 'purged' them. Despite splits and quarrels its membership grew during the 1970s to about 17,500, and it attracted support from disaffected right-wing Conservatives and disaffected Labour supporters in Britain's inner cities. During this period the Front put up candidates for Parliamentary and local government elections, and made significant gains in terms of votes, although it won no seats.

With the election of the Conservative Government in 1979, much of the Front's popular support disappeared, and John Tyndall, Chair of the Front, formed the New National Front.

A series of purges and realignments has seen one group within the party turn away from electoral politics and towards links with extreme right 'direct action' groups in Europe and the USA. The 'political soldier' wing of the Party claims to adopt a 'third position' (neither capitalism nor communism) policy which looks to the regime of Colonel Gaddafi of Libya as their model, and disavows overt racism in favour of 'National Revolution'.

The Flag Group, called after the newspaper around which it groups, meanwhile continues with the more traditional racial politics.

Re-formed by Tyndall in 1981, the British National Party puts more emphasis on national strength, honour and 'purity' and echoes some of the *jingoistic* nationalism of the old League of Empire Loyalists. With some success in recruiting from 'patriotic and vigorous young men', it has organized some protests which have attracted police and media attention, but at present, its organization and support seems patchy.

 What are the main ways in which the parties of the far right differ from each other?

► *Jingoism*: means aggressive patriotism.
It comes from a music hall song which was popular before and during the Boer War (1899–1902)
'We don't want to fight them,
But by jingo if we do,
We've got the ships,
We've got the men,
We've got the money too'.

NATIONALIST PARTIES

For practical purposes, nationalism can be defined as that political doctrine which wishes to see the state – the legal, constitutional entity – based upon the nation – the psychological, cultural, linguistic and cultural entity.

For a fuller discussion of these concepts, see Chapter 2. Irish nationalism will be dealt with at some length in Chapter 13.

Scottish and Welsh nationalism

The main focuses for Scottish and Welsh nationalism respectively are the Scottish Nationalist Party and Plaid Cymru. Both parties enjoyed a significant increase in popular support in the 1960s and 1970s. In the

1980s both suffered a fall-off in this support.

The claim for national recognition and Home Rule, or at least substantial devolution of power from the centre, may be based on all or any combination of the following factors:

• *Economic*. What may be called the 'rip-off' argument. This depends on the assertion that the dominant 'metropolitan' country is using the material resources and layout of the 'subject' country to enrich itself at the subject country's expense.

This line of argument is particularly powerful in Scotland, where it is contended that the English Government has exploited Scotland throughout the last three centuries, as a stag-hunting ground, through clearances of arable farms to make way for absentee-landlord sheep farming, and latterly through drilling for off-shore oil from which Scotland has received few of the benefits.

Less prominent is the Welsh nationalist movement, but it nevertheless surfaces in the shape of challenges to the English use of Welsh water, and ownership of Welsh cottages by English 'weekenders'.

• *Linguistic*. The claim for the propagation of the national language, leading to a bilingual population, is strongest in the Welsh movement, since about 20 per cent of the population of the country speak Welsh, whereas an insignificant proportion of Scots speak Gaelic. In the dying months of the Labour Government of 1974–9, Plaid Cymru were promised an all Welsh TV channel by the Government, in exchange for Parliamentary support.

• *Ethnic*. This is a mixture of historical, cultural and psychological elements which go to make up the idea of 'Welshness' or 'Scottishness' – a feeling that the nation has a distinctive collective personality which is in danger of being extinguished or demeaned by the metropolitan nation.

Rise and decline of the two parties

The Scottish Nationalist Party (SNP) has existed since 1934 and Plaid Cymru since 1925. Both parties have pressed for the setting-up of national assemblies and executives, as a first step to virtual independence from English rule.

Until the 1960s, however, they remained small fringe parties. Support grew in the 1960s and 1970s and rose to the point where in the election of October 1974 the SNP gained 800,000 votes and eleven seats in Parliament and Plaid Cymru 166,000 votes and three seats. The Scottish vote was particularly worrying for the Labour Party which lost voters to the SNP in some of its traditional Scottish strongholds.

The Labour Government came to depend upon the nationalist parties for its continued survival, it made concessions, in the form of a Devolution Bill, which provided for Scottish and Welsh assemblies and a Scottish executive. The measure, however, had built into it a referendum provision which required that 40 per cent of the voters in each country would have to vote for devolution before it came into operation. The referendum in 1978 proved to be a disappointment for the SNP and a disaster for Plaid Cymru. In Scotland about one third

► The left-wing theatre group Theatre 7/84 (Scotland) produced a piece satirizing and attacking the English exploitation of Scotland through the ages, entitled *The stag, the Cheviot and the black, black oil.* It received widespread critical acclaim.

of the electorate supported devolution, a similar number opposed it and the rest didn't vote. In Wales, devolution was overwhelmingly rejected with only about 12 per cent of the electorate voting for it.

The devolution referendum result, and the defeat of Labour in the 1979 election, set the two nationalist parties back. Many of those who voted nationalist, particularly SNP, may have been disaffected former Labour voters, who have since returned to the Labour fold.

Nationalism, however is by no means a spent force in British politics. After a dip in the 1983 election, the SNP vote rose to 417,000 in 1987. Plaid Cymru support, never as strong as that of the SNP, was down to 124,000.

Review – The smaller political parties

1 *The far left*. The Communist Party of Britain has rejected revolution as the way to socialism and small break-away parties have developed, e.g. the Communist Party of Britain (ML), the New Communist Party and the Communist Party of Britain. Heirs to the tradition of Trotsky's Fourth International are similarly split between the Militant Tendency, the Socialist Workers' Party, the Socialist League, the Revolutionary Communist Party and the Revolutionary Communist Group.

2 *The far right*. This is also beset by factions and splits. At present the National Front is split between the 'Political Soldier' movement, adopting a policy of 'national revolution' and the more traditional racial politics of the Flag Group, while the British National Party represents an older jingoistic nationalism.

3 *Nationalist parties*. Two parties on mainland Britain, Plaid Cymru and the Scottish National Party (SNP), support virtually separate statehood for their nations. Arguments for this are:
- *Economic*. Particularly strong in the case of Scotland.
- *Cultural/Historical*. The notion that Welshness and Scottishness should be preserved by Home Rule.

The heyday of the nationalist parties was reached in 1974. The nationalist parties have problems – they are themselves divided between left and right, and most Welsh voters, and about half of Scottish voters, do not support the idea of a national assembly. Nevertheless, the Labour, Liberal Democrat and Green Parties support the idea of devolution to varying degrees in their manifestoes, and the suspicion of government from London by the Scottish and Welsh voters is still there, especially in rural areas.

 Define 'nationalism' in relation to nationalist parties, and parties of the far right. Identify the two nationalist parties of mainland Britain. When did they come closest to achieving their goals?

CHAPTER SUMMARY

1 Political parties form an important part of most liberal democratic systems.

2 They aggregate pressures and ideologies into a programme, give the elector a realistic choice, and provide a means of recruitment and participation in politics.

3 The Conservative Party is the oldest party. It streamlined its organization after 1867, when the franchise was greatly expanded, to cope with the demands of mass politics.

4 Conservative ideology is difficult to define, since Conservatives tend to eschew ideology, but respect for what exists and is working, and suspicion of 'blueprints' for the future, is at the base of much Conservative thinking. It is regarded as the 'party of business', and is supported financially by industrial and commercial firms.

5 The Labour Party was created at the turn of the century, by an alliance of trade unions and pro-socialist groups. Its money and support came from the trade union movement.

6 Labour's ideological basis is partly socialism and partly liberal humanism.

7 Conservative Party structure is oriented towards the Leader who is elected by Conservative MPs. The Conference is an occasion for activists to express their views, and a media event, but not a policy-making body.

8 The Labour Party Conference is technically the sovereign body of the movement. It consists of delegates from trade unions, constituency parties, other affiliated bodies and MPs. Its resolutions are party policy. It elects the NEC, the Leader and the Deputy Leader.

9 The centre in British politics is mainly embodied in the SLD. This party has emerged from a turbulent period (1981–9) during which the traditional Liberal Party formed an Alliance with the SDP, which was formed by four dissident Labour right-wingers after the Wembley conference in 1981.

10 The Alliance did very well in terms of votes in by- and general elections between 1981 and 1987.

11 The ecological Green Party did well in the European elections of 1989, but has had little impact on general or by-elections.

12 The parties of the far left and far right in Britain are small, fissile (inclined to split) and have made little impact in electoral terms.

13 The Scottish National Party and Plaid Cymru increased their support between 1968 and 1975, but have waned since although both remain as minority parties.

The stimulus material, is an article from the *Sunday Correspondent* on Neil Kinnock's attempts to reorganize the Labour Party. Read the passage and answer the questions.

1 Give some examples of the 'damaging confrontations' mentioned in paragraph two, and suggest why they occur more frequently in the Labour Party rather than in the Conservative Party.

2 What criticisms do you think may be aimed at the proposals from within the Party; how might they be justified?

3 Why do you think Kinnock is intent upon changing the Party's constitution in this way?

4 Do you find the article biased in favour of Kinnock's proposals, against, or balanced? Explain your choice using quotations from the article.

5 What other attempts to make major changes in the Party's constitution have been made since 1945? What happened as the results of such efforts?

KINNOCK SEEKS LABOUR OVERHAUL

1 Neil Kinnock, the Labour leader, plans to put the formation of party policy into the hands of a new 170-strong elected national forum in the most sweeping overhaul of party machinery since the first Labour Party conference in 1906. The creation of a new National Policy Forum is designed to avoid the damaging confrontations with annual party conferences which have bedevilled Labour leaders since the war.

2 The plans would create seven new permanent policy commissions on subjects ranging from defence to the economy. They will infuriate the hard left and could be opposed by the party's biggest affiliate, the Transport and General Worker's Union, when they are debated at the party conference in Blackpool this October.

3 A confidential 25-page document to be discussed by the National Executive on Wednesday also opens the way for the Parliamentary Party to have a significant *ex-officio* role in party conference decisions on policy for the first time.

4 The new system will deprive constituencies and trade unions of the right to initiate policy in conference resolutions and is aimed at ending the last minute horse trading which has caused conference fiascos over the past decade. These include the formation of the leadership electoral college in 1981, the defeat of Neil Kinnock's one-person one-vote proposals in 1984 and the TGWU's unilateralist victory in 1988.

5 The policy forum will be drawn from all sections of the party – including MPs – and up to a third elected from the regions. The unions' share of the party conference votes would be cut initially from over 90 per cent to 70 per cent with most of the rest held by constituency delegates who will be elected on a compulsory one-member one-vote basis for the first time.

6 The idea is modelled on the system in European socialist parties – like that of Denmark – which aims to reach consensus before the policies reach party conferences. The Policy Forum would meet quarterly to receive the reports of standing commissions. Constituencies would have the right only to propose amendments to policies already drawn up.

7 While this year's conference will debate the principle, the relevant rule changes would not be enacted until the conference immediately after the general election.

8 Mr Kinnock is said to see the reform as the last and possibly most important 'building block' in his programme of constitutional change.

9 The plans provide for the 70 per cent union block vote share to be progressively reduced if Labour's mass membership campaign succeeds. The constituency share would probably increase by 1 per cent for every 25,000 extra members.

10 The proposals have already commanded wide support among trade unions and constituencies in one of the widest consultations ever mounted by the party.

11 But the TGWU has proposed that the union block vote be no lower than 80 per cent and for the standing commissions to report to the NEC rather than a policy forum.

12 The new left-dominated TGWU executive is expected to be unhappy about the forum proposal. The final decision on whether or not to support the plan could be left to the union's Blackpool delegation.

13 The document, drawn up by Larry Whitty, the Labour Party's general secretary, makes it clear that constituencies voting for the party treasurer, along with the women's section and their own representatives on the NEC, will have to hold compulsory one-member one-vote ballots.

Sunday Correspondent
22 April 1990
Donald Macintyre, Political Editor

Further reading: Chapter 5

McKenzie R.M. 1963. *British Political Parties*. London: Heinemann. This seminal work on British parties is now out of date in its examples but is still interesting for its view on the internal power structure of the two major parties. It is especially interesting on the struggle between Gaitskell and his opponents in the Labour Party.

Beer S.H.M. 1985. *Modern British Politics*. London: Faber & Faber. An overview which takes a view different from that of McKenzie on the essential differences between the Labour and the Conservative Parties.

Rose S. 1980. *Do Parties Make a Difference?* London: Macmillan. An examination of the role of political parties in Britain.

Pelling J. 1965. *A Short History of the Labour Party*. London: Macmillan. Interesting for its concise history of the early years of the Party.

Kavanagh D. (ed.) 1982. *The Politics of the Labour Party*. London: George Allen and Unwin. Useful for further information on the Party in the seventies.

Mitchell A. 1983. *The Case for Labour*. London: Longman. A polemic on behalf of the Labour Party and to be read as such.

Minogue K. & Biddiss M. 1987. *Thatcherism*. London: Macmillan. A look at the influence of this controversial leader and whether her ideas constituted a doctrine.

Patten C. 1983. *The Tory Case*. London: Longman. As with Mitchell, but for the Conservatives.

Now you have completed this chapter, look back to the objectives and check that you have achieved each of them.

Bradley I. 1981. *Breaking the Mould?* Oxford: Martin Robertson & Co. Rather anecdotal, but nonetheless an interesting account of the launch of the SDP.

Taylor S. 1982. *The National Front in British Politics*. London: Macmillan. For further information on the National Front.

Callaghan J. 1987. *The Left in English Politics*. Oxford: Blackwell. For further details on far left groups and politics.

Drucker H. *et al* (eds). 1986. *Developments in British Politics 2*. London: Macmillan. A useful update on all aspects of political parties in Britain.

6   *Elories, voters and political change*

6   *Elections, voters and political change*

Chapter objectives

By the end of this chapter you should:

■ be able to delineate the trends and patterns in voting since 1945 and particularly since 1974

■ be able to give an account of the varying explanations for why people vote as they do, and evaluate these differing explanations

■ be able to describe and evaluate explanations for recent changes in voting behaviour

■ know the meaning of and be able to use the following terms: expressive voting (Butler and Stokes), instrumental voting, ABCDE classification, deviant voters, voting cohorts, class de-alignment in voting, odds-ratio, new and old working class (Ivor Crewe), new and old middle class, post-industrial society, heartlands, north-south polarization, tactical voting.

Media Watch

For this chapter news coverage and analysis of by-elections, local government elections or if you are lucky a general election, would be ideal, but failing that you should pay particular attention to political public opinion polls, especially those which show support for parties and their policies according to social class, age, ethnic group, gender and region of residence.

Introduction

Political scientists have paid close attention to the statistics relating to elections since 1945, and have theorized at great length about what they mean. Surveys have explored the attitudes and intentions of voters before, after and during election campaigns. This is not surprising. A general election provides a wonderful source of information about the politics of the nation, since about three-quarters of its adult population publicly declare their political positions at the same time.

But statistics can be false friends. The obvious conclusion is not always the right one. Avoid assuming that because a factor and a result come together, the one is necessarily the sole cause of the other. For example, when the Conservative Party won the 1983 election with a landslide majority, some commentators pointed to the way Mrs Thatcher's popularity increased (from an all-time low) after Britain's defeat of the Argentinian forces in the Falkland Islands. The *Falklands' factor* was popularly supposed to have gained her and her Party the massive victory in 1983. But there were a number of other factors – the reduction in inflation to the lowest level since 1964, the rise of the Alliance as a credible third group, and the internal problems of the Labour Party. Anyway, the Conservative Party did not do particularly well in terms of its share of the vote. It did not markedly increase its share of the vote over the 1979 election. Labour, however, lost a quarter of its vote.

▶ Another way of characterizing the *Falklands factor* is that it did not so much win the Conservatives the 1983 election as prevent them from losing it. By-elections in 1982–3 seemed to confirm the plummeting fortunes of the Conservatives in the opinion polls. The percentage votes in by-elections in 1982–3 were as follows:

Conservative	27.5
Labour	34.7
Alliance	31.2

In the general election of 1983 the percentages were:

Conservative	43.5
Labour	28.3
Alliance	26.0

While the Falklands war does not fully explain this revival, it was almost certainly a factor.

Even seemingly obvious cause-and-effect relationships may be susceptible to query. Owners of small businesses have consistently supported the Conservative Party rather than any of the other parties in the ratio of about two to one, since 1945. This may well be because they identify their economic interests with the policies and ideology of the Conservative Party. But it may also be because the type of person who starts a small independent business does so because he/she has certain sorts of values and ideas which fit well with those of the Conservative Party. Being a small proprietor may be the product of Conservatism, rather than the other way round.

Bear in mind also that between elections, you are never comparing like with like. Since the last election, some voters will have died, some who did not qualify at the last election will qualify at this election, some who did not vote at the last election will vote at this one and vice versa. Switches in party loyalty will never explain all the changes that occur from one election to another.

This is not to say that you cannot make judgements on the basis of election statistics, just that you need to do so with care.

WHY DO WE VOTE AS WE DO?

Voting is an individual act, performed under conditions of secrecy. Yet there *are* general characteristics of the way we vote that have persisted since 1945.

1 *Most of us vote*. Turnout varies, but between 70 per cent and 80 per cent of those entitled to vote do so at general elections. In view of the facts that most British citizens are not actively involved in party politics, and that, as we saw in the last chapter, many votes are completely wasted in terms of making a difference to the election result, this may seem surprising.

2 *Most of us vote for a party rather than a person*. The personal characteristics of the candidate may affect the result, but not usually by much. Butler and Kavanagh concluded that for the Conservatives in 1987, personal votes were worth about 2 per cent.

3 *Social and economic as well as political factors affect the way we vote*. Much of the analysis and argument by political scientists has been around the extent to which factors in the social background of the voter, including

> Social class
> Family
> Type of work and workplace
> Union membership
> Income and wealth
> Consumption pattern
> Education

affect the way we vote, as compared with more obvious political factors, for example

> Policies
> Specific election promises

► Remember that the voters are never the same group in any two elections.

► The high turnout in general elections contrasts with poor turnout in local government elections, where a 50 per cent turnout is good and around 30 per cent not uncommon.

► Blanket media coverage of general elections may partly explain this difference. It may also have to do with perceiving a general election as a national event, and voting in it as a duty to one's country.

► Butler and Kavanagh (1988) *The British General Election of 1987* (Macmillan). This is one of the most thorough studies of the 1987 election.

Judgement of the fitness of party or leader to govern
Past record
Leadership and/or party 'image'

In the next section we ask what weight we should give to 'social' and 'political' factors, and in particular, how much the balance of their relative importance has changed.

Expressive voting

Butler and Stokes, in their earlier editions of *Political Change in Britain*, distinguished between the 'expressive' and the 'instrumental' motives for voting. Sociological explanations of voting concentrate on the former of the two motives. Voting is seen as an expression of loyalty to and identity with a set of social relationships – family, friends, neighbours, social class, workmates. In this model, I may vote Labour because I see myself as 'working class' and Labour as the party of the working class, and/or out of solidarity with my workmates who are Labour supporters, or with my neighbourhood where nearly everyone votes Labour. I internalize my Labour-orientated surroundings which becomes part of my 'political self-image'. Specific political factors – issues, policies, leadership, past record, future commitments, etc. – are relatively unimportant. Political allegiance is seen as the product of 'socialization' – social learning.

This view dominated the academic analysis of elections between 1950 and 1966, which was based upon the hypothesis that most people would vote 'typically' along class lines. Most such studies used either a straight manual/non-manual worker division, with manual worker typically Labour and non-manual Conservative, or the more sophisticated A, B, C1, C2, D and E classification, as follows:

A   Upper middle class (e.g. heads of large business organizations and the higher levels of the professions, e.g. judges)

B   'Quite well off' (e.g. professional and managerial)

C1 Lower middle class (small tradespeople and supervisory and clerical jobs)

C2 Skilled working class

D   Semi-skilled and unskilled working class

E   State pensioners, casual workers and the unemployed

Many studies of voting behaviour concentrated upon 'deviant' voters, particularly the 30 per cent or so of working class people who voted Conservative. These votes were explained in terms of false consciousness (not seeing themselves as working class), ambition (aspiring to a middle-class lifestyle), or an absence or weakness of the usual factors which socialize most of us into voting typical of our class.

► Butler and Stokes (various editions) *Political Change in Britain*. Butler and Stokes have been charting election trends since 1945.

► Class *objectively* defined is independent of where the individual may think she/he is in the social hierarchy. External criteria, such as income, education, consumption, life-style and/or relationship to the means of production are used to define class objectively. This may differ from an individual's *subjective* view of his/her own class, which may be equally important in determining how they vote.

► There is evidence, in Butler and Stokes and elsewhere, of a conformity factor. Voters are more likely to vote against their class if they live in areas where the dominant class is different from theirs. Doctors who live in mining towns are more likely to vote Labour than doctors elsewhere, and manual workers in seaside towns are more likely to vote Conservative than manual workers in general.

ACT Use a group of colleagues, friends or fellow students as your survey population. Draw up a questionnaire designed to measure their voting intentions, and which factors influence those intentions.

Carry out the survey. Draw any conclusions you can from your results about the relative importance of each factor.

Does the theory of expressive voting fit?

Until the 1970s this type of sociological explanation seemed to fit many of the known facts. During the 1950s and 1960s about two-thirds of both classes voted for the party typical of their class. A dip in Labour support in 1959 was quickly restored. In 1966 the level of 'class' voting was as high as it had ever been. Butler and Stokes and others found strong positive correlations between the way parents voted, and the way their children voted, particularly when the parents voted typically of their class and talked about politics with their children. Reinforcing factors, like trade-union membership and living in a mainly industrial community, were found to have a positive relationship with Labour voting. People who were living in neighbourhoods which were atypical of their class were more likely to vote atypically. The overwhelming majority of voters voted for one of the two big parties.

However after 1970 the picture seemed to change. There was an apparent decline in working-class support for Labour. Figure 6.1 gives the picture in crude manual/non-manual worker terms, up to and including 1983. Up to and including the 1966 election, the 60 per cent plus of manual workers voting Labour held up; indeed, in 1969 it was higher than ever. By 1983 it had declined to 42 per cent.

▶ Decline of class voting for the Labour Party.

Figure 6.1

Class and voting 1945–83

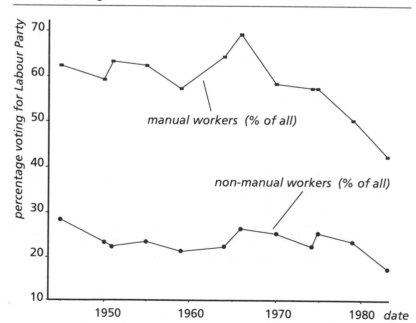

manual workers (% of all)

non-manual workers (% of all)

(Heath *et al.*, 1985)

Butler and Stokes produce evidence concerning 'age cohorts' which suggests that the political situation at the time when people come to political awareness and maturity may affect the strength of their subsequent loyalty to a party. Thus, the generation whose first support was for the 1945 Labour manifesto, with its strong programme for a radical transformation of society in terms of great equality, the welfare state, full employment, tended to remain loyal to Labour for longer, and more consistently, than subsequent generations of Labour voters.

As table 1 shows the 1987 election stayed with the trend illustrated in figure 6.1. In the C2 (skilled workers) group, once regarded as the backbone of Labour support, substantially more voters voted Conservative than Labour. Even amongst trade-union members, large numbers of whom are linked to the Labour Party through dual membership, only 42 per cent voted Labour.

Class voting in the 1987 general election (%)				
	AB	C1	C2	DE
Conservative	54	47	42	31
Labour	13	24	35	46
Lib/SDP	30	26	21	20

Table 1

ITN/Harris Poll
The Independent, 13 June 1987.

A rough-and-ready statement of Labour class-voting support would be this:

> Between 1945 and 1966 Labour could expect to rely on the support of 60 to 65 per cent of manual workers. Since 1970 this figure has diminished to the point where they can expect only 40 to 45 per cent. The decline has been particularly alarming for Labour amongst skilled workers and trade unionists, their former stalwarts.

A decline in middle-class support for the Conservatives, from about 63 per cent to about 55 per cent, also appears to have taken place, although it has been less dramatic than Labour's loss of support among the classes assumed to be its natural supporters.

The fall in the overall level of class voting – middle-class Conservative plus working-class Labour, as a percentage of the total – has been calculated by Crewe as from 63 per cent to 47 per cent, between 1945 and 1983. In 1945 almost two-thirds of voters voted typically of their class, by 1983 this figure was less than half.

One can sympathize with the commentator who said that by 1979 the spin of a coin was a more reliable way of forecasting how someone was going to vote than examining their class background!

There has been some crossing over, with skilled workers voting Conservative and members of what Heath *et al.* call the 'salariat' (the salaried classes) voting Labour.

 What have been the main changes in the relationship between voting and social class since 1945?

► Decline in middle-class support for the Conservative Party

► Until 1966 Labour received between 60 and 65 per cent of the votes of manual workers. Since 1970 this figure has diminished to between 40 and 45 per cent.

► Middle-class support for Conservatives has also declined but not so dramatically as working-class support for Labour – from about 63 per cent to 55 per cent.

The rise of the third party

However, a further change from the stability of 1945–66 has been the increased support for the Liberal Party and then the Liberal/SDP

Alliance. The Liberals gained 19.3 per cent of the total vote in 1974, then after falling back somewhat in October 1974 and 1979 formed the Alliance which polled 26 per cent of the total vote in 1983 and 23 per cent in 1987.

It seemed that we were in a 'three-party' situation, with the third party attracting a quarter of the votes. Furthermore, these votes seemed to come from both classes, only marginally more from the middle class than from the working class.

Explanations for the change in class voting

Those who have studied British political change in detail over the past twenty years have offered explanations which fall into three categories, although the categories are not mutually exclusive. They are:

- Class de-alignment
- An increase in 'instrumental' or 'consumerist' voting
- A redefinition of class boundaries, suggesting that class voting hasn't declined
- Class remains an important determinant of voting but the class structure itself has changed.

Class de-alignment

The working class

This approach is based upon the idea that the old classes, particularly the traditional working class, have fragmented, breaking down the solidarity that once existed. Evidence for this might be drawn from Table 2.

Table 2
How the working class voted (per cent)

The 'new' working class

	Lives in South	Owner occupier	Non union	Works in private sector
	40%•	57%•	66%•	
Con.	46	44	40	38
Lab.	28	32	38	39
Lib/SDP	26	24	22	23

Note: • figures are a per cent of all manual workers

The 'traditional' working class

	Lives in Scotland or North	Council tenant	Union member	Works in public sector
	60% •	43% •	34% •	
Con.	29	25	30	32
Lab.	57	57	48	49
Lib/SDP	15	18	22	19

Note: • figures are a per cent of all manual workers

I. Crewe,
Guardian, 15 June 1987.

Crewe distinguishes the 'new' from the 'old' working class, based upon divisions of geography, property ownership, work and level of affluence. The more affluent working-class Southerner, the voter who owns his or her own house and works in the private sector, was significantly more likely to vote Conservative than Labour in 1987.

It is suggested that property ownership, relative affluence and not being dependent on the state for work might affect working-class people in two ways. First, they might cause individuals who would be objectively identified as working class to subjectively identify themselves as middle class, and therefore support the middle-class party. Second, individuals while still seeing themselves as working class, might identify their interests with the aims of the Conservative Party: that is, private property, low taxes, anti-inflationary policies and a large and thriving private-sector economy.

The 'old' working class, on the contrary, unemployed or on low wages, working for a nationalized industry, living in a council house, belonging to an industrial union, may see their interests closer to the aims of the Labour Party – associated with more public spending, public housing, subsidies, and increased welfare benefits.

Middle-class de-alignment
Erik Ohlin Wright has sought to identify a 'new' middle-class type – a qualified professional working in the public sector, a member of the 'salariat' – who would not easily identify his or her interests with the aims and ideology of the Conservative Party. Table 3, published in 1987, shows divisions within the middle class.

Divisions in middle-class voting behaviour	Public sector %	Private sector %
Conservative	44	65
Labour	24	13
Lib/SDP	32	22

Table 3

I. Crewe,
Guardian, 15 June 1987.

Ohlin Wright claimed that the new middle class found itself in a contradictory situation. While the ideology appropriate to their status in society might be Conservative, their security of tenure as public employees put them in the same position as, or in periods of cuts by Conservative Governments a less secure position than, manual workers.

The growth of the state as an employer since 1945, and its increasing employment of highly qualified professionals, have swelled the ranks of this 'new' middle class. Their interest in seeing a large and well-funded public sector does not fit well with the avowed aim of the Conservative leadership since 1979 to cut public spending, to 'roll back the frontiers of the state' and privatize many publicly-owned operations. Jobs in the public sector which were once regarded as 'jobs for life' are now subject to the threat of redundancy. Large and militant white collar unions within local government, the civil service, and the teaching and lecturing professions are a phenomena of the 1980s – leading to highly qualified and relatively highly paid civil

► Erik Ohlin Wright *Class Crisis and the State* (1975) and 'Class boundaries in advanced capitalist societies' *New Left Review*, (July 1976).

servants and lecturers staffing picket lines.

In sum, the interests of the 'new' middle class do not coincide with the interests of the more traditional middle class.

Another factor affecting de-alignment may be the growth of the 'caring professions' associated with teaching and social work. Here, both the motives which attracted recruits to these professions, and the education and training leading to them, may not fit well with the policies and ideology of the post-1979 Conservative Governments.

Post-industrial society

These trends are sometimes described as typical of a *post-industrial* society: a society in which manufacturing industry ceases to be an important source of employment, and is replaced by service industries such as finance, leisure or health and welfare services. The decline in the number of workers in manufacturing industries (and extractive industries such as mining) and of the communities associated with them is linked to a decline in class loyalties. This process significantly influenced voting habits.

Correspondingly, the rise of the 'service' sector may have increased the number of voters living in mixed, mainly suburban, communities which are not linked to traditional class occupations. Certainly there is evidence that where the old *heartlands* of Labourism and Toryism still exist, class voting is still strong. There are, however, fewer people living in and characteristic of the heartlands.

 Make a list of all the social changes you can think of which might be related to the declining linkage between voting and social class. Add to the list as you continue with this chapter.

More instrumental voting?

The instrumental motive for voting is frequently contrasted with the expressive motive. Where expressive voting is based on loyalty to a social class, instrumental voting is based on specific issues which are important to the voter, and on which there is a perceived difference between the parties. The voter 'shops around' for the party which is more likely to achieve certain goals. So, I might consider economic policy to be of first importance, and seek the goal of low inflation, low personal taxation, and a thriving private sector – in which case I would be likely to vote Conservative. Support for solutions to certain issues does not always fit with the party associated with one's class. I may be working class, and may even have voted Labour in the past, but if I had felt strongly about the maintenance of Britain's nuclear deterrent in 1983, I would not have voted for Labour which at the time put forward a policy of unilateral nuclear disarmament. (Indeed this is assumed by many commentators to be one of the reasons for Labour's poor performance in the 1983 election.)

Franklin and Sarvlik & Crewe both claimed to detect a movement away from many of Labour's traditional policies by its former supporters.

► The term *heartlands* is used to describe areas where support for one party is usually solid and overwhelming. They are characterized by a preponderance of people who by their occupation and lifestyle would hardly be likely to vote for any other party, except perhaps as a one-off aberration.

Review
Voting behaviour

1 Until 1966 the sociological explanation of voting patterns, which saw voting as expressive of loyalty to class and social networks, seemed to fit, with two-thirds of the electorate voting along class lines.

2 Between 1966 and 1987 class, as defined by the manual/non-manual scale or on the ABCDE index, became less and less reliable as a predictor of voting or party loyalty. By 1983 typical class voting was only 47 per cent of the total.

3 As an effect (and partly perhaps as a cause) of this change, there has been a marked increase in 'third-party' voting – a quarter of the voters in the last two elections.

Himmelweit and colleagues argued that issues were the single surest guide to forecasting voting behaviour. This is, however, open to some doubt if you consider the 1987 general election. Butler and Kavanagh concluded that there was evidence that more voters regarded welfare issues as of salient importance in that year, and that Labour was perceived as the party that would deliver the desired goals, yet Labour was roundly defeated. It seems voters are swayed by more generalized perceptions such as 'competence' and 'ability to deliver the goods' rather than particular policies and goals.

Surveys round the time of the 1983 election revealed a 'credibility gap' concerning the competence of the Labour Party. This was not related to any specific issue, but concerned Labour's perceived fitness to govern in the light of its internal squabbles.

Surveys around the 1987 general election found that, on specific issues like handling jobs, health and education, Labour was preferred to Conservative. Conservative manifesto proposals were only weakly backed; only about a third of voters favoured selling water and electricity authorities to private companies, replacing Polaris by Trident or allowing state schools to opt out. And yet the Conservatives won! Again, the surveys suggest that a more generalized perception was important. Conservatives were perceived as being more likely to deliver general prosperity than Labour, and a majority of voters thought that their prosperity was increasing.

 Distinguish expressive voting from instrumental voting.

Class solidarity or consumerism?

Heath *et al.* claim that class solidarity is as strong as ever, and still important; we will examine their view more closely in the next section. Many commentators, however, claim that issues are the most important single factor in determining voting behaviour. Crewe's analysis of the Gallup election survey for 1983 showed that when the voters preferred the policies of one party but the leader of another, they split 5 to 1 in favour of policies; and that if Labour had received votes simply on support for the Labour Leadership, the Labour vote would have dropped by 17 per cent.

The view that voters are purely rational and 'instrumental', however, needs to be taken with a large pinch of salt. As Heath *et al.* point out:

> If people voted purely on the basis of rational calculation about the benefits the rival parties would bring them, they would never vote at all. The individual vote can make so little difference to the outcome of an election that the rational, instrumental elector would never waste his or her time and effort in going to the ballot box. We have to introduce an expressive or moral element to explain the act of voting itself ... So we believe that it is quite unnecessary to decide for or against either theory. Any act of voting must involve both expressive and instrumental elements ...

Heath *et al.* claimed that class solidarity was as strong as ever in the 1983 election. They criticized previous studies on class de-alignment

► Franklin (1985) *The Decline of Class Voting in Britain.* OUP

► Sarvlik and Crewe (1983) *Decade of De-alignment.* CUP

► Himmelweit, Humphreys and Jaeger (1984) *How Voters Decide.* Academic Press

► In their summary of the 1987 general election campaign, Butler and Kavanagh conclude: 'The three major policy areas appear to have been health and social security, unemployment and jobs, and education (which rose strikingly in importance during the election). Labour outscored the Conservatives as the party judged best for handling these issues and managed to get the social agenda across. Yet the campaign did not have much effect on changing the parties' relative standing on these social issues. (The *British General Election of 1987*) Macmillan. Do we attach too much importance to the campaigns as a means of influencing voters?

► Heath, Jowell and Curtice (1985) *How Britain Votes.* Pergamon

► TV and instrumental voting. In a radio discussion with Robert McKenzie, David Butler suggested that television might contribute to instrumental voting because of its treatment of political news in terms of issues quickly and graphically illustrated with pros and cons, and its tendency to avoid presenting broad ideological conflicts in detail.

on the following grounds:

• The studies measured absolute decline in class voting, not the relative probability of people voting against rather than for their 'natural' parties. The proper measure of de-alignment should be an 'odds ratio' made up of the odds of the middle-class voting Labour (rather than Conservative), to the odds of the working class voting Conservative (rather than Labour). On this measure there has been no long-term decline in class voting.

• The definition of class used by most studies is inappropriate. The manual/non-manual categorization is too crude, and ignores important differences within and across those categories. The ABCDE categorization may be suitable for market research, but ignores important differences in relationship to the economy, the labour market and job security, which affect political perception. The self-employed, however low their income, have different economic interests from the employed. Heath *et al.* therefore propose a different classification as follows:

1 Salariat (salaried professionals)

2 Routine non-manual (clerks, salespeople, secretaries)

3 The petty bourgeoisie (farmers, small proprietors, own-account manual workers)

4 Foremen and technicians (the 'blue collar' elite)

5 The working class (rank and file manual workers)

Using this scheme of classes, and the 'odds ratio' method of calculating de-alignment, Heath *et al.* conclude that there has been no decline in class voting.

Heath *et al.* gave the following picture of the changing composition of the electorate:

	1964	1983
Salariat	18%	27%
Routine non-manual	18%	24%
Petty-bourgeoisie	7%	8%
Foremen & technicians	10%	7%
Working class	47%	34%

They claim that these structural changes (particularly the decline in the number of working-class voters) account for nearly half decline in Labour's share of the vote in this period.

• Married women are included as appendages of their husbands in most studies. They are assumed to be of the same class as their husbands. According to Heath *et al's* definitions of class, however, they may well be different, have a different political perspective and vote differently for that reason.

While welcoming Heath *et al's* scheme of classification of social groups, Crewe, in his essay 'On the death and resurrection of class voting' published in *Political Studies* (December 1986, Vol. 34), criticized both the methodology and the conclusions of *How Britain Votes*.

► Recent opinion-poll methods have moved away from this view of women as appendages of their husbands. When women's own occupations are taken into consideration they vote in much the same way as men do.

Major points of criticism were as follows:
- The 'odds ratio' method is flawed. It exaggerates small changes and as Heath *et al.* use it, it ignores movements to a third party. If the odds ratio was reversed and formulated as the joint probability of (1) the working class voting Labour rather than non-Labour and (2) the middle class voting Conservative rather than non-Conservative, it would give a result much closer to the common sense view that class voting has declined.
- Comparing the 1964 with the 1983 election, using Heath *et al's* categories, structural changes in the working class can only account for 50 per cent of the decline in the Labour vote. The rest are explicable by behavioural changes.
- Between 1945 and 1983 the proportion of manual workers voting Labour fell from 62 per cent to 42 per cent accompanying a 20 per cent decline in Labour's share of the total vote. It goes against common understanding to conclude that this shows no weakening of class voting.

 What factors have been cited as important in the apparent decline in 'class' voting?

Summarize Heath *et al's* reasons for suggesting that the decline in class voting has been more apparent than real. What criticisms have been made of their ideas?

Odds Ratio

In *How Britain Votes* (1985) Heath, Jowell and Curtice claim that on this measure there has been no long-term decline in class voting.

The odds ratio is a tricky concept, but if you bear in mind that it is designed to measure relative class solidarity in voting rather than absolute increase or decrease in votes for a party or class it should be easier to follow.

The ratio reflects the combined odds (for example) of a manual worker and a non-manual worker voting Conservative. So if the odds of a non-manual worker voting Conservative were two to one in favour, and the odds of a manual worker voting Conservative were only one to two in favour, the odds ratio would be four to one. If there were no class bias in voting we would expect an odds ratio of 1:1. The bigger the odds ratio the stronger the class allegiance. Heath *et al*'s calculations of the odds ratios for elections 1964 to 1983 are as follows:

1964	9:3	1974 (Feb)	6:1	1983	6:3
1966	7:3	1974 (Oct)	5:5		
1970	3:9	1979	4:9		

► Crewe criticises Heath *et al's* odds ratio method and their claim that there has been no class de-alignment in voting.

► See Crewe 'On the death and resurrection of class voting' *Political Studies* Vol. 34 December 1986.

> ### Review – Class voting
>
> 1 The apparent decline in class voting has been attributed to:
>   - *Class de-alignment*. Economic changes, producing a 'new' working class (southern home-owners, relatively affluent and working in private industry), who are more likely to vote non-Labour than Labour; and a 'new' middle class (the salaried professionals working in the public sector), who are less likely to vote Conservative.
>   - *Less expressive and more instrumental voting*. Salient issues, and the perceived ability of the parties to deliver on them, have become, in the view of some commentators, the single most important factor in voting behaviour.
>
> 2 But instrumental rationality is unlikely to be the complete explanation for peoples' voting behaviour, since if they behaved completely rationally most of them wouldn't vote at all.
>
> 3 Heath, Jowell and Curtice challenge the view that class voting has declined, and attribute the trends in voting to structural and political changes; Crewe contests both their methodology and their conclusions.

GEOGRAPHICAL POLARIZATION

► The north-south divide.

The three general elections of 1979, 1983 and 1987 seem to demonstrate a trend towards a north-south polarization in British politics, with Labour holding almost no seats (outside London) south of a line drawn from the Severn to the Wash, and Conservatives holding very few seats in Scotland and in the five big conurbations of Manchester, Liverpool, South and West Yorkshire and Tyneside.

This effect is exaggerated by the way our electoral system works. In 1983, 61 per cent of the two-party vote for the Conservatives won them 66 per cent of the seats, while 39 per cent of the two-party vote won 34 per cent of the seats for Labour. The Alliance secured 25 per cent of the vote, but only 2.5 per cent of the seats. In the same election there were only 80 marginal seats (compared to 149 in 1979). Of 186 seats south of the Wash–Severn line, outside London, Labour won only three.

► *Marginal seat*:
one which has a history of small majorities for winning parties, and might go either way at another election.

In 1987 the decline in the number of marginals was reversed, but only slightly. Labour's vote increased more sharply in the north of England, Wales and Scotland, and it remained virtually unrepresented in the south of England. In Scotland the Conservatives held only ten of the 72 seats, in Wales eight of the 38. Although Conservatives retained some northern marginals (Bolton North East and Bury South) and Labour made four gains in the Midlands, the pattern remained the same.

In Parliamentary terms Labour is becoming the party of the economically deprived parts of north and north-west Britain, and to a lesser extent Conservatives of the affluent south and south-east. The

Alliance continued to suffer from the electoral system, with 3.5 per cent of the seats for 23.1 per cent of the vote.

What may polarization reflect?

1 *The electoral system* virtually eliminates the centre parties, because their votes are evenly spread, and it causes the substantial numbers of Scottish and northern Conservatives and southern Labour supporters to be grossly under-represented.

2 *Different issues are important.* The higher rate of home-ownership, income, level of consumption and employment in the south and south east may mean that issues like inflation, opportunities to make money and own property, and the prospect of continuing affluence are more important to southern English voters, than welfare, unemployment, council housing and more public spending, which are more important to Northerners.

3 *Changes to the working classes.* If Crewe's division between the 'old' and 'new' working class is accurate, then much of the polarization may well arise from the fact that the 'old' working class are more concentrated in the north of Britain and the 'new' in the south.

 Why might some commentators see geographical polarization as potentially dangerous?

THE THIRD FORCE?

The Liberal Democrats and nationalist parties – making up the third force or the middle ground – are discussed in Chapter 5. Here, however, we may consider what the rise of the 'third force' means in terms of support for the two traditional parties.

Cause or effect?

Has the growth of third parties attracted allegiance, thereby causing a change in voting patterns, or has de-alignment and greater volatility caused voters to have recourse to third parties as better representing their interests? Or is the vote for third parties to be seen as a protest vote against the other two parties by voters without strong class commitments to the Labour or Conservative Parties?

It is likely that some voters indulge in the luxury of voting against the Government or the major opposition party at by-elections, since the question of which party is to govern Britain is not being decided, and then revert to one of the two big parties at the general election. The Alliance seemed to benefit from this fact in by-elections (1982–7), but failed to hold the support in general elections. In by-elections in 1982–3 the Alliance secured 31.2 per cent of the vote, but its support fell to 26 per cent at the 1983 general election. In the 1987 election, in which the Alliance announced its determination to achieve the kind of percentage it had gained in by-elections, it received a creditable but disappointing 23.1 per cent. For the first time the geographical pattern of Alliance voting was uneven. It suffered particularly heavily in working-class areas in the north of England, Wales and Scotland,

► Mrs Thatcher seems to have taken polarization seriously, at least just after the election. Speaking from Central Office on 12 June 1987 she said in an otherwise triumphal speech: *'We have a big job to do in some of those inner cities … to help the people get more choice, and politically we must get right back in there.'*

Is the north-south polarization serious?

Some commentators see dangers ahead if the trend continues. After the 1987 election the *Guardian* and the *Economist* saw it as evidence of a Britain divided politically, reflecting an imbalance in economic prosperity and opportunity. If, as Heath *et al.* and Butler and Kavanagh's 1987 election study suggests, the Conservative Party is more and more representing a national constituency of 'winners' and Labour represents the 'losers' there may be a danger of each party adjusting its policies to suit its supporters. This could have the effect of reducing their claims to be 'national' parties, and causing successive governments to pursue sectional interests rather than consensus policies, thus further exacerbating the divide.

It is also argued by those who favour electoral reform that the Commons is becoming less and less representative. Three-quarters of Labour's 229 MPs are from the north of England, Scotland and Wales. Conservatives have no MPs in the cities of Manchester, Leicester, Bradford, Liverpool, Newcastle-upon-Tyne and Glasgow. Who is to represent the Tories in these cities, and Labour supporters in southern England?

Suggested remedies
The first is to reform the electoral system. As we have seen, proponents of reform hope it would bring more consensual policies and governments.

The second remedy is for parties to pursue more consensual values and policies. 'Wet' Conservatives and 'moderate' Labour supporters have urged their respective leaders to broaden their appeal by going for more consensual policies. The Labour Party, following the defeat of 1983, has been busy modernizing its image, streamlining its organization, dropping what it regarded as some unpopular policies and softening others.

► There is evidence from the 1987 election to suggest that fear of letting in Labour or Conservative candidates was a deterrent to voting for the Alliance. According to a BBC Gallup Poll in 1987, 68 per cent of those who had voted Alliance in the past, or were considering doing so in 1987 and changed their minds, did so for fear that it would let the 'wrong' big party into office (quoted in *The British General Election of 1987*).

indicating that in Labour's heartlands voters had resorted to their traditional class loyalties.

Surveys of Alliance voters carried out after two significant by-election victories (Glasgow Hillhead, 1982; and Bermondsey, 1983) indicated that a majority of Alliance voters had no clear knowledge of the Alliance's policies, and voted for it to express rejection of the Government and the Labour Party, rather than to positively support the Alliance.

The picture is obscured by the fact that in the 1987 election a substantial number of voters voted tactically – not to support their first-choice party, which might not stand a chance, but to block the least preferred party. Thus a Labour supporter in a constituency where Labour stand no chance, may vote for the Alliance to try to block the Conservatives. According to a Harris/ITN exit poll, over 36 per cent of those who switched to Labour from the Alliance from 1983 to 1987 did so for this reason.

There is no class base for the middle ground. In as much as class is still important as a factor in voting behaviour, the centre parties do not have the firm class base that the other two have. However Heath *et al.* suggest that the salariat may form an important component of support for centre parties.

► Bearing in mind the fate of the Labour Party in 1987, despite being ahead on salient issues, one must ask how important are issues and policies.

Another factor affecting the third force is the fluctuating support for national parties. In 1974 the SNP (Scottish Nationalist Party) polled 800,000 votes and won 11 seats; by 1987 its vote was down to 400,000. Much of the SNP vote may have been due to disenchantment with the Labour Party in 1974, rather than a passion or Scottish nationalism.

Has the two-party system gone?

In the sense that that phrase was used to describe British politics between 1945 and 1970, the answer is probably 'yes'. The two parties can no longer rely on the support of more than 90 per cent of those who vote. Nor can they rely on a core of loyal supporters who will support them through thick and thin for the rest of their voting lives.

The fact that the combination of full employment, steady economic growth and effective social services which prevailed in the 1950s and 60s no longer prevails may help to explain why instrumental voters look for an alternative to the two big parties which dominated those decades.

► The SDP has ceased to exist and the Liberal Democrats have emerged as a single party but it is too early to say whether this unity will revive the fortunes of the third force. However results at two by-elections in 1990 (Eastbourne and Bradford) must have given encouragement to the party.

However, the two big parties still get more than 70 per cent of the votes and benefit from the present electoral system. With no credible alternative around they may continue to do so, but perhaps with less authority and confidence than before

 What evidence is there that the two party system has gone?

(ACT) **Essay Discussion Question**

'Social Class is no longer an important factor influencing voting behaviour'. Assess the validity of this statement with particular reference to the general election of 1987.

As a resource for this essay use the list of factors you compiled for the activity on page 110.

CHAPTER SUMMARY

1 Most of us vote at general elections.

2 Most of us vote for a party, rather than an individual.

3 Political scientists differ about the relative importance to voting of long-term sociological factors and short-term political factors.

4 From 1945 to 1970 there was a predictable and apparently steady relationship between social class, defined as working (manual) and middle (white collar), and party support.

5 From 1970, the 'class' model of voting behaviour seemed less and less relevant.

6 Political scientists have ascribed the changes to:
   • Class de-alignment, particularly the division between 'new' and 'old' working class.
   • An increase in instrumental (issue) voting.
   • The result not of class de-alignment, but of political factors combined with structural changes in class sizes.

7 It is difficult to assess whether the rise in support for third parties is the result or the cause of greater volatility on the part of the voters, but indicators seem to point to it being the result.

8 While the two big parties still dominate British politics in terms of seats in Parliament, the model of the two-party system which fitted Britain in the 1950s and 1960s is probably no longer relevant.

STIMULUS MATERIAL

The stimulus material for this chapter is about voting and ethnicity and is taken from the *Independent*. Read the article and answer the following questions:

1 What factors seem, from the article, to have led to the Islamic Party (with the backing of some Imams) to put up council candidates against Labour?

2 What do you think would be the consequences of the development of strong parties representing ethnic and religious groups in British cities where potential backing for such parties existed?

3 What, from the article, seems to be the Labour Party's dilemma in this matter? What, if anything, might the Party do to resolve the problem?

4 How do the events described in the article relate to the argument about Britain's electoral system?

5 Assess the view expressed in paragraph 3, that 'it is better to change Labour from inside'.

TEMPERS FRAY IN TEXTILE TOWN AS ASIANS SWITCH ALLEGIANCE

1 Councillor Brian Iddon sounded distinctly bad tempered on a tour of Bolton's Central ward, which he has held for 10 years: 'The Labour Party will be very angry indeed with the Muslim community if I get knocked off. For those of us that fight for them, it's going to be 10 times more difficult. There would be a backlash.'

2 In the evening, outside the Taiyabah mosque in the ward's Blackburn Road, four young textile machinists had their eyes fixed on the darkening eastern sky. They were looking for the new moon that would signal the end of Ramadan and a month of fasting. All were agreed on what they would do on 3 May: 'It's my religion and my people. We've got to support our own kind. We were Labour, but we are going to vote Islamic Party.'

3 Imtiaz Ibrahim, 22, who works in the electronics industry, said: 'I'll probably vote Labour. I agree that they keep making false promises and also we are not getting our rights in education. But it is better to change Labour from the inside. I don't think the Islamic Party are serious contenders.'

4 But Mr Ibrahim, wearing a white skull cap and just out of evening prayers, was not happy. 'If I don't vote for the Islamic Party, is that against my faith? Is it a vote against God?' This is the aspect of the Islamic Party that upsets Guy Harkin, deputy leader of Bolton's ruling Labour group: 'It's a dreadfully reactionary step in politics and race relations – getting more votes by moral blackmail.'

5 The town's nine mosques seem solidly behind the Islamic Party. Imams are generally giving tacit support – though Labour still courts some of them – and the Party uses the mosques to spread its message. At Idd, the prayer meeting marking the end of Ramadan, candidates intended to advise Bolton's 26,000 Muslims to vote against Labour where there were no Islamic Party candidates.

6 It is the latest escalation in a bitter and dirty campaign, which has seen accusations of racism from both sides. Brian Iddon is worried, not only at what he sees as a political move that can only harm the town's minority ethnic groups, but also about losing his seat. Muslims make up more than half of his electorate.

7 Labour is being challenged in four wards and it could lose Central and Derby wards. Karamat Hussain, Islamic Party candidate in Derby ward, says that if there were any Muslim councillors in Bolton the party might never have been formed. But unlike in Birmingham, Leicester and Bradford, Labour has significantly failed to attract Asian candidates.

8 Mr Hussain and Ayoub Khan, another Islamic Party candidate, have both been Labour Party members – Mr Khan was briefly on the Labour candidates' list. Mr Hussain will recite a long list of grievances – letters ignored, meetings cancelled, support withheld – that led him to withdraw from the Labour Party.

9 On the other side, the Labour leadership talks of apathy among the Muslims in spite of their best efforts – Brian Iddon's ward association even left the Labour club and held alcohol-free meetings to try to bring Muslims in.

10 Might not political expediency suggest the virtues of a little positive discrimination in candidate selection? 'We have to abide by our selection procedures. And there has only been one vacancy in Central and Derby wards in the last 10 years. But I think the next generation of vacancies will, quite rightly, bring out some Asian candidates.'

11 Jameel Ahmad may be one of them. A Labour member for 22 years and the only Asian on the candidates' list, he has been interviewed four times, unsuccessfully, as a potential councillor. His support remains firm and he is not disappointed: 'It is not discrimination. It was in my mind that there may be someone else who was more clever and more experienced than me. Being a councillor is a very responsible job. And Asians should know that the only party is the Labour Party.'

12 But the dispute goes beyond the problem of representation. On his guided tour, Brian Iddon points out a host of benefits for the Asian community that he has achieved as councillor and chairman of the housing committee – land for a mosque here, building grants there, a youth club, a football pitch.

'The indigenous community accuses us of bending over backwards to help Asians.'

13   But all this cuts little ice with the Islamic Party. Concessions for their community have, in their view, been few and far between. There is still no mother-tongue teaching in Bolton schools; halal food in the schools was only won after a long and acrimonious fight. Bolton council is the largest employer in the town, but less than 2 per cent of council employees are Asian. 'What Labour has done for us is only their duty – Conservatives would do the same,' Ilyas Patel, area spokesman for the Party, said.

14   Apart from being the only political group in Britain that wants to return to the rating system, the Islamic Party has a radical agenda based on the Koran that goes far beyond just trying to sting Labour into more action. An economic system without interest on lending is the key platform (there is also a pretty harsh line on homosexuality). But Dr Hany Nasr, deputy leader of the Party, calls the comprehensive manifesto 'a message in a bottle to the British public'.

15   In a few years, he hopes non-Muslims will outnumber Muslims among the membership, currently 1,000. 'We have a comprehensive system, tolerant, benevolent and just, which can expose the deficiencies of the old parties. We want to work together.'

16   Back in Bolton, Mr Patel thinks his party will make an impact. 'Even if we don't take the seats we will have done something to weaken the giant. Next time we will get them. The Labour Party must realize that our votes are not their asset.'

The Independent
3 May 1990

Now that you have reached the end of the chapter, turn back to the beginning, and look at the objectives and make sure that you have achieved each of them.

Further reading: Chapter 6

Butler D. and Kavanagh D. 1988. *The British General Election of 1987*. London: Macmillan. A very thorough study of the election. Read the conclusion and select other parts as you need them.

Drucker H. *et al*. 1986. *Developments in British Politics*, Chapter 2. London: Macmillan. A good summary.

Franklin M. 1984. *The Decline of Class Voting in Britain*. Oxford: OUP. An examination of the apparent decline between class and voting

Heath A. Jowell R. and Curtice J. 1985. *How Britain Votes*. Oxford: Pergamon. Detailed but often difficult account of he ideas summarized in this chapter. Worth reading, but not easy!

Himmelweit H., Humphries P. and Jaeger M. 1985. *How Voters Decide*. Milton Keynes: Open University Press. Good investigation of the issues that influence voters.

⑦ Pressure groups

Chapter objectives

By the end of this chapter you should be able to:

▌ distinguish a pressure group from a political party

▌ explain and examine critically the role of pressure groups in a liberal democracy

▌ identify different kinds of pressure group and classify them according to a typology

▌ describe the role of pressure groups in the terms of models of neo-corporatism, elite pluralism and pluralism in Britain in the 1970s, 1980s and early 90s, using examples from that era.

Media Watch

For this section of the syllabus you will need good up-to-date examples of pressure group politics. Look out especially for situations in which Government consults with various organizations before planning legislation, and for the relationships between Government and the unions, and Government and the CBI. Stories about extra-Parliamentary politics such as demonstrations or riots are also of interest.

WHAT IS A PRESSURE GROUP?

A pressure group may be defined as:

an organized group which seeks to influence the way power is exercised by government and to gain advantage for a particular group or idea, but not to take over power.

The dividing line between pressure groups and political parties is sometimes difficult to draw. Are affiliated unions, who hold the majority of votes at the policy-making body of the Labour Conference and who sponsor Labour candidates at election time, a pressure group or a political party? CND is surely a pressure group – but it has on occasion put up a Parliamentary candidate.

Nevertheless, the differences between pressure groups and political parties remain. Two important features of pressure groups are:

1 *Pressure groups are specific in their aims.* They concentrate on one issue (e.g. homelessness), one group of people (e.g. workers in a certain industry) or one cause (e.g. nuclear disarmament). Political parties offer *general policies* which seek to cover everything – education, the economy, foreign affairs, etc.

2 *Pressure groups aim to influence government, not take it over.* They may favour one political party rather than another, but they will seek to influence whichever political group is in power. A political party puts itself forward as a body which will be willing to govern. Pressure groups may also seek to influence local councils or government agencies such as the NHS.

 How does a pressure group differ from a political party? (Refer back to Chapter 5.)

CND as a pressure group
CND (the Campaign for Nuclear Disarmament) has enjoyed varying fortunes. It reached a peak in terms of membership and media impact in the 1960s, with the massively supported marches to the Government Research Station at Aldermaston. It then declined somewhat with internal quarrels, but grew again in support in the early 1980s. Between 1980 and 1983 there was a tenfold increase in its membership. By 1983 there were over 300,000 members with an annual turnover of £250,000 on booklets alone, and an annual income of £500,000.

Pressure groups in Britain

There are tens of thousands of pressure groups in Britain, ranging from local, ephemeral groups set up to protest at, say, the closure of a school or a proposal to build a motorway, to huge and rich national groups like the Confederation of British Industry (CBI) with an annual income of around £5m, or the Transport and General Workers Union (TGWU) with an income of nearly £20m.

Types of pressure groups

In an effort to make some sense of this diversity, commentators have divided pressure groups into two types, that is, *promotional* groups and *interest* groups.

► Pressure groups are often divided into *promotional groups* and *interest groups*.

1 *Promotional groups* seek to promote a *cause* or *idea*. So, Amnesty International campaigns for the release of political prisoners especially whom they consider to have been cruelly or unjustifiably treated; CND (Campaign for Nuclear Disarmament) seeks to have nuclear weapons banned.

2 *Interest groups* are so labelled because their main purpose is to defend and further the objectives of a group identified in some way, say, by trade or profession. Such groups are defined by the common interests of their members, rather than commonly held views and beliefs. Examples are the trade unions, looking after the interests of workers in a common trade or working in a common industry, or the employers' federations, defending and furthering the interests of firms in a particular area of operation, such as printing.

► In Britain *producer groups* (trade unions, employers' associations) are in general better organized and financed and more effective than *consumer groups*.

Groups may be further divided into *producer groups*, representing those who create a product (trade unions and employers' associations) and *consumer groups* who buy or use a product or service, for instance, the Consumers' Association and 'welfare' consumer groups like the Claimants' Union.

These categories are only a rough-and-ready guide. They often overlap. A trade union, or group of trade unions, will campaign on issues – equal pay, health and safety work while a promotional group such as Shelter (the housing pressure group), may defend the interests of a particular group of people – tenants or mortgagees threatened with eviction, for example. However, if you look at the underlying purpose of a group, and its major activities, it is reasonable to put it into one category or the other. Marsh, in his book *Pressure Politics* re-labels them 'ideological' and 'economic' groups.

 Distinguish between interest pressure groups and promotional pressure groups. Find examples of each.

Why so many pressure groups?

The size and complexity of the pressure-group system in Britain may be attributed to a number of factors:

1 *A complex economy*. Britain is what is usually labelled a *developed* nation. Its economy is based upon a sophisticated and complex division of labour. The division between capital and labour is reflected

respectively in the 'peak' organizations: the CBI (Confederation of British Industry) and the TUC (Trades Union Congress). Both organizations encompass a multitude of factional interests which are often in conflict. Within the TUC a bitter battle arose between the EEPTU (the electricians' union) and other unions, over recruitment and job demarcation. Eventually this led to the expulsion of the EEPTU from the TUC. Within the CBI, the interests of small firms and those of large organizations frequently diverge and some sectors such as retailing, 'services' and financial institutions are under-represented, preferring their own groups.

2   *Liberal democracy.* Britain is not a 'corporate' state in which groups are licensed and controlled by the state and act as extensions of the state machinery. Anybody can form a pressure group, for any legal purpose, organise it the way they want it and, within the laws of defamation, say what they like. This freedom, combined with a literate population and the growth of further and higher education, creates a climate particularly favourable to the setting up of promotional groups.

3   *A large and 'interventionist' state.* Although the three Thatcher Governments emphasized 'rolling back of the frontiers of the state', the state in one form or another remains a potent and pervasive force in British society. It disposes of about 40 per cent of the national income; it is by far the biggest employer of labour in the country, and as the biggest builder and major investor in capital projects its spending decisions spell riches and jobs for some, and ruin and unemployment for others.

During the twentieth century, particularly between 1945 and 1979, the State has intervened significantly in four areas:

- Health, education and welfare.
- The physical environment.
- Management of the economy.
- Industry, to the point of taking over basic industries completely.

It is therefore not surprising that groups form in response to a state which disposes such a large 'cake'.

4   *The rule of law.* The usual method to effect major change is through amendment in the law. Groups seeking change in their favour therefore seek to amend the law. Amendments to the law relating to abortion, homosexuality and capital punishment have been, in great part, the result of pressure applied to Parliament and Government by such groups.

5   *Perceived shortcomings of the political parties.* During the 1960s and 1970s there was a significant increase in the number and variety of promotional groups. Many factors may have contributed to this growth, one of them being the increasing number of people, particularly amongst the salariat, who turned to single-issue politics as the most effective way of getting something changed.

Mass political parties, by their nature, tend to generalize issues. To gain support and avoid alienating a significant group of potential

► In the five years after the 1939–45 war, a number of Acts of Parliament were passed, based upon reports produced during the war, giving the state extensive powers in these areas: in health and welfare, the National Health Services Act and the National Assistance Acts of 1948; in environmental and land control, the Town and Country Planning Act of 1947 and a number of Housing Acts; in industry, laws giving the state ownership and control over coal, electricity, gas, rail, road and air transport.

voters, they compromise. When in office, they drop or water down cherished aims in the face of pressure and conflicting forces. Many articulate and motivated individuals frustrated by the amorphous nature of the Labour Party, turned to single-issue politics as their main focus of activity, although this did not preclude them also working through the Labour Party.

 Why does Britain have so many pressure groups?

Pressure groups within a liberal democracy

A final verdict on where pressure groups fit into the British political system rests partly on your view of the distribution of power in British society, as we shall see later. There are, however, certain functions which pressure groups may perform within any liberal democracy:

1 *The articulation of group demands*. Pressure groups enable a large number of people to 'speak with one voice'. Without this facility the needs and demands of a whole section of society could go unheard.

2 *Agenda-setting*. By ensuring that certain issues continually appear before the eyes of Government, public and media, and by keeping other issues off the agenda, pressure groups contribute to the formation of the political agenda.

3 *Intermediation*. Groups may act as agents of an interest or aim, representing them to Government. This may suit both pressure group and Government, since for the Government:
• It enables them to 'test the water' – assess the likelihood of success of a policy or the degree of resistance to it.
• Pressure groups may provide facts, figures, policies and even draft legislation from which Government can proceed.
• Potentially damaging opposition may be traded off for concessions to pressure groups.

Pressure groups benefit because it gives them access to those who control the levers of power and confers a degree of gravity and respectability. However this is a double-edged weapon, since group members may be wary of their leaders getting too close to Government.

4 *Countervailing power*. Those who support the pluralist view of society see pressure groups as providing counter-pressure to the seemingly enormous power exercised by the state in Britain. By collecting detailed information, pressure groups may provide an authoritative and alternative message to that put out by the State. Well-organized and well-funded pressure groups may employ their own economists, lawyers and planners to present facts and arguments.

 Compare and contrast the role of political parties and pressure groups in a liberal democracy – see also Chapters 4 and 5.

How pressure groups work

The methods used by pressure groups, and the points at which they apply pressure, vary according to the nature of the group, and the nature of its campaign.

To a great extent, the method employed will be influenced by the channel through which pressure is applied. Depending upon their relationship with Government, some pressure groups will use one channel more than another. Typically, groups have the following options:

1 *Direct appeal to the public.* This may take the form of marches, demonstration, leaflets, papers, public meetings and *direct action* – sit-ins, occupation or trespass. This route is used largely, though not exclusively, by ideological or promotional groups. It is appropriate that they should use a channel that reaches as many people as possible since part of their function is to alert people to something of which they were not previously aware, or to change their *perspective* and views.

Another reason why ideological groups may use this route is because most of them are 'outsider' groups – which do not have contacts and established relationships with Government departments, through ministers and civil servants. Thus appealing to the public, as well as spreading the message and gaining supporters, may impress upon Government the idea that the group represents a significant section of public opinion. Since public opinion is difficult to define and assess, active opinion manifested in meetings, petitions marches, etc. may be judged sufficiently articulate to warrant a Governmental response even if it is only a minority opinion.

Ideological and promotional groups do not usually have the ready-made pool of potential recruits, defined by their work or economic function, that interest groups enjoy. Public events therefore, may bring the useful by-product of new recruits. However if the public event produces no change in policy this may bring frustration. Most groups which engage in high-profile public activity combine it with other forms of pressure.

Direct action may include illegal actions. This is often a source of tension and sometimes opens breaches in ideological pressure groups. Those in favour of illegal actions may argue that the law is unfair or discriminatory, and that law-breaking attracts the attention of the national TV channels and newspapers – 'There is no such thing as "bad publicity".' Opponents may argue that in a liberal democracy one should play by the rules, and that illegal actions will alienate more potential supporters than it will impress and attract.

2 *The media.* One of the purposes of the kind of actions outlined above is to attract the attention of TV, radio and newspapers. The British media is highly centralized. Most viewers of TV watch news networked throughout the country: a handful of newspapers can claim between them 20 million readers. Thus a headline or a TV slot communicates to a wider audience than any other method.

► Feminist demands and environmental issues are two examples of *perspectives,* once hardly noticed by those in power, which are now at the centre of the agenda, with practically all politicians finding it desirable to have an attitude on these matters.

► A promotional or ideological group may use its contacts in a powerful interest group to achieve a link through affiliation, declaration of public support or financial support, e.g. some unions affiliated to CND.

► The *Chartists* in the nineteenth century, the *women's suffrage* movement of the early twentieth century, the anti-nuclear movement of the 1960s, and the *animal rights* movement of today, have all at some time been split between those wanting to break the law, and those wanting to stay within it.

As well as promoting events which will attract media attention, groups may seek to get into the media directly. A journalist or celebrity writer who espouses your cause can be helpful in this respect. Establishing a link with newspapers or TV producers may mean that you are asked to furnish a spokesperson for a programme or news item.

Skilful management of newsworthy events to ensure regular exposure in the media is now often a full-time business for employers of pressure groups or for professional media consultants who they employ.

3 *Parliament*. Since Parliament is the place where laws are made, and where Government faces public debate and criticism, it is an obvious target for pressure groups. Ways into Parliament are:

• *Lobbying MPs* (so-called after the Parliamentary lobby where MPs talk to constituents). Lobbying is the term used for seeking to influence MPs and asking them to support you. This may take a variety of forms; a mass lobby at which a large number of supporters seek to talk to their respective MPs all at the same time; or individual approaches, group approaches, letters and mail shots.

Most groups, however, seek to establish a more permanent relationship with MPs sympathetic to their cause. The closeness of this relationship can range from an informal agreement to listen to representatives of the group and put forward its views, to a consultancy by which the MP is paid to look after a group's interests in Parliament. This last has been the subject of considerable controversy. Where money is involved, critics claim, the boundary between proper and improper interest (a euphemism for bribery) becomes blurred. A voluntary 'register of interests' for MPs has been set up in response to this criticism. At the last count 170 MPs on the register described themselves as 'consultants' or 'advisers'.

► Some MPs (notably Enoch Powell) refused to register on the grounds that a voluntary register was absurd, and that it should be compulsory.

• *Legislation*. Although most laws that pass onto the statute book are sponsored by the Government, MPs have the right to promote new legislation as individuals. Since only a small proportion of the Parliamentary timetable is devoted to these *Private Member's Bills*, most of them do not become law because they run out of time before the end of the Parliamentary year, and 'fall'. However, debate, on a Private Member's Bill, may provide valuable publicity.

Governments have been known to undertake to introduce legislation of their own after debate on a Private Member's Bill. Since the priority in the allocation of Private Member's Bill time is done by lot, the MP who draws first priority is a prime target for pressure groups, with many presenting the MP with a ready drafted bill.

► By this route the law on abortion was first liberalized following a private bill presented by David Steel in 1967.

The Government may leave the field free to a Private Member's Bill on what it regards as politically tricky moral issues.

Private members' legislation is not the only area of legislation where pressure groups may get involved. Governments may sponsor legislation as the result of pressure-group activity, or as part of a deal with a group whose support they seek.

Using friendly MPs pressure groups may be involved in seeking to change a bill during its passage through Parliament. There are two stages when this is possible; the *committee stage* (a small all-party grouping of MPs) at which amendments are considered, and the subsequent *report stage*, when amendments are considered by the full House of Commons.

With the Consumer Protection Act, the Consumers' Association persuaded the Labour MPs on the committee to put forward amendments drafted by the Association. These gave the Registrar – proposed by the Bill – powers to prosecute firms and retailers. The Association also persuaded the Labour group to support an amendment which obliged manufacturers to make adequate number of spare parts for their products. Some Conservative members of the Committee were also persuaded and as a result the amendments were passed in Committee. However the CBI (representing manufacturers), acting as another pressure group, pressed the Government to use its Parliamentary majority to throw out these amendments at the later report stage, which it did.

• *Debates and questions*. Much Parliamentary time is spent on policy debates, and an hour a day for four days a week is set aside for Ministers to answer oral questions. The nightly debate on the adjournment, which deals with mundane topics rather than grand policy, presents pressure groups with an opportunity to use a friendly MP to raise issues. MPs may also address written questions to Ministers on behalf of pressure groups. These may receive written answers and can be a valuable source of additional information.

4 *Political parties*. Some pressure groups, particularly those outsider groups with little or no contact with Government, have pursued a long-term strategy of seeking to make their aims and ideas an official part of the policy of one of the political parties – often the Labour Party. This is not an easy strategy to adopt, since it involves deploying groups of members or supporters all over the country, and waiting a long time for results. However the result may be that your aim becomes part of the party manifesto.

5 *Direct influence*. While Parliament *makes* laws, the initiative for most of them comes from Government – ministers and civil servants. The multitude of day-to-day decisions arising from legislation and policy, and much of the crucial discussion and planning of future policy, does not take place in the public arenas of Parliament and the media. Civil servants will not even talk about their discussions with ministers to Parliamentary Select Committees. A route into this secret world may therefore be the means by which a pressure group can hope to do more than score the odd propaganda victory, or piece of legislation. It may enable the group to influence power as it is exercised and policy as it is made.

Some means by which this is achieved are:

• *Formal consultative machinery*. These may be built into a statute, or adopted as policy, a procedure by which the Government is obliged to consult relevant pressure groups before it takes certain decisions. Associations representing local authorities are routinely consulted before the annual grant of money to local authorities is made by

▶ *The Fair Trading Act* (1973) and the *Equal Pay Act* (1970), for example, were introduced after long and effective campaigns by the Consumers' Association, and the Women's Movement respectively. A batch of legislation passed by the Labour Government of 1975–79, including the *Health and Safety at Work Act*, the *Employment Protection Act* and the *Industrial Relations Act*, were part of the 'social contract' between that Government and the major industrial unions, in which the legislation was passed in exchange for union co-operation to limit the size of pay claims.

▶ Skilfully distributed questions, especially those put down for the more informative written answer, might elicit more information, piecemeal, than the Government would be prepared to give as a comprehensive public statement.

▶ The Animal Rights group, in the late 1970s, encouraged their members to join the local Labour Party and put forward the movement's aims, particularly at the time when Conference motions were being considered. The result was that in successive years, motions to Annual Conference on animal rights and blood sports, vivisection, etc., appeared from numerous constituency parties. Although they were not debated at Conference due to lack of time, they were referred to the National Executive, which eventually produced a policy document on the subject, *Beyond Cruelty*. This policy has now been incorporated into Labour's election manifesto in the form of proposals for specific anti-hunting legislation, and would stand a good chance of becoming law under a future Labour Government.

► *Quangos* have been much criticized for being too numerous, too bureaucratic and for not being responsible to Parliament. Nevertheless they still exist in great numbers.

Review – Pressure groups

1 The functions of pressure groups in a liberal democracy are:
- Articulation of demands.
- Agenda-setting.
- Intermediation.
- The provision of countervailing power against Government.

2 Methods used by pressure groups are:
- Direct appeal to the public.
- Use of the media.
- Through Parliament via contacts with MPs, private bills and the amendment of Government bills.
- Through 'infiltration' of the political parties.
- By direct contact with ministers and civil servants, through formal committees, quangos or informal contacts.

central government. Both the CBI and other employers associations, and the TUC and some unions, are represented on a multitude of such 'consultative committees'.

• *Membership of quangos (Quasi Autonomous Non Governmental Organizations).* These are bodies financed from public funds and carrying out government functions but not quite part of a government department. They have an 'arms-length' relationship with government, since the minister is not directly responsible to Parliament for their day-to-day activities – as he or she is in the case of a government department. The TUC and the CBI have been members of many such bodies such as the National Economic Development Council (NEDC) and the Manpower Services Commission (MSC), which administered the Youth Training Scheme (YTS) and other training schemes. Other bodies include the Health and Safety Commission and the Advisory Conciliation and Arbitration Service (ACAS) which conciliates and arbitrates in industrial disputes. Union and CBI representatives also sit on Industrial Tribunals, which act in a judicial capacity regarding employment law.

• *Informal access.* Although formal links may be important to pressure groups, they are no substitute for right of access on an informal basis, to ministers and senior civil servants, as and when each party desires. These contacts have the advantage that they are flexible and often confidential, enabling both sides to explore the views, strengths and weaknesses of the other, without having to commit themselves to anything publicly.

 List the methods a pressure group might use to achieve its aims. From your knowledge of current affairs match your list with examples from real pressure groups.

 Investigate a local or national pressure group. Is it an interest or a promotional group? How does it make decisions and policy? What methods does it use to further its cause?

The changing nature of pressure groups

Insider groups and outsider groups
Groups which establish a close relationship to Government (as outlined above) are referred to by commentators as *insider groups*. Insider groups are mainly but not exclusively in the category of economic interest group, typically employers' organizations and unions and their peak organizations, the CBI and the TUC. The advantage of insider status has already been stated. There are snags, however. Accepting insider status may mean abandoning, or only paying lip-service, to your more radical demands. Ordinary members may complain that they are being undemocratically excluded from decision-making, and accuse their leaders of 'going over to the enemy'.

Outsider groups, which find Governments consulting them, begin to become insiders and thus face some difficult decisions.

Pressure groups and power

As David Marsh pointed out in *Pressure Politics* (1983) power has 'three faces'. First there is 'positive power' – the ability to make Government or people do things they otherwise wouldn't have done. Second there is 'veto power'– the ability to *prevent* things from happening, or to keep some issues off the Government agenda. And third, there is 'ideological power' – the power to create and represent a set of ideas and values which are accepted and dominant at the time.

Pressure groups have at various times exercised all three aspects of power.

Pressure-group power and the state

The power relationship between pressure groups and the state – what it is or what it should be – is the theme of a rich and varied literature. From all this, four models of pressure-group-state intermediation emerge.

1 *Pluralism*. In this model pressure groups are free, numerous and roughly equal in power and influence. The government doesn't have a special relationship with any of them, but acts as an arbitrator between them, listening to their claims, seeking compromise between them and ensuring 'rough justice' by granting each of them some but not all of their claims.

Downe, in his book *An Economic Theory of Democracy*, saw the pluralist political system as resembling a free market with 'demands' and 'supplies' and a 'market price' fixed by government action.

Pluralism is used both as a description of how pressure groups work in a liberal democracy, and as a claim as to how they should work. A flourishing system of free and roughly equal pressure groups with a government listening to all of them but committed to none is seen as a sign of healthy liberal democracy. Citizens have numerous channels through which to express their varied interests and views; governments do not impose their own ideologies, but listen instead to the voices of the people.

2 *Elite Pluralism*. This is a version of pluralism which recognizes the exclusiveness of many pressure groups. It acknowledges that pressure groups are not always open and democratic, but are often dominated by elites with special powers. Many groups in society are not represented by pressure groups. There are those who accept this as a picture of reality and support it by saying that the Government can represent those too poor, too disorganized or too ill-educated to form pressure groups. This is the pluralist idea of competing groups with the Government acting as arbitrator in the national interest. Others are not so favourably disposed towards this situation, seeing elite pluralism as a pattern in which the already powerful and advantaged are able to organize themselves to influence Government to the disadvantage of the powerless and disadvantaged.

3 *Corporatism*. The term corporatism describes a state in which the major pressure groups within the society – interest and promotional

► The BMA (British Medical Association, the doctors' 'trade union') provides examples of positive power and veto power. As Eckstein (in *Pressure Group Politics, the Case of the British Medical Association*, 1960) points out, the BMA substantially influenced the structure of the National Health Service by extracting concessions from Aneurin Bevan, the Minister responsible for the NHS Act. It was to water down to the point of ineffectiveness the Government's proposals to phase out private beds in NHS hospitals, by the threat of the resignation of consultants from the NHS.

► See the insert reading on abortion law reform for an example of *pluralism* in action.

Abortion law reform

The Abortion Law Reform Association (ALRA) campaigned for 32 years to liberalize the law on abortion. In 1967 the Abortion Act, a private member's bill allowed time for discussion by the Government, was passed. As often with successful promotional groups, the times changed to suit its aims. A changed moral climate – the 'swinging sixties' – and a reform-minded Government and Home Secretary combined to assist the group. This is not to play down the role of the ALRA. Although a small group, it had a great deal of expertise, both on the subject of abortion and on the intricacies of drafting and pushing through Parliamentary bills.

The growth of the women's movement in the late sixties and early seventies was reflected in the creation of a wider and more radical movement– the *National Abortion Campaign* – which campaigned for abortion on demand, abortion up to full term, and free birth control, sterilization and abortion services.

By 1975, anti-abortion groups like *LIFE* and *The Society for the Protection of the Unborn Child* were lobbying vigorously. This movement found expression in a series of private member's bills. The White and Benyon Bills (both 1975), the Corrie Bill (1979) and the Alton Bill (1987) all sought to make abortion more difficult to obtain. The first three tried to achieve comprehensive controls on the conditions under which abortion could be obtained. The last, perhaps learning from the defeat of the first three, concentrated upon reducing the period of pregnancy during which an abortion could be legally obtained – from 28 weeks to 24 weeks. The anti-abortion movement, while not as well organized in Parliament as the pro-abortion group, had extensive support in constituencies up and down the country, and proved a formidable campaigning and recruiting organization.

As a response, the pro-abortion supporters formed *CO-ORD*, to co-ordinate action in defence of the 1967 Act. The group's tactics, through sympathetic MPs, was particularly effective in blocking the efforts of the anti-abortion group to get their legislation through Parliament.

Significant support was given to the pro-abortion group by the practitioners' pressure groups – the BMA and the Royal College of Gynaecologists – who after a period of anxiety, accepted that the 1967 Act worked.

Currently (1990) the Government are indicating that they intend to look again at the 1967 Act, with a view to amending it to shorten the period of pregnancy after which abortion cannot be normally obtained.

► The anti-abortion groups have been accused of 'salami tactics' by their opponents – that is, of achieving a goal of making virtually all abortion illegal through a series of one-line or short private member's bills, each designed to take the restriction of legal abortion one stage further.

► *Corporatism* refers to a situation in which pressure groups are controlled by central government or the ruling political party so that they act as state agencies.

– are incorporated into the state machinery. In its ultimate form it is a totalitarian state where the Government registers all groups, controls their internal rules and powers, and does not permit any independent rivals to exist by law. In return for the surrender of all independence, these groups would enjoy both access to the state, and state patronage.

4 *Neo-corporatism.* It has not been suggested that full-blooded corporatism exists in Britain. However, the close *tripartite* relationship that existed between Government, unions and employers in the late 1960s led to a renewed interest in the notion of 'neo-corporatism' which, it was argued, could exist within the framework of a liberal democracy. In this model, the state incorporates the leading economic pressure groups, not by compulsion, but by a *bargaining* process. Groups which represent capital and labour, and some of the 'client' pressure groups of state services, are offered partial incorporation into the

policy and decision-making process, in exchange for co-operation with the Government's policies and control of their members to ensure co-operation with that policy. In addition, the Government may offer special status to some groups which may effectively exclude their rivals. As an example, until recently the Bar Council and the Law Society operated a legally guaranteed monopoly for the supply of legal services.

 Explain the pluralist and the elite pluralist models of pressure group intermediation.

► Proposals in 1990 to 'fuse' the two professions (solicitors and barristers), or at least to allow solicitors to plead in the higher courts on clients' behalf, have so far been successfully resisted by the Bar Council.

The 1980s – from corporatism to dualism?

From 1966 until 1979, aspects of the relationship between Government and the major economic interest groups, represented by the TUC and the CBI, had a neo-corporatist tinge about them. To quote Frank Longstreth ('From corporatism to dualism' *Political Studies* No 36, 1988), during this period

> Britain in particular seemed to present a paradigm case of shift towards neo-corporatism, or at least a more permanent and institutionalised form of political exchange between unions and Government.

► *Paradigm* – example or pattern.

While the emphasis varied, the same could be said for employers and the Government in this period.

The Labour Governments of 1964–70 sought, and obtained TUC and CBI blessing for the ill-fated 'National Plan' which set economic growth targets for the various industries. It set up the National Economic Development Council (NEDC), and the Regional Councils, upon which unions and employers served. The Conservative Government (1970–1974) worked closely with the CBI, and sought union cooperation (though it did not get it!) for its elaborate attempt to structure industrial relations through a Registrar, and a system of Industrial Relations Courts.

Since 1964 both Labour and Conservative Governments had pursued an economic policy which was based upon the idea that economic growth could be achieved and inflation controlled if escalating wage rises could be avoided. To this end, they both sought to 'control' the unions in some way. After the failure of control by law in 1974, the Labour Government sought control by mutual agreement.

The nearest situation to one of neo-corporatism – at least as far as the Government and the unions were concerned – was the 'Social Contract' between the Labour Government and the major industrial unions between 1974 and 1978.

The 'Contract' between the Government and the unions required that the major industrial union leaders should persuade their memberships to moderate their pay claims within a limit agreed with the Government. In exchange the unions were given specific undertakings on future legislation (e.g. the Employment Protection Act 1975), and a consultative role in future domestic policy making, particularly on social and economic matters, through a Cabinet/TUC Liaison

► The Wilson/Callaghan Government attempted to work closely with pressure groups and incorporate them into government. By contrast the Thatcher administration kept at arm's length from most pressure groups, and especially from the unions. Wilson/ Callaghan seemed to move towards corporatism and Thatcher towards dualism – government and pressure groups separate and often opposed.

Committee. A vague undertaking was given by the Government on the control of prices, and a system of Prices and Incomes Boards was established.

The Contract was attacked from the far right, the far left, and even the centre right, with a *Times* editorial describing it as 'social fascism'. The right accused the Government of having sold out to the trade union 'barons'; and the far left within the unions accused their leadership of having sold out to the Government!

As prices continued to rise faster than the limit on wage rises set by the Social Contract the Social Contract was broken.

Those who saw it as full-blooded corporatism exaggerated. The unions were offered consultation, but not real power, and far from being 'incorporated' they withdrew from the Contract once it became clear that their members were suffering more than they were gaining from the Government's economic policy.

The Thatcher Conservative Government elected in 1979 came to power with a different economic policy, and a different view of the relationship between Government and society. Inflation was to be combated not by any deals with the unions, but by curbing the power of the unions which allegedly keep wages artificially high, abolishing the notion of minimum wage, cutting public expenditure and the money supply, and allowing a free market in labour.

The Government acknowledged that this would bring about a higher level of unemployment, but saw this as a necessary readjustment until lower costs created 'real jobs'. Politically, the Government announced its intention of 'rolling back the frontiers of the state', through privatization of some state functions, and encouraging individuals and families to make arrangements for their own welfare.

Thus one whole section of the pressure-group complex – the unions – were not only excluded from any intimate relationship with Government, but their powers to strike, make decisions without secret ballot and to discipline members were severely restricted by new laws. At the same time, unemployment and changing patterns of employment away from the old industries and into the less unionized 'service sector' reduced their power to take on Government and employers via strikes. Whereas the miners' strike in 1973–4 had pushed the Heath Government to a disastrous election, the miners' strike of 1984–5 was greeted by an implacable Government and National Coal Board, and ended in defeat for the miners.

This less compromising style on the part of Government affected other sectors of the pressure-group complex. The dissolution or downgrading of many of the quangos (upon which pressure groups had served), the less cosy arm's-length relationship between Government departments and pressure groups, the reduced willingness to compromise on the part of Government, has all had an effect.

Industrial action has been undertaken by groups not previously renowned for disruption – teachers, ambulance drivers, local government officers, firemen, civil servants. Direct action, such as mass demonstration against and refusal to pay the Poll Tax, is again in vogue. Parliament has again become a favourite battleground for

► Despite this change in ideology, the TUC and individual unions continue to be represented on a number of government and quasi-government bodies.

promotional groups, possibly because in the 1970s and 1980s MPs showed an increasing willingness to 'cross-vote' – a demonstration of an independence of mind, and a lack of deference to the leadership and the whips, both of which can be exploited by pressure groups.

The version of pluralism which recognizes the exclusiveness of many pressure groups is *elite pluralism*. This acknowledges that pressure groups are not always open and democratic, but are often dominated by élites with special powers. It also acknowledges that many groups in society are not represented by pressure groups. Supporters of this view do not see this as a serious problem, however, since the Government can represent those too poor, too disorganized or too ill-educated to form pressure groups. The pluralist idea of competing groups, with the Government acting as arbitrator in the national interest, remains.

None of the models completely fits the British situation at any one time, while some seem to fit parts of the system at different times. We seemed to come near to neo-corporatism in the industrial sector (Labour Government, 1975–79): the pluralistic model seemed to fit the abortion debate (since Governments did not want to intervene on one side or the other). Lately, an elite pluralistic model would seem to fit.

► It would be a mistake to see the 1980s as a decade in which government completely excluded pressure groups, just as it would be a mistake to see the 1970s as a decade of corporatism. The difference is more one of emphasis.

 Compared with the period 1964–78 how did the relationship between pressure groups and government change in Britain 1979–90. Use the terms neo-corporatism and dualism in your notes.

Are pressure groups a good thing?

In terms of a liberal democratic view there is much to be said in their favour:
- By articulating demands, they ensure dialogue between sections of the electorate and Government between elections.
- They provide a means of participation for those who may not want to commit themselves to political parties.
- They enable Governments to test the water by consulting those most affected by a proposed policy, and possibly make it more workable through compromise.
- They ensure a 'rough justice' in the allocation of Government favours and resources.

However, critics would argue that:
- All pressure groups are not equally powerful – some are rich, well organized and influential, often reflecting the power of their members in society, some are not.
- Governments do not always take a lofty detached view of pressure groups. Labour is bound to be closer to the unions, and Conservatives to the CBI, since the unions and big business fund the respective parties.
- The skill and influence of the pressure groups which represents you, rather than the justice of your cause, may be what prevails.

- Many groups within society, by their nature, are not represented or are ill-represented by pressure groups (for example, unmarried mothers, alcoholics, until recently prisoners). Far from rushing to their defence, busy governments are likely to ignore their plight.
- A system of powerful pressure groups may lead to a situation where Government, instead of governing in what it perceives to be the general interest, simply reacts to the particular claims of the most powerful pressure group at the time.
- Many pressure groups are criticized for their lack of internal democracy. Critics would maintain that the views they advance are those of a small group of activists, rather than the whole membership. The trade unions in particular have been criticized in this vein from time to time.

 Why might some people consider pressure groups a good thing and others regard them as a threat?

 'A system of free, articulate pressure groups with access to Government, Parliament and media is the sign of a healthy democracy.'

Assess the validity of this statement, and the extent to which it applies to Britain.

CHAPTER SUMMARY

1 Pressure groups differ from political parties – they seek to influence power, not to take it over.

2 They are broadly divided into interest groups and promotional groups.

3 Because Britain is a liberal democracy with a sophisticated economy and an 'interventionist' state they are numerous.

4 They may articulate demands, set the political agenda, and provide a means of mediation between Government and people and act as a source of countervailing power.

5 They may operate through direct appeal to the public, the media, Parliament, political parties, and formal and informal links with Government.

6 Since 1979, trade unions have been excluded from the near corporatist role they played in the late 1960s and 1970s. Other groups, held at arms' length by Government, have taken advantage of the greater willingness of MPs to vote independently, and some like the Anti-Poll-Tax Union have 'taken to the streets'.

7 Pluralism, corporatism, neo-corporatism and elite-pluralism are models of pressure-group/Government intermediation, which fit parts of the British system at some times and not others.

8 Pressure groups are considered by many liberal democrats as a vital element of democracy – making meaningful dialogue between the Government and the governed possible. Other liberal democrats point to the privileged position of some groups compared with others, and the fact that some groups within society are not represented at all.

STIMULUS MATERIAL

The stimulus material consists of two articles giving different opinions on anti-Poll Tax riots. Both were printed in the Free Speech section of the *Independent* edited by Angela Lambert.

Read the articles and answer the following:

1 Explain and assess the notion of 'democratic violence' put forward in John Williams' article.

2 What is the likely justification for the view (quoted in paragraph 5 of John Williams' article) that 'the right to riot is not an option in democratic politics'?

3 How might a member of the Anti-Poll-Tax Union answer Graham Riddick's fifth paragraph (beginning 'The central reason...')? Who, in your view, is right?

4 How does Riddick answer the point that historically real progress has been achieved by civil disobedience (in your own words)?

5 Which, in your view, is the more convincing argument? Explain your choice.

► The stimulus material and associated questions in Chapter 10 are also relevant to the role of pressure groups.

THIS WEEK: ARE RIOTS SOMETIMES JUSTIFIED?

1   It is no longer necessary to read the Riot Act of 1715 before proceeding to discipline a crowd; that was abolished in 1967.

2   Riots mostly occur in democracies; they are less likely under dictatorships, since penalties are greater. Britain has seen many periods of riot: from industrial unrest of the 1920s to the 1986 Wapping newspaper dispute.

3   Yet it is often claimed that the police provoke violence with their threatening or aggressive presence. Last Saturday's poll tax demonstration was undoubtedly intended as a peaceful protest by more than 90 per cent of those involved; it was only when the bellicose few met the truculent police at the gates of Downing Street that trouble began.

4   During riots people are emboldened by numbers to commit acts that, alone, few would dare. But there must first be a reason for the gathering and its transformation into a riotous mob. Discontent is the necessary trigger.

5   Was the riot against the poll tax undemocratic? People could, after all, have voted against the government that introduced it, and maybe they will. But that is two years hence and two years is a very long time to a rioter.

Angela Lambert

VIOLENCE AS AN EFFECTIVE FORM OF COLLECTIVE BARGAINING

1   The return, after a short absence, of violent civil disobedience to our streets and prisons invariably signals the return, too, of the silly season in the national Press. Consider, for example, *The Sun* doing its best to convert the poll-tax violence to a more familiar game-show format by inviting readers to identify photographs of the 'guilty men'. (A year's supply of lager for the winner?)

2   If you had problems contacting Conservative Central Office for a comment, it didn't matter. All you had to do was pick up Tuesday's *Daily Express*, which condemned the Labour Party and contained instructions from Professor Kenneth Minogue, of the London School of Economics, on the fashionable, but impotent, anger of the 'welfare state parasites' who, inevitably for the right, are at the core of violent disorder such as the riot in Trafalgar Square.

3   This was heady stuff compared with the more prosaic views offered by one of Prof. Minogue's colleagues, who said the events were best understood as the result of 'the interaction of a very hot day, incompetent policing and the fact that many people wanted a scrap'.

4   Angry Tories certainly wanted a scrap earlier this week in the House. But the Opposition, spoil-sports, were having none of it. Even leaders of the left's 'dirty 30' – Labour MPs who pledged not to pay their poll tax – were near-universal in their condemnation of the violence and destruction that took place in London. We were left, instead, with the Conservatives insisting that encouraging tax evasion leads inexorably to setting fire to Porsches in the West End.

5   However, the dominant view was, in the words of the Liberal Democrat Charles Kennedy, that 'the right to riot is not an option in democratic politics'.

6   Playing the 'democracy' card, of course, enables us both to deplore the violent protests in Britain while accommodating or supporting violent insurrection elsewhere in the world and in our pre-democratic past.

7   A number of eminent historians and political scientists have already done so this week by making supportive references to popular uprisings drawn from pre-First World War history or to the recent heroic – and violent – struggles in China, Romania and elsewhere. (The recent violence of the African National Congress in South Africa seems more problematic for the right but, nevertheless, seems to fit into this category.)

8 The basic argument here is that the use of non-state violence may only be appropriate where no properly democratic forms of representation exist and that, by its very nature, violent protest threatens the principles upon which democratic societies exist. Here, the issues become rather more complex.

9 It is clear, as the moral philosopher Ted Honderich points out, that we all believe democracy and violence conflict, but the point is to know how and where. It is also important to recognise the weakness of extravagant claims that acts of violence typically do more to make political systems undemocratic than do, for example, acts of economic power or non-violent infractions of the rules of democracy that derive from wealth and class ascendancies.

10 Honderich convincingly argues a case for 'democratic' forms of political violence, which, in some cases, are the only infractions of democratic practice that serve democratic ends. An example is when a morally insupportable distance between privilege and deprivation will not be appreciably reduced by other means.

11 Such violence is characterised by coercion or persuasion, rather than by force, which allows a government room for genuine reflection and decision-making. (In this case, a wholesale and much needed review of penal policy, perhaps? Further reconsideration of the unpopular and undemocratic poll tax?) This is violence as a mode of address, the 'collective bargaining by riot' that inner-city communities and, indeed, sections of our prison populations, have periodically explored over the past decade.

12 For violence to be 'democratic' it must not be directed at the destruction of the democratic system. It may be revolutionary in rhetoric, but not in reality. This begs the question whether the anarchist groups involved in Saturday's troubles truly believe in the prospects for a popular revolutionary programme in this country. Certainly, the evidence of the past and present strongly contradict such an assumption. Finally, 'democratic' violence should result in the systems in question becoming fuller realisations of democracy in certain respects. Again, this is empirically demonstrable, and a number of democratic systems, as we all know, have had their beginnings in revolutionary violence.

13 None of this is to excuse or, necessarily, to support the violence that occurred last weekend (or, indeed, to argue that aspects of it were anything other than a strategic disaster for more democratic electoral forces). I suspect most people will sympathise with Roy Hattersley's view that inhuman conditions in our prisons encourage inhuman forms of conduct. But only the insane could support the vicious attacks by prisoners on their defenceless fellow inmates or the assaults by the alienated flotsam of Brixton and Hackney on London's affluent 'passers-by'.

14 We should be warned by the words this week of foreign journalists in Britain – 'outsiders' who, perhaps, see us more clearly than we see ourselves – about the 'large populations of alienated, poor Britons who make up entire neighbourhoods in inner-city areas'.

15 The poll tax, or any other tax, will not bring these discards back to the fold. But, as Chesterton remarked, there is 'nothing like a broken head to call philosophies into question'.

The Independent
7 May 1990
John Williams
The writer is a lecturer at Leicester University and co-author of three books on football hooliganism.

WHEN MOB RULE BETRAYS THE PRINCIPLES OF DEMOCRACY

1 The *Concise Oxford Dictionary* defines a riot as an 'outbreak of lawlessness on the part of a crowd'. Lawlessness, in turn, is defined not only as actions that breach the law, but also as wild, uncontrolled and threatening behaviour that does not discriminate in its objectives and choice of targets. Could there possibly be a more vivid and dramatic illustration of this than the horrific scenes last Saturday in Trafalgar Square and the West End?

2 Equally, could there possibly be a more convincing demonstration of the absurdity of the proposition that 'riots are sometimes justified'?

3 Let us be clear about what happened last Saturday. A legitimate and peaceful demonstration against the poll tax was deliberately hijacked by several thousand left-wing hooligans linked to various anarchist groups and the Socialist Worker's Party, who proceeded to engineer a bloody riot, the primary purpose of which was not the airing or redress of grievance, but the infliction of physical injury on the police and the wanton destruction of property.

4 This mayhem was accompanied by several attempts to murder policemen in their cars (by setting fire to them), as well as by theft, looting and the terrorising of tourists and passers-by. Can anyone really believe that riots such as this can ever be justified? The central reason for condemning and discouraging riots is that they always result in injury to the innocent (even when they are a well-motivated response to government repression) and are quite unnecessary in a liberal democracy where abundant opportunity exists for peaceful opposition and change.

5 In a country such as ours, the right response to a damaging policy or an unjust law is to criticise it in Parliament and through the media, and seek change through the ballot box – not to throw bricks at policemen and smash cars and windows. Any other approach invites permanent civil war, for whatever government is in office there will always be minorities who are angered by specific policies or legislation.

6 One of the main questions to arise out of last weekend's riot is how far the declaration by 30 Labour MPs that they would not pay the poll tax contributed to the violent behaviour. I do not suggest that these MPs supported the violence, but they clearly advocated breaking the law.

7 This is always a slippery slope, for once law-breaking of any sort is condoned the vital principle of the rule of law has been breached. Others can then argue that the particular form of law-breaking being advocated does not go far enough and that more extreme forms, including violence as happened last Saturday, are needed.

8 Members of Parliament have a particular and heavy duty to set a good example, and Labour's 30 law-breakers provided justification for the perpetrators of last Saturday's violence. To compare the suffragettes with today's poll-tax non-payers, as Tony Benn has done, is nonsense. The suffragettes could not effect change through the ballot box; poll-tax payers can.

9 Would those left-wing apologists for violence and civil disobedience sing the same tune if thousands of Tories refused to pay taxes to a Labour government or hurled petrol bombs into the homes of Labour MPs and left-wing journalists? Of course, they wouldn't. The air would be filled with denunciations of 'Tory extremism', 'fascist terror' and the need for stern measures against 'enemies of the people'.

10 Even the most cursory glance at history shows the wisdom of adopting a sceptical attitude towards the glib argument, so common on the left, that the growth of freedom and democracy has only taken place as a result of civil disobedience and revolutionary violence in the past.

11 While it is impossible to deny the role of these factors, it can equally be argued that religious beliefs, economic developments and changes in the climate of ideas have exerted an even greater influence on the development of our free and democratic institutions. Furthermore, violence has often retarded, rather than advanced, the cause of freedom.

To give a few examples: can anyone deny that the growing power of Parliament in the seventeenth

12   century was as much due to the increasing wealth of the country gentry, and to Puritan ideas about the supremacy of law over the King, as to the Civil War and the execution of Charles I?

      Would we have seen the growth of democracy and enlightened social legislation during the
13   nineteenth century had it not been for the influence of evangelical Christians, such as Wilberforce and Shaftesbury, and the fact that the ideals of representative government were promoted by liberal thinkers anxious to placate the growing power of the working class spawned by the natural process of industrial capitalism?

      In these instances, it can be plausibly maintained that the 'pen', the 'chapel' and the 'factory' did
14   more for the cause of progress than riots, cannon balls or the executioner's axe. Indeed, the evidence suggests that the violence of the Chartists in the 1840s discredited the cause of universal suffrage in the eyes of the British middle and upper classes and so postponed the advent of democracy in Britain.

      On a larger scale, it can again be argued that the terror and violence of the French Revolution (which
15   cost more than half a million lives) so tarnished the image of democracy in the eyes of contemporaries that it postponed the advent of democracy in Europe for half a century.

      If the use of violence can be double-edged or relatively marginal in pre-democratic societies, it
16   certainly cannot be justified in developed democracies where, through the ballot box, change can be brought about by peaceful means. It is a betrayal of freedom to suggest otherwise.

The Independent
7 May 1990
Graham Riddick, MP
The writer is Tory MP for Colne Valley and a member of the Freedom Association's national council.

Further reading: Chapter 7

All of the following are useful reading on pressure group politics.

Baggott R. 1988. 'Pressure group politics in Great Britain – change and decline' *Talking Politics*, Vol. 1, No. 1.

Bull A. R. 1986. *Pressure and Politics in Industrial Societies*. London: Macmillan.

Cawson, A. (1978) 'Pluralism, corporatism and the role of the state' *Government and Opposition*, 13, 2.

Marsh D. (ed.) 1983. *Pressure Politics*. London: Junction Books.

Moran M. 1986. 'Industrial relations' in Drucker H. *et al*. *Developments in British Politics 2*. London: Macmillan

Now you have completed this chapter, look back to the objectives at the beginning and check that you have accomplished each of them.

(8) Parliament

Media Watch

For this chapter you should pay particular attention to the televised proceedings of parliament or the radio equivalents – see page 5, and/or the parliamentary news pages of the serious newspapers.

► Parliamentary proceedings are recorded verbatim ('word for word') in *Hansard.* You will find back copies of *Hansard* in any large public library.

Chapter objectives

By the end of this chapter should be able to:
▌ fit the concept of an assembly into the notion of liberal democracy

▌ recognize the peculiarities of the British Parliamentary system and its relationship with Government

▌ assess the effectiveness of the House of Commons in the fields of legislation, control and criticism of policy and administration, and control of finance

▌ recognize the problems of the reform of Parliament, and relate the proposals for reform to different perspectives on the role of Parliament

▌ assess the contribution of the House of Lords, and the validity of calls for its abolition

▌ recognize the ideas behind plans for a reformed second chamber, or for none, and the problems involved in such reforms

▌ define the meaning of and be able to use the following terms: Legitimize, working majority, opposition, Speaker, Front Bench, cross voting, Whips, motion, division, lobby, tellers, guillotine, pairing, Confidence debates, adjournment debates, emergency debates, Queen's Speech, opposition days, question time, written questions/answers, standing committee, select committee, Public Accounts Committee, Public/Private/Private Members' Bills, First Reading, Second Reading, Committee Stage, Report Stage, Third Reading, Royal Assent, Second chamber, Hereditary Peers, Life Peers, Lords Spiritual, Lords of Appeal, cross-benchers.

THE IDEA OF AN ELECTED ASSEMBLY

Central to most notions of liberal democracy is that of an elected assembly. Its main functions usually include the following:

1 *Legitimizing the Government.* Whichever body exercises power the assembly makes it legal, acceptable and respectable.

2 *Representing the electorate.* It does this in two ways:
   • By acting as a microcosm of the public; a sounding board for Government actions and policies.
   • By putting forward the grievances and interests of citizens.

3 *Controlling law.* In a system where the rule of law prevails (like ours), the assembly is usually the body whose approval is needed for

any new law or for changing existing law.

4 *Authorizing taxation and spending.* Most things that Governments do require money which is raised by taxation. The origin of Parliament (in Britain) and the Assembly (in France), arose out of the need of Governments to raise more money than they could lay their hands on. They attempted to get popular support for further taxes by naming the assembly the *Commons* in England, and the Estates General in pre-revolutionary France. From authorizing taxation, it is a short step to demanding that the assembly control the *purpose* for which the money is being raised.

► The Civil War of the seventeenth century between Parliamentary and Royalist armies was sparked off by (amongst other things) Charles I's attempts to levy taxes and raise money without Parliament's authorization, and his prosecution of prominent members of Parliament who refused to pay the taxes.

THE BRITISH PARLIAMENT

The British Parliament has features in common with most liberal democratic assemblies, but it also has some peculiarities of its own.

1 *The link between Government and Parliament.* The Government – the Prime Minister and Ministers – are members of the body to which they are responsible: they are MPs or members of the House of Lords. When Government policy is the subject of debate, about a hundred members in both Houses of Parliament (who hold ministerial appointments) will speak for the Government position (and later be voting for themselves).

► The need for the support of a majority of the Commons and the presence of the Government in Parliament means that party discipline and unity are usually (but by no means always) stringent and effective.

This contrasts with (for example) the United States. Here the Government, in the person of the President is separately elected and is outside Congress. He selects ministers from outside the assembly. Similarly in France the President is separately elected.

► See Chapter 2 (pages 16–19) for a general discussion of sovereignty and power.

2 *The link between the Government and the majority party(ies).* It is virtually impossible for a British Government to survive for long without commanding the majority of seats in the House of Commons. Whereas an American President may continue to govern with a Parliament which has a political majority different from the allegiance of the President, it is usual in Britain for the party in Government to enjoy a *working majority* in the Commons. However other arrangements are possible. For instance the Labour Government (1974–79) operated without a majority in the Commons during its last few years in office (1976 on). It survived with the support of the Liberals and the nationalists, but was eventually defeated in a vote of 'no confidence' early in 1979.

► In this century there were wartime coalitions in 1916–18 and 1940–45. Periods of minority Government where one party formed the Government but did not have a majority in the Commons were 1911–16, 1924 (eight months), 1929–31, February–October 1974 and 1976–79. There were two national Governments, where one party shared government with part of another divided party (1919–22 and 1931–35).

3 *Sovereignty.* In Chapter 3, we noted that Parliament is *sovereign*. This means that there is no other body, such as a President, supreme court or provincial government, able to question or overrule Parliament. This fact makes Governments who control a working majority in Parliament potentially all-powerful.

4 *The role of the opposition.* The term 'Her Majesty's Opposition' originated as a sarcastic jibe in the eighteenth century, but it developed into a political reality during the nineteenth and twentieth centuries. It is symbolized by the fact that the leader of the largest opposition party is paid, over and above his MP's salary, for carrying out the function of opposing the Government.

Review – The British Parliament

1 The British Parliament has two chambers, one elected, the House of Commons; one not elected, the House of Lords.

2 Government is not separately elected, but selected by the Prime Minister from MPs and peers supporting the Government party or parties.

▶ Parliamentary procedures and arrangements

▶ The Speaker

▶ *Shadow* ministers are those appointed or elected by the Opposition to shadow the minister by criticizing him/her and putting forward alternative policies.

▶ Front bench

▶ Rules of the House of Commons

Apart from short-lived multi-party, minority or coalition Governments, the norm of British Parliamentary culture has remained consistent. The Government, formed from one party with a majority in the Commons, is faced by the Opposition, dominated by another party with enough support to constitute a credible alternative Government should a few per cent of the electorate vote the other way at the next election.

This scenario means that many of the debates are concerned with each side establishing its own credibility as a Government or potential Government, and seeking to destroy that of the other side. The debates are addressed to the electorate, via the news media.

5 *A non-elected second chamber.* Like the Parliaments of many other countries , Britain's Parliament has two 'Houses'. Unlike many others, however, its second House – the *House of Lords* – is elected by nobody, and responsible to nobody. Nevertheless, it is no mere ornament. It carries out important functions and conducts its business seriously and often very effectively.

 What part does an elected assembly play in a model liberal democracy?

THE HOUSE OF COMMONS

The House of Commons is the senior of the two Houses in function, importance and status, but not in age. It consists of 650 MPs, elected on the basis of one per constituency.

The person who chairs the debates – the *Speaker* – and his (no woman has, to date, occupied the role) deputy, are elected by the Commons from amongst their membership. Once elected, the Speaker becomes strictly neutral, and takes no part in debates or votes. However the Speaker is not only a chairman. He manages the business of the day and may suspend the sitting if in his judgement it has become too unruly. He rules on the procedures of the House, and has disciplinary powers over MPs. These extend as far as the power to expel MPs from the House and to order their suspension for a period of time.

Parliamentary procedure is a labyrinth of precedents and rules. Physically, the arrangements for debate seem to reinforce the two-party system. Two sets of not very comfortable green benches face one another. The row of benches nearest the central aisle – the *front benches* – are by convention occupied by Ministers on the Government side and *Shadow* Ministers on the Opposition side. Hence the term *front-bench speaker* used to refer to them.

Speeches are addressed to the Speaker, not to another MP, and MPs refer to one another in the third person as 'the honourable member for (the constituency)'. If the person addressed is a Minister or ex-Minister the term 'the right honourable ...' is used. Members of your own side are always referred to as 'my honourable friend' or 'my right honourable friend', irrespective of whether they are or not!

Members do not speak from a podium, but stand in their place on the benches. To be called to speak, it is necessary to 'catch the Speaker's eye', although some of the order of speaking will have been arranged in advance. Government and leading Opposition speakers are likely to receive priority, as are back-benchers who have particular expertise or known strong views on a particular topic.

At some point, if a *motion* (proposal) is before the House, a vote may be called. This is referred to as a *division*. After various warning bells have been sounded, summoning members from committee rooms, offices, tea rooms, bars, and in the case of some members nearby flats, members file through one of two *lobbies* – the *Ayes* and the *Noes*, – and are counted by *tellers*.

▶ Motion

▶ Division

▶ Lobby

▶ Tellers

An important part of Commons life is maintaining party discipline and unity, and it is carried out by the party *Whips*. Discipline is particularly important at division time. A single defeat in the Commons, unless it is a motion of no confidence, may not spell the end of that Government, but it will be exploited by the Opposition as a sign that the Government is losing its grip. Opposition defections will similarly be exploited as evidence that the leadership cannot control its followers.

▶ The role of the Whips

The Whips of each party are MPs appointed by the leadership to ensure that MPs support the leadership, and in particular to ensure that they turn up and vote at division time. Where this is not practical the Whips' offices may arrange for *pairing* – one MP who is going to be absent for a division matched by his Whip with an MP from the other side who is also going to be away.

▶ Pairing

Despite pressure from the Whips, *cross-voting* happens from time to time, sometimes on a large enough scale to embarrass the leadership, though almost never on a scale sufficient to bring it down. MPs are warned in advance of crucial debates at which divisions are likely to take place. The 'request' to attend on these occasions is underlined three times in very heavy black ink: a *three line whip*.

▶ Cross-voting

Debate times, topics and speakers are subject to a certain amount of stage management, and deals may be struck between Government and Opposition in discussions that take place 'behind the Speaker's Chair'.

The functions of the House of Commons

The functions of the Commons can be grouped under two main headings:

1 *Legitimization*. Since Governments are not directly elected, their ability to command a majority in the House of Commons is the source of their legitimacy. So there is a sense in which every Commons debate is an affirmation of the right of the Government to continue to govern, until, like the Labour Government in 1979, it loses a motion of no confidence.

2 *Legislation*. The truism 'Parliament makes laws', must be seen in context. Parliament does not spend all its time – not even the majority of its time – debating proposed changes in the laws, or new laws. Much legislation is routine or is to renew existing powers. Other legislation is technical and non-controversial. The controversial

debates on big pieces of legislation are as much about the policy behind the proposed law (since most legislation is in furtherance of Government policy) as they are about the details of the law.

Types of legislation

1 *Public bills.* There are two main types of public bill:
- *Government bills.* Most of Parliament's time for legislation is spent considering Government proposals for legislation to give itself new powers or to renew or alter its existing powers. The Community Charge Act gave the Government new powers to change the system of local government taxation from rates to the Community Charge – the 'Poll Tax'. The annual Finance Bill (the *Budget*) reaffirms the Government's right to set and collect taxes.
- *Private Member's bills.* These were discussed in Chapter 7 and are a happy hunting ground for pressure groups. Most private member's bills run out of time, since only about half a day a week is allocated to their discussion. Even with time, Government acquiescence will probably be needed to get the bill through. If the Government doesn't agree with a bill it may employ the tactic of putting up numerous amendments to exhaust the time available, something the Labour Government did to Clement Freud's Freedom of Information Bill in 1979.

2 *Private bills.* These are sponsored neither by Government nor individual MPs but by outside bodies – usually local authorities. They seek to obtain special legal powers for the body concerned.
- *Hybrids.* These bills contain a mixture of public provision and private powers (e.g. 1946 Bank of England Act).

Going from bill to act

All bills are subject to the same Parliamentary process except that the committee stage of a private bill takes the form of a public enquiry. All bills have to go through the following stages. Most start in the House of Commons before going to the House of Lords for a similar process and then receiving the Royal Assent. Some start in the House of Lords and then go to the Commons.

The stages are:
- *First Reading.* A formality – the long and short titles of the bill are read out. There is no debate.
- *Second Reading.* If the bill is controversial, it is at this stage that the debate on the principles of the bill will take place. It is the main centre of press and public interest for a controversial bill. For a Government bill, the Minister responsible for the Government department which is introducing the bill will open the debate. A vote is taken at the end of the debate (though this might be 'by acclaim' if the bill is non-controversial).
- *Committee Stage.* At this stage the bill is usually examined by a *standing committee*. There may be proposed amendments, which alter the detail of the bill but do not negate it or change its purpose. Away from the attention of the media, committee debates are often more

► Legislation may be preceded by a *Green Paper* – an outline of Government thinking on a topic with suggested changes but no commitment to legislation – and/or a *White Paper*, which is the product of a firm commitment to legislation and is in effect an outline of what is going to appear in legislation. There may be Parliamentary debate on the relevant Green or White Paper preceding the legislation.

► A proposal for a law when it comes before Parliament is called a *bill*. When a bill has passed all its stages in the Commons and the Lords and has received the Royal Assent it becomes an *Act*.

► A Standing Committee consists of some 30 to 40 MPs from all parties, with a built-in Government majority. It meets at a different time to the sittings of the whole House, usually in the morning.

relaxed than those in the House, and amendments may be carried against the Government's advice. Occasionally, the House will decide to take the committee stage in the House rather than in committee.

• *The Report Stage*. The amendments to the bill are considered by the whole House. At this stage the Government may use its control over the majority to throw out amendments that it doesn't like. In the past, Governments have been accused by disgruntled back-bench MPs of giving undertakings to pressure groups that certain amendments that those groups do not want to see in the bill will not go through.

• *Third Reading*. The bill is accepted or rejected as amended previously, with little further discussion.

• The bill passes to the other House.

The Other House

Bills may originate in the House of Commons or the House of Lords, although major and controversial bills usually originate in the Commons. Whichever its House of origin, the bill has to go through the same process in both Houses.

 Construct a diagram or timetable showing the passage of a bill to an act.

The guillotine: time table motion

Parliament has been known to convert a bill into an act in 48 hours, where there was general agreement on the urgency of the conversion. With a long and controversial bill the Government could claim that it needs to get the law onto the *statute book* to further the policies for which it was democratically elected. However the Opposition (and in some cases Government back-benchers) may claim that in order to carry out their duties properly they need time to debate both the principles and the more important details of the bill. But there isn't usually enough time to do both, since much of Parliament's time is already committed to non-legislative debate, and to debate on recurring legislation such as the Budget. This leaves relatively little time to slot in major changes in the law via bills which may have two or three hundred clauses.

This is where that controversial instrument, the *guillotine*, comes in. The guillotine, in its various forms, is a resolution by the House to set a time limit on debate of a bill, or on various stages of a bill, or to debate certain amendments or clauses until a certain time and then close the debate. In effect the Government uses its control to ensure that the bill doesn't run out of time, since bills which are not completed by the end of the Parliamentary session (about 38 weeks) *fall* and must be re-introduced in the next session.

Government ministers habitually justify the use of the guillotine by claiming that MPs are trying to spin out debate in order to cause bills to fall. This they say prevents the Government from getting on with the programme – for which it was democratically elected – and is undemocratic. Opposition MPs habitually claim that the draconian use of the guillotine means that large areas of controversial bills go undebated or inadequately debated and that this prevents MPs

---

Review – The House of Commons

1 The function of the House of Commons is to legitimize the Government, and to pass legislation.

2 Most legislation is initiated by the Government.

3 A Bill goes through the following stages in the House of Commons before going to the House of Lords for a similar process, or vice-versa, and then for Royal Assent. It then becomes an act.

• First reading (a formality)
• Second reading (principles)
• Committee (detailed amendments)
• Report stage (House votes on amendments)
• Third reading (bill as amended)

▶ The Official Secrets Act of 1911 was passed in two days, in the wake of a German spy scare (which turned out to have no foundation). The subject of bitter resentment and controversy, it remained on the statute book for 78 years. The Act transferring the government of Northern Ireland to Westminster was passed with similar speed (see Chapter 13).

► MPs complained at the time of the European Community Bill 1973 – which took Britain into the EEC – about the fact that through use of the guillotine the Bill went to the Lords with hundreds of clauses undebated. The Government replied that MPs had had time but had chosen to use it on ritualistic political debate rather than on detail.

exercising their democratic function – and is undemocratic.

Control of the executive by the legislature

The debate about the legislative process

Academics, journalists and Parliament itself, through its *select committee on procedure*, continually debate the merits and demerits of Britain's legislative process. Some of the criticisms are:

1 *It is too long-winded*. Are all those stages really necessary? Various attempts have been made to shorten the process. Morning sittings on non-controversial business proved wildly unpopular. Taking the second reading of non-controversial bills in committee and merging the report stage and third reading have not gone very far towards solving the problem. The House of Commons continues to insist on its right to consider both the principles and the details of controversial bills in the whole House.

2 *Parliament has no involvement at the pre-legislative stage*. By the time a Government bill gets to Parliament, it may have been discussed by civil servants within the promoting department, by civil servants and ministers, by the department and relevant pressure groups, and by the department and other departments through cabinet committee and/or inter-departmental working parties. What appears before Parliament is but the tip on an iceberg of communication. Parliament may, on some legislation, get the chance to debate a White Paper (see page 144). By this time, however, the Government will have done most of the preliminary work and will be committed to the legislation. The pre-legislative discussions takes place under a cloak of confidentiality, and Parliament is not involved.

For some critics, the answer is a system of pre-legislative committees or the extension of the existing select committee system so that a Parliamentary committee has powers to examine and take part in these pre-legislative discussions.

Opponents of this idea as diverse as Michael Foot (on the left of the Labour Party), and Enoch Powell (Ulster Unionist, to the right of the Conservative Party), have expressed alarm at Parliament becoming a collection of expert committees. They consider that MPs should spend their time in the House debating issues of political principle rather than detail and that once MPs become experts, spending their time in committee, the essentially political function of the House of Commons will be lost.

3 *Parliament tries to do too much*. Bernard Crick, in *The Reform of Parliament* (1960), started a general debate about what ought to be Parliament's role. He claimed that it was not to make policy, initiate legislation or make or break Governments. Policy was the job of the Government, and making and breaking Governments the job of the electorate. He proposed that Parliament's role was to examine, criticise and shed light upon, the whole governmental process. Furthermore he argued that the details of legislation were inappropriate to

the whole House, and should never come there and that Parliamentary committees should look at the policy *behind* legislation, and the events leading up to it.

In practice, Parliament has been reluctant to accept any separation between controversial and non-controversial legislation, and between the principles and the details of a bill. For some MPs the details will involve principles and successive Governments have been equally reluctant to open up the whole process of pre-legislative policy discussion to the prying of MPs.

The debate on policy

An important part of the function of an assembly is to debate Government policy. Debates on crucial pieces of legislation are in great part debates on the policies behind those bills. However, there are other opportunities for policy debate:

- *The Queen's Speech.* This is given by the Monarch at the beginning of each Parliamentary session, but is written by the Government, and is a statement of Government policy and major legislative projects in the coming Parliamentary year. The debate that ensues is about major items of Government policy.
- *Opposition days.* On an Opposition day (about 26 days a year), the Opposition by convention proposes a major debate on a policy area.
- *Emergency debates.* Under one of the House of Commons' standing orders, a number of MPs may require that the House 'adjourn' to discuss a matter of *urgent public* importance. The Speaker, taking into account both the above criteria, decides whether the debate shall take place. The procedure is usually used for 'crisis' debates on unforeseen events, or consequences of Government policy.
- *The Finance Bill.* In practice the Finance Bill (the Budget) is an opportunity to debate the Government's economic policy.
- *Confidence Debate.* A motion of 'no confidence' is in effect a challenge to the Government's whole programme and fitness to govern. Though it was effective against the Labour Government in 1979, it is used sparingly by the Opposition, since success involves the resignation of the Government, or the dissolution of Parliament and a general election. The Opposition may not be ready for an election, or able to take over from the Government. A confidence debate may serve to rally the Government's supporters, and strengthen its position.

The Commons and the control of administration

The *way* in which policy is actually carried out is, for a lot of people, more important than the policy itself, since its impact on the public comes at that point. MPs seek to question and criticize the administration through:

- *Question time.* At the beginning of each Parliamentary day except Friday, a Government minister, representing his or her department, will answer oral questions put by MPs, concerning the work of the department. Although main questions have to be notified in advance, and the answers will have been prepared with the help of civil

---

Review – The function of the House of Commons

The legislative process in Britain has been subject to much criticism, such as:

- It is too long-winded.
- Parliament is not involved in the pre-legislative 'ideas' stage.
- Parliament gets involved in detailed debate on legislation, when it should monitor Government via committees and debate only general policy.

Parliamentary discussion of policy takes place in:

- Debates on the Queen's speech.
- Opposition days.
- Emergency debates.
- The debate on the Finance Bill (the Budget).
- Confidence debates.

► The Parliamentary day starts at 2.30 and goes on till 10.30 unless Parliament votes to extend the day.

servants, *supplementary* questions arising out of the answer may be asked on the spot. (Civil servants, however, try to anticipate supplementaries in their briefings to ministers.) Ministers take questions on a rota basis.

The Prime Minister answers questions in 'Prime Minister's question time', in two short sessions of about half an hour once or twice a week.

Question time has the advantage of direct confrontation, which attracts media attention. It is short, dramatic, and easy to follow. Sometimes an oral question, and particularly the failure of a minister to address some of its implications, will reveal embarrassing gaps in the Government's knowledge or understanding. Attempts to avoid a straight answer often reveal a great deal.

The practice has its limitations, however. Time is too short for the usual number of questions and supplementaries to be dealt with adequately. Ministers and the civil servants have numerous ways of avoiding straight answers. Many sessions, particularly Prime Minister's question time, have become opportunities for ritualistic mudslinging between Government and Opposition, with headline-worthy one-liners thinly disguised as questions.

MPs who genuinely want information usually use the less glamorous but more informative medium of a written question, which receives a written answer.

► *The adjournment* – the historical origin is that before the Commons introduced automatic closure at a certain time a member would propose that 'The House do now adjourn' (finish business and go home). It became habit to use this motion as an excuse for a debate on issues raised by individual members. This has now become part of established procedure.

• *The debate on the adjournment.* This takes place on four nights a week during Parliamentary sessions, after the main business of the Parliamentary day is finished. It is reserved for a mixture of constituency matters and more mundane matters. It gives individual MPs an opportunity to raise with the relevant Government department matters which may be of concern in their constituency.

• *Select committees.* These developed in the nineteenth century when the Commons wished to gain information on a number of social issues, and to exercise some control over the expenditure of Government departments. There are a number of 'in-House' committees dealing with matters such as privilege, procedure, and House domestic arrangements. There are also departmental committees examining the work of the principal Government departments, and the Public Accounts Committee (discussed in more detail later in this section).

► Two examples of *select committee* investigations which made the headlines were the Defence Committee's investigation of the Westland Helicopter takeover in 1986 and the Health Committee's investigation of *salmonella* in eggs in 1989.

MPs from all parties are appointed to sit on select committees. Their brief is to investigate the actual working details of the area for which they are responsible – and produce reports on it.

The structure of departmental committees was created in 1979 and is generally accepted as an improvement on previous arrangements. How effective these committees are, and to what extent their powers and duties should be extended as a way of making Parliament more effective, is a matter of argument.

Contemporary committees have the advantage over their predecessors in having at least one paid professional adviser working for them. Civil servants as well as politicians now appear before committee to give evidence and answer questions. The media give committees' conclusions more exposure now that they issue press statements in advance of their reports, and give press conferences.

Articles beginning something like 'A powerful all-party committee yesterday criticized/called for/condemned ...' are now commonplace. British select committees, however, have a long way to go before they approach the power or influence of the celebrated American Senate committees.

First, select committees have no power to make Governments act on their conclusions. A recent report by the Defence Select Committee (1990) criticized the small proportion of time that a ship in the Royal Navy actually spends at sea, when compared with time in port for leave, breakdowns, repairs and refits. But there is no way in which the Committee can follow up this report to ensure that the Ministry of Defence and the Royal Navy act upon it, unless a public or Parliamentary outcry on the matter pushes the Government into action.

Second, although select committees receive more information than they used to, there is still much that they are not allowed to know. Information may be withheld on the grounds of secrecy, or because its revelation would be 'contrary to the public interest'. Civil servants will refuse to answer questions involving discussions with other civil servants, the minister, or outside groups. They will similarly decline to answer questions concerning the level at which a decision was taken, and which alternative policies may have been considered in discussions leading up to a decision.

Third, members of select committees, who are also members of the Government party, may find that pursuit of the issues may clash with their loyalty to the Government they support. Bitter criticism, by a select committee, of the running of the then nationalized (Government owned) steel industry in Britain during the Labour Government 1974–79 was eventually muted by Labour members on the same Committee. They supported a motion to 'note' the criticisms, rather than carry them as far as demands for the resignation of the relevant minister and the Chairman of the Steel Corporation. This climb-down came after the Government explained that further action would add to pressure for the withdrawal of Government funds to the industry, and to consequent widespread redundancies.

The Public Accounts Committee. This committee is in a class of its own. It addresses itself not to any one department, but to the whole gamut of Government expenditure, and by implication, the policies that may have led to that expenditure. An official, supported by a staff of auditors, reports to it, and it has access to all Government accounts. The committee has scored some notable successes in the past, such as the uncovering of over-payments, of about £4m, by the Ministry of Defence to Ferranti for missile parts in 1964. It works, however, 'after the event', and is no substitute for committees which monitor policy and administration while it is happening.

▶ A guidebook given to civil servants lays down guidelines for answering MPs' questions, and enjoins its reader to limit him or herself 'to explaining the existing policy and defending it'. Select committees do not have extensive powers to demand the appearance of witnesses and documents, although if a minister refuses to produce either, he or she may have to explain such a refusal to the House.

Which parliamentary debates give the House of Commons the opportunity to criticize and examine Government policy, and how?

Explain what a select committee is. What are the strengths and weaknesses of the current system of select committees?

List the functions of the House of Commons, starting with law making.

 Essay/discussion question

Discuss the means available to Parliament in controlling the executive, their limitations and how they might be strengthened.

The reform of the Commons

How you regard the reform of Parliament depends to a great extent upon what you think about the proper role of Parliament.

Bernard Crick insists that Parliament's role is not to legislate (in the sense of originating or substantially altering legislation, or throwing it out); legislation is one of the ways in which the Government furthers its policy. Nor is it to make policy, since Governments do that. Nor is it to dismiss Governments – electorates do that.

In Crick's view, then, Parliament is there to provide the electorate with truly informed comment, and to represent them. To this end, secrecy should be ended except in matters of genuine national security. Research facilities, accommodation, pay and staff assistance for MPs should be improved. Committees should be stronger and more pervasive, genuinely monitoring the work of Government. A second chamber should look at the details of legislation, while a first chamber discusses principles.

Walkland (in *The Commons Today*, [1987] Fontana) on the other hand sees Parliament as a body to which Governments should be genuinely responsible. Parliament has the power. No Government can govern without its support. Walkland sees the root of Parliament's subservience as the two-party system, supported by the 'first-past-the-post' electoral system. The adversary politics of Government versus would-be-government means that, for up to five years, nearly all MPs of the majority party accept the discipline of voting the 'right' way even when they disagree. The alternatives, public humiliation of the Government or an enforced election, are unthinkable.

Walkland proposes that the way out of this situation is to restore the true role of Parliament. He would do this by reforming the electoral system to produce a multi-party Parliament, in which Governments would accept that they have to bargain with Parliament over the policies to follow, in order to survive.

Summarize Crick's view on the proper role of Parliament (see also page 138).

What objections might be made to his views?

Are MPs powerless?

The record of the 1970s and 1980s would seem to indicate that MPs are not the subservient creatures that some commentators have made them out to be. Cross voting (and hence the defeat of the Government, once almost unknown) has become a feature of Parliamentary life.

The role and importance of back-bench MPs

Back-bench MPs, if they do their job properly, do not have an easy life. It is a job that is high on the casualty list for stress, broken marriages and heavy drinking. Apart from travelling, keeping two homes and long hours one could forgive MPs for sometimes suffering identity crises. At one moment they may be pressed to represent their constituency interests as seen by their local party caucus; at another, the same interests as seen by a local pressure group or concerned citizens. Both of these may clash with what the MP sees as the wider interests of the constituency. The party leadership in Parliament may also want MPs to pursue one line while individual conscience, or a group within the party, may propel them in yet another direction.

► During 1974–79, the Labour Government (which had a tiny majority until 1976 and none thereafter) was defeated 43 times. 23 of these defeats occurred because some Labour back-benchers voted with the Opposition.

 Draw up a questionnaire aimed at finding out as much as you can about the work of an MP, how they occupy their time and how they perceive their job. Send it with a letter of explanation to some local MPs and discuss or write a report on the results.

MPs and the leadership

A simplistic master-servant view of the relationship between the leadership and MPs is certainly wrong. While most MPs file through the right lobby in the end, this is the culmination of a process of sounding made by a leadership careful not to introduce something which would alienate too many of their supporters.

The *Parliamentary Labour Party* meets regularly to discuss its leadership's policy. When in Government the Labour Party also has a liaison committee to ensure that the leadership don't move too far away from the back-benchers. The *1922 Committee* is the Conservative equivalent. Each party also has 'subject' committees of back-benchers or a shadow minister concerned with each policy area.

Through the Parliamentary party and the Whips, leaderships sound out feeling and opinion. The fact that they sometimes get it wrong does not minimize the importance of this process. Each group needs the other.

► Between 1979 and 1983 there were four occasions upon which 40 or more Conservative back-benchers voted against the Whip. The Shops Bill of 1986 was defeated on its second reading: 72 Conservative MPs voted against the Whip on this Bill and 38 abstained.

 How and why do governments usually get their way in the House of Commons? Does this mean that the Opposition and Government backbenchers are powerless?

THE HOUSE OF LORDS

Second chambers exist as part of the legislature of most liberal democratic systems. Their purpose differs according to the history and social structure of the country concerned. Some reasons for the existence of a second chamber are:

• To represent *regional*, or *local* governments, particularly in a federal system.
• To be a *chamber of elders* containing elder and more experienced politicians providing stability and continuity.
• To be a *revision chamb*er looking in detail at legislation initiated by the first chamber.
• To act as a *constitutional check* on the first chamber, to prevent it from going too far in its policies or legislation.

The second chamber in the British system is the House of Lords, also known as the 'upper chamber'. Its equivalent in France is called the Senate and in the Germany is the Bundesrat.

The function of the House of Lords

The British House of Lords is a second chamber which has elements of the last three functions mentioned above, although it may also *initiate* legislation. To summarize, it will:

1 *Consider legislation referred from the Commons and suggest amendments*. The Lords may pass bills, reject them totally, or propose amendments. If amendments are acceptable to the Government they become part of the legislation. If not, the Lords may decide to either drop the amendment; or after behind-the-scenes negotiation with the Government, pass a different amendment. Or they may insist on the amendment, and if the Government does not back down the bill will have to be re-introduced in the next session, when it will be passed (become law) whatever the attitude of the Lords. This gives the Lords an effective delaying power of one year.

Review – The reform of Parliament

1 How you regard the reform of Parliament depends upon what you think the role of Parliament should be.
2 In one view (Bernard Crick's) Parliament should concentrate upon 'demystifying' Government and providing well-informed criticism and exposure.
3 In another view (Walkland's), the problem lies in the two-party dominance of Parliament – a government-opposition symbolic conflict with its attendant iron party discipline.
4 A changed electoral system giving a more varied and independent Parliament would, in this view, make governments take Parliament more seriously.
5 MPs are subject to a variety of pressures and not all are subservient 'lobby fodder'; governments react to as well as lead back-bench opinion.

The delaying power, substituted for a veto power in 1911 (after the Lords had vetoed the Governments budget), and reduced to a year in 1949, is used sparingly. The House usually prefers to negotiate. However, it is there, and gives the Lords some 'edge' in dealing with the Government of the day.

In two respects an element of veto remains:

• A bill to extend the life of a Parliament beyond its statutory five years has to have the support of the Lords, as does a bill to abolish the Lords. However, a Government could use its power to create new members of the House of Lords to swamp it with its supporters, in order to get such a bill through. This was suggested by Tony Benn (1980) as a route to abolition of the Lords.

• Statutory instruments (see Chapter 3, page 29) may be subject to a Parliamentary resolution before they become law. The Lords may fail to pass such an instrument.

Usually such 'delegated legislation' deals with matters of detail. However, the Lords considerably upset the Wilson Government of 1964–70 by refusing to pass an 'Order in Council' which would have extended the list of goods in which it would be illegal to trade with Rhodesia (now Zimbabwe).

The amending function of the Lords is not a formality. Sometimes it is carried out at the Government's request, but on other occasions it leads to public debates and conflict between the Government and the Lords.

2 *Initiate legislation*. The Government, several of whose Ministers usually sit in the Lords, may choose to begin the discussion of a bill in the Lords, so that the basic work on it has been done before it comes to the Commons. This is usually reserved for bills which are politically non-contentious.

The Lords have their own equivalent of a Commons' private member's bill, and new ideas have been pioneered in the Lords via this procedure. The liberalisation of the law on homosexuality, abortion and censorship were all discussed around bills originated in the Lords. Latterly (e.g. 1988 – see Chapter 3 pages 43–5) the question of a Bill of Rights has been aired using this route.

3 *Debate policy*. Since some Government Ministers are in the Lords, they face questions in a similar fashion to those in the Commons. As well as the debates on Government policy, the Lords conduct broad policy debates of their own.

 List the functions of the House of Lords.

► The threat of the delaying power can, however, be effective. Between 1979 and 1985 the Lords defeated a proposal to allow local authorities to charge for school transport. The Lords also rejected a clause in the Housing Bill which would have allowed the sale of old people's houses. And they passed an amendment obliging trade union officers to be elected by postal ballot. The Lords blocked attempts by the Government to stop elections due in 1984, in the soon-to-be-abolished Greater London Council.

► Much of the work on private bills is done in the Lords.

► See Chapter 14 for details of the Lords' judicial function.

The composition of the House of Lords

There are about 1100 members of the House of Lords (the number varies). They consist of:

► Between 1958 and 1979 the creation of hereditary peers appeared to have gone out of fashion. Mrs Thatcher, however, created three hereditary peerages during her premiership (1979–90)

1 *Hereditary peers.* The majority of peers are those who have inherited peerages. Most were created in the nineteenth and twentieth centuries. In practice many hereditary peers rarely, if ever, turn up. This gives more influence to the next group who have a better attendance record.

2 *Life peers.* This category was created by an Act of 1958 (the Life Peerages Act) which provided for the creation of peerages for the life of the incumbent only. It included women, to be admitted to the House for the first time, and introduced financial allowances for attendance. The Act was designed to give a 'shot in the arm' to the second chamber by creating a body of notables – men and women of distinction and eminence in the professions, including the arts, academic life, business and trade unions. It seems to have been successful, since from that date the Lords has gone from being a political backwater to an active and high-profile debating chamber. All life peers are appointed on the advice of the Government of the day.

3 *Lords Spiritual.* Twenty-six Bishops and Archbishops of the Anglican Church are appointed to the Lords, some because they occupy certain seats (bishoprics or archbishoprics), and some on length of service.

4 *Lords of Appeal in Ordinary.* These are lawyers appointed to act as judges in the final Court of Appeal in the judicial system – one of the functions of the House of Lords. The Lord Chancellor, who is both head of the Judiciary, and chairman of debate in the Lords, is appointed by the Government from amongst their leading politicians. See Chapter 14 for further details.

The debate on the House of Lords

Criticisms of the House of Lords

The attack on the Lords comes mainly from the left and centre. The grounds for attack include:

► Criticisms of the Lords arise across the political spectrum

1 *Violation of democratic principles.* In a liberal democracy, it seems odd to have a House in which none of the members have been elected (with the exception of the Lord Chancellor who may be a promoted MP) and all of whom are there for life. None of them have a constituency to which they account for their actions – they are in the archaic sense of the word 'irresponsible'.

2 *The indefensibility of the hereditary principle.* Although it may be possible to justify life peers on the grounds that they have ability, it is more difficult to justify putting someone into Parliament because he happens to be a hereditary peer's son.

3 *Elitism.* While many peers exhibit much skill and dedication, they

are representative of the elite of society, with a vested interest in the maintenance of the status quo.

4 *Party bias.* As well as the Conservative Party appointees, the majority of those entitled to attend the Lords are conservatives – with a small 'c'– and tend to support the Conservative Party. There is always the possibility of the 'backwoodsmen' (peers who seldom attend) turning up to defeat a radical measure that has passed the Commons stage. Tony Benn has emphasized how the built-in conservatism of the House could mean that it would use its delaying power to frustrate the programme of any future radical Government.

▶ While it may be that small 'c' conservatives predominate in the Lords, it is difficult to estimate the line-up of party loyalties because many of them are uncertain or undeclared. One estimate, by the Information Office of the House for 1984, is Conservative 418, Labour 136, Liberal 31, SDP 4, cross-benchers (no party allegiance) 219.

5 *It prevents sensible alternatives.* There are those who argue that Britain needs a second chamber, but not this one. Suggestions for alternative systems have included:

- A *Chamber of Trade and Industry,* originally mooted by Winston Churchill. This would represent unions, employers and other pressure groups and look particularly at legislation and policy relating to social and economic matters.
- A *revising chamber,* possibly composed of MPs nominated from the Commons, without any strong powers. It could scrutinize legislation coming from the Commons which had had little or no debate of many of its clauses.
- A *regional or local government assembly* representing geographic areas, with power to initiate or amend Bills inasmuch as they related to the regions, or to provide the detail to 'flesh out' Bills coming from the Commons in outline.

Supporters of the Lords make the following points:

1 *It's irrational but it works.* The Lords' debates are often of high quality, well-researched and informed. Where else would you get an assembly with so many eminent doctors, industrialists, academics, lawyers and trade unionists under one roof? (The charge of elitism is unlikely to worry proponents of this view since they would see such elites as a good thing.) Additionally they argue that all this talent represents no serious threat to the elected Government in the Commons; and carries out valuable functions of legislation, revision and public debate – which the Commons is far too hard-pressed to take on.

▶ In defence of the Lords.

2 *It is a check on an 'Elective Dictatorship'.* Lord Hailsham and others (see Chapter 3, pages 36–8), fear that a Government with control of the Commons, given sovereignty of Parliament, could exercise a dictatorial regime quite legally, even though it might have received the support of less than one third of the electorate. Such commentators see the Lords as a potential guardian of the constitution against such a regime, in that its delaying power could be used to force an election.

3 *What is the alternative?* Assemblies based upon pressure groups, or regional voting, present problems of definition of function and voting rights. An assembly which was democratically elected might either start to claim as much authority as the Commons – leading to

stalemate where they were opposed – or, if it had only minor functions, attract a low calibre of membership.

Do we need a second chamber?

One view is that we don't need a second chamber, because most of the much-vaunted functions of the Lords could be carried out by a better-organized House of Commons with a better committee system.

Another view is that Britain is not a federal country and does not need separate representation of regions.

Last, second chambers are usually conservative, and likely to frustrate future radical Governments whether of the right or of the left. When a second chamber duplicates the views of the first, says this view, it is irrelevant; when it contradicts it, it is a nuisance.

 Draw up a table of defences and criticisms of the House of Lords as it presently operates. Note the proposals which have been made for its reform.

CHAPTER SUMMARY

1 Elected assemblies are characteristic of liberal democratic regimes.

2 The British Parliament:
- Legislates.
- Debates Government policy.
- Authorizes expenditure and taxation.
- Legitimizes, and may bring down, the Government.

3 In Britain, the Government is 'in' Parliament, i.e. Government Ministers are members of Parliament (Commons or Lords). A Government must be able to command a majority in the Commons to survive.

4 The activities of the Commons are divided into debates on legislation; Opposition days; emergency debates; question time; debates on finance particularly the Budget; debates on the adjournment.

5 The Commons is often criticized for its lack of independence. This is likely to continue while party discipline is maintained.

6 The fourteen departmental select committees of the Commons have made some impact, with their public examination of the work of government, but they have no 'teeth' beyond media publicity.

7 The House of Lords is made up of hereditary peers, life peers, the Lords Spiritual and the Lords of Appeal in Ordinary.

8 The Lords debate and initiate legislation, and may delay (but not finally stop) and amend bills coming from the Commons.

9 Though much criticized for being undemocratic and not responsible to any constituent, the Lords remains. Supporters argue that they do a good job without substantially interfering with the Government's programme.

The stimulus material is about the House of Lords and is taken from a *Sunday Correspondent* article by David Blake. Read the article and answer the following questions:

1 Assess the accuracy of the comparison of the Lords to the human appendix (paragraph 1).

2 Why, in your view, has the intention of the preamble to the 1911 Parliament Act (paragraph 13) never been carried out?

3 What is your answer to the question 'Do we need a second chamber at all?', posed in paragraph 9. Give reasons.

4 What is a 'federal constitution' (paragraph 11)? What role might those who support such a constitution see for a second chamber?

5 'But that points to the need to reform the Commons, not keep the Lords'. If the Lords were to be abolished, and nothing replaced it, how might the Commons need to be reformed?

DEMOCRATIC SURGERY TO CURE A BAD CASE OF INERTIA

1 The House of Lords is the constitutional equivalent of the human appendix. It does nothing useful, being the much reduced vestige of a larger organ. Most of the time we do not notice it. Occasionally it grumbles. Very occasionally it becomes seriously inflamed, with grave risks to the patient's health. But medical opinion is nearly unanimous against surgery.

2 Stop and think about it. Because it is really *strange*. In all those lists drawn up to make us feel inadequate (most prisoners per head of any country except Turkey, lowest spending on the arts of any West European Country except Portugal, most embarrassing football manager of any country except Albania) can anything compare with being the only advanced nation where people inherit the right to sit in Parliament? Not just a few, but more than 760 – two-thirds of the House.

3 It is a tribute to our willingness to accept the unacceptable that this is still so. The Parliament Act of 1911, which sets out the power of the Lords, begins 'Whereas it is intended to substitute for the House of Lords a Second Chamber constituted on a popular instead of a hereditary basis but, such substitution cannot immediately be brought about...' Seventy-nine years is a very British use of 'not immediately'.

4 The crisis of 1909–11, which broadly set the present limits of the powers of the Lords, gave us some of our most valued political cliches and moments of the farce to which the British Constitution is prone. Lloyd George, whose Budget started it all, invented the phrase 'backwoodsmen' to describe the Tory peers who tried to frustrate the Liberal Government. The Marquess of Curzon said 'We will die in the last ditch'. The Liberal Government threatened to create another 500 peers including Thomas Hardy and Anthony Hope Hawkins of *Prisoner of Zenda* fame, which would have made the Lords so big it would have taken over Westminster.

5 Yet when it came to it, the Lords chickened out and the last ditchers lost to the Government's determination to take away their powers to block money Bills.

6 There seems no real doubt that last week's Lords' rebellion to defeat the War Crimes Bill was totally in line with the Parliament Act. If they can do anything, they can send Bills back to the Commons to be thought about again. Although I think the Lords were wrong, they were clearly within their rights. But should they have those rights?

7   There have been many cases under this Government of the Lords trying to amend Bills, usually cheered on by the Labour party. Under this Government, opponents of Mrs Thatcher have taken great pleasure in these occasional Lords' defeats of the Government. Most of them have involved social measures, particularly as one cynical 'dry' observed, those of special interest to Catholics led by the Duke of Norfolk.

8   No one can blame opposition peers for trying to frustrate the Government; that is why they are there. But relying on the Premier Duke and Earl of England, created in 1483, to beat a grocer's daughter with a huge majority is a funny way of fighting for democracy and social equality.

9   Do we need a second chamber at all? Among the politocracy, even to ask this question is to invite derision. Sweden seems to manage perfectly well without one, but it is generally accepted a 'revising' chamber is needed to clear up the mess made in the Commons of many Bills. There is no doubt much Commons' legislation is a mess. But that points to the need to reform the Commons, not keep the Lords.

10   The case for abolishing the Lords altogether is seen as soon as we start trying to formulate an alternative. What is it supposed to represent? When the Lords were a powerful class interest, as in the eighteenth century, it is easy to see what their House was for. But that will not do now.

11   It is easy to see what a second chamber is for in a corporate state; it gives representation to all the powerful interests in the land. But corporatism is out of favour so that cannot be the justification. A second chamber has a role in a federal state. It allows the constituent regions, whether they be called states, regions or republics, to have some kind of institutional representation. But we are not a federal state.

12   Many people would like the UK to have a federal constitution and see the second chamber being the place where that could start. Indeed, one of the roles that reforming the Lords plays amongst constitutional theorists is that it allows them to express what they do not like about the way the Commons is elected.

13   Just as the Federalists want the second chamber to give a check to the centralising powers of government, the enemies of the 'first past the post' system in the Commons talk about having a second chamber elected by proportional representation. All of these ideas come from the 'centre' and they all have one basic fault in common. They all try to find a structure of a second chamber which makes it excusable for that chamber to dilute the authority of the Commons.

14   Faced with this hard fact, reformers always run away from doing anything. Like the Official Secrets Act, which was introduced in the same year as the Parliament Act, the fear which holds back reform is that anything new will be worse because we are better off with the present system where the absence of legitimacy means no harm can be done.

15   Maybe so. But building in inheritance is a direct snub to the whole idea of democracy. Mrs Thatcher has made the issue even clearer by resuming the practice of giving hereditary peerages. When she retires, she will presumably become a Countess and hand the title on.

16   Why not get the defenders of a second chamber to justify their position? This could be done by passing a Bill removing the right of anyone to inherit a seat in the Lords without stripping existing peers of their rights. This could be coupled with any kind of study we want – Royal Commission, Speaker's conference – to work out what should be the new shape of a second chamber. It is a hesitant step. But it would at least mean inertia, the greatest of all forces in British politics, would no longer have things all its own way.

The Sunday Correspondent
10 June 1990
David Blake, Political Correspondent

(ACT) Tune in to either the televised or the radio broadcast of Parliamentary proceedings. Identify what is happening in terms of what you have learned in this chapter.

Further reading: Chapter 8

Crick B. 1964. *The Reform of Parliament*. London: Weidenfeld & Nicolson. Now out of date in its examples, but can still form the basis for a stimulating discussion on the proper role of Parliament in Britain.

Judge D. 1983. *The Politics of Parliamentary Reform*. London: Heinemann. An alternative view of parliamentary reform, set in the wider context of politics

Morgan J. 1975. *The House of Lords and the Labour Government*. Oxford: Oxford University Press. An interesting account of how the Lords reacted to a Labour government.

Morgan J. 1981. 'The House of Lords in the 1980s' *The Parliamentarian*, LXII, 18–26. Useful recent examples to illustrate the role of the Lords.

Norton P. 1986. 'Independence, scrutiny and rationalisation: a decade of change in the House of Commons' *Teaching Politics*, 15. A useful summary of Parliamentary changes since 1976.

Walkland S. A. and Ryle M. (eds) 1987. *The Commons Today*. London: Fontana – some of the articles are out of date, but Walkland's introduction is still relevant.

Now you have completed this chapter, look back at the objectives and check that you have achieved each of them.

9 The policy network

Cabinet Diaries

Since the proceedings of the cabinet are secret, our best information comes from the diaries of ex-cabinet ministers. You will find that dipping into one of these diaries will give you a greater insight into cabinet affairs than can be conveyed in a textbook. But remember that such accounts are highly subjective and partial since no one in the cabinet sees the whole game – see further reading on page 179.

► David Easton (1965) *A Framework for Political Analysis.*

Chapter objectives

By the end of this chapter you should be able to:
■ distinguish between values and ideas, policies and decisions based upon policy.

■ identify the stages in policy making and execution, from source to final action.

■ assess the roles of the Prime Minister, the cabinet and cabinet committees in the policy network, and their relationship to one another.

■ assess the Prime Minister–cabinet–committee network in the light of criticisms made of it and suggestions for its reform.

■ know the meaning of and be able to use the following terms: manifesto, mandate, collective responsibility.

POLICY AND THE POLICY NETWORK

David Easton described policy as, 'the authoritative allocation of values'. This definition highlights two important aspects of government policy – *authority* and *values*. Political parties, pressure groups, individuals, put forward values such as 'Concern for the environment', 'Equal opportunities', 'Free enterprise', but such values need to be translated into specific aims and targets before any action can occur. Another prerequisite of the translation of values into action is

The translation of values into policies: a hypothetical example

A party is elected on the slogan 'We care for our children's future'.

This translates into some aims and objectives for education, for example:
- a vast increase in the number of pre-school nursery places to be provided, particularly in some inner-city areas;
- more resources for primary education, and a new look at the primary curriculum;
- a drive to recruit, train and retain more teachers in the primary and pre-school sector;
- a programme of new school buildings.

As well as aims, the policy will generate specific targets or objectives. These can be quantified, for instance:
- x more nursery places by the year y;
- y per cent increase in funding linked to pre- and early school education for a list of areas deemed to have more urgent need.

So policy may be defined as a series of more or less specific aims and objectives, designed to further certain values, put forward by the body which claims to have the authority and the ability to translate them into action.

that someone has to have the authority and the power to get things done.

 Draw up a list of policy aims and objectives to further the values inherent in the slogan, 'We care for our children's future'. You should consider two areas:

a) the environment, and

b) health care.

The Government and policy

The members of the ruling party (or parties) who find themselves appointed to some ministerial office, and thus members of the Government, are all to some extent involved in the policy-making process. Depending on circumstances they may be involved in one of more of three aspects of policy:

1 *Making policy.* Party manifestos do not cover all areas, or they cover some of them in a very vague manner. Unforeseen events may render existing policies useless or inappropriate, or they may require policy decisions that no-one had thought of then. In this case, members of the Government have to make policies to fill the gap. For example, the Argentinian invasion of the Falklands Islands in 1982 was unpredicted and required a rapid development of policy.

2 *Refining and adapting policy.* The route from general policy aims to particular objectives is one on which a number of increasingly specific decisions have to be made.

In our nursery school example, answers to questions like 'How much money?', 'How many extra places?', 'By when?' and 'Where?' have to be provided.

Adaptation may be necessary because a policy that looks fine in theory may turn out not to work. Limitations may be imposed by financial or human resources – you can't suddenly expand education if you already have a shortage of teachers.

Most policies depend upon the co-operation of groups within society other than Ministers and civil servants. If that co-operation is not forthcoming, the policy may be altered or even abandoned. Opposition by the BMA (British Medical Association) to the policy of phasing out 'pay beds' (beds at the disposal of consultants in NHS hospitals which could be reserved for paying patients) caused the Labour Government of 1966–70 to water it down drastically. The Conservative Government (1990) re-thought its education policy on student loans because the banks did not want to administer the scheme, and on the National Curriculum because teachers and educational advisers protested at the burden of work it would create.

3 *Execution of policy.* Carrying out a policy – translating it into action – is not directly the job of Ministers. Full-time paid officials in central and local government do that. Ministers, however will be responsible to public and Parliament for the way in which the policy is carried

► See Chapter 10 for a discussion of the role of full-time officials in central government, and Chapter 11 for a discussion of their role in local government.

► The *party manifesto.*

► *Mandate* implies an order from a higher authority – in this case, the electorate.

► By *salient issues* I mean issues that voters consider to be of importance to them. The perception of large numbers of voters as to 'salience' may not be identical to that of politicians and journalistic and academic commentators. In 1991 European Monetary Union might have been considered vitally important by political leaders (and actually be vitally important) but to many voters the Poll Tax and the National Health Service were far more important in influencing which party they supported.

► Reaction to events as a source of policy.

out, so it is in their interest to exercise a degree of control over the process. This is not easy, and knowing where to get involved in detailed decision-making and monitoring, and where to leave it to others, is part of the art of being a good Minister.

The sources of policy

As you may have gathered by now, the sources of policy vary. First, there is the *party manifesto.* Particularly at the beginning of its term of office, a Government may claim that it has a *mandate* for certain policies.

The reasoning behind the claim to have a mandate is that:
• It was in the programme of the party which gained a majority in the Commons.
• By voting the party into power the electorate endorsed its programme.
• In a liberal democracy, the electorate is the ultimate sovereign, therefore the Government has full political authority for its policy(ies).

The notion of mandate has often been used to rebuff opposition from MPs both inside and outside the ruling party, from pressure groups and from local authorities in opposition who may claim their own 'local' mandate.

However, when examined the concept can look shaky: first, only one Government this century has been elected with a majority of votes cast (that of 1935), and none has secured the support of a majority of those entitled to vote. Second, a vote for a party is not necessarily a vote for every item in that party's manifesto. We saw in Chapter 6 that people vote for a variety of reasons. Many have voted despite certain policy aims, or in complete ignorance of them – since most voters do not read manifestos. And third, Governments are rather choosy about mandates. When they want to do something in their manifesto they claim a mandate to do it. When they want to do something which wasn't in the manifesto they are rarely inhibited by their lack of a mandate.

Nevertheless the notion of the mandate persists and not just among party leaders. On salient issues or general principles there may indeed have been a significant degree of support for the mandate from the electorate. Thus, few have argued with the proposition that the Conservative Government of 1979 had, as a first priority, a mandate to bring inflation down to single figures. Since 1979 the Conservative leadership have used this mandate to justify cuts in public expenditure, particularly against Labour local authorities. Similarly it is widely accepted that a substantial section of the electorate rejected the Labour Party in the 1983 election because of its unilateralist defence policy – in a sense refusing them a mandate.

Another source of policy are particular *events*. Governments are expected to react to events which cause public concern. For instance, changes in the law regarding the safety of sports grounds followed the Ibrox disaster (1974), and further changes are in process of adoption in the wake of the Hillsborough disaster (1989).

And third, *organized pressure* is a source of policy. Much of this will come from organized pressure groups outside Parliament, but occasionally Governments bow to pressure from their own backbenchers. The Labour Government of 1966–70 withdrew a proposal outlawing certain types of strike action from its industrial relations proposals (1969) because of backbench opposition. The Conservative Government in 1988 withdrew its intention of abolishing free school transport for children living more than a certain distance from school in the face of backbench opposition in rural constituencies.

 Where do policies come from? What may cause policies to change?

Review – Policy

1 A *policy* may be defined as aims and objectives designed to further certain values, put forward by a body which claims to have the authority to translate the values into action.
2 The Government may be involved in making policy, refining and adapting it, and providing the resources and machinery by which it can be carried out.
3 Sources of policy are diverse. They include the manifesto of the Government party, reactions to public and pressure-group pressure, and reactions to events.

THE PRIME MINISTER AND THE POLICY NETWORK

The people and groups making up the network of people concerned with the making and carrying-out of policy are:
- The Prime Minister.
- The Cabinet and its Committees.
- Ministers responsible for the fourteen major Government departments, and their junior ministers.
- The central bureaucracy – civil servants, particularly those who advise ministers, and manage the execution of policy.
- Quangos – quasi autonomous non-governmental organizations.
- Local authorities and the bureaucracy which advises them on policy, and manages its execution. See Chapters 10 and 11.
- Other arms of government such as the National Health Service, the police, the military, etc.
- Supra-national agencies such as the United Nations, the EEC and NATO.
- In making rather than carrying out policy, pressure groups of various kinds may be involved.

The Prime Minister

The office of Prime Minister in the British system is largely governed by conventions, rather than laws. It evolved through changing political circumstances. In the eighteenth century, when leading politicians

---

Policy changes following events

The Ibrox disaster (1971) – Celtic fans who thought the game was won started to leave the ground via the stairways, then tried to return when they heard the cheer following a goal being scored. The resulting surge caused crush barriers to collapse, leading to 67 deaths.

Hillsborough (1989) – Fans pressing to get into the ground were admitted when police, fearing death or injury outside the ground, opened the gates. The resulting surge trapped and crushed those already in the ground; 93 people were killed and 200 injured.

Both disasters precipitated inquiries, in the case of Ibrox culminating in the Safety of Sports Grounds Act 1975 (note year).

were becoming more dependent upon parliamentary support and less upon Royal patronage, Walpole was sneeringly referred to as 'Le Premier Ministre' – the implication being that he was running the Government rather than the Monarch who should have been running it. Later, from 1761 onward, George III tried to reassert royal control over Government, and succeeded in ridding himself of Fox as his leading minister. Nevertheless, as Parliament's authority grew and that of the Monarch declined, the importance of a leading minister who could command a majority in Parliament as the *de facto* head of Government grew.

The growth of organized political parties in the nineteenth century (a response to the extension of the franchise), reinforced the importance of the position of the Prime Minister by adding to it the leadership of the party which had received the support of the electorate. By the late nineteenth century, Queen Victoria found herself bound to appoint Gladstone whom she considered 'a half-mad firebrand' because he was the leader of the only party that could command a majority in the Commons.

The office of Prime Minister thus derives its essential authority from three *political* factors: winning a general election, leading the party and keeping a Parliamentary majority.

The functions of the Prime Minister

Because no rigid law controls the office, it is to some extent defined by the style of its occupant, and such styles vary. However, some functions are common to all:

1 *The Prime Minister appoints ministers*. All ministers are appointed by, and may be dismissed by, the Prime Minister. It is a convention that all ministers should be members of one of the Houses of Parliament. Although there are some political restraints this is an important source of power. Once appointed to ministerial office, an MP is obliged to support the Government, whether or not he or she agrees with policy. Thus about a hundred out of the 650 MPs are locked into following the Government line.

The ability to place people in some ministerial jobs rather than others may also be used to shape the Government in the way the Prime Minister wants it. Crossman, a minister in the Labour Governments of 1964–70, records in his diaries his dismay at being appointed not to *Education*, in which he was both interested and knowledgeable, but to *Housing and Local Government*, in which he was not interested and about which he knew nothing.

2 *The Prime Minister is head of the cabinet*. The Prime Minister has significant powers over the cabinet, the premier policy committee of the Government.

First, as *chair of cabinet meetings* the Prime Minister influences the amount of discussion, and can 'steer' the cabinet towards a preferred conclusion. Votes are rarely taken in cabinet meetings, instead the chair will 'sum up' the feeling of the meeting and move to the next discussion point.

▶ Queen Victoria, who reigned from 1836 to 1901, did not fit easily the bland non-political model of a constitutional monarch. At election times, with ticker-tapes providing results, she would ask 'How are we getting on?' – 'we' meaning the Conservative Party. Apart from her detestation of Gladstone's anti-imperialism and his views on Ireland, she didn't like him personally; she claimed that he talked to her 'as though he were addressing a public meeting'.

▶ Although all the major ministerial posts carry important responsibilities some are acknowledged to have more kudos than others. Foreign Secretary, Home Secretary and Chancellor of the Exchequer, particularly, are seen as the most prestigious, while Minister for Northern Ireland is seen as a political graveyard.

▶ Prime Ministers have varied in their approach to running cabinet meetings, some letting ministers ramble, while others have tended to cut speakers short by suggesting a conclusion.

Second, the Prime Minister controls the *cabinet agenda*. The Cabinet Office, the body of civil servants responsible for providing advice to and servicing the cabinet and its committees, is under the direct control of the Prime Minister. Since this body draws up the agenda, the Prime Minister can to some extent influence the outcome of the cabinet's deliberations by determining what they do and do not discuss. Crossman claimed that the Prime Minister used exclusion as a means of avoiding certain conclusions which might flow from cabinet discussion.

Third, the Prime Minister sees the *draft minutes*. The minuted conclusions of the cabinet circulated by the Cabinet Office are policy outputs of the first importance, since they are the basis for future action.

There is some controversy about the extent to which Prime Ministers use their close liaison with the Cabinet Office to frame minutes as they would want to see them.

And fourth, the Prime Minister controls the *cabinet committee network*. The cabinet operates through a system of committees covering major areas of policy, chaired and staffed by cabinet and non-cabinet ministers. Many of the important discussions and conclusions will take place in these committees, rather than in full cabinet, and the cabinet will only be required to ratify decisions reached in committee. Thus decisions about which committees shall exist, who shall chair them (the Prime Minister can do if he or she wishes) and who shall serve on them make this network very powerful.

Critics of 'Prime-ministerial government', like Crossman and Benn, claim that this puts the Prime Minister in a uniquely powerful position. He or she can staff committees to come up with the 'right' conclusions, or take issues away from the main cabinet where a different conclusion might be reached.

Tony Benn claims that he was *not* appointed to a committee on the feasibility of a Freedom of Information Act, during Callaghan's premiership, precisely because he was the one cabinet minister who would have pressed for such an act, something neither Callaghan nor Rees (his Home Secretary) wanted.

3 *The Prime Minister is Head of Government*. We all have the habit of referring to Governments by the name of their respective Prime Ministers – the 'Thatcher' or 'Wilson' Government, etc. Perhaps this reflects part of our culture which sees the Prime Minister as the personification of the Government. Certainly Prime Ministers project themselves at times as quasi-presidential heads of state. Although there is evidence to suggest that major decisions on the Falklands War were discussed in cabinet, the public image of Mrs Thatcher at the time was of a Prime Minister firmly and personally in charge of the whole operation. EEC summits, discussions with foreign Heads of State, public statements on economic policy and serious disasters, often see Prime Ministers appearing to take on the role of 'Head of State'.

4 *The Prime Minister is the Party Leader*. General Elections in Britain are fought to some extent around the images of the Party Leaders.

► In 1986 Michael Heseltine claimed, as one of his reasons for resigning, that Mrs Thatcher had kept off the cabinet agenda effective discussion over the issue of which of two bids for control of Westland Helicopters the Government should support.

► Richard Crossman and Barbara Castle (a minister in two Labour Cabinets) both state in their published diaries that minutes often come out differently from their memory of a meeting, and that the Prime Minister had had a hand in creating the 'official' version. Wilson, the Prime Minister involved, maintains that no such interference took place.

► The impact of Mrs Thatcher as Prime Minister from 1979 to 1990 has been such that she has had a doctrine named after her – 'Thatcherism'. I think this is unique among British Prime Ministers. Will press and public in the 1990s talk of 'Majorism' or 'Kinnockism'? Somehow I doubt it.

► The dissolution power can also be used as a threat against recalcitrant colleagues on the front or back benches. Wilson, at a stormy meeting of the Parliamentary Labour Party, did so in 1965 on the issue of the possible use of force to bring down the Rhodesian Government.

They present themselves on hoardings and in newspapers and TV programmes. An election victory is a confirmation and a consolidation of the position of the Party Leader. This may strengthen the position of the Prime Minister, particularly *vis-à-vis* ministerial colleagues and potential rivals.

5 *The Prime Minister has the power of dissolution of Parliament.* Under the existing law, Parliament must be dissolved and an election held at least once every five years. However, within that time limit, the Queen will dissolve on the advice of her Prime Minister. This power to decide when a general election is to take place can be used to consolidate the position of the Prime Minister, by timing the election when the government of the day is popular – perhaps having pursued popular policies in the period immediately before the election.

Review – The policy network

1 The policy network includes: the Prime Minister, the cabinet and its Committees, the central bureaucracy, quangos and local councils and their permanent officials.
2 The office of Prime Minister is a position whose power and functions is largely governed by convention. The office owes its increasing power to the decline of the Monarchy and the rise of organized national political parties.
3 The Prime Minister:
   • appoints ministers and junior ministers, and controls a host of other appointments and honours.
   • chairs cabinet, and works closely with the Cabinet Office who prepare agenda and minutes.
   • has access to and control of the network of cabinet committees.
   • is *de facto* Head of Government.
   • is Party Leader.
   • within the limits of the Parliament Act, controls the calling of a General Election.

► As with Macmillan, Mrs Thatcher's ruthlessness seems in the end to have contributed to her downfall. Geoffrey Howe, the only one of the ministers left in the cabinet from those appointed in 1979, resigned in November 1990 over Mrs Thatcher's attitude to European monetary union. Among the praise of her in his resignation speech were withering condemnations. Michael Heseltine took this opportunity to challenge her for the leadership (and therefore the Premiership until the next election). John Major and Douglas Hurd felt free to join the contest at the second ballot, and Mrs Thatcher was persuaded to withdraw. Major won.

Prime-ministerial Government?

Crossman in the 1960s and Benn in the 1980s saw the gamut of powers listed above as the basis for government by Prime Minister, rather than collective government by Cabinet. Their hypothesis is based on:

• *The disintegration of the Cabinet.* Real decisions are taken in committees organized by the Prime Minister, or in secret and informal discussions with selected colleagues. The Prime Minister is the only individual in a position to know what is going on in the whole committee network.

• *The 'hire and fire' power.* The power to sack, appoint or reshuffle means that the Prime Minister can dispose of, or sideline, potential enemies or rivals. (Benn would seek to place the power of re-election of cabinet ministers with the Parliamentary Party.)

Macmillan in the celebrated 'night of the long knives' (1962) disposed of a third of his cabinet, including both the Foreign Secretary and Chancellor of the Exchequer.

• *The Prime Minister's special relationship with the civil service*. Both Crossman and Castle have placed particular emphasis on the fact that the two civil servants at the apex of the bureaucracy – the Permanent Secretary to the Treasury and the Secretary to the cabinet – both report directly to the Prime Minister. It is argued that this places control of all three resources vital to the whole system in the Prime Minister's hands, namely information, money and personnel.

• *The power of the public image*. The media often projects the Prime Minister in a quasi-presidential role. To the extent that this succeeds, and they retain popularity, it becomes difficult to remove a Prime Minister since replacement might spell political suicide for the party they lead.

• *The absence of democratic control*. Benn emphasizes the secrecy surrounding the whole Prime Minister/cabinet complex and the absence of democratic control over the cabinet process. In the context of a future Labour Government, he would propose replacing Prime Ministerial right of appointment with approval of the cabinet list by the whole Parliamentary Labour Party and the opening up of the cabinet network by replacing the existing secrecy with a Freedom of Information Act.

Checks on Prime-ministerial power
No-one seriously contests the proposition that the office of Prime Minister carries great potential power. But there are many checks upon a Prime Minister's absolute authority:

• *Prime-ministerial choice of ministers is limited*. Leading members of the Party elected as MPs have public images and may have powerful support independent of the Prime Minister. They, and their followers, expect to be rewarded. This may be particularly so at the beginning of a Government's term of office.

Prime Ministers may appoint ministers from sections of the Parliamentary party unsympathetic to their views, partly in order to reassure supporters of that section, and partly to ensure that its leading spokesperson is debarred – by the convention of collective responsibility – from public criticism of the Government.

▶ Wilson claimed that in his first cabinet only seven members in a cabinet of 24 had supported him for the leadership.

• *The power of the 'public image' is double-edged*. Prime Ministers may receive a boost in their power from a favourable public image, but they are correspondingly vulnerable should their popularity rating slip.

There is, in any case, little evidence to link the success of a leader directly with the success of his or her party. Given that other factors influence voters' decisions, it is unlikely to be decisive.

▶ In the 1970s, voters consistently preferred Wilson as Prime Minister rather than Heath, but Heath won the 1970 election.

• *Prime Ministers do not dominate cabinets*. There is ample evidence, from recent accounts of cabinet meetings, to suggest that Prime Ministers do not get all their own way. If ministers insist, issues go on the cabinet agenda, and once there, the cabinet view may prevail. Barbara Castle, when the minister responsible for Industrial Relations, records how Wilson accepted, very reluctantly, the withdrawal

▶ Mrs Thatcher withdrew from the second round of the Conservative leadership election in 1990 even though she had obtained a majority vote at the first round. Her decision was made after consultation with cabinet colleagues, some of whom pointed to the unpopularity of the Poll Tax with which they thought she was associated in the public mind. Many Conservative MPs, alarmed by the party's poor showing in opinion polls, were convinced that a change of leadership would improve their electoral prospects.

▶ Mrs Thatcher's reservations on full membership of the EEC's exchange rate mechanism (ERM) and monetary system (EMS) resulted in 1989 in the resignation of her Chancellor of the Exchequer, Nigel Lawson. The barely concealed public opposition of some of her remaining ministers, and the open hostility of Michael Heseltine, were the first really serious indications in the media that her position as Prime Minister was no longer unassailable.

In Heseltine's subsequent challenge to her leadership in November 1990 he gained 157 votes on the first ballot, but was squeezed out when Mrs Thatcher withdrew from the second ballot.

of contentious clauses in the Industrial Relations Bill (1969) which would have limited power, after cabinet members had indicated that they were not prepared to risk the embarrassment of a defeat in Parliament. On levels of public spending, privatization and laws restricting trade union power, it is known (partly on her own admission) that Mrs Thatcher wanted to press on with more change in the years 1979–83 but was prevented from so doing by the cabinet.

- *The Prime Minister may face opposition from large powerful departments.* The Prime Minister's support staff, about 75 people, is minute compared with the establishments of the big spending departments like Defence, Health and Social Security. Ministers for these departments have the backing of an army of civil servants, a battery of statistics and carefully planned arguments to deploy. Mrs Thatcher's attempts to secure fast and substantial spending cuts in the early years of her premiership were frustrated by a successful campaign of opposition from the big spenders, who continually and successfully argued that such cuts would adversely affect the operational capability of departments.

Indeed, it has been argued by one ex 'insider', Sir Kenneth Berrill, that the Prime Minister's department needs to be strengthened, with specialist advisers to enable him or her to press departments more effectively to work in line with Government policy.

- *The dissolution threat is also double-edged.* This threat is a bit like offering to pull the bung out of a boat on which you are sailing! Everyone could drown, and ministers stand to lose more than backbenchers should the Party lose the consequent election.

- *A Prime Minister is only one person.* It seems inherently unlikely that any one human being, however little sleep he or she needs, can be simultaneously and continuously involved in even the major areas of policy. Far more feasible is sporadic involvement in matters which the Prime Minister considers politically important.

 Draw up a two column table. On one side list the bases of the power and authority of a British Prime Minister. On the other list the limits on the Prime Minister's power.

Competing elites?

Some variant of elite theory may be opposed to the notion of Prime-ministerial Government, based on the notion that the policy complex is not monolithic, but more a 'patchwork' of power groups whose interests are not identical, all of whom have some power but none of whom have *all* the power. Thus, the Minister, senior civil servants and relevant unions and professional group leaders in say, the Health Service may constitute one 'cluster' of élite groups. The Minister, civil servants, senior military officers and firms with an interest in supplying military hardware may constitute another élite.

In this model the Prime Minister is seen as important, perhaps most important, but not all-powerful. At any time, because of circumstances, one élite cluster may be in the ascendant, while another is 'out' because of conflict within the cluster, or because of events or personalities

The Westland affair

The Westland affair (1985–86) can be considered from the viewpoint of competing élites or Prime-ministerial power. Westland Helicopters was financially ailing and in 1985 cabinet discussion revolved around the question of who was preferred to take it over.

Various power blocks emerged:
1 The Minister of Defence (Heseltine) and Ministry of Defence, pressing for the firm to be taken over by a European consortium.
2 The aviation authorities of other European governments.
3 A consortium of European firms.
4 The Department of Trade and Industry and its Minister (Leon Brittan) who seemed to favour takeover by the US firm Sikorsky.
5 The Board of Westland Helicopters.
6 The Prime Minister and her department, especially the Press Office, who claimed to want to leave the decision to Westland shareholders, but were accused of covertly supporting the US bid.

In a complex series of moves and counter-moves, Heseltine organized European aviation authorities and firms, and pressed for the European solution. This was in defiance of a cabinet injunction not to 'take sides' publicly. Meanwhile, Leon Brittan, Minister for Trade and Industry, leaked a letter from the Attorney General to Heseltine suggesting that inaccuracies in a letter written by Heseltine to a merchant bank could amount to libel.

The Prime Minister remained apparently above these quarrels, although her own office was accused of being the inspiration behind the anti-Heseltine leak. At a subsequent cabinet meeting Heseltine resigned rather than accept that all his future statements on the matter should be cleared through the Cabinet Office. He accused Mrs Thatcher of having stifled debate on the strategic implications of selling to the US the only British firm manufacturing helicopters.

The Attorney General was known to be furious at the leaking of his letter, and subsequently Brittan accepted that the leak was a serious breach of confidence for which he was responsible, and resigned. There were those who claimed that Brittan sacrificed himself to protect the Prime Minister's Office, who were really behind the leak and had covertly supported the American bid.

In the end Sikorsky took over Westland.

Who won politically? We don't know because too much secrecy still surrounds the motives and actions of those involved.

Mrs Thatcher and her cabinet seemed to win in the short term. Heseltine lost, again in the short term, but retained sufficient support to mount a serious challenge to Mrs Thatcher's position as Leader of the Conservative Party in the autumn of 1990. The eventual outcome was that he re-entered Government as a Minister in Mr Major's first round of cabinet appointments in November of the same year. Brittan became an EEC Commissioner. The affair could be seen either as an example of Prime-ministerial Government, cabinet Government, or competing elites, depending upon which aspects you choose to emphasize.

have not created the circumstances for it to occupy the centre of the stage. All compete for their share of time, acknowledgement and resources.

► Bernard Ingham, Mrs Thatcher's famous and pugnacious press secretary claims in his memoirs that he did not authorize the leak of the Attorney General's letter, or give the DTI press secretary the idea that it should be leaked.

During the leadership campaign in November 1990, Heseltine referred to the Westland affair, and claimed that the cabinet were both gagged and fooled by the Prime Minister. He claimed the gagging was carried out by promising a meeting in which full and free discussion of both options would take place, then not convening it, before requiring a cabinet decision not to take sides. The fooling lay in giving the impression that the cabinet committee had met when it had not (*Shoot the Messenger* [1991] HarperCollins).

► The term *cabal* originated in 1668 to describe the group of Charles II's ministers who ran the government after the fall of Clarendon. It was named after the initials of its members; Clifford, Arlington, Buckingham, Ashley and Lauderdale. The word passed into the language to mean a small political clique.

► *Sinecure:* office of profit or honour without duties attached, or with only nominal duties.

 Note down which aspects of the Westland affair you would emphasize if you wanted to use it as an example of:

- Prime-ministerial government
- Cabinet government
- Competing elites

Review – Prime-ministerial power

Prime-ministerial power may be considerable because of: the power of the public image; the absence of democratic control on the PM in the short run; the 'hire and fire' power; control of the cabinet and its committee system; and the special relationship with the apex of the civil service hierarchy.

However the strength of these powers may be limited by: limitations on the choice of appointees to ministerial posts; the double-edged nature of public image; the impossibility of always dominating cabinet; the strength of administrative and financial backing for ministers in charge of the big and important departments.

THE CABINET

Like 'Prime Minister', the word *Cabinet* started life as a term of abuse used to describe the cabal of politicians who surrounded the Prime Minister.

As with the institution of Prime Minister, no law defines it, or states its constitution or functions. It is a body that has arisen out of political and practical expediency, rather than legal or constitutional theory.

Membership of the cabinet

The number of ministers making up the cabinet varies according to the Prime Minister's wishes but generally reflects the number of senior ministers and departments created by the Government. The number of members is usually in the low twenties, and certain ministries will always be represented. Cabinet will usually include:

- The Prime Minister.
- The ministers for the old prestigious ministries – Foreign Secretary, Chancellor of the Exchequer, Home Secretary, Minister of Defence, Lord Chancellor.
- Major functional ministries – Health, Social Services, Education, Transport, Environment.
- The ministries for nationalities – Wales, Northern Ireland, Scotland.
- Sinecure ministries, given for special purposes – Lord President of the Council, Chancellor of the Duchy of Lancaster.
- The Leader of the House, responsible for management of and liaison with the House of Commons.

The cabinet acts in various ways. First, it acts as the senior policy committee of the Government. Policy may not originate in the cabinet, but the cabinet will expect to *clear* major policy initiatives and decisions, particularly decisions that are likely to have serious political repercussions.

Second the cabinet acts as the senior committee of the ruling party (or parties). To retain power British Governments need a Parliamentary majority, and this usually means keeping the Parliamentary party united. The cabinet plays an important party political role: that of presenting a united front both to the backbenchers in the Commons and the electorate in the country.

And thirdly, the cabinet acts as a policy co-ordinating committee.

Most major policy initiatives affect more than one department and the cabinet may act as a committee at which all the ministries involved can express a view about proposals. Cabinet may also act as a final 'Court of Appeal' when ministries disagree, and are unable or unwilling to settle their differences.

Collective responsibility and the need for secrecy

Lord Melbourne, the nineteenth century Prime Minister, is reputed to have said to his quarrelling cabinet, 'Gentlemen, it doesn't matter what damn lie we tell, so long as we all tell the same damn lie'.

While it is to be hoped that cabinet ministers are truthful, Melbourne's admonition sums up one aspect of *collective responsibility*. Politically, it is important that the committee of politicians who lead Government and the Government party (or parties) should tell the same story, or at least not publicly disagree. If more than one line comes from Government, the public might see this as a sign of weakness, the opposition would gratefully take advantage of it, and the Governing party supporters might divide into factions supporting different views.

A less self-regarding reason for collective responsibility is that co-ordination between departments is essential. If cabinet decides on a certain percentage cut in overall expenditure and sets savings targets for each department, it is vital that each department accepts this decision and carries it out, whether or not it agreed with the original proposal. The concomitant is that the department should have had an opportunity to put its point of view before accepting the decision, and it is this opportunity that the cabinet is supposed to afford. (In the Westland affair, Heseltine justified his refusal to accept a cabinet decision on the grounds that he had not been given an opportunity to put his case.)

To make collective responsibility work, secrecy is necessary. It is inconceivable that all Ministers will personally agree with every cabinet decision so, in order to preserve the outward appearance of unanimity arguments in cabinet are kept secret. Cabinet minutes are not published for thirty years after the meeting that they record and Ministers are not supposed publicly to discuss or write about what went on in cabinet.

The executors of the late Richard Crossman, Minister in the Labour Governments of 1964–66 and 1966–70, published his diaries posthumously. (The diaries contained nothing of any strategic significance,

► The cabinet is the senior policy committee of the Government.
► Senior committee of the ruling party.
► Policy co-ordinating committee.

► *Policy co-ordination:* A proposal to allow some non-academic students to leave school at fifteen and go into supervised employment, for example, might involve the Treasury, the Department of Education and Science, the Home Office, the Department of Employment and the Department of Trade and Industry, the Department of Health and the Department of Social Security.

► Prime Minister Melbourne is supposed to have said, in reply to a prospective cabinet member who said 'I'll support you when you're right', 'That's no good, I want someone who'll support me when I'm wrong' – an important aspect of *collective responsibility*.

► Cabinet secrecy.
Some cabinet minutes are kept secret for fifty years or longer.

► A typical gossipy (and rather nasty) passage from the Crossman Diaries reads:
'I don't think the Government can hold together for the rest of this Parliament with Peart and Silkin in charge of discipline, Peart because he lacks authority, Silkin because he's not developed a yard. He is still the Prime Minister's lap-dog. He is squashy, fat Silkin, anxious to please ...'.

► *Benn* records his difficulty in accepting many of the decisions made by the Cabinet of 1974–79 since they seemed to flout the principles on which he believed Labour had been elected.

► The *Independent*, the *Guardian*, and the *Scotsman* have opted out of the Lobby; the quality of their intelligence does not seem to have suffered markedly as a result.

but did contain a good deal of gossipy material about who said what in cabinet, plus some unflattering comments from Crossman about some of his cabinet colleagues.) The publishers, and *The Sunday Times*, who serialized the diaries, were unsuccessfully prosecuted by the Government – whose case was not that these revelations endangered the State, but that they endangered the principle of collective responsibility. If we are all to tell the same story, it is important that we don't reveal the quarrels that preceded the story!

Problems of collective responsibility.

The principle of collective responsibility seems to have become more difficult to maintain in the last thirty years, possibly because:

• *Decision making is fragmented.* Earlier we saw that only *some* decisions are taken in full cabinet. A network of cabinet committees may either take decisions without reference to the cabinet, or do most of the real work on a policy leaving little for the cabinet to discuss.

Also, the Prime Minister may choose to make important policy decisions after limited discussion with an 'inner' cabinet of senior colleagues, or a 'partial' cabinet of ministers chosen for consultation on a particular matter.

Loyalty to the principle of collective responsibility is likely to be strained if ministers find themselves responsible for policy decisions in which they had little or no say and later cannot criticize.

• *The size and complexity of the task.* It is as much as most ministers can do to keep up with the main matters in their own departments, let alone that of others. The scope of Government is both widespread, covering a multitude of decisions, and complex, covering a number of areas where specialist knowledge is required for full understanding. It is difficult to remain loyal to a decision taken by a colleague when you don't fully understand its implications.

• *Intra-cabinet differences.* These arise partly because of the two factors above and additionally because ministers may hold different political and personal views.

Sometimes these breaches are publicly acknowledged; the National Government (1931) 'agreed to differ' on economic policy; the Wilson Government of 1974–79 decided that, pending a referendum, ministers would be permitted to disagree publicly about whether Britain remain in the Economic Community on the terms then offered.

More often the disagreement comes out in the form of selective leaking of information to the press. Journalists who are members of 'the Lobby' are given 'background' and 'non-attributable' information in exchange for an agreement that the source is not revealed. Some newspapers such as the *Independent* have opted not to join the Lobby system but still get 'inside' information via contacts with MPs, Government press officers and other civil servants.

Patrick Gordon-Walker, in his book *The Cabinet* (1973), defends 'leaking' as a means by which ministers may make their views known while avoiding public disagreement with Government policy – so maintaining formal collective responsibility, and avoiding resignation. This seems a poor defence. The problem with 'leaking' is that it is selective and anonymous. The public receives snippets of information, or pseudo-information, without the full story, and without being able to question the source of the information.

 Describe the principles of collective responsibility and explain why cabinet secrecy is difficult to uphold in practice.

Cabinet reform

One approach to cabinet reform, proposed by Benn, is to open up the whole institution, and make it democratically accountable. He proposes:

- A Freedom of Information Act to reduce the secrecy that cloaks the cabinet.
- A Labour cabinet subject to annual re-election by the Parliamentary Labour Party (PLP).
- A Labour cabinet accountable to the PLP for the implementation of the manifesto.

In Benn's view this would change the cabinet from a secret cabal to one that was democratically elected and openly responsible, and whose deliberations MPs and public could judge for themselves. It would reduce the Prime Minister's ability to dominate cabinet.

Some would argue that Benn's proposals would effectively destroy the principle of collective responsibility. How could ministers follow a line if it was known that they had opposed that policy in cabinet? This lack of credibility would then erode the support necessary to keep a Government in office. It is also argued that this might inhibit effective discussion in cabinet were ministers' views to be the subject of party and public debate.

One of the commonest arguments for maintaining secrecy about the discussion which takes place before a commitment is made, is that a minister should not have to take responsibility for something to which he or she is not yet committed. Openness at this stage would put pressure on ministers to commit themselves to a line before any collective decision was made. This argument for secrecy could be seen as a sophisticated excuse for keeping disagreeable differences away from the public eye, and a means of creating an illusion of unanimity which doesn't exist.

The election of cabinet ministers is open to the objection that it would undermine the authority of the Prime Minister, which in a sense is precisely what it is intended to do. One's view of this depends upon whether one considers a strong Prime Minister, with a team controlled by him or her, to be desirable. Cabinet unity might be reduced if cabinet ministers were primarily concerned with their 'constituencies' within the Parliamentary party. The proposal can be seen as a recipe for proper democratic accountability, or chaos, depending upon one's assessment of the likely outcome of such change.

▶ During the Westland affair leaking was used extensively as a weapon against those holding other views.

▶ Objections to Benn's proposals for cabinet reform.

▶ Crossman claims that he and his colleagues put pressure on Wilson to form an inner cabinet: 'Harold lives in his lonely little place and doesn't do anything. We have got to get an inner Cabinet to restrain him and to see whether with that we can steer the Party through the terrible year that is coming' (entry for April 20 1969). A few days later Wilson agreed to the idea, in principle.

Outline Benn's proposals for cabinet reform and the objections made to them.

► Amery's ideas – the Super Cabinet.

In the 1930s *Leo Amery*, a Conservative MP, put forward ideas for reform based upon his assessment of what was wrong with the cabinet operation, although they have never been fully implemented. Amery dealt with the problem he saw arising from the size of the cabinet, and the complexity and number of the matters with which it had to deal. The cabinet in practice deals with few of them in any detail. They are handled by committees, or by the Prime Minister, or by the Prime Minister in consultation with a few senior colleagues. Amery's answer was to have a smaller cabinet, none of whose members would have any departmental responsibilities. They would, instead, oversee the work of groups of departments to ensure that they followed the broad policy guide-lines laid down by cabinet. Cabinet would concern itself not with details; these would be handled by committees and departments. It would, instead, lay down strategies and aims within which departments would work.

Amery said:

1 *Cabinet is too big* – twenty-odd people are too many for a discussion which is primarily concerned with reaching a decision, rather than airing views.

2 *Ministers are too committed to their own departments.* Rather than looking at the broad national interest, departmental ministers are likely to 'fight the department's corner' with briefs from their officials.

3 *Departmental ministers are too busy with their own departments.* Most ministers already work more than a 12-hour day. To ask them to consider matters coming from other departments, having acquired the necessary background knowledge, is to ask too much.

4 *An unofficial hierarchy exists already.* In practice, vital decisions on policy are often taken by the Prime Minister, or by an unofficial 'inner cabinet'. The trouble with this arrangement is that these decisions are theoretically those of the whole cabinet. Those who are really responsible are not identified. The hierarchy should be institutionalized and recognized.

► The problems highlighted by Amery have been addressed from time to time. Churchill (1951–55) experimented with 'super ministers' but withdrew the experiment when MPs demanded to know who was answerable for what. In practice, it proved difficult to separate strategic from detailed decisions. Ministers, if they are to take decisions on matters of importance and be accountable for them, tend to want representation on the most senior policy committee. It is somewhat unrealistic to make decisions on public expenditure in a committee on which the Ministers of Health, Social Security and Defence, whose ministers spend huge amounts of money every year, are not represented.

Amery claimed that his 'super cabinet' would give ministers the time, freedom from bias, and the responsibility for formulating clear strategic policy aims.

This problem has been addressed at times by grouping ministries into 'super departments'. Thus the three service ministries (Army, Navy, Air Force) were grouped into the Ministry of Defence; Health and Social Security into the Department of Health and Social Security; and Local Government, Housing, Land Use and Planning into the Department of the Environment (Transport was later taken out).

Though part of the reason for such groupings was administrative, part was political; to provide a 'super minister' who would represent these areas in cabinet, without expanding the cabinet to an unwieldy size. At times, Prime Ministers have formalized an inner cabinet, to make responsibility clearer. Attlee, Wilson and Thatcher (at the time of the Falklands' War) have all resorted to this.

 What are the attractions of a small 'super cabinet'? What problems are associated with its creation?

How important is the cabinet?

Collective government, in which all senior ministers meeting weekly to consider properly all major matters of concern, make decisions based on equality of status, and subsequently take responsibility for them, is a model more appropriate to the nineteenth century than the twentieth.

Now there are too many decisions and they are too complex for one committee to deal with. Decisions are made and discussions take place in a variety of locations of which the cabinet is only one, and not necessarily the most important. Cabinet ministers are not equal in status, and do not have equal access to information. This could mean that the cabinet has become one of the honorific parts of the constitution, meeting formally, while the real decisions and discussions go on elsewhere. Some commentators (Martin Burch, *Teaching Politics*, 1985) certainly think so. We cannot be certain, while it is surrounded in secrets.

Yet indications are from Crossman, Benn and Castle that cabinet life was still vibrant, alive and kicking. In their time Prime Ministers suffered defeat in it, momentous decisions were made in it, bitter arguments were aired.

The cabinet of today is still important, but not to the degree it once was.

NM How important is the cabinet in the policy network?

ACT Essay/discussion

'The power of the Prime Minister has increased, is increasing, and ought to be diminished.'

Discuss, using recent examples to illustrate your view.

Review – The cabinet

The cabinet is a body governed by conventions based upon political expediency.

Its functions include being:
- the senior committee of the ruling party (ies).
- a policy and decision-making body for decisions of the highest political importance.
- a body which tries to co-ordinate policy for political and practical reasons.
- a 'court of appeal' for quarrelling departments.

The cabinet is surrounded by a network of committees which may take many important decisions themselves and prepare others for cabinet approval.

The twin principles of cabinet government – secrecy and collective responsibility – have proved difficult to uphold in practice.

Proposals for cabinet have ranged from Amery's 'Super cabinet' to Benn's ideas for opening up the system and democratizing it.

CHAPTER SUMMARY

1 Policy may be defined as aims and objectives resulting from values and ideas, or in response to events.

2 The execution of policy involves a series of increasingly specific decisions and realistic actions to make them happen.

3 Prime Minister and cabinet, departmental ministers and officials, quangos and local councillors and officials are all involved in the policy-making/execution process.

4 The Prime Minister plays a number of roles – Party Leader, Head of State, chair of cabinet, controller of a vast number of appointments (patronage) – giving him or her great power.

5 There are powers countervailing those of the Prime Minister and therefore potential for loss of authority.

6 The cabinet is the senior policy committee of the ruling party. It is concerned with major policy decisions of political importance, and co-ordinating the work of the various departments.

7 Its operating principles are secrecy and collective responsibility.

8 These two principles are often difficult to maintain because
• the cabinet is only part of a network of committees which take important decisions and a minister may well not have been in on a decision.
• Prime Ministers often 'rail-road' policies through cabinet.
As a result, ministers often leak their dissent to the media with a thinly disguised anonymity.

9 Some commentators have declared that 'cabinet government' is now a myth and have suggested 'Prime-ministerial government' or some variant of élite pluralism as a more appropriate model for describing what happens.

STIMULUS MATERIAL

The stimulus material is an article taken from the *Independent* newspaper about the relationships between the Prime Minister and the cabinet. Read the article and answer the following questions:

1 What emerges from the article as the possible dilemmas faced by departmental ministers with a strong Prime Minister who wants results?

2 Why, despite her strong leadership, did Mrs Thatcher like other Prime Ministers find 'restraining local government expenditure the most intractable of targets'?

3 Why do Prime Ministers sometimes sack or move Ministers who don't achieve certain objectives (whether they were at fault or not) and sometimes keep them on?

4 Refer to paragraph 6 – 'You have to be strong and say, "it can't be done." But few are'. Why do you think so few say "It can't be done"?

5 To what extent is a Prime Minister justified in ordering departmental Ministers to adopt and deliver policies?

► You will also find the stimulus material and associated exercises in Chapter 10, page 190ff relevant to issues of policy making.

MINISTERS WARNED OVER PERILS OF BEING THATCHER 'YES MEN'

1 Former Ministers yesterday warned their colleagues in the Cabinet who are trying to implement Mrs Thatcher's wishes to learn a lesson from Cecil Parkinson's experience.

2 They said that Kenneth Clarke and Chris Patten, who are handling changes to the NHS and the poll tax, should look carefully at the censure heaped upon Mr Parkinson by a Commons select committee over the aborted sale of the nuclear power industry.

3 Both ministers, like Mr Parkinson, have to deliver policies which were ordered by Mrs Thatcher. And some of her former ministers believe that the past record shows this could be hazardous.

4 Other ministers who became 'victims' of implementing the Prime Minister's wishes, include Patrick (now Lord) Jenkin, who was sacked as Secretary of State for the Environment for failing to deliver on the abolition of the GLC, a task later accomplished by Kenneth Baker, now party chairman.

5 The most spectacular retreat over a legislation demanded by Mrs Thatcher was made by Colin Moynihan, the Sports Minister, when he had to abandon the introduction of the football supporters' identity scheme, in the wake of the report on the Hillsborough disaster.

6 A former colleague said yesterday: 'There is a great deal of pressure on ministers to deliver. Those who say "no" get sacked. Those who don't deliver eventually get shopped by her. You have to be strong and say, "it can't be done." But few are.'

7 Restraining local government expenditure has proved the most intractable of Mrs Thatcher's targets. Michael Heseltine, as Secretary of State for the Environment, was forced into a humiliating retreat in December 1981 when he withdrew the section of the Local Government Finance Bill proposing referendums for councils which were seeking a supplementary rate. It was five years later, as Secretary of State for Defence, that he confronted her over the Westland affair, and resigned.

8 Mrs Thatcher is thought to remain sympathetic to the idea of referendums for high-spending councils. It has been revived and is being pressed on Mr Patten by some Tories as a solution to the problems over the poll tax. Mr Heseltine believes he would be wise to ignore it.

9   Mr Patten inherited the Poll Tax from Nicholas Ridley, now Secretary of State for Trade and Industry. Mr Ridley and Mr Parkinson are Mrs Thatcher's staunchest allies on the right wing in the Cabinet.

10   Another staunch ally, John Moore, was sacked from the Cabinet after failing to win the political debate over the changes to the NHS. He was replaced by Mr Clarke before the legislation was finalised. Mr Parkinson's failure, according to the Commons select committee on energy, was his inadequate preparation for the sale of nuclear power.

11   'Cecil didn't do his homework. He was too anxious to deliver the policy', a former cabinet colleague said. 'Patten and Clarke have got to be strong enough to say "no" if they don't think they can deliver everything she wants.'

12   The cautious approach by Mr Patten and Mr Clarke suggests they do not intend to make the same mistakes as some of their predecessors. In spite of Mr Clarke's assurances that he is sticking to his timetable of 1 April 1991 for the introduction of changes, the pace has slackened.

13   Ministers now point out that the internal market in the NHS will be established gradually. In practice, it is unlikely to take off until after the general election. Mr Patten will announce next month additional money to ease the burden of the Poll Tax next year. But structural changes are likely to be left out of the manifesto.

14   However, the opposition party has failed to attach the blame to Mrs Thatcher for her ministers' failures. Yesterday, Neil Kinnock, the Labour leader, challenged her integrity over Mr Ridley's handling of the Rover 'sweeteners' and Paddy Ashdown, the Liberal Democrat leader, attacked her 'obsession' with the sale of nuclear power. Labour believe the Government has been found guilty of incompetence this week, but making that charge stick on Mrs Thatcher has proved impossible in the past.

The Independent
Friday 29 June 1990
Colin Brown, Political Correspondent.

Further reading: Chapter 9

Amery L.S. 1953. *Thoughts on the Constitution.* Oxford: OUP. Out of date in its examples, but the ideas on cabinet reform are still interesting.

Burch M. 1990. 'Power in the cabinet system' *Talking Politics*, Vol 2, No. 3. A useful and up to date discussion of theories of power as applied to the cabinet.

Two general overviews of cabinet government are

Drucker H. *et al.* 1986. *Developments in British Politics 2*, Chapter 4, pages 88–96. London: Macmillan.

Hennessy P. 1986. *Cabinet.* Oxford: Blackwell.

Norton P. 1987. 'Prime-ministerial power: a framework for analysis' *Teaching Politics*, 16. Discusses different theories of Prime-ministerial power.

Weller P. 1985. *First Among Equals: Prime Ministers in Westminster Systems.* London: Allen & Unwin. A comparative study of Prime-ministerial power.

Diaries of Cabinet Ministers

Castle B. 1980. *The Castle Diaries 1964–70*. London: Weidenfeld & Nicolson.

Castle B. 1984. *The Castle Diaries 1974–76*. London: Weidenfeld & Nicolson.

Crossman R. 1975. (ed. Anthony Howard) *The Crossman Diaries*. London: Methuen.

Benn A. 1989. *The Benn Diaries*. London: Hutchinson

Don't try to read these from cover to cover. Dip into them for information on certain periods and certain topics. They are interesting for the insights they give into political life, but read them critically and sceptically.

Now that you have completed this chapter, look back to the objectives at the beginning and check that you have accomplished each of them.

Government departments – ministers and civil servants

Media Watch

Like the inner workings of the Cabinet (Chapter 9) many aspects of the Civil Service and of the relationships between civil servants and ministers are kept out of the news. However, look out for media debates on the workings of the civil service and for stories on government reforms of the civil service. The memoirs of ex-cabinet ministers also provide an insight into the relationship between ministers and civil servants – see Further reading page 179.

Chapter objectives

By the end of this chapter you should be able to:
- ▌ list the different functional bases for government departments
- ▌ discuss the problems associated with departmental organization
- ▌ critically assess the role of the Minister as head of a government department
- ▌ discuss the controversies surrounding the respective roles of Minister and senior civil servant and the mismatches between bureaucratic and political aims and objectives
- ▌ outline the structure of the British civil service and discuss the criticism that have been made of that structure
- ▌ assess the arguments for and against secrecy in government
- ▌ know the meaning of and be able to use the following terms: Secretary of State, minister, Parliamentary Secretary, Parliamentary Private Secretary, Permanent Secretary, ministerial responsibility.

GOVERNMENT DEPARTMENTS

The ground covered by government departments varies. Departments may be defined in various ways:

- A single activity, e.g. Transport, Employment.
- A theme covering several activities, e.g. Environment covering local government, housing, planning, land use, conservation, and national parks.
- A group of activities – e.g. Defence (containing Army, Navy and Air Force), Agriculture, fisheries and food.
- Geographically, i.e. Wales, Scotland or Northern Ireland.
- Historical evolution, e.g. the Home Office, Lord Chancellor's department.

► A *government department* is an area of government operation, headed by a Minister, with a hierarchical structure of junior ministers and permanent paid officials, and a budget voted to it by Parliament. The minister is directly answerable to Parliament and to the public for the conduct of its affairs and the expenditure of its money.

► Departmental funds are often referred to as coming from the 'Public Purse'.

Departments which have been around a long time may not fit into a logical pattern. For example, 'justice' and 'law and order' are shared between the Home Office (prisons, police, general order and a host of minor licensing and control functions) and the Lord Chancellor's department (responsible for the system of courts). The Chancellor of the Duchy of Lancaster and the Lord Privy Seal have virtually no formal duties left, but these sinecure offices are often used to give special responsibilities to a Minister not covered by an existing department. Lord Whitelaw, in 1987, was appointed Lord President of the Council – in fact he acted as the Deputy Prime Minister.

While certain of the 'old' ministries – the Foreign Office, Home Office, Lord Chancellor's department, the Exchequer – are always with us, others come and go or change form. No separate Minister for Northern Ireland existed before 1968, when the Province became the scene of armed conflict. The Labour Government of 1964–70 created a Department of Economic Affairs arising from its manifesto commitment to medium and long-term economic planning, and a Ministry of Technology because of its commitment to technology. Both were abolished by the Conservatives in 1979.

Like most large and complex organizations, government departments have their problems. The first is their *size*: departments range in size from the giants like the former Health and Social Security (now divided into two ministries), and Defence; through medium-sized departments like the Environment, to minnows like the Northern Ireland office.

► The problem of the size of government departments.

Big departments have advantages, at least in theory, since they should achieve better co-ordination of policy and administration. The creation of a Ministry of Defence meant that the likelihood of the three armed services pursuing different strategic aims was reduced, and administrative and accounting procedures could be unified to avoid confusion and wasteful duplication.

The bigger an organization becomes, however, the harder it becomes to manage. Professor C. Northcote Parkinson, in his amusing book with a serious purpose, *Parkinson's Law*, claims that large organizations have a tendency to generate their own growth, irrespective of what it is they are administering or producing. As examples he quotes two government departments:

►*Parkinson's Law* (1958) – 'Work expands to fill the time allotted to it' and 'Subordinates multiply at a fixed rate regardless of the amount of work produced'.

• The Admiralty – as the number of Royal Navy ships and dockyard installations has steadily reduced, so the number of civil servants (not sailors) has steadily increased.

• The Colonial Office (later called the Commonwealth Office) – the staff was larger when Britain's Empire had virtually disappeared than it was when it covered a quarter of the world's surface.

The second problem area for government departments is that of *demarcation of function* and *co-ordination*. Policy needs do not follow departmental boundary lines. Should sentencing policy for offenders be a Home Office matter, or the province of the Lord Chancellor? Should vocational training be a matter for the Department of Education and Science, the Department of Trade and Industry or the Department of Employment? A case could be made out for each and all of them.

►Problems of *demarcation* of *function* and *co-ordination*.

►Problems of levels of decision making

Co-ordination across departmental boundaries is an allied problem. Departments may regard others with suspicion, or even hostility.

In terms of sheer number, the vast majority of decisions are made within government departments. They are so numerous that no one person can be charged with the job of making all of them. Yet we elect politicians to run and to be responsible for our government departments, as Ministers. One problem is which decisions should be taken by the Minister, and which by civil servants in the name of the Minister.

The case of Chrysler Car Corporation

In 1976, the American *Chrysler Car Corporation* announced the proposed closure of its UK operation, including an assembly plant at Linwood in Scotland, located there with Government encouragement and grants. Two Departments reacted in opposite ways to the suggestion that the Government should spend money to retain Chrysler in Britain.

The *Scottish Office*, concerned about unemployment in Scotland and growing support for the SNP (Scottish National Party), considered it vital that Chrysler should be given financial inducement to stay. The *Department of Industry* claimed that such an inducement was contrary to the Government's industrial strategy, and its investment in British Leyland.

In the event, Chrysler was given financial inducement to stay, but not before a bitter row in Cabinet, and the threatened resignation of the Minister for Industry.

Eric Varley, the Minister for Industry, withdrew his resignation after an interview with Prime Minister Wilson. Wilson permitted Varley to make a statement to the Commons accepting the decision but stating his objections.

▶ The Chrysler case illustrates policy conflicts between government departments.

The case of Vehicle and General Car Insurance Company

The *Vehicle and General Car Insurance Company* went bankrupt in 1972 after having taken on thousands of new policy holders in a sales 'push'. The policy holders lost the money they had paid in premiums and their vehicles became uninsured. A subsequent inquiry revealed that the relevant government department (Trade and Industry) had known that the company's position was shaky, even before the sales campaign, but had not used its powers either to stop Vehicle and General from trading, or to mount some sort of 'rescue' operation.

The inquiry resulted from an understandable outcry from MPs and policy holders who wanted to know *why* John Davies, the Minister, had not acted.

▶ The Vehicle and General Case illustrates that ministers often do not know what is happening in their ministry and that many decisions are made without the minister's knowledge.

The answer was that the minister did not know about it. The civil servant responsible for the insurance division of the DTI had taken the decision not to intervene without referring to the minister, believing that he was following a policy clearly laid down in cabinet of 'hands off' in such cases. The inquiry blamed the civil servant, and he was moved to another job.

In some cases, the answer is clear. If a decision involves the commitment of large amounts of money and resources, if existing policy is not clear or does not apply to the decision, or if the matter is likely to generate political controversy, it needs the minister's approval.

If it is clearly covered by existing policy or recent precedent it may not need the minister's approval. For example, a decision to grant or reject an appeal against a local authority's decision to refuse planning permission for a garage may not require the Minister's attention. A decision as to whether to authorize the building of a nuclear power station certainly would. But there are 'grey' areas between these two extremes.

The Vehicle and General case was unusual in that the public was permitted to see exactly how, and by whom, a decision was made. Normally, the whole business is covered in a cloak of secrecy, and even our elected representatives, through select committees, are not allowed access to such details. Theoretically all decisions are made by the minister.

It also highlights the problem of allocating responsibility in a system where a multitude of decisions have to be made by a number of people operating at different levels. Further discussion of this question requires us to look at the two elements in a government department – the *political* and the *bureaucratic* – the minister and the civil servant – see page 188.

 How could you use the example of Chrysler to illustrate the policy making process dealt with in Chapter 9?

Draw up a two column table to list the pros and cons of having big departments such as Environment or Defence.

THE MINISTER

Ministerial responsibility

The job of a minister can be broken down into a number of functions:
• *Taking responsibility for the department.* The word 'responsible' is commonly used in two ways: (1) *having initiated and carried out* something – I am 'responsible' for this book in the sense that I wrote it. And (2), *answerable for* something – I 'take the can' i.e. answer criticisms and take the blame for faults in the book.
But (1) and (2) don't necessarily go together. A parent may be answerable for the actions of their child, even though he or she will not have been responsible in the sense of (1) above.

A minister is certainly responsible in sense (2), to Parliament, party, public, media and Cabinet (if of Cabinet rank).
• *Taking Parliamentary responsibility.* Every few weeks, a minister will have to defend his department in 'Question Time' in Parliament.

Ministers also have to undertake the task of steering the department's legislation through Parliament (see pages 142–9). For a politically contentious piece of legislation the *second reading* is crucial to making a good or bad impression and answering criticisms about the

► It is not unknown for civil servants, aware of their Minister's poor performance at Question Time, to plant 'friendly' questions with MPs.

fundamentals of the bill.

Policy debates, emergency debates, debates on the adjournment, if they involve the department, all see the Minister defending his or her corner.

As with most departmental matters, this will involve the civil servants. Anxious to project the department in a good light, they will attempt to brief the minister as thoroughly as possible. In the end, however, it is the minister who mounts the public performance on which the department is assessed.

• *Dealing with the media and the public.* Normally it is the minister who will have to face the television cameras and journalists on matters concerning the department, although on major matters of policy or national disaster the Prime Minister may step in.

Each department has a press office issuing 'attributable' statements to the media, and giving background 'non-attributable' briefings. Again, it is likely that the minister's public appearances will have been preceded by briefings from civil servants. Normally their involvement is hidden from public view, although there are exceptions.

For example, during the Falklands' operations, the civil servant who gave the daily reports to the media became something of a TV personality in his own right.

The civil servant sent to Australia to appear for the British Government in court in the *Spycatcher* case, Sir Robert Armstrong, Secretary to the Cabinet, gained world-wide media coverage by denying that he had ever lied, but admitting that he had been 'economical with the truth'.

When she was in office Mrs Thatcher's press officer, Bernard Ingham, become a public figure, particularly after the Westland affair (see pages 169). The increasing visibility of civil servants may reflect their greater involvement in the 'management' of the news.

• *Dealing with pressure groups.* We saw in Chapter 7 that even during Mrs Thatcher's era, when pressure groups were not as close to government as under previous regimes, departments still had a complex relationship with the groups relevant to their work areas. Meeting representatives of the relevant groups formally and informally and listening to delegations, are all part of a minister's work. Attending the conferences of pressure groups may provide an important occasion for a public statement.

• *Dealing with the party.* Civil servants will usually avoid direct involvement with party issues. Ministers regularly talk with and receive views from subject groups of backbench MPs who take a particular interest in the work of the department.

Party conferences may repay the minister's attention, in the sense that his/her popularity with party activists as a leading politician may be influenced by his/her performance as a minister.

• *Dealing with the cabinet.* Even non-cabinet ministers may be involved in cabinet committees. The role of a departmental minister in the cabinet and its committees is twofold; to represent the department in the cabinet and its committees, and to take responsibility for seeing that cabinet policy is followed in the department.

► *Spycatcher* (1989) was written by Peter Wright, a former, and disgruntled, agent of MI5, the internal security agency. It alleged, among other things, that MI5 had tried to bring down the Wilson Government with a dirty tricks campaign, and that the former head of MI5 had been a Soviet spy. The Government's efforts to get it suppressed gave a rather dull book international notoriety and made its author rich.

► At their annual conference Conservative Home Secretaries frequently have to face the hostility of 'Law and Order' Conservative activists, demanding a policy of tougher punishment for offenders; Labour ministers regularly face criticism from left-wing activists at their conference.

► According to Richard Crossman, the departmental civil servants see the Minister's job as being to fight for the department in Cabinet, ensuring, for example, that if cuts in departmental budgets are on the agenda, his/her department suffers as little as possible.

Taking responsibility, although it forms a substantial part of a minister's work, is not all that it consists of. The minister is not just a 'front office' person, there to communicate with public, party and Parliament, while the officials get on with the real work of the department in some back room. The minister's role is far more positive.

► See the Panel on page 188 for the dissonant perspectives of politicians and civil servants.

Ministers: policy and decision making

Policy and decision making are two areas in which the minister is fully involved and responsible in the instigation sense of the term 'responsible'.

• *Making policy*. The minister, particularly at the beginning of a Government's term of office, may bring a collection of manifesto commitments, which may or may not be translated into policies and actions. Policy ideas may also be thought up by the minister, or arise in response to outside pressure, the cabinet or events. Circumstances may change, or civil servants may raise objections which persuade the minister.

► The brilliant TV series, *Yes Minister* and *Yes Prime Minister*, featured a bumbling minister manipulated by his civil servants, who nearly always got their own way. It made some serious points – by all means watch videos or repeats – but take it all with a pinch of salt. It was, apparently, Mrs Thatcher's favourite TV programme.

The process involves a dialogue between the minister as custodian of the party line, and the officials who will be concerned with how the new ideas fit existing policies and commitments, resources and procedures. Neither side in the dialogue is likely to be passive, but the minister's role is crucial. In the end it is for the minister to decide to proceed with, amend or abandon a policy.

• *Decision making*. Ministers are required to make a surprising number of individual decisions. Crossman dubbed this aspect of a minister's work, 'the tyranny of the Red Boxes' – a reference to the red leather dispatch cases which contain papers for ministerial signature. Draft orders, regulations, circulars, decisions authorizing actions each accompanied by an explanatory paper, pile up daily. The extent to which the minister is involved can vary greatly. Crosland (*The Politics of Education*, 1972) claimed that, when he was at the DES (1964), he concentrated on only one issue at a time, leaving the rest to the department. He saw this as a way of having a real influence on the politically important decisions, while not dissipating energy trying to be involved in every aspect of the department's work. The need to adopt this tactic indicates that the sheer volume of decision-making is a problem.

The constitutional doctrine of ministerial responsibility

As the Minister of the Crown appointed to a department, the minister is constitutionally responsible for that department and is expected to 'take the can' politically for the policies and actions of the department. Much debate has taken place around the questions of:

• *How far such responsibility should extend*; in particular whether it should extend to taking the responsibility for the actions of officials which the minister neither sanctioned, nor knew about.

• *What 'taking responsibility' means*: in particular, when it should involve the minister's resignation.

► Dugdale's resignation. Some land had been taken over by the Air Ministry at the outbreak of war in 1939. They passed it over to the Ministry of Agriculture who leased it as 'model' farms. The original promise to the owners to given them a chance to buy the land back was ignored until they brought the matter up in Parliament. The Ministry went through the motions of inviting offers but had already made up its mind who was to get the land.

► Crossman, R. (1978) *The Crossman Diaries.*

• *Whether taking responsibility is often a convenient fiction*, in view of the number of decisions taken collectively by cabinet or committee and individually by civil servants.

The circumstances under which ministers have, or have not, resigned do not follow a consistent pattern.

Thomas Dugdale, Minister of Agriculture (1954), resigned over the department's failure to honour a promise to give the owner of a piece of land that was compulsorily purchased an opportunity to buy it back. The fault was entirely that of the departmental civil servants and Dugdale had not even been minister at the time when the land, in Dorset, was leased to someone else. Dugdale nevertheless resigned, stating that as the responsible minister it was his duty to do so.

This did not create any binding precedent, as the Vehicle and General case illustrates (see page 182).

To suggest that a minister should resign over something which is entirely the fault of civil servants seems harsh and not particularly useful if the objective is to allocate true responsibility. Some commentators at the time of the Westland affair saw Leon Brittan's resignation as a means of ending speculation and avoiding further blame to others involved, rather than as a constitutionally principled solution.

Crossman records reading in the *Daily Mirror* allegations of systematic maltreatment of patients in a psychiatric hospital. As the Minister of Health at the time he was technically responsible. He knew nothing of the hospital, nor of suspicions of ill-treatment. His chief nursing officer reported that the allegations confirmed her suspicions, and would enable an investigation to take place. Up to this time Crossman had not been told of the department's suspicions for lack of proof.

Unless you are going to argue that a minister should know everything that is happening in his or her department, which is impossible, it is difficult to see how ministerial resignation is the appropriate remedy in such a case. Failure of policy, or persistent and widespread maladministration, however, do seem to make the minister a more appropriate target. Policy and the general stewardship of the department are clearly ministerial territory.

Even here, though, the precedents are not consistent. Lord Carrington (Foreign Secretary) resigned at the time of the Falklands' War, ostensibly taking responsibility for Britain's lack of preparedness against the possibility of Argentinian invasion, both militarily and diplomatically.

The recent past also provides plenty of examples of failures of policy which have not been followed by resignation.

The Wilson–Callaghan Government's economic policy had by early 1978 failed to control inflation, or promote economic growth. The social contract was revoked by the TUC and that winter saw a wave of strikes across the whole country. Nevertheless no-one resigned and the Government was eventually forced out of the Commons by a vote of no confidence.

Neither the failed Suez operation of 1956, nor the revelation that the British security service had at least three, possibly four, Soviet agents working within its upper reaches between 1955 and 1963 led to any resignation.

Personal lapses may lead to resignations, but this is by no means automatic. John Profumo, Minister for the Army in the Macmillan Government in 1962, eventually resigned when it became known that he had lied to the House of Commons about his relationship with a prostitute, Christine Keeler, who was also involved with a member of the staff of the Soviet embassy. Macmillan, however, supported Profumo, until the weight of evidence made the accusation undeniable.

In the same government, Thomas Galbraith, a junior minister in the Foreign Office, was vigorously defended by Macmillan when newspapers published letters from him to a junior civil servant facing espionage charges couched in terms which some saw as affectionate. No resignation took place.

During the Thatcher Government, Cecil Parkinson resigned (1988) after his mistress revealed details of broken promises and the existence of a child of which Parkinson was the father. Mrs Thatcher accepted his resignation with reluctance, and later reinstated him as a senior Cabinet Minister.

There are no hard-and-fast rules governing ministerial resignation. The likelihood of resignation is affected by the degree of public and media outcry, the personalities of the individuals concerned and the willingness or not of Prime Minister and Cabinet to 'close ranks' around the individual who is under fire.

 List all the possible meanings of 'ministerial responsibility'. What problems would arise if the convention of ministerial responsibility were followed slavishly?

It is clear that ministers take a large degree of responsibility for the policies and actions of their departments. Determining how far the minister's responsibility does extend or should extend is not made easy by the secrecy that surrounds the policy network. Even a parliamentary select committee will receive no useful answer to questions about who took a decision, or what advice was given or what alternatives were considered.

Yet it is an important part of liberal democracy that areas of responsibility should be clear, and that those who are responsible, in the sense of *instigation*, should be responsible in the sense of *answerable*.

THE CIVIL SERVICE

In a government department many decisions must be taken by *civil servants*, and most important policies will in some way have been influenced by civil service advice. British civil servants, however, are neither elected by the public nor in the main politically attached to the Government of the day (as they are in some liberal democracies). They are in theory neutral technicians, carrying out the wishes of their political masters. As with the theory of cabinet collective responsibility, the theory of individual ministerial responsibility seems inadequate as a framework within which to explain the complexities

► *Civil Service*
For the purposes of this chapter when we refer to the 'Civil Service', we are talking about employees of *central* government departments (local government officers are not included in the definition), who are appointed and employed in a permanent capacity, thus distinguishing them from politicians who are elected and temporary. They are employed in a *civil* as opposed to a *military* capacity, and are working in non-industrial positions, concerned with policy research, advice and administration.

The Politician and the Bureaucrat

• *Different perspectives.* A politician is likely to think in terms of party ideology, to go for short-term visible results which are popular with the electorate, and act in prediction of and in response to public pressure. A bureaucrat may be less interested in ideology, emphasize continuity and long-term and incremental gains. Though not unaware of public and pressure group pressure a bureaucrat is likely to be more interested in practicality than popularity.

• *Different skills.* A successful politician needs media appeal, ability to speak at meetings, to coin memorable phrases and credibility as a leader. A good administrator needs patience, grasp of detail, ability to see long-term consequences and snags and to plan accordingly.

• *Different time scales.* A Minister is likely to be only a few years in office and a matter of months in any one department. S/he has only this short time to make a mark. Most civil servants are in office until retirement, making a life-time career.

• *Different peer groups.* A politician's reputation and self-esteem is dependent on the judgement of the public, the media and other politicians. A civil servant is judged by other civil servants.

---

of British Government in the twentieth century. Such an explanation must include a consideration of the nature and role of the British civil service.

The British civil service has many of the features of the 'classic' model of bureaucracy. It is useful to clarify the nature of bureaucracy as a framework for understanding the role of the civil service in the policy network.

Bureaucracy is often used to mean 'red tape'; unnecessary paperwork, slavish and unimaginative obedience to rules, procedures and precedent. It has in some circles become almost a term of abuse. We are concerned here, however, with the more literal meaning of the word – 'rule by officials'.

Max Weber saw bureaucracy as the characteristic form of administration in the legal rational state: the state in which the source of authority was law passed by an elected assembly, and the purpose of government was to deliver, as efficiently as possible, certain agreed policy objectives for which the government would be responsible. To achieve this, governments employ a corps of officials whose characteristics may include:

• *Professionalism.* In contrast to the priests and landowners of medieval feudalism, bureaucrats do their job, not as a by-product of another position of standing in the community, but as their sole occupation and source of income, with their own professional ethics and rules.

• *Recruitment and promotion by merit rather than political preferment.* The model bureaucrat in a liberal democratic state is picked for ability to do the job, not as an exchange for political loyalty, or because he or she is related to someone important. While professionally loyal, he or she will remain apolitical, prepared to serve whichever set of political masters the electorate chose.

* *Hierarchical structure.* A pyramid structure with seniority marked by rank, salary and importance of function, and each layer reporting to and responsible to the layer above it.
* *Recording and rule-following.* A model bureaucracy follows rules and procedures. For this reason, and because of its accountability to its political masters, decisions and actions are meticulously recorded and filed. Procedures, forms and rules are devised for most situations where repeated decisions are required.

Bureaucracy is often maligned but in a liberal democratic state it has in theory at least a number of virtues. First, it is *efficient*. Officials who are picked for their ability and who are judged by a code of professional ethics should deliver an efficient service.

Next, it is *consistent*. The following of rules and procedures may help to ensure fairness. For example, if entitlement to social security benefit were entirely governed by the moods and prejudices of those individuals who authorized payment, some wildly inequitable results would ensue, and claimants would have little idea of what they were entitled to and under what circumstances.

Then, a bureaucracy helps to maintain *continuity*. Governments in a democracy change frequently, and ministers within the span of one Government even more frequently. Policies and commitments, however, cannot be switched on and off every few years. Current problems will be affected by previous policies and actions. A permanent bureaucracy may provide the element of experience and continuity needed to manage change.

Permanent bureaucrats in the upper reaches like to see themselves as providing a detached, *objective,* view, free from the distortion of political enthusiasm or the desire for political advancement. They provide, they would like to think, a cool view of the realities to temper the enthusiasm of the politician.

Criticisms of British bureaucracy

Yet bureaucracy, and Britain's central bureaucracy in particular, continues to come under fire. One of the criticisms often levelled at it is its *insularity*.

In a case study of planning in Newcastle, *The Evangelistic Bureaucrat* (1974), John Gower-Davis made a trenchant attack on the central and local government officials who handled the redevelopment of Rye Hill. The planners pursued their own vision of Newcastle as 'the Athens of the North' and the architects a 'twenty-first century skyline' without reference to the wishes, interests or feelings of the people who lived in Rye Hill. Gower-Davis highlighted a significant criticism of bureaucracy as a system. Neither planners nor architects lived in or had roots in the communities whose future they decided. Because they have no roots in the communities they administer, bureaucracies, develop their own sub-culture *insulated* from the rest of society.

Weber's model

In Weber's model a bureaucracy

* is staffed by professionals who are
* appointed and promoted on merit
* objective and non-partisan
* it is hierarchical in structure
* is bound by rules and procedures which
* are followed consistently
* and decisions and actions are meticulously documented.

A bureaucracy working properly is efficient and consistent, provides objective and non-partisan advice to politicians, and provides an element of continuity in the political system.

For an account of Weber's ideas on bureaucracy see *From Max Weber Essays in Sociology*, edited and translated by Gerth and C. Wright Mills, 1948, Chapter 8.

►The Northcote–Trevelyan committee had a ready model for their reforms in the corps of officials recruited to administer India on behalf of the British Government.

Another criticism levelled at bureaucracies concerns the amount of red tape, i.e. form filling and procedure following. A consequence of the very procedures which should produce consistency and even-handedness, bureaucracies are often accused of producing confusion and frustration through a multiplicity of forms and procedures which only the bureaucrats themselves can understand.

In a model liberal democracy, the bureaucrats should serve the elected politicians as an instrument of the policies for which the politicians were elected. Real life is more complex. A minister's stay in a department is temporary. Ministers are professional politicians but usually amateurs in the subject matter of their department. Thus they rely on the permanent professionals to advise them and carry out their wishes.

A succession of ex-ministers has accused the British civil service of using their inside knowledge to steer policy in the direction they wanted it to go, delaying or frustrating the implementation of policies of which they did not approve, and even on occasion attempting to subvert whole Governments.

 Essay/Discussion Question

'It is difficult to see how the government of a modern state could be carried out without a large scale bureaucracy and most of the complaints about bureaucracy, are about bureaucracies working inefficiently, rather than about bureaucracy itself'. Discuss.

The characteristics of the British civil service

The roots of the modern civil service lie in the *Northcote-Trevelyan Report* (1854), which was designed to produce an efficient administrative machine, free from political influence and patronage.

The features of the service are:

Permanence

Established civil servants, for the most part, have a career for life. They do not come and go with Governments. The career-service structure is further enhanced by the usual practice of promotion from within the service, rather than recruitment to the top jobs from outside.

Party political neutrality and anonymity

Although departmental ministers and Prime Ministers have temporarily employed political advisers, those career civil servants who work closely with their minister eschew publicity and identification with any political party or its ideology.

A British civil servant must be prepared to serve a Labour Government which wishes to nationalize major industries, increase government spending on the social services, and give trade unions stronger powers under the law, immediately after having served a Conservative Government which has privatized many previously nationalized industries, cut spending on social services and legislated to reduce the power of trade unions.

This continuity of service as Governments come and go could hardly be maintained if civil servants were too publicly and closely identified with the ideas of one party. Too close an identity with a particular regime might lead to the end of a 'permanent' civil service, at least at the top level, and the beginning of a political bureaucracy. Under such a system Ministers would bring with them their own advisers known to be sympathetic to the Government's programme or the ideology of the party in power.

The civil service does not always conform to the strict neutrality of the ideal model. Indeed it is unlikely that any intelligent group of people would be such political eunuchs. During the last twenty years, Prime Ministers have shown a desire to strengthen themselves and their Governments politically against what they anticipated as the countervailing politics of the civil service. One method of achieving this has been the appointment of political advisers, brought in with the Government.

The success of experiments with outside advisers has been limited. Constitutionally, the principal civil servant, the Permanent Secretary (or Secretaries in a big department) is responsible for managing the department and advising and communicating with the minister. He or she is also the Accounting Officer for the department, directly responsible for the proper expenditure of money by the department.

For matters of financial resources, management, and the feasibility of particular policies, the minister is likely to have to rely on the advice of senior civil servants, who are in turn advised by specialist civil servants and officials of lower rank. While this degree of responsibility lies with the permanent civil service, it seems unlikely that outsiders are going to make much impact on the running of the department, although they provide an alternative source of advice which challenges that of the permanent service.

Mrs Thatcher's suspicion that many senior civil servants were politically unsympathetic to the radical right-wing programme of her Government led her to take a personal interest in the filling of senior posts. When making senior appointments arising from retirements or resignations, she asked about prospective promotees 'Is he one of us?', meaning is he or she sympathetic to the Government's ideas.

The very independence and continuity of the service may be seen as a threat by radical governments of the right and left.

With the help of her advisers from Marks and Spencer, Mrs Thatcher succeeded in reducing the size of the service. Her belief that civil servants should concentrate more on managing their departments, and less on getting involved in policy, was reflected in her support for the 'Next Step' reforms, outlined in 1987, which sought to retain only a small number of policy advisers and devolve much of the work of departments to semi-autonomous 'management groups' with their own budgets, and targets for achievement.

► Wilson and Callaghan (1964–70 and 1974–79) introduced 'outsiders' (38 in all) to the team of advisers serving the Prime Minister and major departments.

Mrs Thatcher appointed an efficiency adviser from Marks and Spencers, and an outside economic policy adviser, Professor Alan Walters, amongst others. (Professor Walters, however, resigned soon afterwards.)

► The appointment of political advisers can cause problems. Nigel Lawson, the Chancellor of the Exchequer in the Thatcher Government, resigned in 1989, claiming that Mrs Thatcher supported the views of her adviser (Professor Walters), rather than those of the Treasury, and thus undermined the Chancellor's position.

Note that in the USA, many bureaucratic posts are filled by political appointees or electees so that the civil service changes with each change of government.

What are the advantages and disadvantages of a permanent civil service (and permanent sets of local government officers)?

Hierarchical structure

At the top of the department is the *permanent secretary* (a large department may have more than one), who is responsible for the management of the department, and is also the accounting officer for the department, and the civil servant closest to the Minister, providing policy advice. Below the permanent secretary, deputy secretaries co-ordinate the work of a group of sections, headed by under secretaries.

This is the apex of the pyramid. Although the three top posts are 'open' posts for which any officer can apply, they are most likely to have come into the service originally via the administrative trainee group, newly graduated from university. Statistically they are more likely to have been educated at Oxford or Cambridge than at any other university, and to have degrees in Arts or Social Sciences. Salary and status are commensurate with their rank.

There is a multitude of classes and groups, reflecting the fact that the civil service employs just about every major trade and profession there is. These can be divided into

- *Service-wide groups* which operate across the service, in various or all departments, each having its own salary scales and qualifications for entry.
- *Service-wide* specialist groups.
- *Departmental classes*, peculiar to one department.

The major service-wide group is the *Administration Group*, who provide general management, policy advice, and administration. At the top of the group is the open structure (permanent secretaries, deputy secretaries, under secretaries), below that assistant secretary, senior principal and principal. The grade of principal is filled partly by promotion from lower grades, but likely future 'high fliers' enter the grade via the largely university-graduate Administrative Trainee Scheme; a two-year scheme, during which certain trainees are highlighted for rapid promotion. All these top grades of the Administration Group constitute the 'mandarins' of the service, responsible for policy advice and management.

The next tier down is a middle-management and lower level decision-making function. It is provided by the three executive officer grades, with a graduate or A level entry, and an internal promotion system.

Below this tier clerical officers and assistant clerical officers carry out routine tasks of administration requiring, in theory at least, no great exercise of discretion.

In addition to this administrative 'spine', there are a number of

►Permanent secretary, deputy secretary, under secretary.

►The Civil Service Commission – the body responsible for the recruitment of senior civil servants – has always defended itself vigorously against the accusation of Oxbridge bias. Its members claim that more prospective entrants from the two old universities make the grade. It may be that first-class graduates from other universities are more likely to look elsewhere for employment.

service-wide specialist groups with their own salaries and entry qualifications – the Science Group, Professional and Technical Statisticians, Economists, Information Officers. Theoretically the top 'open structure' posts are open to specialists; in practice they usually go to promotees from the top areas of the Administration Group, who will have had more experience of policy advice.

Civil servants like Tax Inspectors, Customs and Prison Officers and Immigration Officers are confined to one department.

Standardized recruitment and promotion procedures
The Northcote–Trevelyan committee, which established the basis for the modern service, was concerned to find objective criteria for the selection and promotion of civil servants, to get away from political and personal patronage. Since then a mixture of written examinations and interviews – referred to as 'Boards' – has been the standard procedure for most recruitment and selection.

 What are the duties of a permanent secretary? Why and how is a permanent secretary's view likely to differ from that of his/her minister?

The Civil Service: Criticisms and controversies

A Royal Commission, the *Fulton Commission*, was set up to investigate the civil service and reported in 1969. It provided a most searching critique of the structure and ethos of the civil service.

Some of its main criticisms were as follows:

► The *Fulton Commission* on the civil service

• *Amateurism.* Fulton claimed that the service was too dominated by 'the amateur, the generalist, the all-rounder'. He pointed out that 'generalists' – officers with no specific technical expertise, a background in general administration, and an education in philosophy, history, or English literature – dominated the service. It was they who worked closely with the minister and made management decisions, they who might recommend the 'axing' of a project put forward by a team of specialists. The Commission recommended that specialists should be able to attain the highest reaches of the service, so that ministers would have specialist advice direct, not sifted through the general administrator.

• *Too many grades and classes.* Fulton claimed that the profusion of grades, classes and levels inhibited the best use of staff, locking too many employees up in one salary scale and career structure. It recommended a unified scale from the equivalent of the clerical officer up to permanent secretary with a greatly reduced number of *points* on the scale, comparable with ranks in the army. There would be no barriers to movement up and down the new scale.

• *Management skills a low priority.* Too many senior civil servants, according to Fulton, saw themselves as policy advisers rather than managers. More use of modern management techniques and training in such techniques were recommended.

The creation of policy units with a senior officer, not the permanent secretary, responsible for advising the minister on policy, was also suggested.

• *Insularity*. Fulton saw the civil service mandarins as inhabitants of an 'ivory tower', lacking experience of the world of industry, commerce, local government, that they administered. He recommended secondment into and out from the civil service and that more posts at senior level be advertised on the general job market.

Another aspect of insularity touched upon in the Fulton report was the secrecy that surrounds the work of the service. Beyond a vague wish that there should be more openness Fulton provided no guidance as to how this might be achieved.

• *More training and co-ordination needed*. Impressed by the French École National d'Administration, Fulton recommended civil service colleges to provide courses, from degree-level courses in administration, to short in-service and refresher courses. Better co-ordination of the service, it felt, would be provided by the creation of a separate civil service department with a minister at its head.

Response to Fulton

The creation of the two Civil Service Colleges and a Ministry for the Civil Service were the most immediate results of the Fulton report. However, the Thatcher Government abolished the department, dividing its work between Treasury and the Cabinet Office. The Civil Service Colleges remain, but have never acquired the prestige or importance that Fulton envisaged.

The investigation (by a committee chaired by a permanent secretary) of the feasibility of the unified grading structure, resulted in the grouping of classes into Administration, Technical and Scientific, and the introduction of an Open Structure for the three top jobs in each department. A unified structure, it was claimed, clashed with salaries in the specialist grades which should compare with those paid to similarly qualified staff outside the civil service. The civil service unions would object. An administration trainee grade was introduced for promotion from lower grades to higher, and for graduate recruitment.

Management techniques and training, it was claimed, were already being used to a greater extent than Fulton had given the service credit for. However, the 'management versus policy advice' argument resurfaced, in the shape of the *Ibbs Report*, which envisaged a small corps of policy advisers in each department, with the rest of the work devolved to semi-autonomous accountable management groups with their own budgets and production targets. These groups would be semi-autonomous in the sense that they would take complete responsibility for their own day-to-day administration and operational management, and accountable in the sense that they would be given a budget to manage and targets and performance indicators they would be required to achieve.

Lord Crowther-Hunt, a prominent member of the Fulton Commission, writing in the *Guardian* ten years later, confessed himself disappointed with progress since Fulton, and blamed the service itself for blocking progress. He claimed that the essential characteristics of the

► The Civil Service Colleges have certainly not achieved the status and centrality of France's École National d'Administration, which inspired Fulton to recommend such an institution for Britain.

► *Ibbs Report* (1987).

service remained. Élitism, in the form of privileged jobs and promotion routes for starred graduates, still existed despite the theoretical equality of the specialist. The service was still effectively dominated by the generalist mandarin – the Oxbridge graduate who had worked his or her way through the starred path of the Administration Group. Secrecy and insularity from the outside world persisted too.

The defence of the existing structure of the service against the criticisms of Fulton revolves around:

* *The appropriateness of generalism.* A senior civil servant's job is management and policy advice. The former requires extensive experience of the administration of the service, best obtained in general administration rather than, say, scientific research. A specialist might carry out the latter, but only if he or she ceased to be a specialist. Advice has to be given within the context of general policy, the financial budget and political feasibility. None of these involve any single specialism. A specialist who remained so might be dangerous, since his or her knowledge of the specialism would bias judgement in its favour.

* *The inter-dependence of policy and administration.* Fulton's desire to separate policy and administration, and subsequent attempts to introduce policy advisers from outside the service, came against the criticism that policy and administration are inseparable parts of the continuous activity of government. A policy must be judged in the light of whether it can be realized, how much it will cost, and how it will fit into other aspects of government policy. Advice on policy, therefore is best given by those with responsibility for and experience of actually translating it into action.

* *The need for confidentiality.* Apart from matters of State security, the classic arguments for the secrecy that surrounds the deliberations of senior civil servants are that ministers, not civil servants, are publicly responsible for policies and actions, and that premature revelation of discussions before the point of commitment to a policy or action may lead to pressure for the wrong decision.

Support for the former of these two arguments seems to be getting weaker. Civil servants have recently more often been politically identified as being associated with certain decisions. They now regularly give evidence to Parliamentary Select Committees. The *First Division Association* – the top civil servants' trade union – has expressed concern at the position of civil servants who may be instructed to do things they consider of dubious morality or even legality, becoming a scapegoat for the policies of their political masters. They would welcome a system by which civil servants had more opportunities to explain their position publicly.

Nevertheless the cloak of confidentiality remains. Sarah Tisdall, a former officer with MI5, the internal intelligence service, was jailed under the Official Secrets Act in 1983, for leaking to the *Guardian* details of telephone tapping and organizations which MI5 considered subversive.

Clive Ponting, a senior civil servant in the Ministry of Defence at the time of the Falklands operation, was sacked and prosecuted (albeit

---

Arguments against Fulton

Fulton:

* misunderstood the role of the generalist
* took a simplistic view of the grading system, failing to recognize the diversity of jobs within the civil service
* failed to recognize the arguments for confidentiality and made no useful recommendations as to how the need for confidentiality could be reduced
* was over-impressed by 'management science' and did not recognize the importance of policy advice and the close relationship between policy and administration.

► The civil service adage, 'Generalists on top and specialists on tap' reflects the generalists' suspicion of the specialist, which is seen by supporters as reasonable, and by critics as a massive piece of arrogance used to protect the power of a small elite.

► Fulton's recommendations that outsiders should be drafted into the civil service on secondment could face the objection that it would make confidentiality more difficult to maintain. For further details see Chapter 14 of this book and Clive Ponting, *Secrecy in Britain, 1990.*

unsuccessfully) under the same Act for revealing to an MP in 1985 the existence of two versions of a draft answer to a Parliamentary question. There was a 'correct' and a 'sanitized' version of the events surrounding the sinking of the Argentinian cruiser *General Belgrano*, the latter being used.

In 1985–88, the Government went to enormous length and expense to try to stop the publication and sale of *Spycatcher*, the memoirs of Peter Wright, a former MI5 officer, obtaining injunctions against two newspapers who published details, and sending the Cabinet Secretary to Australia to argue (unsuccessfully) for an injunction preventing the book's publication in that country. While Governments maintain that secrecy is a necessary part of good government, critics insist that it is mainly used to cover up embarrassing facts and dubious practices, and give an impression of unity and unanimity where none exists.

 Draw up a two column table. In the first column list the criticisms of the civil service made in the Fulton Report. In the other column write down the arguments used to defend the civil service against Fulton's criticisms.

Review – The civil service

1 Bureaucracy is a system of rule by appointed officials following rules and organized in a hierarchy.

2 It has many critics but at its best, is efficient, incorruptible and consistent.

3 The British civil service is a career service with a hierarchy of grades and classes. Top positions in management and policy advice are usually filled by graduates who have come through the administrative trainee grade: generalists rather than specialists.

4 The *Fulton Report* criticized the British civil service for being dominated by 'amateurs', insular, under-trained and lacking management skills. Some changes have resulted from Fulton, but not as many as the committee would have wished.

5 Experiments with outside political advisers have proved only partially successful.

6 In 1987, the *Ibbs Report* recommended the devolution of much civil service work to accountable management units.

 List the characteristics of the position of a senior civil servant which allow him/her to wield considerable power.

WHO HAS THE POWER?

So, who holds the power – ministers or civil servants? The traditional liberal democratic model, in which the ministers make policy and the civil servants carry it out, seems inadequate to explain the distribution of power between politicians and bureaucrats in Britain. It is necessary to re-examine the evidence to gain a clearer picture of the relationship.

A Marxist view, based upon the notion that the State is the 'executive committee of the ruling class', would see the permanent civil service as a 'veto' group, exercising power mainly in the negative sense of preventing radical left-wing governments from eroding the privileges of the ruling class and the structure of capitalism.

Elite theory (see Chapter 9) sees the civil service as a powerful competing elite with its own aims and interests, using its power to maintain its numbers, its resources, its privileges and 'perks'.

The notion that Britain is a 'constitutional' or 'liberal' bureaucracy is a modification of the traditional liberal democratic model. In this, the bureaucracy has its own aims and powers, but they are tempered and sometimes opposed by democratically elected politicians. The resulting policies are a compromise between ideology and practicality.

Some evidence can be found for each model.

The power of veto

The power of civil servants to delay or stop policies lies first in the minister's *dependence on official advice*. Ministers are birds of passage, lasting usually no more than two years. They seldom have expertise in the matters for which the department is responsible, or alternative sources of advice. Advice may be 'angled' towards a particular conclusion, since civil servants usually make a recommendation as well as providing background information. Unproven assumptions may be slipped in, and awkward facts pointing to an alternative left out.

The second way in which civil servants have the power of veto depends on their control of the 'Whitehall machine'. Civil servants staff the policy network, and the system of cabinet committees is paralleled by a system of official committees, in which the senior civil servants from the relevant departments consider the agenda for forthcoming cabinet committee meetings. Barbara Castle emphasizes that the meetings of officials take place *before* the ministerial meetings, giving civil servants an opportunity to 'co-ordinate' the advice they are to give to their ministers. While this can be seen as a useful way of saving time on inter-departmental wrangling, and smoothing the path to a decision, it has been seen by disgruntled ministers as a means of 'stitching up' a policy most acceptable to the officials.

Crossman maintains that his ideas for a local income tax – to replace rates as a local government tax – were heavily defeated in the relevant Cabinet committee, because his officials had intrigued with their colleagues in other departments to advise their ministers to oppose it.

Benn believes that his ideas for an alternative to the Pressurized

▶ Support for a 'veto' view of the civil service.

▶ Benn emphasizes the importance of the initial briefing given by civil servants to incoming ministers at a time when they are new to the department and therefore vulnerable. He claims his own briefing at the Department of Energy in 1974 assumed that Britain's future energy requirements would be based upon nuclear power, rather than fossil fuels, without any explanation for the assumption.

Barbara Castle, Richard Crossman and Brian Sedgemore, all at some time Ministers in the Labour Government, maintain that civil servants gave the answer 'you can't do that' to proposals which were subsequently realized.

Water Reactor for nuclear power stations, opposed by his departmental officials, were defeated in cabinet because of opposition from the Central Policy Review Staff of the Cabinet Office, prompted by his own officials.

The third way in which civil servants control their ministers is in their day-to-day management of a minister's schedule. A minister's job, taken seriously, is a very busy one. Meetings with civil servants, other ministers in and out of cabinet, pressure groups, the media, speaking in Parliament, maintaining some constituency presence, and appearance at numerous functions, all have to be fitted in. This is the business of the minister's private office, headed by his private secretary.

Crossman and Castle both complained of being over-managed. Crossman compared his office to a 'padded cell' with himself 'surrounded by male and female trained nurses and attendants'. Castle claims that she had to fight for the right to attend her constituency, and walk in St James's Park on her own.

Civil servants as a self-regarding elite

Crowther-Hunt points to the fact that the civil service successfully resisted or watered-down all of the recommendations of the Fulton Committee, except those that increased the number of jobs and promotion opportunities for civil servants – the civil service colleges and the new civil service department. Joe Haines, a former press secretary to Prime Minister Wilson, catalogues examples of over-staffing, over-luxurious facilities and wasteful spending, which he claims the service positively encourages.

A constitutional bureaucracy

Supporters of this view that the civil service is a constitutional bureaucracy would argue that the two perspectives above are over-selective in their examples and unbalanced in their conclusions. Balancing factors include:

• *Ministers have power too.* It is difficult to see how civil servants could in the long run thwart the intentions of a minister who was clear about what he or she wanted. The minister has the backing of the authority of Parliament, the Party, the cabinet and the manifesto. Constitutionally, the minister takes the major decisions, and little can be done without his or her consent.

• *Not all policies are perfect.* Civil servants see it as their duty to point out unpalatable consequences and practical difficulties resulting from a policy objective. It is easy, in this situation, to be accused of being obstructive, when you are trying to be helpful and practical.

• *Advice is not always what Ministers want to hear.* A senior civil servant, interviewed for the series *No Minister* (1982), recalled the occasion when a minister picked up a paper-weight from a desk and threw it at him. (In true Whitehall tradition the civil servant – who had played cricket in his youth – fielded it.) Honest advice rather than sycophancy may be frustrating. Ministers, however, would not thank civil servants for refusing to give guidance, or for merely saying what

► Civil servants control the 'Whitehall machine' and management of the minister's itinerary.

► Support for an elite theory view of the civil service.

► Kellner and Crowther-Hunt, *The Civil Servants*, 1980.

► Support for a 'constitutional' or 'liberal' model of bureaucracy.

► In answer to Labour Government criticisms of the civil service (1964–70 and 1974–79), Dame Evelyn Sharpe, former permanent secretary to the Ministry of Housing and Local Government, argued that policies were often vague and ill-thought out. On some matters there was no clear policy guideline.

they thought the minister wanted to hear. The job of reducing a mass of statistics, reports and conflicting views and priorities to a manageable brief inevitably involves selectivity which lays the civil servant open to accusations of 'withholding evidence'.

• *Change does take place in the civil service.* The British civil service under the Labour Government elected in 1945 built the post-war Welfare State, and nationalized several major basic industries. Under the Labour Government it created the comprehensive education system. Under the Thatcher Governments, it substantially altered the basis of the welfare state, changed the relationship between central and local government, privatized many of the industries nationalized between 1945 and 1950, and radically changed the education system yet again.

In summary, civil servants have on their side continuity, permanence, expertise and the running of the policy machine. Politicians, however, have popular mandate, party and Parliamentary support and access to cabinet, as well as the final decision on major matters. It seems unlikely that one side or the other will prevail permanently. Policies, personalities and circumstances may affect which of the above models is appropriate at any given time.

 Characterize a *veto* model, an *elite* model and a *constitutional bureaucracy* model of the British civil service. Use these terms as headings for a three column table and in the columns enter what seems to support the appropriateness of each model.

ACT Essay/discussion question

The British civil service has been criticized in recent ministerial memoirs as being an over-powerful elite. How far is this criticism justified?

Draw up a person specification for the appointment of an under secretary to take charge of the division responsible for the training and supply of teachers in the Department of Education and Science. Use your own judgement as to what qualifications, experience and personal qualities you require in the successful applicant.

CHAPTER SUMMARY

1 Government departments are areas of operation each with a minister directly responsible to Parliament at their head.

2 Departments vary in size and organization. Each presents problems of size, organization and levels of decision-making.

3 As political head of a department, the Minister takes responsibility for policy, decisions, and the general performance of the department.

4 The principal of ministerial responsibility is important, but varies in application. It is complicated by secrecy and the anonymity of the civil servants who influence many decisions and take others themselves.

5 Political advisers from outside the civil service are used, but their impact and significance had been patchy.

6 The British civil service conforms in many ways with the classic model of bureaucracy: a hierarchical organization of career professionals, independent of any political party and permanently in post.

7 The *Fulton Report* (1969) sought to reduce the influence of the generalist in the service, to reduce insularity, and to simplify and unify the job grading system. Its recommendations for Civil Service Colleges and a Civil Service Department were carried out. For the rest, nothing was done, or there were only token attempts at change.

8 The *Next Step* programme, initiated in 1987, proposed to devolve much of the work of the service to 'accountable management' teams.

9 Ex-ministers have been critical of the way the civil service has used its power to 'steer' policy, veto some policies, and look after its own interests. Ministers have in turn been accused of sour grapes because their ill-thought-out policies were revealed for what they were.

10 The veto, elite and constitutional models for ministerial–bureaucratic interaction are all partly correct. As personalities, politics and situations change, so will the relationship between minister and department.

STIMULUS MATERIAL

The stimulus material is an article from the *Sunday Correspondent* on the development of policy within the Government and within the Department of the Environment. Apart from being relevant to the activities of Ministers, it also gives an insight into policy making and the role of pressure groups in the political process. Read the article and answer the following questions:

What does the article suggest to you about:

1 The influence of pressure groups;

2 Factors which cause governments to take on new policies;

3 The relationship between the personal views of different ministers and policy changes within a department;

4 Compatibility between the Thatcher Government's economic philosophy and the ideas of the Green movement;

5 The making of cabinet policy?

Refer to the article in support of your answer.

WHITEHALL TURNING A PALER GREEN

1   Concern is mounting among environmental pressure groups that the Government's much vaunted White Paper on the environment, due for publication this autumn, is being watered down in Whitehall.

2   Mrs Thatcher backed the decision to produce the White Paper, having been persuaded that retaliation might be needed if Labour brandishes new policies, including a programme of environmental taxation, at is party conference.

3   But senior sources say she is now having second thoughts about its scope. Ministers are struggling to reconcile their belief in freedom of choice with a desire to cut pollution by taxing it.

4   Chris Patten, the Secretary of State for the Environment, had earlier distanced himself from the priority of reducing burdens on business which was central to the thinking of his predecessor, Nicholas Ridley. He had hoped to engineer a document which would integrate environmental considerations into general transport and energy policies.

5   But Mr Patten has already lost some key battles on transport. He also appears to have failed to convince Cabinet colleagues of environmental restraint on energy policy. The Government has recently announced the scrapping of a £2bn scheme for work at coal fired power stations designed to curb sulphur emissions.

6   Drafting of the White Paper is not expected to begin for another two months but a series of detailed position papers has already been produced by the Environment Department.

7   One source said: 'The document will be published just before the Government tries to sell off the electricity industry and so it is unlikely to be heroic on energy policy.' Mr Patten has also lost out to the Ministry of Agriculture over a new national park in the New Forest, which was given Heritage status instead. He was persuaded to continue with the break-up of the Nature Conservancy Council in the Green Bill. According to Whitehall sources, the White Paper will fight shy of setting targets on global warming, with decisions postponed until reports are published by the Intergovernmental Panel

on Climate Change and the United Nations Conference on the Environment and Development.

8 So-called 'green audits' of Government policies appear likely to be watered down. Mr Patten's wish for environmental 'accounts' to be published alongside conventional expenditure balance sheets is not expected to bear fruit.

9 Ideas for controlling pollution through market mechanisms like pollution taxes and charges, and even emission permits, are still on the stocks but sources say their complexity will delay their adoption.

10 Industry is facing higher costs in meeting emission standards after the Green Bill, now before Parliament. The Department of Industry is reluctant to increase the burden by adopting more 'polluter-pays' ideas from Professor David Pearce, Mr Patten's adviser on environmental economics.

11 One Whitehall source said there will be 'lollipops' for the Green movement like a target of 50% for recycling, including a possible ban on one-trip containers such as non-returnable bottles, mandatory deposits and packaging taxes. There is also likely to be a detailed eco-labelling scheme in the White Paper, but its overall environmental philosophy has been pruned.

12 Tom Burke, director of the Green Alliance, said: 'The Government put up the idea of the White Paper to take the wind out of Labour's sails but its clout seems to be dissipated.'

The Sunday Correspondent
22 April 1990
Andrew Morgan, Environment Correspondent

Now you have reached the end of the chapter, turn back to the beginning, look at the objectives and make sure you have achieved each of them.

Further reading: Chapter 10

Drucker H. *et al* (eds). *Developments in British Politics 2*, Chapter 5. London: Macmillan. A useful overall summary.

Fry, G. K. 1985. *The Changing Civil Service*. London: Allen & Unwin. An examination of the changing rules of the civil service.

Gray A. G. and Jenkins W. I. 1985. *Administrative Politics in British Government*. Chapter 6. London: Wheatsheaf. Useful on the politics of the civil service.

Greenwood J. 1988–9. 'Managing the civil service from Fulton to Ibbs' *Talking Politics*, Vol. 1, No. 3. Useful update on recent attempts at reform.

Kellner P. and Crowther-Hunt 1977. *The Civil Service*. London: Macdonald. Critical examination of the service.

Pyper D. 1983. 'The FO resignations – individual ministerial responsibility revived?' *Teaching Politics*, Vol. 12, No. 2. Useful account of ministerial responsibility.

(11) Local government

Chapter objectives

By the end of this chapter you should be able to:

▌ describe the structure of local government in England and Wales and identify and discuss the problems associated with this structure

▌ describe the main functions of local government and their policy and decision-making arrangements

▌ describe and assess the role of local government officers and local authority councillors

▌ outline the most important constitutional and political questions concerning the relationships between central and local government and particularly the clash between the centralist ideology of the government since 1979 and the ideology of municipal socialism held by the ruling parties in many local authorities. (You will need to be able to illustrate this with reference to education, housing, financial control and the Community Charge/Poll Tax.)

▌ know the meaning of and be able to use the following terms:
centralize, municipal socialism
conurbation, metropolitan county, municipal district, shire county, parish or community councils
top tier/second tier authorities, *ultra vires*, default action, surcharging, government circulars, bye-laws, audit, Audit Commission, rates, Community Charge (Poll Tax), council tax, precept.

Media watch

You will probably find that much of the national news on local authorities will be about squabbles between them and central government. Look out for the stories which illustrate the uneasy relationship between central and local government. The reform of the structure of local government is in the air, and government and opposition are both committed to changing local taxation. Unless you live in a very newsworthy metropolitan district or London borough in conflict with central government, you will find that the activities of your own local authorities are very badly covered even by the local media. None the less look out for the stories which illustrate important aspects of local politics in your area.

► The basis of our current local government is the *Local Government Act of 1972*. The new structure began to function on 1 April 1974.

WHO ARE THE LOCAL AUTHORITIES?

The present system was created by the *Local Government Act* (1972), which redrew boundaries around geographic areas of different sizes, over which an elected council would provide a wide range of services.

Authorities were divided in two ways, between conurbations and mixed urban/rural areas, and among the latter between 'top tier' and 'second tier'.

Conurbations and mixed urban/rural areas

Powerful arguments were put forward in the Maud Report (1968), *On the Structure of Local Government in England and Wales,* for treating the conurbations as separate entities with a different type of structure from that of the rest of the country.

▶ *Conurbation*
A large urban area of several contiguous towns, or a major centre and satellite towns.

▶ The Greater London County and its council were created by the Local Government Reform Act of 1965 and abolished in 1986.

▶ *Tiers* – beware the use of this word. Local government in the countryside is often described as *two tier* referring to the county councils and the district and borough councils. But with the parish councils there are really three tiers.

▶ *Shire counties*

In the end, six conurbations were identified by the Act:

1 *Greater Manchester* – Manchester and surrounding towns.
2 *Merseyside* – Liverpool and surrounding towns.
3 *Tyne and Wear* – Newcastle, Gateshead, North and South Tyne.
4 *West Midlands* – Birmingham and the industrial towns on its western side.
5 *West Yorkshire* – the Leeds and Bradford complex.
6 *South Yorkshire* – the Sheffield/Barnsley/Doncaster complex.

In 1974 each of those areas was designated a metropolitan county, and further subdivided into metropolitan districts.

Greater London (from Barnet in the north to Croydon in the south, Barking in the east to Uxbridge in the west) had already been given a separate structure, with a Greater London County further subdivided into London boroughs. The Metropolitan Counties and the Greater London County Council, have since been abolished leaving a single tier authority: Metropolitan District or London borough.

In the rest of England and Wales, boundaries enclose rural, or mixed urban and rural, areas usually referred to as *shire counties*, which are subdivided into *shire districts* (shire districts are either called 'District Authorities' or 'Borough Councils'). There are also 11,000 or so parish and community areas, which may have meetings of all electors to make decisions on minor matters, and for all but the smallest, an elected parish, town or community council.

'Top tier' and 'second tier' authorities

The other way of dividing local authorities is into *top tier* and *second tier* and *third tier*, according to their functions and the area for which they are responsible. Top tier authorities cover a wider geographical area and provide certain services exclusively. Second tier authorities cover a smaller area within that of the top tier and provide other services exclusively. Some services may be shared by both tiers.

Shire county councils (top tier) cover fairly large mixed urban and rural areas, providing those services which are more expensive, and which need to be provided over a wide area – education, police, the fire service and some major roads.

Each shire county is divided into districts (second tier, usually referred to as shire districts, to distinguish them from metropolitan districts), which elect councils and provide local services such as housing, local planning and refuse collection.

In metropolitan districts the district council has responsibility for some services which are provided in the shires by the county council, e.g. education, social services and libraries.

The variety of local areas

English and Welsh local authorities vary greatly in their size, population, wealth and urban/rural mix. A *shire county* may consist of one city and its rural hinterland (Nottinghamshire); several medium-sized towns in a wide rural area (Hampshire); or mainly farmland and villages with small market towns at intervals (Cornwall).

Shire districts range from large cities like Bristol with annual budgets of £100millions, to rural areas with budgets which hardly top £10millions.

Metropolitan districts have in common the fact that they are part of a densely built-up and populated urban area, but they too vary widely. The smallest (Bury) has a population which is about one fifth that of the largest (Birmingham).

Resources, in the form of income per head (and therefore ability to pay Poll Tax) also vary widely. In the *London boroughs*, there is a wide divergence between outer boroughs – mostly affluent commuter country – and the inner boroughs with a large proportion of the unemployed, welfare dependent, and low-income earners. In rural and mixed areas, similar pockets of affluence and poverty are locked inside local government boundaries.

Needs, too, vary. An inner-city district may have demands placed upon it whose nature and extent would not be dreamt of in a rural district. Traffic control, drainage, roads, crime, social services, homelessness, a crumbling urban fabric are cited by beleaguered councillors and officers in inner-city areas to support claims for more resources. Standard Spending Assessments (SSAs, the amount of expenditure per head which the Government believes that an authority needs to spend to provide a reasonable level of service) varied from £178 to £1226 in 1990.

The Maud Report found this diversity presented a number of problems when it was trying to create a system of viable local government units throughout England and Wales.

► *Shire districts*

► *Metropolitan districts*

► *London boroughs*

► *Parish/town and community councils*
Their formal functions are few and small, mainly concerned with local footpaths, lighting and amenities, but many lead thriving lives as pressure groups on district and county councils particularly where planning decisions are concerned. They are third tier authorities.

	Conurbations	Mixed rural–urban areas
	Greater Manchester Merseyside Tyne & Wear West Midlands West Yorkshire South Yorkshire Greater London	
Abolished 1986	metropolitan counties and GLC	
Top Tier	metropolitan districts and London boroughs	shire counties
Second Tier		shire districts and boroughs
Third Tier		parish & town councils *(England)*
		community councils *(Wales)*

► The metropolitan county councils were abolished by the Local Government Act of 1985. They ceased to exist in April 1986.

► Some shire districts are considerably bigger than the average metropolitan district in both population and area, e.g. the cities of Nottingham and Bristol.

The Maud Report on local government structure 1968

The report of a Royal Commission set up to look at the structure of local government in England and Wales. It found the following things wrong with local government:
- too many authorities
- too many authorities which were too small and too poor to provide a wide range of services efficiently
- boundaries did not reflect the social and economic realities of where people lived, worked, travelled and took their leisure
- in the countryside the two tiers of district and county were not conducive to democratic and integrated local government
- there was no local government tier to deal with the special problems of the three big conurbations outside of London – centred on Manchester, Liverpool and Birmingham.

The important recommendations of the Commission were:
- Except for London, Manchester, Liverpool and Birmingham conurbations, local government services should be provided by single 'unitary' authorities – regional planning authorities above and community councils below, but real power with the unitary authorities.
- Minimum population for a unitary authority 250,000, maximum one million.
- Boundaries of new authorities to correspond with contemporary social realities rather than with historic boundaries.
- Manchester, Liverpool and Birmingham and their rural hinterlands to be metropolitan counties responsible for strategic planning, police, fire, major roads and transport and other services to be provided by metropolitan districts: little change for London with the Greater London Council as a metropolitan county and the London boroughs as metropolitan districts.

The new structure for local government established in 1974 owed something to Maud, but the Conservative Government of the time rejected its main idea – unitary authorities – in favour of a two-tier structure for the whole country: shire counties and rural districts in the countryside, metropolitan counties and metropolitan districts (including London boroughs) in the conurbations.

► The Major Government of 1992 is committed to unitary authorities.

 Summarize the arguments for and against:
a) two-tier authorities
b) unitary authorities.

Who does what?

There is an important difference in terms of functions between shire districts and metropolitan districts. In the latter, the metropolitan district provides a number of 'big-budget' services such as education and social services. In the shire districts these are provided at county council level.

The justification for this difference is that metropolitan districts are large enough, in terms of population, to provide these services economically whereas many county districts are not (see *Problems of structure* below).

The table on page 208 summarizes the division of functional responsibility between Shire and County districts. The fact that some functions appear on both lists means that services are provided at both levels.

Metropolitan areas and Greater London

36 metropolitan districts and 33 London boroughs provide all services except police, fire and some transport functions, which, since the abolition of the metropolitan counties, have been provided by joint authorities on which the districts are represented.

(ACT) Find out what kinds of local authority you live in. If you live in a district (or borough) within a shire county, find out what services each provides. The easiest way of doing this is to obtain the leaflets which accompany local tax demands. These usually list the main services provided by each kind of authority, the amount spent on various services provided and the amount of local tax charged by each authority. In addition shire counties and districts produce many pamphlets and booklets describing themselves. You will find these in your local library and in the foyer of the council offices. If you live in a metropolitan district (or London borough) nearly all your local authority services will be provided by the same single authority, but again find out what they are. What services are provided by consortia of local authorities (joint authorities)?

Review – Local authorities

In England and Wales a wide range of services – social, cultural, environmental and protective – is provided by all-purpose elected councils, created by the Local Government Act (1972).

In the six metropolitan areas (formerly metropolitan counties) and in Greater London, most of the services except police, the fire service and transport are provided by district councils.

In the shire counties, county councils provide most of the 'big budget' services including education and social services, and district councils provide the rest, though some services may be provided at both levels.

Allocation of functions for
Shire counties and districts

Shire counties	Shire districts
47 councils *are responsible for:*	333 councils *are responsible for:*
Museums and art galleries	Museums and art galleries
Reserve housing powers	Housing
Town development	Town development
Structure plans	(planning local plans and
Education	development control)
Youth employment	Allotments
Personal social services	Country parks
Libraries	Preservation
National parks	Footpaths and bridleways
Country parks	Local licensing
Tree preservation	Off-street parking
Acquisition and disposal of	Public transport undertakings
land for planning purposes	Footway lighting
development or re-	Environmental health
development	Refuse collection
Footpaths and bridleways	Clean air
Transport	Building regulations
(transport planning,	Coast protection
highways, traffic, all parking,	Markets and fairs
public transport)	Cemeteries and crematoria
Road safety	Bye-laws
Highway lighting	Swimming baths
Refuse disposal	Physical recreation
Consumer protection	Parks and open spaces
Police	Airports
Fire	
Swimming baths	
Physical training and recreation	
Parks and open spaces	
Smallholdings	
Airports	

PROBLEMS OF STRUCTURE

The difficulty in finding a suitable structure for local government arises because of the need to reconcile a number of conflicting objectives.

Economic and functional viability

Local authorities provide a number of services which require a large outlay of money on highly trained personnel and complex capital equipment. Only if the *catchment area* of clients is large enough to justify such expenditure can it usefully be incurred. Specialist courses in further education, police helicopters and sophisticated radar equipment, would not be sufficiently employed to justify their cost in an area with a population of say, 100,000 people. Thus, unless boundaries are drawn around big populations for these services, people will not receive the benefits they may confer.

The physical and economic geography of an area may influence the most appropriate boundary for some services. The existence, for example, of several police forces, or several bus companies with no overall controlling authority, presents problems in a big conurbation. The co-ordination of several different police forces, each with its own command structure, radio wave length and set of procedures, in a conurbation would be a nightmare. Similar problems would beset multiple authorities in fire fighting, drainage, sewerage, transport, roads and environmental planning.

It was the interdependence of the areas within a conurbation which persuaded the Maud Commission to recommend the setting up of metropolitan county authorities with responsibility for police, the fire service, transport, roads and overall planning (though not education – as some experts had recommended). These were abolished by a later Conservative Government in 1986, but for some services (e.g. the police and the fire service) joint authorities, to which the districts would send representatives, were established.

Accessibility and local democracy

Whereas some experienced and expert witnesses to the Maud Commission emphasized the need for 'bigness' to achieve co-ordination and economies of scale, others regarded size with suspicion.

It was pointed out that most people in a city personally identified with a neighbourhood of about 60,000 people. Large remote authorities, with elaborate bureaucratic structures, would alienate electors and tend to provide a standard service which was not adjusted to neighbourhood needs.

In the 'face-to-face' services – social work, primary education, youth work – some of the professionals argued that it was important to be sensitive to local needs. A large bureaucratic structure, it was feared, would undermine flexibility and sensitivity.

They also argued that if local democracy is to be meaningful, people must feel encouraged to participate and communicate with their local councils, and the councils must be responsive to local wishes. Boundaries should therefore enclose 'real' communities, in which the same group of people, or the bulk of them, worked, lived, played and shopped.

Variations in density of population in England and Wales means that an economically viable authority might have a five mile or a fifty mile radius. While the local democracy argument seems to point to small areas, the 'functional and economic viability' arguments need big authorities. Small wonder that the Maud Commission made no pronouncement on the ideal size for an all-purpose authority – one providing all the major services – but said that 'anything less than 250,000 population was probably too small for efficiency and anything more than one million population too big for local democracy'.

Resolving the problem – the two-tier structure

The 1972 Local Government Act attempted to cope with this problem by setting up a two-tiered structure, in which the counties provided the expensive services, and the smaller districts provided what were regarded as the more 'local' services. Thus, in an ideal situation, the

► A major dilemma in planning local government structure arises in balancing economic and functional viability with meaningful local democracy.

► Neither criminals nor car drivers are respecters of local authority boundaries. A traffic foul-up in Manchester will affect the traffic in neighbouring Salford and vice versa. A team of criminals who have carried out a robbery in Manchester are not going to hesitate in driving their getaway car into Stockport!

local elector gets the benefit of a large co-ordinated authority for some services, while enjoying the accessibility of a local council, for more local services.

Alas – nothing in local government is that easy! The Maud Commission tried to avoid recommending two-tier structures, except in three conurbations where they concluded that it was unavoidable, and favoured 'unitary authorities' where one council provided all the main services for the area.

Some of the criticisms of the two-tier structure are:

* *It is confusing*. Effective local democracy requires that electors know who is responsible for what. A system in which one council is responsible for some matters, and another for others is unlikely to gain much sympathy or understanding from the majority of electors.

* *Local services are part of a 'seamless robe'*. One advantage claimed for unitary authorities is that they can provide a co-ordinated policy for the whole area. This is based on the notion that social services, education, housing, environmental planning all affect one another, and in that sense are only artificially separate services, since they all affect the quality of life in one area.

With limited budgets, councils have the responsibility of allocating priorities in spending. According to some commentators, this can only be done rationally if one authority is responsible for all the main services.

* *Duplication and overlap*. In any two-tier system, the problem of exactly who is responsible for what presents itself. The town and country planning function, for example, is divided between county and district. The counties provide structure plans within which the districts are supposed to work. Districts provide local plans and exercise development control (planning permission). Clashes between the two levels are frequent, and the division of responsibility difficult to define. Duplication of staff and paperwork may occur.

* *Large districts could run themselves*. Before 1972, many of the towns of England and Wales were unitary authorities – called 'county boroughs'. While some were small, others such as Bristol, Nottingham, Gloucester, Southampton and Portsmouth claimed that a long tradition of civic achievement, pride and good government was lost when they became districts within Nottinghamshire, Avon and Hampshire, etc.

▶ The Maud Commission recommended fewer metropolitan counties than the 1972 Local Government Act created, but would have set their boundaries much wider to include the rural areas at the fringe of the conurbation.

▶ For planning purposes local authorities have to draw up Structure Plans detailing amounts of housing planned, new road programmes, industrial development, conservation areas, and so on. The structure plans for district authorities have to fit into the broader structure plan of the shire county, but the two kinds of authorities do not always agree with each other. (Structure plans are an excellent source of information about the population and an economy of your local area – they will be in your central library).

▶ Even if social services, housing and environmental planning were the responsibility of a single local authority, this still leaves an awkward division between the local authority and the National Health Service which has responsibilities in these areas.

Draw up a table with three columns. In the first column put the structure of local government proposed by the Maud Report. In the second put the structure introduced in the Local Government Act of 1972, and in the third note how the structure was altered by the abolition of metropolitan counties and the Greater London Council.

Then evaluate the different structures in terms of 'Economic and financial viability', 'Accessibility and local democracy' and 'Avoiding duplication and waste'.

Drawing on the information gathered in the previous activity write a report on your local authority.

1 What type of authority is it?

2 What is the political composition of the council? Does one party have an overall majority?

3 Over which policy areas or projects has there been controversy in the recent past? Give details.

POLICY AND DECISION-MAKING

The legally responsible body in a local authority is the council. This body is elected by registered electors living in the area. Candidates for office must be British subjects or citizens of the Republic of Ireland, aged over 21 years, and either a local government elector for the area, or in possession of certain other property or residential qualifications. Councillors serve for four years.

Local government elections are fought on a party basis, although, particularly in the more rural county districts, there may be a number of 'independent' or 'community association' or 'ratepayers' association' candidates. The metropolitan areas, the bigger towns and the counties, however, are strongly contested by the big parties, who seek to gain a majority in the council chamber, and the chair and majority in the major committees which effectively run the services.

► In county councils the whole council is elected once every four years, in metropolitan districts one third of the council is elected each year (with one 'blank' year). County districts had the choice of timing of their elections – some employing the one-third-per-year system, and some the everyone-once-every-three-years system.

Committees

Local authorities are empowered to delegate almost all their functions to *committees*. Most of the effective policy-making is done in committees, elected by the council from among its councillors, with the whole council meeting ratifying, or referring back, proposals put forward to it in committee reports. Politically, committees are usually microcosms of the councils, with the majority party (if there is one) in the majority on each committee, and councillors of the majority party in the important positions of chair and vice-chair.

A local authority may set up whatever committees and sub-committees it likes. However, it is bound to set up committees to discuss and put forward proposals on certain matters, e.g. education, police, social services (if it is an authority which provides those services).

The Maud (Management) Report 1966

The Maud Commission on Management (1966) should not be confused with the more famous Maud report on external structure (see page 206). Its brief was to look at the internal policy-making and structure of local authorities in England and Wales. It criticized local authorities for having too many committees and sub-committees, and councillors for becoming too involved in the minutiae of administration, generating too much paper-work. In general it found too much 'departmentalism' in local government and too little general management and co-ordination.

It recommended fewer committees, and committees which would have no executive or policy powers, but which would advise a management committee: this would be a small committee with the sole right to report to the Council. Officers would be responsible not to the committees, but to a 'clerk' – a chief executive – who would in turn be responsible to the management committee for the management of the Authority. By this means the Maud Report hoped to encourage a corporate strategy.

Local government officers

As in national government, local government is run by elected representatives – councillors – and paid officials ('local government officers' corresponding to civil servants).

Local authorities employ a permanent staff to carry out their work. Although each local authority is legally a separate employer, local government officers, through their unions, negotiate national pay scales and conditions of services, operated by local authorities. A hierarchy of grades and pay scales is common throughout the country.

Characteristics of local government officers

Unlike the civil service, in local government the specialist rather than the generalist tends to prevail at senior level. Much of local government has evolved as a series of discrete services – education, social services, housing, established by statute. Professional specialisms have developed to provide these services on the basis of special expertise.

▶ The Chief Education Officer is likely to be a qualified and experienced teacher or lecturer, the Director of Social Services a qualified social worker and so on.

Over the past twenty years, prompted by the Maud (Management) Report and the subsequent Bains Report (1971), most of the larger local authorities have sought to introduce the concept of 'general management' into their structure at official level. Many authorities have appointed a chief executive with authority over the whole structure, reporting to central policy committees of councillors. Bains's idea of grouping departments under directors, some of whom would form part of a senior management team around the chief executive, has also been adapted to the existing structure of many authorities.

▶ The Bains Report (1971) was the reaction of a group of chief officers to Maud's proposals for internal management.

Nevertheless, 'departmentalism' remains a strong factor in English and Welsh local government, and is likely to remain so while the individual committees and their chairs keep their role in the system. As Maud saw, as long as chief officers responsible for management and the implementation of policy in individual departments report to committees, which in turn make policy recommendations to council, the individual committees and their chairs are likely to remain a significant force within an authority.

Councillors and officers

As with the civil service and ministers at national level, we are here in the interesting and problematic area of the 'chemistry' resulting from the interaction of bureaucrat and politician. Particularly significant is the relationship between chief officers and chairs of committees.

The chair of a committee is responsible for:
- Overseeing the agenda for committee meetings and the reports and items therein
- Chairing the meetings of the committee
- Maintaining liaison with the chief officer between committee meetings on the management of the relevant part of the service, and the implementation of policy
- In many authorities, making decisions, including decisions on the expenditure of money, on matters delegated to the chair
- Often representing the council to media and public as spokesperson, particularly when a controversial issue has arisen in the area concerned
- In some authorities, membership of the central policy-making committee.

The chief officer's responsibilities are:
- Overseeing and managing the service(s) for which he or she is responsible
- Delivering the council's policy
- Advising the relevant committee on policy for the future, and the progress of current projects, through regular committee reports
- In most authorities, liaising with chair and/or vice chair between meetings.

In theory the relationship between councillors and senior officers is straightforward. The council makes policy, and the chief officer is responsible for seeing that that policy is carried out, and that the service is well managed, through his or her committee.

As you might expect, the reality is often different. An influential local politician who is chair of an important committee and an energetic chief officer together may constitute a formidable team in which both play the 'political' role of contributing ideas and selling them to politicians and public. Chief officers are often publicly identified with certain policies and projects and will publicly defend those policies and projects in a way that most senior civil servants would strive to avoid.

Many of the changes in educational policy since 1945, including comprehensive education, the middle-school system and village colleges, have owed more to the ideas and pressures of officers, who have publicly identified themselves with their ideas, than to councils.

► Differences between local government officers and civil servants.

► A famous example of such a partnership is that of councillor T. Dan Smith, leader of Newcastle-upon-Tyne city council in the 1960s, and his planning officer Wilfred Burns (discussed in *The Evangelistic Bureaucrat* by John Gower–Davis, see Chapter 10, page 189). On his leaving Newcastle, the *Newcastle Evening Chronicle* said of Burns, '... he came to Newcastle, fired with the same sort of missionary zeal that must have seized St Patrick when he arrived in Ireland to evangelize the whole country'.

▶ Chief Constable Anderton of the Greater Manchester Police Force (who is a local government officer) and his committee have frequently and publicly clashed over alleged attempts by the committee to interfere with 'operational' matters . The purchase and retention of plastic bullets and CS gas, and the policing of inner-city areas, are two subjects which have highlighted this controversy.

▶ *ultra vires* – beyond one's legal power or authority.

Such a relationship, while often productive in terms of policy, poses problems for local electors who may be trying to establish who is responsible for what.

A different set of problems arises when councillors and their senior officers clash. Many of our cities have seen the emergence of what some newspaper commentators have dubbed 'the new breed of local politician' – ideologically committed, working full or almost full-time as a councillor, with an interventionist philosophy, not content with the 'arm's-length' relationship with officers which has characterized many authorities in the past.

Friction may arise in a number of ways. While councillors may feel that their aims are being frustrated by unsympathetic officers who are in a position to manipulate the system, officers may feel that the politicians are making their jobs more difficult and blurring the lines of responsibility by interfering in operational matters.

An oppositional council (a council opposed to the central government) may decide to do something which is *ultra vires*, or not to do something which a statute has imposed upon them as a duty. In 1985, a number of authorities contemplated setting a budget in which the income would not meet the projected expenditure. In the event only Liverpool went so far, and such a budget was held by the court to be illegal. The chief officer did nothing, having already warned the council of the consequences of its action – the councillors were surcharged (made personally liable for the money spent as a result of their decisions.). At various times councils have tried to avoid carrying out obligations laid down by statute concerning the provision of civil defence, the cessation of the provision of milk in schools, the sale of council houses and the raising of council house rents. Officers, as

---

Review – Policy and decision making

1 The elected council is the legally recognized body responsible for local government in each area.

2 All councils work through a system of committees, to which many of their powers are delegated.

3 In response to criticism from a Royal Commission (Maud on management) most councils have reduced the number of committees by amalgamation, and introduced a general policy committee and a number of committees whose remit goes across departments.

4 Similar changes have taken place at officer level, with the appointment of chief executives.

5 The chair of a committee is a particularly important figure with delegated powers, usually working closely with the chief officer of the relevant department(s).

6 While, in theory, councillors make policy and officers carry that policy out and manage the relevant departments, in practice the relationship is more problematic. Senior officers may have a substantial influence on policy. Councillors, particularly chairs, may work as a team with chief officers or clash with them.

permanent and non-political employees of the relevant council, are sometimes faced with the option of defying their employers at risk of the sack or discreet premature retirement, or doing something which is legally and/or financially dubious.

 Look at the inset on page 188 of Chapter 10. The difference between civil servants and politicians will be much the same as the differences between local government officers and politicians (councillors). Use the inset and this chapter to make notes on the relationships between local politicians and local government officers.

 The best way of discovering what a local authority does is to look at the council minutes. These are usually in two parts. One part covers the proceedings of council meetings (including committee meetings) to which the public are admitted. These minutes will be available in your public library. The other part covers proceedings of council meetings to which the public are not admitted and are not generally available. If you attend a council meeting as a member of the public there will be a great deal you will not understand if you do not have the minutes of the previous meeting, the agenda and the background papers.

LOCAL GOVERNMENT AND CENTRAL GOVERNMENT

Sovereignty is centralized in Parliament. Since no local authority can override or qualify a law passed by Parliament, local authorities are 'creatures of statute' with no powers outside those given to them by the law prevailing at the time.

A concomitant of this is that the central government, so long as it is in control of a Parliamentary majority, can legislate to remove powers from local authorities, restrict existing powers, add to existing powers or duties, and even abolish local authorities altogether.

The doctrine of ultra vires

The relationship between central and local government is defined by the courts in their rigorous application of the doctrine of *ultra vires*. This means that a local authority can only do those things which are authorized by law and 'anything calculated to facilitate or incidental to the discharge of any of their functions.'

Where the law is silent, you or I as individuals can act without fear of reprisal. A local authority cannot. Any local authority which tries to do something which, though not illegal, is not authorized by law is likely to find itself the subject of a declaration by a court that it is *ultra vires*. This declaration may follow from an application by an individual or group who live in the area, or a decision by the Government Auditor to disallow expenditure on the activity in question.

In Hazell *v*. Hammersmith and Fulham London Borough Council and others (1991), the legality for a local authority of speculating on

► You or I could open a grocery shop. There is nothing illegal about that, provided we get planning permission. A local authority, if it opened a municipal grocery shop, would almost certainly find its action challenged by the Government Auditor and in the Courts.

► *Option-swapping.*
This means swapping a loan repayable with a fixed rate of interest for a loan repayable at an interest rate varying with market rates of interest. If variable interests turn out lower than the fixed rates you win. If not you come a cropper. Hammersmith had got to the point of pure speculation, taking out loans not because it needed the money, but simply in order to speculate in the swap market.

► *Audit* – official examination of accounts.

the *option-swapping* loans market was questioned. Counsel for the Banks who had loaned the authorities money for this purpose argued that it was authorized by the 1972 Act which provided that local authorities should have power to do 'anything which is calculated to facilitate, or is conducive or incidental to the discharge of, any of its functions'.

Allowing an appeal against a Court of Appeal decision by the auditor, the House of Lords declared all 'swap' transactions *ultra vires*. Lord Templeman said that a power was not incidental merely because it was convenient or desirable or profitable.

The local authority audit

Local authority accounts are examined by auditors from the Audit Commission, who may disallow expenditure which is *ultra vires* or 'unreasonable'. The money spent will, if the court upholds the decision, be the subject of a surcharge, and the individuals responsible for the decision leading to the expenditure will have to pay back the money out of their own pockets. An *ultra vires* action may also lead to disqualification from office for five years.

In 1955 Prescott, a local ratepayer, asked for a judicial declaration that Birmingham Corporation were making unreasonable use of their powers as a provider of transport. They were giving free bus travel to old-age pensioners living in the area.

The powers of central Government

As the power of local government is limited and defined by statute, so is the power of central government over local government. Sometimes, as we saw in the Tameside case (see Chapter 3, page XX) central government loses the argument.

The important difference between central and local government, however, is that *central government usually controls the legislature which makes the rules*. Thus after defeat by Tameside Education Authority over the question of changing plans for secondary education at the last minute, the Labour Government in 1976 quickly passed an Act designed to ensure that local education authorities did not so change their plans again.

In practice the statutes which lay out the main powers and duties of local authorities in the big-spending services like education, social services, police and housing have built in to them a number of *checks and controls* which central government may use to try to nudge local authorities in the direction they want them to go. The main controls are:

- *The power to make regulations and orders.* Most of the major Acts concerning services provided by local authorities give the relevant Minister the power to make detailed regulations governing matters like teachers' pay, the powers of school governors, and rules governing police promotion procedures, which have the force of law. Orders relating to specific cases (e.g. the closure of a further education college) also have the force of law.
- *The use of circulars.* Technically, *circulars* are not law but advice and

guidance on the policies to be pursued by a local authority, or the interpretation to be put on the relevant statute or set of regulations. In some cases, though, it is rather like receiving advice from the Godfather; you ignore it at your peril. This is because central government departments may use other controls to back up the 'advice' in the circular.

In 1965, for instance, the Labour Government issued Circular 10/65 from the DES advising that plans for the school organization of each local education system which the ministry required, should follow one of a number of models, each of which was for a comprehensive system abolishing selection for transfer to secondary education. It was later made clear that authorities which did not submit plans in line with the Circular would receive no authorization for new building work. Nevertheless a few Conservative councils hung on without having submitted satisfactory plans. The Conservative Government elected in 1970 let them off the hook with Circular 10/70.

- *Control over plans.* In most of the big-spending services for which local councils have responsibility, the relevant statute obliges local authorities to submit periodically a plan of policy and major projects for the next few years. This plan must meet with the approval of the relevant ministry. Education, town and country planning, and social services are areas where this applies.

- *Approval of specific projects.* As we have seen in reference to education, approval of major building projects and permission to borrow money is required from the ministry in the major spending areas.

- *Vetting appointments.* In education, social services and police, central government exercises some control over the appointment of chief officers.

- *Control over legislation.* Local authorities may pass *bye-laws* relating to their area on minor matters of environmental control and law and order. The scope of these local bye-laws is carefully defined and permission from the relevant central government department is needed before a specific law can come into operation. In order to give itself extra powers, a local authority may promote a private bill, with a view to a private act of Parliament.

The private bill route to new powers is formidable and expensive, involving two resolutions of the council, public meetings, and the employment of Parliamentary counsel (highly paid barristers with expert knowledge of Parliamentary affairs). Ministerial opposition amounts to a veto, and even with ministerial support, a private bill may still fail at the crucial committee stage if MPs are convinced that local opposition is justified.

- *Inspection by central government.* In the areas of education, social services and the police and fire service, the relevant government department employs government inspectors (such as HMIs in education and Inspectors of Constabulary) to ensure that local services are efficient and to give advice.

▶ *Circulars* are issued by government departments to local authorities advising them on the interpretation of policy and law.

▶ In the case of a Chief Education Officer, the short-list is *vetted*, as is that for Director of Social Services. Specific Home Office authorization must be given for the appointment of a Chief Constable, and for dismissal.

▶ Conflict is rare but not unknown. Hampshire were refused permission to appoint a solicitor as Director of Social Services. At the time of writing (1990) Derbyshire county council are in dispute with the Home Office, who have refused to confirm the appointment of their former Deputy Chief Constable to the post of Chief Constable.

▶ Some famous municipal projects have been realized by Private Bills, such as the Manchester Ship Canal and the Birmingham Municipal Bank. Most Private Bills, however, are on minor and uncontroversial matters.

► The department will send an inspector, in the case of large-scale development, to hold a public inquiry and advise the minister, with whom the final decision lies. Departments may also adjudicate between conflicting local authorities as, for example, when two education authorities are in dispute over responsibility for a pupil.

• *Court of appeal function.* Particularly in the area of town and country planning, the central government may act as a sort of 'court of appeal'. If, for example a local authority refuse planning permission for the development or change of use of a piece of land, or if the local authority wishes to purchase compulsorily a piece of land for building or road widening, those aggrieved may appeal to the Department of the Environment.

• *The power to act in default.* If a minister feels that a local authority has failed to carry out a particular function, he or she may have the power to direct another authority to carry out the function, or appoint commissioners to do so. The cost of this action will be charged to the authority or, if they have been surcharged, to the councillors who failed to provide the service.

Such drastic measures are rarely used. Norwich was threatened with default action for only processing 250 council house sales in the first year in which the compulsory sales scheme was operating (1981–2). The courts (Lord Denning) confirmed that Norwich were *ultra vires*, and the threat of a default action proved enough to bring Norwich into line. The urban district of Clay Cross, in Derbyshire, was subject to default action when its councillors refused to conduct 'means' tests' of their council-house tenants, required by the Housing Finance Act (1972).

► The power to act in default will be given by the relevant statute, e.g. the Housing Act (1980) which required local authorities to offer council houses for sale to their tenants, also contained a clause empowering the Minister for the Environment to act in default should a local authority fail to do so.

Default powers are built in to some statutes – Public Health Acts, Town and Country Planning Acts, Housing Acts. The intriguing question of whether central government would put commissioners in to run a whole authority almost became a live issue in 1985, when Liverpool City Council deliberately set a budget in which revenue would not cover expenditure, and the city was set fair to go broke half-way through the financial year. In the event the Council set a new budget after the courts had declared their budget illegal.

• *Finance.* We will look at local government finance in some detail later in the chapter. Here, we may just note that local authorities are dependent upon central government for a large proportion of their total income, and could not run the major, big-spending services from local taxation and revenue at anything like the level required by the various statutes. He who pays the piper, to some extent will call the tune. Since 1979 central government has used its control over grants and has given itself control over local taxation in an attempt to make local authorities reduce their level of spending.

 Take a sheet of paper. In the middle write 'Local Government', then around the outside make notes on the direct and indirect ways in which central government limits the actions of local government.

Where does the power lie?

The list of controls above looks so formidable that you could be forgiven for thinking that local authorities in England and Wales have hardly any freedom of manoeuvre. Before jumping to that conclusion, however, consider the following three points.

First, councils are elected locally. Central government has no say in who gets elected to the council and the council is the body responsible for the provision of local government. Since 1979, Conservative Governments have had to face determined resistance to their ideology, policies and many of their actions. In fact, about fifty pieces of legislation have been passed since 1979 in an attempt to adjust the relationship between central and local government and bring recalcitrant councils to heel.

Although central controls are numerous and frequently irksome, most of them are exercised 'at arm's length' and may prove ineffective against determined political opposition. True, the Government may be able to give itself new powers to deal with recalcitrant local authorities by legislation, but this is a cumbersome and time-consuming process which may involve a tough political battle.

Second, local authorities have considerable discretion over their actions. There are many services, such as cultural services, parks and gardens, and economic development, where central government interferes hardly at all.

Even in those areas where central government does play a heavy role, local authorities vary considerably in how they set about achieving the goals and spending levels required by the legislation and the central government. Even in a big-spending and politically controversial function like education, local authorities were, until recently, in almost complete control of what was taught in schools. Recent attempts by central government, via the 1988 Education Reform Act, to gain more central control over the curriculum have encountered problems, many of which illustrate the difficulties in trying to make detailed prescriptions from the centre.

And third, local authorities have their own source of finance. They get a large proportion of their money from central government in the form of a grant. But for an average local authority, much of its finance is raised locally from local taxation (formerly rates, now the Poll Tax, itself to be replaced by the mid 1990s) and charges made for some municipal services (mainly council housing). Central government has made some inroads on the freedom to set local taxes by introducing the power to 'cap' (set an upper limit to) the level of local tax.

 What factors allow local government some freedom from central government control? In what ways has this independence diminished since 1979?

Agents, partners or opponents?

The answer to this question may be 'All of them at some times and none of them all the time'.

For some projects local authorities may be *agents* in the full meaning

► Local authorities who are supposed to be the political friends of the Government do not always toe the Government line. The Poll Tax has not proved universally popular with Conservative councillors (Oxfordshire group of Conservative councillors resigned *en bloc*). The Thatcher Government backed down from an attempt to abolish free travel to school for pupils living more than two miles away, in the face of Conservative opposition in Conservative dominated rural areas.

► This issue is discussed more fully later in this chapter, pages 220–260.

of the term, carrying out projects which are wholly financed and designed by a central government team.

In education, the ideal-type model is that of a *partnership*. Central government sets broad aims and objectives, within its general policy; local authorities have freedom and discretion in how they achieve those objectives; central government gives 'arm's length' guidance and attempts to ensure that the objectives are achieved.

The views of a central government minister or senior civil servant and those of an oppositional local authority as to the nature of the partnership might well differ. A minister might point to the widely varying standards of local authorities, from the superb to the frankly awful, the immense variations in spending per head, and the stratagems employed by local authorities who do not wish to follow national policy.

An oppositional local councillor might point to the numerous and irksome administrative controls exercised by central government, indicating an absence of the trust that should be fundamental to a good partnership.

More fundamentally, he or she might claim that central government has, of late, tried to turn the relationship from that of partner to that of boss/employee, by preventing local councils from carrying out the programmes and following the principles for which they were democratically elected. For this reason, many local authorities have become active opponents of central government, seeking to subvert its aims, though usually staying just within the law.

► Conflict between central and big-spending Labour authorities is not entirely about conflicting ideologies. It was a Labour Minister who announced the intention of central government to rein in local authority expenditure with the blunt message 'the party's over' addressed to a gathering of mainly Labour councillors.

Local authorities, central government and the economy

Since 1979, the tensions always inherent in the relationship between central and local government in England and Wales have been dramatically stretched, in some cases almost to breaking point.

Local authorities have been a prime target in the attempts of Governments since 1974 to contain or reduce inflation by restraining spending. When the Thatcher Government came to power in 1979, expenditure by local authorities formed 28.2 per cent of total public expenditure, and 12.8 per cent of GNP (gross national product – roughly, the total amount we spend and earn). Since 1945, local authority expenditure had consistently increased at a rate higher than the rate of inflation.

► Thatcherism and municipal socialism

The defence of local authorities to the accusation of overspending is usually based upon the assertion that increased spending has been a response to a rising population, rising costs (particularly labour costs in a labour-intensive activity) and increasing demands for more and better services from the public and, ironically, from central government.

To some extent attempts by Governments to control local government have been a derivative of their attempts to control the economy and to lower inflation.

But only to some extent; since 1979 a more fundamental ideological difference has existed between central government and many, particularly urban, local authorities. Two aspects of the Thatcher Government's economic theory are relevant here:

Thatcher's economic policy

• *Monetarism*. In its early years in office, the Thatcher Government held to the idea, based upon the theories of *Milton Friedman*, that inflation was the result of persistent increases in the money supply, fuelled by increasing state expenditure based on money raised from taxation.

• *A belief in the free market*. Successive Conservative manifestos, and public statements, made this belief clear. For most goods and services, the free market is seen as the most efficient way of serving the consumer. The 1989 Local Government Act obliged local authorities to put many of their services out to competitive tender. The Poll Tax also exemplifies this philosophy in so far as it treats the elector as a consumer buying services and in search of value for money.

Political theory

The Thatcher Government claimed that the political ideas behind the actions of many Labour authorities were wrong, dangerous and even faintly mad. The councils of Brent, Ealing, Hackney, the Greater London Council, Camden, Manchester, Liverpool, Sheffield and other Labour authorities were publicly and scathingly criticized by the Thatcher Government. Added to the accusation of 'political lunacy' was that of illicit expenditure on distributing anti-government political propaganda and financing various anti-government pressure groups.

Favourite targets for this type of criticism are police monitoring units, gay and lesbian support groups, positive discrimination in employment (in favour of ethnic minorities and/or women), peace studies and other 'suspect' teaching in schools, and the declaration of Nuclear Free Zones. The Government has not always confined itself to mere verbal criticism. A clause in the Local Government Act (1989), put forward by an individual MP but accepted by the Government, stated that the 'promotion' of homosexuality, or the idea that homosexual relationships are normal, by local authorities was outside the law.

The Government has also outlawed the promotion of political campaigns using local taxpayers' money (following the campaign by the Greater London Council against its own abolition) and the practice of attaching 'political' conditions, such as union recognition and no links with South Africa, to the acceptance of tenders from businesses.

Another key aspect of conflict arose from Conservative political theory. The Conservative manifesto emphasized that private rather than state services were politically as well as economically desirable.

▶ Milton Friedman, Professor of Economics at the University of Chicago and winner of Nobel Prize for Economics, see page 87.

▶ The Local Government Act 1989 obliged local authorities to draw up specifications for the provision of catering, cleaning, transport, land management and works and maintenance services. The local authority may tender for its own service, but must stay within the tendered budget. The most 'economic' bid must be accepted.

▶ Clause 29 of the Local Government Act 1989 is popularly supposed to have resulted from a book stocked by ILEA (Inner London Education Authority) sympathetically telling the story of the children of a household run by their fathers who had a homosexual relationship with each other. ILEA insisted that the book was not generally available, and was intended to help pupils who found themselves in that situation.

The Government denied that Clause 29 was intended to make gay counselling services *ultra vires*, or to prevent libraries from stocking books by Oscar Wilde, James Baldwin, William Burroughs, William Shakespeare, etc. However, the clause has not yet been tested in the courts.

Accusations of bureaucratic waste

The Thatcher Government consistently maintained that some local authorities (mainly Labour-controlled) employed an unnecessarily large number of people to carry out their functions, and created 'units' and 'projects' staffed by relatively well-paid officers to carry out unnecessary functions.

► This ruling was based on the belief that councillors in some authorities (mainly Labour-controlled) were appointing councillors from neighbouring authorities to these posts. They were then, it was alleged, given light duties with the result that they could effectively become full-time councillors in their own authority.

A local authority is no longer allowed to employ anyone in one of these well-paid positions if that person is at the same time an elected councillor in another authority. Teachers, and some others, are exempt from this rule.

Difficulties with high levels of Poll Tax have been blamed mainly on 'high-spending Labour authorities'. The Government justified the abolition of the metropolitan counties by claiming that they were responsible for an unnecessary layer of bureaucracy and wasteful expenditure. Cynics pointed to the fact that they all had consistent and strong Labour majorities.

 Look at Chapter 5 for passages on Conservative ideology. How does the Thatcher approach to local government illustrate Conservative ideology?

Municipal socialism

There are certain common factors in *municipal socialism*. First, a belief that urban local government can achieve some degree of countervailing power against a right-wing Conservative Government, and that this power can be used, along with the resources at the disposal of a local council, to offset some of the effects of Government policy and achieve some socialist objectives locally. Second, a belief in community politics – closer links with and more involvement in local affairs. Third, a belief in positive action to promote a greater degree of equality and power for those regarded as the powerless and oppressed – women, ethnic minorities, gays and lesbians, the unemployed, the poor. And finally, it brings a style of politics which is high-profile and confrontational. Names like Ken Livingstone (ex-GLC leader) Bernie Grant (Harringey), and David Blunkett (Sheffield) have become nationally known. They have since become MPs.

► Oppositional Labour councils and leaders.

Between them, the oppositional local authorities constituted a national platform of opposition to the Government's policies, which sometimes looked more effective than the opposition in Parliament.

The oppositional councils justified their opposition to the Government by:

• Claiming the authority of a *local* mandate; they were elected by local residents to carry out a programme of reforms and improvements and they claim have been hampered and sometimes prevented from carrying out the wishes of the voters.

► It might be interesting to compare the similarities and differences of some famous left-wing municipal leaders over the last decade to see whether you agree with me.

• Characterizing the Government as being out to destroy effective and democratic local government by starving it of resources, and restricting and removing its powers.

Government ministers (Nicholas Ridley, Kenneth Baker, Margaret Thatcher) replied by claiming that they had a clear *national* mandate to reduce inflation by cutting public spending and promoting market-oriented services wherever possible. In any case, they argued, it is not for a local authority to challenge the authority of the nationally-elected Government. They countered the local mandate claim by pointing to the low turn-out in local government elections, and to the fact that under the local tax system which preceded the Poll Tax, the majority of voters did not directly pay for the services provided by the council for which they voted. These arguments have been the background to a number of radical changes in the functions and powers of local authorities. Three areas which exemplify these changes are housing, education and local government finance.

 What is 'municipal socialism'? How did oppositional authorities justify their opposition to Thatcher Government's policy towards them?

Housing

Paul Durden outlined the housing policy of the Thatcher Government thus: (it)

> can be said to have four explicit objectives: to encourage owner occupation, to minimise local authority housing provision, to target resources more accurately on the most acute problems, and to revitalise the privately rented sector.

With the possible exception of the third, these objectives are in direct contradiction to the idea of massive provision of subsidized 'social' housing for the less well-off, held by municipal socialist councils. Two major Acts have been the instrument of Government housing policy. Both have been the subject of bitter controversy and attack from some Labour councils. Labour councils would seek to preserve their stock of council housing, and if possible extend it. The stock is still considerable with five million tenancies, constituting the bulk of low-price rented housing in the country.

► This is taken from Paul Durden's article in *Talking Politics* (1990) published by the Politics Association. This article gives a thoughtful account of the Housing Act, 1988.

• *The 1980 Housing Act*. This gave local authority tenants the right to buy their houses at considerably less than the going market price. Local authorities were obliged to offer houses for sale. Attempts to get round the requirement by not informing tenants of their right to buy, or by processing applications very slowly, were met by the threat of putting a commissioner into the recalcitrant local authorities to administer the sales, and charge the full cost to the authority. Resistance had been anticipated by putting the power to act in default into the Act.

This Act also sought to revive the private rented sector by replacing 'controlled' tenancies by 'regulated' tenancies and introducing 'assured tenancies' for a fixed period at freely negotiated rents, and 'shorthold' tenancies, of between one and five years at a 'fair' rent.

► The two important Acts are:

• *The 1988 Housing Act*. This aims to reduce the stock of municipal housing still further, first, by allowing rented council accommodation to be transferred to a private landlord approved by the Housing Corporation, or to a co-operative, or a housing association. This can

► The Housing Corporation is a Government quango set up to regulate and give grants to housing associations. For a definition of a quango see page 128.

be initiated by the tenants on an estate, the local authority, or the private landlord. The authority must sell, subject to a ballot of tenants on the estate, in which abstentions count as votes 'for'. If a transfer is made tenants who vote against transfer may remain tenants of the local authority for the duration of their tenancies.

Second, the Act empowers the creation of Housing Action Trusts, which will take over control of estates deemed to be dilapidated or badly run, renovate them and after a period of five to seven years sell them to independent landlords approved by the Housing Corporation, or to the council where a tenant so desires.

The Government saw its job as being to transfer as much of the public housing stock as is feasible to the private sector in the name of freedom of choice, and on the assumption that nearly everybody wants to own their own home if they possibly can.

Labour local authorities claim either that the scheme won't work or that if it does, it will result in decent housing being beyond the reach of those on low incomes or state benefits, resulting in an increase in homelessness which the local authorities will be unable to cope with because of their depleted housing stock.

There has been much criticism of the proposal to take some estates out of the hands of the democratically elected local authority and put them in the hands of an appointed quango.

 Write notes on the way the Thatcher reforms to housing policy illustrate

a) Conservative Party ideology in general.

b) Conservative Party approach to local government in particular.

Education

The 1989 Education Reform Act contains a number of provisions which aim to reduce the control and influence of the local councils. They are:

• *The National Curriculum.* For the first time in this century central government has given itself the power to determine what is to be taught in schools, both in terms of subjects and curriculum within subjects, and how and at what ages progress is to be tested.

The 1944 Education Act, the statutory basis of education until 1989, had left the question of curriculum almost entirely to the local authorities, subject to reaching certain standards, and 'arm's length' direction from the ministry.

There has been much argument over the National Curriculum and the Government has backed off from its original aim, and reduced the number of subjects under detailed control. Nevertheless, the Government is determined broadly to control what is taught in schools.

• *Local management of schools (LMS).* Local council management of the budget, staffing and general management of schools is delegated to the head teacher and the school's board of governors.

- *Opting out.* Where the majority of parents vote for it, a school may apply to the minister to opt out of local authority control altogether. If approved, the school will receive its funds from central government in the form of a direct grant, will be entirely run by its Board of Governors and need have nothing to more to do with the local authority.

- *Parental choice.* Until now parental freedom of choice of schools for their children has, in practice, been circumscribed by the overall plan of the local authority. Under the Act, however, parents will be free to choose.

In the controversy following the Education Reform Act, oppositional local authorities, while by no means its only critics, have characterized it as yet another attempt to destroy true local government. There has been some measure of agreement on the need for a National Curriculum but the initial attempt to prescribe subject areas, proportions of time to be devoted to each subject, and detailed attainment targets and tests, was seen by the Government's critics as a take-over bid rather than an attempt at reform.

Local management of schools has come under fire for removing the co-ordinating and resource allocation role of the council, impairing its ability to discriminate positively in favour of under-privileged areas. It is contended that combined with parental choice and the opting out provision it will lead to a polarization of 'sink schools' and 'elite schools', with schools in poorer areas suffering from low recruitment of teachers and pupils and a consequent low budget.

NM Thatcher/Major education policy has been described by supporters as shifting power from local government to parents and schools and by opponents as shifting power from local to central government. Make notes on education reforms in the 1980s and early 90s to show how both these claims can be supported.

► In higher education, the Polytechnics, previously controlled by local authorities, have been given self-governing corporate status outside the control of local authorities. In 1993 Colleges of Further Education, Tertiary Colleges and Sixth Form Colleges will be given a similar status.

► One authority, Avon, has already successfully challenged in the courts a ministerial decision to allow a school to opt out on the grounds that such a decision would render the authority's re-organization scheme ineffective.

Local government finance

In 1938, 28.9 per cent of the money spent by local authorities was provided by central government, by 1979 it was 60 per cent and local government services accounted for almost 30 per cent of total public expenditure. When the Conservative Government took office in 1979 they committed themselves to:
- Reducing local government spending.
- Making local authorities' level of spending subject to stricter control by central government.
- Increasing the accountability of local authorities to their electorate.
- Abolishing the existing system of local taxation.

In pursuit of these aims, Conservative Governments since 1979 have come into the bitterest conflicts, even with Conservative-controlled local authorities. The first two administrations strove to get expenditure down to the desired level. This was done by a complicated series of legislative changes, among which the following were prominent.

► The rate support grant was a grant to local authorities fixed annually and paid in quarterly instalments. It was based on a complex formula involving three elements and partly calculated as a proportion of actual expenditure.

► Tighter controls on capital expenditure.

► Abolition of supplementary rates.

► The abolition of metropolitan counties.

► Powers to rate cap.

First, the rate support grant was replaced by the 'block grant'. In 1980 the main means by which the Government gave money to local authorities was altered; the new block grant set expenditure targets, beyond which local authorities would be 'fined' by the withholding of grant. The 'leverage' effects on local taxation of trying to make up the shortfall would mean a sharp rise in rates which, the Government hoped, would deter authorities from taking that route or would deter voters from re-electing them if they did so.

Second, the Government proposed tighter controls on capital expenditure. Local authorities spend large amounts on buildings and capital equipment. Virtually all capital expenditure is now subject to Government approval.

The second of these two actions was reasonably successful from the Government's point of view. Capital expenditure fell by more than 60 per cent between 1979 and 1983.

The grant penalties, however, did not produce the desired result in many urban authorities, particularly metropolitan counties and districts. The contribution of central government to local government reduced as a percentage of the total from 60 per cent in 1979 to 48 per cent in 1983. However, many urban local authorities maintained their level of expenditure and made up the shortfall in central government funding by a mixture of raising rates (local taxes) and 'creative accounting' measures such as selling buildings and renting them back to themselves. Electors obstinately continued to elect Labour councils in metropolitan areas.

The Government reaction was to make further legislation:

- They abolished supplementary rates – i.e. the power to add to the level of local taxation at some mid point in the financial year.
- They abolished the Labour-held metropolitan counties.
- In 1984 the Government gave itself the power (by the Rates Act of that year) to direct individual authorities not to set their next rate above a specified level, and a general reserve power to control the level of local government expenditure.

RATES AND THE POLL TAX

After the 1987 election the Government claimed a mandate to abolish rates as a form of local taxation. Rates were a tax, determined by the local authority, on a notional annual value of land and buildings established by the Inland Revenue officers. They had been the subject of frequent criticism on the following grounds.

1 *They were regressive.* They were not related to the ability to pay, and fell harder on the less well-off.

2 *Territorial injustice.* Because of variations in the total rateable value in different parts of the country reflecting economic prosperity, 20 per cent of the local authorities had between them about 50 per cent of the country's rateable value. Often the areas with the need to spend most money per head were the poorest in rateable property.

3 *Businesses were disenfranchised* (i.e. had no voting power).

Particularly in inner urban areas, businesses paid large sums in rates but had no direct influence on the political make-up of the council.

4   *Rates were paid by too few people to ensure accountability.* Only about 50 per cent of the electorate actually paid rates and only about 34 per cent paid the full sum. This figure was lower in some poor urban districts.

Shortcoming (1) led to the massive *subvention* of some ratepayers by a system of rebates and exemptions, while (2) led to central government paying out to authorities with high needs and low rateable values through 'needs and resources payments' in the rate support grant. Since the mid 1950s Governments have discussed the replacement of rates by a better form of local tax, but alternatives such as local income tax, sales tax or capital value tax seemed to lack the virtues of rates. Rates had the following advantages:

► *Subvention* – grant of money from Government, etc., subsidy.

• They were cheap and easy to administer, since they were based on fixed property.
• Evasion was difficult.
• Revenue was predictable.
• They were a genuinely local tax, under local control.

► Advantages of the rates system.

The Conservative Government began to take the idea of a *per capita* tax seriously after protests from businesses in Scotland, some of which were subject to a 50 per cent increase as the result of a revaluation. The result of this reconsideration was the *Local Government Finance Act* (1988). Its main provisions were:

1   *To abolish rates on non-business properties, and substitute a personal tax, to be paid by nearly all adult residents, called the 'Community Charge'* (popularly known as the 'Poll Tax'). The Community Charge is set by district councils. County councils and bodies providing local services

---

Capping

After notification that it is to be capped, expressed as a maximum figure for its Poll Tax, a local authority can either 'seek a redetermination' (appeal to the minister) or make the necessary cuts in its budget. An order confirmed by Parliament makes the capping obligatory.

The formula for capping is, first, that the authority must have an annual budget in excess of £15 million; and second, that its projected expenditure must exceed the standard spending assessment by 12.5 per cent *and* £75 per resident.

The 19 Poll-Tax-capped local authorities sought a judicial review largely on the grounds that the standard spending assessments and the formula for capping were unreasonable and illegal. The Court of Appeal rejected their appeal, and the House of Lords subsequently found against them.

Capping powers were eventually extended to authorities spending less than £15 million, making many more Tory authorities at risk of capping.

'precept', i.e. make a charge on the districts. A single charge per head is declared, but those on low incomes may be entitled to rebates of up to 80 per cent, for example students pay 20 per cent.

2 *To levy a nationally determined and uniform rate on businesses – the 'universal business rate (UBR)'.* Businesses continue to pay rates on their properties. The difference is that the rate is set by central government, not as before, by the local authorities. Payment of the proceeds of the rate are allocated to local authorities in proportion to their share of the adult population.

3 *To introduce a fixed and simplified central government grant.* The new grant is of one payment with no penalties or rebates. Unlike some of its predecessors, it will not be related to the actual level of spending by any local authority. Instead it will be based on the Government's estimate of the cost of providing a standard level of service (SSA).

4 *The power to 'cap' the Poll Tax.* In order to curb the expenditure of local authorities, the Government has retained the power to cap. The Act gives the Minister the power to identify those authorities which have exceeded the Government's SSA by enough to justify a capping order. The only clear restraint on this power is that the minister must apply the same rules to the same category of authority.

Predictably, the first round of Poll-Tax capping in 1990 encountered opposition from most of the capped authorities, particularly since all the capped authorities were Labour controlled. Nineteen of the capped authorities asked for a judicial review of the minister's decision; they declared that it was in excess of his powers and unreasonable, criticizing the low standard spending assessment and the formula for eligibility for capping.

The arguments for the Poll Tax

1 *Everybody pays.* Virtually everybody pays something. This is an improvement on the rates, which were paid in full by little more than one third of the electorate and not at all by almost half the electorate.

2 *It will encourage taxpayers to demand 'Value for Money'.* Significantly, when the Government introduced the Poll Tax, they called it the 'Community Charge' in an attempt to emphasize the idea of local taxpayers as consumers of local authority services. As a result, local authorities should behave sensibly and economically as providers of these services, or face dismissal at the next election.

3 *It is fairer to businesses.* Businesses in high-rated areas in the past frequently complained that they were being put at a disadvantage compared with their competitors in neighbouring low-rated areas.

The arguments against the Poll Tax

1 *It is regressive and unfair.* Rates were not related to the ability to pay, but it is claimed that Poll Tax is even less so, despite the system of rebates. Single householders gain in some areas, but families on a lower income in properties of low rateable value in most cases pay

► There are a few categories of people who are exempt from Poll Tax: the homeless, long-stay hospital patients, people living in nursing homes, prisoners, monks and nuns, and the mentally disabled.

more. Ethnic minorities living in inner cities, who on average have three more adults to a dwelling than the norm, in general pay more. Geographically, too, the impact of the tax is harder on poorer areas.

On the basis of Department of the Environment estimates, Poll Tax is higher in metropolitan areas than in shire counties, and higher in the poorer inner-London boroughs than in the more prosperous outer-London boroughs. The percentage change in a two-adult household, compared with rate bills, is estimated at minus 8 per cent in shire counties, minus 13 per cent in outer-London boroughs, and plus 88 per cent in inner-London boroughs.

2 *It is expensive and difficult to collect.* This is based upon the facts that:
* There are simply more tax points from which to collect.
* People are mobile, buildings are not. Keeping the register up-to-date and keeping track of people who move will require more staff and more expensive information technology.
* Evasion is easy compared with rates and, at the time of writing, widespread in some inner-city areas. Revenue is lost to local authorities through non-payment, the cost of chasing up slow payers and interest paid on money borrowed to cover gaps due to slow paying.

3 *'Consumerism' is not appropriate to local government services.* Critics argue that the purpose of local government is to provide services on the basis of need, not the ability to pay, and that in any case services like street cleaning, parks and roads cannot be packaged into individual benefits for which the individual can realistically pay.

Other criticisms centre not so much on the domestic Poll Tax, as on the way in which the whole system created by the 1988 Act is being applied; in particular

* *Unreasonable and unrealistic SSAs.* Many local authorities have claimed that the standard spending assessments were too low to enable local authorities to carry out even their statutory duties, forcing them to either set a very high Poll Tax and risk capping, or cut services to the bone. Others claim that SSA assessments have been biased against Labour-controlled authorities.

* *The 'capping' formula is politically biased.* All 21 authorities capped so far are Labour-controlled. Some Conservative-controlled authorities fulfil one of the criteria (an increase of 12.5 per cent over SSA), some the other (an increase of £75 per head or more) but none fulfil both. It is argued that many Conservative rural districts increased taxation by more than 12.5 per cent, but since they have small budgets to begin with, either fell below the £15million limit, or the £75 per head figure. Urban Conservative authorities which increased by more than £75 per head were given generous SSAs and therefore did not exceed the 12.5 per cent figure.

* *Too much central control.* The power to set SSAs and the capping formula, combined with a more rigid grant system not related to actual expenditure, and power to set the Universal Business Rate

▶ These figures are extracted from Sylvia Horton's article *The Local Government Finance Act 1988 – The End of Rates*, (taken from DOE figures) in *Teaching Politics.*

> ### Review – Local government and central government
>
> 1 Since 1979 the Government has pursued a policy of controlling the expenditure of local authorities, in pursuit of its determination to control inflation. This has involved numerous pieces of legislation designed to prevent local authority spending from rising above a certain limit.
>
> 2 The Government has sought to encourage market forces in some areas of local government by obliging local authorities to offer council houses for sale to tenants, and opening the way to private landlords for some council estates, and obliging local authorities to put some of its services out to competitive tender.
>
> 3 Directly opposed to the Government's intentions is the philosophy of 'municipal socialism' held by the controlling groups of many of the cities of England and Wales.
>
> 4 The Government has sought to gain greater direction over education through the Education Reform Act, involving a National Curriculum, devolved management of schools and colleges (LMS), and the 'opting-out' provision.
>
> 5 The Community Charge (Poll Tax) was seen by the Government as a way of bringing greater financial and political discipline over local government.

mean, say the critics, that the Government has given itself almost complete control over how much local authorities can spend. Since how much they can spend is closely related to what they are able to do and what level of service they provide, this has been characterized by some critics as 'the destruction of local government'.

 Draw up a table to express the cases for and the cases against the Poll Tax.

The fate of the Poll Tax – a bridge too far?

Even as I wrote about the Poll Tax, the Thatcher Government were running into trouble with it. Whatever its rights and wrongs, it proved widely unpopular. There was a widespread campaign of deliberate non-payment orchestrated by Militant and other far-left groups, and more importantly many local authorities encountered difficulties and expense through non-payment. Some Conservative authorities, as well as Labour authorities complained bitterly of the tax and the administrative complexity and expense of collecting it.

The tax was closely associated with Mrs Thatcher who stoutly defended it, despite its unpopularity with many Tory councils and in the opinion polls. Michael Heseltine on the other hand had rejected the idea of a Poll Tax when he was Environment Minister. Thus when Heseltine challenged Thatcher for the Party leadership the contest could be seen in part as about the Poll Tax. After John Major's victory few of Mrs Thatcher's ex-ministers seemed prepared to defend the Poll Tax.

Michael Heseltine was given the role of Secretary of State for the Environment in the Major Government, with a brief to examine the local government structure in general and the Poll Tax in particular. He made a statement on 21 March 1991 on both subjects.

On structure he announced that a local government commission would evaluate the most appropriate form of government for individual areas with the likelihood that there would be unitary authorities at either the county or the district level.

On finance, Heseltine conceded that the public 'had not been persuaded that the (community) charge is fair' and he stated that it would be replaced by a new local tax under which there would be a single bill for each household comprising two essential elements: the number of adults living there and the value of the property.

▶ Heseltine's proposals mean that all three major parties are now in favour of unitary authorities.

Subsequently, the Government has elaborated its plans: by September 1991 these included:

- banding of properties according to market value: in eight bands: the higher the band the more tax you pay (for suggested bands see page 233)
- fixing a standard council tax, based on a standard level of expenditure expected of local authorities, for each household in each band, graduated so that higher-value households pay more.
- tailoring central government grants so that households of a particular size and band will pay much the same wherever they are geographically, so long as the local authority doesn't spend more than the government thinks it should.
- give discounts to single-person households.
- a complex system of rebates for people less able to pay the tax.

(ACT) Discussion/Essay

'Central government power over local government in Britain has increased, is increasing and ought to be diminished'. Do you agree? How much power should local government have?

CHAPTER SUMMARY

1 British local government is a 'creature of statute' – the 1972 Local Government Act and a host of others.

2 Areas are covered by county councils and their district councils in mixed urban–rural complexes (shire counties), and metropolitan districts in Greater London and the six highly urbanized conurbations.

3 These metropolitan areas had county councils between 1974 and 1986, when they were abolished by statute.

4 Whereas in shire counties the county councils provide the big spending services (police, social services, education, libraries) and the districts the rest, in metropolitan districts education and social

services are provided by the district councils. Police, fire and transport are provided by consortia of authorities in each metropolitan area.

5 The problem of structure in British local government revolves around the questions of 'One tier or two?' and what is the appropriate boundary to ensure both functional efficiency and democratic responsiveness.

6 The three Thatcher Governments made strenuous efforts to curb local government spending and to take more decision-making power out of the hands of the local authorities. They also provided policies in favour of a more market-oriented approach to providing local services.

7 Local authorities get their revenue from local taxation, from local revenue (mainly from council-house rents), and from central government grants, which still form a large proportion of most local authorities' income.

8 The Thatcher Governments were consistently opposed by Labour-controlled authorities in some parts of London and the North of England, with an ideology of 'municipal socialism'.

9 The Poll Tax, which replaced the rates, has proved unpopular with all Labour councils and many Conservative councils. Its unpopularity contributed to the downfall of Mrs Thatcher. The tax is to be replaced by the council tax which is based on banded property values and household composition.

STIMULUS MATERIAL

The stimulus material is taken from an article in the *Economist* in April 1991. It is about the replacement for the Poll Tax. Read the article and answer the questions:

Questions:

1 'John Major has escaped the toils of the poll tax' (paragraph 1). What could be described as the toils of the Poll Tax?

2 Summarize the problems that the proposed new tax is likely to encounter. Try to identify more than are mentioned in the article.

3 Summarize the arguments for and against the system of one-tier authorities favoured by the Government.

4 '..these proposals continue the centralisation intensified in the 1980s' (end of paragraph 8). Which government measures in the 1980s can be labelled as 'intensifying centralization'?

5 Which services 'do not make administrative sense for smaller areas' (paragraph 13) and why?

WITH ONE BOUND, HE WAS ...

1   John Major has escaped the toils of the poll tax. He may soon be caught in other local-government traps.

2   There is something to be said for a government creating horrible problems for itself. The roar of applause when it later rids itself of them may boost its popularity at a critical moment. The announcement of a replacement for the Poll Tax on April 23rd improves the government's prospects in the council elections on May 2nd. The proposed council tax, which offers something to each lobby, is a slick political trick. But the proposals also create a host of future problems by promising to tinker with local government's structure.

3   By returning to a property tax, the government answered the principal objection to the poll tax; its unfairness. The council tax is a sort-of-wealth-tax, with bills determined partly by the value of the biggest asset most people own and partly by how much each council spends. Owners of second homes will pay half the full rate on them.

THE POLL TAX REWORKED

4   On the other hand, the council tax is also a bit-of-a-poll-tax. Single people get a 25 per cent discount under the council tax. This answers Tory demands that the tax should be related to the amount that a household uses local services. So widows in large houses (who always feature prominently in arguments about property taxes) will not do as badly as under the rates. Some Tory MPs feel the discount is not large enough: after consultation, it may increased.

5   Central to the tax are the bands into which homes of different value will be sorted. These are also designed with an eye to reassuring those who did well out of the switch from rates to poll tax. It ensures that the range of possible bills is limited. The top bills will be only 2 1/2 times as much as the lowest bills, and the highest band is for houses worth over £160,000 ($274,000). So the 46 per cent of houses in Barnet that the government reckons will be in the top band will all pay the same amount, irrespective of their value. Barnet is unusual: as the table shows, most households in the country will fall conveniently into the five lowest bands.

Property-value band £	Council tax for standard spending £ *	Properties in band %
Less than 40,000	267	19
40,001–52,000	311	16
52,001–68,000	356	20
68,001–88,000	400	17
88,001–120,000	490	13
120,001–160,000	579	8
More than 160,000	668	7

* *Actual rates will vary among councils depending on local spending.*

Source:
Department of the Environment.

6   In general, the tax will shift the burden towards the south's richer homes and away from the north, because the government intends to tailor its central grants to equalise, roughly, the tax on like houses under like-spending councils. In a place like Kingston-upon-Hull in Humberside, 68 per cent of homes are in the lowest (£40,000 and under) band, and fewer than 1 per cent are in either of the top two bands (more than £120,000). This is politics, not mathematics: Tory marginal seats tend to be in poorer areas – particularly in the north-west – with cheaper houses. There are uncomfortable exceptions, though. In Bath (Chris Patten, party chairman, majority 1,412) the biggest chunk of homes is in the top band. Those with two adults will be £682, compared with a £489 poll tax.

7 Sceptics hunting for flaws in the tax have quickly spotted one potential problem. The banding system looks neat and simple but could lead to a mess. A taxpayer in Lambeth whose house was valued at £121,000, for instance, would save £111 if it were valued instead at £119,000: so councils could find themselves swamped with appeals.

8 The proposed reform leaves councils no more 'accountable' than before. Those who are not responsible for raising taxes are not likely to be responsible about spending them. Under the poll tax, councils raise 11 per cent of the money they spend. That proportion will not change under the new system, and council budgets will still be capped. So these proposals continue the centralisation intensified in the 1980s.

THE NEW SNARE

9 The government has learnt the foolishness of meddling with local taxation. Now, with reckless abandon, it promises to meddle with local-government structure. It wants to set up a local-government commission to review the structure of local government across England. It believes that one-tier authorities would be better than the two-tier authorities that exist everywhere except the metropolitan areas.

10 This is a quiet coup for the Association of District Councils, which has been lobbying hard against the counties ever since the districts lost power to the counties in the 1974 reforms. Although the ADC has a Tory majority, most of the work is done by the 'Big 11' (cities like Swansea and Hull), of which six are Labour, two Tory and the rest hung. The government consultation paper insists that it is not gunning specifically for county or for district councils. But since the thrust of the argument is for grass-roots power and the paper refers implicitly to unpopular counties created by the 1974 reforms, the districts are less worried than the counties that contain them.

11 Already there are mutterings in the shires. Councillors have their pride, their power and their perks, and do not like the idea of being abolished. Most of those under threat are Tories, since the bulk of both county and district councils are Tory-run. So the government risks a revolt by those rural stalwarts who do much of the legwork during general elections, as well as years of ill-mannered squabbles as the two sets of councillors argue their worth to the commission.

12 The government says that the introduction of single-tier authorities will save money. It might; but a forthcoming study by the University of Birmingham's Institute for Local Government on the abolition of the West Midlands Metropolitan County Council in 1985 suggests that it will not necessarily prove cheaper. The study found no savings resulted from the change, and some spending increased.

13 In some areas of council responsibility, there are clear economies of scale. Take food hygiene: it is cheaper for a large council to set up a laboratory to service several districts than for each of the districts to have its own. Other services – like the police and fire brigade – do not make administrative sense for smaller areas. So ad hoc multi-county boards, run by officials accountable to nobody in particular, had to be set up in the metropolitan areas after 1985. Since the officials are not under the thumb of councillors worried about rates increases, they are less likely to be frugal. Critics fear that ad hoc boards, neither accountable nor thrifty will proliferate.

14 The government believes that people will love it for abolishing counties like Humberside, which proud Yorkshiremen have always refused to acknowledge. This is optimistic. Before 1994, the suggested date for introducing reforms, it may decide that the change is not worth the political and administrative pain.

The Economist,
27 April 1991

Further reading: Chapter 11

Dunleavy P. *et al* (eds). 1990. *Developments in British Politics 3*, Chapter 7. London: Macmillan. A good summary of local government in the Thatcher years.

Durden P. 1989. 'Any hope for the homeless?' *Talking Politics*, Vol. 2, No. 1. A thorough examination of the Housing Act 1988 which was one of the Thatcher government's flagship policies.

Gyford J. 1985. *The Politics of Local Socialism.* London: Allen & Unwin. More detailed examination of municipal socialism.

Horton S. 1989. 'The Local Government Finance Act 1988: the end of the rates' *Talking Politics*, Vol. 1, No. 3. Stimulating discussion of the Poll Tax and its likely effects.

Jones B. (ed.) 1985. *Political Issues in Britain Today*. Chapter 4. Manchester: Manchester University Press. General discussion of local and central government in the 1980s.

Jones G.W. and Stewart J. 1983. *The Case for Local Government*. London: Allen & Unwin.

Now that you have completed this chapter look back at the objectives and check that you have achieved each of them.

Media Watch

The most newsworthy matters are likely to be conflicts over proposals for the EEC to increase its powers at the expense of nation states, but look out for more mundane news illustrating the working of the EEC institutions. You may have to look at the financial pages for some of these.

Chapter objectives

By the end of this chapter you should be able to:

▮ describe the historical origins of the European Community

▮ describe the structure of the EEC and the roles and powers of the various institutions which constitute it

▮ discuss the concept of a 'federal Europe', objections to a federal Europe and the problems of trying to realize it.

▮ discuss the obligations which arise from membership of the EEC, the question of national sovereignty and the way in which EEC membership affects the sovereignty of Parliament

▮ discuss the conflicting views about the future of the EEC and in particular the proposals for closer monetary, economic and political union through the European Monetary System, the Single European Act and the European Social Charter

▮ know the meaning of and be able to use the following terms: customs union, Common Agricultural Policy (CAP), Exchange Rate Mechanism (ERM), European Monetary System (EMS), Social Charter, Luxembourg Compromise, European Free Trade Association (EFTA), European Commission, Council of Ministers, European Council, European Parliament, European Court of Justice.

THE CONCEPT OF THE EUROPEAN COMMUNITY

Much of the current argument about the future direction of the Community revolves around the meaning of the word *federalism* (see Chapter 3, page 27). Those who oppose a federal Europe tend to emphasize the implication that overall and ultimate sovereignty would lie in the centre (in Brussels), and that a federation, unlike a 'confederation', does not confer the right of veto or opting out to members. Those who support moves for closer integration emphasize the areas of policy and administration where a federal set up gives guaranteed power and rights to member states.

The Treaty of Rome (1958) is the constitutional authority for the European Community. Jean Monnet and his collaborators who were the driving force behind it, envisaged a number of short and a number of long term developments coming from grouping European countries economically and politically. For this reason the Treaty involved more than most international agreements. It set up supranational institutions with executive and legislative powers, which would override the governments and legislatures of the member

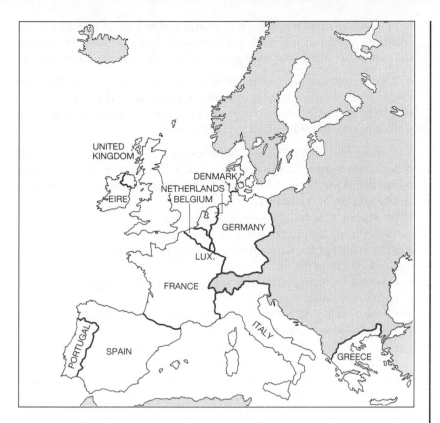

▶ The original six members were the former West Germany, Italy, France, Belgium, the Netherlands and Luxembourg. The Community now consists of the six countries above plus the United Kingdom, Spain, Greece, Portugal, Denmark and Ireland.

countries, implying a voluntary surrender of sovereignty on their part over matters dealt with in the Treaty. Community law would differ from most international law, which affects relationships between states; it would be the law inside the member countries as well as between them.

Among the changes the authors of the Treaty wanted to bring about were:

1 *A customs union.* In addition to abolition of customs duties between member countries, they wanted to set up a common external tariff (the same customs duties on imports from countries outside the Community) and a common policy to the outside world on matters of trade.

2 *A common agricultural policy.* One of the earliest and most ambitious moves by the Community was to create a common agricultural policy, designed to create a free market in agricultural produce in which supply would meet demand at a price that would give farmers a fair return. In order to bring European agriculture to the point where competition was on an equal basis, a supra-national authority was created which would receive contributions from member nations, and use the money received to encourage the modernization of peasant agriculture, encourage the production of some produce and discourage others, buy surplus crops in times of glut and sell stored produce in times of shortage in order to maintain a fair price.

► Currently (1990), the Commission of the EEC wants the British Government to order British Aerospace to repay £44millions of subsidies given to them when they purchased the Government-owned Rover car firm, which the Commission claim was contrary to EEC Law on fair competition.

3 *A regional development policy.* A fund was devised to bring the relatively economically backward areas of the Community nearer to the standards of the rest, by a system of grants from the Community.

4 *Free competition and movement of people, goods and capital.* This has involved the harmonization of laws on transport and taxation, and a whole body of EEC law designed to ensure free competition, with power to prosecute firms and government.

5 *A single free market.* The six countries who signed the Treaty in 1957 constituted a very rich potential market. The twelve who are now members of the Community could constitute the largest and richest single market in the world.

The notion of a fully integrated single market, however, has far-reaching implications for some of its supporters. They would like to run the whole of the Community as if it were one economy. Some of the aspects could be:

* *Common financial institutions* with, in the end, a single bank and a common currency.
* *Common industrial policies.* Since pay and working conditions affect costs and therefore competitiveness, the laws governing hours of work, working conditions, employment, tenure, redundancy and trade union rights would be harmonized. Consumer law, training and qualifications, manufacturing standards and health and safety law would also need to be harmonized.
* *Completely free movement of labour, goods and capital.* All remaining barriers to movement of these factors of production would be removed.

► During the 1960s, General de Gaulle of France insisted on a Europe of Fatherlands (*Europe des Patries*) as the proper goal of the Community. In the 1980s Mrs Thatcher took up this mantle with her insistence on a 'Europe of Sovereign Nations' and trenchant criticism of some of the proposals for integration canvassed by pro-Europeans.

6 *A 'United States of Europe'.* This phrase was first publicly used by Winston Churchill in 1946. Ironically, Britain has been one of the member countries most reluctant to contemplate such an idea. Monnet and his colleagues, however, saw this as the eventual goal. Through economic co-operation could come, they thought, political unity and the end of the nationalist divisions and chauvinism which had been responsible for two horribly destructive wars.

A 'European Federation', in the sense of prime sovereignty being exercised by a supra-national European Government and Parliament, still seems a long way off.

 What were the short and the longer term aims of the founders of the EEC?

Review – The European Community

The European Community was set up by the Treaty of Rome in 1957.

The Treaty created a supra-national institution with legislative and executive powers over member states.

This involved some surrender of sovereignty by the member states.

The early aims of the Community were a full customs union, with the abolition of internal tariffs and a common external tariff, a common agricultural policy and common regional policy.

Current targets (1991) are a single free market with common rules on competition, workers' rights, industrial law and standards, transport, the removal of all barriers to the movement of people, goods, and capital, and a common currency and central bank.

For some committed pro-Europeans, the eventual aim is a sort of 'United States of Europe'.

A SHORT HISTORY OF THE EUROPEAN COMMUNITY

The constitution of the EEC was set up by the Treaty of Rome in 1957, in which six European countries, excluding Britain, built on two existing European Trading Agreements, the *European Coal and Steel Community* and the *European Community for Atomic Energy* (Euratom).

Britain in 1957 was wary of the whole idea, and was not a signatory to the Treaty of Rome; she was instrumental in forming the much more loosely constructed European Free Trade Area (EFTA) consisting of Britain, Norway, Denmark, Sweden, Austria, Switzerland and Portugal, as a counterweight, or as some said a rival, to the EEC.

The Macmillan governments (1957–63) began to make overtures to the Community with a view to joining. Edward Heath was appointed as a special Minister to negotiate terms. At the point when Britain was ready to join as the result of these negotiations, President de Gaulle vetoed British membership. de Gaulle exercised the veto again in 1967, when the Labour Government applied to join.

By this time the Conservative leadership was committed to membership of the Community, especially when Heath took over the leadership of the party in 1964. Many Conservative back-benchers and supporters in the country, however, were bitterly opposed to the idea of joining, seeing membership as an abrogation (cancelling) of national sovereignty, and a relinquishing of democracy to a bureaucracy in Brussels.

The Labour Party was also split on the issue. Conference and the NEC were clearly against joining, but some influential members of the Parliamentary leadership were passionate supporters of EEC membership.

Re-elected in 1970, the Conservative Government, with Heath as Prime Minister, passed the *European Communities Act* (1972), which

► Technically, the administration of the EEC, the Coal and Steel Community and Euratom remained separate until 1967, when the councils of the three Communities were merged into one.

> ### Review – History of the EEC
>
> Britain did not join the EEC at its foundation, but formed the rival European Free Trade Association (EFTA).
>
> Britain applied to join twice in the 1960s but was vetoed by France.
>
> Britain joined in 1973, after the passage through the British Parliament of the European Communities Act in 1972. Labour and Conservative Parties were split on the issue of joining.
>
> Moves towards greater integration have included the agreement to have a single market by 1992, the Single European Act, the Social Charter, the European Monetary System.
>
> Although the Council of Ministers tries to proceed by unanimous agreement through compromise, increasingly decisions on the less sensitive issues are taken by vote.

took Britain into the Community in 1973. The Act passed by a small majority, with some cross-voting – Conservatives voting against the Government and Labour marketeers. The Labour opposition pledged to call a referendum on whether or not Britain should remain in the community.

The Wilson Labour Government (elected in 1974) held a referendum on continued membership of the Community in 1975; the first national referendum in Britain's history. On a 65 per cent turnout, the electorate voted to remain in by 65 per cent to 35 per cent.

The Labour Government justified the referendum on the grounds that such an important constitutional issue should go to the people. Critics saw it as a political manoeuvre by Wilson to give himself the authority to resolve the bitter divisions within his own government and Parliamentary party.

In the intervening years a number of other countries have followed Britain into the Community. Its present membership is Germany, Italy, France, the United Kingdom, Spain, Belgium, Greece, the Netherlands, Portugal, Denmark, Ireland and Luxembourg.

The *European Council* was set up in 1974 to bring heads of Government and foreign ministers together in twice-yearly 'summits'. Though not a part of the formal legalistic structure of the Community, this body has become a policy and decision-making body on matters of grand policy.

Since 1979 the Community has made a number of moves towards further integration, not all of which have been enthusiastically welcomed by the British Government, and particularly Mrs Thatcher (1979–90).

The moves towards further integration include

1 *A single internal market by 1992.* In 1985 a summit meeting of heads of government in the Community agreed to the policy objective of a single internal market by 1992.

This means that all barriers to the movement of goods, services labour and capital will be removed by 1992, and law and procedure

▶ *The Bruges Group*
A group of Conservative MPs who support Mrs Thatcher's concept of a 'Europe of Nations' and are profoundly suspicious of M. Delors and others' concept of greater integration as a preparation for a federal Europe. They take their name from the town in Europe where Mrs Thatcher made a speech opposing a federal Europe.

affecting manufacturing, capital investment, safety standards, consumer protection, quality regulations, technical specifications and a host of other matters are to be harmonized throughout the Community.

 Draw up a time-line to show the major events in the development of the EEC to 1992.

2 *Full economic and monetary union.* The 1985 decision, accepted by Britain and embodied in the *1986 Single Community Act*, has increased pressure for financial and economic integration. The ERM, to which a number of EEC countries belong voluntarily, links currency rates to one another. *The European Monetary System* (EMS) would go further, with a common Central Bank and eventually a common currency replacing national currencies.

Until 1990 the British Government was wary and ambivalent about these proposals. The Labour Party (now apparently committed to the EEC), the Liberal Democrats, and elements within the Conservative Party and the Government, are in favour of closer union. Mrs Thatcher and some of her supporters remained cautious and unenthusiastic.

This is not just an economic and financial issue. Full economic integration could only be achieved by a common economic policy internally and towards the outside world. Economic policy is inextricably linked to foreign policy and even defence policy. For politicians with strong patriotic and nationalistic feelings, the unwelcome spectre of a United States of Europe and loss of national sovereignty looms.

3 *The Social Charter.* The Charter is based upon the idea that workers and their families, if they are to benefit from and co-operate with the single market, need certain guarantees and assurances. These would include worker representation on the boards of directors of companies, a minimum wage, trade union rights, including the right to strike, and redundancy payments. Jacques Delors, the President of the EEC Commission (one of the governing bodies of the Community), has secured agreement in principle to the Charter by almost all nations except Britain.

The Charter has been publicly criticized by Conservative ministers, some of whom see it as interfering with the free market forces in which they believe. Mrs Thatcher attacked the Charter saying it let socialism in by the back door.

4 *The Single European Act.* In agreeing to this Act in 1986, the members of the Community formalized and legalized much of what was already practice, but also extended the power and range of the Community. Regional policy, environmental policy and technological development were incorporated into the Treaty. Foreign policy, while not incorporated into the Treaty, was given recognition as a Community matter by the Act.

Perhaps even more significant for the future is the fact that the Act amended the Treaty to extend unanimous majority voting in the

▶ ERM – *Exchange Rate Mechanism* – a system in which exchange rates of member countries are fixed in relation to one another, within a narrow 'band'. This inevitably means relating economic policy to that of other members.

▶ The *Luxembourg Compromise* adopted in 1966 gives a state the right to exercise a veto when it thinks that 'vital national interest' is at stake.

Council of Ministers. The convention of trying to seek agreement on important policy matters rather than taking a vote still applies, as does the *Luxembourg Compromise*. However the practice of taking votes on all but the 'big' questions is growing and becoming more acceptable. This, combined with the greater number of countries belonging to the Community, should make it increasingly difficult for one or two countries to veto proposals which they consider detrimental to their interests, or to which they are opposed.

 Make notes on full economic and monetary union, the Social Charter, and the Single European Act, noting how they affect the sovereignty of nation states.

 Research and produce a report on the implications of 1992 and the single market for:

• A medium-sized firm selling manufactured goods.

• A student leaving college with a degree or diploma.

You may get help in your local library, from your local Training and Enterprise Council, the Small Firms Advisory Service, bank leaflets, HMSO or even your Euro MP.

THE INSTITUTIONS OF THE COMMUNITY

The major institutions of the Community are the Council of Ministers, the Commission, the European Council, the European Parliament, and the European Court of Justice.

The Council of Ministers

The *Council of Ministers* is the principal decision-making body of the Community. Its membership is made up of representatives from each of the twelve states. It operates at three levels:

1 *Working groups of officials* who examine proposals made by the Commission and try to reach agreement.

2 *COREPER* – a French acronym which has been adopted to describe the *Committee of Permanent Representatives*, i.e. ambassadors from the member states. This body tries to resolve matters not sorted out by official working groups.

3 *Council* made up of appropriate ministers from each state (agriculture ministers if agriculture is to be discussed, industry ministers if industry, etc.). This is the highest decision-making body. If COREPER has agreed on a matter, the decision will probably be a formality, but otherwise a consensus will be sought.

It is when consensus is *not* reached that things become interesting! Where Community law, which is binding upon all states, is to be promulgated, the Council usually proceeds carefully, trying to avoid a situation where a state might feel obliged to invoke a veto on the grounds of 'vital national interest' and where a vote is taken on a politically controversial and sensitive issues.

The voting system

A *simple majority* is required on non-policy procedural matters, such as agriculture or trade.

A *'qualified majority'* is needed in the following areas: non-discrimination; freedom of establishment of business; free movement of capital; mutual recognition of qualifications; completion of internal market. Most votes are taken on a qualified majority system where 54 out of the 76 votes available must be in favour of a given policy.

Unanimity is required on enlargement of the Community, association agreements with non-member countries, extension of the Community's powers, amendments to laws governing training, harmonization of taxation, changes in treaties.

The Single European Act has extended the number of areas where voting may take place, as have the Rules of Procedure. The effect of this is that at least three countries, including one of the 'big' voters, are needed to block a proposal. At present (1990) the Council tends to proceed at the pace of the most reluctant state on controversial matters.

This practice has its advantages. In legal theory the Council could make a law which was binding on all twelve states, but to which five of the smaller states, or two of the big ones, were utterly opposed. In political practice an attempt to enforce such a law could tear the Community apart.

Remember that the Council is *not* a body which initiates policy and the law needed to carry it out. This is done by the Commission, which deliberately does not represent the member states. It was partly to avoid a situation in which the Community departed too far from the policies of the member states that the European Council was set up in 1974.

► Votes are distributed thus: Germany, Italy, France and the UK ten votes each, Spain eight votes, Belgium, Greece, the Netherlands and Portugal five votes each, Denmark and Ireland three votes each, finally Luxembourg with two votes.

 What is the Council of Ministers? Why does it usually try to avoid voting on politically sensitive issues?

The Commission

The *Commission* is a body of bureaucrats (or 'Eurocrats' as some sections of the Press have dubbed them) headed by commissioners appointed for a fixed term by the governments of the member states. However, the commissioners are *not* there to represent the governments who appointed them, nor are they answerable to them. This last point is important. The Commission was envisaged by the creators of the Treaty of Rome as the most truly European of the bodies responsible for running the Community. Commissioners swear loyalty to the Community, and specifically disavow partiality to their own country. The Commission is supported by a corps of civil servants, taken from member countries but working for the Commission.

► Each of the five largest countries (UK, Germany, France, Italy, Belgium) appoint two commissioners, the rest one each – seventeen in all.

What does the Commission do?

- *The Commission protects Community treaties and laws.* To this end it may bring legal proceedings against individuals, firms and member governments. Unresolved disputes may end up in the European Court of Justice (see below).
- *It proposes 'significant' and 'political' legislation to the Council of Ministers.* Ministers representing the member states in the Council of Ministers discuss and decide upon policies and proposals put to them by the Commission. They may accept, reject or amend them. A major policy change will usually involve directives or regulations which are binding upon the member states.
- *It legislates on matters of administration and in 'non-political' areas.* Within the policy laid down by legislation from the Council, the Commission makes many regulations and decisions which have the force of law. However, these tend to be technical in character, not raising major matters of political controversy.
- *It administers policy.* As well as initiating legislation, it is the Commission's responsibility, through a system of committees, to see that the policy inherent in that legislation is carried out.

You may not be surprised to learn, if you don't know already, that it is the Commission which is the main target for criticism of the Community.

Some criticisms of the Commission

- *It is undemocratic.* The Commission is not elected. Its proposals are discussed by the European Parliament and the Parliament's specialist committees, but since the Parliament remains mainly a consultative body, there is no link of direct responsibility to a popularly elected body.
- *It has too many powers.* In addition to not being elected or responsible to an elected body, its critics claim the Commission effectively combines the role of legislator, executive and administrator. Although the Council of Ministers must approve major legislative proposals, it is the Commission which makes those proposals which it then carries out.
- *Commissioners are not always of the highest quality.* In an interview with Dominic Lawson of the *Spectator* (1990), Nicholas Ridley, then Secretary of State for Trade and Industry, described the Commission as being made up of 'seventeen failed politicians'. There is an idea that Commissioner is offered as a consolation post.

The founders of the Community sought to create a body with a powerful influence on the Community's affairs which was quite deliberately *not* tied to any state (or group of states) in the Community. The possibility of being dismissed by one's government, deselected by a constituency, or held to account by a national Parliament, would generate an attitude in which everyone looked to national interest rather than taking the European view. In any case, defenders of the Commission might argue, the democratic element is provided by the need to obtain the authority of the Council of

▶ The tone of Ridley's interview was regarded by fellow Ministers and the quality newspapers as 'over the top' and it was pointed out that many of the commissioners had had distinguished careers as ministers in their own states. One of the commissioners was Leon Brittan, who resigned as Secretary of State for Trade and Industry after the Westland affair. Ridley subsequently resigned over the speech.

Ministers, each of whom *is* answerable to national Parliaments.

 What is the European Commission, and who are the commissioners? Summarize criticisms which have been made of the Commission.

The European Council

The *European Council* meets twice a year. It is a 'summit' gathering made up of the heads of states and their foreign ministers and the president of the Commission and one of the vice presidents.

Originally intended as a body in which to discuss very general policy, it is now used to try to reach agreement and make decisions on specific policy proposals. These decisions constitute not law but a policy framework within the Council and Commission work.

It has to some extent become a 'policy exchange'. Mrs Thatcher used the European Council in 1988 to pursue her aims of reducing Britain's contribution to the *Common Agricultural Fund* and reforming the Common Agricultural Policy, which she claimed discriminated against Britain. She obtained much of what she wanted, but had to agree to a fairly large increase in the Community budget as a price of concession.

 What is the European Council?

The European Parliament

The European Parliament consists of *Euro-MPs* (MEPs) directly elected, and representing constituencies across the whole Community. Usually, but not necessarily, they are natives of the country in which they seek election.

Of the 518 members of the Parliament, 81 represent British constituencies. In all the countries except Britain, they are elected by a system of proportional representation.

Functions of the European Parliament

When you consider the European Parliament, it is probably a good idea to forget all you know about the British Parliament to avoid confusion. The European Parliament is quite different. It does not legislate. Nor does the position of those who run the Community depend upon acceptance by a majority in the European Parliament. Although it does have some power and influence, it is not a sovereign body as is the British House of Commons.

What it can and does do is:
• *Give opinions*. The European Council must obtain the opinion of the European Parliament on all legislative proposals, but is not obliged to concur with them.
• *Question and criticize the Commission*. The Commission is answerable to the Parliament in the sense that is must answer questions about its proposed actions. It is also subject to monitoring by the Parliament's committees, which parallel the work of the commissioners.

► The *Common Agricultural Fund* receives payments from member states as a proportion of their national income. It is by far the largest of the Community's funds. The money is used to give grants to farmers for improvements or to grow certain crops and not grow others, and to buy and store surplus produce which if released onto the market would depress market price below that needed to provide farmers with a fair income. Britain, as a country with an efficient and highly capitalized agriculture industry, pays in far more than it receives in benefits.

► David Steel, former leader of the British Liberal Party, stood for an Italian constituency in 1989, but was not elected.

► No control over the Council of Ministers.

- *Sack the Commission.* But it cannot sack individual commissioners. This power has never been used.
- *Reject or amend the Community budget.* This is probably the most significant power possessed by the Parliament. The budget is subject to the approval of the Council of Ministers, but Parliament may block it and put forward amendments. If an agreement is not reached between Council and Parliament by the date at which the budget is due, the Community must continue with the budget at the level of the previous budget until agreement is reached. Thus increases, decreases or changes in the distribution of the budget between the various headings is negotiable. This power has been used to extract concessions out of the Council, for example, an increase in the regional fund, sometimes with the support of the Commission.
- *Approve treaties and agreements with countries outside the Community.* Agreements and special relationships with countries outside the Community cannot be concluded without the Parliament's approval. The Parliament's major weakness is that it has no direct control over the sovereign body of the Community – the Council of Ministers. Ministers on that Council would claim that they are democratically accountable to their domestic Parliaments, and that accountability cannot be divided. The problem with that argument is that Council may make decisions which have the force of law in all the countries of the Community. If a domestic Parliament disagrees with or wishes to amend those decisions, there is little or nothing it can do about it.

It seems to come down to the question of how countries and their governments perceive their relationship with the Community. While they perceive it as a Europe of Sovereign Nations rather than a United States of Europe, neither governments nor domestic parliaments are likely to relinquish much sovereignty to a European Parliament.

 What is the European Parliament, what does it do and who are the MEPs?

The European Court of Justice

The *European Court of Justice* is the judiciary of the Community. Its judges are appointed by the member states to fixed term contracts and may only be dismissed if in the unanimous opinion of the other judges and *Advocates General* they are no longer fit for office.

Advocates General are appointed to present arguments and advice to the court, based on the public interest, independently of the arguments of the parties to the case. Since the business of the Court is to interpret and rule on Community law, we need to understand the nature of Community law.

Community law

Community law is founded on the Treaties of the Community. The Treaties establish executive, legislative and judicial institutions, as we have seen. They also create rights which can be invoked by

▶ Do not confuse the European Court of Justice with the European Court of Human Rights described in Chapter 14.

individuals in their domestic courts, or in the European Court of Justice.

Although Community law is incorporated into the national ('domestic') law of countries, it is a separate system. National parliaments and governments cannot alter Community law. As far as the European Court is concerned, in the event of a conflict between Community law and national law, it is the Community law which must prevail. The jurisdiction of the Court may cover:

1 *Community Acts.* As we have seen, the Council and the Commission are empowered by various sections of the Community's Treaties to make decisions which have the force of law. These are not called *legislation* in the Treaties (possibly for fear of offending national legislatures).

They are:

* *Regulations* – these are directly binding on the government and the citizens of member states.
* *Directives* – these are binding in the sense that a particular end must be achieved, but it is left to the member governments to decide the means to that end.
* *Decisions* – these are directed to a state, individual or corporate body, and are binding.

2 *Acts of member states.* These include the incorporation of the Community's Treaties into the law of the member states and into international agreements between member states.

3 *Agreements with countries outside the Community.* The agreement can either be with the Community, or where it is relevant to a field such as agriculture or trade covered by the Treaties of the Community, a state or group of states within the Community.

4 *Principles of law. Most* judicial systems have to develop principles of their own, since written law never covers every case. The European Court is no exception.

In carrying out this function the Court will have regard to the principles of law in the member states. It does not, however, feel obliged to stick to the principles of the member nations. What it considers to be the interests of the Community may play a part. So, for example, certain fundamental human rights have been declared as part of the Community law, and Community law which does not harmonize with those principles will be declared invalid by the Court. Equality of treatment has been accepted as one of these principles and it has pronounced against discrimination on grounds of sex and religion.

The Court has also adopted the English principle of the rules of natural justice and the right to a hearing.

The Court may hear cases:

* *Against a member state* brought by the Commission or another member state, for breach of Community law, or an individual or corporation if their interest is directly affected.

▶ In the 'Lamb and Mutton' case, however, France refused to comply with a ruling that British exports of lamb should be given free entry into France. The French government eventually complied, but only after much argument and negotiation, and in exchange for a scheme to protect sheep farmers. Such refusals are bound to weaken the authority of the Court. (Commission *v*. France Case 232/78 ECR 2729.)

- *Against the Council or the Commission.* The Court can review the legality of acts of these bodies, or of unlawful failure to act. The case may be brought by member states, or by individuals or corporations if they are directly affected.

Since the Court has no police force to enforce its judgments, it relies on the co-operation of member states. Article 171 of the EEC treaty provides that if a member state has breached the Treaty, that state 'shall be required to take the necessary measures to comply with the judgment of the Court of Justice'. Compliance is nearly always forthcoming, since not to comply would threaten the whole concept of the Community.

Review – Community institutions

The main institutions of the Community are the Council of Ministers, the Commission, the European Council, the European Parliament and the European Court of Justice.

The Council of Ministers. This is made up of ministers from each of the member countries, representing the subject under discussion. The Council is the sovereign body of the Community.

The Commission. Consists of a President and appointed commissioners – appointed by member states but owing their duty to the Community and not to any member state.
The Commission:
- *Protects* – the Community's Treaties and laws.
- *Submits* – proposals for policies and legislation to the Council of Ministers.
- *Legislates* – on matters of detail.
- *Administers* – and carries out policy through a corps of permanent officials.

The European Council is a 'Summit' of Prime Ministers and Foreign Ministers.

The European Parliament.
The Parliament:
- *Must be consulted* and issue opinions on all proposals of the Commission and Council.
- *May sack* the whole Commission (it has not done this).
- *May refer* back the annual budget. This is its strongest card.
- *Approves* external treaties.

The European Court of Justice. The judiciary of the Community.

The *Community law* is contained in Regulations (written law), Directives (binding as to effect, but member states decide how effect is to be achieved) and Decisions (addressed to individual persons, states or firms, and binding on them).

What law does the European Court administer and how is that law made? What sanctions does the European Court have at its disposal?

THE EEC AND NATIONAL SOVEREIGNTY

Critics of the EEC come from the left and from the right. Both sets of critics emphasize the loss of sovereignty. They focus on:

1 *The loss of Parliamentary sovereignty.* EEC regulations are law as they stand. The British Parliament has some say over the form of legislation resulting from directives, but only as a form of 'delegated legislation'. The principle is laid down somewhere else, only the detail may be discussed.

2 *The loss of legal sovereignty.* As we have already seen, British courts may no longer take British law as the sole source of their judgments. Community law, in part made by the decisions of the European Court, takes precedence.

3 *Loss of political sovereignty.* Critics raise the spectre of democratically elected governments having to pursue policies which are contrary to those on which they have been elected.

During the period when a large section of the Labour Party was opposed to membership of the EEC, it was seen as a body which would impose free market capitalist principles on a future radical Labour government.

While professing themselves 'true Europeans', Mrs Thatcher and her supporters opposed Delors' Social Charter proposals as imposing socialist ideas upon a government elected on a radical 'free market' manifesto. More fundamentally, Mrs Thatcher's idea of a 'Europe of Sovereign Nations' made her oppose moves towards a common currency, a common central bank and a common economic policy, with its concomitant pressures to common foreign and domestic policy generally.

Resistance to some forms of integration may reflect a suspicion of the national ambitions of other countries as much as patriotism for one's own.

Counter-arguments to the loss of sovereignty include:

1 *Parliament is the ultimate sovereign.* Britain entered the Community via the European Communities Act in 1972, and confirmed its membership by the referendum of 1975. While there is no secession clause in the Treaty of Rome, in reality, if a British Parliament decided that its government was to pull out of the Community, that would be that.

2 *Absolute sovereignty is illusory.* The realities of involvement in international politics mean that British governments and Parliaments must accept limitations upon their sovereignty whether they are in the Community or outside. The needs of international trade, defence and diplomacy involve continual compromises with sovereignty.

► Tony Benn remarked 'Parliament is no longer sovereign and can thus be pushed into the background as far as the laws are concerned. If by chance British legislation were to conflict with EEC legislation, the latter would be upheld by the European Court and enforced by the British Courts whatever Parliament said'. (Tony Benn, *Policy and Practice: The Experience of Government*, 1980.)

► For example, in Stoke-on-Trent City Council *v.* B&Q plc; Norwich City Council *v.* B&Q plc (18 July 1990), Mr Justin Hoffman, in assessing whether a section of a British law dealing with Sunday trading infringed Article 30 of the Treaty of Rome, said that the Treaty of Rome was the supreme law of this country, taking precedence over Acts of Parliament.

► In his interview published in the *Spectator* in July 1990 Secretary of State Ridley indicated that while he was not against relinquishing sovereignty on principle, he was not handing it over to 'that lot', by which he meant Germany abetted by France who he labelled Germany's 'Poodle'. He went on to compare it with yielding to Hitler in 1940. Apologies and resignation followed. The apologies were for the tone of the remarks and the offence they may have caused rather than for the basic ideas contained in them. The resignation was delayed to assess public and party reaction. It was obvious that the Mrs Thatcher was reluctant to see Ridley go, and did not want to be seen to sack him.

3 *The power of the Community is exaggerated.* The fact that the Council of Ministers seeks to proceed by unanimous or near unanimous agreement, and the existence of the Luxembourg convention, reflects a recognition that national governments are stronger than the organs of the Community, as does the creation of the European Council.

Much has been made of the power of the undemocratic Commission; however, all its major proposals must be agreed by the Council, consisting of elected representatives, responsible to their national legislatures. Reluctance to give the European Parliament more control over the Commission and the Council may reflect reluctance to give up national sovereignty, rather than concern about democracy.

4 *It will be worth it.* Much depends upon what you think of the idea of a united Europe. Its supporters believe that the political and economic benefits ultimately coming from such a creation will have justified the loss of sovereignty.

► The North Atlantic Treaty Organisation (NATO), the United Nations, the General Agreement on Tariffs and Trade (GATT), the International Monetary Fund (IMF) are just a sample of the international bodies to which, while Britain remains a member of them, it may relinquish some sovereignty.

 Draw up a two column table and make notes on the case for and against giving up some national sovereignty in return for closer European integration.

 Discussion/essay question

In the light of the history of the European Community, is Britain's continued membership of the Community compatible with the notions of 'national' and Parliamentary sovereignty?

CHAPTER SUMMARY

1 The European Community was established by the Treaty of Rome in 1958.

2 Although the initial move was towards a customs union, its founding fathers envisaged eventually a 'United States of Europe'.

3 For this reason the Treaty of Rome is more binding upon signatory countries than most treaties, since its provisions, where they clash with domestic law or policy, are intended to supersede them.

4 Britain joined the Community later – in 1973.

5 The central institutions of the Community are the Commission, the Council of Ministers and the European Parliament, the European Council and the European Court.

6 The Commission consists of appointed Commissioners, who are appointed from each of the member countries. They do not represent those countries and take an oath to serve the Community.

7   The Council of Ministers consists of Ministers from the member countries appropriate to the subject under discussion. It makes major policy decisions and decisions on schemes submitted to it by the Commission.

8   The European Parliament is made up of directly elected MEPs. It does not legislate but has various powers over the Commission.

STIMULUS MATERIAL

The stimulus material is taken from an article in the *Independent* in July 1990 and is about opposition in Britain to further development of the EEC. Read the article and answer the following questions:

1   Explain the first sentence at the beginning of paragraph 5. What are the *'special interests'* referred to?

2   What explanations does the article give for British reluctance to accept the idea of a 'federal' Europe?

3   Why do you think British Governments showed reluctance to become associated with the European Economic Community at its inception?

4   What would be the consequences for the British constitution of a 'federal' Europe?

5   What 'political modernization' is the author referring to in the last sentence? Why does she suggest that a more united Europe might bring it to Britain?

MUFFLED VOICES FROM DEEP IN THE SAND

What good is the EC? Over the next two weeks, leading European statesmen and thinkers explain how their countries benefit. Today, Isabel Hilton bemoans Britain's lack of vision.

1   At a recent conference in London, a man who ranks as one of the thinking anti-Europeans listed what he saw as the advantages of further integration into the European Community for other nations, advantages which did not apply to the UK.

2   The French, he said, had no domestic political agenda and the Community offered a chance to fill the political void. The French Socialists had abandoned socialism and had found their *raison d'être* in Europeanism. The Germans saw the Community as the means by which unification could be made acceptable. But the British, he argued, had a strong domestic agenda which gave their politicians enough to think about without worrying over events beyond the Channel.

3   His audience – largely Community enthusiasts – was sceptical. But the point about diverse national interest within the EC is well made.

4   Why stop at France and Germany? Why not add the Italian special interest in the idea that EC standard of administration will help the Italians towards bureaucratic efficiency? Not trusting their own government, the Italians consistently register high approval of the idea of European government which, in turn, leads to a professional Europhilia among Italian politicians, regardless of party. The Spanish enthusiasm can be explained by the guarantee the EC offers of Spain's escape from political and economic backwardness and cultural isolation.

All of these special interests exist, but adding them together does not diminish the whole. An
5   enterprise that succeeds in advancing the common good while satisfying sectional interests must be
counted a success.

Rather the question remains: if each of these countries can see private and collective gain in a strong
6   Community, why don't the British – or, at least, the British political class?

There are historical reasons, of course, that have made it difficult for the British to adapt to the
7   development of the post-war world. Britain was slow to recognize that its pre-war role was
unsustainable after 1945: the habits of mind of global power lingered long after the show was over.
British trading patterns were more global in scope than those of the founder members of the
Community, for whom it was a more natural step to formalize a set of existing trade relations.

Britain came late to the Community: Clement Attlee refused to participate in the discussions in 1950
8   that led to the founding of the European Coal and Steel Community and Sir Anthony Eden later
withdrew from the opportunity to be a founder member of the Common Market. Britain's refusal
to join in the first instance, followed by its later exclusion by the French, meant it missed the first great
period of growth in the Community and, as bad luck would have it, finally joined as the world went
into recession.

The adjustment was the more painful for that. Unlike the citizens of the founder states, the British
9   do not associate Community membership with personal prosperity. On top of that, when the British
joined in 1973, they did so on the understanding that the priority was to get inside and sort out the
problems later. The subsequent, largely successful sort-out created in the public mind an image of
Britain in constant confrontation with her partners.

But if these explanations can by invoked in defence of the backwardness of the British debate on
10   Europe, there must be added an explicit failure of leadership of British politicians. The battling Britain
myth has been fostered by this government and Mrs Thatcher in particular, as part of her particular
nationalism and political style, but it is increasingly unhelpful to an understanding of the process of
membership so far or of the choices Britain faces.

The most common myth about the former is that Britain joined an economic union and is resisting
11   the encroachment on British sovereignty represented by attempts to transform the Common Market
into a political union. In this argument, repeated lately by Mr Ridley to the Bruges Group, the fact
that Mrs Thatcher signed the Single European Act in 1986 seems to have been erased from the
collective memory.

The Single European Act (SEA) states that European union is the ultimate aim of the Community
12   and enshrines the principle of majority voting on all legislation pertaining to the Single Market. If
British MPs are bent on defending sovereignty at all cost, why did they approve the passage of the
SEA? The stable, if not empty, is less populated than before, but who's counting? Apparently not
many members of the House of Commons. Last year, a Brussels-based polling organisation asked
British MPs what they saw as the most important aspect of 1992. A substantial majority said it was
the harmonization of weights and measures.

This is a pity, because there is quite a lot for them to think about. Essentially, whether the British
13   state, as presently constituted, is compatible with Europe and, if not, what the British are to do about
it.

The question is coming to a head, though shrouded in a cloud of Little Englander smoke. One reason
14   the goal of a Federal Europe is more threatening to the British than to, say the French, the Italians,
or the Germans, is that the foundations of their modern states are republican and ours are not. The
British political system recognizes no higher authority than Parliament in the sense that there is no
supreme constitutional law against which parliamentary legislation can be tested.

But Europe is being constructed on republican constitutional lines: national legislation can be tested
15   against the European constitution – the Treaty of Rome and its amendments. In the republican

tradition, this is entirely normal. In the British tradition, it is not – a point recently brought home by the consternation caused among MPs by the European court ruling in June on fishing licences that said UK courts in certain cases must suspend parliamentary laws pending decisions on EC laws.

16   This is more than a question of getting used to strange Continental ways. It is a question of whether Britain will seek to preserve its system of parliamentary absolutism – or whether it will opt to become a European country, with all the constitutional questions that raises.

17   The political failure has been the failure to acknowledge that the first steps towards becoming a European country have already been taken in the pooled sovereignty represented by the SEA. Even if we stop now, British ministers can still be outvoted in Brussels. If the principle is at stake, the solution is to leave the Community, but, as the European Free Trade Association members are discovering, the price of being outside is that the Community remains a force and its decision count. To have no role in making them, but have to live with them nevertheless, raises issues that are more important to the nation than an arcane vision of sovereignty.

18   In Britain, from deep in the sand, come the muffled voices of ministers arguing that the UK, hovering on the margin, can still play the nineteenth-century game of balancing power in Europe. Those who reflect on it from a twentieth-century perspective see another vision: that Britain's interest in a more united Europe might just lie in the opportunity it offers for political modernization.

The Independent
Tuesday, 31 July 1990
Isabel Hilton, European Affairs Editor

Further reading: Chapter 12

Daltrop A. 1986. *Politics and the European Community*. London: Longman. Discusses the politics behind the arguments and developments.

Hartley and Griffith J.A.G. 1981. *Government and Law*, Chapter 17. London: Weidenfeld & Nicolson. Useful summary of the legal structure of the community.

Nugent N. 1989. *The Government and Politics of the European Community*. London: Macmillan. Useful for insights into the political issues and arguments surrounding the EEC.

Nugent N. 1989. 'The European Community and British independence' *Talking Politics*, Vol. 2, No. 1. Discusses the question of sovereignty.

Now that you have completed this chapter, look back to the objectives at the beginning and check that you have accomplished each of them.

(13) Ireland

Media Watch

Media coverage of Northern Ireland is dominated by reports of violence, although in fact Northern Ireland is not a very violent place by comparison with New York or Washington DC. Avoid this kind of coverage and look instead for news on attempts at reconciliation and background pieces which attempt to explain the troubles in political and historical terms.

Chapter objectives

By the end of this chapter you should be able to:

▮ identify the events and movements in Irish history which have shaped Irish politics and relate them to recent past and the present.

▮ identify the fundamental differences between the politics of Ireland and those of the British mainland.

▮ describe the various political, military and paramilitary groups and parties active in the politics of the Six Counties and their political positions.

▮ describe and evaluate the policies and legislative changes and other initiatives adopted by the British government vis-a-vis Northern Ireland.

▮ critically evaluate the various solutions which have been put forward to solve the problems of conflict in Northern Ireland.

▮ know the meaning of and be able to use the following terms: Unionism, (Irish) republicanism, (Irish) nationalism, home rule, direct rule, power-sharing, sectarian, habeas corpus.

Introduction

For a variety of reasons, not least because violence and death are part of the daily stuff of political conflict, Ireland is a highly charged emotive issue, which produces emotive responses.

Try to distinguish propaganda and abuse (it comes from all sides) from facts and analysis. As well, try to distinguish emotion from objective analysis in your own reactions to Northern Ireland.

Bear in mind the fact that you are looking at a political situation which is *fundamentally* different from that which exists elsewhere in Britain. The broad consensus upon which British politics is based does not exist in the Six Counties. Not only do parties and groups not agree upon solutions, they do not agree upon what the problem is! Whereas in Britain there is broad acceptance of the form of the state and the basic constitutional principles on which it operates, in Ireland there is no such broad agreement.

Look beyond over-simplified polarities like 'North/South', 'Unionist/Nationalist', 'Protestant/Catholic'. There are at least fifty religions in Ireland, and the Unionist and Nationalist communities have divisions within them along political and class lines which are often as serious as those dividing the communities, and which may lead to liaison across the dividing lines. It is misleading to see Irish politics in terms of gun-toting guerrillas and bowler-hatted Orangemen.

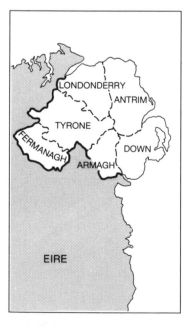

LONDONDERRY
ANTRIM
TYRONE
FERMANAGH
DOWN
ARMAGH
EIRE

THE HISTORICAL BACKGROUND TO 1921

The partial Norman conquest

Perhaps the history of Ireland might have been quite different had she been conquered and politically and administratively 'Normanized' as thoroughly as England after 1066. The Norman hierarchy made only a piecemeal impact on Ireland, beginning with a raid by Richard de Clare, Earl of Pembroke, in 1170. He and others secured territory in Ireland over which they presided as feudal lords. There was, however, no total replacement of the resident nobility by Normans. Irish kings remained in power as earls, nominally giving allegiance to the English, but in many cases continuing as independent lords over their own territories. The political, administrative and legal unity brought to England by the Normans did not run to Ireland.

By the late middle ages, effective English rule had shrunk to an area centred around Dublin and County Wexford, called the Pale.

Colonization

Queen Elizabeth in 1603 crushed a rebellion of Irish earls, but after negotiation, left the earls with their titles, though little power. When the resentful earls departed for Europe to summon support, the British Government confiscated their lands which included the counties of Armagh, Cavan, Coleraine (Derry), Donegal, Fermanagh and Tyrone. Merchants of the city of Derry formed a company to settle and exploit parts of Ulster, and renamed the city 'Londonderry'.

Encouraged by grants, British Protestants, including a great many Presbyterian Scots fleeing from religious persecution in Scotland, settled in the North of Ireland, and formed the predecessors of today's Orangemen.

The Protestant Reformation hardly touched Ireland; most Irish people maintained the 'Old Religion' (Catholicism), and took the side of the Catholic-sympathizing monarch, Charles I, in his quarrel with the English Parliament, which erupted into Civil War. This brought the wrath of Cromwell, the Parliamentary leader, down upon the Irish. In 1649, with 3,000 troops, he captured the Royalist garrison of Drogheda, killing the garrison troops and such Catholic priests as he could catch. This event, doubtless exaggerated in retelling, still retains a powerful symbolism amongst Irish Nationalists, and the name of Cromwell is still reviled. Cromwell, as head of the English Commonwealth, carried out further confiscation and colonizations in an effort to turn Ireland into a Protestant country.

By now only about one-fifth of the land in Ireland was owned by Irish Catholics; before the civil war the figure had been half. Protestants dominated commerce and industry in the towns. Irish Catholic (Jacobite) support for England's deposed Catholic monarch James II was to be responsible for more reparations and losses. Under the Treaty of Limerick of 1691 a million acres of land belonging to Jacobites was confiscated. The Irish Parliament consisted entirely of Protestants, since by an Act of the same year Catholics were barred

► The proposition that you cannot understand a country's present politics without understanding its history is especially appropriate to Ireland. The Irish 'separateness' from Britain is deeply rooted in the history of the two countries, and forms part of the present political argument and mythology of Irish politics. The anniversary of Wolfe Tone, the eighteenth century Irish nationalist, is still celebrated by nationalists, and societies are named after him. Northern Irish Protestant Orange Lodges still mark a battle in 1690, between troops of the Catholic King James II's representative in Ireland and those of Protestant William of Orange, with parades and mass drums. The Orange toast begins 'Here's health to good King Billy'.

► Whether you say Derry or Londonderry may still be seen by Irish listeners as a litmus test of where your sympathies lie.

► Cromwell lingers on too in popular music in Elvis Costello's bitter song about British militarism: 'Oliver's Army'.

► *Presbyterianism* – a branch of Protestantism which rejects the pomp, hierarchy and affluent display of the more 'high' Church of England, in favour of a simpler more egalitarian approach. It is governed by elders who are all of equal status. It is the National Church of Scotland and was brought to Ireland by Scottish settlers.

from membership. Subsequent Acts barred Catholics from all public office; higher education institutions were closed to Catholics; Catholics could not buy land from Protestants, nor will their land to anyone. Although the Irish Parliament legislated for Ireland, the Parliament at Westminster reserved the right to legislate for Ireland. The final say in government rested with the Secretary of State in London. Ireland by now was in all but name a colony in much the same way as the British West Indies or the American Colonies.

By the end of the seventeenth century many of the ingredients for the subsequent 'troubles' were present:

- A *Presbyterian* ascendancy in the North, who were to see themselves as Irish – as French 'colons' in Algeria saw themselves as Algerian, and British and Dutch settlers in South Africa saw themselves as South African.
- Religious, social and economic discrimination against Catholics.
- Effective political power in the hands of the English, or their nominees.

Organized nationalism and the Act of Union

During the eighteenth century, Protestant Anglo-Irish property owners and Northern Presbyterians, as well as Catholics, began to identify their interests with those of Ireland, and resent the political power and powers of taxation held by the Government in London. Many sympathized with the rebellious American colonists. The Irish Parliament softened the laws which discriminated against Catholics. The French Revolution had its ideological impact in Ireland as in other countries.

For a brief period the *Society of United Irishmen*, founded and led by Wolfe Tone to press for reform, looked as though it might unite all religions and classes under the nationalist banner. Conflicts over land between Catholics and Protestants, however, produced virtual civil war between rival farmers. After a bloody clash in Armagh in 1795, with victory to the Northern Protestants, the *Orange Society* was founded.

Despite help from the French, a rebellion against British rule was crushed in 1798 and Tone was executed for treason.

In the face of these events, Pitt, the British Prime Minister, determined that the best course of action was to unite Ireland with Britain. The Irish Parliament was eventually cajoled, bribed and rigged to accept the idea; Roman Catholic bishops and leaders accepted the Union for a promise of Catholic emancipation. The Northern Presbyterians, now distrustful of the Irish Parliament, accepted the idea.

On August 2, 1800, the Irish Parliament ceased to exist, and Ireland became part of the United Kingdom with representation at the Westminster Parliament.

Rural poverty and the Home Rule movement

One of the selling points of the idea of Union had been that closer links with Britain's economy would bring economic prosperity to Ireland. This happened in Ulster, with its prosperous linen industry, but for most Southern Catholics life went on at or below subsistence level.

By 1841 Ireland's population was over eight million. The country had neither enough developed agricultural land nor enough industry to support such a population at a reasonable standard of living. Pitt's attempt to persuade the Government to introduce an assisted scheme of emigration to Canada failed; direct intervention in such problems went against the conventional wisdom of *laissez-faire*. In terms of yield per acre and food value the potato was the most productive crop. It was cultivated in vast quantities and become the staple, sometimes the only, foodstuff of the Irish peasant farmer.

In 1846 a blight destroyed almost the whole crop. Widespread malnutrition, actual starvation, emigration and a legacy of bitterness which still survives, was the result. The census of 1851 revealed that Ireland's population had diminished by about 1,600,000 in the ten years since the last census. Approximately 50 per cent of the drop can be accounted for by deaths through starvation and malnutrition-related diseases, the rest through emigration. The flow of emigrants was to continue for the remainder of the nineteenth century into the early twentieth, building up a potent source of political and financial support for the Irish nationalism abroad, particularly in the USA.

While the Act of Union was not in itself responsible for the plight of Irish farmers, it was against the Union that much of Irish wrath was directed. It was a convenient symbol of real problems – absentee landlords, collecting rents through 'tithe-proctors', tenancies that could be terminated by the landlord at will, no credit for improvement of the land (indeed it often meant a rent increase) and a British Government whose only presence seemed to be in the form of the army and the police, perceived as being there to defend the powers of the landlords.

In 1823 Daniel O'Connell, a Catholic lawyer, founded and led the *Catholic Association*, which aimed to seek the repeal of laws which discriminated against Catholic emancipation. It was funded by the 'Catholic Rent' collected by parish priests.

O'Connell was elected to Parliament in 1828 but could not take his seat because of the legal requirement that MPs should not be Catholic. After the arrival of Catholic emancipation in 1829, the methods of the Catholic Association were used to found the *Repeal Association*, whose aim was to repeal the Act of Union. Highly successful in terms of membership and financial support, it foundered in 1843 when O'Connell, no law-breaker, accepted a ban on a series of mass meetings by the British Government.

O'Connell's mantle was taken up by the *Young Ireland* movement which was crushed, along with an attempted uprising in 1848, by the Royal Irish Constabulary. Veterans of the failed 1848 uprising who had avoided the police and fled to New York founded the *Fenian Brotherhood* in 1858, with a parallel organization in Dublin, which

► Peel, the English Prime Minister, made efforts to alleviate the effects of the Famine, but was hampered by his own followers in the Tory party. The repeal of the Corn Laws which prevented the import of cheap grain, split the Tory Party and lost him his position as leader.

► The Fenian oath pledged to 'the Irish Republic, now virtually established'. The movement was generously funded by money from the USA and Canada.

called itself the *Irish Republican Brotherhood*. The Fenians were committed not to Home Rule or piecemeal reform but to the foundation of an Irish Republic. Some Fenians advocated a campaign of individual acts of violence against the British state as a lead-in to the insurrection, and carried them out.

At the same time, other groups sought more modest changes – Home Rule within the Empire, and land reform. Parnell, president of the *Land League* pressing for agrarian reform through the British Parliament, organized the Irish MPs in Parliament as a cohesive Home Rule Party who would act together under his leadership.

Re-elected in 1893, and again dependent for his majority on Irish support, Gladstone passed a bill giving a limited measure of Home Rule to Ireland through the Commons by a fairly narrow majority, but it was rejected by the Lords. After this defeat, the old man retired from public life.

Until 1906 a period of Conservative Government put paid to hopes of Home Rule. In 1905 Arthur Griffith, a former Parnellite, founded a new movement called *Sinn Fein* ('ourselves') which rejected Home Rule as insufficient and advocated almost complete independence, with only token acknowledgement of the British monarch. Although Sinn Fein did not advocate violence, many of its members sympathized with the Irish Republican Brotherhood.

Sinn Fein at first received little support. This was partly because, with the election of a Liberal Government in 1906, and the removal of the veto power of the House of Lords by the Parliament Act of 1911, Home Rule through Parliamentary legislation became a real possibility.

Home Rule and British politics 1914–1921

Attempts to deal with Ireland periodically put a strain on the established pattern of British politics – they had split the Liberal party and brought down its Government in Gladstone's time. The Home Rule Bill which passed through the Commons in 1912 put a strain upon the whole British constitution.

In the predominantly Protestant counties within Ulster, Protestants of all social classes were united in opposition to Home Rule. 'Home Rule is Rome Rule' was their slogan. An armed force, the *Ulster Volunteers*, was set up and well armed, along with a provisional government for the North, to resist Home Rule. They saw themselves as a beleaguered minority who would suffer religious and economic persecution in a Catholic-dominated United Ireland.

Support for Ulster came from British Conservatives. One senior British Tory (Lord Birkenhead) said 'Ulster will fight and Ulster will be right', while the leader of the Conservatives, Bonar Law, said that he 'could think of no lengths to which the Protestants of Ulster would go, including the use of armed force, that (he) wouldn't support'.

In 1913 most of the officers of the Army unit at the Curragh, including the most senior, signed a statement to the effect that they would resign their commissions rather than be in a position which

► Charles Stewart Parnell, a Protestant landowner, was a charismatic leader who received widespread support in the country, including the support of many Fenians who officially despised parliamentary methods. Until his disgrace and downfall he was frequently referred to as 'the Uncrowned King of Ireland'.

► The Home-Rulers best chance of securing constitutional reform lay with a Liberal Government. This they got in 1889 when Gladstone returned to power. He responded to the widespread boycott of offending landlords, and sporadic acts of violence by members of the Land League, by passing the Irish Land Act through Parliament. Parnell and his followers now held the balance in Parliament. Gladstone committed himself to a watered-down form of Home Rule in 1885, but split his party in doing so.

► The 86 Home Rulers who voted for the 1886 Bill were outweighed by the 93 Liberal Unionists who voted against their leader.

► Until 1911 the Lords had an absolute veto over bills coming from the Commons (see Chapter 8, page 153).

► Parnell lost his leadership in 1890, when he was publicly disgraced because the husband of his mistress, Kitty O'Shea, sued for divorce and cited Parnell as co-respondent.

required them to order their soldiers to fire on Ulster Protestants.

The King (George V) complained bitterly to his Prime Minister (Asquith) that he was being put in an impossible position. If he assented to the Bill, civil war would follow; if he took the advice of some Tories and dissolved Parliament to avoid assent, he would be accused of behaving unconstitutionally.

The war with Germany (1914–18) defused this explosive mixture. Redmond, leader of the Home Rulers in Parliament, agreed to the addition of a clause to the Bill postponing its operation until the war ended. Carson, leader of the Unionists, agreed to stop opposing the Bill on that condition.

The Easter Rising

A great many Irishmen volunteered for service with the British Army during the war and the wartime postponement of Home Rule was accepted by supporters of Home Rule. However it was seen as a betrayal by the Irish Citizen Army and the Irish Republican Brotherhood which were paramilitary groups dedicated to eventual independence for Ireland. Sir Roger Casement went to Germany to arrange arms shipments, and the IRB and the Irish Volunteers, under the leadership of Padraic Pearse, made plans for an armed insurrection. The rising, at Easter 1916, failed. Casement had been arrested on his return to Ireland. MacNeill, the commander of the Irish Volunteers, withdrew and although the Dublin leaders carried on, they were surrounded by British troops in the General Post Office and forced to surrender.

Martial law was proclaimed in Ireland and fifteen of the leaders who had surrendered were court-martialled and shot. British reaction changed an ill-conceived and badly executed operation, which most people regarded as stupid, into a glorious event, with its roll of martyrs. This over-reaction boosted the support of the IRB and Sinn Fein who withdrew their support for the recognition of the British monarch and supported a republic. In the 1918 Parliament, only six Home Rulers won seats with 26 Unionists (mainly from the North) and 73 Sinn Fein candidates.

The newly elected Sinn Fein members refused to recognize the Westminster Parliament, met in Dublin and proclaimed the Republic with a survivor of the Easter rising, Eamonn de Valera, as its President. The Irish Republican Army (IRA) was instructed to make war upon the English.

This declaration of war was followed by 'the Troubles'. Between 1919 and 1921 the Royal Irish Constabulary and auxiliaries recruited from ex-soldiers – the Black and Tans – fought a bitter war, in which each side accused the other of torture and atrocities. In some parts of Ireland the British writ did not run, and the republican forces were, in effect, the Government.

▶ The justification for this apparently unconstitutional defence of violence was that the constitution was 'in suspension', since the preamble to the 1911 Parliament Act which took away the veto power of the Lords, announced the Government's intention to introduce a democratically elected second chamber. Until such a chamber was created, the argument ran, the Liberal Government had no right to make major changes in the constitution of the UK without the consent of the existing second chamber.

1921 – Partition

After some false starts Lloyd George, the British Prime Minister, invited the Irish Republic leaders to discuss a permanent solution. His final offer was made with an ultimatum – refusal would bring military occupation and repression.

The offer was the creation of a Governor General and an Irish Free State, with dominion status within the Empire. The six north east counties of Northern Ireland, given separate status by an Act of 1920, remained within the United Kingdom and were given a devolved Parliament at Stormont. The acceptance of Lloyd George's offer by the nationalist delegation was followed by a civil war in the new Free State. This civil war was between the 'Free Staters' who reluctantly accepted the partition of Ireland, and other members of the republican movement who saw the retention of the Six Counties in the United Kingdom as a betrayal of Irish Nationalism.

Although Lloyd George had talked of an all-Irish assembly, and an eventual referendum on the future of the whole of Ireland, these never took place. The Stormont, which Lloyd George had described as having the 'powers of a County Council', became in reality a Protestant Parliament supporting a Protestant Government. In the words of the Prime Minister of Northern Ireland, it was 'a Protestant Parliament in a Protestant State'.

 Take the review of the historical background to Irish politics and make brief notes amplifying each point.

Review – Historical background to 1921

The present pattern of Irish politics is directly linked with its relations with Britain since Norman times.

Colonization settlement of the North by Scottish Presbyterians and confiscation of land began with Elizabeth I and was continued by Cromwell.

By the end of the eighteenth century, Pitt persuaded the Irish Parliament to preside over its own dissolution and accept union with Britain.

During the nineteenth century the Home Rule movement grew, and Irish MPs were effectively organized into a Home Rule party.

The build up of bitterness was exacerbated by the existence of intense rural poverty on land owned mainly by British absentee landlords, and the failure of the potato harvest in 1845–6, which led to mass starvation and emigration.

Gladstone's attempts at moderate Home Rule were balked by the House of Lords and divisions within his own party. When a Home Rule Bill was introduced in 1914, civil war looked like a real possibility. The war of 1914–18 led to a truce between Unionists and Home Rulers.

Sinn Fein, the Irish Republican Brotherhood and the Irish Volunteers never accepted the compromise of Home Rule but wanted one republic. The Easter Rising of 1916 failed, but British over-reaction created sympathy and support for the republicans.

In 1921 Republican leaders reluctantly accepted Lloyd George's offer of partition, with the Six Counties as a separate statelet as part of the United Kingdom with its own Parliament (Stormont), and the 26 counties as a Free State with dominion status. The acceptance of this compromise led to a bloody civil war in the 26 counties.

IRELAND 1922–72

The British Government was largely content to let Stormont rule in the Six Counties during these years. Northern Irish affairs in London were, until 1968, handled by a small and obscure section of the Home Office.

The overwhelming majority of Northern Irish MPs at Westminster were Unionists, supporting the Conservative Party. Stormont and the Government it supported was Protestant dominated.

The *Royal Ulster Constabulary* (RUC) had an overwhelming majority of Protestant members, whilst the part-time armed *Ulster Special Constabulary*, usually known as the *B Specials* set up in 1920 to counter the IRA, was an entirely Protestant force.

Catholic and civil rights activists in the Province saw this system as a Protestant Government backed by a partisan police force, directed at the repression of the Catholic third of the community. Lord Scarman in 1969, reporting upon the disturbances of that year, rejected the idea that the RUC was a partisan force and praised its even-handedness, but admitted that there was 'a fateful split between the Catholic community and the police'. Of the B specials he said they were 'totally distrusted by the Catholics' who saw them as the 'strong arm of the Protestant Ascendancy'.

Fuelling this mistrust of Government and of the forces of law and order were widespread discrimination in jobs, housing and 'gerrymandering' (fixing boundaries for electoral purposes) to ensure Protestant majorities in cities like Derry which had a majority of Catholic voters.

Here we encounter one example of a common feature of Irish politics – radically different perceptions of what the problem is by different sections of the community. The foundation of the *Northern Ireland Civil Rights Association* in 1967 acted as a focus for the concern of a large number of Catholics, who saw their problem as being that of securing civil rights and fair treatment from a Government which denied them such rights. Considerations of the form of the state and national boundaries were, for many Catholics, of secondary importance.

To a Unionist, however, the whole issue was one of the preservation of the Northern Irish State, which was identified with the preservation of the Protestant religion and the Protestant community. To give more rights to the Catholic community would mean giving power to the leaders of that community, and this would be 'the thin end of the wedge' to annexation by the South or civil war with the IRA.

On 5 October 1968, the growing *Civil Rights Movement* held a march which erupted into violence between marchers, RUC and B specials and Unionist sympathizers. The police, who claimed to be attempting to preserve order, were accused by nationalist groups of attacking them, in support of the Unionist groups.

The Northern Ireland Prime Minister, Terence O'Neill, announced moderate reforms aiming to give Catholics more rights, and Catholic leaders more say. They were attacked by his own supporters including

► As a legacy of the days when Liberals defected to the Conservative Party in protest at Home Rule, it is known as 'The Conservative and Unionist Party'.

► Stormont was modelled on Westminster. The 52-seat Commons was elected from single-member constituencies on a straight vote. The Senate was indirectly elected by the Commons on PR. For most of its history, two out of three of its members were Unionists. All administrations in the Six Counties between 1921 and 1972 were Unionist controlled. Even after a recruiting drive to attract Catholics to the RUC, in 1988 only about 10 per cent of the RUC were Catholics.

► O'Neill was unable to keep his turbulent supporters together (he sacked Craig, who started another party) and he resigned in April, 1969.

his own Minister of Home Affairs, William Craig, for going too far, and by the Civil Rights Movement for not going far enough.

In August 1969 violence in the Bogside area of Derry caused the British Government to send troops in to assist the RUC. The rest of that year was characterized by continual and severe rioting in Belfast, Derry and other towns, with, in some cases, the creation of 'no go' areas protected by barricades where the authority of police and army did not exist.

The period 1969–72 saw growing tension between the British Government and that of Northern Ireland. In 1970 the *Ulster Defence Regiment* (UDR) was introduced to replace the B specials, but violence continued to escalate. Unionists and Nationalist camps had paramilitary groups – the *Ulster Defence Association* (UDA, an umbrella group for Unionist vigilante groups) and the *Ulster Volunteer Force* (UVF) on the Unionist side; the *Provisional IRA,* which broke away from the *Official IRA* in 1969, on the Nationalist side.

The years 1971 and 1972 saw escalating violence and the introduction of internment without trial. In 1971 in separate incidents three Scottish soldiers were shot dead in Belfast, two men were shot by the army in Derry, and 15 people died in an explosion at McGurk's bar in Belfast, for which a UVF member was convicted. In 1972 13 men were shot dead by the army in Derry, the British Embassy in Dublin was burned down, seven people were killed by a bomb at Aldershot barracks, an assassination attempt was made on a British Minister of State, two people were killed and 130 injured in a restaurant explosion in Abercorn. Nine people were killed when 22 bombs exploded in Belfast, eight people were killed by car bombs in Clady, Co. Derry and two people were killed and 80 injured when two bombs exploded while the Dail Irish (Parliament) was debating tougher subversion laws.

Relationships between the Six Counties and the Republic remained officially non-existent, but in 1965 Sean Lemass, Taoiseach (Prime Minister) of the Republic, became the first Taoiseach to visit the Stormont for talks. In 1970 tripartite talks involving the Prime Ministers of Northern Ireland, the Republic and Britain took place at Chequers (the British Prime Minister's country home).

The tension between the British Government and the Government in Northern Ireland came to a head when Brian Faulkner, Northern Irish Prime Minister, said that the Northern Irish Government would not accept any loss of control over law and order. The British Government announced direct rule and the dissolution of the Stormont, with all effective power and control in the hands of a Northern Ireland Department under a British Minister responsible to the Westminster Parliament, and quickly passed legislation to give effect to the decision. Since 1972, with a short break of five months in 1974, Northern Ireland has been so ruled. The fifty-year rule from Stormont has ended.

During the period 1921–72, the Free State moved further away from any direct connection with Britain, remaining neutral during the War of 1939–45, and establishing itself as a fully independent Republic –

► The Official IRA had come in for criticism from Nationalist supporters in Belfast for not protecting the Catholic community with sufficient zeal. Its policy of working through civil rights, and using arms only for defence, was unpopular with many activists. When the IRA army council voted to give some recognition to Parliaments in Westminster, Stormont and Dublin, in December 1969, more militant members split off to form the Provisional IRA, and a similar split occurred in Sinn Fein, the political movement supported by the IRA.

► Article 2 of the Republic's Constitution states 'The national territory consists of the whole of Ireland, its islands and territorial seas' – this nationalist aspiration has however been variously interpreted in the South. Dr Fitzgerald, leader of Fine Gael, has talked of accommodation and a nation of people rather than insistence on territorial unification, whereas Charles Haughey, leader of Fine Fail and Taoiseach (Prime Minister) from 1987, has expressed support for territorial unity. There is no evidence that the idea of taking on the Six Counties, with their ailing economy and internal strife, is popular with the Republic's electorate.

the Republic of Ireland or Eire – in 1949.

The IRA has been illegal in the Republic since 1931 (when it was the Free State), but at various times since then, the British Government has suspected and sometimes accused Republic Governments of 'turning a blind eye' to the IRA and even covertly assisting it.

In 1956 the IRA launched a border campaign of bombing and attacks on the RUC and the B Specials. This was largely unsuccessful, leading to the introduction of internment without trial in the Republic and in the Six Counties. It was called off in 1962.

 '.. a common feature of Irish politics – radically different perceptions of what the problem is by different sections of the community'.

Look at the historical summary 1922–72 and make notes on the way the events exemplify these radically different perceptions.

► Some IRA leaders, notably Cathal Goulding, reformulated their ideas while in prison, and in the 1960s came to the conclusion that the traditional call for a single Republic should take a back seat, in favour of the pursuit of civil rights and socialism. This policy was eventually to clash with the more traditional Nationalism and bring about a split within the IRA and Sinn Fein, between the 'official' and 'provisional' wings.

Review – 1922 to 1972

For the period 1922 to 1972 the British Government was content to leave Stormont (the Protestant-dominated Parliament in the Province) to govern Northern Ireland. From 1972 onwards Northern Ireland has been ruled directly from London.

Catholic and civil rights leaders saw Stormont and its Government and the two police forces (the RUC and the B Specials) as a sectarian force denying them their fair share of civil rights and access to jobs, housing and local government.

The perception of the Unionist Governments and their supporters was that it was of first importance to maintain the border with the Republic and avoid allowing influence from Dublin 'by the back door' by granting privileges and rights to the Catholic minority.

In 1968 a civil rights movement, well organized and supported by Official Sinn Fein and the Official IRA, organized a march which resulted in violent clashes between marchers, police and Unionist bystanders.

British troops were sent in to assist the RUC in the Bogside area of Derry in 1969. The subsequent escalation of violence and growing tension between the British and Northern Irish Governments over who was to control security led to the dissolution of the Stormont and the imposition of direct rule from London in 1972.

The Free State created by the 1922 Act remained neutral during the war of 1939–45, and became a completely independent Republic in 1949. The Republic engaged in tripartite talks with the Northern Irish and British Prime Ministers about the future of Northern Ireland in 1970.

From 1972 onwards Northern Ireland has been directly ruled from London.

THE MAJOR POLITICAL PARTIES AND GROUPS IN NORTHERN IRELAND

To find your way through the labyrinth of Northern Irish Politics it might help if you consider them by two criteria:

• *Their attitude to what should be Northern Ireland's relationship to Great Britain* – on a continuum, 'Unionist' supporting complete union with Britain would be at one end and 'Nationalist' supporting a united self-governing Ireland would be at the other.

• *The methods by which they are prepared to achieve their aims*: from killing and bombing as a positive tactic or as a defensive reaction, through unlawful but peaceful disruption to the completely constitutional route of the ballot box. These categories are not mutually exclusive. The 'Bullet and the Ballot Box' – summing up a phrase used by Danny Morrison, Sinn Fein's former publicity director – refers to maintaining an electoral campaign while continuing the link with the paramilitary Provisional IRA. Constitutional parties may, on occasion, support non-violent action which goes outside the law.

This diagram may help to sort out the relationships.

► The parties are also distinguishable from one another on the traditional Left-Centre-Right spectrum.

► Official IRA and Official Sinn Fein were the original republican movements from which the Provisional IRA and the Provisional Sinn Fein broke away (see page 249). Concentrating more on civil rights and socialism, and less upon armed conflict as time went on, they had ceased to exist by 1982. Though keeping the Provisional label, Provisional IRA and Provisional Sinn Fein are now synonymous with Sinn Fein and IRA.

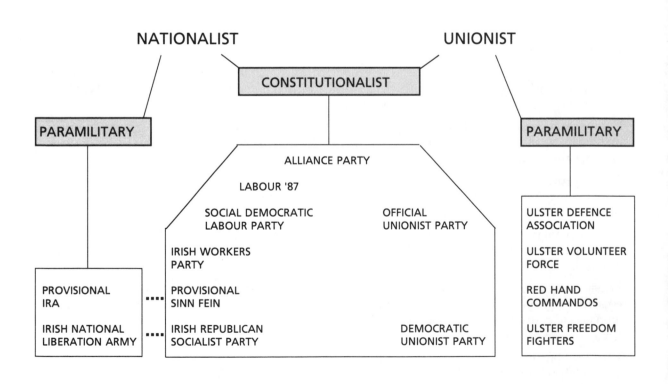

In the space available, I can only give an outline of the Northern Irish parties and political groups. There are many groups and sub-groups, many of them small and ephemeral, arising from splits in existing movements or responses to particular issues. There may be groups and connections between groups whose existence is suspected but which hasn't been proved.

The Official Unionist Party (OUP)

Its official name is the Ulster Unionist Party, but it is popularly known as the *OUP*. It is essentially the post-1972 version of the party that held the majority in the Stormont and which was the ruling party in Northern Ireland from 1921 to 1972. During that period it usually held 10 of the 12 Westminster seats in the Province, and was linked to the British Conservative Party.

As a party which embraced a coalition of political attitudes and whose uniting factor was the maintenance of Unionist rule, it suffered internal strains after 1968 over the attitude to civil rights. Further strains came with direct rule, the break with the British Conservative party and the Sunningdale Agreement. These strains led to the formation of breakaway Unionist parties, notable the Democratic Unionist Party (DUP) and the Vanguard Party.

The party has joined in temporary coalitions with the Democratic Unionists, particularly at the time of the Constitutional Convention of 1975–6, but this broke up when the OUP admitted to talks with Paddy Devlin of the Nationalist SDLP.

From being a party of the establishment, the party has relied since 1972 on working-class support, and has secured a good, though not a decisive, share of the vote. In the 1983 Westminster election it took 34 per cent of the vote and eleven of the seventeen seats.

Critics point to the fact that, despite attempts to eliminate them, the paramilitary groups continue to recruit, organize and kill, often with devastating effect, and the repressive measures can be a propaganda gift to the groups against which they are directed.

The OUP remains opposed to the Anglo-Irish Agreement and committed to the Union, although the 'Charter group' within the party has pressed for progress on devolution, and the party took part in secret talks with the Democratic Unionists, the SDLP and the Alliance at Duisberg in February 1989.

The Democratic Unionist Party (DUP)

The *DUP* was founded in 1971 by the Reverend Ian Paisley and Desmond Boal, the Unionist MP for Shankhill, on the basis of opposition to the 'soft' policies of Terence O'Neill. Boal has described the party's position as 'right-wing in the sense of being strong on the Constitution, but to the left on social policies'.

Its relationship with the OUP has blown hot and cold. In the 1979 Westminster election it gained two seats from OUP; in the 1979 European election Ian Paisley headed the poll with 29.8 per cent of first-preference votes. It disagreed with the OUP over participation in the 1982 Assembly, but the two parties moved closer in opposition to the Anglo-Irish Agreement.

▶ There was a *limited understanding* – an electoral pact for some seats – with the Democratic Unionists during the 1983 election, which mainly benefited the OUP.

Unionist paramilitary groups

The largest of these is the *Ulster Defence Association* (*UDA*), which started in 1971 to co-ordinate the many loyalist vigilante groups. In 1986 one of its recruiting posters showed a member holding an automatic weapon. It concerned itself with violent reaction to Republican demonstrations, demonstrations of strength and revenge attacks on Provisional IRA members in the 1970s. This it did mainly through its military arm, the *Ulster Freedom Fighters* (UFF). Seizure of large quantities of weapons and ammunition intended for the UDA in 1988 led to the suspicion that it was ready for a confrontation with the Provisional IRA. Internal divisions were revealed by the killing of a leading UDA activist, James Craig, whom the UFF accused of treason.

The UDA has, while supporting paramilitary action, put forward political views on the future of Ireland, epitomized by the document *Common Sense* issued in 1987 which proposed an Assembly and Executive elected by PR with an all-party coalition and a Bill of Rights.

The UDA has in the past had talks with the SDLP, which welcomed *Common Sense* but, as with many cross-community initiatives, attitudes to the Anglo-Irish Agreement had come to dominate the agenda.

The *Ulster Volunteer Force* (UVF) is a more specifically Protestant paramilitary force – sometimes called the 'Secret Protestant Army'. It has a long list of armed attacks and killings. In March 1977, 26 UVF men were given a total of seven hundred years' imprisonment. In 1988, a plan to import arms from Canada was frustrated and two men were jailed for organizing it.

The *Red Hand Commandos* are a loyalist paramilitary group sometimes associated with the UVF with a record of sectarian killings.

The Social and Democratic Labour Party (SDLP)

The *SDLP* was founded in 1970; though not a 'Catholic' party in any formal or ideological sense, it has become the party representing most Catholics in the Province. It renounces violence as a means to Nationalist aims. Although it aspires to a united Ireland, it supports it only by agreement, including the agreement of the majority in Northern Ireland. From 1982, it supported the idea of a 'Council for New Ireland' which emerged as the *New Irish Forum*.

In a policy statement made in 1977, *Facing Reality*, it pressed for 'an agreed Ireland – the essential unity of whose people would have evolved in agreement over the years, whose institutions of government would live in harmonious relationship with Britain'. Party spokesmen later denied that this necessarily meant an Ireland united under a single Government.

The British Prime Minister at the time, Mrs Thatcher, sharply rebuffed the New Ireland Forum Report, although it received strong international support, particularly from the United States. This, and the strong showing of Provisional Sinn Fein in the 1985 district council elections, may have moved the Thatcher Government towards

► The *Forum* started as a conference of the four main Nationalist parties, the three from the Republic (Fianna Fail, Fine Gael, the Irish Labour Party) and the SDLP. It reasserted its preference for a united Republic, but expressed willingness to support a federal solution, with authority over Northern Ireland exercised by the British and Irish governments.

the Anglo-Irish Agreement. But it did not bring about the all-party discussions sought by the SDLP, since all the Unionist parties and Sinn Fein rejected it.

The SDLP remains a supporter of the Anglo-Irish Agreement, and of a solution to Northern Ireland's problems by negotiation between the two communities in Northern Ireland, London and Dublin.

The Alliance

The *Alliance* is a centre party which prides itself on having members and supporters from both communities in Northern Ireland. Founded in 1970, it picked up members from O'Neill-supporting Unionists and later from the SDLP.

An Alliance policy statement in October 1988 supported devolved power-sharing government with the Republic as an equal partner in a new Anglo-Irish Agreement.

Labour '87

This party was founded in 1987 out of the remnants of several Northern Ireland Labour parties. The ex-SDLP activist Paddy Devlin is its vice-chairman. It seeks a non-secular trade union base. For the time being it accepts Northern Ireland's constitutional status and calls for a two-chamber assembly elected by PR.

The Workers' Party (WP)

This party emerged from Official Sinn Fein in the Republic and the Republican Clubs in Northern Ireland. The change of name dates from 1982 and signifies a desire to dissociate itself from paramilitarism. The party is Republican, but with a Marxist/socialist ideology.

The WP did not take part in the New Ireland Forum. It reluctantly accepted the Anglo-Irish Agreement in the Republic, but the Northern Irish branches were more critical. In Northern Ireland it supports devolution, worked out by Northern Irish parties. It denies links with, or the existence of, the Official IRA.

Provisional Sinn Fein (PSF)

Provisional Sinn Fein (PSF) is the political party associated with the Provisional IRA. While the two organizations are not completely identical, and differences have sometimes arisen between them, no major policy change is made by PSF without the Provisional IRA's endorsement, and normally at least one member of the PSF executive is on the Provisional IRA's army council.

PSF was formed in 1970, when the Republican movement split over the question of whether to give limited recognition to the Parliaments in Belfast and Dublin.

PSF's policy is to achieve a United Ireland with a single constitution and government. This, it believes, will only be achieved if the British get out of Northern Ireland. In 1987 the Party put out a policy document 'Scenario for Peace' which supported an all-Irish convention to work out a constitution for Ireland, written guarantees for loyalists, and British interim financial aid to achieve a united Ireland, tied to a

► In the 1987 Westminster election the Alliance fielded candidates, hoping to pick up ex-Unionist supporters who disagreed with the Unionist position on the Anglo-Irish Agreement. Its performance was an improvement over its 1983 showing (8 per cent to 10 per cent) but not enough to make an impact in terms of seats.

► The Workers' Party support at elections, local and Assembly, has been small – between 1.6 per cent and 2.7 per cent.

► Behind the break between the Official and the Provisional Wings were a number of issues which divided the Republican movement. The leadership of Sinn Fein and the IRA at the time were accused of lack of zeal in defending Nationalist areas in Belfast against sectarian attacks – a piece of graffiti, '*I ran away*', appeared on walls in Republican areas – and of embracing Marxist-socialism as a priority above national unification under a single government.

commitment to and a date for British withdrawal.

PSF leaders maintain that constitutional political action must be combined with 'the armed struggle' to achieve the removal of 'the Brits'. At the 1981 Ard Fheis (conference), PSF's director of publicity, *Danny Morrison*, said 'Who here really believes that we can win the war through the ballot box? But will anyone here object if, with a ballot paper in this hand and an Armalite [rifle] in this hand, we take power in Ireland?'.

Electorally PSF has never received the support of a majority of the Nationalist community in Northern Ireland, but it has retained the support of a significant minority. In the 1983 Westminster election it achieved its target of 100,000 votes, a percentage poll of 13.4 per cent; in the 1985 local elections it secured 59 council seats and 11.8 per cent of the vote.

In the 1987 Westminster election the PSF vote dropped by 2 per cent, while that of the SDLP increased by 3 per cent.

► The success of the Provisional Sinn Fein may have been a factor in the Thatcher Government's decision to seek an agreement with the Republic, with a hoped for spin-off of increased support for the SDLP by Nationalists and marginalization of PSF.

Provisional IRA

Provisional IRA has been the leading group employing violence in the Northern Irish situation since 1970. Despite some weakening setbacks the organization remains intact and effective. During 1987 and 1988 the PIRA killed 19 RUC members and 18 UDR soldiers. It extended its attacks to Britain and to British servicemen and their families abroad, attacking several housing estates occupied by British servicemen and their families. This was combined with attacks on prominent British figures such as Lord Mountbatten, Lord Chief Justice Gibson and his wife, and Ian Gow, MP (leader of the pro-Unionist group in the Conservative Party). There was a failed attempt to kill Mrs Thatcher and several of her Ministers with one bomb at Brighton in 1984.

The avowed intent is to put pressure on the British to the point where it will become intolerable, and British public opinion will force its Government to withdraw from Northern Ireland. The Provisional IRA and PSF are quite prepared for a long war of attrition.

► Setbacks for the Provisional IRA include 14 of its members shot dead by the SAS in 1987–8 – 8 as they attacked Loughgall RUC station, 3 in Gibraltar (March 1988) and 3 in Tyrone (August 1988). The Provisional IRA suffered 22 casualties within Northern Ireland between January, 1987 and September, 1988.

The Irish Republican Socialist Party (IRSP) and the Irish National Liberation Army (INLA)

The *IRSP* was formed in December 1974 by two breakaway groups, one from the Official IRA, disaffected by what they saw as collaborationist attitudes, and the other from the Provisional IRA who opposed the ceasefire of 1975.

There followed a bitter feud with the Official IRA, with assassinations on both sides. Between 1983 and 1987 the IRSP network was weakened when 25 of its members were named by a 'super-grass', Harry Kirkpatrick. After the discrediting of the super-grass evidence, and the release of IRSP/INLA activists, a struggle for power within the INLA led to a quarrel which was responsible for the deaths of 12 people. Resisting an attempt to disband the organization by a breakaway group – the Irish People's Liberation Organization (IPLO) – the reformed IRSP-INLA projected itself as a Marxist-Leninist party, to the left of PSF.

The network is smaller than the PSF-Provisional IRA, with its main support coming from the Lower Falls and Market area in Belfast and from South Derry.

With something of a reputation as 'wild men', INLA activists killed Conservative MP Airey Neave at the House of Commons in 1979, bombed the Drop-in Well pub disco in Ballykelly in 1982 killing 11 off-duty soldiers and 6 local people, and killed a number of UDA activists.

 Make a copy of the diagram on page 264, and annotate it showing the aims of the parties and groups involved in the politics of Northern Ireland.

IRELAND – 1972 TO THE PRESENT

The British Government's reaction

Since 1972 the Troubles have continued. The level of violence has waxed and waned, but it can be gauged by the figures; between 1969 and 1990 more than 2,500 deaths and 26,000 injuries have been attributed to the Troubles.

Despite military and police attempts to destroy them, paramilitary groups on the Unionist and Nationalist sides have continued to operate. The Provisional IRA and the Irish National Liberation Army (INLA) have at various times extended their bombing and assassination campaign to mainland Britain and to British servicemen and their families abroad. The British Army, whose initial intervention was welcomed by many Catholics, has become a target.

Some Unionists and Nationalists in Northern Ireland, disavowing violence and law-breaking, have formed parties and groups seeking a peaceful and constitutional solution to the Province's problems.

All this has taken place against a backdrop of economic decline in the Province. Northern Ireland's industrial sector (shipbuilding, metal goods, plastic, synthetics) has severely declined during the past 20 years. By 1985 64 per cent of the Province's workers were employed in the service sector. Unemployment generally is the highest in the United Kingdom, but Catholic working-class areas endure an unemployment rate of 35 per cent – two and a half times that of comparable Protestant areas. In the face of these events, various British Governments have tried a mixture of suppression and search for a negotiated solution.

The search for compromise

Governments of both Labour and Conservative Parties have attempted to work within similar policy limits. Neither Party's leadership accepted the option of the restoration of complete Unionist rule in the Province, or of complete British withdrawal from Northern Ireland leaving it to decide its own fate.

Because strong, organized, and often armed groups in the Province

Review – Parties and groups

Paramilitary Nationalist:
- Provisional Sinn Fein and Provisional IRA.
- Irish Republican Socialist Party and the Irish National Liberation Army.

Paramilitary Unionist:
- Ulster Defence Association.
- Ulster Volunteer Force.
- Red Hand Commandos.

Constitutionalist Nationalist:
- Social Democratic and Labour Party.
- Alliance Party.
- Constitutionalist Unionist.
- Official Unionist Party.
- Democratic Unionist Party.

► Not all the killing and violence is across the Unionist-Nationalist or paramilitary-Official lines. Some of it results from internal faction fighting within movements, or punishment, administered at the request of sympathisers, for common crimes.

► There are, however, groups within both parties who differ from the leadership on these 'extreme' options. Ian Gow, Conservative MP for Eastbourne, resigned as a Minister of State in 1983 in protest at the Government's Anglo-Irish Agreement. As trustee of Friends of the Union he was a focus for Unionist sympathy within the Conservative Party until he was killed by the Provisional IRA in 1990. Tony Benn, on the Labour Left, published a Bill to end British Rule in Northern Ireland by 1990, and Labour Party Conferences regularly include motions calling for withdrawal from Northern Ireland, from the Hard Left.

► *Power-sharing* would consist of guaranteed Catholic participation in policy and decision making through a power-sharing executive and guarantees of civil rights and equal treatment (in jobs, housing, etc.) for Catholics.

► The Assembly was to have sixty members – thirty from each Parliament, elected on PR. The Council of Ireland was to have a range of functions including the study of the impact of EC membership, development of resources, trade and industry, public health, sport, culture and the arts.

► In response to a statement by Merlyn Rees (Northern Ireland Minister), that the Government would not be wanting in its response 'if a genuine and sustained cessation of violence occurred', the Provisional IRA extended their Christmas cease-fire in 1974 to February 1975, and at one stage Provisional Sinn Fein set up a cease-fire monitoring centre in liaison with government officials. This did not last long, however, before hostilities were resumed, with each side accusing the other of bad faith.

reject everything but these options, the task of British Governments is difficult if not impossible. Nevertheless attempts have been made since 1972 to achieve a negotiated solution on the 'middle ground'. These have included:

1 *The Sunningdale Agreement (1973).* Preceded by the setting up of an elected Assembly for Northern Ireland, this was the basis of a *power-sharing* constitution following a conference at Sunningdale in Berkshire. Representatives of the Republic, the British Government, the Social Democratic Labour Party (SDLP, the Northern Irish 'constitutionalist' Nationalist Party), the Alliance (centre) Party and the Official Unionist Party were present.

A broad measure of agreement was secured: the Government of the Republic and the SDLP upheld their hope for a united Ireland, but only by consent. The British Government declared that it was its policy to support the wishes of the majority of the people of Northern Ireland.

Proposals for a power-sharing constitution included a Council of Ireland with representatives from both parts of Ireland, a Council of Ministers which was to make decisions by unanimous vote with seven Ministers from either side, and a Consultative Assembly with an advisory role.

There was an agreement that anyone committing crimes of violence should be brought to trial no matter what part of Ireland they might occupy, and that a Joint Law Commission should consider proposals for All-Ireland Courts.

The Council of All Ireland was to consider what further legislation was needed to protect human rights. The British Government accepted that, as soon as some security problems were resolved, consideration would be given to the devolution of policing powers to the new power-sharing executive.

The fate of the power-sharing constitution which followed Sunningdale illustrates the difficulty of trying to apply liberal constitutionalist remedies to the problem of Northern Ireland. The new executive took office on 1 January 1974. It lasted five months. On 14 May the Loyalist Ulster Workers Council called a power strike. Protestant workers responded and practically brought the Province to a standstill. The Unionist members of the Executive resigned, the Sunningdale system collapsed, and direct rule was resumed.

2 *Talks with various parties.* At various points since 1972, the British Government has attempted to move towards a solution by discussion involving one, or some, of the parties involved in Northern Ireland.

On occasion these talks have been bilateral, involving the British Government and one of the parties involved. Ministers from the Heath Government (1970–74) and the Wilson–Callaghan Government (1974–79) had discreet meetings with the Provisional IRA.

3 *The Constitutional Convention 1974–75.* More formal attempts to seek a joint way forward have involved bringing the constitutional parties together. On 4 July 1974 the Labour Government announced

---

The Constitutional Convention

The Constitutional Convention consisted of 78 members elected by PR on the same basis as the former Assembly. It was to consider the question 'What provision for the government of Northern Ireland is likely to command the most widespread acceptance throughout the community?'. The answer seemed to be 'none'. 47 of the seats were held by supporters of the UUUC, who wanted restoration of the powers conferred on Stormont by the 1920 Act. They rejected the idea of power-sharing within a Northern Irish cabinet, and suggested minority representation on departmental committees, which was rejected by the 'power-sharing' parties (SDLP, Alliance and Official Unionists). An attempt to create a 'voluntary coalition' during the emergency by William Craig (leader of the Vanguard Unionists) got no support from other Unionist parties, and not much from his own party. The three Ministers were the Foreign Secretary, Chancellor of the Exchequer and Minister for Northern Ireland.

This meeting followed a meeting between Mrs Thatcher and Mr Haughey at 10 Downing Street on 21 May 1980 which promised closer relationships between the two countries and spoke of a 'unique relationship'.

---

the setting up of an elected Constitutional Convention to look for a political settlement. Elections duly took place, and the first meeting of the Convention took place on the 8 May 1975. It produced no agreement in 1975 and languished until it was recalled on 3 February 1976. Inter-party talks between the United Ulster Unionist Coalition (UUUC) and the Social Democratic Labour Party (SDLP) broke down after an hour, the sitting of the Convention of 3 March ended in uproar, and the Convention was dissolved on 9 March.

4 *The Constitutional Conference 1980*. Organized by the Conservative Secretary of State, Humphrey Atkins, this took place between January and March 1980. The Democratic Unionist Party, the SDLP and the Alliance accepted invitations to take part; the Official Unionist Party declined to take part, but made comments from the sidelines.

There was agreement that there should be devolved government, but there agreement ended. While the SDLP and the Alliance insisted on power-sharing government, the Democratic Unionist Party wanted majority rule, although it allowed that minorities should have 'a meaningful role'.

Atkins tried to find a way forward in July 1980 by proposing two more options, but without success. Atkins' new options were first, an executive made up of parties proportionately to their strength in the electorate, or second, a majority cabinet with an assembly council which would include opposition parties.

The respective fate of these two attempts at a constitutional solution show the difficulty of seeking such a solution when different parties to the discussion have priorities which are so far apart. For the Unionist parties, a government which consists entirely of representatives of the Protestant majority is vital – only that way can their priority objective, the maintenance of the Border and the Northern Irish State, be assured. For the power-sharing parties, only a guaranteed power-sharing executive can assure their priority objective – protection of civil rights and the promotion of equal opportunity.

Another difficulty facing those who seek a constitutionalist solution is that even if the constitutional parties reach agreement, the paramilitary backed parties on both sides would be unlikely to accept it. It might be argued that if agreement were reached by the constitutional parties which are supported by the majority of Northern Irish citizens, active and passive support for the paramilitary groups would wither and die. There is, however, little evidence to suggest that this would happen.

5 *The Irish Dimension and the Hillsborough or Anglo-Irish Agreement.* After the failure of the Constitutional Conference, the British Government sought to approach the problem of the future of the Northern Irish State by talking to the Government of the Republic. On 8 September 1980, Mrs Thatcher and three of her Cabinet Ministers had talks with the Taoiseach (Charles Haughey) and senior advisers in Dublin. They agreed to set up study groups to look at a wide range of common concerns, and the Taoiseach described the meeting as 'a historic breakthrough'.

Two factors influenced this change of tack:
• The apparent hopelessness of trying to get the Unionist parties to agree to a power-sharing constitution.
• Mrs Thatcher's well-publicized determination to 'take on' terrorism, which cross-border co-operation would considerably facilitate.

Early in 1981 Ian Paisley voiced Unionist suspicions that they were about to be abandoned by the British Government in favour of a deal with the Republic when he delivered the 'Ulster Declaration' against the Anglo-Irish talks.

Despite vocal and well-organized opposition from the Unionist coalition, talks continued between the British Government and Garret Fitzgerald, who replaced Charles Haughey as Taoiseach at the end of 1982.

Fitzgerald had already made clear his support for accommodation of the different interests involved in Northern Ireland rather than assimilation or takeover. Fitzgerald clashed sharply with Haughey over support for an all-Irish police force and system of courts to combat terrorism. It was against this background, after intense and frequently secret discussions, that the Anglo-Irish Agreement (popularly referred to as the Hillsborough Agreement) was concluded by 1985. During the run-up to the Agreement, the Republic Government informed and consulted John Hulme, leader of the Northern Irish Social and Democratic Labour Party, whose views were influential upon the outcome.

The features of the agreement were as follows:

Article 1 recognized that change in Northern Ireland could only occur with the consent of the majority in the Province.

Articles 2 and 3 recognized the continued existence of the Anglo-Irish Conference, and that it was concerned with Northern Ireland and North–South relations.

Article 4 characterized the Conference as a framework to accommodate the rights and identities of the two traditions in Northern Ireland,

▶ The Reverend Ian Paisley is the most colourful politician on the Unionist side, with his commanding physical presence and booming oratory. He founded the Democratic Unionist Party, as a breakaway from the Official Unionist Party, and still leads it. He has been MEP for Northern Ireland since 1979, MP at Westminster for North Antrim since 1970 and Assembly Member for North Antrim 1982–86. A Free Presbyterian Minister, he is the scourge of 'Rome' and all its manifestations. He was an influential leader of counter-demonstrations to the Civil Rights marches of the late 1960s, a vigorous opponent of the Sunningdale Agreement and an influence behind the Protestant Workers' strike against it, and a leader and organizer of opposition to the Hillsborough Agreement, and any other negotiations with the Republic. He has been accused of links with the paramilitary Ulster Volunteer Force, but has vigorously denied them.

▶ Garret Fitzgerald was leader of the Fine Gael party, Taoiseach backed by a Fine Gael-Labour coalition in December 1982. This lasted until the election of 1987, after which Haughey returned at the end of a Fine Fail minority government.

recognized that the Government's policy was to devolve power on the basis of 'widespread acceptance' and that the Irish Government would propose schemes on behalf of the minority community in Northern Ireland.

Articles 5 to 10 dealt with the functions of the Conference. These included:

- Consideration of proposals from the Irish Government on matters of concern to the minority population, e.g. electoral arrangements, anti-discrimination measures, and a possible Bill of Rights.
- Security, police and prison policy.
- The administration of justice and extradition.
- Cross-border co-operation in security and economics and social matters.

Article 11 provided for review after three years.

Reactions to Hillsborough

Constitutionalist Nationalists in Northern Ireland welcomed the agreement. The Provisional Sinn Fein President, Gerry Adams, condemned it, saying that it 'copper-fastened' partition and insulated the British Government from international criticism.

Unionist parties issued swingeing condemnations, backed by mass demonstrations, the resignations of fifteen MPs (to create by-elections), the use of their membership of the Northern Ireland Assembly as a platform to argue against the agreement, and a challenge to the legality of the agreement in the Dublin High Court.

Unionist leaders were (and are) particularly concerned with the ambiguous definition of 'the current status of Northern Ireland' which seems to presage a change in its status, the 'rights' of the Republic to make proposals for Northern Ireland and the 'rights and duties' of the two communities. While Unionists may recognize that minority groups in Northern Ireland have legitimate concerns, to enshrine these as 'rights' would seem to give power and influence to a minority equal to that of the majority.

► For details of the Assembly, see section on 'Rolling devolution' later in this chapter.

The Anglo-Irish Agreement since 1985

Between 1985 and 1988 some twenty-five meetings of the Conference have taken place. While cross-border co-operation has improved, the *super-grass* system ended.

The Task Force report by the Department of Economic Development within the Northern Ireland Office laid out a policy for the economic regeneration of the Province and proposed the RUC code of conduct, directed at containing rather than confronting demonstrations. The review of 1988 concluded that it was worth carrying on.

This is, however, small beer. Neither the hopes of some Constitutional Nationalists nor the fear of the Unionists about the Anglo-Irish Agreement seem to have been justified. The influence and activities of Sinn Fein and the Provisional IRA have not been eliminated. Sinn Fein seems to have lost some support to SDLP, but only marginally. The Provisional IRA bombing campaign has escalated and widened

► The *super-grass* system, used by the RUC between 1981 and 1986, involved prosecution on the basis of information from ex-members of Provisional IRA, INLA or UVF (the paramilitary groups) often in exchange for large sums of money and a guarantee of immunity from prosecution. Between 1981 and 1983 evidence from about 30 super-grasses led to charges against some 300 people, but 13 super-grasses retracted their evidence before trial began. In 1986 the Court of Appeal quashed the convictions of 18 men jailed on the word of a Provisional IRA super-grass.

to the British mainland and to British personnel in Europe.

Thus one of the hopes for the Agreement, that by making the SDLP popular it would almost eliminate support for Sinn Fein, has not been realized.

Increased cross-border co-operation was offset by anger on the part of Mrs Thatcher at what she saw as a reluctance to extradite paramilitary republicans for trial in Britain or Northern Ireland. There was most certainly concern in Eire that they would not get a fair trial in Britain or Northern Ireland.

More authoritarian anti-terrorist measures have attracted adverse comment from the Republic. They include:

- the ban on TV interviews with people connected with terrorist groups,
- the abolition of the right to silence of defendants,
- reductions in maximum remission for 'terrorist' prisoners
- the permanency of the Prevention of Terrorism Act (previously subject to renewal)

Though Haughey supported the Anglo-Irish Agreement, the fact that he criticized many aspects of it when it was being discussed indicated that he may not be willing to go as far as Fitzgerald along the road envisaged by the Agreement.

Another respect in which the Agreement has been a disappointment has been its failure to provide a support to the progress of the British Government's rolling devolution policy.

 What are the main points and purposes of the Anglo-Irish agreement? In what ways might critics say that it undermines British sovereignty?

Rolling devolution

Created by Secretary of State James Prior in late 1981–82, this was envisaged as an infinitely flexible system by which elected institutions, at local government level and eventually at the level of the whole Province, would be set up with, at first, few powers. As 'cross-community' agreement and trust grew, more real powers could be devolved to elected institutions. The scheme for the Province is based on a 78-seat Assembly elected by PR in the twelve Westminster Parliamentary constituencies.

Application to the British Government for devolved powers could be made if 70 per cent or 55 members backed the application. This was designed to ensure that no application could be made on the basis of Unionist support alone.

At first the Assembly was boycotted by the SDLP and the Official Unionists, leaving only the Democratic Unionist Party (DUP) and the Alliance. Between May 1984 and November 1985, with the return of the SDLP, the Assembly produced three reports on devolution. From November 1985 until its dissolution on 23 June 1986, the Assembly was dominated by the Unionist protest against the Anglo-Irish Agreement.

Once again a British Government initiative foundered on the problem

► In the 1985 local district elections Provisional Sinn Fein won 59 council seats and 11.8 per cent of the votes. In the 1987 Westminster elections their support fell by 2 per cent compared with 1983, while that of the SDLP increased by 3 per cent.

of trying to work with institutions based upon the assumption of cross-community collaboration and trust, when the basis for such co-operation does not exist.

In March 1991, Brooke, the Minister for Northern Ireland told the Commons of a new initiative involving three stages.

- Talks involving the four 'constitutional' parties in Northern Ireland (DUP, OUP, SDLP & Alliance).
- Discussions between representatives from the above and the Southern Irish parties.
- Talks to include representatives of the British and the Irish governments.

These talks were delayed by objections (mainly from the Unionists) about the venue, the chairperson, and the agenda. Since the Unionists refused to contemplate discussions beyond the pre-arranged Anglo-Irish Conference meeting of 16 July the Secretary of State terminated the discussions while reaffirming the belief in dialogue and expressing hope for the future. Some discussions were held, but no conclusions were reached. Unionists seem to have moved a little, inasmuch as they are now prepared to contemplate a process which might involve Dublin, but they remain opposed to the Anglo-Irish agreement, and the articles of the Irish constitution which affirm that the Six Counties should be part of a united Ireland.

Note down the names of the major attempts to resolve the Northern Ireland problem politically, e.g. Sunningdale. There is no point in trying to remember the details of each. Make general notes instead on why all these attempts have failed.

IRELAND AND THE BRITISH CONSTITUTION

Events in Ireland since 1968 have changed and put a strain upon the British constitution and the British system of government. A liberal democracy works best when disagreement about details is dealt with against a background of agreement about fundamentals, such as the constitution, the source of sovereignty and the legitimacy of the exercise of certain forms of power by the sovereign body and free speech subject to acceptance of the rights of others. Such a consensus does not exist in Northern Ireland, and the search for one has, so far, failed.

The dilemma of a liberal democratic government is how far it can be justified in using methods of government which are anathema to liberal democratic values, in order to maintain itself in the face of opponents who go outside those values.

Some salient examples of these retreats from the liberal democratic ideal are:

1 *Military intervention.* The army intervened on the streets of Northern Ireland in the summer of 1969 when RUC officers claimed that their men were too exhausted to deal with violence in Derry and Bogside. They are still there.

► From a Marxist point of view, Professor Miliband sees the British State's function as that of *containment* of class conflict rather than *liberalization*. Northern Ireland, in this view, is just a special application of containment.
(Ralph Miliband, 1982 *Capitalist Democracy in Britain*)

Welcomed at first in some Catholic areas, the troops were soon regarded with hostility, after the Falls Road curfew of 1970, the warning by General Freeland (GOC) that, after warning, anyone throwing a petrol bomb risked being shot, and the shooting of two men in Derry; this last action led to the withdrawal from Stormont of the SDLP in protest at the refusal of the Government to hold an inquiry.

Operation Motorman, which cleared barricades from Catholic areas, and the shooting dead of 13 men in Derry in 1972, helped to confirm the Nationalist view of the army as being there to deal with the Nationalist side of the population. Criticism has come too from Unionists for ignoring barricades, and failing to deal with known Republican terrorists during the cease-fire of 1975.

Both the role and the size of the army has changed since 1969. Originally there to act as a buffer between the two communities, it was to respond to increasingly devastating attacks upon it by the Provisional IRA, by becoming a back-up force to the RUC in tracking down Republican paramilitaries. The number of troops in the Province has been as high as 20,000. It is now about 10,000.

Backing the Army is the Ulster Defence Regiment (UDR), the successor to the B Specials. A mainly part-time regiment, it is much criticized by Nationalists as a sectarian force, an accusation which it firmly rejects. The discovery of links between some of its members and Unionist paramilitary organizations has not helped its image. Despite calls for its disbandment, the British Government affirmed its support for the continuance of the Regiment in 1988. The Government blames low Catholic recruitment on intimidation by Nationalists.

2 *Direct Rule*. The decision to send troops into the Province led to tension between the British and the Stormont Governments over who controlled security. Since the British troops were answerable to the British Government, and the Stormont Government refused to surrender responsibility for security, the inevitable result was direct rule.

▶ The Stormont departments were Agriculture, Economic Development, Education, Environment, Finance and Personnel, and Health and Social Services

This gave Britain a new department, the Northern Ireland Office, with a new Minister for Northern Ireland. The Minister is responsible for overall policy and key strategic decisions. More detailed decision-making is handled by junior ministers through six departments in Northern Ireland.

Initially, many Northern Ireland politicians welcomed direct rule as a forerunner of devolution. Now, however, devolution on any terms acceptable to both communities seems remote, and the Anglo-Irish Agreement seems to make Northern Ireland a 'conditional' member of the UK supported by Unionists. This is not the power-sharing devolution sought by Constitutionalist Nationalists. Direct rule has few friends in the Province.

▶ *Habeas corpus* – writ requiring person to be brought before judge or into court, especially to investigate lawfulness of his restraint

3 *Powers contrary to the principle of Habeas Corpus*. When a liberal democratic system finds itself faced with determined and armed opposition, a likely casualty is the principle that only those properly

charged with and subsequently tried for an offence recognized by the law should be detained or imprisoned. In the name of the greater good of eliminating organized violence, governments may 'bend' the principles of the rule of law. In the case of the British Government in Northern Ireland, four major changes have illustrated this:

• *The Prevention of Terrorism Act (1974)*. This gives two main powers: first, to exclude from Great Britain, Northern Ireland or the United Kingdom anyone involved in terrorism relating to Northern Ireland, and second, the power to arrest and detain suspected terrorists, without charge or trial, for up to seven days.

The Act also makes it an offence to contribute or try to obtain money for terrorism, and gives the power to *proscribe* organizations (making membership of them illegal).

The Act has attracted criticism from those who consider it as unnecessary and ineffectual in dealing with terrorism, and from those who claim that it is used as a form of 'internal exile' for all sorts of people whom the Government consider undesirable, and not just known terrorists. The European Court of Human Rights ruled that seven-day detention without charge was excessive. However, when the Act came up for review in 1988, it was put on a permanent basis, subject to annual renewal.

• *The Emergency Provisions Act*. The latest version of this legislation dates from 1978. It gives wide powers of search, arrest and, most controversially, internment without trial. Originally used by the

► The Provisional IRA was proscribed in 1974, and the INLA was added in 1979 after the killing of Airey Neave (1979). The list now includes the UFF and the UVF. Calls from Unionists for the outlawing of the political parties associated with both Republican groups, Sinn Fein (with the Provisional IRA) and the Irish Republican Socialist Party (with INLA), have so far been resisted.

Review – 1972 to the present

Since 1972 the 'Troubles' have continued with unabated violence and killing.

This has taken place against a background of economic decline in the province.

British Government attempts to retain control of the Province while seeking a peaceful solution have led to a mixture of repression and attempts at negotiation and liberalization.

Attempts at conciliation have included:
• The power-sharing 'Sunningdale Constitution' (1974) – defeated by a successful power-strike by Protestant workers.
• The Constitutional Convention, 1975 – dissolved in uproar.
• The Constitutional Conference 1980 – agreed that there should be devolved government, but there the agreement ended.
• Talks with the IRA.
• The Anglo-Irish Agreement 1985.
• Secretary of State Brooke's 'three stages' talks in 1991 were wound up at the first stage, but did get off the ground, a fact that some have seen as a softening of the Unionist position.

Attempts at repression have included:
• Military presence.
• Internment without Trial – the last detainees were released in 1975, but the power remains.
• The Prevention of Terrorism Act.
• Diplock Courts – courts to try terrorist offences, without a jury.
• Emergency Provisions Act.
• Broadcasting ban.

► Internees were held at Long Kesh, near Lisburn, Magilligan camp in County Derry, and HMS Maidstone, moored in Belfast Harbour

► In January 1975 the *Gardiner Committee* agreed that detention without trial could only be tolerated in a democratic society in extreme circumstances, then 'chickened out' out of making a recommendation as to whether or not to end internment with these words: 'We would like to be able to recommend that the time has come to abolish detention, but the present level of violence, the risks of increased violence and the difficulty of predicting events even a few months ahead, make it impossible for us to put forward a precise recommendation on timing'.

► In 1989 an increase in violent attacks by the Provisional IRA led the OUP to call for 'selective internment' and the DUP for internment only for Republicans. Mrs Thatcher expressed her 'reluctance' to reintroduce it, but Secretary of State King made clear that it was still a possible option.

Stormont Government to try to eliminate the IRA, internment was followed by an escalation and broadening of violent protest.

A new system was introduced in 1972 involving 'interim detention orders' which after 28 days had to be confirmed by a commissioner in order to continue. A small number of internees were subject to 'interrogation in depth', and the European Court of Human Rights found (1978) that some internees had been subject to 'inhuman and degrading treatment, though not torture'.

Although the last detainees were released by Secretary of State Rees in 1975, the power to reintroduce internment remains in the Emergency Provisions Act. Reintroduction, however, might jeopardize the Anglo-Irish Agreement.

If the intention of internment was to break up paramilitary organizations and reduce violence, it failed. Rather it gave them a propaganda base from which to attack the British Government.

• *Diplock Courts.* These are courts without juries. They were introduced followed the recommendation of the *Diplock Committee* that such courts should be used for terrorist offences because open jury courts would be rendered ineffective through the intimidation of witnesses. Trials are heard by a single judge with no jury. The absence of jury and the ease with which confessions are admitted as evidence have been the subject of criticism.

The justification for these exceptional measures relies upon their success in reducing violence. This effect is difficult to assess, since it is impossible to be certain about whether violence would have been substantially worse had they not been adopted. In 1973, a Government spokesman replied to criticisms of internment by stating that of the more than 800 persons released from internment or detention since direct rule, only 10 had been subsequently charged with offences.

• *Broadcasting ban.* British Broadcasting authorities are not permitted to transmit direct interviews with PSF, PIRA, IRSP, INLA, UDA, UVF, UFF or the Red-Hand commandos.

 The workings of a liberal democracy rely on there being widespread consensus about the legitimacy of the constitution and of the exercise of power by government. This is not so in Northern Ireland. Make notes showing what effects this has had on freedom of speech, freedom of assembly, freedom of movement, habeas corpus and democratic participation.

Alternatives for the future

If you've read the foregoing chapter, I hope you've come to the realization that any solution proposed for the situation in Northern Ireland is to be examined with critical scepticism. The situation admits of no neat resolution, and any plan put forward for the future of Northern Ireland will almost certainly only be carried out at great cost.

With that in mind, here are some of the proffered solutions.

1 *Unilateral British withdrawal.* Support for this policy comes from Provisional Sinn Fein and the IRSP, as well as the 'Troops out' movement in Britain which is supported by some Labour Left-wingers.

It is based upon the view that Northern Ireland's problem is in reality the problem of Britain, who created the artificial 'statelet' to protect a privileged minority and secure a corner of Ireland that might have been strategically useful. In this view, no realistic long-term solution can be worked out while the British remain. Many commentators oppose this policy on the grounds that it would lead to a bloodbath.

It is contended that the Protestant community, led and armed by the UDA, would fight Nationalists led by the Provisional IRA to the bitter end, and many innocent people would be killed. The Republic and other countries, possibly through some UN peacekeeping force might become involved as violence and anarchy escalated.

The alternative to the 'Doomsday' scenario is that, without the British Army, the very possibility of a bloody war would lead Unionists to seek a peaceful compromise. Provisional Sinn Fein (in 'Scenario for Peace') accepted the idea of constitutional guarantees for loyalists in an all-Irish constitution after British withdrawal.

PSF's critics, including the SDLP, claim that the linking of simple 'Brits Out' politics to unification is unrealistic. The most likely outcome of unilateral withdrawal, in their view, is a small, poor and war-ravaged independent Ulster.

2 *The continuation of Direct Rule.* Direct rule is expensive, undemocratic and resented by members of both communities in the Province. However, Unionists might consider it the 'least worst' solution for the time being. Certainly they heard alarm bells when the Anglo-Irish Agreement was concluded, seeing the Agreement as the beginning of Britain's phased withdrawal from responsibility for Northern Ireland.

3 *Full integration with Great Britain.* Though supported by some 'hard-line' Unionists, this commands little support elsewhere. The British Government, of whatever complexion, is unlikely to relish the prospect of Northern Ireland's problems becoming a permanent part of British politics. The Catholic community and large numbers of the Protestant community would resent a situation where the Province was ruled from London.

► Richard Rose termed British withdrawal as 'Doomsday', while commentators in the British press have made comparisons with the appalling death toll in Beirut in 1989 when fundamentally opposed groups were left to fight it out.

4 *Unification with the Republic.* While the majority of Constitutional-ist Nationalists on both sides of the Border pay lip service to the goal of unification, and the Republic's constitution embodies it, there seems little enthusiasm for it outside PSF and IRSP. The New Ireland Forum (1984) supported unification only with the consent of all parties (which would not be forthcoming) and went on to discuss federal and confederal solutions. It is doubtful that the majority of those living in the Republic would want to take on the Province with its economic problems and sectarian violence.

5 *Power-sharing devolution.* This is the preferred option of the British Government. It was embodied in the Sunningdale constitution, and is the aspiration of the present Government's 'rolling devolution' policy. But Unionists are adamant that, while they recognize and may be prepared to accommodate Nationalist aspirations in the Province, in terms of civil rights and equal opportunities, they will not accept power-sharing. For them it is undemocratic, since it gives the minor-ity a privileged position, and gives Dublin a say in Northern Irish government 'by the back door'. PSF would never accept such a solution either.

6 *Anglo-Irish Confederation.* This is an extreme version of the ap-proach tentatively explored by the New Ireland Forum, and even more tentatively indicated by the Anglo-Irish Agreement. Britain and Ireland would assume joint responsibility for Northern Ireland. In the extreme view, Irish people would have joint citizenship or a choice of citizenship, and with increasing co-operation and trade within the European Community, the border would gradually as-sume low, or no, significance.

At present, though, even as lukewarm an approach as the Anglo-Irish Agreement has incurred the determined hostility of Unionists and Republican nationalists.

► *Dual Citizenship.* While resident in Britain, citizens of Eire have the same rights as British citizens – including the right to vote in British elections, but this is not true of British citizens resident in Eire.

Conclusion

All 'solutions' break down on the absence of the consensual basis necessary for a peaceful solution. If that consensus is not reached the Troubles will continue in one form or another. The evidence suggests that a British solution will not achieve that consensus, and that any lasting solution would have to come from the Irish.

 Make notes on each of the proposed solutions to the problems of Northern Ireland and the criticisms which might be made of them. What features of the Northern Irish situation makes any kind of solution difficult?

Review – Possible solutions

British withdrawal – the aim of PIRA, PSF and IRSP and INLA.

Power-sharing devolution – still the policy of the Government and SDLP and Alliance, but opposed by Unionists and Republican Nationalists.

Continuation of Direct Rule likely for the near future, but unpopular.

Anglo-Irish Federation – joint responsibility, including the Republic; resolutely opposed by Unionists, condemned by Republican nationalists.

Full integration into Britain – supported only by some extreme Unionists.

An independent Ulster – little support – likely to be a small, poor and conflict-ridden state.

Unified Ireland with a single system – only PSF and IRSP support this as a practical or desirable aim in the foreseeable future.

The consensual base necessary for a peaceful solution is unlikely to be created by the British Government; it can only come from Ireland.

 Essay/Discussion

'Because Northern Ireland politics differs so from the Anglo-American ideal, it may provide better insights into world-wide problems of authority than does a study of England, America or New Zealand'.
(Richard Rose, *Governing without Consensus*.)

What is the 'Anglo-American ideal' and how do Northern Irish politics differ from it? How do you think Northern Ireland might give better insights into the problem of authority?

 Project

Design a questionnaire to gauge:
How much people know about the situation in Northern Ireland.
How they would like to see the future of the Province settled.
If you have a population available, carry out a survey and produce a report based upon the results.

STIMULUS MATERIAL

The stimulus material is taken from an article in the *Independent* in October 1990 – before Brooke's proposal for a 'three stage' process of talks. Read the article and answer the following questions:

1 What is the 'alternative tendency' that Mr Gray represented, and why did it get such a rough reception?

2 Why do Social Democratic and Labour Party members suspect Mr Molyneaux's motives in engaging in talks about the Anglo-Irish Agreement?

3 Why do you think 'many observers believe that nationalists, while ostensibly supportive of Mr Brooke's initiative, would be privately relieved by its failure' (paragraph 8)?

4 What is the contradiction between the conference slogan, and the contribution of many of its delegates?

5 What do some senior Unionists see as an alternative to devolution? How successful do you think their preferred option would be in bringing order to Northern Ireland?

6 In the light of Mr Brooke's efforts subsequent to the writing of this article, do you consider its tone unduly pessimistic?

UNIONISTS HECKLE THEIR ALTERNATIVE TENDENCY

1 The annual conference of the Ulster Unionists contained little comfort for Peter Brooke, the Secretary of State for Northern Ireland. David McKittrick reports from Newcastle, Co. Down.

2 One particular moment at the Ulster Unionist Party conference this weekend illustrated why many observers are sceptical about the chances of success for Peter Brooke's political initiative.

3 John Gray, a 25-year-old idealist from north Belfast, told the party that all Unionists wanted to maintain their British citizenship and have a peaceful and prosperous province. So far so good.

4 Then he said : 'The reality is that the Anglo-Irish agreement can only be changed by negotiating a better alternative. This will mean talking to all parties in the dispute, which will include the Dublin government.'

5 After a frozen, incredulous moment the barracking began. First came hisses, then shouts. Mr Gray ploughed on to say that a simple majority did not necessarily make for democracy: democracy was government that could include the opinions of both the majority and the minority.

6 By this point a slow handclap was beginning. The chairman appealed for order, saying people would have the right to show they disagreed with the speaker when the vote was taken. The audience duly demonstrated what they thought of Mr Gray's accommodating tendencies : the vote was unanimous except for three people. These were Mr Gray, Mr Gray's mother and Mr Gray's father.

7 The odd thing about the reception given to Mr Gray is that the party leader, James Molyneaux, has in fact formally agreed to do exactly what he had advocated – to talk to Dublin and work out a replacement for the accord.

8 Mr Molyneaux's position is, however, ringed around with preconditions of a type which have caused the Irish government and the nationalist Social Democratic and Labour Party to suspect that his purpose is not to seek accommodation but to damage the agreement. Similarly, many observers believe that nationalists, while ostensibly supportive of Mr Brooke's initiative, would be privately relieved by its failure.

9   There was certainly little sense at the conference of a party poised on the brink of a period of serious negotiations. Rather, there was satisfaction that, at the moment, most of the blame for the anticipated collapse of the Brooke moves looks like being pinned on the nationalists.

10   Some senior Unionists look forward to the establishment of a Westminster select committee to give Northern Ireland MPs more of a voice in the framing of legislation, a move which, arguably, would defuse some of the drive for devolution and make any future talks even more unlikely to succeed. Although the conference slogan was 'British – we shall stay!' many grassroots speakers fiercely attacked British attitudes. John Hunter objected to Unionists allowing themselves to be photographed with 'English colonial ministers', declaring: 'I don't even have the same rights in my country as the Bantu does in Soweto. I don't want to be an Uncle Tom in my own country.'

11   Fred Crowe, a district councillor, also criticized those who cooperated with British ministers: 'Individuals trying to get their names on the Birthday Honours List should think of Ulster. Dublin has no role to play in the affairs of Ulster. British we are, British we stay.'

12   Jeffrey Donaldson was warmly applauded when he described Dr Brian Mawhinney, a Northern Ireland Office minister who was born in Belfast, as 'the lowest form of Ulsterman that exists'. He added: 'There can be no further concessions to the nationalists. We have gone as far as we can. No further must we go.'

13   Walter Lilburn said Britain had a policy of appeasement towards Irish nationalism; both major parties were working for a united Ireland, he said, although the Conservatives were more devious. 'I believe that if this party deviates in its opposition to the Anglo-Irish agreement it is finished. I believe if the Ulster people give way on this one, the province is finished.'

The Independent
29 October 1990

Further reading: Chapter 13

Rose R. 1971. *Governing without Consensus*. London: Faber. This is dated in its examples but still useful in so far as it states and explores the fundamental difference between the politics of Ireland and those of the British mainland.

The following all contain useful summaries of the politics of Northern Ireland. Dunleavy *et al.* is the most up to date.

Arthur P. 1983. *The Government and Politics of Northern Ireland*. London: Longman.

Aughey A. 1990. 'The Troubles in Northern Ireland – 20 years on' *Talking Politics*, Vol. 3, No. 1.

Borthwick R. L. and Spence J. E. 1984. *British Politics in Perspective*, Chapter 8. Leicester: Leicester University Press.

Drucker H. *et al* (eds). 1986. *Developments in British Politics 2*, Chapter 10. London: Macmillan.

Dunleavy P. *et al* (eds). 1990. *Developments in British Politics 3*, Chapter 12. London: Macmillan.

Lyons F. 1990. 'Political stalemate? Policy towards Northern Ireland' *Talking Politics*, Vol. 2, No. 3.

Now you have reached the end of the chapter, turn back to the beginning, look at the objectives and make sure you have achieved each of them.

14 *Justice, the state and the individual*

Media Watch

Watch out especially for cases where the courts hear legal appeals against government actions, and the work of the Ombudsmen – these show you the role of the judiciary in limiting government power.

Look out also for stories which illustrate the relationship between the police and local communities and the conflict between operational efficiency and democratic control in policing.

Chapter objectives

By the end of this chapter you should be able to:

■ assess the relationship between justice and the law.

■ give a reasoned judgement on the independence of the British judiciary having examined the nature of the British legal system.

■ assess the role of police forces in Britain and discuss some of the recent controversies about policing.

■ evaluate the extent to which the legal and political system protects the rights of individuals and groups, given the growth of executive power since 1945.

■ give the meaning of and be able to use the following terms: judiciary, justice, natural justice, judicial review, law officers (Lord Chancellor, Attorney General, Solicitor General), barrister, solicitor, statute law, case law, common law, precedent, criminal law, civil law, indictable offence, stipendiary magistrate, bail, adversarial and inquisitorial systems, legal aim, administrative tribunal, police committees, police complaints procedure. Judicial Committee of the House of Lords, Court of Appeal, Supreme Court, High Court (Queens Bench, Chancery Division, Family Division), Crown Court, Magistrates' Court, High Court Judge, Circuit Judge, Recorder, jury, Parliamentary Commissioners (Ombudsmen), Commissioners for the Health Service and for Local Government.

JUSTICE AND THE LAW

Justice

The *Shorter Oxford English Dictionary* puts together two interesting definitions under *justice*:

- *Exercise of authority or power in maintenance of right; vindication of right by assignment of reward or punishment....*
- *The administration of law, or the forms and processes attending it.*

In the first definition, it is not made clear whether 'right' means 'that which is morally correct' or 'a claim which an individual is morally entitled to', but either or both together fit with the ordinary usage of the word to mean 'fairness' or 'getting what you're entitled to'.

The second definition demonstrates the extent to which our notions of justice are tied up with our idea of law. It is possible to conceive of justice without law; private vigilante groups in some cities of the United States would see themselves as administering justice outside the law. Trade unionists, representatives of welfare claimants, immigrant families and their representatives, and local councillors, have all at some time accused the Thatcher Governments (1979–90) of promulgating laws which offend justice. Nevertheless, the idea that law is there to provide justice is widely accepted.

Law

In the *liberal democratic model of the law*, the rule of law is the means of ensuring justice by providing:

- That the use of power should be based upon an agreed written statute or according to well-known practice, rather than the arbitrary will or whim of individuals or groups.
- That those who exercise power are not themselves exempt from or outside the law, and that the exercise of their discretion in making decisions should be within the boundaries of the law, and subject to legal restraint.
- That a system of applying the law and resolving conflict under the law exists which is independent of direct control by the Government of the day, or any other political group.
- That such a system accords with ideas of 'natural justice', e.g. lack of bias or partiality on the part of judges, an equal and fair hearing given to all parties, charges to be specific.
- That the system is open in two senses: first, that everyone has access to it, and second, that its deliberations are open to public and media scrutiny.

The liberal democratic model of law might be opposed by the *Marxist model* which sees law principally as a means of containment of class conflict, the protection of existing property relationships and the furtherance of the interests of the ruling class. According to the Marxist view, the law may appear superficially independent and fair, and to a limited extent might be so. In the end, however, it is there to preserve the status quo and those who benefit from it.

▶ For one version of the Marxist view see Ralph Miliband (1982) *Capitalist Democracy in Britain*, particularly Chapter 4, 'The Management of Class Conflict'.

A pluralist modification of the rigid Marxist view is that which sees law as an expression of the values and interests of dominant groups in society, which changes with the fortunes of particular parties and groups, and their interpretation of the 'climate of the time'. Case and statute law on abortion, pornography, homosexuality and trade union law make interesting examples.

 Make notes to contrast a liberal democratic, a Marxist and a pluralist model of the law. Note for yourself that there is a difference between the processes through which law is made – legislation, and those through which it is applied through the judiciary, so that paradoxically an 'unfair law' may be 'fairly applied'. Find examples which seem to support each of these models as accurate descriptions of British law.

►*Judiciary* – the judges of a state collectively.

►In 1980 a Labour MP speaking in the Commons described Lord Diplock as a 'Tory Judge'. The Speaker rebuked the MP with a ruling that 'it is offensive to refer to a judge of the High Court by anything other than as a Judge of the High Court'. He went on, 'of course it is wrong for any of us to attribute to any judge a bias'.

►The Lord Chancellor is appointed from the ruling party in the Commons or Lords. He sits in the Lords and acts as chair of debates in the Lords as a Law Lord (see Chapter 8 page 154). He is the Minister responsible for the whole system of courts, judges, etc.

►For the appointment of local magistrates, the Lord Chancellor takes, but does not have to follow, the advice of a local selection committee.

►There hasn't yet been a woman appointed as Chancellor.

►The Law Officers are the Attorney General and the Solicitor General, appointed by the Prime Minister from MPs or Lords.

►There has been no woman as Attorney General either.

The prevalent view of the British judiciary, and its view of itself, is that it is separate from and independent of the Government, and free from any political bias.

Since the Act of Settlement (1701) judges of the High Court have been appointed 'during good behaviour' and can only be dismissed on an *Address* from both Houses of Parliament. Since 1701 only one judge has been dismissed (1803). Thus their security of tenure is virtually unassailable – so they have nothing to fear from the Government – their salaries are guaranteed by statute and they are immune from civil proceedings against them for anything said or done in the course of their judicial duties.

More importantly, perhaps, judges see themselves as independent. As will be described in more detail later in the chapter, the judiciary since 1970 has reversed or set aside several government decisions on the grounds that they were *ultra vires*, unreasonable, or contrary to natural justice, in a process known as 'judicial review', see page 214.

Although the judges have shown themselves to be robustly independent at times, there have been objections and qualifications to the view that we have in Britain complete separation of powers between *judiciary* and *executive*, and that the judges are always unbiased and non-political.

Some of the objections are as follows:

• *Judges are appointed by politicians.* The highest judges (Appeal Court judges and Lords of Appeal in Ordinary) are appointed by the Queen on the advice of the Prime Minister after consultation with the Lord Chancellor. High court judges and lower court judges are appointed by the Lord Chancellor – a member of the Government.

• *The Lord Chancellor and the Law Officers are members of the Government.* The *Lord Chancellor* is head of the judiciary. He is also a member of the Cabinet, and a member of the House of Lords. He may take part in debates in the Lords, as well as chairing them, and sit on the judicial committee of the Lords, which constitutes the highest Court of Appeal. Thus he is a member of the Judiciary, the Legislature and the Executive.

The law officers are the *Attorney General* assisted by the *Solicitor General*.

The Attorney General is a Minister and member of the ruling party, as well as a barrister. He is the chief legal adviser to the Government, and appears on the Government's behalf in Court in important cases. More important as far as the separation of powers is concerned, he can prevent or stop a prosecution, and under certain statutes (notably the Official Secrets Act) his consent is required before a prosecution can be brought. The Solicitor General is also appointed from the ruling party, and is a barrister.

• *The Courts have no power to set aside statutes.* As has already been pointed out (Chapter 2) the British judiciary does not have the independent power of review of legislation that the Supreme Courts of the United States have. Any interpretation of law passed by

Parliament must be on the basis of the words of the statute and an interpretation of what Parliament must have intended by their common-sense meaning. While this gives some room for judicial interpretation, a Government which controls a majority in Parliament can always redress the balance if it does not like the interpretation by passing a new statute.

Although the British judiciary may enjoy a measure of separation from the executive and the legislature, it does not enjoy equal power with them.

- *Judges are drawn from a narrow section of society and this affects 'judge-made' law.* Senior judges are appointed from the ranks of practising barristers.
- *'Judge-made law' is affected by the narrow views of judges.* Neither of the critics mentioned in the inset has suggested that judges exercise deliberate bias in favour of a political party or a government. The

► In Congreve *v.* Home Office (1976), Mr Congreve bought a new TV licence before his old one expired, in order to avoid paying an increased licence fee. The Home Secretary used his powers to revoke the licence, Congreve contested the Minister's power to do this, and the Courts declared the Minister's action unlawful. The Home Secretary promptly gave himself the power to raise licence fees in future without warning.

Background of judges

The British legal profession is divided between *solicitors*, who deal directly with members of the public, advise them and act on their behalf on legal matters (including appearance in the lower courts) and *barristers*, who are approached only by solicitors, and who have exclusive rights to plead in the higher courts. They also give legal advice to clients on more difficult and arcane points of law. Each profession has its own professional body, the Bar Council and the Inns of Court for barristers, and the Law Society for solicitors, and its own system of training and qualification.

To make it as a practising barrister is not easy. It requires several years of full-time education and training, followed by a 'practice-training' and pupillage. After that you need to find a good set of 'Chambers' (barristers' offices) where you might languish for some time until a solicitor, through the offices of the Chamber's Clerk, gives you a 'brief' (a job). Even then it may take some time to build yourself a reputation with solicitors, whose fees provide your income. Rewards for the few at the top of their profession are very high but many barristers rub along on modest and precarious incomes. A private income, good connections and rich parents are not absolutely necessary, but they help. It is much easier to make it as a solicitor where a system of 'paid apprenticeship' (Articles) exists.

Critics point out that because of these restrictions the profession of practising barrister is overwhelmingly male, upper middle class, White and conservative (with a small 'c' – not necessarily a member of the Conservative Party). Griffith in *The Politics of the Judiciary* (1985) points to the fact that a disproportionate number of those appointed as judges went to independent schools and Oxford or Cambridge University. Miliband in *Capitalist Democracy in Britain* claims that 'the profession is notoriously conservative, and barristers who are radical do not become judges'.

► I use the adjective *practising* to distinguish the few who work as barristers from the many who take the qualification for other reasons.

► In Secretary of State for Education and Science *v*. Tameside Metropolitan Borough Council (MBC) (1977), the House of Lords on an appeal by the DES from a judicial review declared that Tameside MBC could change its scheme for transfer to secondary education despite a ministerial order to the contrary. The Government plugged the gap by legislation.

contention is that their background, training and experience leads them to certain conclusions in exercising their strictly judicial function.

The importance of this argument is that, to a certain extent, judges in the higher court *make* the law. The 'Common Law' is a body of principles established in the past by the courts and remains law so long as it is not overruled by statute. In applying these principles to cases judges claim that they are following precedent. In practice they are often re-interpreting them in the light of the circumstances of a new case and 'distinguishing' one case from another so as to create new precedent, and therefore new law. No statute is so word perfect that there is no room for interpretation when applied to cases, and interpretation may substantially alter the way a statute works in practice. A *judicial review* of the decisions of public authorities may have an important effect upon their powers, see page 298.

In three particular areas – industrial relations, the powers of (usually Labour) local authorities and state security – the judiciary has drawn criticism.

Moran says in *The Politics of Industrial Relations* (1977):

> It is no exaggeration to say that with the exception of wartime laws and the 1927 Trade Disputes Act, every significant statute bearing on industrial disputes in the century after 1870 was the result of judicial decisions which had nullified the intended effect of previous legislation.

He was writing in 1977, before the Thatcher Government was elected. Many trade unionists would claim that the courts were rigorous in applying the Thatcher Government's laws designed to restrict the power of trade unions since 1979. In January 1982 the Law Lords decided that the Labour-controlled Greater London Council (GLC) was not empowered to levy a supplementary rate in order to pay for reduction of fares on buses and underground trains. Crucial to the case was the *London Transport Act* (1969) which gave the GLC a duty to provide 'integrated, efficient and economic transport facilities and services for Greater London'. In his judgment, finding against the

---

The Belgrano affair

In 1984 Clive Ponting, a senior civil servant in the Ministry of Defence, sent documents to an MP purporting to show that the Government had misled Parliament on the position and course of the *General Belgrano*, an Argentinian warship, when she was sunk by a British submarine during the Falklands operation in 1982. At his subsequent prosecution under the Official Secrets Act, Ponting's defence was that his action was protected by the Act, since it was in 'the interests of the State', and the Government was acting *against* the interests of the State. The judge was dismissive of the defence case and ruled that the interests of the State were identical with the interests of the Government of the day. Although he all but directed the jury to find Ponting guilty, the jury reached a verdict of not guilty. Ponting lost his job.

The Mark Hosenball case

A deportation order was made in 1977 against Mark Hosenball, an American journalist, on the grounds that he had obtained for publication *'information harmful to the security of the United Kingdom'*. He appealed. No evidence was offered against him but the appeal was dismissed. Judge Lord Denning said:

> 'If it was a case where the ordinary rules of natural justice had to be observed, some criticism could be made of the Home Secretary. It could be said that Mr Hosenball had not been given sufficient information to enable him to meet the charge against him. But it was no ordinary case. It was a case in which national security was involved. When the state was in danger, our own cherished freedoms, and even the rules of natural justice, had to take second place. . . In cases such as the present, where national security was involved, our rules of natural justice have to be modified.'

GLC, Lord Scarman admitted that the term 'economic' could be defined in a variety of ways, 'it is a very useful word, chameleon-like, taking its colour from its surroundings.' Critics of the judiciary's attitude to Labour local authorities pointed out that Lord Scarman and his colleagues chose the free market rather than the social welfare definition of 'economic'.

In its defence, the judiciary might point out:

• That the examples are highly selective, and that examples where the judiciary restrained the over-use of power by both Labour and Conservative Governments abound.

• That the personal political views and backgrounds of judges are irrelevant, since by training and inclination they are concerned with justice and the application of the law as they see it, not politics.

• That Parliament frequently passes laws couched in ambiguous terms. The courts must interpret such statutes, and in doing so they are bound to offend someone.

 Draw up a two column table and in one column note the arguments which have been made claiming that judges are not politically independent, and on the other that they are.

Make notes showing how the Belgrano case (inset) and the Hosenball case (inset) can be used in discussing the political views of judges; and especially their views about the relative importance of justice and state security.

Review – Justice and the law

The notion of 'the rule of law' is closely tied to the idea of justice in our political culture.

Law may be seen as a protection against arbitrary rule or an instrument of class power, depending on your theoretical perspective.

The judiciary in Britain is independent, in the sense that judges are appointed for life, and Governments do not interfere with the proceedings of the courts.

However, the Lord Chancellor, as head of the judiciary and a Cabinet Minister and member of the House of Lords, combines the role of legislator, member of the executive and judge.

Judges have been criticized as being drawn from too narrow a segment of society. This affects, it is claimed, their vital role in 'making law' ('case law') by their decisions.

The system of courts

British courts are distinguished from one another in two ways:

1 *By level of jurisdiction.* Levels of jurisdiction are decided by the seriousness of the crime in criminal cases and the size of the claim in civil cases. The higher the level the higher the status (and pay) of the judge. In this hierarchy the House of Lords is at the top and the magistrates' courts at the bottom.

The levels are indicated in the following diagram.

► *Coroners Court.* This is presided over by an appointed official who is usually legally and medically trained. The coroner sits with or without a jury depending on the kind of case and his or her discretion. Today the main purpose of the coroners court is to decide the cause of death in doubtful cases. A criminal proceeding in the criminal courts may follow a Coroner's verdict of 'unlawful killing', but the coroners court itself has no power to punish. It uses an *inquisitorial* rather than an adversarial method. (See page 293)

► If I rob a bank I may, if caught, be punished by imprisonment – a *criminal matter*. If I enclose a piece of land with my fence which my neighbour claims belongs to him, I may have to give him back the land and pay him compensation – a *civil matter*

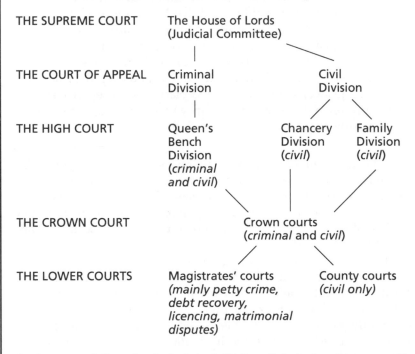

2 *Between civil and criminal jurisdiction. Criminal actions,* usually brought by the Crown Prosecution service, in England and Wales (although it is possible for a private citizen to do so), involve judges as agents of the state hearing charges of crime and deciding upon a suitable punishment. In a sense the state is deciding on behalf of society whether someone has offended against it, and how he or she should pay for it.

Civil actions involve the courts in deciding the rights between one individual or group of individuals or corporate body and another. The remedy in civil cases is not punishment but restitution or recompense by ordering one party to pay damages, or some other form of recompense, e.g. custody of children, handing over of rights to land.

The Courts

The Magistrates' Courts

Magistrates' Courts have both criminal and civil jurisdiction, although most of their work is in the criminal field. Civil jurisdiction is mainly concerned with the recovery of debt, the issuing and revoking of licences locally, matrimonial separation and custody orders.

In criminal matters they have two functions:

• The hearing and determination of *summary offences* – those that do not require a jury – and some offences which may be tried summarily or sent for jury trial. Generally these are less serious offences, including motoring offences, assault and minor theft.

• Conducting preliminary hearings of *indictable offences* which are to be heard in a higher court, to decide whether or not the prosecution has sufficient evidence to justify the accused being committed, on bail or in custody, to appear before a higher court.

Most magistrates are not paid professionals. In some large cities *stipendiary magistrates* (paid lawyers) are appointed, to cope with the volume of work and hear some of the more serious cases, but the rest are 'amateur' volunteers who are paid expenses only, and do the job out of a sense of public duty, for personal satisfaction, the title and honour, or other personal reasons.

The system of unpaid amateur magistrates comes in for periodic criticism, but survives and thrives. Some common criticisms are:

• *Magistrates are drawn from too narrow a section of society.* They are overwhelmingly middle class and White, which does not reflect the social structure of society as a whole or of the bulk of those who appear before them – although recently strenuous efforts have been made to appoint more members of ethnic minorities to the bench.

• *They are too deferential to the police.* Magistrates have been accused of being too willing to believe police evidence.

• *It is not a job for amateurs.* Despite the routine and comparatively trivial nature of some of their work, magistrates often have to make difficult and important decisions on committal proceedings, bail applications, and custodial sentences (they have the power to send defendants to prison for short periods). Some critics say this requires skills and training that most magistrates do not possess.

However it is questionable what calibre of applicant would be forthcoming for the post of professional magistrate, and whether they would be an improvement on lay magistrates. There may be advantages in having magistrates who are carrying out their tasks out of a sense of public duty. Some of the shortcomings of the service could be overcome by more and better training, and a wider and more open selection procedure.

 Summarize the criticisms made of having courts presided over by amateur magistrates. Are there any advantages?

The County Court

County Courts hear smaller civil cases, including actions for damage involving less than a certain amount, and divorce petitions. Small claims may be referred to arbitration to a *small claims court* which has the advantage of speed, informality and cheapness. County Courts are staffed by Circuit Judges. In theory a jury of eight may be employed but this almost never happens.

►There are *Magistrates' Courts* in most sizeable towns. Normally the Bench consists of three lay magistrates or one stipendiary (paid) magistrate.

►*Bail*: a payment (called surety), made by the defendant to the court in a criminal case, upon which the defendant is released until his/her next appearance. Failure to turn up is a criminal offence and would lead to forfeiture of the money. The decision to grant bail or not, and of how much, is made by the magistrate or judge presiding. The alternative is remand in custody.

►After much criticism of their lack of expertise, training of magistrates (an induction course and periodic refreshers) was introduced. This is not, however, legal training. For legal advice, magistrates usually rely on the Clerk of the Court, a permanent official (often a solicitor). Magistrates are appointed by the Lord Chancellor on advice from local committees, whose personnel is kept secret, apparently to avoid 'lobbying'.

►There are County Courts in most large towns.

►*Small claims courts* arbitrate in civil cases involving small sums of money or cases of minor damage or loss. They recommend but have no final jurisdiction. It is for the parties concerned to accept the arbitration.

► There are Crown Courts in all big cities and they hear both civil and criminal cases.

The Crown Court

Crown Courts have jurisdiction over all 'indictable' offences (the more serious crimes, where the trial is by judge and jury) and some non-indictable offences referred from the Magistrates' Courts. They are staffed by High Court Judges, Circuit Judges and Recorders. *High Court Judges* and *Circuit Judges* are full-time and salaried, appointed from barristers of at least ten years standing or Recorders of five years standing. *Recorders* are part-time and salaried judges, appointed from barristers or solicitors of at least ten years standing.

The more serious cases normally come before a High Court Judge. High Court Judges may also hear civil cases, exercising the High Courts' civil jurisdiction outside London.

► The *High Court* is in the Strand, London. The Old Bailey is the criminal wing of the High Court.

High Court Divisions
Queen's Bench
Chancery Division
Family Division

The High Court

The *High Court* together with the Crown Courts and the Court of Appeal constitute the *Supreme Court*. It has virtually unlimited 'original' (meaning 'not appeal') jurisdiction in civil matters. Trial in civil cases is normally by judge only, although in cases of defamation a jury is used ('empanelled').

It is divided into three divisions. The biggest of the three divisions, *Queen's Bench*, deals with civil matters of contract or torts (civil wrongs, e.g. breach of contract, defamation and criminal matters). Additionally it hears appeals, on points of law only, from Magistrates' Courts and Crown Courts. It has, too, jurisdiction over quasi-judicial decisions by local authorities, government bodies, and other corporate bodies, and may issue orders quashing a decision of such a body, order it to carry out its legal duty, or prohibit it from proceeding with something that the court decides is *ultra vires* or unreasonable.

Another division of the High Court is called *Chancery Division*. It has jurisdiction over disputes involving trusts, the redemption and foreclosure of mortgages, contracts concerning land and partnership action, company liquidation, bankruptcy, tax cases and probate disputes.

The *Family Division* has jurisdiction over matrimonial disputes and conflicts involving custody of and access rights to children.

► Master of the Rolls
Lords Justices of Appeal
Lord Chief Justice

The Court of Appeal

As its name implies the *Court of Appeal* has 'appellate' jurisdiction. That is, it hears appeals from lower courts. Appeal may be on the grounds of fact, law, a claim that the original hearing was improperly conducted (e.g. the judge failed to direct the jury properly) or any mixture of those grounds. It has a criminal and civil division.

It is staffed by the *Master of the Rolls* (the President of the Chancery Division), the *Lords Justices of Appeal* and a number of *ex-officio* judges including the Lord Chief Justice, who sits in the criminal division. A Lord Justice of Appeal must be a barrister of at least fifteen years standing. Usually an appeal is heard by three judges in this court.

The Judicial Committee of the House of Lords

The Judicial Committee of the House of Lords is the ultimate *Court of Appeal*. By convention it is staffed from among the *Lord Chancellor, Lords of Appeal in Ordinary* (specially appointed for the purpose) and peers who have judicial qualifications.

Leave to appeal to the Lords must be granted either by the Court of Appeal, from which the appeal will normally come, or by the Lords. A decision of the Lords forms a binding precedent on all lower courts. Until the 1960s the Lords tended to maintain the fiction that its decisions were binding upon itself, but this has been relaxed, and the Lords no longer regard their previous decisions as binding upon themselves.

► See Chapter 8, pages 152–6, for a fuller discussion of the House of Lords.

 Draw up a large version of the diagram on page 290, and annotate it to show the characteristics and functions of the various courts.

CONTROVERSIES AND THE BRITISH JUDICIARY

Some areas of controversy are:

• *The 'adversarial' system*. British cases are conducted as 'X *v*. Y' even when 'X' is the state. The verdict is reached on the basis of evidence and arguments presented in the court, and nowhere else.

It has been argued that in criminal cases Britain would do well to adopt some feature of the 'inquisitorial' system used, for example, in France, in which an examining magistrate interviews all parties, including the police, conducts his or her own investigation, and if he or she decides the case should come to court, presents a dossier on the case.

Some commentators have suggested adoption of this system as protection against convictions based upon thin, partial or fabricated evidence or confessions under pressure. It fits ill with the tradition of the British system, however, since it carries overtones of pre-judgement on the basis of evidence given outside the court.

• *The cost of 'civil action'*. Civil actions in the High Court frequently run up tens of thousands and sometimes hundreds of thousands of pounds in costs. Without some form of 'legal aid', this would mean that redress under the law would only be available for the rich.

► Talking of civil action a former senior judge (Lord Justice Darling) quipped 'The Law is like the Ritz Hotel – open to everyone'. He forbore to add 'who can afford its enormous fees'.

The state-funded legal aid and advice scheme exists to provide assistance to 'litigants' (people in a lawsuit) in civil cases and criminal cases (where it is rarely refused). Its critics contend that because legal-aid applicants in civil cases are 'means tested', persons on higher than average, but not very high, incomes possessing a modest amount of capital are excluded. They don't qualify for aid, but could not afford a lengthy court case.

Also, applicants have to satisfy a local committee that they have a good chance of success. Those paying for their own cases are subject to no such requirement. While it would be wrong to finance frivolous claims from state funds, there are critics who see the committee's criteria as too stringent.

Legal aid is not available for defamation claims (libel and slander). Is this based upon the notion that the poor have no reputation to defame?

Legal aid is not available for appearance before most tribunals (quasi-judicial bodies which make important decisions affecting rights to benefits, and powers to do or not do various things).

 Note how legal action is more easily available to some people than to others.

- *There is no 'administrative division'.* The British judiciary is well equipped and organized to deal with claims made by one individual or group against another individual or group, but not to deal with claims by the individual against the state, i.e. matters belonging to the 'administrative division'.

Since the role of the state in welfare benefits, environmental control, employment law, and many other fields has extended since 1945, so have the number of decisions, ostensibly backed by law, made by state agents. There is, however, no system of administrative courts or body of administrative law to deal expeditiously with the conflicts that inevitably arise, as there is in France. Instead there is a heterogeneous mixture of tribunals, enquiries after tribunals and Ombudsmen established under various statutes which are not part of the judiciary proper.

Some critics see the establishment of an Administrative Division of the High Court as the right response to this development. This will be discussed in more detail later.

 Visit a local Magistrates' Court or a local Crown Court. Try to follow one case through to its conclusion – even though this may mean following it from court to court for a period of months. Write a report in which you express agreement or disagreement with the decisions of the court(s). Give reasons for your agreement or disagreement and assess the strengths and weaknesses of both arguments.

Review – The system of courts

The British system of courts is hierarchical, with Magistrates' Courts at the bottom, and the House of Lords Judicial Committee as the ultimate Court of Appeal at the top.

They are laterally divided between courts hearing civil cases, and those hearing criminal cases.

Criticisms that have been voiced of the British courts include the amateur nature of the Magistrates' Courts, the adversarial system, and the absence of an Administrative Division.

Although the courts have the power of judicial review of administrative action, they do not have the power to review statutes.

THE POLICE

The 43 police forces in England and Wales are charged with the duty of upholding and enforcing the law. Except for the Metropolitan Police Force of Greater London, which comes under the direct control of the Home Office, each force answers to a local police committee consisting two-thirds of councillors from the county council or old metropolitan counties and one-third of magistrates. This responsibility is, however, subject to two major qualifications:

• Police committees receive an annual report, allocate resources, and appoint and dismiss (with the approval of the Home Secretary) their Chief Constable (the most senior policeman). However, they have no control over operational decisions, which includes policing policy and the allocation of resources. These are the province of the Chief Constable.

• The Home Office, although only directly in control of the Metropolitan Police, exercises substantial influence on provincial police forces through their final say in the appointment of Chief Constables, their Inspectorate of Constabulary and the fact that 50 per cent of the cost of policing is borne by a direct Home Office grant.

Contemporary problems

Several senior police officers, including Sir Peter Imbert, Commissioner of the Metropolitan Police, and James Anderton, Chief Constable of Greater Manchester, have made public pronouncements about the role and position of themselves and their officers. Though sometimes conciliatory in tone, these statements have often been defensive and bordering on the angry.

Many senior police officers evidently see themselves and their officers in an invidious position. On the one hand, they claim that the public and some politicians make increasing demands upon them to cope better with what is perceived as a rising tide of crime and disorder. On the other hand, sections of the public and politicians (sometimes the same ones) are bitterly critical of them or overtly hostile to them. Press comments refer to a 'beleaguered' police force.

Some of the factors relevant to this situation are:

• *Larger and better equipped police forces may be distanced from the communities they serve.* The number of police forces in England and Wales has been reduced from 117 in 1963 to 43 in 1991. The greater use of computers, radar, helicopters and cars combined with the larger forces has, distanced the police from the community.

• *Policing of political demonstrations and strikes.* The miners' strike of 1984–5 left a legacy of bitterness between the police and members of the mining communities and other trade unionist and left-wing supporters. The pickets and their supporters claim that, organized on a national basis for the first time, the police exceeded their proper powers in preventing peaceful pickets from going to the areas concerned, displayed blatant partiality and provoked and used extreme violence. Police counter-accusations included deliberate provocation

▶ Now that the metropolitan counties have been abolished, police committees in those areas consist of councillors from the councils of the metropolitan districts.

▶ So far there have been no women Chief Constables.

▶ The police committees of Manchester, Merseyside and South Yorkshire have publicly clashed with their Chief Constables over policy and operational matters.

▶ One of the worst riots on the British mainland happened in 1985 at the Broadwater Farm estate in Tottenham, London. Three men were convicted of the murder of PC Blakelock who died of 43 wounds incurred whilst he was trying to protect a fire engine.
In 1991 the convicted men had their appeals against conviction upheld by the Court of Appeal, on the grounds that the police had fabricated the damning parts of interview notes. Interview notes were the only evidence against them.

►Similar sets of accusations and counter-accusations have surrounded the picketing of the *Sun* newspaper offices in Wapping, a student demonstration at Manchester University in 1985 and the treatment of anti-Poll Tax protesters in London in 1990.

► In July 1991 the six people convicted of bombing a pub in Birmingham were released on the grounds that both police methods and forensic evidence used to convict them were 'unsafe'.

► What is the role of the police?

► In 1986 the Police Complaints Authority dealt with 15,865 complaints. In 12,505 it decided there was not enough evidence to bring disciplinary charges.

and physical intimidation of workers trying to cross picket lines. They deny political partiality and claim that they were trying to uphold the law in preventing violence and intimidation.

• *Dubious convictions*. The decision to free the 'Guildford Four', convicted and imprisoned on faulty forensic evidence of a bombing, and the suspension pending inquiry of the whole of the West Midlands Serious Crimes Squad in the face of evidence of fabricated confessions leading to convictions, have led to demands for more thorough investigations of the internal workings of the police.

• *Accusations of racial bias*. Black and Asian community leaders consistently accuse local police officers of discrimination against ethnic minorities, in the form of day-to-day harassment, particularly of teenage males, failure to follow up racist attacks, and arrests on petty charges. While not denying that a few of their officers have racist views, senior officers point to the provocative behaviour of young males, Black and White, in some areas, and the lack of co-operation with the police in some inner-city areas.

Suggested reforms

Which police reforms you support depends to a great extent upon how you perceive the role of the police.

Community leaders in urban working-class areas, and some on the political left, might see them as responding to the needs and wishes of local communities. A view from the right might see the police as maintaining law and order by whatever means necessary within the law, and staying away from close involvement with 'political' community groups. Liberals might press for maintenance of their traditional role, but with greater accountability and openness to outside investigation.

Among many reforms suggested are:

• *More community policing*. A return to the 'bobby on the beat', on foot or on bicycle, making face-to-face contact with and earning the trust of local people.

• *Democratic accountability*. Local councils to be given greater control over their police forces, in matters of policy and operation.

• *Recruitment from ethnic minorities* – still (1991) grossly under-represented in police forces.

• *Strengthening independent scrutiny*. The 'Police Complaints Authority' (independent of the police force), has statutory authority to hear complaints from members of the public concerning the police. It is criticized because, although the Authority is independent, evidence depends upon internal investigations which comes up against the unwillingness of police officers to 'shop' one another.

• *Recruitment of an 'officer' class*. Some senior police officers have suggested that university graduates should be recruited directly into an 'officer trainee grade', with accelerated promotion and little or no requirement to serve 'on the beat'. Other police officers have reacted with horror, maintaining that all police officers should experience the 'sharp end' and fearing a gap between senior officers and those in the field. Proposers of the 'officer' class claim that it will bring much needed increases in the quality of management.

Whatever the solutions, the problem of a wide gap between the police and some of the communities they are supposed to protect is widely acknowledged, not least by some senior police officers. The prospect of an inward-looking police force facing hostile communities led the Chief Inspector of Constabulary to say in his 1990 report, 'Open-mindedness and the will to listen to the point of view of others are essential qualities for all police officers who have to interact with a complex society'.

 Effective policing depends on the consent of the majority of people to be policed. Make notes summarizing the contemporary problems of policing and suggested solutions. Do so in terms of factors causing mistrust of the police and ways in which reforms might overcome this.

THE STATE AND THE CITIZEN

Charter 88, a pressure group campaigning for a Bill of Rights and a written constitution, stated in an advertisement for members (1990), 'The intensification of authoritarian rule in the United Kingdom has only recently begun'. It went on to say, 'The time has come to demand civil and human rights in the United Kingdom'.

Charter 88's 'constitutionalist' remedy is largely discussed in Chapter 3. What I propose to discuss here is the evidence for its contention that the state is reducing and eroding individual freedom and rights.

In the liberal democratic model, the law is supposed to protect those rights and freedoms. Critics would focus on the following areas: the expanded role of the state, the absence of guaranteed rights, the piecemeal nature of the means of appeal, and official secrecy.

The expanded role of the state

In response to the 'post-war consensus' on the role of government in social welfare, environmental control and a more interventionist role in the economy (see Chapter 9), Governments gave themselves more and more decision-making power.

The absence of guaranteed rights

As we have already seen (Chapter 3) the absence of a written constitution combined with the theoretical sovereignty of Parliament means that a Government that controls Parliament can change the law to suit itself, unfettered by any constitution or bill of rights. So long as there exists a rough consensus about what Governments ought to be doing – as in the 1940s, 1950s and 1960s – this may not present much of a problem. When, however, the consensus begins to break up, individuals and groups are more likely to feel that their basic rights are being invaded by Government, and that the absence of a constitutional remedy is more serious.

In recent years the Government has passed laws restricting the spending powers of local authorities, removing some of their

► Is the state reducing and eroding freedoms and rights of individual citizens and groups?

► The absence of guaranteed rights means the absence of rights which cannot be legally taken away by a particular government. Of course common law and statute law contain a wealth of rights for individuals and for minority groups, women or handicapped people. Some such right are now underpinned by the law of the European Community, which make it more difficult, although not impossible, for a British government to legislate them away.

► The European Court of Human Rights sits at Strasbourg and is *not* the same as the European court of Justice, for which see page 246, Chapter 12.

► Among other items the European Court of Human Rights has criticized interference with a free press (the thalidomide case against the Distiller's Company); the treatment of internees in Northern Ireland; the absence of the right of prisoners to correspond with their lawyers and MPs; the British immigration laws which did not allow women immigrant residents the right to bring their husbands to Britain; the legal protection afforded to mental patients; and corporal punishment in schools.

discretion and some of their functions and abolishing one metropolitan layer of local authorities altogether, in the face of bitter opposition from some local authorities. The Government has put restrictions on the rules and activities of trade unions, with the prospect of sequestration and financial ruin, in the face of fierce opposition from the unions. Clashes between some inner-city communities and the police, and between demonstrators and the police, have also provoked bitterness.

Leaving aside the rights and wrongs in these matters, there is no constitutional definition of the powers and rights of local authorities, no right to strike, picket or organize in a trade union, and no right of assembly or demonstration to which to appeal in these circumstances.

The nearest thing we have to a definition of rights stems from the European Convention on Human Rights. If (and only if) a British citizen fails to obtain a remedy in the British courts, he or she may appeal to the *European Court of Human Rights*, provided the complaint has first been considered by the European Commission and is found admissible. It may be significant that more complaints are made by British citizens than by any other nationality.

In most cases, Britain responded to the European Court by changing the practice criticized, but unlike other signatories, she has not incorporated the Convention into her domestic law.

 What are the European Convention of Human Rights and the European Court of Human Rights? What is Britain's relationship with them?

The piecemeal nature of means of appeal

In some cases appeal against a decision of the state may lie in the courts. This is by the process of *judicial review*, in which the court may pronounce on whether an action by a public authority is *ultra vires*, unreasonable or unlawful. Nevertheless, judicial review as a remedy is strictly limited. It will not normally question the wisdom of a policy or a decision, or assess the balance of private and public interest. It will only consider whether the powers to act existed, and whether they were exercised lawfully.

To some extent, *administrative tribunals* set up by various statutes, have sought to fill the gap left by the courts. Appointed by the Minister, usually with a lawyer as chairman, these are quasi-courts which can make judgments on appeals against decisions on social security benefits, unfair dismissal, decisions of the Inland Revenue, and other matters covered by statutory tribunals. They have the advantage of speed, cheapness and relative informality. However, tribunals do not achieve the consistency and coherence provided by the courts: procedure varies according to the terms and constitution of the tribunal. They may give reasons for their decisions but are not obliged to do so, so their decisions cannot form the basis for a body of law as do those of the courts. While some areas of government decision-making are covered by tribunals, others provide no such remedy.

Some statutes, particularly those regarding town and country planning and the building of nuclear power stations, provide for *public inquiries* before a decision is made. Public inquiries, however, make no final decision; they advise the Minister, who is obliged to *consider* their advice but not to follow it.

Because there were vast areas of decision-taking that were not covered by tribunals and inquiries, the Wilson Government in 1967 created the *Parliamentary Commissioner for Administration* (commonly referred to as the *ombudsman*), with a brief to enquire into complaints of maladministration by central government departments (nationalised industries were added later), but excluding the armed forces, the police, the Foreign Service, the post office and the security services. Complaints to the ombudsman may be received only from MPs (who may pass on complaints from members of the public).

► *Ombudsman*

Although the ombudsman has the power to examine documents and call witnesses, he/she cannot initiate an inquiry. Nor can he/she take action against offending officials. He/she reports back to the MP who made the complaint, and to a select committee.

The ombudsman's terms of reference only allow him/her to inquire into 'injustice arising from *maladministration*', not, you may note, injustice arising from a bad policy, or from a decision which was properly taken.

The ombudsman has since had some notable successes: for example, as the result of his/her investigations, the payment of rebates by the Inland Revenue has been speeded up, the factory inspectorate has been improved, and a scheme of compensation for people who book holidays with firms which fail before they can take the holiday has been introduced. Ombudsmen for the Health Service and for local government have been introduced, to whom complaints can be made direct, although the Health Service ombudsman cannot inquire into matters of clinical judgement or professional medical competence.

Conway v. Rimmer

Since Conway *v*. Rimmer (1968) the courts have demonstrated a wider view of their powers to decide whether the word of government departments or local authorities should be accepted without examination. A probationary police constable was cleared of a charge of malicious prosecution against his Superintendent, during which case the Home Secretary claimed that production of the constable's confidential report would be contrary to the public interest, as it belonged to a class of documents which should not be made public.

Changing an earlier ruling, the Lords declared that they had the power to decide whether the documents should be disclosed, and having read them, ordered disclosure. As we have seen in the case of Secretary of State for Education *v*. Tameside MBC, the Lords decided that they, not the Minister, should decide whether the action of the authority was reasonable, see pages 27–8.

► Since this was written the Major Government has proposed a *Citizens' Charter* which would give people rights to specified levels and qualities of service. However the Charter covers only National Health, nationalized industry and local government services and not services provided by central government.

► In introducing an unsuccessful Private Member's Bill to replace the Official Secrets Act with a Freedom of Information Act, Clement Freud in 1979 commented, 'If one wants to find out how to look after one's children in a nuclear emergency, one cannot because it is an official secret; if one wants to know what noxious gases are being emitted from a factory chimney opposite one's house, one cannot because it is an official secret. A man who applies for a job as a gardener at Hampton Court was asked to sign form E47 in case he gave away information about watering begonias. What is worse, if someone is good enough to tell one, then one is an accessory to a crime. My contention is that Section 2 gives the Attorney General more power than a bad man should have or a good man should need.'

Useful though they are, the ombudsmen remain on the fringe of administrative law. Their powers and scope are severely limited and most members of the public do not know of their existence.

As has already been suggested, this piecemeal collection of remedies against the misuse of state powers is not much of a substitute for a system of 'administrative law' with an accompanying system of 'administrative courts' which would develop a coherent set of principles. It might be argued that such a system would be expensive, legalistic and cumbersome. However, it seems unlikely that the vast area of potential conflict between state and individual could be covered by anything less.

 Make notes on the piecemeal nature of administrative law in Britain – that is the area of law which allows for the decisions of government agencies to be challenged.

Official secrecy

An important pre-requisite of a successful liberal democracy is that the citizen knows what those in power are doing, why they are doing what they are doing, and what they intend to do in the future. Without such knowledge, the citizen cannot properly judge the government or pursue a complaint against it.

Until 1989, the statutory basis for the secrecy of government information was the *Official Secrets Act* (1911) and especially the 'catch all' Section 2 of the Act, which had the effect of making the release or acceptance of any information about a government department an offence. In theory, passing on a copy of the menu in the Home Office canteen could be cause for prosecution under the Act.

The *Fulton Report* of 1968 (see Chapter 10) criticized the 'inward-

The Sachsenhausen case

The distinction between maladministration and policy arose in the first year of the ombudsman's operation in the Sachsenhausen case. A number of ex-prisoners in a concentration camp claimed compensation from a fund set up to compensate the victims of Nazi war crimes. They had been in a kind of annexe to the Sachsenhausen Camp where, they claimed, they were treated as badly as prisoners in the main camp. The Foreign Office refused compensation, on the grounds that the applicants had not been imprisoned in one of the camps which qualified for compensation. Initial reactions to the ombudsman's inquiry were to deny maladministration, since the officials had been quite properly following an agreed rule: that only imprisonment in certain camps qualified one for compensation. The ombudsman's insistence that if, in too rigidly following a rule, you cause injustice, then there is maladministration, eventually won the day. The ombudsman ruled that there was maladministration if injustice was caused by too rigidly following a rule.

looking' secrecy of British Government. The Conservative Government came into office in 1983 pledged to reform the secrecy law. The Labour Government of 1974–79 took over with a firm manifesto commitment to replace the Official Secrets Act with a Freedom of Information Act, which would reverse the principle of the Official Secrets Act – the public would have a right to all information except some protected categories, and the burden of arguing that a piece of information should *not* be released should be on the Government, tested in court.

Despite this, and a growing barrage of criticism of the Act from MPs and journalists, the Act remained on the statute book (i.e. law) until 1989. What seems to have inspired the 1989 Official Secrets Act is not the acceptance of the principle of freedom of information (which the Act does not embody) but a number of prosecutions under the Act, or attempts to stop publication by the civil law device of an 'injunction', which were either unsuccessful from the Government point of view, or when successful, attracted a barrage of criticism and ridicule.

The main point made by the many critics of these prosecutions is that in none of the cases was the information involved strategically important or likely to give assistance to a potential enemy of Britain.

The conclusion was that the Government pursued the cases with such zeal to discourage future 'leaks' which might be embarrassing rather than dangerous. It was also pointed out that Section 2 allowed ministers and civil servants to 'manage' the news more effectively by selective leaks of their own.

The *1989 Official Secrets Act*, which has replaced that of 1911, does a little to placate the critics. The Government, however, claimed it as a liberalizing measure, since it specifies which categories of information would be covered by criminal charges against disclosure, thereby 'de-criminalizing' the remainder. For some areas of information, disclosure will be an *absolute* offence: the prosecution will only have to prove that disclosure took place – this applies to the security and intelligence services. For others some jeopardy has to be demonstrated.

In some respects the new Act is tighter in its protection than its predecessor. A defendant cannot plead public interest or that disclosure was necessary to reveal corruption, dishonesty or inefficiency. Publication of information in the categories covered by the Act is an offence. There will be need to show that any document changed hands.

What Clive Ponting refers to as 'the culture of secrecy' (*Secrecy in Britain*, 1990) remains. It was only recently that the existence of bodies like MI5, the internal security service, and SIS (operating abroad), was even acknowledged. Critics claim that they still remain shrouded in far more secrecy than is necessary for their functional efficiency.

Civil servants, though they may not work under the threat of criminal prosecution for revealing information in many areas, still work under the threat of the sack.

The 'D notice' system of warning newspapers against publication of certain types of information still exists. The flow of public information is still carefully controlled, aided by the 'lobby' system in which

Official secrets

'Official secrets' cases which led to the new 1989 Act included:

The Crossman Diaries. The unsuccessful attempt to prevent publication of the Crossman Diaries, by injunction, on the grounds that they revealed positions taken by Cabinet Ministers in Cabinet.

The 'ABC' Trial (1987). Aubrey, Berry and Campbell tape-recorded an interview involving Berry, a former corporal in signals intelligence. The information given was publicly available in the *Civil Service Yearbook* and the Regimental magazine. The defendants, technically guilty, were given token sentences after a long and expensive trial.

The trial of Sarah Tisdall. Tisdall, a clerk in the Foreign Secretary's office, was in 1983 sentenced to six months in prison for supplying the *Guardian* with documents giving details of the Government's plans for handling press and Parliamentary statements about the arrival of US Cruise Missiles at Greenham Common. She later justified her action by reference to what she saw as the immorality of the Government trying to avoid public and Parliamentary accountability until after the missiles were in place.

The trial of Clive Ponting. See page 288

The Spycatcher affair. Beginning in September 1985, the Government made laborious, expensive and eventually unsuccessful efforts to prevent the publication of a book written by Peter Wright, a former MI5 agent. It contained some anecdotal material about 'bugging' and telephone tapping, the claim that MI5 agents were involved in a plan to overthrow the Wilson Government, and a thinly supported case for the former head of MI5 having been a Soviet agent.

accredited journalists are given 'non-attributable' briefings, provided they co-operate in not attributing the information to any source, and not directly quoting 'background' briefings.

 How does the 1989 Official Secrets Act differ from the Act it replaced?

► The *Independent*, the *Guardian* and the *Scotsman* have all withdrawn from the lobby.

The arguments for and against secrecy

The arguments for secrecy rest on:

• *Ministerial and collective responsibility.* Justification for keeping secret cabinet minutes, Cabinet committee minutes, and the details of discussions between ministers and civil servants rests on the idea that discussions up to the point of public commitment should remain confidential. Until a minister or a Government is prepared to take responsibility for a policy or a decision, it should be able to engage in wide-ranging discussion without the danger of being identified with a view that it is not prepared whole-heartedly to support. The efficiency of collective responsibility would be nullified if ministers were publicly identified with different points of view on a policy which was supposed to be that of the whole Government.

• *Free-ranging pre-policy discussion would be prejudiced by premature disclosure.* It is argued that policy-makers would be reluctant to 'try on' various ideas in reaching policy conclusions if they knew that their discussions were going to be reported and possibly misrepresented in the media.

• *Some categories of information should be protected.* There exist some types of information where the whole category of information should be protected, not because this or that revelation would be harmful in itself, but because knowledge that revelation might take place would prejudice the area of activity covered by the category. Information about police informers is an obvious example. The Government used this argument (among others) to justify its attempt to prevent the sale of *Spycatcher*.

Defenders of the British state would claim that the liberalizing reformers of *Charter 88* exaggerate its authoritarian nature to suit their purposes. Defenders point to the freedom of speech, action, movement, assembly and organization compared with single-party states, the protection afforded by the fact that public bodies must stay within the law, the sovereignty of Parliament which constrains Governments, and the existence of countless pressure groups and points of view.

Still, the critics would argue, the proper comparison is not with the former regimes of Eastern Europe, but with other developed liberal democracies in North America and Europe, where the individual is in a stronger position when confronting the state.

(ACT) Discussion/essay question

'It is well past the time for Britain to have a Freedom of Information Act'. Explain why someone might take this view, and give your own assessment of whether Britain needs such an Act.

  Draw up a two column table and in one column write notes on the arguments for state secrecy, and in the other for freedom of information.

Review – The state and the citizen

Critics of the extent of state power in Britain focus upon:

The expanded role of the State accompanied by the break down of the 'consensus' of the 1950s and 1960s.

The absence of guaranteed rights, combined with the sovereignty of Parliament and a Government with a large majority.

The fact that Britain has been taken to the European Court of Human Rights more often than any other country.

The piecemeal nature of possible remedies – courts, tribunals, ombudsmen – and the absence of any coherent system of administrative law.

The Government's apparent obsession with secrecy, as revealed by a number of cases in the 1970s and 1980s, and its failure to replace the 1911 Official Secrets Act with a Freedom of Information Act.

Review – Defence of the state

Defenders of the British state argue:

That it compares favourably with many states in the degree of freedom of movement, expression and organization that exists.

That the sovereignty of Parliament and the rule of law prevent Governments from becoming too autocratic.

That secrecy is necessary in some areas to support ministerial and collective responsibility, and efficient administration and policy-making.

CHAPTER SUMMARY

1 Law, in the liberal democratic model, is seen as the source of authority and an important provider of justice.

2 Although the British judiciary is independent in the sense that judges are appointed for life, the Lord Chancellor (head of the judiciary) is an elected politician and member of the Government.

3 Judges have been criticized as being drawn from too narrow a segment of society.

4 The hierarchy of courts in Britain is divided by level of jurisdiction, based on the seriousness of the case, and between civil and criminal jurisdiction.

5 Criticisms of the British system of courts have included the 'amateurism' of the Magistrates' Courts, the adversarial system, and the absence of an administrative division.

6 The British police forces have been criticized for taking a 'political' role in events such as the miner's strike and the Wapping dispute. Their defence is that they are being asked to deal with problems without the 'consensus' of society.

7 Suggested reforms of the police range from more local democratic control to an 'officer class' entrant system.

8 Critics of Britain's system of law and justice point to the absence of guaranteed rights, secrecy, and Britain's frequent appearance as a defendant at the European Court of Human Rights.

9 Secrecy is defended as being necessary for good Government, and attacked as being used to cover up mistakes and wrong-doing by Government. The new Official Secrets Act 1989, while less vague and wide ranging than the previous 1911 Act, creates categories of criminal offence and removes the defence of 'public interest'.

STIMULUS MATERIAL

The stimulus material for this chapter is an article from the *Independent* about the role of judges in assessing the legality of the actions of government. Read the article and answer the following questions:

1 How does the article suggest that British judges use the 'three broad grounds of challenge' (paragraph 7) to make 'political decisions'?

2 What problems might arise from British judges adopting the principle of 'proportionality' put forward in paragraph 12?

3 What alternative reforms to those suggested in the article might be put forward as a means of achieving more effective redress against bad state decisions?

4 Why do you think British judges resist the idea of testing cases against the principles of the European Convention on Human Rights (paragraph 13)?

5 On what grounds did a group of local authorities challenge the legality of Poll-Tax capping? What was the result?

CASE WILL SHOW JUDGES' VIEW OF THEIR POWERS

1 Twenty-five years ago the idea of courts adjudicating on the legality of a government minister's use of powers given by an Act of Parliament was anathema to most judges. That view has certainly changed, but next week's challenge to the legality of Poll Tax capping, a move going to the root of government policy, represents the classic test of judges' attitudes to their own powers.

2 The right to question the governmental or administrative action by judicial review is now possible in a host of contexts – immigration, housing, social security, prisons, health, education, planning, legal aid and, where public power is involved, commercial contexts too.

3 But the courts' role, they have repeatedly emphasised, is to scrutinise the legality of decisions, not to substitute their own views on the merits of the case.

4 Their job, as the House of Lords has put it, is to judge the lawfulness, not the wisdom, of the decision. Still less is it to pass judgement on its political rectitude.

5 But while British judges are skilled at camouflaging their actions in the language of strict legal rule, the notion that they no not make 'political' decisions, certainly in the broad sense, is largely a myth.

6 Beneath the metaphysical gymnastics and observance of constitutional niceties, there is a reservoir of judicial power. The upshot can be exciting or dangerous, depending on your viewpoint, imaginative or disappointing, depending on what is at stake.

7 There are three broad grounds of challenge: that a decision-maker acted illegally, or beyond his or her powers; that the decision was 'unreasonable' in the sense of being 'irrational', or, as the late Lord Diplock, the former Law Lord, described it, 'so outrageous in its defiance of logic or of accepted moral standards that no sensible person ... could have arrived at it'; or, there had been 'procedural impropriety', a breach of natural justice, say.

8 Richard Gordon, a public law barrister, said: 'If you get a "right facts" type case, often the one-off challenge without profound policy or practical implications and the court is basically in sympathy with you ... it will apply the reasonableness test flexibly.'

9 'If it is a "wrong facts" type case – a "political" case or one where the courts want to stamp down the amount of judicial review available, it will apply the test in a very strict sense.'

10 Another weapon in the armoury of the conservative judge, Mr Gordon points out, is the discretionary nature of judicial review remedies. 'The court can refuse a remedy using a completely inherent, non-statutory discretion. It is used quite a lot.'

11 As the law now stands, judges have plenty of weaponry to enable them to be restrictive but a number of lawyers believe they have failed to develop principles aimed at improving the quality of decision-making. The 'unreasonableness' ground of challenge has nothing to with reasonableness as understood by most individuals and amounts to having to show that a minister or official has, as one judge once put it, 'gone haywire'. It is now being criticized by a growing number of leading public lawyers as an inadequate check on bad decisions.

12 Reformers are pressing for British judges to adopt the principle of 'proportionality' that is applied in European courts. This would require judges to be satisfied that means used are proportionate to aims, that the exercise of power was a reasonable response to events, that a minister had not taken a sledgehammer to crack a nut. David Pannick, another public law specialist, said: 'It would amount to a half-way house between giving a right of appeal against administrative decisions and the present

approach, which often does not enable courts to deal with manifest injustices.'

13   The stock response to pressure for change is that too much judicial intervention will cause governments to frame powers so that they are not judicially reviewable. Even conservative-minded lawyers are concerned, however, that judges interpret their powers too narrowly. Many deplore their steadfast refusal to accept that the legality of interference with individual rights should be tested against the principles of the European Convention on Human Rights and their failure to develop a general duty to give reasons for administrative action, to enable individuals to divine whether an official may have crossed the line of legality.

14   Other gaps in the law include the shortness of the three-month time limit for seeking judicial review. And in last year's review over whether the remains of the Rose Theatre should be scheduled as a

15   national monument, the court ruled that no-one had legal 'standing' to bring the case. Mr Gordon said: 'It raises the spectre of legally unmeritorious decisions being legally unchallengeable. It strikes me as a classic judicial weapon for reversing the trend of liberalism. It is probably the most dangerous decision of the decade.'

The Independent
30 May 1990

Now you have completed this chapter, look back at the objectives and check that you have achieved each of them.

Further reading: Chapter 14

Brazier R. and Street H. (eds). 1984. *De Smith's Constitutional and Administrative Law* (4th edition). Harmondsworth: Penguin. Good reference work for questions of constitutional law.

Griffith J.A.G. 1977. *The Politics of the Judiciary*. London: Fontana. Challenges the view that our judges are wonderful.

Miliband R. 1982. *Capitalist Democracy in Britain*. Oxford: OUP. Marxist perspective on power and the function of the state.

Ponting, C. 1990. *Secrecy in Britain*. Oxford: Blackwell. Biased but interesting view of secrecy from someone who suffered from the workings of the Official Secrets Act.

Reiner R. 1985. *The Politics of the Police*. Hemel Hempstead: Wheatsheaf. Useful discussion of the police and the community.

Savage S. 1989. 'Crime control, the law and the community' *Talking politics*, Vol. 2, No. 1. Examination of the relationship between politicians, the police and the political climate.

Appendix: Revision and Examinations

REVISION

In an ideal world you would be reviewing and revising your work from the second day of the course. But we don't live in an ideal world and most people leave revision until the last few weeks before the examination. Nevertheless if you have taken some of the advice offered earlier you will have been maintaining good easily retrievable notes and file-cards throughout your course and so be off to a flying start when revision time comes.

Work out a revision timetable, with realistic learning objectives at each stage – you will find many of the chapter objectives in this book useful, but you will have to make up some for yourself.

Use past papers, but NOT to question-spot. Question-spotting is a bad mistake. Use past papers to identify which broad topics and themes the examiner usually asks about and revise them carefully. Analyse past papers for their commands. Make sure you know the differences between 'Describe' and 'Account for', 'List' and 'Analyse' and so on.

What you MUST NOT do is to revise actual questions and prepare model answers. Model questions rarely come up!

Ask yourself questions and answer them. Try to think like an examiner. As you approach different topics ask yourself, 'What questions could the examiner ask me about this?'

Revise actively. Make notes and summaries all the time. Make notes of notes and summaries of notes and notes of summaries. Annotate your notes with notes from a textbook and then produce a tidy version. Convert notes in continuous text to notes in diagram or table format, or vice versa.

As your revision proceeds try to reduce the whole course to a series of trigger words and phrases – just enough to jog your memory.

Practise writing answers under the pressure of time. How much can you get down in the time available? Practise writing answers of that length.

Work in regular sessions, with breaks every hour, but get used to working for three hours at a time before a longer break.

THE EXAMINATION

Think of the Examination as an opportunity for you to give a performance, with an audience of one – the examiner. You are displaying your knowledge, understanding and skills to someone who wants to applaud you.

MAKE SURE YOU KNOW HOW YOU WILL BE EXAMINED. How many exams? How long? What choice of questions? Will there be compulsory questions: essay questions, data-response questions, short answer questions? – all of these require different skills and different ways of revising. Establish, probably with the help of your tutor, just how much of your syllabus you should revise. Check what are usually called the 'assessment objectives' which are printed in the syllabus document produced by your examination board.

READ THE CHIEF EXAMINER'S REPORTS for previous years. These are available from the Examination Board, and should be in your college library. Note well what these reports say. Not only does the Chief Examiner have experience of the mistakes of thousands of students, s/he actually decides what is mistaken and what is correct.

TAKING AN ACTIVE APPROACH to revision is essential. Passive revision, i.e. sitting reading through notes and textbooks is both boring and ineffective. Revise with friends, discussing questions and trying to explain things to each other. Give yourself some time off, especially on the day before the examinations start.

EXAMINERS WANT YOU TO DO WELL. They are instructed to mark your work by giving you credit for everything you do properly, not to penalize you for your mistakes. Your marks start at zero and go on up whenever you do something right. The examiner is looking for opportunities to 'reward positive achievements', so supply plenty of these and make it easy for the examiner to find them. Examination answers are vehicles for you to display your achievement.

IF YOU SUFFER BADLY FROM NERVES, learn to relax through the use of deep breathing techniques. Don't take pills, except under medical supervision. Don't drink alcohol before an examination. It relaxes the wrong parts of your brain.

The most common reason for candidates failing to get the marks they should is not that they lack the knowledge or skill, but because they ignore the golden rule. They usually deal with the right topic but they don't 'discuss' or 'compare and contrast' or 'outline' or 'describe' or they don't 'give the reasons for' or 'explain and account for' when this is what the examiner has asked them to do. Or they only answer part of a multi-part question.

Presentation and layout are important, because they should help the examiner to find your good points easily. Use short sentences and paragraphs.

Here are some key points about exams:

- make sure you know when and where the examination will be held. If it is in an unfamiliar place, try to visit it beforehand and check your travel arrangements;

- the evening before, make sure that you have all the pens and pencils and other equipment you will need;

- arrive in good time, but don't stand around chatting. Go for a walk to loosen up and get the oxygen flowing to the brain;

- when the examination starts, read through the whole paper (or those parts which relate to your options);

- do NOT start writing straight away, but settle down, get the feel of the paper, check the instructions and find the questions you feel OK about. Take the first few minutes and:

- say to yourself for example 'I've got to answer question one, and one question from section B and ...'. A distressingly large number of candidates fail because they don't follow the instructions;

- choose your probable questions, but don't 'firm up' your choice at this early stage;

- the marks allocated to each question or parts of each question are a rough guide to how much you should write on each. If two marks are allocated, make two good points and stop. You will get no more than two marks however many brilliant points you make;

- draw up a rough timetable for yourself – 'by ten thirty I should have finished the first question' etc.;

- start your first question. Now for the golden rule of all exams:

  ANSWER THE QUESTION SET:
  DO WHAT THE EXAMINER TELLS YOU TO DO.

- For all but very short answers make a plan.

- THINK all the time. Don't just try to remember things, but think about how to use and apply what you know TO THE QUESTION SET.

- Answer the number of questions required. You are guaranteeing a disappointing result if you don't.

- Don't overrun your time on a particular question. It takes much longer to get a few more marks at the end of one answer than the first few at the beginning of another.

- Take rests during the exam. Loosen up physically; breathe, stretch, shut your eyes while you are thinking.

- Leave time for checking and polishing your answers. A single additional mark could mean a higher grade.

GOOD LUCK

Index

A New Introduction to British Politics

Peter Madgwick

Stanley Thornes (Publishers) Ltd

Originally published under the title *Introduction to British Politics* in 1970 by
Hutchinson Education
Second edition 1976
Reprinted 1979, 1981
Reprinted with revisions 1982, 1983
Third edition 1984
Reprinted 1985, 1986, 1987

Reprinted 1990 by
Stanley Thornes (Publishers) Ltd
Reprinted 1991, 1992

This edition published in 1994 by
Stanley Thornes (Publishers) Ltd
Ellenborough House
Cheltenham
Glos. GL50 1YD
United Kingdom

A catalogue record for this book is available from the British Library.

ISBN 0 7487 1592 4

Typeset by GCS, Leighton Buzzard, Beds
Printed and bound in Great Britain by Redwood Books, Wilts.

Contents

Preface

This new edition, the fourth, has been completely revised and mostly rewritten; it is well over half as long again as the previous edition. This reflects a fuller treatment of some topics, including ministers, departments and central policy-making, elections and the media, and entirely new chapters on the European Community, non-central government and the courts and the constitution. Many well-loved (by the author at least) extracts have gone, but a few have been retained.

The new edition also reflects some changing perspectives on the study of politics and government and on political activity itself. In particular, there is less confidence about our understanding of the political system and the political values which pervade it and perhaps less confidence too in the effectiveness and general beneficence of political activity.

The general approach of the book, which has proved acceptable to students and teachers, is little changed. It includes illustrative documents, exercises, short assessments of particular topics and issues, and, for this edition, brief explanations of some political concepts and additional case material. The range of information available to the student of politics is now immense; it is hoped that the gathering and focusing of material presented here will assist students to select and make sense of the flow of material, and engage in critical study.

At a time when many of the characters in the drama have been knighted or ennobled, it has seemed sensible and not, it is hoped, discourteous, to avoid 'as he then was', 'as she now is', etc., and to call people by their original names.

A book of this kind owes much to discussions over many years with colleagues and students in Aberystwyth and Oxford and with speakers, teachers and students participating in the excellent conferences of the Politics Association. A word of appreciation is also due to the politicians, members of an under-appreciated profession (like teachers), who do their best, most of the time, to work the British system of democratic government.

Finally I offer my thanks to Olive Madgwick for support and assistance over many years, and to the staff of the publishers and to the editor, Merle Thompson, for their professional skills, generously bestowed on a long and complex manuscript.

P J M
Oxford
November 1993

How to use this book

This book differs from most other textbooks: as well as a straightforward exposition and analysis of the subject, it also contains documents and exercises and some case material. These are designed to encourage the reader to think about the topics for herself or himself and to learn by understanding, not by rote. The book may be taken as a complete text or in individual chapters; or the reader may find specific documents and exercises of value on their own.

The documents are mainly extracts from biographies, commentaries and official publications. They present evidence in a form which may encourage independent thinking. Similarly, the exercises, many of them based on documents, invite readers to formulate their own judgements and assessments.

At the end of each chapter there is a guide to exercises, which suggests answers or advice on possible answers. Then comes a section of assessments, which are short essays on particular themes and problems arising from the chapter. Finally, there are brief explanations of some key concepts and further case material.

The exercises are mainly not of the kind to which an exact answer can be given. They should set the reader thinking and, briefly, writing. He or she may then look up the guide, but should treat the answers given there as a point of departure and not as the final and correct word. They are matters for argument and may provide opportunities to justify conflicting points of view. While it is not cheating to look up the guide, there is obviously much to be said for the reader's thinking about the exercises to begin with. Generally, the exercises and their suggested answers should be read and understood before proceeding with the text, as they are part of the development of the argument.

No textbook on its own is satisfactory for advanced study, and readers are advised to go on from this book to deepen their knowledge of the subject. Most of the books and publications quoted or referred to in the text are suitable for further study, and there is also a select list of books for further study. All these are listed at the end of the book.

Prologue:
The nature of politics and political study

The necessity of politics

Politics is not a wholly respectable word. We are inclined to associate it with excessive partisanship, with devious plotting and unholy alliances, with dishonesty, even, or at least, a lack of straightforwardness. We accuse the other side of 'playing politics', or of 'dragging politics into' an issue which was properly above politics (politics being regarded as a 'low' activity). These pejorative phrases do indicate some of the defects to which political activity tends, but it seems unfair to characterise the whole of an activity by its defects. This is prejudice and no more desirable than the prejudice which characterises a favoured activity like football by all its best qualities, ignoring the defects. We need, for both politics and football, a balanced view.

Such a view must emphasise the necessity of political activity: we simply cannot manage without it. Politics is about society's conflicts and disagreements and it is hardly imaginable that these should not exist. Some small groups with narrow objectives may be relatively harmonious. But even, say, the parochial church council or the Second XI selection committee have their disagreements – young Smith will not accept that Y is badly off form and should be dropped; old Smith will not accept that letting the parish hall for Saturday night gigs is a (fairly) harmless way of promoting community life and paying off the mortgage. That smaller and allegedly naturally harmonious group the family, is notoriously riven by conflict, ranging from trivial matters like pocket money, dress, loud music, to the serious problems of adult life, duties, responsibilities, rights – who does what, gets what, when and

how? Whatever the group, conflicts arise: the nation, being so large and complex, contains within it conflicts both chronic and acute. Politics is the way such conflicts are contained, modified, postponed or settled, the way therefore in which the continued existence, the minimum cohesion, of the nation is promoted.

In many of the groups with which we are concerned in our daily lives, conflict is resolved by quite simple means. In a family of young children, a wise parent will lay down a rule and this will be accepted; in a school or college, the principal will decide many minor questions; in a business, the manager issues instructions. These are all situations in which disagreement is weak, the sense of 'belonging' (social cohesion) quite strong, authority is established and will be more or less readily accepted. In many other situations natural harmony will prevail over conflict, so that a group of friends may have little difficulty in deciding which game to play, or which cinema to go to. However, even these situations in which conflicts are easily settled by authority or goodwill or friendship can easily get out of hand. The Smiths we noted above are not necessarily perverse or obstinate: they simply disagree!

Thus, political activity must take place. It follows that many of the topics which we say are being 'dragged into politics' (like the curriculum or the management of schools) are in fact already in politics: that is, they are fit and proper subjects for political activity, since people disagree about them.

Democracy and authority

So far we have been concerned with definition:

politics is the way a nation (or a group) manages conflicts and disagreements. Beyond this bare definition, the nature of politics depends on value judgements, on whether we broadly favour an authoritarian or a democratic society. These words too, unfortunately, have acquired connotations of approval and disapproval, so that we are all inclined to jump on to the democratic side without waiting to think and 'authoritarian' carries instant disapproval.

In an authoritative society, there is a disposition to settle conflicts through the enforcement of rules and orders by an established authority. This is justified because conflict damages the efficiency and integrity of society and it is argued that the established authority is capable of settling disputes fairly, securing the consent of the protagonists. In this way, a parent's or a teacher's settlement of conflicts may be justified. Few people believe that this is an inhuman or improper method of settling the more violent arguments of the nursery or lower IIb. But for adults – and adolescents – authority is not enough.

In a democratic society, it is assumed that as far as possible conflicts should be resolved by rational discussion among those involved, with the final solution being accepted voluntarily. The process may well be time-consuming and untidy, but is justified because it respects the efficiency and integrity of the individual, the right to consent to the decisions which affect him or her and the need to feel committed to social duties. In the democratic society, the Smiths are valued members, thinking, participating, standing up for their opinions.

Now the authoritative and the democratic assumptions are not wholly antagonistic and mutually exclusive. In an authoritative society, some attempt is made to modify decisions according to the wishes of the people; in a democratic society some decisions are going to be made and enforced whatever the people think. However, there is, especially at the level of nations and states, a fundamental difference. The authoritarian tends to limit the element of consultation and consent to the minimum he or she can get away with. The democrat, on the other hand, tries to maximise the element of consent and to tolerate dissent.

At this point the democrat falls into difficulties. Maximising consent is by no means easy in practice and democratic principles may easily fall into an idealism not firmly based on facts. The authoritarian can usually claim a superior realism.

The problem for the democrat is that on many issues the people's wishes are obscure, inarticulate or even non-existent; on other issues the people will be divided, some for, some against; and in some cases a democratic government may believe profoundly that all or most of the people are mistaken. One solution lies in a liberal pluralism, which restricts the activity of government and leaves people free 'to do their own thing'. Where that solution is not possible (and the proper extent of government activity is a difficult and unresolved question) then government must be based on a system of representation and responsibility. The wishes and views of the people are represented in the government; power rests normally with a majority; the exercise of power is subject to processes of responsibility (answerability) to the people. The device of responsibility allows a government to govern in an approximate and indirect accordance with the wishes of the people. A democratic government may thus, for example, abolish the death penalty despite a popular majority in favour of its retention and expect to justify this decision before the next election (or hope that the public will not feel deeply enough to care or even remember).

This is a relatively crude example of democratic government. Democracy is not simply direct popular government, but neither is it simply government through a system of regular elections and elected assembly. The democratic assumption implies responsiveness as well as responsibility, through a complex range of institutions and processes: political parties, as well as parliament; an elaborate and powerful system of political communications; machinery for the articulation of demands of groups with ideas or interests; a network of committees, habitual processes of consultation, explanation, education; the acceptance of compromise and delay; above all, a respect for opposing views and the ultimate recognition that you may be mistaken.

Thus the rights of opposition are quite fundamental in a democracy. In Britain this is recognised in the official salaried post of Leader of the Opposition. Not everyone would agree that Opposition in Britain is effective. The achievement of the ideals of democratic government is in practice very difficult. Hence the study of politics is difficult and challenging.

Democratic political systems

We should expect to find in a democratic political system institutions of government linked to the governed by systems of responsibility and representation. Briefly these institutions and systems are listed below.

- Head of state: ceremonial or part of the executive government.
- Executive: a small group of directors, usually with one person at their head as chairman, or in a more exalted position as president.
- Representative deliberating assembly, with some control over the executive, but also controlled to some extent by the executive. An important function of the assembly is usually legislation, i.e. the processing of laws, but these may be made (decided upon and fundamentally shaped) by the executive.
- Electoral system providing for the popular election of part, at least, of the assembly and perhaps of the chief executive too.
- Political parties: groups seeking to win power in the government. In a democratic system this means an organisation to secure popular votes and to organise members of the assembly for government power.
- Groups and individuals organised to bring pressure on government in favour of particular ideas or interests.
- A system of political communication, including the press and broadcasting and providing for the intercommunication of parts of the whole political system.
- A judicial system to provide for the arbitration of (mostly) non-political disputes.

These are the basic institutions of the political system. Political activity goes on within and through this framework.

The basic processes of government

- Identification and assessment of a problem and its solution.
- Development of policy ideas by individuals and groups including the government.
- Public ventilation of ideas, problems, solutions.
- Formulation of attitudes within organised groups, including political parties.
- Consultation by government of political and other interested groups.
- Assessment of the policy arguments, both on their intrinsic merits and in the light of pressures and representations.
- Modification of policies by way of compromise with particular interests or adjustment to the general interest.
- Formulation of policy within the administration.
- Formulation and adoption of policy within high executive (decision-making).
- Processing of the policy decided in terms of law, regulation, finance, administration and information to those affected.
- Communication of policy to public to secure acceptance.
- Criticism of policy and scrutiny of its administration, by formal processes (Parliament) and informally (media). This is accountability.
- Adjudication of cases through the courts.

This account of political processes assumes a rational, problem-solving mode of government. It need not be so. Government may also be concerned simply to maintain the governors in power, to protect their favoured interests, to respond to threats to their power, to avoid, resolve or take part in, conflict. Such motives and goals necessarily change the processes of politics. But the account broadly fits the style of British government in the twentieth century – a government of programmes and policies.

The processes do not necessarily take place in this or any set order; sometimes the taking of a decision is the first step, rarely the last; often steps are missed out. The process is continuous, hence in a very rough way circular. But the most complicated lines on a single plane hardly represent the complexity of the political process. It is sometimes said that democratic politics is a dialogue between government and governed (where authoritative politics is mainly a monologue). But a dialogue is too simple a concept. Politics is rather a multilogue, a many-sided, many-centred dialogue.

The study of politics

It is important to take a realistic view of government and politics. Government is about humdrum matters like roads and technical education, not just international summit conferences and the collapse of the British economy. In fact the grand issues include the smaller issues; and the smaller are made up of even more detailed matters. Most of government activity is both detailed and unexciting.

Second, the people dealing with these matters are unlikely to be either heroes or villains. History encourages us to this kind of interpretation and the reformist literature encourages a 'good-guys and bad-guys' approach. This is not to say that there are not some elements of heroism and villainy in politics. But we should not be looking for the joys of praise or denunciation. The heroic and conspiracy theories of politics and history are less persuasive than interpretations which depend on a mixed view of human motives and perceptions and acknowledge the place of accident and mistake.

Third, no quick summing up of British government is likely to be true for very long. The summary characterisations – e.g., 'responsible government', 'elective dictatorship' – seize on one part of the truth and enlarge it. This is stimulating and assists understanding; but it must be followed by the long slow business of detailed qualification.

It is difficult to exclude value judgements from the study of politics. The first task is to discover and describe what actually happens. This is important, worth knowing and not at all easy to accomplish. We shall find, however, that discovery involves selection, description involves analysis; for example, we shall look especially hard at evidence of responsibility, effectiveness, power, or the absence of these. Words like democratic, inefficient, excessive, will slip into our writing and when they do, we must be aware that we are assuming and implying that some forms of political organisation are better than others and be ready to defend our judgement. This involves assumptions about the nature and purposes of government. In the end, that judgement depends on the personal assessment of the kind of society we want to live in; and that assessment must be personal in the sense that it is yours, not the author's.

The setting of British politics

The making of the state

For Britain, unlike many other countries, there is no one point in history which may be seen as formative for the modern nation state and its basic constitution. Yet while there is complexity and uncertainty about the origins of the British state, there is a remarkable continuity – no substantial invasion or conquest for over 900 years, one eleven-year interruption in a thousand years or so of the monarchy, a parliament playing a significant role in politics over 350 years at least; the political integrity of the mainland territory secure for about 300 years. The British state is characterised by longevity and comparative stability and this surely explains the robust and insensitive self-confidence, which has supported Britain in her finest and her less inspiring moments.

However, it is possible to pick out one or two moments in British history which are significant for the making of the nation and the state. These are turning points, moments of historic choice, or simply lurches in the course of history, demonstrating that the stability and continuity of British history is sometimes apparent rather than real and that for the people of Britain the ride has often been quite bumpy.

The early years of modern British history are marked with a series of invasions and conquests, beginning with the Romans (55BC) and culminating with the Normans in 1066. The impact of the French is evident in our names (William, Robert, Richard) and place names and in the language. For two centuries at least after the conquest an educated Englishman needed good French and at least some Latin to supplement his native English. England was at that time a kind of colony. But it should be understood that we are concerned here not with a modern state, but with medieval kingship competing with feudal land-ownership and a powerful church. Even so, the making of the Domesday Survey in 1086 reminds us that the Normans were concerned, like a modern government, with property and taxation.

The Norman Conquest was a disaster because it was a conquest, but also, it has been suggested, because more than any other famous event in British history its fame has encouraged a false view of history.

At least it is incontrovertible that the Norman Conquest was the last successful invasion of England and so determined the nature of the peopling of the country. The next famous date in English history is 1215, the signing of 'Magna Carta'. The famous satire on school history, *1066 and All That* says of the Conquest: '...a Good Thing, as from this time onwards England stopped being conquered and thus was able to become top nation.' (W. C. Sellar and R. J. Yeatman, 1960, p. 25). Of Magna Carta they wrote: 'the chief cause of Democracy in England' (p. 34). Margaret Thatcher seemed to share the same high regard for Magna Carta.

In fact, Magna Carta was essentially a document regulating the relations of the King and his feudal barons. But it plays a significant part in the myth of British history, as the foundation of freedom and the beginning of democracy. There is some truth in this, as long as it is not understood in modern terms. In so far as the King was compelled to come to an agreement with the barons and abide by certain rules, Magna Carta advanced the notion that subjects had rights against kings and that such relationships should be covered by rules, that is, laws. This is a long way from modern notions of representation, government by consent and the rule of law. But an appeal to a false account of history may still support an influential myth.

Jumping over 300 years of history, Henry VIII (1509–47) can be seen as the founder of a modern state, concerned with his authority over the Church and the territories of Scotland, Wales and Ireland, as well as England and committed to effective administration and heavy taxation. He is famous for his six wives – evidence of his defiance of the Church and concern for the dynasty as much as the state and setting an unattainable standard in royal marriage break-ups. Henry had little time for Parliament, but, like all monarchs of the time, often had to bargain and negotiate in order to obtain money and support. Simple autocracy was quite difficult to achieve – some measure of consent was essential. His daughter Elizabeth, who never missed the sixteenth century equivalent of a photo-opportunity, achieved a high reputation for surviving and reigning for over 40 years, without marriage (the Virgin Queen) and in apparent peace and stability. Her actual achievements were less impressive: 'she quietly allowed England to become ungovernable' (J. Guy in K. Morgan, (ed.), 1984, p. 264).

The following century is perhaps the most significant in the development of the characteristic form of British government. In a conflict between Crown and Parliament over religion, taxation and government, the King was defeated, captured, tried and executed (1649). This was indeed a powerful blow for Parliament and against the Divine Right of Kings. But Charles gained much sympathy by his dignified defence of his conduct. A few years later, in 1660, the monarchy was restored and it seemed almost as if there had never been a revolution.

However, the climate of opinion was changed. Religion was less potent, less central, less threatening and the unthinkable act of regicide had been accomplished. In 1688 the 'English Revolution' was completed. James II, a Catholic bigot and an ineffective ruler, was chased off the throne in an astonishing coup d'état and replaced by the Protestants, William and Mary. A 'Bill of Rights' was enacted which affirmed Parliament's monopoly of the power of taxation and ended the Crown's claim to dispense with or suspend the law. This was a coup brought about by the governing class, who hastened to disguise its revolutionary implications. But the events of 1688 were truly revolutionary and confirmed the form of government as parliamentary monarchy.

■ DOCUMENT 2.1
The Glorious Revolution of 1688

a) From A. Maude and E. Powell, 1953, pp. 125–6

Whatever precise view might be taken or description given of the flight of James, William and Mary did not reign by hereditary right. Though they stood high in the hereditary order of succession, William and Mary reigned by the acceptance of those who described themselves as 'lawfully, fully and freely representing all the Estates of the people of this realm' and by virtue of a kind of contract made between them and its representatives, embodied subsequently in an Act of Parliament. Perhaps it might be possible to go on to argue that James was no longer King because he had broken a contract with his people. That, indeed, would be a philosophy which might explain and justify what the vast majority of Englishmen had been forced to accept by the events of 1688; but it would not be that of the High Church and Divine-Right Tories.

In the same ship by which Mary arrived from Holland in 1689, there returned from exile a certain Mr John Locke, who next year published *Two Treatises on Civil Government*, which became the canonical scriptures of the Whig Revolution....

Locke provided the Revolution with the theory of a limited contract, which could be cancelled or revoked and which rested on the ultimate and enduring sovereignty of the people. The theory did duty for most of the eighteenth century in England, though its most striking developments were experienced elsewhere, in America and in France.

b) G. N. Clark, 1934, p. 142

The Revolution as interpreted by Locke was regarded by the majority of the governing class, until the break-down of the old regime in the early nineteenth century, as a masterpiece of political wisdom. The tablets and obelisks which commemorate it in English parks and market-places show how it was accepted as the basis of the prosperity and order in which the squires and tradesmen flourished. It was the Glorious Revolution and it became the object of almost superstitious reverence. ■

EXERCISE
The Revolution of 1688 and modern British government

2.1 Is 1688 a genuine turning point in English and British history?

Since the sixteenth century at least Parliament had been a useful and sometimes an essential support for royal government. If the King needed funds he needed Parliament: most kings fought wars, so they were often short of money. Thus military adventures and parliamentary government went together. In the 'Glorious Revolution' Parliament determined the succession to the throne and rejected the royal claim to suspend or dispense with the law. Parliament thus took a significant step towards establishing its supremacy in the making of law over both the royal prerogative and the common law.

Parliament was then formally supreme but its composition was still heavily influenced by the Crown through the archaic election system. For more than a century Parliament was in fact managed on behalf of the Crown. A full and effective parliamentary sovereignty was not achieved until the series of Parliamentary Reform Acts beginning in 1832. By the redistribution of grossly unrepresentative constituencies and the gradual introduction of universal adult suffrage (completed in 1928), these Acts eventually made Parliament a more or less representative assembly. The Crown was thus compelled to pass the management of Parliament to politicians capable of securing a majority of the popular vote. Parties were organised to accomplish the delivery of support and consent.

The Victorian period was the great age of constitutional transformation. Queen Victoria herself discovered between 1835 and 1841 that she could no longer secure the Prime Minister of her choice. One of the Prime Ministers she liked, Disraeli and another she loathed, Gladstone, became the leaders of modern mass parties. Power had passed to the people, or rather to the people's parties.

The party system has worked in practice to give great power to the political executive, which in effect controls Parliament, by consent of the people. The power of the Monarch diminished, but the power of the political executive took its place. With this understanding the system may still be described as government by the Crown-in-Parliament (see Figure 1).

In this way Britain has preserved medieval forms into the late twentieth century. This history without clear breaks may explain why the British seem to be intensely conservative in their constitutional thinking and firmly committed to their institutions as they have inherited them.

Territory and peoples

The state we refer to loosely as Britain is formally the United Kingdom of Great Britain and Northern Ireland. This includes Scotland and Wales, as well as England; so Britain is a union of four 'countries' or 'national territories', or, some would

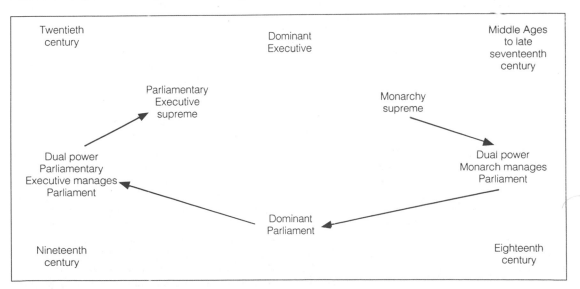

Figure 1 Executive power: a circular process

claim, 'nations'. This raises problems of definition, of formal status and aspiration, which might be regarded differently in the different parts of the union. But if Britain is multi-national, it is not a multi-national federal union like the former USSR, nor a federation with multiple governments like the USA. Britain is more like France, which is unitary in its form of government, but includes within it some groups such as the Bretons claiming cultural and political autonomy and even national independence.

Just as the USSR was dominated by the largest of the constituent nationalities, the 'Great Russians' or Muscovites, so the British Union is dominated by England and the English. But England does not have a strong sense of identity separate from the more inclusive Britain. For example, Bagehot's classic work on the constitution (1867) was called *The English Constitution*. Prime Ministers have described themselves as Prime Ministers of England. This might be regarded as insensitive and imperialist, but Prime Ministers have often been Scottish or Welsh or Jewish in origin. If the English have dominated Britain, it has been by an insidious inclusiveness, not exclusiveness.

The origins of England, both state and nation, are obscure. The modern political entity we know as the state begins as a people or tribe rather than a particular territory. Land ownership and church organisation are at least as old as government. From the beginnings even under the Romans, England seems to have included at least parts of Wales and itself to have been divided into a core and a periphery, a North and South (broadly divided by the Humber). King John at the beginning of the thirteenth century was the first king to describe himself as King of England, not the English and later the Kings of England and France moved to confine their barons to land ownership in one country only. At the same time an English national consciousness seems to have grown, but could never quite be defined and developed, since it was commonly held to include Scotland, Wales and Ireland. It seems the English were determined to be what we should call British.

The modern British state emerged clearly under Henry VIII in the 1530s, with the subjugation of the Church and of Wales, the attempted subjugation of Ireland and dynastic alliance with Scotland. England's French connection – much of Southwest France (Gascony) had been English from the twelfth to the mid-fifteenth century – ended finally when Calais was given up in 1558. In 1601 King James the First of England was also the Sixth of Scotland and officially styled King of France and Ireland too. But he liked to refer to himself as King of Great Britain. (It has been argued, without success so far, that Queen Elizabeth II must be Elizabeth I of Scotland).

The modern form of the United Kingdom was apparent by 1601 – a Union of the four countries under the Crown and Parliament in London, which is not the same as the English Crown and Parliament. The Union with Scotland was formalised in 1707 and with Ireland in 1800. The Irish Union was undone by rebellion in 1922, leaving the larger part of Ulster as a province of Northern Ireland, originally with a fair degree of autonomy in domestic affairs. Scotland and Wales have also been granted a measure of domestic devolution under the Scottish and Welsh Offices, headed by Cabinet Ministers.

For Scotland and Wales this settlement of the territorial and national problems of the United Kingdom seemed to have been accepted. In the 1960s and 1970s nationalist discontent led to demands for greater autonomy and impressive success for nationalist candidates in elections. A Royal Commission on the Constitution recommended schemes of devolution (decentralisation without much diminishing the power of the British Parliament), but in a referendum these were rejected by a large majority in Wales and by a bare minority of the voters in Scotland. Thus Britain appeared to surmount threats to the state by peripheral separatist movements, but Scotland may yet press for a further grant of autonomy – short of full independence.

In Northern Ireland, however, the threat was more severe. For the Catholic minority in Northern Ireland the settlement of 1922 was not satisfactory. Irish Catholics objected to the Protestant domination of the Northern Ireland government, supported by the British government. Republican Nationalists wanted a united Ireland, freed from British rule and governed from Dublin. To that end the Irish Republican Army fought a terrorist campaign against the British Army and an undeclared civil war against the Protestant domination of the province. Britain found itself unwillingly, or at least without enthusiasm, protecting the Unionist majority from the separatist minority. This was a colonial territory which had no wish to be decolonised. Thus, in the end, it has to be said that Britain has on its hands an intractable problem of peripheral, nationalist and separatist discontent (see Case Study in Chapter 24).

Table 1 The national and cultural diversity of the United Kingdom

The Constituent Territories in 1981

Territory	Population (1)	Density (2)	GDP (3)	Agric workers %	Roman Catholics %	Gaelic speakers %	New C'wealth %
England	46.8	376	89	2.8	9	—	3.2
Scotland	5.2	65	93	4.1	14	1.3	0.8
Wales	2.8	136	85	5.1	7	19	—
Northern Ireland	1.54	111	72	5.4	37.5	—	—
Republic of Ireland	3.5	49	64	17.2	94	28	—

(1) Population in millions
(2) Persons per square km
(3) Relative Gross Domestic Product per head (Europe = 100)

Source: Census 1981

These are the problems of the periphery. But England herself has acquired since the 1950s a substantial population of immigrants from the 'New Commonwealth', who with their children now comprise about 5.5 per cent of the UK population – more than the Welsh and over half as many as the Scots. These new peoples tend to be concentrated in a small number of towns, almost half in Greater London and their concentration supports and strengthens ethnic religious and linguistic culture. Thus in the space of a generation England, once determinedly imperial, mono-cultural and indeed metropolitan in outlook (ignoring Scots, Welsh, Irish, non-conformists and so on) has become uneasily multi-cultural – an historic challenge to a post-imperial nation.

EXERCISE
Natural and cultural diversity

2.2 Would you see the diversity indicated in Table 1 as too great to be accommodated in a unitary state?

Unions of diverse peoples – diverse in religion, culture, language, ethnic origin – encounter great difficulties in satisfying conflicting aspirations and interests. The simple solution is territorial: draw boundaries to separate the diverse populations and give them their 'own' units of government. In practice this solution is hardly ever practicable: it is precluded by the mixing and interpenetrating of peoples. This is evident for example in North Wales where Welsh speakers and monoglot English speakers live side by side and indeed throughout Eastern Europe, in Brussels, Canada.... The case of Northern Ireland vividly demonstrates the difficulties of territorial partition – and the consequences of an inevitably unsatisfactory partition.

The English hegemony

England dominates British politics, but its precise standing is ambivalent. There has been only one brief period (1042–66) when there existed a kingdom similar in territory to modern England. There has not been an English Parliament since 1536. There is no Department of State for England and much government activity in England is carried out by departments and agencies which are British or England- and-Wales in scope. The major political parties and the major pressure groups have a regional structure for England, but no 'All-England' body. The BBC takes very little account of England in its structure, except by default. Similarly there are national, that is British, newspapers, but none for England – or the South East, which ranks as a kind of national capital region.

Beyond government and the media, England is a little better represented. There is a Church of England, which since its disestablishment in Wales in 1921, has a special position in England alone. Sport is plainly divided between the nations of the United Kingdom, except for cricket, in which the England team draws on players from the one first-class side in Wales; and recently England has been accorded its own national anthem (*Land of Hope and Glory*) for playing on some sporting occasions.

This absence of institutional identification for England reflects and reinforces an absence of a strong popular consciousness of English identity. In surveys (in answer to the question, Do you think of yourself as...) almost as many English respondents choose their English national identity as the Welsh or Scots choose theirs, but the English identity carries little political charge. There is no English national political culture, except as a counter-culture to Scottish and Welsh nationalism; Irish nationalism inspires a British response. But the substance and force of such an English culture is in London and the South East, that is in the metropolitan and central culture.

This is the most significant 'regional' culture in England, but by definition it is not a culture with which the centre has to deal, it is the culture of the governing centre. Outside the centre there are regional differences and even regional cultures, but not a significant regional political culture.

England is not economically or socially homogeneous and differences between areas abound. Some differences in attitudes are of political relevance. A survey conducted for the Royal Commission on the Constitution (1969–73) showed that feelings of 'regional needs not being understood by the central government' were comparatively strong in the North East and the South West, as well as in Scotland and Wales, with least discontent in the South and Midlands. Interest in devolution was widespread and, despite nationalism and the language discontents in Wales, stronger in the North of England than in Wales. Indeed, when tested by a question about particular services, the demand for devolution appeared

significantly stronger in Scotland and Wales only in the matters of postage stamps and sport. A survey reported by Butler and Stokes in 1970 shows a clearer pattern of discontent with centralisation increasing with distance from London, and Scotland very sharply ahead of England and Wales in this respect.

Such attitudes, revealed to the sample surveyor, might have some political significance if they were to be energised by serious grievances and discontents, closely associated with the region. In fact, there are major economic differences between South and North in industrial structure and in unemployment and depression and in some areas these conditions are intense and of long standing, for example, Merseyside, Tyneside and Teesside. Such discontents cannot be articulated through a regional level of government, since there is none. Nor do the political parties have strong regional structures.

Moreover, the overriding centralisation of British politics has always been resistant to pork-barrel politics on American lines, that is the distribution of public spending as political reward or bribe. The Treasury does not like its extravagance and party discipline ensures a generally national rather than local approach to the distribution of government largesse. This self-denial does not preclude an occasional gesture towards a marginal constituency or one affected by a by-election – hence the Humber Bridge, the preservation of the Central Wales railway and, more recently, a school of military music in Dover and the reprieve of a military establishment in the constituency of Brecon and Radnor (voters in the by-election of July 1985 proved ungrateful).

None of this adds up to a vigorous regional politics based on regional political culture. Nevertheless, there is a centre-periphery pattern to British politics which complicates the class pattern of party conflict. This was evident in the past. For example, between 1885 and 1910 the most anti-

Table 2 Regional views on centralisation of government

	London and S.E. %	Midlands %	South West %	Wales %	North %	Scotland %
Content	72	65	57	55	52	26
Too centralised	21	29	37	38	43	65
Don't know	7	6	6	7	5	9

This table is adapted from D. Butler and D. Stokes, 1977, p.139

Figure 2 A two nation pattern of voting – the constituencies won by the Conservative Party at all three elections, 1979, 1983 and 1987
From R. J. Johnston et al., *A Nation Dividing?*, Longman, 1988.

Conservative areas in mainland Britain were Wales, Scotland, Yorkshire and Northern England. In 1945 Labour won sufficient votes in the South of England to look like a truly national party. But Labour's decline in the 1970s and 1980s revealed what is usually called 'two nations'. In the south of England (roughly south of the line Bristol-Birmingham-the Humber) there is a massive Conservative predominance; Labour seats are almost totally confined to the declining areas of the two big cities of London and Birmingham. In the north of England and in Scotland and Wales the Labour party still holds a majority of seats and votes. It is the party of the working class, but also the party of the periphery. In older terms, it is the party of the Country, while the Conservatives are the Court Party. The 'two nations' pattern of voting is shown in the map (Figure 2).

There is a very evident pattern of division into 'two nations', but some reservations may be made. First, the use of parliamentary voting figures by constituency makes the contrast sharper than it is in practice – there are Labour voters in the South, even if there are few Labour-held constituencies, just as there are Conservative voters in the North. Second, the socio-economic pattern underlying the voting is also patchier: there are, certainly in the 1990s, areas of high unemployment in the South, some of the worst in London, adjacent to areas of great prosperity. Hence, the diagrammatic representation gives an even sharper appearance to divisions, which may not be felt so sharply by the people on the ground. In 'real life' people live in towns, villages and neighbourhoods, rather than in constituencies or regions. Even with such reservations, there is truth in the notion of a divided Britain, but it is patchier than it looks, it is a long-standing product of economic and political history and ironically the most recent depression has struck hardest in the formerly prosperous South.

The 'English hegemony' is evident enough to the historian, to the social scientist and to the politically conscious in Scotland and Wales, but for the most part it is a latent condition of British politics. Nationality in Britain is dual or ambivalent, but the overlay of British nationality is generally acceptable. Patriotism is not wanting, especially at times of external threat and war; and the monarchy has, at least until recently, offered a potent focus of loyalty.

Britain, the island and the empire

Britain is an island which became a great impe-rial power. The record was extraordinary. At its height, between 1919 and 1945, about one quarter of the people of the world were ruled directly or indirectly by the British government. Britain lost only one major colonial war, the American War of Independence. She defeated the French in Canada, the French and the Portuguese in India, the Dutch in South Africa (though the Boers won later on), the French in Egypt, almost everybody in China (and of course the Chinese won later on).

The natives in the colonies were subjugated and exploited economically – harsh words, but the British, like every other imperial power, did not take and hold colonies for the good of the natives. On the credit side there remains the English language (now an international language), the game of cricket, some British varieties of the Christian religion, some elements of democracy and a unique and possibly effective association of nations of the first and third worlds, the Commonwealth.

Like other European empires, except the Russian, which took a little longer, Britain's colonial empire collapsed within three decades after 1945. The Labour government granted independence to India, Pakistan, Ceylon and Burma in 1947, in face of mounting agitation but before the position became quite untenable. Thereafter the process was often reluctant and many of the leaders of the newly independent states had some bitter experience of colonial prisons. British governments of both left and right pursued a world role, especially 'East of Suez' and clung on to colonies and outposts with too little regard for the passing of the age of empire.

The British empire has to be accounted one of the great empires of modern history and it has left its mark on the political culture of modern Britain. The British are strongly but mostly not stridently nationalist, though the tabloid press evinces an unattractive jingoism when foreigners tease the British bulldog. They live on an island and offer a classical example of the meaning of insularity, which is at the heart of British nationalism. The British have little experience of foreigners, except in holiday resorts and at football matches, are notoriously bad at speaking foreign languages and remain suspicious of their fellow Europeans. During the war they were bombed, which made them proud, but not invaded, which would have been humiliating. They are not assertively nationalist; they have a strong sense of national superiority and assume that their superiority is evident and will be accepted without question. The Scots and the Welsh might try to dissociate themselves from this picture of British nationalism, but cannot wholly separate their history from that of the English.

The British imperial experience was not unique, There were eleven major territorial empires in 1900, most of them European, but including Turkey, Russia and China. Only the last survives. The imperial experience has been significant in all of those countries, but there are some grounds for regarding Britain as specially marked by an imperial past. The British Empire was indeed very large and spread across the world. Its exploitation, protection and government were grasped as a profitable and prestigious activity for the ruling classes and humbler folk found work and opportunity in the colonies. The monarchy conferred its aura on the rule of the empire. The imperial outlook and imperial problems engaged much of the time of the government. Despite some nasty experiences as the empire disintegrated, the British people could regard their empire as a success story.

Moreover the imperial experience was linked to and enhanced by Britain's experience as a Great Power. Britain alone among the countries of Europe won all its wars in modern times and escaped invasion and occupation. This enhanced a tendency to the raucous patriotism known as 'jingoism' and to the kind of stolid courage associated with the 'British Bulldog' image of the wartime Prime Minister, Winston Churchill. British patriotism has a strong military side, with soldier heroes and statues of generals and the monarchy is associated with the military profession. History, as in other countries, tells of victories not defeats. Defence expenditure remains comparatively high, suggesting continuing illusions of grandeur.

Imperialism in Britain was a complex collection of ideas and sentiments. There was much arrogance, self-aggrandisement and simple greed; but there was also an element of noble striving and idealism, good intentions, though marred by a patronising insensitivity. Consider the imperialism expressed by Churchill in Document 2.

■ DOCUMENT 2.2
Churchill's late nineteenth century imperialism

a) *From a speech by Winston Churchill to the Southsea Conservative Association, October 1898, quoted in R. S. Churchill, 1966, pp. 422–3*

To keep our Empire we must have a free people, an educated and well fed people. That is why we are in favour of social reform. That is why we are in favour of Old Age Pensions and the like.... You have two duties to perform – the support of the Empire abroad and the support of liberty at home.

So the great game goes on...it shall not be interrupted until we are come through all the peril and trial and rule in majesty and tranquillity by merit as well as by strength over the fairest and happiest regions of the world in which we live

b) *From M. Gilbert, 1988, pp.1040–1*

[Over half a century later, in 1954, Prime Minister Churchill wrote to the American President Eisenhower:]

I read with great interest all that you have written me about what is called Colonialism, namely: bringing forward backward races and opening up the jungles. I was brought up to feel proud of much that we had done. Certainly in India, with all its history, religion and ancient forms of despotic rule, Britain has a story to tell which will look quite well against the background of the coming hundred years.
He added:.. I am a bit sceptical about universal suffrage for the Hottentots.... ■

EXERCISE
Churchill's imperialism

2.3 Do you see much that is noble and good about Churchill's ideas on imperialism as indicated here?

Britain emerged triumphant from the Second World War with much to be proud of and an apparent place as one of three great powers. But this was self-deception and Britain has only slowly adjusted (if indeed she has) to a humbler place as a second rate power at best, with a quite altered place in a post-colonial world dominated by the two super powers. Victory in the Falklands war in 1982 gave temporary new life to the delusions of grandeur, as perhaps did the easy victory in the Gulf war in 1991.

Industrial revolution

Britain was the first country to experience an industrial revolution, the transformation of a mainly rural and agricultural economy into an industrialised and urban economy, initially based on the heavy industries of coal, iron and steel and textiles. The British industrial revolution had two consequences for modern Britain. First, it helped to make nineteenth century Britain 'top nation', indisputably a Great Power in Europe and a naval and imperial power across much of the world, backed by its unrivalled industrial power as 'the workshop of the world'. This position was under challenge by the end of the century when other countries, notably Germany and the USA were developing rapidly and the European Powers were competing for colonies and for the domination of Europe. Britain gained from this early economic and international superiority a strong sense of national self-confidence, touched with a self-deluding vanity and disdain for other countries. This has lasted well beyond the economic strength which first gave rise to it.

Second, the industrial revolution had social and political consequences for Britain. The 'revolution' was rapid and brutal – though not when compared with Stalin's attempt to transform Russian industry in the 1930s – but its social effects seem to have been moderated in many ways. The standard of living rose slowly but substantially, agriculture was productive enough to avoid starvation if not malnutrition, social reform brought some improvement in working and living conditions.

The revolution produced an urban working class, as Marx and Engels observed. But it never developed into the revolutionary proletariat which they foresaw. Radical movements like the Chartists did not aim to overthrow society and government; rather they struggled to reform the political system and use it for their own social purposes. When working men had the vote they supported the Liberal party, if not the Conservatives; and when they turned more radically to the new Labour Party, that turned out to be committed to the Parliamentary system of government and to the capitalist economic system.

Altogether Britain was able to flourish and adapt to very rapid economic and social change with little violence and without much disturbance of the external pattern of institutions and society.

The industrial revolution changed the class structure of modern Britain, producing a new working class and a new middle class of entrepreneurs, financiers and industrialists. But the old aristocracy was not destroyed; rather it was strengthened by the incorporation of the new money. The monarchy and the House of Lords remained as a support for the aristocracy and for a society conscious of social difference and still broadly deferential to the gentry. The British working man aspired to 'better himself', to attain 'respectability', to join the system, not to destroy it. The comparative prosperity of the decades following 1945 completed the transformation of this conservative, non-proletarian working class into a new, property-owning, affluent lower middle class, which appears to have no historical connection with the Chartists, or the Labour Party of the first half of the twentieth century.

■ DOCUMENT 2.3
Social class in Britain in the late nineteenth century

From H. C. G . Matthew, The Liberal Age, *in K. O. Morgan, 1984, pp. 488–91*
As the British economy became gradually as much commercial as industrial, it created a vast army of white-collar workers to manage and serve in the retailing, banking, accounting, advertising and trading sectors. The management of factories passed from a paternal family tradition to a new class of professional managers and the bureaucracies of manufacturing industry grew swiftly. The civil service, both local and central, began to expand rapidly as government spent more on new responsibilities, especially on the education system created by the Act of 1870. Shops, offices and telephone exchanges offered new opportunities for the employment of women.... Suburbanisation was the characteristic innovation of city life in the second half of the century: rows of neat houses, terraced or semi-detached, with small gardens, often both at front and rear of the house, testified to the successful propertied aspirations of this new society ■

EXERCISE
Social class in Britain and abroad

2.4 Would you expect social class in Britain to differ from other countries?

The political tradition and political culture

Peaceful change
An apparent characteristic of British history is peaceful or non-revolutionary adaptation. This is true in part, but in part an influential myth. There is no equivalent in British history of the French,

Table 3 Some aspects of the 'civic culture'

Some comparative results obtained by sample survey.
The number of interviews in each country is approximately 1000.
Interviews were carried out 1959–60.

	US	UK	Germany	Italy	Mexico
Percentage who say they are proud of:					
Government, political institutions	85	46	7	3	30
position in international affairs	5	11	5	2	3
economic system	23	10	33	3	24
Percentage who say national government improves conditions	76	77	61	66	58
Percentage who expect serious consideration of their point of view from a) bureaucracy	48	59	53	35	14
b) police	56	74	59	35	12
Percentage who say the ordinary man should be active in his local community	51	39	22	10	26

Derived from G. Almond and S. Verba, The Civic Culture, 1965, pp. 48, 64, 72, 79, 127

Russian or American Revolutions. Instead there is a remarkable continuity. The major break of the 1640s was repaired by the Restoration. The revolution of 1688 brought about a major shift in government with little upheaval, although it was not 'bloodless' (particularly in Ireland) and hardly justified its title of 'glorious'.

Indeed there was bloodshed, violence and tyranny in British history. The Chartists and the early trade unionists might have been much more troublesome if they had not been often surrounded by police and troops on horseback, or if it had not been raining; and Britain still faces in Ireland a bloody civil war against the most enduring guerrilla army in modern history. Even so the point about institutional continuity remains. The essential structure has been bent and bruised but not broken. This is the first and fundamental element in British political culture.

The civic culture

In a famous study made by two American political scientists in 1959–60 Britain emerged as a model of the 'civic culture' (G. A. Almond and S.

Verba, The Civic Culture). The British people, it was argued, were proud of and attached to their political institutions, were generally satisfied with the outputs of government (what it did for them) and combined deference towards the system with confidence and competence in participating in and using it. The British had reached by the good fortune of the historical development an ideal mix of active and participant citizen and deferential and passive subject. This attractive theory fitted well with liberal interpretations of British history, which are reflected above and was incorporated into the tradition. The secret of stable democracy, much sought after at the time, had, it seemed, been found.

EXERCISE

The civic culture

2.5 What are the significant differences between the countries? Is there any evidence of a 'civic culture' in Britain?

The theory was supported by sample survey evidence drawn from five countries. The evidence has been much criticised both in conception and on technical grounds. So the civic culture theory as applied to Britain remains an unsubstantiated but illuminating sketch. This is frustrating since it seems likely that some explanations of politics are to be found in 'political culture', if only we could find an adequate research method. Leaving aside the difficulties of conducting surveys in four languages in five countries, it is plain that the theory is sketched rather than specified and there are problems about specifying the components of the civic culture – for example, what does deference actually mean?

Further difficulties arose when the civic culture which characterised Britain in the 1960s was alleged to be in decline in the harsher climate of the 1980s. It appeared there had been significant changes in social customs and outlook in Britain as in other developed countries – 'pop' music, a brash and assertive new youth culture, the loosening or liberalisation of sexual behaviour, trade union militancy and some street rioting, football hooliganism.... It is possible to argue about the magnitude of the changes but difficult to deny any change at all.

But what was the significance of such cultural change for political culture in general, the civic culture in particular? Recent survey evidence shows the British as fairly cynical towards government; and there seems to have been little change in this respect since the 1970s. It may be argued that Almond and Verba's study of 1960 failed to detect cynicism and that a healthy scepticism has long been part of a British citizen's armour. (Interesting evidence for this could be adduced from accounts of the British soldier in two World Wars, stoic and cynical, lacking the commitment and obedience of the Germans, and the French combination of patriotic ardour and a tendency to mutiny). But there is much to be said for the view that the elements of deference which Almond and Verba claimed to find have changed along with other changes in the social climate.

The tentative conclusion seems to be that support for political institutions in Britain is high. The power of 'the Government' personified by the Prime Minister, is made democratic by its Parliamentary support and legitimated by the crown. Democracy is confused by the pomp of Parliament and mystified by monarchist sentiment. The resulting democratic 'good feeling' is strengthened by confidence and competence in making use of the institutions. The quality of deference is difficult to locate. The authority of the squire, the

boss, the parent or the school master is no longer undisputed, but social life is still marked by discipline rather than disorder. Similarly the authority of government may well have diminished, but citizens are sceptical and uninterested rather than actively protesting or rebellious.

This conclusion finds some support in political events and non-events. It is evident that attempts to influence government by non-parliamentary means (strikes, demonstrations) especially violent means, are not widely approved; and that the elected government, even when it represents a minority of the voters, is still widely regarded as legitimate. This is not to deny that there have been times in the 1970s and 1980s when some small groups have edged towards 'unparliamentary' action, and non-payment of the unpopular community charge or poll-tax was widespread. Most people most of the time express little confidence in politicians but without wanting to overthrow the system of government.

Politics and social class

Politics in Britain is centred on social class. There are limits to this broad generalisation. Other political divisions – ethnicity, culture, religion, geography – play some part in politics, or have done so in the past; and in Northern Ireland politics is based on religion and culture. But on the mainland class is the major division by which politics is structured – insofar as it is structured at all. This is unusual in a world in which ethnic, linguistic and religious cleavages are most salient and politicised. In France religion still has a noticeable effect on politics and is evident in the pattern of support for parties. In the USA religion and ethnicity affect political allegiance.

Social class is a broad, umbrella-like or basket-like term, which is easy to use and difficult to define. It refers to the range of social differences which begin with occupation and income but embrace education, life-style, outlook. In Britain the urban working class created by the industrial revolution could be fairly clearly identified, comparatively poor, living in council (public) housing, organised in trade unions, attending non-conformist chapels and voting for the Labour Party. This ideal type existed in sufficient numbers to support a Labour Party able to take office twice, in 1945 and 1966, with substantial majorities.

However, social differences were still not simple enough, nor felt so sharply, to provide a solid, unchanging base for a class oriented Labour Party. Some people were objectively working class but did not share a working-class outlook. Some moved away from 'pure' working class, for example by moving into one of the many 'white collar' occupations which industrial revolution had also developed and/or by acquiring more extended education in the schools, which had also arrived with industrialisation. Such people, a lower or middle 'middle class', could join politically with the established middle class, propertied, prosperous and well-educated and support the Conservative Party, which has been in power for much of the twentieth century and is in effect Britain's governing party.

The pattern of party support has never been quite as neat as this. The terms 'middle class' and 'working class' are too rough to carry such a weight of social and political significance. There are no clear boundaries and there is a good deal of movement. Yet few observers of British life deny the pervasive influence of perceptions of class. There are many evident supports to a class system – the monarchy, the aristocracy and the House of Lords, the 'public' (private fee-paying) schools, the many petty distinctions of social life – and some substance can be given to the notion of a 'governing class' in Britain, an English governing class which rules Britain. One significant test of the existence of class in politics is the fate of centre parties: they find great difficulty in getting a grip on popular support without the guide of an obvious class support. The British political imagination is still dominated by images of class.

The effect on British politics of this fixation on class is interesting. Politics lags behind changes in social class, but at least a class-shaped society provides a comparatively diverse and fluid basis for politics and changes more rapidly than religion, ethnicity and the cultural sources of political cleavage. Moreover, class divisions, even when they exaggerate actual social differences, do indicate relevant problems, equality, employment, welfare, for the attention of politicians. There is in fact a good deal to be said for Britain's old-fashioned class politics, especially for those who are at the bottom of the class system.

Social class in politics can be measured among voters, Members of Parliament, the Cabinet, though the significance of the measurement – the 'so what?' question – is open to debate. The analysis of voting by social class throws up distributions which may plausibly be presented as showing cause and effect, that is, class position leads to a particular vote. This was evident in post-war Britain. However, later analyses of class voting are less certain in their conclusions – the analysis is more subtle and the behaviour apparently more complex (see Chapter 18).

Table 4 Social class and politics in Britain

Proportion (%) of manual and non-manual classes voting for each party 1951

	non-manual	manual
Conservative	75	34
Liberal	3	3
Labour	22	63

From A. Heath et al.,1985, p.30

EXERCISE

2.6 Does the Table demonstrate that voting in Britain in 1951 was based on social class?

Analyses of the social background of Members of Parliament (Chapter 11) show up differences between the parties, as might be expected. But no political party is anywhere near reflecting the social composition of the electorate. In these matters, the middle classes rule – OK? The Cabinet naturally reflects Parliament.

Thus, about three-fifths of Conservative Members of Parliament were educated at the public (private, fee-paying) schools and one in ten at just one school, Eton College. Almost one half of Conservative and one sixth of Labour Members of Parliament attended Oxford or Cambridge Universities. This is an extraordinary concentration of educational background, which is paralleled in other 'top' professions.

But in politics at least there is some change. Etonians in the Conservative Cabinet sank from twelve in 1962 to three in 1983. Recent leaders of the Conservative Party have been grammar-school educated and middle class in origin. John Major is notably more humble in class background than many of his predecessors – but his Cabinet is still largely solid middle-class, three-quarters from private schools and three-quarters Oxbridge-educated. By contrast the Labour and Liberal Democratic parties now tend to draw leaders from the Celtic universities.

GUIDE TO EXERCISES

2.1 Yes. The effective intervention of Parliament in the matter of succession marked and strengthened Parliament's power at the very centre of government. Of course this was not completely unprecedented – consider what had happened in 1649. But the regicide of 1649 was the work of rebels and the monarchy was later restored. In 1688 the King was replaced and this was presented as a legitimate, almost normal act. It was this seeming unrevolutionary quality which made the events of 1688 so revolutionary and so permanently significant.

2.2 This is a matter of judgement. Both the USSR and the USA encompassed much greater diversity, but within formally federal and de-centralised constitutions. The collapse of the USSR as a federal union demonstrates the difficulties of containing diversity. France contains some linguistic, cultural and ethnic diversity, notably in Brittany and in parts of the South, but has maintained a unitary and in some respects centralised government. The position in Britain may be easier to handle because of the predominance of England – in the simple sense, understood by the English if not the others, that much the largest part of the Union has no strong feelings of diversity. The parts which are potentially centrifugal are too small to influence the matter. But this is not the understanding of the Scots, Welsh and Irish, for whom some measures of devolution have been devised.

2.3 This is not of course a representative sample of Churchill's views, though it is significant that the speech seems to reach so easily, almost thoughtlessly, for the rhetoric of empire. The 23 year old aspiring politician seems to see a national mission for Britain in ruling an empire and providing social welfare for the British people. It was a characteristic view of the time and is based on the idea of the mission of a British governing class to promote the blessings of its rule at home and abroad. Little here about self-government, so it is patronising though not ignoble. The casual phrasing of the 1954 letters is revealing, but some historians would argue that the British record in India was good, at least by the standards of the imperial powers.

2.4 Yes and no! All modern developed, that is, industrialised, countries share some similar economic and social experiences. But there are both differences in the original condition and in the experience of development. In the case of Britain industrialisation came early to a country with a distinctive class system, dominated by a powerful landed aristocracy. This may have had an influence on the emergence of the commercial, high finance class described in the Document. Suburbanisation, on the other hand, was a development common to all industralising countries.

2.5 There are some substantial differences in every row of the tables and you may speculate freely about their significance. A rough case for civic culture can be made for both Britain and USA on these figures, but the Table shows how difficult it is to devise questions which uncover the elements of a civic culture.

2.6 Yes; and the pattern is clearer than in any other Western country. But some reservations must be made. The distinction between manual and non-manual is very rough and the two categories include but hide other factors such as religion. Voting behaviour is known to be more complex than the simple class-party link indicated. Note that one third of the very large manual class votes for the Conservative party. Both class and party have changed since 1951. The topic is further discussed in Chapter 18.

ASSESSMENT

How helpful is the study of history, tradition and political culture for the understanding of contemporary politics?

The present is not randomly related to the past: there is a thread of continuity, a process of development and change and some lines of causation. At least this is the way we think about the past and it seems to accord with experience. There are obvious ways in which a country's past makes a difference to the present — for example, invasions, wars, famine, economic change, population growth and movement. In politics, the past lays down territorial boundaries, institutions, ideas and assumptions.

Thus the past has bestowed on contemporary Britain:

- a peculiar mix of peoples and territories, making up a multi-national state

- a formally sovereign Parliament and a constitutional monarchy, fashioned by early political struggles and only partly adapted to the requirements of a modern democracy
- a political tradition embodying a liberal constitutionalism, highly revered, but vague and ineffective in detail.

The realm of ideas and traditions seems particularly significant but disappointingly elusive. The term 'political tradition' implies a set of ideas and assumptions which can be identified and recognised at least by political elites and which to some extent modifies behaviour. It is arguable that Britain has such a political tradition, as Chapters 2 and 3 try to demonstrate. Such a tradition is reinforced by the conscious promotion by moralising politicians and indeed in books such as this (writers and teachers believing that there ought to be something to be said under this heading, before getting down to practical detail).

The term 'political culture' is more problematic. It implies popular or mass political assumptions, beliefs, attitudes, modes of behaviour. These are by their nature not written down and can be discovered only by observation, analysis of actual behaviour, or, in recent times, by sample survey. It is difficult to demonstrate that there is one general British political culture, or even a collection of cultures shifting under the impact of time, place and social conditions.

Bagehot's interesting observation that 'the English are a deferential people' has been shown to be difficult to define and 'operationalise', as the researchers say and so incapable of validation. This is not to say that it is meaningless, or untrue. For it is a fact of some significance that the English (and the Scots and the Welsh) have not risen up in revolution as have the French, the Germans, the Russians. National differences plainly exist but are difficult to explain. If we conclude that the different behaviour is related to differences in political culture – or 'national character' – we may be simply restating the existence of unexplained differences.

The problems of identification and demonstration are complicated by the pace of change. History does not stop and contemporary events flood in to change or obliterate the heritage of the past. This was plainly the case in the recent history of Germany. The experience of the war of 1939–45 was severe enough to modify the thrust of German history. For Britain the war probably reinforced some elements in the political culture – insularity, imperialism, the sense of superiority. Economic decline may eventually bring about a parallel decline in self-confidence and civility.

Concepts

State and Nation

These are basic political concepts, yet hard to pin down. The British, famous for their pragmatism, are particularly casual in their attitude to these concepts.

The state

In Britain 'state' and 'government' are difficult to distinguish: the state appears to be the government of the day. However, there are references to 'the Queen's government' ('the Queen's government must be carried on') and to the Crown (for example, as the Crown-in-Parliament). Such references seem to extend the notion of government to a more general concept incorporating the totality of governing authority and legitimacy, of which the government is by far the larger part, but not the whole. The state thus conceived is usually associated with a particular territory, personified by a monarch or president and symbolised by flags, monuments, ceremonies and the like. The broader concept of the state can include the law and the judiciary, the police and the armed forces and even citizens, alongside the government of the day.

Thus government may be seen not as the state but as the chief wielder of the authority of the state. This may enhance or restrain government power, depending on the nature of the state. In European history the state has been endowed sometimes with mystical, semi-divine authority; but that is not a necessary connotation of the term. Indeed, the state can be associated with citizenship and hence the idea of individual rights. Still the most common usage of the state is in interstate politics, which are known as international politics.

For students of British politics, the chief significance of the term is that it is little understood and not often used except in the context of nationalisation and public provision (state industries, state schools etc.) often with a pejorative implication. Historically the British have governments but leave to continental philosophers such abstractions as 'the state'.

The Nation

The term 'nation' also presents difficulties for the British. A 'nation' is a collection of people who feel themselves to belong together because of certain common factors – history, occupation of, or claim to, a particular territory, culture, including language and religion. 'Ethnic' character or 'race' could be added, but raises problems of identification. It is difficult to distinguish Anglo-Saxons, Normans or Danes in Britain, though Celts and Scots may insist on their own identity.

However that sense of national identity is variable and strongest where it reflects challenge and conflict between peoples, as to some extent in Scotland, Wales and Ireland. Even there, the serious differences are cultural, linguistic, religious or economic. Hence a nation is most clearly seen as such when conflict elicits the self-assertion known as nationalism. The nation matters to nationalists; the loyalty of others is to country and state and may be called patriotism.

Britain is properly regarded as a multi-national state and includes five different nationalisms – two Irish, Scottish, Welsh and the peculiar English nationalism which gently but patronisingly assumes that everyone is British. Government arrangements have not so far taken much notice of this problem. Here again the British settle for practical arrangements, ignoring theoretical complexities.

The principles of government in Britain

The public philosophy

Britain has no great and widely known statements of constitutional and political principles, such as the Americans' Preamble to the Declaration of Independence. The documents arising from the crises of British history, notably Magna Carta, 1215, and the Bill of Rights, 1689, are comparatively specific settlements of immediate problems rather than historic statements of principle, with a resonance and relevance for all time. So in that sense Britain has no avowed public philosophy. There are institutions and the assumptions which sustain them, political parties and their doctrines, and some political philosophers of repute and influence. But there is no accepted political tradition or a generally agreed collection of political values and aspirations. Like the constitution itself, Britain's political values have to be read into the historical experience.

Britain's national anthem, God save the Queen and what has become the English national song, Land of Hope and Glory, reflect monarchical and imperialist sentiments. But the 'Land of Hope and Glory' was also the 'Mother of the Free' and national rhetoric stresses freedom alongside references to parliament and the rule of law. Document 3.1 offers one recent statement about the British political tradition, made significantly enough in a speech concerned to distance Britain from supra-national developments in the European Community.

■ DOCUMENT 3.1
The British political tradition
From a speech made by the Prime Minister, Margaret Thatcher, at Bruges, September, 1988

We are rightly proud of the way in which, since Magna Carta in 1215, we have pioneered and developed representative institutions to stand as bastions of freedom. And proud, too, of the way in which for centuries Britain was a home for people from the rest of Europe who sought sanctuary from tyranny. But we know that without the European legacy of political ideas we could not have achieved as much as we did.

From classical and medieval thought we have borrowed that concept of the rule of law which marks out a civilised society from barbarism. And on that concept of Christendom – for long synonymous with Europe – with its recognition of the unique and spiritual nature of the individual, we still base belief in personal liberty and other human rights....

We British have in a special way contributed to Europe. For over the centuries we have fought and died for her freedom, fought to prevent Europe from falling under the dominance of a single power. Only miles from here lie the bodies of 60 000 British soldiers who died in the First World War. Had it not been for that willingness to fight and die, Europe would have been united long before now – but not in liberty and not in justice. It was British help to resistance movements throughout the last war that kept alive the flame of liberty in so many countries until the day of liberation came. ■

EXERCISE
Margaret Thatcher's Bruges speech

3.1 On the evidence of Document 3.1 assess Margaret Thatcher as historian and philosopher.

A modern 'Declaration of Rights' for Britain might

take from history, from Parliamentary institutions and from constitutional myth-making four fundamental principles.

1 *Resistance to arbitrary government*. This derives from the long but sporadic history of resistance to the monarchy, and the Protestant and Nonconformist struggles against the Catholic and the established Anglican churches. It may also draw encouragement from other historic battles for a free press, for the extension of the suffrage and for trade union rights. Each of these has its heroes and martyrs.

'Resistance to arbitrary government' may be a more appropriate formulation than a more positive reference to freedom; for freedom in Britain arises from the defeat or limitation of arbitrary government and the British constitution offers no precise guarantees of freedom.

2 *The rule of law*. The rule of law, according to the Conservative Party manifesto of 1983, is 'the foundation of all our liberties'. In one sense this is true, in that the rule of law must protect citizens from arbitrary rule or chaos. But the phrase is used, as in this instance, to carry a great weight of liberal or democratic principle; the phrase has potency but an imprecise substance and content.

Again, the concept arises historically from the struggles of Lords and Commons against arbitrary monarchs. It implies that government must be 'by the rules', according to established law, government itself being under the law, the citizen having entrenched rights of protection and redress against an arbitrary government. This is not exactly the case in Britain, since citizen 'rights' derive from the precedents of common law rather than an entrenched Bill of Rights, as in the USA. Still it is true and valuable in Britain's political arrangements that the judiciary is formally independent of the government, that judges are free to interpret the law as they are able to understand and expound it and that imprisonment and other punishment may be inflicted only for a breach of the law, established in court. In that specific sense government is 'under the law' and the citizen enjoys 'equality before the law', though this valued concept takes no account of executive power and privilege, not to mention the high costs of the law and the bias which may arise from the nature and peculiar practices of the legal profession.

The rule of law might by extension (it is a vague enough concept) convey the great liberal freedoms of speech, publication and assembly. In fact the judiciary can promote such freedom only if the law allows; and where there is any scope for discretion judges have quite often come down on the side of the executive. Hence British governments have succeeded in becoming the most secretive in the Western world without hindrance from the rule of law.

3 *Representative institutions*. Parliament is central to the British understanding of government, and 'parliamentary sovereignty' does duty in the political culture for democracy, state and even nationhood. The British people are committed to their parliamentary institutions and by implication to the underlying historic principle of 'no taxation without representation' or the redress of grievances before the granting of supply. The commitment is uncritical and unenthusiastic. There is little strong popular concern about the representational defects of the electoral system on which Parliament is based, its evident weakness or the absurdity of the continued existence of the hereditary and nominated House of Lords.

Parliament is not a regular place of holiday pilgrimage for British families and a high proportion of its visitors seem to be foreigners; in contrast the Congress building in Washington is thronged with American families come to pay their respects to a great institution of American democracy, to enjoy the excellent facilities including two public restaurants and to compete with Senators to ride on their underground railway.

Representation in Britain follows the majoritarian principle. The ballot-system awards the seat to the candidate with the highest vote, a system which can have very disproportionate effects in the country as a whole and which discourages third parties. In Parliament the government is formed by the majority party, coalitions are abhorred, minorities are excluded and may console themselves with the thought that their turn may come later. In Britain there is little of the concern for minority opinion and interests, which is normal in other European countries where coalition is accepted as a device for taking account of the minority.

4 *Toleration*. The British would like to believe that they have a tradition of toleration. History lends some support for this belief. A degree of toleration in religion was established by the

Protestant revolt against the Catholic church in the sixteenth and seventeenth centuries; and the hold on opinion of the Anglican church was later challenged by the non-conformist denominations. Thus protest and refusal to conform provided significant drives in British history and challenged the grip of orthodoxy. But the process was long and at times bitterly fought and it is only in this century and as religious faith itself declined, that full and open religious toleration was approached. Religious faith is by its nature uneasy, to say the least, about differences in belief and Britain has never attained the wholly secular state of many other countries.

Political freedom developed alongside religious freedom. There has been no arbitrary power of arrest in peacetime for political offences since the 1760s, when a general warrant for the detention of John Wilkes was held to be unlawful. However, the right to express political opinions is not formally guaranteed and is subject to a number of restrictions, for example, under laws of defamation, sedition and blasphemy and police powers over public meetings. Speakers Corner in Hyde Park in London is often used to demonstrate the extent of freedom of speech in Britain. Such an illustration is misleading in detail but reflects the strong tradition of and practical commitment to, free speech.

Even so, there is in Britain, as in most countries, a strong tendency to conformity in social and political life. People in Britain holding and trying to propagate eccentric, radical, non-conformist or even simply unusual ideas may well be regarded as trouble-makers but at least they are unlikely to be prosecuted, or persecuted.

Toleration of other ethnic groups does not come so easily to the British people. Their own concept of nationality is inclusive and the absence of a public philosophy equal to the American Preamble to the Declaration of Independence has not been helpful. Hence the British have experienced some difficulty in coming to terms with the immigration of substantial numbers of peoples (their former colonial subjects) from Asia and the Caribbean in the last forty years.

Forms and principles of government

No written constitution

Britain, notoriously, has no written constitution. This is a consequence of its history. Of its constitutional revolutions one was followed by a restoration; and the more successful revolution of 1688 preserved old forms. So there was no clear break and no opportunity for a new basic document. There is, nevertheless, a constitution and some of it is written down. This lack of codification has consequences.

1 *Flexibility.* The form of government has developed and adjusted to new conditions, notably universal suffrage and the growth of mass political parties.
2 *Inflexibility.* Old and inappropriate forms and institutions survive, for example, some part of parliamentary procedure, the House of Lords, perhaps the monarchy.
3 *Uncertainty.* There are many parts of the constitution which are obscure and imprecise e.g. the conventions on responsibility.
4 *Limited scope.* Many other modern constitutions include provision for civil rights. These arise in Britain under Common Law and may be regarded as more restricted and less certain than is appropriate.
5 *Absence of 'entrenchment'.* So no part of the constitution is specially protected from change by the legislature.
6 Overall, *the absence of a framework* of support for and restraint of, government power.

■ DOCUMENT 3.2
'Archaism' and the unwritten constitution
From C. Leys, 1985, pp. 250–1

[One] way in which accountability is avoided is through mystification, of which a chief form is archaism. The original archaism is the absence of a written constitution itself, which helps to preserve all the others. It would at least be harder to perpetuate the mockery of democracy...if the constitution were written.... An 'unwritten constitution' also affords scope for resistance to reform, since any unwelcome reform can be pronounced 'unconstitutional'.

After the unwritten constitution the chief fount of archaism is the monarchy. The 'convenient fiction' that the Queen rules allows the government to hide behind the 'Royal Prerogative' in refusing to give details about a large range of its actions...which would hardly be tolerated if the refusal were explained as an exercise of 'Prime Minister's prerogative'. Moreover, the Royal Family and the court...legitimate several of the more archaic elements in the culture of the British capitalist class .... Next to the monarchy the legal system is the most elaborately archaic branch of the state.... ■

EXERCISE
Archaism and an unwritten constitution

3.2 Do you agree that there is a connection between the unwritten constitution and 'archaism'?

A unitary constitution — centralisation with fragmentation.

The British constitution is unitary, not federal. It seems that the British abhor federalism (the Commission on the Constitution rejected it rather disdainfully) although forms of federalism were sometimes proposed for the colonies.

Sovereign power rests in Parliament, so formally Britain is centralised. This formal centralisation is reinforced by a substantial development of practical centralising measures, for example, the unified civil service, the close financial control of local government, the national parties, the concentration of the media. Thus the unitary constitution supports a centralised government.

Even so, there is some fragmentation of the system — some limited devolution to Scotland and

The centre

United Kingdom departments of state

Scotland
Scottish Office
Wales
Welsh Office
Northern Ireland
Northern Ireland Office

Intermediate bodies

National Health Service,
Public Corporations (e.g. BBC, British Coal)
Quangos (e.g. Arts Council, Sports Council)
and so on.

Local government

(different systems in Scotland,
Wales and Northern Ireland)

Figure 1 The constitutional structure of the United Kingdom

Wales and formerly to Northern Ireland, a system of local government and numerous agencies and quasi-non-governmental bodies. (The latter are sometimes called 'quangos', standing for quasi-autonomous, non-governmental bodies). Hence centralisation is moderated by non-central implementation and some elements of non-central government.

EXERCISES
The structure of the United Kingdom

3.3 Is it reasonable to describe the structure as unitary but fragmented?
3.4 Why do you think there is no English Office?

Government by the Crown-in-Parliament
This is the constitutional form of modern British government by a powerful executive of Prime Minister and Cabinet, backed by the departments of state and managing, even controlling, Parliament through a party-based majority. Historically, over the last 300 years, power passed to Parliament and was arrogated by the political executive, which arose from Parliament. Government by the Crown-in-Parliament has become government by the Executive-in-Parliament. Thus the structure reflects the pattern of history. Parliament never broke the executive, but contrived instead to claim an indirect share in executive power.
These are the elements of the modern British system of government.

1 *The sovereignty of Parliament.* Parliament is sovereign, that is supreme. Its authority arose historically from the revolutions of the seventeenth century. Parliament won the struggle against the Crown and the Royal Prerogative. There was no constitution or basic law to limit its powers and as the only legislature and as the 'High Court of Parliament', it has asserted its superiority over the judiciary.
2 *The Cabinet.* Parliament was supreme but was never directly the government. Historically the government was and is carried on by the Crown-in-Parliament. This reflects the slow yielding of authority by the Crown and the practice of government by a Prime Minister and Cabinet managing Parliament on behalf of the Crown. In effect the Cabinet arises from the legislature as a committee of Parliament, but takes on the functions and powers of the executive, on behalf of, or in place of, the Crown.

■ DOCUMENT 3.3
The Cabinet system

From W. Bagehot, The English Constitution,
1867, Fontana 1963, pp. 63–9
The efficient secret of the English Constitution
may be described as the close union, the
nearly complete fusion, of the executive and
legislative powers.... The connecting link is the
Cabinet. By that new word we mean a committee of the legislative body selected to be the
executive body. The legislature has many committees, but this is its greatest.... We have in
England an elective first magistrate as truly as
the Americans have an elective first magistrate.... Nevertheless, our first magistrate differs
from the American. He is not elected directly by
the people; he is elected by the representatives
of the people.... A Cabinet is a combining committee – a hyphen which joins, a buckle which
fastens, the legislative part of the State to the
executive part of the State. In its origin it belongs to the one, in its functions it belongs to
the other.... ■

EXERCISES
The Cabinet system

3.5 Most countries have some kind of Cabinet.
What is so distinctive about the English
Cabinet system perceived by Bagehot?
3.6 Would you expect the system to have
changed fundamentally since the mid-
nineteenth century?

3 *Responsibility to Parliament.* The Cabinet/ex-
ecutive is responsible to Parliament; but 'responsibility' is a term of constitutional art. Its
meaning ranges from strict accountability to
giving an account to speaking to Parliament to
silence in Parliament. It also means authority
(legitimised by responsibility). Despite its ambivalence the term 'responsibility' is the key to
the theory if not always the practice of the British Constitution.
4 *A competitive electoral system.* This is the most
significant democratic element in the British
system of government. Elections are genuinely
competitive. They determine the composition
of the government and indirectly influence the
policies of government. The openness and fairness of the electoral competition may be diminished somewhat by factors such as the control and manipulation of opinion and the bias
of the simple plurality ballot system.

5 *A two-party system and an official Opposition.*
Two coherent and disciplined parties compete
for power. In the classical theory they alternate
in power and thus check and balance each
other. This is the pendulum theory of the British constitution. In practice the pendulum
sticks on the right; and the symmetry is further
disturbed by the rise and decline of third and
minor parties (see Figure 2).

EXERCISE
The pendulum stops swinging?

3.7 Construct a diagram for elections since
1945 (see Chapter 14, Table 1) and consider whether the pendulum still swings.

The pendulum theory of British politics is significant in the theory of British democracy. It is
assumed that the minority party will form an
official Opposition in Parliament (enjoying certain privileges including a salary and a government car for the Leader of the Opposition) and
offer an alternative government, bidding
through Parliament for the support of the electorate and likely in due course to take its turn
as the government. Thus the government was
accountable and removable and, it was implied, alternation of parties in power was indispensable to a healthy democracy. Single party
rule was inherently undemocratic.
This is the essence of majoritarian two-party
democracy, British style. Any country claiming
to be democratic has to provide for minorities,
opposition and the peaceful replacement of
governments. Britain can meet these tests.
However, the pendulum theory has been
damaged, though not yet destroyed, by the
fourth consecutive victory of the Conservative
party in the election of 1992. Since 1945 Labour has won a working majority only twice –
but the theory, and British democracy, is safe
as long as there is serious competition with a
dominant party.
6 *A powerful central bureaucracy.* Britain, like all
developed countries and indeed many less developed ones, has a large and powerful bureaucracy which plays a significant part in the
day-to-day business of government and to some
extent in policy-making. This is for reasons
which are common to all bureaucracies; they
are large, permanent, comparatively expert
and well-informed and control the implementation of policy.

Figure 2 The pendulum theory of British politics
From W. I. Jennings, *The British Constitution*, CUP, 1947.

The bureaucracy in Britain is probably not as powerful as in France (where the bureaucracy has high prestige and is closely integrated with politics). But the upper level of the British bureaucracy forms a close and self-conscious community, jealous of its position as guardian of the interests of the state and unchallenged by a provincial or local or party bureaucracy. This is not the case in the USA, where the upper levels of the bureaucracy may be recruited from business and the professions and there are state and local bureaucracies to rival the federal bureaucracy.

7 *Limited judicial review.* In most modern states the government is subject to some degree of judicial review, that is, government policies and decisions as well as legislation may be challenged in the courts and declared illegal or unconstitutional. This usually amounts to impropriety in substance or procedure, for example an act going beyond constitutional or statutory powers, or involving inadequate or improper procedures.

The judgement of the courts is thus different from the political judgement. The courts do not say, your policy is wrong or not to our taste, but your policy, whether good or bad, goes beyond your constitutional powers, involves an illegal infringement of individual rights, or an unjust or burdensome procedure. However, it is evident that the line between the political and the judicial may be indistinct. This has been notoriously the case in the USA, where the powerful Supreme Court has sometimes very clearly judged on the basis of political values – either its own values, or what it perceived to be the values of the elite or the people.

In Britain there is only limited scope for judicial review, since there is no constitutional provision for judicial review, no written constitution to set a standard for the review of the decisions of government or Parliament and an established parliamentary supremacy. Nevertheless, the judges have from time to time reviewed the acts of government, basing their judgement on the precise powers granted by statute.

The weakness of judicial review in Britain clearly adds to the power of the central government. If the government has a secure majority in Parliament, no challenge from the courts and no rival provincial or local jurisdictions, then it may well be, as critics have charged, an 'elective dictatorship'. On the other hand, crit-

ics of the unchallenged power of British governments may regard the courts as unrepresentative, biased towards the propertied classes and the executive, archaic and expensive.

The constraints of an international setting

International organisations and the EC. If the extent of diffusion of power through the United Kingdom is in question, there is less doubt about the loss of power by central government in the international sphere. Here national sovereignty is more clearly open to challenge. In domestic matters, within limits (e.g. the precise number of houses and level of rents), central government in the end can expect to implement its policy throughout the United Kingdom. But in economic and defence matters, policy is the outcome of bargaining and negotiation, in which the United Kingdom government is not (as with local governments) a heavy-handed senior partner.

Since 1945 international organisations have become more numerous, more formal in structure and much wider in their scope of influence. Britain, like other European countries, voluntarily conceded power in foreign and defence policies to bodies like the United Nations Organisation, the North Atlantic Treaty Organisation and various bodies for economic co-operation (e.g. the Organisation for Economic Co-operation and Development and the European Free Trade Association).

Britain's accession in 1972 to the European Economic Community (EEC or Common Market, now the European Community) was a significant further step, involving much greater transfer of power in a much wider area of policies. Britain as a member of the Community has a voice in the taking of decisions, which are subject to a prolonged process of bargaining, ending in an agreed package of decisions. But the locus of policy-making is Brussels and the machinery is that of the EC not of the United Kingdom.

There is no doubt that membership of the EC infringes the sovereignty of the British Parliament. That, after all, was the intention of the creation of this supra-national organisation. Parliamentary sovereignty is saved in theory by the power of Parliament to repeal the Act of Accession and in practice by the bargaining and veto power of United Kingdom Ministers in the EC's Council of Ministers. But citizens of the United Kingdom are now subject to EC laws; hence sovereignty has been weakened.

A governing class

Behind governments lie governing classes. This is true in two ways. First, the profession of government is not completely open; like most professions it is hard to get in and entry is to some extent controlled by those already in or with interests in the composition of the profession. Second, government, the general direction of a country's affairs, is the concern of many groups not formally making up the government – bankers, financiers, industrialists, trade unionists, leaders of the professions and so on. It may be argued that some of these groups and notably the major economic groups, wield substantial power in closed circles intimately related to the circle of government itself.

This interpretation is true to some extent in all developed countries, though there are obvious differences between the capitalist and the communist systems. Britain is a particularly good, or bad, example of a country with a system of government overlaid or interpenetrated by a governing class. It is a familiar observation that in Britain holders of positions of power share a common social and educational background. A study by *The Economist* of one hundred 'top' people in 1972 and 1992 showed that at both dates two-thirds attended private ('public') schools and over one half 'Oxbridge' – and almost all were of course middle-aged men.

Characterisations of British Government

Responsible government

British government is responsible, that is to say answerable, government. It is not and does not try to be, direct popular government. The government is responsible to Parliament and Parliament to the people, in general elections. Within government, the administration (the departments, the civil service) is responsible to Ministers, through the Cabinet to Parliament. Thus in theory a line of responsibility runs from the humblest civil servant, via Cabinet and Parliament, to the people, and popular sovereignty is assured.

This is, of course, an overstatement. The line of responsibility is much too tenuous to support the supremacy of the people. Responsibility means answerability and this implies something weaker than control, weaker because it is discontinuous, tentative, general; because it indicates rather than commands. Answerability is rightly seen as a way of providing for freedom and restriction, scope for initiative and independent action, but without

complete loss of control.

Responsibility is a powerful myth in British government. At its best it has emphasised democratic accountability to Parliament and people; but it has also enhanced the power of government to act independently under a cloak of responsibility. The more general meaning of responsibility – reliable, trustworthy – has covered up this diminution of answerability.

Where the choice of words and their connotations are so important, diagrams are plainly misleading. We can draw a line of responsibility with electorate at one end and a humble civil servant at the other as shown in Figure 3.

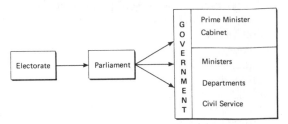

Figure 3 The flow of responsibility (1)

We can stand this on one end or the other, height signifying power as shown in Figure 4.

Or we can escape from this dilemma and draw a circle instead of a line – this is sensible, for government is a continuous process as shown in Figure 5.

However, these diagrams are all unsatisfactory, for they do not show the importance of the Cabinet, nor indicate any differences in the relations of the parts of the system. Nor do they take account of the pressures upon government.

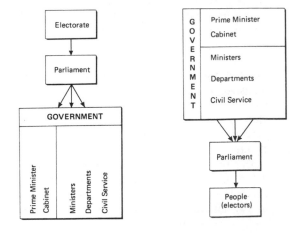

Figure 4 The flow of responsibility (2)

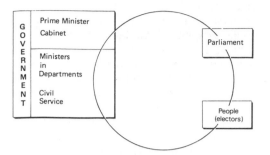

Figure 5 The flow of responsibility (3)

The diagrams might imply that a government in harmonious relationship with Parliament and people is free to govern. But in politics the problems fight back. Our diagrams are insufficient, but so too is the characterisation of British government simply as 'responsible government'.

Strong but restrained and responsive government

The constitutional foundation of British government is the sovereignty (i.e. supremacy) of Parliament. Strictly and historically, the Crown-in-Parliament is supreme; in practice Parliament has wrested power from the Crown; but also in practice Parliament hands that power to its executive committee (Prime Minister and Cabinet) to exercise on its behalf. There is an apparent paradox in that the sovereign Parliament is powerless. Herein lies the strength of the British government.

The distribution of power in the British political system is transformed in this way by the operation of political parties. It is normally possible for one of the two major parties to secure from a general election a majority of Members of Parliament. From these is drawn a government which can normally expect to control Parliament. The electorate itself cannot be controlled, but the government has up to five years before it has to hold an election and has substantial advantages in the electoral contest, including some influence over relative prosperity and a free choice of date for the election.

Clearly, the majority party has very considerable power. Within the party the leadership and particularly the Leader himself as Prime Minister, is dominant. There is a possibility here of unrestrained power ('dictatorship', to use an old-fashioned and emotive phrase) in the hands of Prime Minister or Cabinet. But for most of the time restraints seem to operate: the personal restraints of regard for principle and need for approval; the perhaps more dependable restraints of political colleagues and senior civil servants; the desire and the need to retain the ungrudging support of the party in Parliament; the pressures and persuasions of interest groups, journalists, advisers (asked and unasked); the constant reminder by the opposition that the electorate is the final arbiter.

British governments are enmeshed in this network of restraints, whether they like it or not. But mostly governments take a more positive attitude and are willingly responsive to these restraining influences. This is not simply a matter of accepting the necessary or the inevitable with good grace; it springs in part from a genuine acceptance of democratic principles.

Big government and the illusion of power

Alongside these constitutional characterisations it is necessary to keep in mind the overall feature of modern government to do with its size and scope, its ambitions and aspirations, hence its power, but also, paradoxically, the impotence which arises because its reach exceeds its grasp.

Sheer size can be demonstrated in various ways. For example, there are about ten times more civil or public servants now than in 1900; almost one half of the adult population derive their income directly or indirectly from the government; the proportion of Gross National Product spent by the government has risen from 9 per cent in 1870 to over 40 per cent in the 1990s. It is clear that the full development of the 'Managed Economy/Welfare State' has brought about a condition which may reasonably be characterised as 'big government'. This is not peculiar to Britain and it does not mean that governments in earlier centuries did not intervene at all in the lives of citizens. Nor does it mean that governments have grown against the wishes of citizens; the contrary is true.

Centralisation and the diffusion of power

British government is centralised as well as big. It acts over a great range of the nation's affairs. The constitution is undeniably unitary, not federal: there are no units or levels of government with the standing to compete with the centre. Parliamentary sovereignty and Ministerial responsibility deliver formal power to an executive derived from, but controlling, Parliament.

In practice, power is more diffuse than this constitutional model suggests. A great deal of government is carried out at one remove at least from the centre, by local government and by a host of corporations, councils and committees. Some of these are clearly 'government', some are 'non-government' but government-assisted; and some are hybrid, 'quasi-governmental' bodies. The distinctions are not always clear. 'Government' is thus a network of bodies, governmental, quasi-governmental and 'non-governmental', overshadowed by the central government itself. Governing at one remove, or through the network or at arms length, can modify the centralisation of government. There is a shift of function and execution, while overall financial control remains at the centre. In recent years the central government has insisted on tight financial control, notably in the case of local government and the nationalised industries. In consequence, the system of partly indirect government has been operated as a direct and centralised system.

Still it does not follow that British government is normally and naturally a single system totally controlled from the centre. The government meets both inertia (the system tends to go on doing what it has always done) and counter pressure (the people working the system resist and fight back). Moreover, the government's weapons for close control are comparatively crude.

Thus government is a bit like an elephant. If it plays football, it will not score many goals; but if it sits on you, you are dead.

Change and reform in British government

British government has changed a good deal in the last fifty years. The international dimension is one aspect of change. Contrast the high drama of Chamberlain's famous visit to Europe in September 1938 (Munich) with the constant round of negotiation abroad which takes place now. Local government once had an honoured place in the system and grew assertive; now it has been humbled and restrained by central government. In the 1940s and 1950s, Britain had a stable two-party system, apparently supported by a fairly stable electorate. Since then allegiance has become less certain and the two-party system seems to have become a three- or four-party system with a single governing party. In 1945 the Labour Party knew what it stood for and politics was organised around Labour's stance. Since then political principles have been obscured by immediate crises and a sea change in political thinking. The 1940s and 1950s were characterised by a strong confi-

dence in the government's duty and capacity to provide peace, prosperity and social welfare. The economic problems of the last two decades and the evident inefficiencies and high costs of state bureaucracies have weakened that confidence.

The consequence for British governments has been that they face insoluble problems before sceptical and critical spectators. Dissatisfaction with the performance of governments has dissolved some of the old trust in the constitution. The revered constitutional principles of sovereignty, responsibility and the rule of law seemed inadequate compared with the new critical characterisations: 'elective dictatorship', 'Prime Ministerial power', 'overload', 'ungovernability', 'governing under pressure'. These were all criticisms from within the conventional liberal pluralist approach: beyond lay the heavier guns of Marxist analysis and the diagnosis of an oppressive, late capitalist system in decline. Margaret Thatcher's decade restored authority to government and ended talk of 'ungovernability', but at some cost in consent, despite election victories.

British government in the 1990s looks to be uneasy. Its power is restricted by the sheer intractability of the matters it tries to control. 'Decisions' are not always very decisive: 'Let us stop talking and try this and see what happens; you never know, it might help.' Policy is often no more than a set of loose understandings about a general approach to a problem. Sometimes the great mountain (the structure and processes of policy-making) labours only to bring forth 'a ridiculous mouse'. Yet the great mountain is still worth studying, for some of its mice are less ridiculous than others and sometimes its labour is not in vain. We do not study a barren mountain.

Modern governments perhaps try to control too much, but this seems now to be expected of them. But if expectations are high, interest and participation in politics are relatively low. For most people the vote in a general election is their only political act. Thus governments seem sometimes to be trying to sell goods they do not stock to customers they cannot see; the customers maintain the shop, but sometimes throw bricks through the window. The governing of a modern mass democracy is indeed a difficult art and we do well to remember that the world is littered with the debris of political failure.

GUIDE TO EXERCISES

3.1 Margaret Thatcher studied chemistry and

law, not history. Perhaps a Pass, not a Distinction (unless it fails as not being her own work). None of the ideas is wrong, but there is a lack of precision and scepticism. The connection of Magna Carta with representative institutions is tenuous; the concept of the rule of law requires definition. Britain's historic relationship to Europe is not adequately conveyed in the otherwise moving reference to the 60 000 British soldiers.

3.2 There can be little doubt that the British system of government and British public life are shot through with 'archaisms' and it seems unlikely that such archaism is merely decoration and has no effect on the substance and working of the system. The connection of the unwritten constitution with archaism is less clear. There has never been a grand sweeping away of the legacy of the past as in France or Russia; on the other hand, there has never been a new constitution to acquire itself over a period of time the aura of the ancient. It is indeed often argued that the British constitution is uniquely flexible. But, as the Document asserts, an unwritten but revered constitution may be very difficult to reform, both because it is ancient and revered and because it is obscure and elusive. It may be further argued that the absence of a written constitution has discouraged serious, detailed and practical thinking about the constitution in Britain. In that way Britain has come to rely on the relics of the past and this might well be called constitutional archaism.

3.3 Yes, this seems to be indicated by the diagram. But it is well to remember that overriding authority remains at the centre. This is not the case in the USA. The question of comparative degrees of centralisation is further discussed in Chapter 24.

3.4 The absence of a Ministry for England may be explained partly on the practical ground that England is so large a part of the UK that it can be governed satisfactorily by a UK ministry; but also and significantly by the national history of the English, explained above – the English see themselves as British.

3.5 Yes, Bagehot was and is, correct about the significance of the legislative origins and support of the British Cabinet. For all that

has to be said about the power of the executive in Britain and the weakness of Parliament, the Cabinet is at the centre of the structure of the executive and is at the same time at the centre of the structure of Parliament. The Cabinet is characteristically a team of party politicians who have served for some time and with some distinction (enough to be picked out by the leader) in Parliament.

3.6 Of course the system has changed since the 1860s – for example, a massive expansion of government and the bureaucracy, the consolidation of parties, the development of the media, the internationalisation of politics. Such change has strengthened the executive and drawn the Cabinet away from Parliament. But the link with Parliament remains important. Bagehot thought that Parliament could withdraw its confidence from the Cabinet, but the Cabinet could respond by threatening dissolution. This balance of power has been destroyed by modern party solidarity.

3.7. This you do for yourself. Has the clock stopped? – see text.

ASSESSMENT
Models of British government

There are roughly three kinds of model of British government.

1 The classic Westminster model
   This is best explained by an extract from Sir Ivor Jennings.
   From W. I. Jennings, *The British Constitution*, 1941, pp. 209–10:
   '[There is a] close relation between the policies followed by the Government and the general ideas of the majority of the electorate. It is a consequence of the simple principles upon which the British Constitution is based. The Government governs because it has a majority in the House of Commons. It possesses that majority because the party which it leads secured a majority of seats in the last general election. The parties are not mere electioneering organisations...but are truly based upon competing political principles. In preferring one party to another, therefore, the electorate not only prefers one Government to another but prefers one line of policy to another. Its choice is of course made at

infrequent intervals, but always the Government in power has the prospect of having to appeal to the electorate at no very distant date....

Since in fact the division of support between the two major parties is extremely small, any Government must have profound respect for movements of opinion. Nor can it fail to be aware of such movements, for every member of the House of Commons is in close touch with his constituency and is aware of the currents that tend to lose him votes....He sounds the alarm in the House when the bell begins to ring in his constituency.'

2 Capitalist Democracy

The constitutional forms of government serve to hide the real power of a governing class, or the political power of capitalism. Here is a characterisation of British government as 'capitalist democracy'. Note that this falls short of a simple Marxist interpretation, which would see British democracy as 'bourgeois democracy', democracy for capitalists not for workers.

From R. Miliband, *Capitalist Democracy in Britain*, 1984, p. 1:

'... if democracy is defined in terms of popular participation in the determination of policy and popular control over the conduct of affairs, then the British political system is far from democratic....the political system has served, so far as was possible, to prevent rather than facilitate the exercise of popular power either in the determination of policy or in the conduct of affairs. Democratic claims and political reality do not truly match.

On the other hand, the British political system does incorporate a number of democratic features, which make it possible for "ordinary people" to make themselves heard, and which compel those in power to take some account of popular concerns and expectations. Indeed, the people in power may find themselves out of it as a result of a shift of opinion as expressed in a general election. This may be of much smaller consequence for the actual structure of power than is alleged or believed; but it may also have substantial policy implications and cannot be dismissed as of no consequence.

The term "capitalist democracy" is... intended to denote a permanent and fundamental contradiction or tension, in a capitalist society such as Britain, between the promise of popular power, enshrined in universal suffrage, and the curbing or denial of that promise in practice. Democratic institutions and practices provide means of expression and representation to the working class, organised labour, political parties and groups, and other such forms of pressure and challenge from below; but the context provided by capitalism requires that the effect they may have should as far as possible be weakened.'

3 'Contemporary realism'

This is a tendentious label for a perspective which tries to improve on the idealistic Westminster model without fully conceding the domination of economic interests.

Compared with the Westminster model the sceptical realist perspective emphasises::

- the power of the majority party to control the Parliament
- the consequent weakness of Parliament
- the dominance of the executive and within the executive of the Prime Minister and senior Ministers
- the pervasive influence of senior civil servants
- the significant influence of the major pressure groups, especially financial and producer groups
- the capacity of the competitive electoral system to deliver a degree of genuine democracy, including a good deal of government which is plainly in the interests of the a majority of people.

The contemporary realist model incorporates the critical understanding of the 'elective dictatorship' view, while allowing for constraints in detail (as does the capitalist democracy model).

A contemporary realist view (to which this account aspires) would be uneasy about characterising British government simply as 'responsible government', though that description is technically correct. It would be more acceptable, if just a little complacent, to use the description: 'strong but restrained and responsive government'. This formulation suggests some difficult tests to be applied in the study of British government and recent political history. What indications and evidence can be found to suggest strength, restraint and responsiveness?

Concept

Legitimacy

Legitimacy implies a measure of acceptance and consent as well as legality; hence it refers to the qualities beyond legality which induce or encourage consent. Acceptance of a regime can arise from coercion – 'legitimacy out of the barrel of a gun' – but such involuntary acceptance does not constitute consent.

In the Middle Ages legitimacy could be derived from the doctrine of the Divine Right of Kings. For a medieval king legality was derived from birth, legitimacy from God – and anyone in doubt could be referred to the Tower and the axeman. In Britain since the seventeenth century legitimacy has come to be associated with the approval of Parliament. Behind that lay significant ideas about the conditions of legitimacy: representation, responsibility and the imputation of a contract between government and governed.

The idea of contract allows for appeal against even a parliamentary government and is potentially a revolutionary doctrine, as the American Colonists demonstrated in 1776. In a modern liberal and pluralist state it would be accepted (within limits) that a government may default on its implied contract, lose legitimacy and suffer justifiable protest – short of its overthrow. (There follow difficult problems about the justification of forms of protest involving disobedience, illegality and violence).

The idea of legitimacy raises problems for the courts too: are they concerned simply with legality or should they venture into quasi-political judgements of legitimacy?

● CASE STUDY
The Monarchy and British politics

Do we need a monarchy?
The monarchy is a distinctive feature of the public face of British politics and enjoys high popularity and public esteem. But its political value may be questioned. The case for the monarchy rests on the following:

1 Its actual constitutional utility. It is a necessary element in the constitution and machinery for choosing governments, but this could be done in other ways, for example, by a President, or by the Speaker of the House of Commons.

2 The monarchy symbolises the nation and the state and so plays a significant part in the symbolic side of politics, both at home and more especially abroad. This is notably so in the Commonwealth, for which the Queen provides a symbolic unity which belies its conflicts and tensions. (Critics argue that the Commonwealth serves no purpose anyway). It is also worth noting that Margaret Thatcher thought it worthwhile to prevent the Queen visiting the European Parliament, thus bestowing prestige upon it.

3 The monarchy has stood for social and personal ideals, in particular family life and religious faith. This is less convincing as Britain has become secular or multi-faith and royal marriages have collapsed. Further the Royal Family has not been able to hide from public view its massive wealth and the far from modest life styles which go with it.

4 It may also be argued that the Monarchy provides a storehouse of political wisdom, accumulated over many years and available to the nation in times of crisis. (This does not convince those who believe the Royal Family to be almost wholly cut off from the real world their subjects inhabit.)

The case against the monarchy rests on the rejection of these supporting arguments but goes beyond this.

It is argued that the monarchy reinforces undemocratic and elitist elements in British society – wealth, aristocracy, snobbery, living on unearned income, militarism, preference for horses over art. The monarchy contradicts the sound Thatcherite principle that people should work for a living and reinforces an aristocratic version of the 'dependency culture'.

Further, the existence of the monarchy encourages the preservation of medieval ritual which is meaningless in itself but can be damaging politically – the Queen's Speech at the opening of Parliament, the whole absurd notion of the House of Lords and the use by government of unfettered executive power disguised as the 'royal prerogative'.

Finally, the monarchy imposes on members of the Royal Family heavy personal and social burdens which it is evidently difficult for many of them to bear with grace, equanimity and success; monarchy is a cruel system.

Clearly the case for the monarchy is weak. But the problem, as with the House of Lords,

is what to put in its place? The most ingenious suggestion is that Prince Charles should
become the first elected President of the
United Kingdom.

The constitutional uses of the monarchy
Who chooses the Prime Minister? – the role of
the monarchy.
The monarch has an essential part in the formalities of establishing a new government, but
normally has no influence on the choice of
Prime Minister. The Prime Minister must have
the support of a majority in the House of Commons and it is there and in the electoral procedures of the parties, that the essential choice is
made. It is always possible that the House
might not produce a clear majority, but less
likely in such circumstances that the choice
would in practice lie with the Queen. For the
monarch cannot choose a Prime Minister; she
must invite to form a government the person
most likely to carry a majority in the House. On
this point she must take advice, being in no
position to judge; and the House, in the end,
would surely not abdicate its prime duty to ensure that the Queen's government goes on.

There have been occasions recently when
the Queen may appear to have exercised some
choice of her own. In January 1957 she invited
Harold Macmillan to succeed Sir Anthony
Eden, though R. A. Butler was the expected
heir. During the time when the choice was being made, the Queen received in audience two
elder statesmen of the Conservative Party, Sir
Winston Churchill and Lord Salisbury. But it
seems the invitation to Macmillan was the result of a hasty and informal poll of the Conservative Party. The consultation with Churchill
and Salisbury was presumably by way of confirmation.

In 1963 the Conservative Party had once
more to choose a new Leader/Prime Minister:
and this time there was even greater confusion
about the available candidates, following the
unexpected announcement during the party's
Annual Conference of Macmillan's retirement.
Again there was a hasty informal poll and the
Queen was advised to send for Lord Home
(who was to renounce his peerage). Lord
Home was not acceptable to some Conservatives and two former Ministers refused to serve.
The party was indeed in disarray; there was no
obvious candidate for the leadership, but some
were less in disfavour than others.

It has been argued that the Queen in effect
intervened in the choosing process by sending
immediately for Lord Home: had she waited,
Home's opponents in the party would have
been able to make their preferences known.
This may be so; but it seems much more likely
that the Queen and her advisers acted with
unusual speed in order to end the uncertainty
and secure a new government. She was surely
right to think that further delay might make
choice more, not less, difficult; and it was still
open to Parliament to reject her choice. Subsequently, in 1965, the Conservatives adopted a
formal election procedure for the choice of
leader; so the monarch would not again face
the problems of succession which arose in
1957 and 1964.

In February 1974 the monarch had at last to
face what had been in recent times only a textbook speculation: no party gained an overall
majority in the House of Commons. Again it
seems that the Queen was not compelled to
intervene, because the politicians chose to
manage the crisis themselves. The Conservative Prime Minister failed to make an alliance
with the Liberals; he resigned, advising the
Queen to invite the Leader of the largest single
party, Labour, to form a government. A Labour
government was formed and its opponents in
the House of Commons did not combine to use
their majority to bring the government down.
Another election in October solved the problem
(just) by providing the Labour government with
a bare majority.

Can the monarch refuse a dissolution?
The problem of dissolution arose again in
1974–5. Could the Queen refuse a dissolution
to the minority Labour Prime Minister? ('We
have just had an election; another one may
make no difference; go away and form a coalition'). The answer is that the Queen will not
intrude into the government of the country, unless the politicians are in deadlock or otherwise
abdicate; and the politicians together with the
Queen's advisers collaborate to protect the
Queen from political embarrassment. In practice this means that a Prime Minister of a government with an uncertain parliamentary
majority may ask for and expect to receive a
dissolution a few months after the previous
election – unless it seems (and here the
Queen's advisers have to take a view) there is
an alternative majority already available. (In

July 1993 John Major threatened his party with a general election if he lost a confidence motion. He seems to have assumed, correctly if discourteously, that the Queen would grant a dissolution if he lost the confidence of the house – and provided no other potential Prime Minister was at hand).

Can the Queen insist on the dissolution of Parliament and the holding of an election – which is equivalent to the dismissal of a ministry? No monarch has done this since George III (or possibly William IV). Theory, constitutional law and precedents, including a recent Australian precedent, give some support to such monarchical power. But, again, the conditions of modern politics go right against the possibility. First, the monarch must find a government with a majority in the Commons; a forced dissolution would be acceptable only if the government had lost its majority and a dissolution was likely to provide a new majority. But, second, the monarch cannot insist on a dissolution in circumstances in which the move might fail to provide a majority administration, thus damaging the prestige of the Crown. Third, the monarch cannot act in a way which may appear to be partisan – these are conditions of survival, not conventions; matters not of constitutional right but of what the monarch can 'get away with'. It is difficult for the monarch to 'get away with' insisting on a dissolution.

It should be understood that 'the Queen' in this political context is, like the Prime Minister, an office, not just a person. The Queen has senior advisers and secretaries and in any political crisis they will advise her and deal directly with politicians. This de-personalisation or institutionalisation strengthens rather than demeans the monarchy.

These incidents and considerations show that the monarch is an essential part of the mechanics of government formation, but normally has no discretion. However, the possibility of a 'hung' Parliament is comparatively high, because of the working of the electoral system and the success of minority parties. Hence it is now a little more likely that the processes of government formation will not be straightforward. In practice the parties are likely to act so that the monarchy is protected from political intervention and will be told ('advised') whom she must choose. ●

Prime Minister and Cabinet: the structure

Approach and analysis

The executive in the British Constitution

Prime Minister and Cabinet, together with the Departments of State and the civil service constitute the main part of the executive branch of British government. The executive is the dominant part of British government. The executive power of the Crown was challenged by Parliament, and then, in effect, taken over by Prime Minister and Cabinet backed by a political party, in the name of Parliament (see Chapters 2 and 3). The British constitution includes none of the checking and balancing of the executive that is a feature of, for example, the United States constitution.

The executive element in British government is best described as 'Cabinet government'. The Prime Minister wields substantial power, and attracts a significant share of public attention. There is, therefore, a case for labelling the system 'prime ministerial government', or even 'presidential government' (though the American connotation is misleading). However, this emphasis on the personal power of the Prime Minister neglects the continuing force of the collective and Cabinet elements in the structure of government. These arguments are reviewed below.

Prime Minister and Cabinet do not constitute the whole of the executive centre of British government. The Prime Minister is surrounded and supported by the Cabinet Office, the Prime Minister's Office, including the Policy Unit and other personal advisers. The Cabinet is a collection of colleagues and a system of committees and small groups, as well as the formal full Cabinet. Both Prime Minister and Cabinet swim in a pool of officials.

All of these, politicians, advisers, officials, live and work in what might be called the Central Executive Territory – about 400 people occupying buildings in and around Downing Street and Whitehall. The Central Executive Territory is clearly, by its physical and constitutional location and by function, central and executive. The designation 'territory' has the advantage of avoiding institutional shapes and formal relationships. Of course, these exist, but the Territory is a network of shifting relationships, as if in the London Underground railway, or the Paris Metro, the maps as well as the timetable were not entirely reliable.

Analysing the office of Prime Minister

This chapter is concerned with the office of Prime Minister, the person and the office. The following scheme of analysis tries to order and make sense of the abundant and confusing evidence.

1 *Style*

This word has been much used, especially in relation to Margaret Thatcher – 'it is not what she did, but the way that she did it!' 'Style' is, indeed, a treacherous term, which can easily become a large basket for various items, a catch-all for the left overs (residuals). Style includes the following elements.

a) Stance, or approach to the job, including choice of policy objective and strategies; the choice between popular and party leadership and bureaucratic management.

There are alternative models, which might be labelled 'Chairman' and 'Chief Executive', the former taking a more collective and consensual approach, the latter the hard-driving 'boss'.

Chairman	Chief Executive
consensus building	decisive leadership
reactive	pro-active
'hands-off'	interventionist
looking to survival	pursuing specific aims

gradualist   purposive
keeping convoy together   racing ahead

The two models are not mutually exclusive. Prime Ministers do not consciously choose one or the other; they can take something of both; or work in between; or switch from one to the other over time or for different areas of policy.

b) Methods, mode of work. Prime Ministers read, write, talk, like all senior managers. Prime Ministers might be characterised by their general commitment to work (Thatcher a notable workaholic, Baldwin notably relaxed), and their division of time between the three basic activities of reading, writing and talking. Behind this lie questions of how the Prime Minister chooses to brief himself or herself, and how much he or she works alone or in company. Such distributions may be significant for the emphasis he places on collegiality and consent. But there is not much evidence on which we can make a judgement.

c) Personal style. This includes what we understand as 'personality', in the proper sense of character, temperament, disposition, values, together with the mode and manner of social or public presentation, which include less fundamental elements, voice, hair, make-up. We say, 'He or she strikes me as nice, warm and friendly, or cold and unfriendly'. Personal style is what does the striking, makes that impact between persons, causes an immediate, irrational response.

Alternatively, we say that leadership depends partly on an elusive personal 'chemistry' – hence one leader regularly gets more work and commitment out of his team than another.

Gender and age are also significant elements. Political leaders throughout the world are frequently old men. Of recent Prime Ministers Churchill was 76 when he took office in 1951, Macmillan 63 in 1957. By contrast Wilson was 47, Major 46 on taking office, and Margaret Thatcher, feminine and 55. Margaret Thatcher had the strongest personal style of recent Prime Ministers – an advantage and a disadvantage in that she attracted some and repelled others.

These elements of prime ministerial style are significant for the conduct of the office of Prime Minister, in so far as it is an office for an individual, with scope for personal action. But the office is also locked into the Cabinet structure. Recent commentary especially on Margaret Thatcher, has perhaps exaggerated the importance of personality and personal style in the long-term understanding of the office of Prime Minister.

2 *Prime Minister and Government: working relationships*

a) Officials and advisers. The Prime Ministership is in practice a set of offices and persons, not an individual – just as the US President is the Presidency, and the Queen is for constitutional purposes 'the Queen and her advisers', not the Queen as an individual. Prime Ministers since Lloyd George (1916–22) have developed their supporting offices into a substantial institution, including Prime Minister's Office, Cabinet Office, personal advisers and 'kitchen Cabinets'. Prime Ministers differ in their use of these supporting offices, but the Prime Ministership can function for a short period without the Prime Minister, who might be absent abroad, ill, absent or merely indolent.

b) Cabinet colleagues. The Prime Minister's relationship with his ministerial colleagues, especially members of the Cabinet, is the crucial relationship, determining the political quality of the government, and its effectiveness. There are two dominant but uneven elements in the relationship: the Prime Minister's power to hire and fire his colleagues; and the capacity of discontented senior ministers to make trouble.

c) Managing the system. The Prime Minister is the manager of the Cabinet and the support and advisory systems centred in 10 Downing Street. These expand his potential but complicate his professional life.

3 *Prime Minister and political leadership: party, Parliament, people.*

The Prime Minister has to build consent for his government; specifically, he has to win the next election. He is already leader of his party, and must secure continuing support, in Westminster and in the country. In Parliament he must keep his own side happy, partly by the generous use of favour and patronage, partly by blasting the Opposition (voting them down will normally present no problem).

Relations with 'the people' lie largely with the party and the media. A Prime Minister has massive advantages over his colleagues and opponents in access to the media. He makes news and gets two or three minutes of prime television time just by walking out of his front door and making a statement – and ten seconds just by walking out or arriving.

Questions and puzzles

Study of Prime Minister and Cabinet raises a number of significant questions about the nature and workings of British government:

- the recruitment and dismissal of a Prime Minister
- the exact nature of the Prime Minister's functions – political leadership, policy management
- the extent of the Prime Minister's power or force, within the Central Executive Territory and beyond; the impact and achievement of Prime Ministers
- the nature, functions and power of the Cabinet system.

The bases of Prime Ministerial force

The Prime Minister is powerful: he is a prince, even a king, within the Central Executive Territory. However, there are countervailing forces, and there may be restrictive circumstances. The Prime Minister's personal power is rooted in the Cabinet and the Cabinet system. The Prime Minister's relationship with his colleagues, whether dominant or collegial, is inescapable.

These are the persistent bases of a Prime Minister's power.

■ DOCUMENT 4.1
The major factors in Prime Ministerial power

Factor	Likely effect on Prime Minister's power
PARTY	The Prime Minister is leader of the party, and is expected to exercise leadership in policy and organisation matters and in election campaigns. But the party in parliament and in the country still expects to be listened to.
COLLEAGUES	The Prime Minister has the power to appoint and dismiss Ministerial colleagues. This was extended in practice by Margaret Thatcher (quite legitimately) to senior civil servants. There are a number of other public appointments within the

Prime Minister's gift, including peerages and other honours and membership of many public bodies.

But senior Ministers still have their own political standing and bases of support, civil servants may resent any apparent interference with their non-political tradition; in any case, there are prudential limits to the free use of the power of patronage.

CABINET	The Prime Minister chairs the Cabinet, controls its agenda, and manages the processing of issues within the Central Executive Territory. She can make bi-lateral deals with Ministers and thus divide and rule. But there is both a constitutional tradition and a political necessity for an element of collectivity, and in a complex network of relations there is scope for resisting Prime Ministerial domination.
PUBLIC FIGURE	The Prime Minister is the most prominent figure by far in the government, and has continuing opportunities to appear as national leader and world statesman (for example in summit meetings). He has easy access to the media, and ample facilities for the management and exploitation of the media. The Prime Minister has the potential to achieve high personal popularity. But continuous exposure brings continuous vulnerability. If things go wrong the Prime Minister 'carries the can'. The polls show that Prime Ministers can be very unpopular as well as very popular.
DEPARTMENTS	The Prime Minister is free of day-to-day departmental

responsibilities, which tie up many of her colleagues.

But much government policy making necessarily emerges from the detailed work of departments, which must be mastered. ■

EXERCISES
Major factors in Prime Ministerial power

4.1 Would you expect the Prime Minister's power to have increased in the last two decades?

4.2 Would you expect the personal qualities of the Prime Minister to make a substantial difference to his power?

Figure 1 The modern Cabinet

The chart shows one model of a modern Cabinet. But the tendency of such charts is to tidy up essentially overlapping and conflicting responsibilities. For example, the Chancellor belongs with the 'economics team'; Environment spreads over both social and economic functions; and the Prime Minister might well count as a 'non-departmental grandee'. The position and ranking of some departments depends on the personal standing of the Minister and the salience of the policy area. For example, in John Major's 1992 Government the Secretary for Trade and Industry, Michael Heseltine, belongs with the 'Great Of-

fices'. The Ministry of Defence is less important after the end of the Cold War but is still a high spender with a massive impact on industry.

How to become Prime Minister

In contrast with presidential systems, political leaders in Britain do not emerge from nowhere; they are not unknown. The three major parties all elect leaders through formal electoral arrangements. The Liberal Democrats alone give equal voice to all members. The Labour Party adopted in 1981 a system which gave votes to Trade Unions, Constituency Parties and the Parliamentary Labour Party, in the proportion 40:30:30. These arrangements compel candidates for leadership to appeal to the trade unions and the party in the country, as well as to Labour Members of Parliament. The Conservatives adopted an electoral system in 1965, based on Conservative Members of Parliament. This followed dissatisfaction with the choice of Lord Home by the 'customary processes' of the party elite, denounced by aggrieved Conservatives as 'the magic circle'. Margaret Thatcher rose and fell by this new and complex ballot system. Ironically, it seems likely that in a system which included representatives of the constituencies she would not have won in 1975, nor lost in 1990.

Advice to the politically ambitious is obvious enough: join a political party; become a Member of Parliament; work hard, show ability, please people and so become Leader; win a General Election. This advice reflects a significant characteristic of the British constitution – the recruitment, training and selection of political leaders goes on through the operation of political parties and in and around the House of Commons.

Such advice to candidates cannot guarantee success. The record shows that a politician is assisted in his ambitions by:

● patronage, support in high places
● association with, or dissociation from, significant tendencies and factions
● good luck, in particular being around, and coming up, at the right time.

When these last factors play a part, the unexpected candidate may win – and this is often the case. John Major, who succeeded Margaret Thatcher in 1990, is a good example of the unexpected and largely unknown Prime Minister. But Home's accession was even more surprising; and few people predicted Margaret Thatcher's election to the party leadership in 1975.

Table 1 The path to power

The length of parliamentary and Cabinet service of Prime Ministers

	(1)	(2)	(3)	(4)	(5)	(6)	(7)
Prime Minister	MP	Cabinet office	L'der	PM	years from first MP*	years from first Cabinet office*	Total Cabinet service*
Churchill	1900	1908	1940	1940	40	32	15
Eden	1923	1935	1955	1955	32	20	11
Wilson	1945	1947	1963	1964	19	17	4
Heath	1950	1959	1965	1970	20	11	5
Callaghan	1945	1964	1976	1976	31	12	8
Thatcher	1959	1970	1975	1979	20	9	4
Major	1979	1987	1990	1990	11	3	3

* Before becoming prime minister

EXERCISE
The path to Prime Ministerial power

4.3 Can you explain the 'odd man out' in the Table?

In his study of American politics in the late nineteenth century Lord Bryce wrote a chapter on 'Why great men are not chosen as Presidents'. In the USA the processes of presidential selection are indeed somewhat haphazard. In Britain the process seems better adapted to the selection, if not of great men and women, then of experienced politicians who have earned the confidence of their parliamentary colleagues and of the party. A conclusion about whether the Prime Ministerial selection process works well requires judgements on the quality and performance of Prime Ministers, and on the actual working of the selection process. With regard to quality and performance, the text offers some evidence of Prime Ministerial strengths and weaknesses and success and failure. But in a highly competitive trade there is often a feeling that there is a better potential Prime Minister in the Cabinet or on the back benches; and the fact that this is impossible to prove does not make it an unlikely speculation.

The selection processes differ in each party (see Chapter 14). In the Conservative Party only Members of Parliament take part in the leadership election; in other parties the membership is involved directly or, in the case of Labour, indirectly (with a substantial voice given to the trade unions). The selection of a party leader inevitably reflects the nature of the British political system, and indeed the nature of democratic politics. Politicians rise to the job of Prime Minister by being good at party and popular leadership; but the job demands a good deal more than the skills by which it was won.

There is here a built-in 'Peter principle', that is, the nature of selection processes tends to advance people to the level of their incompetence; thus good teachers or surgeons or plumbers become bad managers, good batsmen make bad captains, and successful party politicians fail to become great statesmen. However, a less sceptical view would be that in the case of politics a selection process which is part rational, part haphazard, has worked surprisingly well, judged by its products; and that the quality of the whole organisation may be as important for success as the quality of the person at the top.

The day-to-day work of a Prime Minister

■ DOCUMENT 4.2
A day in the life of a Prime Minister

a) From an article by Simon Hoggart in The Observer, *2 January 1983*

Margaret Thatcher
Margaret Thatcher's morning generally begins the previous night. One of her Ministers describes a typical encounter. 'It's 1 a.m. and you've had a hell of a day, so you're tottering down a Commons corridor... when you see this vision in blue drifting along looking as if she's just emerged from the beauty parlour... "Ah," she says, "How are you, dear? Now tell me what you think about these new statistics! And what do you propose to do about them?" It is absolutely terrifying.'

Probably no Premier in history has devoted so long to the [Red] Boxes. She is obsessively industrious, a source of much resentment to those who work with her. 'I regard it as quite unwholesome,' another Minister says.... 'She thinks that she must know everything that is going on, every single detail,' a Cabinet Minister says. 'It can be infuriating. She just will not allow you to get on with it.' She might spare a moment to glance through the newspapers, but certainly no longer.... [Later Margaret Thatcher came to depend on summaries of the media prepared by her Press Secretary.]

Meetings begin at 9 o'clock, and, on Tuesdays and Thursdays, the first session is devoted to plotting Prime Minister's Questions. This fifteen-minute session is regarded as of crucial importance, partly because she permits any topic at all to be raised. 'She thinks that Questions are her hotline to the British people'....

Most of her day is spent in meetings, sometimes of a distinctly argumentative nature.... In the evening there might be a reception at Downing Street. Whisked between official residences in official cars, Prime Ministers soon become sealed off from the real world and begin to place exaggerated store by their meetings with ordinary people whether across a factory bench or a gin and tonic....

If she has no official dinner, she will return to the Commons to chat to Conservative MPs. She is much better at this than Ted Heath ever was. Sometimes she will take a quick snack in the cafeteria, the only Prime Minister to make a habit of this.... [Later Margaret Thatcher abandoned this 'habit' which was not always welcomed.]

It is late at night and she is still scurrying around. Unlike, say, Harold Wilson, she does not try to fix her Cabinets beforehand. There are no sessions with old pals swigging brandy at Number 10. 'This is not a late-night drinking club,' says one official, severely. She might occasionally see a recalcitrant MP if the whips ask her, but this is rare...

b) From H. Wilson, 1976, pp. 84–5
Harold Wilson, ten years later, on briefings and engagements
[Wilson analysed his diary for the three months October to December 1975 as follows.]

Audiences of the Queen	8
Cabinet meetings	11
Cabinet committees	24
Other Ministerial meetings	43
State visits	1
Other head of government visits	5
Other foreign VIP visits (deputy Prime Minister, finance, foreign ministers etc.)	8
Visits abroad	2
Visits to Northern Ireland	1
Meetings with industry, prominent industrialists etc.	28
Official meetings	27
Ministerial speeches	17
Political speeches	9
Visits within Britain	13
Official lunches and dinners	20
Political meetings — no speech	11
TV or radio broadcasts (excluding party conference)	8

Christmas apart, I was not able to record a single private or social engagement ... ■

■ DOCUMENT 4.3
The pell-mell of politics

From D. Hurd, 1979, pp. 113–4
[Douglas Hurd worked as Political Secretary to Edward Heath when he was Prime Minister. In his account of that time he wrote of 'the pell-mell of politics'.]

'Because historians tend to analyse one subject at a time they sometimes lose sight of the pell-mell of politics. Problems crowd in on top of each other, competing for scarce time. The immediate topic crowds out something more important. The principal actors thrive for a time on the excitement of this way of life. They do not notice the onset of fatigue... they begin without realising it to move through a fog of tiredness'.

This happened, he says, in the Winter of 1973 when the Prime Minister was concerned with Stage 3 of the Incomes Policy, the onset of the Yom Kippur War, a government reshuffle, the Party Conference; a visit from Chancellor Brandt and from the ruler of Abu Dhabi. ('Rulers from the Gulf were not men to be bowed in and out in ten minutes or half an hour. They required coffee and much ceremonious chat'), four by-elections and the beginnings of the Miners' Strike which was to bring about the fall of the government. ■

EXERCISE
Job satisfaction for Prime Ministers

4.4 How and why can Prime Ministers cope with the heavy demands of the job?

The Downing Street complex: The Prime Minister's Office

At the heart of the Central Executive Territory is the 'Downing Street complex'. This comprises the offices, advisers, support staff and 'friends' who work alongside, to and for Prime Minister and Cabinet. (The precise working relationship is for discussion.)

The Prime Minister's Office
The Private Office (secretariat)
Policy Unit
Political Office
Special Advisers

Efficiency Unit

Kitchen Cabinet or 'Friends' and Family

Cabinet Office

Figure 2 The Downing Street complex

This complex has developed since 1916 and mainly since 1945. Before Lloyd George Prime Ministers were assisted by two or three Private Secretaries. The Principal Private Secretary was a personal and political appointment and served as an intimate friend as well as a political assistant. Downing Street was not then seen as a major centre of government but rather as the London home and office of a senior gentleman politician.

Lloyd George, coming to power in 1916, in the middle of a world war, took the first steps to transform No. 10 and the office of Prime Minister into the executive centre of British government. Lloyd George established the Cabinet Secretariat and a team of advisers, for which huts were built in the garden of No. 10 (the famous 'Garden Suburb'). After the end of the war the advisers were dispersed and the huts dismantled. But the Cabinet Secretariat was indispensable. The complex grew again during the 1939–45 war (evidence again of the impact of war on government), faltered and was then developed and solidified under Wilson and Heath in the 1960s and 1970s.

Thus, over a period of 50 years Britain acquired an established support structure to underpin the basic institution of Prime Minister and a score of Ministers meeting in Cabinet. Both Prime Minister and Cabinet are now properly to be seen as two closely intermeshed systems.

The Private Office
This is the main official support for the Prime Minister. It comprises six senior officials headed by a Principal Private Secretary (PPS). The latter is of Deputy Secretary rank, and so one step below the Permanent Secretaries of the Cabinet Office. Nevertheless the Prime Minister's PPS is of high significance and his continuing access to the Prime Minister gives him a strategic advantage in the work of the complex.

The nature of the work and the atmosphere of the Private Office is conveyed in the following documents. These offices are not all accommodated at No. 10 Downing Street but the official home of the Prime Minister is much larger than its modest facade suggests; altogether more than 130 people earn their living within it. The famous door of No. 10 gives access to three houses and 160 rooms.

■ DOCUMENT 4.4
The Prime Minister's Private Office

Harold Wilson from an interview with Mr Wilson by Dr Norman Hunt, 1964, pp.18, 20
I am very worried about what I feel is the amateurism of the central direction of the Govern-

ment. I think the right thing is to build up the Cabinet Secretariat to its proper strength. You see, perhaps the effect of having been a civil servant is that one is, to some extent in a Whitehall phrase, 'house trained', and one wants to see any experts properly dovetailed into the administrative machine – on an organisation chart, not floating about in a somewhat irresponsible way....

The traditional job of the Cabinet Secretariat is, of course, to brief – to service the Cabinet committees, provide secretaries for the Cabinet committees and see that the papers are properly circulated and a certain amount of co-ordination done by those means. I think they will also have to do much more in the way of briefing the Prime Minister, not only briefing him on the machinery of Government and briefing him on the work of any Cabinet committee, but also providing a briefing agency, so that he is right up to date and on top of the job in respect of all these major departments of State.

[In the event, as Prime Minister 1964–70, Wilson did not much enlarge his personal staff, but he brought into Downing Street a personal Political Office to deal with parliamentary matters. Following the views expressed in the Document he came to regard the Cabinet Office as a part of the Prime Minister's staff, and it doubled in size between 1964 and 1970. ■

■ DOCUMENT 4.5
The Prime Minister's Private Office

From B. Donoughue, 1987, pp. 17–19
The Prime Minister's Private Office is the single most important section of the administrative support services in No. 10. It is the communications centre of Downing Street, and is in regular contact with all the Ministerial private offices.... The Private Secretaries sift through the flow of papers and decide – based upon their experience of central government and upon their knowledge of a particular Prime Minister's interests and priorities – which to put before him urgently, which to delay, and which not to bother him with but to answer themselves. They fill the Prime Minister's red boxes for his nightly or his weekend reading. The Senior Secretaries will periodically sit with him in the study or in the flat discussing how to respond on certain issues. ■

EXERCISE
The Prime Minister's Private Office.

4.5 What strikes you as the most significant features of the Private Office?

James Callaghan wrote with respect and affection of the Private Office which served him as Prime Minister. He lists their functions as 'including sorting out essential items from the daily flood of papers; assembling material and drafting speeches, briefing before Cabinet and other meetings, acting as eyes and ears, and as a filter' (J. Callaghan, 1987, pp. 405–6).

These functions can be summed up as:

● gate keeping
● shadowing
● 'minding'.

The Policy Unit
The Policy Unit was established by Harold Wilson in 1974, and has survived to the 1990s, unlike the CPRS and the Civil Service Department. The Unit's survival, even under Margaret Thatcher (who did not love government institutions) indicates that Wilson's move to strengthen and systemise the Prime Minister's advisory and support system was correct.

It is interesting that Wilson's original diagnosis, made before he became Prime Minister for the first time in 1964, referred to the building-up of the Cabinet Secretariat. In the event Cabinet Office and Prime Minister's Office have developed side by side but separate; and the Policy Unit has been separated again because it is personal and political in appointment and functions, not official.

The Policy Unit is mixed in membership – academics, businessmen, civil servants – specialists and generalists, partisan, sympathetic, independent but all of high calibre. Its main function is advice, direct and personal to the Prime Minister; and it has the advantage and disadvantage of having no departmental base to act as launch pad or prison.

The Unit is generally committed to the objectives of the government, but in an independent rather than a partisan manner. Bernard Donoughue, the first Head of the Policy Unit under Wilson issued the following call to his staff.

■ DOCUMENT 4.6
The political function of the Policy Unit

From B. Donoughue, 1987, pp. 21–2
The Unit must ensure that the Prime Minister is

aware of what is coming up from departments to Cabinet. It must scrutinise papers, contact departments, know the background to policy decisions, disputes and compromises, and act as an early warning system.... The political dimension in its work was underlined: 'The Prime Minister has assumed responsibility as custodian of the Labour manifesto. The Unit will clearly be aware of the political dimension in Government. It must maintain good relations with the party organisation. The individual Ministries must not become isolated from the Government as a whole and lapse into traditional "departmental views" '. ■

EXERCISE
The politics of the Policy Unit

4.6 Is such an exhortation likely to compromise the independence of the advice of the Unit?

A major problem for a semi-independent Unit is to fit into the structure of government so that it can acquire information and build influence. Donoughue fought hard and successfully for access, and obtained the right to attend official committee and Cabinet committees chaired by the Prime Minister. He was also able to attend the weekly meetings of the Cabinet Office Deputy Secretaries.

On this crucial question of access and influence a member of the Policy Unit in the 1980s has written of a 'virtuous circle'.

■ DOCUMENT 4.7
The virtuous circle of advice

From D. Willetts, 1987, p. 454
Any person trying to break into the world of Whitehall policy advice wants to get into the virtuous circle of being recognised as influential, and therefore worth providing with information, which in turn increases one's ability to provide influential advice.... To get into the virtuous circle it is important to have good relations with knowledgeable, conscientious, and intellectually honest Whitehall officials.... Over the past few years the Policy Unit has successfully got into this virtuous circle without surrendering its prime loyalty to the Prime Minister and its commitment to this Government's strategic objectives'. ■

EXERCISE
The virtuous circle

4.7 What exactly is meant by 'virtuous circle' in this context?

The Press Office
Prime Ministers have always been concerned for favourable treatment in the press and have employed professional Press Secretaries since 1929. In face of the development of truly massive media, dominating the distribution of news, Prime Ministers and governments have worked energetically, sometimes obsessively, to shape media reporting. This was evident under Harold Wilson and Margaret Thatcher.

Wilson's Press Secretary 1974–6, Joe Haines, a skilled *Daily Mirror* journalist, became a close confidant of the Prime Minister, writing many of his speeches, and advising on policy. Margaret Thatcher's Press Secretary, Bernard Ingham, achieved notoriety similarly for his closeness to the Prime Minister; also for his vigorous promotion of the government's interests.

The Press Office under Bernard Ingham showed its capacity to boost prime ministerial power. Ingham used his professional skills and vigorous personal style in the service of the Prime Minister but in a manner which revealed the inherent tensions of a formally non-political office. The centralisation of information services further increased prime ministerial power. The Press Office is particularly conducive to the Prime Minister's power since there is no Cabinet Press Office, so no countervailing power. This is true even under John Major, whose first Press Secretary, a former Treasury official, did not seek the high public profile of his predecessor.

The Political Office
No. 10 includes a small Political Office, which deals with the Prime Minister's relations with the party – backbench Members of Parliament, the national party organisation, the Prime Minister's own constituency and correspondence from supporters. The Office is staffed by temporary outsiders but is officially recognised in the Civil Service Yearbook.

The Political Office is clearly not at the centre of national policy-making, but is an important support for the Prime Minister, and may provide one of the Prime Minister's Friends or a member of the Kitchen Cabinet.

Special Advisers

Prime Ministers appoint special advisers in addition to the Policy Unit – up to eight or nine advisers covering several fields but normally including an Economic Adviser. This looks reasonable enough but raises in acute form the general problem of the relationship between the prime ministerial support and advisory team and the Cabinet and Departments. For example, the Chancellor of the Exchequer may feel that he, backed by the Treasury, is the Prime Minister's chief adviser on economics. The resignation of Nigel Lawson, the Chancellor of the Exchequer in October 1989, arose directly from a dispute with a Special Adviser, and well exemplifies the tensions between the Downing Street complex and Cabinet Ministers (see Case Study in Chapter 7).

The Kitchen Cabinet: friends and family

All Prime Ministers have 'friends' and supporters who may be close to the Prime Minister but do not occupy any formal office, or belong to any unit. They associate with the Prime Minister as individuals, but they are often part of an informal group around the Prime Minister. They are close, unofficial, political, friendly and supportive, rather than formal advisers participating in decision making.

The term 'kitchen Cabinet' may be applied to the Prime Minister's friends. This conveys the informality of the association and the function – personal support, companionship and sympathy, a relaxed chat at the end of a tiring day, exchanging information and gossip, trying out ideas. There is nothing sinister about this: it is necessary that the Prime Minister has a life 'off-the-record' and indeed a private and family life. But there is always the possibility of influence behind the scenes, the improper influence of the eminence grise, the power behind the throne.

The influence of such friends is difficult to assess. They come and go quickly (especially in Thatcher's case) as prime ministerial favour ebbs and flows; but some seem to have exercised a significant influence at particular moments, for example, Sir John Hoskyns, Charles Powell and Bernard Ingham for Margaret Thatcher, Marcia Williams (Lady Falkender) under Harold Wilson. It is likely that such influence mainly confirms the Prime Minister in moving in a particular direction; and of course, the Prime Minister is subject to other countervailing influences.

The prime ministerial friend or confidant is not a recent phenomenon. Indeed some earlier Prime Ministers, lacking the support of the now expanded Downing Street complex, were even more dependent on close personal friends and confidants. 'Neville Chamberlain, on becoming Prime Minister, was told it is essential to have the friendship of someone outside the Cabinet whose loyalty and discretion is beyond question' (see Davidson's memorandum to Chamberlain, in R. R. James, 1971, pp. 421–2). Chamberlain kept closely in touch with Geoffrey Dawson, Editor of *The Times*. Churchill sought advice from the Oxford physicist, Lord Cherwell and later brought him into the government in a special 'statistical office'. Macmillan had a close confidant in John Wyndham.

All Prime Ministers have had friends and confidants, as well as policy advisers. Chamberlain's relationship with Dawson, Wilson's with Joe Haines and Thatcher's with Ingham show up both the vulnerability and insecurities of Prime Ministers, and their political concerns and skills. A Prime Minister is careful to develop personal relations with media people, and even to incorporate one or two in a kitchen Cabinet.

■ DOCUMENT 4.8
Prime Ministers and media confidants

a) From J. E. Wrench, 1955, pp. 373, 376–7
Neville Chamberlain and Geoffrey Dawson
Geoffrey [Dawson] remained in close contact with Neville Chamberlain during the latter's premiership.... A study of the records available certainly gives the impression that Chamberlain valued the Editor's opinion and was strengthened in his own views by the knowledge that Geoffrey agreed with his policy and would support it in *The Times*.
[Extracts from Dawson's diary.]

Sept. 14. Prime Minister decides to visit Hitler, Edward [Lord Halifax] imparted this momentous news to me at the Foreign Office in the afternoon under seal of secrecy till released but it enabled me to prepare for it, writing headlines and diplomatic notes and getting a leader started....

Sept. 22. The Prime Minister's 2nd meeting with Hitler...drove down to see Neville Chamberlain off to Germany.

b) From R. Harris, 1990, p. 122
Margaret Thatcher and Bernard Ingham
Margaret Thatcher's relations with her Chief Press Officer, Bernard Ingham, became very close. He was for good professional reasons

always early and fully informed about her thoughts, actions and intentions, and at her side in encounters with the media. These for a modern Prime Minister are more important than encounters with Parliament. Here are some illustrations of the working relationship.

- The banning of trade union membership at the GCHQ. The Foreign Secretary and the Cabinet Secretary had negotiated a compromise (short of a complete ban). Margaret Thatcher was doubtful and consulted Ingham. He said: 'It will look like a U-turn. It will be a U-turn'. So the compromise was rejected (R. Harris, 1990, p. 122).
- The editor of the *Sunday Express* reported that Ingham was present at a conversation he had with Margaret Thatcher during the miners' strike of 1984. He wrote: 'It was evident that Ingham was now very much part of the inner Cabinet. He intervened from time to time in our talk and it was obvious from the way the Prime Minister listened to what he had to say that she respected his judgement' (J. Junor quoted in R. Harris, 1990, p. 122).
- There is other evidence of Margaret Thatcher's dependence on Ingham and her high regard for him. He was lavishly praised in public (and awarded a knighthood in Margaret Thatcher's resignation honours); he was placed in charge of the whole Government Information Service (a position normally occupied by the Director of the Central Office of Information); he was allowed, perhaps encouraged, to criticise members of the Cabinet; and he was forgiven in 1985 when he failed to understand or foresee that the Chancellor was about to change his mind about exchange rate policy. ∎

EXERCISES
Prime Ministers and media confidants

4.8 Do these extracts from Dawson's diary support the view that Dawson influenced Chamberlain, or that Chamberlain used Dawson to secure support of *The Times* for his policies? (Answer briefly, unless you are able to consult the book itself for further evidence.)

4.9 Do you see anything wrong in a Prime Minister's seeking advice from a newspaper editor or the Press Office?

The Downing Street Complex: The Cabinet Office

The Cabinet Office is essentially an official body, not at all like the personal and political entourage of the Prime Minister in No. 10. Indeed the Cabinet Office is in all but name and size a Department of State, now rivalling the Treasury in its influence in British government. It connects by a locked green baize door to No. 10 Downing Street, but spreads around the block and has an entrance on Whitehall. The Cabinet Office is at the very centre of the Central Executive Territory and its job is to make Cabinet government work.

The Cabinet Secretariat owed its origin to the pressures of war. Until 1917 the work of the Cabinet had been conducted with what looks like terrifying informality. No minutes were taken and sometimes Ministers were not at all sure what had been decided. The only official record was that sent by the Prime Minister to the Queen. Lloyd George, a 'master of the art of getting things done', changed this amateur and gentlemanly system. Taking over the Secretary of the Committee of Imperial Defence, he established a small team of civil servants to expedite the work of the Cabinet. Henceforth, the Cabinet Secretariat was responsible, under the Prime Minister, for preparing the papers for Cabinet meetings (agenda and supporting papers), making a record of the meeting and seeing to the initiation of action arising from Cabinet decisions.

The main work of the Cabinet Office (leaving aside the scientific, historical and statistical sections) is to act as the Cabinet Secretariat. This is to use Secretary not to indicate typing and clerical work, but the servicing of administration, the arrangement of meetings and the provision of agenda, supporting papers and minutes. This secretarial function expands into the preparation of matters for Cabinet, and the processing of decisions made. Servicing procedures shade into policy development: the management of policy. The Cabinet Office is thus deeply involved in this pre-processing, trying to iron out disagreements and resolve conflicts. The Cabinet process itself may then be a registration of decisions already prepared through the network of departments and the Cabinet Office.

The Cabinet Office includes 30 or so senior civil servants, headed by the Cabinet Secretary, who is also (but not ex-officio) Head of the Home Civil Service, and the most powerful official in the land. Under him, the Cabinet Office is organised in six sections under Deputy Secretaries. These relate to the major areas of Cabinet business and the permanent Cabinet Committees:

- Economic
- Home (including legislation)
- Overseas and Defence
- European
- Science and Technology
- Security and Intelligence.

The Cabinet Secretary holds regular meetings with the Deputy Secretaries and the Prime Minister's Principal Private Secretary. This meeting is in effect the Steering Committee of British Government, though it has a partner or rival in the regular meetings of all the Permanent Secretaries, and the official Steering Committee on Economic Policy. These three committees of officials are at the core of British government.

Harold Wilson paid tribute to the significance of the Cabinet Office, especially after his first experience of office.

■ DOCUMENT 4.9
Harold Wilson as Prime Minister on the Cabinet Office

From an interview between Mr Wilson and Dr N. Hunt, The Listener, 6 April 1967, reprinted in A. King, 1969, pp. 94–6
...in addition, the Cabinet secretariat is the private department of the Prime Minister. Each member of the Cabinet Office staff services and serves the whole Cabinet, but they are also my own staff...the Permanent Secretary of the Cabinet – he is the servant of the whole Cabinet and attends all its meetings; but he is also my Permanent Secretary in the same sense that any other Minister has a Permanent Secretary/Chief Adviser. He advises me, briefs me, not only for Cabinet meetings and other Cabinet committees over which I preside, but on the general running of the government so far as policy is concerned....

The Cabinet Office has been greatly strengthened....

I think one thing I underrated [in the 1964 interview, see Document 4.4] was the extent to which the Cabinet office itself briefs the Prime Minister. It is pretty well in touch with all the departments. But the brief I get from the Cabinet secretariat...is an independent brief for me. ■

In the book Wilson published ten years later, after five more years in 10 Downing Street, he was careful to emphasise again the relationship of the Cabinet Office to the Cabinet as a whole. 'The secretary of the Cabinet is, in a sense, the "Prime Minister's permanent secretary", to use a phrase [of a former Cabinet Secretary],...but his loyalty is, no less, to Cabinet and the doctrine of Cabinet government.' (H. Wilson, 1976, p. 96.) Wilson's predecessor, Harold Macmillan, described the role of the Cabinet Office in similar terms. The Cabinet Office does not serve the Prime Minister exclusively but, given the pre-eminence of the Prime Minister, 'the Secretary to the Cabinet acts in effect both as co-ordinator and friend in a very special degree' (Macmillan, 1971, p. 193).

The influence of the Cabinet Office derives not from the conspiracies of senior civil servants lustful for power, but from the processes of servicing the Cabinet and the skill with which these are carried through. The Cabinet Office prepares a handling brief: 'it is not primarily a brief about political advice; it is a chairman's brief' (so the Cabinet Secretary told the Expenditure Committee in 1977). The preparation of such a brief involves talking with departments, identifying and reconciling points of difference. This is policy management rather than policy-making; much of it is humdrum, to do with the detail of policy, not its basic shape. The influence which arises is what Donoughue called 'influence through process' – influence in the shaping of the detail of decision.

In the following Document two American researchers who penetrated the centre of British government give an account of the work of the Cabinet Office.

■ DOCUMENT 4.10
The work of the Cabinet Office

From H. Heclo and A. Wildavsky, 1974, pp. 314–5
[If the Treasury and Cabinet Office were preparing briefs for the Prime Minister on a disputed policy] the Cabinet Office will try to balance evenly the pros and cons, extracting the main points from the mass of papers provided by the rival departments.... Though the official committee will probably have a chairman and/or secretary from the Cabinet Office, they must deal essentially with what the protagonists put before them....

[Mostly the Cabinet Office official] is a talented layman trying to relate the issues to a wider context.... For the most part the Cabinet Office has been (and must be) preoccupied with day-to-day pedestrian work – writing briefs, keeping minutes, checking up on progress, getting papers from departments, arranging for legislative proposals to come forward, clearing everything with the main participants. At its base, any man with experience will tell you, 'The Cabinet Office is a high-grade machine.' Only in rare periods,...may the Cabinet Office become a seed-bed of change. ■

Harold Wilson referred to an improved process of Cabinet Office clearance of major papers with departments, thus expediting Cabinet discussion and approval (H. Wilson, 1976, p. 53). He also paid tribute to the contribution of the Cabinet Office to the preparation by clarification of Cabinet decisions, thus facilitating summing up by the Prime Minister.

The Cabinet Office is influential but there are some ambiguities in its role:

- does it advise the Cabinet as a whole, or simply the Prime Minister?
- is the Cabinet Secretary or the Downing Street PPS the Prime Minister's chief adviser?
- how do both relate to that other Prince of the Territory, the Permanent Secretary to the Treasury?
- how to draw the line between policy management and policy advice?

There are no short answers to these questions (so this is not an Exercise!). Such ambiguities are inherent in the political system.

However there is no doubt that the Cabinet Secretary is now of the highest importance in the system of Cabinet government. He is the head of the Cabinet Office, the official Head of the Home Civil Service, and in effect the Prime Minister's Permanent Secretary and Chief Adviser. He is literally at the Prime Minister's right hand. Macmillan paid tribute to Sir Norman Brook as 'a tower of strength'; Wilson and Heath were accompanied by Sir Bruce Trend for international 'talks' and Sir William Armstrong was so often at Heath's side during economic crises that commentators began to call him a deputy Prime Minister. Sir William himself resisted this interpretation – 'serving the public has always been done through service of Ministers': (*The Listener*, 28 March 1973). Crossman complains in The Diaries of the influence of the Cabinet Secretary as drafter of the

minutes, a point which no minutes secretary would be inclined to doubt. Under Margaret Thatcher Sir Robert Armstrong occupied this high office and attracted criticism for his alleged political role.

Sir Robert Armstrong served as Cabinet Secretary and Head of the Home Civil Service from 1979 to 1987. He was in many ways a typical 'mandarin', educated at Eton, Oxford and the Treasury, and serving as Principal Private Secretary to two Prime Ministers, Wilson and Heath. His later career was marked by a series of events which drove him on to a public stage, revealed the stresses in the non-political role assumed by the higher civil service, and breached the curtain of secrecy which normally hides the stress. Thus an essentially private and non-political servant of the government was seen defending in public controversial political decisions.

The 'happenings' included:

- the banning of trade unions at GCHQ, a decision which turned out to be legally imperfect
- the Ponting case in which a middle-ranking civil servant leaked confidential information to Parliament, and was acquitted when prosecuted under the Official Secrets Act
- the Westland Affair in which Armstrong was put up by the Government to explain the leaking of a confidential document before a Select Committee of the House of Commons, thus defending the Prime Minister as well as the civil service
- the 'Spycatcher' Affair, in which Armstrong was put up by the Government to support its attempt to secure the banning of a book by a former agent.

In all these cases Sir Robert performed as a good professional. He disagreed with the Government over GCHQ, but (of course) defended the decision. Over Ponting, he took a firm civil service line: 'leaking' was unprofessional. In Westland he defended a difficult position with great skill, converting the alleged faults of politicians into reprehensible but forgivable official misconduct. Only in the alien and disrespectful environment of the Australian courts did he give a less than polished performance, which included his famous admission that he had been 'economical with the truth'.

Other sources of advice for the Prime Minister

It is necessary at this point to remind ourselves,

because even Prime Ministers sometimes forget, that the Prime Minister is not, or should not be, isolated within the Downing Street complex. He is a politician, leader of a political party and a prominent member of the House of Commons.

There are many other sources of advice he can draw on; indeed, advice will be thrust on him from many quarters.

EXERCISE
Sources of advice to the Prime Minister

4.10 What other sources of advice are there?

GUIDE TO EXERCISES

4.1 The salience of the Prime Minister has been increased by the growth of 'summitry' and of television exposure, and by deliberate exploitation of both; but salience is not the same as power, and indeed the salient Prime Minister is more vulnerable. At the same time the high expectations of the Prime Minister give him a standing and a leadership role which lift him above his colleagues.

4.2 Personal qualities make a difference, a) to the manner of going about the business of Prime Minister (and thus affect the appearance and perhaps the understanding of power); b) to the drive or aspiration of the Prime Minister (whether he tries to be powerful or not); and c) to the interpersonal skills of persuasion, persistence, strength (pushing for his own lines of policy).

4.3 This is John Major. He came early and inexperienced to the office of Prime Minister because of the resignations and dismissals of senior Ministers, the determination of Margaret Thatcher to be succeeded by 'one of her own men', the inevitable change of generation at the top, hostility to other candidates, and of course the support of party colleagues for an acceptable candidate. But it was a remarkable promotion. If Labour had won the election of 1992, Prime Minister Kinnock, like Ramsay MacDonald in 1924, would have been without previous Cabinet experience. A further column could be added to the Table to show years in opposition. Major would be the only one without any experience of opposition.

4.4 Through the selection process they should be suitable, trained and experienced; they have a support staff; and they are spared the detailed administrative responsibilities of a departmental Minister. Macmillan claimed he had more leisure (and time to read classical novels) as Prime Minister than ever he had as a Minister. Stamina and temperament are necessary, and the good manager's skills of time and stress management.

Why do they do it? A Prime Minister is an ambitious politician at the peak of a chosen profession, enjoying high status, many comforts and exercising great power. If they really want to spend more time reading novels they should not be Prime Minister. Fortunately most Prime Ministers do not stay in the job for more than a few years; Margaret Thatcher's eleven year reign is unusual, and perhaps her last years showed the disadvantages of holding such an onerous post for so long.

4.5 It is small; close to the Prime Minister; and of high calibre. Thus it provides an extension of the Prime Minister personally, rather than an external office. Thus it may be fitted into Wilson's organisation chart.

4.6 That could be so, if the Unit followed the Manifesto slavishly. On the other hand, a government does legitimately have party objectives, and these are just as likely to be compromised by the weight of civil service inertia?

4.7 Vicious circles are better known. It is a matter of continuous reinforcement: if you are denied access once, you will be shut out again and again, but if you gain access, other doors will open for you. As in many similar situations, the first few weeks or months may set up a pattern that is difficult to change.

4.8 The latter, but it might be inferred that such a close relationship would be reciprocal. (Of course, as indicated by Wrench at the beginning of the document other evidence confirms this.)

4.9 No. But it should be expected that the Prime Minister would regard such advice as a small part only of the advice on which he or she should base policy. In particular, a Prime Minister should look to his political colleagues and his senior professional advisers.

4.10   The following would not like to be ignored by the Prime Minister:

- the Cabinet and other ministerial colleagues
- Ministers without Portfolio' or similar figures, specially appointed as advisers within the Cabinet
- the Party Manifesto, the Party Research Department and policy committees; the party in Parliament
- Parliament itself. Prime Ministers do sometimes learn from the Opposition
- Think-tanks such as the Centre for Policy Studies
- Royal Commissions and Committees of Inquiry – a source neglected by Margaret Thatcher.

ASSESSMENT
The qualities of a Prime Minister

If a key to effective politics is to find men and women of high quality for top political jobs, we need a good selection process, and the selectors need to have some idea of what they are looking for. If the selectors/electors of party leaders and Prime Ministers drew up a list of qualities for the ideal candidate, what should they prescribe?

Many of the qualities required might be deduced from the nature of the Prime Minister's functions. He or she requires the capacity to work effectively with colleagues and through the Cabinet and Parliament, to develop appropriate policies, to win popular consent and so on. This much is obvious enough and not very helpful: a Prime Minister needs to be able to do the job of Prime Minister. Each occupant of the office shapes the job to his own capacities and style and to the demands of a changing political situation. Drawing up specifications for an ideal Prime Minister is therefore hazardous work for the political scientist, and perhaps more appropriate for a party game. So this section is mainly a do-it-yourself one: make your own list of qualities. There are, however, a few general points to be made.

- There is no agreement that a Prime Minister must be of the highest intellectual calibre. Some judges plead for a certain ordinariness of mind, and Bagehot called for 'a man of first-rate capacity and second-rate ideas'. Some recent Prime Ministers – Eden, Macmillan, Wilson – have held first class degrees; others

– Baldwin, Douglas-Home – third class degrees; Lloyd George, MacDonald, Churchill, Callaghan, and Major did not enjoy a university education. It looks as if academic distinction is not essential, but some force or nimbleness of intellect is needed. These considerations apply to Ministers too – and managers – for the most intelligent may see too many sides of the question and find decision difficult.

- Besides vigour of mind, there must be a certain attack. A Prime Minister should be industrious, but ought to avoid excessive detail.

  But hard work is not enough; a Prime Minister must have the strength to push other people along and around. He must not, like Asquith, earn Amery's harsh comment: '...for twenty years he has held a season ticket on the line of least resistance'. Margaret Thatcher offers a good illustration: plainly not an intellectual or a philosopher, yet with a powerful mind and a formidable capacity for work, and a relish for meeting problems head-on. On the other hand Margaret Thatcher had a short attention span, and did not like to ruminate long on a problem before making a decision.

- A Prime Minister should not need to be liked and should not mind criticism, and certainly should not, like Chamberlain, resent it. More, he should accept the troubles and difficulties of politics as a necessary part of the job. The point is well made by Vansittart in his book *The Mist Procession* 1958, p. 354. He disagreed with Churchill's judgement that Baldwin was 'an adroit and relentless politician'. 'Adroit, yes, relentless no. Winston liked trouble; SB eschewed it. The difference was unbridgeable.'

- A Prime Minister needs self-confidence, self-belief. This should run as far as a readiness to be totally unreasonable but fall short of a complete unwillingness to accept that you might be wrong.

- A Prime Minister needs courage to cope with bad times as well as good and not to show that he is rattled.

- A Prime Minister must want, indeed relish, power. There is nothing ignoble in this, since principles, policies, programmes have to be applied, enacted, and executed. Power is a substantial source of motivation and reward for politicians, and it is possible, to say the least, that it will be sought and cherished for its own sake. This indicates another requisite quality.

- A Prime Minister needs some kind of political purpose, even a moral purpose, a vision of a better Britain or a better world. This provides the drive to push him through the hard times, and an overriding principle of decision when the choices are agonisingly difficult.
- A Prime Minister does not need to be a great orator and there are speech writers to produce great speeches. Nevertheless speaking is the prime art of a politician and a capacity for effective, easy communication is essential. In particular a Prime Minister must come over well on television, a matter of performance rather than looks. Here training, grooming and briefing help, but in the end the Prime Minister is alone in front of the camera.
- Success – which may well mean good fortune. Here the clichés are apt. Nothing succeeds like success. A good Prime Minister makes her own luck. Both these apply to Margaret Thatcher's Falklands triumph.

Much was written, especially in 1993, about John Major's fitness or unfitness to be Prime Minister. The harsher judgements spoke of his 'not being up to the job.' The points set out above provide a check-list for the assessment of his being 'up to the job'.

Concept

Leadership

In most walks of life it is assumed there is a need for leadership. Employers of all kinds – the army, the schools, Marks and Spencer – advertise for and seek out persons of leadership quality. Captains of the England cricket team are sometimes chosen for their leadership qualities, neglecting their skills in batting and bowling. Similarly Prime Ministers are expected to be 'great leaders' (the word 'great' is always suspect).

What is leadership and does the country need it? The cases of Churchill and Attlee (see Case Study) illustrate the answer. In times of crisis, stress and confusion most groups and organisations (school, army, country) need 'a lead', that is someone to maintain morale and point out a way forward or backward, or order a standstill. This can be clearly understood in a fire or a battle, or on the fifth day of a test match you might just avoid losing. In most other situations, leadership

is either not required or has to be more subtle. If the team has scored over 500 for 3 wickets by tea-time on the second day, all the captain needs to do is decide when to declare. He might be a better captain if he had contributed a very fast 100 runs himself: that would be leadership by example.

The question of leadership by a Prime Minister was raised by Margaret Thatcher's tenure of office, and by the succession of a much milder, more consensual Prime Minister. Bold moves in the right direction are fine – if the direction is correct and movement is actually required. If not, you would do better with a leader who did not think her job was to make bold moves, or one who knew better which was the right direction. The virtues of persuasion and consent had been undervalued in the Thatcher years. Other Prime Ministers, from Attlee to Major, remind us that persuasion and consent – and a patient 'wait and see' – make for good leadership – unless the enemy are at the gates.

Mr Attlee and Mr Churchill are both regarded as 'great' Prime Ministers. But they were very different in their approach and style. These extracts offer some evidence of the differences, and raise the question, on this evidence which one would make the better Prime Minister and why?

- CASE STUDY

Two great Prime Ministers

a) The qualities of a Prime Minister: Mr Churchill on being appointed Prime Minister from W. S. Churchill, 1948, pp. 526–7

Thus, then, on the night of the 10th May, at the outset of this mighty battle, I acquired the chief power in the State, which henceforth I wielded in ever-growing measure for five years and three months of world war, at the end of which time, all our enemies having surrendered unconditionally or being about to do so, I was immediately dismissed by the British electorate from all further conduct of their affairs.

During these last crowded days of the political crisis my pulse had not quickened at any moment. I took it all as it came. But I cannot conceal from the reader of this truthful account that as I went to bed at about 3 a.m. I was conscious of a profound sense of relief. At last I had the authority to give directions over the whole scene. I felt as if I were walking with destiny, and that all my past life had been but a preparation for this hour and for this trial. Ten years in the political wilderness had freed me from ordinary party antagonisms. My warnings over the last six years had been so numerous, so detailed, and were now so terribly vindicated, that no one could gainsay me. I could not be reproached either for making the war or with want of preparation for it. I thought I knew a good deal about it all and I was sure I should not fail. Therefore, although impatient for the morning, I slept soundly and had no need for cheering dreams. Facts are better than dreams.

b) The qualities of a Prime Minister: Mr Atlee on being appointed Prime Minister from C. R. Attlee, 1954, p. 148

As the day wore on, country results confirmed our victory and by the middle of the afternoon it was clear that we had won a great victory.

Lord Portal, who was Chairman of the Great Western Railway, gave the family tea at Paddington, and presently I was told by the Prime Minister that he was resigning. A summons to the Palace followed. My wife drove me there and waited outside for me. The King gave me his commission to form a Government. He always used to say that I looked very surprised, as indeed I certainly was at the extent of our success. We went to a Victory Rally at Westminster Central Hall where I announced that I had been charged with the task of forming a Government, looked in at a Fabian Society gathering and then returned to Stanmore after an exciting day. •

● CASE STUDY
The Central Policy Review Staff (CPRS)

Between 1971 and 1983 the Cabinet Office included a Central Policy Review Staff (CPRS). The CPRS was established following a White Paper by Edward Heath's incoming administration on The Reorganisation of Central Government (Cmnd 4506 of 1970). In setting out the purpose of the CPRS the Paper referred to strategies, priorities, new options, underlying implications and, specifically, participation in the new public expenditure survey procedures. The basic notions were to do with overall or corporate strategy, government policy in the round, a collective perspective. The unit was intended to remedy one of the persistent weaknesses of modern government, tunnel vision, a concern for the short run, the tendency to develop policy compartmentally, backed by the strength of separate departments. Hence the CPRS endeavoured to brief non-departmental Ministers to penetrate the smooth and well-armoured departmental briefs. An early member of staff talked of his mission 'to think the unthinkable'. In pursuit of these exciting notions, the unit was sometimes referred to as the 'think-tank'. There was little doubt that if it were to contribute effectively to the formulation of government policy, the CPRS would need to be close both to the politics and the mechanics of government and thus in a sensitive position. It was not clear how this could be achieved, even at the practical level of access by CPRS to the departments.

The aspirations of this reorganisation were indeed larger than the actual impact of the CPRS. The work of the unit depended on the quality of its staff and the flow of issues, as well as the readiness of Whitehall to accommodate this young cuckoo in the nest. The staff (up to twenty, all temporary) were partly drawn from outside the civil service, from the universities and industry, and were intended to be 'multidisciplinary' (a phrase which implies a function different from that of the ordinary civil servant administrator). Directors included a scientist, an economist and a businessman. The CPRS produced reports on, for example, the research councils, counter-inflation and regional policy, the computer industry, the Concorde project, the motor-car industry.

In September 1973 Lord Rothschild, the first Director, aroused displeasure, even wrath, by stating in public that Britain was in danger of becoming the poorest country in Europe by 1985. This can be regarded as precisely the kind of gritty realism the system needs; or an inconsequential over-dramatisation of a dubious and by no means novel speculation. (It would have been acuurate to say one of the poorer countries of Europe). In December 1975 the unit produced a highly critical report on the car industry on the very day the government announced a policy of aid for the Chrysler company which was not consistent with the report. Similarly, its advice on the building of power stations was not followed. Under Margaret Thatcher a report on the reduction of the Welfare State, requested by the government, was publicly disowned by Margaret Thatcher.

Yet this situation is understandable. The CPRS could improve the government's information and thinking but it could not replace the government. The 'think-tank' label may have encouraged illusions about the value of sheer brainpower. But government decision taking is more complex and CPRS was not an integral part of the formal processes for policy development – hence the limits on the scope of CPRS. Its weakness was not casual or easily remediable: it was a weakness inherent in the structure of central government. Either the CPRS was superfluous (the Cabinet Office and the Downing Street complex are already on the job) or it should have become a very influential centre of decision-making (partially replacing the Downing Street complex). This fundamental lack of fit may explain the disbandment of the CPRS in 1983. It interfered with the departments without serving the Cabinet effectively. There were other explanations: it was invented by Margaret Thatcher's predecessor in the Conservative leadership; like much of government in the 1980s, it leaked; there was no demand for independent thinking. According to one high official observer the CPRS had become 'more and more the creature of the Prime Minister'. If so, then its original justification, in terms of independence and challenge, had

been lost. But for Margaret Thatcher it was simply superfluous. She did not need it for herself – she had her own sources of advice – and she certainly did not want 'independent' advice.

The problem of advice and support at the centre remained. One possibility often raised (by Margaret Thatcher among others) was the development of a Prime Ministerial department. The despatch of the CPRS seemed to mark the end of Margaret Thatcher's interest. The Cabinet Office view of the centre of British government had triumphed. This is an important question in the organisation of central government. It is not simply a question of Prime Ministers' presidential ambitions. The problem is how to arrange the central direction of the large and complex machine of modern government. British government has wavered between the old collegial tradition of the Cabinet, and another tradition, going back beyond Churchill and Lloyd George, which looks to a strong Prime Minister working on behalf of government by Prime Minister and Cabinet. Behind both traditions is the substantial reality of government by departments and their Ministers. ●

Prime Minister and Cabinet: working relations

The Cabinet

British government is 'Cabinet-shaped' – that is to say, the Cabinet is the organising principle and provides the basic structure of government. The Cabinet is therefore not best understood as twenty or so Ministers sitting around the Cabinet table on Thursday mornings. Rather it should be conceived as:

- the whole network of interactions of those Ministers individually, in their departments and in small groups
- processing the policies and decisions (and non-policies and non-decisions) which are finally ratified as the policy of the Cabinet
- working under the overall management of the Prime Minister and
- the administrative servicing of the Cabinet Office.

The shape of the modern Cabinet is shown in Figure 1.

The weight of the departments in the Cabinet is significant; the non-departmental Ministers, including the Prime Minister, may be weighty individually but are far outnumbered by the heads of the major departments – see diagram. Nevertheless the Cabinet is a team or collectivity. It embraces a complex of people and processes.

1 The Colleagues. Ministers as individuals carrying major departmental responsibilities, and as members of a team.
2 The Cabinet Council. The full Cabinet, the twenty or so Ministers meeting once or twice weekly around the Cabinet table. (The term 'Cabinet Council' has not been used since the

eighteenth century, but ought perhaps to be revived!)
3 The Cabinet committees.
4 Bilateral and other less formal meetings.
5 Officials surrounding and supporting the Cabinet, including the Cabinet Office and senior department officials.
6 The Prime Minister: heading, chairing, managing the system.

This development of the Cabinet is an expansion and multiplication rather than a fragmentation. The full development of this 'multi-plex' Cabinet is recent – since 1945; but the shifting away from the full Cabinet or 'Cabinet Council' has a longer history. Clearly Prime Ministers have always had some discussion with colleagues outside the Cabinet, and prior to meetings. Lloyd George (1916–22) certainly went further in the neglect of the full Cabinet; and Chamberlain (1937–40) notoriously made and conducted foreign policy on his own or with one or two personal advisers, with little reference to the Cabinet or even the Foreign Office.

■ DOCUMENT 5.1
The Cabinet Process 1

From Reflections on Cabinet Government, Lord Butler interviewed by Norman Hunt in V. Herman and J. Alt , 1975 , pp. 206–7
The 'pre-processing' of Cabinet business
LORD BUTLER: *The Education Act, the Budget, and the Common Market are the three examples where practically all the work, and practically all the initial part of the decision was taken before it came into the Cabinet. On the other hand, the final jumping over the fence, as in the*

	The Cabinet 1902	The Cabinet 1992
The Big Five	Prime Minister Chancellor of the Exchequer Home Secretary Lord Chancellor Foreign Secretary	Prime Minister Chancellor of the Exchequer Home Secretary Lord Chancellor Foreign Secretary
Empire	India Colonial	
War	Admiralty War	{ Defence
Economy	Board of Trade Agriculture (Board)	Trade and Industry Agriculture (non-Cabinet) Employment Transport
Social welfare	Education (Board)* Local Government (Board)	Education (Dept for) Environment Health Social Security
Government utilities	Postmaster-General First Commissioner of Works	
Non-departmental	Lord President Lord Privy Seal Chancellor of the Duchy of Lancester	Lord President Lord Privy Seal Chancellor of the Duchy of Lancester (includes Office of Public Service and Science)
UK territories	Ireland (Chief Secretary) Lord Chancellor of Ireland Lord Lieutenant of Ireland Scottish Office	Northern Ireland Scotland Wales National Heritage

* The President of the Board of Education was held by
Lord Londonderry who was also successively Lord Privy Seal
and Lord President of the Council

Note: Trade and Industry absorbed
most of the former Department of Energy
in 1992

Figure 1 The modern Cabinet

case of the Common Market, was a very big political decision for any government.

HUNT: But in a sense...on all these questions that we have been discussing the Cabinet was really faced with a pretty well unanimous recommendation to move in a certain direction. And so, even on political issues like these, the Cabinet really wasn't in a position freely to take a decision?

LORD BUTLER: I think if you take the Cabinet as covering the Cabinet committees and the committees of Ministers under it, you get a rather better conception of what the Cabinet is. If you just take the Cabinet meeting itself, you have to come to the conclusion that unless the people are very alive that day, and very political, much of the decision has already been taken before it reaches them. ■

Cabinet Minutes (Conclusions)

The Minutes of a Cabinet meeting summarise the discussion but focus on the conclusions.
This is the pattern.

1 The Minister speaks briefly to his proposal (submitted as a paper).
2 The Chancellor comments on financial implications (again there may be a note from the Chancellor submitted as a paper).
3 A general debate, controlled by the Prime Minister, with some regard for tactics, for example, influential negative voices to be disposed of early or brought in near to the moment of summing-up).
4 Summing up by the Prime Minister, who judges the balance of opinion (but not on a simple head count) and proceeds to a decision, positive, negative or fudged or deferred (for example, agreed in principle, but further consideration by a committee of practical problems and timing).

This account offers a model of a Cabinet deliberation; much well-prepared business goes through in this way, with potential disagreement and controversy carefully contained, if not squeezed out. However, Cabinets may also be less disciplined, lively, angry, especially when they take up a controversial matter which is still raw and unprocessed. Cabinets have to deal with disagreement, even at the cost of the smooth flow of business.

Here is an account composed by Hugo Young, the journalist and biographer of Margaret Thatcher – evidence in itself that Cabinet proceedings do not remain confidential, especially when Cabinet Ministers are angry, hurt or alarmed. It also throws light on the question of Prime Ministerial power.

■ DOCUMENT 5.2
The Cabinet Process 2

From H.Young, 1991, pp. 218–220
The Cabinet of 23 July 1981
[The main item on the agenda was the Chancellor's projections for the next year, in particular the cuts in public spending required to meet his financial targets. Despite a tough budget and incipient civil unrest Howe demanded an overall reduction of five billion pounds.]

Now, for the first time, the wets' unease at the economic strategy spread far beyond the usual dissenters. Heseltine... said that Howe's proposal would cause despair in the cities and elec-

toral disaster for the Tories. If the situation demanded rigour, he inquired, why didn't the Chancellor consider a pay freeze: a remarkable suggestion for any Thatcher Minister to put forward but one which others took up.

Peter Walker, likewise, reached for remedies that smacked of the dreaded days of Edward Heath..... Pym declared that employment not inflation was the issue, and a political rather than an economic strategy the prime requirement. Gilmour quoted Churchill: 'However beautiful the strategy you should occasionally look at the results...'

[Ministers previously thought to be loyal argued strongly against the Chancellor: enough is enough, the Treasury does not understand. Only two Ministers sided with the Chancellor and Prime Minister. In the end the Prime Minister, after belligerently joining in the debate, concluded in prudent managerial style by asking the Chancellor to produce another paper setting out both sides of the argument.

Young concludes that the Prime Minister was persuaded by this meeting that she had no alternative but to use the ultimate weapon and sack some of her dissident colleagues. ■

EXERCISE
The Prime Minister in face of a hostile Cabinet

5.1 How can the Prime Minister assert her dominance of the Cabinet in such circumstances?

The Cabinet as the colleagues

The Cabinet is a group of colleagues. The Prime Minister's relationship with them is based on his power of appointment and dismissal, and the frequently employed 're-shuffle'. This appointing power is exercised by the Prime Minister alone, and is formally unlimited. He may take advice, and prudence may indicate, sometimes even compel, particular appointments. Senior colleagues expect posts commensurate with their seniority and predilections. Representation of groups and tendencies, young and old, men and women, left and right is desirable. For some posts lawyers and lords must be found; Scotland and Wales must be represented and governed. Within these limits the Prime Minister is free to choose. He has thus an immense power of patronage: on him depend the political careers of perhaps a hundred or more serious contenders for office. But, more important, on the quality of his choice depends the quality of his government.

The Prime Minister has the power to break as well as to make the colleagues. He can dismiss members of his Cabinet with no effective right of appeal against his decision, and with the approval and gratitude of the newly promoted replacements. The extent of this power was demonstrated in July 1962 by Harold Macmillan's sudden, brutal dismissal of seven Cabinet Ministers at one sweep, and by Margaret Thatcher's regular and drastic reshuffles, which in the course of a decade, removed a whole Cabinet-full of Ministers.

Here again, however, prudence indicates a more cautious approach by the Prime Minister. He is not a 'dictator'. He must live and work with his colleagues. He can lose the confidence of his colleagues, and build up resentment. Macmillan never quite recovered from his 'putsch' in 1962; he had exceeded his powers. Margaret Thatcher's eventual fall owed something to the accumulated resentments of dismissed colleagues. John Major's delayed dismissal of Norman Lamont, gained him no new friends and at least one enemy.

The colleagues form a team, with the Prime Minister as captain and manager. The team has a certain cohesion and solidarity arising from its common political objectives and long service together in the political struggle and in Parliament. This 'team' quality of the members of a British government is a significant feature of the system and contrasts with the USA, where an incoming President puts together an administration of outsiders and strangers (in some cases people not personally known to the President). In Britain this group loyalty is re-inforced by the convention of collective responsibility, but exists already and does not depend on that re-inforcement.

The team of colleagues, like a football team, has its fissures and tensions to modify its cohesion. Some colleagues are 'more equal than others', have a higher standing and greater influence. A few are disappointed with their posts. Wilson tried to contain within his Cabinet the ideological and personal divisions inherited from the Gaitskell-Bevan split of the 1950s and the emerging left-right divisions of the 1970s. Some of his Ministers were in Crossman's phrase, 'independent and free-wheeling'. In Margaret Thatcher's early Cabinets she was in a minority. John Major's Cabinets were divided by ideology, policy and personality.

Personal and political rivalries are soon extended by gains and losses in Cabinet battle, over policy and spending. The pressures of a Ministerial post are heavy, and exhaustion does not encourage brotherly love. From time to time solidarity breaks down, and there are leaks, counter-briefings, intrigues and occasionally a resignation. This may be best explained as the final collapse of toleration of one's colleagues, and especially the Prime Minister; the departing Minister says in effect, 'Enough is enough!'.

Resignations are dramatic and public demonstrations of the breakdown of relations among the Colleagues, and are specifically associated with the convention of collective responsibility. They are plainly significant for the working relationships within the government, and they offer evidence, if rather ambiguous evidence, of the power of the Prime Minister. Resignations are considered at several points in the chapters on the executive.

A Minister may resign on one or more of the following grounds.

1 *Collective responsibility*. Resignations associated with collective responsibility (policy and personal disagreements) should be distinguished from resignations under the convention of ministerial responsibility (ministerial fault); also from the involuntary resignation of a dismissed minister or the surrogate resignation of a re-shuffled minister.
2 *Personal dissociation*. The Minister feels he cannot go along with a particular major policy and/or cannot bear to continue working with his colleagues. Sometimes this is a matter of honour, sometimes of anger, often quite simply a fundamental disagreement. Resignation might also be triggered by the temporary collapse or disarray of the departments concerned (Heclo and Wildavsky, p. 131, referring particularly to Thorneycroft and his associates in 1958). Personal dissociation is grounded in constitutional considerations.
3 *Constitutional*. The constitutional obligation to observe collective responsibility and so preserve the unity of the Cabinet. But this is preserved outwardly if a dissident Minister keeps silent. Plainly, there are many occasions when a Minister accepts defeat and lives on to fight again or fight on some other issue. There is nothing dishonourable in this – it happens all the time in professional life – unless the matter of disagreement is one of high principle.
4 *Tactical*. This is evident only when it fails. The Minister has threatened resignation as a means of persuading colleagues, but his threat has failed and he cannot extricate himself. Alterna-

tively, he may wish to appeal beyond the Cabinet to party or country. Such appeals are rarely successful. The best place to fight for policies is in the Cabinet, where you may hope eventually to persuade some of your colleagues that you are right. (A Minister would be unwise to threaten resignation frequently, for few ministers are indispensable and no committee works harmoniously when subjected to bullying tactics.)

In any case the Prime Minister has the weapons of dismissal and reshuffle to preserve collectivity and ensure a Cabinet united behind her. A wise Prime Minister can, like a rugby player, 'get her retaliation in first' by moving a discontented Minister, sideways or out. In a few cases the resignation of a Minister would damage the Prime Minister – so it does not happen. The best examples are Callaghan in 1969 over trade union legislation (see Document 5.11), and Lamont in 1992, following enforced devaluation (he was later dismissed).

Document 5.3 gives three serious cases of resignation from the Thatcher Cabinet. These are unusual in representing a kind of serial break-up of the government. Howe's resignation led directly to the fall of the Prime Minister in 1990, after Heseltine stood against her. Lawson backed both Howe and Heseltine. For once a Prime Minister had suffered one resignation too many.

■ DOCUMENT 5.3
Margaret Thatcher's three musketeers

a) *Heseltine resignation January 1986*
Michael Heseltine resigned in January 1986 in the middle of the Westland affair. He resigned because he disagreed with the Government's policy towards the Westland helicopter company; and objected to Margaret Thatcher's non-collegial mode (as he thought) of conducting Cabinet business, and specifically to an attempt to silence him (or as the Prime Minister thought, the imposition of the restraints of collective responsibility).

b) *Lawson resignation 1989*
Nigel Lawson resigned in October 1989 because he objected to Margaret Thatcher's (alleged) preference for the advice of her personal economic adviser, Sir Alan Walters, over the Chancellor's advice. Specifically Lawson favoured a more rapid approach to the European Exchange Rate Mechanism. Critics believe the

impending failure of his economic policies precipitated his resignation.

c) *Howe resignation 1990*
Sir Geoffrey Howe resigned in October 1990 over disagreements with the Prime Minister's brusque and sceptical approach to European policy, and her continuing humiliation of him following his dismissal from the Foreign Secretaryship. ■

EXERCISE
The significance of the three musketeers

5.2 What do these resignations demonstrate – the power of the Prime Minister or the persistence of collectivity?

Resignation is still quite rare, as it is in ordinary professional life. We all have doubts about the boss, but do not see why we, not he, should resign. Peter Walker put the usual and persuasive case for carrying on despite disagreements.

■ DOCUMENT 5.4
The futility of resignation

From P. Walker, 1991, pp. 159–60
[After the Budget Cabinet of 1981] a number of us discussed again what we should do. We were faced with an impossible dilemma. If we decided we could not accept the budget and must resign, we had to take into account the damage this would do to sterling and the economy. You had to ask: is it worth it? If you did it, you knew it was unlikely the government would change the budget. It would be too late.

Immediately after the budget Cabinet, in the hallway of No. 10, a number of us chatted for 10 minutes. I had a longer conversation with Ian Gilmour, who was a close personal friend, but there was no formal group. You simply knew a large proportion of the Cabinet was troubled and hardly anyone had expressed enthusiasm for the budget. We decided we could not get it changed, and resignation would do more harm to the economy. ■

The Prime Minister is thus protected from resignations most of the time; it is an unattractive prospect for his or her colleagues. In any case she has the weapons of re-shuffle and dismissal to use against dissident or otherwise unsatisfactory Ministers. The dissatisfied colleague may conclude that it would be best to stay and fight; the Prime Minister may decide otherwise. for example, the persistently dissident (but non-disruptive) Peter Walker was later appointed Secretary of State for Wales, a post he occupied with great success and much deviation from Thatcherite principles – but it was clear that he was in political exile.

Thus resignations are only part of the continuing uneasy relations of senior politicians. There are also dismissals, re-shuffles, non-resignations, and the normal tensions of a hard-working life among competitive professionals working in the fierce gaze of publicity.

■ DOCUMENT 5.5
The Prime Minister's uneasy relationships with colleagues

a) From Thomas Jones, p. xxvii
[MacDonald] did not delight in the company of his colleagues.

b) From Baldwin to Dawson, Editor of The Times, *quoted in Lord Vansittart, 1958, p. 354*
It is easier for me to talk these matters over with you than with any of my colleagues.

c) From LLoyd George, quoted in Thomas Jones, p. 52
There can be no friendship between the top five men in a Cabinet.

d) From Macmillan, 1971, p. 209
[Macmillan commented on the isolation of the Prime Minister compared with a departmental Minister.] Now I found myself alone, solitary....

e) From J. Haines, 1977, p. 89
Whenever [Wilson and Callaghan] met, the tension that exists between top competitors was always there. ■

EXERCISE
Prime Ministers and their colleagues

5.3 Would you expect a Prime Minister's relations with his colleagues normally to be better than those indicated above?

Cabinet Committees

The Cabinet works through a system of subcommittees and with the assistance of a small but powerful Secretariat. Most of the Cabinet's work is thus done outside the Cabinet itself. Only this pre-processing enables the full Cabinet to meet for just a few hours each week, and still remain, in theory at least, ultimate master of the system.

There have always been informal committees: the first formal committee was that for Imperial Defence established in 1904. Thereafter committees were set up from time to time; for example, one on foreign affairs in the 1930s. From 1942, first under Churchill and then Attlee, the committee system has been developed and formalised. Depending on definitions, there may be a score of standing committees, and many more *ad hoc* and temporary. These are mostly paralleled by committees of officials. The Cabinet system is thus not twenty Ministers round a table in Downing Street, but an intricate double-layered honeycomb of committees..

The system of Cabinet committees is private, if not now wholly secret, so full information is lacking. Normally, it seems, there have been standing committees on Defence and Overseas Policy, Economic Policy and Home Affairs, a committee on Future Legislation (or ad hoc committees on a particular piece of projected legislation). Such committees are usually composed of two or three Cabinet and senior Ministers, other Ministers concerned in the committee's agenda, and sometimes high civil servants. The chair is taken either by the Prime Minister or by a senior colleague.

The function of the system is that of any subcommittee: to consider in detail matters for which the Cabinet itself would have no time. The Cabinet committee system has the particular purpose and advantage that it can bring into the discussion non-Cabinet Ministers and civil servants, including some who are only indirectly concerned in the agenda. This ensures effective communication and a measure of co-ordination, and, so it is officially argued, 'buttresses the principle of collective responsibility'.

A system of subcommittees is by definition subordinate to the parent committee, in this case, the Cabinet. Committee decisions are reported to the Cabinet for ratification, and the Cabinet has the right of veto. The Cabinet comes thus to function as a court of appeal, rather than a board of directors. In practice, objections to a committee's line of policy are likely to have been uncovered and met during its deliberations, and Cabinet approval is thus ensured. But where this is not the case the members of the Cabinet who do not sit on the committee are not in a strong position to resist its conclusions.

Thus the development of the committee system

has lessened the importance and power of the Cabinet as a whole. At the same time it may have increased the power of the Prime Minister, for he or she is at the centre of the system, taking a leading part in some committees and keeping in touch with the rest. But most Prime Ministers share their authority with a few senior Ministers acting as committee chairmen, and thus operate a kind of collective leadership.

EXERCISE
The function of Cabinet Committees

5.4 What can a Minister do if he has an interest in an issue but is not a member of the Committee dealing with it?

Senior Ministers, who sit on and even chair important committees, seem to approve of the committee system (they would, wouldn't they?). They complain about Ministers who have not mastered their briefs. Whitelaw wrote of his 'irritation as some Minister carefully reads out a dreary departmental brief which he obviously only partially understands', Whitelaw himself being already fully briefed by the Cabinet Office on that department's views (W. Whitelaw, 1989, pp. 328–9). Joel Barnett similarly complained that the Minister reading out a departmental brief 'sounds terrible, but it also offends colleagues' (J. Barnett, 1982, p. 17).

Another complaint is about absence from important meetings. Roy Jenkins was particularly angry when a junior Minister, attending in place of the Foreign Secretary, tried to reserve the right of the Foreign Secretary to raise a matter at Cabinet. Barbara Castle recorded this incident in her diary: '"That was the most gross abuse of the procedures of Cabinet in his experience", Jenkins said icily. If one member of the Cabinet who had not even taken the trouble to be present, found himself in a minority of one on a committee and then claimed the right to re-open the matter in Cabinet, he really could not see any point in committees meeting at all' (B. Castle, 1980, p. 72).

Such senior Ministers, the heavies and trusties of the Cabinet, can exert influence through the committee system and share in or constrain the Prime Minister's power. For lesser Ministers, and excluded Ministers, the system supports prime ministerial dominance. Michael Heseltine's reactions during the Westland Affair show the frustrations of the excluded Minister.

The 'Cabinet Council'

The full Cabinet (or Cabinet Council), may be regarded as at the apex or centre of the Cabinet system, and it is at least formally the summit of authority in British government. As part of the Prime Minister's management of policy decisions through the Cabinet system, he or she must determine the time and the form in which matters come to the full Cabinet (the Cabinet Council). Specifically the Prime Minister determines the agenda of Cabinet and chairs its meetings.

There are two simple answers to the question, what comes to the Cabinet?
1 Not much, there is not enough time.
2 Whatever the Prime Minister says.

In fact the answer is more complex. The Cabinet routinely considers foreign affairs and the programme of legislation in Parliament. Major policy is at least ratified in Cabinet, it cannot go by default. But policy tends to be made up of individual decisions. The Cabinet also considers matters of dispute across and between departments (but may not hear of disputes inside departments), and matters of high political sensitivity or salience (but these may need to be settled quickly and quietly outside the Cabinet).

Thus a decision to build Concorde, or go ahead with a new airport for London, or to settle on the route of a rail-link from the Channel Tunnel to London all come to the Cabinet for final decision, because they require substantial public investment and carry political disadvantages. The siting of major public or subsidised projects is always difficult, since people welcome employment prospects but not the loss of amenity. Hence the building of a nuclear waste dump in England (and even perhaps in Scotland and Wales) is a matter for the Cabinet. These examples emphasise matters of political sensitivity. This is only slightly misleading: since most issues are 'pre-processed' within the Cabinet system, the full Cabinet does end up with a mix of formal ratification and political trouble.

A Minister may propose an item for the agenda, and it will be accepted if it has 'Cabinet-resonance': but the Prime Minister may well say, sort that out in committee first, so that Cabinet can have a paper setting out options and a recommendation. In some cases 'Cabinet-resonance' will be misjudged and political trouble not be foreseen; then the Cabinet is brought in when an issue 'blows up in their face'. Thus in October 1992 a proposal to close half of Britain's remaining coal pits was agreed in a Ministerial meeting and announced before Cabinet approval was obtained. It was assumed the policy was not controversial, but angry opposition, popular and parliamentary, including Conservative back benchers, led to a series of concessions by the government. This was a classic example of the dangers of neglecting consent. But it is still unlikely that the full Cabinet would have foreseen the intensity of the public reactions.

The Prime Minister chairs the Cabinet Council. Chairmen like to say, 'I am in the hands of the meeting', but unless the Chairman has lost his way, the reverse is true. The Prime Minister, as chairman, selects the speakers, ensuring that opposing views are aired, preferably early in the debate, so that they may be effectively countered or smothered. The Chancellor's view, one way or the other, must be fitted in. The Prime Minister chooses when to close the discussion (whether to push it to a conclusion or defer a decision), and how a conclusion shall be formulated. In summing up the Prime Minister has the help of the Cabinet Office brief, which indicates appropriate conclusions. This is not quite the same as writing the minutes before the meeting, but a brief for a well-prepared meeting properly includes at least an indication of the lines of the conclusion. Some chairmen can sum up with such precision that they are in effect dictating the minutes.

There is not one style of chairmanship for Prime Ministers, and each Prime Minister varies over time and with the issues. Attlee, by reputation at least, established an ideal of brisk and efficient chairmanship, no wasted words, dissent briefly expressed and dealt with; financial and international implications considered and a conclusion shortly made out. Other Prime Ministers did not always attain the Attlee ideal.

Prime Ministers speak too much themselves (Churchill) or too little (Heath); or allow others to ramble and ruminate (Wilson). The ten minutes before lunch should not bring a welter of hasty decisions or the postponement of urgent matters. Here are some illustrations of Prime Ministers in the Cabinet Council.

■ DOCUMENT 5.6
Prime Ministers in the Cabinet Council

a) From Lord Hill of Luton, 1964, p. 235
I thought Harold Macmillan's chairmanship of the Cabinet to be superb by any standards. If he dominated it (he usually did), he did not do it by ex cathedra pronouncements or by laying down the law or by expressing his views too early in a discussion or by any of the arts of repression which skilful chairmen are tempted to cultivate. It was done by sheer superiority of mind and judgement. He encouraged genuine discussion, provided it kept to the point. If he found himself in a minority he accepted the fact with grace and humour. If I have a criticism it is that now and again, the Cabinet was consulted at too late a stage in the evolution of some important line of policy: he seemed to forget that many of us had not been present at the Cabinet committee concerned with the topic.

b) From F. Williams, 1965, p. 147
Hore-Belisha told Francis Williams that to sit under Chamberlain in Cabinet was like being a departmental manager in a firm in which the chairman owned all the shares.

c) From Thomas Jones, 1954, p. xxviii
[Bonar Law] was an admirable chairman of Cabinet and was not unlike Neville Chamberlain: painstaking, methodical, unhumorous, a master of detail, not entirely unconscious in a quiet way of his own competence. He gave clear, positive directions and summed up a discussion in Cabinet with such precision that his words were taken down verbatim by the secretary as the permanent record in the Minutes.

d) From Peter Hennessy, The Times, 16 May 1983, quoting senior officials
I think Ted [Heath] dominated to a greater extent than the others, including Margaret Thatcher. Ministers were frightened of him.... Ted did not really believe in Cabinet government. He was never happy in Cabinet....

e) From an ex-Minister's summary of a Thatcher Cabinet meeting, in Harris, 1988, p. 97
In Cabinet she spoke first, outlining what she proposed to do, what the policy of the Government was going to be. The dissidents came next. They did not always get a chance to complete their case because she would interrupt them, sometimes offensively in that she would tell them in very simple language that what they were advocating was simply not on. Then she would sum up. The summing up would be a restatement of the action she had proposed at the beginning of the meeting. The Cabinet minutes, when circulated to those Cabinet Ministers who had been present, would reflect what

the Prime Minister had told the Cabinet that her Government was going to do.

f) From D. Healey, 1989, p. 448
James Callaghan as chairman
Like all good chairmen, Callaghan tried to restrain the talkative, encourage the reticent and 'preserve the theme of the conversation'. Healey admired his technique, 'never content simply to preside', but, having read his briefs, knowing what outcome to steer for, sometimes making his own view clear early, sometimes 'allowing his colleagues to exhaust themselves in argument before forcing a decision'. ■

EXERCISE
Chairing the Cabinet

5.5 Do you see any ways of typifying these Prime Ministerial chairmen? Where do you think Harold Wilson (not represented here) would fit in?

The Prime Minister and the Cabinet System

The Prime Minister's position in relation to the whole Cabinet system is crucial to his role and influence. He is manager of the system, captain of the team and referee of the game. Almost he is in the position of the boy who owns the bat and ball: if he walks off that ends the game. But that is a dangerous bluff for the Prime Minister; for if he walks off (resigns or dissolves Parliament) his game ends too, and he may not be captain any more. This is the bluff that John Major carried off with apparent success in July 1993. The Prime Minister needs the Cabinet, though not quite as much as they need him.

Most of the time Prime Minister and Cabinet struggle with difficult matters which are not at the centre of partisan politics, and which are unlikely to yield dramatic political dividends. Most public expenditure issues are like that. The Prime Minister's task then is not to engage in a clever deal with a few colleagues, or stampede the Cabinet with a brilliant tour de force. Rather it is to set a course for the matter through the Cabinet system, drive it on week-by-week, and finally bring it to Cabinet carefully shaped and treated for a clear and consensual decision.

The Prime Minister's Cabinet style thus divides into:

● the approach to and use of the Cabinet system

● the conduct of the full Cabinet or Cabinet Council.

A Prime Minister's style varies with the issues. He is concerned about some matters, and is competent and feels comfortable with them, but in other matters he may know and care less, leaving others to bring the matter to resolution. The concerns and competencies of long-serving Prime Ministers change over time, as their policy agenda shifts.

It is evident that all Prime Ministers use the Cabinet system of committees, bilaterals and informal discussion: these are a normal and integral part of what is understood as 'the Cabinet'. But there is variation in the role accorded to the full Cabinet in this process. The Cabinet may be used:

● as a discussion arena in the early stages
● as a development workshop in the middle stages
● as a decision point in the final stage
● as a final court of appeal
● as a registration process only.

Harold Wilson (1964–70 and 1974–6)
Accounts of Wilson's Prime Ministership show that he used the Cabinet in all five modes. But normally he expected preparatory work to be done in committee: matters coming to Cabinet should be fully prepared, processed for decision.

■ DOCUMENT 5.7
Harold Wilson and the Cabinet system

From an interview with Mr Harold Wilson by Kenneth Harris in The Observer Magazine, *24 October 1965*
PM: *I've followed very closely what I learned from Lord Attlee when I was a member of his Cabinet: circulation of papers before the meeting; decisions not satisfactorily cleared at departmental level to be referred to the Prime Minister; extensive use of Cabinet sub-committees so that we can economise on the use of the time of the full Cabinet; re-introduction of his insistence – I say re-introduction because the practice seemed to have lapsed at some time since his day – that all Cabinet reports must have a price tag, meaning that the financial and economic implications must be previously agreed with the Treasury – which is a great time-saver in Cabinet, and a solvent of possible tensions outside it.*
[Wilson stressed that his Cabinet had 'talked a good deal less than Clem's did'; did not vote; had got through a good deal of work without

bad temper or personal clashes. The sub-committees had been invaluable.]
This Cabinet, like every other, owes a great deal to the non-departmental Ministers. I've come to believe that the strength of a Cabinet is in its non-departmental Ministers. They are the half-backs of the government team. They don't often score goals, or hit the headlines, but no team can be a success without a good half-back line. ■

Note. For Attlee himself on his Cabinet see F. Williams, 1961, pp. 79–91 (reprinted in A. King, 1969).

EXERCISES
Wilson and the Cabinet

5.6 What importance does Wilson appear to attach to the Cabinet?
5.7 Does the preparation of issues for the Cabinet determine the decision to be taken?

It should not be assumed in the light of this discussion that Wilson governed wholly within the formal Cabinet system. Alongside the accounts of stormy Cabinet meetings are many complaints that Wilson was too close to his personal staff, advisers and confidants, leaving Cabinet in the dark. In a long working day a Prime Minister is likely to spend less time with members of the Cabinet than with others of his entourage. It is certainly easy and natural for a Prime Minister to neglect his Cabinet colleagues, and even easier for his colleagues to suspect him of conspiring against them.

Margaret Thatcher (1979–1990)
Margaret Thatcher was unusual as a Prime Minister in the extent to which she side-stepped the Cabinet. This was partly because of her temperament, quick and decisive, disliking rumination and disagreement; partly because she had a distinct policy agenda but no majority in Cabinet to push it through. Her first Cabinet was 'probably the most divided in twentieth-century British government' (K. Harris, 1988, p. 88), and also 'the most unhappy' (ibid. p. 96). Margaret Thatcher was frequently defeated in full Cabinet in her early years. Hence she came to depend on small groups outside the formal Cabinet system, an economics group (which Young called 'the secretive cabal at the heart of government' (1989 p. 151), and shadowy triumvirates of Principal Private Secretary, Parliamentary Secretary and Press Secretary or Party

Chairman. In July 1984, the Economist commented, No. 10 Downing Street had become 'a curiously empty place'.

■ DOCUMENT 5.8
Thatcher and the Cabinet system

From P. Jenkins, 1987, p. 183
Her dominance of the government was achieved partly through the force of her personality and partly by the technique of side-stepping the Cabinet whenever she could....
She ruled through a web of *ad hoc* committees manned by trusties.... John Biffen, when he fell from her favour, was virtually excluded from the government [while still Leader of the House].... It was a style well-suited to crisis management – the Falklands War, the miners' strike – but less so to crisis prevention. ■

EXERCISE
Thatcher and the Cabinet system

5.8 Why do you think Margaret Thatcher's Cabinet colleagues tolerated (put up with) this treatment of the Cabinet, even when they were in a majority?

James Callaghan (1976–79)
Callaghan held that the four senior Ministers should normally not disagree in Cabinet; if they must then the Prime Minister should know beforehand, so that he could consider carefully his own position, and decide whether or not to 'lay his authority on the line' (David Owen reported in K. Harris, 1987, p. 86).
In pursuit of this strategy, Callaghan took care to know Crosland's position and intentions during the long Cabinet negotiations over the IMF deal in 1976. Callaghan finally pinned Crosland down while flying back from The Hague in an 8-seater aircraft. At the next Cabinet meeting, he told Crosland, 'Ministers must now reach a conclusion on their general strategy. I knew where I stood. What would he do?' This was gently but firmly to 'lay the Prime Minister's authority on the line'. Crosland responded as Callaghan hoped, reluctantly promising to support the IMF package (J. Callaghan, 1987, p. 438).
The experience of the IMF crisis led Callaghan to seek more 'space' for decisions in exchange and interest rate policy, freeing himself from dependence on the Treasury or too close a confinement within the Cabinet. So he moved the key discussions into a small group including just the Prime

Minister, the Chancellor and one other Minister (Lever), and a handful of senior officials from the Treasury, the Bank of England, the Cabinet Office, the No. 10 Private Office and the Policy Unit and the CPRS. This was a secret decision-making group disguised as the 'Economics Seminar', and unknown to most of the Cabinet. Callaghan, like most Prime Ministers, operated both collectively, and in small personal groups.

Collective Responsibility

If British government is shaped by the Cabinet, it is also shaped by the conventions of responsibility to Parliament. The degree of responsibility or accountability has been much diminished in practice by the operation of party majorities loyal to the government. Nevertheless the procedures and the constitutional rhetoric of the system are shaped by the notion of responsibility to Parliament. At this point you may reasonably feel that there is a good deal of facade about the British Constitution – a set of elaborate fronts hiding shacks, like a cowboy town in the American mid-West or even a film-lot version of the same.

There is it seems a constitutional principle of Parliamentary Sovereignty, disguising executive dominance; a Cabinet system dominated by the Prime Minister; and conventions of responsibility which protect irresponsibility. There is clearly some validity in the 'facade' critique of government in Britain, even allowing that most formal institutional arrangements disguise rather different practical arrangements.

The convention of collective responsibility now applies not just to the Cabinet but to all members of a government, including junior Ministers, and it is concerned with the solidarity of the government in face of Parliament, press and public. The convention of Ministerial responsibility relates to the accountability of individual Ministers to Parliament for their official duties. This convention of individual Ministerial responsibility is discussed in Chapters 6 and 8.

The meaning of the convention of collective responsibility is indicated in 'Questions of Procedure', the rule book for Ministers, once secret, but published by the Cabinet Office in 1992.

■ DOCUMENT 5.9
Collective responsibility

From Questions of Procedure, *Cabinet Office, 1992*

18. Collective responsibility requires that Ministers should be able to express their views frankly in the expectation that they can argue freely in private while maintaining a united front when decisions have been reached....
17. Decisions reached by the Cabinet or Ministerial Committees are binding on all members of the Government....
The internal process through which a decision has been made, or the level of Committee by which it was taken, should not be disclosed....
87. Ministers cannot speak publicly for themselves alone. In all cases they speak as Ministers; and the principle of collective responsibility applies. They should ensure that their statements are consistent with collective Government policy and should not anticipate decisions not yet made public. Ministers should exercise special care in referring to subjects which are the responsibility of other Ministers.... ■

The document *Questions of Procedure* is handed to new Ministers when they take up office, and is a codification of the rules for Ministers. So unusually we have a written-down part of the unwritten constitution, incorporating a convention (though that term is not used) based on custom and practice. The convention thus acquires some formality and precision, but it remains a working custom, defended by Prime Ministers and breached by Ministers, mostly with impunity. Other countries seem to manage quite well without a similar rule, since all groups in power work naturally under some minimal commitment to solidarity.

The convention of collective responsibility developed originally as Ministers united in face of the Crown and the modern notion of a solidary government emerged. The centre of power then shifted to the Commons and the electorate, and it is in face of them that the modern Cabinet strives to retain its unity. Thus the convention serves a political purpose – otherwise it would, no doubt, have been modified. Prime Ministers are quite clear and confident about the convention; some Ministers are more sceptical.

■ DOCUMENT 5.10
The convention of collective responsibility

Lord Salisbury, 1878, House of Lords, 8 April 1878 Parliamentary Debate, 3, *Vol. 239, pp. 833–4*
For all that passes in Cabinet each member of it who does not resign is absolutely and irre-

trievably responsible, and has no right afterwards to say that he agreed in one case to a compromise, while in another he was persuaded by his colleagues.... It is only on the principle that absolute responsibility is undertaken by every member of the Cabinet who, after a decision is arrived at, remains a member of it, that the joint responsibility of Ministers to Parliament can be upheld, and one of the most essential principles of parliamentary responsibility established. ■

EXERCISE
The convention of collective responsibility

5.9 What do you see as the advantages and disadvantages of the convention?

The convention of collective responsibility is now applied to all members of the government, including junior Ministers, and indeed the opposition have adopted it for their Shadow Cabinet. The operation of the convention has significant consequences for British government.

1 Ultimate responsibility of the government to the House of Commons. Prime Minister and Cabinet, the whole Government, fall when defeated on a specified vote of confidence in the House. Under a two-party system, with disciplined parties, this happens rarely – only three times this century, 1924 (twice) and 1979, times when the two-party system was in disarray. However, it may be fair to say, the relationship of Government to House of Commons is affected by this ultimate deterrent; the Government tries to keep its own side happy, even if it knows that the ultimate deterrent (like nuclear weaponry) destroys its user.
2 Solidarity. The acceptance of this collective responsibility has led Prime Ministers to impose unity or solidarity on all members of the Cabinet. Solidarity is supported by secrecy or confidentiality. Prime Ministers love the convention, since it clearly supports their power by enforcing solidarity.
3 Excessive secrecy about policy development. Disagreement, which is at the heart of politics, is ruled out, and governments pretend that every member is agreed on everything, now and in the past. The public is educated to believe that this is so, and the media are encouraged to hunt out disagreement and shout 'Party Split'.
4 Hence some hypocrisy or dissembling by Ministers struggling to pretend that they agree fully with every item of government policy. Lord Birkenhead, a more robust politician with the advantage of a seat in the House of Lords, confessed in 1928, when commending an Equal Franchise Bill he personally opposed:

'I have been a member of a Cabinet with a very slight interruption for thirteen years, and I can hardly recall a single measure of first-class importance on which all members of the Cabinet had precisely the same views.....

I have spent nearly the whole of my political life in giving wise advice invariably disregarded, and if I had resigned every time that my wise and advantageous advice was rejected I should seldom, indeed, during that critical period, have been in office.'

5 Persistent challenge to the convention's restrictions. The Cabinet and the Government form a team pursuing broadly agreed political goals, and anxious to retain power. Hence it is not unreasonable to expect a high degree of natural solidarity. On the other hand, politicians thrive on disagreement (among their colleagues, as well as with the Opposition), and cultivate their own public personalities. They may well resent a Prime Ministerial order to be seen and not heard, or at least, to say nothing on a favourite and controversial subject except the official line. In practice the convention is challenged and breached.

On two occasions there has been a formal 'Agreement to Differ' – one in 1931–2 over free trade, the second in 1975 over Britain's accession to the EEC. The latter was most startling, since politicians crossed party lines to join vigorous public campaigns before the Referendum. Political opponents appeared on the same platform to denounce their friends as well as their enemies. Curiously, it may be thought, no Minister on the losing side felt unable to continue to serve the government, despite disagreement on a major item of policy.

Apart from these formal arrangements, Cabinets are frequently unable fully to resolve disagreements, and they rumble on, sometimes in private, often in the half light of the leak, occasionally in the full light of day. For open dissent and defiance of the convention a Minister may be re-shuffled, dismissed or (rarely) may choose to resign – later to write his memoirs.

Thus leaks and memoirs are the other side of the coin, the inevitable complement to the imposition of solidarity under the convention. The convention is 'honoured in the breach'. It is a device to resolve the unavoidable stresses and tensions of Cabinet government in favour of the Prime Minister and the Cabinet majority. Challenge to such enforced resolution is neither surprising nor dishonourable.

Nor is it surprising that total secrecy is not maintained, when about 200 people see even the most restricted Cabinet papers. In practice only quite specific pieces of information can be kept secret: budget tax proposals, the date of the invasion or a Prime Ministerial visit to Northern Ireland. There is a constant tension between proclaimed Cabinet convention and actual practice.

There are accounts in other chapters of disagreements in the Cabinet, resignations, dismissals and even the overthrow of a Prime Minister. We should not expect politics to be continuously peaceful and uncontentious. This would be unnatural. The convention of collective responsibility like most rules goes against nature; but then that is the justification for rules.

Here are two illustrations of challenges to the convention.

■ DOCUMENT 5.11
Collective responsibility and Cabinet management

a) Callaghan and Wilson, April 1969
In 1969 Barbara Castle, backed by the Prime Minister, Harold Wilson, tried to secure legislation on industrial relations which was to include legal sanctions against trade unions. This was to be based on a White paper, 'In Place of Strife'. The proposals were highly contentious and had not been fully discussed and agreed within the Cabinet system. Several Ministers were unhappy about the proposals, and Callaghan was openly critical in well-reported meetings of the Labour party's NEC. He regarded the attempt to rush through first the White Paper, then a Bill, as at best 'the reckless gallantry of the Light Brigade at Balaclava'. Dissident Members of Parliament approached Callaghan about replacing Wilson as leader, though they received no encouragement from Callaghan.

It was apparent that Callaghan was in breach of collective responsibility, though he was entitled to argue, as Heseltine did over Westland, that there was not a fully agreed Cabinet position. However, the Prime Minister could argue that there was an emerging position, and the

time for campaigning outside the Cabinet was past.

In the event, the Prime Minister decided to impose discipline on the Cabinet, even at the risk of Callaghan's resignation. Wilson's reprimand turned out, to disappointed observers like Castle, to be generalised and conciliatory. However, Wilson briefed the press about a 'dressing-down' administered to the erring Minister. Castle commented that Wilson had 'compensated to the lobby for what he had failed to do in Cabinet' (1990, p. 318, 5 April, 1969).

Benn's account of this incident is critical of Callaghan, but not flattering to Wilson or Castle. Wilson, he wrote, 'allowed Callaghan to get away with an explanation which was simply not true. I am afraid I was rather sharp with him. Barbara was vague and woolly and didn't want any action taken, although if I were her I would have been absolutely furious with Jim.' The Prime Minister then 'asked the Cabinet to reaffirm their belief in the White Paper' but Callaghan objected, and Wilson said 'it was all subject to consultation'. Benn commented: 'We left the meeting without knowing more about where we were than at the beginning. I am afraid Jim is winning'. Benn regarded Wilson's subsequent briefing of the press about kicking Ministers into line as 'disrespectful'; 'what a very small man [Wilson] is' (1988, p. 158).

Wilson shortly removed Callaghan from the inner Cabinet he was then using. But it might be thought Callaghan did win this battle. The 'In Place of Strife' proposals were dropped later in the year, and Callaghan went on to become Foreign Secretary in 1974 and Prime Minister in 1976. Ironically his government fell after the 'Winter of Discontent' (a rash of strikes in the public sector) 1978–9, which arguably might have been restrained by the kind of legislation Barbara Castle proposed ten years earlier.

b) Callaghan and Benn, February 1979
Tony Benn was a 'difficult' minister from a Prime Minister's point of view – that is, he had an independent mind, personal courage and a political following. He also had a seat on the Labour party's NEC and so claimed a right to speak out on policy. This is always a constitutional problem for Labour.

Callaghan had used his position on the NEC against the Cabinet in the 'In Place of Strife' crisis of 1969, but both Wilson and Callaghan as Prime Ministers had done their best to ignore the NEC.

In February 1979 a disagreement arose over the sale of Harrier jet fighter aircraft to China. The Cabinet approved, but Benn promoted a resolution in the NEC calling for reconsideration. Callaghan summoned Benn for what turned out to be over an hour of blazing row.

As recounted in Benn's diary Callaghan said in the course of the interchange:

'What about collective responsibility?' 'Do you really want to be in the Cabinet?'

'If we were in calmer waters I would sack you...'.

Callaghan called Benn 'calculating', and 'self-righteous', asked 'Why do you write all these notes in the Cabinet?', and then, rather like a caring and desperate parent or headteacher: 'Why is it always you who's in trouble? First it was Harold and you, now it's me and you.'

Benn gave as good as he got. To the last point he countered: 'Well, before that, Jim, it was Harold and you!'

Benn pointed out that Cabinet was not always fully informed, and other ministers made speeches going beyond approved Cabinet policy – 'Even you admitted that collective Cabinet responsibility only applies when you say it does.' Prime Ministers used to 'get on to' Callaghan, then to Roy Jenkins. 'Maybe it's just what PMs do.' (Benn, 1990, pp. 458–9). ∎

EXERCISE

5.10 How do the strength and skill of the Prime Minister show up in handling these Cabinet crises?

Departmentalism in the Cabinet

Discussion of collective responsibility and the Prime Minister's relations with his political colleagues distracts attention from consideration of the Cabinet as an instrument of management. Tested by managerial effectiveness the Cabinet does not always score high marks. Critics like Douglas Wass, a former Permanent Secretary, do not see in the Cabinet, small or large, and the committee system, a sufficient capacity to deal in detail and with adequate expertise with the range and complexity of government business. Theirs is the complaint that British government has a 'hole at the centre': government by political amateurs, at a level of expertise far below that employed in the management of a multi-national company. Wass' own favoured solution was the establishment of a substantial policy review staff, 'free-standing' but working to the Cabinet Office.

■ DOCUMENT 5.12
Departmentalism in the Cabinet

From D. Wass, 1984, pp. 24–6
Ministers in Cabinet rarely look at the totality of their responsibilities, at the balance of policy, at the progress of government towards its objectives as a whole.... Cabinet's staple diet consists of a selection of individually important one-off cases or of issues on which the Ministers departmentally concerned are unable to agree.

The form and structure of a modern Cabinet and the diet it consumes almost oblige it to function like a group of individuals, and not as a unity. Indeed for each Minister the test of his success in office lies in his ability to deliver his departmental goals.... Cabinet does not have adequate safeguards against a strong departmental Minister.... Cabinet can be too easily rail-roaded. ■

Thus, in this critical view, Cabinet collectivity or solidarity disguises actual departmentalism; and disguised departmentalism, however effective politically, is disastrous for the effective direction of UK plc.

GUIDE TO EXERCISES

5.1 With difficulty! – and the account shows the Cabinet can stop the Prime Minister in her tracks. In the short term the Prime Minister can give way (but that is to abandon the strategy and the Chancellor), play for time (standard practice, if the decision is not urgent), then attempt to fashion a compromise which would not look like a climb-down on her part. In the medium term Margaret Thatcher chose as indicated to dismiss some of her colleagues, and to make less use of the full Cabinet.

5.2 They demonstrate both the power and the ultimate weakness of the Prime Minister, and the persistence of the ideal of collectivity in the Cabinet. They were all resignations partly motivated by discontent with Margaret Thatcher's dominant conduct of her office: they were protests in favour of greater collectivity, hence showed the persistence of the preference for collectivity. Margaret Thatcher does not seem to have been much influenced by them. But these resignations led eventually to her fall from office, and the Prime

Ministerial mode of her successor was quite different, and plainly more collective.

5.3 One may hope for a fruitful tension at the top. But there is no reason to expect that articulate and ambitious men, who have been fighting for power in the same organisation, will be compatible and naturally amicable. Remember that in other spheres promotion often takes a person to another organisation.

Often tensions and resentments will be overcome for the sake of the common cause – but not always. These considerations help to put in perspective the evident troubles of Wilson, Callaghan, Thatcher and Major in maintaining the unity of the Cabinet.

5.4 One answer is 'not much'. He will be neither popular nor effective if he tries to raise it at Cabinet itself. He could put in a paper to the Committee, setting out his views. Appointment to Committees is a significant element of Prime Ministerial control of the Cabinet.

5.5 Some Prime Ministers are dominant, others more consensual; some are masters of the agenda, either by industrious briefing, high intelligence, or both. James Callaghan emerges well from this evidence as the ideal chair. not too strong, not too weak. For Wilson see below. His prime ministerial career, stretching over twelve years and two terms in office, is recounted in detail in three Ministerial diaries. The evidence is that he played every type at different times, and that might be true for any Prime Minister observed in detail over a long period.

5.6 On this evidence Wilson expected Cabinet to take decisions, get through work and apply some balance to department Ministers.

5.7 No, but preparation with options considered and assessed comes very near to determining the outcome. Cabinet Ministers who participated in the pre-Cabinet discussion are likely to support the prepared papers; and others must study the matter carefully if they are, late in the day, to produce effective counter-arguments.

5.8 Good question. Something to do with personalities, perhaps; in any case it is always difficult to defy the Boss.

Departmental ministers may choose to concentrate on their departmental objectives. These are the general reasons for the dominance of the Prime Minister. Further, after the Falklands War and the 1983 election victory, Margaret Thatcher's 'political standing' was high. Jenkins, making this point, comments *when Prime Ministers are up they are very, very up....'* (1987, p.184) – a significant comment in the light of Margaret Thatcher's later fall.

5.9 Solidarity and confidentiality do have advantages, and not just in making life easier for Prime Minister and party managers. The virtues of coherence and team work are secured; Parliament and public may reasonably attribute policies to the government and judge it as a whole. In practice the operation of the convention is weakened by leaks, memoirs and diaries; and Ministers evade retrospective responsibility for their governments. For example, it seems Margaret Thatcher disagreed with Heath's policies, Tony Benn with Wilson's and John Major (and most of his Cabinet) with Margaret Thatcher's. Thus the imposition of solidarity is not wholly effective; and it does diminish public information and understanding. That is the chief disadvantage. See following text.

5.10 In the first Wilson was in difficulty because he was pushing a controversial policy not fully agreed in Cabinet, and against the determined opposition of a powerful Cabinet Minister. His timing was not good; after a rushed White Paper the matter was allowed to drag on, as the Parliamentary and election timetables closed in. Yet the next fifteen years were to show the possibilities and the advantages of legal restraint of 'industrial action'. The affair was badly handled by Wilson, though the best strategy for the Labour Party may have been to leave this kind of legislation to a Conservative government.

For all the comments on the Prime Minister's power of appointment and dismissal, it is evident that Wilson felt that the costs of dismissing Callaghan were too high. Similarly in 1979 Callaghan was reluctant to dismiss Benn. Callaghan's candid remarks on the subject are significant. In the last months of a government without an assured majority, an angry reprimand is more appropriate than dismissal. Both Prime Ministers, for different reasons, were in a weak position and had little scope to display their political skills.

ASSESSMENT
Is the Cabinet an ineffective directing body?

It must first be emphasised that 'the Cabinet' is in practice the 'Cabinet system'. The 'directing body' of that system is, formally and ultimately, the Cabinet. But in normal working of the system the directing body is the Prime Minister-in-Cabinet, and this connotes a shifting structure of relationships of Prime Minister, senior colleagues, and four or five central committees, conducted by the Prime Minister but reporting to and legitimised by the whole Cabinet.

So the question has to be re-formulated to refer to the Prime Minister-in-Cabinet pattern of government. This could be answered by reference to its practical consequences and achievements. Has this structure proved capable of providing good and effective executive government over the last, say, fifty years? This is impossible to answer briefly, but at least it can be said that Britain has enjoyed remarkably stable government, and the system has accommodated to very different kinds of political leadership, and different types of political problems – war and peace, economic change and shifts in ideology.

This is a rather modest testimonial and sharper criticisms may be made. In the end these can be assessed only after a study of the whole system, not to mention a fair tranche of recent history. Briefly the criticisms of the Cabinet system focus on a democratic deficit and managerial ineffectiveness. The democratic critique is concerned with the high concentration of power, secret and largely unaccountable, and the scope for effective pressure by interest groups, party elites and the bureaucracy. Much of this study offers evidence for and against this critique.

The managerialist case against the Cabinet system focuses on the formlessness of the system (who is in charge?), the absence of clear lines of responsibility, the confusion between departmental and government responsibilities, and the weighting of the full Cabinet with departmental Ministers.

The managerial critique might point to the advantages of a small 'super-Cabinet'. This idea has a long history (it was advocated by the Haldane Committee in 1918), and significant trials in the War Cabinets of 1917–18, 1940–5 and in the Falklands War (Margaret Thatcher loved her Falklands War Cabinet). Harold Wilson tried out a small super-Cabinet; and most Prime Ministers have used similar informal groups.

The idea of the small super-Cabinet is attractive, but it is based on the facile assumption that governments can develop long-term strategy in a body cut off from departmental responsibilities and the day-to-day detail of government. 'Strategy' and 'policy' are simply umbrella terms for specific strategies and policies. Hence it is by no means clear that a concern with departmental responsibilities is a disablement for higher policy-making. The implied dichotomy between 'entanglement with administrative detail' and 'creative forward thinking' is much exaggerated. A good deal of government is about administrative detail; forward thinking and higher policy cannot be divorced from day to day concerns.

In any case, given an alternation of government between the parties, there is plenty of time in opposition for long-term planning divorced from administrative responsibilities. And the quality of some of it suggests the validity of the argument that administrative responsibilities provide a necessary starting point and background for long-term planning.

Further, it is a function of the Cabinet to represent and this the larger Cabinet does better than the small. Prime Ministers who have persisted with large Cabinets have probably been most influenced by this need to represent sections of the party. In wartime this is not necessary. Politics of the usual kind are in abeyance and there is a general agreement on a single objective – to win the war. Hence the experience of small super-Cabinets in wartime is in a fundamental way irrelevant.

All of this is rather negative. Surely the Cabinet system as it stands is neither perfect nor incapable of change? The existing system does meet the need to incorporate the departments and to be broadly representative of government, party and people. But improvement in detail is possible. In particular the democratic critique would indicate much more open and accountable procedures of policy development, making more use of

Parliament. The managerial critique identifies the 'hole-in-the-centre' of British government, the weakness of support and advice for Prime Minister and Cabinet. The strengthening of the Downing Street complex is a contribution to this. The establishment and achievements of the Central Policy Review Staff demonstrated the nature and limits of the need, and its failings and abolition showed the difficulties of changing the system. It was a lost opportunity.

Concepts

Cabinet
The term 'Cabinet' denotes a structure, a set of procedures and thus a principle of organisation for government in Britain. It is a powerful term, and may be regarded as a grand idea which floats above and around British government. Beyond its meaning as structure and procedure, 'Cabinet' connotes the collective nature of British government, compared with systems headed by a single individual chief executive, for example, the President of the USA or the Mayor of New York City. Both of these have Cabinets, but they are advisory only. The collective nature of the Cabinet is re-inforced by the constitutional standing of the departments, hence of their Ministerial heads, by the responsibility of the group to Parliament, the cohesion of the Cabinet as a working team and the absence of a system of direct election of the chief executive.

There are still powerful pressures (considered in the text) to move the Cabinet system towards a more presidential mode. If it is true that Cabinet is the underlying concept of British government, then that development has limits, and anything approaching presidential government in Britain could only be a temporary malformation.

Collective responsibility
Like 'Cabinet' the term 'collective responsibility' has a resonance beyond the rules and procedures specifically associated with it (see text). It appears to re-inforce the collectivity or collegiality implicit in the Cabinet, and particularly emphasises the relationship of responsibility to Parliament. In the case of the Cabinet the resonance or penumbra, the grand idea, still seems to count. The resonance of collective responsibility is to some extent misleading, since the relationship to

Parliament involves dominance as well as responsibility.

● CASE STUDY
Westland and the Cabinet

The Westland Affair (December – January 1985-6) was significant for what it showed of the relations of Prime Minister and Cabinet and the convention of collective responsibility; also for the relations of ministers and Cabinet, the convention of ministerial responsibility, and the role of the House of Commons Select Committees. Hence it is noted as a case under the three heads of Cabinet, Ministers and Parliament.

The Westland helicopter company was in financial trouble, and needed rescue by finance and orders, hence either government subsidy or amalgamation or take-over. The government, represented by Leon Brittan at the Department of Trade and Industry, professed neutrality but expected the company to accept take-over by the American Sikorsky company. Michael Heseltine, Secretary of State for Defence, favoured the construction of a European consortium, on grounds both of defence procurement policy and a general leaning towards Europe. Heseltine picked up the issue late but then campaigned vigorously in Cabinet and in public for his favoured solution, while rapidly getting together the 'consortium'.

At this point (early December 1985) Heseltine believed he had a case to make on a matter of high importance on which the Cabinet had yet to come to a conclusion. To the Prime Minister it seemed that Heseltine was intervening late and with excessive force on a matter of middling importance, on which Heseltine was in a minority and on which the Cabinet's position was virtually decided. For both Heseltine and Thatcher collective responsibility was at issue. The affair blew up after clumsy management of the Cabinet system by Margaret Thatcher – the processing of the issue through an informal committee and the failure of a 'pencilled-in' meeting to take place.

Up to that time two points were clear.

1 Heseltine's argument (whatever the facts in his case) that collective responsibility implied a contract: solidarity following collective decision.

2 The Prime Minister's reluctance to dismiss him despite what was (not only in her eyes) a gross breach of collective responsibility and proper Cabinet discipline and courtesy. This was not an example of the Iron Lady in command, or rampant Prime Ministerial Power.

The inflation of the disagreement into a domestic political crisis, headlines, a resignation, and later an anguished Prime Minister happened because Heseltine had determination, political clout and access to the media. He made it happen not because the issue itself justified it (though Europe was to become a damaging issue) but because he was already discontented, and his relations with Margaret Thatcher were edgy.

At the Cabinet of 9 January 1986, ministers were asked to clear public statements on the matter with the Cabinet Office – because of commercial sensitivity. In answer to a question from Nicholas Ridley the Prime Minister ruled that the restriction applied to the reiteration of past positions, not just new statements. Thus at last corralled, Heseltine walked out of the Cabinet room and the Cabinet.

The story as far as we know it does make it look as if Ridley in particular was determined to stop Heseltine. Margaret Thatcher was unsure: despite, or even because of, her reputation, she was soft, hesitant, reluctant to dismiss Heseltine, and indecisive as well as clumsy in her management of senior colleagues.

Heseltine's resignation, like most such resignations, marked the deterioration of his relations with the Prime Minister – evidence of the central role of the Prime Minister in the Cabinet system. For Heseltine his resignation marked a reaffirmation of the necessary collectivity of the Cabinet.

Margaret Thatcher, like her predecessors, survived this reaffirmation, but it caught up with her in the end. After Lawson and Howe left her government in 1988–9, Heseltine challenged her for the leadership and that challenge brought her down. Thus, in the light of later events Margaret Thatcher's reluctance to dismiss Heseltine is understandable. ●

● CASE STUDY
Managing the Cabinet

The threat to resign countered by the threat to dismiss, July–December 1976

The Cabinet spent the Autumn in a marathon series of meetings debating, negotiating and finally accepting the harsh restrictions on public spending proposed by the IMF as the price of a loan.

In the end none of the five major dissidents resigned. At the final Cabinet meeting on 7 December Tony Benn said: 'I don't support this. I am only going along with it out of loyalty to the Government....' By this time it was clear that the Prime Minister himself was 'going for broke'. The Cabinet package would be submitted to the Party and to Parliament, and would in effect be an issue of confidence in the Prime Minister.

Callaghan's conduct of these arguments is a classic exercise in Cabinet government and in the management of the Labour Party. His own account is characteristically dry and unemotional. 'News reached me that two groups were intending to hold separate meetings outside the Cabinet to plan their next moves.

Neither group made its existence known to me directly, but it is surprising how much information filters through to Downing Street and I had a fair idea of the state of play. The two groups were distinct, and I am sure their motivations were good, but they were playing a dangerous game which I determined to circumvent. It was apparent that if the two groups were to coalesce the Chancellor would not have a majority in support of his negotiating stance.... At a pinch we could afford to lose the Secretary for Energy, or in extremis even the Foreign Secretary, but the Government would not have survived the resignation of the Chancellor.

The best possibility of avoiding this was to set aside other business and bring the arguments into the heart of the Cabinet' (1987, p. 435).

Callaghan then called 'a series of dreary Cabinet meetings' to agree specific programme reductions, summoned the Whips to report on the constituencies and finally faced down the left wing of the Parliamentary Labour party by the direct question, 'Do you want us to go on?' (pp. 442–3). ●

6

Prime Ministers and governing: functions and force

Prime Ministers and the government

The Prime Minister is at the head of the government – not only the Cabinet but the non-Cabinet Ministers and their departments. The Prime Minister is:

1 The creator of the government, having powers of appointment and dismissal over all Ministers. His powers over the civil service are more restricted, but his approval is necessary for appointment of Permanent Secretaries. But the element of power should not be over-emphasised. He is personnel director of a very large organisation and his concern will be with efficiency, with finding the right jobs for the right people. Necessarily he will look to one or two senior colleagues including the Leader of the House, and the Chief Whip, for advice about filling over a hundred posts on the political side of the government; and to the Head of the Civil Service for official appointments.

2 The 'full-time executive chairman' of an immense organisation. Like any individual in such a position he cannot himself attend to very much in detail. His job is to appoint an efficient staff, and see that they can get on with their work according to the general directions of the government. He must encourage, even inspire; he must co-ordinate, preserve a balance, keep the convoy moving steadily. Frequently he must step in to unravel acute problems and see that opportunities are taken. For all this he needs to keep in touch with his Ministers without taking over their work or involving himself too deeply in one department.

This is to ask a great deal of one person; not surprisingly, some Prime Ministers have not been good in this crucial role. Here are some illustrations of Prime Ministers at work, and in their relations with colleagues.

■ DOCUMENT 6.1
Prime Ministers and Ministers

a) From Lord Simon, 1952, p. 275
When Home Secretary for the first time I occasionally asked for an interview with Asquith to tell him of an impending difficulty and to ask his advice. Asquith would bring his sledge-hammer mind to bear and in a few minutes would express his view, usually, I am glad to say, agreeing with mine, but sometimes, as a matter of prudence, deciding that the question should be brought before the Cabinet. Baldwin, when I was Home Secretary for the second time, was equally considerate. But, in my experience, his method was to ask what I proposed and then, after a series of grimaces as he pulled in silence at his pipe, to say, 'well, carry on'. Neville Chamberlain, on such occasions, adopted a method different from either of these. He would go into the matter as though it was his personal problem, test it at every point, listen in a businesslike fashion to what one had to say, and then state his conclusion with the finality of a general manager conducting a company's affairs.

b) From a letter written by Ernest Brown, Minister of Labour, to Neville Chamberlain in 1940, quoted in K. Feiling, 1947, p. 303
You cannot know what a comfort it has been to hard pressed departmental Ministers to know that, when their subjects have to be discussed, whoever else has not read their papers and digested them, one man had – the Prime Minister.

c) From G. M. Young, 1952, p. 100
Sooner or later every one of [Baldwin's] colleagues could report the same experience. 'Why come to me? I have perfect confidence in you'. Letters laying some problem of administration before him for decision are answered always promptly, but not so helpfully: 'Go ahead as you propose in your letter just received' or, not infrequently, 'The P.M. has no time to study these papers, and leaves the matter to Mr A's discretion.'

d) From an interview with Harold Wilson by Kenneth Harris in The Observer Magazine, *24 October 1965*
P.M. No. 10 should be a power house not a monastery. And though you've got to let departmental Ministers get on with their job, you've got to know what is happening....
...The levers of power are all here in No. 10. In the Cabinet Room. The ability of the Prime Minister to use them depends on the Prime Minister being in touch with what is going on – and not going on.... The more things you take an interest in, the more information comes back to you. A Prime Minister governs by curiosity and range of interest.

e) From Davidson's memorandum to Neville Chamberlain on becoming Prime Minister quoted in R. R. James, 1969, p. 421
The Prime Minister must cease to look at questions with the eyes of an advocate. He must be the judge before whom the case is argued.... ■

EXERCISES
Prime Ministers and Ministers

6.1 What do you think Lloyd George meant when he said of Chamberlain: 'a retail mind in a wholesale business'?
6.2 Is there a case for preferring the Baldwin method of leadership to Neville Chamberlain's?
6.3 How does Wilson's method in extract d) differ from Baldwin's, and Chamberlain's?

■ DOCUMENT 6.2
Margaret Thatcher and her Ministers

a) The general approach
From Simon Hoggart, 'The Thatcher Phenomenon', The Observer, 2 January 1983
...She has always preferred to make up her own mind without troubling her colleagues for their views. Her notorious 'swamping' remark on immigration came from the top of her head during a TV interview. Willie Whitelaw, who had to build a policy around the phrase, first heard of it from the Press Association tapes. Nor was the Cabinet consulted in 1979 when she and Sir Geoffrey Howe decided to remove exchange controls. She often likes to give the impression that her Ministers are actually nothing to do with her. You half expect her to say "If you ask me, blame the Government,"' an MP says.

b) The responsible Minister excluded
From Harris, 1988, p. 89
Jim Prior had 'assumed [Mrs Thatcher as new Prime Minister] would take things gradually' He was soon disillusioned.
Only three weeks after Mrs Thatcher arrived in Downing Street, Prior, as her Secretary of Employment, sent her a paper suggesting the outlines for a suitable wages and incomes policy – the staple diet of consensus, managerial politics. Within hours it arrived back on Prior's desk with...the message, as Prior read it... in short, that the new Government was not going to have a wages and incomes policy. If the Prime Minister required a paper on the subject...it would come to her from the Treasury. No more was heard of Prior's paper. It did not get to Cabinet or even to a Cabinet committee. ■

These extracts raise the question of the proper role of the Prime Minister in the day-to-day business of government. There is much to be said for Lloyd George's view: the Prime Minister is in a wholesale not a retail business. The Prime Minister's role is a bit like that of a sheep-dog rounding up his flock by a mix of running around, standing still and yelping. Simple practicality indicates that the Prime Minister had best limit his concerns: he has no time for detail. Further, Ministers are likely to do better if given scope and autonomy. It may even be argued that constitutionally government rests with the Minister, in the Department, not the Prime Minister.

This view is clearly set out by Bernard Donoughue.

■ DOCUMENT 6.3
The Prime Minister's policy role

From Bernard Donoughue, 1987, p. 6–7
The Prime Minister's basic policy role, when he or she chooses to exercise it, in the face of all

the constraints, is not related to a specific policy area, but is rather to sustain and co-ordinate the coherence of government policy-making as a whole. In addition, frequently his or her contribution is to introduce a dimension which is wider than departmental. It may often be seen as a national dimension, something called the national interest, difficult though that may be to define.... Ministers sometimes 'go native' in their deprtments and the Prime Minister may feel compelled to introduce a degree of party political realism into that Minister's proposals.

However, it is open to a Prime Minister to intervene with personal initiatives in specific areas of micro-policy. ∎

Thus the Prime Minister is more and less than a manager. He needs to know what is going on in the departments, to understand their problems, and to ensure that government policy is driven through. But he has functions away from and above the work of the departments – to do with morale, vision and popular consent. Sir Ian Gilmour's judgement on politicians is thus appropriate for Prime Ministers: they 'should not be mere managers. Their place is halfway between the counting house and the pulpit' (1978, p.170).

The Prime Minister, Parliament, party and people

Within the Central Executive Territory the Prime Minister is the leader of the Government; beyond that Territory he is the leader of the people. The two functions are not totally distinct. Within the Territory the Prime Minister is concerned with the management of government, but cannot neglect the building of support and consent. Outside the Territory he builds support, but ought not to forget his responsibilities for governing.

Popular leadership is exercised in and through the party, in Parliament and in the party-in-the-country, and directly through the media. Popular leadership requires different qualities from those of the manager of government, and not all Prime Ministers have been good at both kinds of leadership. The system normally provides a substantial parliamentary apprenticeship and a slighter Ministerial apprenticeship for Prime Ministers, though long periods of opposition upset, but may also enhance, this learning process.

In Parliament the Prime Minister is the chief spokesman and leader of his party on the floor of the House, taking part in major debates, making statements, answering Questions twice a week. Prime Ministerial Question Time now provides the most frequent, regular and well-attended prime ministerial occasion in the Commons. Participation in debate is occasional but there may be a number of Prime Ministerial statements.

The significance of Prime Minister's Question Time is much exaggerated (see Chapter 12). It occupies only 15 minutes twice a week, and is mainly used for adversarial combat and abuse. But it takes place before a crowded House and a comparatively large television audience. Extracts are often used in news programmes. A Prime Minister who was regularly worsted in this combat would lose standing among his colleagues and to some extent in the country.

There are few other big occasions for the Prime Minister in the House of Commons. Major speeches are infrequent, up to six each year, but Margaret Thatcher made very few speeches and passed three sessions, 1985–8, without any debating intervention at all. She was 'far and away the least active Prime Minister in the Commons for the last hundred and twenty years' (Dunleavy et al., 1990).

For the Prime Minister, as for the government as a whole, Parliament means in effect the majority party's backbenchers; the Opposition matters much less, it will be voted down anyway. So it is necessary for the Prime Minister to keep in touch with his own parliamentary party, through the Whips and the parliamentary committee, but also informally by circulating, talking and listening. Some Prime Ministers have not been very good at 'keeping in touch'; it requires qualities of social ease, empathy, 'clubability' and a willingness to sacrifice time which might be spent on apparently more urgent matters. But the main work of keeping in touch is done in regular meetings with the 'business managers', the Government Whips, the Leaders of the two Houses, and the party chairman.

A Prime Minister needs to be 'a good House of Commons man'. The House is still an essential part of the metropolitan arena of politics, feeding the endless commentary, speculation and gossip of the corridors, bars and studios of Westminster and its hinterland. However, Parliament is no longer the undisputed centre of politics. Prime Ministers like Churchill and Attlee expected to address the nation through the House of Commons (though Churchill in wartime wisely made his radio speeches too). Herbert Morrison, a senior Labour Minister was shocked to hear Ramsay MacDonald, Labour's first Prime Minister, say he hated the House of Commons.

Most Prime Ministers perform well in the House, by virtue of their office and experience, not because they love the place. But it seems likely that Margaret Thatcher had no great affection for the House, and neglected it when she could: the male-dominated, talking shop and drinking club was not her style at all. She demonstrated that successful leadership of the party and the country exercised through the media would satisfy her backbenchers – as long as it was successful.

Prime Ministers since Gladstone have been leaders of a political party, a nation-wide as well as a parliamentary organisation. The Prime Minister's relations with the national or exterior party differ according to the ethos and structure of the party. A Conservative Prime Minister stands apart from the party, while a Labour Leader is enmeshed in the party; a Liberal Leader lies somewhere between these positions. This relationship is discussed in Chapter 14.

The relationship with party is mainly an aspect of the media projection of the Prime Minister. Party conferences for all parties are now organised as media events. The prolonged standing ovation marks the vulgarisation of the relationship, and the triumph of the media over serious politics.

A Prime Minister has therefore to project an image of himself or herself, which will be acceptable to millions of people. The medium of projection was once the public meeting and the press, reporting the parliamentary feats of the Prime Minister. Since 1959, television has supplanted both as the most important medium, projecting the Prime Minister directly in interviews and at meetings, reporting his parliamentary performances. Television also makes much of the Prime Minister as the embodiment of the government. He is seen arriving at and leaving No. 10 Downing Street, addressing the nation from a lectern set up outside the front door, greeting distinguished visitors, departing from airports, visiting foreign potentates. Much of this is purely visual news, available only to cameras, thin in substance but its cumulative effect quite potent.

The content of the 'image' has been much worked on recently by public relations experts. Previously, Prime Ministers from Gladstone through Lloyd George to Baldwin and Churchill had done their own public relations work. The productions of the experts have

not been markedly different, but it may be said that most politicians have treated their image as something closely related to their own political selves, and have regarded political issues as still quite important. One consequence of the business of image projection is that other party leaders must be presented as unattractively as possible.

The results of this work at election times may be studied in the pictures issued by the parties. Prime Ministers are presented, according to the possibilities of the raw material, as persons of distinction and authority, as friendly chaps anyone might talk to over the garden gate, as trustworthy, as determined, as (whatever it may mean) sincere; or, in the case of Margaret Thatcher, as a masterful but still womanly woman. All of this is understandable. Politics has to be reduced to very general terms and humanised, bearing in mind that the attitudes and policies which lie behind the faces should not be neglected.

Prime Ministers so far have not given their media advisers full freedom to create whatever electoral success requires. The media component in Margaret Thatcher was certainly high but it seems to have been a development of, not just a fantasy on, her own political personality. Similarly, the famous election film of 1987 about the Labour Leader, Neil Kinnock, was confected from his own ingredients. The impact of the media on politics is further discussed in Chapters 19 and 20.

Prime Ministers as national leaders like to speak to and for the British people. The existence of the monarchy as symbol of the nation still leaves the Prime Minister with a role as national leader, perhaps a necessary role (as in time of war or crisis), certainly a role which may be exploited for party advantage. Here are three illustrations of Prime Ministers attempting to get in touch with the people of Britain.

■ DOCUMENT 6.4
Prime Minister and People

a) From G. M. Young, 1952, pp. 54, 56–7
Baldwin was an Englishman not casually, by accident of birth, but deliberately and by election. To be an Englishman was the part he had undertaken to play... a fond projection of everything that the common Englishman still believed himself to be.

He was Prime Minister because none better could be thought of. But of all the gifts which that office seems to require, there was one he believed himself to possess in pre-eminent degree. 'My worst enemy could never say that I do not understand the people of England.' And it was in corresponding terms that he conceived his duty. Whatever else the Prime Minister may do, or be, he must bring that knowledge into the Cabinet room....

b) Wilson in the shipyards of the North East 1965
From P. Jenkins, 1970, pp. 143–4
Wilson trudged through the shipyards. He participated in a question and answer session with shop stewards. It was poorly attended and not a success, but imagine! – here was a Prime Minister, the leading citizen, successor of Pitt, Gladstone, Disraeli and Churchill, chatting away, one northerner to another, with real live shop stewards in a real clanking shipyard. The more cut off a public man becomes from the daily world the more he is moved and impressed by his contacts with it: no amount of political intelligence, reports and opinion polls, are substitute for a politician's personal encounters: for all the social science tools which assist them nowadays in their trade they remain impressionists – one opinion from an aproned housewife on a scrubbed and chalked doorstep is worth a thousand Dr Gallups.

c) Margaret Thatcher
From BBC radio interview 17 Dec 1985 in D. Kavanagh, 1990, p. 252
Her brand of conservatism was 'radical because at the time when I took over we needed to be radical. It is populist.... I would say many of the things I've said strike a chord in the hearts of ordinary people. Why? Because they're British, because their character is independent, because they don't like to be shoved around, because they are prepared to take responsibility....' ■

EXERCISES
Prime Minister and people

6.4 In what sense, if any, do people need a national leader in the sense indicated here?
6.5 In what ways in practice can a Prime Minister discern the views of the people?

The Prime Minister: functions and styles of leadership

It is time to turn from the consideration of the Prime Minister's working relationships to focus on his functions, the job he does, and his force. This provides a context in which the problem of power can be properly addressed.

Functions
The Prime Minister's daily round of reading, talking, meetings is directed to the accomplishment of his political and governmental purposes. These might be analysed as follows.

1 Managing policy in the senses indicated above – initiating, or selecting initiatives, and guiding them through the Cabinet process, offering encouragement and support, or criticism and restraint.
2 Managing crises.
3 Maintaining morale.
4 Building consent, specifically winning the next election.

These essential functions force the Prime Minister into endless choices.

1 Choices between policies; and between policy and non-policy.
2 The judgement of priorities, action and inaction: intervention and non-intervention; decisive action or 'wait and see'; a 'broad brush' or detailed approach.
3 The timing and rationing of authority. All Prime Ministers have a minimal authority. They have to use it with skill, know when to close debate, how to deal with challenges from colleagues of high calibre, when to offer leadership, support, direction, to push faint-hearted colleagues in new directions.
4 A Prime Minister must choose whether and when to have a crisis. Unlucky Prime Ministers will have crises thrust upon them by events, the media, the economy; but a crisis surmounted triumphantly has positive effects.

A Prime Minister certainly does not have to do everything himself: quite the contrary, he is spared the continuing burdens of running a department, and can, and should if he is wise, manage his time to allow space for thought, reflection and relaxation. Nor is he responsible for everything. His ultimate responsibility for the government does not mean that he is personally responsible for the work of all his colleagues. His responsibility relates to:

● the overall performance of the government
● its standing with the people and its re-election prospects and performance
● major policy (but he has some choice over what counts as major)

• matters in which he has been personally involved.

It is not true that the person at the top carries the can, stops the buck or whatever over the whole range of policy. (Football is the only profession in which the failure of the enterprise leads to immediate dismissal; and that is quite irrational, for the failed manager normally gets immediate re-employment at a higher salary).

The non-interventionist view of the job of the Prime Minister was set out above in Document 6.3 above. Document 6.5 emphasises the ministerial basis of British government, while Document 6.6 takes a different line.

■ DOCUMENT 6.5
The ministerial basis of British government

a) From G. W. Jones, in W. Plowden 1987, p. 64
In the British constitution, government is ministerial government. Powers and duties are laid on ministers, not on the Prime Minister. They come together in Cabinet to resolve disputes between themselves and to determine a common line. The Prime Minister's task, among others, is to help colleagues reach agreement, to promote collegiality and a collective strategy.... Personal initiatives come up against the constraints of Cabinet government. The urgings of the Prime Minister's own policy may hinder the achievement of a united Cabinet. The logic of the British Constitution is that Prime Ministers do not intervene in the policy responsibilities of specific ministers in order to advance personal prime ministerial objectives. Their intervention makes constitutional sense only if it is to enhance collective Cabinet responsibility.

[Professor Jones allows that the Prime Minister may need to check a colleague, not by taking over that policy area, but by efforts 'to confine and redirect the Ministers through the Cabinet and a Cabinet committee, or else to replace the Minister'. A Prime Minister should not allow the promotion of a personal policy to damage Cabinet consensus.]

b) From W. I. Jennings, 1941, pp. 160–1
Indeed a Prime Minister in peacetime ought not to have a policy. If he has able Ministers he ought to rely on them, and policies should come from departmental Ministers, assisted as they are by the knowledge and experience that their departments can offer. The qualities which made Lloyd George a great Prime Minister in wartime made him a disastrous Prime Minister in peacetime. ■

The non-interventionist model suits most Prime Ministers. They like to be above the battle, avoiding heat, smoke and injury – and the blame for defeat. Life is more comfortable back at staff headquarters, and you may get a better view of what is going on. On the other hand you may not; and in the end wars are decided on the battlefield, by fighting soldiers not generals (though generals take the credit or blame). So a Prime Minister who wants to win the war has to take some part in the battle.

A former Cabinet Secretary takes this view and emphasises the need for an active, interventionist, directing Prime Minister.

■ DOCUMENT 6.6
The active, interventionist Prime Minister

a) From Lord Hunt of Tamworth (formerly Cabinet Secretary) speaking in November 1984, and printed in W. Plowden, 1987, pp. 66–8
[Mr Callaghan] 'did not want to involve himself in every issue; he would have liked almost an Attlee role – presiding as chairman of the Cabinet and concentrating his efforts on the things of greatest importance and interest to him. He found this was impossible, however, and he had to get involved in all sorts of detail. Why?

1 The change came with the extension of the public sector...the government feeling it was responsible for everything...it increased the co-ordinating and strategic role of the Prime Minister.
2 [Lord Hunt refers to the dissatisfaction with advice to Ministers despite CPRS advisers and new management methods.]
   Under the present system there is a Cabinet which has collective responsibility, without sufficient information or power to exercise it. This is partly because of the lack of adequate collective briefing, and partly because of the impossible overload on Ministers in their own departments and the very little time that they can give to their collective responsibilities. Hence, again, the tendency to involve the Prime Minister more.
3 Other pressures...underline the difficulty of running a collective executive. These include modern communications and the pressures of the media, which make governments feel – rightly or wrongly – that they have to react to everything very quickly.... That necessarily

involves the Prime Minister... there is also Prime Minister's Questions, an 'extraordinary arrangement'.

Another development has been the rise of summitry... [and] joining Europe.

[Civil servants no longer feel] – such loyalty... to their own department...and to the Treasury. Nowadays this kind of Treasury power is weaker and the role of the Treasury in holding the show on the road is correspondingly less.

All these changes mean that the role of the Prime Minister, as distinct from the power of the Prime Minister, has inevitably evolved.
[Lord Hunt lists the role as including:

- a need to keep informed, not waiting for trouble to come along
- a need to initiate and to call others in for collective discussion
- acting as the guardian of Cabinet strategy, ensuring consistency and coherence, although not necessarily its architect.

Lord Hunt sums up his view]:
I do not think it is possible any more – regrettable as it may be – to think of the Prime Minister in this country simply as holding the ring as a neutral chairman. This has nothing to do with whether there happens to be a pushy Prime Minister or a less pushy Prime Minister....

[These views of a former Cabinet Secretary are supported by others, for example, a Victorrian Cabinet Minister and a recent Professor of Politics who was also a Member of Parliament.]

b) Sir William Harcourt, quoted in A. G. Gardiner, 1923, Vol. II, p. 612
...on a question of policy there can be no doubt that the most successful administrations are those in which there is a strong Prime Minister and a subordinate Cabinet.

c) From J. P. Mackintosh, 1962, p. 384
A Premier soon imparts his own tone to his government and if he fails to bind his Ministers together, to tackle contemporary problems, or to ensure action, then there is no-one who can, so to speak, steer the bus from the back seat. ∎

The choice for the Prime Minister between intervention and non-intervention is crossed by the choice of styles in the senses suggested in Chapter 5. Three general types of prime ministerial leadership might be discerned (Document 6.7).

■ DOCUMENT 6.7
Types of prime ministerial leadership

a) The manager (or civil servant)
From Peter Hennessy in The Times, *16 May 1983, quoting a senior civil servant*
Ted (Heath) was a technocrat, felt he had to be on top of everything. He would have been a jolly good permanent secretary.

[Heath and Wilson had been civil servants. Margaret Thatcher had not. She disliked the civil service and did not approach politics as a civil servant.]

b) The healer or fixer (or party leader)
From John P. Mackintosh (ed.), 1978, pp. 213–14
...although (Wilson) left behind him no major legislative or diplomatic triumphs, he nevertheless did have his achievements, and they were in party and electoral terms. He made a warring set of factions look like an alternative government in 1963...After 1964, Wilson made Labour the party of government.... Though he lost in 1970, he held the Labour Party together through another period of divisive in-fighting....
Whether these positive factors are held to be of great importance, whether they mitigate or outweigh the defects that have been described really depend on how much value is placed on holding the Labour Party together and keeping it in government.

c) The crusader (or heroic leader)
Churchill is the best example. Margaret Thatcher cultivated, or had cultivated for her, an image of crusading, moral and patriotic fervour and strong conviction. The public phrases encapsulated the image – the Iron Lady; the Lady's not for Turning; There is No Alternative. In fact, the image fitted reality mainly in the period of the Falklands War. The long and bloody struggle with the British economy brought less elation, but the approach was still heroic. Like a general in the 1914–18 war, Margaret Thatcher met the enemy head-on, and kept going despite the mounting casualties. ■

Of these types the Fixer and the Crusader are far apart. The Fixer minimises disagreements and pursues damage-limitation politics, the Crusader maximises differences and marches into danger. The Fixer hopes to end arguments, the Crusader wants to win them. John Major is evidently a

Fixer, in contrast to his crusading predecessor. Even so, these types are not mutually exclusive, and a wise Prime Minister might mix them shrewdly, managing all of the time, fixing some of the time and crusading when a crisis looms. The reality differs from the image. The nature of the office imposes some flexibility on the strong and some firmness on the weak.

Prime ministerial force

The long-running debate on prime ministerial power began in the 1960s The thesis of prime ministerial power was first forcibly stated by R. H. S. Crossman in 1963 (1963, p. 51):

The post-war epoch has seen the final transformation of Cabinet Government into prime ministerial Government. Under this system the 'hyphen which joins, the buckle which fastens, the legislative part of the state to the executive part' becomes one single man.

Academic weight was offered by Professor John Mackintosh. In his classic study of the British Cabinet (1977, pp. 428, 458) he wrote, 'The position and power of the Prime Minister has been the focal point of modern Cabinets...overall direction can come from no other source'. Even in times of criticism and weakness, the authority of the office stands up. Curiously, Crossman soon joined the government, and modified his view: Mackintosh went into Parliament, and strengthened his view. Margaret Thatcher's long tenure of the office fuelled the debate with abundant new evidence about the possibilities of 'Prime ministerial despotism of a formidable kind', as *The Guardian* wrote in March 1981 (even before Margaret Thatcher's Falklands and later triumphs).

In fact, the evidence was more mixed than is implied. Earlier Prime Ministers and senior Ministers have never agreed on the extent of prime ministerial power.

■ DOCUMENT 6.8
How powerful is the Prime Minister?

a) From Lord Morrison, 1964 (preface to 3rd Ed.), pp. 9–10
I have not thought it necessary to refer to exaggerated beliefs as to the role and status of the Prime Minister. He is clearly the most important member of the Cabinet unless – as has happened in some cases – he subordinates himself and prefers to leave the heavier burdens to some of his colleagues.

b) From Lord Morrison, 1964, pp. 51–2
The first and most important non-departmental Minister is the Prime Minister himself.... As the head of the Government he is primus inter pares. He is the leader of his party...he must know enough to be ready to intervene if he apprehends that something is going wrong.... He is not the master of the Cabinet.

c) From Stanley Baldwin, quoted in Reith, 1949, p. 129
No matter how much imagination or vision or energy the Prime Minister may have, it's like being stuck in a glue pot.

d) From Earl of Oxford and Asquith, 1928, Vol. II, p. 207
There is not and cannot be, from the nature of the case, any authoritative definition of the precise relation of the Prime Minister to his colleagues. 'In practice', as Sir William Harcourt says, 'the thing depends very much upon the character of the man....' The office of Prime Minister is what its holder chooses and is able to make of it.'

e) From Harold Wilson, 1976, pp. 9–10
The arguments in support of the prime ministerial government thesis entirely fail to allow for almost 180-degree differences in the style of individual, indeed successive, Prime Ministers. ■

EXERCISES
The power of the Prime Minister

6.6 What might be the precise possible meaning of primus inter pares (first among equals)?
6.7 What is the 'glue' Baldwin refers to?

The debate is interesting and highly relevant for the understanding of British government, but is unsatisfactory in some respects.

● The central proposition is not closely defined: power in relation to whom? and to do what?
● The evidence is hard to come by, and by its nature, anecdotal and unsystematic.
● prime ministerial power is difficult to isolate, changes over time and circumstance, and differs radically between individual Prime Ministers.
● The prime ministerial role is central in government, so trying to sum up prime ministerial power is like trying to sum up the nature of British executive government in one bite.

However, the subject of prime ministerial power cannot be set aside: it just needs to be approached with care. It is helpful to 'unpack' the term 'power' at least into two of its elements, 'force' and 'impact'. 'Force' is understood as a potential to move other objects (like the wind blowing); 'impact' is the action of the force on an object. Force and impact equal 'power'.

The basic elements of prime ministerial force arise from the Prime Minister's political position. These were summarised in Chapter 4, Document 4.1. They constitute the Prime Minister's resources for power, and these are without doubt substantial. But the Prime Minister's force is diminished, diverted or blocked by elements of counter force – colleagues, the Cabinet, ministerial and official systems.

The consideration of the job of Prime Ministers, the day-to-day work, throws light on both force and impact. These two chapters on the Prime Minister have shown him at once managing the Cabinet and locked into its procedures. The Prime Minister is characteristically an individual leader in a collective context. There is push and pull, an ebb and flow between the two. The Prime Minister is not King in the Central Executive Territory; but he is the eldest Prince, or the senior Baron.

The impact of the Prime Minister is the resultant of the application of force, minus counter force, both on his Colleagues and the conditions and events of his time. These are two different tests. A forceful Prime Minister may dominate his colleagues but not his problems, and so have a low impact. A dominant Prime Minister facing an insoluble problem may make little impact. But almost any Prime Minister can exert a high impact on simple conditions and events, and easy problems. (There is an obvious comparison with a general facing a weak army.) Hence the ultimate test of power for a Prime Minister is the making of an impact on an intractable problem.

Here is a selection of evidence about the power of two recent Prime Ministers.

Prime ministerial power
Harold Wilson
1 Government by an inner group. In Wilson's first administration (1964–6) power was exercised largely by a small inner group (Wilson, Brown, Callaghan), which took the major decisions on economic policy, including the establishment of the Department of Economic Affairs, the refusal to devalue the pound and the July 1965

economic package – 'dumped without warning on the Cabinet table the morning it was due to be announced, and Ministers were given three hours to discuss and agree it' (C. Ponting, 1989, p. 33).

This looks like a key to success for a Prime Minister: share power in a close alliance with two or three of your Cabinet heavyweights. Thus a Prime Minister may hope to secure substantial power, but at the cost of giving some of it away.

EXERCISE
The power-sharing strategy

6.8 So why do not all Prime Ministers settle for this strategy?

2 In Place of Strife, 1969 (see Chapter 5, Document 5.11). The Prime Minister encouraged Barbara Castle (Secretary of State for Trade and Industry) to develop legislation on trade unions and industrial relations. After a long-running battle in the Cabinet, in the party and in the trade unions, the proposals were eventually withdrawn. A compromise agreement with the trade unions was purely cosmetic: Wilson and Castle had been defeated.

The incident is a bench-mark for the limits of prime ministerial power. It began with what must be regarded as a normal example of modern Cabinet government: the Prime Minister propelled forward a ministerial policy initiative, which was judged to be likely to secure Cabinet approval later. In the event the policy was aborted by the opposition of the trade unions, the parliamentary party and a majority of the Cabinet. The Prime Minister might have won over, or forced down, one or two but not all three of these groups; in practice, the Cabinet, backed by dissident back benchers blocked the way.

EXERCISE
In Place of Strife

6.9 Is this a representative example of the limits of prime ministerial power?

3 Waiting for the Prime Minister – policy paralysis. In 1974–5 an economic crisis developed (or continued). Cabinet and the Treasury waited for the Prime Minister to act, but Wilson, pre-occupied with the problems of governing without a secure majority, delayed action. This

is a good – though not encouraging – example of the negative power of the Prime Minister, the power to hold up action. Bernard Donoughue, then head of the Prime Minister's Policy Unit wrote (A. King, 1985, p. 55–6):

The most striking feature of the first months of Harold Wilson's third and fourth administrations in 1974–5 was the almost total absence of collective discussion of economic policy.... A senior Treasury official told me in the Summer of 1974 that the Treasury was holding its hand and waiting till after the second General Election clarified the political situation and that then it would bring forward a crisis package of economic measures. [But after the October 1974 Election the Government was distracted by foreign affairs and devolution.]

4 'National security' – secrecy as a support to power. The 'Chevaline' programme. In matters of defence ('national security') the Prime Minister enjoys substantial power because defence expenditure and dispositions are decided partly in secret, and within very broad guide lines. This is especially true for all governments in the matter of nuclear arms.

The 'Chevaline' programme for 'modernising' Britain's Trident missiles was first reported orally to Cabinet by Wilson, who then hurried off to a public engagement. There was no debate. The cost was then estimated at £24m. By 1976 the cost had risen to £595m; expenditure on Chevaline was not cash-limited. But the project did not come before Cabinet again. The Chief Secretary to the Treasury learned about it when he was in opposition, and Chairman of the Public Accounts Committee. The cost by then was £1 billion.

National security is not unique in being surrounded by secrecy. High economic policy (e.g. exchange and interest rates) is also subject to some necessity for secrecy, and again it may be exploited to evade open discussion and challenge.

Harold Wilson was concerned to build a consensus, avoiding rows, resignations and party splits – but of course retaining as much of his own policy inclinations as he could. In this way he managed to confirm Britain's accession to the European Community, frustrate Benn and the left wing, and edge towards an incomes policy.

By contrast Margaret Thatcher, certainly in her later years, appeared to be the model of the powerful Prime Minister. If the prime ministerial power theorists needed an example this was it. Margaret Thatcher did indeed demonstrate, first, that the office of Prime Minister could be pushed a long way towards personal dominance of the Cabinet system; and, second, that a Prime Minister with a talent for political leadership could make a significant impact on the country. Measured by personal dominance and impact, Margaret Thatcher must be adjudged a powerful Prime Minister.

■ DOCUMENT 6.9
Margaret Thatcher as a powerful Prime Minister: the evidence

1 Personal relations with colleagues. The dismissal of a whole Cabinetful of colleagues. The undermining and by-passing of colleagues (Pym, Biffen, Howe).
2 The 'by-passing' of the full Cabinet in favour of committees and bilaterals and a kitchen Cabinet (though this is to some extent a normal feature of the modern Cabinet).
3 The standing firm in face of Cabinet disagreement over for example, the 1981 budget, the Community charge, Westland – Hugo Young wrote: 'sheer prime ministerial will [as a] substitute for orderly decisions logically arrived at' (1989, p. 462).
4 Personally taking, and not retreating from, tough decisions, for example, giving permission to President Reagan to use British airfields for the bombing of Libya (H. Young, 1989, pp. 475–8, 481).
5 Successful mobilisation of opinion in winning three general elections, but also in shifting the basis of British politics away from the old 'social democratic consensus' ■

Margaret Thatcher's Prime Ministership constitutes a formidable argument for prime ministerial power. However, there is something to be said on the other side, about the limits of prime ministerial power, and the persistence of collective constraints. The Thatcher Cabinets sometimes disagreed, and she lost arguments in Cabinet (that is why she tried to bypass it). She accepted some policies which she did not positively favour, for example, the Anglo-Irish Agreement, the Rhodesian settlement, the slow drift towards Europe, the failure to go further in the privatisation of Education and the Health Services, continuing high public expenditure.

Moreover Margaret Thatcher showed some

signs of a fundamental weakness of character: she did not tolerate strong and competitive personalities around her. She dismissed her strongest ministerial colleagues, unwilling to accept the stress that Harold Wilson took in his Cabinet of 'heavyweights'. The persons closest to her were subordinates, officials, advisers and Friends. At the end she had retreated to a bunker – not a mark of inner confidence and strength.

Even so, Margaret Thatcher was never able wholly to dispense with the Cabinet system. Perhaps she never wanted to, though plainly her style was well suited to a presidential system. An 'observer' quoted by her former senior civil servant Sir Leo Pliatzky, said of Margaret Thatcher: 'The Cabinet system has remained intact but... she has operated it so as to get her own way' (L. Pliatzky, 1989, p. 12). That phrase might be an unhelpful paradox, like the 'primus inter pares' formula. If the Prime Minister got her own way consistently, could the Cabinet system be truly said to remain intact?

Nor was Margaret Thatcher wholly successful in converting the British people to her way of thinking. She won three general elections, it is true, but without increasing the Conservative share of the vote; and she helped to push the Labour Party back towards the centre, a move Labour was ready to make. Margaret Thatcher transformed thinking about the trade unions, nationalisation and public expenditure, but without converting the majority to her own sharp hostility.

The persistence of collectivity was demonstrated under Margaret Thatcher by the resignations of three senior Cabinet Ministers, Heseltine, Lawson and Howe, and her eventual downfall. The defenestration (literally ejecting through the window) of Margaret Thatcher in November 1990 was a remarkable event, which ought to tell us much about the power of the Prime Minister.

■ DOCUMENT 6.10
The defenestration of Margaret Thatcher

[Margaret Thatcher had been in power for over eleven years with hardly a hint of retirement to encourage the ambitious among the new generation; some of her policies, notably the 'poll-tax' and reform of the National Health Service, were unpopular, and the economy was moving into sharp recession. She had made many enemies and few warm friends. Read on...]

Here is the course of events, October–November 1990

1 Polls showed Labour in a 16 per cent lead. Eastbourne, Conservative majority almost 17 000, was lost to Liberal Democrats in by-election; Conservatives did badly in two later by-elections in Bootle and Bradford North.

2 Margaret Thatcher was in a minority of one at Rome meeting of European Council. On her return she reported to the House of Commons and, once through her carefully prepared text, spoke with passion, or at least an unstatesmanlike vehemence, about the iniquities of the European Commission. To any hint of a united Europe, she shouted, 'No! No! No!'. Hugo Young described this as one of her most 'electric' parliamentary performances; she was 'high on power and rectitude' (1991, p. 577).

3 Sir Geoffrey Howe resigned on 1 November, responding directly to Margaret Thatcher's performance in the House, when she had abandoned positions agreed with colleagues, and to months of isolation and humiliation. His resignation speech two weeks later was the most devastating resignation speech ever made. He concluded: 'The time has come for others to consider their response to the tragic conflict of loyalty with which I have myself wrestled for perhaps too long'. Nigel Lawson sat near to Sir Geoffrey, and clearly supported him.

4 Enter, or re-enter, the First Musketeer, Michael Heseltine. He restated his disagreements with Margaret Thatcher, and after two weeks of hesitation, announced that he would be a candidate in the forthcoming election for the leadership of the Conservative Party.

5 In the first ballot Margaret Thatcher won 204 votes to Heseltine's 152 – just 4 votes short of the necessary 15 per cent majority required.

6 There followed a confused 40 hours at the end of which Margaret Thatcher informed the Cabinet that she would step down. In those 40 hours of high drama, sometimes in front of the world media, excited meetings took place all over Westminster. One, composed mainly of Ministers, at the nearby house of Tristan Garel-Jones, a Conservative junior Minister, is reported to have constituted a conspiracy to drive Margaret Thatcher from office. But what is a conspiracy? The meeting was a conspiracy in so far as it was not accidental, the people present were certain to claim a

voice in the determination of the leadership crisis, and most people present were pessimistic about Margaret Thatcher's chance of survival. In effect the meeting concluded that it was necessary to stop Michael Heseltine. This tactical consideration sealed Margaret Thatcher's fate.

7 On the day after the results of the first ballot were announced Margaret Thatcher called in her Cabinet Ministers one by one. The occasion was tense, sad and for some tearful. The message was clear: the Prime Minister was told that she could not win. Later that night she decided to resign, and prepared to appear in the Commons next day as a soon-to-be-replaced Prime Minister. (Like all tough and aggressive leaders Margaret Thatcher showed up most admirably when anything less than iron would bend and snap.)

8 Other candidates, John Major and Douglas Hurd, joined the contest for the succession. The campaigns of Major and Heseltine particularly were run with great skill, energy and resources. This was a contest between ambitious professionals. In the event, on 27 November 1990, seven days after the declaration of the first ballot, it was announced that John Major had secured 185 votes, Heseltine 131 and Hurd 56. Major, too, had failed by two votes to get the 15 per cent lead required, but the other two in effect withdrew from the contest. There was no third ballot. Thus Britain acquired a new Prime Minister by defective pursuit of the unsatisfactory procedures of the Conservative Party, defined for this purpose as all Conservative Members of Parliament. John Major was Margaret Thatcher's preferred successor, but her threat to be 'a very good back seat driver' came to nought. In her last week in power, the extent and the limits of her prime ministerial power were demonstrated once again. ∎

EXERCISES
The defenestration of Margaret Thatcher.

6.10 Who was primarily responsible for the defenestration of Margaret Thatcher – Cabinet, Party, Parliament or People? Or an individual?

6.11 Does the defenestration prove that Prime Ministers are not after all very powerful?

The lesson of these events seems to be:

- that only continuously successful Prime Ministers can manage without the support of colleagues: so, in the long run, all Prime Ministers need the support of colleagues
- dominant and interfering Prime Ministers who bypass the Cabinet risk coming to sticky ends – Lloyd George, Chamberlain and Thatcher are all examples.

Yet, when all that is said, it is evident that Margaret Thatcher's ultimately rebellious colleagues put up with her dominant ways for a long time. Prime Ministers, it seems, can exceed the collegial limits for a good many miles before they are gonged down.

EXERCISE
The Thatcher Prime Ministership and the power of Prime Ministers.

6.12 What reasons are there for judging that Margaret Thatcher's Prime Ministership was not a representative indicator of prime ministerial power?

It is evident on the one hand that the office of Prime Minister has a potential for high personal power, if not anything approaching autocracy; and at the same time that the countervailing power of the collective elements in the system cannot be suppressed for ever. But Margaret Thatcher remained uncollectivised for ten years. With the party and enough of the country behind her she passed her MOT in 1983 and 1987, and fell when it looked as if she might be adjudged unroadworthy next time.

GUIDE TO EXERCISES
6.1 Too much attention to small-scale transactions, too little concern for the broader strategy.

6.2 Baldwin's method has the merit of delegation: much was left to individual Ministers, who were encouraged to use their own discretion and initiative. The disadvantage is the lack of any control or guidance and support to weak and bewildered Ministers.

6.3 It seems that where Chamberlain intervened to take decisions and Baldwin left his Ministers on their own, Wilson tried to keep himself well-informed. This might allow him to influence decisions, but perhaps short of detailed intervention.

6.4   This is really a matter of complex psychology. People need security, protection, someone watching over them, especially in times of crisis and stress. Such needs can be met in various ways – religion, the 'community', neighbours, family, friends. The monarchy offers a protective symbolism. A more rational view is that political leaders should attend to the needs of the people for public policy and programmes, leaving their emotional needs to vicars and pop stars. However, a purely rational view of political leadership is inadequate. Politics is also about feelings such as loyalty, trust and confidence. Napoleon Bonaparte, hearing the bells at Malmaison, said, 'Men are governed by magic'. Prime Ministers more modest than Napoleon endeavour to build a relationship of warmth and good feeling with 'the people'.

6.5   This is quite difficult. A Prime Minister can read the papers, talk to colleagues, travel about and ask questions, deal with constituency problems, study opinion surveys, generally 'keep his ear to the ground'. Despite such efforts a Prime Minister remains isolated, cut off in a narrow world, even more than most professionals.

6.6   This is an unhelpful paradox, since the contradiction in it needs to be resolved. It must mean in practice that the Prime Minister is ahead, or on top, but not by very much.

6.7   All the restraints on prime ministerial action arising from colleagues, and party, plus the intractability of political problems. John Major's prime ministership demonstrated some of the truth of Baldwin's remark .

6.8   First, the strategy is not attractive to a Prime Minister looking for unfettered personal power. Second, the strategy is not always available, and may soon break down, because the inner group will run into disagreements. This was the case in the Wilson government. The inner group was divided by rivalry and policy disagreements. The Prime Minister can then follow the 'divide and rule' tactic; but this is not easy – the divided tend to fight back. Altogether a prudent Prime Minister tries to include the whole Cabinet in the circle of his close advisers.

6.9   Obviously not. The 'In Place of Strife' proposals were a radical change for a party traditionally committed to trade union interests; and they were inadequately prepared by consultation and discussion. It is conceivable that a more dominant, less consensual Prime Minister like Margaret Thatcher would have pushed the proposals through, in defiance of Cabinet, party and trade unions. But the political cost would have been high.

6.10   There are two questions: who wielded the axe? Who compelled the mob?
       Clearly all four had a part. The opinions of the People, as shown in the polls were crucial. If Margaret Thatcher had looked like winning the next election, she would have been secure. The Party was divided, but there remained substantial support for her in the constituencies. Conservative Members of Parliament made their views public in the first ballot of the election. It may be assumed that some voted for her only as an alternative to Heseltine, and many would not wish to depose a respected leader. Overall Conservative Members of Parliament demonstrated a massive loss of confidence in Margaret Thatcher's leadership.
       The final execution was carried out by members of the Cabinet. In that way the Cabinet finally re-asserted its lost authority. But their moment came almost by chance after years of submission, and even then depended on the resignation of Howe, and his defiant speech, and the candidature of Heseltine. They – or Heseltine at least – may be said to have acted positively to overthrow Margaret Thatcher.

6.11   No. It shows only that there are some limits to Prime ministerial power. Margaret Thatcher was a forceful Prime Minister with a strong ideological commitment, and with substantial support in the constituency parties. Hence her overthrow was more than a personal assassination; it amounted to a peaceful but radical revolution.

6.12   Margaret Thatcher was unusually dominant and aggressive in her personal style, and acquired a clear policy agenda. There were few political 'heavyweights' in her Cabinet. These factors are unusual. Further, her exercise of the Prime Ministership aroused much hostility, leading to her downfall, and a welcome to her successor on the simple ground that he was not Margaret Thatcher. There is clear discouragement to would-be autocrats.

ASSESSMENT
John Major and prime ministerial power

John Major was elected in succession to Margaret Thatcher as Leader of the Conservative Party and Prime Minister (November 1990). The reasons for his election are complex, but there was agreement, even outside the Conservative Party , that John Major was a 'nice' man, gentle and with a sense of humour, and that his style of leadership would be less abrasive than Margaret Thatcher's. John Major had served as a Whip and both his inclinations and his skills made him a master of moderation and compromise, the conjuror of agreement out of discord. He was, as was suggested above, a Fixer, a maker of deals. His approach to Cabinet and colleagues was collegial and consensual, and Ministers rejoiced that open discussion was encouraged in Cabinet. His predecessor's dominant style was admitted even by some of her admirers to have led to policy mistakes through inadequate discussion.

By 1993 John Major was widely perceived as a weak and ineffective Prime Minister. The Conservative Party was divided, partly but not exclusively over Europe, and there was open and organised rebellion in Parliament; economic policy had collapsed, the government's annual deficit had reached £50bn., and there were a series of policy U-turns (so despised by Margaret Thatcher) and fumbled crises. Polls showed Major to be the most unpopular Prime Minister of modern times. The media, especially the 'Tory tabloids', who had supported the Conservatives and John Major so vociferously in the 1992 election, led the outcry. Major was declared to be 'not up to the job'; even his Chancellor (and former campaign manager), having been unjustly dismissed, said that the government was 'in office but not in power'. John Major himself admitted that he had come too early to the highest office. A general view at the end of 1993 was that the Prime Minister was 'on probation'.

Inevitably there was some unfairness in these judgements. In particular John Major's best political qualities showed up on private rather than public occasions. The public arena no

longer included obvious Public Enemies (Galtieri, Scargill) so helpful to Thatcher's style; and the Conservative Party , in power since 1979, was plainly responsible for the condition of the country. So John Major faced severe political problems. But of course that is what Prime Ministers are for. All this was very far from the notion of high prime ministerial power associated with Margaret Thatcher's reign, and provides interesting evidence for the great debate on prime ministerial power.

1 Was John Major markedly less powerful than Margaret Thatcher? In terms of personal power the answer is clearly, yes. He did not choose to exercise highly personal power, and lacked the drive and personal style and political support to sustain personal power. In terms of principles and policies the answer is less certain. It may be that the whole record of the Major prime ministership (not yet available) will demonstrate a consistent approach and the achievement of a coherent set of relevant and effective policies – despite U-turns and an apparent loss of direction on the way. However, the evidence of the third year of Major's leadership, and indeed of some of the previous fifty years of British government, not excepting Margaret Thatcher's, is that consistency, coherence and effectiveness are not normal characteristics of government. By that test of substantial achievement, few Prime Ministers measure high on the scale of prime ministerial power.
2 Does the Major experience show that theories of prime ministerial power were mistaken or over-stated at least? In the simplest form – all Prime Ministers are very powerful all of the time, dominating policy, getting their own way without challenge – this is true. The Major prime ministership clearly demonstrates limits on prime ministerial power; but so, if we look carefully, did Margaret Thatcher's, Harold Wilson's and any other we choose. John Major confirms that prime ministerial power is variable, falls short of omnipotence and can drift into impotence.

However, it is important not to move to the other extreme position. There is a substantial block of power which every Prime Minister inherits – management of the central machinery of government and a formidable support staff, the power of appointment and dismissal, a public standing and excellent media opportunities. A Prime Minister has a substantial power at least to hold up policy development and action, and (despite Margaret Thatcher's experience) he is protected by the sheer difficulty of unseating a party leader.

Some Prime Ministers have been able to add to the basic block of power additional and very substantial elements: the support of an undivided party, some policy opportunities to provide success and popularity (Thatcher very fortunate in that respect), and high skill in exploiting media interest. (See the analysis of prime ministerial power in Document 4.1).

John Major's prime ministership has been undermined by the absence of these factors. Such a judgement means that Prime Ministers do not all automatically inherit the full comple-ment of power. That is partly the fault of circumstances, the political and policy situation. However, it may be argued that some Prime Ministers dominate or change the circumstances. If that is so, then it would seem that some Prime Ministers (make your own list) exercised some significant if elusive qualities of leadership, which for them en-larged the power of their office.

3 Is that extra quality of leadership an advan-tage in a democracy? Margaret Thatcher may have given strong leadership a bad name, but it may be that other Prime Ministers have shown or do show the case for strong leader-ship.

The case for a strong prime ministership.
- *Popular and national leadership* We may assume that a country like Britain faces serious problems which cannot be solved without effort and sacrifice. The winners and losers of the system will change. If radical change is to be accomplished without grave social and political tension, then political leaders will need to persuade, bully, cajole, stand firm in face of privilege and self-interest, and convey to the people a sense of direction, of a journey with a purpose. That kind of leadership could come from a collec-tive Cabinet and a vigorous political class; but it seems likely that a Prime Minister at the centre of the action could offer an invaluable element of what is usually called political leadership.
- *Direction of the government* The Cabinet system is not self-starting, nor self-steering, and requires direction and co-ordination.

Prime ministerial force is needed too to overcome departmentalism and 'short-termism', and to impart the dynamism required to overcome resistance and inertia and drive policies through. (See Document 6.6.)

The argument against the strong Prime Minister depends on:
- doubts about the true advantages of strong and active leadership. It is not always and necessarily better than 'weak' leadership. On the contrary, 'wait and see' or Micawberism (hoping something will turn up) is often wise and requires courage. Activity, still less, hyperactivity, are not the true essence of leadership. There may be further doubts about the disadvantages of strong leadership by one person, its narrowness, its burdens and its corruptions.
- acceptance of the ministerial and departmen-tal basis of British government as both effective and constitutionally proper. (See Document 6.5.)
- concern for the collegial nature of Cabinet government, and the securing of consent.
  'Wise Prime Ministers are careful not to flaunt the dictatorial powers granted them by the British constitution. They pay attention not just to presentation but to the political proc-esses through which decisions must pass to gain public consensus. They respect the residual pluralism in the constitution – collec-tive Cabinet responsibility, local government, the House of Lords, the status accorded to pressure groups and the press – as a counterweight to their own power.' (The Economist, July 7, 1984.)
- A lack of confidence about the personal qualities of likely holders of the office, given the narrowness of the political career in Britain and the workings of the selection process. The choice of party leaders neces-sarily reflects intra-party accommodations, deals, compromises as well as prime ministe-rial potential. (This may be sensible since party support is a necessary element in prime ministerial performance.)

The choice between the strong and the weak views of the Prime Minister ought to depend not on personal taste ('what a nice person our Prime Minister is!') but on an assessment of effective-ness in government, including the winning of consent for necessary policies. It may be argued that, just as Churchill suited the circumstances of 1940, so Margaret Thatcher met the needs of the 1980s, after two decades of relatively unsuccessful government, which had diminished the authority of the state. This is the 'horses for courses' view of the office of Prime Minister: different times require different styles.

However, this is not the whole of the truth. The office of Prime Minister is an office for an individual, and he or she must work in part according to personal capacities and style, and in relation to the particular chemistry of personal relationships with colleagues. This is to say that there are many ways of being Prime Minister, and no certainty that there is one way to suit particular times. This reverses the old adage: it does matter what you do, not how you do it!

Concept

Power and the measurement of power

Power is the capacity or force to make others (people, things) do as you want. So there is a range of power from total command and instant obedience to powerlessness, the point at which others do as they want. The range can incorporate measures of extent and frequency – e.g. how many people and how often respond to the source of command.

Such a scheme is rather crude and mechanistic. In politics, even in small and simple organisations, direct command and obedience is rare. (This would be true even of a family). Power is exercised within relationships, usually continuing and complex networks of relationships; and the goal of the exercise of power is diffuse, ill-defined, long-term. Thus, in a family the command 'tidy your room before you go out,' seems immediate and specific, but 'tidy' is not well-defined; further, the objective probably includes securing general tidiness in the longer term – which is a matter for promises, threats, and deferment.

The power of a political leader is mainly to do with similar but infinitely more complex relationships (with colleagues, officials, party, people, organisations, other countries etc.) and with complex, ill-defined and continuously re-defined goals (including negative goals, stopping things being done). Hence the politician is involved less in command relationships (though there are some, including appointments and dismissals), more in the relationships of persuasion. These range from the strong (negotiation or bargaining) to the weak (pleading).

Measuring power

Students of politics are concerned about the exercise of power, and relative amounts of power. They make judgements about power – X is very powerful, or more powerful than Y. Sometimes the argument is pressed hard – 'Stalin was a dictator', 'British government is prime-ministerial government', 'the civil service is a state within a state', and so on. Even if you have overcome the problems of definition (what precisely are you looking for?) there are still problems of methodology (how do you go about finding it?). Many examples of kinds of evidence and argument about power are to be found in this book. Roughly these comprise evidence and argument about power:

- in relation to competing bodies and colleagues, and in party and people
- in relation to the achievement of objectives
- by reputation
- by analysis of resources and mechanisms of power.

- CASE STUDY
The Madrid 'Ambush', June 1989

The Madrid 'Ambush' is a good illustration of the late Thatcher Cabinet. It arose over Britain's attitude to the developing European Community. The Delors Plan, proposing the extension of economic and monetary union (EMU) was thought likely to arise at a meeting of Community heads of government in Madrid in June 1989.

The Cabinet was in increasingly open disagreement about the Government's European stance, following a poor performance in the elections for the European Parliament (May 1989). Margaret Thatcher took little trouble to hide her hostility towards European unity and what she called 'the Belgian Empire' (a very British insult to the smaller nations hidden in that phrase). The disarray of the government over the issue was evident in Thatcher's plainly false public support for the Chancellor, Nigel Lawson – she supported him, she declared, 'fully, fully, fully, fully'.

Lawson and Howe (the Foreign Secretary) now saw that Britain was likely to be isolated at the summit on the issue of further integration. They moved from the existing strategy of deferment or fudge (Britain would join 'when the time was ripe') to advocacy of acceptance in principle to be followed by implementation, subject to some not impossible conditions. Their advice was put formally to the Prime Minister in a long memorandum.

Margaret Thatcher's response was to assemble a meeting of the whole Downing Street advisory staff, including officials, the Policy Unit, the Economic Adviser, Walters, and the Press Secretary, Bernard Ingham (H. Young, 1991, p. 557). Margaret Thatcher was the only Minister present. This group included several shades of opinion, both for and against joining ERM. The Prime Minister concluded that she could work on the conditions element in the strategy. This allowed her to accept in principle, continue to resist in practice, and avoid any appearance of total capitulation. Such is the version of events offered by Sir Alan Walters, who claims to have drafted the new 'Madrid conditions'. In another account the final version was drafted by Charles Powell, the trusted Private Secretary for Foreign Affairs, in Madrid.

At this point, on the Sunday morning before Margaret Thatcher's departure for Madrid, Howe and Lawson saw her at their request. In this 'nasty little meeting' (as the Prime Minister later wrote), they affirmed that they would resign unless in Howe's words, 'a specific commitment to join the ERM was made'. This was the 'ambush' – Nicholas Ridley's term. Howe claims that the Madrid conditions were a response to this meeting.

Minds are never made up with quite the immediacy and finality that historians might wish. It seems likely that Margaret Thatcher had already accepted that the conditions strategy was a possible way forward, but still wished to avoid commitment, both as a matter of principle and as her normal negotiating stance (1 Say No! 2 Continue to say No!). The 'ambush' showed her that continuing resistance would be politically damaging, so she had reluctantly to pick up the conditions strategy.

Nicholas Ridley's account of this incident is wholly favourable to Margaret Thatcher. Ridley was even more hostile to European integration in general and the ERM in particular than the Prime Minister. In his book he denounces the Howe-Lawson demarche as 'a shameful episode'. 'It was not a collective decision to join [the ERM] taken in Cabinet. They had forced their policy on her by an ultimatum. If a large majority in the Cabinet had been behind them, such a strong-arm approach might have been easier to justify... (1991, p. 209).

Ridley takes the opportunity to put forward his unusual view of prime ministerial government:

'In reality, the Prime Minister is the head of the executive. Other Cabinet Ministers are hired and fired by her, in order to spread the great burden of decision-taking over a wider number than just one person. The Cabinet forms a useful forum for discussion as well as providing a collective executive.... But the responsibility for governing the country is the Prime Minister's and she alone must be allowed to take the ultimate decisions which are important.'

Ridley adds that the right course for Howe and Lawson was to resign, not threaten to resign 'as a weapon in the day-to-day conduct of business'. This is an unusual approach to resignation, opening up the possibility that a resignation would come as a complete and unwelcome surprise to the Prime Minister. (In any case a resignation is formally offered to the Prime Minister, not executed until accepted.)

Who won this sharp little encounter? The Prime Minister appeared to win the immediate battle by a tactical evasion. However, the issue had been conceded in principle and the practice followed fifteen months later, though to Margaret Thatcher's timetable, not Lawson's. So the Prime Minister lost her policy, but more serious for her, she began to lose her Cabinet. The following month Howe was moved from the Foreign Office (demoted in effect) and from his favourite country residence, Chevening; Lawson kept his job but had to give up his country residence to Howe. Within a year and a half Howe, Lawson and (by accident) Ridley had resigned, and then Margaret Thatcher was herself bundled out of office. Her successor was clearly determined to be more conciliatory towards Europe, though the question continues to divide the party and remains to be resolved.

This was a messy episode, and the lesson seems to be that Cabinets need to be managed if they are not to come apart on divisive issues. The evidence is that in Margaret Thatcher's late period the Cabinet was not well-managed, and senior Ministers lost goodwill and ceased collaborative participation in the managed collectivity. There was a breakdown of this aspect of good government. As for prime ministerial power, the Prime Minister has the power to manage well or to manage badly; if the management is bad, power disintegrates.

[Britain joined the ERM in 1990, when Margaret

Thatcher was still Prime Minister and John Major was Chancellor. In September 1992 the pound was too weak to sustain its position within ERM, and Britain withdrew; by then John Major was Prime Minister and Norman Lamont, Chancellor. So it could be argued that Margaret Thatcher was right in her resistance to joining the ERM; and some economists are of that opinion. However, the matter is more complex:
– i) Britain did join while Thatcher was still re-sponsible ii) at a rate judged by many to be far too high and iii) no serious attempt was made in the summer of 1992 to negotiate with partners an agreed adjustment (a devaluation in effect) in face of the problems arising for the ERM from German re-unification. No-one emerges with much credit, and it is not certain that a Labour government would have done any better. Lawson's detailed account of the episode is in N. Lawson, 1992, Chapter 74 ●

Central Government: the Departments of State

The structure of governing

Governing is concerned both with governing in the sense of controlling, and governing in the sense of delivery of programmes and services. Hence the structure of government, including controlling and delivery of programmes, is huge, complex and stretched out through the country. Central government is only part of this structure, though its function of controlling makes it the more important part.

Much of the work of central government is carried out not by Prime Minister and Cabinet but by the Departments of State. In that way Prime Minister and Cabinet lack the power to do much directly themselves. The Departments of State are 'closer to the action': they have a more direct part in the work of governing. Generally any government activity that goes on anywhere is connected by a line of 'responsibility' to a department of government; and thus in British constitutional theory is linked to a Minister who is responsible to Parliament.

However, this may give a misleading picture of a solid, centralised, all-embracing structure of government. In fact, Government activity is carried on through a structure which is large, sprawling, illogical, and messy. Thus many government activities are remote from the Department, and not carried on in the name of the Department. All local government activity, including education, is linked to a central Department, but not carried on in its name. We can add to the list of linked but indirect government activity the National Health Service, the remaining nationalised industries (including Coal and Rail but also the BBC); private industry and especially recently privatised industries, which are more or less regulated by central government; and the newly established Agencies such as the Stationery Office (HMSO), which carry out their functions within structures which are not of the government, but are regulated by government (see Figure 1).

Such a brief description of government activity throws up a number of problems of vocabulary – the words we use, and the ideas or concepts behind them.

- 'Governing' implies direction, control, choice; but much of 'government' is activity or programmes.
- The links between 'the government' and its activities are complex and elusive. It is sometimes said loosely that a ministry is the 'sponsoring department' for a particular activity. But we need to know what the relationship is more exactly in respect to:
  a) command and control
  b) regulation, inspection, oversight, accountability
  c) funding directly by grant, or indirectly by purchase of goods and services. Since there is no money without strings, this leads to a bargaining or negotiating relationship.
- The nature of the minister's 'responsibility'. This is a notoriously slippery term. In English usage it encompasses both 'authority' and 'accountability'. In the Parliamentary context it conveys the constitutional accountability to Parliament and raises a question about the nature of the convention of ministerial responsibility (see Chapter 9).
- The Departments themselves are not solid

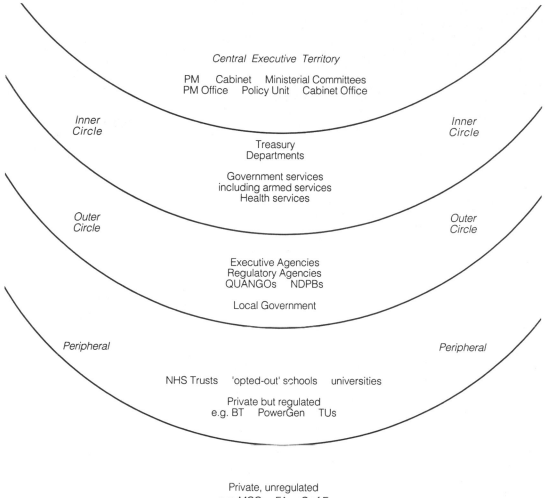

Central Executive Territory

PM   Cabinet   Ministerial Committees
PM Office   Policy Unit   Cabinet Office

*Inner
Circle*

Treasury
Departments

Government services
including armed services
Health services

*Outer
Circle*

Executive Agencies
Regulatory Agencies
QUANGOs   NDPBs

Local Government

Peripheral

NHS Trusts   'opted-out' schools   universities

Private but regulated
e.g. BT   PowerGen   TUs

Private, unregulated
e.g. MCC   FA   C of E

Figure 1 The structure of Government

blocks, but are divided into 'operating divisions', many of them self-contained and within limits, separate. Altogether the major departments of state include about 400 such divisions – a sharp indication of the multifarious nature of 'the government'. It is, further, misleading to perceive the departments as very simple structures, arranged in the hierarchies and pyramids favoured by organisation charts, which seem to show that the person at the top carries heavy 'responsibilities' (and so is entitled to a large salary!).

● The meaning of 'nationalisation' and 'privatisation'. These terms have been used to excess in party propaganda, and exaggerate the significance of ownership as distinct from control and regulation.
● Governments make policy, so it is believed. But policy is another elusive term, and is considered under 'concepts' at the end of this chapter.

Thus the activities or programmes of government stretch out through the nation from Cabinet and

Parliament to the school classroom, the water in the tap, the bypass, or the traffic lights at the centre of the town. But governing, in the sense of controlling and regulating, takes place more continuously and most powerfully at the Centre, in the Central Executive Territory and within the Departments. In that perspective government may be seen as a federation of departments; but, as in all federations, there is a centre of national power. That centre in Britain, the equivalent of Washington, is the Central Executive Territory, including the Cabinet Office and Downing Street Complex and the one Super-department, the Treasury.

The shape of this central power has changed over the last 30 years, and its power has increased. In 1964 about 19 or 20 'operating' departments faced the Treasury and, beyond, the Cabinet. Since then several developments, already noted in Chapter 4, have enhanced the power of this centre.

● The number of operating departments has been reduced to about 12.
● The Cabinet Office and the 'Downing Street complex' have grown in weight and significance.
● The capacity of the Prime Minister has been enhanced by these developments, and by the growth of television as a medium for politics.
● The Treasury has survived as a key player, though its influence is now shared with the Cabinet Office, and in particular, the Cabinet Secretary is the Prime Minister's chief official.

The rise and fall in this period of the Central Policy Review Staff and the Civil Service Department show, if anything, that the tendency of these developments is towards a tighter and coherent structure at the top. The establishment of a few 'giant' departments has not produced a new class of super-minister, barons in the Central Executive Territory. The barons have been too heavily committed in ruling their departments to challenge the King.

The Structure of Departments of State

The Departments of State
At the head of the huge sprawling collection of departments, offices, agencies, corporations which deliver the programmes of government stand a dozen or so 'major' departments of state. They are called variously Departments, Offices or Ministries, apart from the Treasury (which has the Chancellor of the Exchequer as its chief Minister).

Despite the look of permanence which Whitehall wears, there has been much demolition and construction. The changing position at two dates is shown in Document 7.1.

■ DOCUMENT 7.1
The Departments of State, 1902 and 1992

1902	1992
Treasury	Treasury
Foreign Office	Foreign Office
Home Office	Home Office
Lord Chancellor's Department	Lord Chancellor's Department
India	
Colonial	
Admiralty	Defence
War	
Trade (Board)	Trade and Industry
Agriculture (Board)	Agriculture
	Employment
	Transport
Education (Board)	Education
Local Government Board	Environment
	Health
	Social Security
Post Office	
Works	
Ireland	Northern Ireland
Scotland	Scotland
	Wales
	National Heritage ■

Some major trends in twentieth century government are evident – the loss of empire, and the expansion of government into the management of the economy and the provision of a range of welfare services (the Ministries of Pensions and Health were established in the period 1916–19). The number of economic ministries was higher under Labour in 1974 – Trade, Industry, Prices, Employment, Energy, Transport, Agriculture. Some of the changes reflect a Prime Minister's efforts to fit colleagues to suitable ministries. In terms of government structure two tendencies are apparent in these changes. One is the endeavour to unify blocks of government responsibility in 'giant' or 'federal' departments. The Department of Health and Social Security, created in 1968, set the trend; and in 1970 Edward Heath established the Department of the Environment (comprising the old Ministries of Housing and Local Government, Transport and Public Buildings and Works); and the Department of Trade and Industry (comprising the Board of Trade and the Ministry of Technology). The second is the attempt to signal a new priority, to emphasise the importance and independence of a particular field of work; hence the (short-lived) Department of Economic Affairs, the Ministries of Land and Natural Resources, and of Technology, a Department of Prices and Consumer Protection, and in 1992 a Department of National Heritage.

The second tendency contradicts the first and in two cases Heath's new giant departments were partially unscrambled by Harold Wilson in 1974. The Department of Trade and Industry was divided into three, and the Ministry of Overseas Development separated from the Foreign and Commonwealth Office. Neither of these changes lasted for long. Margaret Thatcher was less interested in the remaking of institutions, but divided the giant DHSS and slimmed down the DOE by taking out Transport. In 1992 the Department of Energy was absorbed mostly by Trade and Industry.

The departments vary in size from a few thousand (but only about 1700 in the Cabinet Office) to 10–15 000. Some departments are far larger, Defence and the Home Office for example, but this is because they include large operating sections like ordnance factories or the prison service (both now subject to forms of privatisation). Discounting these functions the departments are massive bureaucracies, and gross size is a highly significant feature of the work of the civil service.

Function and size

It may seem at this point that the central organisation of government is untidy and illogical, or that the changes suggest no clear principle of organisation: Whitehall is shaped and reshaped by politicians in a hurry, and having regard only to persons and political gestures. Only the makers of brass plates and letterheads have had cause for rejoicing.

Seventy years ago the Haldane Committee thought it had found the answer – a principle for the allocation of functions. They reported: 'There appear to be only two alternatives, which may be briefly described as distribution according to the persons or classes to be dealt with, and distribution according to the services to be performed.'

The Haldane Committee rejected the first, recognising the impossibility for example, of unifying the administration of all government services for children or insured persons. But the alternative is not much easier, especially as the range of government activity has broadened. Education may look set apart, but is in fact caught up with training, employment and social policies. Similarly transport and housing are bound up with the economic and social policies of government. No area of policy is independent of the constraints of public expenditure. Interrelationships seem to be more valuable than independence.

The search for a general principle has been abandoned, and recent governments have attempted to secure coherence and co-ordination through the establishments of the 'giant' or 'federal' departments and the expansion of the Cabinet and Downing Street Offices as an 'executive centre'.

The question of size itself is a relevant consideration for all kinds of governments and organisations, and crops up in for example local government, the organisation of industry, the Health Service, schools and so on. It used to be said that in the best schools the Head teacher should be able to recognise by name every pupil. This meant a maximum size of 500 and a Head with a retentive visual memory. Research in local government in the 1960s failed to demonstrate any systematic relationship between size and efficiency. Similarly little seems to have been gained by the construction of giant departments, except in the case of Defence, where the unification of the management of the three armed services was clearly essential.

The structure of departments: secretaries, advisers and committees

The Ministers At the head of each department is the Secretary of State (or Minister) and below him Ministers, or Ministers of State and Under-Secretaries of State. In the larger departments there is in effect a team of Ministers. In the Department of the Environment the Minister may be supported by two Ministers of State, four Parliamentary Under Secretaries and three Parliamentary Private Secretaries. Michael Heseltine, in his first period as Secretary of State in the Department of the Environment valued his team and used it in the running of his Department, dispensing with policy advisers. This is one clear advantage of a 'giant' department – balanced by the enormous range of its responsibilities.

The Permanent Secretary The official side of a ministry is headed by the Permanent Under-Secretary of State (the Permanent Secretary). Below him come the Deputy and Assistant Under-Secretaries, each supervising a defined section of the ministry's work. The Minister is also well supported by his Private Office, and his official Private Secretary.

In this scheme the part of the Permanent Secretary is crucial. He is in the highest grade of the general administrators of the Civil Service (see Chapter 10) and is the highest official in the department, responsible to the political head for all its work. Given the Minister's absorption in political work and lack of time for any but the most important departmental business, then the Permanent Secretary's responsibility amounts to the direction and supervision of most of the department's normal work. If these things could be measured, 'most', in terms of quantity but not significance, would here mean perhaps 95 per cent. The Permanent Secretary's administrative responsibility is fixed not only by his place at the top of the hierarchy, but also by his being formally the department's accounting officer. As such he appears before the committees of the House of Commons.

Apart from these duties as chief administrator, the Permanent Secretary has a close and special relationship with the Minister. This has two aspects. One is advising the Minister on the other highly significant five per cent of business, the major departmental decisions, the formulation of new policy, the handling of politically live issues. The other is advising and assisting the Minister on the parliamentary and political business of the department – speeches, questions, legislation, committees. The Minister will of course deal with other senior civil servants, but he will normally do so through the Permanent Secretary. Indeed, in some departments, the Permanent Secretary is the department, as far as the Minister can see. However, the Minister is supported in his departmental work and relationships by the Private Office, a substantial official support force – Richard Crossman's at one time included sixty people. There will also be one or two personal and specialist advisers to the Minister – temporary outsiders, not permanent officials.

■ DOCUMENT 7.2
A Permanent Secretary on his responsibilities

From a lecture, by Sir Douglas Allan, Head of the Civil Service, 1978, quoted in Crowther-Hunt and Kellner, 1980, pp. 178–9
He is responsible for the efficient organisation of his Department, for instance its division into operational blocks of work, the allocation of efficient staff (and no more) to different areas of work.... It is his duty as Accounting Officer to keep the Department's activities and expenditure within the bounds set by Parliament.... He is responsible for the management of his Department's staff including their training and career development.... On all this kind of work he is directly answerable to Parliament.... He will also be responsible for ensuring that the Minister is provided with the kind of service he wants from the Department; of which the elements most likely to be of interest to the Minister are the general organisation of the Department, the disposition of senior officials and the arrangements for providing the Minister with his support services, including briefing him on both Departmental and general Government matters and handling his correspondence. The Permanent Secretary will also be the Minister's chief policy adviser but by no means the only one.... Official Heads of Departments also share in a collective responsibility for the Civil Service.... ■

This is the professional civil servant's view of the proper relationship of Permanent Secretary to Minister. In practice relations vary and may sometimes be tense; this does not mean that they will not be fruitful. The Document gives one example of such a tense and competitive relationship. Other illustrations are to be found in the Case Study at the end of Chapter 10.

■ DOCUMENT 7.3
Minister and a Permanent Secretary

Margaret Thatcher at the Ministry of Education, 1970
From H. Young and A. Sloman, 1986, pp. 24–6
In an interview with Hugo Young the then Permanent Secretary at the Ministry of Education said:
'Within the first ten minutes of her arrival she uncovered two things to us; one is, I think, what I would call an innate wariness of the civil service, quite possibly even a distrust, and secondly a

page from an exercise book with eighteen things she wanted done that day. Now these were two actions quite unlike anything we'd come across from predecessors and later on I think we saw that this was only the beginnings of the revelation of a character that we'd have to get used to and that we hadn't run into before.'

Sir William judged that such a clear political directive should be obeyed immediately. But subsequently he and his colleagues 'followed our old traditional course of speaking up for what either the Department had always done or what we thought the Department should do, as opposed to what Ministers were going to tell us to do....' ■

Sir William thought that it was his professional job to offer advice; Margaret Thatcher was self-sufficient, stubbornly refusing to acknowledge facts and arguments put forward by her civil servants.

Thus two views of the Minister-civil servant relationship were sharply opposed.

EXERCISE
The good Permanent Secretary

7.1 Does a good relationship of Minister with Permanent Secretary depend on the Minister 'showing who is master'?

The Private Secretary The Minister's Principal Private Secretary (not to be confused with Parliamentary Private Secretary, an unpaid office filled by a Member of Parliament) is an important link between the Minister and the department. The Private Secretary is usually an able young civil servant, marked out for rapid promotion but still relatively junior. Thus he does not fit neatly into an hierarchical chart, for he is by rank junior, and very much the servant of both political and official heads, yet access to the bosses gives opportunities for acquiring information and influence. We need not look here for powers behind the throne: rather we may discern how the machine actually works, or more modestly is nudged into getting by. Tony Crosland wrote of the value of the able Private Secretary who will talk about the department with intelligent indiscretion. 'This is one of the quickest means whereby a Minister can learn about the strengths and weaknesses of his Department' (1971, p. 158). The process also works in reverse, not necessarily to the detriment of the Minister. This complex and even intimate relationship of Minister and Private Secretary is one key to the understanding of the work-

ing of British government at the top.

The following account of the work of a Principal Private Secretary is by Sir James Grigg, later both a Permanent Secretary and a Minister.

■ DOCUMENT 7.4
The work and influence of a Principal Private Secretary

From Sir James Grigg, 1948, pp. 56–7
It was the business of the Principal Private Secretary to take a pre-view of all drafts and memoranda.... He was (or so I held) entitled to offer suggestions to the authors of the documents for making them more acceptable or convincing to Ministers or more calculated to meet their requirements. In my view, the Private Secretary was never justified in revamping the work of his official superior and the most I ever permitted myself was to give the Chancellor a short written summary of the case.... I could also supplement the official recommendations by oral exposition of them and if the Chancellor was still unconvinced I could get him to send for the expert concerned. In course of time one actually acquired great knowledge and experience and in consequence great influence both with the Minister and with the office hierarchy. But...it was essential that the Private Secretary...should strictly confine himself to being an efficient link between the Minister and the machine.... ■

This extract conforms to the classic pattern of a civil servant and Minister, servant and master. But the hierarchical relationship is confusing since the Private Secretary serves two masters, his service superiors and the Minister. One is reported as saying: 'A good private secretary sometimes has to anger the Permanent Secretary' (Kellner and Crowther-Hunt, 1980, p. 150). Denis Healey saw the Private Secretary as the Minister's 'eyes and ears' and the essential gate keeper, deciding which people and documents actually reached the Minister. Crossman was inclined to see the Private Secretary as the Department's man in his office, set to watch over him. The views of Sir Nicholas Henderson are more subtle.

■ DOCUMENT 7.5
Two views of the Private Secretary

a) From R. H. S. Crossman, 1975, p. 385
The Private Office is the heart of the Ministry... the Private Secretary... really does try to get my ideas across to the Department.... I have got to face it that his main job is to get across to me

what the Department wants. The Private Office is the Department's way of keeping a watch on me, of making sure I run along the lines they want me to run on, of dividing my time and getting the Department's policies and attitudes brought to my notice.

b) From Nicholas Henderson, 1984, p. 1 and passim
Henderson recalls Charles II's description of the Private Secretary as 'never in the way, never out of the way'.

The Private Secretaries to Ministers are the impresarios of Whitehall; and in their Private Offices the drama and friction between politics and the machine are theatrically audible... [The Private Secretary] is the hinge between the Minister and his Ministry, and his loyalty is really a double one – to both Minister and department. It is this duality that gives him his exceptional influence; he represents to the Minister the opinion of the Office and to the latter the will of the Minister. Neither commission would carry the same weight if it were not balanced by the other. ■

EXERCISE
The Minister's Private Secretary

7.2 Does the Private Secretary serve the Minister or the department?

Ministers have not always been satisfied to be surrounded and served entirely by officials of their department. Envious glances have been cast at the American practice of appointing 'political executives' at the highest levels, and at the French Ministerial Cabinet or private office. Harold Wilson in his first administration introduced a number of 'irregulars', that is personal advisers, appointed to temporary posts by the Minister himself. In the 1974 government there were about 40 such appointments, including those in the Prime Minister's offices as well as the other departments. Since then it has become normal for most Ministers in charge of departments to have two or three advisers.

The role and value of such appointments is now accepted. Some reports suggest that the 'irregular' does not fit into the structure of the established civil service, and the service itself, it is suggested, is not co-operative. 'The irregulars', wrote one of them (who resigned after three years) 'inevitably run with leaden boots, in any race against the professionals.' Nevertheless, it seems

likely that able advisers can at least mitigate the 'loneliness' which some Ministers complain of, the isolation from their political colleagues.

A Minister's life is not determined simply by his relationships with Permanent and Private Secretary and personal advisers. While the Minister is bound to his Cabinet and party colleagues, the civil servants are tied into an official committee system. This shadows the Cabinet committees, and works through the business at official level. Any gaps in the formal committee system are covered by the continuous network of informal communication. All this may sound sensible and indeed supportive. But again Crossman was a hostile witness.

■ DOCUMENT 7.6
The official committee system

a) From R. H. S. Crossman, 1975, p. 168
In addition to the Cabinet committees which only Ministers normally attend, there is a full network of official committees; and the work of the Ministers is therefore strictly and completely paralleled at the official level. This means that very often the whole job is pre-cooked in the official committees to a point from which it is difficult to reach any other conclusion than that already determined by officials in advance; so if agreement is reached at the lower level of a Cabinet Committee, only formal approval is needed from the full Cabinet. This is the way in which Whitehall ensures that the Cabinet system is relatively harmless.

b) From R. H. S. Crossman, 1972, p. 73
When I was Minister of Housing I was very keen to substitute local income tax for local rates as the main basis of our local taxation. So I made a speech or two about this before I squared my officials. What happened? An official committee was established which did a tremendous lot of work in order to prove that rates were the only practical form of local taxation. And so before I could get to my colleagues and argue the case for the local income tax, every one of my colleagues had been briefed by his officials that there was no alternative to the rates. So that was that! If Whitehall gangs up on you it is very difficult to get your policy through, or even get a fair hearing for a new idea.

c) From D. Owen 1981, p. 137
The most dangerous embrace of all is the grow-

ing reliance by Ministers on committee decision-making which ensures that the Whitehall view is inserted into every meeting. Far too many decisions are made collectively by Ministers and the degree of Ministerial discretion is being eroded on the seemingly unobjectionable grounds of democratic control and Departmental views. The weekly meeting of Permanent Under Secretaries which is a relatively recent development, ensures the co-ordination of attitudes. It is claimed that no decisions are made at these meetings but it is here that the co-ordinated civil service view is evolved and a sense of direction maintained. Copies of departmental briefs are clandestinely exchanged, and officials may thus be encouraged to take a departmental view distinct from the Minister's viewpoint and the 'departmental' view continues across different governments. A powerful civil service, with its own ethos, can easily incorporate Ministers and drag them further away from their political party, parliament and their constituents. It is this bureaucratic embrace which a politician has most to fear. ■

EXERCISE

7.3 If official committees are so powerful, how can you explain the replacement of the rates system in the 1980s by the community charge (poll-tax)?

The place of the Minister in his Department is further discussed below – see Chapters 9 and 10. But it can be seen already that the Minister is fitted into a formidable structure of support and control – the Ministerial team, the Permanent Secretary, the Private Office, and beyond them the Cabinet and official networks and committees.

EXERCISE
The Minister in the Department

7.4 Is the Minister inevitably 'cocooned' within his Department, losing all independence?

The administrative process
The work of government departments is conducted according to the general principles of administration.

First, the processes of administration take place within certain horizontal and vertical divisions – as the Treasury organisation chart in Chapter 8 shows. The horizontal divisions indicate specialisation, and the vertical divisions are levels within a hierarchy. This simple pattern determines the location or routing of each problem, with important and general problems going towards the top of the pyramidal structure. The pattern is modified by a general but imprecise commitment to flexibility, and against the routine referring of decisions to a higher level.

Second. the system works by communication, in letters, meetings, personal discussion by telephone or face-to-face, but characteristically in the circulation of a file. This is simply a folder containing the relevant documents, to which are added 'minutes' (that is, notes or comments) as the file goes around (up, down or sideways). Its destination is the officer who must take the final decision based on the contents of the file – or pass it up to a higher level. Most large bureaucratic organisations are based perforce on these two principles.

EXERCISE

7.5 Do these principles look entirely sound?

Characteristically, the senior bureaucrat works at two or three removes from the object of his administration, (whether it be coal mining, the manufacture of cars or the social services). This is not just a physical separation: the bureaucrat works at a structural and cultural distance from the field.

In these ways the civil service is like any other bureaucracy. But this is a government bureaucracy in a parliamentary democracy. Two further principles affect the administrative process. First, the service is accountable to Parliament. For every problem, and at every point, there is the awareness that the department must be ready to defend all its actions in Parliament. This, for the public administrator, is the equivalent of a businessman's 'bottom line', the need to make a profit. Hence some of the civil servant's tendency to make written records, and some of his caution. Second, and related to that is Ministerial responsibility. This means for civil servants that they normally do not take public responsibility for policy. Thus the government bureaucracy is both answerable and not answerable. Characteristically, the civil servant's power to take independent action is heavily circumscribed.

EXERCISE
The level of decision-taking

7.6 A distinguished former Permanent Secretary

complained of 'the drift upwards of decision-taking'. 'All officers should assume the
maximum responsibility and take the largest
number of decisions that they properly and
rightly can.... Sometimes "I should have
been consulted" means "I should have
been told"....' (quoted in R. Clarke, 1971,
pp. 123–4).

    a) If you were a middle-ranking official,
what kinds of decision would you feel
you should not take yourself?

    b) How often would you worry about
answerability to Parliament?

The nature of departments of state

Most departments of state are massive. Only a
handful of departments employ less than 10 000
civil servants, and half-a-dozen currently employ
more than 30 000. Only the Law officers spend
less than one billion pounds each year. Even the
Welsh Office, which acts as a kind of intermediate
administration for the 2.5 million people of Wales
employs over 2000 civil servants.

At the same time most ministries are fragmented by the range of their activities and responsibilities. This can be illustrated by organisation charts. Only the Minister and the most senior
officials see the whole of the department's activities. But such an overview does not overcome
fragmentation; they are still a collection of disparate activities, loosely joined in the overall functions of the ministry. For example an official in
MAFF dealing with milk may not have much to
do with fisheries, especially because milk is dealt
with as an agricultural commodity, not as a food.
This raises the question whether in this case a
ministry serves the producer, the consumer, the
tax payer or a model citizen concerned with the
public interest. The constitutional answer (not entirely convincing) is that officials serve the Minister who is responsible to Parliament.

The Department for Education is less fragmented; every section is concerned in some way
with Education. But even here officials dealing
with, say, teachers' pensions have little in common with those dealing with nursery education.

One of the most fragmented departments was
the Department of Health and Social Security, established as a 'giant department' in 1968. At its
peak this colossus employed nearly 100 000 civil
servants, and managed expenditure of 65 billion
pounds. It was a good example of 'stretched out'
or 'arms length' administration, since most of its

work was done by the health authorities, hospital
and medical practitioners, and, on the social security side, by the 500 or so local offices which
deal with social security 'benefits'. DHSS was a
characteristic creation of the 1960s and 1970s. In
the late 1980s the Department was divided into
two dealing with the two major responsibilities,
and significant moves were made towards independence for medical and social security services. The DHSS once the triumphant creation of
the state in the service of the people, was seen as
a bureaucratic monster, and destroyed, or rather,
cut in half.

The Foreign and Commonwealth Office differs
by its nature, traditions and functions from other
departments. It has its own civil servants, the Diplomatic Service, a Secretary of State of high political standing, and what it regards as a high and
exclusive mission to represent Britain and defend
the national interests. It knows a great deal about
foreign countries and not so much about domestic affairs. In some ways it has been overtaken by
history: Britain is no longer a world power, its foreign relations and its problems are mainly
economic. Rapid air travel and good communications mean that an Ambassador is no longer on
his own as a diplomat. Officials speak gloomily of
the management of decline – and of the problems for diplomats posed by holiday makers, football hooligans and drugs.

If functions have changed, the Foreign Office
still aspires to be the Rolls Royce of the departments, has successfully resisted attempts to reform
it (see Chapter 22 Case Study) and has found in
Europe a new destiny, and some more or less exclusive administrative territory. Some Ministers
have found the Foreign Office 'difficult', to the
point where self-confidence becomes arrogance.
David Owen, Foreign Secretary 1977–79 wrote:

■ DOCUMENT 7.7
The Foreign Office is different

*From David Owen, Personally Speaking to
Kenneth Harris, 1987, p. 131*
I found that the attitude of the Foreign Office to
the Secretary of State making the decisions
was quite different to that of the DHSS. At the
DHSS you felt that they were much more relaxed about the idea that the Minister made the
decisions. Some of the Foreign Office found it
immensely difficult to accept that diplomacy
could be subject to the same degree of Ministerial authority. They thought that diplomacy was
a different thing from normal everyday politics,

and that special skills were required for it which they had and the Secretary of State did not. ■

The Ministry of Defence was the first of the giant departments. It was established originally in 1946 to co-ordinate the three armed services, and was transformed in 1964 into a mega-ministry embracing the three services. The Ministry of Defence is responsible for defence policy, the armed forces, and the 'procurement' of weaponry and equipment – a difficult policy area, a massive management task and a spending programme with enormous consequences for industry, research and the tax-payer. The Defence budget seems to enjoy a protected status (Britain spends proportionately more on defence than other European countries, despite the loss of empire and the end of the Cold War).

The armed services themselves enjoy a privileged status, with special access to the Prime Minister. Successive Defence Ministers have fought in vain to contain inter-service rivalry and reduce expenditure. The assaults of the 1980s on restrictive practices and self-serving professionals faltered with the lawyers and stopped short of the soldiers. Every Minister in charge of a department of state learns that it has some of the characteristics of a giant oil tanker: almost impossible to steer or stop and dangerous to manoeuvre. The MOD is the biggest and grandest tanker of them all, the only department of state to enjoy 'royal appointment' status, and to receive from time to time religious services of national thanksgiving.

Michael Heseltine's sharp and moderately successful struggle with the services are recounted by him (perhaps with some understandable enhancement of his own role and influence!).

■ DOCUMENT 7.8
Cutting a department down to size

a) Cutting staff in the Department of the Environment, based on M. Heseltine, 1990, pp. 16–19
The Conservative Government had come to power in 1979 determined to reduce the number of civil servants, which had reached its highest post-war level. Cabinet agreed that each Minister would examine options for cuts of 2.5, 5 and 7.5 per cent. Civil servants set about demonstrating that even the lowest rate of cuts would do serious damage to the essential services provided by the department – and it was suggested to the Minister's career (the careers of civil servants were not mentioned).

Heseltine reported, with he admits just an element of parody, that the catalogue presented to him of cuts at the 5 per cent level was harrowing, and included increased levels of raw sewage in the rivers. The Secretary of State was advised that none of his colleagues would be considering the 7.5 per cent level of cuts, and he himself might be unwise 'so soon in his political career... to be out there alone, taking risks, sacrificing standards, abandoning the fruits of decades of social improvement.'

Heseltine, undaunted, then asked how many people were allowed to recruit to the department. The answer (after investigation) turned out to be 57. Heseltine immediately reduced this to one, the Secretary of State himself. Four years later the department was 29 per cent smaller, and employed 15 000 fewer people.

Heseltine comments: 'Looking back, it seems incredible that a department which was supposed to be efficiently managed could lose a quarter of its manpower and still in other respects be the same department.'

b) Disciplining the Service, from M. Heseltine, 1990, pp. 30–32
I discovered to my astonishment that the three service chiefs were not directly answerable to the Chief of the Defence Staff. Business was conducted through the Chiefs of Staff committee and rested on consensus.

The fiercely protected prerogatives of the Royal Navy, the Army, and the Royal Air Force, had produced and sustained for 20 years something which was indefensible not only by modern standards of management in the world beyond the services but by every rule of command taught to the humblest uniformed recruit....

The chiefs, steeped as they were in loyalty to their own services, disliked my proposals...and on my suggestion exercised their right to take their objections directly to the Prime Minister. She put her authority behind me.... ■

EXERCISE
The Minister as administrative reformer

7.7 Why is the kind of reform undertaken by Mr Heseltine so difficult? To what would you attribute any success by the Minister?

These examples of ministries in different areas of government, illustrate the diversity of government activity, hence of government departments. It is evident that no two ministries are much alike. They vary by:

- the nature of their work
- number of staff
- level of expenditure
- need for legislation
- clientele
- direct or indirect operation
- political sensitivity and partisan divisions
- generation of publicity
- relationship to Cabinet system
- attractiveness in a political career.

Most ministries are large, high-spending but concerned for much of the time with the indirect oversight of largely uncontroversial areas of state administration.

The Minister acquiring his 'own' department for the first time is caught between the primary political ambitions which have driven him through his career to this apparent point of success, and the imperatives of the departmental structure and culture which he is expected to head. The force of political ambition can never be discounted – behind the Minister on his first day in his new office lie long years of toil in Parliament and constituency, party conference and television studio, as well as an apprenticeship, hurried or tediously slow, in junior office. Ahead lie Ministerial re-shuffles and the threat of the next election, a rough performance appraisal and the possibility of instant dismissal (softened for a Conservative by the consolation of City directorships). The wise Minister keeps his eye on the next election and the next Ministerial post. If he aims for the top then the route lies through a major economic or social ministry to one of the Treasury, the Foreign Office or the Home Office.

The ethos of departments
The Minister thus surveying his position in politics, stands on the edge of another political system: the structure and culture of departments. Every department has its own strong sense of identity, culture, pride in achievement and territory.

■ DOCUMENT 7.9
Departmental ethos

a) A former Minister's view
From Shirley Williams, 1981, p. 184
Departments develop a character of their own.

This is formed partly by their last great achievement or reform.

The character of departments is...also formed by their relationships with the particular interest groups with which they normally work. The danger is that departments will get too close to their particular interest groups, to the point of advocating their interests against the interests of the wider community. Agricultural departments, for instance, often seem much more concerned about farmers' interests than about consumers' interests. Industrial departments tend to be soft on monopolies and mergers, even though the wider public interest may suffer.

b) A former Head of the Civil Service
From Sir Edward Bridges, Portrait of a Profession, *1950 reprinted in R. A. Chapman and A. Dunsire, 1971, pp. 50–1*
By degrees, then, as Civil Service organisation got into its stride, there has been built up in every Department a store of knowledge and experience in the subjects handled, something which eventually takes shape as a practical philosophy, or may merit the title of a departmental point of view.... An original scheme has been altered to meet acknowledged difficulties...it is something which has been fashioned by many hands...it is something which works, and which works better than anything else so far devised. And in making and reshaping it, things have been learnt which could only be fully grasped by practical experience.... These departmental philosophies are of the essence of a Civil Servant's work. They represent an acceptable, middle point of view after the extreme divergencies have been rooted out. ■

EXERCISE
Departmental philosophies

7.8 Is there not a danger that 'departmental philosophies' harden into a rigid point of view, in conflict with the needs of Government policy – or of the country?

Territorialism, the jealous guarding of a department's territory or 'turf', is an integral part of the departmental philosophy. Territorial disputes between departments arise from the inevitable confusions and overlaps in the statutory or traditional responsibilities of departments in a highly interventionist government. Thus the objectives of conservation (Department of the Environment) clash with the Ministry of Agriculture's concern (until recently) for production and the interests of farmers. The interests of industry, employment and defence procurement overlap and compete; the interests of energy policy may conflict with employment policy – and so on.

Such disputes reflect a conservative but arguably sensible concern for the proper location of administrative responsibility, as well as some departmental *amour-propre*. The Minister steps unsuspecting into a well-developed set of departmental attitudes and jealousies, a visiting amateur in a club of hardened professionals. He is likely to become 'domesticated' or 'go native'.

There are many examples of such domestication, including most Ministers of Defence. The Foreign Office notoriously converts its Ministers to enthusiasm for Europe; the Treasury beats out enthusiasm for public expenditure; Agriculture, in the unlikely event of acquiring a Minister who is not already a farmer, converts its Ministers to Farmers' Friends. Good Ministers defy domestication: they have to be experienced and tough, and know what they want to do. This means selecting a few matters for their own influence and initiative, refusing to be smothered by the rest, and leaving all the detail to officials.

■ DOCUMENT 7.10
The Domestication of Ministers

From J. Bruce-Gardyne, 1986, pp. 58–60
Ministers, regardless of party, are expected to absorb as rapidly as may be the ethos of the departments to which they happen to be assigned.... Most politicians are...swiftly domesticated. (p. 58)....

A long-standing bone of contention between Energy and the Treasury concerns the price of fuel. The Department of Energy likes it low.... The Treasury, by contrast always wants to get fuel prices up....(p. 59).

... in the early Spring of 1983 Nigel Lawson, Energy Secretary, commissioned a report from the accountants Coopers and Lybrand, which showed – to nobody's surprise – that the Treasury's estimates of the 'long-run marginal cost' of electricity supply were far too high. Five months later Nigel Lawson returned to the Treasury as Chancellor. He lost no time whatsoever in demonstrating, beyond a peradventure of doubt, that Coopers and Lybrand were incapable of adding two to two correctly. (pp. 59–60).... ■

EXERCISE

7.9 Comment on this evidence of departmental management.

The Department's first loyalty is to itself; its second, to the Whitehall 'village'. Senior officials know one another, and act as if they grew up together. Like public figures in a village, they refer (and defer) to village opinion (rather than public opinion). To the villager the Minister is an outsider, a temporary resident; his proposals must not disturb the village community, which is permanent.

This was the view of two American observers of Whitehall (see H. Heclo and A. Wildavsky, 1974). A former Treasury Permanent Secretary has responded bluntly that the Whitehall village is dominated by the castle known as the Cabinet (L. Pliatzky, 1982, p. 38). The Minister's task is to sally forth from the castle and impose his political priorities on the proud department family and the enveloping village. The Case Studies below indicate some of the problems for the temporary resident in the Whitehall village. Thus we approach the centre of the business of governing.

GUIDE TO EXERCISES

7.1 It looks as if this may be helpful in some cases. But the ideal relationship is not of master to servant (see Case Study in Chapter 10). Comparative power is not a matter of continuing, still less of obsessive, concern. Minister and Permanent Secretary have different functions and should aim at collaboration and partnership; they can be mutually supportive. The Permanent Secretary should recognise the Minister's political priorities, the Minister the civil servant's continuing commitment to the work of the department.

7.2 Both. The Minister has got to work with his department, and the Private Secretary is an essential link. It does not follow that the Minister is 'managed' by the department – but that is clearly one of a range of possible relationships.

7.3 A determined Prime Minister with some ministerial support insisted on the abolition of the rates. The officials cannot win against a determined Prime Minister. It seems likely that the civil service helped to delay the introduction of the poll-tax by setting out the arguments against. It turned out that they were correct.

7.4 The department clearly puts the Minister into a massive structure which must inhibit his freedom of action. The structure is a 'co-coon' in that it supports him comfortably; he can relax and do very little if he chooses. Crossman found that simply shifting the contents of his 'In' tray to the 'Out' tray ensured that all his work would be duly completed. The Minister can still act for himself if he wants to, but he is no longer an individual, and he must act 'corporately', taking his 'cocoon' with him. The 'cocoon' may resist – courteously, rationally but firmly.

7.5 They look much too simple. The second contradicts the first. Most large and complex organisations (and that would include large schools and colleges) are based on a simple structure, including a hierarchy of management, but can only function effectively by communication and action across the vertical and horizontal divisions. Some modern management theorists favour 'flat' organisation, with few steps in the hierarchy and much responsibility devolved to the base. Communication by 'net-working' is much valued.

7.6 a) Those entirely without precedent; involving high or unpredicted costs; or of some political delicacy.
b) Civil servants do not relish parliamentary exposure, so there is at least a continuing prudence and caution.

7.7 Large bureaucratic organisations are always difficult to move, and their senior members see change as threatening to their status (it often is). The civil service has some advantages over the Minister, notably in expertise and experience, and can play the game long – they have time on their side. The armed services enjoy a special status as the potential saviours of the nation and can call up support from the highest quarters.

Much of his success was due to his own determination and energy; but it was necessary that he was following the general objectives of the government and had the support of the Prime Minister. Even so, Heseltine's success was quite limited, and the three services remained heavily manned at the top (e.g. an Air Marshal for every squadron of aircraft) to fight the inter-service battles Heseltine objected to.

7.8 Shirley Williams does not say this directly but perhaps implies that it is so. Sir Edward Bridges posed the question himself at another point but without mention of the needs of the country. (Perhaps that omission is significant!) Sir Edward's answer was that the problem existed, but had been transformed by frequent transfers of officials between jobs. This looks a little optimistic given that such transfers tend to be at lower levels, and young newcomers usually feel they must adapt to, rather than subvert, the prevailing philosophy. Some of the more radical reforms of the 1980s may have had some impact on the problem.

7.9 First, the worst and most picturesque examples are quoted, and we need to be cautious about interpreting the evidence. Second, these phenomena are natural enough, to be expected in any organisation, not part of a wicked conspiracy. The departments as the permanent professionals in their area are justified to some extent in developing and asserting their own views and traditions. However, third, the minister, as political head, is entitled to assert his own preferences and priorities. The relationship ought to be tense, not cosy.

ASSESSMENT

Departments of State – do we need them? Is this the only way there is of arranging government?

The work of the Departments could in some cases not be done at all (which?); or done privately by individuals, groups and companies (which?). This reverses the assumptions of over 200 years of the growth of government; but that assumption has been challenged since the 1970s and in some cases quite successfully. The work of the Departments could also be done by other public bodies, local or regional governments and public or semi-public corporations, boards or commissions. Again this was exemplified in the 1980s. In Britain local and regional governments have not been favoured as alternatives to the central government department, but the Local Management of Schools and the establishment of Hospital Trusts indicate the possibilities of a tentative diminution in the work of government (though in these cases power is lost at the local rather than the central level). The new Executive Agencies (see Chapter 10) indicate another form of government department.

Indeed the present forrn of the department of state could be radically changed, possibly with advantage. Some features are peculiarly British: the high level of official posts, the responsibility to Parliament of the Minister. By contrast local councils in Britain work with a committee-based executive, and the chief executive officers play a more public and more influential role. Thus the relationships of Minister, Permanent Secretary and Private Secretary are peculiar to the British form of the Department of State.

Whether any other arrangement would be better is another question. The characteristic faults of Departments of State in Britain – departmental self-importance, territorial jealousies, inertia, arise and flourish in other forms of organisation.

Policy making
Throughout the study of politics we encounter the notion of policy-making. Policy is the main product of government; the power to make it is an appropriate test of power, and the processes of making it show the institutions of government in productive motion. Government is thus a kind of policy factory (or should it be a farm?).

All this assumes we know what policy is. But often policy is not precise, firm, and written down; more a collection of understandings – or even hopes. Again policy has a time dimension. Few policies begin as fully-articulated and coherent choices, laid down at one moment of time. Policies are backed into, put together piece by piece, discovered and written down, 'formalised', only after they have been practised for some time. This is plainly the case in daily and domestic lives: we do develop rough 'policies' about say, cycling to school in the Winter, or writing essays after midnight, but these are a matter of recollecting and stating what appears to be our practice. Governments, being large organisations dealing with complex matters, have to act more deliberately than this. Even so, policy is often the sum of what happened in the past, rationalised for presentation purposes, and garnished with optimism.

Policy making can be fully understood only when the study of the political system is complete. Every part of the system, by definition, has a potential influence. But some general points can be made.

1 Policy-making at the centre is a result of the interaction of two kinds of persons in different roles: the permanent official with his career drives and service socialisation, and the temporary Minister with his political drives, both personal and ideological, and his parliamentary and partisan socialisation. The official has behind him the weight of his department; the Minister has the party and (with luck) the Cabinet at his back.

2 That interaction takes place in a structure characterised by the size and nature of government (large and federal) and the nature of Parliament (organised by the executive, disciplined by party).

3 Policy-making takes place in an environment of pressure, mainly from groups, some of which have consultative status, a few being almost incorporated into the structure of government (see Chapter 21).

4 A great deal of policy is highly technical. It is necessary for a policy-maker to know the detail; it may be necessary for him to understand technical data. It may still be impossible to do more than make an informed guess about the consequence of alternative policies.

5 Problems are rarely new; nor are policies. Policy-making mainly requires shifting perceptions about the agenda of issues, changing priorities and promoting existing policy-ideas.

6 Discussion of policy-making is often based on highly optimistic assumptions about the potential of government. Limitations on the capacity of governments to influence events may well lie in the nature of events, rather than in the structure or personnel of government. Change is often marginal, government is 'a percentage game'.

(For a fuller discussion of policy-making see Chapter 22.)

● CASE STUDY
The Ministry of Defence: The Defence School of Music
Based on C. Ponting, 1986, pp. 181-6 – Ponting was personally concerned as a civil servant with some part of this story
The services spent over £60m per year on music – far more than all public and 'civilian' music. Each of the three services maintained its own music school, all three being unsuitable and neglected.

In March 1982 Ponting submitted a Report,

recommending establishment of one School of Music at Eastney (Portsmouth). The services responded by requesting a report by a military officer. One year later the officer reported his agreement with the civil service report. The services agreed 'in principle' to a new school, but called for a further report on location, the site at Deal being ruled out. Further negotiations were obstructed by services; there was intensive lobbying by MPs, briefed by services.

On Christmas Eve 1983 the new Minister of Defence (Michael Heseltine) after a long delay and without any discussion of the previous reports, decided that there should be a new School of Music, but it must be 'north of Birmingham'.

February/March 1984 A site in Edinburgh was found. This was part of an Army complex, and the Army now supported a Defence School of Music. However, Peter Rees, Chief Secretary at the Treasury, intervened. Rees as Chief Secretary was responsible for cutting public expenditure; but he was MP for the Dover constituency, which included Deal. Further investigation confirmed that Deal would cost £2.5m. extra, while Eastney would save £4m.

Faced with this dilemma – save public money or displease a powerful Cabinet colleague – Michael Heseltine decided to establish the new School of Music at Deal. The Permanent Secretary was concerned about how to justify this decision to the Public Accounts Committee, asked for a direct order from the Minister. This was refused, and, instead, the costs were hidden by a re-working of the figures.

Ponting, in his account, draws out the lessons of this story and comments that in such decisions: 'Political expediency dominates everything else' (p. 186). Is that fair comment?

A further lesson may be that for the defence services cuts never quite take place. In 1992 the three schools of music still existed. •

● CASE STUDY
The Department for Education: middle range politics

Politics may be roughly divided into 'low' and 'high'. High politics includes the grander responsibilities of the state, the management of the economy, defence and foreign policy; low politics includes the welfare services, roads, health and education. Formerly, high politics offered prestigious activity and pleasant foreign travel for an aspiring statesman who could han-

dle problems directly, making policy as he went, and perhaps making history too. By contrast low politics meant travelling to the North to talk with local governments or health authorities, having only an indirect influence on policy, still dealing with awkward problems but enjoying little prestige.

This distinction is now much less clear. High politics is different for a second-rank power, enmeshed in international alliances; there are endless photo-opportunities, but less scope to make policy. Meanwhile low politics has become more politically salient – more expensive, more controversial, and with some opportunities for serious policymaking – and serious mistakes.

Education has shifted from its former lowly position. When Churchill made Butler President of the Board of Education (there was no Ministry until 1944), he was surprised that Butler was so pleased with the appointment. Butler was to attach his name to a major education reform act, the Act of 1944. Since then Education has become a politically interesting ministry, particularly in the 60s and 70s when the comprehensive re-organisation of schools was undertaken and a rapid expansion of higher education began; and again in the 1980s, when doubts grew about the management and the effectiveness of education. Margaret Thatcher, a former Minister of Education herself, appointed one senior Cabinet colleague to the ministry (Sir Keith Joseph) and one rising star (Kenneth Baker). Education seems to have ascended to a middle order of politics.

Education reflects some of the characteristics of the social programme ministries:

● high cost
● indirectly administered, through local government
● active and influential professional groups
● active interest groups, though the consumers (parents rather than children) have never exerted their full potential
● subject to waves of theory, which may become fashionable, and may also be taken up by political parties
● subject to conflicts of value, basically over equality or equality of opportunity (to become unequal) and over the purposes of education (preparation for work or more liberal and cultural goals).

In addition to these general characteristics

Education has its own special character. Education itself is a subject on which most adults are ready if not well qualified to pronounce; professional expertise is not held in high esteem and the teaching profession does not have the prestige or political 'clout' of medicine and the law. Its unions are fragmented and defensive. Parent power could be a formidable pressure against teachers, education authorities and governments. But affluent middle-class parents, including most Conservative Ministers, opt out of the public system of education, and have no strong motive to improve it. Student power is formally organised and not without influence. Pupil power has no formal structure but, along with financial resources, is the 'bottom-line' determinant of what can and cannot be done. ●

The Treasury, the Chancellor and public expenditure

Public expenditure

Over much of government, policy is a matter of what you can afford to spend, coupled with the question of how the money will be raised (taxation). These are closely related to economic considerations, the production of the wealth to be taxed, and the consequences for the economy of the programme to be financed. Policies which are based on taxation and expenditure always involve either redistribution or a refusal to redistribute from rich to poor, or from poor to rich; hence they are politically sensitive, for no-one enjoys being taxed, and the beneficiaries of government programmes are rarely satisfied or grateful. There still remain some policies which, in the short-term at least, are cost-free – for example, variations in foreign policy, and some regulatory functions. But for much of a Minister's time he is concerned with questions of expenditure, hence with the distribution of wealth, hence with the spread of content and discontent.

The proportion of the national wealth spent by government has risen steadily over the years – about 10 per cent of GDP in 1900, passing 40 per cent in the 1914–18 war, and 60 per cent in 1939–45. Since then it has moved between 35–47 per cent. In the 1980s a peak of 47 per cent was pushed down to 39 per cent.

Public expenditure is the immediate responsibility of the Treasury and its political head, the Chancellor of the Exchequer. The Treasury also has responsibility for the management of the economy. The public expenditure function carries responsibility for government manpower, hence indirectly for the Civil Service itself, which in the past has been a direct responsibility of the Treasury. Thus, the Treasury is the 'super department' of British government, and a major part of the work of Ministers in other departments is to deal with the Treasury.

Public expenditure is at the centre of contemporary political argument. The election of 1992 turned in part on competing claims about taxation and expenditure; and there was unusually some recognition that the two were related. British domestic politics since 1945 can be understood partly by reference to changing attitudes to spending on government programmes. The post-war, 'social-democratic' consensus included a strong commitment to public spending, in sharp contrast to the 1930s, and all previous history. Sometime in the 1960s and 1970s, the failings of the British economy raised doubts about its continuing capacity to support massive government expenditure. Dissatisfaction with the performance of the public industries and services re-inforced these doubts.

The Labour governments (1964–70, 1974–79) fell into difficulties especially in the mid-70s (the IMF crisis 1976). In the 1980s Margaret Thatcher's government set about the reduction of public spending, and succeeded only in reducing the rate of growth and changing the distribution. Nevertheless this fundamental change in ideas and approach, initially and essentially driven by the Conservative Party, is now broadly common ground between the parties, though with significant differences in emphasis. The change in ideas is illustrated in the Document.

■ DOCUMENT 8.1
Changing attitudes to public spending

From L. Pliatzky 1982 p. 2
*[Sir Leo Pliatzky rose to be Second Permanent
Secretary in the Treasury at a time of crisis in the
control of public expenditure. He began his
service in 1947 when the assumptions were
quite   different.]*
During those early days I attended a week's
induction course for new entrants to the
Ministry of Food. Practically every lecturer
referred with pride to the fact that the Ministry
was spending £1 million a day on food
subsidies. Since I did not see everything in
public expenditure terms in those days, I did
not react in any particular way to this
information. There was still a physical shortage
of food in the war-devastated world, and food
subsidies were part of the apparatus of controls
and rationing designed to ensure a fair
distribution of supplies.

In retrospect I came to see the food
subsidies as a budgetary millstone round the
post-war government's neck. [By 1992 that £1
million a day would have been about £10
million a day, or £3.6 billion a year] – a major
expenditure programme exceeded by only the
few largest programmes. In the impoverished
circumstances of 1947, it was an enormous
amount to find. ■

EXERCISE
The virtue of public expenditure

8.1 How can the change in attitudes to public
expenditure be explained?

The Chancellor and the Treasury are at the heart
of this fundamental political controversy.

The Treasury

The Treasury as a super-department
The Treasury is a 'super-department' because of
its functions and historical status. Its origins can
be traced back to the beginnings of English government in the courts of the medieval monarchy.
Its constitutional standing and function were established by the beginning of the eighteenth century, when all proposals for expenditure were
arrogated to the government. By the 1920s any
proposal for expenditure had to be discussed in
draft with the Treasury. In the last 25 years that
status has been modified by the rise of the Cabinet Office and the loss of full responsibility for the
civil service. The Treasury now has a rival.

The great period of Treasury supremacy was
from 1919 to 1968. Until 1919 each department
looked after its own staff, and was a miniature
civil service on its own. This was probably not
good for efficiency, since it bred departmental
narrowness, and it was bad for careers because
there were no short cuts to the top. The regulations of 1919–20 changed this. There was to be a
single service, with movement and promotion
across departmental boundaries, and the Permanent Secretary of the Treasury became Head of
the Civil Service. Appointments to the top post in
every department could be made only with the
Prime Minister's consent – which meant in practice the consent of the Head of the Civil Service.
Thus, the Treasury acquired as a substantial part
of its functions a 'Pay and Management side' –
the control and management of the public bureaucracy. This was the basis of 'Treasury supremacy', which was not seriously challenged
until the Cabinet Office acquired independence
(from 1962) and the management of the civil
service was withdrawn from the Treasury, in
whole or in part, after 1968.

In economic matters the Treasury has retained
its dominant position with less difficulty. It is responsible for:

● the raising of revenue
● the control of public expenditure
● the oversight or management of the national
economy.

The removal of part of this function to the Department of Economic Affairs was short-lived (1964–
9). The structure of the Treasury reflects these
major concerns for the National Economy and
Public Expenditure. There are four or five Ministers, two of them, the Chancellor and the Chief
Secretary, in the Cabinet. The detailed structure is
indicated in the diagram (Figure 2). The Treasury
has about 25 working divisions and 3500 civil
servants. This is not large by Whitehall standards.
However there are attached to the Treasury two
Boards – Inland Revenue and Customs and Ex-
cise – which employ altogether almost 100 000
civil servants.

The Treasury's long history and high governmental functions have helped to create the
strongest departmental culture in Whitehall. This
is sustained by the deliberate recruitment of 'the
best and the brightest' of young officials attracted
by the Treasury path to positions of strategic

(a) *General government expenditure (excluding privatisation proceeds)*

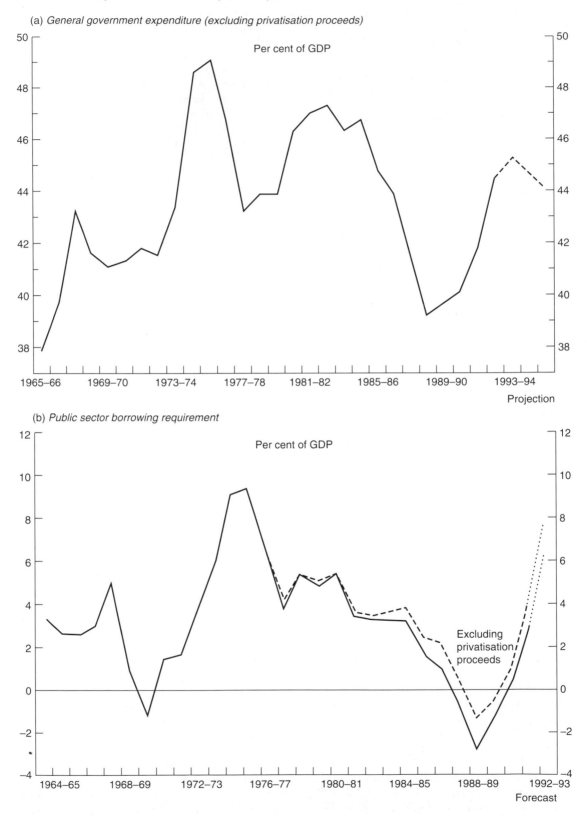

Per cent of GDP

Projection

(b) *Public sector borrowing requirement*

Per cent of GDP

Excluding privatisation proceeds

Forecast

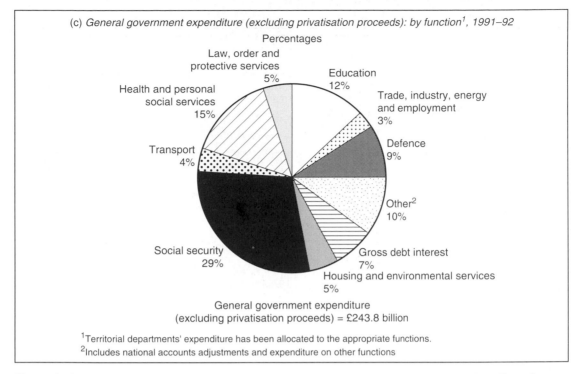

(c) *General government expenditure (excluding privatisation proceeds): by function[1], 1991–92*

Percentages

Law, order and protective services 5%

Education 12%

Health and personal social services 15%

Trade, industry, energy and employment 3%

Transport 4%

Defence 9%

Other[2] 10%

Social security 29%

Gross debt interest 7%

Housing and environmental services 5%

General government expenditure (excluding privatisation proceeds) = £243.8 billion

[1]Territorial departments' expenditure has been allocated to the appropriate functions.
[2]Includes national accounts adjustments and expenditure on other functions

Figure 1 a), b) and c) The functions of the Treasury: spending, borrowing and the allocation of expenditure

Source: HM Treasury

policy-making. Bernard Donoughue, as Head of the Prime Minister's Policy Unit 1974–9, found the Treasury formidable and difficult to work with. Clive Ponting, formerly a rising civil servant of middle rank, comments more sharply.

■ DOCUMENT 8.2
Critics of the Treasury

a) From B. Donoughue, 1987, pp. 33–4
[The Treasury had created] 'a departmental culture of monastic unworldliness. They appear to spend too much of their lives mixing only with other Treasury men. They are often foolishly proud of being untainted or uncorrupted by contact with or practical knowledge of the soiled outside world into whose fiscal and monetary affairs they intervene with devastating effect'

b) From C. Ponting, 1986, pp. 101–2
The Treasury is the most Olympian and detached of all departments and encapsulates in dramatic form the weaknesses of the Mandarin elite....

The whole philosophy of the Treasury is built round hostility to public expenditure. It is not interested in what public expenditure buys in

the real world, it is simply interested in the total amount of public expenditure. Whatever the economic problems facing the country...its remedy is always the same: cut public expenditure. ■

This atmosphere of detachment from the hard world of real public expenditure decisions is reinforced by the domination within the Treasury of the views of the City of London, transmitted through the Bank of England, and also of the international financial institutions. They pay more attention to the exchange rate, the interest rates and the stock exchange than to measures of the real economy – output, unemployment, etc.

Treasury dominance was based not only on constitutional position and intellectual dominance but also on the colonisation of other areas of Whitehall and close links with the Cabinet Office (usually headed by a former Treasury man) and the Bank of England. The Treasury builds 'a fundamentally cohesive world of insiders', linked by 'overlapping, criss-crossing and repetitive channels of communication', a purposive kind of 'village gossip' (H. Heclo and A. Wildavsky, 1974, pp. 68, 78). Thus the Treasury, while doing little

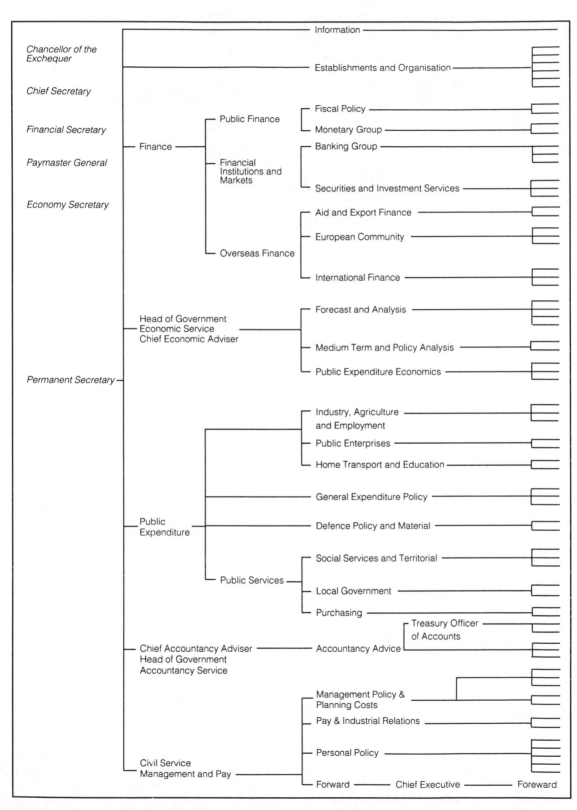

Figure 2 HM Treasury Organisation

directly itself, establishes a system of Treasury control of what other departments aspire to do.

The Treasury and public expenditure

In the field of 'public expenditure' the Treasury is notoriously tight-fisted, concerned literally in former days for candle-ends and carbon paper. There is some foundation for this view. Before 1939 no department could hire an extra cleaner without Treasury approval. The tyranny of management by accountants with defective tunnel vision is well-known (not least in schools and colleges). The Treasury's problem, not always recognised as a problem, is that it has to take a view about a whole range of policy – education, transport, social policy, defence and industry – on which it has no 'natural' or specialist understanding. But these days accountants, sometimes disguised as management consultants, do this all the time.

But there is something to be said for the Treasury position. Public expenditure has to be controlled, and, department Ministers hardly ever limit their own demands. Cabinet Ministers favour restraint in general, but not in their own case, at least, not yet. If the political masters will not take the big money-saving decisions, then the Treasury is left to save on the candle-ends. The Treasury would say (in a favoured civil service phrase) that it 'stands for reality'.

In the pursuit of 'reality' (or cutting a department's programme) the Treasury can be maddeningly persistent and sceptical, altogether too well-informed about a department's 'own' business. It has developed hundreds of ways of saying 'no', of which the most common is simply and firmly, 'No!'. The Treasury is opposed to thin ends, open ends, the setting of precedents, the disguising of expenditure, and facile assumptions about economic growth (to justify rising expenditure). It may seem the Treasury is a formidable obstacle to a spending Minister. Yet its actual record is mixed. Increases in public expenditure have proved difficult to restrain, facile assumptions are made, and thin ends and open ends abound (Concorde for example). It sometimes seems the Treasury is not so powerful, but rather like a man walking slowly in front of a steam-roller of public expenditure, going down hill ever faster.

Denis Healey, once a high-spending Minister of Defence, later a tight-fisted Chancellor, testified to the capacity of the Treasury to exploit the committee system for its own purposes.

■ DOCUMENT 8.3
The conservatives in the Treasury

From D. Healey, 1989, p. 376
I doubt whether any other country has so fully developed a committee system as Britain. Because no decision can be taken until every departmental interest has had its say, this system has a natural tendency to produce a soggy compromise. The Treasury lies at its heart; it is represented on every committee which might conceivably take a decision leading to the spending of money. Its central role, however, is to control the existing apparatus of government rather than to initiate change. Precisely because its representatives are so often the ablest on any committee, they find it too easy to stifle the initiative of others. As Defence Secretary I had felt that the Treasury knew the price of everything and the value of nothing. Though I was now poacher turned gamekeeper, this suspicion remained at the back of my mind. ■

EXERCISE
The Treasury maligned?

8.2 Criticisms of the Treasury, often accompanied by admiration for its intellectual qualities, are common. Is there anything to be said in the Treasury's favour?

The Treasury and the Management of the Economy

In the management of the economy the Treasury faces even more difficulties than in the control of public expenditure. Problems with public expenditure are manageable in the short term by compromise, 'phasing' (delays) and the fudging of figures among ministerial colleagues. The management of the economy is less amenable to deals of that kind.

Briefly the problems are.

1 Doubts about the methods and even the possibility of economic management, including doctrinal disputes about Keynesian and Monetarist approaches, and technical disputes about such matters as exchange and interest rate. Modern economics offered no certain answers. Former Chancellor Healey wrote that 'Economics is not a science.... [It] has acquired a spurious respectability through the use of numbers.... [Economic] theory can give you valuable insights into what is happening, [but] it can rarely offer clear prescriptions for government action (1989, pp. 377, 379, 383).

2 Unreliability of the figures which purported to describe the economy. Again, Healey claimed 'the most important numbers were nearly always wrong.... As Chancellor I found it impossible to get accurate figures of our national output the previous year, or of our imports and exports' (ibid, p. 380).

Healey claimed that the IMF crisis of 1976 arose mainly from the inaccuracy of the figures used to measure public expenditure.

The margin of error in economic statistics crucial for policy-making, for example, domestic demand or the balance of payments, was often so great as to make a nonsense of rational policy-making. Ignorance would have been no disadvantage.

3 Inadequate control over the behaviour of managers, workers and consumers in Britain (and abroad of course).

4 Lack of control over the financial markets which behaved 'like hysterical school girls' according to Healey (p. 27). To balance this male chauvinist remark (which however has an etymological justification) he adds that the markets were advised by 'clever young men who were particularly susceptible to changes in academic fashion – "teenage scribblers" as Nigel Lawson (a later Chancellor) was to call them after he had ceased to be one himself' (p. 434). Healey complained that Chancellors and bankers had to take seriously whatever nonsense (including monetarism) the financial markets took seriously.

5 The political sensitivity of much of what the Treasury was able to do – levels and kinds of taxation, as well as of public expenditure, interest rates, exchange rates, incomes policy. Policies which were demonstrably correct on technical grounds were often regarded as unacceptable on political grounds. Hence the frequent resort to optimistic assumptions about economic growth. The Treasury finds it is much easier to make enemies than friends; and since success eludes it so often, there is no comfort in the glib phrase of another Chancellor, John Major, 'if it isn't hurting, it isn't working'.

The spectacular collapse of economic policy in September 1992 (leading to Britain's withdrawal from the ERM and the forced devaluation of sterling) emphasised and advertised what sceptics had been saying for some years. Governments and great economic experts lacked the understanding to control the national economy. Subsequently a group of seven distinguished economists was appointed to advise the Treasury. They were genuinely independent; indeed, some had been previously denounced as quacks. One of these had by far the best record as an economic forecaster. Such a group is certain to offer conflicting advice, some of it unacceptable to the Treasury and/or the Chancellor. The appointment of advisers demonstrates the problem without ensuring its resolution. But something would be gained if the self-confidence of the Treasury was moderated and the arrogance of Chancellors undermined.

In the management of the economy the relations of the Treasury (and Chancellor and Prime Minister) with the Bank of England are crucial but uneasy. Formally since nationalisation in 1947, the Bank has been subordinate to the Government. As the Chancellor said in appointing the new Governor of the Bank (January 1993): 'The Bank's central responsibility should be to support the Government....' The Treasury should determine exchange and interest rate policy and give directions to the Bank; and the Bank's job is to carry out those policies by operating in the markets.

Naturally the Bank does not relish this position, and claims a voice in these matters. The relations of the Treasury and Bank are sometimes tense. 'Treasury men resent the Bank's airs and graces, and are loath to miss a chance to remind it of its subordinate constitutional position. The great men of the Bank, in their turn are riled by the Treasury's reminders of subordination, and tend to see themselves as men of the world obliged to humour a bunch of theoreticians and hobbledehoys at the other end of town' (J. Bruce Gardyne, 1986, p. 93).

Donoughue comments: 'The Bank of England considered its own mode of working to be both perfect and nobody else's business' (p. 144). Denis Healey took a similar view: the Bank [saw itself] 'as the guardian of mysteries which no ordinary mortal should be allowed to understand.... [It regarded itself] as the only authorised channel of contact between the City and the Treasury' (1987, pp. 374–5). Tensions have persisted between Governors, Chancellors and Prime Ministers, even when the Governor, appointed by the Prime Minister, is politically sympathetic to the Government.

The Governor of the Bank has sufficient standing, especially in the financial community, to be a formidable constraint on the Chancellor and the

Treasury. For example, in the spring of 1991 the Chancellor might well have liked to reduce interest rates quickly. The Governor made it clear in public speeches around the world that a reduction was premature. So the Chancellor was caught. He was free to do as he wished, but the financial markets were certain to react unfavourably, and so frustrate him.

EXERCISE

8.3 Is it desirable that the Bank of England should exercise influence independent of the Government?

The Chancellor of the Exchequer

The Chancellor, like other Ministers, works as head of his department and in parallel with it; that is to say, most of his policy development work and his decision making is prepared and negotiated through the Treasury's channels to the departments. But there is a difference. The Chancellor's responsibilities affect all other Ministers and indeed the whole performance of the government; he has, as Nigel Lawson said, 'a finger in every pie'. The Chancellor more often than most other Ministers has to struggle with colleagues – to control and restrain them, or defy them. Hence a Chancellor has few friends, except, with luck, the Prime Minister. Enoch Powell, once a Treasury Minister, said, 'If the Prime Minister is not on the Chancellor's side, no-body is on his side' (quoted in Hennessy, 1989, p. 394). The Chancellor soon learns that British Cabinet government is competitive rather than collective.

Some Chancellors have spoken of the immense burden of their office. Roy Jenkins came to the Treasury after the Home Office and wrote that while the Home Secretary experienced 'sudden, tropical storms, fading away', the Chancellor endured 'a long, dark, Arctic Winter'. The Chancellor had to attend all major ministerial meetings, 'and nearly always be either protagonist or antagonist'. His responsibilities were especially burdensome because of the 'endemic nature of the Treasury crisis; the size of the stakes if things go wrong; and the amount of time which has to be devoted to dealing with one's colleagues....' (*Sunday Times* 17 January 1971).

Nevertheless there are compensations for the Chancellor in terms of power and prestige. The Chancellor is normally a politician of some seniority; in any case, once in office, he carries 'clout'. Prime Minister and Chancellor need each

other; in alliance they are unbeatable, in dispute, things go badly wrong (as between Margaret Thatcher and Nigel Lawson; John Major and Norman Lamont). 'A Treasury man's dream of bliss', said Sir William Armstrong, was 'Prime Minister and the Chancellor locked together like a centaur' (S. Crosland, 1982, p. 203). He was thinking of Harold Wilson and Roy Jenkins.

The Chancellor is further buttressed by a team of Ministers including the Chief Secretary usually in the Cabinet, and a formidable civil service team. If the Chancellor can forge an alliance with the Prime Minister and work well with his officials in the Treasury, then he is well placed to confront, if not to overcome, the horrendous problems of economic management and public expenditure. The Chancellor also has excellent information over the whole range of government activity. James Callaghan wrote of his sense of deprivation when he arrived in the Home Office, after serving as Chancellor.

It is further to the Chancellor's advantage that much of his work can plausibly be regarded as unsuitable for open discussion. The unsuitability is no doubt often exaggerated, but it is true that the management of the economy requires much confidential international negotiation, and the development of Budget (taxation) proposals must always for the most part be conducted in secret. In the determination of public expenditure there can be full discussion on aggregate totals, but departmental spending is regarded as a matter for confidential bilateral negotiation.

Hence Chancellors may frequently be heard declining to engage in consultation, refusing to accept Cabinet decisions, imposing policies on departments. For example, in a Cabinet of July 1975, Healey 'snapped out', 'I must say to you, Prime Minister, that these matters cannot be decided by a majority in Cabinet' (B. Castle, 1980, p. 474). On that occasion Healey appeared to lose the immediate argument, but won the issue later on – a not at all unusual illustration of 'serial' decision making – this week's episode has a (sometimes unexpected) sequel.

Healey's predecessor as Chancellor, Roy Jenkins, in the earlier Labour government, had in similar fashion, 'hit the roof' at what he said was 'an intolerable pre-emption of budgetary policy and no Chancellor could be expected to stand for it – this was a proposal, not the Chancellor's, to raise employers' contributions to National Insurance to fund the Health Service (B. Castle, 1984, p. 725).

The Chancellor's claim to privileged authority does not go unchallenged by Ministers. Barbara Castle claimed that Chancellors, like Foreign Secretaries, developed 'God complexes' (1984, p. 671). She was as irritated by James Callaghan as she was by his successors. The Budget procedure '[gave] the Chancellor almost dictatorial power in matters greatly affecting other Departments, [and] is inconsistent with effective planning.' (B. Castle, 1984, p. 121).

Similar complaints were made by other Ministers. For example, in 1968 Tony Benn, having complained about 'the absolute exclusion of Cabinet Ministers from important decisions', declared 'I am not prepared to accept the Treasury's right to dart into individual Minister's Departments and find savings to suit their particular policies' (1988, p. 2). Two years later Tony Crosland (Secretary of State for the Environment) had a sharp exchange with the same Chancellor, Roy Jenkins, over funds for housing. 'It's up to me as Chancellor to decide.' 'On the contrary. It's up to the two of us to decide, as it's my Department that is under discussion'.

The Prime Minister interceded in his mollifying way, and the Chancellor amended his attitude. Tony Crosland thought his civil servants could have done more to help him, but were too concerned to protect other 'traditional relationships with the Treasury' (S. Crosland, 1982, p. 209).

EXERCISE
The power of the Chancellor of the Exchequer

8.4 Is the Chancellor the most powerful Minister after the Prime Minister?

The Financial planning system

The Government spends about £250bn each year, and the raising and allocation of this huge sum form a substantial part of the government's domestic policy. The choices to be made are therefore highly political (arousing disputation and requiring consent) as well as formidably technical (requiring the mastery of a mass of complex detail). The Cabinet, or the Prime Minister and Chancellor of the Exchequer, at least, set a broad target for expenditure at the beginning, approve the detailed allocations in the middle, and the revenue proposals (the Budget) at the end. The influence of the full Cabinet diminishes as the year goes by, figures harden and the Chancellor

goes into his Budget mode of silence and restricted access.

The public expenditure process is sometimes known as the PESC process, after the official Public Expenditure Survey Committee which since the 1960s has done the hard preparatory work, and produced the outlines and the options. The process takes about a year, but is part of a continuous programme of review, taking a three-year perspective, rolling forward each year. Before the plans for Year One (next year) are formally endorsed, planning of Year Two has begun. The planning year runs as follows, with a climax in December as the expenditure and taxation plans are presented to Parliament.

■ DOCUMENT 8.4
The course of the financial year

Winter into Spring: Cabinet agrees overall spending target for following year, with menacing assertions of the government's determination not to exceed the target.

Spring into Summer: Departments work on their spending programmes and negotiate with Treasury over departmental allocations and programmes.

Summer into Autumn: Cabinet agrees on modifications which if the total is fixed means re-allocation, and blood on the carpet. Negotiations are conducted by the Chief Secretary with individual Ministers, and final settlement is by a Cabinet committee chaired by the Chancellor. Previously the final decisions were made either by the Chief Secretary or by a special Cabinet Committee known as the 'Star Chamber' (see below), or in extremis by prime ministerial intervention.

Mid-Winter (December): Publication of Chancellor's Autumn Statement (dealing with the state of the economy and overall economic and financial plans) and Public Expenditure Departmental Reports. At the same time (from 1993) a Financial Statement (the 'Red Book') and Budget Report is published – this is the Budget statement about the government's revenue and taxation proposals.

Continuing: Under the National Audit Act of 1983 the National Audit Office, under the Comptroller and Auditor General scrutinises the accounts of departments and reports to the Public Accounts Committee of the House of Commons.

The recent bringing together of the two great

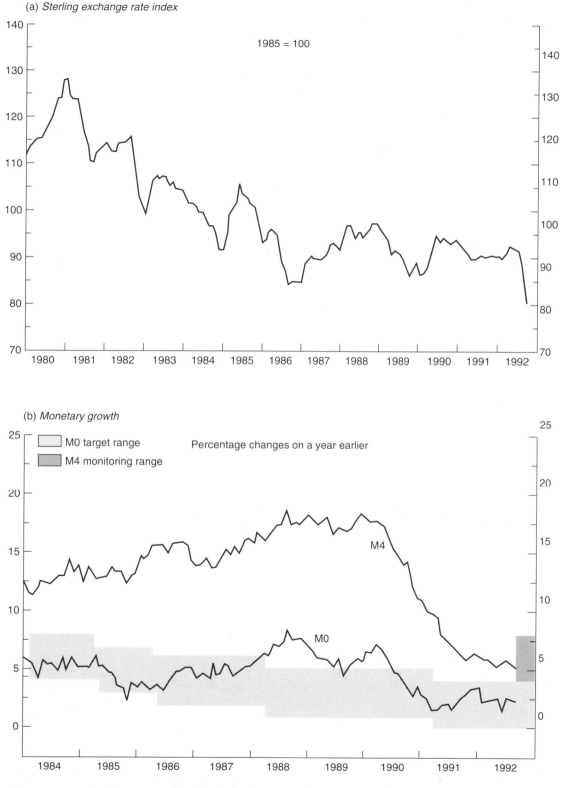

(a) *Sterling exchange rate index*

1985 = 100

(b) *Monetary growth*

MO target range

M4 monitoring range

Percentage changes on a year earlier

M4

M0

Figure 3 a) and b) Instruments in the Chancellor's cockpit

Source: HM Treasury

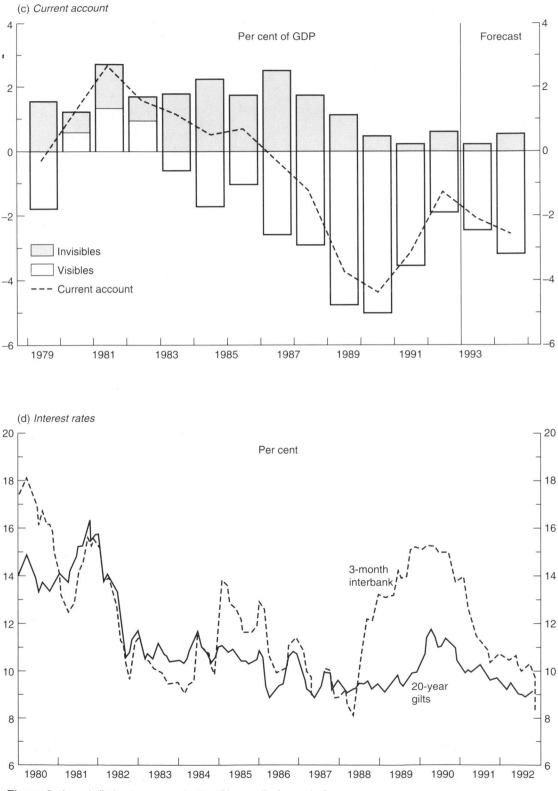

Figure 3 c) and d) Instruments in the Chancellor's cockpit
Sources: HM Treasury

financial occasions, the expenditure plans of the Autumn statement and the revenue (taxation) proposals of the Spring budget was a long overdue move to rationality in financial planning, or at least in its public and political presentation. In the past, expenditure plans never attracted the high publicity given to tax proposals, and popular understanding of the economics of government was in consequence quite limited. ■

It is evident that these financial procedures are largely in the hands – and under the influence – of the Treasury and the Chancellor, with the Prime Minister by his side or at his back, to support or restrain. An old treasury hand, Sir Leo Pliatzky, confirms this.

■ DOCUMENT 8.5
The Chancellor and non-collective government

From L. Pliatzky, 1989, p. 75
All the things which are at the heart of economic management – the Budget balance, interest rates and the exchange rate – are in practice matters for the Chancellor under our system, in consultation with the Governor of the Bank of England on interest rates and the exchange rate, and reporting to the Prime Minister who, over at least the last few administrations, has had the last word. (Roy Jenkins, however, consulted Harold Wilson hardly at all on the Budget.) These derogations from the doctrine of collective Cabinet responsibility go back as far as one can remember and have nothing to do with the alleged recent Presidential style of government. ■

Further, the role of the House of Commons is quite limited. Matters beyond the control of the full Cabinet are even less likely to be influenced by Parliament. In practice, what little influence the House of Commons has in financial affairs rests mainly with the Select Committees, especially the Treasury and Civil Service Committee and the Public Accounts Committee.

EXERCISE
The making of financial policy

8.5 Is it satisfactory that financial policy is largely in the hands of the Chancellor and the Prime Minister?

Chancellor and Ministers in conflict
In the inevitable contests between Chancellor and Ministers rationality is mixed with other factors, sometimes called 'political'. The Chancellor has a view of the economy and the government's strategy and spending priorities. But he is also aware of the reputation and 'clout' of particular Ministers, and the flowing tides which favour some kinds of expenditure most of the time (defence, agriculture) and others only some of the time (health, education). The Chancellor knows too that he has little freedom of manoeuvre arising from the buoyancy of the economy, but a great deal arising from the 'assumptions' (Joel Barnett called them guesses) he builds into his estimates. An economic crisis gives him a hold over Ministers, but at a cost in the economic and financial standing of government.

Ministers, for their part, tend to identify with the interests of their Department, rather than the government; so they 'fight their corner', struggle at the expense of others to win more for themselves. Their officials naturally share these ambitions, subject only to agreements made through the official networks, and a prudent reluctance not to damage their standing with the Treasury. Departmental tactics in fighting off the Treasury include the sore thumb, the long bounce, the sacrificial lamb and, on a few well-judged occasions, going over the top (you may guess the meanings or see H. Heclo and A. Wildavsky, 1974, pp. 92–4, 121–2).

The departmental Minister argues the grave consequences of cuts – as near as one can get to babies starving to death on television, homeless mothers camping in the streets, or, a different kind of politics, angry generals and admirals commenting in endless television interviews on the betrayal of the armed forces, Members of Parliament in marginal constituencies fearful for their seats. Officials and Ministers concentrate on the defence and advancement of their own interests, not on appraising competing claims from other departments. Labour's Chief Secretary in the 1970s told Susan Crosland: 'Each time a spending Minister argued with the Treasury, except for Tony [Crosland], not one of them offered to sacrifice a low priority for a high priority' (S. Crosland, 1982, p. 307). The simple logic of balancing increases here with cuts elsewhere is not voluntarily and vigorously pursued, since spending Ministers never agree on cuts, for themselves or anyone else. The Minister is not encouraged to make judgements in a Cabinet perspective – though the establishment in 1992 of a fixed total in advance of final departmental negotiations applies some discipline to ambitious Ministers.

Governments have struggled over the years to deal with the problem of controlling public expenditure and in most years have succeeded only in slowing the pace of increase. On the technical side procedures have been thoroughly and repeatedly reformed since the Plowden Report (1961) on the Control of Public Expenditure. The Report reflected the Treasury's alarm at the lack of control of public spending, and laid down two obvious principles which had been not so much neglected as difficult to enforce: 'decisions involving substantial future expenditure should always be taken in the light of public expenditure as a whole over a period of years, and in relation to the prospective resources' (*Plowden Report*, 1961, para. 7).

Following the Report, a new procedure, the Public Expenditure Survey Committee (PESC) was instituted. This is an interdepartmental group of finance officers and Treasury officials, chaired by a senior Treasury official. The Committee endeavours to secure realistic projected costings of current programmes, looking four years ahead and taking account of implications and consequences. Total projected expenditure is considered against likely resources, and different expenditures within the total are compared.

PESC reports in May-June each year, providing the material for the Chief Secretary and Ministers to wrestle over until November. However, PESC has not resolved the problems for three reasons. First, the figures on which they work and the assumptions (guesses) about the performance of the economy are unreliable. Second, the fundamental problems are to do with political values, on which agreement is difficult. Third, most of the Ministers concerned do not perceive and follow a collective interest or a government strategy. Perhaps they should, but it is often the fate of public interest that it is defined only by the conflict of sectional or private interests. Thus the expenditure process is highly political.

Governments have tried new approaches to the political problem. The Cabinet itself proved inadequate to the task, since the spending Ministers out-numbered the rest, and could not consistently be out-gunned by the Cabinet clout of Prime Minister and Chancellor of Exchequer (Prime ministerial power here met its limits). A committee of non-spending Ministers did not work because most non-spending Ministers want 'less work and more friends', not working harder to make enemies (H. Heclo and A. Wildavsky, p. 372). A senior Treasury official (quoted in H. Heclo and A. Wildavsky, pp. 186–7) said 'Ministers live by supporting each other. Dog doesn't eat dog.... Any big spending operation is a political operation. This is something Plowden overlooked, or underestimated, with its technologist view. Who will you get as 'non-spending' Ministers? The Foreign Minister? He knows he needs the support of his Cabinet colleagues for things he wants to do, even if he's not spending a lot of money. What's more the Cabinet is a personal business. 'There may be four or five 'non-spending' Ministers the Chancellor can try to line up, but they may hate his guts – you know what I mean'.

The first effective step in the control of public expenditure was the imposition from 1976 of 'cash limits' to spending. In effect expenditure was approved as a sum of money, not as a commitment to particular programmes of spending, so the Minister could not ask for more money to complete his programme if costs had risen. The second step was to take a Cabinet decision on total spending, the only variation lying in the contingency reserve.

The procedure adopted in the 1980s centred on the Chief Secretary, promoted to the Cabinet as part of this reform. Once the total spending programme had been agreed by Cabinet, the Chief Secretary held a series of bilateral talks with the spending Ministers, to squeeze departmental claims into the agreed Cabinet total. The only appeal lay not to the Cabinet or another senior committee but to a specially constituted Cabinet Committee known as the 'Star Chamber'. Here the Chief Secretary was backed by a senior Minister in the Chair (not the Prime Minister, but the Deputy or equivalent) other senior Ministers and a high-powered team of officials from the Treasury and the Cabinet Office. This was the last court of appeal: the discontented Minister could acquiesce or resign. In some years proceedings in the Star Chamber were prolonged and acrimonious; in other years Ministers settled quietly. In one case the Prime Minister intervened personally to arrange a settlement in advance of a meeting of the Star Chamber; and the procedure was not always used.

Thus the Star Chamber procedure worked as a deterrent to persistent fighting up to Cabinet level which was normal in Wilson's Cabinet. Collectivity was the product of restraint and discipline, rather than of armed struggle and 'going down fighting'. However, the procedure appeared to separate both Prime Minister and full Cabinet from the public expenditure decisions, in order it seems to exclude appeals and impose a conclusion.

In 1992 a new procedure was adopted which meets this criticism. The Cabinet determined a total sum for public expenditure, the Chief Secretary conducted the detailed negotiations, but the Chancellor presided over the supervising committee. Apart from the inevitable growth in government expenditure arising from unemployment, and perhaps some disposal of assets and creative accounting, the total was set in concrete; any increase for one department must be re-couped from another.

The principle is not, of course, novel, and indeed is a normal part of most financial planning. The committee arrangement is new, and places the responsibility for the control of public expenditure where it must belong, with the Chancellor and a major Cabinet committee.

■ DOCUMENT 8.6
Cases in the politics of public expenditure: Ministers and the Treasury

a) A Chief Secretary's gloomy view
Joel Barnett as Chief Secretary reported the approach of different Ministers to discussions on expenditure. For Barbara Castle 'it was almost a matter of principle not to concede anything in bilaterals but to go down fighting in Cabinet. I doubt if it really helped her case, but it certainly made my life more difficult' (J. Barnett, 1982, pp. 65–8). Crosland, after fighting in vain against a whole package of cuts, accepted his own in an 'urbane and civilised' way. Defence then as later refused to accept, or even discuss, cuts, taking a high moral stance (B. Donoughue, 1987, p. 61).

b) Crisis expenditure cuts
From H. Heclo and A. Wildavsky, 1974, p. 212
[Sometimes under severe financial pressures orderly negotiation breaks down. Here is a report of officials at work on cuts in July 1966. This is perhaps the civil service at its most dynamic, working under pressure and under clear political direction – and, some would add, doing what they like doing best, cutting government spending.]

A senior Treasury official recalled that cuts were made in ways 'totally contrary to the rules of the game. Undertakings entered into in a

proper way with the Treasury were broken. Cutting was done by horse-trading by political push and pull.' They quote an article from *The Sunday Times* of 24 July 1966:

[By now the three Permanent Secretaries, Treasury, DEA, Cabinet Office] 'were flat out: keeping the lights on in the Cabinet Office all night, taking hardly any sleep at the weekend.... No Ministers were involved. It was a concentrated exhibition of pure Civil Service virtuosity. The three men rang round the Civil Service heads of all the spending departments and said: give us your cuts. Cannily they went light on the departments of political heavyweights like Dick Crossman, Tony Crosland and Barbara Castle.
Minor figures...had their appropriations wiped out without a tremor....' ■

EXERCISE
The Minister and money

8.6 If the Secretary of State for Health were faced with a large number of resignations from the National Health Service by doctors going to work in the USA because of low pay in Britain, what case should he or she make to the Chancellor and the Chief Secretary for increased funding to provide higher pay?

If this were rejected what should the Secretary of State do? – accept the situation, appeal to Prime Minister and Cabinet, appeal to backbenchers, leak the case to the media, encourage the doctors' organisations to threaten to strike, or resign?

The Budget
Public expenditure is thus dealt with in a specially modified version of Cabinet government which allows participation by Cabinet and spending Ministers, but within a framework which imposes discipline. By contrast taxation proposals are prepared by the Chancellor in conditions of great secrecy and unveiled ceremonially in the Budget, traditionally in March but since 1993 in November or December. The Cabinet holds an early general discussion. Then the Chancellor falls silent until the eve of Budget day, except for carefully designed leaks, intended to raise or lower expectations.

In this period of 'purdah' the Chancellor does not consult outside the Inner Treasury circle (including the Prime Minister). However, since variations in taxation can be helpful or damaging to

Table 1 The Chancellor's problem

Revenue 1992–3   *Planned spending 1993–4*

*The Budget 1992–3: the government's income to
meet its expenditure for 1992–3*

	£/bn		£/bn
1 Income Tax	60	1 Defence	23.5
2 VAT	40	2 Foreign/Overseas	3.5
3 Community charge	8	3 Agriculture	2.8
4 Corporation tax	17	4 Trade and Industry	2.6
5 Petrol	12	5 Employment	3.7
6 Social security receipts	39	6 Transport	6.4
7 Interest and dividend	5	7 Environment	38.8
8 Drink	5	8 Home Office	6.1
9 Business rates	14	9 Legal departments	2.6
10 Tobacco	7	10 Education	9.25
		11 National Heritage	1.0
Total:	207	12 Health	29.9
		13 Social Security	65.0
		14 Scotland, Wales, N.Ireland	26.7
		15 Chancellor's departments	3.4
		16 Cabinet Office	1.7
		17 EC	1.4
The gap between income and expenditure has to		18 Reserve	4.0
be filled by borrowing, taxation or sale of assets		19 Local authority self-financed	11.1
(privatisation).		Total:	243

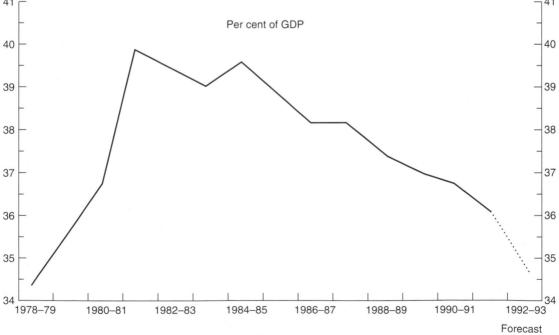

On a national accounts accruals basis, including community charge

Figure 4 Taxes and Social Security contributions

business and charity, the Chancellor is subject to a good deal of lobbying. Of course taxation is helpful or damaging to individuals too, but they must look to political parties to represent them. Here is an illustration of pre-budget lobbying.

■ DOCUMENT 8.7
Lobbying the Chancellor

From J. Bruce-Gardyne 1986, pp. 155–6
...during the run-up to the Budget of 1985, word got round that Chancellor Lawson had two targets in his sights. One was the zero-rating for VAT of books and newspapers. The other was the tax privilege of pension funds. Both targets swiftly took evasive action. Booksellers and newspaper publishers made common cause in denunciation of a 'tax on knowledge', led by Lord Macmillan [the well-known publisher and ex-Prime Minister].... The campaign in defence of the tax on exemption enjoyed by the pension funds was even more high profile, and comprehensive. Tory MPs were snowed under with complaints about both subjects; and the CBI did its best to ensure that no politician could visit a boardroom without being deafened by denunciations of the Chancellor's evil intentions towards the senior citizens....
[The Chancellor got the message, did not make the changes feared by these lobbies, and claimed he had never had such intentions.] ■

EXERCISE
The Chancellor and the Lobbies

8.7 How should the Chancellor deal with the lobbies?

Drives for efficiency in government

Since the 1960s there have been a series of attempts to make the civil service more efficient, more cost-conscious, concerned with value for money, managerially oriented. They were all new and special programmes, readily identifiable by their acronyms, and carrying a fair weight of top-down management discipline.

Efficiency drives were rooted in cost cutting, and began with the improved and formalised procedures for the control of public expenditure introduced in the 1960s (PESC). Programme Analysis and Review (PAR) was introduced as a supplement to PESC. The latter was the overall review, PAR was selective within departments. The aim was to measure output in relation to

costs, by asking not simply is this operation reasonably priced, but what does it achieve? and is that worth doing at all? These awkward questions about objectives and achievements are always much resented when asked by persistent outsiders – who will certainly be accused of arrogance and ignorance.

PAR was very much in tune with the times (the late 60s, early 70s) when American ideas on 'scientific' management were in fashion. These were all elaborated versions of the kind of management a housekeeper, say, employs when considering how to provide hospitality for two weekend house guests, or a large children's party, except that the stakes are so much higher – massive investments, serious consequences for good or ill for millions of people.

PAR petered out in the mid-1970s, for good and bad reasons. Departments did not like such searching and, it seemed, impertinent questioning. Governments liked it in theory, but in practice preferred to go on spending without awkward questions. But the difficulties with PAR go to the heart of the dilemma of government. It is comparatively easy to identify a good car by its sales; it is much more difficult to identify a good policy, and define a meaning for that facile formula, 'value for money'. PAR did not provide a magic procedure or a new and powerful analytic tool, and the problem of securing efficiency remained.

In the 1980s Margaret Thatcher established a vigorous drive for efficiency based initially in her Private Office and subsequently in the Cabinet Office – but still with her strong support. There were four elements:

1 An Efficiency Unit was set up under Sir Derek Rayner (of Marks and Spencer) whom Margaret Thatcher treated as an alternative Head of the Civil Service. The Unit used able (and preferably not too sensitive) young civil servants to conduct 'scrutinies' of selected areas of departmental work. The savings were reckoned to be almost £1 bn in the first seven years, though dramatic savings obviously get harder as the process goes on, some recommendations were never implemented and questions about policy (is this worth doing at all?) were neglected.
2 The Financial Management Initiative (FMI) was introduced (1982) and affected all departments. This drew in part on the MINIS (Ministerial information systems introduced by Michael

Heseltine in the Department of the Environment. The object was to collect, order and present information to managers to support strategic and accountable management. There was no mystery really about FMI – define your objectives, relate resources to achieving them and monitor performance. But there were practical problems – too much useless information, a shortage of the qualitative information that is only available by personal contact with the work, a tendency to centralise and thus waste local knowledge, a confusion of budgetary procedures with sound policy making. There was some resistance among top civil servants to FMI, as formerly to PAR; it was not 'their scene' or perhaps 'their cup of tea'; and it did look as if the intention was to cut costs and jobs (it was). The culture of the higher civil service was modified but not transformed by FMI.

3 The National Audit Office was established in 1983 to strengthen the work carried out by the Comptroller and Auditor General for the Public Accounts Committee of Parliament. For example the NAO report for 1989 complained of vague and general objectives 'providing a ready excuse for missed targets'. Managers were criticised for failing 'to maximise revenue or achieve a reasonable level of return on public sector investments'. The Department of Social Security had been shown a way of 'saving £55 million a year forever [a nice touch!] by ceasing excessive generosity towards disabled people already awarded large sums in damages.

4 The Next Steps (1988) programme for the 'hiving off' of government activities to non-departmental, semi-independent agencies marked the recognition that there were limits to the efforts to make the departments more efficient. The culture of the civil service had not been transformed. It might be better to confine government departments to work which was characteristically government work, and to move other activities of a commercial or quasi-commercial kind to agencies designed on more commercial lines. The Next Steps initiative is further discussed in Chapter 10.

The new pressure for efficiency raised two challenges for the Treasury. For older hands this was an intrusion into the traditional Treasury territory of cheese-paring and candle-ends. For the more enlightened it was an ill thought-out and clumsy attempt to impose the imperatives of efficiency and accountable management where political priorities and sensitivities properly applied. Running a country is different from running a company – as Leo Pliatzky, former second Permanent Secretary at the Treasury points out in the following Document, referring to PAR.

■ DOCUMENT 8.8
The difficulties of applying management theory to government: the case of defence

From L. Pliatzky, 1982, pp. 104–5
[Pliatzky, a former Treasury Permanent Secretary, argues that PAR was unrealistic in assuming that] the whole organic process of policy formation could somehow be subordinated to a mechanical review procedure....

[In practice policies were often determined, apart from manifesto commitments, by events and the prevailing ethos of party or senior ministers.]

Further, defence is also a good illustration of the fact that there is a great temptation for people to believe what it suits them to believe. Traditionally, those concerned about footing the bill have tended to argue that the need for a large defence budget is exaggerated, sometimes contending that there is nothing much that Britain can do about Russian aggression anyway and that only the United States can provide the counterweight, while those concerned about the country's defence have tended to play down the problem of financing it, and if ever a choice had to be made between a more and a less optimistic assumption about the growth of resources, naturally they would support the high growth assumption. Both of these lines of argument are of course wishful thinking. There is a problem about defence, and there is a problem about paying for it. ■

EXERCISE
The Treasury and the policies of other departments

8.8 How far can and should a Treasury official get involved in the policies as distinct from the costs of other departments?

GUIDE TO EXERCISES

8.1 The attitude towards public expenditure identified by Pliatzky was a product of the wartime reaction to the depression of the 1930s and to wartime economic and social measures. The mood of public benevolence lasted until the 1970s, when a strong reaction set in. 'Throwing money at problems' went out of fashion, and the advantages of 'the market' replaced the tarnished virtues of public provision. Public expenditure needs to be supported either by a prosperous economy or by high taxation, willingly paid by socially inclined citizens. The prosperous economy and the socially-inclined citizens were lacking in Britain after the 1960s. Further it was evident that public expenditure was sometimes (critics said, often and inevitably) wasteful, inefficient, perverted by the public sector unions.

8.2 Yes! Every government, indeed every organisation, needs one – that is, needs a firm control of expenditure, a guardian of what should always – not just when you do not favour a particular object of expenditure – be called 'taxpayers' money. The case for the Treasury is first that its reputation partly reflects the failure of the British economy to produce enough wealth to fund public services; second that it tries hard to discriminate between the worthwhile projects and the extravagant; third, that expenditure has not in fact been tightly controlled; fourth, that the pattern of expenditure still largely reflects political choices.

One of the Treasury's problems in sustaining its case is that it is also responsible for the management of the economy, so it can be blamed for the government's shortage of funds.

However, most Chancellors of the Exchequer would challenge the assumption that the Treasury is so powerful. If Chancellors are so powerful why do they always seem so hard-worked and harassed?

8.3 In an ideal world the will of the democratically elected government should not be frustrated. In practice it is now frequently argued that elected governments are too sensitive to popular opinion to take the hard decisions required. Hence there is a case for an independent central bank. This does not say much for democracy!

8.4 Potentially yes; in practice, not always because the problems are so difficult and the constraints severe. In any case there are often other senior Ministers who by reason of experience and standing, or special responsibilities, carry significant influence, for example, William Whitelaw in Margaret Thatcher's government. See also Assessment 1 and the case on Nigel Lawson's resignation.

8.5 Cabinet Ministers do complain frequently of exclusion from the making of economic and financial policy; in most governments it is in the hands of a small inner group. It could be argued that the Cabinet never has played a significant part in financial affairs or more positively a) that the overall policy framework for finance (the broad levels of expenditure, taxation and borrowing) is settled openly, b) that the detail has to be settled behind closed doors, and in more open systems like the USA it is extremely difficult to make a budget at all.

8.6 Argue the particular merits of the pay claim (high skill and workload, comparability); the unfairness of solving the government's (the country's) economic problems by cutting the pay of particular groups of public sector workers; the possibility of a breakdown in the Health Service, with serious political consequences. The latter is the most persuasive argument especially if clamour in the press can be arranged. If this fails try everything short of resignation; then hope to be moved to the Foreign Office in the next re-shuffle.

8.7 He must first choose which ones he is going to receive and listen to. The advantage of the budget procedure is that he cannot be expected to say much at all in advance of presenting the budget; and thereafter his decisions are fairly well protected from lobby pressures since any variation will have to be made in public. Ideally the Chancellor should make a firm judgement about economic efficiency and justice and stand by it. In practice the Chancellor is not so clear-sighted, and efficiency and justice not so easy to identify, and as a politician he must be concerned with consent. Of course this includes less noble, more immediate and practical objectives, like not upsetting his Cabinet and party colleagues, and constituency loyalists, nor disturbing potentially trouble-making interest groups, nor appearing to be profligate or mean, for or against whatever it is unfashionable to be for or against.

8.8 This is a basic and insoluble problem in all administration; for example, how far should accountants have a say in the running of a hospital or a college? Sir Leo Pliatzky offers no answer; he is content to draw attention to the problem. The Treasury official operates from a difficult position, but he has to know enough and guess a little more in order to challenge, say, the Ministry of Defence about the real need and true cost of a particular disposition of troops or new weapon system.

ASSESSMENTS

1 The Chancellor of the Exchequer

For all the prestige of the office of Chancellor it is the 'bed of nails' of Cabinet posts. It is essentially a post in which scope, reach and potential exceed grasp and usable power. Most of the Chancellor's advantages are cancelled out in practice. As Denis Healey wrote:

'When I was responsible for the nation's defence, I had the power to see that my decisions were carried out by nearly a million military and civilian personnel under my direct control. When I was responsible for the nation's economy, the success of my policies depended largely on people over whom I had no direct control whatever, and over whom no one had any central control – the workers and managers in British industry, and the men and women who bought what they produced, both at home and abroad. My central problem was to discover which of the decisions open to me as Chancellor were most likely to get these people to behave as I wanted' (1989, p. 377).

The Chancellor can free himself from the constraints of Cabinet collectivity as indicated above, but only by working under the close observation of the Prime Minister, the Bank and the City and the international financial network. Even his Cabinet colleagues might be preferable, though Chancellors never seem convinced of this.

The Prime Minister is a powerful ally for the Chancellor: together they are unbeatable, as rueful spending Ministers complain. But Chancellors do not always enjoy an easy partnership with the Prime Minister. The resignations of Thorneycroft and Lawson, noted below, show this to be the case. Butler and Macmillan did not always get the support of Churchill and Eden. Callaghan had an uneasy relationship with Wilson. Major and Lamont

disagreed over fundamentals, the policy collapsed and Lamont was eventually dismissed, a scapegoat for the Prime Minister's policy. Jenkins and Wilson, Thatcher and Howe show the relationship at its best. But Prime Ministers unlike most Chancellors retain political sensitivities about the popularity of expenditure and prosperity, and the unpopularity of financial restraint.

The ambivalence of the Chancellor's position is reflected in his relations with his department. The Chancellor heads the most powerful department in Whitehall. But the Treasury is a difficult department to master. Only a very tough and independent-minded Chancellor can impose himself fully on the formidable Knights of the Treasury and their Economic Advisers.

If the Chancellor's job is ambivalent in its power, it is also ambivalent in its politics. The Chancellor as Head of the Treasury is concerned with financial honesty, integrity and rectitude. However, a Chancellor has to please not only the international financial community but the voters, at least his own party's supporters, plus a few more. He is expected to provide a measure of prosperity or at least the perception of economic well-being. Public expenditure must not be so tightly controlled that there is widespread dissatisfaction with public services. So the Chancellor, normally a stern and parsimonious bank-manager, sometimes behaves like a rich and benevolent uncle.

The Chancellor's benevolence is particularly directed to the periods preceding general elections. Only one Chancellor since 1950, Roy Jenkins in 1970, has introduced a wholly responsible budget in an election year. He actually raised taxes, Labour lost the election, and the two events may have had some connection. By contrast, in April 1955 Butler reduced income tax by 2.5p. (6d.) only to re-impose taxes with the same yield in October. He is reported to have said privately: 'Surely the most inflationary budget would be one that just let Labour in?' (The Economist, 21 March 1987).

2 The Treasury

The Treasury, more than any other department, is regarded as a force independent of its Minister. It is also a department much complained against. These complaints centre on its power – its constitutional and strategic position, its network of communications to Prime Minister and Cabinet Office and through the departments, its right of entry to departments and 'their' business, its uses of bilateral processes to exert its influence, and its close relationship with the Bank of England. The Treasury, the critics claim, has 'seen off' a series of rivals, institutions and persons – DEA, CSD, CPRS, a marauding Minister, Harold Lever, an overmighty Permanent Secretary (of CSD), Sir William Armstrong....

Further, critics assert that the Treasury's undoubted power is used to further its mistaken purposes – the interests of finance capital (the City), and the close restraint of public expenditure (the candle-ends approach). The Treasury, say its more perceptive critics, lacks political feel. Referring to the IMF crisis of 1976, Bernard Donoughue, then Head of the Policy Unit, wrote: *'Invariably [the Treasury] would come forward with a list of expenditure cuts which no Labour government could conceivably accept for political reasons, or which totally reversed major manifesto commitments....' Yet, he added, 'not all the [Treasury] mandarins were political innocents'.*

The mandarins themselves might argue that their duty is to identify and advocate the correct economic policy, not the most politically acceptable policy. It is for the politicians to find and strike a political balance. But it would be unrealistic and certainly unproductive for the Treasury to disdain political considerations. There is a necessary dimension of acceptability and consent to any policy, and it is not corrupt or perverse to take account of that dimension. (Similarly a factory manager has to concern herself with the acceptability of an industrial policy to workers as well as customers).

There is a case to be made on behalf of the Treasury. First, it is not nearly as powerful as its critics claim. It can do very little itself directly, and must work through other departments. Under the newly developed 'Downing Street complex' and the Cabinet Office, official power at the top is shared, and the international linkages preclude a concentration of national power. The record of the economic policy of recent governments (rising public expenditure and swings in approaches to economic management) does not indicate the dominance of Treasury orthodoxy. Second, it is not conceivable that any government can manage without some discipline in expenditure and some regard for international finance. Hence, if the Treasury did not exist, a ministry carrying out

its functions would need to be invented. Third, the Treasury, alone among the departments has an overview function, which is more than passive co-ordination. Here the separate pieces of government policy are fitted together and moulded into an affordable, if not a coherent, whole. The function is served by the Treasury's network mode of operation.

Further, the redistribution of finite resources sets the most severe problem for government, as for any organisation, and the real difficulties are often evaded. Priorities are not defined and implemented; change occurs only incrementally. The Treasury is smart enough to recognise that its policy field is shot through with political values. The Treasury's job is to 'reconnect' (in Pliatzky's phrase) the technocratic and the political; to bring its technical expertise to bear on the political issues, and as far as possible analyse and assess the political values – so that its political masters can make judgements combining technical rationality and coherent political principle. In practice the process is never so clear: Treasury and Government get in each other's way, and the policy package is a mixture of expertise, principle and expediency. But that, you might say, is what politics is about.

Thus, the institutional arrangements for the making of Treasury policy look to be an unavoidable mix of technical and political pressures. Two reforms have been advocated. The first is to separate the two main functions of the Treasury, economic management and public expenditure, into two separate ministries. The two functions are connected logically, but do not need to be connected operationally. So there is some advantage in breaking up a centre of power, and lessening the burden on the Chancellor. Chancellors do not favour this reform, though they have been pleased to pass much of the Public Expenditure work to the Chief Secretary (a Treasury Minister).

The second reform is to grant independence to the Bank of England. This, it is argued, would enable the Bank to serve the national interest by taking necessary decisions, painful to the people, which governments avoid. Curiously the Bank was nationalised in 1947 so that it would serve the national interest by taking necessary decisions painful to the international financial community, which an independent Bank avoided. Thus the argument raises a serious question about democracy and finance capital. Experience suggests that no great area of public interest, for example, education, health, law, defence – should be left in the hands of an unaccountable professional monopoly. In practice the relations of the Bank and the government have fluctuated over recent years, and some Governors have given some Chancellors (especially Labour Chancellors) a hard time.

Concept

Efficiency

Some critics of government are concerned about, even obsessed with, efficiency. The Treasury historically has been more worried about economy. It is also as well to look for effectiveness.

Efficiency is best tied to its meaning in physics – the ratio of useful work done to energy expended. The Treasury's alleged zeal for saving on candle-ends is to do with economy – expending as little as possible, without regard for adequate office lighting or the costs of procedures for control. Effectiveness raises similar relevant questions: does what we are doing make a useful difference, achieve desired ends? Beyond that lie questions about the choice of ends, that is, policy and strategy. This does not mean that a concern for efficiency is not needed, but it has to be pursued in relation to economy and effectiveness. Often the big savings arise from getting objectives and strategies right. Pliatzky has pointed out that better policy advice and policy choices could have prevented the Falklands War, thus saving billions of pounds (and some lives too) – far beyond any savings arising from the various schemes for greater efficiency pressed on the Ministry of Defence. This is a reversal of the proverbial advice to look after the pennies, the pounds will look after themselves. Similarly the unsuccessful attempt to defend the pound sterling in September 1992 cost the country well over £1bn.

● CASE STUDY
Chancellor of the Exchequer disagrees with the Prime Minister

a) *Chancellor loses the argument but does not even threaten resignation.*
Based on K. O. Morgan, 1990, pp. 20–1
ROBOT. Early in 1952 Butler as Chancellor, together with three senior civil servants, proposed a scheme for 'floating' the pound (ending fixed exchange rates). The scheme was called ROBOT, after the names of the three officials. ROBOT was likely to raise food

prices and unemployment at home, and antagonise other countries, including the USA. The Prime Minister did not like the scheme and his personal adviser, Lord Cherwell was a fierce critic. The Foreign Secretary, Anthony Eden, was opposed, the more sharply because he had been abroad when the plan was first proposed. (This is a common managerial phenomena, known as 'Not Invented Here'). The government's economic advisers were also critical.

Given this line-up of forces, the discerning reader may guess that the Chancellor lost. But, despite his anxieties about the economic situation, he did not resign. The ROBOT episode illustrates the balance of forces that can make life difficult for a Chancellor; and the dominance of political considerations. Further, and significantly, the resolution of this argument marked the commitment of the Conservative Party to the socially oriented economic management of the so-called post-war consensus. Kenneth Morgan comments: 'It was an historic moment in post-war Conservative history. A party devoted to decontrol and encouraging the private market decided firmly in favour of control and management' (K. O. Morgan, 1990, p. 122).

Three years later, in 1955, under Anthony Eden as Prime Minister, Butler was again forced to retreat on some of his Budget proposals. In particular, Butler had wanted to abolish the bread subsidy. Other Ministers argued that the unions would press for higher wages, and that National Assistance rates would have to rise.

Ironically Butler was later blamed for not introducing a tough budget. Butler was shortly replaced by Macmillan as Chancellor, and, a few weeks later, Macmillan beat him to the office of Prime Minister.

This story shows well enough that the Minister who fails to resign when he loses his policies still carries the responsibility, and if necessary the blame, for the alternative policies forced on him – and may at the same time acquire a reputation for weakness and lack of principle. Butler enjoyed the consolation of staying in high office, losing another contest for the Prime Ministership in 1963, and serving 'loyally' under Douglas-Home until the election of 1964.

b) *Chancellor resigns 1958*
The Chancellor, Peter Thorneycroft, was

concerned about the economic and financial situation in the Summer of 1957, and began to argue for restriction of the money supply (what later came to be called monetarism) and reductions in public expenditure. The Prime Minister, Macmillan, and other Ministers were more concerned about the Government's social programme, and particularly about unemployment, on which Macmillan was especially sensitive. Butler, then Deputy Prime Minister, supported Macmillan. This looks like the classic scenario of post-war British governments, except that the Permanent Secretary to the Treasury did not support the Chancellor's line [Treasury officials were divided on the issue].

The argument went on through the Autumn – most big issues coming before Cabinet are settled over months and even years, not days or weeks. The crisis came early in the New Year when the public expenditure programme had to be agreed.

The word 'crisis' is for once quite apt for Cabinet even met on a Sunday. In the end the Cabinet would not accept the full programme of economies which the Chancellor called for. The Cabinet Conclusions [Minutes] significantly stated that the proposed abolition of the family allowance for the second child was 'contrary to the traditions of the Conservative Party' (quoted in K.O. Morgan, 1990, p. 174). Thus the post-war consensus was saved again. The Chancellor with his two Treasury Ministers, Enoch Powell and Nigel Birch, resigned. Macmillan dismissed the affair as 'a little local difficulty' over a matter of just £50m. Thorneycroft and Powell returned to office two years later, though their careers never flourished.

The episode illustrates again the classic conflict between Chancellor and Cabinet; the difficulties of finding the right moment to dramatise the issue; and the capacity of the Prime Minister to manage the issue within the Cabinet context. For the Treasury and the Civil Service the episode was demoralising, and demonstrated clearly that when Cabinet was fully engaged in the argument, Treasury and Civil Service were not dominant but simply players in the game, and the Treasury itself was divided.

c) Chancellor threatens resignation and wins
From D. Healey, 1989, pp. 430–1
[In October 1976 the Chancellor, Denis Healey, in the throes of the IMF crisis, asked the Prime Minister to approve the raising of interest rates by two per cent to what was then an unprecedented fifteen per cent. Callaghan refused.]

I said I wanted to take the matter to Cabinet that morning. 'All right,' he replied, 'but I will not support you.' Nevertheless I insisted on taking it to Cabinet. I knew I had no chance of persuading my colleagues without Jim's support. We both knew that I would have to resign if I was defeated.

I walked through to my office in No. 11 and put through a call to Edmund Dell, the only member of Cabinet on whom I could count. Before Edmund came on the line, the door opened and in came the Prime Minister's Private Secretary, Ken Stowe. 'Excuse me, Chancellor,' he said, 'the Prime Minister has asked me to tell you that he was only testing the strength of your conviction. Of course he will support you.' This was the only time I have ever used the threat of resignation to get my way, though I had made it clear to Jim that I would not remain Chancellor if he insisted on splitting the Treasury.

d) Chancellor resigns 1989
Nigel Lawson, Chancellor of the Exchequer in Margaret Thatcher's government since 1983, resigned in October 1989. Like many such events in politics this one had a general and long-running cause and a particular occasion. The cause was the classic one for resignations, a sharp deterioration in the relations of Minister and Prime Minister. Lawson objected to what he saw as Margaret Thatcher's mode of running Cabinet government. As he said in his resignation speech in the House of Commons, 1 November 1989:
'For our system of Cabinet government to work effectively, the Prime Minister of the day must appoint Ministers that he or she trusts and then leave them to carry out the policy. When differences of view emerge, as they are bound to do from time to time, they should be resolved privately and, wherever appropriate collectively.'

The occasion which precipitated the resignation was the growing public evidence that the Prime Minister was looking to her own Economic Adviser, Sir Alan Walters, for guidance on economic policy, and getting from him advice on exchange rates and, in particular, entry to the Exchange Rate Mechanism contrary to the views of the Chancellor.

Thus Lawson was able to base his resignation on what appeared to be a very reasonable constitutional position, in opposition to the familiar 'bossy-boots' Margaret Thatcher. In fact it was all more complicated than that. Like most Cabinet Ministers – and most administrators in other fields – Lawson believed most strongly in a collective approach when he was not getting his way in bilateral talks. Further it does seem the Prime Minister made concessions to him in the previous Summer, in what is known as the 'Madrid ambush' (see Chapter 6). This was a negotiation between Prime Minister, Chancellor and Foreign Secretary outside the Cabinet. Behind the push and pull of this power struggle lay the growing awareness on all sides that the economic miracle of the mid-80s, for which Lawson could claim some credit, was collapsing into recession, for which Lawson – who else? – had to take the blame. Hence Lawson may have been content to go at that time, and Margaret Thatcher may well have been happy to lose him.

There was no clear winner. A year later Lawson's support of Sir Geoffrey Howe in his resignation helped forward the move to replace Margaret Thatcher. Prime Minister and Chancellor need each other – but the Chancellor's need is normally the greater. As for the policy, Britain joined the ERM in 1990 but at some cost to the 'real' economy and at a parity which proved impossible to sustain – leading to withdrawal in 1992. ●

Ministers in their departments

Ministers and their functions

The government now contains well over one hundred posts. These may be divided by rank into:

- Prime Minister
- Cabinet Ministers, including some non-departmental Ministers (the Lord President, the Lord Privy Seal, the Chancellor of the Duchy of Lancaster); departmental Ministers (entitled Secretary of State except for the Minister of Agriculture, the Lord Chancellor and the Treasury Ministers)
- Other Ministers mostly entitled Minister or Minister of State, but including four Law Officers
- Junior Ministers, mostly entitled Under-Secretary of State
- Government Whips, holding appointments as Lords Commissioner of the Treasury or as Assistant Whips. The Chief Whip is Parliamentary Secretary to the Treasury. (For the duties of Whips see Chapter 12).

Most Ministers are members of the House of Commons, but a few (about fourteen) are in the Lords. This is a consequence of the statutory limitations on the number of Ministers in the Commons (Ministers of the Crown Act 1937, as amended). In any case a government needs some representatives in the Upper House.

With remarkably few exceptions, Ministers qualify for promotion by several years of service in Parliament, and Cabinet Ministers normally have behind them a period of ministerial service outside the Cabinet. Obviously this is less true when a party attains power after a long period in opposition, as in 1964. Parliament and junior offices thus serve as a school for the training and selection of senior Ministers.

The functions of most Ministers are both political and administrative. On the administrative side they have responsibility for departments of state, or else may engage in the overseeing or co-ordination of a sector of public activity. On the political side they contribute directly or indirectly to the formulation of policy at Cabinet level, and to the representation of the government in Parliament and outside. The constitutional conventions of collective and ministerial responsibility define and sustain the role of Ministers in the Cabinet and in the departments.

A Minister heading a department has certain essential functions. In his day-to-day work he must as a minimum:

- take responsibility for the work of his department by approving a mass of papers. This requires that the Minister 'goes through' the papers – a careful critical reading may be beyond his time and capacity
- secure the minimum needs of his department within the Cabinet system; in practice this means agreement to expenditure plans and parliamentary time and general approval for any proposed legislation
- speak for the department in the House of Commons, including Parliamentary Questions, and in the media.

A more positive and creative Minister will go beyond these minimal functions, into leadership and innovation, setting objectives and motivating others to pursue them.

A Minister is a temporary occupant of his post; the average tenure is less than two years. This has two obvious disadvantages. First the Minister cannot possibly master his job; second, he is encouraged to think in the short term, knowing he will not have to live with his mistakes, or enjoy the fruits of any success.

The Minister fits awkwardly into his department. He is a professional politician not a manager; his personal career drives have been political, focused on elections, parliament, party, constituency; his reputation will be made in the political arena, in the media and in Cabinet and ministerial meetings. He will need six months to find his way in the business of his department (to 'get his head above water', as Tony Crosland said), and he is likely to move on in less than two years.

The Minister's dual role is a necessary consequence of the system of responsible government, but it is not at all easy to carry out. The Minister is like, say, the chairman of a football club, experienced largely in board rooms, committees and business, who is suddenly asked to act like a manager, and direct the team from the 'dug-out'. The comparison is not quite exact because the Permanent Secretary is the player captain. Certainly a Minister has to get to grips with the work of a department, and so take part in management, with little experience and no training to help him. In practice the prudent Minister chooses carefully how best to distribute his time, energy and talent between the four major functions.

1 Policy – initiating, developing and implementing policy.
2 Management – in the sense of oversight of the effectiveness and efficiency of the operations of his department.
3 Representation and responsibility – in Parliament, media, party and with the public.
4 The integrative political function of relating the work and policy of the department to the overall political aspirations of government and party.

How to become a Minister: qualifications and routes of entry

Normally a politician must prove himself in Parliament before getting office, and prove himself again in office before entering the Cabinet. This is an important aspect of British government, for it means that there is a built-in system of training and selection, and continuous experience of colleagues working together. As a consequence, most politicians reaching high office are long-service professionals, who started their political careers at a comparatively early age and who have on average already passed about fourteen years in Parliament. However, the training is general and the Minister is usually given little time to work into a departmental post. They must be ready, like the advocates they often are, to mug up a new brief in a hurry.

Occasionally non-politicians are appointed to the Cabinet for special purposes without any previous parliamentary or ministerial experience. This is normal in USA but abnormal in Britain. Many of these appointments can be explained by the special circumstances of war, the weakness of the early Labour Party and Mr Churchill's penchant for wartime colleagues. But there are later examples of such unorthodox appointments notably Lord Young, at Employment then Trade and Industry, which demonstrate the continuing possibility. It may be argued that the experience of such Ministers outside the closed world of politics is valuable; but parliamentary inexperience is a handicap, and some appointments of this kind have not been successful.

The 'career profile' of a senior politician is likely to differ from that of the modern executive. The executive may expect a coherent pattern of development, promotion following experience and proving. The pattern of the political career is upset by periods in opposition, with only 'shadow' responsibilities, by occasional resignations or less obvious disagreements, but also by unexpected promotions. The political career is unpredictable, and quite often unrewarding, especially if a party spends long periods in opposition.

As in most careers 'getting on' requires more than talent and ambition. The best do not get to the top without luck and patronage – the favour and backing of influential persons. Few politicians attain high office without talents of some kind, but, as in other areas of professional competition, the top prizes are distributed without a fine discrimination. That at least is the opinion of the losers; and they are probably right in thinking that personnel selection is an inexact science. Yet in most governments the best five or six Ministers would make a mark in any public or managerial post.

Ministers fit awkwardly into departments of state for two good reasons; they are politicians making a political career, and they are politicians with a political not a managerial perspective. This raises problems of motivation and selection and training.

■ DOCUMENT 9.1
The professional perspective of a politician

From R. Rose, 1974, pp. 73–4
A Minister is a professional politician before he is a Secretary of State; the statement is accurate as a description of personal priorities as

well as of his career.... An MP will spend as much time thinking about who governs as about what government does.... From the perspective of an individual politician, what a ministry can do for his career is as important as what he can do for the ministry. Ministries work best when the skills and ambitions of Ministers run parallel with the requirements of the ministries that they head. The need to match individual and institutional goals is not unique to politics. ■

EXERCISE
The professional perspectives of a politician

9.1 Should a politician not have other motivations than those of a career?

An unavoidable weakness of the process of selecting Ministers is that the qualities required cannot be fully tested in political activity before getting the job. In this matter, politics is like other professional activities: you qualify for promoted job A by demonstrated capacity in the different and lesser post B. The dual demands on the Minister, as political head of a department of state, determine the qualities required of the Minister. However it may be argued that these demands are not at all of equal weight, and that the political role, of which the new Minister has most experience, is the one that matters.

■ DOCUMENT 9.2
The Minister as politician

From R. Rose, 1987, pp. 245, 273
A Minister is not a manager, involved in co-ordination for the sake of gains in administrative efficiency. A Minister is a politician, concerned with reconciling conflicts between competing political interests and objectives. Within a ministry, a Secretary of State is concerned with political not administrative co-ordination....

The first priority of democratic politics is consent. A Minister is an MP, not an MBA.... If the practice of government were solely a question of management efficiency, then elections would not be necessary, the civil service could be disbanded and public programmes provided by private sector firms on a fee-for-service basis! Giving direction to government is first of all about popular representation; managerial efficiency is a secondary concern that arises after

political decisions are made about the ends of government. ■

It is not easy for the Minister/politician to fit himself into the upper levels of a Department, where the main business is management. But it is possible, as the experience of many Ministers demonstrates. The demands of politics and departmental management are not totally incompatible, and the parliamentary and public roles may sometimes complement and enhance the administrative role.

The work of a Minister

The Minister day-to-day

■ DOCUMENT 9.3
The life of a Minister

a) A year in the life of a Minister
Mr Benn's diary for 1977 showed that he had as Cabinet Minister:
attended 42 Cabinet meetings, and 106 Cabinet committees; submitted 4 Cabinet papers and 45 Cabinet committee papers; receiving 1750 Cabinet papers himself; as Secretary of State for Energy been concerned with 3 bills, 59 statutory instruments, 33 explanatory memorandums, made 8 speeches, 5 statements, answered 51 oral Questions, held 154 meetings with non-governmental groups.

In addition he carried out the normal work of an MP in the House of Commons; the PLP, the NEC and the constituency; made 19 visits abroad; and took part in 140 broadcast interviews.

b) A Cabinet Minister's working week
Adapted from B. Headey, 1974, p. 36

	Min	Max
Cabinet and Cabinet Committees	7	11
Informal ministerial meetings	1	2
Office meetings	5	10
Parliament	10	15
Party meetings	1	2
Interviews (deputations, MPs, media)	8	10
Formal receptions etc	6	8
Visits, inspections	10	12
Constituency responsibilities	2	3
Papers	10	20
Total	60	93
Weekend (mainly papers)	6	15 ■

A Minister's day is likely to be long and heavy – possibly too heavy for the efficient conduct of an office over a long term. A typical day might include reading, face-to-face briefing and consultation with officials, encounters with delegations of various interests, and formal and informal meetings with colleagues and backbenchers. Eating and drinking and travelling are incorporated into the day's activities. In a tightly 'time-managed' day a Minister has few moments to himself. (But only an American President is recorded as conducting official discussions while on the lavatory.)

This may give an impression of a more rationally planned day than a Minister can expect. It may be, as one Minister – and former businessman – Ernest Marples, complained, 'a dog's life. Policy and thought inevitably come last on his agenda' (*Sunday Telegraph*, 22 November 1964). Nor can a Minister's life be confined to Westminster and Whitehall (or wherever his ministry is situated). An energetic Minister will want to investigate some of his department's problems on the spot, to hear local opinion at first hand, generally to keep in touch, to 'keep an ear to the ground'. But outside the office, and often inside too, the Minister may spend too much time talking, not enough reading and thinking.

■ DOCUMENT 9.4
Ministers on their rounds

a) Neville Chamberlain in the North
From K. Feiling, Macmillan, 1947, p. 135
In 1927 his Lancashire and Yorkshire tour took in 30 institutions, 15 housing estates, and 6 slum areas. As of old he made a brief, legible, meticulous commentary. This town clerk is 'deservedly popular, but too old', this chairman 'old, deaf and feeble', this medical officer 'kind-hearted and sympathetic', 'an excellent matron here'. At Bradford 'the worst slums I have come across yet', at Halifax 'rich and liberal citizens', at Liverpool 'the usual tale of nothing done by the Landlord'.

b) Crossman in East Anglia, February 1969
From R. Crossman, 1977, pp. 389–90
Crossman's activities included visiting social security offices; a press conference at a hospital and lunch; visiting flats for the elderly; seminar on geriatric services at another hospital; dinner at a holiday camp with 590 Labour Party members. To bed at 1.30 am, having started out at 9 am, after an all-night sitting. ■

EXERCISE
Ministers and their rounds

9.2 Is activity of this kind wasteful of a Minister's time and energy?

There is general agreement by Ministers and former Ministers that the work of a Minister is very heavy. For all Ministers work eats up time, with weekend reading as well as constituency engagements added to long days during the week – extended by the late working hours of Parliament and the need to read papers. The amount of reading is formidable. William Whitelaw claimed that as Home Secretary he needed three or even four hours each night between 10.30 pm and 8 am to get through his reading. As he also needed eight hours sleep, and never worked after midnight he suffered from early rising and deprivation of sleep!

The weekends offer little relief – James Callaghan refers to ten to twelve hours of weekend reading. Even with speed-reading and skip-reading the Minister must often feel like an examination candidate unsure of the facts and hoping some questions do not come up. But at least the Minister has a team of officials to read and summarise for him.

Most Ministers live busy and highly programmed lives, the diary filled to the minute by assiduous secretaries. There is little time for family, or relaxation. The job provides its own esoteric pleasures, gossip, food and drink, comradeship, enmities, occasional triumphs. Most Ministers seem to enjoy it. Barbara Castle in her Diaries conveys the pressures and tensions of ministerial life, but also the exhilaration. Fifteen hundred pages of diary are clearly not the work of a desperate and unhappy politician. Denis Healey recalled the long hours and hard work, but found it exhilarating, 'like a man who, after driving his Jaguar for hours behind a tractor on narrow country lanes, finally reaches the motor way....' (1989, p. 253).

The actual burden of ministerial life arises not from long hours (though these do not help) but from the stress of making and defending difficult decisions or non-decisions, carrying grave consequences. Many Ministers enjoy long periods of quiet, interrupted by occasional periods of pressure or moments of crisis. The Home Secretary is especially likely to sudden squalls. For Chancellors there is little relief. The nature of different departments is illustrated in the Case Studies in Chapter 7.

The Minister's life is made harder by his isolation. This is especially true for Ministers not in the

Cabinet. They are cut off from the agreeable ca-maraderie of the House of Commons, and the stimulating irresponsibility of party warfare; but they are still excluded from the ego-enhancing Cabinet club. The isolation is diminished by the support of the Department and in particular the service of the Private Secretary and the Permanent Secretary. Private Secretaries earn high marks from Ministers: the support service is clearly first class. They act as the Minister's eyes and ears, and as gatekeepers. Their qualities include, wrote Denis Healey, 'a first-class brain...inexhaustible tact, demonic energy and an understanding wife – for he must arrive at the office an hour before his Minister and leave an hour later' (D. Healey, 1989, p. 267). In this and other ways the minister enjoys a total, high-quality support service, ranging from lucid policy advice to a chauffeured limousine.

Relations with Permanent Secretaries are less cosy and supportive, for the functions of the official Head of the Department go beyond merely supporting his Minister. The relationship was noted in Chapter 7 and is further explored below and in Chapter 10. The potential for difficulty is evident in the diaries of Benn, Castle and Crossman, though Castle and Crossman at least learned to build a constructive and mutually respectful relationship. Healey pays tribute to the sheer technical capacity of senior civil servants, and Heseltine expressed admiration and gratitude for the ability and readiness of a Permanent Secretary to come to the aid of a Minister who could see no way through his problems. Thus a Permanent Secretary is part of a Minister's support team.

A Minister can to some extent isolate himself from his department. Yet the Minister and the department are bound together, capable of doing each other some harm and a little good, until parted by resignation, or re-shuffle. Since Ministers measure their service in departments by months rather than years their marriage to the department is not 'till death us do part'.

The Minister and his department

Most senior Ministers are at the head of major departments of state. This imposes on them a dual responsibility – as politicians with duties in or towards Cabinet and Parliament, and as administrators directing a major organisation. Thus they direct, represent and answer for their departments, but also manage them or assist in their management. The initiation of policy is involved in both

roles, but for many Ministers this will not be a frequent or continuing activity. A Minister comes to his department as a trained and experienced politician, but with only his native abilities as an administrator and often with no special knowledge or experience of the work of the ministry. More than nine-tenths of the work of his department will not come before him. In two years he may move elsewhere. Nevertheless, the temporary, part-time, 'amateur' politician is responsible for his department.

This sets an obvious problem. Most departments are large. Altogether there are about 500 000 non-industrial civil servants of whom about 2000 may be regarded as senior policy-makers. So, on a rough average, a score of senior Ministers are each responsible for 25 000 staff, 100 of them senior. A Minister can hardly know what most of them are doing; but he is nevertheless 'responsible' for them. Even when civil servants move into 'agencies' (see Chapter 10) the Minister retains formal responsibility.

This arrangement is central to the British system of responsible government; for it provides a line of responsibility from the humblest section of the administration to Parliament. The line may be tenuous at times, but the principle of its existence is important. This political answerability is most significant at the higher levels, and there it depends for its effective working on the maintenance of a special kind of relationship between the Minister and the senior administrators of his department.

The relationship is not one of master and servant. Rather it is based on the administrators' recognition of the political concerns and the final responsibility of the Minister: and on the Minister's respect for the information, advice and professional competence of his administrators. For the senior administrator is not concerned simply with the execution of policy but also with its formulation. This is the classic understanding of responsible government in Britain as it applies to the relationship of Ministers and civil servants. It is plainly somewhat idealised, and sceptics regard it as a myth.

Clearly, there will be many variations of this relationship, depending on the capacities and temperament of the Minister, and the nature of the department's work. The administrators, too, though carefully trained, will not have achieved complete homogeneity, and will also vary in talent and temperament. Yet an effective relationship is achieved more often than not. A distinguished wartime temporary civil servant, Sir

Oliver Franks (Lord Franks), has testified to a paradox. Ministers could keep themselves informed and take decisions on a very limited number of topics: yet 'the effect of a change of Minister on headquarters was considerable' (O. Franks, 1947, p. 13).

On the other hand, Aubrey Jones, with experience as Minister, civil servant and industrialist, has written more sceptically: 'I had been a Minister; but what was a Minister? The occupant for a couple of years of a Department of State, numerous in its layers of staff, tenacious in its traditions, and massive to move. One scarcely in fact moved it...' (A. Jones, 1973, p. X). Others have testified to the capacity of the civil service both to resist change, and, if they were so minded, to organise change.

Of course there is not a common conspiracy of civil servants against Minister, or even a conspiracy at all – but rather a various collection of relationships, centred on policy and power. Here are two illustrations of the relationship of Minister and civil servant; see also Chapter 7, Document 7.3 and Chapter 10, especially the Case Study. Alan Clark (Diaries, 1993) gives an entertaining account of sparring between a new junior minister and his officials – see entries for June–December 1983.

■ DOCUMENT 9.5
A Minister and his department

a) *Hugh Dalton imposes himself on his department*
From Hugh Dalton, *1962, pp. 15–16 and 1957, p. 435*
A Minister has many necessary relationships which can be managed well or ill. First, his relations with his officials.... A Minister should show his officials at the start that he has a mind of his own. Perhaps by refusing some early piece of official advice...[or] by making a fuss about the secretarial arrangements of the Minister and his Chief Adviser...or in sharply reversing previous policy.... But, having established an independent personality, the Minister should try to get all the help he can – and it will generally be a lot – out of his officials. There is great knowledge, naturally enough, and also great wisdom, not quite so naturally, in the Civil Service. But not in every Civil Servant equally.

[Dalton, admitting that officials could be helpful in putting the Minister's own ideas into good shape, warned that officials might point out

'formidable difficulties'. The Minister should] face these in a calm and honest mood, but may sometimes usefully invite those who have indicated the difficulties to indicate also how these can best be surmounted, or evaded. For it would be going too far to deny that the Civil Service contains a few congenital snag-hunters.

b) *Ernest Bevin and his officials*
From Lord Strang, *1956, pp. 292–3*
[Ernest Bevin, Foreign Secretary in the postwar Labour Government, was a man of powerful but untrained mind. He demonstrated that a Minister does not need a first class degree, or even good A-levels. In expertise in the use of words, in diplomatic finesse, his officials were his superiors. But he had the force of mind and personality, they had the skill, training and willingness to efface themselves. The result, suggested in this extract from Lord Strang's book was a remarkable combination which, in Strang's view, left the final decision to Bevin. Strang was Permanent Secretary of the Foreign Office at the time.]

He would call his advisers together and go round the map with them and look at the question at issue from the point of view of each of the other governments concerned. Again and again he would perceive connections which none of us had thought of; and if, as was sometimes the case, they were invalid, he would expect us to tell him so. In his exploratory peregrinations he had no ordered method of procedure. He might start from some remote point, wandering round and round the subject moving gradually nearer the centre, making up his mind as he went along, opening up his perplexities to us. These were the fruit of cogitations in the watches of the night or of perusal of the papers in the early hours of the morning. Before going in to him, we would ask ourselves: 'Where is he going to start from this time?' But wherever the starting point might be, however unrelated it might seem, we learnt that it could not be lightly disregarded. As his mind cleared, he might put up some unacceptable solution and wait for us to give him our reasons for knocking it down. When these preliminaries had been exhausted, he would gather himself together and come to his conclusion. It might not always be very accurately formulated, but we knew his mind well enough to be able to inter-pret it and to translate it into executive terms. Some Secretaries of State stimulate; others devitalise; Bevin nourished. ■

EXERCISE
Ministers and departments

9.3 In different ways these extracts draw attention to the sheer difficulty of being a good Minister heading a department of government. What briefly are the difficulties?

Working relations

In the pursuit of his political and departmental functions a Minister needs to build relations with his colleagues in government and Parliament, and with the world outside.

Prime Minister and Cabinet

This crucial relationship has been discussed above. The Minister works 'for' the Prime Minister just as other people work for a boss, employer or manager. In government the relationship is normally more collegial than the boss-worker relationship – say rather like a professional partnership, though the Prime Minister's power to dismiss goes beyond the gentlemanly terms of a partnership contract.

Further, the Minister shares in the political objectives of the government, and the general aspirations of the party. There is an implied contract. The Minister advances the general purposes of the government (and avoids departmental disasters). In return the Prime Minister supports the Minister in advancing his personal and departmental objectives. However, these purposes are not identical. The Minister is not happy to see his departmental interests go down in Cabinet; the Prime Minister may withdraw his full support if the Minister runs into trouble. The collectivity of the Cabinet is not solid; and as in most such organisations there is competition to take credit for success and avoid responsibility for failure – to win the crown or carry the can. Ministers should not be surprised that in a system managed by the Prime Minister he finds others to carry the can.

The relations of the Minister to Prime Minister and Cabinet are governed by the convention of collective responsibility. This was discussed above (Chapter 5) in considering the working of the Cabinet. In relation to the working of a department, the convention gives the whole Cabinet some ill-defined responsibility for the major policies of each department. This encourages the Cabinet to take an interest in the departments – or, to put it more strongly, this forces the Cabinet to exercise a general oversight of the departments. A Cabinet will not wish to remain ignorant of and unconcerned with policies for which it may be answerable.

In practice, however, this effect is not always very strong. The convention of individual Ministerial responsibility lays on the departmental Minister the formal responsibility for his department. The Cabinet's function is to give or withhold collective political cover. Hence the Cabinet, or rather the Prime Minister leading the Cabinet, has a choice: to apply its majority in defence of an erring Minister or else dissociate the Cabinet, either by removing the Minister; or, more often, by keeping heads down while the responsible Minister faces critics in Parliament or in the media.

The convention of collective responsibility has another important effect for all Ministers. If a Minister is overruled by the Cabinet, he should not speak outside the Cabinet for the policies he prefers. He must submit – or resign. Normally he submits; occasionally he threatens to resign; more rarely he carries through his resignation. Since 1945 less than a score of Ministers have resigned in this way – the figure for Cabinet Ministers only is 8 or 9. But Ministers may be moved or dismissed by the Prime Minister, as an alternative to a volunteered resignation, but for the same reason, a lack of fit between the Minister and the Prime Minister/Cabinet. Usually a move or dismissal follows some time after a particular occasion of disagreement.

Examples of resignation were given in Chapter 5. Such resignations often reflect a general discontent with the direction of government policy as a whole, as well as specific dissatisfaction with the policies as they affect the Minister's department. Though resignations are rare, it is evident that able and ambitious Ministers, in vulnerable public posts, and open to instant dismissal, do see resignation as an available last resort. This is particularly so for Conservative Ministers, who can earn far more outside than in office. (A Labour Minister may see no other way of paying the mortgage.)

A resignation does disturb a government, and may cumulatively damage it, as happened to Margaret Thatcher. Hence Ministers may more frequently threaten to resign, using the threat in its veiled form ('I might have to consider my position'). The threat of resignation, rather than resignation itself, is a regular element in the relations of Ministers and the Prime Minister. Document 9.6 gives illustrations of the threat in play.

■ DOCUMENT 9.6
The threat of resignation

a) Francis Pym, 1980
Pym, as Minister of Defence, threatened resignation in November, 1980, in protest at demands for spending cuts. The Chiefs of Staff exercised their right to a personal hearing from the Prime Minister, and in the end Defence 'got very nearly all the money it was asking for.' For once, Margaret Thatcher 'had, to her great discomfort, been worsted by the Defence Secretary' (Young, 1989, p. 210). Pym was, and remained, a leading 'wet' Tory, believing that the Government's monetarist strategy was mistaken, in face of a world recession, and thought the Prime Minister 'a walking disaster' (see Pym, 1984, pp. 24–5).

Pym won his point at the time, but he was moved sideways to be Leader of the House, while Margaret Thatcher promoted enthusiasts for monetarism. Pym was later moved to the Foreign Office (after Carrington's resignation at the onset of the Falklands War) but was dismissed after the 1983 election. So it may be thought that Pym's successful threat of resignation led shortly to dismissal and failure.

b) Macmillan as Chancellor, 1956, urges stringent measures
Summarised from Macmillan, 1971, pp. 10–44
Macmillan was appointed Chancellor of the Exchequer in December 1955. He inherited an inflationary crisis which conventional measures had failed to remedy. Macmillan felt that more drastic measures were immediately necessary including intensifying the credit squeeze, cuts in defence spending and abolishing government subsidies on bread and milk. The Cabinet (20 January 1956) agreed in principle but many wanted to postpone action until the Budget. The dissenters included the Prime Minister, Eden, who was particularly critical of the proposed abolition of bread and milk subsidies, especially since there were important wage negotiations coming to a head. The subsidies thus became the central issue, and discussion continued into February. Since the Cabinet was hesitant Macmillan decided to clinch the matter in a letter to Eden. Part of this read:

'*I must tell you frankly that, if I cannot have your confidence and that of your colleagues in handling this problem which you have entrusted to me in the way that seems to me essential, I should not feel justified in proposing measures which seem insufficient for the purpose. Nor should I be any good to you and the Cabinet in such circumstances* ' (quoted p. 13).

Discussions continued. Macmillan was trying to humble the Prime Minister but Eden did not deal directly with him, only through other Cabinet members. A compromise was finally suggested (14 February 1956) in the face of Macmillan's apparent determination to resign. This proposed some reduction of subsidies immediately and abolition later. Macmillan discussed his position with the Governor of the Bank of England: 'Which would do most harm? My resignation or a compromise? The Governor had no doubt. My resignation would cause a panic in the City.' (quoted p. 14, from the entry to Macmillan's private journal made 14 February 1956). Consequently Macmillan agreed to compromise and the anti-inflationary measures, rather less than Macmillan had wanted, were agreed by the whole Cabinet on 15 February 1956. The subsequent budget was notable mainly for the introduction of 'Premium Bonds', justified as encouraging savings, but denounced as state-sponsored gambling. ■

EXERCISES
The political effect of resignation

9.4 Why do you think Pym threatened resignation on this issue, but stayed in the government nearly three years despite major disagreements on economic policy?
9.5 Why did Margaret Thatcher give way to Pym on this occasion?
9.6 Was Macmillan bluffing?
9.7 Crossman commented on the 'fatality' of resignations. Perhaps he meant 'futility'. Is either of these words appropriate?
9.8 Resignations by Cabinet Ministers on policy grounds are not frequent. Why is this so?

Ministers and the Treasury
The Minister recognises, as Heclo and Wildavsky say, that 'the way to gain respect and advance himself is to enhance some of the great purposes of his department. And great purposes cost money' (1974, p. 135). For money the Minister needs the support of the Chancellor – and the Prime Minister. The Minister's relationship with the Chancellor and the Treasury have been explored above. It is a crucial relationship. In most policy areas the Minister can do only what the Treasury will provide the funds to do. To the

Minister it seems all Chancellors speak to the theme of an early Labour Chancellor, Snowden: 'It may shorten discussion on the matter, Mr Prime Minister, if I say there is no money for it'. To the Chancellor, it seems he has few allies in a never-ending struggle with eight or nine extravagant spending Ministers, determined to build their reputations on the Chancellor's weakness.

■ DOCUMENT 9.7
Ministers and the Treasury
From an address by Sir Edward Boyle, Bart, MP, at a conference on 'Who are the policy makers?', reported in Public Administration, Autumn 1965, p. 252
When performing this vital function [of getting money out of the Treasury] Ministers have really got to know their stuff and have got to be able to argue in detail. The Minister must in my view do that very important homework himself. He must know and be ready to refute the sort of objections that the Treasury are likely to raise. I think, with great respect, that Ministers (particularly ex-Ministers) are far too inclined to abuse the Treasury. The truth is that Ministers – if they are to do their stuff – must know how to argue with the Treasury and must know their facts well enough to be able at any rate to get a reasonable settlement. ■

A Minister should not fight for his department without regard for government policy as a whole: but a Minister who does not fight at all will often unduly weaken his department. Sir Edward Boyle notes the comment of a colleague who divided Ministers into 'those who habitually get their way and those who do not... Ministers are strikingly different in their success at getting things through'.

This view of the spending Minister – the 'macho' view – is very characteristic of one version of British government, and seems to be part of the culture of adversary politics. Clearly the control of public expenditure requires that Ministers sometimes recognise the necessity to reduce their own department's spending. In the 1980s a few such Ministers appeared on the scene, ready to sacrifice the work of their departments for the greater good. They soon discovered that this was a hard road for the politically ambitious.

All this may reinforce the impression that Chancellors are always iron men disapproving in principle of all expenditure. This is not always the case, of course; but a Chancellor must tread warily. Ministers will not be pleased with a Chancellor who seems to favour expenditure by one department but not another.

Ministers and Parliament
In a Parliament normally dominated by the governing party the Minister can be certain that his major policies and legislation will be approved. This is a substantial and effective policy-making power, envied by Ministers in countries such as USA where legislative majorities are not easily available to the executive. Nevertheless the individual Minister in Britain must promote and protect his standing with his own side in the House of Commons. He must show himself to be master of his brief, put down the Opposition, perform effectively on television and avoid the 'banana-skins' which make him and the government look foolish. Failure in these matters leads to a slump in standing, trouble on the detail of legislation, awkward Parliamentary Questions – and damage to the Minister's career prospects.

Headey quotes a Conservative Minister saying: 'It is essential to remain a House of Commons man. Remember you belong to this place. You've got to have a nose for matters that arouse Parliament's attention' (p. 67). Some Ministers might not accept the implication of ancient mystique, but they must still take the House seriously, and keep in touch with opinion on their own back benches. In this they are assisted by a Parliamentary Private Secretary, the unpaid and junior member of the Ministerial team, and the 'eyes and ears' of the Minister in Westminster, like the official Principal Private Secretary in Whitehall.

Speaking in Parliament is of 'vital importance to a Minister', according to Roy Jenkins, a good but nervous performer. Barbara Castle argued that 'a superb parliamentary manner will get anyone, from Left or Right, out of trouble': she instanced Callaghan, Benn, Crosland and Foot (1980, p. 486, 5 August 1975).

Parliamentary Questions and Select Committees provide further tests and opportunities for the Minister. Neither is too difficult for a well-briefed Minister, as long as he can think quickly and speak fluently on his feet (or his seat). These are the basic skills of the politician, who unlike many other executives must be a professional public performer (see also Chapters 12 and 13 on Parliament).

Ministers and interest groups
Dealing with interest groups is at the sharp end of a Minister's job. This is where governing by con-

sent becomes a political imperative. The two major parties serve broad interests (trade unions, in the case of Labour; finance and business, for the Conservatives). But many more specific interests lurk in these clusters, and a Minister may easily be ambushed or bounced by some vocal and well-supported cause, demonstrating its desperate needs on prime-time television.

In handling the pressures of the interest groups as with much else of a department's business, the Minister can depend on his officials to make a deal which satisfies the lobbyists and is just about acceptable to the department. The Minister intervenes at his peril. For example, Bruce-Gardyne moved to scrap a scheme to enable horse-traders to escape VAT. But this had been approved already by his predecessor, and with the support of a senior Tory backbencher. Bruce-Gardyne reported: '... I was accosted by one of my senior Tory colleagues in the corridors of Westminster. "I hear", he told me in a voice full of menace, "that you're being bloody minded about our horse-trading scheme. Well forget it. It was all fixed up with your predecessor, and I can assure you that if you muck it around we'll make your life a misery." I had second thoughts' (J. Bruce-Gardyne, 1986, pp. 152–3).

This is an example of a comparatively marginal interest group to which victory is conceded for the sake of a quiet life. But a Minister is likely to face more serious problems with a major group, such as a Minister of Health with the British Medical Association. Here is a group of high prestige, well able to mount an expensive publicity campaign and to mobilise patients' opinion throughout the land. The Minister cannot run the Health Service without their co-operation, but he may well judge that the price of co-operation is too high. Barbara Castle's dealings with hospital consultants, and Kenneth Clarke's with the BMA, show the Minister in a duly elected government negotiating desperately with a group carrying an effective power of veto. This is the brutal reality of pluralist politics.

The Minister is in a stronger position when there are competing interest groups, and no strong party alignment. For example, the plan (1985) to impose a levy on blank recording tape was promoted by the record companies, and opposed by the manufacturers of recording equipment, disguised as the Home Taping Rights Campaign. Ministers came and went, each reversing his predecessor's stand, and in the end the equipment manufacturers (mainly Japanese)

carried the day.

A Minister's struggle with an 'insider' group is illustrated in the case at the end of the chapter (David Owen). Interest groups are fully explored in Chapter 21.

Ministerial responsibility

Ministerial responsibility is the convention that each Minister is answerable for all the actions of his ministry whether done with his consent or knowledge or not. All is done in his name: the officials begin their letters, 'The Minister directs me to say....' In Parliament the Minister must speak for his department, giving information and rebutting (or occasionally accepting) criticism. This is a fundamental element in the political system, securing answerability (of Ministers, not officials) to Parliament. Answerability here means at the minimum acceptance of responsibility; beyond that, an obligation to explain; and further, to offer remedy, disciplining wrong-doers and/or putting things right. In the strongest form of the convention it is indicated that a Minister whose department commits a grave mistake is obliged to resign his office. In practice, this form of the convention does not operate consistently or often, and there is some dispute about its actual status.

The convention of individual ministerial responsibility, like that of collective responsibility, is regarded as an important and operative part of the British constitution. Both are conventions, that is non-statutory rules, but both operate in a manner largely determined by the underlying political condition of modern British government: the achievement of invulnerable government through Cabinet and party solidarity. Cabinets remain united, as far as possible, in order to present a bold front to Parliament and public. Just as Ministers do not resign on policy grounds every time they are in serious disagreement, so Ministers do not resign simply because an official in their department has blundered.

This somewhat indeterminate position has come about because the conventions have no definable meaning. 'Responsibility' is a notoriously evasive word, though its political usage would suggest it must be held to imply answerability or accountability. There is another source of confusion in the margin between ministerial and collective responsibility, that is, between the work of a department and the policy of the government. Nor have the conventions any strong sanction.

They operate only if the Prime Minister and the majority party can force a resignation. Since a resignation is a breach of solidarity, neither convention often operates in that way. The dissident Cabinet Minister is persuaded or persuades himself not to resign, and similarly the departmental Minister does not resign. Instead he accepts responsibility either by defending his department in the House or by criticising it, or just 'accepting responsibility'.

In the last century or so, only twenty Ministers have resigned in response to the convention of ministerial responsibility. Now, it seems likely that departments have made major blunders rather more often than once every five years. Where such blunders have become public, either the minister has 'accounted' to Parliament, defending himself, by admitting or not admitting error, but not resigning; or the Minister himself has blamed his officials and promised disciplinary measures; or the Minister has been quietly removed in a reshuffle. In the comparatively few cases where Ministers have resigned, this appears to be due to additional factors: either the Prime Minister or the party or both wanting the Minister to go, or the Minister himself feeling he should go; media and popular agitation may play a part. In all these cases considerations of constitutional propriety are never entirely absent, but political motivations are powerful, and constitutional considerations are marginal in the determination of the resignation.

The resignation of Sir Thomas Dugdale in 1954 is the classic example of the convention in operation, in a case in which errors were arguably (but not certainly) more departmental than ministerial. More recent history provides many examples of the non-operation of the convention. Lord Carrington's departure from the Foreign Office in April 1982 was an isolated example of the classic convention (see below).

The question of ministerial resignation is important but has confused the understanding of the convention. Resignation is the ultimate but rare consequence of the convention. It is not quite as rare as it seems since Ministers may be moved in a later re-shuffle, rather than resigning at the time. But, still, few people accept that the resignation of the Minister is a proper response to departmental fault or error, especially when this is plainly not a direct consequence of the Minister's actions. Rather, the convention confirms that Ministers account to Parliament for the work of the departments. In practice this means:

- that Ministers answer in public and civil servants remain anonymous. In fact the names of some senior civil servants are now well-known, along with some information (or guesses) about their particular policy approaches. Further, civil servants appear before Select Committees; what they say is reported and they may even be televised
- that Ministers account in a form ranging from a brief acceptance of responsibility to explanation to amendment (undertaking to put matters right, discipline offending officials and do better in future). The ultimate point in this scale of accountability is resignation – the sacrificial or 'heads must roll' form of the convention.

'Classic' resignations – the convention applied

1 *Departmental or ministerial fault: Sir Thomas Dugdale, 1954*

Sir Thomas Dugdale was Minister of Agriculture in the Conservative government. During his tenure of the office, some land on Crichel Down, Dorset, belonging to the Ministry, was sold to the Crown Land Commissioners. The land had a history: it had been compulsorily acquired in 1937 for military purposes and taken over by the Ministry of Agriculture in 1950. The (independent) Land Commission had advised that it should be equipped and sold for farming as a single holding. Representatives of the former owners then asked for the land to be sold back to them, to form part of existing farms. This request was refused, and after much delay and confusion, the land was sold to the Crown Land Commissioners who were to rehabilitate and re-equip the land as farming land and then lease it. Other applicants were not given an opportunity to bid for the land. The Minister was himself aware of the problem of the disposal of the Crichel Down land, but was not fully informed of the matter early in the dispute. The decision to sell was taken on the grounds of the national need for efficient farming, but it looked as if the claims of the former owners were not considered with due care. The problem was not a simple one of black-and-white; tyrannical bureaucrat against long-suffering landowner. Much depends on what rights a landowner should have in these matters, and this is a matter of opinion, not law.

In the event, the Minister resigned, saying:

'I, as Minister, must accept full responsibility to Parliament for any mistakes and inefficiency of officials in my Department. Any departure from this

long-established rule is bound to bring the Civil Service right into the political arena.... [But] it should not be thought that this means I am bound to endorse the actions of officials, whatever they may be, or that I or any other Minister must shield those who make errors against proper consequences.' (H. C. Deb., Vol. 530, 20 July 1954, col. 1186).

The Home Secretary, Sir David Maxwell Fyfe, added to the theory of convention in his speech, which was based on a draft prepared by the Permanent Under Secretary at the Treasury (Sir Edward Bridges):

'We all recognise that we must have that principle [ministerial responsibility] in existence and that Ministers must be responsible for the acts of civil servants. Without it, it would be impossible to have a Civil Service which would be able to serve Ministries and Governments of different political faiths and persuasions with the same zeal and honesty which we have always found.... There has been criticism that the principle operates so as to oblige Ministers to extend total protection to their officials [who in consequence] cannot be called to account and are effectively responsible to no one. That is a position which I believe is quite wrong...[the civil servant] can be dismissed at any time by the Minister; and that power is none the less real because it is seldom used (the only exception being a small number of senior posts)' (H. C. Deb., Vol. 530, 20 July 1954, cols. 1285–7).

Sir David then laid down categories of error which amount to two:
a) The Minister must protect and defend a civil servant acting on his explicit order or in accordance with the policy laid down by the Minister.
b) In matters of which the Minister has no prior knowledge the Minister 'accepts responsibility', tells Parliament and 'renders an account of his stewardship', and disciplines officials as appropriate.

Sir Thomas Dugdale's resignation has often been held up as the classic (if not only) example of the strong form of the convention – resignation for other people's faults. In fact its motivation was probably more complex than this. At the beginning of the affair Dugdale was not in office, but it seems, in the later stages of a prolonged affair, he had gone along with his officials' decisions on the Crichel Down land, and felt he shared in the responsibility. At the same time and paradoxically, he disapproved in general of the damage done to individual property rights (a position he had

taken in opposition), and he recognised and fully sympathised with Conservative Party reaction to what was seen as high handed bureaucracy infringing individual freedom.

Thus Dugdale 'stood by' his department's decision, and so did not admit error; but he resigned because Conservative Members of Parliament believed the decision to be wrong. Dugdale acted out of loyalty to his departmental and ministerial colleagues and his party, and these conflicting loyalties compelled him to observe the convention of ministerial responsibility.

Altogether Sir Thomas Dugdale seems to have been an honourable man, and a Conservative politician, caught in a situation which had both constitutional and political implications. His resignation, whatever he intended, remains an isolated affirmation that the convention of ministerial responsibility exists and is enforced by political circumstance and constitutional morality, and may extend to the 'sacrificial' resignation of a responsible but personally innocent Minister. There is confirmation of this position in the evident fact that Ministers defending errors who do not resign go to some lengths to explain why they should not resign. The convention is thus honoured in the carefully explained away breach.

The Crichel Down affair is significant in another way. During the inquiry, civil servants had to give evidence and submit to questioning in public. This was one of the first occasions when they have been submitted to public scrutiny – an ironical consequence of a convention designed to protect them.

2 *Ministerial fault: Lord Carrington and the invasion of the Falkland Islands, 1982*

Lord Carrington and two of his colleagues in the Foreign Office resigned in April 1982 after Argentine forces had invaded and taken possession of the Falkland Islands. The invasion was a serious defeat for British foreign policy: it should have been prevented. Lord Carrington felt that someone should take responsibility in face of a national outcry over a national humiliation. He added that it seemed important to end recrimination before the onset of war (BBC radio interview, 18 January 1983).

Ironically, the Foreign Office had argued for some years that Britain's claim to sovereignty over the Falklands was open to doubt historically, and difficult to sustain in practice. The Foreign Office had pursued negotiations with Argentina (not very energetically it is true) but wished to preserve a

British military presence (in the shape of HMS Endurance) until negotiations were concluded. Lord Carrington was overruled on this in the Cabinet's Overseas and Defence Committee, where he was opposed by the Prime Minister in the chair, and the Defence Minister. The Endurance was withdrawn and the invasion followed. So Lord Carrington resigned not because he was wrong, but because a resignation was needed. It was a sacrificial resignation, offering a scapegoat to the public. This fitted Carrington's history. He was a junior Minister under Sir Thomas Dugdale in 1954, and had offered his resignation then.

The Committee set up by the government to inquire into the Falklands War set out the diplomatic errors, but still concluded that no-one was to blame – the invasion would have happened anyway. This was a curious position to take: if policy made no difference then there can be no responsibility, but no reason to have a policy at all.

Carrington's resignation was a political as much as a constitutional event; it drew 'responsibility' and criticism away from the Cabinet as a whole, the Prime Minister and the Defence Secretary. It fitted the political strategy of damage-limitation, the underlying convention of minimum vulnerability. One other element in the resignation was probably Lord Carrington's unease in the Thatcher Cabinet. Nevertheless, there was an element of constitutional morality in the resignation: without the convention Carrington might well have remained in office.

Non-resignations and non-accountability

Non-resignations are more frequent than resignations for reasons which by now are evident (the Minister does not admit culpable error, and does not want to lose his job; the government does not want to lose a Minister, and so admit error). There are several alternatives to resignation:

- deny error
- admit error on the part of officials, not the Minister, and promise to 'take appropriate action'
- while not denying error (which is not the same as admitting it) the Prime Minister moves the Minister by re-shuffle or dismissal – normally a Minister's stay in one department is so short that it is unlikely that he will still be there when his mistakes are revealed
- while not denying error, say as little as possible and hope the problem will go away.

Even resignation does not lead to full accountability, for Ministers who have resigned may refuse to account to the House of Commons.

Here are examples of the evasion of responsibility in these ways. Denying error is a daily occurrence in the adversarial exchanges of the House of Commons , and no example is necessary.

1 *The De Lorean affair – Ministers deny error and move on.* In the years 1978–82 about £80 million was invested in the De Lorean car enterprise in Northern Ireland. The investment was made for good reasons, to help Belfast's ailing economy and thus perhaps diminish the bloody antagonism of its two warring communities. However few cars were made and the company was soon wound up. Most of the money ended up, as Jock Bruce-Gardyne wrote, in numbered bank accounts in Switzerland or on the ski slopes of Colorado, and Mr De Lorean himself ended up in the hands of the FBI, accused of drug trafficking.

Meanwhile the first Minister concerned had left office along with his government, and the second had been removed in a re-shuffle. There was no-one to take responsibility for a gross waste of public funds.

2 *Prison break-outs – not the Minister's fault.* In 1984 thirty eight Republican prisoners broke out of the Maze prison in Northern Ireland. The Secretary of State, James Prior, offered his resignation but the Prime Minister believed such an escape was a risk inherent in the conditions of Northern Ireland. Prior himself was satisfied that the Inquiry showed that no policy decision contributed to the escape. There was no serious call for Prior's resignation and he stayed. Yet it might be thought that the escape of so many prisoners in a province racked by terrorism was a serious matter, and the Minister might have looked more carefully at the day-to-day running of the prisons.

This policy/operations distinction was used again by Kenneth Baker as Home Secretary when two 'high security' prisoners accused of terrorist activity escaped from Brixton prison in London. In this case it appeared that the Home Office had earlier received an intelligence report about a possible break-out.

EXERCISE
The policy/operation distinction

9.9 Do you think the distinction between policy and operations or administration is satisfactory for the assessment of ministerial responsibility?

3 *Resignation but no accountability – Edwina*

Currie and Leon Brittan. The case of Leon Brittan is part of the Westland Affair and is dealt with as a Case Study at the end of the chapter.

Edwina Currie's resignation December 1988

On 3 December 1988 Edwina Currie, the junior Minister of Health said in a television interview:

'We do warn people now that most of the egg production of this country, sadly, is now infected with salmonella'.

The statement properly drew attention to a serious problem in food quality, but the wording was imprecise and ambiguous. Consumers could well be grateful to a Minister concerned for their interests rather than the farmers, but such a vague but sweeping statement was not helpful. The producers were naturally angry as egg sales fell off dramatically. At this point it might have seemed easy for Edwina Currie to explain her remarks with more detail and precision, and apologise for misunderstandings and damage. But, after one interview in which she repeated her views, she fell silent under instructions from her Minister. The only reasonable explanation for this is that any elaboration of the statement would concede some grounds for her views.

After further agitation by the producers and both the government and opposition parties, Edwina Currie resigned. It seems probable that the Prime Minister would have preferred to retain her, but a hastily prepared compensation scheme for egg producers put an embarrassing price, £19m, on the indiscretion. Conservative backbenchers, always sympathetic to farming interests and resentful of Edwina Currie's talent for provocative speeches, called for her resignation.

Edwina Currie made no statement about her resignation. At first she refused to appear before the Select Committee on Agriculture. When under threat of compulsion she did appear she said very little; her performance would have seemed obstructive if the Chairman had not been remarkably complaisant. (See Chapter 13 for her appearance before the Select Committee.)

The episode is interesting as a revelation of the influence of the agricultural interest and the Conservative backbenchers. It is especially significant as an illustration of the operation of the convention of ministerial responsibility to produce a resignation but no accountability.

4 *Responsibility for regulation of financial and commercial affairs.* There are a number of cases which raise the question of the responsibilities of the relevant department (Trade and Industry or the Bank of England) for regulating commercial and financial affairs – the Vehicle and General Affair (1972), Barlow Clowes (1988), Bank of Commerce and Credit International (1992) and the Maxwell companies (1992). The typical pattern is : a company collapses, due possibly to negligence or fraud, and causing substantial losses to investors. The department responsible for oversight and regulation is accused of failing to intervene to protect the public; the department pleads that intervention destroys confidence and so brings about the collapse which it is intended to avoid.

There are clearly special problems about this kind of regulating activity, which does seem to be intermittent and 'light touch', and the civil servants concerned might well feel that theirs was responsibility without power. That is of course unsatisfactory. The Minister's position is equally unsatisfactory. The Report on the Vehicle and General case exonerated Ministers specifically and in general: in the absence of a reference by the official to the Minister, he was entitled to assume that the official was not in doubt as to the course of action, and could be relied on to take the appropriate decisions.

This wholesale exemption of the Minister from responsibility does not look adequate under the convention of ministerial responsibility, for the Minister must carry the final responsibility for the efficient operation of the department. In speaking on the Report in the House the Home Secretary tried both to confirm ultimate responsibility and to minimise indirect responsibility.

■ DOCUMENT 9.8
The contradictions of Ministerial responsibility

From a speech by the Home Secretary, Reginald Maudling, H. C. Deb., Vol. 836, 1 May 1972

Ministers are responsible not only for their personal decisions but also for seeing that there is a system in their departments by which they are informed of important matters which arise. They are also responsible for minimising the dangers of errors and mistakes so far as possible, and, clearly, they are responsible for the general efficiency of their departments. This is still the right doctrine of ministerial responsibility....

One must look at this classic doctrine in the

light of modern reality. In my own department we get one and a half million letters a year, any one of which may lead to disaster. No Home Secretary could be expected to supervise all those one and a half million letters. It is no minimising of the responsibility of Ministers to Parliament to say that a Minister cannot be blamed for a mistake made, if he did not make it himself, and if he has not failed to ensure that that sort of mistake ought not to be made. ■

It is difficult to define the convention of ministerial responsibility. At one end of the scale it is clear, and no cause for concern, that a minor mistake made without the Minister's knowledge should not lead to blame for the Minister, still less to resignation. At the other end of the scale, a gross blunder by an official acting on the instructions of a Minister must be accounted for to Parliament and may lead to resignation. In between (which is where most cases fall) there is a large area of doubt about the gravity of, and the degree of responsibility for, error; the point at which loss of office by voluntary or involuntary resignation is appropriate, and the circumstances in which it may be enforced. Accountability in a weak form is normal, immediate resignation is rare. Nevertheless there is a commitment to the convention of ministerial responsibility and even to resignation as the ultimate sanction; but the constitutional doctrine is all but overwhelmed by political judgements of Prime Minister and party leadership about party and public unrest.

EXERCISE
Ministerial responsibility

9.10 In the light of the argument does it seem that the convention of ministerial responsibility still operates, and is a valuable part of Britain's democratic system?

The question of resignation, though significant as a measure of the operation of the convention, distracts attention from the fundamental issue, which is the provision of adequate accountability of government to Parliament. Even resignation does not necessarily secure full accountability. The protection of civil service anonymity, which is regarded as a virtue of the convention, further diminishes the possibilities of accountability. Parliament faces the reality that officials do not account since they are not expected to, and Ministers do not account since they do not want to, and are protected by the party majority.

Despite the weakness of accountability it is still true that British government is based fundamentally on the convention of ministerial responsibility. Derogation of power from the Minister, whether to courts or devolved authorities or to the European Community, is resisted on the grounds that accountability to Parliament would thus be diminished. The effectiveness of the convention at the heart of the British Constitution depends on the capacity of Parliament to rise above partisan loyalty and exact accountability. The question is taken up in the chapters on Parliament.

The roles and influence of Ministers

There is no single relationship of Minister and department which sums up actual or ideal relationships. Ministers fill a variety of roles according to their choice, abilities and opportunities: initiating, or at least selecting, policies; managing their department; dealing with the outside world. They may be positive, maximising their potential; or negative, doing what is necessary and keeping out of trouble. Departments vary too. Some are technical in subject matter and complex in organisation; some are crisis-prone; some work only in the long term; some are politically safe, and plainly some are regarded as desirable, others not. These characteristics vary with the period and the political situation.

The nature of this conjunction of Minister and department is summed up in the document on page 144.

Such analyses help understanding but in practice most Ministers do a little of each, according to their own talents and dispositions, the current needs of the department and the demands of politics. No Minister can avoid carrying out the minimum roles and engaging in some public relations (which will be forced on him, whether he or she likes it or not). In practice Ministers may be characterised as primarily:

- caretakers (which may be a passive role but can include energetic fixing)
- executives (in a weak sense, equivalent to managers)
- policy makers (but often more generally initiating and positive).

The caretakers may be genuine minimalists, doing as little as possible, and hoping to move on quickly. Caretaking arises from the nature of the department as well as the drive, or lack of it, of the Minister. But the caretaker Minister may be busy in other directions, outside of the depart- ment, as an all-purpose fixer (normally on behalf of the Prime Minister) or as an all-purpose phi- losopher, guide and friend. (The Prime Minister may give the Philosopher rather more or alto- gether less work, especially if the Minister is more of a Diarist than a Philosopher, saving his best advice for future readers.)

Ministers setting out to be good executives are likely nowadays to see themselves as managers in a modern style, cutting costs and imposing the disciplines of modern management science. It may be objected that by experience and training Ministers are not suited to the management func- tion, and that their proper role is political. But the Minister does not need a Harvard MBA degree to alert his officials to management per- spectives, and push them hard towards new thinking. They may argue back that government is not at all like business, true enough, but it is for

them to identify the differences, and justify their management methods. With regard to the second objection, the Minister's proper role, as the politi- cal head of a department of state, may reasonably be held to include a responsibility for efficient management. The Minister does not have to do the managing himself, but must see that manage- ment is efficient.

The Minister's policy-making role looks obvious and natural. Politics is about policy surely? In the long run this is so. But in the short run (in which most political activity takes place) there is not so much policy-making as policy-adjustment and cri- sis management. The outlines or framework of policy are in place, derived from the past, party doctrine and decisions, interest group pressures. Radically new policies, such as privatisation and the community charge, are neither frequent nor numerous, and do not depend on the initiative of a single Minister. Hence the job of the Minister as

■ DOCUMENT 9.9
Ministers and departments

The table below is adapted from B. Headey, 1974, p. 170

Department differences affecting ministerial role performance

Type of Minister	Type of Department *	
	favourable to role	*unfavourable*
1 Policy initiation and selection	Fragmented Non-technical	Single subject Technical
2 Management roles	Non-complex organisations	Complex organisations
3 Public relations roles to obtain	Newsworthy	Publicity difficult
4 Minimum roles		
a) Legitimating decisions, clearing in-tray	Light workload	Heavy workload
b) Mobilising Cabinet support	High status	Low status
c) Parliamentary trouble-shooting	Politically safe	Politically sensitive

* Note: examples of departments are given in the original, but you should be able to supply your own ■

Policy Maker is to step into a continuing process. He rarely makes a policy from beginning to end but he may:

- select and push forward. The Minister 'must select his points of attack and throw all his available weight and attention there' (J. Enoch Powell quoted in P. Cosgrave, 1989, p. 179)
- stir or, in Enoch Powell's word, 'upset'. 'The essence of a Minister's initiative is to alter what otherwise would have happened – to upset, in a word' (ibid p. 179).
- reflect – thinking is an unusual activity for Ministers ('Decision making is the greatest enemy of thought', said a Minister quoted by Headey (1974, p. 37).
- put forward a moral and intellectual basis for the policies of the department. This neglected function of the Minister was done, it has been suggested, rather well by Sir Edward Boyle when he was Minister of Education 1962–4.

■ DOCUMENT 9.10
The moral and intellectual function of the Minister

From M. Kogan in A. Gold ed., *1991, p. 99*
[Edward Boyle's] role was charismatic and moral rather than that of an outstanding policy innovator...he changed the ethos, level and style of discourse within which policies were made. He put his enormous authority behind such themes as the widening of opportunity in society and increasing the level of civilisation for all citizens. He staunchly supported policies, even if he did not invent them, which would compensate for the inequality of home environment of children over the country.... In this he was moving to the edge of Conservative policy.... ■

EXERCISE
The moral, intellectual, and charismatic function

9.11 Why do you think this function may be often neglected, and does it matter?

GUIDE TO EXERCISES

9.1 Career motivations are not dishonourable, nor are they disadvantageous for the country, as long as ambition is focussed on recognition for doing a good job and meriting promotion. This kind of career drive is normal in most occupations. Thus ambition is normally constrained and disciplined, by the demands of the job, expectations of colleagues (including the Prime Minister and the party) and the need to win their good opinion.

9.2 No. It is valuable for any manager to have some direct contact with the work he is meant to direct, in order to get a 'feel' for the work 'on the ground', and so better understand the mass of information conveyed to him on paper. But the Minister must take care, for visits are time-consuming, and may give a misleading snap-shot of diverse activity.

9.3 Dalton is perhaps excessively concerned to master his officials, but this is understandable for the Minister is dependent on them and they can frustrate change. Strang's classic piece on Bevin is intended to show how the ill-educated Bevin triumphed over his literary deficiencies, but the triumph was clearly arduous and painfully achieved, and Bevin was in the hands of his officials.

9.4 Probably because he thought (correctly) that the threat would work. He stayed in the government because he hoped to influence policy. In the long run this turned out to be a mistake, but he had more influence inside than outside the government.

9.5 Margaret Thatcher was not in a strong position in her Cabinet in 1980, and so needed to avoid the resignation of a senior Minister. Nor would she be very happy about cutting defence, one of the few public services she warmly approved of.

9.6 Probably. He was trying to assert himself as Chancellor, and this and other actions indicated that he saw himself in line for the Prime Ministership, ahead of Butler. His threat was tactical: he was negotiating strongly, but Eden was able to call his bluff. The episode clearly gains from Macmillan's over-dramatic account; the 'panic in the City' line is almost caricature.

9.7 'Futile', in that it did not help to win your argument, and may indeed have reinforced the determination of the Prime Minister not to concede. 'Fatal' seems to be the case for senior Ministers near the end of their career. But for younger Ministers it might help if circumstances changed (as they did for Eden 1938–40), or if there were time to come again (Wilson resigned in 1951 on the eve of Labour's thirteen years in opposition, and returned as Prime Minister).

9.8 Ministers may have learned that resignation does not help their cause, that disagreements are normal and can be lived with; also for full-time professionals with no other career or source of income, resignation is personally damaging.

9.9 No. A Minister should be responsible not only for major policy, but for the proper running of his department. For example, it may be argued that the Minister responsible for prisons does not have to patrol the cell blocks himself, but he should check that procedures are appropriate and are being followed – again he does not have to do it himself. But there are fine distinctions to be drawn. For example, a Minister of Transport might think that safety was the responsibility of British Rail managers. Of the Baker case the Financial Times wrote: 'A Minister is not responsible for policy alone. He must also make certain that his department is well-run'.

9.10 It does still operate, in that it is referred to, even when not followed, and it does still play a part in some resignations. As for democracy the convention is inadequate, not only because it is obscure and open to evasion, but also because it does not provide for a proper system of accountability. See following text.

9.11 Perhaps because few Ministers have Boyle's moral and intellectual qualities; and moral and intellectual debate are not a feature of some policy areas as they were in education at that time. Further the style of adversarial politics in Britain discourages such debate. Does it matter? Yes!

ASSESSMENT
The power of a Minister

The Minister stands at the centre of a triangle of contending forces: the concerns and interests of the Department, the Party and the Public. He or she has to bring these into some balance, in the light of personal assessments, and under the pressures of personal drives and ambitions.

Ministerial power is related to ministerial problems and aims. The Caretaking Minister will with some luck achieve his objectives – power enough. The policy-making Minister, aiming high, may well lack the power to succeed in his transformative aims. On his own, and without good fortune, he is likely to be frustrated. Few Ministers admit to their impotence.

Tony Crosland, looking back over a year as Secretary of State for the Environment, recorded his achievements modestly.

a) Getting Land White Paper through....
b) Excellent programme of legislation, but others did all the work.... Doesn't seem much! Perhaps the main thing is having presided over vast and politically sensitive Department and avoided cock-ups!
(S. Crosland, 1982, pp. 272–8.)

Crossman wrote more dramatically of George Brown: 'Whatever Ministry he's in at the moment is a booming, zooming Ministry' (II, p. 110, 6 Nov. 1966). But, of course, despite the booming and zooming, Brown's achievements were not substantial.

There are tides and flows in opinion, in Parliament, party and country. For every idea 'whose time has come', there are a dozen which are judged untimely, inappropriate, too difficult, or simply mistaken. Few policy ideas can flourish independently of other policy areas; most cost money, and so involve the Treasury, and carry technical complexities beyond the Minister's grasp. Change for the most part can only be marginal, and few problems and policies are new. The Minister, is a temporary amateur, facing a massive department, with entrenched programmes, served by a permanent professional staff. A ministerial intervention, as Healey said, is like trying to stop or re-direct a supertanker.

Nevertheless, in a situation in which no-one has very much power at all, the Minister at least has much more power than most other actors. He can normally expect to gain the backing of Prime Minister and Cabinet, and hence the approval of Parliament. The government's control of the legislature is a formidable instrument of governing power. Any Minister in the USA, for example, would envy a British Minister his capacity to push legislation through.

In sum, a Minister of high standing, facing a soluble problem at an affordable price, can get his way. How then to define standing? Perhaps best to fall back on a circular argument. A Minister of standing is one who, faced with a soluble problem at an affordable price, can get his way. Higher standing allows a higher price. Political standing, the most valuable of ministerial assets, is a prophecy based on perceived achievement. Standing is necessary for achievement; achievement is necessary for standing.

Concept

Responsibility

The concept of responsibility is fundamental to the understanding of British politics and government, and is discussed in the text. It is an elusive concept with at least three meanings or zones of meaning with a 'penumbra' added.

1 'Responsibility' is literally answerability and so refers to accountability (normally in the British context accountability to Parliament).
2 'Authority 'in the usage: X has the responsibility to do this or that. Thus accountable power slides into plain power.
3 'Proper' as applied to behaviour ('now that you are in the sixth form/a teenager/a senior student etc., I expect you to behave responsibly').

In Britain responsibility in government refers to the system of accountability to a representative Parliament, and so is fundamental to the idea of democracy achieved indirectly through Parliament – representative and responsible government.

In practice responsibility in its strict and literal form is much weakened especially by the executive's control of Parliament through party discipline. So 'responsibility' has always to be scrutinised carefully and in detail; answerability to whom? for what? when? and with what consequences and sanctions? These questions should underlie the consideration of the conventions of ministerial and collective responsibility.

● CASE STUDY
Westland again: Leon Brittan's resignation

In the course of the Westland Affair Michael Heseltine resigned over collective responsibility, Leon Brittan over ministerial responsibility for the leaking of a confidential letter from the Solicitor-General. The whole story is complicated and obscure. Michael Heseltine in pursuing his campaign for a European solution to the problems of the helicopter industry warned Westland that their joining with the US Sikorsky company might lead to their exclusion from European collaborative projects. The Solicitor-

General was asked to comment on the accuracy of this letter, and parts of his letter damaging to Heseltine were then leaked. *The Sun* headline next day screamed: YOU LIAR. The leak had hit its target. Both sides were playing the game hard.

Though leaking goes on all the time, the advice of a Law Officer is strictly confidential. In the end Brittan took responsibility for the leak and resigned. It seems most likely that he asked his Press Officer to clear the leak with Downing Street, and Downing Street (the Prime Minister's Private Office and Press Officer) cleverly avoided giving explicit sanction. Margaret Thatcher herself wanted the leak to be made but was not told of the practical arrangements. So the Cabinet Secretary undertook an inquiry to discover what almost everyone concerned already knew. This helped to keep the Prime Minister at a distance from the incident. Leon Brittan was trapped, resigned, thus formally accepting responsibility but without ever conceding his guilt. He had been 'stitched up' by Downing Street.

The Affair is rich in constitutional significance.

1 The Minister under the convention of ministerial responsibility. The Minister resigned but without a proper accounting. Political rather than constitutional factors weighed heavily. Brittan's reputation had been further damaged by his dealings with the aircraft industry, his vigorous lobbying for his own cause and a humiliation in the House of Commons. Brittan was not popular with his own side (he had perhaps risen too quickly) and a scapegoat was needed to deflect criticism from Margaret Thatcher. Brittan's resignation was in consequence more a political manoeuvre than an act of constitutional propriety.
2 The civil servant under the convention of ministerial responsibility. Further doubt was raised about the anonymity and the accountability of civil servants. Civil servants involved in the leak were named and criticised, but their conduct was not fully explained by the Minister or by the Cabinet Secretary who appeared before the Defence Select Committee in their place (see Chapter 13 Case Study).

The question of the conduct of a civil servant faced with an unacceptable instruction arose too, and it was confirmed that a civil servant in such a case should consult his or her superior officer, up to the Permanent Secretary. The Press Officer concerned in the Westland leak was unable to contact her Permanent Secretary. But she knew that her Minister and Downing Street wanted the letter 'in the public domain' (as they said to avoid the word 'leak'). Faced with such a professional dilemma, what would you do? Well, if you were a Whitehall Press Officer paid to feed favourable information to the press by fair means and foul, you would go for the professional foul, wouldn't you? •

• CASE STUDY
The negotiating relationship

Governing often involves negotiating with partners in the governing process. Government is not divided simply into the governors and the governed – a command relationship. Those whom Ministers would like to command claim instead to participate in the governing process. Some are already within the circle of governance, at least on its margins. Others, outside the circle, may have ample spoiling or even veto power to back the claim to participation. The government, that is, the Minister, is then involved in persuading and negotiating, not commanding.

The negotiating relationship applies to the Minister's department and to other departments – this is clear from this chapter and the next. It also applies to some groups which are formally external to government but which work closely with government in a relationship of interdependence. Some trade unions fitted this description under the Labour governments of the 1960s and 1970s. Here is an illustration of a Minister in negotiation with the Navy, an awkward and well-connected inside group, possessing what has been called 'dining power'.

Dr Owen and the Royal Navy based on K. Harris, 1987, pp. 43–49

Dr David Owen was appointed Under Secretary of State for the Royal Navy in 1968. The Navy had just had a planned aircraft carrier cancelled, but had been offered a cruiser in compensation. Soon the Navy asked that the cruiser be designed with a 'through-deck' ostensibly for helicopters, in practice for other aircraft: the cruiser was to be a small aircraft carrier. Owen, as junior Minister, supported the admirals against the Minister of Defence (Denis Healey), arranged for Harrier aircraft to be flown on and off the cruiser by RAF pilots initially, and justified it all as good for defence and good for export orders for the Harrier. The first of these through-deck cruisers, carrying Harriers, was later used very effectively in the Falklands. So perhaps the junior Minister was justified in siding with the Admirals against the Minister for Defence. But there is an alternative interpretation, less flattering to Dr Owen: after all a clear decision by the Defence Minister had been reversed by subterfuge at some cost to the taxpayer.

In his time as Navy Minister Dr Owen was also concerned with the ending of the Navy's traditional rum ration – a daily allowance of a special rum equivalent to four and a half whiskies. The Admirals wanted to abolish the rum ration. Dr Owen agreed. But he had a political problem. He was a Member of Parliament for a naval constituency, in a government which was accused of being 'anti-Navy'. It was necessary, therefore, to persuade the Admirals to take the lead in public and for other measures to soften the blow e.g. a new welfare fund for sailors. Thus the Minister negotiated with the professionals about the political conditions under which they could gain their policy. This was government by negotiation not command. •

The Civil Service: the policy managers

Introduction: meanings and assumptions

It is notoriously difficult to define the civil service. The term itself is not of great antiquity. It is a nineteenth century usage, first applied in India.

There is no entirely satisfactory definition, but the problem need not be serious as long as it is acknowledged and worked around. First statistics about the numbers of civil servants (a matter of some political interest) have to be scrutinised with care. Some, but not all, of the reductions achieved in the 1980s depended on definitions and re-organisation – the workers were still there. Second, the definition of the civil service has to be seen as part of the problem of the definition and boundaries of government itself – government and not-quite government and non-government (see Chapter 24).

Third, the focus of political study certainly in this book, is on the central political processes of government. Hence we are concerned with the higher ranks of the civil service, 600 in the three highest grades and altogether not more than 2000 officials engaged in the higher management of government, adjacent to Ministers, concerned in the development of policy and crisis-management and so acting to some extent as policy advisers. One term suggested as appropriate to this kind of function is 'policy-administrator' or 'policy-manager'. But to avoid too large an assumption the term 'higher civil servant' may seem better. This is roughly equivalent to the popular and mildly critical terms 'mandarins' or, following the hero of the television series, 'Yes, Minister', 'Sir Humphrey's.'

Terms like 'civil service' convey meanings and connotations, a 'penumbra', apart from any precisely-defined meaning. 'Civil service' originally distinguished civilian from military service. This is no longer of much significance, but there is some indication of a unified 'Service' with traditions, loyalties, disciplines, like the Navy, but without the rum ration. There is also an indication of appointment by merit – which is the American usage of the term. More significantly there is an implication that the civil service does work which is fundamentally different from that of private firms and industry. This is true of course, but the senior civil servant has nowadays to think of himself as a manager doing a job comparable in many ways to that of his counterpart in private industry.

Beyond these connotations of the term 'civil service' lie the common assumptions and stereotypes, many of them false. For example, the civil service is not alone in having conventions and even some regulations, about dress; or in taking tea-breaks; or in preferring 'not to do anything for the first time'; or, in being sometimes unhelpful and 'bureaucratic'. The latter has become a thoughtless term of abuse. Parts of the civil service are certainly overmanned; but few areas of work are not at some time, except perhaps, supermarket checkout desks, school class rooms and one-person ice-cream vans – and one-author books.

The aim of this chapter is to give an account of what the civil service actually does. This is the basis for an examination of the role of the civil service in the system of government, in the context of concerns about its power and reform proposals. It is accepted that the higher civil service is very powerful, but this in itself is neither good nor bad. Nevertheless, there are problems about fitting a powerful civil service into a democracy – problems of accountability in a system protected by party majorities, the doctrine of ministerial responsibility and an enveloping secrecy.

History

1 *The Northcote-Trevelyan Report 1854*

The modern civil service dates only from the nineteenth century. The first movement toward a modern form arose, characteristically it might be thought, from the development of the Indian civil service and the provision of pensions in Britain. The civil service was not invented, it grew haphazardly over decades to meet the growing needs of government. Victorian reformers took government seriously and deplored the inefficiency and corruption of the civil service. Such criticisms led to an inquiry and a historic report, the Northcote-Trevelyan Report of 1854. Trevelyan, the senior figure in this duo, had served in India and in the highest post in the Treasury.

The Northcote-Trevelyan Report made important recommendations which have become the basis of the modern civil service in Britain.

- Separation of the 'intellectual' from the 'mechanical' sides of administration.
- Recruitment by competitive examination, not patronage; the examination to be 'literary', that is, in the arts and humanities, not professional or technical subjects. Recruitment of young men (the gender assumed of course in 1854), to be trained on-the-job, not men of 'experience in other walks of life'.
- Promotion by merit.
- Unification of the service, through a uniform procedure for recruitment and some movement between departments.

The Northcote-Trevelyan Report marked a fundamental reform and at the same time laid down some of the characteristics of the service which were to be criticised a century later: the Oxbridge arts graduate, 'gentleman-amateur', administrator, part of an isolated elite in a service dominated and protected by the Treasury.

The Report's conclusions were recommendations only, but in the next 70 years (a timescale on which a cynic might think British governments always work) they were virtually all adopted. A civil service Commission to supervise recruitment was set up with commendable speed in 1855 and in 1870 the first competitive recruitment was established. Fifty years later, the service was in effect unified under the Treasury. By 1920 the process of converting nineteenth century clerks to administrators had been completed, while the introduction of typewriters (from the 1880s) and mainly women to do the typing had depressed the status of copying work – and the quality of handwriting.

The process from clerk to administrator is nicely described in this piece by one of the architects of the modern civil service. The process is important because it reflects but at the same time significantly reinforces the 'clerical' nature of all administration – the dominance of words and paper.

■ DOCUMENT 10.1
From clerk to administrator

From Sir Edward Bridges, 1953, p. 14
The Clerk who at first had done nothing except copy letters, despatch them and file them, makes himself useful in collecting precedents and previous papers. The next stage is that he becomes a clerk who can describe accurately what has happened in the past, who can collect together the information required by the officer who is going to reach a decision on the matter in hand; and before long you have an adviser who presents his senior colleagues or his Minister with a carefully documented appraisal of the position, who tests all the statements made and sets out what seem to him the possible courses of action and the likely consequences of each. There remains a final step. To sum it all up and say which course has behind it the backing of all the knowledge and the experience that the Department can give to its Minister. ■

2 *Growth and centralisation, 1900–39*

The development of the civil service reflects the growth of government. Critics of the civil service should note that the growth of government was in response to popular needs and demands; hence a large civil service is a popular and inevitable institution. The industrialised and urbanised Britain of the nineteenth century required more government than ever before – not just for the historic functions of domestic and international security (though these both expanded) but for the provision and regulation of public services, transport, health, education. Even a narrow self-interest required educated workers and a contented population living in sanitary towns. The social legislation of the early twentieth century notably the National Insurance Act and the economic and military mobilisation of the war of 1914–18 accelerated the growth of government; the depression and the second world war then completed the process.

At the beginning of the nineteenth century the

number of civil servants was roughly 20 000. The figure doubled by mid-century and almost trebled again by 1901 (to 116 000). The total then rose rapidly by the 1920s (306 000+) and doubled again by 1950 (almost 700 000). The number of civil servants peaked in the 1970s at well over 700 000 and then fell back in the 1980s to about 500 000 (the reduction reflects in part 'hiving-off' and re-description).

Such rapid growth to a massive total forced changes in structure and control. In 1919–20 the service was reorganised under Treasury control. In 1919 the Permanent Secretary of the Treasury, Sir Warren Fisher, was designated Permanent Secretary of the civil service and the Treasury set up an Establishments Division to deal with civil service pay and personnel matters throughout the service. In 1920 the dominant position of the Treasury was formalised and strengthened by an Order-in-Council which gave the Treasury authority to 'make regulations for controlling the conduct of His Majesty's Civil Establishments'. The Treasury now controlled the apron strings as well as the purse strings.

3 The Fulton critique 1968
The civil service, thus strengthened under the Treasury, coped well with its rapid enlargement and the burden of new tasks arising from the slow but almost complete conversion of Britain to the Managed Economy Welfare State. It reached its peak in the War of 1939–45 and under the Labour government of 1945–51. This adaptation to high spending, close regulation and a large public sector was impressive. It was what the people wanted; but it was also in the interests of the civil servants.

It was all too good to last. By the 1960s there were serious doubts about the health of the British economy and its capacity to sustain the Welfare State. The civil service was exposed by the evident decline in performance, the loss of confidence and the breakdown in a broad political consensus. It was further challenged by a new emphasis on management and managerial skills. The ideal senior civil servant no longer seemed to be one who could write verse in Classical Greek, turn an elegant memorandum and never hold a firm view of his own about policy goals. Such criticisms lay behind the establishment of the Fulton Committee on the civil service (1966–8).

The Fulton Report is a major document in the history of the British civil service, though its immediate effects were quite limited.

■ DOCUMENT 10.2
The Fulton Report 1968: the diagnosis

The Committee wrote in its opening paragraph: 'The Home Civil Service today is still fundamentally the product of the nineteenth-century philosophy of the Northcote-Trevelyan Report. The tasks it faces are those of the second half of the twentieth century.'

Specifically, the Committee noted six major defects:
● the Service is too much based on the philosophy of the amateur, that is the gifted and experienced layman, called pejoratively the generalist or all-rounder
● the system of classes impedes the efficient use of individuals
● the specialist classes, e.g. scientists, accountants, are denied opportunities for full administrative (managerial) responsibility
● too few civil servants are, or see themselves as, skilled managers
● there is not enough contact between the Service and the community it serves
● personnel management and career planning are inadequate. ■

The Committee proposed a basic guiding principle for the development of the civil service: 'look at the job first'. (Translated into official English: 'The civil service must continuously review the tasks it is called upon to perform and the possible ways it might perform them....)

EXERCISE
'Generalists' and 'specialists'

10.1 The use by Fulton of the mildly pejorative word 'amateur' may have been a mistake (it was used only three times but it attracted attention and came to label the argument). The word was resented and it was inaccurate. Why?

In the light of this general diagnosis the Fulton Report made substantial proposals for reform:
a) The higher direction of the civil service
A new civil service Department should be established, replacing the Civil Service Commission and the Pay and Management side of the Treasury.
b) Classification, training and recruitment
(i) All classes should be abolished and replaced by a single grading structure for all non-industrial civil servants. The existing rather rigid boundaries, both horizontal and

vertical, would disappear and the differences in qualifications, skills and kinds of work between specialists and general administrators would be diminished.

(ii) A Civil Service College should be set up, to provide courses mainly in administration and management and to conduct research into problems of government machinery and policy.

(iii) Recruitment. There should be greater mobility between the civil service and other employments by means of late entry, temporary appointments and interchange.

A majority of the Committee considered that, in the recruitment of some graduates, 'more account should be taken of the relevance of their university courses' to their prospective jobs. All agreed that increasing importance should be attached to 'numeracy'.

c) The organisation of departments

(i) The principles of 'accountable management' should be applied to the work of departments. Accountable management was defined as a 'system in which individuals and units are held responsible for performance and output measured as objectively as possible'.

(ii) Departments should establish planning units, with comparatively young staffs. 'The Unit's main task should be to identify and study the problems and needs of the future and the possible means to meet them.

(iii) Most departments should have a 'senior policy adviser' to assist the Minister. He would normally be Head of the Planning Unit and his job would be similar to that of the unit. He should be an authority in the department's field of work, familiar with other experts and new trends in thinking and practice in that field. Such advisers would usually, but not invariably, be career civil servants. The Permanent Secretary would retain overall responsibility for the department, under the Minister.

(iv) The administrative process should be more open, with less secrecy and more consultation. 'The convention of anonymity should be modified and civil servants, as professional administrators, should be able to go further than now in explaining what their departments are doing, at any rate so far as concerns managing existing policies and implementing legislation'.

(v) The 'hiving-off' of responsibilities from government departments to autonomous public boards (like the BBC and the nationalised industries) was tentatively approved and further inquiry recommended.

The Wilson government accepted immediately the proposals for a new Civil Service Department, for the modification of the grading structure and for the establishment of a Civil Service College. This gave the impression that Fulton was about to be implemented. In many respects this was not the case.

EXERCISE
The Fulton Report on the civil service

10.2 Why do you think the Fulton Report has had only a slight effect on the civil service?

The Fulton reforms actually carried out were soon modified and little was done about the radical proposals for the structure of departments. However, in the long run, the ideas for radical structural reform have survived and two of them, accountable management and 'hiving-off' have been implemented to some extent.

4 The 1980s: Margaret Thatcher's reforms

The Fulton Report brought about few immediate and radical changes but served notice that reform was on the agenda. Edward Heath, like Wilson a former civil servant, continued Wilson's reforming thrust, but was mainly concerned with structural matters – giant departments and a more effective advisory and policy development system. By contrast Margaret Thatcher was impatient with institutions, distrusted civil servants and disliked the large public sector. Her general distrust of public bureaucracy reflected a large segment of opinion, disillusioned with the apparent inefficiencies of the post-war welfare state. This shift in opinion proved to be a good basis for quite radical change in the civil service.

■ DOCUMENT 10.3
Margaret Thatcher's reforms

1 Reduction in numbers by more than 20 percent in a decade, though this was partly by hiving off and re-description.

2 Intervention in senior appointments (quite legitimate) to achieve promotion of more active, committed officials, goal-oriented 'doers', rather than the smooth committee men, who could set out the options, secure a compromise and devise a form of words to

please everybody. This is not the same as promotion on political grounds.

3 Abolition of the Civil Service Department on the grounds that it was too concerned with protecting the privileges of the civil service.

4 Support for a vigorous drive for efficiency, particularly through the 'Efficiency Unit', originally led by Sir Derek Rayner.

5 Support for the proposals in the Ibbs Report, 'Improving Management in Government, the 'Next Steps' (1988) for the 'hiving-off' to separate quasi-autonomous agencies of much of the civil service's functions of service delivery, as distinct from policy advice. (See below for a full account of the 'Next Steps' proposals).

6 In the 1990s, further steps, not signalled by a report of that name, go beyond agencies towards complete privatisation. ■

EXERCISE
The Thatcher reforms

10.3 How, if at all, do Margaret Thatcher's reforms relate to the Fulton proposals?

Structure, recruitment

Structure
Who runs the civil service? Such direct questions about British government are always difficult to answer. There is no doubt that the Prime Minister and Ministers are 'responsible' for the civil service and their policies determine the funding and activities of the service. But the politicians have traditionally distanced themselves a little from day-to-day management. This lay in the hands of the Permanent Secretaries of the Departments and the formally designated 'Head of the Civil Service', a post held by the Permanent Secretary to the Treasury (1919–56) and then successively by the Cabinet Secretary, the Permanent Secretary to the Treasury again, the Permanent Secretary to the Civil Service Department (1968–81) and recently by the Cabinet Secretary again. The administration of the service lay with the Treasury until the CSD was established and after its abolition was divided between the Treasury and a small special section of the Cabinet Office.

The shape of the civil service, in the sense of distribution or spread, reflects the size of the departments, the largest being Defence, Social Security, Health, Employment and the Inland Revenue. Most 'industrial civil servants' (e.g. ordnance factory workers) are no longer within the civil service. The largest numbers are clerical officers and this is the only grade with a preponderance of women employees.

The clerks are at the lowest levels of the Administration Group. Above that are the senior officials in an 'open structure', so-called in deference to a recommendation of Fulton that senior administrative posts should be open to specialists such as accountants.

The 'open structure' includes less that 20 000 civil servants altogether. Of these less than 3000 at the grade 5 level and above (assistant secretary through to permanent secretary) are concerned with advice and support to Ministers and the higher direction of government. These are the greater and lesser mandarins referred to generally as 'the civil service' in the political and constitutional context.

Recruitment
Recruitment of the higher civil service is the most politically significant of the internal management functions of the civil service and arouses criticism of the kind and quality of person appointed. Recruitment is carried out by the Civil Service Commission which is set slightly apart from the civil service management and the departments.

Recruitment lies behind the basic Fulton critique of the 'gentleman-amateur'. At its simplest, it is contended, the higher civil service tends to recruit graduates educated at Oxford or Cambridge, who are both socially unrepresentative and unsuited to the active goal-oriented managerial role now required of the service.

Recruitment methods for the higher civil service are intensive and rigorous. All candidates take a written examination, including tests in precis writing, the interpretation of statistics and the drafting of policy advice. About four fifths of candidates go no further. The remaining one fifth then go through group and individual tests and interviews, lasting three days. Tests include taking part in and chairing meetings of small groups and an extensive exercise in the preparation of policy advice, based on documents and statistics. Assessors include a retired senior civil servant, a younger civil servant and a psychologist. The Final Selection Board usually includes a Civil Service Commissioner, two senior civil servants, an academic and someone with experience of industry.

There is no doubt that the selection process is well-designed according to the criteria of modern personnel management and is rigorous and structured to be fair.

EXERCISE
Civil service selection procedures

10.4 Do you see anything wrong with the selection procedures described above?

In the 1970s the typical recruit to the administration trainee grade was not quite an Oxford classicist, but certainly an Oxbridge arts or social science graduate. For example in 1975 about 80 per cent of administration trainees had taken arts or social science degrees, about 60 per cent of them at Oxbridge and about 50 per cent had attended fee-paying schools. In the years 1989–91 the representation of Oxbridge among administration trainee recruits has varied between 46 per cent and 55 per cent – higher if the Diplomatic Service is included, much lower (34 per cent and 41 per cent) if specialists (economists, statisticians, scientists) are included. The hold of the Oxford classicist and his successors has not yet seriously weakened – though Oxbridge's best and brightest may now find employment in high finance more attractive than the poorly paid public service.

There are two major lines of criticism of the recruitment to the higher civil service: the dominance of Oxbridge and the preference for the generalist.

The dominance of Oxbridge can be explained and even justified (but not with entire conviction). The explanation must be, first, that Oxford and Cambridge were over-represented among candidates (perhaps because of tradition, the high chance of success and prior selection, i.e. the people who choose Oxbridge tend to choose a career in government); second, that these were or seemed to be the best candidates. The justification must depend on the acceptance that Oxbridge gets and/or develops the qualities most suited (or apparently most suited) to the civil service. There is probably something in this argument, for Oxbridge seems to 'cream off' talent from schools. Here the civil service may simply reflect how meritocratic selection works in British society (and if Labour Cabinets were dominated by Oxford arts graduates, how is the civil service to be blamed for a similar bias?)

Even so there are valid criticisms of the over-representation. The selection process is open to criticism. It is a rough instrument; though there is no obvious alternative. Oxbridge and the public schools are well represented among the selectors and there may well be a tendency for like to choose like. The candidate who seems fully matured by the early 20s plainly has an advantage; potential is more difficult to judge. The present system may be unfair to many good candidates who, in the long run, would make good administrators. In any case, the highest ranks of government administration ought to be widely representative of Britain. The educational bias reflects a class and regional bias. The civil service ought perhaps to reach across this bias.

There are limits to the applicability of this point. A Cornishman or a Liverpudlian would presumably prefer to be administered by an Oxford-educated Londoner of sharp intellect and sound judgement, than by a local lad who had neither. The effects of the bias are difficult to establish or measure. In the long run the ethos and drives of the service itself must be of greater consequence.

The generalist/specialist argument is more worrying. For example, a Treasury civil servant may need to acquire his own grasp of Economics. But does a DTI civil servant need to have a specialist understanding of say the generation of nuclear power, or should be or she depend on specialist advice. Should an official who has never taught in a school (and never set foot in a state school) assist in the development of the National Curriculum? Firm and precise answers are difficult. The development of the Concorde aircraft (costing the taxpayer £1bn) illustrates the difficulties of specialist advice: the specialists were much too enthusiastic about their technological marvel and over-optimistic about the economics of the project. What was needed was a sceptical generalist capable of discussion with aircraft builders and operators.

Specialists may be radical or conservative as policy advisers: their peculiar faults are narrowness of vision and unconscious self-interest. The debate about generalists and specialists has been won by the generalists, but with some concessions to the specialists and to the critics of the 'gentleman-amateur'. The case for the generalist has been quietly re-affirmed.

■ DOCUMENT 10.4
The case for the generalist civil servant

a) Administration is an art or skill on its own and may be equally discovered or developed in the classics graduate as in, say, the biochemist.
b) Higher education provides a broad intellectual training. What is required of the subject matter of this training is that it should involve clear thinking, judgement, precision and some force of written and spoken expression. If

anything, these may be better developed in arts subjects than in sciences. In particular, it may be argued that some arts subjects help to develop judgement, both in respect of other people and in situations where the evidence is incomplete and untested.

c) It is not possible in many cases to arrange that an administrator should confine himself to certain special fields. Indeed, if he does so, he may be less useful as an administrator for co-ordination and communication among specialists.

d) It is by no means certain that the special knowledge acquired by a first degree is usefully 'special' by the standards of government. (And as with most specialisms, it will go out of date very quickly.)

e) The non-specialist recruit can acquire relevant special knowledge after entry to the service.

f) Moreover, civil servants in the specialist classes can work alongside the generalist, providing all necessary special knowledge and techniques. ■

These points are not of course the whole of the argument. There is more to be said for the specialist and about the problem of fitting him or her into the civil service. But governments have not accepted the (not unanimous) Fulton recommendation for recruitment by 'relevance' of a university degree.

So the highest ranks of the civil service are still largely the preserve of the generalist, but the 'gentleman-amateur' label is not accepted by civil servants. The senior civil servant is expected to be knowledgeable in the affairs of his department. Hence the Treasury official, whatever his background, must be at home in aspects of economics. The senior civil servant works alongside specialists and is expected to be able to understand and deal with specialist expertise. He or she is expected to understand and apply where relevant the ideas of modern management science. Finally there are training programmes which are especially concerned with numeracy, statistics and management.

The civil service would claim that it now has 'about the right balance' in the quality and capacities of its highest ranks, 'the best of both worlds'. This is, you may think, a typically middle-of-the-road civil service view. But it may well be correct nevertheless. The real problem may lie in the insulation of the civil service, the fact that like many other professions, it is pursued for too long, with too little opportunity for experience of the world outside.

Characteristics of the higher civil service in Britain

The higher civil service in Britain has a number of distinguishing characteristics.

1 The civil service is massive. Figures have been quoted above. Much depends on what you refer to. The total number of civil servants is plainly very high and contributes about one tenth of the quarter of the workforce which works in the public sector (local government contributes about one half of this quarter of the total work force). The cost is high, too – getting on for 4 per cent of the GDP and 7 per cent of public expenditure. This is equivalent to roughly £270 each year for every person in Britain. Of course a similar calculation can be made for other kinds of public (or private) expenditure, for example, education, health, advertising, motor cars, alcohol, pet food; and they all seem shocking. Spending tax-payer's money is the major activity of the modern state and the sums are large.

Much of civil service manpower is devoted to the delivery or regulation of services. The functions of governing or higher management are carried out by a comparatively small cadre of senior civil servants – not more than 2–3000 in all. This might be regarded as quite modest in size and cost for the government of 55m people and the annual expenditure of about £250bn.

2 The civil service is a self-consciously professional public service, recruited by merit, hierarchical in structure and supported by a strong ethos of public service. Modes of recruitment attract the pejorative labels of 'meritocracy' and 'elitism'. The civil service itself might prefer to be described as 'aristocratic' in the literal sense of government by the best. There is an intense concern, an obsession even, for personal quality in the service, with reputation and performance. There is little wrong with this, though coupled with isolation in a life-time career, the sense of superiority can lead to arrogance and even to 'elitism'.

Like most self-conscious professions the civil service is confident of the value of its own contribution to the public weal. The cynical view that all professions are conspiracies against the public interest is not echoed in Whitehall, but there is a natural bias towards government activity, public services and the privileges of the civil service.

The hierarchy of the service is a normal feature of such organisations and is a necessary element in control and co-ordination – in the simple sense that a football team needs a captain and probably a manager too. Again there are disadvantages if the hierarchy is steep and many-layered and if the freedom of action of the lower levels is strictly controlled. The junior or middle-ranking official is inclined then to avoid initiatives and refer everything up to a higher level, taking no decisions himself. Such 'buck-passing' seems to be characteristic of the civil service and is further encouraged by the sensitive relationship with Ministers.

One aspect of the public service ethos which is little noticed but altogether creditable is the commitment of the civil service to honesty and probity. There is very little corruption in the civil service, though in many other countries bureaucracies are notoriously corrupt. This is not to say that the British civil servant does not support Governments in their efforts to deceive the public; nor that they do not engage in relations with client or interest groups which are closer than a proper neutrality requires; nor that they do not move on retirement into well-paid employment with companies with which they have had an official relationship. All that lies within the broad band of professional ethics. But the British civil servant is not corrupt in the sense of taking open bribes, or working for private gain. It is significant in this connection that 'hiving-off' and privatisation have led to some episodes indicating a weakening of the strict public service ethos.

3 The civil service is committed at the top to the ideal of administration as an art. This has been discussed above in considering recruitment and the Fulton critique of the 'gentleman-amateur'. For the civil service the effectiveness of the ideal administrator is based in general intellectual calibre, facility in drafting, skill in communication, steadiness of judgement, together with a sound understanding of the issues and knowledge of the relevant information. The essential skills begin on natural talent and are developed by experience. Special knowledge and training, in contributory skills such as accounting and in basic skills, represented by scientific management are not so highly valued.

4 The civil service forms a community. Two American observers, investigating the Treasury in the 1960s, perceived the Treasury and by extension, the higher civil service as a whole, as a village community, people who have grown up together, enjoying kinship, a common culture and common experience. There is a 'shared and exclusive group life', which by definition excludes outsiders (H. Heclo and A. Wildavsky 1974 passim). In this interpretation the service has all the best and worst features of village life – the warmth of 'community', the distrust of outsiders, tensions and jealousies within the community, an obsession with reputations, malicious gossip, the fear of disgrace.

5 There is something of a civil service philosophy, or point of view or approach. This includes the sense of profession and of the Whitehall community referred to. It may also include a general commitment to government intervention, regulation and provision, to 'good government' in the bureaucratic mode and to a preference, a political preference, for a middle or common ground, for a 'realism' and 'pragmatism' falling short of the more radical proposals of the parties. This is a view of critics: most senior civil servants would deny that they have a political position. But, of course, not having any political position or outlook is to take up a political position of some significance.

These points 2,3,4 and 5 together make the civil service into something of a 'caste', a superior class set apart and conscious of its own special qualities. This would, if true, justify the use of the word 'mandarin' (originally a Chinese bureaucrat). Some of this sense of a superior class is conveyed in Sir William Armstrong's account of how he looked for future Permanent Secretaries:
'I tried to look several years ahead. I did a great deal of it personally, starting in 1968. I built up a big chessboard, with departments listed along one side, using counters for people and moving them about to see what could happen.... I often used to spend most of Sunday at home playing with different possibilities' (from an interview with Peter Kellner, quoted in P. Kellner and Lord Crowther-Hunt, 1980, p. 174).

6 The civil service works under the convention of Ministerial responsibility (see Chapter 9). This makes the service formally 'non-political'; and the individual servant enjoys the protection of

anonymity. The British civil service is unusual in that the very highest level of officials are 'non-political' career civil servants committed to serving whatever government is in power. Andrew Shonfield has called this the 'sterilisation' of the British civil servant. 'Having decided, somewhat belatedly, on the need for a non-political body of officials, the British proceeded to make their divorce from the world of politics more complete than it is anywhere else' (A. Shonfield, quoted in R. Chapman and A. Dunsire, 1971, p. 409).

In other countries, for example, France and USA, the highest level of the civil service is occupied by political appointees, coming and going with the government of the day. The introduction of special advisers to Ministers (one or two for each Minister) and the Prime Minister's Policy Unit has only slightly modified the position. The Permanent Secretary is still the Minister's weightiest adviser within the Department.

The civil servant is non-political by appointment. He is politically neutral in the sense that his own party political opinions are irrelevant and that he is expected to serve the Minister without reservation. Most of the official's work will not require him to promote the government's case in public, but he will have to appear before Select Committees, hence on television. Press officers are in a different position. Their job is precisely to promote the government in a public forum. This raises a question about the proper stance of press officers. Margaret Thatcher's Press Officer, Sir Bernard Ingham, was notoriously regarded as one of her closest advisers and apparently an enthusiastic supporter.

The 'non-political' civil servant remains by convention anonymous, protected from the public gaze by the all embracing convention of Ministerial responsibility. In practice anonymity is now far from complete. Civil servants have been named in official inquiries, or have become known through investigation by the media. Occasionally a senior civil servant talks in an academic or professional forum. Retired civil servants have written books and given interviews. Peter Hennessy's classic work on Whitehall draws on some notable inroads into the anonymity and secrecy of the civil service.

7 It follows from this that the civil service is necessarily secretive, since the civil servant is formally anonymous and not publicly responsi-

ble. Civil service advice to Ministers is jealously guarded: it has no substance except as Ministerial policy. This professional secrecy of the civil service intensifies the government secrecy which Ministers activate for their own reasons.

Civil servants: the job at the top

Top civil servants are thus expected to play a difficult and frustrating role – Vicars of Bray, no matter who is king. Most senior civil servants adapt to the role (or they would not have become senior civil servants). They are rather like barristers in that they have to accept the brief of their clients. They have some limited independence in that it is their right and duty to offer advice, even unpalatable advice to their Minister – but he does not have to listen to it for one moment. Then the civil servant unlike the barrister, cannot decline to take the brief. Some civil servants are emotionally in tune with the Minister. A few become emotionally engaged. This was true notably of Sir William Armstrong when as Permanent Secretary to the Civil Service Department he worked closely with Prime Minister Heath in the industrial crises of 1973–4. But most senior officials cultivate a professional detachment.

Detachment is a characteristic of the British civil servant and for some critics a characteristic weakness. The system, wrote Michael Heseltine, produces 'thinker-advisers', not 'thinker-doers'; 'Whitehall ladders are most easily climbed by "sound" men of high critical intelligence, but too often without creativity of any practical kind' (M. Heseltine, 1987, pp. 9, 45). The ship of state is kept afloat but is not going anywhere. Performance tends to be assessed by 'behaviour' rather than 'achievement'. Detachment, it is suggested, produces good government but not dynamic government, compromise, 'fixing', elegant and clever memoranda but no strategic vision or problem-solving drive. In the British system these must come from the politicians.

The non-political nature of the civil service clearly indicates the proper relationship of Minister and civil servant. The Minister is 'responsible', the civil servant acts as a subordinate, under the authority of the Minister. 'The whole machine is geared to finding out and acting on the Minister's mind', said a Permanent Secretary quoted by B. Headey (1974, p. 128). Of course the Minister's mind may be empty, distracted, uncertain, indecisive; and his senior civil servants must then judge how forceful their advice should be. Thus civil servants enjoy a special version of the dilemma of all subordinates with bosses who are not quite up to the job — should you say something, do something, or shrug and choose a quiet life?

The elusive non-political character of the civil service is best seen in the Permanent Secretary, who works at the peak of administration and policy advice and in regular communication with the Minister. The political and the non-political come together in the Permanent Secretary.

The role of the Permanent Secretary was first considered in Chapter 7, in the formal and cautious terms of a serving Permanent Secretary following the official line. Document 10.5 gives a comment on the role of the Permanent Secretary, by one who had become a Minister.

■ DOCUMENT 10.5
Permanent Secretaries and policy
Minister and Permanent Secretary: the differences From Sir James Grigg, 1948, pp. 351–2
Sir James moved (in wartime) from Permanent Secretary to Secretary of State in the War Office.
[When I was Permanent Secretary] I could get nothing done without persuading those whose primary concern it was that it was the right thing to do. After that we had to go hand in hand to the Secretary of State and convince him that it was the right thing to do. But once he had decided...they became his own and he assumed the entire responsibility for them urbi et orbi....

Those of us who had advised or pressed the decisions upon him hid ourselves behind the cloak of the unique but universal accountability of the Secretary of State.

Now I was myself Secretary of State. I had no longer to go through a whole chain of private persuasions. In the administrative sphere I could decide things for myself and I could give orders in any sense and at any time I liked. But I had to recognise that I might be called on to justify what I had done to the Prime Minister and the War Cabinet or to defend it publicly in the House of Commons. From now on it was I and not another who had to answer for everything that went on in the War Office and the Army. ■

EXERCISES
Minister and Permanent Secretary

10.5 What are the chief differences between the two jobs indicated by Sir James Grigg?

10.6 Do you see grounds for scepticism about this classic view?

Thus, it is misleading to describe civil servants as non-political. This is true in the sense that in his official work he should not be a partisan (committed to a political party). At the same time the civil servant may hold firm policy commitments, for example to roads rather than railways, to cutting the costs of the health service or education in particular ways, to the community care of the mentally handicapped, to the reform of the tax system or the strengthening of local government. He is entitled to advocate these with due regard for relevance, rationality and proportionality. At least, commitment to a departmental line is not uncommon and one former Minister, Shirley Williams, has said that departments tend to fly their last great achievement like a banner. This is commitment, but not partisan commitment. In the end, of course, the Minister has the power to end the argument as he or she pleases. At that point the civil servant must acknowledge that he is servant, the Minister is master.

Criticisms and concerns

Weakness and inadequacy to the task
Civil servants, it is argued, are weak, because they lack the will and the power to do anything, their power is the power of inertia, they are powerful but passive, influential in defending the status quo and the common ground, never pushing the Minister towards new thinking, or pressing an unpopular line, keeping the Minister out of trouble and avoiding embarrassment at all costs.

■ DOCUMENT 10.6
Douglas Hurd on the inadequacy of the civil servant
From D. Hurd, 1979, pp. 36, 117–8
[Douglas Hurd served as a political adviser to Prime Minister Heath, 1970–4, later rising to Cabinet posts under Margaret Thatcher and John Major]
a)...in rough times, when existing policies have collapsed, a Prime Minister will find that the senior civil servant fell silent. I saw this happen once over Ireland and three times over incomes policy. They busy themselves at such times with the usual agendas and meetings, the corridors are full of scurrying figures, but nothing substantial emerges. They are, quite reasonably, waiting for the new course which only politicians can set. It is then that the political advice becomes all-important (p. 36).

b) [Hurd comments on the role of civil servants in a meeting in No. 10 Downing Street on 27 November 1973 to brief the Prime Minister for his encounter with the Miners' Executive the next day.]

It should have provided a chance for that clear-headed analysis of the options before the Government, which was by then badly needed. Instead there was silence on the big issues and a confused, bitty discussion of trivial, tactical points. I felt critical of the senior civil servants present, whose duty it should have been to force the discussion into some coherent channel. This was the third and final occasion when I felt that at a crucial moment they fell below what was required. The others had occurred after Bloody Sunday in Londonderry in 1972 and during the discussion of inflation in the summer of 1973. No one who was present at any of these three meetings could believe that the civil service runs this country (pp. 117–8).

[Other illustrations could be given. Richard Crossman reported an experimental Cabinet meeting in October 1966, with officials present, to discuss the EEC. None of the officials gave views independent of their Ministers. But, given the system, civil servants could hardly be expected to diverge from and so undermine, the Minister.]

EXERCISE

10.7 Is Hurd's comment unfair and misleading?

c) *From William Plowden, then Director General RIPA in Parliamentary Affairs, 38,4, Winter 1985, pp. 393–414*

What C. H. Sisson called the 'nonentity of the administrator' (Sisson, 1966) seems to me a psychological nonsense. That is to say, I do not believe that thoughtful individuals, with their own established practices and values, can, in fact, support with equal enthusiasm governments with totally dissimilar ideologies; or that they can prevent the relative intensity of their enthusiasms from influencing their behaviour. Alternatively, an intolerable strain can be placed on conscientious officials compelled to implant policies with which they personally disagree (p. 403).

Instead of instinctively resisting in principle any increase in political control of the civil service, we ought now to start thinking about how to bring this about in a controlled and constructive way (p. 405).

[Plowden suggests a greater frequency of requested moves to other posts, without the official being marked down as 'unsound'].

EXERCISE
Civil service neutrality

10.8 What are the advantages of preserving 'neutrality'?

d) From Sir John Hoskyns, former soldier and businessman, who headed Margaret Thatcher's Policy Unit 1979–82, in Parliamentary Affairs, 36,2, Spring 1983, pp. 137–43.
[Sir John was highly critical of the 'passionless detachment of the civil servant, 'goal-free policy-making', the lack of strategic objectives, the cynical acceptance of the inevitability of failure'].

Conventionally, an official can preserve his neutral status provided he concerns himself with policy and not with presentation. On closer inspection, this distinction is almost meaningless. All the big problems facing government, especially at a time of discontinuity, require it to do things which are essential, but which are regarded as "politically impossible"....

I suggest that policy, events, political messages and public debate are all part of a single behaviour-changing process. You cannot separate out the components of this process. But the civil servant must try to do so, so that his conduct – forget the results – conforms to the code of political neutrality....

If you agree with me that many of the problems confronting present-day governments can only be solved by shifting the boundaries of political possibility, then you will see that it is precisely at these boundaries that the officials may begin to feel uneasy and may start to withhold that last five per cent of commitment.

I am suggesting that the concept of political neutrality puts senior civil servants in an impossible position where they have to become passive, doing what they are told but no more, just when a supreme effort of will and imagination is called for. ∎

Power
The allegation of excessive power fits awkwardly with the first line of criticism, but it is not incompatible.
Senior officials are powerful for many good reasons.
● Civil servants, compared with Ministers, are permanent; skilled and experienced in the

business of the department; virtually independent of the Minister in appointment; in control of the department's channels of communication and access to the Ministers; operating within Whitehall into departmental networks; able to shape the Minister's engagements, his diet of papers and the timing (including the endless deferment) of decisions.

- The Minister, by contrast, is a transient amateur, in a hurry and with many other pressing matters on his mind.
- The convention of Ministerial responsibility largely disguises and protects the influence of the civil service.

Here are some views of civil servants and former Ministers, who in different ways attest to the power of the civil service.

■ DOCUMENT 10.7
The power of the civil service.

a) From a statement by Lord (Sir William) Armstrong in The Times, *15 November 1976*
Obviously I had a great deal of influence. The biggest and most persuasive influence is in setting the framework within which the questions of policy are raised. We, while I was in the Treasury, had a framework of the economy which was basically neo-Keynesian. We set the questions which we asked Ministers to decide arising out of that framework and it would have been enormously difficult for my Minister to change the framework so to that extent we had great power. I don't think we used it maliciously or malignly. I think we chose that framework because we thought it the best one going.

b) Sir Antony Part, former Permanent Secretary, in an interview with David Jessel, The Listener, *11 December 1980*
'The civil service always hopes that it's influencing Ministers towards the common ground. Now, that's not to say influencing them towards some piece of ground which the civil service has itself constructed; it is the civil service trying to have a sense of what can succeed for Britain and trying to exercise its influence on Ministers to try to see that they do capture the common ground with their ideas from whatever origin they start.'
[Sir Antony denied that the common ground was either the status quo or the centre.]...
'judgement of where the common ground is, or

might be, is a quite sophisticated matter and it is one of the most intriguing and difficult parts of the job of a civil servant.'...
'the centre is literally half-way between the two poles, while the common ground is the ground on which, or to which, the majority of people can be persuaded to move. You have to remember that in recent times neither of the main political parties has been elected by a majority of the electorate.'

c) From Barbara Castle, 'Mandarin Power', The Sunday Times, *10 June 1973*
I have no doubt that the civil service is a State within a State to an extent that the trade union movement could never aspire to be....

I believe that you have the absolute power as a civil service, because of your excellence, to make life impossible for any government which radically tries to alter the civil service. We are talking about government by consent. This is what the current democratic argument is about and your consent above all is necessary.

I think you have the largest negative power any organisation has in this country. Britain experiences negative power all the time. I think you've got negative power; you can work without enthusiasm.... ■

The structure of government
The structural critique of the civil servant is implied in the criticism of power and inadequacy. The civil service is as it is because its operation is determined by the structure of government, in particular the system of Ministerial responsibility coupled with the political neutrality and formal anonymity of civil servants. Ministerial responsibility remains the basic form of administration in Britain and preserves the fiction of government by Ministers and strengthens the illusion that civil servants do not govern. Civil servants are constrained by the structure to eschew innovations, creativity.

The Fulton Committee made some recommendations about structure – hiving off, planning units and policy advisers and the modification of anonymity. These were relevant but radical and so made little progress in the 20 years after Fulton reported.

Little has been done to meet the structural critique, except for the appointment of political advisers to Ministers. The Next Steps Report (1988) went further. In particular it proposed to separate and 'hive-off' the service delivery functions of the civil service from policy-advice and apply modern performance-related management to the hived-off operations. See below for the detail of the Next Steps proposals.

The nature of civil servants
This was considered above in relation to recruitment and training. The senior civil servant tends to be an able 'policy-administrator', neither a manager, nor a Minister. He or she is good at words, minutes, memoranda, meetings. Policy is arrived at by the well-turned phrase and the well-honed, well-marshalled argument. Policy development is literary and forensic, work for a barrister-don.

The civil servant is formed by his education, which wins recruitment to the first post at the age of 21 or so. Thereafter, he or she is shaped by lifelong immersion in the culture of the service and the metropolitan area. A certain insularity and insensitivity to other institutions is inbred. British civil servants rarely write books and articles, or give lectures as French civil servants do. Nor do they participate actively among groups and circles of the political class, as do their counterparts in Washington.

The civil service as a whole is not free of the faults associated with bureaucracy – an excessive concern for procedures and precedents, caution, a lack of initiative and creativity, a devotion to status and hierarchy. Some of this is clearly justifiable. We all deplore excessive caution in civil servants, until an energetic, creative, imaginative official does something positive to us; then we talk of excessive zeal, high-handedness, dictatorship. But there is abundant evidence too of time consuming routines thoughtlessly adhered to. Senior civil servants have not always intervened vigorously to combat bureaucratic inertia.

Again Sir John Hoskyns is a hostile witness, concerned at, indeed contemptuous of, the enclosed, inbred 'rather small world' of Whitehall, Westminster and the media.

'To an outsider, then, the overwhelming impression of government is of a rather small world: perhaps too small for what it has to do. A small policy-making monopoly, with salary tariff barriers to repel outsiders; a Cabinet formed from a tiny pool of talent... the key posts filled again and again from the same cast of players. Cabinet Ministers this time were the junior Ministers last time; the Permanent Secretaries this time were the Private Secretaries last time; a few remarkable people, on whom too much depends; all linked by the shared experience of past failure.'
(Parliamentary Affairs, 36,2, Spring 1983, p. 144)

Reform: the civil service in the 1990s

The civil service has been subject to persistent criticism and frequent attempts at reform. The radical proposals of the Fulton Report were largely neutralised at the time. Margaret Thatcher's blunter attacks on the service in the 1980s had a more substantial impact. This included a reduction in size and some 'hiving-off' of work to agencies or the private sector; a vigorous drive for efficiency, value for money or simply cost-cutting and intervention in appointments, in particular to promote 'doers' rather than 'thinkers', positive, goal-oriented managers. Under this assault the service may have lost some certainty about its role as a public service and its traditional ethic of non-commitment was perhaps weakened by the unbroken rule of one party and the obsessive defensiveness of government against intrusive media – not to mention contamination by private sector business ethics.

The thrust of civil service reform in the 1980s was embodied in the 'Next Steps' document (the Ibbs Report), published by the Prime Minister's Efficiency Unit in 1988.

The main and radical recommendation was that a substantial amount of government business should be 'hived-off' into agencies. These are 'quasi-autonomous'. They work within a 'policy and resources framework' set by a department, but within that the chief executive has freedom to manage against performance targets. It is evident here that the proposals aim to secure a modern business-style management, while retaining departmental oversight and Ministerial responsibility. It is envisaged that the civil service itself would be much smaller and would concentrate on servicing Ministers, managing departments and, at the highest levels, advising on policy.

The main themes and recommendations of the Next Steps Report are set out in the following Document.

■ DOCUMENT 10.8
The Next Steps Report

Extracts from a Report to the Prime Minister by the Efficiency Unit, HMSO, 1988

[Diagnosis]
3 First, the management and staff concerned with the delivery of government services (some 95 per cent of the civil service) are generally convinced that the developments

towards more clearly defined and budgeted management are positive and helpful.

4 Second, most civil servants are very conscious that senior management is dominated by people whose skills are in policy formulation and who have relatively little experience of managing or working where services are actually being delivered.

6 Third, senior civil servants inevitably and rightly respond to the priorities set by their Ministers which tend to be dominated by the demands of Parliament and communicating government policies.

7 Fourth, the greater diversity and complexity of work in many departments, together with demands from Parliament, the media and the public for more information, has added to Ministerial overload.

8 Fifth, the pressures on departments are mainly on expenditure and activities; there is still too little attention paid to the results to be achieved with the resources.

9 Sixth, there are relatively few external pressures demanding improvement in performance.

10 Seventh, the civil service is too big and too diverse to manage as a single entity. With 600 000 employees it is an enormous organisation compared with any private sector company and most public sector organisations.

[Recommendations]
First: The work of each department must be organised in a way which focuses on the job to be done; the systems and structures must enhance the effective delivery of policies and services.

Second: The management of each department must ensure that their staff have the relevant experience and skills needed to do the tasks that are essential to effective government.

Third: There must be a real and sustained pressure on and within each department for continuous improvement in the value for money obtained in the delivery of policies and services.

[Further]
The delivery of services
19 We recommend that 'agencies' should be established to carry out the executive functions of government within a policy and resources framework set by a department. An 'agency' of this kind may be part of government and the public service, or it may be more effective outside government. We use the term 'agency' not in its technical sense but to describe any executive unit that delivers a service for government. The choice and definition of suitable agencies is primarily for Ministers and senior management in departments to decide. In some instances very large blocks of work comprising virtually a whole department will be suitable to be managed in this way. In other instances, where the scale of activity is too small for an entirely separate organisation, it may be better to have one or even several smaller agencies within departments.

20 These units, large or small, need to be given a well defined framework in which to operate, which sets out the policy, the budget, specific targets and the results to be achieved. It must also specify how politically sensitive issues are to be dealt with and the extent of the delegated authority of management. The management of the agency must be held rigorously to account by their department for the results they achieve. ■

Once accepted and backed by the Prime Minister, the Next Steps Report became an action plan, to be forwarded by a project team based in the Cabinet Office and headed by an official of Permanent Secretary rank. The implementation of the proposals began immediately and by 1992 over 70 Agencies had been established, employing almost 300 000 civil servants. (These include, for example, the Civil Service College, HMSO, Meteorological Office, Ordnance Survey, Patent Office.)

Privatisation
The Executive Agency was devised to bring the virtues and disciplines of private enterprise and management into the public services, but without letting go of the ultimate responsibility of the Minister. In the 1990s the Government took further steps towards a more whole-hearted privatisation of government services. Some parts of government activity were designated for 'market testing' (assessment by experiment of the value of market disciplines) and plans were made and in some cases implemented for the contracting out of services such as prisons, the Royal Mint and even parts of the Inland Revenue.

As these proposals went ahead the civil service, as an organisation delivering government programmes and services, shrank.

At the top the policy advice and co-ordinating functions remained, for the shrunken public sector was still large and there was still a need to regulate or oversee the hived-off, contracted out or privatised public services. But even policy advice is available in the market and governments are already frequent buyers of expensive 'consultancy'. Are we witnessing the end of the Victorian civil service?

EXERCISES
The Next Steps

10.9   Do the Next Steps proposals relate in any way to the Fulton Report?

10.10 The Agency appears to be a 'half-way house' between a department and complete privatisation. How can this be justified?

10.11 Can Ministerial responsibility be preserved under the Agency scheme?

Politicisation

Margaret Thatcher was sometimes accused of 'politicising' the civil service. This was not true in a partisan sense, but she did make the civil service aware of the political priorities of the government. She was fully entitled to do that and, indeed, it was in accordance with some previous Labour Party criticism of the civil service. There is a case for some degree of politicisation.

Politicisation is sometimes denounced as damaging to the proper constitutional neutrality of the civil servant. Yet that neutrality, unusual in extending so high in Britain, puts the senior official in a false position, suppressing his own sharper judgements, yet accused of excessive power. Alternatively critics of the civil service argue that the real power of the high official is disguised by the 'neutered chameleon' image. One remedy for the problems of civil service power and civil service inadequacy is to create a layer of policy advisers and planning sections next to the Minister and alongside the senior managers. This would be an extension and formalisation of the present arrangements for special (political) advisers in the departments; and it fits the Fulton proposals for policy planning units and the Next Steps recommendation that the functions of management and policy advice be separated. There is no insuparable objection to senior civil servants working in the policy planning sections.

Such a scheme would be most valuable if it opened up the policy debate, challenging both departmental and political certainties and counter-balancing the pressures of the interest groups. An additional and complementary reform would be the opening up of all top civil service jobs to outside competition.

Red tape, plain words and a Citizens' Charter

The civil service suffers from the normal problems of large bureaucracies – size unrelated to output, rigid hierarchies, caution, conservatism, respect for precedent, addiction to forms and legalistic and impenetrable prose – all the defects associated with 'red tape'.

The problems of size and output are addressed by the Management and Next Steps reforms. The 'red tape' criticisms are often exaggerated. Forms, precedents, conservatism are necessary for information, consistency and predictability. Creativity, imagination and innovation may threaten the efficient conduct of routine administration. On the other hand, forms can be (and often now are) written in plain English, civil servants answer enquiries courteously and even informatively and the manager of a Social Security Office may choose to install carpets and bright curtains and purchase his own supply of paper-clips.

The civil service is affected by a new and broader sensitivity to the 'rights of citizens' (as in John Major's Citizen's Charter announced in 1991) and interest in mechanisms for the claiming of rights and redress of grievances (see Chapter 25).

GUIDE TO EXERCISES

10.1   Quite simply that civil servants are professionals in the strict sense and they would argue that they are also professional, that is technically accomplished and expert, general administrators.

10.2   There are three possibilities – a bad Report, a resistant civil service and a lack of political drive. All three are relevant. First the Report was perhaps too glib in its condemnation of the gentleman-amateur, too dismissive of the formidable qualities and technical accomplishments of the professional administrator. Some of the Report's structural proposals look too radical for easy implementation. Second, the civil service, like any large bureaucracy, distrusts change and has the resources to resist. Third, the government faced many other problems and the Prime Minister did not wish to apply his already shaky political resources to driving through reform

10.3   One major difference is that Margaret Thatcher got on with her reforms, without calling for a Report and so had much greater freedom of manoeuvre and met less resistance. But the Thatcher reforms reflected Fulton's concern with 'amateur-ism' and 'accountable management' and picked up the idea of 'hiving-off'. This suggests that Fulton may have been a useful preliminary to reform.

10.4   They aim to be rigorous and fair. The best candidates do very well in their later service careers (though this could be evidence that bias in selection continues as a bias in appraisal and promotion). It may be objected that the selectors will tend to choose candidates rather like themselves; also that the procedures favour candidates who are already mature, socially at ease, self-confident (these do seem to be desirable qualities but potential may be neglected).

10.5   The Permanent Secretary had the task of formulating policy and persuading the Minister. The Minister had the ultimate decision-taking and the responsibility.

10.6   Yes. It is altogether too neat a division and too facile a view of the development of policy. It is not as simple as that. Both Minister and civil servant have to wrestle with difficult problems and everything is shared except final authority and public responsibility.

10.7   The episodes cited were critical or turning points, when policy needed to be sharply changed or reversed. Civil servants, he suggests, are not good at breaking out of settled policy and routine. It may be argued against this, first that such crises are not representative of the general run of government problems (but that seems unlikely); second that the devising of new policies is properly a matter for Ministers, not civil servants. This argument is not entirely convincing either. Senior officials may be expected to devise and present options, leaving the Minister to decide. Of course the options might be politically difficult, administratively impracticable or

ineffectual. That is a difficult line for an official to argue – 'in effect, Minister, you can only solve this problem at a high political cost'. (Sir Humphrey, of 'Yes Minister' fame, would be inclined to say, 'That would be courageous, Minister'). This is when most civil servants may fall silent. Should they?
The constitutional answer may be, yes; the practical answer has more regard for solving problems than for preserving proprieties. Even Barbara Castle, a trenchant critic of civil service power, once complained of the fatuity of 'either-or' analysis, when the Minister desper-ately needed a firm recommendation.

10.8   The traditional arguments are that neutral-ity avoids 'politicisation', preserves a proper relationship with elected politi-cians, allows a Minister to hear 'unbiased' advice and fits a practicable distinction between policy and administration. You may think these arguments look like a rationalisation of the existing situation. See the following extract by Sir John Hoskyns.

10.9   Yes. See the Fulton proposals under 'Organisation of Departments' for 'hiving-off', for accountable management and for policy advisers and planning units.

10.10 The government did not rule out the later privatisation of Agency work. At issue here are gradations of control, account-ability and regulation. The Agency is intended to provide a 'halfway house' between autonomy and government oversight, perhaps the best but possibly the worst of both worlds – but we shall see. It may be that any gains in efficiency are balanced by a loss of accountability and the ethos of public service.

10.11 Ministerial responsibility fits rather awk-wardly, since an Agency is more distant from the Minister than a department and deliberately so. The Next Steps team prefer that ministerial responsibility is not seen as a central issue.

ASSESSMENTS
The power of the civil service

Denunciation of the evils of bureaucracy is easy enough and satisfying for those (most of us) who like conspiracy theories. The evidence and arguments set out above have shown both that bureaucracy is necessary and that it can get in the way of good government. But it is important to keep in mind the purposes of government – briefly, effective rule by consent. The civil service has to be judged by its capacity to serve those purposes.

Evidence was presented on both the power and the weakness of the civil service. Its power lies primarily in its permanence and expertise and its control over the machinery of government. It can and does run the country within the broad settled lines of custom and precedent and, like all such institutions, it is well able to delay and obstruct change. The weakness of the civil service – which may be appropriate constitutionally – is that it cannot govern in the strongest sense of bringing about radical change. Only politicians can do that – and Margaret Thatcher demonstrated in the 1980s that a determined Prime Minister can override the inertia and predispositions of the civil service.

However this is not a convincing demonstration of civil service weakness. If it takes a determined Prime Minister to overcome civil service power, that suggests very substantial power is normal. Thus, for example, we know that a Chancellor of the Exchequer complained that the Treasury was obstructing his programme of cuts. The Prime Minister summoned the Second Permanent Secretary and obstruction ceased (or at least diminished). The indication here is that the civil service is very powerful but not all-powerful.

It is realistic to accept that this must be so. The civil service carries out at least nine tenths of governing and plays an influential part in the remaining one tenth. Within that one tenth the scope for rapid and radical change is limited – Hennessy compares the civil servants to small tugs nudging an ocean liner through a narrow channel. It may be more helpful in securing good and democratic government, not to denounce civil service power as a conspiracy, but to recognise it and endeavour to reconcile it with a proper accountability to Parliament and public. This would indicate the need for less secrecy and a more open system of policy advice and development. The British civil service, like most bureaucracies, is better at effectiveness than at consent – but its

effectiveness is limited by the enormous scale of its operations.

Is management science enough?

Britain in general, and the civil service in particular, have been slow to adopt management science (or theory or technique). Civil servants thought of themselves as administrators rather than managers and their professional arts (not 'skills') were derived from general abilities and intellectual force, personal qualities and long experience. In the eyes of the managerialists the civil service view looked like a self-serving and elitist version of apprenticeship, or, in its traditional British form, as operated in nineteenth century textile factories, 'sitting next to Nellie' (actually if Nellie is a good instructor this is an effective way of teaching skills: compare the training of teachers).

In the 1980s Thatcherism, the mood of the Conservative right wing and the personal commitment of the Prime Minister, brought businessmen and business culture to bear on the civil service and the whole public sector including schools and the Health Service. The accountants and the strategic planners pushed aside the classicists and their elegant memoranda. The Age of the Word gave way to the Age of the Number. The consequences were seen in the FMI and MINIS and The Next Steps. The case for this radical shift in the civil service approach to management has been set out. The civil service always had reservations and the case against 'managerialism' (that is, the wholesale impact of the approach and techniques of business management into the public service) has some validity.

The case against management science as perceived by the civil service is as follows.

1   Political and constitutional matters are not at all like private business and they require more than managerial techniques aimed at profit-maximisation. The civil servant has to keep in mind political values, ideology and interests expressed through Cabinet and Parliament. Organised interests and general or particular public opinions have to be taken into account. In short political priorities may clash with simple considerations of efficiency and accountable management has to be fitted into the framework of ministerial power and responsibility to Parliament.
2   Management science itself as sold in the 1980s in Whitehall is inadequate. It is

insufficiently concerned with the sensitive motivation of people, with the facing of uncertainty with courage and energy, with the cultivation of values and commitment; and excessively concerned with economy, with cuts in manpower, simple, not to say crude, performance indicators and performance appraisal. Management science is not a value-free technology and its values, if appropriate at all, must be adapted to the public service.

3 The civil service already knows about and practises 'management science', even if few civil servants hold degrees in Management or Business Administration.

These arguments are stated in a more absolute form than is necessary. Some compromise is possible, once the differing contexts of business and the public service are appreciated. It is still of the highest importance in government to get policies right. A bad policy can waste billions of pounds, while good administration in detail (like the old Treasury pre-occupation with candle-ends) can at best save thousands. (The former permanent secretary, Leo Pliatzky, takes the (slightly unrepresentative) example of the Falklands and comments that better policy advice might have saved more money than 'any number of new management methods in the Ministry of Defence' (1989, p. 96). There are many other examples, including the management of the economy.

Concept

Bureaucracy

Bureaucracy is a word carrying a penumbra of pejorative meaning. At its simplest bureaucracy refers to the large corps of officials or administrators in all large organisations (not just governments) who 'run' the organisation. A small village primary school has no bureaucracy, a large comprehensive school or a university has a large and powerful bureaucracy. The bureaucrat is characteristically a specialist administrator, appointed on merit, organised in a hierarchy and following routine procedures – altogether an indispensable person.

However, the term is not much used in this neutral way. More often bureaucracy and bureaucratic are used as terms of criticism and denigration. Bureaucracy, it is said, is inherently self-aggrandising, wasteful and inefficient, addicted to routine procedures, precedent, paper and 'red tape', hostile to change – nothing must be done for the first time. These criticisms have a special force in government, since the bureaucracy is very large, public expenditure high and the power of the bureaucrats in relation to elected politicians is open to criticism on democratic grounds.

● CASE STUDY
Ministers and permanent secretaries

Michael Heseltine
From M. Heseltine, 1990, pp. 10–11
I freely admit to the moments where the pure gold of the perceptive permanent secretary shone through. I have as many faults as the next man but I can, by and large, take decisions. Sometimes, however, your powers fail. You are tired. It is late. The issue is of secondary importance, only half understood, and you know in your heart that you have lost control of that meeting of civil servants waiting for the firm hand of government. You ramble, hesitate and suddenly the voice at your elbow takes over: 'I think that's most helpful Secretary of State. We'll proceed as you have outlined which, if I follow your argument correctly, I would summarise as follows....' And the permanent secretary pours out a string of elegant phrases and concise instructions as tears of gratitude well up within you. And private secretaries – the permanent secretaries of tomorrow – make no mean fist of the same process. ●

(See also Chapter 7, Document 7.3 and Chapter 9, Document 9.8.)

● CASE STUDY
Roy Jenkins at the Home Office 1965

Based on Lord (Roy) Jenkins, 1991, pp. 180–4
Jenkins had a short experience as Minister of Aviation before appointment to the Home Office. More important, he had thought about and published ideas about the reform of Home Office policies; he had in effect 'a published personal agenda of what I wanted to do'. He immediately perceived that the approach, style and ideas of the Permanent Secretary, Sir Charles Cunningham, would not do and decided on a 'high-noon shoot-out'. 'It was at once the most difficult and the most crucial encounter that I ever had with any high-ranking civil servant'. Jenkins put forward twenty-two

'organisational demands', including some changes in staff and crucially a radical change in the department's advisory system. The structure was completely hierarchical and produced for the minister just one or two pages of advice over the initials of the Permanent Secretary, all background material, dissent and options being excluded.

Jenkins reasonably enough objected (though his three predecessors had not done so) to a system of advice which excluded alternatives and offered the choice of accepting or confront-

ing the Permanent Secretary. Sir Charles resisted, tried most unprofessionally to enlist the support of junior ministers, cried tears of rage (so Jenkins later concluded), Jenkins wavered but stood firm.

This is a good account of victory by the minister over a Permanent Secretary. This Permanent Secretary sounds in Jenkins' account rather old-fashioned. Perhaps they do not make them like that any more; or perhaps long experience, high status and power make all senior bureaucrats a little like that? ●

The elements and functions of Parliament

Parliament in decay?

A recent authoritative book on Parliament states: 'the key to understanding how the constitution works still lies in the relationship between the Government and the House of Commons as the representative body' (J. Griffith and M. Ryle, 1989, p. 5).

This is true, yet there is a paradox. Parliament is at once the fundamental institution of British government, the repository of constitutional sovereignty, political legitimacy and the major theatre of politics (supported but also challenged by the media). At the same time Parliament is arguably ineffective, grotesquely inefficient and lacking substantial political influence.

Parliament enjoys high prestige and persistent criticism, a strange mixture of the reverence in general and contempt in particular which the British bestow on their historic national institutions, the monarchy, the weather, football and cricket teams, the BBC.... Such ambivalence is not unreasonable, at least in the case of Parliament, for the British Parliament may justly claim a place in history as a practical and effective form of government through representation and by consent of the governed. In the light of this great and original contribution the imperfections of parliamentary government should perhaps be condoned. Yet Parliament in Britain at the end of the twentieth century is plainly in need of repair and renewal. Its main defects, according to its critics, are:

- it is poorly representative, being forced by the electoral system into a false two-party pattern
- it is dominated by party and, through party, by the government, thus restricting ('excluding' would be too strong?) individual opinion and dissent

- it has little effective capacity to challenge or monitor the actions of government
- the private Member of Parliament has yielded independence to party and to interest groups.

This substantial set of criticisms will be tested in the following account of Parliament.

Composition: the Members

1 Parliament is composed of two chambers, the House of Commons and the House of Lords. The Lords, made up of hereditary and appointed peers, is an anachronism in a modern legislature. It is treated at the end of the chapter as a subject for reform or abolition. It shows the English talent for making do with old institutions, which is not the same as making the best of old institutions. The House of Commons is composed of 651 members, (comparatively large by international standards) – 524 for England, 72 for Scotland and 38 for Wales, both slightly over-represented, and 17 for Northern Ireland. Members are elected by universal adult suffrage in a simple plurality ballot system. The system favours two parties and since 1945 Conservative and Labour Members have made up over 93 per cent of the House (though since 1970 only 70 to 80 per cent of the popular vote).

2 The profession of Parliament. Members of Parliament are professionals, though in a profession of unusual character:

- entry is quite difficult, requiring long service in humble capacities in local parties and local government, the cultivation of influential patrons and the struggle to secure adoption for an unwinnable seat and the fiercer competition for a safe seat. In a safe seat, by definition, job security is good, but 60 or more seats may change party allegiance at a general election and the Member may thus suffer 'compulsory redundancy'

- the whole profession of politics in Britain is very small, because there is no intermediate level of government (as in the states of the USA) and no very serious system of local government
- professional rewards are not great. Parliament offers a modest salary (by the standards of the City and the private London-based professions). There are quite generous allowances for research and secretarial assistance, (the average Member now has 2 staff assistants) and excessive car allowances, poor but improving office accommodation and good facilities for a 'gentlemen's club'
- promotion is hard to come by. There is a long and treacherous climb through the ranks from back bench to front bench. The ambitious politician needs talent, luck and patronage; timing is crucial and a long period in opposition may ruin a promising political career
- the work of a Member of Parliament is hard during the six months or so of the parliamentary session, up to fourteen hours a day about the House, (not often in the Chamber itself) with a weekend of activities in a distant constituency and a fair amount of drudgery on committees and dealing with constituency grievances. The average working week is over 60 hours with the House itself in session for 40 to 45 hours a week. However, for many Members, especially Conservatives without high political ambitions, membership of Parliament can be combined with the pursuit of professional and business interests and indeed may serve those interests very well. Even so, Parliament is no longer the profession for gentlemen it was a century ago, when it adjourned on Derby Day; but then there are few gentlemen's professions left.

For most Members of Parliament political and parliamentary activity provides its own satisfactions. In this it is like other occupations. It is attractive enough for those who do not make cold calculations about their prospects, but satisfactions diminish over the years and cynicism creeps in. The turnover is quite high; only the successful and the very determined and some who have nothing better to do, make parliamentary politics a lifetime career.

EXERCISES
The profession of Parliament

11.1 There is no shortage of candidates for Par-

liament. Why? For what reasons would you consider or reject going into Parliament?
11.2 Should Members of Parliament be given the salaries and conditions appropriate to a high professional post in the public service?

3 The Members themselves

There is no average Member of Parliament – they are a various collection of people from many walks of life, but the following tables of occupation and education show some major classifications within the variety. A majority of MPs are middle-class by occupation and have had a university education. Almost two out of three Conservative MPs are from the public schools; a handful of Labour members finished their education at the elementary stage. There are notable clusters in each party – barristers and businessmen in the Conservative Party; trade unionists and teachers in the Labour Party. Liberal Democrat Members tend to be nearer to the Conservatives in these respects. One half of Liberal MPs are public school educated, almost one third (6 of 20) from Oxbridge and 6 are lawyers; but the Liberals resemble Labour in drawing about 30 per cent of their candidates from among teachers.

In recent years in terms of social status the Conservative Party has come down and the Labour Party has risen, but there is still overall a social gap. Conservative Members of Parliament are more often drawn from or connected with the high middle class – one test would be attitude to the parliamentary salary, pocket money for the successful barrister but princely to the teacher.

Women are as seriously under-represented in this area of public life as in so many others and mainly for the same reasons. In the 1992 Parliament 58 women were elected (35 Labour), the previous highest being 41 in 1987. In this and in other ways the House of Commons is not a true image of the nation and its capacity to represent the nation may be diminished.

EXERCISES
The social representativeness of Parliament

11.3 What are the notable features revealed by the Table and what has changed over the last thirty years?
11.4 Should Parliament be more socially representative of the nation?

Table 1 The social background of Members of Parliament

a) Occupations of Members of Parliament, 1964 and 1992

[The table shows the major occupational groups in each party, as a percentage of all members in that party: information from D. Butler and A. King, The British General Election of 1964, 1965, and D. Butler and D. Kavanagh, and The British General Election of 1992, 1992.]

Occupations	*1964*		*1992*	
	Cons	*Lab*	*Cons*	*Lab*
Barristers, solicitors	26	15	18	6
Teachers, lecturers	2	6	7	8
Armed Services	9	0.6	4	–
Business	26	11	38	8
Journalists, publishers	7	9	8	4
Farmers	12	0.6	3	0.7
Housewives	–	0.2	0.2	–
Manual workers	0.7	32	1	22

(Note: there is an element of inaccuracy in a table of this kind because some members have more than one occupation, for example, a barrister who accepts a directorship after election to Parliament, or a miner who became a trade union official before election – and others do not reveal all their activities.)

b) The educational background of Members of Parliament, 1964 and 1992

[The categories are shown as percentages of all members in that party: Source as above.]

Education	*1964*		*1992*	
	Cons	*Lab*	*Cons*	*Lab*
All universities	63	42	73	61
Oxford and Cambridge	52	19	45	16
All public schools	75	18	62	14
Eton	21	0.6	10	0.7
Secondary only	11	16	6	12.5

The building

'We shape our buildings and afterwards our buildings shape us' – so Mr Churchill said in the debate of October 1943 on the rebuilding of the House of Commons. The oblong shape symbolises the division of the House into two parties, Government and Opposition and the structuring of most of its business around this division. But it is not the cause of that division, which is to be found in British social and political history and in the electoral system. Three parties existed for a time between the wars, despite an oblong chamber; and so did coalition government, which would best flourish, it might be supposed, in a semicircular chamber. (The chamber of the Northern Ireland Parliament was changed in 1975 from oblong to horseshoe layout, to encourage the sharing of power – an unsuccessful venture into the politics of carpentry).

A second point made by Mr Churchill in the debate of October 1943, about the size of the chamber and its effects on speaking styles, is less open to challenge. The chamber is small, seating under 450, on benches, not individual seats and desks ('with a lid to bang', as Churchill said). There is no rostrum – 'harangues from a rostrum would be a bad substitute for the conversational style in which so much of our business is done'. Backbenchers are discouraged by the lack of desk or lectern, as well as by convention, from reading their speech. This informality of style is supported by the conventions of the House, notably that all remarks are addressed to the Speaker and no Member is addressed by name; and there are interjections and interventions.

There is a third point which Mr Churchill omitted, but which was raised by backbenchers: it concerns the facilities of the House of Commons outside the chamber. These were, and still are, inadequate for a profession which at its best demands both learning and administrative skill. A backbench MP, lamenting his lack of an adequate private office, a telephone, an interviewing room, might well mutter to himself 'we shape our buildings and afterwards our buildings shape us'.

Facilities have been much improved in recent years, notably by the provision of office accommodation in a nearby block. However, the Palace of Westminster, historic but much re-built, despite 1100 rooms and its excellent hospitality facilities, cannot match the needs of a modern legislature for professional legislators and their support staffs including Library and Research Divisions. For a backbencher a room of his own is still a luxury and many assistants do not have desks of their own. The more radical young professional Members might even look to the abolition of the House of Lords, or its removal to Liverpool or Leeds, as a necessary beginning to the creation of a modern parliament for Britain.

But do they really need such professional facilities? There is not complete agreement that the Member of Parliament should be seen as the thoroughly professional legislator fully equipped like a business executive. It may be argued that a simpler operation is more appropriate and effective (and that may be true for the business executive too).

The weakness with this argument is that the present Parliament is neither business-like nor simple but effective. The mock-medieval building, like the procedures of the House, is complex, baroque, convoluted and above all oppressive. As in all such buildings, cathedrals and Oxbridge colleges and courts of law, the individual is charmed, captivated, made captive. Any pupil in an old-established school with a high regard for itself would know the feeling. As in schools, such intangibles can be powerful agents in moulding the pattern of life and in setting standards and codes of conduct, but they can also be powerful in inhibiting critical thought and innovation and in ritualising the vitality out of life. Both kinds of view appear in the following document.

■ DOCUMENT 11.1
The Atmosphere of Parliament

a) From Hugh Dalton, 1953, pp. 156–7
Parliament is a very comfortable place. The historic dignity of its procedure and its precincts is very soothing. The sense of unreality in debates, where speeches turn no votes, is enervating. The physical atmosphere of the House itself, through which no fresh wind ever blows, seems designed to subdue the will and banish discontent...

b) From Sir Thomas Moore's speech, H. C. Deb., Vol. 393, 28 October 1943, cols. 460–1
There has been something in the atmosphere of the whole House and of the surroundings as a whole that has managed to discover the best that is even in the worst of us. I, and most other hon. Members, have seen great reforming spirits come down to this House as new Members. They have come possibly from the Clyde and the Tyne and from Ipswich, where they have been inspired or embittered by social injustices prevailing in their own districts. They come with an exaggerated idea of what they are determined to do, sometimes even to destroy not only the constitutional structure, but the material structure of our Chamber. I have watched for years and seen the way the atmosphere has got hold of these wild spirits, has tamed them and brought them into a constitutional frame of mind in which they become proud of the structure, of the atmosphere and of the constitutional methods adopted by this ancient Mother of Parliaments. ■

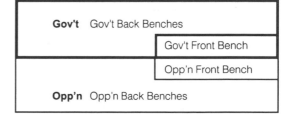

Figure 1 The formal divisions of the House of Commons

EXERCISES
The building and the atmosphere

11.5 What is the case for a mock-medieval Parliament building?
11.6 Which of the following facilities would you regard as important in a Parliament building?

- seats for each member in the chamber
- offices for each member
- desks for each member in shared writing-rooms
- telephone booths
- dictating rooms
- research facilities (including the preparation of briefs).

11.7 Can you think of any arguments against regarding the House of Commons as a workshop?

11.8 Do you find Sir Thomas complacent or perceptive?

Discussion of the buildings of Parliament and facilities for Members raises questions about the proper functions of Members. The modern position is that the Member is an expert professional, able to challenge the executive and its army of officials on their own ground, especially in the specialist Select Committees. The traditional view is that the Member is an amateur not an expert and should not try to participate in a professional contest he cannot win. One of the most vigorous exponents of the traditional view, Enoch Powell, spent hours in the Library doing his own research, but no time at all in Select Committees, which he regarded as irrelevant to the proper purposes of Parliament. However, the dichotomy implied by the terms expert and amateur, may be misleading; the role of the Member is primarily to do with political representation, principles and values.

Principles and functions

Organising principles

1 *Party*

The place of Parliament in British government is largely determined by the operation of party. In effect the majority party chooses a government and hands the parliamentary power of its majority to the government, which thus acquires the command of Parliament. Ministers are Members of Parliament. This is an unusual arrangement in legislatures which are mostly based on the principle of separation of powers. The inherent conflict is resolved by party majority in favour of Ministers: they dominate the legislature. Thus the sovereignty of Parliament is ceded to the executive. This was the consequence of the extension of the suffrage and the development of political parties in the nineteenth century: a House of Commons disciplined by party is not a recent development.

In the eighteenth century political parties in the modern form did not exist, but were foreshadowed by groupings or connections of political friends. These were shifting, ill-organised groups lacking common and defined political attitudes and without connection or support in the country. In this situation, the King could usually secure the nominal co-operation of Parliament, which was a prerequisite of government, by the judicious use of patronage and political management. Parliament could be persuaded not to obstruct, if not to support either, the course of royal government.

In the first half of the nineteenth century, due to the decline of patronage, the growth of a democratic public sentiment and the slow enlargement of the electorate, the Crown found it increasingly difficult to arrange a majority in the House: political power had slipped into the hands of the Commons.

The changed distribution of power became apparent in 1835, when Peel found he could not go on as Prime Minister with the support of the King but not of the Commons and again in 1841, when Queen Victoria found that holding a general election was no longer a guaranteed method of arranging parliamentary support for the royal candidate for Prime Minister. In 1868 Disraeli resigned after defeat in the general election without meeting Parliament; this is the modern practice which acknowledges the decisive power of the electorate.

The keys to this newly defined political situation were:

- the organisation of a majority of voters in the constituencies
- the organisation of a majority of Members in the Commons.

Modern political parties have developed in order to grasp and use these keys. The change is a profound one, indeed a revolution: the source of government had been the throne and was now the people. The purpose of the political party became, and still is, to make and sustain a government in the name of popular sovereignty. Parliament, which itself had never been the government, had become the direct support of government. It was that, much more than it was a critic, overseer or scrutineer of government. The authority of Parliament was exercised by the Government Whips – on behalf of the Government.

The consequences for Parliament of this

imposition of party organisation have been fundamental and, so it may be argued, damaging. The party organisation of Parliament has been criticised on the grounds that it has made Parliament powerless in the face of the Cabinet; that the individual MP has become 'mere lobby-fodder'; that the range of political choice is unduly restricted; that adversary style politics and 'instant opposition' are destructive and often hypocritical. There is some truth in all these points. Nevertheless there are major advantages arising from the operation of political parties and in particular from the two-party system.

- The system imposes a limit on discussion and expedites the taking of decisions on policy.
- The decision-takers may be identified and are answerable in the end for their decisions through the House of Commons and to the electorate.
- The elector is confronted with a clearly marked set of choices – he knows for what as well as for whom he is voting. These points reflect the 'pendulum theory' of British democracy, as long as the pendulum retains the potential to swing.
- Government is relatively stable (and this is not simply an acceptable way of saying that government is immune to criticism and inflexible).
- There is strong incentive for each party to seek majority support, rather than appealing to a single group or interest.

It may be that the validity of these arguments has changed in recent years and the argument is reconsidered at the end of the chapter. The distribution of power between Government, Opposition and backbenchers is examined in Chapter 12.

2 Opposition
The governing majority party dominates the proceedings of the House of Commons but minority parties are allowed by the custom and procedures of the House to oppose. The largest minority party forms the official Opposition and its Leader has formal standing, a government salary and a car. The opposition parties and especially the official Opposition, have some rights and privileges in the conduct of parliamentary business, subject to the overriding limit that the majority party gets its way. The Opposition endeavours to harry and embarrass the government and to stake its claim as an alternative government. In this winner-takes-all system the contest is inevitably one-sided, but it is

pursued with vigour. Politics in the House of Commons is partisan, adversarial, unconstructive and, to an outsider, manic.

The division between government and opposition is the most obvious division in Parliament; but it is crossed by the gap created by a disciplined and solid party majority between the 'front bench' of party leaders and their 'back bench' followers. In this four-way division (see Figure 2) the front bench of the majority party is the gang of heavy weights, the governors. The machinery and procedures of the House are shaped by their power.

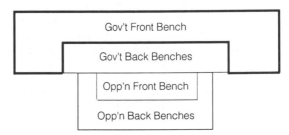

Figure 2 The forces of the House of Commons – the relative power of the four divisions

The functions of Parliament

■ DOCUMENT 11.2
The purpose of Parliament

a) From W. Bagehot, (1867), 1963, pp. 150–3
The House of Commons is an electoral chamber; it is the assembly which chooses our president...our House of Commons is a real choosing body; it elects the people it likes. And it dismisses whom it likes, too.

Because the House of Commons has the power of dismissal in addition to the power of election, its relations to the Premier are incessant. They guide him and he leads them. He is to them what they are to the nation. He only goes where he believes they will go after him. But he has to take the lead; he must choose his direction and begin the journey... [a Minister should say firmly], 'Parliament has maintained ME, and that was its greatest duty; Parliament has carried on what, in the language of traditional respect, we call the Queen's Government; it has maintained what wisely or unwisely it deemed the best executive of the English nation.'

The second function of the House of Commons is what I may call an expressive function. It is its office to express the mind of the English people on all matters which come before it....

The third function of Parliament is what I may call... the teaching function. A great and open council of considerable men cannot be placed in the middle of a society without altering that society. It ought to alter it for the better. It ought to teach the nation what it does not know....

Fourthly, the House of Commons has what may be called an informing function. In old times one office of the House of Commons was to inform the sovereign what was wrong. It laid before the Crown the grievances and complaints of particular interests. Since the publication of the Parliamentary debates a corresponding office of Parliament is to lay these same grievances, these same complaints, before the nation, which is the present sovereign.

Lastly, there is the function of legislation, of which of course it would be preposterous to deny the great importance, and which I only deny to be as important as the executive management of the whole state, or the political education given by Parliament to the whole nation. There are, as I allow, seasons when legislation is more important than either of these.'

b) From R. H. S. Crossman, H. C. Deb., Vol. 738, 14 December 1966, cols 479–80

The physical conditions under which we work and many of our main procedures are survivals from a period when parties were weak, when the making and unmaking of Ministries still rested with the House of Commons, not with an electorate based on universal suffrage, and when the Cabinet was merely the executive committee of the Commons. Procedurally, we still behave as though we were a sovereign which really shared with the Government in the initiation of legislation, which exercised a real control not only of finance, but of the administration of the Department.... The House of Commons too, has surrendered most of its effective powers to the Executive and has become in the main the passive forum in which the struggle is fought between the modern usurpers of parliamentary power, the great political machines.

In this transformation of the parliamentary scene the House of Commons has largely lost the three functions for which its procedures were evolved and to which they are relevant, the making of Ministries, initiation of legislation shared with the Cabinet, and the watchdog con-

trol of finance and administration....

It is no good trying to reform ourselves by harking back to ancient days. An effective reform must be an adaptation of obsolete procedures to modern conditions and to the functions we should fulfil in a modern highly industrialised community. Today, for example, it must be the electorate, not the Commons, who normally make and unmake governments. It must be the Cabinet that runs the Executive and initiates and controls legislation, and it must be the party machines that manage most of our business, through the usual channels, as well as organising what was once a congeries of independent backbenchers into two disciplined political armies. Since this is the structure of modern political power, the task of the reformer is to adapt our institutions and procedures to make them efficient. ■

EXERCISES
The functions of Parliament

11.9 Bagehot's first two paragraphs, on the electoral function do not seem to fit the contemporary House of Commons. Why?

11.10 In the light of these extracts and what has been said so far, list the functions of Parliament.

The functions of Parliament are as follows.

1 Choosing and sustaining a government

This is the most significant constitutional function of the House of Commons, though it acts in practice only as an electoral college registering the popular vote. As part of this function, the House provides a training and selection system for Ministers. With a few exceptions the government is made up of Ministers who have gained their qualifications for office by performance in and around the House. This is a party government chosen by the majority party; but it is also a parliamentary government and government Ministers remain active members of the Parliament.

2 Making laws

Parliament provides both the overriding legitimacy of law and the machinery for the making of law, derived from its legislative sovereignty. Parliament's legislative function is mainly to do with the processing, not the initiation and shaping, of laws.

3 Representation

Parliament's historic role was to grant money in

return for the redress of grievance. Representation was implicit in both these functions. Representation includes Bagehot's three functions of expression, teaching and informing; alternatively it might be said that Parliament remonstrates and demonstrates. In the pursuit of this function Parliament relates to the local party and constituents and also interest groups.

4 *Opposition*
In the Westminster model of British government the job of the minority in Parliament is to oppose the government, thus compelling the government to make its case, subjecting the government to critical scrutiny and appealing to the electors as an alternative government.

5 *Oversight, scrutiny*
Parliament as a whole is entitled to call the government to account for its conduct of affairs. In practice the challenge to major policy is left to the Opposition, but the whole House participates, notably through the Select Committees, in the scrutiny of the government's administration (as distinguished not very satisfactorily from policy).

EXERCISE
The functions of Parliament

11.11 Which of these functions is restricted and weakened by the operation of a disciplined party majority?

Business, procedures, management

The business of the House
The House of Commons works broadly in four ways.

Work	by/for (mainly)
legislation	Government
debate	Government and Opposition
scrutiny, monitoring	backbenchers
representing individual grievances and demands	backbenchers
representing group grievances and demands	backbenchers, parties Opposition

The work of the House of Commons takes place:

- in sessions of the Commons in the Chamber
- in committee in the committee rooms of the

House (there is a corridor of committee rooms sometimes referred to as 'upstairs')
- about the House, in offices and corridors, outside the House and in the constituencies

The main business conducted in the Chamber can be roughly divided into:

- government legislation (about one third of the time)
- motions by Government or Opposition for general debate, including the debate on the Queen's Speech (the government's programme) at the opening of each session of Parliament
- Private Member's motions on the adjournment – a half-hour debate each day led by a backbencher normally chosen by ballot and raising particular matters of concern
- oral questions
- ministerial statements, followed by questions for example, reporting on recent negotiations, or an emergency or catastrophe (significant by subject, but not taking up substantial time)
- emergency debates under Standing Order No. 20 which may be requested of the Speaker to consider a matter which is 'specific and important and should have urgent consideration'. Such requests are hardly ever granted, but secure media attention anyway.

The work of the House outside the Chamber, in Committee, is important, though assessments of its significance and value vary. This committee work is further discussed below, but it may be noted here that the Standing Committees (which are actually ad hoc, not standing) deal with legislation and the Select Committees (which are standing for each Parliamentary Session) deal with administrative oversight or scrutiny.

In the formal business of the House, as distinct from private interviews and meetings, the disposal of time and the right to initiate are essential. Not surprisingly the Government is most generously provided, but it does not have a monopoly of either time or initiative. There is a struggle at the margins for both. The Government's mastery of the House is not undisputed.

The Government has the lion's share of time on the floor of the Chamber and dominates the nearly one half of the time devoted to legislation. In some of the time under its control, initiative lies with backbenchers, but some of backbench-initiated business is late at night in an almost deserted Chamber.

Table 2 Share of time and initiatives (%
Session 1985–6)

	Government	Opposition	Backbenchers
	%	%	%
Time	75	12	13
Initiative	55	10	35

Source: J. Griffith and M. Ryle, 1989, p. 12

Managing the business of the House

The management of the business of the House, and especially what goes on in the Chamber, is the responsibility of the Speaker, as the presiding officer of the House, and also of the Leader of the House, who is the Cabinet Minister charged with managing parliamentary business on behalf of the government. The Speaker, though a Member of Parliament, serves the House of Commons, not the government. The House is also served by officials, headed by the Clerk.

Parliamentary business amounts to a massive industry of speeches, debate, committees, minutes and reports. The paper itself is daunting – over 10 000 pages each year of legislation and Standing Orders (double the product in the 1950s). On most days of the session Parliament in effect produces a substantial book.

Effective debate requires some elementary rules of procedure about, for example, who shall speak and when, what kind of remark or action shall be regarded as inappropriate and 'out of order' and if and at what point a conclusion should be reached. A chairman is necessary to control the discussion and enforce the rules. The House of Commons has rules of this kind, though in more complicated form and the office of chairman is filled by the Speaker.

Many chairmen hold positions of authority and exercise leadership functions in the organisation over whose committees they preside. This is true, for example, of a chairman of a school's board of governors and of the Prime Minister in the Cabinet. Their position as captains of the side may overlay their position as umpires. The Speaker of the House of Commons, however, has no governmental responsibility and is able to act as umpire impartially with respect to contenders in the House of Commons, committed only to the preservation of parliamentary methods and manners. This is a position which has evolved since the eighteenth century. Originally the Speaker was

the Spokesman of the Commons and a person of influence with King and Commons. His or her importance lay in his political role: now it lies in her non-political character. The house now has its first woman speaker.

A good Speaker is a Member able to gain respect from all parties, but not, or no longer, required for high office by her own party and preferably with a good presence and voice. In general, the Speaker ensures fair play, gives rulings on the proper conduct of debate, suppresses disorder and has some regard for the rights of the backbenchers. Some arrangements – for example, the order of speaking, or notice by a backbencher of an intention to raise a point of order – may be made privately 'behind the Speaker's Chair'. Speakers keep records of the activity and interests of Members, so that her calling of Members to speak may be reasonably fair, taking into account personal, and constituency interests and party position.

To enforce the orderly conduct of debate the Speaker may call for order; call for the withdrawal of 'unparliamentary' language or for a Member's withdrawal from the Chamber; or, in extreme cases of general disorder, she may suspend the sitting. These sanctions against disorder depend on the moral authority of the office, supported by the House, whose servant the Speaker is. The House has some sense of self-discipline, though it accepts interjections, heckling and barracking as part of legitimate political conflict. Indeed, the House of Commons in recent years is disorderly by post–1945 standards and the number of Members 'named', that is reprimanded or ordered out of the Chamber has markedly increased.

The Leader of the House, together with the government Whips, plans the timetable of the House, in some degree of consultation with the opposition Whips. These are the 'usual channels' through which informal agreement is made. The Leader of the House is bound to respect the sentiment of the House as a whole, whilst not forgetting that he is the agent of the government. The government has a majority and, in case of disagreement, the sentiment of the House is what the majority says it is.

Occasionally, the government has to show its procedural teeth. A guillotine procedure provides for the ending of debate according to a timetable and is the complete answer to opposition 'filibustering'. The filibuster is the American device of talking at length to delay and perhaps prevent government action and can be effective in the

American Senate, with its tradition of unlimited debate.

Normally, in Britain, the government controls most of the time of the House, just as it controls its parliamentary facilities, its information and its work. It is a peculiarity of this Mother of Parliaments that the full weight of parliamentary sovereignty lies with the government to which parliament has conceded its power.

The business of the House is also managed on behalf of the government and the parties by Whips, well-named as the whippers-in, sergeant majors or minders of party discipline. Their work is considered in Chapter 12 as part of the Government's control of the House. The Liaison Committee of the Chairmen of the Select Committees is also considered in Chapter 13. Both are noted here to complete the pattern of the management of the House based on Speaker, Leader, Whips and Liaison Committee. Of these only the Speaker (with the Clerks) is truly the servant of the whole House, undiminished by party.

The sources of legislation

Governments arrive in office committed to making changes – all the more so, because the election campaign will have exaggerated the differences in the policies advocated by the parties. A good deal can be changed without legislation. For example, new financial priorities might switch spending from defence to education, or vice versa: this change in policy would go through the House in the estimates. Foreign or economic policy can be changed by new initiatives or a new emphasis, or have changes forced on it: these again would be debated in the House – though not necessarily immediately. Similarly changes in, say, weapons procurement or development, the disposition of troops or the social security regulations can be made 'administratively', Parliament might be informed, but would not be consulted.

None of these cases involves making a new law. Similarly all governments lay heavy hands on economic affairs without recourse to Parliament (or even the Cabinet); for example, influencing the lending policies of banks and building societies, prices in industry, salaries in the public sector. There is a limit, however, to what a government can do without legislation. Only laws can provide for enforcement in the courts and only laws can provide a regular authority for spending money.

The process of legislation begins a long time before it reaches the stage of formal introduction in Parliament; indeed by that stage the process is almost complete. There are five main sources for the policy ideas which become Bills:

- the party
- interest groups
- 'think tanks', official committees and Royal Commissions
- government departments
- the government itself (Cabinet, Ministers).

These sources may work in informal combination, but Parliament itself, its Members and its Committees make very little direct contribution to the genesis of legislation.

The draft Bill which comes to Parliament has proceeded from original ideas through lengthy consultations with departments of state and interested groups; its general provisions may have been commented on by the majority parliamentary party; and it will have gone to the Cabinet via a ministerial committee. The parliamentary stages of legislation constitute the final amending and registration process. But the legislative process is much longer than the parliamentary process and much more important; and it takes place mainly outside Parliament.

EXERCISES
The sources of legislation

11.12 Discover all you can about the sources of legislation currently passing through Parliament, or in a particular period, for example the first or last year of a government. Assess the relative importance of party, departments and interest groups.

11.13 The necessity and the difficulty of drafting laws in exact and meaningful language is often underestimated. Try drafting a clause which would compel employers to provide somewhere to sit down for those employees who could reasonably sit from time to time in the course of their work – a shop assistant serving at a counter for example.

(Do not spend more than ten to fifteen minutes on your draft – long enough to appreciate the problems.)

The legislative machine

Bills are of two kinds, public and private. Private bills are concerned with private interests, for example, local authorities seeking new powers, or a company seeking power to acquire land. The rest are public bills, except for a few which are deemed hybrid. Public bills may be promoted either by the government or by a private Member. Thus a private Member's bill is a public bill.

All bills go through the following procedure or a variant of it:

1 Introduction and first reading. The Clerk reads out the short title of the bill and the Minister names a day for second reading. This is a formal signification that the government intends to bring in a bill. No debate takes place.

2 Second reading. This is the main debate on principles, the only amendment being one amounting to complete rejection. The amendment may be in the simple form 'declining to give a second reading'; or it may be in the form, 'that the bill be read a second time upon this day six months' (meaning that the bill be rejected). The latter is a good example of the characteristic and baffling procedural convolutions of the House of Commons.

3 Financial resolution. If the bill involves expenditure, then the expenditure must be authorised by the House.

4 Standing Committee. Most bills are then sent to a Standing Committee for detailed consideration and amendment.

The House appoints seven or eight Standing Committees. They have no specialised functions. Indeed, in the ordinary sense they are not 'standing' committees at all, for they are reconstituted for each bill as it comes up. Usually between twenty five and forty five members are appointed by the all-party Committee of Selection run by the Whips. The membership is roughly in proportion to the balance of parties in the House, with the government always in a majority (if it has a majority in the House). A chairman is appointed by the Speaker from an all-party panel.

The Standing Committees meet in the morning, twice a week, but sometimes for longer and more often. The Minister in charge of the bill will go through the bill clause by clause, sometimes himself proposing amendments and urging the rejection of opposition amendments. The Minister works from a set of detailed briefs and officials are on hand to offer advice. Government backbenchers read their correspondence and call out 'Aye' or 'No' at the Whips' command. Dissidents, opposition Members and those 'representing' particular interests busily move amendments – which are promptly rejected. Most bills are not highly contentious and will be approved by the committee in one or two sittings. Others may be fought clause by clause. The record for consideration in standing committees is about 140 hours.

The committee stage is an important part of the legislative procedure of the House. It is unlikely, given party-based government, that bills will be rejected on principle at second or third reading. In effect, the electorate has empowered the government in advance to enact certain broad policies and to meet other problems as they see fit. The function of the House is to make the execution in detail as effective and as just as possible. This is a quite restricted function. Of the few amendments approved by the Committee about half are withdrawn at the report stage and almost all of the rest are then voted down by the government majority. A study of three sessions in the period 1967 to 1971 showed only 1.5 per cent of amendments passed against the government (J. A. G. Griffith, 1975). Apart from this rather thin tally of public victories, the committees do have modest influence – bringing about, or helping to bring about, government changes of mind without adverse votes. Recent Parliaments have been only a little less docile.

5 Report stage. The bill as amended by the standing committee is formally 'reported' to the House. The government may introduce further amendments, based on its second thoughts, or the prompting of the committee's discussions. Often the House proceeds directly to the third reading.

6 Third reading. This is a general debate on the bill in its final form, rather like the second reading. For that reason this stage is sometimes taken without debate.

7 The bill in the Lords. The bill goes through similar stages in the House of Lords, except that there is no financial resolution (the Lords cannot deal with financial matters) and the committee stage is usually taken by a Committee of the whole House.

The bill may be amended in the Lords, often on the initiative of the government. These amendments must be submitted to the Commons. If they are not accepted, the Houses exchange messages and, if there is still no agreement, the Commons may resort to the procedure of the Parliament Acts and thus override the Lords. Normally bills pass through the Lords quite quickly.

8 Royal Assent. The bill has then completed its journey through Parliament and shortly receives the Royal Assent.

Although the Government controls the legislative machinery, legislation is still time consuming and laborious. There is a limit to its capacity to put through legislation. This is a practical rather than a political restraint on government.

EXERCISES

The legislative procedure of the House of Commons

11.14 In the light of the above account of legislative procedure, what points can you make for and against the procedure?

11.15 Can you devise better procedures for the making of laws?

The government's control of a bill's timetable

Parliamentary procedure provides the government, through its majority in the House, with several weapons to expedite the passage of its bills. These are all to do with the closure of debate, which may be moved at any time, though the Speaker may refuse to accept the motion if he thinks the matter has not been sufficiently debated. If he does accept the motion, it will be decided by vote, normally, of course, in the government's favour.

These arrangements clearly might not meet the needs of a government in a hurry, faced with an opposition determined to fight every inch of ground. So the government has some reserve weapons, dating from the 1880s when the Irish used obstructive tactics in the Commons. The government may propose a restrictive timetable for the consideration of a bill. This is known picturesquely as the 'guillotine' and it may be operated by compartments (grouping clauses and amendments) or by 'kangaroo' (leaping from one selected amendment to another). For example, a guillotine was applied to the Telecommunications Bill (1983) after over 300 hours of unconstructive (or even destructive) debate. The effect of obstruction followed by guillotine is to destroy serious debate, though both sides claim their devotion to parliamentary democracy.

These devices are normally used only when the government is in serious difficulties with its legislative programme, or has 'emergency' bills to enact, or when the opposition is engaged in obstruction (see Chapter 12, Table 1). Of course, the judgement of what constitutes an emergency and what obstruction, lies with the government. The devices are unpopular, restricting valuable criticism and amendment as well as obstruction and negating the legislative role of Parliament. Hence governments use these closure procedures with some 'respect for the rights of the House as a whole' and a prudent awareness that they must do as they would be done by (the latter a diminishing basis for parliamentary ethics by the 1990s).

The problems for a government unable to impose a timetable (because of small majority, party rebellions and the high constitutional significance of the matter) were shown by the protracted process of legislative approval of the Maastricht Treaty in 1992–3. This stretched over 14 months, involving 300 hours of debate and over 70 divisions.

Financial business

Financial business in the House of Commons is similar to legislation in its politics. Historically the grant of supply (money) is the source of Parliament's power against the Crown; but in practice that power is now exercised by the executive, on behalf of Parliament, not the Crown. The processing of financial legislation is tightly controlled by the Whips on behalf of the government in the same way as ordinary legislation.

The financial business of Parliament is notable in some respects. By a rigid convention, only Ministers may propose expenditure. The Lords play no part in financial matters. In the past expenditure has been considered in December and raising funds by taxation in the Spring Budget. The latter has always been accorded much publicity, without reference to spending or the state of the economy and has not encouraged a proper public understanding of government finances ('Chancellor hits beer drinkers and motorists' etc.). From 1993 expenditure and taxation are dealt with on one great occasion, in November or December each year.

The financial procedures of the House of Commons are complex. Taxation proposals are first incorporated in 'Ways and Means Resolutions' (which have immediate effect) and then into a Finance Bill and Finance Act. Expenditure proposals begin as Estimates and a Vote on Account and end as the Consolidated Fund (Appropriation) Act. Actual expenditure by the departments is subject to the scrutiny of the National Audit Office and the Select Committee on Public Accounts.

One seemingly insurmountable problem in the control of finance is the sheer size and complexity and elusiveness of the data. Anyone with experience of trying to understand and discuss a budget of more than a few thousand pounds can testify to the problems of accounting, timing, allowing for inflation, predicting under-spending and over-spending. At the same time, public finance is complicated by enormity – approaching 250 billion pounds in the 1990s – and indirectness. Money may be raised not only by taxation but, for example, by selling nationalised industries, or raising national insurance payments ; and much of it is spent by other bodies than the government itself – local councils, nationalised industries, general practitioners of medicine, people having babies or falling out of work and so on.

Governments now endeavour to present to Parliament a coherent picture of their plans for public expenditure. The autumn financial statement is by previous standards a revolution in the financial information available to Parliament. But the margins of error in accounting may be as large as the scope for policy change.

Financial business is laborious and takes hours of parliamentary time, much of it concerned with undramatic, not to say boring, detail. It does demonstrate the principle that the government cannot spend except with the approval of Parliament. But a British government never suffers the embarrassment of American administrations, which cannot secure their budgets against Congressional raids. Some Washington agencies have been left without funds to pay the monthly salary cheques. Parliament does not have that power to make bureaucrats jump (what a pity, you may say?).

Pressures on Parliament

Heavy pressures fall on Parliament. The chief oppressor is the government, but interest groups and the media also pursue their own ends in and through the House of Commons, parties endeavour to exert a continuing influence and, behind them, the voters await, mostly without great interest, their four-to-five year opportunity for a performance review of their masterful servants.

The dominance of the government, in effect Prime Minister and Cabinet, has already been indicated. In the normal situation of a majority government, the government demands, and the majority party in the House willingly concedes, a full authority to govern broadly on the accepted lines of party policy, traditions and interests, subject to consultation, occasional modification of proposals and an assurance of success in the next election.

The 1992–3 Parliament was quite exceptional in that an organised group of Conservative rebels opposed to the Treaty of Maastricht, generally lacking confidence in the party leadership and exploiting a thin majority, were able to mount an organised and persistent campaign of opposition. The rebels were finally called to (temporary) order by a confidence motion (July 1993).

The system of a government dominated legislature is not in itself and by definition contrary to good and democratic government. Such a system plainly restricts the freedom of the individual legislator and the authority of the House as a whole. But the system is not designed to be government directly by Members of Parliament individually (a practical impossibility) or collectively (that is, government by assembly). Rather the system provides representative and responsible government through a party-based Cabinet structure. This is one way, more or less satisfactory, of conducting the business of the state; there are other ways, again more or less satisfactory. The less and the more is a matter of detailed argument. The system of dominant Cabinet and subordinate legislature is not in itself doomed to produce an elective dictatorship and a pointless parliament. However, you may feel that the evidence is quite suggestive of such a conclusion!

The other oppressors of Parliament, interest groups, the media, parties and electors are dealt with in Chapter 12 and in other relevant chapters. Most Members of Parliament serve their party and their constituents, even their country, well enough, without much deviation from political principle or gross abuse of conscience. We have come a long way from Burke's famous address to the electors of Bristol in 1774, asserting the Member's right to exercise his independent judgement (see Chapter 15).

Burke was concerned about the Member's freedom from constituency pressures, though not necessarily from the highest constitutional motives – on another occasion he wrote to his constituents to say that they should not expect to see him often, as he lived a hundred miles away and was often tired by his work on their behalf! The modern Member has many more pressures to deal with, including distance and exhaustion, but especially those arising from his allegiance to a party. That overriding allegiance is the basis of functioning of the House of Commons.

Nevertheless, a handful of awkwardly independent Members of Parliament survive, mavericks who enliven and often enlighten the House. They bring joy to the parliamentary reporters and irritation to the party managers. Such mavericks have sometimes secured minor legislative change or directed media attention to government error, but few have changed the course of history. One exception might be Winston Churchill's sustained private campaign during the 1930s to draw attention to the threat from Hitler's Germany, but government and public opinion was changed in the end by Hitler's rather than by Churchill's actions. Some illustrations of back bench independence are given in Chapter 13.

GUIDE TO EXERCISES

11.1 Probably because some people see politics as the highest form of public service, giving opportunities to take part in the shaping of society; because, too, some people find politics a peculiarly satisfying activity both intellectually and emotionally; because quite a few people come from backgrounds which encourage a political career, e.g. trade unions, journalism, the forces. (Lord Boyle gave his reasons for entering politics in Boyle and Crosland, 1971, p. 69.)

The second part of the question is for you to answer unaided.

11.2 Some Members may be attracted by the financial reward alone and be in other ways unsuited. But that only makes Parliament comparable to most other professions, except perhaps schoolteaching and the Church. We do not expect, say, ICI, to attract better executives by paying them low salaries.

The more serious objection is that some Members may not be able to afford antagonising their party or their constituents, or they may be reluctant to resign or retire.

These arguments derive from the notion that membership of Parliament should be different from that of other professions, even that it should not be considered a profession at all. This does not seem to be a good way of attracting into Parliament persons of high calibre.

11.3 Broadly the Conservative Party tends to be high middle class in character, with

lawyers and businessmen making up over half of the parliamentary party; the Labour Party tends more to the lower/public sector middle class, with a quarter of its MPs drawn from the teaching profession. Even so there is some indication that the parties have moved slightly nearer one another over the last thirty years, judged by these social measures. Ironically, social goodwill and collegiality has probably declined in the House of Commons in that period (the decline of 'noblesse oblige' in the Conservative Party and a general sharpening of political ill-will in the 1980s).

11.4 This echoes the debate about the social background of civil servants. On the one hand, Members of Parliament need for the practice of their profession the education and skills normally associated with middle class professionals; at the same time, they should reflect in their own experience and understanding the conditions and outlook of all 'walks of life'. Parliament is not socially a mirror of the nation; but it is far more representative than the upper levels of the law, the church, the civil service and financial and business corporations.

11.5 It encourages an awareness of the great history of the institution of Parliament and this ought to be a constant factor in the activities of the House. It should serve as a warning to governments tempted to apply their majority in defiance of the rights of the House and an indication, also, to new and inexperienced members that some of the irritating convolutions of parliamentary life might be a proper institutional adjustment to complex and contradictory functions. An historic-looking building may also secure the respect and affection of the people, demonstrating the continuity of their institutions. It may be good for the tourist trade too.

11.6 Not perhaps the first, for the good reason given by Churchill – in any case, seats for each member would not often be in demand. Similarly some Members do not need elaborate offices, but, for those who do, a shared desk or a shared writing-room is not a satisfactory substitute. On research facilities, it might be argued that the Member should aim to be an informed layman, not an expert and that he ought to do his own 'homework'. But without research, how is a Member effectively to tackle the Minister with his departmental brief?

11.7 That Parliament's function is separate and different from that of the executive. It ought not to concern itself with expertise and administrative detail, but with the wider more philosophical criticism implied in the word 'deliberation'. Given the expansion and complexity of government activities, this amateur view now seems out of date.

11.8 Complacent rather than perceptive; but Sir Thomas does demonstrate an important historical position, that Parliament has contributed to the diversion of radical and rebellious tendencies in Britain into constitutional and non-violent forms.

11.9 Bagehot was writing about the House of Commons in the 1850s and 1860s, when it worked without a solid party majority and selected and dismissed Prime Ministers freely, though not as frequently or as capriciously as he implies. This was an unusual period of parliamentary government. Bagehot's electoral function has remained the prime function of the House of Commons, but in a party context which transforms the relationship.

11.10 See following text.

11.11 Functions 2, 4 and 5; and probably 3 too.

11.12 This you must do for yourself. Shrewd guesses are not ruled out. You should discover that a great deal of legislation is not related to party programmes or ideology. Organised interests are likely to have their say, often by invitation, but their influence on the shape of legislation is difficult to measure.

11.13 You might assess the effectiveness of your draft clause by pretending to be an inhumane and grasping employer. Do you see a loophole?

The actual provision of the Offices, Shops and Railway Premises Act 1963 reads: 'Where persons who are employed to work in office, shop or railway premises have, in the course of their work, reasonable opportunities for sitting, without detriment to it, there shall be provided for their use [at suitable places conveniently accessible to them] suitable facilities for sitting sufficient to enable them to take advantage of those opportunities.'

The phrase in brackets was inserted by the government at the committee stage in the Lords.

11.14 The procedure is complicated, repetitive and long, yet still does not ensure full consideration of proposed legislation. On behalf of the procedure it may be countered that the length of the procedure does enable Parliament to give adequate consideration (that is why it is so long) and a substantial amount of amending does go on, (mostly by the government, but in response to criticism, as well as its own second thoughts). Moreover the procedure is logical. Behind this argument lies the question of the proper role of Parliament in legislation – a major development role, or, as governments prefer, just tidying-up and formal registration?

11.15 The answer reflects these conclusions. If Parliament is to play a bigger role in legislation, then it would need to enter the procedure earlier, with a debate on general principles, and do far more work in the legislative Standing Committees. However, this would depend on a fundamental change in the present division of labour and power; for party and Cabinet deal with general principles, and the departments deal with detail, for which Parliament is not equipped. Other possibilities are that Parliament should sit for longer and a (reformed) second chamber could do more work.

ASSESSMENT
Party diminishes Parliament

It is evident from the account so far – and what is said in the next two chapters does not much modify the position – that the operation of a disciplined party majority diminishes the role of Parliament. This could be put more strongly: the influence of Parliament is annihilated. In a system characterised by its critics as 'elective dictatorship', 'government by dogmatic minority', or 'winner-takes-all', there is no independent role for Parliament; the majority party obediently supports the Government, the Opposition rages impotently.

There are three responses to this fundamental criticism of the British Parliament.

1 The criticism is exaggerated. Parliament does have a role and significant influence; there is scope for independent and worthwhile activity by Opposition and backbenchers, within the limitations of a party-based system.

2 The criticism is based on a misunderstanding. Party organisation of Parliament is inevitable and wholesome: it gives effect to the will of the people as expressed in elections. This argument begs a number of questions about elections and the nature of political parties, to be examined below (Chapters 14–18). But, leaving these considerations aside, the contention is that party strengthens Parliament - indeed, party is the very life-force of Parliament.

3 The criticism is well-founded and indicates the need for reform. Reform could be fundamental (changing the party system by the introduction of proportional representation); or procedural (modernisation and improvements in procedure to favour Private Members); or, alternatively or additionally, the moderation of party control by the relaxation of party discipline (calling off the Whips) and the extension of free (unwhipped) votes.

The extension of free voting looks attractive, but it does raise political and constitutional problems. At the moment free voting is limited to a very few issues of 'conscience' (for example, abortion, Sunday closing and the death penalty). If free votes are to be extended to substantive policy, the business of government becomes more complex and 'messy'. Policy development and decision in large groups is time-consuming and untidy; it may lead to less clear-cut decisions, compromises, retreat to cautious gradualism, 'phasing'. All this may be true, though the record of Cabinet decisions has not been so brilliant and better to be right gradually than wrong decisively.

Free voting also runs up against the ideas of collective and ministerial responsibility. If Parliament takes the decision, then Cabinet or Minister cannot be responsible in the accepted way to Parliament and people. But we know that relationship of responsibility is in fact mostly a disguise. Under a system of free voting the Cabinet or Minister would account in a way familiar in other organisations, working to the instructions, broad or specific, of a higher body. Cabinet would operate as a committee of Parliament, which is what in theory it is.

Of course, it might be argued that the process would proceed in full circle and the committee would organise and dominate Parliament. That may be so: the party organisation of Parliament is a rational response to the demands of representative government.

Still it does seem practicable and desirable that Parliament should insist on more free votes on matters in which options are developed and presented to it. It could be open to governments (subject to parliamentary comment) to restrict matters for free votes to the less central issues, for example, restricting economic, financial and foreign policy to 'confidence' (therefore whipped) votes, but leaving to free votes matters such as the school curriculum, the management of schools and the Health Service, the general shape of the road programme, the Social Security regulations....

In fact, trying to distinguish matters appropriate for free votes shows up the difficulties. All of the matters given as examples have been subject to sharp party disputation and, it may be argued, justifiably so, since they can reflect different approaches and philosophies. Subjects like road programmes raise another problem – the corrupt distribution of local benefits, or what the Americans call the 'pork-barrel'. Again there are answers: first, that there is no point in allowing free votes on matters on which there is no dispute; second, that the 'pork-barrel' exists already and openness would make it less corrupt. Free voting also makes it more difficult for Members to resist the pressures of interest groups.

Altogether, this consideration of the extension of free voting demonstrates the party controlled system is not without a certain sharp practicality. The question of the role of Parliament and possibilities of reform are taken up again in Chapter 13.

Concept

Sovereignty of Parliament

The British constitution is based on the principle of Parliamentary Sovereignty. It could alternatively be called a doctrine, precept, notion, general idea. It is, indeed, the chief and perhaps the only clause in the constitution, but since formally there is no constitution, its actual status is obscure.

Parliamentary sovereignty was asserted by a Parliament in 1688, in the course of a power struggle; so it rests on something like a coup d'etat (not unlike the disposition of power in the USSR in 1991–2). However, parliamentary sovereignty has been recognised by the courts, though that raises the question of the source of the authority of the courts.

Whatever the origin and status of parliamentary sovereignty and, leaving aside the problems of a constitution derived from a representative assembly, the British system of government is based on parliamentary sovereignty as a working principle. However, in practice the power of Parliament, as explained in Chapter 3, is handed over to, and exercised by, the government. Thus parliamentary sovereignty is, paradoxically, the basis of executive dominance. This is evident in much of this account of the work of the two Houses of Parliament.

The principle of parliamentary sovereignty raises problems in relation to the sharing of power with international bodies, especially the European Community, and the devolution of power to Scotland, or to local government.

● CASE STUDY
Norman Fowler and the abolition of SERPS

Based on N. Fowler, 1991
This case study gives a rough indication of the relative significance of Parliament in the total work of ministerial policy making. The policy is already made: the Minister drives it off the production line and displays it to a partly hostile audience....

Norman Fowler, Secretary of State for Health and Social Security, 1981–7 wanted to reform the social security system and in particular to abolish SERPS, the State Earnings Related Pension Scheme. There was a good demographic reason for this: as the number of pensioners increased and the number of contributors decreased, so the scheme would become horrendously expensive.

Like most major projects of social legislation, this one stretched over the years. Fowler was appointed in September 1981, announced a review of social security in April 1984, took his conclusions to a Cabinet committee in February 1985 and to Cabinet in May 1985. There followed a Green (consultative) Paper and in

December a White Paper (firm proposals). Legislation took another six months, to July 1986 and a scheme, considerably amended from the original, was introduced in April 1988. Thus ended not less than four years work – but Fowler believed another round of reform was required.

Fowler's proposals faced a number of obstacles.

● Cabinet committee. The ad hoc committee was chaired by the Prime Minister and included half of the Cabinet. This looked to be the crucial decision area – as it usually is.
● But the Chancellor, Nigel Lawson and the Treasury were difficult. Every paper going before a Cabinet committee required clearance by the Treasury. But the Treasury had already vetoed any consideration of social security and tax policy together (which Fowler favoured), and Lawson further objected to any proposals on National Insurance which, he said, was a budget matter for the Chancellor alone. Lawson was especially concerned about the cost of tax-relief for private pensions to replace SERPS. Since Lawson also wanted to get rid of SERPS, it was possible for him to work together with Fowler. But it then appeared the Treasury wanted a saving of £2 billion on the social security budget by 1987–8. Fowler regarded this as impossible.

Chancellors are difficult to 'square' or put down. Lawson intervened again just two days before Cabinet was to consider the recommendations of the committee. Fowler was angry at this intervention which he regarded as 'unconstitutional'. It was, rather, contrary to normal procedure and courtesy, for the recommendations had been cleared with the Treasury and agreed by the Cabinet committee. Under Margaret Thatcher and, indeed, most Prime Ministers, the full Cabinet was not an appropriate place for fights over policy, except when prior resolution had proved impossible. From the point of view of a Minister promoting a policy, a show-down in Cabinet is likely to damage both his policy and his reputation. In this case Fowler arranged to take the item off the Cabinet agenda and endeavoured to come to an agreement with Lawson before re-submitting it. However, the Chancellor's position prevented the more radical reform which Fowler might have preferred.

- House of Commons. Fowler records two occasions in the House which he found difficult – especially because some of his own backbenchers were uneasy about his proposals. On the first occasion he was forced by an accurate leak about the proposal to abolish SERPS to defend himself in the Commons – before the policy had been before the Cabinet. 'The forthcoming debate promised to be a highly uncomfortable occasion with my defence alternating between "no decisions have been taken" and "wait and see". Neither defence was likely to go down conspicuously well in a crowded House' (1991, p. 218). But Fowler believed he was saved when the Opposition spokesman put forward controversial proposals of his own, not agreed by his shadow Cabinet colleagues.

  Again Fowler expected trouble in the House when he made his statement on the publication of the Green Paper.

  'The atmosphere was more like the Budget than an announcement on social security... the predictions were that I was in for a stormy time. Even stout warriors like Kenneth Clarke felt that all the rows, the leaks and the speculation were going to make my task difficult. Yet, as often happens in the House of Commons, the predictions of a major confrontation proved false....' Fowler was again, so he thought, saved as the Opposition launched into a denunciation of the reforms as 'a new Victorian Poor Law'. The legislation was hard fought, but the government's majority remained secure, except in the House of Lords.

- Consultation and negotiation. As the Minister moved through the long process of policy development, he was compelled to make many concessions. After the publication of the Green Paper this was a fairly open process, good for democracy perhaps, but making life difficult for policy makers. The Treasury remained anxious about costs. The pensions industry (who had much to gain) and employers (who had much to lose) were both concerned about compulsory occupational pensions. The party and many social welfare groups pressed that the new Family Credit be paid direct to the mother. This was conceded and SERPS was reduced, not abolished, and occupational pensions were encouraged but not made compulsory.

- Social legislation is like painting the Forth Bridge. As soon as you have finished it is time to start again. There was another major social security bill, two years after Fowler's – the fifth since 1979. ●

The House of Commons at work I

The Government

The Government sees in the House of Commons:

- a legislative machine, as indicated in Chapter 11
- a continuing, statutory press conference to which it is obliged to give some information and one forum (not the most important) in which it must make its case
- the main source of support, a prop of its standing and a channel of communication to the party and the country
- There is also an element of reverse influence which has low but variable and disputed significance – Governments respond to 'negative feedback' from Parliament. But they are just as concerned with feedback from the media, the polls and the interest groups.

The Government acknowledges the majority party in the House as the source of its power and indeed the very substance of its being; but, after acknowledgement and flowing from it, Government expects to control the House.

Control of the party
The major political parties in Britain are coherent and disciplined. Parties support their leaders for the most part voluntarily. The leaders are elected, the main policies are agreed and the rewards of party unity in the prevailing party and ballot system are high. Members of Parliament as members of a party are therefore well-disposed towards the Government, enthusiastic for its main work and ready to forgive minor deviations. Members of Parliament as individual aspirants to office have further cause to follow their leaders: promotion is not won by persistent awkwardness.

This natural coherence of parties qualifies all talk of imposed discipline. Nevertheless, the parties employ 'Whips' to keep the troops happy and in line and they act to reinforce natural cohesion and, when it fails, to replace it with sharper discipline. The Whips on the Government side enjoy government posts; that is, they are paid and the Chief Whip may attend Cabinet. Whips are not Ministers, but have good prospects of promotion (Edward Heath was a Chief Whip and John Major a Whip).

The day-to-day job of the Whips is to organise attendance in the House, keep in touch with Members and communicate their views and concerns to Ministers and to promote support for the Government. As a matter of routine, the Chief Whip (in all parties) sends out to his members each week a document, also known as a 'whip', which sets out the business of the coming week and indicating with one, two or three heavy underlinings when attendance is essential, necessary or requested. A Member may 'pair' with a member of another party and thus be excused from all but the most vital of votes.

Absence from a debate with a three-line whip will be noticed and, indeed, may be the subject of prior negotiation in which the Whip moves from comradely persuasion to the more menacing terms and tones of the sergeant-major. The rebel member's 'card will be marked'. He will not get promotion, or even election to office in the parliamentary party; he will not get pleasant expense-paid trips to sunny and salubrious countries and his request for better office accommodation will be mislaid. At worst the chairman of his constituency party will be told of the disloyalty and, exceptionally, he may be denied membership of a Select Committee he desires in order to pursue his special interests or justify his consultancy fees; ultimately the threat of 'de-selection' may be put in play.

Thus the Whips plainly deal in discipline: they are the prefects of the parliamentary parties. The following Documents put rather different views of the role of the Whips. Lord Morrison, a leading figure in the Labour Party of the 1940s and 50s, writes like a headmaster, trying to soften and disguise his absolute power. Edward Pearce, a sharp observer from the press gallery in the 1980s, sees the whips as something of a tyranny.

■ DOCUMENT 12.1
The Whips

a) *From Lord Morrison, 1964, pp. 184–5*
It is a widespread belief that the Whips have no other duty than to bully and coerce Members against their will into voting in the party lobby and speaking in accordance with the 'party line'. This is an inaccurate and incomplete picture of the functions of the Whips. It is persuasion rather than bullying that is the rule; it is reasoning with a recalcitrant Member rather than coercion that is the general practice. The good Whip seeks to avoid a situation in which the troubled or troublesome Member is driven to choose between humiliating conformity and flagrant revolt, which may raise all the difficult problems of formal disciplinary action. There are extreme cases from time to time which may justify and, indeed, necessitate straight speaking, but peaceful persuasion, friendly reasoning, and argument based on the need for keeping the party together, are far more normal and effective.

b) *Conservative Whips*
From E. Pearce, 1991, p. 96
...the Conservative Whips inherit a position of strength nowhere equalled in the English speaking world. Deferential associations, a parliamentary party about eighty three per cent ambitious, if only for budgerigar-seed, persuasive authority over all junior appointments which, since in Britain they are the pre-condition of higher appointments, means guardianship of the ladder to the top, a shameless traffic in honours with knighthood as the parliamentary party's long service medal, also a brisk bourse in committee places and free trips...list the means to hand and we are talking power.

The Conservative Whips enjoy in their small but influential kingdom, a power which, compared with the lot of a middle eastern despot, armed only with life and death and control of the press and television, might fall short in crude overkill, but which in its finely nuanced way suffices. ■

EXERCISE
The Whips

12.1 Which of these descriptions of the Whips is the more convincing?

■ DOCUMENT 12.2
John Major as Whip

John Major was, like all Conservative Whips, allocated an area and a department. He needed to know the strengths, weaknesses and aspirations of his Members and the detail of his department's business, including legislation. He did not go so far as to tell the Minister his business, but he should know enough about, say, a department bill to spot trouble and warn of it. Major was good on the detail and earned the respect of backbenchers. He was able, tough but not hyperactive – 'he knows how to do nothing'. ■

The distribution of power between front bench and back bench is obviously and, no doubt justifiably, uneven. The front bench will be dominant most of the time and especially when in office, for the following reasons:
● through its superior information, experience and ability
● through the force of the general agreement that underlies a party's thinking and the general desire to preserve party unity as an electoral asset
● through the absence for most of the time of issues of contention within the party
● through the prudent restraint of the ambitious backbencher
● in the case of the Conservative Party, through the ready acceptance of the principle of front bench leadership. This must be true in the long run, though the rebellions of 1992–3 over Maastricht indicate a temporary loss of cohesion and discipline.

Lord Morrison argues that this balance (or imbalance) is right and proper. It may at least be considered efficient.

There is some evidence that the Government, through the Whips, cannot exercise total control of backbenchers. Members take a more professional view of their role; some can afford to spurn the favours of the Whips and hold that independence of mind is not a disqualification for promotion. They may rightly believe that there is safety in numbers and even that the authority of the Whips is partly based on bluff. But there are casualties among backbenchers to show that persistent independence and awkwardness meet with punishment. The authority of the Whips is after all more than a friendly bluff.

The role of rebel backbenchers is discussed further below, but their influence, as distinct from their interest, should not be exaggerated. Judged by what Governments get out of Parliament, it is evident that Government control of Parliament goes without serious challenge. In particular Government controls the legislative machinery and the flow of information.

Control of the legislative machine
Modern governments require vast amounts of legislation – at least, they think they do. Even Margaret Thatcher's Government, while claiming to be non-interventionist, enacted in 1989 three times the volume of the (minority) Labour Government of 1977. A major reform bill like the Education Reform Bill of 1988 was almost twice the length of its predecessor the 1944 Education Act (it tackled many more problems) and included 238 clauses. Hence Governments 'push through' the House substantial legislative programmes. Governments can do many things without legislation, or even without the immediate approval of the House, but changes in law, institutions, expenditure and taxation all require legislation, that is, the making of statute law. Most governments add at least 30–40 new laws and about 1500 pages to the Statute Book each year. The size of the Statute Book is a weighty tribute to the power of governments to use Parliament as its own law-making machine.

This is not to say that the legislative process is smooth, rapid and uncontested. A Bill may be fought 'line-by-line' through all its stages' but the Government can apply its majority and arrange for the limitation of debate by closure or 'guillotine' (a pre-fixed time-table). For example, on three days in 1988 the Government 'put through' altogether over 900 amendments (almost all government-sponsored) to the Education Reform Bill and the Local Government Finance Bill, most without debate. The use of the guillotine has increased in recent years. According to the researches (with the help of the Commons Library) of a Conservative back

bencher, Richard Shepherd, who qualifies as a 'rebel', the number of guillotine motions was as follows:

Table 1 Number of guillotine motions 1945–90

1945–50	3	1974–79	21
1950–60	10	1979–83	30
1960–70	13	1983–87	10
1970–74	8	1987–90	28

EXERCISE
The guillotine

12.2 Comment on the significance of Table 1

Governments control the outcome as well as the timing of the legislative process. Most of the amendments to Bills represent the government's own second thoughts, further negotiation with interest groups and occasional concession to its own backbenchers. Concessions to the Opposition are rare.

For example, the 220 pages of the Finance Bill, 1984, including the Government's main taxation proposals, were considered line-by-line in committee for 150 hours. The Opposition, without expert advice, raised complex issues like the taxation of woodlands or landladies' flats. It was a fine demonstration of professional parliamentary opposition – but virtually nothing was changed against the Government's will. Government backbenchers stayed silent and voted when they were told to.

To take another example, in the Standing Committee considering the Bill to privatise the electricity industry (1988–9) in 110 hours of consideration, amendments were dealt with as shown in Table 2 and Figure 1.

Table 2 The Government's legislative machine

Amendment moved by	moved	accepted
Government	114	113
Opposition	227	0
Gov't backbenchers	22	1

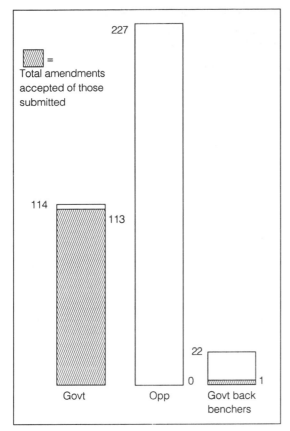

Figure 1 Amending the bill to privatise the electricity industry 1988–9.

The Figure gives the bare facts about controversial but comparatively straightforward legislation; crudely you were for it or against it, the detail followed from these contrary positions, and the Government could regard itself as entitled to privatise, as a Labour Government had previously been entitled to nationalise. (You may think that what is acceptable constitutionally still makes an odd way to run an industry!). In the case of the Conservative Government's massive Education Reform Bill (1988) there is some evidence of the Government's making concessions on the way through about 370 hours of the legislative process. Some concessions were made to interest groups, notably the Church of England, the Universities (both well represented in the House of Lords) and local authorities. Altogether 5000 amendments were tabled. The Government itself had many changes of mind. According to the Opposition spokeman, the original Bill gave government 175 new powers and when amended conferred 240 more. Even allowing for some

partisan arithmetic, the Bill is significant in this respect, as an indication of the uses and abuses of the House of Lords and above all as a triumph of government-dominated legislation.

Control of information

The Government controls the flow of information to Parliament. It would be churlish and untrue to say that it gives as little information as possible. Ministers collectively spend a good many hours in the House, there are shelves of verbatim reports and a Minister rarely refuses an invitation to talk to the media. Still, the Opposition and all backbenchers may well feel that in spite of best efforts they do not know much of what is going on.

The Government has many advantages in the information game.

- The conventions of collective and ministerial responsibility preclude the revelation of official advice and of current Cabinet discussion. It is customary to deny all disagreements among Ministers, so Parliament is excluded from discussion of policy at the crucial stage of development, precisely when it is open to modification.
- The culture of government secrecy reinforces and protects this position. The government may deny information to Parliament in matters in which it appears the main consideration is the avoidance of government embarrassment (see Chapter 13, Documents 13.3 and 13.4).
- The government has an enormous advantage over backbenchers and Opposition in all complex and technical matters. For example on the committee stage of the Finance Bill the government can field up to four Ministers, all fully briefed and supported by Treasury officials, up to seven parliamentary secretaries and a score of tame backbenchers. The Opposition must cope with no official and little research support; symbolically one assiduous Labour member used to bring his files in Marks and Spencer plastic bags (very sensible of course but it may illustrate the difficulties of not being the Government).
- The government manages the flow of information and does not regard Parliament as having much priority or rights to information. Government news is dispensed to the lobby of journalists, announced in public speeches or leaked selectively. For example, in November 1988 the Chancellor of the Exchequer, Nigel

Lawson, briefed Sunday newpaper correspondents to the effect that he was considering means-testing pensioners' benefits. This was then denied by the Treasury and later in vigorous terms by the Chancellor in answer to a question from the Leader of the Opposition. The Government refused a request for a debate.

The standing of the Government

The Government's control of the House is not absolute and cannot in any case guarantee its standing, that is its reputation among political and media people and others seriously interested in politics, readers of 'quality' newspapers, listeners to Radio 4 at breakfast time and academic students of politics – the kind of people sometimes called the attentive public or the chattering classes. The Government's standing in and around Westminster counts for the most, since that is likely to be projected into the mass media and so around the country.

Standing is open and public and yet quite obscure. It may easily be discounted and bold politicians may conclude that there is no virtue in standing well in the House and with the media. But most politicians conclude prudently that this intangible, undefinable standing may count when times are bad. If so, then the House, as a central part of this struggle for standing, also counts and so has influence.

The extent and limits of Government control of the parliamentary legislative machine

In the Session 1988–9 Parliament passed 33 Bills, 12 of them major legislative projects, including the privatisation of water and electricity. Eight of the twelve were strictly curtailed by timetable motions. The Government had a secure majority, but there were rumbles of discontent, particularly on European issues, leading finally to the resignation of the Chancellor, Nigel Lawson.

There were significant rebellions in the Commons, over:

- official secrets
- child benefit
- football spectators' identity card scheme
- dog registration scheme (Government refusal to set one up).

The House of Lords defeated the Government on:

- compliance with EC drinking water standards
- and laying pipes over private land (both in a Water Bill and subsequently reversed by Government)

- Electricity privatisations – also criticised by the Commons Select Committee on Energy
- a private inspection system for schools

The Government also 'climbed down' or made forced concessions on:

- nuclear power stations. The Government reversed its previous stand and withdrew the nuclear power stations from the sale – an embarrassing demonstration that nuclear power was not economical
- some restriction of party political activity by local government officers (Local Government and Housing Bill)
- the football spectators' bill.

Despite these examples of opposition and concession, overall the Government pushed through a massive programme of legislation, some of it highly controversial. The programme included the two major privatisations, a new Official Secrets Act, a new and permanent Prevention of Terrorism Act, a Dock Work Bill abolishing the National Dock Labour Scheme (rushed through in advance of a strike in defence of the scheme), a Social Security Bill and a Companies Bill.

EXERCISE

Government and the parliamentary legislative machine

12.3 Does this record show that Government has secure control of the Parliamentary legislative machine?

The two Oppositions

Governments face two oppositions in Parliament, the official Opposition and their own backbenchers. The Opposition harries the Government without mercy, but also without effect. The backbenchers of the majority party are full of goodwill but do occasionally express discontent and may go so far as to embarrass – but not defeat – the Government. Hence they do from time to time exert a modest influence.

Government backbenchers

Government backbenchers do not make up much of an opposition. They are loyalists, their loyalty reinforced in many cases by ambition. They aim to make a mark by steady and skilful support of the Government and occasional brilliant destruction of the Opposition. If their efforts are rewarded by advance to the lowest rung of office as an unpaid 'Parliamentary Private Secretary' then they join the silent ranks of 'the Government', their career as Parliamentarians done. But beyond the ranks of the promoted or the obsessively ambitious, there are genuine parliamentarians and occasional dissenters.

Governments can be defeated only when their own Members join with the Opposition. Given the solidarity of governing parties, such defeats are very rare. But government backbench opinion is taken account of continuously 'behind the scenes' and, especially so, if dissent is pressed beyond the persuasions of the Whips as far as abstention or contrary voting.

Such open dissent has increased in the last two decades. In the 1950s the proportion of divisions involving dissenting votes was 2–3 per cent. In the 1970s this measure of dissent rose to more than 20 per cent and as high as 28 per cent in the period of minority or near-minority Labour Government, 1974–9. In that Parliament Labour members dissented in 309 divisions. This intra-party opposition was highly organised by the dissident Tribune Group. In 44 of the divisions over 50 Members voted against the Government, which was defeated on 42 occasions.

The two issues which most aroused dissent were membership of the European Community and the Government's proposals for devolution to Scotland and Wales – interesting evidence of the divisive power of these 'cross-cutting' issues. The Government was able to shrug off defeats as well as embarrassment and survived for a full term, despite never having a majority of more than three. The Government finally fell when its voting coalition fell apart on a division accepted in advance as carrying its fate.

Parliamentary dissent seems to have reached a peak in the period 1974–9. The Labour Government was in an unusual political position – a bare majority, a divided party and a stream of difficult issues. In the 1980s Margaret Thatcher ruled a more united party with a sharp discipline. But her radical measures provoked intra-party division and distress, so the new tradition of parliamentary dissent, for what it was worth, occasionally barked.

For example, in the 1979–83 Parliament there were 18 occasions of serious dissent; four of these involved over 40 Members. On two occasions the issue provoking dissent was immigration and the Government was defeated once over immigration

rules. On a score of matters the Government is known to have withdrawn or modified its position, under the threat of defeat in the House. Many of these incidents show that the chief dissenters were the moderates or 'wets', resisting the Government's radical policies in matters such as the Health Service, local government and education. Concern about charges for school transport demonstrated sympathy for public education and the problems of rural areas. Thus dissent arose from ideological disagreement (the 'wets') and constituency or group pressures. The Government was also defeated over its proposals to 'stage' or phase increased pay for Members of Parliament – no complex explanation required!

Dissent continued in the 1983–87 Parliament, despite Margaret Thatcher's high political standing after a second election victory. Again the concerns of the 'wets' and constituency and other pressures were evident and the 'dries' sometimes urged the Government to the right, notably on trade union reform. The Government was defeated over Sunday trading in a Shops Bill and modified its position on parental contributions to students in higher education. Once more Members of Parliament defied the Whips in their determination to improve their own conditions of work, in this case their allowances for support staffs.

The retreat on parental contributions to university fees (December 1984) was spectacular and revealing. One commentator described it as 'one of the swiftest and most effective assertions of backbencher power over the executive' since Wilson's retreat over trade union reform in 1969 (Ian Aitken in *The Guardian*, 7 December 1984). The Minister, Sir Keith Joseph, faced angry backbenchers (of his own side) at Question Time and a humiliating mass meeting of Conservative members. The Chief Whip was in hospital and the Prime Minister was in Dublin for the day. Joseph was a monkish intellectual rather than a political bruiser (otherwise he might have become leader of the party). The Conservative backbenchers were ferocious in their defence of what may be called a class interest (just like Labour in 1969). Some observers found the episode, with its undertones of bloodlust, distasteful: but the sudden assertion of power by the normally frustrated and powerless is often 'distasteful' in that way.

In the 1987 Parliament Margaret Thatcher's Government was a little less secure, not least because her backbenchers included 39 of her former Ministers. The most notable parliamentary battles were fought over the Community Charge or poll-tax. There is clear evidence of backbench misgivings and a modest record of attempted amendment; but it is equally clear that the Whips responded firmly if not ferociously to dissent and the Bill was passed with few concessions to its many critics (The Act was finally abandoned after the fall of Margaret Thatcher).

The Community Charge – and many other of Margaret Thatcher's radical policies – help to put parliamentary dissent in perspective. Defeat of the government on significant issues is very rare. The most notable occasion in recent years was the vote on the Second Reading of the Shops Bill, 1986; but this concerned Sunday opening and is clearly a special case. In October 1992 the Government retreated rapidly on its proposal to close down coal mines, buying time but without fully conceding the principle.

In July 1993 John Major's Government was defeated in a vote on the inclusion of the Social Chapter in the Maastricht Treaty. This was in form at least a serious defeat on a matter of high policy, although the dissident Conservatives took a different position from most of the Labour and all of the Liberal members with whom they had joined. The vote reflected the persistent opposition to the Maastricht Treaty of an organised group within the Conservative Party, as well as a more extensive loss of confidence in the government and the Prime Minister and also the Government's vulnerably thin majority. The conjunction of these factors was unusual in the Conservative Party and, while these conditions last, there has to be a tendency for modest parliamentary rebellion. However the force of the Maastricht rebellion was immediately diminished by the Government's victory in a confidence vote. This was a rare glimpse of the bottom line of rebellion in the majority party: it collapses at the point at which it threatens the standing, and certainly the survival, of the Government. Rebellions within the governing party may win battles (secure concessions) but never win the war, because the Government is not the enemy.

Thus Governments get their way in all matters central to their purposes, subject to continuing minor modifications and very occasionally more substantial amendment. Governments trim, backbenchers know their place. There is a partnership recognised by both sides to be mutually beneficial; but, as in normally steady relationships, the partners can get out of phase and drift out of sympathy. This is the opportunity for the Whips to display their gentler, agony-aunt side.

The modest increase in dissent over the last two decades reflects some changes in Members themselves and in the pressures upon them.

- There are fewer party loyalists, Tory squires and Labour union officials, content for the most part to lead a quiet and docile parliamentary life. The new MPs are more often professionals looking for the professional challenges and scope for independent action to which they are accustomed. But of course their natural ambitions may impose discretion rather than dissent upon them, just as it does on junior professionals and executives. It may be just as relevant that the new professional Member is not totally dependent on Parliament to make a living, now or in the future and, in the case of Conservatives, the financial prospects are far more attractive outside than in Parliament.
- Pressures on Members from the constituency and interest groups may be more imperious, expecting some response from the Member, and forcing him to balance the terror of the Whips against the displeasures of the constituency Chairman or local businessmen, workers, housewives, parents. British politics are in effect nationalised by the major parties, but the defence of local interests is not wholly neglected (contrast the USA where local interests are paramount).
- The new constitutional understanding, particularly born of experience of minority government in the 1970s, that a single defeat need not bring a government down.
- The polarisation of parties in the 1970s and 1980s extended the possibilities of intra-party dissent – there was more to object to. This is evident in the Conservative Party in 'wet' dissent from radical Government policies, but also occasionally in the expression of disappointment among the 'dries' at the Government's alleged backsliding. Meanwhile the Labour Party was deeply divided to the point of serious defection; the party is characteristically a volatile coalition of disparate tendencies with mutiny a respected custom.

The Opposition

The historic duty and the partisan disposition of the Opposition is to oppose; and, in so doing, to present itself as an alternative government. The Opposition conducts three dialogues – with

Government, with itself and with the electorate. This is all depressing work: the government always wins the vote, if not the argument; the minority party without power or patronage easily disintegrates into bickering; the Opposition has a hard time with the electorate trying to look like a government when it is not. But the Opposition cannot do nothing and wait for the election – though attendance in the House is not a high priority for most Members.

Procedures give the Opposition some opportunities for initiating business – priority in about 12 per cent of business – in particular in about 20 Opposition Days (formerly Supply Days). The Opposition's main weapon (apart from giving a good account of itself) is time, the denial to government of the time and co-operation necessary to transact the government's business – delaying tactics, obstruction of the normal arrangements made 'behind the Speaker's Chair' (through discussion between the party managers). Beyond that are the filibusters, procedural ambushes, points of order and lobby rebellions carried out by Private Members. Thus the denial of time and obstruction are the major weapons for a near-impotent Opposition; and the Government very occasionally makes concessions to exhaustion.

Parliamentary Questions are also used as a weapon of opposition as well as by Private Members in pursuit of their own concerns (see below). In particular Prime Minister's Question Time has become a regular 15 minute twice-a-week confrontation between Prime Minister and Leader of Opposition. This is a phenomenon of the last 20 years and follows the development of the so-called 'open question' about the Prime Minister's engagements. Prime Minister's Question Time is well reported and usually broadcast live on television. Hence readers may judge for themselves whether Prime Minister's Question Time is a triumph of the art of parliamentary government or a demonstration of the degradation of parliamentary government by unthinking partisan confrontation and vulgar abuse. (This counts as an Exercise and the Guide to Exercises would say that there is much to be said for the latter view.)

Within the limits that procedure and permanent minority place upon the Opposition, it is still possible for an Opposition to make something of a case against the Government. A good example is the campaign by Robin Cook, as Labour 'Shadow' Health Minister. In the two years before the 1992 Election he exploited very effectively the unpopularity of the Government's radical reforms of the National Health Service. He used both the House of Commons and the media to make his case and it seems likely that he won the argument and had some influence on the election. However, this is an unusual case: he was 'batting on a good wicket' in that the health issue favoured Labour; and he might have done as well without parliamentary appearances at all. Cook was a well-informed Shadow Minister and a highly skilled debater.

Most of the time the Opposition is restricted not only in time but in choice of subject. Given the Government's control of the timetable for its legislative purposes, it is difficult to shift the attention of the House, and hence the public, to matters of current urgency or controversy (at least those favoured by the Opposition). There are ministerial statements, 'Private Notice' Questions and, more rarely, emergency debates (for example, on Social Security changes in April 1988 and on the Ambulance strike – Robin Cook again – in November 1989). But normally there is not a direct and immediate connection between great matters and House of Commons debate. In particular, periods of policy development, when policy is 'under advice' or 'in consultation', are regarded by government not as most appropriate for parliamentary consideration, but, on the contrary, a 'no-go' area. Government policy is never revealed until it is fully formed, all objections and qualifications dismissed and Ministers are and, it is implied, always have been, of one mind. In such a system there is no place for much serious work by Parliament, either Opposition or Government backbenchers, in the development of policy.

A Grand National Debate?

Backbenchers on both sides take part in debates in the House and so, it may be argued, contribute to a 'Grand National Debate', improving political information and awareness and generally contributing to the political education of the nation. This comprises Bagehot's expressive, teaching and informing functions. There was room for doubt about the effectiveness of this educational process, on the grounds that hardly anyone knew what went on in Parliament. But the introduction of broadcasting, especially television since 1989, counters that argument.

The more important debates as well as Parliamentary Questions are now broadcast live and reported in news programmes. What a pity that some of the great occasions of the past were not broadcast and recorded – the Falklands invasion for example, or the Miners' Strike of 1984–5 in recent times, or the debates about Munich 1938 or the fall of France in 1940.

However, there are some reservations to be made. Much of the business of the House is undramatic, not to say, boring. There are very few great occasions (perhaps that is as well) and most debates are poorly attended. The front benches dominate proceedings and all Privy Councillors (Ministers, former Ministers and Opposition leaders) are accorded priority. In a six-hour debate it is unlikely that backbenchers will be called in the first two hours and the last hour will be taken up by winding-up speeches from the front bench. With luck perhaps 15–20 back-benchers can make short speeches, many around dinner time; and with persistence an aspiring backbencher might thus speak once or twice a year. He will get a bigger and possibly better audience by offering his comments to a radio or television programme.

The regular reporting of Parliament is hardly adequate or lively enough to catch the attention of the public, but for the student there is abundant and comparatively accessible material. So it is worth finding and studying your own documentary material. The 'quality' press gives some space to reports; but no newspaper now attempts anything like a comprehensive cover-age. The BBC, fulfilling its statutory duty, gives an excellent summary of the day's proceedings in both Houses each sitting day. Best of all, of course, get hold of copies of Hansard and listen to broadcasts from Parliament.

You might even visit Parliament, but that is of course easier for those who live in the South East. Parliament is not as welcoming to ordinary visitors as the US Congress and is beginning to resemble Wimbledon or Lords cricket ground in being most accessible to the executive entertain-ment industry!

EXERCISE
Parliament and the 'Grand National Debate'

12.4 Take one day's proceedings in the House of Commons and check how they were reported by the daily newspapers and by the broadcasting authorities. Avoid Fridays. You will need *The Times* report at

least as a control. Consider:

- the amount of reporting
- the prominence given
- the selection made
- the total 'slanting' or bias introduced by selection, editorial comment and headlines.

You could supplement this analysis with an informal survey among your acquaintances: ask them questions designed to elicit how much they know about the previous day's proceedings.

In the light of your analysis would you say that the reporting of Parliament is:

- in amount and prominence given adequate, barely adequate, inadequate, grossly inadequate?
- in selection and treatment perfectly fair, just about fair, a little unfair, quite unfair?

The Lobbies

The MP is pursued by two groups or lobbies, the lobby of interest groups and the press or media lobby. The interest lobby wants to influence the Member to support and advance its particular interest; the media simply want a story, an interview, a comment. Both are willing to reward the Member for his services – the interest groups with fat fees and 'perks', the media with small fees and a little fame (useful in the constituency, and perhaps to the ambitious).

The main effect of the media lobby, including the broadcasting of Parliament, is to reinforce the dominance of the government and of the front bench of Ministers and shadow Ministers. However, a few political discussion programmes (notably 'Any Questions' on radio and 'Question Time' on television) have enlarged the audience for the discussion of current politics and helped to make a few political reputations. The am-bitious Member learns that fluency and effective-ness on camera are essential for a successful political career; the modern politician is a television public relations professional before he is a parliamentarian and a Minister (and Ministers are fully briefed by the civil service and party officials for their public appearances).

A more serious conflict of interest for MPs is raised by the work of the interest group lobbies. Interest groups play a preponderant part in British government and it is reasonable to see government as mainly a negotiation between government, in effect the bureaucracy, and interests, with Parliament and parties marginalised and the Cabinet much diminished. (The question is discussed in Chapter 21.)

The marginalisation of Parliament can be illustrated by almost any issue discussed in Parliament, except those to do with the internal working of Parliament. The Commons includes spokesmen on most significant public activities, for example, hairdressers, tyre distributors, teachers, policemen, engine drivers, numerous lawyers. The Conservatives usually represent trade associations, Labour trade unions. Here are two illustrations of major interests.

■ DOCUMENT 12.3
Interest groups and Parliament

a) *The Labour Party and the TUC*
In 1976 the Chancellor in the Labour Government proposed income tax reliefs conditional on the TUC's agreeing to a voluntary pay limit. This they did, more or less. The following year the Chancellor offered a similar arrangement, the TUC failed to respond adequately (or indeed much at all) and the Chancellor made only half of the tax cuts he had proposed.

EXERCISE
Interest groups and Parliament

12.5 This kind of bargaining was denounced as damaging to Parliament. Was it?

b) *The Conservative Party and the farmers*
The National Farmers' Union is one of the most successful lobbies in Britain and the farming lobby has evidently substantial influence in the European Community. The farmers have been well-served by all governments since 1945, but the NFU has especially close links with the Conservative Party. On one occasion in 1987 the NFU, dissatisfied with government policy on agriculture (that is, the amount of taxpayers' money passed to the farmers), formally called on the Minister of Agriculture (himself a farmer) to resign. The NFU president was summoned before a meeting of the Conservative backbench (1922) committee and reprimanded. 'From henceforth', said the chairman, 'we will regard the NFU merely as a trade association' – non-farmers had always assumed that was exactly what it was.

Less than two years later Conservative backbenchers forced the resignation of Edwina Currie after she had damaged the interests of egg producers by her imprecise remarks about salmonella infection in eggs. A generous compensation scheme costing up to £20m was hastily drawn up, but few voices were raised on behalf of consumers, who still had serious grounds for doubt about the methods used by the food producers. ■

EXERCISE
Representing interests

12.6 Is it not a proper function of Parliament to represent interests as well as individuals?

These examples illustrate the Members working in a disciplined party in support of favoured interests. The questions raised relate to the normal operation of party majority government. But there has grown up a substantial practice of lobbying by individual Members, working for fees on behalf of client companies. The relationship is not necessarily as sharp as the payment of fees might imply and can be presented in the more appropriate terms of advice and consultation. In principle this kind of interest representation is not very different from the unacknowledged direct representation of interests by virtue of the Member's own occupation or interest – the land and the church from the beginnings of Parliament, industry, the railways, the City in the nineteenth century and later the trade unions. We all have our personal interests. But there is a difference in practice between a personal interest arising fron profession or background and the contracted commitment to an outside interest. There exists a possibility of the re-shaping or corruption of the Member's representative function. Conceding that there was cause for concern, the House was moved in 1975 to establish a Register of Members' financial interests in order to display, if not to condone or limit, improper influence.

■ DOCUMENT 12.4
The Member of Parliament as a lobbyist

● In 1991 there were 384 MPs, holding 522 directorships and 452 consultancies. A Member with a directorship and a consultancy can easily double his salary. Most of these business connections are on the Conservative side.

- At the end of his parliamentary career Sir Geoffrey (Lord) Rippon held 48 directorships, for one of which he was paid £60k per year.
- Over half of Labour MPs are 'sponsored' by trade unions, who pay about £2–3000 towards election expenses, plus help in kind (e.g. office facilities) and small amounts to the constituency in return for unspecified sympathy and support.
- About 20 MP's research assistants are full-time employees of lobbying companies.
- There are about 40 companies trading as parliamentary consultancies, claiming to be able to arrange meetings with Ministers and officials as well as MPs and to influence administrative decisions, major legislation and government policy (the more serious the business, the higher the fee).
- Passes to the House of Commons are made available to lobbyists.
- Lobbyists have been present at meetings of party committees.
- At one time the Chairman of the Commons Committee of Selection (which allocates Members to Committees) was a director of a public relations company; a member of the Transport Select Committee was at the same time a consultant to the National Bus Company; a chairman of the Defence Committee acted as consultant to a Defence public relations company concerned with the securing of contracts; another member of the Defence Committee was a 'parliamentary adviser' to British Aerospace, a major defence contractor; a member of a Committee dealing with the Channel Tunnel was a paid consultant to a company with a significant interest in the outcome.
- It is mainly but not exclusively business interests which can afford to buy the services of MPs. Well-financed lobbies do so too. For example, David Alton was provided with a full-time research assistant by anti-abortion groups when he was promoting his Private Members Bill restricting abortion. The splendid – and subsidised – entertainment facilities of the Houses of Parliament are hired out, through Members and Lords, to lobbyists and other outside bodies. ∎

EXERCISE

12.7 Is this growth of 'consultancy' defensible or corrupt?

The practice of 'sponsorship' of Labour Members by the trade unions is a special historical phenomenon, reflecting the origins of the party as the political wing of the trade union movement, the difficulties of service of working men as Members before payment was instituted (1911) and arguably the capacity of trade unions to represent broadly the interests of working people. The proportion of sponsored Labour Members has risen from just over one third in 1970 to well over one half (56 per cent) in 1992. One large union, the TGWU, sponsors 38 Members in the 1992 Parliament. The relationship involves modest financial support of the constituency party and its campaign funds by the trade union and an unspecified concern by the Member for the interests of the union.

The main influence of the trade union lies probably in the selection of Parliamentary candidates, thus helping to ensure Members of Parliament who are acceptable and sympathetic to the union. (Trade unions favour the safer constituencies for their sponsorship). Altogether sponsorship by trade unions does raise questions about the nature of the Labour Party and the corruption of true representation. In a notorious case the Yorkshire Area of the National Union Of Mineworkers tried to bind the actions of its sponsored Members.

∎ DOCUMENT 12.5
Members and their sponsors

Resolution of Yorkshire Area Council, NUM, 25 June 1975
That we can no longer tolerate the position where a 'sponsored' MP can oppose his Union's policy on major issues.

Therefore it is agreed that the following guidelines shall apply to MPs sponsored by the Yorkshire area.

1 No Miners' MP shall vote or speak against Union policy on any issue which affects the Coal Mining industry.
2 No Miners' MP shall actively campaign or work against the Union policy on any other major issue.
3 If any Miners' MP refuses to agree to the 'guidelines' or violates these guidelines, the Area Council shall withdraw sponsorship from that MP. We wish to make it clear that the Yorkshire Area will no longer tolerate a situation where a Miners' MP accepts the 'Privilege' of sponsorship and then demands

the 'luxury' of independence from Union policy. ■

EXERCISE
Members and their sponsors

12.8 Do you regard this statement as an inappropriate interference with the independence of the Member?

The Committee on Privileges was quite certain that this kind of claim on Members' loyalty and services was improper, but accepted the assurance of the President of the Union that the Yorkshire Area's position was not accepted by the Union itself. Thus the convention was upheld (see also Chapter 21, especially Document 21.5).

This is not to say that a Member of Parliament must be a remote judicial person, whose only contact is with his constituents (all 60 000 of them). Of course, this view is unrealistic: a modern MP is no more set apart from his own background and experience than an eighteenth century knight of the shire. However there is no reason why the background and experience represented in the House should be limited to that already available to Members themselves. The representation of other outside organisations is quite proper; indeed, such organisations are often more meaningful than the territorial constituency. There is, in short, no objection in principle to such representation unless it is plainly disturbing the balance of representation in the House.

Even so, there is still a good deal to be said for the maintenance of the traditional view of Parliament as a collection of independent judicial individuals. Though out-of-date and unrealistic, the continuing assertion of an ideal that never was helps to achieve a balance between independence and outside control. In this matter there is much to be said for observing the proprieties.

The House of Lords

It is convenient and realistic to deal with the House of Lords as an adjunct of the House of Commons: another case of political realism overcoming historical impropriety. The House of Lords is one of Britain's peculiar institutions, indefensible by the standards of modern democracy and proof, according to one critic, of life after death. Tony Benn has called it 'the Madame Tussauds of British politics'. The House is made up of hereditary peers, life peers (following the Act of 1958), bishops and Law Lords. The Table sets out the composition in rounded figures.

EXERCISE
The composition of the House of Lords

12.9 Judged by composition, is the House of Lords suitable as a legislative chamber in a modern democracy?

The House as a whole is grossly unrepresentative – one third were educated at Eton, two fifths at 'Oxbridge', three quarters at 'public' schools; only one in twenty is a woman. The introduction of

Table 3 Composition of the House of Lords

Total 1200 of which:

Life Peers	*Working Peers	**average daily attendance	never there
400 + 26 Bishops + 20 Law Lords	3–400	c 300	c 300

* say, attending over half of the time and likely to respond to a 2-line whip
** on about 130–140 sitting days

Cons	Lab	Libs	crossbench***	other
460	110	80	250+	300

*** dividing about 2:1 to Conservatives

Note: figures are approximate for 1992

Life Peers and a generous attendance allowance have improved attendance and the active peers are more representative. They include former politicians and persons distinguished in public life (not that this makes them very representative). The Conservatives are not predominant in the 'working' House, but when it comes to voting there is a safe Conservative majority. The 'cross-benchers' (not accepting a party whip) in practice divide their votes 2:1 in favour of the Conservatives.

Although the atmosphere is less partisan and adversarial than in the Commons (the manners are better) the voting is whipped in over 90 per cent of the divisions and, if a close vote is foreseen, the Whips call up a posse of 'backwoodsmen'. In the crucial vote on Britain's accession to the EEC in 1971 over 500 peers voted, but that was a record. The Conservative majority is particularly vulnerable at and after dinner time, when an 'ambush' by hidden (and hungry) opposition voters can be mounted. However, this is not serious long-term politics. The Lords have sometimes been troublesome to Conservative governments, but trouble always falls short of serious damage to government proposals.

Since the Parliament Acts of 1911 and 1949 the House of Lords has had very little power. It may delay legislation, except Money Bills, and thus make itself a nuisance to governments in a hurry, especially to governments with small majorities or near the end of their term. For example, the House defeated the Conservative Government of 1979–83 over 40 times, on issues such as rural school transport, BBC foreign language broadcasts, housing, jury secrecy and British nationality. It did rather more to the preceding minority Labour Government, defending it on nearly 350 occasions, e.g. the Shipbuilding Bill of 1975, the Trade Union Bill of 1976.

The Lords won general approval (except in government circles) for its frustration in 1984 of Margaret Thatcher's proposal to cancel elections to the GLC and Metropolitan Councils prior to their abolition; and for resisting the identity card scheme for football spectators (1989). In June 1986 the Lords devoted almost 20 hours, a post-war record, to debate on the controversial Gas (privatisation) Bill. On the other hand, in May 1988 over 300 peers turned out to vote down an amendment to the Community Charge bill designed to relate the tax to ability to pay. The following year over 200 peers were mustered to defeat a Labour amendment to a Companies Bill (1989) which would have given to shareholders the right to decide company donations to political parties.

Thus the reputation of the House for independence and debate of high intellectual quality looked to be ill-founded. In any case, the Lords have very shaky grounds in democratic theory for acting independently of the elected Chamber. The post-1945 'Salisbury doctrine' claimed the right for the Lords to intervene when the government went beyond the principles of the Party manifesto, but that was to assert an improper function for a hereditary chamber and gave the manifesto an inappropriate status and solidity.

The provisions of the Parliament Act for the overriding of the Lords have been used only three times altogether and twice since 1945 (to amend the Parliament Act itself in 1949 and to pass an unusual piece of retro-active legislation, the War Crimes Bill, 1991). In most cases, the government chooses to respond to the possibility of delay and embarrassment and even to reasoned argument and its own second thoughts by making concessions, especially when it is already meeting criticism elsewhere. But a government still has the power to override the Lords and the Lords recognize that they lack the constitutional authority and political 'clout' to press their case. The moderate constitutional argument is that the delaying power is valuable in ensuring reconsideration, even if the outcome is unchanged.

The Lords' claim to represent independent opinion or high intellect is diminished not only by their evident partisanship but also by the indications of favoured interests. The Lords represent, and inevitably over-represent, the land-owning, countryside and farming interests, the legal profession, the armed services, the universities, the Church of England, some charities. For example:

- in a debate in 1986 on drug patents, nearly all those taking part had worked in the pharmaceutical industry or as patent lawyers.
- in a later debate on the regulation of financial services most speakers were connected to the industry to be regulated
- the Lords' much praised interest in European matters derives in part from the presence of farmers and lawyers
- the Archbishop of Canterbury led a successful move to insert an amendment in the Further

and Higher Education Bill (February 1992) requiring the former Sixth Form Colleges to provide religious education.

At the same time the Lords showed their more liberal concerns by deleting the Secretary of State's powers over appointments, admissions and duration of courses – again an amendment accepted by the Government.

- on the other hand, in the debate on the Privatisation of the Gas Industry, the interests of consumers were well represented – only to be voted down.

Apart from its restricted independent legislative power, the House of Lords carries out valuable functions as a chamber of the legislature, on behalf of the government – initiating non-contentious bills, revising bills. Mainly this is detailed work in which the Lords act as a government agency for amending its legislation, correcting and tidying up ill thought-out or badly drafted clauses. In most sessions the Government moves over 1000 amendments of this kind, sometimes twice as many. Since there are no Standing (legislative) Committees the Lords spend much time in divisions – up to 40 hours in the session 1985–6 (A. Adonis, 1988, p. 164).

The Lords also hold debates on matters of general concern and do useful work in committees, notably on EC legislation. The House is in fact a necessary part of the whole parliamentary process and has become more active and more self-confident in recent years. The House has influence enough to attract the attention of the professional lobbyists and to attract some peers into paid consultancies. Mainly the House of Lords serves as an accomplice or instrument of government but it exercises a limited independent capacity to be awkward, especially to Labour governments.

Thus given an indefensible composition and a valuable function, there is scope for several approaches to the reform of the Lords.

1 *Simple conservative.* 'It works, so let it be'. The 'it works' argument is always less convincing than it sounds since it begs questions about purpose and performance.
2 *Traditional conservative.* This is the Enoch Powell argument about institutions and history. An example of this kind of argument is given in Document 12.6 below.
3 *Pragmatic inertia.* This may be a reinforcement of conservatism, or simply a failure to see an alternative. More seriously many critics of the

House of Lords fear that reform must be a threat to the primacy of the Commons, so better to leave the Lords looking ridiculous. (That is why the radical Michael Foot combined with Enoch Powell to frustrate the reform projected by the Labour Government in 1968).
4 *Modification.* For example, the reforms proposed in 1968 would have restricted voting to created life peers, all hereditary peers being non-voting. The government of the day would have a small majority over opposition parties (but the House would include peers without party allegiance and Law lords and bishops). The power of the House would be limited to delay.
5 *Root-and-branch reform.* This really means abolition and starting again, with a system based on election. Here is an opportunity for some do-it-yourself constitution making (see Exercise 12.11 below).

■ DOCUMENT 12.6
The traditional or historical justification of the House of Lords

From article by Lord (Max) Beloff The Times *1 Nov 1982*
What both the monarch and the House of Lords represent in their different ways is the belief that there should be in a balanced constitution organs that do not owe their whole being to the device of popular election; that if there is to be stability, there must be room for institutions expressing continuity as against the ebb and flow of opinion. The emblems of royalty, the robes of the peers are not just decoration; they express a desire for visible links with the national past.

These institutions – wholly in the case of the monarchy and partially in the case of the House of Lords – also embody the idea that hereditary succession can itself be an instrument of continuity.... Both the monarchy and the House of Lords are seen as some kind of substitute for our lack of a written and limited constitution or Bill of Rights. ■

EXERCISES
The House of Lords: justification and reform

12.10 Is Lord Beloff's argument convincing?
12.11 Draw up proposals for radical reform of the House of Lords, taking into account the composition, mode of selection and

powers of a new chamber and its relation to the existing House of Commons.

Beside the questions of function and composition, there is an intriguing constitutional problem about the mechanism of reform. According to the convention, Parliament is sovereign; and in practice the courts accept without question the validity of an Act of Parliament duly passed and assented to. Suppose the Lords refused to pass a bill radically amending or even abolishing their own House? This presents no problem: the existing Parliament Act provides for the passage of a bill after delay, without the Lords' assent. But this is disturbing to a constitutionalist, since the effect of using the procedure of the Parliament Act is to destroy the possibility of using the procedure again. (In theory another Parliament could restore the House of Lords but that would be farcical.) An alternative would be to follow the precedent of 1910 and ask the Queen to create sufficient peers to pass the legislation. But that would be disturbing to a royalist!

In the end the constitution is more or less what Parliament says it is. If Britain were not a very conservative country, constitutionalists would have a very disturbing time.

Parliamentary Questions

Question Time is often regarded as one of the glories of the British Parliament. More sceptical observers believe it is 'useless', 'a charade', 'a fake instrument of democracy'. But, at the very least, it is an important opportunity for the backbench member to probe aspects of the government's administrative record.

Question Time takes place from Mondays to Thursdays each week (except at the beginning of the session), immediately after Prayers and Private Business. It begins at about 2.35 p.m. or soon after and goes on until 3.30 p.m. Members 'put down' Questions, giving not less than forty eight hours notice (and no more than ten sitting days). Questions for oral answer are 'starred'. Members are limited to two oral Questions each day, priority being decided by lot. There is special provision for raising urgent matters by Private Notice.

Ministers reply on a rota system, with the more important Ministers appearing frequently, the Prime Minister twice a week for up to twenty minutes. Further Questions may be asked after the Minister has given his reply. These Supplementary Questions (with supplementary answers) take up a good deal of time. If the later Questions are not reached, the Minister will furnish written answers. The number of Questions asked has more than doubled since 1970 to about 50 000 in each session, of which between one quarter and one third are for oral answer.

A Parliamentary Question is much more than simply a question. It must indeed be interrogatory in form, and not, in substance, a statement or speech. It must be new and necessary. It must seek information or press for action on a matter within the responsibility of the Minister to whom it is addressed. It must not be argumentative, or a rhetorical question and it must not refer to a debate in the current session or be critical of a decision of the House. It must not be based on rumour or unauthenticated reports. A Question must not contravene constitutional usage or parliamentary etiquette.

The rules of admissibility are based on precedent and are sometimes difficult to apply. The list of barred subjects includes security matters, the nationalized industries, commercially sensitive matters, government research contracts and the work of 'non-governmental' bodies like the Sports Council. Answers may also be refused on grounds of disproportionate cost, triviality or vagueness, or of raising questions of policy too large to be dealt with in an answer. The 'Table Office' assists Members in redrafting Questions to meet the rules. In recent years Questions have tended to be more general and open, at least allowing for more open supplementaries, intended to score political points rather than raise specific grievances. Broadcasting has encouraged this development.

EXERCISE
The admissibility of Parliamentary Questions

12.12 Which of the following Questions would you regard as admissible under the above rules?

a) To ask the Secretary of State for Defence if he is aware that the government's defence policy is both costly and wholly irrelevant.
b) To ask the Secretary of State for Trade and Industry what plans he has for a co-ordinated national fuel and energy policy.
c) To ask the Secretary for Education what action he proposes to take to improve discipline in the Long Puddleton

Secondary School.

d) To ask the Prime Minister if he would consider resigning in order to restore the country's international standing.

e) To ask the Secretary of State for the Environment what plans he has to provide that the national stockpile of 500 million bricks will be used for building houses.

f) To ask the Heritage Secretary to give directions to the ITC to discontinue the programme known as 'Spitting Image'.

g) To ask the Chancellor of the Exchequer if he would agree that Britain now bears a burden of taxation so high as to cripple incentive and productivity.

h) To ask the Secretary of State for Health whether she will make a statement on the present outbreak of influenza.

i) To ask the Home Secretary if he will confirm that the number of cases of telephone-tapping by the security services has sharply increased in the last year.

j) To ask the Secretary of State for Education if he is satisfied with the standards of primary education.

k) To ask the Prime Minister if he will list his official engagements for Tuesday 7 December.

l) To ask the Prime Minister if he would give an estimate of the likely cost of the Labour Party's expenditure commitments.

Answers to Parliamentary Questions are prepared in the departments as a matter of urgency. Information may be refused on grounds of security, difficulty in finding out or cost – or, of course, unadmitted political embarrassment. In 1987 the cost of answering an oral question was £75 and £43 for a written question. So the minimum costs of the whole procedure, or of serving Tony Banks, a Labour MP who asked 992 written questions in the session 1985–6, can be calculated.

EXERCISE
The costs of answering Questions

12.13 Is the expenditure on answers to Parliamentary Questions justified?

The Minister answering Questions is also briefed to answer supplementary questions. Here the civil servant preparing the Minister's brief will assess political factors, as well as giving additional departmental information (for example, what is the questioner's usual political line? how will he attempt to score a political point in a supplementary? who else may join in?). The Minister reads the first (prepared) answer from his brief; very rarely he gets his answers in the wrong order – even the well-prepared Margaret Thatcher was caught out once.

The supplementary is the Member's chief weapon against an unsatisfactory reply, or to take advantage of a supposed chink in the governmental armour. The Minister will find some support in his brief, but he will also need to know his business and to be quick in thinking on his feet as well as in repartee and judicious shots in the dark. However, if all this fails him, he can simply refuse to answer (not necessarily by remaining silent). In the last few years, Speakers have been generous in allowing supplementaries and sometimes 'mini-debates' have taken place. But this is at the expense of later Questions.

Table 4 The Questioners

Backbenchers asking PQs Session 1985–6

No of Questions	1+	40+	300+
No of Members asking			
Written Qs	557		20
Oral Qs	508	24	

The maximum number of Written Questions asked by one member was 992 and Oral Questions, 95

Source: House of Commons Library 'Polis' quoted in J. Griffith and M. Ryle, 1989, p. 72

Most backbenchers and opposition Members ask Questions occasionally, but comparatively few make regular and substantial use of Question Time. With some variation, fewer than 100 members provide half the Questions; and 150 or more (including all Ministers) rarely put down Questions for oral answer at all. Some backbenchers specialise in this kind of harrying of the government and a few, like Tony Banks, have tabled 500 or more Questions in a session.

Opposition Members, as might be expected, ask more Questions than the government side. Generally there is little difference between the parties, except for a slight tendency for Labour to ask more Questions than the Conservatives and for the latter to oblige their own governments by asking only for written answers when the party holds office. One or two Members conduct long campaigns through Questions. Sir Gerald Nabarro, for example, mounted a marathon campaign against the anomalies of purchase tax. Some Questions, on the other hand, are inspired (that is, arranged) by the government, a practice the Speaker deplores but cannot prevent. Some Members conduct research by means of Written Questions (and why not?), but it is open to the Minister to refuse an answer on grounds of disproportional cost.

Time is limited and as many as two thirds of Questions for oral answer are not reached and are instead given written answers. It is easy to obstruct Question Time, by accident or design and to reduce it to inanity by the planting or 'orchestration' of Questions.

Question Time is one of the more effective ways in which the backbencher may participate in the scrutiny and criticism of the government – which is not to say that it is highly effective. It is a moment in the parliamentary week when the rights of backbenchers are dominant. Questions do not have to be arranged 'through the usual channels' (the Whips' Office), although sometimes the Whips may intervene to place or to block a Question.

However, in the last few years opposition frontbench spokesmen have taken an increasing part in Question Time and the Leader of the Opposition has exercised the conventional right to ask supplementaries. Hence, at times, and especially if the Prime Minister is answering, Question Time becomes party confrontation. This is now the case with Prime Minister's Questions. Only a few Questions will be called (between 3 and 5); an 'open' Question will ask about his engagements and will lead to supplementaries, some of which, it is hoped, will catch out even a well-briefed Prime Minister. A noisy party knockabout ensues.

Sometimes the supplementaries are prearranged, for example, would the Prime Minister confirm that the Government's proposal to do this or that would be of the greatest advantage to the country? – to which the Prime Minister happily responds with a short, prepared party political broadcast. Both Margaret Thatcher and John Major have read carefully scripted answers to 'spontaneous' supplementaries.

It would be an exaggeration to say that reputations are made and lost in these sometimes farcical proceedings – though the reputation of Parliament itself suffers in the minds of viewers and listeners. No votes are taken; since there is no vote there is no decision – but then, if there were a vote, the government would win. Here, as with committees, the Commons must accept that divisions (votes) reflect the function of Parliament as support and servant of the executive, and Members can operate independently only in business without divisions and therefore without victories – and without high significance for policy.

Even without a vote, Questions make Ministers and, through them, departments, answerable in public over a wide range of their responsibilities; answerable, too, in conditions which attract publicity. For Question Time takes place conveniently for journalists and the evening television news programmes. There is advance notice of topics and the exchanges are comparatively short. Moreover, there is always the possibility of minor sensation, the revelation of maladministration, or a Minister caught out in ignorance or incompetence.

For all this, the effectiveness of Questions should not be exaggerated. Government policy is not often changed by a Question. Occasionally a Question uncovers some administrative discrepancy, inefficiency or injustice and secures a remedy, or simply provides information.

Governments do not rise and fall in Question Time and Ministers rarely gain or lose in reputation. Their performance is part of a necessary relationship with the House and most Ministers, having risen through the House, can cope satisfactorily with this modest test. For the few Ministers who have entered office without a parliamentary apprenticeship, Question Time is perhaps the severest trial. The answers themselves usually present no problem: they are prepared by highly skilled civil servants, with all the resources of the department at their call. Here the private member is at a disadvantage. It is for reasons of this kind that an experienced Minister can go down to the House for Questions with a serene air and a jaunty step.

Illustrative material on Question Time is abundant and easily obtainable. It is often featured in live broadcasts and in news bulletins. The newspapers with full parliamentary reports usually include some account of Questions and answers. Copies of the daily or weekly Hansard, or of course the bound volumes, include Questions.

EXERCISES
Question Time

Study some examples of Parliamentary Questions and answer the following:

12.14 In each case, say whether the Question is:

a) local or b) national
a) of major importance or b) comparatively trivial
a) straightforward or(b) with an 'ulterior motive', to get at something else
a) based on special investigation or b) general knowledge or local information
a) probably suggested by an outside body or b) the Member's own work.

12.15 Why do you think a Member raises an individual case, when he could write to the Minister about it?

12.16 Do Ministers avoid answering some Questions? If so, why? and how?

12.17 If you were a Minister, how would you look forward to Question Time:

● with apprehension
● with cautious pessimism
● as a routine parliamentary chore of no great consequence
● with cautious optimism
● joyfully?

Why?

12.18 Would you recommend the introduction of a Question Time in any organisation with which you are connected?

Other opportunities for backbenchers

Question Time in a House dominated by the Government and the front benches is pre-eminently a time for backbenchers (leaving aside the 'planted' Question and the punch-ups between the front benches). Other procedures give time to the back benchers to make a case – usually airing a local or constituency grievance.

● Adjournment debates. Backbenchers ballot for the daily opportunity to open a half hour debate at 10 pm or at the end of business, sometimes in the small hours, and a junior Minister responds – to a near-empty House.
● Private Members' motions are taken on eleven days, usually Fridays, each session; again, Members, selected by ballot, choose their subject.

Neither of these procedures does more than 'ventilate' a grievance, interest or case.

In addition Members may subscribe to 'Early Day Motions'. These are printed but never debated and are used to gather and publicise opinion again on local matters, or on more serious national matters, reflecting interest group pressures or opinion across the parties or dissident opinion within the party (as for example on the Maastricht Treaty in the Summer of 1992). The number of Early Day Motions has increased tenfold since the 1950s and they have been called parliamentary graffiti. Well, why not?

GUIDE TO EXERCISES

12.1 They apply to different periods and different parties and so might both be true. It could be that the harsher discipline of the 1980s reflects the apparently greater independence of Members, or, more likely, the rule of a less tolerant government. Julian Critchley, Conservative backbencher of independent temperament, speaks of the Whips Office as representing an old fashioned Tory Party, mostly old Etonian and totally male. One commentator, Hugo Young, wrote in 1988 that 'the imagination of the managers [of the Conservative Party in the House at that time] stretches no further than a requirement of total acquiescence, unless it be to the orchestrated stamping and booing which drown out Labour speakers'. But Labour Whips, though very different socially, are equally concerned with discipline, not brotherly (or sisterly) love. The question is pursued in the following text.

12.2 A complete answer would require more information, particularly on the nature of the Government's legislative programme and the size, disposition and tactics of the opposition. However, it is evident that Attlee's radical post-war government managed a substantial and radical programme without much recourse to the guillotine. A change seems to have come about in the mid-70s, when party politics became polarised. Margaret Thatcher's first and third administrations were particularly radical and impatient of opposition. In 1984 the Clerk of the

House commented that the 'purely mechanistic approach' of the House in the legislative Standing Committees was 'in danger of bringing the House...into disrepute'.

12.3 Plainly the control is not complete. The legislative programme was large and controversial. Most of it was pushed through successfully, though not without some concessions, much hard work by the Whips and occasional embarrassment. The record illustrates well that extreme judgements cannot be sustained. The government does not wield absolute power, Parliament is not totally impotent. On a scale stretching between these poles, Parliament clearly sits near to the impotence end – an occasional and occasionally significant influence, perhaps a nudge or a push, hardly ever an imperious command or veto.

Here as elsewhere it is only too plain that the study of politics is not a 'hard' science and, without scope for quantification, we are dangerously dependent on the use – and abuse – of words.

12.4 This you must do for yourself!

12.5 It certainly excluded Parliament from the bargaining process. But this was to do in public what is normally done in private, Parliament always being excluded. The process, whether public or private, was damaging to the unrepresented public and the public interest. But Parliament works as the guardian of party dogma rather than the public interest.

12.6 Yes. Both major parties are 'aligned with' major interests. But inevitably it is the highly organised and well-financed producer groups who mount the most effective pressures. It does seem proper that Parliament should make a more serious effort to represent the unorganised and the minorities.

12.7 It is defensible but it is potentially corrupt. Defensible on the grounds that MPs need the money, should be active in the 'world outside' and are incorruptible especially if it is all made public. Corrupt on the grounds that Members undertake to serve special interests (for reward, sometimes related to relative success) which must conflict with the service of constituents, party, government or country – sometimes at least. The information given in the Register is incomplete and the House is more concerned with regulating lobbyists than its own Members acting in effect as lobbyists. Many MPs have always represented interests in themselves, as landowners, farmers, railway builders, trade unionists. They are now for hire. The corruption of the service of the public interest is no greater, just more venal.

But perhaps this is a harsh judgement. Members of Parliament peddle access and influence, but little more. Unlike the government itself, and local government, they cannot dispense honours, contracts, jobs, permissions – and their influence is less than that of a Committee Chair in a County Council.

12.8 Yes; if applied rigorously it would replace the normal relationship of a Member with his constituents over major sections of policy. The House Committee of Privileges agreed.

12.9 No-one now would design a Chamber like this and its justification must lie in history and tradition ('You don't ask what an oak is for', said Enoch Powell); the pragmatic judgement that 'it works'; and simple inertia ('it's there, can't think of anything better'). The political composition of the House undermines the argument that it protects us from the unchallenged hegemony of a single Chamber.

12.10 The value of symbols for stability and continuity should not be under-rated; but in a democracy this argument applies better to the politically powerless monarchy than to the second chamber of the legislature. Similarly it may be conceded that popular election is not the source of all good, but in a pluralist polity there are other ways of modifying the potential tyranny of the electorate – and for most of us that is all the power we have.

12.11 You should look at the published proposals of the political parties and bodies such as IPPR, Charter 88 and the Constitutional Reform Centre.

Note the possibility of relating, or the need to relate, a reformed House to regional and local government and to the European Parliament (or to MEPs from Britain). Abolition and single chamber government would be an unusual solution. (Denmark has no second chamber, but it does have a Bill of Rights, a Supreme Court and a right to referendums). Abolition and replacement by a system of regional assemblies is a possibility and would make for space in the crowded Palace of Westminster.

12.12 The following would not be admitted: a) argumentative, not seeking information or pressing for action except in a very indirect manner; also d) and g) on similar grounds; i) has to do with security.

The following would be admitted and were actually asked: b), e), h), j) and k). The latter is the normal form of the 'open' Question to the Prime Minister.

The following would probably be admitted, but unless they were very serious or embarrassing, the Minister would probably claim that such matters were either beyond his responsibility, or beyond the area of his normal intervention; or the government's responsibility: c) and f).

Question l) is outside the Prime Minister's responsibility but similar Questions have been asked – and answered – as supplementaries to an open question.

12.13 Of course. It is a major source of information for MPs and still cheap by the standards of government expenditure. In the USA the provision is much more lavish and the Library of Congress even offers answers to students' essay questions. Questions have some value for departments and Ministers, too, in that their attention is drawn to the detail of their responsibilities.

12.14 This you do for yourself.

12.15 Probably he had written to the Minister about it and received an unsatisfactory or dilatory reply. A Question normally secures immediate attention at a higher level among officials and of course some attention from the Minister himself. If the case has no special features, this procedure will not secure a different answer, only a quicker one. So Members would tend not to put down straightforward or routine cases as Questions.

12.16 Yes: they may not know the answer, or believe that revealing the answer, or speculating about it, may be harmful to the public, party or personal interest. A Minister may simply refuse to answer, or speak vacuously, or turn aside the Question by a partisan jibe.

12.17 Perhaps a personal question which only you can answer. Clearly much would depend on the Minister's career position and status and the state of his department's business. An experienced Minister, on top of his job and enjoying parliamentary combat, would perhaps admit to 'joyfully'. The text implies that no Minister worthy of his post would be pessimistic, still less apprehensive, about Questions.

12.18 QT works best as point-scoring or detailed probing into administration; the latter may be better done by other procedures. So you might enjoy yourself occasionally, but would you achieve anything worthwhile?

The House of Commons at work II

Select Committees

The House of Commons does a good deal of work in committees, not on the floor of the Chamber itself. The committees may be called standing or select committees, but these terms are misleading. It is more meaningful to describe them by function as either legislative or scrutiny committees. In addition there are a number of other committees, some temporary, for specific purposes.

The standing, or legislative, committees discussed in Chapter 11 are concerned with the revision and amendment of legislation. The Minister in charge of the bill directs the work of the committee, applying his party majority to secure his objectives. Select committees are more varied in function and their work is not wholly determined by party differences.

The Select Committee on Public Accounts (PAC)

The PAC is the oldest of the Select Committees. It was first established in 1861 and has been reappointed annually since then. It has fifteen members, all backbenchers, appointed in accordance with the balance of parties. The chairman is a member of the Opposition, usually with Ministerial experience on the financial side.

The PAC is served by 'clerks' who are from the staff of the Clerk of the House (equivalent to Administration Group civil servants) and an official from the Treasury is in attendance. In addition, the committee has the services of the Comptroller and Auditor-General and the staff of the National Audit Office, consisting of over 800 auditors specialising in government accounts. Under the National Audit Act of 1983 the Comptroller and his staff are employed in effect by the House of Commons and are not civil servants. They work under the direction of the CAG not the Treasury. The

Comptroller and his staff audit the accounts of each government department, present reports to the committee and act as its expert advisers. So, unlike other Select Committees, the PAC is able to base its inquiries on the extensive preliminary work of an expert and authoritative staff. The committee, as a select committee, has the power 'to send for persons, papers and records and to report from time to time'.

The PAC deals with accounts (of money already expended), not with estimates (of proposed expenditure). Its inquiries are concerned with the auditing function of seeing that the money has been spent as appropriated (in amount and purpose); with excess votes; with the exercise by the Treasury of the power of virement, that is, transfer of money by departments from one Vote (head or category) to another; and with the method of presentation of the national accounts. In practice, the committee does more than carry out this rather limited and technical audit. Its remit, in the words of the Act, is to carry out 'examinations into the economy, efficiency and effectiveness with which any department...has used its resources in discharging its function'. The Committee was warned off questioning 'the merits of the policy objectives' of departments. However, the value-for-money inquiries of the PAC were given statutory support and the inevitable exclusion from 'policy' did not completely blunt its investigation and conclusions. If a government activity is found to be poor value for money, then the question is raised whether it is worth doing at all, or whether an alternative course would be better.

The Committee works hard, meeting twice a week during the session. Its reports are produced in attractive format and given publicity in the media. PAC reports often appear in the headlines and Parliament debates the reports for one or two days each session. It must be assumed the PAC has some influence, but the committee has not yet run out of examples of financial mismanagement to uncover. It seems likely that the scale of government expenditure is so vast that it is virtually out of control. Here are some illustrations of the work of the Committee.

■ DOCUMENT 13.1
The work of the Public Accounts Committee

a) In 1988 the Public Accounts Committee, following an investigation by the National Audit Office, criticised the failure of the departments to improve their purchasing policy. Many recommendations of a reform initiative had not been implemented and the departments fell almost £200m short of the lowest target for savings.

b) Defence contracts are persistently discovered to be overspent and late on delivery. This is an old and shameful story, in which defence contractors working in advanced technology, have been allowed to operate in effect on a cost-plus basis. For example, a helicopter estimated to cost £513m eventually cost not less than £835m and was delayed for five years or more; a missile estimated to cost £28m for development cost at least £60m; a submarine projected to cost £187m actually cost £322m; and many more. The Comptroller, through the Committee, has tried to identify the reasons for persistent cost overruns (especially under-estimation of technical problems and poor control of contractors) and may have brought about some improvement in defence procurement procedures. (Michael Heseltine as Minister of Defence was also concerned with this problem – see Chapter 7).

c) In 1991 the Transport Department was criticised for selling off the National Bus Company without taking proper account of the value of its property. For example, the bus station in Keswick valued by the government at £55 000 was sold by the new private owners for £750 000.

d) In January 1992 the National Rivers Authority was criticised by the Public Accounts Committee following a report by the National Audit Office. This showed that the refitting of offices had cost £2.7m, more than twice as much as intended. The chief executive responsible had resigned with a leaving payment of £125 000. ■

EXERCISE
The work of the Public Accounts Committee

13.1 Do these examples demonstrate the effectiveness of the Public Accounts Committee?

Every large organisation is guilty of carelessness with money and requires an auditing process of this kind. There is a special need to keep watch on government spending, because the money is the tax-payers', the scale of the operation is enormous and there are particular difficulties in dealing with secret and highly confidential defence contracts and with some clients of government, for example, farmers, or benefit claimants.

Hence the work of the PAC as the government's auditor is necessary and valuable. But the PAC's work goes beyond that of the auditor of a private company. Leo Pliatzky, a former Treasury Permanent Secretary, claims that the PAC works rather like management consultants than auditors, except that the PAC is at liberty to inquire wherever it wants and reports, not in confidence to the management, but to the House of Commons in public. Pliatzky wrote:

...as seen from Whitehall, the NAO has from the first been pushing at the frontiers of its remit and encroaching on policy issues – an encroachment which, from the point of view of the executive, has to be discouraged if the National Audit Office and the Committee on Public Accounts are not to develop into a court of appeal sitting in judgement on government policies (L. Pliatzky, 1989, pp. 89–91).

If Pliatzky's perception is correct then the PAC is pressing the potential of the Select Committees to the limit; and the limit is set by the government at the point at which they begin to have an impact on government policies.

The Departmental Select Committees

In 1979 the old Expenditure Committee was succeeded by fourteen scrutiny or Select Committees (in addition to the PAC). Of the fourteen new committees, twelve are strictly departmental and two are on Scottish and Welsh Affairs. In addition to the legislative and scrutiny committees there are committees such as those on Statutory Instruments, European Secondary Legislation and the work of the Parliamentary Commissioner for Administration. One committee only, the Committee on Public Accounts, is now specifically dedicated to finance; but among departmental committees, the Treasury and Civil Service Committee is much concerned with financial matters. Further there are committees on the affairs of the House itself – privileges, procedure, catering – and occasional ad hoc committees, for example on Members' Interests or on a particular bill like the bill to develop the Maplin air and sea port.

Between one third and one half of Members take part in committee work and the most energetic of these begin to look like a new kind of Member, new political 'stars' in a minor league. All this adds up to a large and various collection of committees, rather lacking in system. The changes of recent years responded to reformist arguments that the place of Parliament in relation to the executive must be asserted (or reasserted); and, it was implied, the place of the backbencher within Parliament must be enlarged. The record of the first decade of the new departmental committees suggests that the committees may do good and useful work, but they are unlikely to change the course of governments. It is in the nature of the British system of government that their potential is limited.

The Select Committees are empowered by the Standing Order 'to examine the expenditure, administration and policy of the principal government departments...and associated public bodies'. This remit was a substantial extension of previous formulations. The old Expenditure Committee and its predecessor, the Estimates Committee, were confined to estimates and expenditure. The novelty for the new Select Committees lay in the specific reference to policy. This had been a 'no-go' area. In practice there is still a problem since civil servants do not discuss policy much at all and Ministers will only discuss settled policy. In any case the Committee's discussion of controversial policy is inhibited by party loyalties. Bipartisanship is a necessary condition of functioning for the Select Committee – in a system in which a party majority is the only source of independent power. The Committees choose to be bipartisan and weak, rather than partisan and powerless.

Membership of the Committees is proportionate to the parties and some chairmanships are allocated to Opposition members. Selection is in the hands of a Committee of Selection, which acts on the advice of party Whips. In 1992 the power of the Whips in selection was made apparent when Conservative Whips invented a new maximum service rule for their own side in order to

exclude a troublesome Member. The Chairmen make up a Liaison Committee which from time to time has pressed the rights of the Committees against the preferences of the majority Whips. The House has the power in this as in all business to assert the supremacy of Parliament not party, but it never does.

Each Committee is served by a Clerk and one or two specialist advisers. The chairman and the clerks play an important part in the work of the Select Committees especially since there is a significant turnover of membership, roughly 20 per cent in a session and on average 44 per cent over the 1979–83 Parliament. The clerks guide the chairman and draft the reports. The chairman leads the questioning. The effectiveness of the committee depends a good deal on how well he has studied the papers and briefed himself for the sitting and how skilfully he presses the questions. But the task is not easy for a lay and part-time chairman faced with professionals.

Even so the standard of question and answer is reasonably high, in comparison, for example, with committees of the US Congress. The lay committeemen probe with some acuity and obstinacy and the expert witnesses marshal and present an impressive array of material. Sometimes, however, the weight and complexity of information suffocate the committee; members are unsure of what they are looking for and their questioning lacks coherence.

Occasionally sharpness and challenge lie behind moderate words. The civil servant says to a persistent Member, for example, 'that is not the direction in which I would look, if I may say so, if I wanted guidance on the point that I think the Member is seeking to ask about'...which could be translated into a fairly blunt rebuke. Or the chairman urges on an apparently unforthcoming witness: 'The question I asked, and I hope I do not have to repeat it... have you or have you not got that information?' Sometimes the official must plead his subordinate and non-political status: 'I do not think this is a question that an official could be expected to answer.... I cannot forecast what the Minister will say.'

The distinctive features of the Select Committees are set out below.

● The committees do not form a coherent system. There is overlap between the committees and a diversity of approach. Specialisation is uneven. The scope of target departments is large and committees have not consistently pursued narrow subjects in depth to the point of specialisation. Topics have been picked up by passing interest, rather than long-term strategy

- The committees are characteristically backbench committees, with all that implies in the House of Commons – independent, but separated from government (or even in many cases, experience of government) and lacking consistent influence.

- The committees are also mostly and necessarily bipartisan, not divided by party lines, and presenting agreed reports. There is no formal party whipping, the focus is on information and the style is rational and not adversarial and theatrical as in the Chamber. For some of the time, at least, backbench solidarity prevails over party solidarity. Unfortunately for the committee, in the House of Commons influence goes with party; bipartisanship indicates lack of influence, and partisanship brings the automatic government majority into play.

- The committees engage in a dialogue with government, mainly civil service officials, but also with Ministers. This last has been described by a former Head of the Civil Service as a 'drastic constitutional change'. Politically neutral officials naturally resist any public exposure in connection with controversial issues; civil servants work to and for Ministers, not Parliament. Civil servants have been officially instructed not to discuss advice given to Ministers, nor matters of public controversy – a fairly broad no-go area. The committees also talk with representatives of bodies outside the government. Thus, the system does formally compel powerful persons, mostly unknown, to make a case in public.

- Governments are still inclined to shelter behind the convention of ministerial responsibility and the tradition and practice of secrecy. The civil service was initially inclined to regard the committees as 'the enemy' – a normal professional reaction to the interfering lay outsider. But officials have become more responsive and, in some cases, when the 'chemistry' (of interpersonal relations) is right, there is active co-operation between committee and department.

The reports of the select committees are submitted to the relevant department for its observations. After some delay the department may accept or 'note' some of the committee's strictures and recommendations, or it may indicate disagreement, adding a brief justification. Unless Parliament itself intervenes, the committee's recommendations carry no sanction. But they do not go quite unheeded, for the department has had to explain itself before the committee, a salutary proceeding, and will not wish to attract the committee's further notice by a show of unconcern. But, unless the executive itself chooses to take up the findings of the committee, the department can normally go back to its work, fairly confident that its policy interests and standing have not suffered serious damage.

Parliament itself does not spend much time in the Chamber on the proceedings of the select committees and the participation of frontbenchers on either side is sparse. The political rewards of service on these committees are slight; modest reputations may made, but service is not essential for promotion. There is little incentive for the energetic and ambitious Member to devote himself to committee work. These conclusions indicate a rather modest role for the Select Committees.

Illustrations of the work of the Departmental Select Committees

1 The House of Fraser

The Trade and Industry Committee inquired into the dealings of the Department (DTI) and the Bank of England with the take-over of the House of Fraser (including Harrods) by the Fayed brothers (1985). The Committee criticised one Minister for refusing to appoint inspectors to investigate, and another (Lord Young) for not referring the matter to the Monopolies and Mergers Commission, and the Bank of England for not taking action over Harrods Bank. The Fayed Brothers were being pursued at the same time by the Lonrho company which had been unsuccessful in their bid for the House of Fraser. (The Lonhro comany owned The Observer and issued a special midweek edition to publicise its case.)

Thus the Committee was intervening in a struggle between two groups of capitalists and Conservative members were as cheerfully engaged as Labour. The Committee's proceedings won headlines: 'Governor in the Firing Line'; 'Tory Fury Erupts'. Lord Young, who suffered as a businessman turned non-elected politician, isolated in the House of Lords, had an uncomfortable time before the Committee and believed that his reputation suffered. So the Committee made an impact and alerted the Department to its responsibilities, though the Fayed Brothers remained in control of the House of Fraser.

2 British Aerospace and Rover

Lord Young was in trouble again with the same

committee over the British Aerospace purchase of the state-owned Rover Group. Lord Young, concerned to conclude the deal and, so he beleived, save 200 000 jobs threw in 'financial sweeteners' to induce British Aerospace to make the deal. These were contrary to EC competition law and had not been fully disclosed to Parliament. Lord Young was roughly handled by the Public Accounts Committee and the Select Committee on Trade and Industry. The latter's report, Lord Young said, gave him 'the worst day of my life apart from the day my brother died.... I was accused of having the morals of a barrow-boy. What's wrong with barrow-boys?.... Everyone in the business world understands what I did; noone in politics understands' (*The Guardian*, 13 March 1991).

The episode is of interest both for the work of Select Committees, the impact of the EC and the experience of businessmen in politics.

3 *The National Health Service*

The NHS has been the subject of several reports by the Social Service Committee, which has demonstrated some of the values of the Select Committees. It had had an able and experienced chairman (Frank Field). It has included members with relevant experience (for example, in health authorities). Its witnesses include people working in the Health Service. It has been able to clarify and publicise some of the crucial financial statistics. But the Committee's actual impact on the Government's running of the Health Service has not been substantial. In particular, the government went ahead with its radical reform of the management of the Service, despite the reservations and comparative caution of the Committee.

4 *Pit closures 1992–3*

This is an unusual case of a Select Committee apparently playing a part in policy-making – of course, in unusual circumstances. In October 1992 the Department of Trade and Industry (there was no longer an Energy Department) announced the immediate closure of 31 coal pits. This was in face of a rapidly declining market for coal, much affected by the preference of the privatised electricity generating industry for gas power stations and cheap imported coal.

There was a public outcry against the severe loss of jobs at a time of heavy unemployment. This affected the economic case for the closures since unemployment cost the government about £9000 per person unemployed. Many Conserva-

tives shared this concern. The Government retreated and promised a further review. In the time thus made available the Trade and Industry Select Committee conducted its own inquiry and produced an agreed report arguing for a substantial reduction in the number of proposed closures. The Committee was backed by the Conservative Coal Group; the group's attitude was headlined by one Sunday paper as: 'SAVE 20 PITS OR ELSE, SAY REBEL MPs'.

The Government did not accept the Committee's recommendations, but it is evident that the Government modified its proposals in face of widespread criticism on its own side, to which the Committee provided weight and precision. In the end the rebels did not persist (that is the nature of rebellions) and the forces of the market (whether re-structured or 'rigged') triumphed – few pits survived for long.

The power to send for persons and papers

The Select Committees have the power 'to send for persons and papers'. In theory the Committee's powers, if fully backed by the House, are sweeping. If the Committee summoned the Prime Minister he would come. In practice, of course, the Committee's powers are restricted in the interests of the government which controls Parliament. The Prime Minister by (what seems now to be) convention, does not appear; Ministers attend, though Wilson ordered one not to do so, on the special ground that the matter was outside that Minister's responsibility. It is more difficult to compel witnesses to speak at all or to speak freely. The Documents show how Ministers and civil servants can frustrate the committees. The more politically sensitive the matter, the less the committee learns about it. This is not the same as saying, the more significant the matter, the less the committee learns about it.

Other 'lay' witnesses are generally more open, except where there are special reasons for confidentiality, commercial, financial or, in the case of the Maxwell brothers in January 1992, the possibility of criminal charges.

■ DOCUMENT 13.2
The silences of Ministers

In two notorious cases former Ministers have conspicuously failed to answer the questions of a Select Committee.

a) Defence Committee – Leon Brittan

Leon Brittan appearing before Defence Committee 30 January 1986

From Defence Committee Minutes of Evidence, 1985–6, p. 169, HMSO, 1986

This was Brittan's third session with the Committee which was investigating the Westland Affair – see Chapter 9 Case Study. The Minutes show sharp and persistent questioning in particular by one Member of the Committee, Dr John Gilbert, and Brittan's effective resistance. These discontinuous extracts give the flavour.

Dr Gilbert: [about a telephone call] 'It is quite significant, is it not?'

Mr Brittan: 'No, it is of no significance whatsoever and you know it.'

In the next passage of interrogation Mr Brittan is to be heard blocking questions briskly and even brusquely.

'I cannot answer for the Prime Minister.... I understand what you are reading.... That is what she said in the House.... That appears to be correct.... It depends what you mean.... I am not going to add anything.... It depends what you mean by 'the facts'.... That is a comment that you make: I hear it with interest.'

In the course of these many refusals to be drawn Mr Brittan did say:

'I accept full responsibility for what was done.... I would particularly stress that it all had to be subject to the agreement of No. 10'.

Dr Gilbert: 'I would like to get a list of questions you are not prepared to answer.'

Mr Brittan's subsequent answers included the following statement while answering several other questions.

I have accepted there is an infinity of questions that could be devised by an astute and intelligent questioner to probe these matters further, but the answer will be the same.

b) Agriculture Committee – Edwina Currie

(First Report of the Agriculture Committee on Salmonella in Eggs, Vol. II, Minutes, H. C.108–11, 1988–9)

Edwina Currie had resigned as Junior Health Minister in December 1989 following a statement by her in a television interview that 'most of the egg production of this country, sadly, is now infected with salmonella'. For further detail see Chapter 9.

The Select Committee on Agriculture inquired into the matter, but met with stonewalling by Ministers, including Edwina Currie.

First, she refused to attend. At the end of a long exchange of letters the Chairman of the Committee wrote:

'The Committee was of the view that you should not be excused from giving evidence; and believes it is for it, not you, to decide whether such evidence is relevant.

I would be grateful if you could indicate by 2.30 pm tomorrow whether you intend to accept this invitation. If you do not do so, the Committee will have no option but to take formal steps in the House to seek to secure your attendance. I hope you will agree that it is in everyone's interest to avoid this course.'

Mrs Currie replied: 'I am bound to say that I was surprised (as many colleagues will be) that your Committee should feel it is able to decide whether or not to 'excuse' me from attendance.' The rights and immunities of individual Members were established long before the rights and powers of Select Committees to compel certain witnesses.

The House was very wise not to give Departmental Select Committees the power to require individual Members to attend. This power the House reserves for itself and to exercise it would be a very serious matter for which I believe there is no precedent since 1690. In those circumstances it could well be that the House would wish to seek the advice of the Select Committee on Parliamentary Privilege before discussing any such proposition or considering any further action....

When finally and reluctantly Mrs Currie appeared before the Committee sparks flew, but little new information was revealed.

Mrs Currie was understandably a little edgy, especially after being kept waiting outside the committee room for 50 minutes. Her manner, according to the BBC reporter was of 'chilly disdain', despite very conciliatory protection by her friend the Chairman of the Committee. Mrs Currie repelled questions for 30 minutes, protected by the Chairman and her own brisk and combative manner. Since she was no longer a Minister she no longer carried responsibility; and in any case, as she pointed out: '...as a former Minister, the content of any discussions that I might have had with officials, or of any papers that I might have seen other than published information, is subject to the usual convention which is that I would not discuss it now'. ■

EXERCISE
The silences of Ministers

13.2 Do these episodes show the weakness of the Select Committees?

■ DOCUMENT 13.3
The silences of Civil Servants – the principles

Memorandum of Guidance for Officials Appearing before Select Committees, 1980 (sometimes known, after a civil servant, as the 'Osmotherly Rules')
Officials appearing before Select Committees do so on behalf of their Ministers.... [An official is] subject to ministerial instructions as to how he should answer questions....

The general principle to be followed is that it is the duty of officials to be as helpful as possible to Committees and that any withholding of information should be limited to reservations that are necessary in the interests of good government or to safeguard national security. Departments should, therefore, be as forthcoming as they can (within the limits set out in this note) when requested to provide information...

Committees' requests for information should not be met regardless of cost or of diversion of effort from other important matters....

Officials should not give evidence about or discuss the following topics.

a) In order to preserve the collective responsibility of Ministers, the advice given to Ministers by their Departments should not be disclosed, nor should information about interdepartmental exchanges on policy issues, about the level at which decisions were taken or the manner in which a Minister has consulted his colleagues. Information should not be given about Cabinet Committees or their discussions....
b) Advice given by a Law Officer....
c) The private affairs of individuals or institutions on which any information... has been supplied in confidence....

Officials should also, where possible, avoid giving written evidence about or discussing the following matters....

d) Questions in the field of political controversy....
e) Sensitive information of a commercial or economic nature.

f) Matters which are, or may become, the subject of sensitive negotiations with governments or other bodies, including the European Community, without prior consultation with...the Ministers concerned....
g) Specific cases where the Minister has or may have a quasi-judicial or appellate function....

Official witnesses...should as far as possible confine their evidence to questions of fact relating to existing Government policies and actions. Officials should be ready to explain what the existing policies are and the objectives and justification, as the Government sees them, for those policies.... It is open to officials to make comments which are not politically contentious but they should as far as possible avoid being drawn, without prior Ministerial authority, into the discussion of alternative policy. ■

■ DOCUMENT 13.4
The silences of Civil Servants – an example

From Hearing of Select Committee on Defence, October 1988 (First report of the Defence Committee, H. C. 68, 1988–9)
These exchanges are between the witness, a senior civil servant and the Chairman, Michael Mates MP. The official, Mr Bevan, begins:
'In giving evidence to this Committee we want to be as helpful as we can in responding to your questions and indeed in providing information which is relevant to your study. I am sure you will understand, however, that we are to a degree constrained by the conventions which apply to officials giving evidence to Parliamentary committees and, to some extent, we shall feel inhibited when questions are raised which relate to future policy options and indeed to work in hand, which is designed to support future ministerial decisions....'
'Mr Chairman, Ministers, of course, will take the decision on the future of the Gurkhas and I think I wouldn't wish to comment on the way in which departmental advice to Ministers is formulated or where consideration has got to, other than to make a fairly obvious point, which is that it can be expected that the Government's principal military advisers' views will have been sought before a decision is taken...'
Chairman: 'What I am trying to get a feel for is where are we in this process and I don't think

you can tell me nowhere, can you Mr Bevan?'

'No, as I have already said, studies have been in hand for some time. What I do find difficulty in giving you a straight answer on is precisely where in the Ministry of Defence those studies have reached.'

Chairman: 'And you can't tell me whether the Chiefs of Staff have taken this problem formally or not.'

'No, I do not wish to answer that question.'

'Can we assume then that they have? It seems reasonable given your reluctance to answer.'

'I don't think that is a fair deduction.'....

'Please, it is perfectly clear advice to Ministers is sacrosanct. But possible advice to Ministers is not, because it is in the general area and the general domain of the considerations of the Ministry of Defence and I really do not think we can be satisfied with that kind of response.'

Member of the Committee: 'Mr Bevan is looking for an announcement which is underneath his file! Perhaps that will be helpful.'

'Well no, indeed, I was merely reminding myself of the constraints which are imposed upon us by the rules.'

Chairman: 'You seem to know the constraints all too well, Mr Bevan, if I may say so.'

'Well, I am sure, Mr Chairman, you will understand that we take care to prepare ourselves before coming to this Committee.'

Chairman: 'The rules everyone are looking at are not ones that were approved by Parliament or in fact voted by Parliament, they are internal Civil Service rules which we have not accepted.'....

At this point the exasperated Chairman suspended the sitting for the Committee to consider how to proceed and, after further unfruitful exchanges, it was agreed to summon the Minister the following week. That was not very fruitful either. ∎

EXERCISE
The silences of civil servants

13.3 What line or distinction is the Civil Service attempting to draw in Documents 3 and 4? What are the consequences for Select Committees?

The influence of the Select Committee

There are two indications that the new Select Committees do have an impact on government.

First, some of their work is 'newsworthy' and gains the attention of the media. A controversial session or report can win headlines on an inside page of a quality paper. Chairmen of Committees are called on for broadcast interviews, the standard introduction being, 'Chairman of the influential cross-party committee'. Such attention from the media is not to be discounted.

Second and more significant, against a background of generally comfortable relationships, distant, cosy, or co-operative, there is some friction and awkwardness in the relation of committees and government. In particular civil servants are unhappy about their increased exposure, especially after the Westland Affair, in which civil servants were named by the Prime Minister, but not allowed to defend themselves before the Defence Committee. Ministers, through the Whips or directly, sometimes take steps to influence a Committee's deliberations or conclusions.

In 1991–2 it appeared that the American research assistant of a member of the Health Committee had passed a draft report on NHS reform to the Minister's Parliamentary Private Secretary. Subsequently the report was amended, criticisms of the Government were withdrawn; five Conservative members who had previously approved the draft voted against the original draft. It seems the Committee had been 'got at'. The Privileges Committee decided that it was all very deplorable – which will not prevent it happening again. The incident shows that governments may care what Select Committees say about them, but also that they can intervene to influence what is said.

It is evident that the work of the Select Committees is severely limited by the British system of collective and ministerial responsibility in an executive-dominated Parliament. There is virtually no restraint on the application by the government of its majority to preserve itself and its policies. Party discipline and loyalty ensure that the Committees have no serious power to challenge the government. The Committees can choose to be partisan and so powerless except to support the government, or bipartisan and so powerless. The highest aspiration of the Select Committees is to have influence on the margins or in the detail of government. Such influence is not without constitutional value, and it is inappropriate to condemn the committees by comparison with those of the US Congress.

Within these limits it may be said of the influence of the committees.

● They are no longer provisional and experimental, but an established part of the parliamentary process.

- Information about government has been improved, though you need to be an assiduous reader to discover and absorb it all (the figures are startling – in the first four years, 1979–83, the Select Committees asked almost 100 000 questions, received 5000 memoranda, questioned Ministers on 230 occasions and civil servants on 1800). The Trade and Industry Committee's investigation (1991–2) of the notorious Iraqi 'super-gun' (made in Britain) offers a striking example of the information function of the Committees. Either the government knew and was not going to tell, or it did not know, and should have known.
- Government policy making takes into account the consequences of interrogation by the Select Committees, so there is greater concern with the detailed justification of policy – hence the influence of the committees may be anticipated and so difficult to identify, but none the less significant.
- In a few identifiable cases government policy has been modified by the Select Committees. For example, the Home Affairs Committee had some part in persuading the government to repeal the 'sus' law (arrest on suspicion); and the Foreign Affairs Committee seems to have persuaded the government to cede Britain's residual rights over the Canadian Constitution. There are other examples, none highly significant. In 1980 the Education Committee under an energetic chairman intervened in a musicians' strike and so saved the Promenade Concerts – a quite untypical intervention in a typically marginal affair. In 1992 the Social Security Committee argued vigorously for a reform of laws relating to pensions, following the collapse of the Maxwell business empire, but the effect is not so far apparent. In 1993 the Energy Committee gave voice and precision to public and parliamentary concern about the closure of coal mines (see above).
- Members ambitious for office can reasonably take up committee service (preferably conspicuous) as a first career step. But any government office or Opposition front bench responsibility disbars, so few politicians of weight, or rather weighty reputation, are to be found in the Committees.

There are more sceptical views of the influence and proper role of the Committees.

- The work of the Committees is not always impressive. There is no clear focus or continuing strategy in inquiry. There is weak or unskilful chairing, inadequate preparation, poor attendance. A well-briefed witness finds no difficulty in stonewalling or evading. Mainly this reflects the inequalities of the two sides – on one side laymen supported by a clerk and perhaps two advisers, on the other a team of senior professionals backed by scores of officials. Reports of the committees are drafted by an inexpert clerk under extreme pressures of time, politics and personalities.
- The Committees offer another point of access and platform for sectional interest groups and professional lobbyists.
- The Committees have added to the workload of Members and, for better or for worse, taken them away from the Chamber.
- Committees do not and should not change the course of governments. The proper role of the Committees is exaggerated by ambitious members and constitutional radicals. The work of Parliament lies mainly in the Chamber (Enoch Powell's view) and in supporting the government (the realistic interpretation of the British constitution). Policy is properly a matter for the parties, including party committees. The Select Committees should restrict themselves to the scrutiny of administration.

A precise summing-up is not possible. The Select Committees have proved themselves useful and have a very modest influence. Perhaps the search for precise evidence of influence is vain. Consider the Document.

■ DOCUMENT 13.5
The influence of Select Committees

From L. Pliatzky, 1989, pp. 79–80
Leo Pliatzky reports the following conversation
Well-known journalist: 'What decision has ever been changed by a Select Committee report?'
Well-known Minister: 'What decision has ever been changed by one of your leading articles?' ■

EXERCISE
The influence of Select Committees

13.4 What, if anything, does this exchange suggest about the influence of Select Committees?

Private Members

The role of Private Members independently and 'in their own right' is clearly limited by the dominance of government and the demands of party, limitations which Members freely accept when they seek election to the House on a party ticket. This does not mean that the backbencher is merely 'lobby-fodder'; their commitment falls a little short of vows of poverty, chastity and obedience. But it does mean that the political work of backbenchers is for the most part shaped by service of a party and conformity to its disciplines and a strong desire to be re-elected. The scope for independence is small.

The backbencher has other personal drives besides those of party and re-election and a mix of these drives modified by the overwhelming pressures of party and re-election produces five models of Member of Parliament according to the different priorities.

The priorities of the backbencher

Basic

1 *Re-selection and re-election.* All Members, but especially those from marginal constituencies (up to 100 or so) are concerned to hold on to their vote in the constituency. This entails conspicuous service of the constituency, visiting it most weekends, holding advice 'surgeries', attending dinners, opening bazaars and so on and responding speedily to the grievances of constituents, even when the matter is not the responsibility of central government. Some Members are with good reason almost as frightened of their postbags as of the Whips.

In defence of local interests Members act as case workers, grievance chasers and interest lobbyists.

- Case working means taking up the problems of constituents, often to do with local government (for which the Member has no responsibility) or the welfare services – a house, a school, planning permission, the care of old people, crime or other nuisance. The Member listens sympathetically and may forward details of the case to the appropriate authority. In the case of a department of central government he is likely by his intervention to get a quicker but not usually a different response.
- Grievance chasing means taking up in the House or directly with Ministers (through official or party channels) the more general griev-

ances expressed in the constituency – student grants, Sunday trading, the latest crime wave, the maximum earnings rule for pensioners (now abolished through just such complaining).

- Interest lobbying means defending and promoting specific major interests – an arms factory (never mind about defence policy), a local industry menaced by foreign competition (never mind the interests of the consumer), a railway line (never mind the party's transport policy). This kind of 'localism' is in fact much diminished by the disciplines of party; national considerations and priorities prevail over the local interest – for better or for worse. By contrast an American Congressman would not dream of subordinating local to national interest.

In a marginal constituency the Member may be unseated by the voters. In every constituency there is some danger that the Member may be 'de-selected', that is, tactfully or more brutally invited to retire; so he needs to be particularly solicitous of his constituency party, its committee and officers. Some illustrations of this potentially difficult relationship of a Member with his constituency are given in Chapter 15.

2 *Party commitment.* For most MPs commitment to party is the basis of their political life and work; the chains and burdens of service are accepted with a light heart and good cheer. The form and intensity of commitment ranges from zealous activism through docile loyalty to a critical commitment. Most – but not all – Members do not resent, and may not even be aware of, the hypocrisy involved in believing that your own side is always right and the other always wrong.

For perhaps a third of Members these two priorities, the service of constituency and party, constitute the main professional drives. Others are less easily satisfied.

Additional

1 *Hope of office.* Those who choose a political career may honourably aspire to the higher forms of service and the greater satisfactions of office. Almost one in three of the majority party may expect office of some kind and even the lowly unpaid office of Parliamentary Private Secretary may lead on to ministerial comforts and splendours. But the Member who aspires to office binds himself more tightly to the party and the Whips; the path of ambition is not the

path of independence.

The pre-war careers of Winston Churchill or even of Macmillan demonstrate the incompatibility between independence of mind and rapid or continuing preferment. Lloyd George solved the problem by forming a personal coalition; for Enoch Powell, ambition was subordinated to principle and independence; most of the people promoted by Margaret Thatcher had to be 'one of us'.

2 *Professional backbenchers.* A minority of Members find satisfaction in their work as backbenchers without thought of office or complementary outside activity: they are professional backbenchers. Most Members spend long hours on parliamentary business. A survey carried out in the first three months of 1988 showed an average working week of 69 hours – the late hours for business and the weekends in the constituency raise the average and some Members can clock up over 100 hours a week during the six months of the session. Over 80 per cent of Members voted in at least half of the divisions. But Members vary sharply in their devotion to parliamentary work. The score of Members who voted, according to the 1988 survey, in over 95 per cent of divisions is balanced by a score who voted in less than 30 per cent. Debates are not well attended; the Chamber empties after Question Time and usually does not fill again until the 10 p.m. division approaches.

Of course, Members have many other and perhaps better things to do. Many judge that they can contribute more to their party, political cause, personal advancement or income by busying themselves elsewhere and doing other work. Although the House has a strong sense of its own importance, it does not have a sense of corporate purpose, for a good and obvious reason. Nevertheless, there are always a few who swim against the tide of indolence or cynicism and pursue with pride the profession or vocation of Private Member. They pursue no other employment, accept no 'free lunches' and other pleasing inducements, do their parliamentary work in Chamber, committee and constituency with unstinting devotion and earn the admiration but not the imitation of their less single-minded colleagues. Their indispensable contribution is to demonstrate that there is a serious purpose and work for the Private Member of Parliament to do.

3 *Service of a specific interest.* The Member's relations with interest groups was discussed above in the section on lobbies. No MP serves a specific interest exclusively, but there are many whose most vigorous work, after attending to the constituency, is the defence and promotion of a particular interest. This may be justified on the grounds that a particular interest, for example, farming, textiles or mining, is essential to the economy of the constituency; but the decline of traditional industries, including agriculture, and economic diversification, makes this identity of interest unlikely. Sometimes contributions to a debate in the House can be classified by an observer according to the particular lobby of which the Member speaking is known to be the paid or otherwise retained or sponsored 'consultant'. Parliament represents interests as well as territorial constituencies and voters and Members play their part in this system of representation.

4 *Diversion and additional income.* In contrast to the professionals, many Members are driven to find other and more diverting and preferably better paid work. The section on the lobbies indicated one range of activities pursued by Members. Others practise their professions, law, business, the metropolitan financial professions and journalism. (Winston Churchill, the great commoner, made a fortune out of his writing in the 1930s from his base in the House of Commons). Insider accounts, such as those by Julian Critchley, a journalist MP who cheerfully defies both his party and his constituency, record the seamier side of this London Gentleman's Club, where some at least of the seven deadly sins are believed to flourish. Members pursuing additional income do not give anxiety to the Whips, as long as they turn up to divisions. Those pursuing other diversions had best avoid scandal. The files in the Whips' Office are not restricted to the Member's political behaviour.

5 *Rebel or maverick.* This category includes those who are not only dedicated backbenchers, but are driven to assert their independence by persistent and public refusal to go along with the party line and a constant harrying of the government or the party leadership. They are, honourably, the trouble-makers of Parliament and every democracy needs them. One awkward parliamentarian (but a Minister nevertheless) Alan Clark said on his retirement in 1992 and his decision not to seek re-election: 'trouble in its various forms is really the only solace left for backbenchers'.

Normally such trouble-making stops short of a threat to the government itself, which can only occur in a closely divided parliament on a vote of confidence recognised as determining the fate of the government. Even so trouble is not made easily; governments are almost invulnerable. The trouble-maker needs to do research, prepare his case, exploit procedure and persist in the face of the pleadings and anger of the Whips and sometimes the indifference of his colleagues. Here are some illustrations of the trouble-makers.

Rebels and mavericks: Parliament's trouble-makers

1 Tam Dalyell specialises in the harrying of government on specific matters. His most famous campaign was about the sinking of the Argentine warship, the General Belgrano, just before the outbreak of the Falklands War in May 1982. The case achieved a justifiable notoriety because a civil servant, Clive Ponting, was tried – and acquitted by a jury – under the Official Secrets Act for disclosing confidential papers to a Member of the House of Commons. There remains a dispute about the legitimacy and the morality of sinking the 'Belgrano' at that particular moment, but there is little doubt that the government was less than forthright in its account of the incident. Parliament was deceived and Mr Dalyell has fought a long campaign to have the record put right. He has failed, of course. Governments rarely admit error and the crucial evidence of a naval log book is strangely missing. But Dalyell – he is a Labour Member and would not expect a knighthood – has made a contribution to history; the 'Belgrano' affair cannot now be expunged from the record of what governments do to avoid embarrassment and one commentator said, perhaps with some exaggeration, that Dalyell had 'more effect on the way this country is run than most Cabinet Ministers ever do'.

Tam Dalyell has a long and honourable record of parliamentary awkwardness. He pursued Margaret Thatcher's government over Westland, the US bombing of Libya, the miners' strike, the Spycatcher affair. He was the instigator of the 'West Lothian' question (West Lothian is his constituency) during the devolution debates of the 1970s. This is a question to which there is no easy answer: if significant powers are devolved to a Scottish Assembly –

and so removed from the London (UK) Parliament – what right have Scottish MPs to vote on matters concerning England and Wales? Dalyell makes trouble for his own party as well as the other side. His case is always well researched and pursued with vigour. In the three year period 1983–6 he made 306 speeches in the House and asked 170 Oral Questions and 1559 for written answer; only two of his colleagues, Dennis Skinner and Tony Banks, both also distinguished trouble-makers, could match that record. Dennis Skinner makes a point of accepting for himself only the average industrial wage, refuses all invitations to eat and drink at the expense of interest groups and does not 'pair' with a Conservative Member to avoid taking part in divisions (voting).

2 Other trouble-makers. On the Conservative side trouble-making is less frequent and disciplined loyalty to the leadership (tempered by occasional assassination) is maintained. But Members of strong principles and convictions, once they have given up hope of preferment, do sometimes take a stand on principle. Michael Mates, a valiant defender of Margaret Thatcher over the 'Belgrano' and 'Spycatcher' affairs, was an independent Chairman of the Defence Select Committee and led a revolt over the Community Charge. A score of his colleagues joined him in the lobby in support of an amendment designed to make the tax a little more equitable. Another normally loyal backbencher, Dame Jill Knight (so loyal that she had already earned her equivalent knighthood), led a campaign in 1988 to protect the old and the poor against the new charges. Both Michael Mates and Jill Knight were removed from backbench office by their colleagues, at the command of the Whips, for these demonstrations of independence and concern for the poor, but Mates gained overdue promotion to office under John Major after the election of 1992.

Trouble-making is different from 'cussedness', making mischief for its own sake, for fun or for spite and partisan malice, and different from the normal discourtesies of the Chamber of the House. At its most noble, trouble-making involves hard work, persistence and courage in face of both gentle dissuasion and arm-twisting. Sometimes trouble-makers feel the pull of party and personal loyalties and have to wrestle with conscience. Richard Shepherd, a rebel over official secrets and the EC, has spoken of the need to apply a sense of right and wrong to the demands of the party whips. Emma Nicholson, a 'poll-tax' rebel, said:

'It's commonly perceived as a virtue to stick to someone through thick and thin. But the Charge of the Light Brigade always seemed to me to be a mistake. I had no feeling of disloyalty because I'd realised...that my principles and the needs of my constituents meshed' (interview in *The Guardian*, 13 March, 1991).

EXERCISE
Disobeying orders

13.5 What is the significance of the reference to the Charge of the Light Brigade?

The rebel MP defying the Whips chooses an honourable course. In the British parliamentary system the course of party loyalty is also honourable, though it requires less effort and usually less courage. Nevertheless private criticism and resistance behind the scenes may be more effective than public rebellion, since the Minister wishes to avoid a public concession or retreat.

Membership of Parliament is an honourable profession, but it has its less honourable side. It is acknowledged by the Procedure Committee that there has been a recent decline in what may be called parliamentary manners. Parliamentary discourtesy includes 'low-grade abuse' (the term used by the Clerk of the House), barracking and the kind of low muttering not unknown in other institutions which renders the speaker inaudible while the mutterers are unidentifiable. It is usually said in defence that the House was always an unmannerly place – no more convincing than the usual 'what was good enough for grandad' argument.

In any case the number of Members 'named' by the Speaker for indiscipline has increased significantly. There is no doubt some frustration on the Labour benches after so many years in Opposition and some triumphalism among a new class of Conservative members lacking the genteel upbringing and courtesy of the old Tory party. Whatever the explanation, such behaviour helps to explain the low regard we have for politicians as distinct from the institution of Parliament.

Government and the rebels
Governments do not regard persistent individual rebels and trouble makers with respect and affection. They are concerned to push their business through and regard the criticism of opposition, media and public opinion as quite enough to

cope with. While governments look so powerful to us and to rebellious backbenchers, they feel vulnerable. Hence, governments invoke loyalty and threaten discipline. Mostly the Whips endeavour to restrain the rebel. Sometimes, rebellion spreads and the Government seems to face not an individual rebel, but a party rebellion. The heavier guns may be used.

This was the case over the Maastricht Treaty 1992–3. Individual rebels, combining personal courage (perceived by the Whips as bloody-mindedness) with principled disagreements on policy (also perceived by the Whips as bloody-mindedness), coalesced into a rebel party within the party, with its own sources of finance, support staff and headquarters. The Prime Minister was forced in the end to bring out his ultimate weapon, the threat of dissolution.

EXERCISES
The effectiveness of backbench rebellion

13.6 In what conditions would you think backbench rebellions are likely to be successful?

13.7 What is the Cabinet's trump card against a rebellion?

A rebellious party, or even sections of a party, presents a serious problem. Individual trouble makers can be tolerated, just because they are individuals and do not threaten majorities. Faced with a more substantial dissent, party leaders must find a mix of discipline and concession, that is, they must exercise the skills of political management.

Private Member's bills

Private members do not spend all their time being rude to one another, or in slavish obedience to, or heroic defiance of, the Whips. Much of their time is spent, as indicated elsewhere, in useful work in Committee or in the constituency, or attending to the problems of constituents, or, perhaps of less parliamentary value, in pursuing their own professional work or the political interests of the lobbies which employ them. There are too some limited opportunities for the private member to promote legislation through the procedures for private Member's bills.

Nine tenths of Parliament's time is devoted to the business of the government and the official Opposition (technically this is all government business). In the brief remainder of time, the private member can take the initiative in asking Questions and in introducing bills and motions. Here, above all, the private member has his day. In the context of British government-dominated politics, this meagre ration of time may look fair; compared with the system which operates in the United States, the scope allowed to the British private member acting on his own seems ludicrously inadequate. The restrictions are not of recent origin, the present position having been almost reached by 1902.

Private Members normally have about twenty Fridays for introducing bills and motions. Some time is taken up by the later stages of bills, so there is time for no more than 2–3 new bills to be introduced on any one day. These times are shared by ballot and a Member has about a 1:20 chance of being successful. It is also open to a Member under the 'ten-minute rule' to introduce a bill with a ten-minute speech at certain specified times. A ten-minute speech may be made in reply and the House then votes, or accepts the bill unopposed. The ballot procedure is the more significant for serious legislators.

Of the bills going forward from the ballot roughly 10 per cent are 'party-political'; about 60 per cent are either not controversial at all or cut across party divisions. The remaining 30 per cent are government-drafted, departmental bills favoured by the Member (J. Griffith and M. Ryle, 1989, p. 388).

Thus the Member is able at least to 'ventilate' a subject, to publicise a cause or grievance, to show a need for legislation and test the extent of support. This leads only infrequently to the enactment of legislation, for which the obstacles are considerable. The ballot is an initial hazard and, even with good fortune, the time available on the allotted days is short for a bill to go through all its stages and it is easy for opponents to obstruct and destroy. No bill may propose the spending of money (a government prerogative). Official help with drafting is not normally available.

If the bill antagonizes the majority party, the Cabinet, or a powerful pressure group, it is likely to be sunk. A bill may be talked out if the debate is kept going until 4 o'clock and the Speaker refuses to put the question; it must anyway be supported by at least a 100 Members; the committee considering it must keep a quorum; and, like all other bills, if it is not completed in one session it lapses.

Even in this area of apparent independence for the Private Member the Whips rarely yield their control. For example, on Friday 24 January 1992 a handful of Members talked with enthusiasm and at length about a bill to promote 'traffic calming' measures. The trams of Blackpool were warmly praised. But the Whips had been at work. The objective of the long-winded enthusiasm for traffic calming was to ensure that there was no time left for the following bill on freedom of information, which was soon 'talked out'. (The record for obstructive marathon speeches is probably Sir Ivan Lawrence's 4 hours 27 minutes in a debate of March 1985 on a water fluoridation measure).

Despite such obstruction, the difficulties are not insurmountable. In the 1987–92 Parliament 65 Private Member's bills were passed, about 1 in 7 of those introduced by all procedures; for balloted bills the success rate was 41 out of 99. Sometimes a bill has widespread sympathy, both in and outside the House, and the government itself may step in to facilitate its passage. Governments often prefer that legislation on controversial matters of conscience, for example to do with private and sexual morality, be promoted by Private Members – a position of benevolent, but not entirely reliable neutrality. No bill succeeds unless it is granted time by the Government.

About two fifths of the bills which are balloted do in fact become law, either as separate acts or by later being incorporated in government legislation. There has been a long line of minor legislation, on fireguards, litter, protection of birds, pool betting, mock auctions and so on, as well as one or two outstanding laws, introduced by private members. Of these the most justly famous are the Murder (Abolition of Death Penalty) Bill of Sidney Silverman (1965), Duncan Sandys's Civic Amenities Bill and David Steel's Bill on Abortion Law Reform (1967).

These bills were fought over by competing groups, with the government holding the ring. In other cases – for example, Graham Bright's Video Recordings Bill, 1983 – the government offers active encouragement and help. In the case of David Alton's Abortion Amendment Bill (1988) the Government remained neutral and it was 'talked out' by a coalition of opponents including Dennis Skinner, who spoke for three hours.

Enoch Powell in a long career in the House was once successful in carrying a Private Members bill (to make it compulsory for motor vehicles to carry two tail lights) and once (1988) unsuccessful (with a bill to prohibit the use of human embryos for experimentation). He was supported by a majority in a free vote, but the Government refused to make more parliamentary time available. Mr Powell accepted that this was entirely proper: 'any law which raises the slightest objection anywhere must be backed by the Government'.

EXERCISE
Private Members' bills

13.8 Do you see a case for the extension of facilities for private members' legislation? What about Enoch Powell's principle?

A 'servile' Parliament?

The overriding working force in Parliament is party. When account is taken of the complexity of Members' drives and the multiplicity of pressures falling upon them, the primacy of party is still apparent. Nigel Nicolson's summing-up is interesting in this respect. Nicolson was a Conservative MP of independent mind, who rebelled over the Suez intervention (1956) and lost a struggle with his constituency association to retain the nomination (see Chapter 15).

■ DOCUMENT 13.6
The primacy of party

Based on N. Nicolson, 1958, p. 66
Nicolson lists the pressures on the Member of Parliament

a) Pressures from outside Parliament:
● constituents
● party central office
● associates in business, profession or trade union
● friends
● national organisations.

b) Pressures from inside Parliament:
● colleagues
● Whips
● Ministers or Shadow Ministers
● party committees. ■

EXERCISE
The primacy of party

13.9 How do these pressures balance between party and non-party?

Nicolson summed up these pressures as follows:

'The resultant of this parallelogram of forces is almost always the same: [the Member] votes as he is required to vote by the Whips. But the reasons why he does so, and what can be the different methods and consequences of not doing so, are not so simple'. He thought that unfulfilled ambition and laziness (common to all professions) converted the early enthusiasms of the backbencher into calm docility. Thus Nicolson, a distinguished rebel himself, confirms that the rule of the Whips is always more than a simple tyranny, and the behaviour of Members is more complex than blind obedience – but in both cases, not much more.'

The Economist said (on Guy Fawkes Day 1977) that Parliament was 'inglorious' and 'servile'; being a Member of Parliament 'is a whipped, degrading and self-perpetuating profession'. Clearly there is something to be said for Guy Fawkes' plan to blow up Parliament. Contemporary Members of Parliament must accept the political subordination of their position. There is no scope in the system for the great parliamentarians of the past, a Chatham, Fox or Gladstone, nor for the powerful independent legislators to be found in the United States Senate.

Within the limits of party loyalty and discipline (or servility) most members settle for a mix of the priorities set out above. Like most other professions membership of Parliament is characterised by much honest, hum-drum, unimaginative and unambitious toil; there is purposive drive and cynical sloth, solid integrity and a hint of corruption.

GUIDE TO EXERCISES

13.1 The Public Accounts Committee has the best professional support of any parliamentary as distinct from government operation. The Reports, based on the work of the National Audit Office, are consistently more searching than those of any other committee. It may be assumed that they have some effect on the future conduct of the financial affairs of particular departments and divisions. However, if the effect of the Public Accounts Committee were truly substantive, it would find less evidence of financial inefficiency. Its best efforts seem only to hold back the tide of extravagance.

Further, the Public Accounts Committee deals with the implementation of policy, not policy itself. For example, it does not challenge directly the wisdom of acquiring high technology defence hardware which so frequently exceeds estimated costs. The Public Accounts Committee concentrates on 'looking after the pennies' when it seems clear the greater savings would arise from 'taking care of the pounds'. But that really would be to intrude on policy.

13.2 Yes and no! These were unrepresentative episodes; the political temperature was high and the media were preparing their headlines. You can argue on one side that these are precisely the occasions for the Select Committees to assert their role, show their mettle. On the other hand, in the British constitution, the proper and useful role of Select Committees cannot be in the harrying and embarrassment of Ministers. But that does sound a little complacent?

13.3 Follow the text closely and write down in two columns what civil servants will and will not do. In general they are ready to talk about settled policy, but not policy that is in process of development. The discussion of alternative policies or policy options is ruled out. For civil servants policy is either an accomplished fact or a void of silence.

In consequence the Select Committees, in their dialogues with civil servants, cannot play a serious role in policy development. They may do a little better with outside groups and with Ministers. This position is in accord with the constitutional conventions of collective and ministerial responsibility.

13.4 The Minister could be saying: Neither journalists nor Select Committees change government decisions; they, like you, are powerless. But he might be inferring more subtly that specific decisions are not sharply changed but there may be influence on a climate of opinion – unspecific but significant and impossible to demonstrate.

13.5 The Charge of the Light Brigade was a military disaster in the Crimean war (1854). It raises the moral issue of the right of subordinates to disobey orders, a dilemma that arises in all hierarchical organisations, including government, schools and colleges, industry as well as the army. If

things go wrong who is responsible? And if the command is perceived to be morally wrong (in matters ranging from the treatment of Jews in Germany in the 1930s to, say, the neglect of safety procedures in a mine or a railway, or the leaking of a confidential government paper) do you have the right to refuse the order? And should you be blamed if you obey? And do you think 'war criminals' (Germany in the 1940s, Iraq in 1990–1, Bosnia in 1992) should be pursued?

Plainly these moral dilemmas are more serious than those of a rebellious backbencher, but the principles are similar. In each case the costs and benefits of the alternative courses of action need to be precisely calculated. Generally the Member of Parliament has more time to do this than the cavalry officer in the Crimea.

13.6 When the rebellion is widespread and coherent (discipline is difficult to apply against large numbers) and reflects dissent or discontent in the country, in the party and in the media, or in a major interest group close to the party. It helps the rebellion if the Cabinet is itself divided; it does not help much if the rebels have a good case.

13.7 Making the issue one of confidence, that is, if we are defeated on this we resign. But a government can only do this if it is certain to win the vote. Otherwise it is risking bringing itself down along with the rebels. The sword is two-edged. So Prime Ministers rarely make this threat as John Major did in October 1992 and again in July 1993. Normally even difficult and contentious issues are settled long before this stage.

All these factors were present in 1992–3 for the Maastricht rebels and the strength of their case was recognised. Were they successful? Apparently not on the immediate issue of the ratification of the Treaty; but the rebellion contributed to changes in the longer term to Conservative policy on Europe – and incidentally towards greater public awareness and even understanding of the issue.

13.8 Yes. The history of Private Members' bills suggests that there are a number of matters demanding legislation on which government has no wish to legislate: they are preoccupied with other matters, or reluctant to interfere in matters like divorce or Sunday observance for fear of antagonising vociferous pressure groups. Private Members may step in and do good where governments fear to tread. In many cases, these are matters which do not excite opinion on party lines and the prestige and authority of the government is not at stake. The possibility of making laws is also important for the morale of the backbencher.

The overall case for the extension of these facilities is indeed a good one, but it comes up against the problem of shortage of time. There is too the problem of finance. Private Members cannot propose the expenditure of money. If they could, they would doubtless be hounded by pressure groups wanting a share. So the scope of Private Members' legislation must necessarily be limited and the problem of time remains unsolved.

Enoch Powell's principle is one view of the operation of the British constitution: the sovereignty of Parliament is entrusted to the government, carrying its responsibility to the electorate. An alternative view is that a majority of the House legitimately exercises the authority of the House. In practice there may not be much difference, since it is difficult to build a majority against the firm opposition of the government.

13.9 Some of the outside pressures may be non-party, but even that is not certain. As to the relative force of pressures, those inside Parliament have the advantage of proximity; in the constituency the party is the Member's main contact. A major non-party pressure could be a factory or other commercial interest threatened by party policy. See following text.

ASSESSMENTS
Change in Parliament

Parliament in the 1990s differs from the Parliament of the 1950s. The fundamentals remain – dominance by the government through the majority party, mock-medieval atmosphere and ritual, the sense (in part an illusion) of being at the centre of events, survival as an arena to make and challenge political reputation.

Parliament remains, too, a fine London club for gentlemen. But it is now more business-like and more influenced by the media. The 'more business-like' reflects:

- new kinds of Member
- a greater readiness to dissent, coupled with undiminished partisanship
- a more active House of Lords
- the new Select Committees
- enhanced role for PAC working with NAO
- the introduction of television, which has raised the public impact of Parliament, for better or for worse.

While Parliament has changed, the whole system of politics in which it must operate has changed too. This is indicated throughout this book. At many points – for example in the development of the executive, the Europeanisation of government, the clamour of lobbies and the imperiousness of specialist expertise – the claims and capacity of Parliament to a role in government are challenged and diminished.

The House of Commons is more 'instrumental', even brutally so, than before, reflecting a shift from an academic, Senior Common Room culture to a business, Board Room, culture. Decision and action counts more than reflection and rumination. Lord (Roy) Jenkins described himself as 'by modern standards (particularly those now applying, in the Conservative Party) an old-style member' (1991, p, 81), – pursuing a metropolitan career related to political life, but not notably assiduous in his constituency or the House of Commons. Jenkins believed there was 'a significant change in the style of the House' in the late 1970s; 'Except on rare occasions debate had ceased to be central to the parliamentary process...there developed a parliamentary style with a rhythm like a game of snap.' (p. 565). Jenkins ascribes the change to Margaret Thatcher's style (preferring Parliamentary Questions to debate and 'sustained rational argument') and the needs of the media to finish their reporting by 9 p.m. Jenkins and perhaps many others, did not feel at home in a House characterised by short, sharp thrusts and wrecking asides by 'Skinner and co'. The reference is to Dennis Skinner, 'the Beast of Bolsover', typical of a new kind of mainly Labour Member, who fought with gritty and sometimes offensive integrity, against the power structure of Parliament and Britain.

The place of Parliament in British government

We may now return to the criticisms of Parliament raised at the beginning of Chapter 11.

It is evident from the above account that the place of Parliament is limited by the support of the party majority for the government, which converts Parliament into an instrument of the government. Three fundamental questions may be raised about the role of a legislature. In the case of the British Parliament they can all be given qualified negative answers.

1 Does Parliament control its own procedures?
2 Does Parliament have a substantial influence over policy?
3 Does Parliament secure a significant measure of accountability of government?

Of course, all these questions are worded or loaded – ('control', 'substantial', 'significant') to justify a negative answer.

1 *Control of procedures.* An independent legislature needs the control of its timetable, the capacity to secure debate on matters considered immediate and urgent, to set up investigative committees on matters it chooses and to secure information. These matters are for the most part in the hands of the majority party.
2 *Influence over policy.* The evidence set out shows Parliament has only a modest capacity to exert influence on policy and certainly does not normally 'make' policy. A determined government can drive through policies on which there is at least serious misgiving in a majority of the House – the Community Charge is one example. Parliament's role is essentially reactive rather than initiating.
3 *Accountability.* There is no doubt that governments have to make a case in Parliament, in the Chamber and in Committee. But it is overstating the case to say that Parliament can 'call the government to account'. Ministers are likely to find a long interview on television more demanding.

Reformulating the question

It may be objected that these questions are not only loaded in favour of negative answers, but also excessively concerned with the distribution of power, rather than with consent and effectiveness in a system of government. So the question may be reformulated: does Parliament contribute to the effectiveness of British government?

If you approve in general of the executive-dominated system, then the answer is, yes. Alternatively, it may be argued that too little is made of the potential of Parliament to contribute to policy development and accountability. An unusually large assembly is restricted to the margins of the governmental process. Further, it may be contended, Parliament has failed to adjust to the demands of governing a complex society on which government itself spends about £250bn a year. The adversarial partisan combat which characterises the House of Commons is not appropriate to the governmental task.

Reform of Parliament

These comments raise the question of reform. For those who accept the fundamental criticisms of the last paragraph, only fundamental reform will do. This means:

● proportional representation
● replacement of the House of Lords
● devolution to the nations and regions
● diminishing the responsibilities of governments
● the re-assertion of the authority of Parliament in face of the executive.

These reforms amount to a constitutional revolution and are unlikely to be broached in the short term – or ever. An alternative menu of minor reforms can be composed by reference to the account given above of the shortcomings of Parliament. It might include, for example:

● improving facilities, including accommodation and support for backbenchers
● establishing a full support service for the Opposition
● rationalising working hours, procedures and voting,
● strengthening of the committee system and in particular extending its remit into pre-legislative consideration. There is a case for fusing the functions of scrutiny and legislation, but the crucial reform is to bring committee consideration to bear before government has determined policy – this is a radical reform, most unlikely to be accepted by governments.

The uses of the Opposition

Much of what has been said about the functions of Parliament and the role of the backbencher applies with most force to the majority party in the House. The majority party chooses and sustains a government, does its legislative work, defends it in the House and in the country, and may hope for the material and political rewards of power. Altogether, the work of the most humble backbencher on the government side may be useful and satisfying, even if occasionally dull.

For the Opposition, the situation is different and even the frontbencher may feel at times that his daily work is largely without reward or purpose. This is not the case, however, for Opposition has its uses too.

1 Criticism by the Opposition has some influence on government, especially in the same conditions in which rebellions have a hope of success and when party principle or tradition or emotion are not at stake.
2 The Opposition's part in public political education is also an appeal to the electorate. The Opposition has up to five years to show that it is a desirable alternative government. It may regard itself as involved in a continuous election campaign.
3 An occasional period in opposition is essential if a party is to rethink its policies. (By the 1990s the Labour Party had enjoyed too much time and, it may be thought, the Conservative Party, not enough!)
4 Finally, opposition Members of Parliament can participate in the undramatic work of the legislature, the parliamentary party and the constituency. In any large organisation, the number of persons able to take big decisions is necessarily small: they also serve who only sit and wait – for the next election.

However, even for front benchers, Opposition is frustrating. Five years may be tolerable but the Labour Party has had to endure more than that – two long periods (13 years and at least 17 years) since 1945. It is hard to sustain purpose and morale through such barren times.

Concept

Parliamentary Privilege

Parliamentary privilege refers to the peculiar rights of Parliament developed historically from its struggle for independence of the Crown and its status as the 'High Court of Parliament'. Parliamentary privilege is recognised by the courts as rightfully asserted by Parliament and based on the common law or political fact, or both. Whatever the constitutional status might be, Parliament assumes or claims its privileges, and enforces them, and indeed could not carry out its functions without some elements of legal immunity.

The most important privileges are Parliament's right to regulate its own composition and affairs and freedom of speech. The Member of Parliament is secure from action for defamation for what he says in Parliament, though there are awkward questions about what constitutes a proceeding in Parliament and what privilege the Member has in his personal capacity as a Member of Parliament.

The offence of Contempt of Parliament derives from the concept of privilege or special status and covers offences against the authority and dignity of the House. For example, John Junor, the journalist, was arraigned at the bar of the House in 1957 for raising questions about how Members were using their petrol allowances following the Suez crisis. Students at Essex University who interrupted a hearing of a select committee held at the university in 1969 were committing contempt, though the House took no action. Members may themselves commit contempt, for example by misleading the House, obstructing its business or disclosing confidential information.

● CASE STUDY
Westland yet again: Parliament

See Case Studies in Chapters 4 and 9 for details of the affair
The Westland Affair offers an interesting test of the influence of the House of Commons. Here was an affair which raised significant political issues, brought about the resignation of two Cabinet Ministers, damaged the relations of Ministers and civil servants, threatened the Prime Minister's hold on office and for a time destroyed the credibility and standing of the Government. The media reported and helped to create the crisis. What part, if any, did Parliament play?

The answer offers a good rough guide to the role of Parliament. The extremes of a scale of influence can be excluded. The House of Commons did not remove Margaret Thatcher from office, nor effectively investigate the improper leaking of the Attorney-General's letter. (Of course, the House had the power to do both and, it may be said, under the party majority system, freely chose not to go so far). At the other end of the scale, Parliament did not act simply as an unconcerned and impotent bystander. The House acted in the Westland Affair in a livelier, rowdier version of its normal role in great affairs – like a theatre in which the audience cheers and jeers, but also occasionally leaps on the stage, changes the script and tries to oust the players.

There were moments of that kind during the Westland Affair, moments in which not the fate but the standing of the government rested in the House of Commons. The first half of the Affair was fought out within the Cabinet and in the media, while Parliament was in recess over Christmas. In January (1986) there were several dramatic episodes in the House of Commons theatre. In a sub-plot about a letter from the Chairman of British Aerospace, Leon Brittan was discovered to have misled the House. In a sharp and dramatic intervention Roy Jenkins attacked both Brittan and the Prime Minister.

'For the Prime Minister to sit there for half an hour and allow the Secretary of State to mislead the House was a most extraordinary procedure. Although what the Secretary of State said may just be within the formal bounds of the truth, the margin is so narrow that we shall count our spoons quickly whenever they are together again' (H. C. Deb. 13 Jan 1986, col 874). It was clear then that Brittan had lost the confidence of the House and would have to go.

Two weeks later Margaret Thatcher faced a major debate with some trepidation. She won the vote of course, perhaps aided by an unskil-ful opposition; but her 'standing' was damaged. In the following three or four months her authority in the party was weak and, as one senior backbencher said, the government caved in to the backbenches three times a week. The House cannot stop the show, but some of the glitter fades.

The House also dealt with Westland in the Defence Select Committee – see section on Select Committees. Again the government may be said to have won the encounter, but rather – to change the metaphor – as the defenders of a castle resist attack, with casualties, damage and a collapsed drawbridge.

Invulnerability, in the defence analogy, or playing to acclamation in the theatre, are indicators of political standing. Governments flourish or fade in the light of their 'standing' – a continuous judgement of capacity, competence and record – made initially in the political world of Westminster and Whitehall and in the media and, eventually, in the wider world of 'public opinion' and the electorate. Parliament is one of the arbiters of standing. It is a theatre, both stage and auditorium, for the government. On a good night it can do no wrong, on a bad night it just repeats its lines grimly. If the Government's standing falls, its command of the House falls too: authority depends on standing. For the government, as Westland demonstrated, there is a condition. Whatever happens, the show goes on: even with a flop, the backers are committed to a five-year run. ●

Political parties: functions and structure

Analysing political parties

The value of political parties

From Houghton Committee Report on Financial Aid to Political Parties, Cmnd 6601, 1976, p. 53
Effective political parties are the crux of democratic government. Without them democracy withers and decays. Their role is all pervasive. They provide the men and women and the policies for all levels of government.... The parties in opposition have the responsibility of scrutinising and checking all the actions of the Executive. Parties are the people's watchdog, the guardian of our liberties. At election times it is they who run the campaigns and whose job it is to give the voters a clear-cut choice between different men and different measures. At all times they are the vital link between the government and the governed. Their function is to maximise the participation of the people in decision-making at all levels of government. In short they are the mainspring of all the processes of democracy. If parties fail, whether from lack of resources or vision, democracy itself will fail. ■

Phew! – is there anything left to say?: the answer is, of course, yes!

Parties pervade the political system: there is no chapter in this book to which they have no relevance. There are two great areas of party activity – at the centre of government, in Parliament and the Cabinet; and in the country, that is to say, in the exterior party. The party-in-Parliament and the party-in-government have been studied in earlier parts of this book. This chapter deals with the party as a whole, emphasising and assessing the role of the exterior party.

In the accepted model of Western democratic politics, political parties compete for political power in an election-based representative system. To do this they must recruit candidates, produce leaders and develop a programme of policies. In the struggle for power, the party must engage in the 'market-place' activities (sometimes literally a market-place) of political communication and brokerage: discovering and assessing the needs, interests, prejudices and levels of tolerance of people and of groups; identifying issues, developing and adjusting policies; finally, seeking support for candidates and a programme.

In power, the party must continue with its market-place activity, but it is also deeply concerned with the parliamentary activity of sustaining a government. The Government itself is at once 'the Government of the United Kingdom' wielding the powers bestowed on it by the constitution and at the same time an emanation or product of party.

This phenomenon of 'party government' raises questions about the actual relationship of party to government and what is gained or lost in the relationship. Historically, across the world the political party has been both a guarantor of democracy and the instrument of totalitarian control. Britain's competitive two-party system appeared to be a prop of democracy and to provide an essential mechanism for representative and responsible government.

The inquiry into this broad proposition proceeds along the following lines.

- the nature of the British party system and the functions of political parties
- the relationship of political parties to social classes or groups
- the structure and organisation of political parties and the work of the constituency party
- the relationship of political parties to major in-

terests and the associated matter of financing political parties

- the principles and programmes of parties and the recent history of ideological change
- the part played by parties in government and specifically in democratic government.

Finally, it has to be considered whether political parties in Britain are changing and are, in some way, in decline. Is a two-party system giving way to a single party system and would coalition politics be preferable?

Party systems and the functions of parties

Britain's two-party system

From 1945 until the 1970s Britain had a two-party system. This was not always the case. Until the 1860s political parties were only loosely organised: the great split of 1846 over the Repeal of the Corn Laws was followed by the split of 1886 over Ireland and then over free trade (1903). Meanwhile the Irish Party had grown strong enough to modify politics by its alliances. Then the Labour Party weighed in and the Liberal Party began to decline. In the 1920s Britain had three major parties; in the 1930s it was reduced to one super-party and two minor ones; only in 1945 was there a clear return to a system with two major parties competing for office and alternating in it.

Between 1945 and 1970 the two major parties between them took not less than 87 per cent of the vote and well over 90 per cent of the parliamentary seats. In 1955, most constituencies had only two candidates. The system faltered in 1974 when there was a temporary surge of nationalist voting and Liberal voting was high too. The two-party share of the vote fell to 75 per cent, but recovered to 81 per cent in 1979.

Then the system received a damaging blow. In 1981 the Social Democratic Party was established by the defection of a few leading Labour 'right-wingers'. In the election of 1983 the Alliance of SDP and the Liberal Party won 25 per cent of the vote. This was only two points less than the Labour Party, though the peculiarities of the ballot system gave Labour 209 seats to 23 for the Alliance. Thus it is arguable that Britain then had a multi-party or a three-party system. In terms of seats, the two major parties were still dominant (they held 93 per cent of the seats). In terms of votes they held only 70 per cent. Britain's two-party system was broken - except in the House of Commons, where it mattered most.

The 1983 election was a high point for the Liberal Alliance, but the Alliance itself and the SDP collapsed after the 1987 election. However, the Liberals did not fall back to the insignifiance of the 1950s and, together with the Nationalists, they have ensured that the two 'major' parties did not re-establish their hegemony. In the 1992 election Conservatives and Labour together took only 77 per cent of the vote, though they still inevitably dominated the House of Commons with 94 per cent of the seats.

Table 1 Britain's party system since 1900: votes as per cent share of total vote, selected elections

Party and Allies	Cons	Liberal	Labour
Date			
1906	44	49	6
1918	48 (Coalition)	12	22
1923	38	30	1
1929	38	23	37
1931	67 (National)	1 (Independent)	31
1935	54	6	38
1945	40	9	47
1951	48	3	49
1964	43	11	44
1970	46	8	43
1974 (Feb)	38	9	37
1983	42	25 (Lib Alliance)	28
1992	42	18	35

Table 2 Britain's party system since 1900: seats

Party and Allies	Cons	Liberal	Labour
Date of election			
*1906	157	400	30
**1918	478 (Coalition)	28	63
1923	258	159	191
1929	260	59	288
1931	554 (National)	4	52
1935	432	20	154
1945	213	12	393
1951	321	6	295
1964	304	9	317
1970	330	6	287
1974 (Feb)	297	14	301
1983	397	23 (Alliance)	209
1992	336	20	271

*Parliament included 85 Irish Nationalists
**Parliament included 23 Independent Conservatives and 105 Irish Members (73 Sinn Fein)

EXERCISES
Britain's party system

14.1 What are the main features of Britain's electoral politics displayed in the Tables?
14.2 Has Britain had a two-party system in the twentieth century?

These results indicate one explanation of the two-party system. It is sustained by the electoral device of the simple majority single ballot (see Chapter 17). Thus, in February 1974 the Liberals' 6 million votes (about half the size of the vote for each of the major parties) gained only 14 seats. In 1983, similarly, 8 million Alliance votes gained only 23 seats. The ballot system strengthens the two-party system by undervaluing minority party votes, especially if they are evenly spread throughout the territorial constituencies. Given this ballot system and the concentration of the Labour vote, the further weakening of Conservative/Labour dominance in Parliament is a possibility rather than a probability.

This simple majority system reinforces the tendency of societies to divide into two – a lower and an upper class, employer and worker, town and country, Catholic and Protestant, private and public and so on. There may be in all this a natural tendency to bipolarity, easily convertible by electoral devices into a two-party system. But social conflict is usually more complex than bipo-

larity allows, so the whole system is often under strain.

Two-party systems are by no means normal throughout the world and most countries seem on the whole content with rather different systems. Some Western political scientists were inclined to regard the British pattern with favour, seeing in competition and alternation between parties and the coherence and responsibility of party-based governments, the best fulfilment of the democratic functions of a party system. But there is room for doubt about the alternation and the realities of 'responsibility' and about the virtues of competition and the alleged disadvantages of multi-party coalition.

In Britain, it may be argued, the party in opposition is impotent and damagingly divorced from government. The party contest may lead to a harmful adversarial style of politics and sharp reversals of policy; alternatively it may lead to the obscuring of differences, an immobilising centrism, or often, vacillation between the two. It does not even guarantee the alternation of the two major parties in office, as the record since 1979 shows, thus damaging the essential democratic mechanism of alternation in office.

If 'conventional wisdom' approved of the British system in the 1950s, the fashion moved against it in the 1970s and there was criticism of 'adversarial politics' and 'elective dictatorship'.

The dominance of the Conservatives after 1979 reinforced the 'elective dictatorship' argument. What had previously been regarded as the system's special virtues were now seen as vices. In sample surveys respondents sometimes favoured a distant prospect of coalition government, especially of course if the existing single party government was unpopular. At the same time voting for 'third' parties increased, notably in by-elections.

The phenomenon of third party voting is related to:

- protest against the government of the day, mainly a passing gesture of protest in by-elections
- a more complex gesture of sympathy and protest, evident in the case of support for the Green party in the European elections of 1989
- dissatisfaction with the two major parties, which do not always (or ever) represent well the divisions and discontents of the electorate
- positive support for third parties, especially in the case of the Nationalist parties in Scotland and Wales and the 'confessional' (religious or cultural) parties of Northern Ireland
- positive but in practice insecurely based support for the Liberal and Social Democratic parties of the 1980s Alliance, now the Liberal Democrats.

The functions of political parties

A party, simply defined, is an organised group seeking political power, at least partly through a representative system and aiming to form, or form part of, a government. For the British system it might be tempting to add as a characteristic feature that the party is mainly a programmatic one, concerned to develop a programme in a process of two-way communication with the electorate, subsequently submitting the programme to the electorate at a general election and, if elected, governing according to its main lines. But this is an ideal view and may give a misleading impression of party activity, which is in practice more varied, more diffuse and less effective than this wholesome democratic model allows for.

First, it should already be clear from other chapters that the processes of policy formulation are more complex than the notion of a policy-making party suggests and that policy is the product of more forces than are involved in the relationship between party and electorate. There is a historical measure for this – how far can the history of modern Britain be written in terms of party conferences, party programmes and general elec-

tions? Thus 1906 and 1945 seem to be turning points based on elections and party programmes, although the election of 1906 hardly anticipated the great series of state welfare laws of 1908–12, which were rather the personal promotions of two energetic and skilful politicians, Lloyd George and Churchill. The election of the Conservatives under Margaret Thatcher in 1979 was another turning point.

In many other cases, including 1966 and 1970, the relationship between election programme and actual policies seems to have been tenuous. Frequently, major changes in government policies have depended rather on economic and international trends and crises, slumps and wars, on overriding domestic political processes and on changes of dominant generation among politicians, or the departure of a dominant individual.

Second, parties are not groups of people with identical ideas, interests and objectives. Even similarities are complicated by the existence of divergent tendencies which may be articulated from time to time by independent-minded individuals or discontented groups. Political parties are by nature coalitions. Hence the internal processes by which policy is formulated are often as important and decisive as the party's public activity centred on elections.

Third, the simple description of the democratic political party neglects the range and complexity of a party's functions.. These may be described as generalised functions: socialisation, mobilisation, recruitment, communication, policy development and the support and control of government. In the perspective of the local party, these may be translated into more down-to-earth language and grouped as follows:

1 keeping the organisation going:

- recruiting members;
- running essential committees and meetings;
- arranging social functions to raise money and/or keep members happy.

2 relating to the national organisation:

- by correspondence
- by attending area or regional committees and annual conference, or sending resolutions
- by liaison with the MP.

3 electoral:

- selecting a candidate
- nursing the constituency

- campaigning and vote-getting.

4 political communication and policy formulation:

- keeping in touch with local opinion
- keeping in touch with local interests
- participating in the formulation of policy in this light
- promoting the party's programme.

5 activities directed at local government under all of these headings.

EXERCISES
The functions of political parties

14.3 Which of these functions of political parties may contribute fundamentally to a democratic system of government? and why?

14.4 Do you see any ways in which:
(a) a single-party system may be democratic?
(b) a multi-party system may be democratic?
(c) a two-party system may be more effectively democratic?

14.5 In the light of this account of their functions, is it desirable that political parties should have a substantial mass membership?

Social Bases

The British party system has for long provided the model of a two-party system based on distinct social classes.

Britain, it was argued had a simple class structure with a substantial and coherent working class; and the political expression of class was not complicated or obscured by other cleavages – race and locality as in USA, religion and locality as in France. However, the class basis of British politics has weakened in the last fifty years.

The class basis of party support is conveyed in Table 3

EXERCISE
Class and Party

14.6 Does the Table show that the Conservative and Labour parties were still 'class parties'?

Class survives as a significant cleavage, which gives shape to political parties; but the class analysis needs to be refined and developed. Social class itself can no longer be plausibly represented as consisting of just two more or less clearly defined groups, perceived to hold conflicting interests. For example, a miner may have a wife with a 'white collar' job and children in higher education; the miner – and there are not many left – is likely to be a well-paid and highly skilled technician and who knows where, socially, the children will move – up, down or sideways? In a changing and confused society it is unlikely that voting can be explained wholly in terms of class, except by stretching that term into a large and vague category.

In the study of the 1983 election carried out by Heath, Jowell and Curtice (1985), the research team developed a fivefold classification, as follows:

Percentage of adults

28	The salariat – managers, supervisors, professionals
24	Routine non-manual – clerks, salesworkers, secretaries
8	Petty bourgeoisie – farmer, proprietors, own-account manual workers
7	Foremen and technicians
32	Working class – rank and file manual employees

The analysis based on this classification is shown in Table 4. In interpreting the Table it should be remembered that Labour secured only 28 per cent of the vote in the 1983 election (Conservative

Table 3 The class basis of British politics

Proportion (%) of manual and non-manual classes voting for each party

Election	1951		1970		1983	
	Non Manual	Manual	Non Manual	Manual	Non Manual	Manual
Conservative	75	34	64	33	55	35
Liberal(All'ce)	3	3	11	9	28	22
Labour	22	63	25	58	17	42

Sources A. Heath, et al 1985, p. 30

42 per cent, Alliance 25 per cent). The overall Conservative lead was 14 per cent. Look for the deviation from the norm.

Table 4 Class and vote in 1983

Conservative lead over Labour in class categories 1983	
Salariat	40
Routine non-manual	21
Petty bourgeoisie	59
Foremen, technicians	22
Working class	-19

Based on Heath et al, 1985, p. 20

EXERCISE
Class and party

14.7 Does the Table suggest the weakening of the class basis of British politics?

Social class is attractively simple, but a little misleading as an explanation of voting behaviour. Other factors within the hold-all concept of class and some social factors outside class seem to be at work. Employment, housing and education are part of social class, and differences in those factors are related to differences in voting. One of the major social differences between Britain and other Western countries and notably, USA, is the large proportion of people living in council housing (public housing). This proportion has remained substantial, but the number of owner occupiers has rapidly increased (sharply reducing private renting) from about 30 per cent in 1950 to 67 per cent in the 1990s. Among people who are working class by occupation, more than twice as many owner-occupiers voted Conservative in 1992 than Labour.

The British political parties (apart from the nationalist parties in Scotland and Wales and all parties in Northern Ireland) have always regarded themselves as national parties. British politics, it was claimed, was largely free of the debilitating, fragmentary regional loyalties to be found in France and the USA. This argument was rather disdainful of regional loyalties and pessimistic about their consequences. In any case, a regional pattern is now evident in British politics. The Conservative Party's support is highest in the south of England, Labour's in the North and in Scotland and Wales. Outside London Labour holds very few seats in the South and in some constituencies the Liberal Democrats are the effective challengers. However, this picture is derived from electoral analysis only and focuses on parliamentary seats. In fact the parties are national in form, organisation and appeal and there is no strong regional loyalty in England (where over four fifths of the population live) to bring about a fragmentation or even a decentralisation of the parties.

The social bases of parties have been analysed here in terms of the social and class character of voters. It is also relevant to consider the nature of members, representatives and leaders. Would an observer attending a conference of one of the political parties know immediately, without listening to speeches and opinions, which party he was concerned with? In Britain the answer is, yes, for the Labour and Conservative parties. Speech, dress, newspapers, evening social activities would all give clues. The social characteristics of Members of Parliament and Ministers also reflect differences in social background. A Labour front bench still differs markedly from a Conservative front bench when measured by social background, education and geographical links. In 1991 only three of the Labour Shadow Cabinet came from southern England while only three of the Conservative Cabinet did not come from the South. The differences are not as sharp as between cloth-capped manual worker and pin-striped city gentleman, but still there are significant differences in income and life-style between the classes or within the broad middle class.

Even so it seems that the social bases of the British parties are no longer as simple and solid as they were. It may be that the strength based on class-fit of Britain's two-party system belongs to a short period, 1945-1970 and we must expect the relation of parties to social base to be complex, shifting and unstable.

Among the traditional models of political parties the stable class-based two-party system made for effective and responsible government – so much so that the American Political Science Association issued a statement in 1951, expressing its admiration for the British system and recommending it to the American political parties. This argument takes in more of the nature of political parties than the social base; but the social base was an essential part of the two-party system. Britain's parties derived coherence, stability and relevance from their base in class difference. A main function of political parties is to articulate social division and grievance. The British parties effectively expressed, and so made available for political resolution, the fundamental conflict in British society.

This admiring interpretation of British politics may have been true for an earlier period. It seems less relevant to the 1990s. In a changed and still changing society the political parties have to search for and adapt to real conflicts of culture and interest. The problem for political parties then – and for a representative and responsive political system – is to make a majority out of a society which is most likely to be made up of a collection of minorities.

Note: the social bases of the parties in relation to election is further considered in Chapter 18.

The structure of parties and the distribution of power

Power in political parties

Like most bodies with a large 'mass' membership, political parties are managed by a small 'cadre' of leaders and officials. The relationship of 'cadre' and mass membership is tense, sometimes productive, sometimes destructive. This is a complex and difficult version of the relationship of, say, the managers or leaders of a football club or a church with members and supporters. The organisation of a political party is complicated by the existence of voters as well as members and supporters. The voters set special problems, since their support is essential, but they are not participant members of the organisation.

Thus political parties are shadowy organisations, that is organisations of leaders, members and an enormous shadow of supporters, some of them reliable, most of them not quite sure they are with you. It helps if there is a high membership, acting as a token or representation of supporters. But membership is in fact quite low. In the 1950s the Conservative Party claimed 2.8 million members, Labour at least one million. By the 1990s, despite membership drives and, despite (or even because of) computer membership records, the Conservative Party was down to 0.75 million members and Labour perhaps 0.25 million members and the Liberal Democrats about 70 000. The Labour Party has in addition some 4.5 million members paying the political levy through an affiliated trade union. Such membership is not now quite involuntary, but most of this affiliated membership is inactive and indeed some part of it votes for the Conservative Party.

The problem of party organisation then is to hold the structure together in continuing support of the party's parliamentary activity and available for intensive mobilisation for elections, particularly parliamentary elections. It seems reasonable that the organisation of a political party in a democracy should itself be democratic – representative, consensual, not dominated by the leaders. At the same time it seems likely that political parties will conform to what the German sociologist, Michels, called the 'iron law of oliigarchy': power tends to concentrate in the hands of small groups of people in positions of authority and is not broadly devolved to the membership.

In practice the Labour Party's problems have been more complex, a perpetual struggle between the parliamentary based leadership and the two bases of membership, the trade unions and the constituencies. It is a curious paradox of democratic organisations that they are open to take-over by well-organised and active minorities, hi-jacking a passive majority. This is a serious challenge to the leadership of the political parties and it is a mistake to dismiss as of little account the party management element in our assessment of political leaders.

The structure of the Labour and Conservative Parties

The distribution of power in the two major political parties can be roughly illustrated in the diagrams.

Diagrams of this kind simplify highly complex relationships. The real problems are to discover and define the nature of the relationships indicated by the lines. These may be one- or two-way; neutral or weak relationships of communication and information, ranging up through advice and persuasion to the leadership relations of influence, pressure or command. At some points the line may indicate election or appointment, with their associated power relationships.

There are three main views about the distribution of power within the parties:

- a traditional view that the Labour party is more democratic than the Conservative Party, in the sense that the exterior party is much more powerful, for historical and constitutional reasons.
- dominance by the Leader in both parties. In his classic study of British political parties first published in 1955, Professor McKenzie argued that the Labour Party was remarkably similar to the Conservative Party in the distribution of power. 'No major parliamentary party in the modern period has allowed itself to be relegated to the role of spokesman or servant of its mass organisation.' It was experience of office which

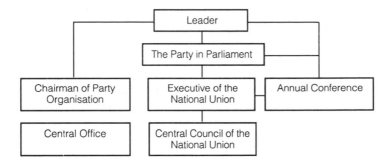

Figure 1 The structure of the Conservative Party leadership

Note: formally the Party in Parliament is separate from the National Union of Conservative and Unionist Associations. The 'Party Organisation' is separate again. Thus it would appear that the notion of the 'Conservative Party' as such is difficult to place.

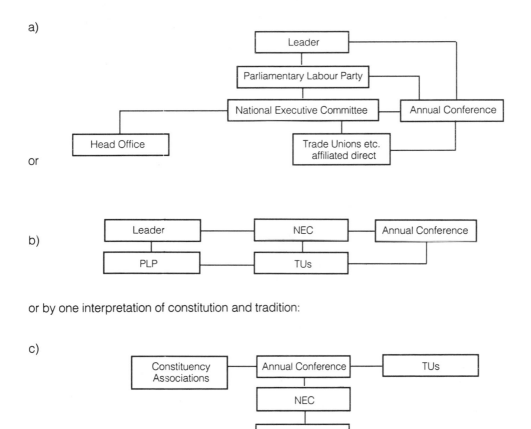

Figure 2 The structure of the Labour Party leadership: alternative views.

Note: there is room for disagreement about the exact distribution of power in the Labour Party. The position of the NEC and Annual Conference is crucial in relationship to the leadership and is discussed in detail below.

had transformed the Labour Party from a mass movement to a party centred like the Conservative Party on the Cabinet and parliamentary system and above all, the Leader/Prime Minister.

Richard Crossman took a similar view about the distribution of power in the Labour Party, but gave it a more Machiavellian background. Where McKenzie on the whole approved of a concentration of power at the top, Crossman deplored it.

● a middle view, while not regarding any parliamentary party as controlled by its mass organisation, sees the mass organisation as having a more significant influence than McKenzie and Crossman would allow.

This is especially true when the party is in opposition. The period of opposition is particularly important in the formation of future party policy. In this view, there are significant differences between the parties. In particular, the tradition and ethos of the Labour Party is regarded as important in restraining the ultimate power of the leadership. Further, the structure of the party formally divides power and reflects the origins of the party as a popular movement before it was a parliamentary party.

The recent history of the two major parties just about confirms this middle view, though not without ambivalence. The 'lurch to the left' of the Labour Party in the 70s and early 80s reflected the power of the exterior party over the parliamentary wing. Neil Kinnock campaigned for the leadership in the country – the unions and the constituencies – rather than in Parliament. Once elected Leader Kinnock re-organised and firmly controlled the party organisation and drove through a revision of policy far removed from the aspirations of his original backers on the left. But Kinnock's power was based on a slim majority in the NEC – the party's constitution was used, not defied.

Margaret Thatcher demonstrated the dominance of the Leader in the Conservative Party, yet her fall showed how dissidence could survive and finally triumph. The party in the country accepted meekly the results of the parliamentary putsch. Altogether the 1980s showed that the McKenzie thesis overstated the similarities between the two parties. But they are complex organisations and the ebb and flow of the struggle to manage them does sometimes bring about a convergence.

Leaders, party organisation, conference
1 *The Leader*
The position of the Leader is set out in the following Document.

■ DOCUMENT 14.2
The position of the Leader in the Conservative and Labour Parties

Looking at figure 14.2 overleaf, the Conservative Leader clearly has more constitutional authority than the Labour leader. It may be added that the ethos of the Conservative Party encourages deference to the Leader – an aspect of the general Conservative disposition to authority. Notwithstanding the deferential ethos the Conservative Party is brutal – more so than the Labour Party – in removing failed leaders. The ethos of the Labour Party may be more 'democratic', at least in the narrow sense that there are persistent challenges to the parliamentary leadership; but the tolerance of minorities, which is a necessary element in democracy, is often lacking.

The position of the Leader is further investigated under 2 and 3. ■

2 *The Party organisation*
The Conservative Leader heads the party organisation – it is his party. In practice the Leader appoints a Chairman to run the machine and the work of Central Office and the Research Department reflects the Leader's wishes. The Conservative Party has no existence, or little active life, apart from the Leader. Members of Parliament make up the Parliamentary Committee of the party; members in the constituencies belong to the National Union of Conservative and Unionist Associations. This elusiveness of the Conservative Party neatly preserves the position of the Leader and evades any constitutional dispute, by denying any constitutional standing to members.

The Labour Party does not enjoy this freedom from constitutional tension. Historically the party developed from a movement of trade unions and socialist organisations in the country into a party with bases in the constituencies, a cadre of Members of Parliament and eventually a government. Constitutionally it is and has to be a federation in which 'bottom-up' forces contend with the growing 'top-down' authority of a party forming or aspiring to form, a government. The structure was not designed to be restful: indeed, it was hardly designed at all (good evidence against the argument that constitutions which 'just grow', like the

	Conservative Party	Labour Party
Mode of election	Ballot of Conservative MPs replaced 1965 informal 'emergence' of Leader. Re-election required, after further reforms of 1975 and a contest may be triggered by 10% of MPs	Until 1981, ballot of PLP, not usually contested. From 1981 by an electoral college voting in ratio 40:30:30 by trade unions, constituency parties and PLP; changed to one third each in 1993. Contest difficult to trigger without a vacancy.

In ballot both parties require an absolute majority and use a second ballot

Choice of colleagues	Complete discretion	In opposition the Parliamentary Committee ('Shadow Cabinet') is elected by the PLP, but includes Leader, etc. ex officio. (The Leader may still designate others as 'spokesman'.) Under a reform in 1981 if the party forms a government the elected Shadow Cabinet becomes the first Cabinet.
Relations with private Members of Parliament	Prime Minister, occasionally attends the meetings of the Parliamentary (1922) Committee. In opposition, the leader attends more frequently, but is not constrained to do so.	As Prime Minister, he attends meetings of the PLP, at his request or theirs, but not usually any other committees of the PLP. As Leader in opposition, he is Chairman of the Parliamentary Committee of the Labour Party – thus tied in to a committee system, which can however be led, if not dominated, by the elected Leader.
Relation to the national committee of the party	The Leader is an important member both of the Executive Committee and of the Central Council of the National Union. Neither of these bodies has a major policy-forming role. The Leader appoints the Chairman of the Party and thus controls the 'Party Organisation'.	He is an ex officio member of the NEC and obviously an important one, but he can be outvoted. The NEC is primarily concerned with party management, but insists on a role in policy making though not necessarily a decisive one.
Relation to Annual Conference	Mr Heath was the first Conservative Leader to attend the Conference, a fact which remains of some significance for the Leader's place in the Conference. But the Conference behaves as a rally, expressing enthusiastic support for the Leader.	The Leader is compelled by constitution and tradition to be responsible to Conference, but may be able to evade conference decisions. Conference influences but does not make policy.

Figure 3 The position of the Leader in the Conservative and Labour Parties

British constitution, necessarily work well).

The essential part of the federal structure is the National Executive Committee. There is no equivalent in the Conservative Party (it is worth reflecting how Prime Ministers Heath and Thatcher would have dealt with such a body). The NEC has 29 members. The Leader and Deputy-Leader are members ex officio, and a youth representative elected by the Young Socialists. The rest are elected at the Annual Conference to represent various groups in the party: twelve by and for the trade unions, seven by and for constituency parties, one by and for socialist and co-operative societies; and five women elected by the whole Conference. In addition, the Treasurer is elected by the whole Conference.

The trade unionists virtually control the election of these last six members. Altogether they appear to make a formidable bloc, but in fact members of the General Council of the Trade Union Congress (top-ranking trade union leaders) may not stand for NEC and several trade union members of NEC are always Members of Parliament (with competing or even overriding loyalties to the PLP). The functions of the NEC are to do partly with the management of the exterior party, partly with policy. As party manager, the NEC is responsible for the work of the local parties including the endorsement of candidates, for research and propaganda, for party finances and for the formal machinery of discipline. Second, the NEC decides, jointly with the Cabinet or Shadow Cabinet, which items of the party programme shall be included in the election manifesto, subject in practice to veto by the Leader.

Thus the NEC is concerned with policies and programme, including indirectly the implementation of the programme in Parliament. Altogether the NEC has a formidable set of functions and hence scope for considerable influence. In particular, it controls the financing and preparation of propaganda. In the case of serious disagreement with the Leader or the PLP, it can refuse to co-operate in propagating policies it disapproves of. Gaitskell was embarrassed by this kind of non-co-operation in 1960.

There is considerable scope for tension, especially between the NEC and the leadership of the Parliamentary Party when the party is in office. Cabinet and NEC are fundamentally different bodies, the one enmeshed in government but concerned for parliamentary forms, the other without governing responsibilities, but with a strong sense of loyalty to 'the working-class move-ment' and interests.

The PLP is also distinct from the NEC, formally and in operation; it provides (but no longer elects) the Leader, hence the Prime Minister; elects the Shadow Cabinet and the Cabinet on the formation of a Labour government; and provides most of the personnel of the Cabinet. Thus, the PLP shares in the constitutional powers of the state, from which the NEC is excluded.

Harold Wilson emphasised the distinction by staying away from NEC meetings and sometimes calling the Cabinet to meet at the same time. One crucial aspect of Wilson's policy in the 1974 government, the 'social contract' with the trade unions, was conducted through a special Labour-TUC Liaison Committee, circumventing the NEC which had rejected the policy. The convention of collective responsibility was specifically applied by Wilson and Callaghan to Cabinet Ministers who were also members of NEC.

In the late 1970s and early 1980s, government failure and electoral defeat, as well as disagreements on policy, sharpened tensions between the leadership and the NEC. James Callaghan complained bitterly that for him NEC meetings were 'like going to purgatory being cross-examined and vilified' (November 1979). There are, of course, quieter periods, when the NEC gets on with the work of party management and liaison and supports the parliamentary leadership which, after all, shares broadly the same objectives. Neil Kinnock, elected leader in 1983, fought hard to secure a majority in the NEC and used it ruthlessly to re-build the Party. As Leader of the Opposition he was able to concentrate on this task, without the responsibility which Wilson and Callaghan carried, for governing the country at the same time.

The question remains, how powerful is the NEC? Callaghan suffered 'purgatory' partly because he would not give way. But the pressures cannot be totally resisted. Policy tends to be pushed and pulled and confused. For example, in 1973 the NEC approved a policy of nationalisation involving 25 named companies. At the Conference a motion advocating the nationalisation of 250 companies was heavily defeated, but the NEC programme was still approved in general. The subsequent election manifesto referred in general terms only to a quite wide-ranging extension of public ownership. In office, the Labour government pursued a selective programme of nationalisation, probably more than some members of the Cabinet wanted and less than the fundamentalists who were associated with the NEC policy. Thus the NEC influenced but did not dictate Labour policy.

⅟The ambiguities of the situation are illustrated, indeed formalised, by the ambivalent terms used to describe policy-making: proposals are converted by Conference into a programme, which is converted by the NEC and the leadership into a manifesto, which may be converted by the Cabinet and PLP into government policy.

The claim of the NEC to challenge the PLP is illustrated in the Laski Case (at the end of the chapter). This shows the NEC being swept aside by the constitutional weight and power of the Cabinet. But, more often than not, Labour is not in power and must work within the constraints of its own constitution, not that of the British government.

Of course, there is no one normal relationship between the Labour Party's centres of power and it is unlikely that the nature of the whole relationship could be inferred from one incident fifty years ago. The Laski episode is a special case, but it has come to be regarded as setting a precedent. Twenty years later Mr Wilson seemed to follow the precedent in claiming that he held his office from the Queen, not the party. When asked what the government would do after the conference defeats of 1967, he said, 'Govern'. In this Attlee–Wilson constitutionalist view, the NEC and the Cabinet are fundamentally different bodies. Later, after the fall of the Callaghan government in 1979, the NEC pressed with more success for influence against what its majority regarded as a right wing parliamentary leadership. But then it did not have to challenge a Cabinet.

3 Party conferences

The Annual Conferences of the two parties display the differences between them. As Edward Pearce noted in 1985, the Conservatives are conformists proclaiming individualism, while for Labour conformism is 'urgently demanded by ungovernable and fiercely competing private souls' (*The Times*, 7 September 1985). For both parties the conferences are arranged for television. The Conservative Conference is staged as a mass rally in support of the leadership, the agenda is rigged and only a score of carefully chosen resolutions are selected from the hundreds submitted. The Conference, with delegates mainly elderly and female, only comes to life in adulation of the Leader (long standing ovations) and only expresses heat and anger over old-fashioned causes

of the Right, Rhodesia and South Africa and 'law and order' ('bring back hanging'); and in the unusually disturbed conference of 1992, the European issue. The strongest resolution begins by congratulating the government and goes on to regret that.... The ideal resolution reaffirms its strong belief in this or that and calls on the government to convince the electorate that it is best served by a government devoted to the national interest rather than short term party advantage....

The Labour Conference, dominated until recently by middle-aged male trade unionists, is much more unruly than the Conservative, but still controlled as far as possible for the television cameras. Resolutions are selected and, where appropriate, 'composited' and voting on the floor is dominated by the massive block votes of the big trade unions. Debate is often in the style, now old-fashioned or at least inappropriate for television, of the factory gate harangue, shouted, despite amplification, angry, vituperative, denouncing treachery (usually by the leadership). Politics is a battle between good and evil, fought with religious fervour; no prisoners are taken.

The Kogans describe the Labour Conference of 1979 in highly critical terms: 'No equivalent group of established leaders has to put up with the sustained venom displayed by many of the constituency delegates.... There is no guarantee of even the politest and mildest form of applause for those who oppose the left. Some speakers are condemned by their audience before they even open their mouths. It is not only deference but some of the ordinary conventions of public debate that have gone'. (D. and M. Kogan, 1983, p. 69.)

This was the Labour Party in hard times, trapped in its past, apparently taken over by activists and trade union militants. A more sympathetic view is that the Party was never, or not for very long, 'taken over' and that the activists and militants represented significant strands in the Party. The problem for the Party – and for democratic politics – was that the activists and militants were not at all representative of the Labour Party's potential voters.

The nature of the party conference shows up even in caricature the differing nature of the parties (how would you sum up the differences?) A more precise test of the distribution of power lies in the question of policy-making: does the Conference make policy? and in particular who drafts and authorises the Manifesto? The policy-making role of conferences is illustrated in the Documents.

■ DOCUMENT 14.3
The Conservative Conference and the making of policy

a) The Conference of 1950

The Conference was debating housing and had before it a rather vague resolution condemning Labour's record and calling for an increase in house-building. A delegate from the floor proposed a specific target – 300 000 houses a year under a Conservative government. Support for this figure gathered like a wave. The platform, unwilling to make such an ambitious commitment, was embarrassed and hesitant. Finally, the Chairman, Lord Woolton, rose and conceded the point. In the event the target was reached in 1952, the second year of the Conservative administration. Thus Conference modified a major item of policy.

b) The Conference of 1965

Rhodesia was on the brink of its 'Unilateral Declaration of Independence'. Lord Salisbury and a group of Conservative MPs were concerned that the interests of the European population should not be neglected by the British Government. The crisis developed rapidly at the time of the Conference. This made the issue at once more delicate but more pressing. Old colonial issues of this kind were very close to the heart of a certain old-fashioned Toryism. The scene was set for Lord Salisbury to demonstrate the power of the Conservative Conference.

But the platform beat him. The executive committee responsible for arranging the business of the Conference scheduled the debate on Rhodesia for late on Friday, the last full day. Lord Salisbury was not permitted to move a resolution on his own. Instead he proposed an amendment to a platform motion, but this had been toned down – 'deeply deplore' instead of 'totally oppose' sanctions against Rhodesia.

Salisbury's seconder had scored some success with an emotional speech. ('Do you support the Socialist Party to transfer power to African Nationalist leaders – almost immediately?' 'No', the audience roared back. 'Then', cried Mr Wall, 'make your voice heard and you may yet change history.') A temperate speech criticising Salisbury's point of view was heckled and slow-handclapped. The atmosphere was highly charged and the platform grew anxious. In desperation they finally invited Lord Salisbury to withdraw his amendment. He refused and appealed to Conference to decide whether there should be a vote. There was a resounding shout of 'No!', and the platform's day was saved; but it had been a very near thing. ■

EXERCISES
The Conservative Conference 1965

14.8 Would you agree that Lord Salisbury's move failed in conditions that were unusually favourable?

14.9 Can a single conference provide evidence about the influence in general of Conferences?

It was 27 years (1992) before a conference of comparable mutinous anger took place. In 1992 the Conference was disturbed by the European issue (the Treaty of Maastricht), the continuing recession and the evident collapse of the Government's economic strategy (the pound having just fallen out of the ERM). There were open attacks on the leadership, notably by the Thatcherite 'old guard'. Altogether the Conference resembled the Labour conferences of the early 1980s. John Major rallied the Conference at its close in a patriotic speech mentioning 'Britain' or 'British' over fifty times. However, the 1992 Conservative Conference was quite untypical – it happened to fall at a time of calamity for a government unknown since 1931.

The Labour Party Conference and the making of policy

It is clear already that the Labour Conference has more influence than its Conservative equivalent. Formally, it has an important place in the constitution of the Party. Historically, it derives influence from the nature of the Party as a mass movement originating outside Parliament. Philosophically, the characteristic posture of the Party, its principles, myths and slogans, are democratic. However, the place and importance of the Conference are neither as definite nor as substantial as this would imply. In particular, when Labour has been in office (about twenty of its first ninety years) the Conference has had to accept the final responsibility of the Labour Cabinet. For example, in the period 1964–70, Conference rejected the government's position ten times; six of these occasions were in 1968 and concerned economic questions. But the government was inclined to carry on regardless.

Such disregard of conference votes can easily

be justified (apart from constitutional and policy arguments) by reference to the peculiar block or card voting system. This gave trade union delegations five million votes on behalf of their members, compared with under one million for the constituency parties. But constituency parties may be unrepresentative too and the leadership often depends on the support of the union block vote. So leaders express respect for the Conference, but may still go their own way.

■ DOCUMENT 14.4
The Labour Conference and the making of policy: the constitutional position

The Constitution
From Clauses V and VI of the Constitution of the Labour Party

● The Party Conference shall decide from time to time what specific proposals of legislative, financial or administrative reform shall be included in the Party Programme.
● No proposal shall be included in the Party Programme unless it has been adopted by the Party Conference by a majority of not less than two thirds of the votes recorded on a card vote.
● The work of the party shall be under the direction and control of the Party Conference.
 [The Party Programme is not the election manifesto, but is the source of most of the manifesto proposals. The manifesto itself is drawn up by the Parliamentary leadership and the NEC, the Leader himself having substantial influence.] ■

■ DOCUMENT 14.5
The Labour Conference and the making of policy: the Conferences of 1959, 60 and 61

a) The Conference of 1959
The Leader of the Party, Hugh Gaitskell, opened a debate on the lessons of the Party's defeat in the general election of 1959 and urged reconsideration of the famous Clause IV of the Party's constitution. This clause seems to commit the Party to nationalisation ('the common ownership of the means of production, distribution and exchange').

Gaitskell's apparently ill-prepared attack on a hallowed principle of the Party met with a good deal of criticism at the Conference and was firmly rejected by the NEC a few months later. Gaitskell perhaps intended only to introduce the

idea into discussion, to ventilate it: but the conference proved quite the wrong place to do so. Clause IV lay next to the old-fashioned heart of the Party and, as with the Conservatives, it is the old-fashioned heart that is worn by many conference delegates.

b) The Conference of 1960
Next year Gaitskell was again in trouble. The Party was divided over Britain's possession of nuclear armaments. The PLP and the leadership, including the NEC, accepted their necessity: many of the delegates, especially from the larger trade unions, favoured their abandonment by Britain ('unilateral nuclear disarmament'). The extent of the constitutional authority and actual power of the Conference was crucial and was also fought over. Thus a delegate from Nottingham, speaking in support of a resolution that '...Labour policy is decided by the Party Conference which is the final authority', declared: 'There will be those who say we are seeking to tie our Parliamentary members hand and foot. Yes, that is exactly what we do want.' The motion was carried.

Gaitskell, aware that the vote on nuclear arms might be won by the disarmers, stated his intention not to accept the decision of Conference as final:

'It is not the end of the problem because Labour Members of Parliament will have to consider what they do in the House of Commons... what do you expect them to do? Change their minds overnight?... Do you think we can simply accept a decision of this kind?... there are some of us... who will fight and fight and fight again to save the Party we love....'

Gaitskell did lose the vote, but by comparatively small margins, none more than 407 000 in a total of 6–6.5 million. The voting included of course the block votes of the unions. In this case, the decision of Conference was determined by Frank Cousins, the 'unilateralist' who led the giant Transport and General Workers Union. Cousins and his executive controlled over 800 000 votes at the Conference and it was their decision to support the unilateral policy which swung the Conference decision. Thus arguments based on the superior democratic rights of Conference obviously have their weakness.

c) The Conference of 1961
Gaitskell and his supporters did fight back with

a highly organised intra-party campaign, the so-called Campaign for Democratic Socialism. Gaitskell himself survived the challenge to his leadership by Harold Wilson (the first time the annual re-election of a leader had been contested). Several large unions abandoned the cause of nuclear disarmament. The 1961 Conference reversed the unilateral decision of the previous year. Conference resolved nevertheless that the American Polaris base in Scotland should be removed, but this was ignored by Gaitskell and later, with Labour in power, by Wilson. ■

EXERCISE
The influence of the Labour Party Conference

14.10 Crossman considered that the events of 1960 and 1961 demonstrated the supremacy of Conference. Do you agree?

The Liberal Democrat Party

Like the 'major' parties the Liberal Democrat Party (and for that matter the Nationalist and the Irish parties) encounter problems in finding a constitutional balance between leaders and members. The Liberal Democrat Party is federal in structure (based on Scotland, Wales and English regions). Policy is developed by a federal policy committee, partly elected by the Annual Conference and, through a consultative process, proceeding from draft to final papers. The Liberal Democrat Leader is elected by all members through a postal ballot and is in a good position to build an effective relationship with the party.

Inevitably, there is tension. Liberal Democrat traditions emphasise local autonomy, while the Leader, with only a handful of parliamentary colleagues, needs the party in the country to give him substance. On the other hand the party needs a Leader rather more than he needs them, particularly to appear in the national media as an equivalent to the 'major' party leaders. So the Liberal Democrat Party enjoys the same creative tensions as Labour, but with a weaker tendency to damaging 'splits'. Liberal Democrat quarrels are not enlarged or resolved by any equivalent of the trade unions' block vote. Conference is tightly controlled, there is a well-designed policy process and this most modern of the parties has a clear and positive policy on the representation of women.

A brief comparison between the three parties shows up the peculiarities of each. The Leader is weakest in the Labour Party. The Parliamentary Party alone elects the Leader in the Conservative Party – this now sets it apart from the other parties. The exterior party is concerned with policy in every party except the Conservatives. Interest groups (in the shape of business and the trade unions) provide finance for Conservatives and Labour and are built into the constitution in the case of Labour. The Liberal Democrats are independent of such pressures. Such brief summaries are of course misleading and the evidence of this chapter qualifies the summary statement.

GUIDE TO EXERCISES

14.1 There are three parties but with a 'hole-in-the-middle', or a saucer-shaped depression made by the fall in the Liberal vote between 1931 and 1974. One of the causes of the Liberal decline is indicated in the two coalition governments, of 1918 (formed 1916, led by Lloyd George) and 1931 (led by MacDonald but dominated by the Conservatives). The extraordinary persistence of the Conservative vote is clear; both Conservatives and Labour have suffered from the growth of the Liberal vote, but Labour has suffered the most.

14.2 Measured in seats, the answer could be, no; though, taking 20 as a reasonable minimum there has been a three-party system since 1983. Measured by votes the development of a three-party system is clearer: the proportion of votes supporting the Liberals is substantial and the Liberals are in second place in about one quarter of seats. In Scotland and Wales support for the Nationalist parties creates a four-party system.

14.3 All except a) and that is of course essential for the carrying out of other functions. Why? Because all of these functions are to do with representation and with the political communication, education, persuasion and control that go with democracy.

14.4 All of these functions, so valuable for democratic politics, can be carried out in single and multi-party systems. The special merit of a two-party system lies in the competition, the clear choice and the possibility of alternation. By comparison, the single party restricts choice, though it may well include competitive factions, and many parties complicate it. But a two-party system may impose an unnatural pattern of choice.

14.5 Desirable for what end? If for good or democratic government, the answer would seem to be, yes: representation, communication and so on are democratic in so far as they involve a substantial proportion of the people. This leaves the problem of what constitutes a substantial proportion. It cannot be expected that all, or nearly all, the people will wish to belong to and take an active part in political parties – and the theory of democracy does not require this. The present individual membership of the parties is about one million (not counting affiliated trade unionists in the Labour Party). This is less than 1 in 40 of the electorate and is rather low from the idealistic point of view of this exercise.

14.6 Not exactly, but the proportion of 'class voters' (Conservative non-manuals and Labour manuals) as a percentage of all voters declined over those years from 67 to 60 to 47. The major change is the growth of the Liberal vote – which might be seen as evidence of the weakening of class. However, the significance of the analysis depends on the validity of the class categories used – see following text. For an analysis for 1992 see Chapter 18. The significance of this analysis could be demonstrated graphically by plotting Conservative non-manuals, Labour manuals and both sets of Liberal voting figures.

14.7 Broadly; yes, but with the necessary reservations about the meaning of this kind of statement. It is evident, too, that in the 1980s a more complex collection of parties is related to more complex class divisions. This is not simply a result of more elaborate analysis. The class structure is itself changing quite fast. Rapid economic changes have expanded the upper two classes (the salariat by one half since 1964) and shrunk the working class by almost a quarter since 1964. Hence a class party based on the working class was bound to shrink. The vote of the small 'petty bourgeoisie' is heavily skewed to the Conservatives (why?). For class and voting in 1992 see Chapter 18.

14.8 It failed at the time, but registered a point of view which had much sympathy and has had at least some influence on Conservative policy since then. This was not absolute failure, therefore. But conditions were certainly favourable for success: there was a crisis; the issue was important to party philosophy and to party interests; Salisbury was of high, even though by then waning, prestige; the party was in opposition and not therefore cramped by practical considerations; and the platform had shown little positive leadership.

Another explanation of the 'failure' is that the fuss about sanctions had the function of signalling that any policy beyond sanctions (military intervention) was absolutely unacceptable and the effectiveness of the signal did not depend on the ultimate rejection of sanctions (which some conferees may well have regarded as likely to be ineffective anyway). Indeed, Salisbury's move did not fail completely, since it later turned out that oil sanctions had been regularly evaded, with the knowledge of the British government.

14.9 Of course, but in isolation the evidence is bound to be partial and misleading. This is particularly true because policy-making is a cumulative and ragged process; policy emerges not simply from particular units in the party structure but from the total ideology or collection of ideas which 'floats above' the party at any time. On a specific issue conference may encourage or discourage – adding a small weight to the balance of opinion (thus the 1987 Conference favoured the early implementation of the poll-tax).

14.10 No. Gaitskell quite openly and specifically rejected the decision of the 1960 Conference. The presumption is that, in office, he would not have acted upon the decision, leaving his critics to unseat him if they could. But, as he well knew, the leadership was a matter for the PLP; so the ultimate power lay there and not in Conference. (But the leadership is no longer in the hands of the PLP). On the other hand, the fight to rescind the decision implied a certain respect for the authority of Conference. Note that the Polaris decision of 1961 went unheeded.

The incidents of 1960 and 1961 show well the power of small groups of activists working through the machinery of mass democracy. This may affect the ultimate judgement on whether a Conference decision is more 'democratic' than a decision of, say, the PLP.

ASSESSMENTS

a) The influence of the exterior party: general
Exterior parties in Britain do not have a substantial or decisive influence. There are good general reasons for this. First, it is in the nature of the political system that government is the initiating force: it is responsible to, but not directly controlled by, the people. The opposition, as an alternative government, tends to operate in the same way. This fundamental aspect of the system is reinforced by the practical possibilities. The parliamentary leadership is in a decision-making position: it has information, a national viewpoint and the requisite machinery. The local parties are better equipped to gather votes than to formulate policy.

Further, a division of work exists and is perpetuated by traditions and institutions. Finally, all parties accept in practice a form of 'democratic centralism'. Democracy is not contradicted by discipline and central control: rather these are necessary props of an effective democratic movement. Moreover, party loyalty, not 'rocking the boat', is a natural enough characteristic in a party's supporters.

However, this is not the whole of the matter. Exterior parties do have some influence and for good reasons. First, the parties need the constituency associations. They depend on the local party loyalist for essential electoral work. Second, being, or at least looking, democratic ensures a certain approval – the reverse leads to murmurs of complaint and headlines about dictatorship. This is true for all parties. The Labour tradition of democracy is strong, but it is modified by the embattled revolutionary tradition of democratic centralism. If the Conservative tradition of democracy is weaker, it draws force from the social strength and independence of its constituency associations.

Third, and perhaps most important, policy is rarely made by a single decisive stroke; it is built up over time in a discontinuous and uneven process of accumulation of pronouncements and undertakings, often very ragged at the edges. To this process, the exterior party can clearly make a contribution, perhaps the more substantial because it will often not be plainly attributable to the party in the country. This point reminds us that a party is not simply a structure, but a collection of people, a tradition and a (loose) collection of (somewhat vague) ideas.

There is another consideration. The party out of office is much less of a central decision-taking machine, much more open to pressure from below. Compared with the governing party, the Parliamentary party in opposition is a weak administrative machine, and may well be rivalled by the central organs of the exterior party. Periods out of office promote intra-party democracy: this has an obvious significance for all parties in a prolonged period of Conservative rule.

All this is the argument in specifically political terms. It is well to remember that the relationship will be determined for much of the time by more human considerations – respect for the leaders, loyalty to the party, ignorance and some bewilderment among the ordinary members – but crossed and modified occasionally by notions of independence and assertiveness, illumined by bright ideas and strengthened by sturdy, if sometimes cantankerous, principle. Frustrated opposition backbenchers – from different motives – may seek a substitute for power in the exterior party.

These human considerations appear to reinforce the verdict of political reasoning: the influence of exterior parties is weak, uneven, discontinuous, but rarely negligible and occasionally of some significance. Michels's 'Iron Law' is not wholly acceptable in this context. The controversy over the role of the exterior party is still a live one in British politics.

In the Labour Party, disputation continues. The new arrangements for the election of the leader introduced in 1981, represented a victory for the party as a whole, against its parliamentary wing. The further reform of these arrangements in the 1990s is based on the principle of 'one member, one vote', which is already enshrined in the Liberal Democrats' constitution. Democracy based on party membership would represent the triumph of the exterior party – though it is not quite the outcome fought for over the years by Labour's exterior party elites, in the Unions, the Conference and the NEC.

b) Party leadership

The leadership of a great political party is a demanding, ill-rewarded yet essential contribution to democratic government. It is easy to forget this, for political leaders are easy targets for denigration; indeed, an adversarial form of politics seems to require that political opponents are routinely accused of stupidity, hypocrisy, dishonesty and any of the seven deadly sins that seem at all plausible.

In face of such familiar insults it is worth stressing the necessity and value of political leadership. In particular it has to be understood that the binding together of divergent political tendencies, the building of consent by concessions and compromise, while fighting not to abandon principle altogether – these are the essence of democratic leadership.

Harold Wilson, who acquired an exaggerated reputation for deviousness, defends himself well on these lines:

'*To bridge a deep political chasm without splitting a party...is sometimes regarded as...political chicanery. The highest aim of leadership is to secure policies adequate to deal with any situation, including the production of acceptable new solutions and policies, without major confrontations, splits and resignations....*

To produce a policy on which the party could remain united...inevitably evoked the phrase "devious". But in my view a constant effort to keep his party together, without sacrificing either principle or the essentials of basic strategy, is the very stuff of political leadership. Macmillan was canonised for it. No Labour leader can expect such an outcome: indeed in an articulate party such as Labour, formed out of so many diverse views and pressures, it would be folly to expect it.'

(Harold Wilson, *Final Term: The Labour Government 1974–1976, 1979,* pp. 121, 234)

Macmillan could have made a similar defence of his habit of facing one way and proceeding in the other direction; Heath could justify his U-turns; and perhaps Margaret Thatcher would admit and defend the bouts of shrewd pragmatism which moderated her famous tendency to proceed by conviction (that is, her own conviction).

c) Should political parties be democratic?

This is like being asked whether you are against sin, or in favour of motherhood. Of course parties should be democratic, but the difficult question is, how?

A democratic party should properly ensure accountability of the leadership, a diffusion of influence and an active participation; policy development should be consensual. All that is difficult to achieve in a party, a country or any institution. Political parties are peculiarly difficult to organise at all, let alone in a coherent democratic form. Parties are immense but very thin on the ground; shadowy, weak structures, energised by strong currents of interest and ideology, constantly open to partial, temporary colonisation; an army of corporals and colonels, an elected general and hardly any troops; an army unsure of its objectives and facing hostile civilians. But one of these armies takes over the centres of power and rules the kingdom.

If this picture is near to the reality, then the structure of the party is less important than the working of the national political system. Political parties are democratic in Britain insofar as the system of responsible parliamentary government imposes on them continuing and effective accountability to the people.

Concept

Party

After a lengthy consideration of political parties it seems unnecessary to raise the question of definition: but the concept remains elusive. A political party necessarily breaks out of its formal structure. It may be embodied for the time being in the government, the parliamentary party, the party organisation centrally and in the country, the annual conference; or the shadow party of supporters, sympathisers and voters; or some part of a television audience for a political broadcast. Parties must be comprehended by their spirit as well as their structures, and the spirit flows, invades, takes over other institutions. Hence the observer of politics can never be certain what is on show: is that the Prime Minister or the party leader? is this the House of Commons or the Conservative Party? The Queen's Speech, which is not really the Queen's speech, serves as a metaphor for the take-over of institutions by party – and occasionally the take-over of party by institutions.

● CASE STUDY
The NEC and the Laski episode

This is the classic illustration of the NEC

challenging the Parliamentary Labour Party and it shows that when Labour is in government the NEC cannot always and easily overcome the constitutional weight and power of the Cabinet.

In 1945, the Chairman of the Labour Party's National Executive Committee was Harold Laski, a distinguished Professor of Political Science. Laski took the view that the Leader of the Party was responsible both to the PLP and to the National Executive Committee and could not act in certain important matters without consulting those bodies.

In the wartime election of 1945 there was an abnormally long interval between voting and the declaration of the poll. Prime Minister Churchill therefore invited the Leader of the Opposition, Attlee, to attend the important Allied Conference at Potsdam, so that there would be continuity of major foreign policy if Labour were to win the election. Laski, speaking as Chairman of the NEC, hastened to say that Attlee could attend only as an observer and could not commit the Labour Party to decisions on 'matters which have not been debated either in the Party Executive or at meetings of the Parliamentary Labour Party' (Kingsley Martin, 1953, 169–70).

Churchill seized on this curious statement and inflated it for electoral purposes. Attlee, thus challenged on his position as Leader, conceded only that he must consult the NEC. In his own version of the incident, Attlee comments that the Chairman of the NEC 'does not make authoritative pronouncements of this kind'.

A few weeks later, Attlee's position as Leader was again challenged. Laski and some of Attlee's parliamentary colleagues, including Morrison and Cripps, considered that Attlee could not accept the King's commission to form a government until the new Parliamentary Party had met to elect a leader.

This was not a wholly unreasonable view, since there had been no election for ten years and the new Parliamentary Party of 1945 was markedly different from the tiny party which ten years previously had chosen Attlee as Leader. However, Attlee at once rejected the suggestion of a new election. Later he commented: 'If you're invited by the King to form a government you don't say you can't reply for forty eight hours. You accept the commission and you either bring it off successfully or you don't and, if you don't, you go back and say you can't and advise the king to send for someone else...' (F. Williams, 1961, p. 4).

Attlee's blunt and simple (possibly inappropriately simple) language conveys an important if old-fashioned interpretation of the working of the British constitution. The royal invitation to form a government is regarded as the essential initiating procedure; thereafter it is for Parliament to grant or withhold its confidence. Thus Attlee asserted the primacy of the British constitution over the Party's constitution.

It could be argued against the significance of the episode that Attlee was not a fully legitimate and acceptable Leader for several reasons, notably the lapse of time since Attlee was elected and the absence of normal party politics during the war. On the other hand, Attlee had the prestige of his long service as wartime Deputy Prime Minister and his convincing and unexpected victory in the election of 1945. These factors, and the still continuing war against Japan, weighed the situation in Attlee's favour. In the eyes of the voters he was fully accepted and legitimate; he was the people's choice and he knew it. ●

Political parties: constituencies, finance, government

The parties at work

Constituency parties

Most of the discussion of political parties so far has been concerned with the distribution of power. This is an important question, but there remain other equally important aspects to be studied. Pressures and programmes are dealt with in the next two sections. First, though, it is worth considering what local constituency parties actually do, for the-day-to day job of keeping an organisation going often obscures for the harassed practitioner the nicer problems of power, and hence modifies the struggle for power.

Thus, the local party committee may well be more concerned about the attendance at the next meeting, or the weather for the garden fete, than about its own influence on the development of policy. The business of keeping the organisation going is, in fact, a prime task of the local activists. There are meetings to call, minutes to write up, subscriptions to collect, someone to be coaxed into taking on the treasurer's job next year. This round of activity is the dynamic centre of any voluntary organisation, producing its own experts, its own sense of group endeavour and its own justification. Its ethos is corporate loyalty, not intellectual wrath and insurgency. From all this, the national party may hope to gain faithful toil or, as second best, cosy loyalty, or, a not uncommon third, ineffectual bumbling.

One of the most important jobs of the local party is to gain and hold members, the source of support, funds, help in constituency work, and a small pool of candidates for office. None of the major parties has an individual membership of more than a fraction of the voters who regularly turn out on their behalf at elections, and the total number of individual members of any political party is not more than 1.2 million. Thus a political party outside Parliament has four sections; supporters, members, elected officers, professionals. Supporters range from habitual voters to those who feel more deeply committed without actually joining.

The major parties employ full-time professional agents in the constituencies, the Conservatives having one in over half the constituencies, Labour in under one sixth. On their broad if sometimes threadbare shoulders fall the routine chores of organisation – for the Conservatives, general supportive activity and fund-raising, for Labour, political activity and the building of relations with the unions. Agents are particularly important in maintaining communication with area and national parties, where the professional element is much stronger. The party with the sitting Member of Parliament has an advantage in the possession of further professional support, and a figure of some prestige and importance to address meetings, open the garden fete, attend to grievances and generally to give the impression of serving all constituents of whatever party.

But the life of the party locally is not confined to routine chores and social events. Elections happen just often enough to keep activists active. Again, there is an immense amount of routine work – writing out envelopes for election literature, arranging meetings, canvassing, radiating confidence. In marginal seats the excitement keeps the parties going. Where, as in four out of five constituencies, the result is fairly certain, the parties fight on, believing reasonably enough that no seat is won or lost until 10 p.m. on polling day. Local government also provides stirring work and most local elections are now (since the 1970s) contested by political parties, with the party organisation fully engaged. There is much evidence for the recent period that such local elections are in practice decided by the electorate's judgement on national issues and the national government. Hence they count as a kind of referendum on a government's performance. The government's hold on Parliament is not of course affected by the result, but in some policy areas – education, housing and transport for example – the local implementation of its policies may be checked or hindered. Hence the local party organisation is likely to regard the local elections as an important battleground.

Little of this round of activity has a direct place in the development of policy. In the Conservative Party there is a tacit acknowledgement that the local association selects the candidate and runs an election campaign, while the centre has a free hand with policy. Labour constituency parties claim a voice in the development of policy. Ideally in both parties members inform themselves about local interests and points of view, discuss party policy and pass on their thoughts. A strongly held viewpoint could be formulated as a resolution to an area or national conference.

In practice, the processes of communication are more haphazard – a chance discussion with a local shopkeeper, a question to the visiting speaker, a resolution proposed by an articulate stranger and cheerfully passed on because it is nice to have a resolution down. These are the processes of democracy, operated, as they must be, by mostly ordinary people.

This is a picture of a cosy and friendly organisation, not very efficient, and far from dynamic. In safe seats this must often be so, for voluntary organisations are like that. However, active party workers are likely to have stronger political views than other electors, and will be further from the soft neutral centre of politics – otherwise, there would be no point in joining and working for the party. Some of the active members with strong opinions will hold views at the far ends of the political spectrum. Give such people a sense of mission, a touch of impatience and some organisational skills, and you have the extremist activist or zealot, whom party leaders may see as troublemakers.

It is a pity that the term 'activist' has thus become a term of abuse, but there may be some justification for it. The Labour Party, and to some extent the Liberal Democrat Party, have both been beset by activists in recent times. In the case of the Labour Party some of the activists have also been 'entryists', deliberately joining a party with which they had little sympathy in order to convert it from within to their own way of thinking, or use it for their own political purposes.

There is a real difficulty here for democratic organisations. If members are apathetic and inactive (and they often are) the organisation is open to take-over by more highly motivated people. Democratic procedures may allow such activists a swift rise to power, even though their views and objectives are not at all representative of members, still less the voters. Most voluntary organisations, including trade unions, function in this way – attend a meeting and you are on the committee; speak, and you are Secretary or even Chairman. No problem arises if other members are active and committees are aware of their representative function. But the possibility of a democratic hijack is there.

Political parties are peculiarly vulnerable because they offer a genuine opportunity to influence national policy. The response of the political leadership is to plead the higher democratic legitimacy of the voters. But they still need party members, and especially the active ones, to do the work of the local party, and must needs grant them some democratic legitimacy.

The selection of candidates

Two thirds of parliamentary seats are safe over long periods for one party or the other; in these constituencies, selecting the candidate means selecting a Member of Parliament. The processes of selection are therefore of great importance.

Formally the process is local in operation, but all parties have to approve candidates and there is scope for the centre to exercise influence and, occasionally, even a veto. The business of joining a candidate to a constituency association has been likened to marriage guidance, but with the significant difference that the 'guide' has a stake in the success of the union.

Tests of political opinion count for more in the ideologically sensitive and sectarian Labour Party than in the Broad Church of the Conservative Party. Local roots and connections are helpful, but localism is not a dominant sentiment. Trade union sponsorship, including financial support to the constituency party, is attractive to Labour selection committees. Conservative candidates are not asked about their financial standing, and are strictly limited in their contributions to party funds.

The study of formal procedures does not yield much evidence about selection. There is keen competition for selection in the two major parties. Inevitably constituency 'activists' in constituency management or executive committees wield substantial influence, and neither Conservative nor Labour parties follow the 'one member, one vote' principle.

Direct and open veto by the national party is rare in the Conservative Party and infrequent in the Labour Party. Since 1945 there are two known cases in the Conservative Party and a dozen or so in the Labour Party (mainly concerning Communist or near-Communist candidates and members of the 'Militant Tendency'). In the 1970s and 1980s the Labour Party met increasing difficulty in controlling active and assertive local parties, but Conservative local associations can be very firmly independent too.

The study of the results of the procedures – who was selected and who failed – throws more light.

- Party efforts to promote particular kinds of candidate are not very successful. The Conservative Central Office has had only limited success in asking for more trade unionists, more members of ethnic minorities and more women to be adopted.
- The importance of the local constituency association in the selection of parliamentary candidates does not mean that local candidates are preferred. A majority of candidatures still go to non-locals. There is no hidden 'locality rule' as in the USA, restricting candidature to natives and residents of the locality. Thus, there is no restriction by selection procedures of the opportunity to embark on a political career. A Londoner may seek a seat in Lancashire or Devon, and not expect his geographical connections to count much against him.
- Mostly, constituency associations are concerned with general qualities, background, manner and speaking ability, knowledge of or suitability for the constituency. Within broad limits selectors do not test political leanings and candidates are careful not to stray too far from the party's central positions. Exceptionally, and especially in the Labour Party, a selection committee applies narrower political tests.

- Trade unions have significant influence in the Labour Party. Over one quarter of candidates are 'sponsored' by trade unions, that is, supported politically and financially, and about three quarters of these are elected (making up almost one half of Labour MPs). The trade unions choose the safer seats but do not confine their support to their own members or officials. Apart from the effect of sponsorship, trade unions locally controlled up to 40 per cent of the vote in the constituency selection process. At the 1993 Conference the party resolved by a narrow margin to restrict participation in candidate selection to members (including trade union levy payers who paid an additional membership fee). This was part of the drive towards the principle of 'one member, one vote' (OMOV) aimed at diminishing the privileges of membership given automatically to members of affiliated trade unions (including members and supporters of other parties), and exercised by union leaders as a 'block' vote. The influence of the trade unions is not consistently in one political direction and has more often favoured the national party; but in left-right terms the unions are divided.

To sum up, there is naturally a potential conflict between the central party and the local association. But both sides have equally naturally a common objective – to secure able and attractive candidates, loyal to the party. These qualities may of course be assessed differently at the centre and locally by, say, a retired colonel or miner, but tact and skill from the professionals normally solve the differences. Dictation from the centre may be impossible, but defiant revolt by the constituency association is also rare.

It is sometimes argued that selection of parliamentary candidates is too important a function in a democracy to be left to quite small groups of party officers and committee men – a 'selectorate' which it is alleged is not representative in any way of the electorate. There is indeed a problem here. One solution lies in much more vigorous political parties with large and actively participating memberships – but that seems an unlikely development. Another is the primary election, as practised in USA, which is an intra-party election to choose candidates. However, most candidates are certain losers, and their selectors wield no great political power, and it seems unlikely that a primary election would attract much interest. The Labour Party has a special problem about widening selection, because of its two classes of membership, individual and the far larger indirect membership through the trade unions.

The continuing relationship of candidate or member and constituency

In hopeless seats, candidates move on as soon as they decently can to more fruitful pastures and the problems of a continuing relationship are thus avoided. But a constituency is stuck for some years at least with its sitting member, and the relationship between him or her and the party constituency association is of some importance. The normal relationship is no doubt an easy one, shaped by party solidarity and dominated by the Member, descending from Westminster at weekends, full of prestige and half-disclosed inside information. But such normal relationships are always shaped to some extent by the possibilities of abnormality. What happens when tensions and disagreements arise?

The constituency association's influence then depends on its ultimate weapon, a refusal, or a serious threat of refusal, to re-adopt the member as their candidate for the next election. This has happened occasionally in the past – about one in a hundred cases. 'De-selection' is rare in the Conservative Party. For example, Sir Anthony Meyer (Clwyd North West) was de-selected after contesting the leadership against Margaret Thatcher in 1989; but despite many threats no Member was de-selected for voting against Thatcher in 1990 (though many Members prudently took soundings in their constituencies). Recently Labour Members of Parliament have encountered more difficulties, mainly from 'left-wing' constituency associations. The adoption of 'mandatory re-selection' in 1980 threatened sitting members but only six or seven fell by this method before the 1983 election, another seven before 1987 and four before 1992 (though another ten faced severe contests).

In a notable case in 1989, Frank Field, a Member of high reputation and Chairman of one of the most effective Select Committees, was de-selected by his Birkenhead constituency and then re-selected when the national party insisted on a new and more strictly conducted ballot. This indicates the power of the national party in the last resort to overrule the constituency associations. Similarly in 1992 Dave Nellist, the Member for Coventry South East, was expelled from the party by the NEC, fought the election as an independent and was beaten by the official candidate. Thus the weapon of a refusal of party endorsement may be wielded by the centre against the constituency party.

■ DOCUMENT 15.1
The Member and the constituency association: the threat to refuse re-adoption

a) Nigel Nicolson and Bournemouth East, 1956–9
In this case, the member was beaten in a long-drawn-out fight with the constituency association and lost his seat. As is usual in the Conservative Party, the national party was reluctant to intervene, openly and directly at least, in disputes between a member or candidate and his local association. Local autonomy counts for a great deal. There is of course no guarantee that what is decided locally will be wise and tolerant, any more than that national intervention is bound to be the opposite.

Nicolson opposed the Eden government's intervention in Suez (October 1956) and abstained in crucial votes in the Commons. He was censured by his constituency association and a new candidate was adopted. There was no election, however, and Nicolson remained in Parliament. At the end of 1958 the new prospective candidate resigned his candidature and Nicolson was able to re-enter the fight. He asked for a poll of all party members in the constituency and this was accepted. Members voted by post for or against Nicolson's re-adoption. By a few hundred votes in several thousands, Nicolson lost. This was as near as Britain has been to a primary election.

b) Reg Prentice and Newham North East 1975–76
Reg Prentice was in effect disowned by the constituency party while he was still a Cabinet Minister. There were serious political differences between the new ruling group in the party and the Member, differences between left and right, which reflect the Labour Party's normal tendency to split between near-Marxists and 'Social Democrats'. The Prime Minister supported Reg Prentice, but the NEC chose not to intervene and in the end Reg Prentice withdrew. Wilson had mentioned the possibility that unofficial candidates might in fact run as parliamentary Labour Party candidates. This recalls the massive and fatal split of the Liberals in the 1920s.

As in other cases there was much talk of a 'coup' by constituency activists and later there was a counter-coup. But this is a normal feature, or hazard, of democratic politics, as trade union and student politics show. The risks go with the freedom and opportunities of democracy. ■

In the Conservative Party, it would seem that deviation to the right is tolerated more easily than deviation to the left. Four of the seven rebels opposed to the 1956 attack on Egypt were not re-adopted. A few months later, another set of rebels, this time in the other direction, opposed the resumption of the use of the Suez Canal. None of them experienced much trouble with his constituency association. In the Labour Party, tolerance seems to extend to the left in the constituencies, but until recently the NEC has been inclined to back loyalists not rebels. Good constituency members may survive policy differences, especially in the Conservative Party.

The business of re-adoption is crucial to party coherence and discipline. It is virtually impossible in Britain now to win an election as an Independent, without the financial and organising help and the label or cue to voters which the major parties alone can provide. To be refused re-adoption is almost equivalent to being dismissed from the profession of politics. Recent evidence suggests that the Member rejected by or rejecting his local party and standing as an Independent, has only a slight chance of temporary success. Thus Dick Taverne had a dramatic success in a by-election in Lincoln but lost the seat in 1974. Dave Nellist, a good constituency Member, did not survive one election as an Independent in Coventry South East in 1992.

Life can be uncomfortable for a Member of independent mind. The Member of Parliament can find himself serving too many masters. Joe Ashton MP, spoke against 'mandatory re-selection' in the Conference debate of 1978:

'You are asking us to try all the time to serve five masters – to do what Conference tells us to do, to do what the constituency tells us to do, to do what our trade union tells us to do, to do what the government and Whips tell us. Then there is the electorate telling us what to do....'

This discussion brings us again to the question of the proper loyalties of the Member of Parliament.

There is in this connection a famous pronouncement by Burke condemning 'authoritative instructions' (Document 15.2), which runs quite contrary to the claims of the modern party activist.

■ DOCUMENT 15.2
Burke on 'authoritative instructions'

From E. Burke, Speech to the Electorate of Bristol, 1774, in *Speeches and Letters on American Affairs*, 1908, p. 73

Your representative owes you not his industry only, but his judgement; and he betrays instead of serving you if he sacrifices it to your opinion...authoritative instructions arise from a fundamental mistake of the whole order and tenor of our constitution. Parliament is not a congress of ambassadors from different and hostile interests...[it] is a deliberative assembly of one nation, with one interest, that of the whole.... You choose a member indeed; but when you have chosen him, he is not a member of Bristol, but he is a Member of Parliament. ■

EXERCISE
The duty of an MP to his constituency

15.1 Consider the Burke quotation and attempt to justify the action of the Bournemouth East Constituency in virtually dismissing Nicolson.

The political parties, interests and party finance

In the British political system, groups with interests or ideas to promote work mainly in direct relation with the executive, and to a lesser extent with Members of Parliament (see Chapter 21). These direct approaches to governing circles seem more effective than approaches to the political parties for the purpose of pressing specific policy changes or administrative action, revising legislation, or obtaining an increased subsidy. But political parties can have some influence in these matters, participating at an earlier stage in the formulation of policy, and occasionally modifying government action by last minute protest. So the parties are not neglected by the pressure groups.

Of course, relations with MPs provide good channels of communication to the party, and for most groups this suffices. The parties are clearly somewhat unwieldy instruments for the promotion of specific causes. However, two massive interest groups press continuously on the political parties. The Labour Party has the trade unions as a permanent built-in force, and the Conservative Party has close if less formal links with industry. The crucial relationship is financial, so it is necessary first to consider the general question of party finance.

Party finance

Both major parties have difficulties in financing their work at a level regarded as appropriate in a modern democracy. The minor parties have even greater difficulties. Some countries (for example, West Germany, Sweden and Finland) have established state subsidies for political parties. So far in Britain the government has offered modest grants (about £1.1m a year to the opposition) for the maintenance of essential parliamentary work, but nothing more.

Political parties are essential to democracy and the work they do is expensive. Therefore it is proper for the state to give them financial support. This is the broad argument for the financial subvention of political parties by the state. It was put forward by the Houghton Committee in 1975, pointing to the example of other countries. Houghton argued that state finance was necessary to the effective operation of parties, and would diminish dependence on special interests. The Houghton majority recommended the state contributed 5p per vote, subject to a minimum threshold.

The minority argued vigorously against, on the grounds that:

- organisation for political ends is essentially a voluntary activity
- state subvention could not be limited to the existing major parties (what about Trotskyists or the National Front?)
- money raising is a cohesive activity, (so helpful to a voluntary organisation)
- links with traditional sources of support would be weakened
- public money would not be more 'neutral' than existing funds
- state funding might well strengthen central bureaucracy and add to already heavy expenditure on national advertising.

Overall, the Houghton minority felt that state finance would not improve the performance of political parties, and might increase cynicism about

politics. Democracy was not in danger; indeed, if anything, the British economy was in greater danger.

The Houghton recommendations were not implemented, but the parties were allowed modest support for their parliamentary work. By 1993 the Labour Party was entitled to about £985 000, the Liberal Democrats about £190 000. Labour has used these funds to expand the Leader's staff into an 'Executive Office'. In fact political parties do better than this since they get free postage for election literature and free access to television and radio. The latter is extremely valuable, and the prohibition on the purchase of advertising time does much to reduce the expenditure of the parties on elections (notably compared with the USA).

Detailed accounts of income and expenditure are not available for the Conservative Party but it is clear that the party is much richer than the Labour Party. Annual income fluctuates but roughly the Conservatives receive twice as much as Labour and ten times as much as the Liberal Democrats. A simple test of comparative affluence lies in the employment of professional agents. In 1992 the Conservatives had about 300, Labour under 100 and the Liberal Democrats only a handful. Expenditure on elections provides another indicator. According to research by the Hansard Society, in the 1987 election the Conservatives spent twice as much as Labour. If expenditure by the three parties is adjusted to allow for free broadcasting and postage, Conservatives are ahead, but not so far.

Table 1 Election expenditure 1987 and 1992

a) 1987 actual (estimates)

b) adjusted to allow for free broadcasting and postage

c) 1992 (estimates by parties)

	Conservative	Labour	Liberal(All'ce)
a)	£12–15m	£6m	£2m
b)	£24.9m	£19.7m	£16.5m
c)	£10.1m	£7.1m	£2.1m

The Labour Party is heavily dependent on contributions from the trade unions in cash and the provision of organising assistance in some constituencies. Quantitatively this financial dependence for central income may be as high as 90 per cent. The Conservatives draw substantial donations from business and industry, directly or through propaganda organisations, such as Aims of Industry. In cash the total may be similar to the unions' contributions to the Labour Party. But as a proportion of total party income, the corporate contributions to the Conservative Party are much less significant. The secret source of Conservative affluence is really the local income derived from the garden fetes and coffee mornings (and the personal prosperity they reflect) of the constituency associations. This is no doubt unfair. But the Conservatives are not so dependent on one source of finance as the Labour Party.

Houghton found that people (that is, respondents to a survey) appreciated the value of political parties. But few of them (few of us) join, contribute, participate. There are no doubt many more attractive things to do than taking part in politics. In consequence the two major political parties are trapped in potentially difficult relations with financial backers.

The trade unions and the Labour Party

The trade unions are the basis of the Labour Party. Historically they created it in the famous decision of 1900 to set up a Labour Representation Committee. It is true that much was due to the vision and initiative of Keir Hardie of the Independent Labour Party, while some trade union leaders were happy to continue their bargaining relationships with the existing parties. But the party could not have been viable without union support. Constitutionally, through political affiliation, the unions provide the bulk of the membership, a majority (about four fifths) in Conference and over half the NEC. By the reforms of 1981, they gained the largest share (40 per cent) in the election of the Leader. Even after the reforms of 1993 their vote is equal with the constituencies and the PLP. Further, they sponsor almost one half of Labour's Members of Parliament (1992).

The trade unions contribute to the finances of the Labour Party through the political levy paid by members of affiliated unions, and by direct donations, especially for election campaigns. The total trade union contribution is always more than two thirds of Labour's still inadequate income. The sponsorship of Members of Parliament carries substantial financial aid for campaign and constituency expenses.

There can be no doubt that the party is financially dependent on the trade unions, and particularly on a few large unions like the public employees, engineers and the transport workers. That dependence is not often used brutally by the unions to secure their interests, but clearly it has a profound effect on the relations of party and unions. The contributions of the unions are not paid to the party automatically and predictably, and the Labour Party Treasurer has often to appeal to the unions to hand over money already collected.

In the light of the historical, constitutional and financial position of the unions in the Labour Party, is the Party the prisoner of the unions? They are at least related in a way which makes it difficult for the Party to act independently against the special interests of the unions: there are some 'no-go' areas for the party. Historically, the party's origins lie at least partly in the trade union movement. Professor Rose has called the party, perhaps with some exaggeration, 'the sponsored offshoot of the trade union movement'. But it is quite usual to see the party as the political wing of 'the Labour movement', which also has an industrial wing (the unions) with an equal claim to status and power. Constitutionally the unions plainly have substantial powers through the Conference and the NEC, which in effect they control. But these are centres of power in a federal system of separate but linked institutions, of which the Parliamentary party is still probably the most influential.

Recent history offers examples both of trade union influence, and its limits. In 1960–1 Gaitskell fought the conference and won; in 1966–68, the Labour government operated an incomes policy in face of trade union hostility, but in 1968–69 was forced to withdraw industrial relations legislation. In 1973–75, the 'Social Contract' between the Labour Party (subsequently the government) and the unions accorded the unions immense gains in economic and social policy in return for ill-defined promises of co-operation in the moderation of wage claims. Outside that narrow but important area, the trade union influence on the Labour Party has led to a profound and damaging neglect of consumer interests. The wages of the miner cutting coal aroused more concern than the price of a bag of coal to the elderly poor. The Labour Party has been by-passed in concern for the consumer by the Conservatives.

In the 1980s trade union influence in the Labour Party was less evident. The unions were weakened by Conservative legislation and the Labour Party shaken by three heavy election defeats.

The Labour Party adopted centrist policies, accepting most of the Conservative trade union legislation, and even abandoning the closed shop, in defiance of union pressure. Some Labour policies still reflect the union interests and pressures – the minimum wage, hostility to compulsory competitive tendering, and a reluctance to intervene in 'free collective bargaining'.

By the end of the decade it seemed that the unions were no longer behaving as if they owned the Labour Party – but they still were the majority shareholder. On its side the Labour Party has successfully claimed its right and need to seek and serve a majority of voters, and not trade unionists exclusively. This can be argued on grounds of social democracy, pluralism, the changing social structure and aspirations of a capitalist economy; or, pragmatically, it can be argued in terms of electoral arithmetic – there are simply not enough Labour voting trade unionists to support a major party.

EXERCISES
The trade unions and the Labour Party

15.2 Should trade unions avoid 'getting mixed up in politics'?
15.3 What is the case for accepting that the trade unions should have a considerable influence in the Labour Party?
15.4 Do you see any justification for the view that the Labour Party leadership in its relations with the unions 'gets the worst of both worlds'?

It is doubtful in any case whether a great party, once in office, can respond exclusively to any one pressure upon it. The collective strength of the Cabinet, the corporate force of the civil service, as well as the nature of the problems, force a government to a viewpoint which is necessarily wider than that of any single element in the political world. Nevertheless the Labour Party needs the support of the unions, and cannot oppose them too openly or too long. If the union connection deters some voters, then it helps to ensure that the Labour Party never wins the government power which would enable it to lessen its dependence on the unions. So it may seem without the unions there is no Labour Party; with them there can be no Labour government.

Industry and the Conservative Party
The Conservative Party has no formal links with industry equivalent to the Labour Party's relationship with the trade unions. Nevertheless, there is a strong informal connection. Conservative policies and principles are clearly more sympathetic to the needs and desires of industry, more precisely to the owners and managers of industry and business. Many Conservative Members of Parliament have a business background and continue to hold directorships and other positions in industry. Conservative Cabinets usually include one or two members with strong business, finance or, more rarely, industrial links.

In 1987 over 300 companies raised about £4.5m for the Conservative election campaign and a similar amount was raised before the 1992 election. Contributions are made by companies or by individuals. Some contributions are made indirectly to organisations sympathetic to the Conservative Party. In the past special companies, named after rivers, were set up to enable the party to benefit from wills, trusts and covenants. Very few companies – Marks and Spencer a notable exception – consult their shareholders about political donations. Recently substantial donations have been made by foreign businessmen, especially from Hong Kong, and by a Greek shipping magnate. As shown above the total contributions of industry to the Conservative Party are substantial, but not so dominant proportionately in the total income of the party. It still raises a good deal of money for itself, and is not heavily dependent like the Labour Party on one source of income.

The question arises, as for the trade unions, does industry by its donations acquire an unfair influence on policy? It is impossible to say with any confidence. Industry, like the trade unions, is entitled to the consideration of its interests by government; and the Conservative Party would be inclined by its ideology to be sympathetic. Again, the Conservative Party, like Labour, has to win a majority in a mass electorate. The Conservatives at times have pursued policies against the interests of business and industry, for example, high interest rates, resale price maintenance. In any case, the interests of business and industry are various and often irreconcilable: there are conflicts of interest between big and small industry, manufacturing, finance, and retail, exporters and importers and so on.

However, there are many examples of 'policy generosity' by the Conservative Party towards business interests. For example, the government has not pressed for rigorous regulation of high finance. It retreated from its determination to force the brewers to modify their tied house system or 'vertical integration', after the brewers (the 'beerage', traditional supporters of the Party) held back their normally generous donations. British Airways, too, stopped its usual generous donation to the party when the government modified BA's monopoly of many routes. This example argues both ways: a Conservative government was proved capable of acting against the interests of a donor industry; but the expectation of that industry was clearly that donations purchased sympathetic government action.

The case of the businessman, Asil Nadir (1993), raised further concern about the relations of the party, hence the government, with businessmen making large donations to the party. Asil Nadir, facing fraud charges and jumping bail, had secretly given over £400 000 to the party; he had been entertained six times by Margaret Thatcher and three ministers had approached the Attorney-General on his behalf. None of this was illegal; the Conservative Party is committed to the interests of business as a matter of principle and policy and perhaps ministers take up the grievances of humbler people in high places. But it does look as if large donations to the party secure the attention of ministers – just as they do in the Labour Party.

Big business and high finance are indeed well represented in the party, but there are spokesmen too for small business, farmers, lawyers. There is little evidence of the pressures of big business at the party's Conference, but of course this indicates that these groups operate more discreetly than the trade unions in the Labour Party, rather than that they do not operate at all. In office the Conservative Party is bound by the same political and constitutional constraints as Labour. It must work within the framework of Cabinet and civil service, and secure support from a mass electorate. On the other hand, for both parties the major interests are so closely bound in with the party that they will not always be seen as external forces. Following such interests may seem natural, and not a concession to a pressure group at all.

EXERCISE
Business interests and the Conservative Party

15.5 Should business stay out of politics?

A special further question arises in the case of the Conservative Party and its related interests: is there a link between donations and 'honours'? This is evident in the case of the press: the owners and editors of the Conservative press have been well-rewarded with peerages and knighthoods by a grateful Conservative government. This can only be justified on the politically sound if amoral principle that a prudent government must reward its friends. (The principle would be well understood in USA where it is accepted that patronage is a normal and necessary instrument of politics). In the case of industry, there is evidence that donations to the Conservative Party are associated with, if not directly rewarded by, the grant of honours. Thus two thirds of the industrialists given peerages and one third of those given knighthoods by Margaret Thatcher (1979–90) worked in private companies which had donated to the party (figures based on research for a Radio 4 programme, January 1991).

Finally, the Houghton arguments for the public subsidy of political parties can be evaluated.

EXERCISE
State subsidy to political parties.

15.6 Indicate briefly the arguments for state subsidy to political parties, taking into account the arguments of the Houghton Minority Report summarised above.

Parties and government: do parties make a difference?

In the traditional 'Westminster' model of British government, political parties appear to be the essential link between the people and the actions of government. In that model two parties compete by their record and programme for the favour of the voters, and the elected government then governs according to the wishes of the electorate. The voters are deemed to have studied the party manifestos, and indicated their preference, and thus given the government a mandate to carry out its advertised programme.

This is the theory, but it can hardly be matched by practice. In restaurant terms, some of the dishes are off the menu, some are said to be available but are a long time coming, some are overcooked, missing vital ingredients and so on. This is government as 'Fawlty Towers', dissatisfied customers are bullied by the crazy proprietor and of course overcharged.

The record is, fortunately, a little better than this. Governments do keep many of their promises, but there is evidence of some failings:

● some promises are too vague and ambitious to be fulfilled, or in general and limited form already available, for example, peace, prosperity, and freedom

- external pressures, particular world economic conditions, prevent the realisation of optimistic promises about prosperity and public expenditure
- internal pressures of trade unions, industry, disadvantaged interests, outraged citizens, divert government from its objectives
- bureaucratic pressures or inertia block government initiatives
- change in the problems and opportunities, and in the government's own thinking lead to changes in its priorities
- in any case the manifesto is only one of many indications of a party's general approach and its policy commitments, most voters do not read the manifesto and a majority does not vote for the winning party, so there are no indisputable grounds for regarding the manifesto as a binding contract.

Thus there may be good reasons for a government to diverge from its promises, in face of changing circumstances or a more realistic appreciation of the problems. However, the citizen-voter may reasonably complain – as in Fawlty Towers – if performance bears little relation to promise. For example, there was no mention during the election of 1979 that the Conservative government would almost double VAT – indeed, any such change was denied for good electoral reasons. The Conservative 1987 pledges on community charge and child benefit were imprecise; there was no mention of joining the EMS, even as an option. In 1983 the Conservative manifesto made no mention of the fundamental review of welfare policies later carried out by Norman Fowler. The privatisation of British Gas was not mentioned, though this was one of the major acts of Margaret Thatcher's second term of government.

Indeed, the whole privatisation programme, which was one of the great political and – more controversially – economic successes of Margaret Thatcher's governments 'came from no-where': there were only brief and timid references in the manifestos of 1979 and 1983. This was probably not deliberate deception, and may show that governments get their best ideas in the course of governing, and should not be tied to a programme sketched out for the purposes of election. This looks to be a realistic argument, though if pressed it becomes little more than an invitation to deception of the electorate – not 'trust the people' but 'trust the government'. Thus, there are evident defects in the processes of policy development in a democracy conducted by adversarial party competition.

The disconnection between party and government is made obvious by reference to the election manifestos. These inevitably reflect divergent currents of opinion within the parties, especially in the case of the Labour Party (because of the comparative weakness of the Leader). The manifesto is ostensibly designed for the voters, but in practice registers a temporary settlement of intra-party dispute. Manifestos do contain specific and realistic pledges which parties endeavour to keep. (For example, it is known that Margaret Thatcher on one occasion stopped pressing for a particular line of policy when told it contradicted a specific commitment. In 1992 the Conservatives withdrew some proposed manifesto pledges in face of the Chancellor's warning that they could not be afforded).

However, for the most part manifestos deal in broad generalities and short-term electorally motivated appeals, which make them useless as guides to policy, and unattractive to read. The most eager readers of the manifestos are opponents looking for points to attack.

The civil service studies the manifestos carefully in the period before a general election, thus increasing the small readership of these documents, and prepares itself, without reference to the existing government, for the possibility of change. If government changes hands, incoming Ministers will be presented on their first day in office with substantial briefs outlining the department's position and the implications of new lines of policy as indicated in the manifestos. Some discussions with the opposition also take place prior to the election. Thus the civil service takes the party manifestos seriously – but sometimes too sceptically if not cynically. Civil servants appreciate what they call 'reality', and are inclined to believe that incoming Ministers, fresh from a heady election campaign, and brandishing the manifesto, need to be persuaded to face up to a harsher reality than they have talked about on the hustings.

The discussion so far of the impact of party on government has concentrated on the nature of the party programme and the reasons for a divergence in performance – unreality of the programme, resistance of bureaucracy and other interests, intractability of problems. Leaving aside the relationship of promise and performance, it is relevant to ask whether parties make any difference at all to what governments actually do. If the performance or output of governments is measured, is it possible to detect significant differences arising from a change of party?

This raises large issues, requiring a review of recent history. The case that parties do not make any – or much – difference rests on two arguments.

First, despite an adversarial mode of politics, there is a substantial agreement between the parties about the fundamental objectives of government. This argument looked more convincing in the 1950s and 1960s, when, so it was contended, there existed a consensus ('the post-war consensus') broadly about the managed economy and welfare state, and a pluralist polity in which local government pushed up public expenditure and the trade unions and industry were consulted, even incorporated, in the process of government. Margaret Thatcher's three governments broke the consensus, with radical new policies for the management of the economy (by monetarism), the privatisation of industry, the exclusion and restriction of the unions, and the introduction of market practices into some social services. Yet public expenditure continued to rise, the Welfare State was not dismantled, and after 1990, under John Major, the Conservative government adopted policies particularly in the expansion of public debt which looked distinctly Keynesian. At the same time the Labour Party appeared to have been converted to strict economic disciplines, and was committed to the restrictions of the ERM. The consensus was, it seems, partly restored, though it had moved.

Hence, again, the question could be raised do parties make a difference? – with the expected answer, not very much.

Second, even if the parties would like to disagree, the hard facts of economics and international politics, drive them together. Whatever a government might like to do, it ends by doing what its resources allow, and no more. Such gross limitations on governments have not figured much in party manifestos and propaganda. Governments are doomed to default on their fine promises and disappoint their more enthusiastic supporters. The most dramatic recent illustration was the collapse and reversal of economic policies in the Autumn of 1992, just six months after the election.

The Thatcher governments offered the best demonstration since Attlee's post-war Labour administration that parties do sometimes make some difference. Here are three simple demonstrations in terms of public expenditure of the impact of a party determined to make a difference.

EXERCISE
Parties and public expenditure

15.7 Study Figure 1, p. 256. What conclusions can be drawn about the impact of parties in government on public expenditure?

GUIDE TO EXERCISES

15.1 Burke was a Dublin lawyer without roots in his constituency, speaking before modern parties were organised. There are two possible lines of argument. a) Burke is wrong, at least for the twentieth century. Party is a fundamental principle of organisation. The electorate votes for a party, rather than a candidate, and the winning party may reasonably expect conformity to party principle. Individual conscience may properly be subordinated to the higher principle (in this context) of party solidarity. b) While Burke is in general acceptable, his principle does not apply to this particular case, for Nicolson was either clearly wrong, or just as clearly in conflict with basic Conservative principle, or both. This is to imply that the constituency association is a proper judge of the scope of individual conscience.

15.2 They are 'mixed up in politics', whether they like it or not, for they are organised specifically to protect and press interests and views on which there is certain to be disagreement and conflict. But it does not follow that they should ally themselves with one political party.

15.3 But why not have such influence? There can be no objection in political morality unless the result were gravely to distort the processes of representation. Over a half of all trade unionists are affiliated to the Labour Party, and altogether trade unionists make up at least one sixth of the electorate, and their interests are of some importance in the community. Hence, even if they exercised considerable influence in the Labour Party, this would not amount to 'grave distortion'.

Of course, the Labour Party ought to represent other interests as well as those of the trade unions – for example the interests of the professions and of consumers, which might be in conflict with those of the unions. If it were consistently

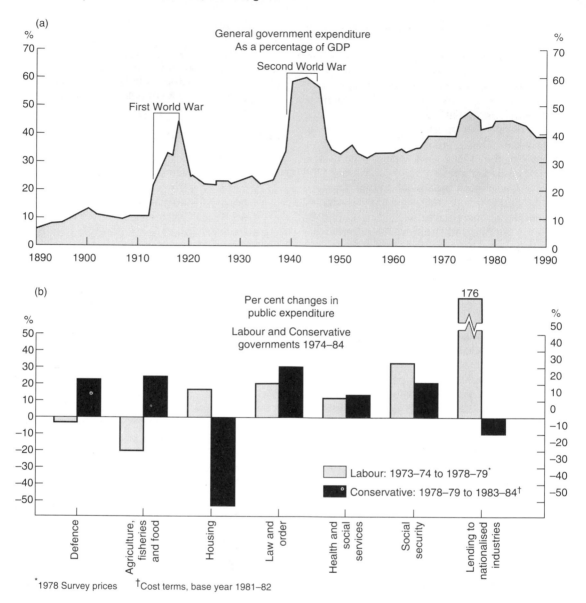

Figure 1 Do parties make a difference to the pattern of public expenditure?

prevented from doing so, then distortion might occur. The constitution of the Labour Party, by giving such weight to the trade unions, seems always in danger of permitting distortion.

15.4 In this question the argument changes from considerations of morality and propriety to considerations of political tactics. The party gets a great deal from the unions – particularly money, sympathy, support. But, of course, the support is not guaranteed: no votes are delivered, and trade unions have been known to wreck a Labour government's policies. Their influence sharply restricts the Labour Party's freedom of action, and drives voters away. For all this, however, the credit balance is substantial: the trade unions are still the rock on which the Labour Party is raised.

The argument also needs to be considered from the trade union side: it is open to doubt whether the modern trade union movement serves its members well by staying so close to one political party, especially one that is not often in office.

15.5 No: in a modern industrial state, business, like the unions, forms one of the great interests involved in society. Of course, it will certainly be in conflict with other groups and with society as a whole. But such conflicts are the agenda of politics, and business has a right to engage in political activity. Moreover, since these conflicts are among the most important in any modern society, a political party may properly seek to defend or promote the interests of one side. But we should expect this to be done with a reasonable regard for other interests, and the need of a party for mass support normally ensures this.

15.6 The case for should be clear from the text. Parties perform vital but costly activities essential in a participatory democracy. The present methods of financing from sympathetic corporations encourages an undue dependence, without providing an adequate income. The case against is that the state ought not to subsidise an essentially voluntary activity, and that subsidies would encourage dependence on the state and perhaps the bureaucratisation of the parties. (Not very convincing you may

think.) There are problems of cost and practicality (how much? how assessed? must a party be large and democratic?)

The Conservative government proposed (1983) to reform the trade union political levy procedure to make it easier not to pay the levy. This can hardly be done without raising the general question of party finance, not to mention the particular question of company contributions to the Conservative Party.

15.7 The overall tendency shown in Figure 1a) is clearly ever upward. Wars push up total expenditure spectacularly, and leave it higher; in a hundred year perspective there are minor variations related to governments. Figure 1b) shows marked differences over the short term in expenditure by head – the 1979 change of government really did make a difference (*The Economist* heading, the first time it presented these figures, was 'People lose, cows win'!). However, Figure 1c) shows that some of the government's radical drive (but not all of it) is modified by brutal reality. In particular, continuing heavy unemployment leads to increased expenditure on unemployment and training, and social security; similarly heavy demand for health and social services, and the fear of unpopularity leads to increased spending. Even education gets a modest increase.

So, measured by public expenditure, do parties make a difference? – yes, but not as much as they might expect or claim.

ASSESSMENTS
The uses of political parties

1 It is evident that political parties provide essential machinery for the organisation and articulation of elections, parliament and government. Much of that political activity could conceivably be carried out by individuals, or by ad hoc groups. However the rewards of power are so high that there would be a strong drive to build the ad hoc group into a solid and permanent organisation capable of forming a majority government. Hence, it may be said, parties do have functions and are a natural and inevitable development in the political system.

2 Nevertheless, the British party system and the political parties fall far short of perfection in

the fulfilment of their functions.

a) Participation and representation. The record is at best modest. Membership is low and inactive. The parties are not vibrant centres of political education, though to be fair, they must stand out as beacons of light in a politically apathetic nation. Mainly they provide a shadowy local presence for the national parties and help to get out the vote in local and national elections.

b) Policy development. The machinery and procedures for policy development within the party are rudimentary in the case of the Conservatives, clumsy and open to hijack in the Labour Party. The Liberal Democrats have a more carefully structured system, though much still depends on the leader.

c) Political leadership. Party leaders are the only national leaders Britain has. No business, trade union or church leader, nor the monarch, can match the salience of the majority party leader, who is also the Prime Minister. The Leader of the Opposition also has a high public profile, though his standing is inevitably diminished by his evident powerlessness. However, Britain's leaders are forced by the adversarial party system into partisan rather than national leadership. This was true, for example, of Margaret Thatcher and Harold Wilson, who could both in different ways electrify an audience of faithful partisans. Only Churchill among post-war Prime Ministers could make an impact on the uncommitted. It may be that a 'mature' democracy does not need much national leadership of this kind, except in time of war; but it could be argued that the persistent and fundamental problems of Britain's economy and society do require some degree of mobilisation of opinion and effort if they are ever to be effectively resolved. And it would appear that adversarial party politics precludes that kind of national awakening.

The decline of political parties?

It is tempting to argue that political parties are in decline – though that sets the problem of establishing what the 'before' and 'after' conditions of parties were. Parties do now have fewer active members, and a diminishing number of committed supporters (in the sense of regular and undeviating voters). There is less certainty and solidity about the great interests and ideologies they represent. While the form and

procedures of Parliament symbolise and emphasise the confrontation of political parties, the media provide a more popular forum in which the politician seems often to appear as an individual performer.

At the same time interest groups and single issue campaigns have further shifted the ground of politics away from the parties. For example, a Minister and an Opposition spokesman debating transport policy in a television studio may seem to represent competing interests, the ministry itself, the road users, the transport unions, and particular campaigns. The party dimension in the debate is most evident only just before an election, when the various and complex strands in the argument are pushed and pulled and squeezed into partisan shapes.

So much may be conceded to the argument that political parties are in decline. They have been challenged by alternative forms and forces and pushed away from the centre of politics. But they have not been replaced or even marginalised. Political parties are still indispensable. It is impossible to finance a campaign and get elected without the support of a party. There is an interesting comparison with the USA, where individuals campaign and raise much of their own finances; even so they carry a party label. The name of a party is a necessary cue to voters.

The problems of managing without parties can be seen in elections in some rural local authorities in the past, where 'non-partisanship' was associated with inertia and corruption, and in companies, trade unions and student unions. Parties give the voter a crude choice, and that is better than no choice at all. (To appreciate the difficulties of voting in mass electorates consider the practical problems of choice for say an election for school prefects – not that it is necessarily a good idea – among all pupils in the school, not just the senior pupils who might be expected to know the candidates).

Multi-party politics?

An alternative form of the argument is that, while parties may not be in decline, the British party system is ineffective and weak. The two major parties, Conservative and Labour, which have dominated post-war politics no longer represent an adequate range of interests and ideologies. The simple confrontation between capital and labour, rich and poor, public provision and private freedom reflects nineteenth-century conditions and assumptions. These divisions are now more complex and there are many other issues which cut across the traditional political divide. Hence there is a need for more than the two parties through which the British have tried to conduct politics. This is demonstrated by the relative decline of Labour and the growth of third parties.

The two-party system itself no longer serves the needs of the people, and is preserved only by the artificial simple plurality electoral system. The debate about alternative ballot systems is considered in Chapter 17. Here it should be noted that the debate is essentially about the kind of party system and the form of government.
In sum the argument is:

- the two-party system has failed because of the defects set out above (representation, participation, policy development, leadership), and has led to a false and debilitating adversarial mode of politics. The claimed advantages of choice and accountability have not been achieved.
- persistent support for 'third' parties, the Alliance, Liberal Democrats, Nationalists, represents more than an occasional protest vote. There is substantial support for such parties, now hidden and frustrated by the ballot system. Multi-party politics, if allowed to escape from that artificial constraint, could provide a fairer representation of popular opinion. The coalition governments which would inevitably stem from the change could be as strong and decisive as the majority party government is claimed to be, and much more representative.

This argument is controversial. If the alternative to the present party system is coalition government then many critics of the party system give up and settle for the devil they know.

Coalition government
Politics and political parties are not in great favour. It is an old and popular notion that political parties distort government, making it doctrinaire, bigoted, inflexible, and concerned with sectional advantage rather than public interest. Since it is difficult to get rid of parties altogether, one favoured remedy is that governments should be based on a coalition of existing parties (survey evidence shows a strong

popular support for this in principle, but there was less enthusiasm for a hung Parliament in 1992 when that became a practical possibility).

The case against coalition government
Although the coalition argument looks attractive, government by a single majority party has substantial advantages in the settlement of political disputes.

If politics is a necessary mechanism for arguing out disagreements, coalition politics (certainly in the form of a national government) restricts the argument, encourages a complacent sense that there is not a case to be made on the other side. This is satisfactory in wartime: the only recent peacetime experience of coalition – the National Government of 1931 – is less encouraging. Effective opposition was destroyed while the government carried out policies which are now seen to be wholly mistaken.

Where there are political differences (that is, differences about policy), government by a single majority party makes for a clear decision. One side of the argument is deemed to have won and its preferences will prevail. This is praised by opponents of coalition as 'strong government'.

Moreover, a government based on a majority is in effect chosen by the electorate, while a coalition is based on a post-election negotiation by politicians – it is usual to add 'behind closed doors, in smoke-filled rooms'. Thus opponents of coalition government portray it as both ineffective (not strong) and undemocratic.

These arguments do not of course imply that party government has no faults and unerringly ensures both good and democratic government. Plainly it does not. The faults ascribed to it by coalitionists are all true in part. Its justification depends on these being outweighed by its advantages.

In the light of the recent political history of Britain this basic case against coalition government is not totally convincing. Coalitionists can advance arguments against the present system and in favour of their preferred alternative.
The case for coalition government
The case for coalition government is based on the defects of the existing party system, in particular the unrepresentative nature of the two-party system, and the distortion of popular will inherent in what amounts to government by an

arrogant minority. Coalition emerges not so much in its own right but as the acceptable consequence of a reformed proportionate ballot system and multi-party politics.

The case for coalition government can be made more strongly than that, and arguably has been strengthened by recent history.

- The performance of governments since the 1960s is adjudged to be poor, and is blamed on the nature of government, rather than the severity of the problems.
- The thin majorities of the 1970s (and 1964) and the fat majorities of the 1980s have distorted popular opinion and harmed good government.
- Policies have changed unpredictably and not in accordance with party programmes, (the 'U-turns' of, for example, 1972, 1976 and 1992), or they have been unduly influenced by partisan rivalry and the need to court the electorate (for example, the policies towards trade unions and income restraint of the two major parties). Despite the claims that the British form of party government makes for decisive government, single parties elected on a minority of votes are beholden to major interests and oversensitive to popular opinion (a good example being tax privileges for house-ownership).
- The 'adversary' form and style of British politics has strengthened the characteristic defects of competitive party government – an unthinking acceptance of traditional policies (doctrinaire rigidity), an excessive enthusiasm for gladiatorial contests, and destructive politics, a lack of respect for minorities and opponents. All governments include diverse opinions; coalition governments recognise rather than disguise diversity.
- The two-party system of the 1945–70 period was based ultimately on the conflicts of interest between the working class and the business and propertied class. If that division of society is now less important, the political parties should reflect that change.
- Finally, the record of coalition governments elsewhere in Europe (West Germany, Scandinavia) demonstrates the possibility of stable, effective and responsive government under coalition.

Supporters of the two-party system are not without counter arguments. Economic performance is independent of a particular form of government. The occasional dysfunctions of the system do not condemn it totally. The major parties are already coalitions, and the system works by channelling diverse opinion into alternative coalitions – avoiding fragmentation and presenting the elector with an effective choice. The record of coalition government elsewhere is not uniformly impressive (Italy?).

For all the doubts about coalition government, which come so easily to the British, elsewhere government by coalition is frequent and sometimes normal, and appears to satisfy the governed. So one may suspect that the defence of the competitive two-party system exaggerates its virtues.

Concept

Party government

Party government implies that the leaders of government are drawn from one or more political parties and the actions of government are guided or determined by the doctrines or tendencies of the parties represented in government. This is not very helpful since there is evidently a wide range of characteristics included in the term. In the old Soviet Union an authoritarian single party monopolised office and power. In the USA government leaders use the labels of loosely organised parties with no clearly defined doctrine, but this is mainly an electoral convenience. Britain lies between these two examples. Government is based on the personnel and policies of comparatively solid parties, and is normally monopolised by the largest minority party (usually known as the majority party).

However, it is evident that the statement 'British government is party government' has to be 'unpacked' into a number of subsidiary questions about the nature of the parties and their relation to governing. Alternatively such questions can be passed over in favour of a conclusion about what governments do: 'In Britain the outputs of government are heavily influenced by the personnel, pressures and policies of party'. This kind of statement may appear in an examination paper, followed by the command 'Discuss'. It should be apparent from this and other chapters that the statement requires qualification.

16

Political parties: ideas

The recent history of the parties

Polarisation and convergence

In the 1950s and 1960s the two major parties seemed to move closer in their outlook. While an American diagnosed an 'end of ideology', commentators in Britain coined the term 'Butskellism' to indicate the large area of agreement over economic policy between the Conservative and Labour Chancellors, Butler and Gaitskell. Economic problems were disguised by 'affluence' and a whole area of political dispute was removed. Crosland (1956) argued that nationalisation was no longer relevant, while Crossman (1960) denounced such revisionism as offering merely 'an alternative board of management for the affluent society'. Wilson's appeal in 1964 was to modernisation rather than Socialism.

During the 1970s and early 1980s the influence of the Left in the Labour Party increased sharply, both in the constituency parties and in the trade unions. Traditional deference to the leadership, never whole-hearted, was abandoned, the position of the PLP in the selection of the Leader was diminished, the individual Member of Parliament was subjected to re-selection and the role of Conference in policy making was re-asserted.

This was the age of the political activist, often young, educated beyond school age, unemployed, or employed in the public sector, with bases in local government, devoting all spare time to political activity, skilled in the exploitation of party rules and trade union support – at best, hard working and committed to the poor and socially deprived, at worst, ruthlessly coercive and even sometimes corrupt. When a few of this new type of Labour politicians arrived in the House of Commons as Members of Parliament they were distinguished by their non-traditional dress (jeans and tee-shirt) and non-traditional commitment to the hard grind of Parliamentary work on behalf of their principles and their constituents. One right wing Labour Member of Parliament said the SAS had replaced the Old Contemptibles.

This new Left stood against 'revisionism' and social democracy, against any compromise with the existing power structure, and for a class-based politics, an open and vigorous struggle on behalf of the poor, the unemployed, council tenants, public sector workers, shop stewards, ethnic and other minorities. The cry was locally for 'Jobs and Services', nationally (in Labour's Programme for Britain, 1973) for systematic intervention in and control of industry.

The Left is a normal tendency in the Labour Party, which has Socialist, Marxist and militant strands in its collection of traditions or tendencies. The capture of the party by the Left in the 1970s and early 1980s reflects the apparent failure of Wilson's governments between 1964 and 1979 (despite or because of the abandonment of radical policies) and the collapse of the social democratic cause in the constituencies and unions. At the same time the Conservative Party also reacting to failure and defeat, moved to the Right, first and hesitantly under Heath and then with conviction and vigour, under Margaret Thatcher, so justifying and providing an enemy for the Left.

The Wilson-Callaghan government (1974–9), in difficult parliamentary and economic circumstances, scored no continuing and evident political success and went down to defeat in 1979, following the rash of public sector strikes known as the Winter of Discontent. The Left moved in to achieve its constitutional gains (1981) and to drive out the dissident Right to form the Social Democratic Party. Michael Foot was elected Leader and duly went down to massive defeat in the election of 1983. At that point British politics moved from polarisation between Right and Left to a broken backed or bifurcated system comprising one dominant party and a collapsed and divided opposition.

But politics does not stand still. In a party democracy based on competitive elections political parties respond to the pressures of the electors, and seek a centre ground where a majority of votes can be achieved. This was evident in the Labour Party, which moved by 1992 to a centre, social democratic position, the Left vanquished and militant trade unions acquiescent. At the same time the Conservative Party, fearful that Margaret Thatcher would lose them the election, also retreated towards the centre.

Ideology, principle and interest push the parties apart (a perfectly wholesome process), but electoral pressures push them together again (also a perfectly wholesome, indeed, democratic process). In particular, the Labour Party has to recognise that the old class rhetoric will not run in a Britain which has been transformed economically and socially in the last 40 years; that trade unions and strikes are unpopular; and that British political culture is conservative in spirit and lacking in breadth and generosity. On the other side, the Conservatives have to recognise (indeed seem to have long recognised) that Britain is not composed of Old Etonian landowners and city financiers, and that most people approve of the public provision of a minimum level of public services, including health, education and public transport.

This broad area of economic prosperity and its distribution in social provision is the main battleground of the parties, yet it is one in which compromise is possible. For many of the issues are not resolved on the basis of either/or but rather more/ or less. Thus, all parties are committed to massive expenditure on health, education and social welfare; and party propaganda obscures differences which lie in relative enthusiasm or reluctance, managerial philosophy and the nice calculation of less and more. Many other issues, for example, 'law and order', immigration, the Irish problem and perhaps Europe, are more fiercely divisive but less crucial in popular political choice.

Overall, political competition flickers and flares. There is a tension between the demands of ideology and the pressures of practical politics. Conference rhetoric enlarges the differences, government and general elections tend to reduce them. Hence overall on many matters the parties

do not sit around opposite poles, and the pressures of democratic government pull their principle and policies towards the centre.

Thus a simplified model of a two-party system in Britain would show not two points each side of a divide, but a scale or spectrum along which the parties are stretched. The distance from left to right of the Labour Party might well be larger than that in the Conservative Party; this means that a right wing Labour position may be much nearer, in ideological terms or policy consequences, to a left wing Conservative position than to a far left wing Labour position. In the middle is an ill-defined area of 'overlap'. (But a one-dimensional scale hardly does justice to the complexity of political opinion (see Ideological maps and models pp. 268–9).

Political parties have more or less coherent sets of ideas. These may be referred to loosely as 'ideologies', though the term has a special meaning particularly in Marxist theory, and may have a generally pejorative implication (you have ideas, your political opponents have an ideology). The term 'doctrine' is neutral and to be preferred.

The 'post-war consensus'

There is some agreement that in the 1950s and 1960s at least there was a broad agreement across the parties on what might be called 'the post-war settlement'. This developed out of the wartime reaction to the Depression of the 1930s, the wartime experience of a regulated economy and imposition of 'fair shares', and the coalition government's foreshadowing of 'post–war reconstruction', notably in the Beveridge Report on Social Insurance (1942), the Education Act (1944) and serious discussion of town planning and a health service.

Although most of the legislation of the Labour government (1945–51) was hotly opposed by the Conservatives, it does seem that the Conservative Party which took office in 1951 had come to accept the 'Managed Economy/Welfare State' more or less as it stood. Hence, despite some fraying at the edges there appeared to be a broad consensus based on the following ideas.

The 'post-war consensus'
- active government
- managing a mixed economy
- providing for full employment
- and social welfare
- in consultation and collaboration with major interests, including the trade unions

- foreign policy based on NATO and deterrence of USSR.

The consensus tended towards benevolent bureaucracy and corporatism; it was not overly concerned with 'getting the economy moving', nor with a radical drive towards equality. It was a bureaucrat's pragmatic balance rather than an idealist's vision. The consensus stretched from Macmillan's 'One-Nation Toryism' to Crosland's and subsequently Wilson's 'revisionist Socialism'.

The ideas of the political parties

Ideas in political parties

A political party is a collection of people and a collection of ideas. The people are leaders, candidates and Members of Parliament, workers and active supporters and voters; also, interest groups aligned with the party. The ideas range from philosophy through tradition and rhetoric to specific policy proposals and actual performance in office. People, policy ideas and actual policies interact.

The people of the parties are active throughout the political system, and are considered in other chapters, as leaders and Ministers, Members of Parliament, members of interest groups, and voters. The party's ideas pervade all that activity. The background of Members of Parliament is particularly significant for the development and presentation of political ideas. But these are not elaborate ideas in the sense of philosophy or of policy detail. They are a rough but often powerful awareness of what the party stands for.

There are four levels at which the parties reveal what they stand for. At a literary and philosophical or doctrinal level there are expositions of party principles. In political speeches, particularly during elections, there emerges a more general exposition, based more on marketing strategy than philosophical principle, and tending towards caricature, especially of your opponents. At the same time a party will put forward a more specific programme. And if it gets into power its principles may be inferred (subject to some qualification) from its performance.

At all levels, however, a rough bipolarity tends to arise. Partly this is natural – one is for or against, right or left, good or bad. But the movement to opposite poles is reinforced in Britain by the electoral system; parties must show themselves to be different in order to compete. At the same time they must not move far from the centre where

converts must be won. Differences between the parties are often more evident in doctrine or political rhetoric than in performance. Even so, the Liberal Democrats are squeezed by the 'rough bipolarity', and the centripetal tendency; hence they find it difficult to develop a distinctive philosophy or brand image; then they are squeezed by the electoral system.

There is no single, simple guide to the philosophies of the great parties, for each is in reality a coalition (cynics would say a ragbag) of ideas and policies, based on a philosophy which is eclectic and pragmatic, picking up ideas here and there and dropping them if they do not work or do not appeal. Thus, the Conservative Party is not devoted merely to avoiding change; the Labour Party caters for interests wider than those of labour and may leave its opponents to call it socialist; the Liberal Democrat Party is not sure of the ways in which it is liberal (economic or political), though it might claim by its own structure and its commitment to constitutional reform to be distinctively democratic.

From time to time it is possible to discern clear tendencies to left and right in each party – assuming that 'left' and 'right' can be identified and defined. These tendencies are most evident when they relate to particular policies, but also have some basis in philosophy. The question of private education and private health care offer examples of such 'litmus tests' of political position, which may be harder to discern in complex arguments over central areas of policy like economic management or foreign policy.

The Case Study at the end of the chapter offers a brief anthology of the ideas of the parties at the more philosophical level. Here, nearer to the hustings than the philosophy seminar, there is an attempt briefly to identify what the parties stand for and to distinguish between them.

The Conservative Party

■ DOCUMENT 16.1
What the Conservatives stand for

a) Free market Conservatism
Main ideas of free market conservatism
- Hostility to government activity, the public sector in general and the civil service.
- Confidence in a free market, including a monetarist approach to economics, the privatisation of industry, or the introduction of markets into the public sector (e.g. health, education).

● Hostility to trade unions.

b) Margaret Thatcher's Conservatism

Margaret Thatcher accepted the free market principles and added a personal gloss, derived from her past as the striving and successful daughter of a small-town, Methodist Alderman, and owner of the grocery shop. Margaret Thatcher believed in:

● individual responsibility – people should solve their own problems
● recognition of the difference between right and wrong
● prudent house-keeping, not borrowing or spending more than you can afford
● public money is tax-payer's money and must be carefully husbanded
● firm discipline, a strong state, 'law and order' (including the death penalty) at home, and strong defences
● English nationalism, distrust of Europe but not USA, hostility to immigration
● strong foreign policy, high defence spending and a reluctant withdrawal from empire.

The latter is a significant theme in Conservatism, not confined to the right wing, though the 1930s policy of appeasement has to be explained in other ways. Imperialism is no longer relevant, but Conservatism is nationalist, militarist in that national security is understood as an exclusively military problem.

c) John Major's Conservatism

This is roughly Margaret Thatcher's Conservatism, minus Margaret Thatcher herself, and the Poll-Tax, and plus the Citizen's Charter and a greater concern for public services. In the Party's Manifesto, 1992, which he claimed was largely his work, and has a large picture of him on the cover, he stressed:

'Only Conservatives can truly claim to be the party of opportunity; choice; ownership and responsibility. Socialists like to keep people under the government's thumb. Conservatives want to give them independence. But we also want to put government at your service, giving you what you've paid for – good public services, responsible to you.... We can be free of old prejudices and class barriers. We can encourage diversity, not division; achievement, not antagonism.'

d) Freedom and Community: David Willetts' conservatism

From D. Willetts, 1992

Margaret Thatcher's government showed that the Conservative enjoys the luxury of being able to stick to his principles knowing that they also work in practice. A Conservative in government, equipped with a commitment to freedom and to a sense of community, is able to meet people's everyday aspirations – including their desire for greater prosperity (p. 61).

The Conservative Party's achievement is to show how apparently contrasting political principles can in practice be reconciled .... we have a tradition of individualism ... freedom is the way to prosperity. The tension between market and communities is resolved because they help to sustain each other (p. 186). ■

EXERCISE
Markets and communities

16.1 What might the last sentence mean?

■ DOCUMENT 16.2
The appeal of the Conservatives 1983

This is a summary of a leading article in the *Daily Express* of 9 June 1983 (the day of the election). It offers a shrewd assessment from a highly sympathetic newspaper of the appeal of the Conservatives.

● Margaret Thatcher as leader
● the sale of council houses
● improving the standards of teaching and discipline in schools
● reducing taxes and encouraging enterprise
● the promotion of 'law and order'
● facing the cost of the health and other welfare services
● silencing the 'union bully boys'
● reducing inflation
● laying the foundations of a prosperous economy
● rolling back the frontiers of the state
● maintaining national defences
● recognising the limitations of political activity.
■

EXERCISES
The appeal of the Conservatives 1983 and 1992

16.2 Are all of these appeals characteristically Conservative?
16.3 Does the leader writer show his bias?
16.4 How does this compare with the Conservative appeal of 1992?

The Labour Party

■ DOCUMENT 16.3
What Labour stands for

The New Labour party of the 1990s as re-formed under Neil Kinnock had moved a long way from its earlier socialist commitments.

a) 1950s Socialism
A study of backbench opinion in the 1950s, as expressed in Early Day Motions in the House of Commons (Finer et al, 1961, pp. 49–50) concluded that British Socialism was then made up of the following broad attitudes:

● pacifism
● anti-colonialism
● humanitarianism
● zeal for the welfare state
● libertarianism
● faith in public enterprise and control of the economy
● desire for social equality.

b) In the early 1980s the party stood for:

● Keynesian management of the economy, including price and import controls, job subsidies, re-nationalisation, compulsory planning agreements
● high taxes on income and wealth
● legal immunities (privileges) for trade unions
● withdrawal from Europe.

By 1992 none of this remained on the agenda. The party accepted the primacy of markets (subject to regulation), prudence in public expenditure, a concern for citizenship rather than social class and full commitment to Europe, including the Exchange Rate Mechanism and NATO.

c) The appeal of Labour 1992
Labour no longer talked of Socialism, though sometimes of democratic Socialism, thus moving towards social democracy (which is regulated, welfare-oriented capitalism). However, there was still a distinctive appeal evident in its 1992 election campaign.

● The regeneration of the economy, by an emphasis on investment and training. Of course, the Conservatives aimed to regenerate the economy too, and the most obvious difference was that the Conservatives had presided over/brought about a major recession.

● A move towards greater equality by adjusting taxation in favour of the less well-off, the Conservatives having favoured the better-off.
● Commitment to the public services, especially health and education, in contrast to the Conservatives' (alleged) underfunding and commercialisation of such services. This is a matter of intense dispute, though two points are clear (i) the Conservatives favoured private rather than public services (ii) a Labour government's spending priorities differ from the Conservatives – if there is any money to spare at all.
● Constitutional reform, in particular the establishment of a Scottish Assembly and the replacement of the House of Lords. ■

The basic differences between the Conservative and Labour Parties

■ DOCUMENT 16.4
The basic differences between the Conservative and Labour Parties at the beginning of the 1990s are shown in Figure 1.

EXERCISE
The differences between the Conservative and Labour Parties

16.5 The document reflects the traditional and actual positions of the parties in 1992, after the fall of Margaret Thatcher and during the 1992 election. Since then the Conservatives, under a newly confident John Major, and Labour, in the aftermath of defeat and under a new Leader, have shifted their positions. What modifications need to be made to the Document to bring it up-to-date?

The Liberal Democrats

What the Liberal Democrats stand for

There are serious problems for a third party in British politics, quite apart from the massive obstacle of the ballot system. These are the problems of ideology and interest, finding a distinctive set of ideas, and appealing to a substantial and identifiable interest.

The fundamental conflicts of British politics have related in the past to the issues defined by the Labour Party and Socialism – the management of the economy and the provision of public services in the interests of the 'have-nots', the working class, the unions. There was very broadly

	Conservative Party	Labour Party
Economy	For private property and free enterprise: hence outright opposition to nationalisation and lack of enthusiasm for planning. Suspicious of power of trade unions.	In the past for common ownership now favours regulation. Enthusiastic planners and inventors of quangos to do the regulating and planning. Accepts the power of trade unions as proper if sometimes inconvenient, in a modern social democracy.
Taxation	High taxation regarded as discouraging enterprise and choice.	'Robin Hoods' (robbing the rich to feed the poor) but some reluctance for this after 1992.
Welfare	Prefers 'individual self-reliance' and 'freedom of choice' to state welfare; keen to cut costs and 'privatise'.	Enthusiasm for 'fair shares'. Helping the weak, concern for a national minimum wage. Reluctant to reduce spending or jobs in welfare services. Prefers 'universal' benefits (no 'means test').
Social equality	Favours private education and selective grammar schools; also private health care. Sees the ideal society as based on distinctions of merit and wealth, a society in which there must be leaders and led. Competition for reward a necessary incentive. Equality of opportunity to acquire privilege.	Against both private education and health care. This is one of the sharpest distinctions now between right and left, and is related to fundamental ideas about social equality, as against Conservative notions of a society which is necessarily unequal to some extent because this reflects natural inequalities and encourages effort and enterprise.
Foreign policy and defence	Strongly patriotic, favouring a world role for Britain; willingly high spenders on defence; suspicious of UNO, but not of USA.	Tendency to split on this, particularly when the Party is in power. Strong tendencies to 'little Englander' policies' colonial withdrawal, distrust of NATO and nuclear weapons.
Law and order	For strong police force, sharp justice (Conference favours hanging).	'Tender-minded'. Riots caused by social conditions.
Constitution	Against reform, hostile to local government; prefers privatisation to decentralisation.	Edging towards constitutional reform, including an Assembly for Scotland and some reform of ballot system.

Figure 1 Basic differences between Conservative and Labour Parties at the beginning of the 1990s ■

a conflict of interest and ideology based on social class. This conflict has always been complicated and confused by rapid economic and social change, the diminution of older proletarian and capitalist values and the intrusion of new issues, such as Europe and the environment.

It has proved difficult for the Liberal Democrats (and previously the Alliance of Liberals and SDP) to take an exclusive stand on a clearly

marked part of this territory. Yet if the old class based division is declining, it ought to be possible for a third party to identify itself with a new territory and new issues. The success of the Alliance in the 1980s demonstrated the possibilities of such a political development, especially when television could be exploited for the promotion of party leaders.

But the Alliance was destroyed by its own internal disagreements (partly personal but also related to the political orientation of the party); and the revived Liberal Democrats found that the gap between the Thatcher Conservative Party and a Left dominated Labour Party was closing rapidly. By 1992 there was little space left for the Liberal Democrats to colonise. They looked to outsiders like a moderate, sensible Labour Party, not tied to the trade unions – a social democratic party. But both Kinnock's Labour Party and John Major's Conservatives claimed to be just that.

The party manifestos 1992

1 *Labour's general approach*
Foreword to Labour Manifesto by Neil Kinnock [Compare with the extract from John Major's Foreword to the Conservative Manifesto, Document 16.1 c) above]

At the core of our convictions is belief in individual liberty.

We therefore believe:

First, that for liberty to have real meaning the standards of community provision must be high and access to that provision must be wide.

Second, that those rights of the individual must, like all others in a free society, belong to all men and women of every age, class and ethnic origin and be balanced by responsibilities of fair contribution and law-abiding conduct.

Third, that for rights and responsibilities to be exercised fully and fairly, government in Britain, as in other industrialised democracies, must work to build prosperity by properly supporting research, innovation, the improvement of skills, the infrastructure and long-term industrial development.

Our vision for Britain is founded on these values.

2 *The 1992 Manifestos compared*
The Constitution
The Conservative Manifesto has nothing to say directly about the Constitution, but has sections on 'choice and the Charter','Freedom under law' and 'A United Kingdom' – an interesting emphasis concerned with less government and efficient government rather than the shape of institutions.

The Citizen's Charter 'will be at the centre of government's decision-making throughout the 1990s': its aim is informal choice by the citizen as customer of public services, clear performance standards, proper response to complaints and

competition in the public services. 'Whitehall' will be re-organised, devolved, contracted-out or otherwise reduced.

'Freedom under the law' deals mainly with crime. The section on the UK rejects any weakening of the Union. 'Our constitution is flexible, fair and tolerant'.

The Labour Manifesto promises a Charter of Rights, including a bill of rights; a Freedom of Information Act; a Parliament for Scotland, an elected Welsh Assembly, a regional tier of government in England, and a Greater London Authority; a Department of Legal Administration; a Ministry for Women; a new elected Second Chamber; and – here the reformist drive falters – a public debate on the electoral system.

Education
Conservative Further encouragement to schools to become grant-maintained (i.e. opted out of local education authorities), and to vary their character (e.g. becoming grammar or technology schools). More City Technology Colleges. More rigorous testing; less assessed course work. More practical teacher-training. More students in higher education, and an expanded loan scheme.
Labour Spend extra £600m on 2 years of nursery education for all by 2000; reduction of primary classes to 30 or less; more books and equipment. New Advanced Certificate for 18 year olds to include technical subjects. Education Standards Commission. Abolition of selection at 11, assisted places, grant-maintained schools, City Technology Colleges, student loans. Encourage employers to spend on training.
Liberal Democrats Spend extra £2bn within a year; abolition of grant-maintained schools, City Technology Colleges, assisted places. A new 14–19 year old curriculum. Training levy of 2 per cent of payroll for training.

3 *The Liberal Democrat Manifesto 1992*
The Main Themes
The Manifesto begins with a section headed – What Liberal Democrats stand for.
'Liberal Democrats put people first. We aim to create a society in which all men and women can realise their full potential and shape their own successes.... We must change our political system to give the citizen more power and the government less; our economic system to confer power on consumers and to provide employees with a share in the wealth they create; our public service to guarantee choice and dignity to each of

us; and our education system to equip us better for the modern world.

Liberal Democrats recognise the importance of the things we own in private but we also know the value of what we hold in common. We believe that people are at their best as members of communities....

In the economic sphere we know that the free market is the best guarantee of responsiveness to choice and change. But we believe the market should be our servant not our master....'

Much of the Liberal appeal is not markedly different from Conservative and Labour positions; but two points stood out in the campaign:

● constitutional reform, including 'fair voting' (proportional representation), devolution, a Freedom of Information Act and a Bill of Rights
● increasing spending on education by £2bn in the first year, funded by raising income tax by one penny in the pound – a bold move, unlikely to be accepted in the Treasury, towards 'hypothecated' taxes (i.e. objectives specified).

Ideological maps and models

It is clearly relevant for both politicians and political analysts to know how voters receive and respond to the range of political ideas represented by the parties. A simple Left-Right scale however defined is plainly inadequate to encompass the complexity of current political ideas. If challenged we could suggest some measures which indicate leftness or rightness (for example, in economic or social policy, health or education). But some issues are difficult to identify in this directional way, notably attitudes to Europe; perhaps, for example, there should be a Europe/British nationalist dimension?

An alternative approach is to construct a matrix, which give two dimensions and four defined sectors. For example, economic issues can be combined with social and moral issues. The former may be scaled as conservative or radical, and the latter as tough-minded or tender-minded (following Professor Eysenck) We can use attitudes to planning or income redistribution, and generosity of welfare benefits or the death penalty – though already these are not entirely satisfactory as single measures of values and opinion. But having thus reduced complex sets of ideas, we can construct a matrix as in Figure 2. (For this purpose, Thatcherist ideas on the economy are assumed to be 'conservative', rather than 'liberal' in the old Manchester School sense).

Economic issues		
conservative	tough-minded conservatives	tender-minded conservatives
liberal	tough-minded liberals	tender-minded liberals
	tough-minded	tender-minded

social or moral issues

Figure 2 A matrix of political attitudes

The measures indicated could represent the attitudes underlying the 'free economy and strong state' interpretation of Thatcherism, thus allowing for two partial forms of Thatcherism. The matrix can be adapted for other sets of ideas, and in the analysis of sample survey data statistical techniques (factor analysis) are available to identify the grouping of opinion.

The complexity of individual opinion, or more accurately its failure to fit either the analyst's or the politician's categories, was shown in the British Election Study survey of 1983. Taking two measures which were regarded as reasonable reflections of 'class' and 'liberal' values the following table is produced. Note that these were high profile issues in the early 1980s and marginal by the 1990s.

Table 1 A map of ideological position

Proportion of respondents (voters) accepting certain key opinions (N = 3636)		
Nuclear weapons:		
reduce	11	11	12
no change	3	12	18
increase	5	6	23
Nationalised industries: more	no change	sell off

Notice that 6 of the 9 cells are occupied by 11 per cent or more of the voters. However, if the cells are analysed by vote, opinions do fit party positions in a more expected way

EXERCISE
An ideological map

16.6 In which cells would you expect to find the

highest proportions of Conservative and Labour voters? And Liberal/Alliance?

GUIDE TO EXERCISES

16.1 Nothing very much, but consult David Willetts' book.

16.2 Yes – interestingly, this makes a good, short statement about modern Conservatism.

16.3 Yes, of course. In particular, 'facing the cost' of welfare services might be regarded as a nice way of saying 'cutting the services'. Taxes for most people were not reduced by Margaret Thatcher's government. Law and order were not promoted, though there were more and better paid policemen. The third point – about schools – is very odd, but it is interesting that it is so high in the list.

16.4 There is remarkably little change, except for a greater emphasis on the public services.

16.5 For contemporary Conservatism consider what John Major's government has actually done. For the Labour Party, consider its developing position under new leadership. Few party supporters would agree with every point in the summary.

16.6 Conservative voters form the largest proportion of the three cells in the right hand column, while Labour voters predominate in the left hand column; Alliance voters are spread fairly evenly. In the far NW cell 78 per cent were Labour voters; in the SE cell 77 per cent were Conservative voters. The highest number of Alliance voters in one cell are in the top middle cell. Roughly 11 per cent of all voters, divided almost equally among the three parties, are in the central (no change at all) cell.

ASSESSMENT
The end of ideology or the renewal of a Socialist alternative

The political weakness of the Labour Party in Britain and of parties of the left in Europe (even leaving aside the collapse of the rather different phenomenon of Communism in Eastern Europe) raises the question whether there is a political role, and in particular ideological space, for some version or development of a coherent non-Conservative Party.

The question 'Must Labour Lose?' raised after the second consecutive defeat in 1959 seems even more relevant after the fourth consecutive defeat in 1992.

Of course, it may be argued that Britain can do very nicely without the Labour Party. But considerations of democracy and efficiency indicate that at the very least the government should be challenged by an Opposition carrying credibility as an alternative government. The Labour Party could improve its leadership, organisation and campaigning, and as a minimum present itself as better able to manage the present system more effectively than the Conservatives. This does not look very convincing as a potent new appeal to the electorate, for whom the incumbent government, the 'devil you know', is likely to prove attractive. In any case the interesting problem for the analyst of democratic party politics is the question of ideological space or stance.

The traditionalists' diagnosis is that nothing fundamental has changed, and the mission of the post-war Labour Party, whether or not described as Socialist, is still highly relevant. The interests of the workers and the poor remain to be served, market forces need to be checked, public services to be re-vitalised; fairness, even equality, need to be set as overriding goals. Such a diagnosis leads to the 'one more heave' response to the electoral problems of the Labour Party.

A more radical approach rejects this diagnosis as too complacent, too rooted in the past, and not constituting a serious challenge to John Major's new Conservatism, which claims to accept a good deal of the old Labour social agenda, though with a different emphasis and rhetoric. The radical diagnosis emphasises profound social change, the diminution of the old working class and its outlook, and the spread of 'affluence'. Professor Galbraith's thesis of a 'culture of contentment' is accepted: there is now a majority, perhaps two thirds, who are relatively affluent and content, and little disposed to sympathy with, let alone generosity towards, the under-privileged one third, the underclass of old, unemployed, single parents and the like. The newly contented majority is not disposed to be altruistic. Indeed, earlier support for a re-distributive welfare state was based on the self-interest of the still discontented, non-affluent majority. Self-interest is the driving force of society, and Socialism must somehow accommodate itself to selfishness.

This is a neat, plausible but bleak and sweeping analysis. The one third/two thirds division may well over-estimate the size of the contented majority. Insofar as the analysis is valid, then a party of the left has a necessary but difficult task of political education. This is not so much to re-think traditional doctrines, but to re-vitalise the argument, sharpen the rhetoric and rebut the self-interested society. For example, most people are still totally dependent on the public provision of education and health, and no private citizen can provide a safe and clean environment. The case for public services is almost as strong as it was in the days of Victorian municipal Socialism.

There is still much here that could be cheerfully accepted by the wetter sort of Conservative, and perhaps by John Major. Is there still a coherent set of ideas to be constructed left of the soft centre of British politics, or have we at last, and happily for some, arrived at the end of ideology in Britain, democracy without fundamental political conflict? Such a conclusion seems unlikely, given the existence of an underclass of poverty, a good deal of social and inter-ethnic tension, massive and continuing unemployment, shabby and ineffective public services, the problem of Northern Ireland.... There appears still to be relevance if not much vigour and popular acknowledgement in the old agenda of the left.

Moreover, there are some new themes to be explored:

- the individual as an individual, not as a member of a socio-economic group, exercising choice and responsibility, as people are accustomed to do when shopping in supermarkets
- the advantages of the market for the individual: exercise of free choice (though the individual may still need to be protected from exploitation)
- economic opportunity for the individual, to improve the initial distribution of income, rather than to remedy inadequacies and unfairness later, by means of state intervention
- the individual as consumer (replacing Labour's traditional close concern for producers), including the consumption of public services and the environment
- the individual as citizen, exercising rights and

responsibilities in a system of government extending participation and choice into the regions, localities and neighbourhoods
- women in the home and in the workplace, as an undervalued and underprivileged majority.

Some of this looks very attractive, but not very distinctive, so New Socialism may turn out to be quite like New Conservatism. However, one lesson arising from the study of party politics is that there is a remarkable fluidity in the perception of political and social problems, and in public moods relating to them. The task of a party is to catch the mood of the time.

Concepts

Socialism

Socialism has a specific meaning in Marxist thought as the stage of historical development between capitalism and Communism. In its less precise meaning in Western countries and liberal thinking, Socialism still has its origin in the struggle against the oppressive nature of the capitalist economy. Hence it is related to the betterment of the condition of the people, embracing working and living conditions, and striving toward economic equality and political freedom. The characteristic strategy and objective of Socialism is to diminish the power of private capital by the action of the state.

In Britain the Labour Party has historically pursued the Socialist mission, but not without substantial differences about what constituted the essence of Socialism. By the 1990s Socialism did not figure in major public statements about Labour policy, though some Labour leaders still defiantly claimed the historic title.

The nature of Labour's doctrine is indicated in the text. It would seem reasonable to regard Socialism as characteristically concerned with:

- the intervention of the state as the guardian of the worker, the poor and the under-privileged
- such intervention involving acquisition, control or regulation of economic activity
- the re-distribution of income
- all directed towards a greater degree of equality and fairness and the extension of the freedom of the individual.

The latter political aim may be seen as a contradiction of the inevitable increase in state power involved in the achievement of other aims.

Conservatism

Conservatism is even more difficult to pin down than Socialism, but the task may be evaded on the grounds that Conservatism is characteristically pragmatic, and avoids a commitment to ideology. This comes near to proposing the absence of principle as the only tenable principle, but Conservatives have struggled, like Socialists but in a more relaxed way, to lay down some basic ideas.

The term 'Conservatism' is taken to convey, not a literal objection to change, but a respect for custom and tradition and a suspicion of change based on elaborate theory. Conservatives are inclined to pessimism, believing that self-interest is the motive force of individuals. 'If it ain't broke, don't fix it' is a good Conservative motto, based on these understandings of individuals and society.

The text indicates that Conservatism in practice, judged by what Conservative governments do, or aim to do, is much more complex. Socialists and many others would regard the British Conservative Party as essentially the protector of the propertied classes. Margaret Thatcher's 'Free economy and strong state' may be regarded as a logical development of Conservatism against the quasi-socialist 'post-war consensus'; but critics regard it as an aberration, seeing Conservatism as properly concerned for conciliation, the diminution of gross inequality, the care of the less fortunate.

Conservatives do have much less trouble than the Labour Party in re-defining what they stand for; thus differences in approach between the parties are made plain. The Conservative Party is more like a club, the Labour Party like a church. The Conservatives are concerned for membership, facilities, money-raising activities and winning; Labour is concerned for the true faith.

● CASE STUDY
The ideas of the Conservative Party: an anthology

a) The Tory tradition
From Quintin Hogg, 1947, pp.10, 11, 13, 14 and 97
i) Conservatives do not believe that political struggle is the most important thing in life.... The simplest among them prefer fox-hunting – the wisest religion.
ii) The Conservative does not believe that the power of politics to put things right in this world is unlimited.

iii) Conservatism is not so much a philosophy as an attitude.... Indeed history records no example of a fixed political theory, however successful, which does not appear wrong, and even ridiculous, in the eye of succeeding generations.
iv)...private property is to the interest of the community since the desire to obtain it provides an incentive for work which is morally legitimate, and at the same time sufficiently material to operate on natures which in most of us contain certain elements not entirely spiritual or unselfseeking... private property – including some large fortunes – is the natural bulwark of liberty because it ensures that economic power is not entirely in the hands of the State.

b) Moderate Conservatism
i) From Sir Ian Gilmour, speech to Tory Reform Group, 12 October 1983
Without presuming to give an exhaustive, still less an infallible, definition of Toryism, I will briefly mention some of its most relevant features:

● a realisation of the State's duty to protect the weak
● a readiness to use the power of the State to guide the economy and a refusal to leave the steering to market forces alone
● a recognition that in many areas public expenditure is thoroughly desirable
● a prejudice against compulsion and a bias towards agreement
● a willingness to be guided by the real world, which means paying attention to 'circumstance' rather than dogma, adapting policy to facts not vice versa.

ii) From Timothy Raison, Why Conservative?, 1964, pp. 24 and 30
The fundamental injustice of class comes when it deprives any man of the right to make the most of the talents which he may possess.
The Tory party has an instinctive understanding that a government must have authority. Democracy does not work if there is weakness in the centre.

c) Right wing Conservatism
i) Sir John Nott, then a Conservative Minister, 13 September 1982
I am a minimalist. It is the function of governments to remove specified causes of unhappiness. But governments cannot create happiness and they cannot create wealth....

ii) Sir Keith Joseph, 1974

There are limits to the good which governments can do to help the economy, but no limits to the harm.

iii) Michael Portillo, from The Times, September 17 1993

I believe it is the first duty of government to help people to become what they wish to become, to fulfil their potential; above all to be individual and independent. The evil of poverty is that it removes people's choices. They have no opportunity to be independent and so poverty affects not only their way of life but also their spirits and their humanity. It robs them of their dignity.

Christian teaching urges us to be generous and to share our wealth with others. But it does not tell governments that they should be generous with money which is not their own... It is, I believe, a great confusion to stigmatise governments as somehow less Christian if they demur before removing money from people who have earned it, even if the intention is to give it to others. Taxation, by reducing people's disposable income, removes choices which are rightly theirs. By taking money from people in order to provide for their wants, we deny them the right to provide for themselves and their families and to make the moral choice of assisting others.

For many people the role of government has sapped from them – one might almost say confiscated – their sense of responsibility towards other people.... We expect the state to regulate and take full responsibility for everything.... The state must not be allowed to substitute for individual conscience and responsibility.

d) Greed: a Thatcherist analysis
From Peregrine Worsthorne in The Sunday Telegraph, 15 May, 1988

What distinguishes today's greed from the greed of the three preceding decades is that instead of making Britain poorer it has made Britain richer. All human societies are greedy and acquisitive – envy is merely passive greed – and in those moral respects there is not much to choose between them. The difference lies in the use to which greed is put. To my mind Mrs Thatcher has put greed to better use than did her predecessors.... Socialism pretends to be above greed. Capitalism is more honest and open. It admits the importance of greed.

e) Michael Heseltine's interventionist Conservatism
From M. Heseltine, 1990, pp. 5–6

...The laissez faire idealists may hold that all government action, to the extent that it inhibits the free exercise of the citizen's will, must threaten his liberty and weaken his spirit. This is too romantic and impractical a guide for men and women who hold public office, and it has nothing to do with the Tory Party.

Conservative Ministers and their officials, as in all previous governments, today intervene habitually and on an immense scale to limit the citizen's freedom of action and constrain the working of markets, and ordered government would be impossible if they did not. The need, surely, is not to wrestle with making respectable the idea of intervention but to make the reality of it more responsive and effective, so that a whole range of activities which at present seem haphazard and sometimes shamefaced are in future co-ordinated and pursued with conviction. ●

● CASE STUDY
The ideas of the Labour Party

a) The great tradition
From R. H. Tawney, 1952, p. 49

So to criticise inequality and to desire equality is not, as is sometimes suggested, to cherish the romantic illusion that men are equal in character and intelligence. It is to hold that, while their natural endowments differ profoundly, it is the mark of a civilised society to aim at eliminating such inequalities as have their source, not in individual differences, but in its own organisation, and that individual differences, which are a source of social energy, are more likely to ripen and find expression if social inequalities are, as far as practicable, diminished. And the obstacle to the progress of equality ... is the habit of mind which thinks it, not regrettable, but natural and desirable, that different sections of a community should be distinguished from each other by sharp differences of economic status, of environment, of education and culture and habit of life. It is the temper which regards with approval the social institutions and economic arrangements by which such differences are emphasised and enhanced, and feels distrust and apprehension at all attempts to diminish them.

b) Revisionist Socialism

Anthony Crosland, formerly a Fellow of Trinity College, Oxford, was a member of the Labour Governments of 1964 and 1974. This is a brief summary of part of the main argument of Chapters vi–x of *The Future of Socialism*, first published in 1956, dealing with the idea of social equality. The book marked a serious attempt to revise or reinterpret (some might say abandon) socialist ideas.

Crosland contends that the economic welfare argument for equality no longer applies with much force: 'to make the rich less rich would not make the poor significantly less poor'. The case for equality rests now rather on 'certain value or ethical judgements of a non-economic character'. These are:

- the need to diminish social antagonism ('collective resentments')
- the achievement of social justice – equitable rewards for ability and effort; and the diffusion of power
- the avoidance of social waste (barriers to mobility).

Thus far, Crosland's ideal society is one of equality of opportunity, and social mobility. But he accepts that this must be modified to avoid the replacement of the old elite of birth and wealth by a formidable new elite of brains and examination distinctions (meritocracy, as it was called).

c) Modern Socialism

From a statement of the National Executive Committee, March 1960

Labour Aims. The British Labour Party is a democratic socialist party. Its central ideal is the brotherhood of man. Its purpose is to make this ideal a reality everywhere.

i) It stands for social justice, for a society in which the claims of those in hardship or distress come first; where the wealth produced by all is fairly shared among all; where differences in rewards depend not upon birth or inheritance but on the effort, skill and creative energy contributed to the common good; and where equal opportunities exist for all to live a full and varied life.

ii) Regarding the pursuit of material wealth by and for itself as empty and barren, it rejects the selfish, acquisitive doctrines of capitalism, and strives to create instead a social community based on fellowship, co-operation and service in which all can share fully in our cultural heritage.

iii) Its aim is a classless society from which all class barriers and false social values have been eliminated.... ●

The electoral system and the campaign

Political function of elections

Elections and politics

A general election is part of the whole, complex, continuing process of political communication and adjustment, in which government, parties, pressure groups, the mass media and the public are all engaged. It is an important, but not, on its own, a decisive factor in this process. Its importance lies in the making and unmaking of governments, though this occurs at other times too (e.g. 1940, 1963, 1976 and 1990). A general election determines which party shall have power. The leadership of the party and its general policy leanings are evident; policy in detail and in practice has still to be determined. But the name of the party, and hence of the Prime Minister, normally emerges from the election, and is ratified by the process.

The importance of general elections is increased by the regard, even fear, which politicians have for them This is understandable enough, since the electorate is in a sense the politician's employer – a somewhat capricious and stern one at that. The politicians do not fully understand what behaviour alters the judgement of the electorate, so, taking no chances, they assume a politically conscious and censorious electorate, and play to it so far as they can. This process of assuming and allowing for critical judgements has been called the 'law of anticipated reactions' and applies generally in politics (and indeed in life). It accounts, for example, for the playing down of the trade unions in Labour's 1992 campaign, and the Conservative Party's abandonment of its last three Leaders. All were regarded as electoral liabilities. In this way assumptions about the likely relations of political decisions to electoral support endow a general election with substantial influence.

The politicians are certainly right that the general election is for them a kind of employee's review board. They may be right too that the board (the electorate) makes a highly political judgement, based on a closely remembered and well understood record of political performance – after all some political happenings must influence electors' opinions. It seems likely at least, that the temporary events and conditions of the election period engage with longer-term factors, mobilising or countering, developing (in the photographic sense) or wiping out. In any case, general elections are major public events, well-reported, and impinging on the lives of most adults. About three-quarters of the electorate turn out to vote (the figure is lower than in many other western democracies, but much higher than in the USA). General elections raise a certain excitement, as with a major sporting event, ending with massive broadcast programmes going on for half the night. The public perception of politics is thus raised and enhanced.

The scale and intensity of activity during a general election gives the process a further significance. Its outcome is accepted without question and the resulting government gains legitimation and a certain allegiance. In this way, an election is a major political ritual, equivalent to the coronation of the monarch.

The process and the ritual get their intensity from the competition and conflict of an election. This is genuine: important matters are at stake, and partisanship is sharp and bitter. But the contest takes place against a background of comparative cohesion or apathy, in which the intentions of the other side are seen by most electors as not wholly disastrous. Hence the decision of the poll is accepted, and life goes on.

Politics takes place, as it were, in a fenced-off arena, not in the High Street or in Laburnum Grove, the streets where we live.

The frequency and extent of elections

Elections are not as frequent or as extensive in Britain as in, for example, the USA or even France. The proper frequency of elections is a matter of nice judgement. The five-year limit to the duration of a Parliament was laid down in the Parliament Act of 1911. This shortened the interval between elections by two years to compensate for the reduction in the powers of the House of Lords over the Commons. (The people must replace the peers as the guardians of the constitution – so ran the argument.)

In practice, many Parliaments have lasted for much less than five years, and the average interval is well under four years. But many decisions of government, for example on defence and on major public investment, are long-term, and work themselves out over years. Clearly, a government needs time to prove itself, time to govern without undue concern for temporary popularity; time, too, simply to govern. For the object is good government, not continuous answerability to the electorate. The answerability must be frequent enough to be effective: an interval in practice of four years seems about right.

For central government, elections are held for membership of the legislature only. There are no direct elections for the executive, as in the presidential elections of the USA and France, and there are no primary elections within parties to decide on candidates. Elections for local councils and the European Parliament do not have anything like the salience or significance of parliamentary elections.

The first point is a fundamental one in the British system. A Prime Minister has no national constituency of his own, like an American president, and no route to, or source of, power outside the House of Commons. This situation is slightly modified by the nature of general elections, with the party leaders prominent in drawing support to their party.

The doctrine of the mandate

The doctrine of the mandate is the strongest form of the notion that a government draws a set of instructions from a general election. A programme, both general and particular, has been submitted to the electorate, and winning a majority indicates popular approval for carrying the programme out. This is the mandate, which includes an element of command (a precise instruction) and a weaker element of trust (do as you think fit on these general lines). Governments may justify unpopular policies by reference to the 'mandate', while oppositions and restive supporters complain of 'broken promises' and novel policies; or, in the case of a government with a small majority, say that it has no mandate at all.

The democratic theory, British version, is in outline fairly clear. A general election would be meaningless if it included no presentation of policies. What takes place is in a crude way equal to a conversation or dialogue: the elector is given an opportunity to acquaint himself with party policies before casting his vote. The difficulty lies in delimiting the process. Should a party present its policies in practical detail? (Too little means an ill-informed elector, too much an over-committed party.) Should the party feel bound in all circumstances by its campaign presentations? (Again the dilemma of meaningless choice or over-commitment.) Is a party bound to present to the electorate all the options, and its own choices, as it sees them? If a major issue arises after the election, what then? What about the constitutional morality of 'winner-takes-all' – should the majority party, whatever its mandate, take account of the minority (actual majority) views? In Britain the answer is, No!

In theory, the status of the mandate would seem to be this: some relationship between party programme and government action is necessary, but a close and detailed mandate is not essential for democratic politics. The mandate may lead to mistaken policies through commitment of a party prior to its engagement with the problem as a government. On the other hand, most policies gain from subjection to extensive and critical discussion. Moreover, there is a good case for the mandate as a necessary support to 'grassroots' power in political parties, and hence to party democracy – as radical activists in the Labour Party have argued. For them the mandate is a contract with the party, not the electorate.

The more limited view of the mandate is supported by some practical considerations. The electorate as a whole is not really sophisticated enough to give an informed judgement on, say, the devaluation of the pound or British nuclear strategy; nor could it be enlightened about such matters in the course of one election campaign.

Political parties cannot foresee in detail which (if any) of their policies will be practicable or even appropriate. The movement of events and ideas abroad as well as at home, and the activities of individuals and of masses, seem to determine a large part of government policy.

There are many historical examples of this. The welfare state owes a good deal to Lloyd George, Winston Churchill and two wars – not to a party with a programme. Economic policy often seems to be an improvisation in the face of crisis. In recent years both parties have reversed apparently firm policies (the U-turn). Social and health expenditure is affected by the survival of old people, and the invention of new medical technology. For this kind of reason it is probably impractical as well as undesirable that a political party should feel bound closely to every item of a detailed mandate.

This rather soft view of the mandate appeals to party leaders and Ministers, but is less acceptable to party members in the constituencies, particularly those who are dedicated, hard-working and passionately interested in political ideas and policy. These are the 'activists' whose enthusiasms make life difficult for those in power. For them the mandate is hard; it is their hold on their leaders. Hence they will fight over the contents of the party's election manifesto, which becomes the mandate. The more democratic a party claims to be in its internal arrangements, the more seriously it must take its manifesto-mandate.

The referendum
The referendum is a form of the election mandate. A specific question is posed and the government responds to the electorate's expressed wish. Clearly this does not fit the 'soft' tradition of the general election mandate; nor does it fit the constitutional theory of responsible government. So it is surprising that the Labour Government of 1974–9 held two referenda, on membership of the EEC and, in Scotland and Wales only, the establishment of assemblies (devolution). These were not entirely without precedent: there had been referenda on local matters, on the opening of public houses on Sundays in Wales (held every seven years), and on the Northern Ireland border (1973). Still the two major referenda were a marked constitutional departure.

Explanation is easier than justification. Both these issues, membership of the EEC and devolution, cut across party ideology and

loyalties. The referenda were an appeal to a higher authority; the people's will would be accepted and the unity of the party maintained. The justification lay in the need to secure a firm and legitimate decision on a constitutional matter on which there was no apparent national or party consensus. It should be added that the Labour Party had said in its election manifestos in 1974 that it would negotiate the terms of British accession to the EEC and submit the results to the people at the election or in a consultative referendum. So the government had a 'mandate' for its constitutional innovation.

In the event the referenda of 1975 and 1979 did not work well. The EEC issue was settled for a time, but within a few years public opinion wavered and the Labour Party committed itself to withdrawal. The issue was decided again by the defeat of the Labour Party in the election of 1983. The devolution referendum of 1979 settled that question in Wales where the government's proposals were heavily rejected. In Scotland there was a small majority in favour of an assembly, but the 'Yes' vote did not pass the 40 per cent limit which had been set as a minimum. So the Scotland Act fell. It seemed the government had organised a popular veto to defeat its own proposals in which it only half believed. The proponents of devolution had been given their chance and failed. But the issue did not go away, and was back on the political agenda in the 1990s.

Opponents of EEC membership and devolutionists might well feel that their cases had not been given an entirely fair hearing. Constitutionalists might wonder how the principle of parliamentary responsibility could be breached so lightly. The first objections are raised in the following exercise; the latter are considered in an Assessment in Chapter 18.

EXERCISE
The referendum as the verdict of the people

17.1 Why should opponents of EEC membership and devolutionists feel that the referendum had been unfair?

The alternation of parties
General elections bring about changes of the party in power. In constitutional theory this figures as an alternation, but the common description of it as a 'swing of the pendulum' is inaccurate. Table 1 shows the governments of Britain by party and Prime Minister.

EXERCISE
The swing of the pendulum

17.2 What is wrong with the idea of a pendulum?

The pendulum theory of British politics does not fit much of political history in the twentieth century, and lost the remnants of its credibility in the 1992 election. The half century between 1945 and 1995 will have included only 19 years of non-Conservative government, and only 9 years when Labour had a working majority. The failure of the pendulum theory is highly significant for the British constitution, since the democratic quality of the constitution depends so much on the opposition as an alternative government (see also Chapter 3).

The electoral system

Dissolution of Parliament
The decision to hold an election is taken by the Prime Minister subject only to the five-year limit on Parliaments. He or she may, of course, consult anyone at all, but some Prime Ministers (not John Major) have tended to keep this matter to themselves. The decision will be formulated as advice to the Queen to dissolve Parliament – advice which the monarch can not normally refuse to accept; nor can she insist on a dissolution (see Case Study in Chapter 3).

Since political parties have had to face a mass and virtually incorruptible electorate, the time of a dissolution has been a difficult tactical exercise. Prime Ministers have naturally been concerned

Table 1 Parties in power in Britain since 1900

General election	Party in power	Prime Minister (date of formation of government)	General election	Party in power	Prime Minister (date of formation of government)
Oct. 1900	Con	Salisbury (Jun. 1895) Balfour (July 1902)	Nov. 1935	Con	Baldwin (Nov. 1935) Chamberlain (May 1937)
Jan. 1906 (Dec.1905)	Lib.	Campbell-Bannerman Asquith (May 1908)		Coalition Con. ('Caretaker')	Churchill (May 1940) Churchill (May 1945)
Jan. 1910 Dec. 1910	Coalition	Asquith (May 1915) Lloyd George (Dec.1916) Lloyd George (Jan. 1919)	Jul. 1945 Feb. 1950	Lab.	Attlee (Aug. 1945) Attlee (Mar. 1950)
Nov. 1922	Con	Bonar Law (Oct. 1922) Baldwin (May 1923)	Oct. 1951 May 1955 Oct. 1959	Con	Churchill (Oct. 1951) Eden (April 1955) Macmillan (Jan. 1957) Douglas-Home (Oct. 1963)
Dec. 1923	Lab.	MacDonald (Jan. 1924)	Oct. 1964	Lab.	Wilson (Oct. 1964)
Aug. 1924	Con.	Baldwin (Nov. 1924)	Jun. 1970	Con.	Heath (Jun. 1970)
May 1929 Oct. 1931	Lab. Coalition	MacDonald (Jun. 1929) MacDonald (Aug. 1931) Baldwin (Jun. 1935)	Feb. 1974 Oct. 1974	Lab.	Wilson (Mar. 1974) Callaghan (Apr. 1976)
			May 1979 Jun. 1983 Jun. 1987	Con	Thatcher (May 1979) Thatcher (Jun. 1983) Thatcher (Jun. 1987) Major (Nov. 1990)
			Apr. 1992		Major (Apr. 1992)

The horizontal lines indicate a change in the party in power. Dates after name of Prime Minister are dates of formation of the government for the electoral prospects of their party. The pursuit of Keynesian economic policies has usually enabled the government to provide some economic improvements, at least a sense of well-being, before an election. In some cases the manipulation of the economy for electoral purposes has been blatant. Only one Chancellor, Roy Jenkins, in 1970, abstained from this modern form of corruption. In 1992 the Chancellor claimed that the economy was in a better state than turned out to be the case, and the govern-ment committed itself to unusually generous public spending before the election.

The choice of date for the election has also been made easier by the application of sample survey techniques, and the publication of 'polls' of voters' intentions. These are not an infallible guide, especially when the parties are close, the voters volatile and inclined to deceive the pollsters and perhaps themselves too about their true voting intentions. In 1970 electoral calculations went wrong; in 1992 time ran out for the government but it won nevertheless. In most elections the Prime Minister and his advisers are able to pick a favourable time for the election; hence incumbency is an important factor in elections and electoral behaviour.

EXERCISE
Fixed terms for Parliament?

17.3 Is there a case for introducing fixed terms for Parliament?

The franchise
The franchise (the right to vote) formerly inhered in property, not in persons. By a series of Reform Acts in the nineteenth century, the vote was given to householders, but the electorate in 1910 still numbered under eight million, little more than one quarter of the adult population. The Representation of the People Act of 1918 extended the vote to all men on the principle of residence, and to women over 30 on the principle of occupation of land or premises worth at least five pounds annually (or being married to such an occupier). Occupation implied payment of rates on property and is of course more limiting than residence – apart from campers and tramps, we all reside (and in 1983 even the Greenham Common peace campers were adjudged to be resident and entitled to vote). The reform of 1918 almost trebled the electorate – to over 21 million at one stroke, three quarters of the adult population. In

1928 the franchise for women was assimilated to that for men – being over 21, and 'residence'. The voting age was reduced to 18 in 1969 and the electorate grew from 36 million in 1966 to 39 million in 1970 and 43 million in 1992.

The old Chartist aim of the 1830s, 'One man one vote' was finally achieved in 1949, for men and women. Until then two classes of person had an extra vote: university graduates and occupiers of business premises. University graduates voted in special constituencies of universities. Most university Members of Parliament were somewhat independent Conservatives, with, notably in 1945, a number of genuine Independents. A few, like A. P. Herbert, made a distinguished contribution to the work of the Commons. There were no Labour university MPs.

EXERCISES
'Fancy' franchises

17.4 What justification do you see for university and business votes? Is your justification sufficient?
17.5 Would you regard any other 'fancy' franchises as justified?

The ballot system
The ballot system employs simple plurality in single-member constituencies. This is the first-past-the-post system, in which the contestant with the most votes wins the seat. It is the simplest of all electoral systems, and some would say the crudest. In two-member constituencies (common until 1885; a remaining 15 abolished in 1948), the crudity of the system was modified because two votes gave the elector a greater range of choice – you could vote for both parties if you wanted to. In practice the voter was often deprived of any choice at all by agreement between the parties to share the seats and avoid an election altogether. Since 1945, virtually all seats have been contested and the elector has had a choice – if a rough one.

The effect of the ballot system is normally to over-represent, in terms of seats won, what may be quite small majorities in votes, and seriously to under-represent minority votes. Thus in a constituency of 60 000 with 50 000 voting and two candidates, a vote of 25 001 secures the seat, and 24 999 voters are left unrepresented. With three candidates it is theoretically possible for a vote of one third of the electors, plus one, to secure the seat, and winning on a minority vote is quite common. With a substantial third party vote the

Table 2 Election results October 1974, 1983 and 1992

| | 1974 (Oct.) | | 1983 | | 1992 | |
Party	% of seats	% of votes	% of seats	% of votes	% of seats	% of votes
Con.	43.5	36	61	42	52	42
Lab.	50	39	32	28	42	34
Lib. (All. 1983)	2	18	3.5	25	3	18

effect is magnified: in 1983 over half of Members were elected on a minority. In 1992, the remote Scottish seat of Inverness, Nairn and Lochaber, was held by the Liberal Democrats with a record low of 26.0 per cent of the vote, in a four party contest in which each party gained about one quarter of the vote.

The effect may be seen in the election results of October 1974, 1983 and 1992.

Table 2 shows clearly the exaggeration of a majority and the under-representation of a minority party. The result in 1983 was particularly unjust. The Sunday Times said: 'No general election result in this country since universal suffrage has been so flagrantly unfair. The Prime Minister sits in triumph in Downing Street not on a surge of popular support but as the result of unjust electoral arrangements' (12 June 1983). It should be noted that a proportional distribution of seats might have led in all three cases to coalition government; that seems to represent the wishes of voters 'as a whole', but not necessarily the wishes of most voters.

The system does not often change the overall result of the election; it simply hands out bigger

prizes to the winners, and bigger penalties to the losers. The elections of 1951 and 1974 (Feb.) were exceptional in that the overall majority was due to the system and the quirks of the distribution of votes within it, and not to a movement of opinion on the part of the British people. If this happened more often, the two major parties would be more interested in changing the system. (The Conservatives gained less from the system in 1992, due to tactical voting.)

The distortions that arise locally, and the impact of reform, can be illustrated in the results for the County of Suffolk in 1992 (see Table 3).

EXERCISE
Voting in Suffolk 1992

17.6 Calculate votes per seat in the existing and proportionate system, and comment.

The defects of the system are significant enough to give rise to a persistent movement for electoral reform, especially among Liberals who lose most by the system. Defenders of the system argue that the unfairness is occasional and not too serious;

Table 3 Voting in Suffolk in 1992

Total vote	386090	% of vote 100	seats	redistributed proportionately*
Conservative	192333	50	5	3
Labour	110665	29	1	2
Liberals	78683	20	0	1

*But it should be understood that in a different system electors would vote differently.

that it makes for single party majority government chosen by the people, rather than a coalition arranged by politicians; and that the smaller parties simply have to grow beyond a threshold. Reformers believe the present system to give rise to unacceptable injustice and they do not see coalition government as at all undesirable.

Schemes of reform have won official support in the past, for example, in an all-party Speaker's Conference in 1918, and in votes of the House of Commons in 1918 and again 1931. Those who win power by the existing system have little incentive to change it. But the Liberal Democrats and recently the Labour Party are attracted to reform on grounds both of justice and self-interest.

A completely proportional system would require a national list of candidates, to be elected in a prescribed order for a certain quota of votes. Such a system would destroy the territorial constituency system, and pose difficult problems in drawing up the lists; it would also mean that any party or group which could collect, say, 50 000 votes out of the whole of the country would secure a seat in Parliament. This prospect frightens some people and delights others.

However, there are ballot systems which secure a measure of proportional representation within a constituency system. These involve preferential voting and either eliminative counting (the alternative vote) or quota counting (single transferable vote – STV). In the alternative vote system, votes for candidates at the bottom of the poll are redistributed according to the second or subsequent preferences. In the STV system a five or seven member constituency is used and candidates are elected as they reach a minimum quota of votes. It is feasible to use a mixed system as in Germany – half by simple plurality, half by PR from a national list. One form of this, the Additional Member System, has been widely canvassed as the main alternative to STV.

The Liberals are committed to the introduction of a system of proportional representation, and advocate a system of 'Community Proportional Representation', which is, in effect, the Single Transferable Vote (STV) within 'natural communities' varying between one and eight members (mostly 3–6). The Labour Party has established a study group, and so far favours a form of proportional representation for Scotland and for Europe, and even for a reformed House of Lords, but is uneasy about reform for the House of Commons.

EXERCISES
Proportional representation

17.7 It helps the appreciation of the problems and possibilities of PR to organise and take part in an election on these lines. You can vote in this way for a students' representative body, or for the most (or the three most) popular television programmes or what you will. The ballot form must provide for voting in order of preference, 1, 2, 3 etc. In counting, eliminate the candidate with the least number of first choices and redistribute the vote according to next preferences. Alternatively, where several places are to be filled, first determine the quota:

$$\frac{\text{no. of electors}}{\text{no. of places} + 1} + 1$$

Then in counting, redistribute surplus votes (votes above the quota) according to the second preference of all the votes for that candidate – and so on until all places are filled by candidates reaching the quota.

Compare the results with those obtained by counting first preferences on a simple majority basis. Note that a different ballot system may elicit different electoral behaviour. For a true comparison it is therefore necessary to hold a completely new election by the other ballot system.

17.8 What do you see as the main advantages and disadvantages of proportional representation?

The case for reform

The case for reform rests largely on the preferred form of party government, for there is little doubt that proportional representation leads to the strengthening of 'third' parties and coalition as the basis for majority government. The advantages and disadvantages of coalition government were reviewed in Chapter 15. Much depends on the claim that the present system provides 'strong and decisive' government. The claim may be contested on the grounds that it is ill-defined; not an exclusive consequence of the simple plurality electoral system; and that it is in any case undesirable (consider the Poll Tax; what about consensus?). The Conservatives may claim with more justification that the present system provides accountability since the voters normally choose the government, and that the single-member constituency of about 60 000 voters is a valuable part of our political arrangements (sceptics think it is greatly over-valued).

The reformers have on their side the persisting failure of the first-past-the-post system to reflect adequately what has become a multi-party system. The ultimate argument is that without reform Britain is blessed with, or condemned to, permanent single-party Conservative government. Should even Conservatives think that might not be a good thing?

The debate on proportional representation is necessarily complex. A voting system must have several qualities.

- 'Fairness' related to individual voters, groups (e.g. women, ethnic minorities) and regions.
- 'Comprehensibility' to the ordinary voter, though the voter need not understand the detailed counting procedures.
- Effective choice of government (proportional representation may remove choice of government to inter-party negotiation 'behind closed doors').
- Accountability of elected to electors (the single member constituency is valued in this respect).

■ DOCUMENT 17.1
Alternative voting systems

The main systems proposed are as follows.

1 Simple plurality or first-past-the-post – only used now in countries with historical links with Britain.
  Advantages: clarity, accountability, discourages small parties.
  Disadvantages: unfair to third parties, many votes are 'wasted', majority government not guaranteed.
2 Single transferable vote (STV) – the quota system (see Exercise 17.7), used in Ireland, where it was introduced by the British government, in Northern Ireland for European elections, and for university MPs until 1948; advocated by Liberal Democrats and many reformers. Requires larger, multi-member constituencies.
  Advantages: proportional within a constituency, but not helpful to very small parties (with less than 15–20 per cent of vote); voters have choice of candidates within same

party.
  Disadvantages: does not guarantee a proportional vote nationally; bad for small parties; encourages cross-party voting and so damages party solidarity (a disadvantage?); destroys much-loved single member constituency.
3 Alternative voting (AV) – preferential voting with bottom candidate eliminated (as in Exercise 17.7). Used in Australia and (by second ballot) in France.
  Advantages: no wasted votes, all candidates elected by a majority.
  Disadvantages: elevates second preferences above first and might still leave non-Conservative voters in Suffolk and non-Labour voters in Glasgow under-represented.
4 Additional Member System (AMS) – used in Germany. Combines single member constituency, which can retain simple plurality, with a second vote for a party list. Seats are adjusted to secure proportionality.
  Advantages: proportional; flexible – system can be adjusted between the two groups of seats.
  Disadvantages: gives power to large parties in drawing up lists; constituencies are single-member but large; one class of Member is accountable to party rather than constituency.
  AMS encourages small parties which may be a disadvantage (extreme parties) or an advantage (ethnic or 'green' parties).
5 List system – voters choose a party list: there is absolute proportionality, but the system relates to party lists, not to territorial constituencies. To counteract the proliferation of small parties, a threshold is used but this is only one per cent in Israel and the Netherlands. Most countries use regional lists with much higher thresholds (Spain, Portugal and Greece). ■

EXERCISE
Systems of proportional representation (PR)

17.9 Which system do you prefer and why?

The boundaries of constituencies
Under the single ballot simple plurality system the drawing of the boundaries of the constituency is crucial. The inclusion of, say, a rural area with part of a city can swing a seat from Labour; the addition of a city centre to a residential suburb

can move a seat from the Conservatives. In a highly stable system in which two thirds of the seats are safe for one party, the redrawing of boundaries is a major element of instability and an alarming professional hazard for the MP.

The old Chartist ideal of 'equal electoral districts' has been accepted in principle since 1885. With continuing rapid social change, notably the recent growth of suburbs, regular and radical redistribution is essential. Thus, for example, in 1989 the new town of Milton Keynes had grown to over 100 000, over 30 000 above the average size for English constituencies, and it was unusually divided into two for the 1992 election. (This explains why there are currently 651 Members of Parliament.)

Under legislation consolidated in 1986 re-distribution is carried out by four boundary commissions for each of the countries of Great Britain. The commissions include the Registrar-General and the Director of the Ordnance Survey, and are chaired by the Speaker, but the work is done by civil servants, with the help of professional advice and public submissions. Redistribution now occurs at intervals of eight to twelve years. A generous allowance of seats is provided for Scotland and Wales, and a few for Northern Ireland (which had its own Parliament for home affairs until 1972). The Commission aims to keep the number of electors in each constituency as near as possible to the quota. Local government boundaries are respected where possible.

The Commissioners have a difficult task, and have not escaped accusations of gerrymandering, that is, shaping constituencies with an eye to political advantage. This is not the case, at least as far as the commissioners are concerned and their work is a remarkable illustration of the capacity of British public life for incorruptibility. By contrast, gerrymandering is a normal part of American political life. But the political parties resist vigorously any damage to their interests, and deals with other parties are not unknown. Inevitably many constituencies have odd shapes and obscure names.

The British tradition of incorruptibility of public life is in fact always vulnerable to the pressures of party advantage. In 1969 the Labour government rejected most of the Commission's recommendations. The justification offered was the pending reform of local government boundaries, but it seems fairly clear that electoral calculations were involved. The revised constituency boundaries were accepted after the 1970 election and may well have been slightly unfavourable to Labour.

The revision which came into force for the 1983 election was the most sweeping ever. There were 650 seats in the new Parliament, an increase of 15, and almost 600 were redrawn, 541 by more than 5 per cent. The redistribution was to the advantage of the Conservatives, since Labour lost some of its safe but depopulated inner city seats. In this way, the new boundaries reflected demographic change and that change was against Labour. In addition, the over-representation of Scotland and Wales was retained, and extended (favouring Labour), and Northern Ireland was allocated 17 seats. The redistribution due in the 1990s will for good demographic reasons be unfavourable to Labour, and for that reason is unlikely to be delayed by the Conservative government.

The nature of the campaign

This section is mainly concerned with the way in which a political appeal is made to the elector; the next chapter, on electoral behaviour, deals with the voter's response to that appeal.

The significance of the campaign

There is continuing uncertainty about the significance of the campaign in the voter's decision. In the 1950s and 1960s it seemed that a substantial proportion of voters were 'stable partisans', solid loyalists over a lifetime. The prime object of the campaign was to motivate these loyalists and 'get out the vote'; secondly, to capture a small group of 'floating voters', and only thirdly to convert opponents. The candidates themselves were never entirely convinced of this view. Voters might after all waver in their loyalty, a few, but enough to be decisive. If the voters were once at least fairly stable, by the 1970s and 1980s they were plainly less so: volatility replaced stability. Opinion polls showed up much greater movements of voting intention than were evident in the election itself. Third party voting increased substantially. Surveys revealed that about one fifth or more of the vote moved during the campaign.

In these conditions the election campaign should have been crucial. Curiously in the 1983 election, which registered a massive movement of votes since the previous election, the overall result of the election was foretold in the earliest polls, and throughout the campaign. The campaign itself seemed to make little difference; the volatile electorate was struck by a paralysis.

Moreover, small movements in voting made less difference than before, since the number of marginal seats had declined. Altogether, the conclusion for the political analyst is that volatility is not quite the word for electoral movement: there are strong movements in a sticky medium, and no bounce. For the politician the safe assumption is that opinion may move at any time, including an election campaign; the campaign is at least the cashing of a credit balance built up over the years.

The campaign cannot be separated from the continuing activity of political argument and appeal. It is a brief but intense part of that activity, in which the audience for politics is at its maximum. This was evident in the two years preceding the 1992 election. The election campaign proper runs from the announcement of dissolution to polling day, a period of about four weeks. The expectation of an election may give an electoral atmosphere to much longer periods. It is likely that in the pattern of political activity these pre-election periods are as important as the campaign in the determination of the vote, and in practice there are three campaigns, the permanent campaign, the medium-term and the pre-election.

The pre-election campaign is significant in shifting or confirming votes, and in providing a procedure or ritual for choosing a government, and for registering and legitimating that choice. It follows that we should expect the campaign to display the minimal qualities of high purpose, seriousness and rationality appropriate to a mature democracy. If we make some allowance for the limits of interest and understanding of the voters, the ambitions, self-deceptions, and desire for power of the politicians, and the dominance of television and a philosophy of political marketing, then the expectation of these minimal qualities will not be high.

The campaign in the constituency

The campaign is a national campaign organised by the parties centrally, and played out by the national leaders on platforms provided in effect by the London-based media, especially television. The movement and speeches of the leaders are well-reported; further material is fed to press and broadcasters through specially arranged press conferences. In addition, party leaders figure prominently in the special party political broadcasts. The voter in the constituencies is much more likely to see a party leader for a few minutes on television than to hear his own local candidate; though there is a good chance that he will read at least one of the election addresses sent out by the candidates. The candidates do indeed prosecute vigorous campaigns in the constituencies, addressing meetings, speaking on street corners and outside factory gates, calling on voters, encouraging the party workers. All this is very impressive, considering that three-quarters of candidates have no chance of success at all; of the rest, three-quarters will win anyway, and for the last quarter of hopefuls the result seems to depend mainly on the national campaign..

So why does it go on? The rational answer is that no election is won or lost until the votes are cast, and getting the vote out is in part a local street-by-street job. In conditions of electoral volatility, it is assumed that the local campaign has some influence. There is evidence that votes may be affected by the quality and appeal of candidates (especially the sitting Member), the thoroughness of canvassing, and the organisation of the postal and overseas vote, which may be worth 2 per cent of the vote in some constituencies. (The Conservative overall majority in 1992 depended on 11 seats won by less than 600 votes.)

The shift of even a few hundred votes can be decisive in marginal seats; and the loss or gain of a few seats is decisive in narrowly balanced Parliaments. Further, it is clear that the local campaign is a necessary element in the national campaign, alerting people to the campaign and relating it to their locality, for a local connection is always a vital ingredient in news value. The local campaign enhances interest and information, and involves the citizen in a crucial political ritual.

In the nineteenth century elections were notoriously corrupt, voters were bribed and intimidated and huge sums spent on securing a seat. The average sum spent in each contested constituency by the Conservative Party in the 1880s seems to have been £2–3000, equivalent now to perhaps £100 000. Expenditure on this scale, and the corruption that went with it, has now been eliminated. All kinds of undue influence are illegal, and a candidate must avoid even casually buying a meal or a drink for a voter not actually working for him. Expenditure is restricted to about £7–8000 in counties and less in boroughs. The candidate is also entitled to some personal expenses. These are very severe limits. They are generally observed, though skilled management and accountancy make for some latitude.

These limitations apply only to the constituency and the campaign period, thus excluding the much larger sums spent by the national parties on poster and other advertising in between and during elections. In that way, financial resources still have some influence on the conduct of elections, and possibly on their outcome. The Conservatives maintain many more agents than other parties and spend far more on electoral activity (see Chapter 15 for a full consideration of party finance). It may be too that the resources of party supporters – cars, telephones, leisure – count for a little. On the other hand, broadcasting is shared between the parties without regard for money. British elections are not now corrupt in the nineteenth-century sense, but undue influences may arise from differences in resources and the operations of the mass media. Such possibilities are discussed below.

The presentation of policies

A general election elicits a great flood of propaganda for the parties – the manifestos and major speeches of the national party leaders, the addresses and speeches of the candidates, broadcasts and articles, leaflets and posters. It is impossible to encompass this mass of material easily in formal analysis, though the election surveys (co-authored by David Butler and published by Macmillan) attempt to do this for parts of the material (manifestos, addresses, broadcasts, posters). A general impression of the material may be obtained by reading one or more of the surveys, or better, by experiencing a general election 'live'.

The party manifestos are significant among the piles of election literature, not because they are widely read, or even readable, but because they represent the party's deliberate election appeal, its general outlook and orientation and more specific programme and policy commitments. These are expressed in language designed both to cover disagreements within the party and to appeal to the people.

The titles of the 1992 manifestos give the flavour: 'The Best Future for Britain', 'It's time to get Britain working again', 'Changing Britain for Good' (which parties are these?). Only Labour did not feature a picture of the Leader on the cover. Few people read these manifestos. They are quoted during the campaign sometimes more by opponents. They may enshrine major policy commitments, sometimes bitterly fought over, and do not shrink from promising all things to all men and women (not to mention animals). Statistics are manipulated shamelessly (e.g. by the choice of base dates or design of diagrams).

Through the hastily drafted, redrafted and amended language emerge some major and relevant themes. Labour repeated in 1983 its old commitment to a 'fundamental and irreversible shift in the balance of power and wealth in favour of working people and their families'. The Conservatives referred to Britain's having 'recaptured much of her old pride', and offered a basic Tory philosophy: 'It is not for the government to dictate how men and women should organise their lives.'

In 1992 all parties promised to improve public services, the Conservatives while reducing taxes, Labour and Liberal Democrats by putting taxes up. Labour repeated that many of its promises would be delivered only 'when resources allow'. None of this was dishonest. Indeed the debate on public expenditure and taxation was more extensive, candid and even honest than in previous elections, though the Conservatives misrepresented Labour's tax plans, and their own performance in government did not match their stated intentions. Yet the room for manoeuvre was very narrow, and a sceptical observer might still doubt whether there could be any significant improvement in public services without much more radical change than any party dared to contemplate (much lower unemployment, reduced defence expenditure, phasing out of tax privileges for mortgagors and private pensioners....).

The election propaganda of the parties is both seriously political and relevant, but is also highly partisan and softened and sweetened for popular consumption. This is evident in the national campaigns conducted mainly through the media. The harsher words of politics are avoided – the Labour Party favours families and fair shares, not socialism, the Conservative Party stands for the nation, responsibility, choice and free enterprise – and also families – not the virtues of hard work, 'getting on' and income differentials. Parties present themselves as capable and 'national', avoiding awkward problems and specific policies. Incumbent parties especially like to stand as 'the government', serving the national interest and almost above politics.

In recent elections the promotion of the personality of the leader through visits, 'walkabouts' and other media events has restricted the number of major political speeches, and hence serious political ideas. Even so, political parties do from time to time put forward policy proposals which are not designed to be universally popular. In 1983 Labour made a highly political appeal, aimed well to the left of the middle ground. In 1992 both Labour and Liberal Democrats were committed to the raising of taxes to maintain and improve public services. Their fate will not encourage others to move far from the middle ground, where issues are softened and the spotlight plays on the Leader.

Political marketing

In modern election campaigns the politicians yield substantial influence to marketing professionals, who package and present the politics by the standards and techniques of commercial advertising. In Britain broadcasting time is allocated and not open to purchase; and the form and length of the Party Election Broadcasts discourages some of the crudity of the 15–30 second advertisement. Nevertheless, political campaigns now reflect all the skills and most of the salesman's ethics of the advertising profession. This is true for all parties; the only difference is that the Conservatives can spend twice as much as Labour, and both far outspend any other party.

All political campaigns involve marketing, advertising and public relations. Queen Elizabeth I was an early skilled practitioner of public relations and it has done much for her 'Gloriana' reputation. Gladstone and Lloyd George knew a good deal about appealing to public opinion, and both were skilled and shameless in emotional appeals to mass meetings. Most of this was regarded as acceptable, though the Fascist dictators went to far greater lengths, with the aid of new amplification equipment, to manipulate the mass meeting.

In Britain doubts about the possible corruption of politics by the use of the techniques of advertising developed in the 1950s, especially with the coming of television. The ethics of political marketing raise difficult questions. It is easy to make the extreme cases: political marketing is wicked, or politics in a mass democracy is the art of persuasion.

Here it is assumed simply that there are degrees of propriety in advertising, ranging from the perfectly acceptable to the deplorable. The criteria of legitimacy and impropriety must clearly relate to the methods as well as the political content and reasonableness of the appeal. The nature of the criteria, and the difficulty of defining and applying them, may appear from the following exercises.

EXERCISES

Advertising as legitimate political campaign or improper manipulation?

17.10 Is the hiring of a commercial public relations firm to manage a party's election campaign:
- improper in itself
- likely to lead to improper advertising
- a serious diminution of the political nature of the campaign
- a sensible attempt to improve the party's propaganda?

17.11 There are illustrations of election posters in the Nuffield surveys, published by Macmillan. There may be a poster campaign on now. Consider some examples of political posters and say whether you regard any of them as making an improper appeal.

■ DOCUMENT 17.2
Criticism of advertising in politics

a) From Henry Fairlie, Daily Mail, 9 June 1960
The Conservatives at the last election treated the electors as conditioned morons, who could be won by the methods used by commercial advertisers on TV.... This was my first criticism of the Conservatives at the last election. My second was that they had introduced into British politics a professionalism which should be automatically rejected by anyone who cares for the health of a free society.

b) From The Times, 22 April 1965
The real risk is that we are moving towards the day when market research, opinion poll findings, techniques of motivational persuasion and public relations and even the analyses of political scientists will be crudely and cold-bloodedly used to govern party strategies in government and out.

When that day comes – sometimes it already seems to be here – the point of politics will not be the conviction of politicians about the rightness of their principles, policies or beliefs. It will be to discover the degree of prejudice or gullibility in the electors.

The point of leadership will not be to lead, but to follow the crowd. ■

The Document indicates anxieties current as the television marketing of politics was developing in Britain. Such anxieties about advertising, market research and professional public relations in politics may exaggerate the potential of the persuasion industry. People go on worrying about wages, prices, housing and peace, whatever the persuaders say; and the evidence of the wage packet, the shopping basket or the mortgage statement is immediate, powerful and convincing. The persuaders have a hard task. Moreover, they may have difficulty in exploiting the full power of their propaganda machines. The politicians may insist on using their own judgement; they may well be concerned for their political principles; they may be distracted, ill-prepared and inefficient. In short, they will act for some of the time like people and politicians, not like the powerful propagandists they might be.

All the same, advertising pays in commerce, and it pays in politics too if the advertiser has a moderately good product which fills a perceived need. Advertising can change the perception of need and enhance the appreciation of the product. But advertising cannot carry a certain loser to victory.

The ethical question hangs over the modern campaign, partly because of its high cost, partly because politicians retain political principles, and insist on some independence from the marketing professionals; also because the voter too may resist the most blatant manipulation. But there is another reason for the prevalence of ethical doubts: the media themselves, while reporting the campaign as presented to them by the parties (far beyond the call of fairness), do at the same time encourage scepticism by showing the marketing techniques as well as its product. For example, the cameras draw back to show that the leader is simply posing for 50 photographers, or that the crowd of eager voters is in fact a carefully corralled handful. In this way the media signal to the viewer that he or she is watching a carefully planned marketing operation, not spontaneous politics.

Media events

In the 1960s daily press conferences replaced the major speech as the target for the media. Now the media event has challenged the press conference. The media event is the happening which is arranged for the media, especially the television cameras, and has little justification apart from that. Hence it is timed to suit the networked news programmes, and is designed to look well on film, and of course to show the politician and party in an attractive light. The activity itself is not in general new; it is an expansion and elaboration of shaking hands and kissing babies. But it does mean that a major political leader is always accompanied by at least half a busload of journalists. The 'walkabout' is the basic exercise, but is full of hazards – too few or too many people, political opponents, elderly and infirm ladies who want to do their shopping in peace, television cables to trip over.... The planned visitation is better, and yields film of the candidate chatting to workers, showing grave and intelligent interest, trying out machinery, wearing a hard hat and so on.

The classic of this kind was Margaret Thatcher's visit to a Suffolk field in 1979. There, surrounded by eighty journalists and fifty of her entourage, she held a calf on her lap. Not much to go wrong there, you might think, and anyway the media professionals will always do a retake if the event goes wrong. On a visit to Harry Ramsden's fish and chip shop near Bradford (the only fish and chip shop in the country with chandeliers), customers struggled to eat their lunches amidst the crowds of media men, while party aides called desperately for children to come forward to be served fish and chips by the Prime Minister in the take-away bar. A Labour leader is more likely to be seen comforting patients and staff in an (allegedly) under-funded NHS hospital.

Accidents and incidents

Accidents and incidents upset this carefully structured process. When Macmillan was asked what he most feared as Prime Minister, he said, 'events!'. Actual events can have a powerful effect on election campaigns, and perhaps on their outcome. For the politician they are an unpredictable hazard which may be turned to advantage. For the public they are like case studies or exercises, in which the politicians must demonstrate their skills.

In post-war elections the most significant incursion of events was in 1951, when a crisis arose over Persian oil. The Labour government clearly faced serious setbacks in its foreign policy, in the middle of an election campaign. The opposition tried to exploit the situation, but was outflanked by Labour's counter-attack – the 'warmonger' campaign. The electoral result was probably a draw, with some slight gain in public political education.

In 1959 Macmillan managed to appear on television with the visiting President Eisenhower. But events did not match these promotions of personality. In 1964 the election provided ironic examples of events happening too late to benefit the government. On polling day itself the Russian leader, Khrushchev, fell from power; next day China exploded an atom bomb. The effect of crises relating to national security is normally to rally support to the government of the day, of whatever party. Thus the Conservative government was possibly deprived of power by this failure of events to match its needs.

Since then television coverage of elections has been increasingly desperate to find or create news, and events have had a prominent part in the campaigns. In 1970 the announcement of adverse trade figures three days before the poll, and even the defeat of England's football team in the World Cup, seem to have affected the Labour vote. In February 1974 the election itself was part of the government's response to a miners' strike. During the campaign a mistake in calculating miners' pay was revealed, and it appeared that the government's confrontation with the miners (and hence the 'snap' election) had been based on a false statistic.

During the 1983 election, Margaret Thatcher travelled to a 'summit' conference in the USA, but spent so little time there that a sceptical observer might conclude that the real-life incident was being turned into a media event. The *Daily Mail* and *The Sun* ran enthusiastic headlines: 'Maggie wins all the way'; 'Maggie flies home from summit triumph'; but the *Financial Times* was unimpressed by the achievement of the conference. In 1987 Margaret Thatcher's visit to a summit conference in Venice was exploited to demonstrate her undoubted experience in international affairs, but the exploitation became part of the news too.

The role of the mass media in elections

The broadcasters and the editors of the less committed newspapers have to choose which of the material thrust at them should be reported, with what prominence, slant and style. Mostly they follow the leads of the parties, and the broadcasters try hard to 'balance' their reporting both in quantity, and in neutrality or balance of comment. The normal editorial judgements of 'news value' are to some extent suspended, unless a new and significant story breaks outside the election campaign. Since the broadcasters, and especially the BBC, are being watched by the parties (every broadcast is recorded, timed and assessed for 'fairness') editors may have a hard time.

EXERCISES
The editor's dilemma

If you were the editor of a television news programme, how would you react to the following:

17.12 The Labour Party in its press conference runs the health issue for the fourth time in two weeks. It is boring and throws no new light on the issue. The Labour Leader is due to visit a hospital later that day. Do you decide on minimal coverage (short, late in the bulletin) because we have heard it all before?

17.13 Your Chief Economics Correspondent has produced a long 'Panorama' type programme about the recession, demonstrating authoritatively that the government's claim that it is a world recession is wrong, and that the recession was in part caused by the government's errors. You are in the middle of the election campaign. Do you cancel the broadcast?

17.14 It is an important day in the election campaign, and there is much good material. Buckingham Palace announces that a Royal couple are to separate. Do you lead with this item and how much time do you give it?

17.15 The Prime Minister is hit by an egg thrown by a protesting voter. Do you report the incident prominently?

17.16 The US President tells reporters that he has little confidence in the Labour Party's defence policy. How much prominence do you give to this item?

The crusading tabloids

There are four crusading tabloid newspapers, *The Sun*, *Daily Mail* and the *Daily Express* for the Conservatives, and the *Daily Mirror* for Labour. Readership is in the proportion 2.5:1 in favour of the Conservatives. None of these papers hides its political commitment, and the three Conservative-inclined papers work very closely with Conservative Central Office.

This is not a recent development, though the rise of *The Sun* newspaper since the 1970s has affected the political balance and perhaps coarsened the style of popular journalism. A highly partisan press is legitimate in a free society, but it does raise some doubts about fairness in a democracy, mainly among Labour supporters. The shrill partisanship of these papers was evident, and for once much commented on, in the 1992 election which appeared to be very close and likely to end with Labour ahead. For example, typical bold headlines on the front pages just before the election included:

- Kinnock Blunder
- Nightmare on Kinnock Street (with 9 pages to follow)
- Don't throw it all away
- I was wrong, wrong, wrong (of Mr Kinnock's admissions of past errors)
- The Kinnock Mask slips
- If Kinnock wins would the last person to leave Britain please turn out the lights (on election day in *The Sun*).

The Conservative papers all savaged Labour's taxation plans, which were misrepresented. Here they joined forces with the Conservatives in a major strategic attack on one of Labour's most vulnerable positions. In one case the *Daily Express* used tax-tables from a Conservative Party propaganda leaflet.

None of this was very different in style from the anti-Conservative material to be found in the *Daily Mirror*, but the Tory tabloids are more numerous, and possibly – it is a matter of judgement – more ruthless. There was no pause during the election, or indeed in the previous months, except to cover such matters as the breakdown of royal marriages. One of the less obvious factors which adds to the power of the press is that it helps to create an agenda for the rest of the media, including the much more neutral and 'balanced' broadcasters.

Did it all make a difference? A former Treasurer of the Conservative Party, Lord McAlpine, thought so. He wrote in *The Sunday Telegraph* of 13 April, 1992:

'The heroes of this campaign were Sir David English, Sir Nicholas Lloyd, Kelvin McKenzie and the other editors of the grander Tory press. Never in the past nine elections have they come out so strongly in favour of the Conservatives. Never has their attack on the Labour Party been so comprehensive.... This was how the election was won, and if the politicians, elated in their hour of victory, are tempted to believe otherwise, they are in real trouble next time.'

Neil Kinnock repeated these words in his resignation speech after the election. The Member for Basildon agreed and he represented an area full of the Conservatives' crucial voters ('Essex man', the skilled working class) half of whom took *The Sun*. His expression of gratitude to *The Sun* led to a Sun headline: 'It's the Sun wot won it'.

Soon, however, the tabloid editors struck back, claiming their papers had no influence, their

readers were too intelligent, only read the sports pages and so on. This does not look entirely convincing. History showed that Labour had won elections despite the efforts of the tabloids – but not very often. It could be argued that the tabloid readers were already disposed towards the Tories, but they were certainly not given much of a chance to change their minds. Survey research showed that, for example, about one third of *Daily Mail* and *Daily Express* readers did not vote Conservative, but again that might have been higher if the papers had not battered and blasted them with Conservative propaganda.

Survey research in 1987 suggested that the Tory tabloids may have converted 2 per cent of undecided voters. In 1992 research by Mori showed swings to the Conservatives in the last week of the campaign – 4 per cent among *The Sun* readers, 3 per cent for the *Daily Express*, 2 per cent for the *Daily Mail*. In a close election such movement was enough to change the result. These findings are still not conclusive, for readers of the pro-Labour *Daily Mirror* also switched late and in comparable proportions (2.5 per cent) to the Conservatives. So there is still a puzzle about the power of the popular press.

A rule of advertising is that even the most skilful advertising cannot sell a bad product. There is much evidence (look around you) that this is not true; or at least, that advertisers can sell goods which people do not actually need. However, the rule, dubious though it is, does point to a more neutral interpretation of the role of the tabloids. It is evident that some of the most vicious attacks on Labour focused on their tax plans and the quality of the leadership. These were vulnerable points in Labour's appeal. Both were seriously misrepresented, but the criticisms which the Tory tabloids presented with wild exaggeration and malice were not inherently unreasonable.

Television and elections

The influence of the press on elections is modified by television, which does not display the persistent bias and hyperbole of the popular press. Since 1955, television has transformed electioneering, and has now replaced the press as the major source of political information and opinion. This conclusion is significant because television operates in this field under quite different rules from that of the press. Newspapers are commercial enterprises involved in severe competition for readers (as the demise of some newspapers has shown) and following a tradition of political partisanship. Television on the other hand is so far much less competitive, and observes statutory rules of fairness and non-partisanship, and a tradition of impartiality and integrity. In consequence the background and style of a British general election is no longer dominated by the screaming headlines of the popular dailies, but rather reflects the comparative reasonableness of the television screen and studio, and the family living room in which the broadcast will be received. This is not to claim that all television electioneering is a model of rationality.

Broadcasting time on television or radio is not open to purchase, but some time is allocated to the parties (in proportions determined by the votes received at the previous election) for party political broadcasts. Programmes of news, comment and discussions are designed under the more flexible rules of fairness and balance.

This rough apportionment of time according to votes received inevitably works to the disadvantage of minor parties. The broadcasting arrangements, like the ballot system itself, tend to confirm the dominance of the two 'big' parties, and especially of the government.

Negative campaigning, stunts and dirty tricks

'Negative campaigning' is an accepted part of modern political marketing. Negative campaigning is not much to do with rational argument: it implies exaggeration and distortion, personal attacks on integrity and trustworthiness; the other side is unfit to govern, and their policies would be disastrous. This is the kind of debate which would not be acceptable outside politics, and might indeed lead to legal action for slander; and may not be appropriate in a democracy in which the Opposition has a constitutional role as an alternative government.

Negative campaigning is a product of the application of professional marketing, television and mass circulation newspapers to political campaigning. It existed in earlier times in simpler forms, as an early English form of dirty trick, or as a 'stunt' mainly connected to the popular press. In the days of rotten boroughs, bribery and corruption, a 'dirty trick' might be to lock up your opponent's supporters in a pub and buy them free drinks all day. In the USA, the original home of dirty tricks, the tricks may include the disruption of the other side's campaign arrangements (e.g. causing a traffic jam in the middle of town

before the candidate arrives), the burglary of your opponent's national headquarters (Watergate) and the unending and shameless search for, and revelation of personal matters, 'scandals' connected with drink, sex or money (presented as a serious concern about his judgement and trustworthiness).

Britain cannot match the American repertoire of dirty tricks, – though the Liberals have specialised in vigorous constituency campaigns, which have included, for example, bogus leaflets for an opposing party. Personal revelations are pursued indefatigably by the popular press, but there is some restraint on publication, arising from libel laws and the threat of new legislation on privacy.

Modern negative campaigning at the national level goes back to the 'stunts' of the 1920–50 period. These were a response to the extended suffrage, which substituted persuasion, the bribery of promises and threats for the nineteenth century's simple and direct rewards of money, drink, jobs or housing; also to the 'sensationalism', and political bias, of the new mass circulation newspapers. The classic stunt involved heavy promotion of a dubious proposition in order to frighten the voter. It is quite evident that the classic stunt lives on in a form much less crude, but more regular, indeed routine, and probably more effective.

The classic stunt of modern times was the so-called 'Red Letter scare' of 1924 (the Zinoviev Letter). MacDonald's Labour government of 1924 went to the country after less than a year in office, in an attempt to improve its minority position. Just before polling day, *The Times* published a letter said to be in the possession of the Foreign Office, and containing instructions from the International Communist organisation to the Communist Party of Great Britain. The instructions provided in detail for a communist take-over of Britain. The government fumbled the issue badly and after a delay admitted the existence of the letter. The incident dominated the last few days of the campaign, and on polling day itself the *Daily Express* splashed in red across the top of every page:

DO NOT VOTE RED TODAY

The whole truth of the matter is still obscure, but two points seem clear: first, the letter was certainly a forgery, produced for electoral purposes. Second, a letter of this kind may have indicated the aims and activities of international communism, but there was nothing except fear and prejudice to link MacDonald's moderate government with red revolution. Nevertheless (and despite an increased vote overall), MacDonald's government fell, the victim of a wave of opinion which had perhaps been strengthened by the Red Letter Scare.

The 1992 campaign: Labour's 'Double Whammy'

The 1992 campaign was vigorously contested under the rules of modern political marketing (or warfare), and including much 'negative campaigning', especially by the Conservative Party attacking Labour in general, Neil Kinnock in particular, by the Labour Party attacking the record of the government and the state of the economy,. and by the Liberals (which meant in practice Paddy Ashdown) attacking the other two parties for attacking each other.

Here is one major episode of allegedly negative campaigning, which might earlier have been described as a stunt. Note that another major stunt, 'the War of Jennifer's Ear' is described in a Case Study at the end of Chapter 18.

Labour's double whammy (an obscure American phrase, which seems to convey its own meaning) was alleged to be rising prices and higher taxes. Higher prices, Conservatives argued, would arise inter alia from higher interest rates (probably necessary to defend the pound against hostile markets – unfair but true), higher inflation (because Labour governments always caused higher inflation), public sector wage increases (because Labour was the public sector's friend), the introduction of a minimum wage (specifically promised by Labour). Most of this was plausible, some of it unfair, little of it unacceptable in a robust election campaign.

The other element in the double whammy, taxation, was more controversial. Labour has been historically a party of comparatively high taxation, for good doctrinal reasons, and inevitably has suffered vigorous attacks, some exaggerated and unfair. As it happened the burden of taxation under the Conservatives had not diminished, though this was not so evident since income tax had been reduced, very obviously in the budget preceding the 1992 election.

Labour then chose quite deliberately to publish a budget, with great ceremony, in the early stages of the election campaign. This included some increases in pensions and child benefit but also substantial increases in taxation, hitting high income earners hard, and middle income earners very hard indeed (by the extension of the National Insurance charge). The total effect was presented by Labour as benefiting eight out of ten families (true, but some of them by very little), and by Conservatives as imposing the highest ever tax rise in peace time, and establishing punitive rates for high earners by European standards (true, but for many of them the Labour plan was simply a return to the pre-1988 levels). The Conservatives chose to plug away at this gift for their propaganda.

The crusading Tory tabloids had crucified Labour over taxation in 1987. In 1992 they were presented with enough evidence to mount continuous scare stories throughout the election, thus re-inforcing the Conservatives' own campaign. Indeed, the party and the tabloids could not be distinguished; the tabloids did the campaigning for the party. Opinion polls suggested that the campaign was effective. The voters were for once given a choice about whether to pay more taxes or not, and they declined, just as they had done over the Poll-Tax.

The moral of this story is that the only way to sell a tax increase to the British people is to get the tabloids to do it for you.

Stunting at elections seems to be a declining sport. There are several reasons for this. First, successful stunts are difficult to bring off. For example, the Jennifer's Ear 'stunt' (if such it was) might have worked, on the no-smoke-without-fire principle, in a climate of hostility to the Conservatives; but in that case it might not have been necessary. Similarly, Labour failed in two clumsy attempts to fix blame on the Conservatives for 'glorying' in the Falklands War. Labour supported the war and could hardly complain if the Conservatives enjoyed winning it. The stuntman needs to start from a secure position.

Second, stunts were diminished by the shrill denunciation of stunts; every stunt came with its own antidote, and accusations of stunting seem to cancel out any possible gain from the stunt itself. Third, it seems likely that the voters were becoming a little better informed, and less vulnerable to the scare which was characteristic of the true stunt. Fourth, the successful stunt required the amplifications and distortions of the tabloid press so even modest election gambits were likely to go far beyond the control of the electioneers themselves. Politicians have no need to produce stunts themselves: they are likely to have stunts thrust upon them.

Finally, as a response to these developments, the parties modernised their campaign strategies, hired advertising and marketing professionals, surveyed public opinion and set about the persuasion of a mass electorate with an expertise and ruthlessness which make the stunts of the 1930s and 1940s look very crude indeed. One consequence is that the stunts of the modern campaign are smoothly enfolded and hidden in the continuing processes of negative image management.

Questions about the consequences and the ethics of 'negative campaigning' can now be re-considered. The 1992 campaign showed that there are limits to negative campaigning.

- The politicians themselves have some scruples; at least some of them hold political principles above the desire to get elected at all costs.
- The advice of the professional marketeers may be rejected.
- There is evidence anyway that their judgement is unsound: the Conservative campaign was heavily criticised, but proved effective. Mr Major's revisiting of Brixton and his bar-stool chats with the faithful lacked credibility; his hastily contrived and awkward soap-box appearances proved attractive. Some of the posters which were intended as advertising blockbusters, turned out to lack impact or even a clear message.
- There is a sceptical climate, hostile to the more outrageous distortions of the campaign. This is encouraged by television, and may reflect sceptical voters, better educated and informed than those of the 1920 to 1950 period.
- There is some relation between the 'stunts' and reality. This is true in the cases cited above. The advertisers exaggerate, distort and sensationalise – but they rarely invent.

However, in the end a different and brutal reality overtakes the parties' optimistic self-deceptions and their deliberate deception of the voters. In the case of the 1992 election the economic situation turned out to be far worse than the Conservatives admitted (or perhaps even knew), and within a year they were compelled to increase taxes and then devalue the pound (both quite contrary to their election pledges).

Polls

Since 1966 polls (forecasts of the election result) have played a dominant part in election campaigns. In 1979 twenty six national polls were reported; in the 1980s and 1990s over 40, with a cluster at weekends. Polls are usually reported as lead stories, though in 1992 the BBC decided not to lead with poll results. Most of the reporting is careful, and running averages of polls are used. But the margins of error, though reported, are largely discounted; so too the possibility of error due to the technical problems of sampling and field work, and the tendency evident in 1992 for respondents to deceive the interviewer (and perhaps themselves too).

Overall the impression given is of a real election, and the politicians find themselves either floating on, or fighting, the results. In 1970 Mr Wilson, and in 1992 Mr Kinnock floated triumphantly into defeat. In 1983 and 1987 Margaret Thatcher's substantial lead hardly faltered, and her opponents lost credibility. There is no doubt that the polls affect the campaign; hence they must have some effect on the result. But the effect on voters is obscure. The polls may induce apathy in electors on the losing side; or encourage them to join the winners; or set up a resistance to the winners. Much still depends on the political context. In the three-party conditions of the 1980s and 1990s the polls may encourage and assist tactical voting. In that way they provide the uncommitted voter with valuable information, though so far tactical voting is not very significant.

The polls failed spectacularly in 1992 to predict the correct result, even in 'exit' polls taken as voters left the polling stations. This failure related to an underestimate of the Conservative vote and seems to have several explanations. Some voters deceived the interviewers (in particular wavering Conservative voters dismayed by Labour's precise tax proposals but not willing to admit it). Others moved late from a Labour inclination to voting Conservative; this may have been a consequence of the polls' continuing demonstration that Labour would win (ironically the polls helped to disprove their own predictions). There may be a methodological bias towards the Labour Party. The error of the polls, at about 4 per cent, is large enough to signify the wrong winner in many elections.

The dominance of the polls in the reporting of elections, coupled with their apparent inaccuracy, lead to demands that polls should not be published at all during an election, or during the last part of the election (as in France). However, this seems a gross interference with freedom of speech, and difficult to apply in practice. It would be more appropriate to understand polls and report them less emphatically.

These then are aspects of the election campaign seen from the transmitting end. The campaign must now be observed from the elector's point of view: how is it received and what is its impact?

GUIDE TO EXERCISES

17.1 The wording of the question is crucial and in both these cases the popular vote was heavily on the conservative side, for leaving things as they were (though the devolutionists gained a slight majority in Scotland). Moreover, the referendum required Yes/No answers to complex questions, to which there were a range of answers, including conditions and qualifications.

Resources for campaigning – finance, people, organisation – vary. There was clearly more money on the side of the EEC than against.

The question gets caught up with other matters, notably, in the case of devolution, with the general standing of the government.

17.2 The pendulum swings unevenly, tending to stick on one side or hardly to pass the vertical. For some parts of the twentieth century, the pendulum would have to swing three ways -- a very odd clock. Further, the metaphor implies a steady alternation in opinion and in policy and obscures the substantial continuity and overlapping in both.

17.3 The freedom to choose when to have a general election (up to the limit of five years) is mainly an advantage to the government, which can get its unpopular measures out of the way, and manage the economy to gain favour before an election. Most governments have done this – and would still try to do so in fixed-term parliaments. It may be thought that governments have advantage enough in publicity and prestige, without the added bonus of choice of date of election. A stronger argument for fixed terms is to avoid the uncertainty, prolonged electioneering and prime ministerial teasing of the Opposition and the country.

17.4 For university votes, the superior political judgement of graduates – but this is plainly absurd, whatever the subject of graduation.

For business premises, having a stake in another constituency – but many other people work in another constituency: should they have an extra vote too?

17.5 There is a case for giving additional votes to those with superior political judgement, but it is impossible to define or detect this rather vague quality. In any case, it is consistent with the theory of democracy to regard a vote as representing a person, his interests, emotions and prejudices, not his political wisdom.

17.6 The existing system is clearly unfair to Labour and Liberal, but an example drawn from, say, Glasgow would work the other way. It may be regarded as unfair and unhealthy for politics that in such areas of party predominance the minority party hold very few seats or no seats at all. Redistribution has its dangers, but over the country as a whole a proportionate system based on large multi-member constituencies tends to balance out.

17.7 This you do for yourself.

17.8 See following text.

17.9 The pros and cons are indicated in the text. Note that a preference needs to be based on a balance of advantage in a particular system, and likely consequences in Britain. It is not enough to dismiss PR in general, as some politicians do, with 'Look at Israel or Italy'. Similarly advocates of PR may overrate the difference it would make; in particular, it is not clear how voters in Britain would respond in a new electoral system, and how parties (including some not yet invented) might respond to the opportunities. PR is not just about dishing the Tories.

17.10 The last, but with some danger of the alternatives ranging down to impropriety. The advertiser is trained to sell, and is interested primarily in the marketability of the product which may include its quality. The politician is expected to have a prime concern for the quality of the product, even if it damages sales. There is a conflict of objective here, which the politician may not be able to control. No serious politician can disclaim a concern for marketability.

17.11 Remember that posters only permit brief cryptic statements. It may seem legitimate to link Labour with higher taxes, and the Conservatives with neglect of public services. Opponents might not accept these sweeping claims, but they do not represent gross distortion of the intentions of the parties. It may not be improper, therefore, to use a poster which, briefly and pictorially, conveys these points.

17.12–17.16 These are all matters of fine judgement about news value, the right (reasonable claim anyway) of the parties to put forward their own ideas not the news

editors', and the practical business of maintaining good relations with the parties.

17.12 A middling solution is possible.

17.13 Arose in 1992, the programme was postponed and that decision was much criticised.

17.14, 17.15 and 17.16 all happened and news-value ensured prominent reporting.

Note: Assessments and a Case Study on Elections are to be found at the end of Chapter 18.

Elections: the voter

Electoral behaviour – the nature of a voter's choice

The mobility of the vote

About three quarters of the electorate turn out to vote in general elections – a fair indication of a commitment to a minimal participation in the democratic system. Most of the rest choose, deliberately or more often by default, not to vote. The voter's action or inaction looks simple enough, but before we can explain electoral choice we need to 'unpack' it, break it down into its component parts. For example, among those who voted both in the 1983 and 1987 general elections, roughly four out of five were 'loyalists', voting for the same party; but the 'loyalists' include 'waverers', who return to the fold after experiencing doubts. The other one fifth are the 'switchers', most of whom switch to a Liberal vote, or abstain; the long switch between Conservative and Labour is for a tiny minority only (perhaps one per cent in 1987). Thus there are five categories of voter: firm loyalists, wavering loyalists, short and long switchers and abstainers. Much of this movement is 'self-cancelling' and does not show up in the aggregate change in votes: the picture of a largely immobile electorate is misleading, especially if the time period extends over three or more elections.

The vote, when it finally happens, reflects a variable strength, for one party and against others, and a variable direction – towards the party's policies, leaders, traditions and philosophy, or alignments and alliances. In a multi-party system switching and wavering and abstaining represent a complex mobile battle, not a static war between two entrenched armies. The vote also varies in its sources, from social or group-based response, e.g. by class or occupation, to an individual response to politics, or even an intellectual assessment of values and issues.

Studying voting behaviour

Voting behaviour is a rich but frustrating subject for social science research. The sample survey has opened up the possibility of intensive study of voting, and more is known about it than many other forms of social behaviour. There is no doubt of the advances in our understanding. Compare the analysis of, say, the election of 1906 with that for any election since the 1960s, and the difference is clear. Yet along with new understanding comes a recognition of the limits of knowledge. Hence political behaviour retains an ultimate mystery. Perhaps that is as well.

There are good reasons for the continuing puzzles and perplexities about voting. First, voting is a complex act, reflecting a social and political context, and a medley of current influences. Second, for all the technical sophistications of modern sample surveys, the evidence they yield is necessarily imperfect. In particular, hard statistical techniques are applied to relatively soft survey data; respondents are honest but inevitably less than accurate about the past and the future, and about their attitudes to complex matters which are not often or at all in their minds. (However surveys like those for the British Election Studies since 1964 which repeat questions over many years may show up significant changes in responses, and so have validity in their own right.)

A third problem lies in the difficulty of proving causation. Sample surveys reveal associations between say housing tenure and vote; but it is impossible to prove that one affects the other. Often other factors are involved in a complex process of pre-disposition and disposition and change. For example, a couple buying their council house change their vote from Labour to Conservative. But they may well have been already pre-disposed to make the voting switch;

and the factors behind the voting behaviour may be similar to those behind the housing switch.

There is here, as often in this search for significant association, the problem sometimes referred to as 'chicken and egg'; which came first, which was the cause, which the effect. We can recognise that voting and house purchase are complex acts; people do not resolve to change their vote as they sign the house purchase contract. The statistical association demonstrated by the survey shows inter-relationship, in which we may with due caution read a process of linked shifts. We are entitled to assume that voting is not random behaviour.

Trends in voting behaviour and the social and political context

We are on much surer ground in studying aggregate statistics (not dependent on sample survey interviews) for voting. The Table shows the vote (by percentage of poll) in selected elections since 1951.

Table 1 Percentage of the vote by party in selected elections

	Con	Lab	Lib*	Other**
1951	48	49	3	1
1974(Feb.)	38	37	19	6
1983	42	28	25	5
1992	43	35	18	5

* Alliance (with SDP) in 1983, 1987; Liberal Democrats in 1992
** Includes Nationalists in Scotland and Wales, and the Northern Ireland parties

EXERCISES

The pattern of voting since 1951

18.1 What are the notable features of the Table?
18.2 How does it appear to explain the decline of Labour?

The pattern of voting shown in the Table seems to be self-explanatory, but is not as simple as it looks. First, aggregate figures hide a great deal of movement which 'cancels itself out'. Second, that movement takes place in a radically changing context so that the political significance of a party vote changes too. Third, the simple observation that Liberal and Nationalist voting has depressed the Labour vote raises the question why the Labour vote was so vulnerable to the 'third parties'. Altogether we have to explain:

- the comparative steadfastness of the Conservative vote
- the substantial decline in the Labour vote
- the sudden rise of Liberal and Nationalist voting.

These questions can be summed up in relation to the Labour Party, specifically the question first raised in an academic analysis after the 1959 election: 'Must Labour Lose?'

EXERCISE

Studying voting behaviour by introspection or interview

18.3 It is useful at this point to reflect on your own voting behaviour, past or prospective, or talk with others, family, friends, enemies; or even mount a simple survey (you need a schedule of questions, some notion of a sample and an understanding that many people do not like talking about politics to strangers). Try to discover when, how and why the choice of party or no party was made.

Changes in the context of voting

Britain in the 1980s and 1990s is very different from the 1950s. There are scores of different measures of social change, or change in life-styles. Notably house, car, television and telephone ownership and higher education have substantially increased – so too have 'one-person households'. Manual and manufacturing work has sharply decreased. Since the working environment and experience, education, family life and the media have changed, so influences on opinion formation in daily life have changed (parents, employers, colleagues, journalists and politicians).

Changes in the political system in which the voter lives and votes would seem to be at least as significant as social change for the voter's choice of party. Here are the most important:

- the electorate has increased in number from 35 million people in the 1950s, to 42 million in the 1990s; most of the increase arises from the enfranchisement of the 18–21 year olds in 1968. These young voters are comparatively not much interested in politics, but when they do vote, tend slightly to favour non-Conservative parties
- the Liberals (and allies) have put up a much larger number of candidates since 1950; they

did not exceed 300 candidates until 1964, but contested over 600 seats in October 1974, and from 1983 onwards. Even assuming that the old 300 seats were their best prospects, this doubling of the opportunity to vote Liberal has an obvious direct effect on voting (though the chicken and egg problem arises here, since the Liberals' decision to contest most seats was partly a response to perceived shifts in voters' opinions). For the voter the contending party in second place in about one quarter of the constituencies is now likely to be a Liberal or Nationalist

- the parties have shifted their ground from the sharp opposition of 1945 into a period of 'consensus' in the 1950s and 1960s; then a period of polarisation in the 1970s and 1980s, as Labour moved left and the Conservatives moved right; and more recently, under John Major and Neil Kinnock, back to the centre ground in pursuit of 'electability', a kind of false consensus. Voters would be very insensitive if they did not notice some of this change and perhaps reconsider their vote.

These changes in the political parties are the most obvious sources of change among voters, and the availability of sample survey data may have shifted our attention from them. However, the parties were in part at least responding to changes in the voters, so a complete explanation of voting requires the study of voters as well as parties.

Explanations of voting

The changes shown above indicate two broad sets of explanations of voting, social and political. Social determination of voting may be thought of as a 'bottom-up' approach: voting is changed by matters outside the immediate area of politics ('exogenous' factors). Conversely, political determination of voting is a 'top-down' approach: voters respond to politicians (as Gladstone might have thought, just as if sociology had never been invented). However, most theories of voting assume some combination of factors, but vary in their emphasis. The process is broken down for analysis, but in practice it is circular and interwoven: voters and politicians, social and political context, are mixed up together as cause and effect.

Here are some of the main theories of voting behaviour.

1 Class and party identification and alignment (D. Butler and D. Stokes). Voting was based on a division between middle and working class, voting predominantly Conservative and Labour respectively, with stable identification with a party in a stable two-party system. This reflected American understandings of voting behaviour, and appeared to fit both the class and the two-party system prevailing in Britain from 1945 until the 1970s.

2 Class and party de-alignment (I. Crewe and the British Election Study based at the University of Essex). Social change undermined the old class-based stability, and political loyalties crumbled. A new working class and a new middle class emerged alongside the old. In politics volatility replaced stability. This was evident in the rapid shifts of party support showing up in opinion polls in the 1970s and 1980s, and in the sharp reversals of normal voting displayed in by-elections; also in the decline in the proportion of 'strong' party identifiers (down from 88 per cent in 1964 to 71 per cent in 1987). The two-party system weakened, and multi-party politics proved especially damaging to the Labour vote.

In the dealignment theory the voter has moved from firm commitment towards hesitation and a more deliberate choice, thus opening the way for political appeals.

3 Political explanations. The 1987 British Election Study (Heath et al, 1991) combined social with political explanations, but put more weight on the political. Such theories emphasise the competing appeals of the political parties, and the voter's response to them. 'Issues', that is, salient policy areas on which parties have different positions, are significant. Economic conditions are important, especially for the voter's judgement of competence, or his disposition to optimism, the 'feel-good factor'. Responses to party leadership also count, both in summing up competence and experience and in the less rational responses of individuals and groups to projected 'personality'.

In all of these cases, both the parties and the voters behave autonomously, rather than in the determined (deterministic) way of the social explanations. The voter, it is proposed, is rational. This perception leads to an 'economic' view of electoral behaviour. The voter, like a consumer and shopper in the market place, seeks to maximise his own interests and desires. Similarly, the parties compete for the middle ground, where the last 5 or 10 per cent of voters can bring them a majority.

This is plausible, even convincing, as one explanation of party and voting behaviour. Evidently the Labour Party after 1983, and the Conservative Party after the fall of Margaret Thatcher, moved back from 'extreme' ideological positions, to woo the voter in the centre. 'Electability' replaced ideology; the Conservatives held on to ground they might have lost under Margaret Thatcher, and Labour painfully regained a little of the ground they had lost in the disastrous election of 1983. Such rational, market behaviour is deplored by the more committed party members, who rightly feel that a party must sustain its principles, while the pragmatists feel just as strongly that principles without power are useless.

4 The campaign and other short term factors. These offer additional rather than exclusive explanations of voting. A majority of voters do not change their vote in the course of the campaign. But many do switch, and even more waver, venturing away from their favoured party but returning on polling day. So the election campaign seems to matter. Yet it matters only in the total social and political environment, and in the context of the long election campaign which begins after the previous election, and the 'medium-term' campaign which affects the one or two years before the next election. Since Parliaments in practice last only about four years, there is a period of about three years before the onset of the 'medium' campaign. For the 1992 election this began with John Major's election as Conservative leader 16 months before the election of April 1992.

Thus political campaigning is a continuous process of persuasion, appeal and marketing, intensified in the final three weeks, and its impact on the voter is likely to follow the same course. The final three weeks, the campaign proper, brings an intensification of political news and comment in the media. Given the continuing heavy bias of the press towards the Conservatives there are grounds for arguing that the media determine voting behaviour, hence, the outcome of elections. This is plausible, as long as the argument is set in context. Voting behaviour is the outcome of many complex conditions and drives, and no single factor on its own can provide a full explanation. On the other hand governments win elections on

the last 5 per cent of their vote, and any factor which produces that 5 per cent must share in the multiple responsibility for the voter's choice.

These explanations or theories of voting behaviour are not mutually exclusive. The best strategy is to accept the most convincing and construct a composite picture. But it is not helpful for understanding if the picture is a random jumble; we need as far as possible to indicate the positions and weight of each factor.

Social explanations of voting

Class voting

Voting is still related to social class; but the relationship is complex, and there is less confidence about the significance of the term. Certainly the simple formulation, middle class votes Conservative, working class votes Labour, as in the formulations of original class and party alignment theory, is no longer appropriate. The twofold division of class, and, of course, of partisanship, is too rough to be more than broadly indicative, and the second part of the proposition has particularly weakened.

An analysis of vote by class in 1983 and 1992 is shown in Table 2.

Table 2 Voting by class 1983 and 1992

	1983			1992		
	Con	Lab	LD	Con	Lab	LD
AB – professional	60	10	28	56	20	22
C1 – white collar	51	20	27	52	25	19
C2 – skilled worker	40	32	26	38	41	17
DE – semi or unskilled	33	41	24	30	50	15

Source: MORI

EXERCISES
Voting by class

18.4 Is this evidence of class-based voting?
18.5 What major shift in voting is indicated?

The major shift in votes has been from the Liberals to Labour, a shift evident in all social classes. If the analysis is pursued further back it is clear that Labour lost heavily to the Conservatives among the C2 skilled working class in the 1980s. This is the origin of talk of 'Essex man' or 'Basildon man' – the newly affluent worker in the South to whom

Margaret Thatcher's materialistic conservatism was particularly attractive.

In 1992 Labour re-established its 1979 share of the vote of the C2s, though this was less than its almost 50 per cent score in October 1974, while the Conservatives held on to their improved vote in this class, which had been only 28 per cent in October 1974.

This movement in working class voting is the basis of the class and party dealignment theory. It proposes a divided working class, in which there is a new, relatively affluent section, inclined to the Conservatives, and an old working class, maintaining its traditional allegiance to Labour. In such an interpretation, social class is modified and reinforced by other factors.

Patterns' of reinforcement and modification can be observed in the 1983 result, as analysed by Ivor Crewe. Within the working class (manual workers) council tenants were more likely to vote Labour than owner-occupiers; public sector workers more likely to vote Labour than private sector workers; those who lived in Scotland and the North were more likely to vote Labour than southerners. The reverse applied in every case to Conservative voting. Of these comparisons, housing tenure makes the most difference. Liberal (Alliance) voting is not related to these social differences.

A new working class?

It has been argued that this pattern reflects the growth of a new working class, independent of the state in housing and occupation, and more likely to be found in the more prosperous South, rather than the old 'smoke-stack' industrial areas of the North. This is an improved version of the 'embourgeoisement' thesis in which the working class is seen as increasingly middle class in its condition and outlook. In these terms the working class is not fully 'bourgeois', but it is no longer 'proletarian'. Within a class-conscious society some kind of upward mobility has taken place. It should be noted that these explanations present a refinement not a denial of class theories of voting, though the terms of the argument are broad and ill-defined.

EXERCISE
A new working class?

18.6 Does this table demonstrate the emergence of a new working class?

A similar analysis for 1992 (see *Politics Review* 2,1, September 1992) shows a narrowing of the gap in voting between the two classes. Thus voting behaviour remains fluid and the boundaries of the two classes are blurred. They are, of course, 'merely' analytic constructs, but they do illuminate, have a basis in reality.

One factor missing from this analysis is trade union membership. This used to be a major reinforcement of working class support for Labour. That is still the case for the old-style unions in the heavy industries (and this shows up in the public sector and North figures). But for trade unionists as a whole, including the large number of middle-class 'white collar' unionists, Labour declined from the 55 per cent support of 1974 to 46 per cent in the trough of 1983 and 47 per cent in 1992.

In the 1983 Table housing tenure is clearly a powerful differentiator. This can be seen again in the 1992 election.

Table 3 The votes of a new and old working class

	New working class			Old working class		
	Owner-occupier	Works in private sector	Lives in South	Council tenants	Works in public sector	Lives in North
Con	47	36	42	19	29	32
Lab	25	37	26	57	46	42
Lib/SDP	28	27	32	24	25	26

Source: BBC/Gallup Survey; 8–9 June 1983, analysed by Ivor Crewe, *The Guardian*, 13 June 1983

Table 4 Housing tenure and vote 1992

	Con	Lab	LD 100%
Middle class			
home owners	56	21	20
council tenants	34	40	8
Working class			
home owners	41	39	1
council tenants	22	58	15
All home owners	49	30	19
All council tenants	24	55	15

Source: MORI polls during election, aggregated and adjusted to outcome

EXERCISE
Housing tenure and vote 1992

18.7 Does the Table show that 'a property-owning democracy is a Conservative democracy'?

A new middle class?

While the working class has been changing or dividing, the middle class too show signs of division as well as expansion. This may explain a slight drift from the Conservatives since 1983, and a sharp increase (from 14 per cent to 20 per cent) in the Labour vote in the AB professional class. A substantial percentage of Labour voting professionals is not new; it has been as high as 29 per cent in 1970. However, such a shift is significant for the Labour Party, given its 'proletarian' tradition. The factors behind 'middle class-ness' are less familiar than in our understanding of 'working class-ness'. They include further and higher education, employment in the welfare and 'creative' occupations (teaching being both?), membership of trade unions and professional associations (still strong in the public services).

Socio-political explanations of voting

Altogether there is much evidence in these tables to support a theory of class and partisan dealignment. Indeed, to observers of politics who have lived in Britain through the 1970s and 1980s, it seems reasonable to posit changes in social class factors coupled with changes in political attitudes. These might be summed up in the notion of 'affluence', the spread of comparative prosperity and comfortable life-styles in the skilled working class and the lower middle class and self-employed. Affluence has been coupled with an increase in the number of women working, some social mobility and the development of ma-

terialism and acquisitive individualism. Television has expressed and encouraged this culture, and personalised and (by diminishing faith and doctrine) secularised politics and political appeals.

This at least is a plausible account of the social and political history of the 1970s and 1980s. But statisticians and scholars are rightly cautious about such impressions, which do easily acquire the status of undisputed 'conventional wisdom'. The main critics of the dealignment theory, Heath et al (1991), suggest that change in social class has been slow and that the political behaviour attributable to social-class factors in the 1960s was not so different from the 1980s. Bring back politics! they cry.

They argue that changes in voting over the period are better explained by changes in the size of classes and by political factors, the extension of the franchise, the apparent failure of Labour governments and the political consequences of polarisation and the intensification of the Liberal challenge, and the establishment of the SDP.

Table 5 Combined effects of social and political change 1964–1987 as calculated by A. Heath et al 1991, pp. 209 and 220

Percentage shift in vote 1964–87 omitting shifts of less than 1.0 per cent			
Source of change	Cons	Lib/All	Lab
a) Social Class	+3.8	-	4.5
Housing	+4.6	-	-5.0
Ethnicity	-	-	+4.1
Combined social factors and including higher education and religion	+2.7	+1.8	-4.0
b) Political Number of Liberal candidates	-2.4	+6.7	-4.3
Formation of SDP	-	+1.3	-
Ideological polarisation	-2.0	+4.0	-2.0
Combined political factors including extension of franchise and tactical voting	-5.0	+12.0	-7.6
Total of social and political effects	-2.3	+13.8	-11.6
Actual change	+1.7	+12.8	-15.3

It does look as if class interpretations of voting have concentrated too much on the presence or absence of a large, solid Labour-voting working class. But the evident decline of such a class is not the same as the decline of all class influence in voting; and indeed some of the political factors, notably the rise of the Liberal Alliance were in part a response to social change. It is prudent for the analyst of voting to resist the temptation of a dramatic headline conclusion – Bring Back Politics, or Triumph of Essex Man, or even Disraeli's Two Nations.

Heath's conclusions are evident in the simple class/vote pattern shown in Table 3 in Chapter 14. All of the change shown can be attributed to the intervention of the Liberals since the 1970s. However, the attractive simplicity of such tables hides much complex movement. Table 5, p. 299, sets out Heath's own attempt to estimate sources of voting change between 1964 and 1987. Notice that political factors outweigh social factors. The message of this Table is that Labour and Liberals should fight each other, or, of course, ally with each other.

EXERCISES
Social and political change

18.8 What appear to be the most significant factors in the shifting of votes?

18.9 How can you explain why the Conservatives did better and Labour worse than predicted?

Political explanations of voting

The Table and other evidence suggest that there may be a New Politics in a New Society. Political factors are prominent in the range of short-term influences on voting which arise in the campaign. The politicians assume that voting is not totally determined by social factors; politics counts and political persuasion is worthwhile, for the election is decided by a comparatively few floaters, waverers and loyalists in marginal constituencies, and voters will be swayed by the policies offered by the parties.

Voting directed towards policies looks to be a plausible explanation of voting. It fits the model of the rational voter, and the election campaign as a kind of prolonged promotion of the best buy in a policy supermarket. In practice the voter responds to broad issues rather than specific policies and the record of government. An issue is a broad

policy area of concern to voters and where the parties are seen to hold differing positions, either in substance, or in degree of enthusiasm or competence to do something about it.

The evidence on voters' response to issues is complex. In surveys respondents are happy to rank issues in order of importance to them, but voting is not closely related to such perceptions. For example, in 1987 it appeared that Labour won on most issues – but still lost the election. Opinions on specifics do not always add up to a coherent set of opinions aligned with a particular party. For example, in the 1980s some voters obstinately favoured both nuclear disarmament and privatisation, a combination which was not on offer. In 1992 voters responding to survey questions favoured higher taxes to provide good public services; but still did not vote Labour. (There are, of course, many other explanations for this, including acceptance of the Conservative claim that they could provide the services without raising taxes.)

An alternative version of issue-voting is that it is based on political values and attitudes, a general outlook rather than specific opinions on matters of current concern, a more general philosophy rather than opinion on specific issues. This sounds rather old-fashioned but nevertheless true – Gladstone would not have been surprised. But again, philosophy may be too strong a word; the voter's philosophy has some of the character of a 'feeling', an 'instinct' (in its vaguer sense) or a mood.

There is a problem here, for voters and politicians, as well as students of politics, about how to distinguish between an opinion or value and a response to an issue. In practice, the voter faced with rival policies about individualism and community on the one hand, and equality and justice on the other, is likely to respond to more practical concerns, such as how much tax will I pay, or how soon shall I get my hip operation, or when will the school be able to buy some more text books.

The voter's decision may be composed of quite specific concerns of this kind together with general feelings about comfort and prosperity (the 'feel-good factor') and trust in a party (especially the governing party). The 'feel-good' factor is mainly related to economic matters, wages, inflation, interest rates for mortgages, and the experience or threat of unemployment. This is a judgement about one's own condition, with little concern for others. 'Feeling good' is linked to 'pocket-book voting' ('pocket-book' is American-English for 'wallet'). Voting in local elections in high and low poll tax areas demonstrated a direct link between vote and taxation; people prefer lower taxes with little regard for policies or party. It is clear that the Labour Party lost some votes in 1992 following its precise budget proposals to raise taxation on middle and high incomes.

Trust is directed mainly to the handling of the economy, though in some elections defence and national security are prominent (as in 1983 and 1987 when Labour favoured unilateral disarmament and withdrawal from the European Community). Judgements about the economy are not of course objective judgements, for even the economists do not agree! Under the influence of politicians, rather more than economists, the criteria for a layman's quick opinion on the economy has moved from balance of payments to inflation to 'Public Sector Borrowing Requirement' (a government term for debt) to interest rates and the value of the pound, and back to inflation. Since unemployment began its inexorable rise in the 1980s, governments do not propose it as a measure of the health of the economy.

Hence the voter's trust in the government's handling of the economy is likely to reflect the government's actual performance and its propaganda, the voter's general disposition towards the governing party, and a more informed assessment of his own prosperity and prospects. In the 1992 election voters showed an inclination to trust the Conservatives, despite their record, only partly acknowledged, of serious mismanagement of the economy in their third term. (The recession was blamed on world conditions, or on Margaret Thatcher's government, not on John Major's 'new' government.) The voter 'feeling good' is inclined by prudence and inertia to 'trust' the incumbent government, despite serious doubts about its record. There is here an incumbency factor at work – either choosing 'the devil you know' or else a tendency to trust the Conservatives in all conditions short of disaster.

Table 6 shows how the 1992 election campaign changed the dispositions of floating voters on certain major issues and on party leadership.

EXERCISES
Floating voters

18.10 Assuming these voters were decisive, why then did Labour lose the election?

18.11 Did the campaign make a significant difference?

Table 6 Floating voters changing their min

How floating voters changed		
Con lead over Labour		
	Before election	After election
Party with best policies on:		
Inflation	+29	+44
Unemployment	-28	-20
Health	-23	-22
Education	-1	+2
Taxation	-19	+40
Party best able to handle Economy	+18	+41
Whose tax plan and spending plans would make you feel better off	+4	+19
Most capable Prime Minister	+19	+36

Source: MORI On the Record panel of floating voters, quoted by John Curtice in *The Guardian*, 13 April 1992

Other factors in voting behaviour

Region and neighbourhood

There has developed since the 1970s a distinct geographical pattern to voting in Britain. This reflects old and new influences.

1 There have been since the late nineteenth century areas inclined to vote Liberal, often rural areas, strong in religious nonconformity.

2 Scotland and Wales have nurtured Nationalist movements, again since the nineteenth century and these began to support parliamentary candidates with some vigour and effect notably from 1974. In the election of October 1974 'third' parties (Liberals and Nationalists) were supported by roughly one fifth of voters in England, one quarter in Wales, two fifths in Scotland and just over a fifth of all voters.

3 The Conservative vote came to dominate the South of England, Labour the North, Scotland and Wales. The effect was most striking in 1983 when Labour held only 4 seats in southern England, south of Birmingham, apart from London. This North-South divide was even more evident in Parliament and in the Cabinet. This was a new version of the 'Two Nations' (Figure 1).

4 Northern Ireland remained politically another country. Religious or cultural loyalties in the Catholic and Protestant 'communities' largely

determine voting, and politics reflects sectarian conflict over national boundaries and status. This reminds us that the broadly economic conflicts within Britain are by comparison amenable to bargaining, and can be managed within a political system which is still – just – accepted by the contestants.

This regional pattern incorporates many factors, economic, social and political, so it is not appropriate to see region as a single and dominant cause of a particular pattern of voting. Yet there is substantial truth in that view, certainly in parts of Scotland and Wales, where regional or national consciousness is high. Elsewhere the regions begin to look like the old American 'Sections', which were central to the understanding of American politics, and perhaps there is a creeping consciousness of localities within regions.

One important consequence of the new regional division of voting is that there are fewer marginal seats (since voters are more concentrated territorially), so large shifts in seats at a general election are less likely. In the 1990s there is a greater chance of a continuing Conservative majority or a 'hung' Parliament.

The Table shows regional voting patterns in 1992.

Table 7 Regional patterns of voting 1992

Region	Cons	Lab	Other
Scotland	25	39	35
Wales	29	50	21
North	38	44	17
Midlands	42	41	17
South	50	26	25

Source: NOP

Within regions there is a neighbourhood effect, which again reflects social conditions and values. Where a neighbourhood has a marked economic, social or cultural character, it may have a characteristic vote which exaggerates normal tendencies. For example, a miner in a South Wales or Durham colliery village (if there are any left) will be more Labour-inclined than his income and total social position might indicate; similarly a businessman living in a prosperous Surrey suburb will be more Conservative than a businessman in a Yorkshire mill town. Race may have a stronger effect where there are large communities of coloured immigrants.

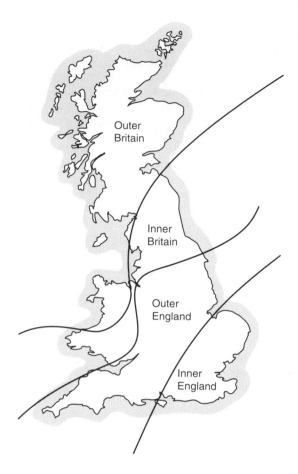

Figure 1 Two nations – or more?
Conservative voting and average income decreases from SE to NW and unemployment and mortality rates increase. See also Chapter 3, Figure 2

Thus there is a neighbourhood reinforcing effect. However, this effect depends on the existence of communities of comparatively homogeneous character. Changes in economic structure, notably the decline in mining and heavy industry, suburbanisation of the countryside and variation in the class structure, may all diversify neighbourhoods and weaken or at least change their political effect. For example, villages which develop as 'dormitory' suburbs change their social and political character. The much talked of 'mining communities' have broken down in areas where it is normal for miners to live at a distance, and drive to work.

Party image
There is still much to be said for the notion of

party 'image', or basic perception or understanding. We know that the analyses presented here do not reflect the processes in the voter's mind. Voting is not highly self-conscious behaviour, and many of the longer-term influences on it, especially the social elements, are part of the individual's settled personality and outlook. As with much individual behaviour, outlook and disposition are organised into simple rules, self-understandings, predispositions, frameworks for perception. The term 'image' does duty for all this, rather inadequately, but there is a parallel for the process in the development and fixing of an image in photography.

The Document shows images of the parties in the 1959 election. This is based on research in Leeds, but it is broadly representative of Britain in the 1950s and 1960s, and is still relevant in the 1990s.

■ DOCUMENT 18.1
Elements in the voter's image of the parties (1959)

Derived from J. Trenaman and D. McQuail, 1961, pp. 42–8
a) Conservative Party image
   i) among its supporters:
   - national ('out for the nation as a whole')
   - strength (clear policy, keeps promises, no squabbling)
   - individualism (opportunity, prosperity).
   ii) among Labour supporters:
   - national ('out for the nation as a whole')
   - upper-class party
   - prosperity.

b) Labour Party image
   i) among its supporters:
   - betterment of the common people
   - a divided party
   - national ('out for the nation as a whole').
   ii) among Conservative supporters:
   - weakness (e.g. absence of a clear policy)
   - not national (e.g. identified with the working class). ■

The document throws light on voting behaviour. The images include judgements about capacity to govern as well as assessments of policy; there is some awareness of social class. It is noticeable that Labour supporters held some favourable views of the other party; this is significant for the appeal of Conservatism in the 1990s. Images of this kind vary in quality and definition depending on the interest and information of the voter. But the image remains broad and general, a rough framework of feeling, rather than a precise perception. The voter characteristically thought of a party as 'the party for people like me' – thus bringing together a rough party image with a rough self-image. This was the mechanism of the process of 'party-identification', which appeared to underline and stabilise electoral behaviour at that time.

The image interpretation of voting is helpful and fits the insights of the psychology of perception. We perceive what we have learned to perceive: the real world is mediated by the images in store. But this is a rather simple model of behaviour which is in fact complex and obscure. Moreover, the image itself is a picture or metaphor, not strictly an explanation. It does not have an independent existence and it changes over time. An account of voting in terms of images best suits a stable political condition, in which images acquire a certain strength. In the more volatile 1970s and 1980s voters moved fast. In 1983, a third of 1979's Labour voters switched to another party, or abstained, and similarly a quarter of Conservatives moved. The posited relationship between self-image and party-image seems less firm and assured, and again this is valid for the 1990s.

Age and Gender
Age and gender make a great difference to personal lives, for example, in work experience, relative prosperity and culture; so it might be expected that they would influence the vote. Age reflects a particular personal political experience, as well as changes in work and status, and psychological changes. The latter may make for conservatism, but insecurity, poverty, and memories of old political loyalties may press in the other direction. In recent elections the pattern of age and voting is clear and unsurprising. The distribution of the middle-aged (35–54) vote is very close to the overall distribution. The young vote more heavily Labour (5–6 per cent above the average) and the old are more Conservative than the average (by 5–6 points). This still does not give the Conservatives an overall majority among pensioners. The differences in voting between age groups appear to be due to ageing rather than generation; that is, the radical younger voters grow more Conservative as they grow older. If this were not

so, the electorate would be steadily radicalised; it is possible that as people live longer so there will be an advantage to the Conservatives.

Differences by sex are less significant than these age differences. Women are more Conservative than men, for reasons which you may speculate about – home-centred? family-centred? more genteel? It was suggested after the 1992 election defeat that the Labour Party was too 'macho' for women voters, but this may be another way of saying that the Labour Party is not southern and bourgeois. If the Conservatism of age is combined with the Conservatism of sex, it follows that old women are very Conservative, 8 points above the average – and women live much longer than men. Observe the ranks of elderly middle-class women at a Conservative Party Conference – compared with the Labour conference.

Political perceptions: the political psychology of voting

Voting is the political act of an individual; indeed, for most people the most highly political action in their lives. So it seems best at the end of this analysis to return to the individual voter – or non-voter – confronted with a general election, watching, and deploring, endless politics on television, believing or disbelieving the morning paper, talking with neighbours or colleagues or evading the subject with defensive and sceptical remarks like 'They're all the same, politicians', or 'I can't stand x' or 'x seems to be doing all right'.

Most voters are not well-informed about, or interested in, politics. This is entirely understandable and not in the least discreditable, unless they are studying politics. At the lowest the voter simply votes; this is his only participation in the system, and his social awareness and political information are negligible. At the next level the voter is aware of at least some aspects of his place in society, and of the nature of the parties (but what does the jargon 'place in society' mean in practice?). Above this the appeal of the parties enters more clearly into the process, and the voter's reaction becomes more specifically political. At this point a vote may be said to have a substantial and specific political content, and the electoral campaign becomes more relevant.

The minimal voter, even the ill-informed voter, still makes a complex judgement as he or she relates a 'place in society' to the record and appeals of the party, and casts a vote. This is a difficult judgement to make, and it is not invalidated by the inarticulate voter's inability to explain and justify his vote. Democracy depends on voting as a minimal measure of participation, but does not require high political interest and activity. Indeed, democratic government soon becomes unworkable if everyone joins in – as in NIMBY protests (see Chapter 21).

Here are some indications of the political mind of the voter.

1 *The context of the election.* General elections differ in their political context and significance, and it seems likely that this is appreciated by voters. An election reflects specific political circumstances. The election of 1945 is the most striking example of an election with a dominant political context; other lesser examples are 1979 (after the 'Winter of Discontent'), 1983 (after the Falklands War, and in a reviving economy). In 1955 and again in 1992 the Conservatives had changed their leader and were allowed to proceed; and this was almost true in 1964. It might have been true in 1978 for Mr Callaghan.

2 *The standing of government.* The overriding political circumstance of an election is the standing and appeal of the government in power. This may be judged neutrally in party terms: the government is the government, the Prime Minister's government, but not the Conservative government. So in this context the critical questions are to do with trust (of the government compared with the opposition) and whether it is 'Time for a Change' (Labour's appeal in 1992). Unfortunately for Opposition parties, it is in most circumstances not time for a change, and the future will resemble the past. This is a special version of what in the USA is called the 'incumbency factor'. The British are not at all 'opposition-minded'. They have only elected a Labour government with a working majority when it already is the government (1966, and October 1974, but only just, and 1945, when the Labour Party had been part of the Coalition government in office until just before the election).

3 *The voter's experience of the campaign.* Voters receive the campaign mainly through television. In 1950 about 30 per cent of voters attended an election meeting; in 1987 only 3 per cent. Instead the voter-viewers watch television in quite significant numbers (news bulletins retain at least two thirds of the normal audience, but video rentals increase by about one fifth in a flight from election television). In consequence the viewing voter is presented with

politics as designed for television, characteristically originated in London, leader-oriented, dominated by images and 'sound-bites', packaged for political marketing. This is in the idiom of television and fits reality as routinely produced and presented by television. In the triangle of forces, politicians, media and viewer-voters it is not clear who if any one dominates. (see Chapter 17 for discussion of the campaign and the media).

4 *Elections as a sporting contest.*. Parliamentary elections are the most important and the most salient of all elections. Voting in other elections, local and European, do not attract the same interest, and the turn-out of voters is much lower. Parliamentary elections have a significant horse-race quality, which appeals to the British sporting and gambling instincts. A general election is the third most popular race of the sporting calendar, and rivals snooker in its capacity to attract an all night television audience. Ironically, the interest generated by the thrill of the competition has little political spill-over, and quickly subsides. The publi-cation of polls throughout the campaign en- courages the horse race view of elections (see Chapter 17.)

5 *Political memory.* Political memory is notoriously short and highly selective. In any case young voters have limited direct experience of politics. By 1992 only pensioners had adult memories of the 1939–45 war. By 1996, no voter under 40 will have voted in an election won by the Labour Party. Some incidents may stay in this 'folk memory' and retain some political energy: perhaps the Great Depression of the 1930s, more certainly Churchill, the Great War Leader; perhaps Margaret Thatcher and the Falklands. The 'Winter of Discontent' seems to stick uncomfortably for Labour (but with some justification) in the popular consciousness. Party propaganda clearly plays a part in shaping the 'folk memory'; political myths are made, but they are based on some part of reality, and are related to dominant political values. In politics, as in everyday life, people choose what they remember.

6 *The appeal of political leaders.* People love leaders. This is confirmed by history, and is evident in religious life. General elections are about leaders, both in themselves, and, much more important, for what they embody – for magnetism, charisma and the sub-Nuremberg emotions of political loyalty, and for summing up neatly, in an obviously human way the complex factors of political competition. The voter is able to put aside the manifestos and the interminable broadcasts, abandon the study of electoral behaviour, and respond simply with mental relief and a warm glow to a leader seen both as convenient summary of current politics and as icon.

The appeal of leaders is potent but is set in the context of party and current politics; leadership is not separable from the per-formance and promise of parties. Hence it is possible for a party with a less popular leader to win elections (as in 1970 and 1979), and for the Liberals with comparatively popular leaders to lose elections consistently. An unusually good or unusually bad leader may be worth a few points one way or the other, but the perceived success or failure of governments is more important. So leaders do not win or lose elec-tions on their own. Nevertheless, the Labour Party seems to have been damaged electorally by its leaders, Michael Foot and Neil Kinnock, who both did badly in a survey about 'who would make the best Prime Minister?'; while John Major's popularity improved Conservative prospects.

Political parties most of the time choose electable leaders, but this is not their only consideration when selecting a leader. Political parties, like most organisations, have their own internal drives, tensions, confusions and misinformation. They do not act consistently and rationally to maximise votes, just as voters do not act consistently to maximise political satisfaction.

7 *Dominant ideology.* In social interpretations of voting the behaviour of the voter is seen as largely determined by impersonal forces. In political interpretations the voter seems to enjoy and exercise significant autonomy. This is misleading for in practice the voter is constrained by the political system too – by the power of the elites, the government and the political culture to modify the context and define the choices of the election. This still falls short of controlling the individual's vote. For the voter Free Will remains – but it has many enemies.

Conclusion. It should be clear from the foregoing sections that voting is a complicated activity, the product of the interaction of an individual with his home and work background and his life history, with political principles, attitudes and policies formulated and promoted by a complex organisation called a political party, modified by events and magnified by the media. Figure 2 conveys a little of this extraordinary process.

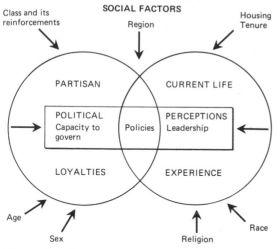

Figure 2. Influences on the voter's choice

It seems likely that most British voters are not very interested in politics, except as a background soap opera and occasional sporting contest; that their values are related to home, family, work, income, with occasional bursts of moral outrage or patriotism; and that they do not have high expectations of politicians. There is not much emotion here, but just enough rationality. It is all very low-key, low profile. Then a general election bursts on the placid scene, and both emotion and rationality are put under strain. This is not an ideal scenario for the making of major political choice. Yet democracy depends on this process being at least a little reasonable and relevant. One critic described a general election as a 'ramshackle and haphazard procedure'; but then many choices in life, business, sport, love and politics are inevitably a mixture of rationality, inertia and leaping in the dark.

GUIDE TO EXERCISES

18.1 The comparative stability of the Conservative vote, the decline of Labour and the rise of third and fourth parties.

18.2 The rise of third and fourth parties (especially Liberals and Nationalists) appears to have damaged Labour far more than the Conservatives, but see following text.

18.3 Check your findings with the conclusions of this chapter.

18.4 Yes, at the top and bottom of the scale, the pattern is clear enough. But the C2 category and all Liberals are 'class-neutral' zones. Still keep in mind a general health warning: voting is complex behaviour, and class is an 'umbrella' term. Although every vote can be assigned to a class category, the strength of the class motivation of the vote is uncertain.

18.5 A shift of votes from Liberal Democrats to Labour, spread over all classes and reflecting the decline of the Alliance and the reformation of the Labour Party under Neil Kinnock.

18.6 It is suggestive at least, though it is well to be cautious about hypothesizing anything like a solid and coherent class. The figures for housing tenure and for region are especially notable and there is here some indication of the emergence of the Two Nations of Disraeli's rhetoric of the 1870s. Remember, too, that the 1983 election was especially bad for Labour, so the exaggeration of anti-Labour tendencies is helpful for analysis but misleading.

18.7 Yes, there is a strong association between home ownership and Conservative voting, and council tenancy and Labour voting. But we know that this association is not the same as cause and effect, and is set in other social relationships and political attitudes. Predisposition rather than conversion is at work, but also reinforcement.

A similar comment is appropriate in relation to new share owners, the purchasers of shares in the privatised companies in the 1980s. Most purchasers were already comfortable financially and inclined to vote Conservative.

18.8 All the factors with a score of 4 or more – class, housing, religion, the number of Liberal candidates and polarisation. The last two political factors have as much impact as class and housing combined. Religion is unexpectedly salient in this analysis, and is related to the emergence of a 'new' middle class.

18.9 Perhaps best by not expecting figures like these to be so accurate. But the tendency for the Conservatives to out-perform the polls was noticeable in 1970 and again in 1992. It may be there is a lag or gap between the social and political scene perceived in a social science analysis and the reality as experienced or felt by voters, a kind of inarticulate extra disposition towards the Conservatives.

18.10 The Table is not exhaustive, but on this evidence, Labour was not trusted to handle the economy, its tax plans were unpopular and the Conservatives had the better Prime Minister. Labour was preferred on health and unemployment.

18.11 Except on health and unemployment the campaign appears to have made a significant difference; though it is possible, indeed likely, that some of the apparent effect reflects not campaign influence but a process of voters making up their minds and returning to their serious, 'when-the-chips-are-down' opinions.

ASSESSMENT
The referendum

The first national referendum in British history was held in June 1975 to decide whether Britain should remain a member of the European Economic Community. The government's case for holding a referendum was that the issue involved a fundamental constitutional change, even a shift in sovereignty, but it was also true that the Labour leadership faced difficulties in securing the support of the Labour Party. In 1992 the issue of a referendum arose again when the Treaty of Maastricht was submitted to referenda in some other countries and was rejected in Denmark. In Britain it seemed that popular consent to a major constitutional change was not at all firm, both major parties were divided, and the absence of informed public debate on such a fundamental issue was disturbing.

In 1975 the government secured a majority of two to one in favour of staying within the EEC. This 'wholehearted popular acceptance' of the EEC contradicted the views of some organisations, particularly the trade unions, which claimed to speak on behalf of the people. Thus, it seemed, the true voice of the people was heard loud and clear, and for once it determined policy. Where the parties had failed to develop a clear position, the referendum offered a decisive and legitimate judgement. In

the process many people must have learned a little about the issues.

Herein lay the classic democratic case for referenda, government by consent of the governed. There is a further argument in favour of the referendum arising from a point of view of British party politics. The old party divisions, it may be said, are stale and irrelevant, the 'dogfights' are unproductive, and disheartening to all but the party faithful. The referendum cuts across these divisions, and restores meaning to the political contest. At the same time Parliament is weakened by party control, the democratic quality of the system now depends mainly on general elections; so, it is argued, if we have to be content with a form of plebiscitary democracy, let us at least have more plebiscites!

However, there is a powerful case against the referendum, and one which seemed to have the sympathy of many citizens in June 1975, grumbling on their way to the polls. It is clear from the discussion above that specific questions of policy may be too fine a task for the blunt instrument of a mass electorate. Even if the issue is well understood, it may be entangled with other current but not wholly relevant matters, and may not be accurately reflected by the phrasing of the question. Most serious political issues require complex answers, taking account of qualifications, priorities, conditions.

Moreover, the theory of democracy requires representative and responsible government, but not direct popular government. Indeed, there are times when a responsible government quite properly defies popular opinion, or gives a lead where popular opinion is silent. There is evidence from countries where the referendum is used that it is rarely on the side of change, and may often be on the side of reaction. One striking though unrepresentative example is that in Britain today a referendum would almost certainly favour the re-introduction of the death penalty, against all the evidence that it has virtually no deterrent effect.

Opponents of referenda can point to the result of the EEC referendum, as an almost exact confirmation of how Parliament had already voted on the people's behalf. So trust Parliament to make the right choice! Certainly the question put in the 1975 referendum was complex, indeed unanswerable with any degree of confidence. Much depended on the form of the question, seeking approval for an existing situation, not a radical new move.

Further, other events and circumstances plainly affected the vote. The issue was obscured by an economic crisis and tangled up in divisions in the Labour Party. Arguably, the sovereign people in their fluctuating wisdom would have voted Yes in 1967 but No in 1972–73. Thus it is naive to think that a Yes or a No vote in June 1975 meant just Yes or No to the EEC. A referendum is always more than a simple question and answer.

Such complications are unavoidable. The referendum divides, and divides in unexpected ways. For all the argument about the irrelevance of the political parties, we still need an effective party system; and the effect of the referendum is not to reform or improve the system, but to put almost unbearable strains on it.

The same may be said about the consequences of a referendum for Cabinet government. The convention of Cabinet responsibility is well entrenched. It means normally that Cabinet ministers argue out their disagreements in private and accept the agreed policy – or resign. This system has the virtue (much over-rated it is true) of forcing Cabinet to take a line and stick by it: the Cabinet plays as a team. During the EEC referendum campaign this entrenched convention was suspended, and some Cabinet ministers denounced as disastrous a major policy they later had to support and carry out. This is not 'responsible' government as understood in British constitutional theory.

In 1992 there were renewed calls for a referendum on the Treaty of Maastricht which confirmed and developed the European Community. It was argued that the Treaty confirmed and extended a major constitutional change, which had not been presented to the people in any detail. Since all parties apparently agreed, there was no discussion during the election, and there had been little public discussion when the Single European Act was passed in 1985. Yet there remained serious divisions in both Conservative and Labour Parties. Opponents of the EC tended to favour a referendum, but not on purely constitutional grounds.

These arguments for and against referenda are not easy to weigh. Here again a simple answer, yes or no, does not do justice to the complexity of the issues. At the heart of the problem lie value judgements about the present state of British government. If you answer 'yes' to the following questions, then the referendum is for you worth serious consideration.

Do you think government is not sufficiently responsive to the views of the people?

Do you think the present party system is irrelevant and ineffective?

Are you prepared to modify the constitutional principle of responsible government and the Cabinet's collective responsibility?

Do you think some issues, notably significant constitutional change, require a special procedure of popular appeal?

Can a satisfactory question be devised?

Can adequate arrangements for campaigning be made?

It might be wise to avoid answering such difficult questions with a simple yes or no. If so, then perhaps the referendum too is best suited to straightforward questions, of the kind which figure in local referenda – Do you want a village hall? Should bus fares for the elderly be subsidised? Should public houses be shut on Sundays? On the other hand, the public debate about difficult choices improves information and understanding, and challenges the normal artificiality and hypocrisy of adversarial politics; the referendum refreshes the parties which parliamentary procedures can never reach!

Concepts

Participation

Participation is generally regarded as a 'Good Thing', indeed an essential, in a democracy. People (ordinary people, not 'The People') consent to what governments do to them and for them, but by a process in which they should play a part. In Britain the minimum participation is to abstain in a general election. But most people vote; and a tiny minority, not much more than a million, join a political party and engage in political activity. Many more people belong to, or support, interest groups, and so contribute indirectly to political activity.

This is a very thin basis of popular activity for a vigorous democracy. It may be defended on the grounds that democracy requires no more, and that the sanction of a general election every four or five years economically ensures the responsiveness of government. Further, it is against human nature that we should all take up political activity. So political apathy is fine...?

Majoritarianism

This inelegant and not much used term refers to the doctrine of majority rule. This is a good and economical basis for decision making, but it carries with it the possibility of coercion by a majority, and the insensitive treatment of minorities. Many countries, containing substantial minorities and profound cultural divisions, have had to arrange their system of government to allow the living together of minorities, the sharing of power, and a continuing concern for proportionality (for example, in government posts). Government is conducted through fairly stable coalitions. Such political systems are sometimes called 'consociational'.

Britain, or rather, British governments, prefer rule by a majority (they would, wouldn't they?). This works, so it may be argued, except in Northern Ireland, where there are deep cultural divisions. There power-sharing has been tried, but so far the Unionist and Protestant majority has not accepted it. Power-sharing has to be based on the mutual respect of the groups, and the abnegation of majoritarian politics. Majorities are reluctant to give up the advantage of their position, but the legitimacy of small majorities exercising absolute power is open to question.

● CASE STUDY
The War of Jennifer's Ear 1992

A Labour Party election broadcast told of two young girls, both suffering from a painful ear condition; one was quickly cured by a private operation, the other endured 12 months of pain and misery while waiting for an operation under the National Health Service. The film, skilfully produced (at an estimated cost of not less than £200 000) to wrench the heart, was 'faction', a story based on a real case. 'Faction' allows a great deal of dramatic license, while conveying a sense of authenticity. Some critics think 'faction' is inherently deceiving. So it is; but the degree of deception varies. No-one sees Shakespeare's Henry IV as a source of historical truth, but it may well be a source of insight and underlying general truth. But then, a Shakespeare play does not look like a history book.

There is a problem with a television programme which looks like a documentary but does not have a commitment to authenticity in detail. The truth, underlying, general or specific, of Labour's film became a matter of debate, but no-one could deny that the film was a dramatic statement, and therefore an overstatement, of one easily exploitable aspect of the problem of National Health Service funding.

On the following day the name of the owner of the painful ear, Jennifer, was accidentally (but perhaps carelessly?) revealed to one newspaper. At the same time, Jennifer's family, Mum, Dad and Grandfather, turned out to be politically committed and active but divided. Dad had first informed his Member of Parliament and the Labour Party; Mum and Grandfather now told their concerns to the Conservative Party, thus (perhaps inadvertently) ensuring that details of the case were more widely known. The consultant concerned entered the fray, claiming the facts were not as portrayed in the film; but Jennifer's father produced an earlier letter which appeared to justify the account given in the film.

Labour then had to spend time defending the broadcast, not attacking the government's record of support for the National Health Service. The imputation of deception was seized on and added to the increasing flow of insults to Neil Kinnock: a Sun headline ran: 'If Kinnock will tell lies about a sick little girl, will he ever tell the truth about anything'. There were two unusually dramatic press conferences. In one, Neil Kinnock's Press Officer intervened to make an emotional but effective speech defending the handling of the case. In another, the Health Secretary had to admit that Conservative Central Office had passed their information to one of the Tory tabloids. By then all of the media were in hot pursuit.

The row over Jennifer's Ear (a reference to a war with Spain known as the War of Jenkins' Ear, 1739) erupted over the campaign for three days. Every one directly involved was damaged, except Jennifer herself, who being only five years old rose calmly above the storm, and was much more excited about her new tropical frog called Rupert. Her parents seemed to survive, with their politically incompatible partnership intact for the time being; though they had to endure an intrusive attention from the press which is little understood outside the ranks of the royal or famous. (The press really does 'camp on the doorstep' – that is, if you are lucky.) The reputation of the press for intrusion and harassment was further damaged, though a British two-tier morality seems to apply – we all deplore the behaviour of the press, but buy the papers.

Television for the most part followed the press, without the headlines but, of course, with film cameras. The *Daily Express* accused television of its customary Labour bias, but if television never reported misleading claims by the political parties, it could give up reporting elections – (and why not? you may say). Some local television, often neglected in national commentaries, followed up the Jennifer case with local cases comparable with Jennifer's. Viewers, like readers of the newspapers, were still unlikely to acquire a well-informed understanding of the funding problems of the NHS. But, then, this was an election in a mass-democracy with a liking for soap-operas, not a series of lectures on politics and economics.

The Labour Party had most to lose, and lost it. Its campaign on the health issue, one of its strongest issues, was overwhelmed by the row over the broadcast, and may well have suggested that this particular tactic had been used too often (in the previous month and in the 1987 election, for example), and the form of argument ('waving the shroud') did not address the real problems. (Most families could quote a relative or friend who had received excellent treatment in the NHS for a serious and life-threatening condition; and another with a non-urgent condition who had waited months, or been invited to 'go private'.) Labour lost, not so much on the health issue itself, but on its credibility and reputation for fair and honest campaigning.

The Conservative Party should have gained from the affair on an issue on which their credibility was thin, especially after Margaret Thatcher's firm support for private medicine. But the revelation of their direct dealings with the tabloid press showed that they too were ready to join electoral battle over Jennifer's Ear. The Liberals were able to take their high moral line, attacking the other two parties, for attacking each other, and the Liberals' standing in the polls rose.

Later, Jennifer's Dad complained to the Press Complaints Commission about the publication, by *The Independent* and the *Daily Express*, of Jennifer's name, without permission. The Commission ruled that 'publication was in the public interest'. How would you assess the rights and wrongs of the whole of this bizarre episode?

It is acceptable in political argument to dramatise a case in personal terms e.g. unemployment or inadequate education or strikes have or had such consequences for these particular people. So the intention was not improper. However, the execution was careless, for there was clearly a risk of press harassment if the child's identity became known (but the family were party to some of the publicity). A more serious charge is that the film was trivial and irrelevant to the serious problems of funding health care, and rationing by means other than money. ●

Political communication and the media

Public opinion and private opinions

A triangle of forces

Communication between the government and the people is an essential process in a system of government claiming to be democratic. Communication is necessary not only for effective command but also for accountability, responsiveness and consent. But this crucial process of political communication is rarely direct. A Prime Minister may address a crowd in a market place, or a party conference, but he would need to travel and speak everyday for ten years to reach an audience the size of a single evening television news programme.

Hence political communication depends on an intermediary – the 'mass media'. But the media do not act simply as a screen or transmitter; they take a positive part in the communication process. At the same time 'the people' are not passive receivers of government communications (except perhaps at party conferences!). So there is a triangle of forces engaged in political communication – government, media, people.

A triangle is acceptable as a rough characterisation, but in fact the processes of communication are more complex.

- the government here stands for all the institutions of government and politics, the executive, parliament and political parties, including the opposition parties
- the media includes press and television but also in theory everything that counts as communication and affects politics – for example, the teaching of history or politics in schools, a sermon on charity by a local minister of religion or symbols such as the Union Jack
- the people includes articulate individuals and groups, of many kinds, from angry motorists

protesting at stubble burning to 'major' interest groups like the National Farmers Union.

Thus the 'triangle of forces' is not simple or shapely. Nor is the process of communication always to do with communication. It includes non-communication and secrecy on the government's side as well as selection, distortion, management and manipulation by government, the media, the interest groups and even some of the people. Political communication is a crucial part of the struggle for political power. In this perspective 'public opinion', which older politicians used to respect, flatter, cajole and woo, is to be assaulted and refashioned.

The nature of public opinion

Formerly politicians regarded 'public opinion' as an entity, to be judged or estimated, mainly by politician's hunch, and to be taken account of. The sentiment was a little patronising; so too the notion that politicians might have, to quote Lord Morrison, 'an extensive knowledge of the outlook of the people in various walks of life and an understanding of how their minds work'. Since Lord Morrison wrote in the 1950s, sample surveys have replaced the politician's 'ear to the ground' or weekend in the constituency as a guide to public opinion. But, except on particular issues at one moment in time, public opinion remains complex, variable and obscure.

There is a major problem with the term 'public opinion'. The 'public' includes private individuals, who may be aggregated into sections of the public; this is the true mass public, but it is often divided into a majority, a minority and the 'don't knows'. Apart from such aggregated opinion there are many little publics, interests and groups, contributing to the general clamour of 'opinion' (watch or read the news to discover the sound of the little publics).

'Opinion' is more difficult to unscramble. Opinion is a spectrum. At one end lie the ill-defined perceptions, images, values, prejudices which are part of traditional political culture. At the other end are the more precise formulations of opinion on specific issues, taxation, say, selective schools, or dog registration. Attitudes to the parties lie somewhere in the middle.

Generally the less specific elements in the spectrum of opinion persist over time, but on specific issues people have no views until there are headlines and opinion polls. Hence an opinion poll on an unfamiliar or obscure topic has to be interpreted as precisely that: 'X per cent of people, when confronted by an interviewer and asked about a matter on which they had no opinions at all in the previous week, said that...'. This is not without validity, but it indicates that 'public opinion' on some issues is insubstantial.

Analysing political communication

The media may be analysed as institutions or organisations, and the product of the media – news, opinion, persuasion – assessed as political communication. The influence of the media is more difficult to assess and must be measured against the counter-influence of the government as a powerful player in the political communication game. The people, it must be assumed, are not passive receptacles for the messages of government and media.

Insofar as relative influence in the triangle of forces can be identified and measured, and the imputation of bias sustained, then questions of democratic values arise. Broadly there are three positions.

1 Liberal – let the market decide. There should be freedom to publish newspapers, subject only to laws of libel, obscenity and so on. Publishers and readers have freedom of choice. Government intervention is abhorrent, and impractical anyway. The market freedom enjoyed by the press should be extended to broadcasting.
2 The media as entertainment and political persuasion. Entertainment is the main function, but persuasion, even political crusade, is entirely legitimate. The imbalance between Left and Right in the press probably reflects opinion, is much exaggerated and may be temporary. (This second position justifies what appear to be the consequences of trusting to

the market).
3 Public service or public interest - there is a responsibility to inform and educate, as well as persuade and entertain. The model here is the BBC and what has become known as public service broadcasting. The application of this model to an expanded system of broadcasting has not proved impossible so far, but further commercial expansion raises problems. The privately owned, commercially competitive press would not accept the notion of public service as exemplified by the BBC, and would assert that it does serve the public interest.

These three positions raise questions about for example

- the nature of the bias
- the extent of influence
- the relative power of producers and consumers in the market
- the value of the public service tradition
- the feasibility of regulation in the public interest
- the use and abuse of freedom.

The media – the mass and monopoly

The Press

The mass media of the mid-twentieth century are, above all else, massive. In the nineteenth century journalism was dominated by *The Times* with a circulation of 50 000. In 1896 Lord Northcliffe (Alfred Harmsworth) published the *Daily Mail*; by 1900 it was selling nearly a million copies at 1/2d (about 25p now) a copy. By 1947 both the *Daily Mirror* and the *Daily Express* were selling nearly 4 million copies each. In the mid 1960s the *Daily Mirror* topped 5 million. But both these giants fell back in the 1970s, the *Daily Mirror* to under 4 million, the *Daily Express* to under 3 million, at which point it met the rapidly rising *Sun* (formerly the *Daily Herald*).

By the 1990s *The Sun* and the *Daily Mirror* (with the *Scottish Daily Record*) topped the charts at just over 3.5m copies each; the *Mail* and the *Express* were 2m below at just over 1.5m copies each. Of the 'quality' newspapers, only *The Telegraph* at over 1m copies approached these tabloids. The Sunday newspapers displayed a similar pattern. *The News of the World* beat all comers at 4.7m copies, and 12m readers – a world record, one of the few which Britain now holds.

Table 1 National Newspaper Circulation 1992 (millions)

	May-Oct 1992
Sun	3.56
Daily Mirror/Record	3.58
Daily Star	0.81
Daily Mail	1.72
Daily Express	1.54
Today	0.53
Daily Telegraph	1.04
Guardian	0.41
Times	0.38
Independent	0.37
Financial Times	0.29
News of the World	4.70
Sunday Mirror	2.72
People	2.10
Mail on Sunday	1.95
Sunday Express	1.76
Sunday Times	1.19
Sunday Telegraph	0.57
Observer	0.53
Independent on Sunday	0.40

The figures for circulation May–October 1992 are given in the Table. Readership is between 2.5 and 3.0 persons per copy. On average the British 'consume' about five times more newspapers than other countries.

These very high circulation national newspapers are without parallel in the Western world. Of the popular papers, only the *Daily Mirror* and *The People* are sympathetic to the Labour party. Hence there arises a peculiar bias in British, or rather, English, politics: for better or for worse, the Tory tabloids are part of the political culture. Every weekday morning three Tory tabloids attract about 17m readers; on the other side, the *Daily Mirror* musters about 8m.

Such massive circulations have been built up at the cost of destroying many small newspapers. The Liberal-inclined *News Chronicle* collapsed in 1960 and the *Daily Herald*, a Labour paper, in 1964. However, the launch of new titles has kept the number of national dailies almost unchanged – 12 in 1921, 11 in 1993. The great slaughter was among the provincial morning papers – 41 in 1921, only 16 in 1993; in the same period provincial evening papers have been reduced from 89 to about 64.

This process is mainly a consequence of the harsh economics of the industry. Newpapers are a fiercely competitive industry. Proprietors have made and lost fortunes. Production costs are high – until the 1980s because of old technology, overmanning, and restrictive trade unions; and in the 1990s due to the cost of new technology and newsprint. The costs of gathering news have risen sharply. Advertising revenue, which accounts for 40 to 70 per cent of the income of national papers, fluctuates with the economy, and favours the papers with the highest or the richest readership. In consequence, newspapers with circulations comfortably above one million (the *Daily Herald* and the *News Chronicle*) proved not to be viable, and some of the quality papers with much lower circulations lose money and are subsidised by other activities.

The ownership of the press is even more restricted than the small number of independent newspapers suggests: multiple ownership compounds the effect of the concentration of readership, so that the British press is characterised by monopoly. By the 1990s seven groups owned newspapers accounting for over 80 per cent of the readership; three groups controlled just over one half – the highest concentration in the western world. Rupert Murdoch's News International owned *The Sun, The Times, Sunday Times, News of the World*, and altogether almost ninety newspapers around the world. Rupert Murdoch also has substantial interests in television, including the merged satellite channel, BSkyB. However, while Murdoch has restricted competition, he has enhanced the viability of a diverse press by destroying the monopoly power of the print unions.

The monopolistic proprietors have sometimes figured as the villains in the history of the press. In their high period – between about 1900 and the 1930s – the press barons (Northcliffe, Rothermere, Beaverbrook) seemed both to make substantial fortunes and wield considerable political power. This was, in Baldwin's celebrated phrase, 'power without responsibility' – 'the prerogative of the harlot', as he said quoting Kipling. Since 1945 the power has been challenged, and the fortunes diminished. Some newspapers lose money, but the popular press is still capable of making good money for its owners and its workers.

Broadcasting

The lack of diversity in the British press is virtually unmatched in any other western democracy. It would be cause for concern if the press were not itself subject to keen and effective competition from the other mass media, radio and television. Wireless broadcasting began in 1922, and in 1927 the British Broadcasting Corporation was established as a public corporation with a monopoly of broadcasting. By 1945 almost 10 million wireless sets were licensed annually. But in the 1950s television rapidly became a rival to radio for public attention. In 1958 the number of licences for television and radio surpassed those for radio alone. In 1973 there were over 17 million television licences. By then, well over 90 per cent of the British people had access to a television set, and at any time in the evenings a third of the adult population was viewing television.

Audience figures demonstrate the massive scale of television broadcasting. Average viewing per head is about 27 hours per week, nearly 4 hours each day (though a surprising number of other activites are combined with viewing!). 'Soap-operas', like Coronation Street and Neighbours, are seen regularly by 15–20 million viewers - far more than the readership of the *News of the World*. Light entertainment programmes may attract audiences of 8–12 million or so. On special occasions television can create a massive national audience. The World Cup Final of July 1990 was seen by 25 million in Britain (and an estimated 400 million in the whole world). The live broadcast of Princess Anne's wedding was seen by almost 28 million in Britain; and three-quarters of the population saw live or recorded coverage.

At Christmas time popular comedy shows may rival Princess Anne. None so far has reached the 20 million people in Britain (and 750 millions altogether) who watched the wedding of the Prince of Wales to Lady Diana Spencer in the summer of 1981. Eleven years later over 13 million watched the sadder story, 'Diana – End of a Fairytale'. For the record, it is claimed that Bob Geldof's Live Aid concert of 1985 was viewed by 2000 million people world wide. Beat that! News and current affairs programmes are less popular. Even so, the major news bulletins can reach 7–8 million people. Newspapers with very high readership can just about match these figures for news programmes.

In ownership and control broadcasting is no more diversified than the press. The BBC lost its monopoly in television in 1954 with the establishment of commercial television under the Independent Television Authority; but the commercial companies co-operated in what was for some of the time a national network. The resulting duopoly was loosened somewhat by the Broad-

casting Act of 1990 and the advent of cable and satellite television which attracted about 5 per cent of viewing by the early 1990s. Channel 4, which is operationally independent takes 10 per cent, leaving the rest to be divided between the two BBC channels and ITV. Regional stations, which are the norm in other countries, 'opt out' of the national networks for comparatively short periods. Radio broadcasting is happily much stronger in the regions and localities; the BBC now has commercial competitors locally, and the BBC's national monopoly of sound broadcasting was ended by the establishment of the admirable Classic FM station (1992). Still, despite increased competition, broadcasting in Britain is characterised like the press by mass and monopoly.

Broadcasting, especially by television, is now the most important source of political information and opinion for most people. In terms of massiveness and monopoly it has far outdone the press. The BBC is a massive organisation, with a staff of over 20,000 and annual expenditure of about £1bn. Its undoubted massiveness and a strong tendency to monopoly raise problems in an industry which serves the information needs of a democracy, as well as its tastes in entertainment.

Mass and monopoly in the media go with a dominant national organisation. This is centred in London and reflects the dominance of the metropolitan culture of the United Kingdom. Scotland and Northern Ireland, and Wales enjoy limited autonomy, having a strong national or regional press and broadcasting. But the main evening news still originates in London. There are signs of a more vigorous development of regional broadcasting and a local press, but there is little serious politics at that level to sustain it. If the dominance of London in the media is to be weakened, the challenge is likely to come from Australia and the USA rather than from the provinces of Britain.

Nature of the press

The nature of the press

Though the tabloid press is treated with some disdain by liberal middle-class commentators, it has to be said that it attracts readers, makes a profit and has an impact. It is essentially a popular press with a broad appeal. In particular the Mail and the Express both draw readers from across the social classes, taking not less than one fifth of their readers from each of the four socio-economic groups (AB, C1, C2, DE).

The press is a commercial enterprise, and exists to make a profit; indeed, it cannot exist for long without making a profit. Its costs, especially in newsprint and labour, are high. Hence it needs a high circulation to bring in the pennies of the millions and the pounds of the advertisers, or, alternatively, a readership with high purchasing power to attract up-market advertising. The British press reflects the commercial alternatives: a small-circulation 'quality' press and a mass-circulation popular press. To secure a high circulation, the popular press must cater for the tastes of the masses, 'giving the public what it wants', or at least what it is prepared to buy.

■ DOCUMENT 19.1
Editors aim at the masses

a) Extract from National Union of Teachers, 'Popular culture and personal responsibility' *(verbatim report of a conference held in October 1960). Speech by Mr Cecil King, chairman of the* Daily Mirror, *p. 253*
Of course you have got to give the public what it wants, otherwise you go out of business as we have seen recently in the case of two or three newspapers. You try and raise its standards as well. The trouble is the critics imagine the great British public is as educated as themselves and their friends.... In point of fact it is only the people who conduct newspapers and other similar organisations who have any idea quite how indifferent, quite how stupid, quite how uninterested in education of any kind the great bulk of the British public are...

b) Arthur Christiansen, former Editor of the Daily Express, *quoted in F. Williams, 1959, p. 191*
I journeyed from Rhyl to Prestatyn on Sunday past lines of boarding houses, caravans, wooden huts, shacks, tents and heaven knows what else. In every one of them there were newspaper readers. Happy citizens, worthy, fine people but not in the least like the reader Fleet Street seems to be writing for. These people are not interested in Glyndebourne or vintage claret or opera or the Sitwells or dry-as-dust economics or tough politics. It is our job to interest them in everything. It requires the highest degree of skill and ingenuity.

c) A place in The Sun
The Sun purchased by Rupert Murdoch in 1970, has become the quintessential British tabloid newspaper – characterised by high circulation, commercial success, crusading and heavily biased politics, robust in its popular appeal, and according to its critics, crude, vulgar, and sexist. Its headlines have included GOTCHA for the sinking of the Argentine warship, the Belgrano, and UP YOURS DELORS (1990) in criticism of the then President of the European Commission. It takes a jingoistic attitude to foreigners, especially the French – HOP OFF YOU FROGS. *The Sun* has been a fervent supporter of Margaret Thatcher and the Conservative party, but not of the monarch; the prime interests of the paper are sex, sport and money. Altogether *The Sun* seems to confirm the ancient wisdom that no-one ever went broke through underestimating the taste and intelligence of the British people. ■

EXERCISE
Editors and their readers

19.1 Are these editors wrong to estimate so low the intelligence and interests of their readers?

News as a product
Newspapers sell entertainment, and much of the content of the popular press is not very serious. But they are still newspapers rather than picture or story magazines or comics. News, in the sense of up-to-the-minute information on a matter of high public interest, is what sells newspapers. The scoop, the high impact exclusive story, is the pot of gold. Editors select according to a scale of news values which becomes instinctive. Alastair Hetherington, a writer, broadcaster and former editor of *The Guardian* set out what he called his 'seismic scale', which could be adapted to any newsroom.

■ DOCUMENT 19.2
A measure of news values

From A. Hetherington, 1985, p. 8
Significance: social, economic, political, human.
Drama: the excitement, action and entertainment in the event.
Surprise: the freshness, newness, unpredictability.
Personalities: royal, political, 'showbiz', others.
Sex, scandal, crime: popular ingredients.
Numbers: the scale of the event, numbers of people affected.
Proximity: on our doorsteps, or 10 000 miles away.
[for television an extra factor]
Pictures and visual attractiveness. ■

EXERCISE
News values

19.2 Would a news editor or reporter find this advice restrictive?

News is a highly perishable commodity. The best news is the newest; for a morning paper this means the news that happened too late for either the evening papers or the evening television bulletins. Sometimes the newest news is speculation about what is going to happen – not always presented as speculation. Newspapers are produced at speed, reports may be written by people with inadequate information, sub-edited and headlined by people with no relevant information at all. The amount of news available has expanded substantially, and rapid selection is necessary; little wonder then that the standard of accuracy is not high.

The editor of a national Sunday paper admitted to the Royal Commission of 1947–49: 'I do not wish to be hypercritical, but the plain fact is – and we all know it to be true – that whenever we see a story in a newspaper concerning something we know about, it is more often wrong than right.' The Commission in its Report considered this statement 'extreme' but also 'in our experience it has a substantial element of truth' – and many people can confirm this. This situation is not entirely the fault of the newspapermen; it is a consequence of the conditions of their work. Indeed, the competition of television in hard news is so intense that some newspapers have become magazines, looking for stories of 'human interest', not national concern.

News is an artefact, that is, literally, it is artificial. Selection and slanting are built into the reporting, so often there is no clear divide between fact and comment. When you receive 'the facts', you receive a framework of interpretation.

News has three components:
1 happenings, events
2 accounts by interested parties, leaks, briefings
3 accounts by the media adding their own slant.

If you read that the Foreign Secretary had a very bad time over the Maastricht Treaty at a meeting of back benchers in June 1992, you are reading a story put to the media by back benchers. If, on the other hand, you read that the Foreign Secretary handled a lively meeting skilfully, successfully reassured dissident back benchers, and so on – you have the story from the Foreign Office press officer and the Foreign Secretary's aides. Both stories are likely to be true in part; neither is the whole truth. Again if you read that the Prime Minister scored a great diplomatic success at Maastricht (December 1991), you are not reading a French newspaper; if you believe it, you have not studied the Maastricht Treaty....

However, these examples do not include much of the third element, the media's own contribution to 'artificial truth'. This may best be illustrated in cases where the political partisanship of the press shows up strongly in reports of the same events by the *Daily Mail* or *Daily Express* and the *Daily Mirror*. Examples can be found most days.

News is expensive. The revered journalist's motto was: 'Facts are sacred; comment is free'. This has been transformed into the more practical wisdom: 'Facts are expensive; comment is free'. Facts have become even more expensive as new technology has created the 'global village' in which a meeting in Washington, a speech in Moscow, a disaster in Bangledesh and a small war in the Balkans all have to be served up with pictures, interviews and 'on-the-spot' reports in the evening news broadcasts, and these have to be improved on in the next days papers. Today's news is stale, tomorrow's news is better.

The popular press: style and content
Writing for the popular press calls for communicating skills of a very high level. It is easy to criticise the views expressed in Document 19.1; the fact remains that the mass circulation papers are attempting to provide reading for people who do not read much at all and have little interest in serious public affairs. Research into the reception and understanding of quite simple messages demonstrates the difficulties of communicating anything at all. (Consider the communication failures of say, weather forecasts or official forms).

The popular dailies neglect any responsibility for raising the level of their readers' tastes and appreciation; but they have some success in inducing their readers occasionally to attend to serious public affairs. The *Daily Mirror*, for example, rightly boasts that its leading article is read by a greater proportion of its readers than *The Times*'s leading article (by *Times* readers). Such readability is secured sometimes at a heavy cost in bias, sensationalism, or trivialisation. But the alternative may be no article on a serious theme at all. Writing of this kind is extremely difficult, as the following exercise may show.

EXERCISES
Writing for the *Daily Mirror*

19.3 This is your chance to find out whether you would make a good reporter or sub-editor on the Daily Mirror. Decide on a treatment and devise a headline for a leading article based on the following story: the wife of a Church of England vicar (herself happily married and mother of two children) refused to join the Mothers' Union, because the Union did not accept divorced women as members. Do not spend too long on this; just a few minutes, and then look up the guide to exercises.

19.4 Journalists write to short deadlines. Try writing a leading article for a quality paper, say 6–700 words, beginning with an editorial conference in the morning to choose a subject and agree a 'line', and deliver the copy 2–3 hours later.

EXERCISE
Analysis of a newspaper

19.5 The analysis of newspapers by content and style is a useful piece of research which may be easily organised.

Here are some general points: decide which kinds of newspaper you wish to study – dailies, national, local – and whether you wish to examine all the papers on one day or on several days; or whether you will compare two or three papers.

A little time (but not too much) may usefully be spent in measuring the amount of space devoted to news, comment, features, pictures and advertisements. What are the proportions of political and other serious matter compared with human interest and trivia?

Analyse lead stories – which have been chosen, and how they are presented (length, detail, headline, slant, comment). Compare the selection and treatment of other matter. How are parliamentary proceedings reported? Are there substantial differences between 'quality', popular and 'tabloid' newspapers?

All this will show you what a newspaper is like in total, but it will not tell you how it is used by its readers. So you could go on to design a survey to test the quantity and quality of reading (who reads what? and do they understand?)

Proprietors and editors

In most cases, proprietors or principal shareholders do not act formally in an editorial capacity. Obviously proprietors tend to employ editors whose views are at least compatible with their own, and then leave the editor to work with his staff and within the general lines of the newspaper's established outlook. Tensions arise when an independent editor falls out of line with a strong-minded proprietor; the editor, as in Document 3 (c), may be dismissed.

There are many illustrations of the power of proprietors over editors, and hence over the content and stance of the paper. Arthur Christiansen, Editor of the *Daily Express* quoted above, may have terrorised his journalists, but he was in turn terrorised by the proprietor, Lord Beaverbrook. 'The Lord' was, to his credit, a newspaperman before he was a businessman, and took an active part in the editing of his newspapers. A 'policy man' sat beside the 'night lawyer', and while the latter read for libel the policy man read for consistency wth Beaverbrook's views.

More recent evidence of proprietorial influence includes Rupert Murdoch's pressing of the faked Hitler Diaries on *The Sunday Times*, and the *The Observer*'s occasional difficulties arising from the African business interests of its otherwise liberal 'hands-off' owners. Robert Maxwell notoriously worked on his own newspapers, calling himself 'the publisher' or editor-in-chief, and sometimes contributing his own pieces. He liked to see a proof of the *Daily Mirror*'s front page at the same time as the editor – even on his yacht.

Why not? you may say; a proprietor is surely entitled to write in his own paper? This would indeed be acceptable if there were many more newspapers, and you did not have to be a millionaire (at least) to own one. The more liberal view is that the editor should be given independence within broad limits – conservative proprietors are entitled not to appoint socialist editors. This moves the question down to the powers of the editor – what about the staff, the printers, the readers? The answer has to lie in a plurality of newspapers – which in fact Britain does not enjoy.

However, the evidence on proprietorial influence is not all on the side of proprietorial domination of weak editors. Consider these cases.

■ DOCUMENT 19.3
Proprietors and editors

a) The Sunday Times
The *Sunday Times* is owned by Rupert Murdoch, edited by Andrew Neil. The Editor resisted pressure from Murdoch to support Margaret Thatcher against Michael Heseltine (November 1990) and continued happily through the 1992 election to feature articles by Robert Harris who was distinctly unsympathetic to Major's as well as Thatcher's Conservatism. Neil supported Murdoch's TV interests, but he was already opposed to the TV duopoly which Murdoch was challenging. *The Sunday Times* serialised a book about Princess Diana's marriage, but *The Times*, also owned by Murdoch openly criticised the project.

b) The Sunday Express
From Robin Morgan editor of the Sunday Express, *in* The Guardian, 15 July 1991.
At the *Sunday Express*, the public assumption was that [the proprietor] and not I, as editor, would decide who the paper backed to succeed Thatcher last November. I suspected as much myself when the car-phone rang. 'It's Norman Lamont, here, Robin. I've talked to Lord Stevens and now I'm calling you to ask if John Major can count on the *Sunday Express*'s support.'

Had a decision been reached already between Lamont and my proprietor, Lord Stevens? If so, would I be malleable or mutinous? I told Lamont, truthfully, that I was undecided. Then came the inevitable call from the proprietor. 'Norman Lamont asked if John Major could count on your support,' said Lord Stevens. 'I told him to talk to you, it's your decision.'

The unpopular truth is that most proprietors concede a considerable amount of independence to editors and invest millions in their instincts and views with only one condition - commercial success rather than political subservience.

c) Harold Evans and The Times
From Harold Evans, Good Times, Bad Times, 1984, 355–7
Harold Evans was eventually dismissed as editor of *The Times* by the proprietor, Rupert Murdoch. Here, in Evans's racy account, are two dramatic episodes in his battle with the proprietor and the managing director.

...in my early months there had been growls about Margaret Thatcher being the only British politician who was any good and 'those pissing Liberals' who did not support her. He lobbed newspaper clippings across the Atlantic, mainly from the *American New Right*. He asked me to note an article contributed to the *Wall Street Journal* which said there was no plausible alternative to Thatcherism and compared Margaret Thatcher to the wartime Churchill...

Gerald Long (the managing director) exerted himself to get a better Press for the Government. He wrote me a 'private and personal' two-page memorandum protesting that *The Times* should not give prominence to reports unhelpful to the Government. What produced his outburst was a report by David Blake, the economics editor, based on figures released by the Central Statistics Office. They showed that output had fallen for the sixth successive quarter. It was not much of a fall, about half a percentage point, but it belied the Chancellor's statement in the spring that the recession was over and recovery would begin in the early summer. Blake said the figures were embarrassing for the Government and we ran it under the headline 'Recession goes on with sixth drop in output'.

Long wanted an answer from me why our treatment was bolder than other papers. He did not get it. I was not going to let the managing director get me on the run on editorial matters. It was an important story, our report was accurate and fair and Blake's interpretation was sound. It was certainly vindicated by events. The recession that Long would have liked *The Times* to play down went on and on.
[Murdoch and Evans drove together to dine at Evans's home.]
'Why d'ya run that stuff?'
'Well, it's timely.'
'And it's wrong! Wrong! What does he know anyway?'
We spilled out on to the pavement.
'Come on,' I retorted, 'He won the Nobel Prize.'
'Intellectual bullshit!'
'Well, what do you know?' I demanded, jabbing the doorbell to my home.
'You said inflation would be down in single figures by now and it isn't. I don't know why you go for this monetarist stuff. All the high interest rates you're paying....
[Evans's wife] opened the door. 'Hello!' she

said cheerfully, only to discover the proprietor and the editor of The Times about to start a street brawl. ■

EXERCISES
Proprietors and editors

19.6 Was Lord Stevens remarkably liberal in his attitude to the Conservative leadership election?

19.7 Was Rupert Murdoch wrong to try to influence the editor of The Times?

Like most commercial organisations, newspapers are controlled by a few men at the top, especially the chairman of the board and the editor. Some newspaper proprietors, such as Lord Beaverbrook, have notoriously directed the editorial policy of their papers; others, such as Lord Thomson, granted considerable discretion to the editor. Proprietors are not always independent potentates – boards and, in some cases, trusts may be involved. For example, Mr Cecil King, chairman of the *Daily Mirror* published (May 1968) a front page article calling for Mr Wilson's resignation – under the banner headline 'Enough is enough'. A few weeks later Mr King was himself summarily dismissed. The day of the proprietor/editor/politician, like Beaverbrook has perhaps passed. Press lords and knights may still take telephone calls from 10 Downing Street, and lunch at Chequers, but the most powerful are caught up in international finance and the conglomerate world of mass communication, too busy making or losing money to play domestic politics.

Editors may fight for independence from proprietors, but freedom for editors does not necessarily mean freedom for the editorial staff. Thus, in the 1930s *The Times* rewrote or suppressed despatches from its Berlin correspondent criticising Hitler's regime in Germany. On the other hand, some writers have been permitted to write in a sense opposed to the policy of their paper. Leading articles are often developed collectively in an editorial 'Cabinet'.

Still, in general, newspapermen, like the rest of us, work for bosses and do not have a free hand. This is not to say that newspaper offices are battlegrounds or prisons. As in other organisations, the staff tends to include like-minded people, who do not need to be dragooned by the editor. Such organisations acquire civilised relationships and traditions which discourage (while not precluding)

dictatorial direction. At the same time economic pressures make recognised and imperious demands on all sections of the staff. Mainly these are the demands of the proprietors and the market; advertisers are influential mainly in requiring a particular and substantial readership.

Partisanship

Most newspapers are politically partisan and news is normally reported, selected and presented with a bias intended to secure approval for the paper's favoured party. This includes selection of favourable and suppression of unfavourable news, headlining and treatment. News and comment are inevitably mixed. The tendency of newspapers to become magazines rather than political journals has perhaps modified partisanship somewhat; but on major political events most national newspapers are predictably, and in some cases shrilly, partisan. Some of the bias is not deliberate political manipulation, but proceeds again from the nature of journalism. An extreme statement attracts the reader more than a moderate statement. An account of violence in the streets is news; a rehearsal of the arguments involved in the dispute is dull.

The political alignment of the press is towards the right. Only two of a dozen national dailies, and five of twenty national daily and Sunday papers, are sympathetic to Labour. Almost three quarters of the circulation of the national press is anti-Labour. For a short period in the 60s both *The Sun* and the *Daily Mirror* were Labour papers, and for the first time, Labour enjoyed the favours of a substantial press. But the *Sun* moved to the right, and the Labour party is isolated, with the Mirror as its one daily supporter. The *Daily Mirror* is a 'crusading' paper (no question of impartiality) with a circulation of well over three million; but it is a lonely Labour voice in the tabloid jungle.

The Conservative press, led by the *Daily Express*, *Daily Mail*, and *Sunday Express* (all with editors knighted by Margaret Thatcher), is reliably partisan, and during elections works closely with Conservative Central Office. The *Daily Express* announced quite early in the 1983 campaign: 'we stand four square and 100 per cent behind Margaret Thatcher'. Seventy of the *Daily Mail*'s editorial staff later protested about the bias of its coverage of the election. In recent elections the partisanship of the press has made Labour's already difficult task look quite impossible.

There is one remarkable exception to this account of the loyalty of the Tory tabloids. In the political crisis of Autumn 1992 the tabloids led the whole of the Conservative press in acrimonious criticism of the government's incompetence and mismanagement (following the withdrawal from the ERM). For once the Conservative party was treated to the kind of vituperation normally reserved for the Labour party. This temporary treachery by the Tory tabloids can be explained by the evidence and scale of government failures, especially in economic policy, opposition to the development of relations with the EC implicit in the Maastricht Treaty, lingering attachment to Margaret Thatcher and a loss of confidence in John Major. For all this, it is inconceivable that the Tory tabloids would remain hostile in a general election.

There is a marked tendency for readers to agree with the general political leanings of their newspaper. This presents a chicken-and-egg problem. The likely solution has to take account of a triple relationship: readers choose newspapers which fit their existing tendencies to partisanship (this is probably not a very deliberate process); newspapers promote and reinforce that partisanship; and readers have some influence on their newspapers.

The partisanship of the press is evident wherever political stories are in the news. Hence during elections partisanship becomes vigorous political propaganda.

Here are some examples of partisan electioneering in the British press.

■ DOCUMENT 19.4
Partisan electioneering by British newspapers

a) The Daily Mail *attempts a stunt, 1983*
The Mail reported on its front page (16 May) that the Japanese car company, Nissan, would scrap plans for a £500m. assembly plant if Labour won the election ('35 000 jobs lost if Foot wins'). Nissan denied this; their denial was published next day – on page two, in the fifteenth paragraph of a story which began on page one under the headline, 'Car Jobs Row Boils Over'. (A similar rumour was floated in 1992).

b) The Daily Mail *in the 1987 election campaign From an article by Dave Hill in* The Guardian *of 9 March, 1992 – a month before the election.*
One ex-Mail writer recalls the atmosphere during the 1987 campaign. 'You felt as if you were in Conservative HQ. One day after Labour had scored a particularly good point against the Government, one of [the Editors'] deputies

stood up in the middle of the newsroom and shouted: 'We must hit back! We must hit back!' They did, too, breaking the damaging story that Denis Healey's wife had made use of private health care.

c) The 1992 Election
For the 1992 election, and in particular, 'Labour's Double Whammy' and 'The War of Jennifer's Ear', see Chapters 17–18. The latter case raises the problem of privacy as well as political bias. ■

EXERCISE
The Tory tabloids

19.8 If you were a Labour politician, should you worry about the Tory tabloids?

Labour may find some consolation for its weakness in the press from the growth of the quality press, which includes one sympathetic paper, *The Guardian*, (circulation over 400 000) and papers of some independence. The *Financial Times* actually backed the Labour party in 1992. Further, there has developed a much greater awareness of the nature of the press and it may be that Labour should try to educate the public about the partisan tendencies of the tabloid press, Left and Right.

Broadcasting

The nature of broadcasting
The press is basically competitive and partisan, organised and operating for the most part like a commercial venture in a market-place. Broadcasting has been quite different in style, working with some sense of public service and cultural responsibility, and within a long tradition of political impartiality. These qualities derive from the history of broadcasting and from its statutory obligations, but are challenged in the 1990s by the Broadcasting Act of 1990, and the Conservative party's dislike of the BBC and enthusiasm for 'market forces'.

Broadcasting was from 1922 until 1954 a monopoly of the British Broadcasting Corporation, which began as a company licensed by the Postmaster-General but was established as a public corporation in 1926. The BBC's Charter underlines its responsibility as a public service, and the Corporation's first Director-General, Sir John Reith, gave it a tradition of high morality, propriety and political impartiality. Possibly Reith, a Scots Presbyterian, went too far. In his day, newsreaders (on radio) wore evening dress, Sunday was entirely given over to serious, mainly religious, programmes; on days of thin or trivial news, no news bulletins were given at all. Still, Reith's achievement was substantial: he founded and sustained one of the most distinctive and widely admired features of twentieth-century Britain, public service broadcasting.

Radio remained a BBC monopoly, until the establishment in the 1980s of local commercial stations. In television, the monopoly was broken in 1954 with the establishment of commercial companies, financed by advertising but operating under the supervision of the Independent Television Authority. Thereafter, the BBC and the commercial companies competed for viewers, rather as newspapers compete for readers, and with similar effects. But the BBC can still afford to ignore viewing figures or at least feel less bound by them than the commercial companies; its long-standing Reithian traditions have not entirely crumbled, and have even had some influence on commercial broadcasting.

In the political field, the Independent Television Act laid down standards of impartiality similar to those of the BBC. However, if commercial broadcasting has benefited from the BBC's public service tradition, the BBC appears to have learned from the commercial drives of the independent sector. In television only the advertisements now distinguish the programmes of commercial and BBC television.

The historical and statutory basis of the public service tradition in broadcasting is illustrated in the following document.

■ DOCUMENT 19.5
The public service tradition in broadcasting

a) The BBC's Charter and Licence
Under the terms and conditions of the Charter and Licence of the British Broadcasting Corporation:

- the Broadcasting Service is recognised as 'a means of information, education and entertainment';
- the Corporation is charged with the duty of broadcasting each day an impartial account of the proceedings of Parliament, and announcements by Government Departments;
- the Corporation is not permitted to broadcast its own opinion on matters of controversy. [This convention means, in effect, that the

BBC has no editorial policy or 'line' of its own, unlike newspapers; but its correspondents do now offer comment as well as 'facts', implicitly or explicitly.]

b) Relations of BBC and government
The Corporation must comply with the directions of the government, and the government specifically has the right to 'require the Corporation to refrain from' broadcasting particular matter. In practice, the responsible Minister normally refuses to answer for or intervene in matters of content and style of programmes. The independence of the BBC is substantial, though a little bent and chipped by government pressures (see Chapter 20).

c) Lord Reith on the influence of broadcasting
The tradition established by the first Director-General, Sir John (later Lord) Reith was strongly one of public service. Two extracts from Reith's Memorandum to the Broadcasting Committee of 1949 convey the flavour and the fervour.

'Objective
The exploitation and development of Broadcasting were (haply) under control from the outset; and in the public interest; without prejudice to entertainment functions, under a feeling of moral responsibility, moral in the broadest sense - intellectual and ethical; with determination that the greatest benefit possible would accrue from its output.'
'Conclusion
... It is in terms of moral effect that the influence of Broadcasting will eventually be judged ...'
[Reith regarded listening figures with some disdain.]

d) From evidence of Sir John (Lord) Reith to the Broadcasting Committee, 1949 (Report, Cmnd 8116, 364)
...It was the brute force of monopoly that enabled the BBC to become what it did; and to do what it did; that made it possible for a policy of moral responsibility to be followed. If there is to be competition it will be of cheapness not of goodness. The usual disadvantages and dangers of monopoly do not apply to Broadcasting; it is in fact a potent incentive...

e) The Television Act 1954
Independent television inherited the tradition of the BBC, but is also guided by the provisions of the Television Act 1954. Section 3 of the Act

requires inter alia:

'that nothing is included in the programmes which offends against good taste or decency or is likely to encourage or incite to crime or to lead to disorder or to be offensive to public feeling...';

that news is 'presented with due accuracy and impartiality';

that 'due impartiality is preserved on the part of the persons providing the programmes' on matters of political controversy;

that programmes might include 'properly balanced discussions or debates'.

Broadcasting time cannot be purchased for political purposes. The political parties are allocated time on both BBC and ITV (simultaneously) for 'party political broadcasts'.

[The legal obligation of due impartiality was maintained in the Broadcasting Act of 1981, while giving Channel 4 responsibility for innovation and experiment.] ■

EXERCISES
Monopoly and public service broadcasting

19.9 Are Reith's views on monopoly control in the public interest acceptable in a democracy?

19.10 What are the arguments against monopoly?

19.11 Do the arguments against monopoly amount to an argument for the introduction of 'commercial' broadcasting (i.e. produced by companies seeking a profit through the sale of advertising time)?

In 1926 Reith declared that the BBC was 'an institution within the constitution' - this was in the special circumstances of the General Strike and a national emergency. But for Reith the status and mission of the BBC was always to do with the constitution, the state and the public good as he saw it. For the promoters of commercial broadcasting Reith's vision was false and damaging. The competition of the market was appropriate for broadcasting as it was for the press and publishing. Margaret Thatcher's enthusiasm for competition was enhanced by a particular dislike of the BBC, which she regarded as a nest of radicals who talked down Britain and distrusted her government. She would have liked to switch the financing of the BBC to advertising; but the idea did not win favour, not least in commercial television, where it was feared its own advertising revenues would be diminished. However, the Broadcasting Act of 1990 opened independent broadcasting more fully to commercial competition by the auction of franchises, and there is continuing pressure on the BBC to compete for its funding.

So far the 'public service tradition' has preserved broadcasting from the worst excesses of the press. There is a greater regard for the standards of fairness and balance, and a genuine mission to inform and educate as well as entertain. However, there are reservations to be set against this wholesome view of broadcasting.

First, as indicated above, television is massive and monopolistic on a scale undreamed of by the barons of the popular press. The control of television rests in the hands of one large corporation and a network of a dozen or so independent companies. The controllers and editors wield enormous influence, especially outside the sensitive and closely monitored areas of political balance.

Second, the relations of government and broadcasters have not been settled beyond dispute by the framework of Charter and Licence in the case of the BBC, the Broadcasting Acts and supervisory commissions in the case of commercial television. Television is too important to politicians to be left alone. In matters of national security or high political sensitivity – Suez 1956, Ulster, the Falklands War 1982 – governments have exerted heavy pressure.

Some Prime Ministers have had notably uneasy relations with the broadcasters. The BBC's desire in an inflationary economy and in competition with high-spending commercial companies for continuing increases in licence income has been a lever in the hands of government.

Third, the output of television is not all sweetness and light. Television has some of the faults of the press, and a few of its own. There is an element of competition for viewers; low figures for the BBC would affect its prestige and its chance of increasing the licence fee. Mostly the BBC is in 'show-business': political and current affairs programmes are a small part of a vast entertainment operation. If the press had its over-powerful barons in Northcliffe and Beaverbrook, broadcasting had its authoritarian knight, Sir John Reith. Now, possibly, excessive power lies in the hands of a few producers, administrators or performers. The star interviewers can at best – like the press – help to secure the answerability of politicians, but at their worst they can cast suspicion on an honest statement.

Television seems much more than the press to give rise to a spurious, superficial air of concern and omniscience. It suffers like the press from the necessity for speed and brevity; but, dealing in pictures, not the printed word, it can exaggerate and distort simply by illustrating rather than narrating or analysing. It is a little like a cartoon strip. Its message is less structured, less organised, than the newspapers. It is good at showing the announcement of decisions but not the grounds and the process of decision.

EXERCISE
Analysis of television

19.12 There are obvious practical difficulties in the analysis of content and style of television. A video-recorder and a stopwatch would obviously help, but are not indispensable. Answers should be sought to some of the following questions:

- News programmes. Do BBC and ITV tend to treat the same items at roughly the same length? Are there variations in the selection of the lead story? What use is made of film and interviews? Is the report just a report, or a comment, or a judgement? Is the presentation easy to understand, moderately difficult or suitable only for comparatively well-informed people? How does the treatment compare with that of the newspapers?
- Other current affairs programmes. Similar questions. Also, what is the effect of interviews? – to elucidate or to obscure? to press the person interviewed hard or not? fairly or not?

Refer to the books on television for academic analyses.

GUIDE TO EXERCISES

19.1 It may well be an underestimate, and therefore no service to public education and communication in a democracy. On the other hand it may be realistic, since newspapers have to survive in a competitive world. Of course, characteristically the point is overstated – Glyndebourne and claret are not appropriate measures. Notice that the extracts do concede some commitment to raising standards and heightening interest.

19.2 It depends on the paper or programme and what the editor (or proprietor) might mean by some of these suggestions. A serious-minded young reporter, wanting to write about environmental issues or prison reform, might have a hard time.

19.3 The Mirror's editorial was headed: MESSAGE FROM ST PAUL. The text referred to 'faith, hope and charity . . . and the greatest of these is charity'. Clever? (Joe Haines, a distinguished Mirror leader-writer, said that a 200-word leader was more difficult to write than 400 words; he added that the first paragraph of a leader can often be cut without loss of meaning - true too of some student essays!).

19.4 If you choose the right topic you can compare your efforts with those of the next day's newspapers.

19.5 These you must do for yourself. You should have discovered differences in treatment, length, style and headlines ('Recovery hopes dampened' or 'Tory cheer as economy takes off'), both between papers and between the press as a whole and broadcast news. On the face of it is one more likely to have a persuasive effect than another?

19.6 Yes, but it was not, after all, a general election. Note the assumptions of a politician about press support.

19.7 It seems legitimate and realistic that the proprietor should have some influence; at the same time the editorial staff are entitled to the exercise of their professional expertise and integrity. But they have no absolute right to do as they please (except to go and work for a more congenial proprietor). A compromise position is that the proprietor's views should be contributed to the editorial pool - note that Murdoch accepted this position for the time being at least (but soon after this incident, Murdoch appointed a new editor, and the paper moved to a 'radical right' position).

Most newspapers, unlike the broadcasters, do have a particular bias, but this ought not to exclude other opinion. Ideally a 'free' but capitalist-owned press achieves freedom and plurality in the expression of opinion through the competition of the market; in practice freedom and plurality depend on the restraint and altruism of the wealthy businessmen who own the press.

19.8 It would be prudent to be concerned, but there is not much you can do about it. Neil Kinnock had as little as possible to do with the tabloids, and his campaign in 1992 was designed to shield him from what some regarded as the predatory 'rat-pack'. There is no doubt that any minor 'gaffe' or 'banana-skin' would have been headlined. Margaret Thatcher did not hand out all those knighthoods to the Tory editors for nothing. For further evidence on the influence of the tabloids see chapter 20 Table 1.

19.9 A monopoly in broadcasting may have been technically necessary in the 1920s, but is no more appropriate than a monopoly in the press or publishing. Monopoly in information and communication is not to be trusted, however noble the intentions of the monpolist. Reith wanted, and to some extent created, a positive force for good - but this was good as he saw it, including a solemn Presbyterian Sunday. Freedom may lead to the sacrifice of Reithian values, but is a great value in itself. Better free and nasty than controlled and wholesome?

The alternative to monopoly is not unrestricted competition; regulation in the public interest is acceptable. For example, there are obvious justifications for limiting pornography (if you can define it), incitement to racial prejudice, or violence.

19.10 Briefly size, rigidity, exclusion of alternative employers or publishers, lack of diversity, excessive power. It is as if there were only one state publishing house (hence only one text book on politics).

19.11 No. But it may be argued that the profit motive involved in seeking high audiences for advertising would necessarily lead to the provision of a service appreciated by a large audience. Other kinds of non-commercial competition would not provide this incentive to wide public appeal.

19.12 This you do for yourself. You should discover among other things that the picture may determine the story and that the differences between television channels is not great, but differences between television and press treatment of public events is marked. Does television seem to be effective in conveying information? or influencing attitudes?

ASSESSMENT
Theories of media inlfuence on politics

Note that the section on the influence of the media in Chapter 20 is relevant to both chapters on the media.

The influence of the media is disputed and research is difficult. There are three positions.

1 The media has very little or no influence. The position lays stress on the complexity of the processes of communication and persuasion. The consumer is not an empty vessel waiting to be filled. Rather the consumer has his own views and attitudes, assumptions and scruples, and in any case lives in a dense context of predispositions and values. Listening and viewing is never open and passive, but is confused by the needs and interests of the consumer - he or she needs or does not need, seeks or is not seeking, information, education, help.

2 The media have a massive influence. Whatever the complexity of the consumer's own motives and objectives, he or she is in the end open to persuasion, with very little resistance. The effectiveness of most advertising confirms this position: advertising can sell products which meet human needs and desires, but these can be created.

3 Middle positions.
These stress:
- the constraints on undue influence, arising from the autonomy or obstinacy or obtuseness of the individual, and the density of the social and political context in which he or she acts.
- the influence of the media short of simple conversion, in particular the capacity of the media to 'set agenda', that is determine the content of political debate, and to reinforce pre-dispositions.
- some evidence of direct, independent and significant influence, beyond agenda-setting and reinforcement, and despite the constraints.

Whatever position is taken there is a prior question about the proper role of the media in a democracy. It is a reasonable assumption that a democracy requires information and debate based on evidence and reason, and that the media must be a main contributor to that debate.

In Britain, the contribution of the media to democracy is based in the case of the press on market competition, and in the case of broadcasting on market competition constrained by regulation in the interests of 'public service'. The press offers competitive prejudice, and unequal competition in the tabloids, but with some commitment to reasoned argument in the quality press. Broadcasting, so far, offers impartiality (no overt partisanship or editorial line), 'balance' and 'socio-centrism', with some commitment to pluralism. The incoherence of the system probably aids the cause of democracy, but democratic values are not well served by the tabloid press.

Here again Britain suffers from the centralised form of its polity. Democracy would be served better by more vigorous provincial media, so that English regions might enjoy the relative freedom from metropolitan dominance available in Scotland. It would help if London ceased to be the only theatre of politics in the kingdom. Such intense concentration corrupts the media as well as government itself.

Concept

Public service (broadcasting)

This refers to all that the old Reithian BBC stood for. It implies provision not by a commercial organisation but by a public corporation of some kind, with non-commercial objectives. The latter are difficult to define; as indicated in the text, they include service of the public interest (also undefinable), some commitment to information and education as well as entertainment, and (on very shaky ground) some recognition of the proper bounds of 'good taste'. It is not surprising that the free and competing commercial press is seen, or at least sees itself, as a better model for a democracy. The true libertarian resists the enforcement of standards of entertainment and culture, as long as the consequences offend only good taste. But that simply shifts the argument to the nature of 'taste' and 'enforcement'.

● CASE STUDY
Media policy-making

Media policy has never been a prime concern for governments; indeed the notion of 'media policy' is a recent invention, more academic than political. The media do not figure largely in party politics, within or between parties. No department of state regarded the media as a major responsibility, and no senior Minister staked his reputation on a media policy initiative. Media policy hardly appeared in party manifestos, and the departmental responsibility for broadcasting has shifted from the Postmaster General to the Home Secretary and now to the Minister for Heritage.

In the 1930s and 1940s Britain had a 'free' press and the British Broadcasting Corporation, and was proud of both. However, newspapers and broadcasting mattered too much for governments to stand aside. Concern about monopoly and standards in the press led in 1947 to the first of (so far) seven major inquiries into the press and broadcasting. The onset of inflation gave governments frequent opportunities to encourage or squeeze the BBC by the setting of its licence fee. At the same time the development of television opened up the issue of commercial broadcasting, and gave rise to one of the first modern lobbying campaigns which succeeded in breaking the BBC's monopoly.

The duopoly in television created in 1954 survived until the 1980s. All governments worried about the media, intervened with the broadcasters to secure more favourable reporting, and cultivated relations with the press. But until the 1980s there was concern but no new policy. The Conservatives were broadly satisfied; for Labour, intervention in a free press looked to be politically costly and ineffective. The position thus preserved was a curious, incoherent mess: regulated broadcasting, non-partisan and with some commitment to public service, and some public funding for the BBC; a 'free' commercial press, partisan and dominated by a few large groups. It could be argued that this incoherent mix of media policy was in fact satisfactory – and might indicate other areas (health, education?) where a mix of public service and commercial competition would have advantages.

However, two developments led to the breaking of the status quo. First, technological development, in particular, satellite broadcasting, broke through the limits of nationally controlled air-waves (just as the national framework of radio broadcasting had been broken by off-shore pirate stations and some continental stations like Radio Luxembourg). Second, the Conservatives of the 1980s strongly favoured commercial enterprise rather than public service. So, for once, a government, pushed by technology, but also by its own ideology, developed its own media policy, embodied in the Broadcasting Act of 1990. This amounted to a substantial element of commercialisation ('market forces') added to the old public service-commercial duopoly in broadcasting.

The logical complement might be to inject a stronger public-service element in to the already commercialised press. A Conservative gov-rnment sees no reason to do this. Its only concern has been the infringement of privacy, especially in the case of the Royal Family.

Overall, the recent history of the making of media policy indicates that rapid and radical policy change is infrequent, that technical change may prod government into action, but the most powerful propellant of policy initiative is a mixture of technical or other change making new policy necessary or desirable and practicable, plus ideology and the pressure of organised interests. ●

20

Government and the Media

Government and the media: a tug of influence

The influence of the media in the British political system is substantially modified by the inaccessibility and secretiveness of British government. The conventions of party solidarity, collective responsibility, and civil service anonymity combine to form almost impenetrable barriers around the centres of power. The secretiveness of government is reinforced by a prudent regard for the Official Secrets Act and the laws of libel.

Governments see themselves, with some justification, as vulnerable to the media, always likely to have their position misrepresented, their success challenged, their failures exaggerated, and their reasonable disagreements headlined as 'Cabinet splits'. This is what Bernard Ingham, Margaret Thatcher's Press Officer denounced as the 'Le Carré Syndrome': 'Government is inevitably up to no good and guilty as charged.' Even Conservative governments, normally assured of preponderant favour in the press, still harry the broadcasters. The BBC may not be biased systematically to left or right, but it works on the assumption (unacceptable to governments) that the government might be mistaken.

The government's defence against the media involves management of the news as well as secretiveness. This is not new. There is much evidence in the 1930s of government's systematic endeavours to influence the press, notably on the policy of 'appeasement' of Germany. Earlier politicians, like Lloyd George, regarded the assured support of a major newspaper, preferably secured by ownership, as essential to political leadership in or out of government. The development of television with mass audiences has promoted media management into a serious and substantial arm of policy making.

The government now employs about 1200 officers in the Government Information Service. Part of their work is to do with advertising and news management. The budget for advertising quadrupled in the 1980s to about £170m annually; some of this was for information (drug abuse and AIDS for example) but some, notably on privatisation, had a propaganda effect. News management was more directly political.

News management means that the news you read or hear is often not the product of forays by an intrepid reporter, but the result of a special briefing in the Minister's room – or a convenient restaurant. The reporter's 'I understand that...' covers a variety of sources of information, from guesswork to the Prime Minister's Press Secretary. The arranged 'leak' is part of this system. Policies can be tried out by leak; a budget may be defused in that way by diminishing expectations; the humiliation of a Minister can be arranged; a report which is in part critical, like the Franks Report on the Falklands War, can be presented as wholly favourable. All of these examples have happened. Deliberate leaks seem to have increased in recent years, but examples can be found at all times since the invention of the newspaper.

One former Minister has complained that the civil servants whose advice he found most restrictive and irksome were the public relations officers, with their judgements on what could or could not be said in public (as distinct from the full truth). Harold Wilson emphasised the 'presentational' aspects of a policy, implying, realistically enough, that presentation affected substance. Information officers, official briefings and press conferences all provide formal channels from government to newsmen. The parliamentary 'lobby' (journalists attached to Parliament) has privileged access to Ministers as well

327

as to private Members. Ministers try to win friends among the press, exchanging exclusive information for the promises of sympathetic treatment: the press as a whole may resent, but individual pressmen cannot always resist, such blandishments.

In the case of the broadcasting authorities, and especially the BBC, government management often amounts to heavy pressure, bullying and arm-twisting, based on the government's ultimate power over the BBC's Charter and licence fee. Politicians do use that power. Harold Wilson whose relations with the BBC were often tense and occasionally bitter, appointed the Chairman of the rival Independent Television Authority as Chairman of the BBC's Board of Governors. Margaret Thatcher's appointments to the Board reflected her own predispositions. In 1987 when the Director-General had been summarily dismissed, *The Sunday Telegraph* reported that 'senior party figures are confident that the final choice of the 12-strong Board of Governors, all...appointed since Margaret Thatcher came to power, will be "acceptable"'. That might sound like the old Soviet Politburo at work.

Managing the media is a routine operation for government. 'Management' includes the selection of information, the timing of its release and the arrangement of effective presentation. In itself this kind of operation does not deserve sinister interpretations. It is to do with persuasion not 'manipulation'; and a government is entitled to present its policies or position as persuasively as it can. Even allowing for that, governments do engage in deception in the presentation of information and the management of the media.

- Governments do not admit to failure, disagreement, not knowing what to do or the superior wisdom of opposing parties. Governments never cause disasters. This cannot be true all the time.
- Governments do not give all the facts. This is the notorious 'economy with the truth' referred to by the Cabinet Secretary in the Spycatcher trial. It amounts to not telling the truth, but not actually lying.
- Governments impart a slant or spin to the facts, for example, 'the rate of increase in unemployment has slowed down' – not 'unemployment has gone up again but not so fast'. The complex assessment that needed to be made about the Maastricht Treaty is reduced to John Major's diplomatic triumph ('game, set and match').

- Governments influence opinion indirectly through leaks and the unattributable briefings of the 'lobby'.
- Governments exert influence on the construction of political programmes on television, the participants, the order, the subjects to be treated.

The management of the media: the lobby

The lobby
The lobby is a collection of about 200 journalists who report Parliamentary affairs and have privileged access to the areas of Parliament (except the Chamber itself) reserved for Members of Parliament. Up to forty or fifty also attend the twice-a-day briefings by the Downing Street Press Office. These briefings are 'unattributable' and reports are ascribed to 'Downing Street sources', or something similar, or else may be disguised by a phrase such as 'I understand that....' The procedure has aroused controversy; some newspapers withdrew from the briefings for a period, and opposition parties say they would change the system. Ministers, and opposition leaders for that matter, also brief or leak unattributably, usually at a lunch or other social occasion. The consumption of food and drink seems to be essential to the processes of politics. The constitutional basis for leaks is that Ministers may authorise themselves to dispense information which is strictly an official secret. (Next time someone in authority challenges your right to do something, you could try responding, 'I authorised myself'.)

The case for unattributable lobby briefing is clear enough. Governments are held responsible for everything they say, so they are inclined to say very little, especially about the background of policy discussions, disagreements and emerging policy ideas, and their assessments of the politics of particular proposals. The unattributable briefing offers an opportunity to float these matters without responsibility, indeed with complete, or almost complete, 'deniability'. Since governments must report accountably to Parliament, so it is argued, the lobby briefing provides background information, useful to the journalists – as is proven by their continuing attendance and support for the system.

The case against the lobby briefing is that it practises a deception; the information it dispenses is given an aura of truth and importance which may not be deserved and cannot be challenged; and the existence of the lobby briefing is a barrier to the development of an alternative system of on-the-record briefing. The briefing is used for deliberate manipulation of opinion, for example, damaging the standing of particular Ministers (as practised by Harold Wilson and Margaret Thatcher); bouncing the Cabinet by letting it be known that for example the standard rate of income tax would not rise (Margaret Thatcher, 1981, before the matter had been agreed in Cabinet), or reducing expectations of a budget (so that the actual budget will be better than expected). The lobby briefing is thus part of the government's management of opinion, not part of 'open government'. What else would you expect?

The critics of the lobby system prefer on-the-record briefings, and even press conferences on the lines of the White House press conferences faced by the President and his colleagues. These are not always impressive as sources of full and accurate information. The truth is that governments, like top managements everywhere, feel entitled to protect themselves from what they regard as hostile and ill-informed criticism. Journalists do not expect to be told the truth; they must find out by research.

Margaret Thatcher's Press Officer, a close adviser, acquired a high reputation as a master manipulator of the lobby and a bluff Yorkshire bully (the county of Yorkshire has a peculiar reputation, especially among Yorkshiremen). He claimed his influence was quite limited.

■ DOCUMENT 20.1
The limits of lobbying

From B. Ingham, 1991, p. 188
News management, in the sense of ensuring that nothing is allowed to get in the way of the story the Government wants to get over, is impossible in the modern world. A chief information officer...is not in charge of events, or journalists. Nor has he any influence over a Minister who suddenly goes ape and commands the front pages.... An earthquake here; a famine there; an horrendous aircrash elsewhere; or quite simply some appallingly visual event anywhere – and his news management cause is lost. The real news managers today are the media themselves. It is television which predominantly dictates news values for the masses: either there are pictures or there are not, and if there are not pictures there is no news. It is the editors of this world who receive the raw material in the form of reports from the

journalist on the spot. Then they get to work on it: developing it, exploiting it, angling it, massaging it and eventually presenting it as polished fact and unvarnished truth. And they dare to accuse Government press officers of news management? ■

EXERCISE
The limits of lobbying

20.1 Are the media 'the real news managers'?

Cases of news management
1 *The Falklands Islands Review*
The review of the events leading to the Falklands War posed a tricky problem for news management. The Report was critical of the conduct of affairs in the body of the text, but concluded with what might be taken as a broad exoneration (see Chapter 9; also P. Madgwick, 1991, pp. 220–4).
Bernard Ingham wrote:
'Margaret Thatcher was adamant that the report would be published without advance copies to the lobby or any other journalists. She – like me – was fed up with the way journalists leaked advance copies of reports to anyone who might usefully express a destructively newsworthy view on them....'(B. Ingham, 1991, p. 303).

He later agreed to identify key paragraph numbers to the lobby 45 minutes before the report was available. This arrangement was leaked, the Opposition made a fuss. So Margaret Thatcher ruled no briefing before publication. In the House of Commons she read out the exonerating paragraphs, making no mention of the criticism. This was a triumph of political and news management.

2 *The GLC – a case of failure?*
Sources: James Curran: The Boomerang Effect: the press and the battle for London 1981-6 in J. Curran et al, 1987 and R. Harris, 1990, pp. 117–8.

The Conservative government was pledged in 1983 to abolish the Greater London Council, along with other Metropolitan Councils. This was unpopular with a majority of Londoners, and was not much favoured by many Conservative Councillors, MPs and peers.

Bernard Ingham wrote a seven-page memorandum setting out a campaign aimed to 'treat dissident elements among the Government's own supporters to ensure they are neutralised if not positively harnessed to the Government's cause', and to take 'remedial action with troublesome journals'. This was news-management of a positive, active character, perhaps appropriately termed 'manipulation'?

The government's campaign was not wholly successful. The 'Tory tabloids' supported the government and made much of the record of 'loony left' councils and 'Red Ken' Livingstone, the leader of the GLC – there was evidence enough of wasteful administration and the funding of unpopular minority causes, summed up as black lesbian street theatre workshops and the like. But the GLC fought back effectively, basing their case on the support of Londoners for an elected authority, and Red Ken's evident charm and reasonableness. The GLC could afford an advertising campaign, and exploited their riverside site opposite the Houses of Parliament with roof top banners, visible to television cameras as well as Members of Parliament. It was all very irritating to a government accustomed to having its own way with the media.

The GLC lost in that it was subsequently abolished, but it gained publicity for its cause, and much sympathy even among Conservative voters. However, it would be unwise to read too much into this case. The government lost the argument, but still had its way. It would be difficult for other objectors to high-handed government to fight back as the GLC could.

But it is not impossible – is it?

EXERCISE
The GLC resists the government

20.2 Is the GLC resistance a special case?

Secrecy

Government secrecy
British Government has the reputation for being the most secretive in the Western world. There is some substance in this reputation. Secrecy has of course a persuasive justification in the needs of national security, and the necessary confidentiality of some part of the process of policy making. Beyond that, secrecy in Britain is supported, almost certainly to excess, by some features of constitution, politics, culture and law.

1 *Constitutional and cultural supports of secrecy*

- A unitary and centralised constitution without competing jurisdictions.
- Executive dominance based on majority party control of parliament.
- A powerful civil service deprived of political salience by Ministerial responsibility.
- The limited accountability (or non-accountability) of major forces in the state, the 'City'

and the Bank of England, the armed forces, the police.
- Cabinet 'solidarity' enforced by the convention of collective responsibility and an obsession with political invulnerability derived from adversarial party politics.
- A political culture supportive of government by a metropolitan elite, and heavily influenced by the assumptions of the high military about security.
- The absence of any constitutional commitment to freedom of speech or information.

2 *Specific legislation protecting the government*

- Official Secrets Act 1989.
- Security Service Act 1989.
- Legislation relating to privacy and confidentiality.

Additionally:

- the informal D-notice system of advice on security matters and more or less voluntary self-censorship
- the absence of a Freedom of Information Act.

3 *Uncertainty of the freedom of speech of the citizen under the common law*
Without the support of any constitutional commitment to freedom of speech, much depends on the disposition and interpretations of the judges. These have tended to give weight to the needs of national security as claimed by the government. One judgement specifically rejected any notion of the interests of the state as differing from the government of the day. The responsibilities of the media toward free speech have been diminished by the claims of the government to govern without obstacle or embarrassment. No test of national security has been developed equivalent to the US formulation of 'clear and present danger' or the European Convention's 'pressing social need'.

Secrecy: some illustrative cases
1 *Suez*
A striking but abnormal example of government secrecy and deception about collusion with Israel. The record of an official meeting at Sevres in France between Britain, France and Israel was destroyed, and both the Prime Minister and the Foreign Secretary lied to the House of Commons.

Cabinet papers (18 October to 2 November 1956) have not been revealed after the statutory 30 years. In fact, government papers are carefully sifted and much remains secret. Ironically, there are two exceptions: any matters involving dealings with the USA may be discovered in the USA by use of the US Freedom of Information Act, and any matters uncovered by Russian spies (quite a few it seems) may now be revealed in the newly-opened files of the KGB.

2 Select Committees

See Chapter 13 for official recommendation to reticence on the part of civil servants, and some discretion and reticence by the Select Committees themselves. The Public Accounts Committee, following the work of the National Audit Office, does better, but is concerned with matters of administrative detail long after the event, and accept government guidance on matters affecting security – and the Royal Family.

3 Windscale nuclear accident of 1958

The Cabinet papers show that the Prime Minister and senior Ministers were obsessively concerned, not about damage from nuclear fall-out, but about the maintenance of secrecy, and how much to reveal.

3 The war in Dhofar 1965–75

This was largely hidden from the press and disguised by the government's management of the media, so that hardly anyone in Britain was aware that British troops were engaged in a small but costly war.

Restriction of freedom of speech by the British government

Northern Ireland

The politics of Northern Ireland raise acute problems for a government aspiring to be democratic. The violent conflict of the two cultures has led to a condition of near-civil war (see Chapter 24); the (Catholic) Republicans fight the (Protestant) Unionists and the British government and army: the Unionists fight the Republicans and the army. Caught literally in the cross-fire the British government has to maintain peace, law and order by methods bounded by law and falling short of the licence to kill of an open and full-scale war. It is relevant to the reasoned argument – and more than just a plea for sympathy – that five or six of Margaret Thatcher's close colleagues and friends were murdered or grievously wounded by the IRA. The response of the government has been to restrict any media reporting of the Northern Ireland 'Troubles' likely to assist the terrorists, and especially the IRA, in their waging of war against their fellow-countrymen.

The 'Death on the Rock' case (see end of chapter) shows government distaste for a programme which had the effect, whatever the intentions, of presenting IRA members as oppressed by a British anti-terrorist operation. The softer liberal view is that even IRA members are innocent (except of membership of the IRA) until proved guilty. A more pragmatic judgement is that there is a political advantage to Britain in acting in Northern Ireland as a civilian police power, and refraining, despite provocation, from waging war. In Northern Ireland itself attitudes are harsher on both sides, and shooting to kill is the Irish way of death.

Faced with this cruel dilemma the liberal aspirations of British governments have been tested to destruction. Government believed all publicity for terrorists sustained terrorism. There were major rows with the broadcasters as they tried to report a problem with two sides. For example in 1985 the Home Secretary called for the cancellation of a BBC film on Northern Ireland called 'Real Lives', showing two people from each of the cultures, speaking of their beliefs and attitudes. The programme was postponed and shown a month later with 30 seconds added. This incident was a part of Margaret Thatcher's long-running conflict with the BBC.

In 1988 the Home Secretary moved to ban all broadcasting of direct speech by members of Northern Ireland terrorist groups, under the Broadcasting Act of 1981 and the BBC Licence. The banned groups included Sinn Fein, which is a political party not proscribed in Northern Ireland, so the ban had to be lifted for the election of 1992. The ban was judged by the Court of Appeal to be lawful and not perverse or absurd. The Home Secretary was not required to be 'impartial between the terrorists and the terrorised' (an interesting judgement which a liberal might say begs the question?). The European Convention's provision (Art. 10) for freedom of speech was deemed not to preclude the ban, though it might at least have indicated a lack of proportionality in the Home Secretary's heavy-handed act. Later the European Court of Human Rights specifically upheld the government's action.

There is clearly much to be said for the government's view – so the English Court of Appeal believed. The practical effect is quite strange, for the ban applies only to direct speech, not to reporting or even hearing an actor read what the 'terrorist' said against an unsynchronised film of the terrorist saying it. So the ban is of little practical consequence.

The liberal case depends on bringing into the frame not just the government, the media and the 'terrorists' but the listening and viewing citizen. Does he or she not have rights in this matter? The point was put persuasively by Hugo Young (see also Chapter 25).

■ DOCUMENT 20.2
Banning the bombers

Hugo Young in The Guardian, *17 November 1988*
[The Adams referred to was then a Sinn Fein MP and frequent advocate of the cause of the IRA.]
...the principal victims of unfree television are neither the people who produce the programmes nor those who would appear on them, but the people who watch them in the hope of enlightenment. What is at stake is not Adams's freedom to speak but our collective right to be told the truth. Those who have been deprived are not, as our leader would have it, a handful of gunmen but an entire citizenry.... Quite apart from the fact that all censorship is bad for freedom, to censor the IRA and their friends is to exclude from view not the irresistible glamour but the self-convicting brutality which the terrorist almost unfailingly conveys.... All the same, one expects better of serious politicians. Here is a Prime Minister, a Government, a whole governing class perhaps, who apparently cannot see that the freedom of the press is not about the freedom of journalists but the liberty of the subject. ■

EXERCISE
Banning the bombers

20.3 Do you find Young's argument convincing, that is, would you support the ban?

It may be that the Northern Ireland case is special. Governments cannot be expected to act liberally towards their opponents in a civil war. Liberals would argue in general that freedom of speech is of little value if it does not extend to the expression of opinion hostile to the government and the state itself. Tolerance stops short only of specific incitement to violence and the overthrow of the state. Thus the argument must be brought down to specifics.

The dilemmas of toleration are by no means confined to Ireland. Violence occurs in other contexts - street rioting, strikes and pickets. To liberal opinion, violence 'cannot be condoned' but is evidence of discontent and grievance, which must be attended to. For the non-liberal supporter of 'law and order' violence excludes the perpetrator from consideration. One position allows too much, the other has little room for the expression of dissent. This is a version of the child's catch-22: Those who don't ask don't want, those who ask don't get. If government does not act, it evades its responsibility; if it does act, it exceeds its powers.

Official Secrets Acts, 1911 and 1989 and confidentiality
The history of the Official Secrets Act lends support to the view that British governments are obsessively and excessively secretive. Their concern for national security extends beyond the threats from Russian spies to what Margaret Thatcher called 'the enemy within', 'bolshie' shop stewards, CND activists, even Members of Parliament. Some of this reflects the obsessions of unaccountable and unreliable security services, who at one time were pursuing Harold Wilson, the Prime Minister. But it also reflects the tendency of governments to paranoia and defensiveness, so that Prime Ministers deliberately suppress the truth and Ministers argue seriously not to provide any information because 'they will only ask for more'!

The original Official Secrets Act was passed in a panic one afternoon in 1911 during an Anglo–German naval crisis (the post-Victorian version of the cold war). It was so broadly drafted that almost any information derived from government employment was an official secret (choose your own example, – the price of tea in a ministry canteen or the number of daffodil bulbs planted at Kew). The Act fell into disrepute and was condemned by judges and other high authorities. Successive governments, Labour as well as Conservative, seemed in no hurry to replace it. Then in 1984 Clive Ponting, a civil servant in the Ministry of Defence, 'leaked' an official document relating to the controversial sinking of the Argentine warship, the 'Belgrano'. He sent a copy of a 'Minute' to Tam Dalyell, a member of the Commons Select Committee on Defence. The Minute set out, so Ponting believed, a strategy for misleading the Committee and blocking any further enquiries (see Ponting's account in C. Ponting, 1985).

The Committee returned the document to the Ministry, and Ponting was prosecuted under the Official Secrets Act. To the dismay of the government, and in defiance of the judge's direction, the jury returned a verdict of 'Not Guilty', convinced it seems that Ponting had acted 'in the public interest'. The government decided to reform the Act, though at the same time they began to use the law of confidentiality, which did not require trial by (unreliable) jury.

The new Official Secrets Bill was pushed through Parliament by the use of the guillotine, so debate over six days was very uneven. However, on behalf of the government it could be said that the Bill was based on a well-publicised White Paper. Notable features of the new Act were:

- some restriction of the information covered, but its scope is still wide, extending for example to international relations and information received from foreign governments (also the civil service disciplinary code has been tightened in relation to information)
- in prosecutions under the Act a degree of harm has to be proved, but those who disclose secrets cannot plead public interest or prior publication
- in general the nature of an offence under the Act is broadly drawn, and defence is more problematic.

Clive Ponting believes that under the new Act the government's position would be easier in all the 1980s cases. Ponting himself would have no defence. In the case of Sarah Tisdall (a young, junior clerk who was sentenced to six months imprisonment for leaking a document about the presentation of the arrival of Cruise missiles at US bases in England), *The Guardian* too could be prosecuted. Any reporting of the work of the security services would be illegal.

These cases indicate the problem of the 'whistle-blower', the official or employee who feels he or she must draw attention to wrong-doing, despite professional obligations of confidentiality. Suppose a security official informed a Member of Parliament that the Member's phone was being illegally tapped (it has happened). The official would be committing an offence; and if the Member publicised the information, so would he. When this point was put to the then Minister of State, Home Office, the Minister was unabashed.

There are other related features of official secrecy legislation which are unsatisfactory. Ministers may disclose information legally, because they are held to be 'self-authorising' – that is they may do what seems to them reasonable and necessary, or if you like, just as they please. At the same time Ministers refuse to disclose information on grounds which may confuse national security with simply avoiding embarrassment to the government.

A new Security Services Act was passed at the same time as the new Official Secrets Act. The Security Services were at last put on a statutory basis, though the Act does not set out the relationship of the government and the service. There is no formal provision for parliamentary scrutiny, though two years later Questions on the security services were permitted, the new head of MI5 was named, and the MI6 headquarters was identified (it was quite difficult to hide a large new building in central London). The D-notice system of voluntary censorship by the Defence Press and Broadcasting Committee was not mentioned in either of the 1989 Acts. It seems characteristic of secrecy in Britain that the existence and practice of secrecy are themselves secret.

There were several well-publicised security incidents in the 1980s which suggested an obsessive and illiberal concern for security on the part of the government. In the GCHQ case (1984) the government, anxious about the threat to the work of the Government communication or spying centre (which operated closely with the USA's Central Intelligence Agency) posed by unionised workers, rejected all compromise and banned trade unions at the Headquarters. Margaret Thatcher's concern for security was here joined to her distrust of trade unions (see Chapter 25, Document 25.4).

In the Zircon case (1986) the government was anxious about a series of television programmes on security matters. Since the programmes were made by the BBC the government was angry as well as anxious; the project seemed to confirm that the BBC was 'a nest of communists'. The most sensitive of these programmes related to a spy-satellite called Zircon, for which expenditure of £471m had been planned but concealed from Parliament. The existence of Zircon was not secret, and the Ministry of Defence had co-operated in the making of the programme.

In the cause of bringing about the banning of the film the security services (the Metropolitan Police Special Branch) searched the houses of the writer and two researchers, the offices of the New Statesman, and the headquarters of BBC Scotland. Tapes and film were seized and carted away in scenes thought to be characteristic of Eastern Europe rather than Britain. The Zircon film was shown, despite government objections, in the

House of Commons and, two years later, it was transmitted. The BBC admitted that its position in matters of the kind had been weakened by the heavy attacks on it by the Prime Minister and senior Cabinet Ministers since the Libya bombing (for that incident see the Case Study at end of chapter).

In the Spycatcher case the government endeavoured to suppress a book written by a former member of the security services. This, like Zircon, revealed very little that was not already known, and usefully gave just a little more substance to the stories of the attempted 'destabilisation' of Harold Wilson by members of the security services. The government used the laws of confidence and contempt, and a series of applications for injunctions and prior restraint orders which effectively prevent publication and do not run the risk of an embarrassing trial by jury.

In this case the book was already published abroad and by the time the government sent the Cabinet Secretary to fight the case in Australia, anyone who really wanted to read Spycatcher could find a copy in Britain. The author and former spy, who it seemed held a grievance about the paucity of his government pension, made a fortune from his book, with its sales boosted by the government's public pursuit of it. The new Official Secrets Act laid on members of the security services a life-long duty of confidentiality.

British governments in the 1980s seemed very ready to resort to the courts, and the courts (in Britain not Australia) seemed ready to be persuaded by the government's claim to secrecy, and the overriding value of national security as defined by the government. The independence of the courts was not in doubt yet the courts were open to criticism for their judgements. The government's position acquired ambiguity from the peculiar dual nature of the Attorney-General's position as Minister of the government and its chief prosecutor, but also a high judicial official, and guardian of the integrity of the courts. The treatment of the government's case in the Australian courts was in marked and refreshing contrast to the respect shown in British courts to claims to government secrecy and privilege.

However, in the Spycatcher case Mr Justice Scott demonstrated the true independence of the judiciary and asserted the need for a balance between the demands of security and the demands of freedom: the Crown must demonstrate damage to the public interest. His judgement was upheld in the Court of Appeal and the House of Lords.

■ DOCUMENT 20.3
The balance between security and freedom of the press

A. G. v Guardian Newspapers Ltd. and others (No. 2) [1988] 2WLR 805

- The judge referring to the evidence given by Sir Robert Armstrong, Cabinet Secretary, declared that the absolute protection of the security service that Sir Robert was contending for could not be achieved this side of the Iron Curtain.
- The purpose of the 'duty of confidence' was to do with the efficiency of MI5 and not to save the Government of the day from pressure or embarrassment.
- '...the ability of the press freely to report allegations of scandals in government is one of the bulwarks of our democratic society. It could not happen in totalitarian countries.'....
- A balance had to be struck between two competing public interests. The price to be paid for an efficient and secure security service would be some loss in the freedom of the press to publish what it chooses. The price to be paid for free speech in a democratic society would be the loss of some degree of secrecy about the affairs of government, including the security service.
- 'It is open to Parliament, if it wishes to impose guidelines. The United States Congress has done so in the form of the First Amendment. Parliament has not. And so it is for the courts to strike the balance.' ■

EXERCISES
Security and freedom

20.4 What kind of guidelines could be developed to make more precise the 'balance' between government and press?
20.5 Is it appropriate that such guidelines be developed in Parliament or the courts?

These security cases attract much publicity and tend to distort the argument about secrecy. Clearly in security matters there is a case for a substantial measure of secrecy. Sceptics may feel concern for secrecy is overdone, especially given the ending of the Cold War, the evident inefficiency of the security services, and their own insecurity which seems to make them conduits of information. Still, in any situation which includes the possibility or the actuality of war, it may be conceded that secrecy is a necessary protection.

On the other side, the liberal critics of excessive secrecy find easy targets in the operation of the security services beyond the accepted standards of legitimacy and natural justice.

Altogether the argument about secrecy in government is 'blown up' by the security cases, and attention is diverted from the routine employment of secrecy in the civil functions of government. The adversarial nature of British political life makes governments avoid political trouble, any hint of failure or disagreement, any possibility of embarrassment, anything which could be used in evidence against them. The media feed on political trouble and embarrassment, and they encourage governments to go into hiding. Secretiveness is the normal condition of British government.

Hence, alongside the headlined security cases must be set first the routine, day-in, day-out, practice of secretiveness and information management, normal in all policy making; and, second, a long list of special examples of policy making, in which secretiveness has included the deliberate suppression and distortion of the truth. The list would include many defence procurement decisions, especially concerning atomic and nuclear weapons (the British atomic bomb, the Chevaline programme); Suez; the Westland affair; the inclusion in the sale of Rover to British Aerospace of payments ('sweeteners') of over £40m, not revealed to Parliament or the European Community; and the sale of arms to Iraq (revealed in the Scott Inquiry 1993–4).

Government, the media and society: regulation

The freedom of the media is constrained by the government's management of information and imposition of secrecy, in the cause of its own and the nation's security. The media are further subject to the law, to the imperatives of the market, and to regulation.

The constraints used by the government have been discussed above. These include laws relating to secrecy and the security services, and the laws of confidence and contempt. The media are also restricted, like everyone else, by laws of libel, obscenity and privacy. The law of libel is highly restrictive in Britain, and politicians enjoy far more protection than is afforded in the USA, for example. A politician whose reputation is defamed (except on the floor of the House of Commons) can silence a newspaper by the threat of legal action, which may end in heavy damages and costs for the paper concerned.

On the other hand, privacy is little protected and the same politician might have no redress against the intrusion of the press into his private life (camping in the front garden, late night telephone calls, cameras in the house opposite and so on). The media, and in particular the tabloid press, do not consistently live up to the ideals of a noble profession serving the public interest by the fearless but unintrusive pursuit of the truth.

The dominance of the market largely determines the behaviour of the media – the need to attract readers and audiences and to survive in a competitive commercial world. The market secures accountability, though not necessarily 'in the public interest' as that would be understood by readers of *The Guardian*. The provision of formal regulation of the media offers a significant example of a different kind of accountability, which lies between government control and market freedom. The process is significant because it is the only practicable response of government to securing the service of the public interest by public or private enterprise, whether in monopoly or competitive conditions. It is the recognition of governments that both public ownership and commercial competition require a framework of accountability if the public interest is not to be neglected.

In the case of broadcasting, regulation is in the hands of the BBC's Board of Governors, the Independent Television Commission and the new Radio Authority. These are typically government-appointed bodies, not directly responsible to the government, but with duties defined by statute, and beyond that a healthy concern not to offend too often the government or the 'public' as represented by the press and bodies such as the Viewers and Listeners Council. In addition the broadcasters are subject to a Broadcasting Complaints Commission and the Broadcasting Standards Council. The Complaints Commission may be effective in particular cases, though it does not monitor programmes on its own initiative.

The Broadcasting Standards Council (1990) was given statutory powers in the Broadcasting Act of 1989. It is concerned with matters of taste and decency, sex and violence on television. It has established a code of practice and its adjudications are published. It does not see programmes before transmission. The Council's code is inevitably unspecific, and differs little from the codes already operated by the companies. The Council, first chaired by a former editor of *The Times*, looks like a characteristically 'establishment' device to safeguard the morals of the people; but the actual effect of the Council is to act as a buffer between the broadcasters and the vociferous pressure groups. The Council might further wish to protect Britain from the pornography programmes available in other countries, but broadcasting technology is likely to override the censors.

The press is much less watched over than television, because it is privately owned and deemed to be competitive and accountable to the market; also because it appears to have a less powerful cultural impact than television, and because most of the press is sympathetic to Conservative governments. The Labour Party, for good reason, shows some hostility to the press, especially the 'Tory tabloids', and even more to those owned by Rupert Murdoch, the hammer of the print unions.

The press has been left so far to regulate itself, first in the Press Council, notoriously an in-house 'toothless watchdog', now in the Press Complaints Commission, established in 1991 under threat of statutory intervention. The Commission is intended to curb the grosser violations of truth and decency in the press, especially inaccuracy and intrusion into privacy. The press is more sharply restrained by the libel laws, to the point where the threat of legal action, and the use of injunctions, may silence the legitimate investigation of the journalists. This was true in the case of Robert Maxwell, who effectively excluded the press from the reporting of his business empire. In this area as in most others the existing law serves mainly as a protection for the wealthy; but there is a case for the extension of privacy law at least to restrict physical intrusion, spying and telephone tapping (or the publication of material discovered thereby).

Both press and television are also regulated by the Advertising Standards Authority, which require that advertisements be 'legal, decent, honest and truthful'. Readers and viewers will note that the standards of truth and decency in advertisements are higher than in some of the editorial matter – though most advertising is inevitably intended to seduce or deceive and falls short of full and precise truth. Party political broadcasting is excluded from the ASA's code.

For politicians to complain about the media is like sailors complaining about the sea – so wrote Enoch Powell. But, of course, the sea has a serious effect on the security and comfort of sailors, and so too the media for politicians. Many senior politicians appear to be obsessed with the media, as is evident in the records of Harold Wilson's government, and the frequent rows between Margaret Thatcher, her Ministers and the BBC. Presentation dominates policy: how will it play in the Nine O'clock News? The substance of policy is excluded or marginalised for the sake of media presentation. Thus the profound constitutional issues raised by Britain's commitment to Europe have been hidden by stories of a series of British diplomatic triumphs – 'Maggie says No!', 'Game, set and match' and so on.

Despite the exasperations and temptations of their daily encounter with the media, British governments have accepted the basic democratic commitment to a free press. Systematic government control of the media has operated only in wartime – though the extent and vigour of wartime censorship has worried libertarians. At other times governments have respected the freedom of the press but have not refrained from threats and bullying, especially in the case of the BBC. Numerous inquiries into both press and broadcasting have not resolved the problems inherent in government-media relations; nor so far has the opening of broadcasting to the market.

The influence of the media

The influence of television

Television now plainly has a powerful effect on our lives, a pervasive cultural effect incorporating the political. This is evident in many ways, for example:

- the figures for viewing, the daily average and the massive audience for some programmes, in particular the 'soaps'
- the salience of television as the essential medium of great events, politics, sport and disasters; and the extraordinary fame that is available from television
- the creation of the global village in which a war, an assassination, a famine, an earthquake on the other side of the world is delivered within minutes to our living rooms.

Television has in some ways created an arena for our lives, and it follows, an arena at least as important as Parliament for politics. Indeed, Parliament is now incorporated into the television arena. The political impact of television is dominated by the power of pictorial illustration.

Examples abound:

- a protest march or occupation or stunt gains most of its effect through pictures on television
- the strikes of the 1970s, the 'Winter of Discontent' of 1979, and the Miners' Strike of 1984–5 (with its violent scenes of clashes between police and pickets) created potent images, which stay in the public mind, and are recycled for political purposes
- pictures of bombing in Libya and in the Gulf War offered strong images of destruction, though with ambivalent political consequences.

Television has changed the job and the professional requirements of politicians: they must be acceptable and effective on television in interviews and public situations and in Parliament. Some politicians have made their careers by television, others with considerable talent but no television 'personality' have fallen by the way.

Television is able to stage or create events – both artificial events like 'walk-abouts' and real events, like the selection of a Labour Party leader, which both in 1983 and 1992 was a television rather than a party event, indeed not much of an event at all, because television rapidly confirmed the preference of the major trade union leaders.

Television does not convey the crusading partisan bias of the tabloid press, but it does inevitably convey inclinations and values of its own.

- Its careful impartiality and concern for balance incorporates a bias towards the government of the day (which inevitably dominates the news) and the conventional consensus of the day. It is not open to the broadcasters to be unconventional or radical.
- There is a bias towards major interests. For example, the threatened cancellation of the European Fighter Aircraft in the Summer of 1992 was covered by interviews with representatives of defence, the aerospace industry and the trade unions; not with the Treasury or the tax-payer – while The Times newspaper, enjoying the freedom bestowed by Rupert Murdoch, ran a leader questioning the value of a '20 billion pound job creation scheme'.
- Beyond this there may be a bias towards the Right on defence and trade union matters, though that is difficult to establish. On economic affairs the broadcasters employ a formidable array of 'independent' economists, most of them employed in the City, and if anything reflecting City rather than government

interests.
- There is always a bias towards pictorial news values. A news cameraman has said: 'You have to give the wrong impression: in a crowd in Cyprus you film the one woman who is weeping, and even if you film the rest of the crowd, the editor will pick out the weeping woman.'

The influence of the press

Despite the evident power of television the press still carries substantial political influence. There are several reasons for this.

- Some newspapers convey a persistent heavy bias by the characteristic tabloid techniques, selection, sensational treatment, headlines, repetition. These newspapers are partisan crusaders, engaging in vigorous propaganda.
- Newspapers 'stay around' for longer than television programmes, and include political items packaged with human interest and sport.
- Newspapers often 'set the agenda' for television: newspapers create news more openly than television.

Can newspapers actually shift opinion? Here is some evidence which suggests a positive answer.

1 The Suez crisis 1956
The press generally followed the party it normally supported, Conservative papers for intervention, Labour and Liberal against it.

The *Daily Mirror* criticised the Prime Minister with all the customary force and brilliance of its front page. But it did not carry along all its readers – circulation dropped by 70000. The *Daily Mirror* then trimmed its policy slightly, and confused the political issue with admiration of the British soldier. 'Heads high', it wrote. 'The British Army could have wiped out the Egyptians within forty-eight hours. Everybody knows this, including Colonel Nasser and all the other Egyptians.' A historian of the Mirror, Maurice Edelman, commented: 'It was an editorial which skilfully reflected the changing mood of the British public....' (M. Edelman, 1966, p. 163).

Thus, it seems the *Mirror* did not lead its readers, it followed them. But too much should not be made of this one incident. On war as such (not foreign policy), the public knows its own mind, thus restricting the influence of the press.

2 Enoch Powell and the Race Issue
This account is based on C. Seymour-Ure, 1974, Chapter 4

One Saturday afternoon in April 1968, in

Birmingham, Enoch Powell, MP, made a public speech about race in Britain. He spoke of the social threat arising from uncontrolled immigration into Britain of peoples whose own background and culture could not easily be assimilated or contained within British society. Powell's speech was composed and delivered in an emphatic rhetorical style. He spoke to an audience of under one hundred, but within a few days he received 45 000 letters and his speech was known to 96 per cent of the entire adult population.

This massive amplification of the speech was not of course fortuitous. Enoch Powell intended that his speech should reach a wide audience. He was an eminent and controversial figure (already exiled from the Conservative leadership for his views on immigration) and he was one of the very few original and stimulating speakers in British politics. The theme he dealt with was peculiarly suited to amplification by the media. It aroused strong feelings hitherto largely neglected, and it dealt in conflict within communities and between leading politicians. The press had for once a subject strong enough to rival sex, violence and football as a popular attraction. Powell's theme, dramatic enough in itself was treated in a way likely to arouse alarm.

'Mr Powell's earthquake', as it has been called, could not have happened without the press; but it illustrates rather more than the power of the press, the power of a striking political personality to develop and exploit a particularly flammable issue.

Enoch Powell's impact on and through the media continued. In the 1970 election he was quoted more often on television and radio than anyone else except the three party leaders. 'His views and their reverberations took up about one fifth of all broadcast election coverage' (C. Seymour-Ure, 1974, p. 133). In the press, except for *The Guardian*, he received more coverage than the entire Liberal Party.

EXERCISE
Enoch Powell and the Race Issue

20.6 Is this a convincing example of the powerful influence of the press?

3 *Influence of the press on partisanship*

EXERCISE
Influence of the press 1987

20.7 What is the significance of the analysis presented in the Tables?

Table 1

Conservative lead over Labour in votes (%)	
Amongst Conservative identifiers who	
– read right-wing papers	90
– did not	83
Effect of right-wing paper on Conservative identifiers	7
Amongst Labour identifiers who	
– read right-wing papers	–76
– did not	–81
Effect of right-wing paper on Labour identifiers	5
Amongst Alliance identifiers who	
– read right-wing papers	16
– did not	–7
Effect of right-wing paper on Alliance identifiers	23
Amongst those with no party identification who	
– read right-wing papers	33
– did not	5
Effect of right-wing paper on those with no party identification	28

Source: W. L. Miller, Media and Voters, Clarendon Press, Oxford, 1991, p. 189. Professor Miller's study is based on the analysis of data from the 1987 British Election Campaign Study, using a five-wave panel survey, coupled with a media content analysis.

EXERCISE
The press and partisanship

20.8 Does Figure 1 show that your newspaper affects your party preference?

Family	Newspaper	Party
Conservative	Conservative	79% Conservative (n=259)
	Labour	44% Conservative (n=85)
Labour	Labour	86% Labour (n=221)
	Conservative	62% Labour (n=141)

Figure 1 The influence of the press on partisanship, 1963
Based on D. Butler and D. Stokes, 1974, p. 118

The percentage is the percentage of respondents in the first and second columns, e.g. respondents with a Conservative family, and taking a Conservative newspaper.

In the light of these case studies it appears that the press does have political influence, modest though still significant where readers already hold steady political allegiance, and substantial and highly significant for those with weak political allegiance. This fits a 'common sense' appraisal of the everyday processes of persuasion. Newspaper persuasion goes with the grain, not against it.

This conclusion applies to partisanship and voting, and to other issues on which there may be a ready formed opinion, or a predisposition, or an absence of opinion. The Enoch Powell case showed how opinion on race and immigration could be developed. Other prejudices (prior opinion) ready for dramatic expansion by the press might include, say, 'welfare state scroungers', 'picket line bullies', 'bolshie school teachers', or, from the left, 'greedy businessmen', 'a casino-style stock exchange'; and for all popular papers, English jingoistic attitudes can be called out to defend John Bull against the French. The press may then defend itself as expressing no more than what people are already thinking; but this is not an entirely convincing justification of the articulation and exploitation of latent prejudice.

The impact of the media
The overall impact of the media on politics is invigorating and enlivening but it is also damaging in some respects.

1 Personalisation
Politics is presented through 'personality'. Margaret Thatcher's exploitation of personality is well-known and was judged by some observers as both effective and wholesome. Neil Kinnock's election as leader of the Labour Party provides another example. It was accompanied by the full media treatment, including breakfast with a television crew, and a walk on the promenade (with wife), preceded by twenty photographers and two television crews, all walking slowly backwards. One commentator, at least, thought this was a landmark in the modernisation of the Labour Party:

'...Mr Kinnock's victory...marks the final acceptance by the Labour Party of the sovereignty of television...the fact that both the Kinnock hardware and software were American products also highlighted the extent to which the candidate and his advisers had absorbed the lessons of campaigning, US-style. Stay clean-cut, smile a lot, keep a well-scrubbed family up front, look decisive, offend nobody – well, nobody with block votes anyway, look modern, go-ahead, unstuffy. And

never, ever get overweight...' (J. Naughton, The Listener, 5 October 1983).

On the other hand, it is contended that television has given the citizen unprecedented opportunities to observe politicians at work, under close and persistent questioning. It is certainly true that some broadcast interviews are far more challenging for politicians than Question Time in the House of Commons. One caller on a radio phone-in programme is credited with being the only person to have flustered Margaret Thatcher in public over the sinking of the Argentine warship, the 'Belgrano'.

An American observer of the 1983 election wrote: 'Sir Robin Day, Mr Jimmy Young and others provide a true service, unimaginable in American media politics. Their interviews may not always provide substance, but they do elicit true personalities from normally protected politicians, especially ones as well-managed as Margaret Thatcher.' (Steven Erlanger, The Economist, 11 June 1983). Peter Jenkins confirmed this view: 'One important consequence of television is that voters know their leaders far better than was possible in the age of mass meetings and popular newspapers.' (Peter Jenkins, The Guardian, 2 June 1983).

The consequences of the personalisation of politics are negative when personality excludes substance, and when able politicians are marginalised by the lack of 'personality'. But it should be said that the personalisation of politics is based on the willing collaboration of the politicians with the media, and elicits a response from an otherwise politically apathetic public.

2 Conflict and the adversarial style
The media demand conflict and encourage the conflictual tendencies of the Westminster model of politics. Complex issues – the economy, the health service, relations with Europe – are reduced to simple Left-Right, Government-Opposition conflict. Each side aims to 'rubbish' the other in ritual warfare which would be unacceptable in industry and commerce and social life. General respect for politicians is destroyed since it seems they have no respect for each other.

The vigour of the media in seeking out disagreements and presenting them as 'splits' threatening the future of the government or party has reinforced the obsession of governments with solidarity and secrecy. This has imposed the most severe restraint on free discussion, so that, for example, the serious constitutional implications of Britain's accession to the EC have never been fully debated. Observe too the transformation of former Ministers from smooth-talking public relations functionaries in office, always less than candid if not actually deceiving, into backbenchers of sharp mind, stimulating speech and intellectual honesty. The contrast does not encourage confidence in British democracy.

3 *The pursuit of 'news-values' or, pejoratively, trivialisation*

This arises from the journalistic style of the press and the domination of television by the picture, and of all media by personality and conflict. The tabloid newspapers lead the way from news values to trivialisation. Hence, for example, the European issues are reduced to the all-purpose denunciation of Brussels 'bureaucrats', prying into 'nooks and crannies' to destroy the British sausage; the problems of health service finance are reduced to the dramatisation of heart-rending but unrepresentative cases; the issues of post-Cold War strategy are reduced to questions of particular weapons systems. Again, the politicians encourage rather than resist the media approach to the framing of political debate.

4 *Closed government*

British government is secretive; this is evident from the cases reported above. The media have not succeeded in opening up government to full public scrutiny. Indeed, they have not always tried. The news values required by the media flourish best on leaks, lobby-briefings and gossip from a secret system. There is a collaboration if not a conspiracy between government and the media: they are engaged in the same trade of selling information to the people - information which gains in value from its scarcity.

GUIDE TO EXERCISES

20.1 Ingham characteristically overstates the case in this extract. It is true that the media will pursue news values in earthquakes, striking pictures, a Minister talking loosely; and in any case will put their own gloss, slant or frame on the Press Officer's story. But a Chief Information Officer is a major if not a monopoly source of information, and journalists need his co-operation.

20.2 Yes. It had funds, a good cause with cross-party or non-party support, it got itself into the news and it had in Ken Livingstone a skilful media operator. This was an unusual combination of advantages against a government entrenched behind party loyalties and heavily armed with the 'Tory tabloids'. This is the normal David v Goliath line-up, in this case, Ken v Bernard, and the Davids always get beaten up.

20.3 Not easy to answer in terms of political morality. In practical terms, what is thought or known to be the effect of broadcasts by 'terrorists'? If broadcasting conferred standing, increased sympathy, made converts, that would perhaps justify a ban? If broadcasting increased understanding of the problems of Northern Ireland - and did not make hundreds of converts - that would indicate no ban. Most broadcasts of 'terrorists' in Northern Ireland and elsewhere reveal the passion of their beliefs rather than the violence of their behaviour.

20.4 'Balance' sounds fine but is very difficult to define, and if not defined does not carry much significance at all. As indicated earlier in the text the US formula is 'clear and present danger' to the constitution. This suggests a test incorporating a clearly evident, immediate and urgent threat to the stability of government, the maintenance of minimal law and order and the peace of the nation. By such a rough test CND was not a threat (it was never banned but its leaders were kept under surveillance including telephone tapping); the IRA was a threat. Spycatcher was a threat only if it is right to insist on the absolute integrity of the security services. Sceptics may feel that the whole business of spying is a fantasy world, and that peace is better served by openness.

20.5 It is difficult in practice for Parliament to devise more than very general guidelines. Then the courts may develop the guidelines on a case by case basis. This is the normal division of labour between courts and Parliament. It has the advantage of practicality, precision and sensitivity; and the disadvantage that Parliament yields power to the courts, and the lawyers will take a long time and make a very expensive meal of it.

20.6 It is a good indicator of the conditions in which the press can exercise influence –

in this case with an emotional issue, a forceful personality and a speech made for tabloid headlines and exploitation. Powell needed the issue and the press; the press needed Powell and the issue.

20.7 Reading a right-wing paper has a modest, but electorally significant effect on the voting dispositions of Conservative and Labour identifiers. On those with a weaker party identification the effect is substantial.

20.8 The diagram inevitably simplifies complex relationships. It appears to show a quite marked influence of newspaper on vote. However, there is no indication here of factors involved in that choice. For example it may be that a person of Conservative background choosing a Labour newspaper is already moving away from the Conservatives (just as a Labour voter buying a house and changing his vote is not reacting simply to the house purchase). As usual, analysis of this kind shows association, not causation. The number of respondents in one row is quite small.

ASSESSMENT
Open government and freedom of information

These are two contemporary slogans, ideas converted into 'buzz-words' or propaganda terms. 'Open government' means making public the processes of government, including the information and considerations on which policy is based, options for change and the monitoring of the implementation of policy. 'Freedom of information' implies a statutory right of access to information held by the government, limited only by national security, international relationships, and the safeguarding of necessary privacy and confidentiality.

Many countries, including USA, Australia and New Zealand, now have Freedom of Information Acts – and without the collapse of national security or the constant embarrassment of governments. But openness and freedom of information, even hedged about as they are, make government more difficult, and British governments happily use their party-based power to diminish the embarrassments arising from adversarial politics.

The case for open government is to do with democracy and justice, but also the efficiency that arises from vigorous accountability to a well-informed opposition and press. A statutory provision for open government would shift the balance of power towards the citizen, who would gain a right to information against the goverment's present right to secrecy. The culture of secrecy would be diminished, and the approach of the courts would necessarily change.

The case against open government is that policy making has to be confidential:

- to allow the trims and turns, hovering and backing necessary and normal in making policy in complex situations
- to protect the anonymity of civil servants advising on policy
- to protect the prime responsibility of governments to account to Parliament.

Opponents of open government would argue that government is open enough already, through the procedures of Parliament including the Select Committees, and through briefings and leaks.

The statutory provision of Freedom of Information is even more controversial. Information which may reasonably be held to be in the public interest, for example, a health hazard in farming, safety in shops and motor cars and nuclear plants, remains confidential in Britain but not in USA. But a comprehensive Freedom of Information Act is opposed on the grounds that it would be impractical and costly and provide more information than people really need or can cope with. The experience of other countries is that information under Freedom of Information Acts is mostly sought by companies; some kinds of information, for example on drug enforcement, is sought by criminals; and there is a threat to privacy and confidentiality.

So what should be done? Governments in Britain are reluctant to do much at all. The 'Croham directive' of 1977 encouraged departments

'to publish as much as possible of the factual and analytical material used as the background to major policy studies.... In the past it has normally been assumed that background material relating to policy studies and reports would not be published unless the responsible Minister or Ministers decided otherwise; henceforth, the working assumption should be that such material will be published unless they decide that it should not be'.

It is not evident that the directive has been acted upon with vigour, and the obvious starting point, the Select Committees, have often been blocked or ignored by government. Lord Croham himself, like some other senior civil servants, was converted after retirement to the cause of greater openness and even a Freedom of Information Act.

If government is to be made more open then:

- there is a need for the strengthening of parliamentary procedures
- the extension of other procedures for the remedy of maladministration (see Chapter 25)
- Freedom of Information legislation
- some protection for the 'whistle-blower' who feels compelled by conscience to reveal government secrets.

But such reforms are unlikely without a change in political culture from government invulnerability, omniscience and omnipotence to the frank recognition that governments are often and rightly divided, uncertain of the way ahead, rightly unsure of their power to solve their problems, as distinct from their power to silence their opponents, and sometimes simply wrong. What would all this mean for the media? Ideally the relations of media and government would become more candid and honest. But the interest of the more sensationalist media lies in penetrating, not removing the veil of secrecy.

Concept

Impartiality and balance

Applied to the media these terms propose not so much never taking sides in a controversy, but not persistently and with prejudice (pre-judgement) leaning in one direction, and not giving reasonable consideration to contrary views. No newspaper is fully impartial and balanced in this way, though one or two of the 'quality' papers would claim that major controversies are openly argued out, both in editorial conferences and in the newspaper itself. By contrast the older broadcasting organisations (BBC and ITV) are committed to these values. Since perfect impartiality and balance is unattainable, perhaps meaningless and not even informative and educative, the ideal system of media is pluralist and

competitive, far more than is the case in Britain now.

● CASE STUDY
Westland yet again

Information officers were concerned in the leaking of the Solicitor-General's letter to the press – for details of the Westland Affair see Case Studies at the end of Chapters 5 and 9. The leaking of the letter, though defended as providing necessary and urgent information for the Westland Board, was intended to damage Heseltine, the Cabinet rebel – and sympathetic newspapers took the cue.

The Chief Information Officer at DTI, Colette Bowe, had the job of leaking the letter but felt reasonably enough that she needed the authority of No. 10. Miss Bowe spoke with Bernard Ingham by telephone in a conversation which must have been fraught with anxiety and ill temper.

a) Ingham's account
From B. Ingham, 1991, p. 335
[Colette Bowe] told me that she had been given Ministerial permission to 'leak' the Solicitor-General's letter to Mr Heseltine.... I expressed grave reservations about the plan.... Colette Bowe made it clear to me that the DTI hoped that Number 10 – namely myself – would do the leaking. I refused to do so point blank. I had no authority to disclose the Solicitor-General's letter. I told Colette Bowe that I had to keep the Prime Minister above that sort of thing. At no time was I asked to approve of the disclosure.

What I ought to have done – and regret to this day that I did not – was advise Colette Bowe, regardless of her Minister's permission, to have nothing to do with the ploy herself.

b) Robert Harris, biographer of Bernard Ingham and a distinguished political journalist, gives Colette Bowe's account or point of view
She had misgivings, as the Cabinet Secretary later confirmed, but could not consult her Principal Personnel Officer or the Permanent Secretary, because neither was in the building. According to friends of Miss Bowe, quoted in the press at the time, Ingham told Bowe in characteristically blunt language, 'to do what you're **** well told'. The Cabinet Secretary's inquiry did not reconcile this discrepancy between Ingham's and Bowe's accounts. Both in effect, claimed passivity; the other took the responsibility. Harris concludes that 'it was in [Ingham's] power during that crucial telephone

call to put a stop to the whole business – and he did not do it' (R. Harris, 1990, p. 132). The conclusion, but not the detail of the account, accords with that of Ingham.

c) Leon Brittan, the Secretary of State, DTI kept his silence in 1986 and resigned, bearing but not positively accepting, the responsibility
Three years later he said in a television interview that the leak was approved both by Ingham and Charles Powell, the Private Secretary: 'there would have been no question of the leaking of that document without that express approval from Number 10.'

Altogether the leaking of this letter, intended to discredit a Cabinet Minister, the lack of candour about the incident, and the difficulties of civil servants caught up in the matter, all support the argument that the management of press relations falls easily into manipulation and deception. A greater openness is (in this view) more honest, less corrupting. •

• CASE STUDY
Conflict between government and the broadcasters

a) The bombing of Libya, April 1986
Libya was bombed by US aircraft based in and flying from Britain. The Libyan President, Col. Gadaffi was a target, but he survived (one of his children was killed). The British government endorsed the action by giving permission for the flights. The reporting of the bombing aroused controversy.

Conservative Central Office complained that where ITV emphasised Libyan terrorism, the BBC emphasised (led off with) worldwide condemnation, and civilian casualties, mentioning Libyan terrorism 'only in the last breath'. The BBC refuted most of these charges.

The Central Office complaint appears to exaggerate but not invent differences in presentation. The complaint concluded that 'the BBC's coverage was riddled with inaccuracy, innuendo and unbalance'.

Leaving aside the assessment of detail what, if anything, can be said by way of general defence of the BBC?

The bombing episode was controversial and it is the responsibility of a public service broadcaster to reflect the controversy. All reports (ITV and the press) showed pictures which drew attention to damage and civilian casualties. In wartime it may be acceptable that coverage is

not balanced between the nation and its enemies, but this was not wartime. It might be added that even in wartime some concern for justice and humanity is still appropriate, as over the bombing of Dresden in February 1945 (and the moral point is raised by the war crimes trials, in which obedience to orders was not an accepted defence). But that point indicates that there is a sharp conflict of values here, just as there had been over the Falklands War. Margaret Thatcher did not expect the BBC to be neutral between Britain and Argentina – and Libya was in her eyes an enemy too.

b) Death on the Rock
In 1988 Thames Television broadcast a programme about the shooting by the SAS of three IRA members in Gibraltar. The programme suggested that the shooting might have been unlawful, in that at the moment the IRA members were shot they were not doing anything illegal, nor were they threatening the SAS, and may have been about to surrender. Thames Television and the IBA had resisted pressure from the Foreign Secretary not to transmit the programme. Such pressure is illegal and curiously, was not applied to newspapers, which had printed long speculative articles on the shootings.

An independent inquiry by Lord Windlesham, a former Conservative leader in the Lords, concluded that the programme was well-researched and did not offend against the requirement of due impartiality; nor did it prejudice the inquest in Gibraltar. Witnesses had not been bribed, bullied or misrepresented. Overall the programme 'reflected the virtues and limitations of television journalism in the late 1980s'.

The government did not agree and made its displeasure known. The government did not like the way the evidence for the programme had been collected, believed that it contained inaccuracies and risked prejudicing the inquest.

Leaving aside the assessment of detail, what, if anything, can be said by way of general defence of the Government's attitude?

The possibility of prejudice ('contamination of the evidence') to the inquest is important, even though the programme was not transmitted in Gibraltar (it was known about, reported in the press and videos were available). The best case for the Government is one that cannot be put openly: there is a war on against the IRA, and IRA members ('terrorists') were not in Gibraltar as tourists. The difficulty about that argument is that there is strictly not a war on, and it is important for Britain to act within the law in resisting the IRA. That is perhaps a tactical rather than a moral point, and should be reworded to say 'Britain should be seen to act within the law'. It may be doubted whether British 'public opinion' was heavily in favour of the point made by the programme, but that is not decisive either for law or morality. Evidently, Ireland poses difficult problems for broadcasters. ●

Interest Groups

Interest groups – what they are, what they do

Definitions
Interest groups, or pressure groups, are groups or organisations which seek to change government policy, in its fundamental or in its administrative aspects, by various forms of persuasion, but without themselves taking over government power.

'Changes in government policy' are sought because the group has an interest to protect and foster, an idea to promote – or something of both. The group might be concerned with fundamental government policy, such as exchange or interest rates, privatisation or European integration, or with an administrative detail, such as the modification of a regulation, help with export credits or a government contract or the application of a lower rate of tax to domestic pots and pans. Most of the work of interest groups lies in administrative detail; we are for the most part not concerned with the great swings of policy which concern the cabinet and the politicians. But, then, policy is often built up or modified by the accumulation of minor decisions on points of detail. So what may look to be routine and humdrum 'administration' may turn out still to be the lower slopes of high policy.

'Persuasion' includes methods ranging from rational argument in a joint committee, a pamphlet or a restaurant to a threat of withdrawal from the Health Service or a parade of taxis blocking Parliament Square. Interest groups do not want to take over government themselves: if so, they would be political parties.

There is a problem of terminology. The term 'pressure group' may be regarded as unsatisfactory because 'pressure' is a loaded word. We should all be happy to persuade but not to bully –

pressure may always seem undue and much pressure group activity is not pressure at all, but routine collaboration. The best alternative, 'interest group', has the same kind of defect and omits the group which has an idea or an attitude to promote.

The word 'group' is also inaccurate, and in this context covers a wide range of organisations and people including individuals. The use of the term 'lobby' is again not quite appropriate, for the lobbies of Parliament are not so much frequented by serious pressure-groupers, and 'lobby' is not a neutral word for Americans. It seems that any term we use will at best be a shorthand expression requiring elaboration if it is to be useful.

It is easy to regard all interest groups as outside government, not part of government, but part of the forces which play upon government. This is misleading – as indeed it is misleading to consider parties or the media as wholly outside government. The most successful interest groups are to some extent incorporated in government, taking part in the processes of government, in consultation, advice and in some cases policy-making and implementation. They are an accepted part of the political system, apparently legitimate and almost constitutional, not part of some political equivalent of the black economy.

Interest groups are not new. The barons at Runnymede in 1215, persuading King John to sign Magna Carta, were in a very different political context a kind of pressure group (unless they were an early form of political party). The Church has always been a force in government. In the nineteenth century the Anti-Corn Law League and the powerful 'railway interest' were recognisably modern interest groups. As the scope of government has expanded, so the pressures on government have grown. Hence one intended consequence of the retreat of government in the 1980s (most notably in the matter of incomes policy) was the relief of government from intolerable pressure.

Interest groups may be roughly categorised as follows:

1 Groups which seek to protect and foster sectional interests, characteristically economic organisations, with a great deal at stake, competitive, well-funded, and with ready access to government. These include:
   - manufacturing, commercial and business interests: e.g. Confederation of British Industries, the Association of British Chambers of Commerce, the Champagne Association; but also single companies working on their own behalf as well as through trade associations
   - employers, professionals and employees: e.g. The National Federation of Building Trades Employers, British Medical Association, National Union of Mineworkers.

2 Groups with an idea, ideal or cause to promote: e.g. the Lord's Day Observance Society, Royal Society for the Protection of Birds, Howard League for Penal Reform, Campaign for Nuclear Disarmament.

3 Other groups having interests and ideals which may suffer from or benefit by government action: e.g. Country Landowners' Association, Income Tax Payers' Society, National Federation of Women's Institutes, British Legion; associations representing the Churches, ethnic groups, sport and many more.

   The distinction between interests and ideals is rough, and in any case interests are presented as ideals.

4 Single issue, 'one-off', campaigns, usually to protest at a particular government decision (e.g. a planning decision) or a proposed piece of legislation (e.g. on Sunday trading), or to urge immediate action (e.g. to prevent the closure of a steel works). Such campaigns tend to be angry protests by people who have no regular access to government.

A list of interest groups could be very long indeed: there are very few activities which are not the subject of 'pressure' of some kind. It is evident that these categories overlap; in particular interests and ideas are not distinct, both are 'causes'. The groups can be further sub-divided: large or small, rich or poor, accepted or excluded, insider or outsider (in relation to government), open or focused in strategy, and effective or ineffective.

Most of the groups, except the single issue campaigns, are organisations with continuing responsibilities apart from exerting pressure on government. This is true not only for the major economic associations, but also the social welfare organisations such as Shelter or Mind which en-gage in substantial work in their chosen field, while campaigning for more support from government.

Illustrations of interest group activity

1 The Confederation of British Industry (CBI) is the major spokesman for industry. It was represented on the National Economic Development Council, the government's main forum for consultation with industry and the trade unions (until its abolition in 1992), and well over a hundred other bodies including the Advisory Conciliation and Arbitration Service and the Equal Opportunities Commission.

2 As an example of individual industries, the British Plastics Federation is in regular contact with appropriate ministries, mainly the Board of Trade, over statistics, exports, machinery, plastic fitments for housing, freight rates, taxation and similar matters.

3 In some cases the industry-government relationship is indirect. Thus the government's concern for standards of conduct in the selling of insurance and investment, specifically, disclosure and advice, were carried out through discussions by the regulating bodies, the Securities and Investments Board and the Office of Fair Trading, with the Association of British Insurers and directly with major insurers. Any agreement reached might require the authority of the minister and legislation; so government is involved at one remove. The Consumers' Association made comments on behalf of consumers, and the 'watchdog' bodies had a specific remit to protect the interests of consumers. This may be done more effectively by such bodies, rather than by department officials, who may settle for an easier life and a friendly relationship – in what is called a 'policy community'.

4 Threats to what is known as 'the British Sunday' bring into action both 'cause' and economic interest groups. The churches and the Lord's Day Observance Society are joined by the shop workers' trade union, USDAW, and many small shopkeepers, to fight the superstores and the entertainment industry, and perhaps many of

the would-be Sunday shoppers. On issues of this kind politicians cannot win, and Members of Parliament and ministers 'keep their heads down'. Nowadays the problem can be referred to or blamed on the European Community.

5 The Royal Society for the Protection of Birds is perhaps the most powerful single-interest lobby in the country, powerful, that is, in relation to its limited objectives. Birds should be grateful for such protection. Birds migrating North through the unfriendly skies of Italy and France should sing a song of praise to the RSPB as they reach the safer shores of England. Some other charities can match the RSPB in influence and exceed it in wealth, for example, the National Trust, Oxfam and the Royal National Lifeboat Institution.

The RSPB (the Royal approval is a valuable asset) began as a late Victorian campaign against the trade in rare feathers for hats. In recent years it has grown to a membership of over half a million, with an income to match, expanded by professional marketing. The Society draws on the support of nature lovers and environmentalists, and is well represented in the House of Lords. Prudently the Society does not seek to protect game birds, rather, as the RSPCA re-defines cruelty when it comes to hunting.

The RSPB is a successful interest group because it pursues limited objectives of broad appeal and makes few demands on government funds and none which threatens government's popularity, standing, or principles. It can plausibly claim to be non-political and it never needs to resort to militancy. The RSPB is the ideal interest group. Unfortunately, most other groups serve clients who lack the universally acceptable grace of the birds.

6 VAT on books, 1987. The book trade fought hard to retain their privilege (and ours) of exemption of books from VAT. To avoid appearing simply as the defenders of commercial interests the campaign stressed the potential harm to education, and so enlisted the support of the DES, educational organisations and many Members of Parliament, as well as the media. Apart from the educational argument, it was suggested to the Treasury that the fall in book buying would diminish the returns from the tax. The government did not bring forward a firm proposal, but it was probably on the Treasury's list of options. The trade claimed a victory; the Chancellor claimed innocence of

any such intention. In the game of pressure politics the government can leak or float policy options to test reaction, and then withdraw or deny. The Chancellor is particularly subject to lobbying while he prepares taxation and expenditure proposals, but he is well protected by secrecy and collective responsibility.

Strategies and resources of interest groups

To gain their objectives, interest groups must influence governments. Generally the more direct methods are the best, so the most powerful groups do their work in Whitehall, in the departments and with ministers. Thus the groups endeavour to influence decisions at the point at which they are taken. But Parliament and public are not neglected by the powerful, for it would be tactically unwise to allow hostile opinion to develop. Less important and less powerful groups may find Whitehall less accessible, and for them Parliament and public may be the only targets for their activity. Street demonstrations are a sign of the powerlessness, of the lack of access to the corridors of power. The major strategies of the interest groups are these:

- membership of standing joint official committees
- regular formal contact with officials, in meetings and by correspondence
- informal contacts with ministers, ranging from private interviews and telephone conversations to dinners and golf
- delegations to see the minister and his senior officials (a touch of desperation about this: other means of persuasion have failed)
- regular representation through Members of Parliament
- occasional attempts to secure the support of Members, through meetings, dinners, written material
- management of the media – feeding news items and comment, being available for interviews to respond to criticism
- public campaigns to draw attention and win support, including advertising, feeding material to the press, and demonstrations: e.g. parade of farmers on tractors; unemployed lying down in the middle of Oxford Street at rush-hour (that was in the 1930s); all London taxis converging on the Houses of Parliament, causing a traffic jam in Parliament Square; carrying a coffin to the ministry (the coffin symbolising the ministry's alleged destruction of something or other

and containing either a petition or the bearers' packed lunches).

The listing of these activities indicates the major resources of interest groups. Access to government is clearly essential, but is itself partly the product of some factors beyond the group's control. Finance, for organising and campaigning, and access to the media are also essential. Popular approval of the group's goals encourages government benevolence, while control of a scarce resource such as coal (in the past) or surgical or exporting skills, increases the group's bargaining capacity. Defending an existing position is always easier than promoting change.

Of all these resources, access to government is probably the most significant for group influence. But the initial grant of access is likely to depend in part on the government's independent assessment of the value and power of the group. Hence access is not so much a resource in the competition, as a reward for having won. However, it is still conceivable that some groups enter the competition already endowed with access, for example, corporations headed by political or social notables; associations with existing governmental links. In this and in other ways, groups are not equally endowed with resources, and to that extent the competition for influence is unequal.

Professional lobbying

Much of the lobbying activity required by companies can be done either by specialist 'in-house' public relations or government affairs departments, or by the hiring of professional lobbyists. Professional lobbying has a long history – there was a lobbyist working for a Channel Tunnel in the 1920s – but grew in the 1970s and 1980s to a substantial sector of business. That development indicates that, despite the rhetoric of non-intervention, government is a powerful actor in commerce and industry, and that lobbying must be presumed to be reasonably effective to justify its fees. So here, as elsewhere, money can buy access and influence. In the Document a professional lobbyist reveals some of the tricks of his trade.

■ DOCUMENT 21.1
Lobbying Government

Based on Charles Miller, 1987, pp. 122, 129–31
Five lobbying 'myths', that is, false conventional wisdom.
● Parliament is all-important.

● Pressure gets results (referring to 'high profile pressure' – he instances mass lobbying of Parliament).
● Start at the top (better start at Assistant Secretary/Principal/Policy Unit level).
● MPs and officials should be entertained, or 'Eat your way out of trouble'. (The author adds primly, 'No-one would ask their lawyer to wine and dine a jury' – but the courts are a different battle ground).
● Working with government is an extension of public relations (He treats public relations as image-building, and emphasises the need for information, understanding, access and advocacy – lobbying is more than advertising). ■

EXERCISE
Lobbying government

21.1 Do you agree that these notions are all 'myths'?

The professional approach of the lobbyist comprises at best the skills and strategies that anyone engaged in making a case would use: move early to influence the context of decision-making; find out who has an influence on the decision and how they might be persuaded; make a case that is sustainable (so be at least honest enough to meet a sharp challenge); understand the priorities and procedures of government, and in particular the role of officials; be ready to adapt or moderate, prepare your own compromise, be courteous at all times....

It all sounds very civilised, a tolerant and unprejudiced discussion among reasonable people. But of course the issues are too complex, the interests too committed and the stakes too high to allow total rationality. Some arguments will be suppressed, others given an undue emphasis, the calculation of economic or political advantage will determine the outcome of argument. How could it be otherwise? Politics is a conflict of interests masked by reason rather than a competition of rationality tainted by interest. So we should not expect the influence of the professional lobbyist to strengthen the force of reason in public affairs.

Interest groups and government: governing as interest group competition
Interest group activity is continuous and inclusive, and operates across the whole range of government activity. Much of it is collaborative rather than invasive or aggressive. For groups like say

CND or Greenpeace, government is the fortress they besiege, and the fortress dominates the territory. But for many industrial and commercial and even some welfare groups, government is co-participant in a continuing collaborative project. This may still be warfare of a kind, and the government has the bigger guns, but this is a long-running civil war, in which the objectives are not surrender and conquest, but local territorial gains, and living to fight another day.

This continuing more or less civilised competition of groups makes up a substantial part of the process of governing. In this perspective governing is about competing in and umpiring the competition of interest groups. Government itself is both player and umpire, and is itself made up of competing interests, the departments themselves and sections within them. This system of governing as interest group competition has three important characteristics.

1 Departments and divisions of departments work as interest groups, competing with other departments for territory or funding (the Treasury is a powerful player in the game). Ministers themselves represent interests, their clients. Much of this competition is confined to the corridors of government, but departments may themselves harness outside pressures to their cause. This has been done most blatantly and effectively by the three defence services, competing with each other, and by the Foreign Office, defending its privileges. This phenomenon of intra-government sectionalism is more highly developed and evident in the USA, where sections of government (departments, bureaux, the defence forces) openly bid for Congressional favour and funding. In Britain the legislature has fewer favours to hand out, and lobbying is less extensive and certainly more discreet.
2 If government is not a fortress, the civil service does not work simply as the castle guard or security cordon. The civil servant is either engaging in the in-house competition of interests, or more often, negotiating with the accepted groups. The official's task is to listen, probe, research; the aim is not just to fend off the group pressure or refer to the minister, but to make a deal within the accepted limits of the department's policies and practice. The tendency of bureaucratic negotiation with interests is to make a deal with regular clients and stand by it. (The good civil servant likes to clear his desk and stay out of trouble.)

3 In face of the continuing necessity to meet and accommodate a multiplicity of interests, governments have resorted to a range of intermediate bodies, or quangos, consultative committees, advisory and regulatory bodies. Their function, one way or another, is to collect, aggregate, deflect, represent or suppress interests.

Thus the government, perceiving that it faces a complex of interests and pressures, engages in strategies to deal with them, and by doing so regularises and legitimates governing as a competition of interests.

EXERCISES
Current activity by pressure groups

21.2 Go through not more than three issues of a daily paper and note cases of the current activities of pressure groups.

  a) Objective:
    i) an interest to protect or foster
    ii) an idea, ideal or cause to promote.
  b) Strategy:
    i) discreet e.g. contact with a government department
    ii) open, e.g. through Parliament, press or a public campaign.
  c) Resources:
    i) ample in finance, expertise, access, respectability
    ii) deficient.
  d) Effectiveness: Is there any evidence to suggest (or would you judge) that the group:
    i) will get its way
    ii) will have a substantial influence
    iii) will have its point of view taken into account
    iv) will have virtually no effect?
  e) Concern for the general interest:
    i) exclusively self-interested
    ii) self-interested but responsible
    iii) some concern for the public interest some of the time
    iv) strong concern for the public interest most of the time.

21.3 Analyse some of the longer BBC radio or television news programmes and check how often group spokesmen are reported or interviewed. Try to guess which news items were provided by interested bodies.
21.4 Devise a lobbying campaign on behalf of some mildly controversial cause in a

school or college, club or association with which you are connected. Assess your chances of success.

A number of Case Studies dealing with interest groups are given below.

● CASE STUDY
Agriculture

The relationship of the government and the National Farmers' Union is very close – 'unique in its range and intensity' (P. Self and H. J. Storing, 1962, p. 230). Total public support for agriculture, including EC funds, ran in the early 1990s at about £250 each year for every man, woman and child – very large sum for a privately owned and controlled industry which accounts for only 2–3 per cent of Gross National Product.

Government and National Farmers' Union engage in a close and continuing process of consultation. The union's representatives frequent the Ministry of Agriculture – and not merely its corridors. They sit on committees, they inform, advise, persuade, stand firm; they are adamant. The Minister and his officials normally attempt to secure agreement before acting. The official description of this relationship is 'partnership'; some political scientists call it 'symbiosis', or living together; or it may be called colonisation (of government by the interests).

Since Britain joined the EEC the relationship has been extended and strengthened through the Community's Common Agricultural Policy which takes up the bulk of the EEC's funds, and administrative effort. If the British government were already locked into a system of its own devising, it is now double locked into a continental system.

There are two ways of assessing this relationship, by its economic and social results, and by its political method. In both cases, some balance has to be struck between the interests of farmers and the interests of consumers, the two interests which make up the elusive 'public interest'.

An assessment of the first kind, social and economic, is not a special concern of this book, but it clearly has some relevance. It would seem that since 1939 the close partnership between government and NFU has brought about a great increase in the productivity and prosperity of the countryside; both were lacking previously and highly desirable for the community at large as well as for the farmers and farm workers. But these gains are not unmixed and certainly not cost free. As the cost of agricultural support has grown, so the number of people working on the land has diminished – by about two thirds since 1945. Subsidies and support have benefited the prosperous farmer without always saving the poorer farmer. The consumer has gained abundant, indeed over-abundant, food, but he, or usually she, has paid twice, in taxes and food prices, in some cases for absurdly uneconomic arrangements (e.g. growing wheat in a hostile climate, while excluding cheap American wheat).

Modern tax-supported farming has also been damaging to the environment, and when the environment has been protected the tax payer has footed the bill. Thus, under the Wild Life and Countryside Act of 1981 landowners were offered generous compensation for preserving sites of special concern to conservationists. In some cases already wealthy landowners were able to claim large sums for not doing what they would not have done anyway. Farmers are also paid to 'set aside', that is not cultivate (though still caring for) land; and sensible farmers choose to set aside their least fertile tracts of land.

Farmers cheerfully plough up footpaths (ramblers are entitled to walk through the growing crop), and put so much fertiliser on their fields that the water is polluted (but that is regarded as the responsibility of the water authority and its customers, not the farmer); and if limits are placed on the farmers' use of fertiliser, he will be entitled to compensation. Farmers are effectively not subject to planning control, and again may be compensated for not doing what the ordinary citizen is simply forbidden to do. And so on.

Such privilege is difficult to understand, yet it has been bestowed without a struggle. This is the great strength of the farming and landowners lobby. It does not have to fight for its privileges: it is accepted, established and entrenched. Altogether the balance of government-bestowed privilege seems to have been tipped heavily towards the farmers and landowners.

The government's relationship with the farmers in the 1990s is under challenge, but not yet in decline. Agriculture remains the only industry with its own ministry, and a commitment to support and subsidy on a scale which has been denied to other industries such as car manufacture or coal mining. Environmental concerns have given a new justification to the public support of agriculture. The salmonella in eggs affair in 1988 demonstrated that the farming lobby could wring £20m (and even the scalp of a Minister) out of the government as quickly as the Royal Navy; and the reforms of the CAP, tardily agreed, in 1992 will pay farmers as much in compensation as they lose in prices.

Despite the recent decline in their privileges it would seem that the farmers and the NFU have enjoyed an undue influence with governments. There are several explanations for the government's service of the farmers to the neglect of the consumer's interest.

1 *History and inertia.* State support to agriculture developed during the Second World War, after a long period of depression in the countryside, and when the production of food was a vital national necessity. The Ministry of Agriculture in the post-war Labour government continued and developed the policy, so that by the 1950s financial aid to farming depended on government inertia in the face of established interests, rather than on a continuing assessment of national needs.

2 *Perceived desirability of the policy.* Governments have regarded the support of agriculture as a proper policy anyway, on social and economic grounds. This is to imply that governments still have some choice in the matter, and have not merely capitulated to a vociferous pressure group. Thus the effect of the pressure group is to increase the pace and intensity of the government's pursuit of a policy, and to make it more difficult for the government to slow down, turn aside, or stop.

3 *Mutual interest of government and farmers.* The Union is a necessary instrument or associate of government. The government has in the NFU a source of information and advice; it has also an instrument, a channel of communication at least, through which it might influence the industry, for example to greater efficiency.

The farmers have an instrument too, for communicating with and influencing the government. They have virtually exclusive rights. There is some advantage in this for the government, in that it has only one body to deal with, and that body must itself effect compromise between the sectional interests of its own members. Moreover, the union, having got itself into a privileged position, has much to lose by recalcitrance. But, if the arrangement saves the government some diplomatic labours, it precludes some diplomatic manoeuvres, and concedes the NFU the strength of a monopoly.

4 *Representation of farming interests in Parliament.* The apparent political weight of agriculture has declined – fewer farming voters, farming constituencies and farmer Members of Parliament (38 in 1964, 12 in 1992) and Ministers. But the farming interest is well-organised and articulate locally (and not sharply divided like industry between managers and workers), and the House of Lords is stiff with land-owning peers. Naturally some members of government have been farmers, and others have had a stake in farming through land-ownership. It is not unusual for Ministers of Agriculture to be farmers. This is not to suggest that Members of Parliament or Ministers have improperly advanced their own interests; but it is to suggest that close personal involvement in an activity makes for understanding and sympathy, insight and perception, a greater facility for seeing a point of view and adjusting action to it.

5 *Close collaboration with the civil service.* Apart from parliamentary representation, the NFU has been well represented in Whitehall itself, in committees and in office in the Ministry itself. Senior officials from MAFF have moved easily into top positions in the NFU. Thus the traditional representation of the farming interest at Westminster is matched by a carefully built-in partnership in Whitehall. This is a most effective foundation for a successful pressure group.

6 *Popular goodwill.* A farming 'community in danger' gets more sympathy than a mining 'community'. Farming has usually enjoyed popular goodwill, based on an appreciation of its economic value, and a somewhat romantic view of the rural way of life. But goodwill is declining as the costs to taxpayer and shopper and the environmental disadvantages of modern factory farming and tax-supported over-production are appreciated. ●

EXERCISES
Representation and negotiation

If you were the Minister concerned with a

particular interest group:

21.5 Would you be concerned to discover whether the group you were dealing with was genuinely representative of the interest it claimed to represent? If so, how would you do this?

21.6 How would you distinguish between consulting with the group, and negotiating with it? Would you regard negotiation as improper or not? Why?

● CASE STUDY
The Consumers' Association versus the Law Society

The consumers' movement began in Britain with the establishment of the Consumers' Association in 1957, publishers of one of the first and few consumers' guides totally independent of producers and advertisers. Within a few years the Association had over a quarter of a million members. The Association's original main function was testing of products and the distribution of information, but it soon moved into the representation of consumer interests with government, and contributed to improvements for the consumer in hire purchase and credit, contracts, unsolicited goods and service and generally to the setting of standards by government and the British Standards Institution. In 1972 the government appointed its first Minister for Consumer Affairs and in 1981 the EC established a Directorate-General for Environmental and Consumer Protection.

In 1983 the Labour Member of Parliament, Austin Mitchell, won a high place in the ballot for Private Member's Bills. Less than two hours after the drawing of the ballot the Consumers' Association delivered letters to the 20 successful Members. Mitchell responded positively to CA's proposal to end the solicitors' monopoly of property conveyancing. The 'conveyancing' (that is, legal transfer) of property is a comparatively simple procedure, especially in a system of land registration and computerised records, for which solicitors charge fees which seem to hard-pressed house buyers to bear little relation to the work done. This seems to be half admitted by solicitors, who argue that their income from conveyancing is necessary to subsidise their litigation work – an unusual tax on house-buyers.

The Law Society has about 60 000 members, a substantial income, high standing and about 300 staff (plus 1200 more to run the Legal Aid scheme in civil cases on behalf of the government). Margaret Thatcher's government was ideologically opposed to professional privilege and monopoly, but it did not act against institutions and associations of high status with the conviction and courage it showed in face of, for example, the miners and print workers. So, though Austin Mitchell's Home Buyers Bill was enacted in 1984, with the support of the Consumers' Association and the press, it was seriously weakened. The solicitors fought hard and with some success. They had the advantage of a hundred lawyers in the House of Commons (80 of them Conservative), and Lord Chancellor Hailsham in the Cabinet. The solicitors succeeded in restricting the new profession of licensed conveyancers, and later the right of banks and building societies to establish their own conveyancing service. Thus the case nicely demonstrates that some entrenched interests are too well protected to fall easily, and that producer groups are usually stronger than consumer groups. ●

● CASE STUDY
The roads lobby

The roads lobby appears to be one of the most successful lobbies. If you want the evidence, drive around Southern England, or through the middle of Coventry or Glasgow. Motorways have been built while the railways have decayed. Why? because people wanted it so – at least, until recently when 'people' as car owners and drivers have shown more concern for the environmental costs of cars and roads. Since car owners were also voters the politics appear to be simple. The car-owning voters got what they wanted without being asked. But they were not really presented with alternatives, and the commercial roads lobby forced the pace of road building with little concern for the vehicle saturation which accompanied it.

The roads lobby is powerful because of its dual base of private car owners and multiple commercial interests – road haulage, motor manufacturing, bus operators, the oil industry and the motorists' organisations. These are numerous, large and rich, and well-entrenched in the Department of Transport. The Department is responsible for transport policy as a whole, but historically it has been concerned with roads because it has a full responsibility for them, which it cannot have with the railways.

Roads are the 'property' of the Department, the nationalised railways belong to British Rail.

In particular, the Department has its own roads engineers, and as elsewhere, technologists have a heavy influence on their 'technological property'. The engineers and the administrators as well as Ministers, have favoured the economic arguments (costs and competition) against the environmental arguments. The maximum weight of lorries has been periodically increased, taxes have been kept low (in relation to damage caused by heavy lorries) and safety regulation is comparatively light. A senior civil servant (in a leaked document) argued that the purpose of the Armitage inquiry, which cleared the way in 1983 for the 38-tonne lorry, was to 'get round the political obstacles': 'the establishment in the public mind of a clear, overwhelming case on balance for heavier lorry weights is seen as the main end of the inquiry'. Thus the purpose of an inquiry was to establish and legitimate an option already selected by the Department.

The railways, their users and their workers, also constitute a lobby, and quite effective judged by the amount of subsidy. Curiously London commuters complain bitterly about the conditions they endure each day on their rail journeys to work, but their anger is directed at, or deflected by the government towards, British Rail. Subsidies are not the answer says the government, try kicking British Rail. Political attitudes and culture are significant here. Nationalised industries and public sector unions are unpopular, certainly in Southern England, and not without reason. Somehow, money given to the railways is taxpayers' money; but money spent on roads is government money, or is not noticed, certainly not resented.

Altogether, it looks as if the effectiveness of the roads lobby should not be exaggerated. Policies favourable to that lobby emerge from a complex of political factors, not least the desire of car owners to drive their cars. ●

■ DOCUMENT 21.2
The charity lobby: Bob Geldof and Live Aid
Based on Bob Geldof, 1986, pp. 392–3
The Live Aid concert at Wembley in 1985 was then the biggest ever televised concert and fund-raising event. It went on all day and all night; mobilised opinion worldwide and raised over $100m. Geldof's success, talents and skil-

fully cultivated notoriety gave him enviable political clout and access. He met Margaret Thatcher at a newspaper awards ceremony. She said:

'I think it's wonderful what you've been doing with the Band Aid record'.

Geldof, with more courage than many a Cabinet Minister, responded by suggesting it was ridiculous to dispose of EEC surplus butter at a cost of £10m when, in another part of the world, people were dying of starvation.

Margaret Thatcher responded briskly, first:

'There's nothing ridiculous about a healthy agriculture...'
and :'Mr Geldof, they can't eat butter'.

The exchange ended icily.

Margaret Thatcher: 'It's not as simple as that'.

Geldof: 'No, Prime Minister, nothing is as simple as dying'.

Geldof tried with the support of leading politicians to persuade the government to exempt from VAT the proceeds of the Band Aid Christmas record. The government refused, and finally agreed to spend an equivalent sum on aid for Africa. ■

EXERCISES
Live Aid

21.7 Was government right to refuse to grant a VAT exemption?
21.8 Was Live Aid successful?
21.9 Why are there not more campaigns like that?

EXERCISE
Cases of interest group activity

21.10 What can you learn about the nature of the interest group process from these cases?

The examples and cases considered so far offer some indications of the nature of interest groups and interest group activity. These include the following:

● the working of 'policy communities'
● climates of opinion
● the influence of experts and technologists
● the value to the interest group of popular approval, respectability and access to the Minister
● history and inertia as determinants of the legitimacy of groups
● national security as a prime, indeed, an overwhelming objective of governments

- the uses, but also the limits of Parliament
- the EC as a necessary focus of lobbying
- the primacy in the long term of government, especially a government which has firm political goals.

There are limits to the reach of governments. If you want to know how to preserve a privileged position, study the farmers and the lawyers; if you want to pursue a particular kind of charitable cause, ask Bob Geldof.

Campaigns on a single issue

In the areas of public life discussed above, pressure groups are more or less permanently organised and continuously active. In addition, pressure groups arise from time to time to fight for or against some new direction of government policy or intention. Often they lapse when the struggle is decisively won or lost but some struggles are never finally decided and there is a discernible tendency for some campaigns, on housing, social welfare and pollution for example, to give rise to permanent organisations.

The best example of a single-issue campaign is also an early one, the Anti-Corn Law League, active from the late 1830s to its triumph in the repeal of the Corn Laws in 1846. The League drew on the energies and finances of the new manufacturers, and mounted a massive public and parliamentary campaign. This was planned as deliberately and even as skilfully as any contemporary campaign mounted by public relations experts. Victory came when the Prime Minister himself, Sir Robert Peel, confessed himself convinced by the League's arguments, and introduced the Bill to repeal the Corn Laws.

One of the first campaigns of modern times to claim equal success and to draw attention to the potential of organised pressure is the campaign for commercial television of the early 1950s. (For an account of that campaign see H. Wilson, 1961, and, in summary, P. Madgwick, 1984). The outcome of that campaign demonstrated that, however forceful the pressures, one condition of success is some support within the Cabinet and the ruling party.

Here are two examples of recent campaigns on a single issue. A feature of such campaigns is their concentration on parliamentary and public activity: there is no time, and usually no basis, for the development of close relations with a department. Indeed, there is a tendency for groups lacking the ordinary means of political influence to resort to militancy or direct action. For example, the number of 'demos' in London increased ten times between 1973 and 1983. The case studies below illustrate and raise questions about this tendency.

Some examples of campaigns on a single issue.

- CASE STUDY
CLEAR – The Campaign for Lead-free Air 1981–83

In 1981 the Government took a final decision that Britain would not have lead-free petrol. The decision was based on expert advice which was later discredited. Des Wilson, a noted public crusader (Shelter, Friends of the Earth, Freedom of Information, more recently the Liberal Democrats), established a campaign for lead-free petrol. It was opposed by the Government, the car manufacturers and the oil and 'additives' industry. In a little over a year, the Government reversed its position and by the end of the 1980s, lead-free petrol was widely available, and its use encouraged by lower taxation. The success of the campaign was due first to the fact that it won the argument, through good research, the assembling of expert testimony, and the countering of the negative argument ('there is no firm evidence that...') by stressing the risks ('we ought to act as if...'). Second, for winning the argument is never quite enough, Wilson was a skilled campaigner, good at organising support among other respected and potentially sympathetic organisations (PTAs for example) and among political parties. Third, and crucially, the Royal Commission on Environmental Pollution recommended in favour of lead-free petrol, and then decisively, the Prime Minister, a former industrial chemist, was persuaded by the scientific arguments.

Was the campaign necessary after all, or would Margaret Thatcher have been persuaded anyway? ●

- CASE STUDY
The Anti-Poll-Tax Campaign 1989–90
For an account of the Poll-Tax see Case Study in Chapter 24
The Community Charge, always known as the hated Poll-Tax, was unpopular because it proved to be heavier than the rates (property tax), fell on individuals who had not previously paid local taxes directly and was not related to ability to pay. It gave rise to a number of local

protests and a national Anti-Poll-Tax Federation organised by Militant and other radical left-wing groups. In Scotland a movement was established to oppose payment of the tax; demonstrations and marches took place and council chambers were invaded. In Trafalgar Square, London, in March 1990 a demonstration turned into a riot, with scores of arrests and casualties. There was even a modest riot in Tunbridge Wells, thought to be the heart of middle-class England, and in the heart of rural England there was a demonstration in Somerset and a mass resignation of Conservative councillors in West Oxfordshire.

The unpopularity of the Poll-Tax contributed to the downfall of Margaret Thatcher, and her successors moved to find a new form of local taxation. So the protestors won? ●

EXERCISES
Pressure by direct action

21.11 How would you distinguish between 'direct action' and 'violence'?
21.12 Were the Poll-Tax protests justified? Were they effective?

Direct Action
In planning cases, local protest often runs into 'direct action', ranging from marches and demonstrations (burning the Minister in effigy), through civil disobedience (refusing to pay the poll-tax) to physical force, either passive (standing in front of the bulldozers) or active (a brick through the Minister's window).

'Direct Action' is used here loosely to encompass several kinds of physical activity, going beyond meetings, speeches, letters and deputations. The distinctive measures are:

● actions rather than words, e.g. a 'mass' lobby of Parliament compared with a deputation of three people
● direct effect, a favoured form being an occupation of premises to obstruct or, say, to prevent closure
● illegality, beginning with passive civil disobedience
● violence, starting with, say, sitting on a pavement, ending with the assassination of the ruler.

These forms of protest activity have grown in Britain, and elsewhere, since the more contented and passive post-war period. The Campaign for Nuclear Disarmament led the way (literally), and

protests over the Vietnam War intensified the public expression of hostility. The year 1968 was the Year of Revolutions, notably in USA, France and Czechoslovakia, and most universities in Britain suffered or enjoyed, violent protest.

The new outbursts of protest activity from the 1960s onwards marked a distinct change in British politics, the extension of the range of pressures to which government must respond, even if only to neglect or suppress. Such protest is by its nature uneven. There are always grounds for discontent, though, fortunately for governments, those with grounds for discontent are often passive (the unemployed, for example), and may not even feel discontented. Protest requires an occasion, a focus, leadership, an example. The respectable, bourgeous British political culture is hostile to most forms of violent protest, though with some sympathy for non-destructive occupations.

In an unpromising political culture the growth of protest activity requires explanation. Protest arises from a subjective sense of grievance which might be as strong in 1990 because a man could not afford a car as in 1930 when he could not afford to feed his children. There is a greater dependence on government and a great resentment of its failings, hence much criticism of impersonal government, 'faceless bureaucrats' and so on. Standards of contentment changed; there was a lower degree of tolerance of misfortune, and economic performance lagged behind higher expectations.

However, that lower tolerance itself requires explanation. It would seem to be associated with the lifting of the intense fear of poverty and the ending of the disciplines of war and military service. It was also associated in time with the rebellion of youth in the 1960s, a break-out from dependence, subordination and discipline. Evidence of participation and leadership of protest movements suggests too that the highly educated and the unemployed, sometimes the same people, were likely protesters. Finally, one indisputably new element in British politics, race, and another which had only briefly appeared before, women's liberation, added objectives, motives and willing demonstrators to the protest movements.

For all its vigour, rage and ingenuity, protest activity did not often change the course of governments. Indeed, protest on the streets meant that the group lacked an entry to the corridors of power. So government could brush aside the protest, unless the protesters had a good deal of public sympathy, some support in party and Parliament or high places, or an awkward capacity to disrupt. For these reasons, in varying proportions, strikes were by far the most effective weapon of protest. In other cases governments sometimes made concessions which carried virtually no economic or political cost; for example, the government's retreat from motorway building in the late 1970s in response to an effective if unscrupulous campaign of disruption of planning inquiries was not very painful for a government desperately short of money.

There is and was a justification in democratic theory for such protest activity, when democracy fails to take proper account of all interests and reach a fair compromise. History may seem to confirm the necessity of direct action, since many of the great social and political reforms of history owe something to its use – aggrieved and obstinate people mounting the barricades. To deny the possibility that direct action might sometimes be justified seems to deny the movement of history and to choose a static society.

There is still some room for doubt whether the quality of British democracy was always served by the protest activity of this period. Protest movements were not always representative, since people vary in their willingness and capacity to take part in protest, and the variation is not in proportion to the grievance. The young and the middle classes were often overrepresented; and the issues fought over were of a special kind. Nuclear weapons, and later nuclear power, Vietnam and South Africa, abortion and the Welsh language were frequent subjects for militant activity, but not poverty in old age or the community care of the mentally ill. Perhaps these priorities are right but a concern for priority was not characteristic of protesters.

The balance is difficult to strike. Governments had taken immense powers to influence the lives of ordinary people in countless ways. The constitutional machinery for ordinary people to talk back to governments was not, or was not thought to be, adequate. The protesters seemed to give voice to the voiceless, power to the powerless. But the politics of protest was in practice much cruder than that neat and comforting formulation suggests. Protest was a necessary element in freedom of speech, a proper complement to parliamentary processes. But the power which militant protest sometimes gave was unevenly distributed, and challenged the minimal order and authority on which all governments must depend. In general, therefore, the assessment of protest groups is similar to that of interest groups: the power lost to government was not distributed in ways which were representative, equitable and accountable.

In a democracy the case for direct action is not entirely convincing. The principles of democracy justify at most the sparing use of minimally violent forms of direct action as a last resort. Even so there are grave difficulties. The use of direct action is not easily limited, and will be used by reactionary as well as 'progressive' forces (that is, by people you disagree with), and by the state itself for protection or in retaliation. Since democracy is ultimately government by persuasion, the use of force in any cause, including the government's, damages the networks of reason on which democracy is based.

Militant activity on the streets raised another issue, the role and power of the police. By the 1980s this had become a matter of political concern, and the 'law and order' issues formed a new divide between soft left and hard right.

Analysis: relationships and issues

Industrial pressure groups and incorporation

Industrial pressure groups – finance, management and labour – surpass all other groups in their size and significance, and in the closeness of relations with government which they have sometimes achieved. There are good reasons for this. Governments, endeavouring to manage the economy, need to secure the co-operation of industry in order to get their policies right, to adjust them to the practical problems perceived by the groups, and to secure their implementation. Governments seek co-operation by consultation, persuasion, exhortation or by pressure, threats and the ultimate force of legislation. Industry and the unions have their own resources to persuade or threaten. They too may refuse to co-operate. A process of bargaining and mutual accommodation ensues, governed by the balance of forces, and modified by the ideological commitments of the major parties. The relations of government with industry offer a model of governing under pressure as the normal and routine pattern of governing – there is no other, though the pressures vary. Government attempts to exert its authority in a range from commanding or regulating, through negotiating and consulting to the softer persuasions of advice or laissez-faire and ultimately concession and acquiescence. The interest needs to respond proportionately, fitting acquiescence to command and using high force against only the softer approaches of the government. Much of governing lies in the middle area where compromise and consensus are reached.

In the 1970s there was a more determined effort to establish and consolidate the middle area. In an economy beset with problems, government needed the co-operation of industry (owners and managers) and the trade unions for even minimal economic planning, improved efficiency and the moderation of earnings.

The attempt to build both sides of industry into partnership with government began with the establishment of the National Economic Development Council in 1962, the institutional expression of what came to be called tri-partism, or more portentously, corporatism. The strategy, if such it was, ended with the election of the Conservative government in 1979, though curiously NEDC survived until 1992.

Industry was cautious and reluctant about incorporation. The trade unions, their leaders increasingly yielding control to militant shop floors, resisted any arrangement which infringed 'free collective bargaining' and the right to strike. The Labour government of 1974–9 took a long further stride towards corporatism by agreeing a 'Social Contract' with the unions, and establishing a Labour-TUC Liaison Committee to monitor and sustain the relationship. There followed major concessions to the unions in two Acts of Parliament, and massive wage increases. The trade unions had become a part of government, literally incorporated, their leaders glimpsed nightly on television entering and leaving Downing Street. These arrangements with the unions collapsed with the collapse of incomes policy in the 'Winter of Discontent' in 1979, and the return of a Conservative government determined to curtail the power of the unions.

The corporatism of the 1970s was thus mainly an attempt to deal with the problems of trade union power by consent, through the consolidation and legitimation of the negotiating relationship. The experience of the 1970s suggested that this kind of corporatism could not work; in this area at least government was expected to govern.

For Labour the unions were favoured by ideology and tradition and already incorporated in the party structure. The Thatcher governments carried no such commitments and vigorously pursued legal restrictions on the unions, the free play of market forces and the meeting of force with force in the year-long battle with the miners 1984–5 and then the printing dispute at Wapping. The alternative to the pursuit of consensus through incorporation proved to be effective but bloody.

Trade unions are a special case among interest groups because of their size, functions and the unique capacity of a few of them to disrupt economic or social life. The attempt by governments in the 1970s to come to terms with the unions is thus a special case of incorporation or corporatism, and harassed Ministers might have been surprised at the pretentious label put on their desperate stratagems.

However, the unions, for all their disruptive capacity, are only a small part of the total economic power which bears upon governments. There is still the general problem of the government's dealings with banks, investment companies, transnational companies and the like. Here again, the government's power, that is the power of the state, is at issue. Governments resort to some variation of the negotiating relationships at the centre of government by consent. These could be summed up as quasi-corporatism, though there is really no need to invent an 'ism'. What goes on is partial incorporation. The government, faced with economic powers it cannot simply command, and with whom it does not choose to engage in bloody conflict, seeks to 'come to terms' in a working or bargaining relationship. Here the government clearly acts not as the fortress dominating the tribes in the surrounding territory, but as the keeper of the territory, engaging with the tribes in a kind of partnership, incorporating the tribal chiefs within limits in the business of government.

Such is the normal relationship of government and economy. It is routine, and can be exemplified any day of the week. However, the development of government-industry relationships in the 1970s as governments struggled to control incomes and prices led to criticism of the corporatist relationship – 'corporatism' became a negative term, helped by its historical association with the Fascism of the 1930s. Here is a summary of a critique of corporatism from the left of the Labour Party.

■ DOCUMENT 21.3
Corporatism and democracy

From B. Sedgemore, 1980, p. 34
Corporatism is characterised as:

1 Government which seeks to reconcile the interests of big institutions and corporations

with each other where they are in conflict, in the belief that if this can be done then everyone else will have no option other than to accept what has been done, and in the belief that in such circumstances dissent in society can be contained. Corporatism may not be the antithesis of individualism but it is certainly incompatible with it.

2 Government in which the leaders of the big institutions in our society see their role as that of bringing or keeping their members in line with government policy rather than necessarily expressing the views of their members. Democracy is a system of government which comes up from the people whereas corporatism is a system of government handed down from on high.

3 Government in which the leaders of the big institutions in society, in return for carrying out the role which has been assigned to them, whether tacitly or overtly, and through a variety of pressures and inducements, are given a say in the decision-taking process, or more likely a veto over the framework within which policy is discussed, as well as over certain government decisions. ■

EXERCISE
Corporatism

21.13 What do you see as the advantages and disadvantages of corporatism?

There were important consequences for government of the quasi-incorporation of the 1970s, which persists in a weaker form in the 1990s, without the special relationship with the trade unions.

● Government was extended and 'pluralised' within limits but the 'pluralisation' was selective, so some interests were excluded.
● Problems get solved, mainly by compromise, 'the institutionalisation and regularisation of compromise' (Jordan and Richardson, 1982, p. 92) and by a process of reduction of large issues to matters of technical detail, or what may pass as such. Inertia rules, and radical policy-making is not possible.
● The system co-exists with other networks and policy communities and does not override the Cabinet system, if Ministers choose to intervene.
● Government gains from the consultative relationship information, policy ideas and a measure of consent, or at least insurance against accusations of high-handedness; those who are

consulted gain a modest influence.
● The system is largely de-politicised; Parliament, parties and voters are put to one side by government, though Parliament may be brought back to the scene by the interests themselves (see next section).

Corporatism seemed in the end little more than a portentous term for government's normal consulting relations with industry, intensified by the Labour government's attempts to govern in close partnership with the unions, under the 'Social Contract'. But the unions could not deliver their part of the bargain, and this union-biased 'corporatism' (if that is what it was) collapsed in a series of strikes in the 'Winter of Discontent' (1978–9). Any kind of further partnership between government and the unions was swept aside by the new Conservative government. This was the end of corporatism in the heavy sense, but not the end of the normal lighter relationship between government and industry.

Interest groups and parliamentary politics
Interest groups focus on government, specifically the executive branch of government, because in Britain that is where power lies. However, the rest of the political system is not wholly neglected. Interest groups pay a tribute to the processes of democracy, as a re-insurance, because those processes count at least for something, and because the interest groups wish to be, or at least appear, democratic.

Interest groups value the approval of the public, but mainly they are concerned with the approval of the government, and the assurance of advantageous policies and favourable decisions. There are close relations between some groups and the political parties (see Chapter 15) and with Members of Parliament (Chapter 12). Parliament is therefore at least an arena of some significance for interest group pressures. Interests have always appeared in Parliament in their own right, as bishops and barons, landowners, knights of the shire and burgesses from the towns. The agricultural interest, the railway interest, the manufacturing interest, the university interest have spoken directly. Parliament has always been about the representation of interests, but in the twentieth century the new interests of a mass and pluralist democracy have claimed a voice, through the parties and through individual Members. The lobby traditionally associated with the US Congress, and not quite British, has become a significant feature of the modern Parliamentary process.

The pressure of special interests in Parliament is now intense, routine, normal. Members' mail has doubled in the last decade; they are pressed by constituents and groups, their services are not only sought but bought. The sphere of the work of Parliament has expanded: the interests have come in, the Members have gone out. The lobby is as important to some MPs as the constituency. The scale and frequency of lobbying of Parliament is the best evidence we have of the influence of Parliament – at least important groups believe that it makes a difference. Consider the following examples:

- a company promoting a Private Bill hosts a party in the Commons
- the companies concerned with cable broadcasting briefed members of the Standing Committee considering the legislation so thoroughly that they were almost a match for the Ministers briefed by the civil service
- Tottenham Hotspur Football Club, anxious about the effects of a proposed ban on alcohol in football grounds on their 'executive entertainment' suites (where, unlike the fans on the terraces, they come for the alcohol rather than the football) invited Members of Parliament to their ground and secured Adjournment Debates, Early Day Motions and eventually the modification of the Bill
- Kentucky Fried Chicken lobbied against a proposal to compel 'take-aways' to close at 11 p.m.

Although lobbying is now a routine part of the work of Members of Parliament there remains a question about its legitimacy. Within limits lobbying has advantages for Parliament. There are matters of technical and administrative detail, particularly in legislation, which Members could not handle effectively without the advice and briefing of concerned interests. The lobby's alternative briefing offers Members a counter to the Minister's civil service briefing and so enhances their independence. But such independence is gained at the risk of dependence on the interest group, particularly when the Member receives some reward, a fee, a research assistant, a paid consultancy, for accepting the briefing.

Like Burke, Members think of themselves as persons of principle and independent judgement, not party hacks, or slaves to constituency zealots (though such roles are usual and legitimate). The hiring-out of Members' services does not fit the noble aspiration, though it helps to pay the mortgage.

Parliament stands for the voters and the parties as well as its own structures and procedures. Voters in the mass cannot easily be appealed to by interest groups, and certainly cannot be 'delivered', even by trade unions, which appear to be committed and active in politics. At constituency level issues may arise which could move the voter. There are few constituencies now dominated by one interest, except perhaps agriculture in the wholly rural areas, but most constituencies contain some significant local interests, for example a particular industry like car manufacturing, whisky distilling or tourism. The Member of Parliament could be approached by the concerned interests and would happily pursue their cause in the House by means of a Question or a Motion, directly with the Minister or through a party committee.

However, localism in British politics is weak (in contrast to the USA where it dominates the behaviour of Congressmen), the Member normally accepts the party line, knowing that his re-election depends mostly on the national standing of the party. This is less true where regional parties are strong (Scotland, Wales and Northern Ireland) and would be modified by a change to proportional representation in some forms.

Political parties offer better prospects for interest group pressure, and are open to the strategy of an indirect approach to the voter. The relations of parties and interest groups was discussed in Chapter 15. Some groups have a naturally close relationship with particular parties, for example, the Country Landowners and the Conservatives, the Child Poverty Action Group and Labour. These are mainly to do with the parties in Parliament, not the party in the country.

In the Conservative Party the relations of interests and party are powerful but informal and private, though they are revealed in some Parliamentary activities. In the Labour Party the trade unions have a formal and powerful constitutional and historical position, and their influence on policy has been evident, particularly in the 1970s. At the height of the relationship, under the Labour government of 1974–9, trade union leaders went directly to Downing Street; the support of Parliament, and the consent of the voters was taken for granted. No interest has enjoyed better access, though when matters came to a crunch the international bankers demonstrated that they could over-rule government – and the electors subsequently showed their ultimate power too.

The following Document illustrates the activities of Members of Parliament in assisting interest groups in Standing (legislative) Committees, in asking Questions, and in raising issues through Early Day Motions. All this is the small change of parliamentary politics. The citizen is unlikely to find major policy has been overturned by a lobby working through Members of Parliament; but if, for example, he or she objected to the brewers' allegedly monopolistic grasp on the kinds of beer available in pubs, then alas, the brewers' lobby has often proved more powerful than the beer drinkers' lobby!

■ DOCUMENT 21.4
The relations of interest groups and MPs

a) The pharmaceutical industry is one of many industries which is 'political' in the sense that it is dependent on government as its major customer and regulator. The Association of the British Pharmaceutical Industry has been concerned to defend the industry from allegations (e.g. by the Public Accounts Committee) of overcharging. It has the services of a Conservative MP acting as parliamentary adviser, and has sought actively 'to expand and strengthen our contacts with Parliament'. Several Members of Parliament are in fact already directors of major drug firms.

b) *From A. King, 1974, pp. 76–7, quoting a Member of Parliament*
In 1968, on the committee stage of the Race Relations Bill, there was a body set up called Equal Rights, which did a very good briefing job of Members on the committee, and they were extremely well organised. Their views about the shape the legislation should take happened to accord with mine to a very large extent, and every morning at 9.30 a.m., when the committee was about to sit, one was briefed on what was coming up that day: both orally and with pieces of paper and so on. If they happened to be pushing a particular point that I disagreed with, I opted out. When I agreed with them, I did what I could. It was a total service: I went into that committee briefed on every amendment that was going to come up in a way that I've only ever seen a Minister briefed or an opposition spokesman.

c) *From S. Hoggart,* The Guardian, *31 October 1978*
[A professional lobbyist tells of his tactics when trying, for example, to secure a reduction of tax on a client's product:]
First I would identify the interested MPs, those whose constituents stand to gain from what we are trying to do. Then I would convene a meeting of MPs to explain the facts of the case, choosing a good time from parliament's point of view. There certainly wouldn't be any caviar lying around, but there probably would be a drink – nothing to make people feel they were being bought.
Then I would get a few sympathetic MPs to go on the record. Perhaps they would put down an Early Day Motion (the standard technique for raising an issue), and we'd try to get some written Questions down. Then I would explore the issue with civil servants. Best of all, I'd get at the Minister if I could.
You have to learn some of the tricks. There are some MPs who would be the kiss of death to any campaign, people whose help would actually hinder you....
Recently I had to do a job on the road issue and the civil servant I wanted to talk to wouldn't meet me. So I arranged for our MPs to draft something like twenty written Questions, questions which I knew he would have to do the work of answering. He soon got the message. You might call that blackmail. I call it a triumph for inspired democracy. ■

EXERCISE
Professional lobbyists

21.14 Should a democrat be concerned about the work of the lobbyists?

The above quotations illustrate the sort of connection a pressure group may have with Parliament. In some cases, a Member is 'sponsored' by the group, and receives some financial assistance for his election campaign and for his subsequent activities, and in return is expected to look to the interests of the group. About one half of Labour members are sponsored by trade unions. In other cases, the connection is rather different. A Member may take a part-time salaried post as an adviser or 'parliamentary consultant' to a group and thus come to brief himself on its work and problems. Again, a Member may be invited to take honorary office in an association, as a vice-president or as a co-opted member of the managing body, for example, and thus, by taking an interest, come to support that interest. A number of MPs may form a parliamentary group, having links with an outside body. Such relationships are very common. Some Members, about 100, mostly Conservative, go into business as free-lance parliamentary consultants, available for hire (though the MP/lobbyist is still free to choose his clients).

It is possible broadly to take three views about such relationships:

1 The traditional view: that a Member's first duty is to his judgement and conscience, or to his constituents, or to his party. These variations might be combined by saying that a Member's duty is to Parliament. Formal relationships with other bodies inhibit the Member in the discharge of his parliamentary duty and are therefore undesirable, indeed, improper.

2 The opposite view: that the purpose of Parliament is to represent the community and this representation may be done through associations as well as through the territorial constituency and the party.

3 A middle view: that outside relationships may be valuable in bringing relevant information and opinion to the notice of Parliament and in communicating parliamentary opinion to the outside world. At the same time the relationship needs to be open and acknowledged and subject to the overriding duty of the Member to represent his constituency and his right to autonomy. The danger that the Member may be unduly influenced can be exaggerated.

The latter, middling, view is not necessarily the correct one, especially as it endeavours to reconcile divergent objectives for the MP. Some general criticisms which apply to all pressure group activity apply to that in the House of Commons. Too much is, if not secret, then hardly acknowledged; too little voice and weight is given to unorganised causes and unassociated people.

The formal view of the House of Commons was stated in the case of a Member, W. J. Brown, who acted as 'Parliamentary General Secretary' of the Civil Service Clerical Association (previously he was General Secretary) on his election as MP in 1942.

■ DOCUMENT 21.5
The House and contractual agreements

From H. C. Deb., Vol. 440, 15 July 1947, cols 284–5

[It] is inconsistent with the dignity of the House, with the duty of a Member to his constituents, and with the maintenance of the privilege of freedom of speech, for any Member of the House to enter into any contractual agreement with an outside body, controlling or limiting the Member's complete independence and freedom of action in Parliament or stipulating that he shall act in any way as the representative of such outside body in regard to any matters to be transacted in Parliament; the duty of a Member being to his constituents and to the country as a whole, rather than to any particular section thereof. ■

This resolution was used by the Committee on Privileges when deciding a later case arising from a resolution of the Yorkshire Area Council of the National Union of Mineworkers, 1975 (see Chapter 12), which specifically asserted that the sponsorship of MPs required adherence to Union policy.

Disclosure is so far the only response by Parliament to the proliferation and intensification of relationships with interest groups. This was the objective of the Register of Members' Interests established in 1975. The disclosure of a member's interests (including employment, sponsorship, consultancies, directorships, shareholdings and overseas visits) was intended not to diminish the holding of such interests, but to demonstrate concern about the possibility of improper influences arising therefrom. The Member is left to be his own judge of propriety.

A sceptic might conclude from all the evidence that the last thing the Member uses is his own judgement and Parliament has been taken over by the 'interests'. However, Parliament is more complex and more elusive than that implies. To take it over you must first catch it. The influence of the interests is limited if not by the integrity of Members, then by the primacy of party and the dominance of government. The parliamentary procedures which are open to outside pressures through individual Members – Standing and Select Committees, Questions and Motions – are the marginal procedures from a governing point of view.

Moreover, at the margins of government policy, the political culture or public opinion prescribe what can or cannot be done. Farmers, lawyers, dog-owners, sabbatarians and anti-fluoride zealots can expect Parliamentary favour; trade unionists will be looked after by a Labour majority, the 'financial services' industry by a Conservative majority. No interest is protected or promoted in the teeth of public disfavour. Old interests fade slowly; new interests, women, the disabled, gain favour even more slowly. Yet even a slow response to new interests justifies Parliament as a mediator of interest group pressures and as a democratic institution.

Interest groups and the courts

Interest groups in Britain do not make much use of the law. This is in notable contrast to the USA where the constitution and the political culture encourage resort to the courts. That strategy has been spectacularly successful in some cases, notably in the campaigns for civil rights. The struggle in the courts served as a focus for organisation, and a platform for propaganda, and established precedents for the interpretation of the law and the constitution.

In Britain the courts figure less prominently in the strategies of the interests. Legal action is costly, slow and uncertain in outcome. There is no constitution to appeal to, legislation is drafted to exclude appeals on broad principle and to protect the Minister's discretion. An interest group may not be granted legal standing (not being an aggrieved person); and the decision in a single case, even if favourable to the interest, may not serve as a precedent for future cases, or may even be reversed by changes in the law.

Nevertheless, interest groups have acted directly or on behalf of individuals in matters such as sex or racial discrimination, welfare benefits and planning decisions. They may seek redress in the courts on the grounds of illegality, irrationality or improper procedure. Questions of procedure may also be raised with the Parliamentary Commissioner for Administration (Ombudsman – see Chapter 25).

The Child Poverty Action Group was particularly active in litigation on behalf of claimants of Supplementary Benefit, as part of a strategy of public education ('consciousness-raising') about welfare rights. The National Council for Civil Liberties has also followed that strategy. Winning individual cases may be less important (except to the individual concerned) than the longer term propaganda effect.

The courts have been cautious for several reasons about intervening in cases pursued by interest groups. The groups are not personally aggrieved and are not always representative of an aggrieved class. The judge may feel uneasy at what may be seen as the political exploitation or at least exaggeration of grievance (by Claimants Unions for example). A more reasonable objective for the courts is the avoidance of a flood of cases in which the court in effect replaces the ministry, agency or tribunal.

In a welfare rights case Lord Denning declared that 'Parliament intended the Supplementary Benefit Act should be administered with as little technicality as possible. It should not become the happy hunting ground for lawyers.... [The Courts] should leave the tribunals to interpret the Act in a broad reasonable way, according to the spirit and not the letter.....'

Parliament will anyway have the last word. If the interests were often successful in litigation, then the law could be changed. This happened to an educational pressure group in Oxfordshire. They successfully demonstrated in court that the law set a duty upon the local education authority to provide nursery education. The government then changed the law to make the provision of nursery education discretionary. The moral for interest groups contemplating litigation was clear.

Excluded groups

No-one, or hardly anyone, is now excluded from participation in the interest group process. Forty years ago the list of the excluded would have been long: the poor, the unemployed, the old, consumers, the polluted.... But the development of radical interest groups and street level protest groups has brought almost anyone with a cause or grievance the possibility of action to protest and persuade.

In practice such advance in participation may not be worth much. Everyone may have a voice, but the question is, who is listening? Access, acceptability and command of the media vary enormously between those who can telephone or lunch with the Prime Minister and those who might find it difficult to get a headline on the local radio station. Everyone may enter the race, but few gain prizes. Hence a pluralist political system is not necessarily an equitable one.

GUIDE TO EXERCISES

21.1 The first, second and fifth as interpreted may reasonably be regarded as 'myths'. The third is normally a myth. Top people have to be cautious about responding to an approach, but it does happen, perhaps more often with Prime Ministers and Ministers, than with permanent secretaries. But the author is advising only not to start at the top. The fourth, entertaining, is used so regularly, it must be helpful sometimes!

21.2 You must do this for yourself. You are sure to find good examples of the multitude of minor groups at work trying to persuade or press the government; and perhaps fewer of the major groups, who work mostly in private. Press publicity through news items is a frequently used method, cheap but not very effective. This happy glimpse of busy citizens having their say should not obscure our understanding of the giant groups going about their more effective persuading labours.

21.3 In the course of a week you should find many instances, solicitors, doctors, and the Stock Exchange are usually invited to answer any criticisms made of them. News about house prices going up or down is usually provided by estate agents (who have an interest); news about sheep buried in snowdrifts is not provided by shepherds or intrepid reporters but by the National Farmers' Union Press Office.

21.4 Beware of over-confidence, and over-aggression. Des Wilson's advice includes: 'Be right, make friends; address the world as it is.'

21.5 Yes, of course, it is reasonable to ask a body like the NFU for details of its membership. Associations concerned with a clearly defined role, particularly an economic one, are usually representative in that they have a substantial membership (substantial in relation to the potential numbers). 'Cause' groups are naturally not representative in this way, and some may draw on quite narrow sections of the populace. Thus, for example, the claims to representation of sabbatarians and of pedestrians are difficult to assess. The Campaign for Nuclear Disarmament was supported predominantly by educated middle-class persons.

21.6 Consulting means asking for advice and implies a readiness to listen to that advice. Negotiation implies discussion between two bodies, both of whom must consent to the outcome. Usually the bodies are nearly equal in power: otherwise the more powerful will tend to impose a settlement.

'Improper' is another difficult word. All government is in the last resort by consent of the governed, but we cannot live all the time in conditions of last resort. Governments need the co-operation or goodwill of some important groups within the community. Is it improper for you to refuse to help with the household chores? No, but it may be destructive of the conditions of family life, and therefore open to objection – and overruling by established authority.

21.7 Governments are unwise to vary rules, except in very special (and unlikely to be repeated) cases. Was this such a case? Probably not....

21.8 Yes, financially and in raising consciousness world wide. It brought pressure to bear on government. But of course the problems are massive and remain unresolved.

21.9 Geldof was a man of unusual talent, and a pop star (the two do not always go together). The 'pop' youth culture could be exploited for a cause with an immediate emotional appeal and without political embarrassment. Poverty at home in Britain has less appeal. Seems easy? But Geldof took great risks, worked hard and travelled far to make a continuing impact on the problem. He did rather more than fill Wembley for a pop concert with added moral uplift. So Geldof's project is not so easily repeated.

21.10 Remember that cases offer examples and illustrations, but, unless they are shown to be representative, they do not constitute a systematic analysis, from which firm conclusions may be drawn. With that qualification, what the cases show is set out in the following text.

21.11 Both terms are now used rather loosely, and often polemically, and are not easy to define. 'Direct action', strictly, means doing for yourself what the government has refused to do: 'squatting' in unoccupied premises by the homeless is the best example. There is a rough progression from demonstrations (marches, sit-downs, camping outside a nuclear air base as at Greenham Common) through direct action (especially occupations) into violence (obstruction, destruction and, inevitably, fighting with the police).

A refusal to pay the poll-tax is clearly non-violent (but illegal) direct action, like the time-honoured refusal to pay rates.

Some of the poll-tax demonstrations were violent, whatever the intention, because of clashes with the police (raising the question, who started it?). All these protests are attempts to use a demonstration effect in place of persuasion: direct or indirect may not matter very much, violent or non-violent may be a crucial distinction.

21.12 Justification is a matter of judgement about the iniquity of the tax (see Chapter 24). Protests were certainly widespread, but refusal to pay taxes, however unjust, is not only illegal but unwise under the do-as-you-would-be-done-by rule. The government was persuaded by a range of pressures, including its own unpopularity as an election approached, and the difficulty of actually collecting the tax. On its own, protest in the streets was not persuasive; the resignation of 18 Conservative councillors was more worrying.

21.13 The advantages arise because governments need a close relationship with industry for information, the resolution of conflict and implementation of policy. It is a major function of political institutions to resolve conflicting interests and secure co-operation with government. Parliamentary institutions do not do this well, because the form of representation, territorial and partisan, does not fit the pattern of group conflict. Perhaps Parliament should try harder.

The disadvantages are indicated in the Document. Corporatism was undemocratic or even anti-democratic. It was closed and exclusive; private and public bureaucracies resolved conflicts out of the public eye, and not certainly in the public interest. The establishment and institutionalisation of the relationships tended to 'solidify' the decisions. The role of Cabinet was diminished, Parliament marginalised, and non-incorporated interest groups excluded.

21.14 Yes. In theory this sort of activity is acceptable (and difficult to restrain) in a pluralist democracy: information and persuasion are legitimate, and are better done skilfully than badly. But in practice the resources to do such work are not equitably distributed; and skilful advocacy may become undue pressure. But

Members of Parliament, Ministers and civil servants ought to be able to defend themselves.

ASSESSMENTS

1 The case for interest groups

a) Interest groups are both natural and necessary. It is arguable that individuals have very few political needs which cannot be expressed and mediated through representative groups. Indeed, it is likely that there is no other way in a large community of meeting the demands of the individual and extending the opportunities for citizen participation. In this way interest groups supplement the constitutional provisions, such as they are, for legitimacy, and strengthen democracy.

b) Interest groups may serve as acute critics and goads of government. They are highly motivated and well informed, even if not disinterested. Even a democratically elected government needs to be subjected to and checked by, influences of this kind, to improve its sensitivity and moderate its power.

   Indeed, the major interest groups can be a source of political movement and innovation in a political system tending to stagnation. This is true, for example, of the rise of industrial interests, of the weakening of the hold of the church, and of changes in attitudes to the environment and women.

c) The organisation of a group imposes some discipline on the members of the group: they must reach compromise among themselves. Thus government, by dealing with a group, ensures a measure of self-discipline within the group; also, a unified source of information and centre for consultation. But this does not guarantee moderation.

d) The access and influence of an interest reflects its public standing and is in accord with the basic assumptions and values of society. (This view no doubt flatters the interest groups, and overstates the capacity of the political system to restrain an interest which is not in accord with society's basic values.)

e) Interest groups do not operate as an irresistible force in a vacuum, without friction, hindrance or check. Other interest groups provide countervailing power. A case pressed too hard may lead to counter-group activity. Government itself, while not an immovable object, has inner and outer defences against assault and infiltration:

- The civil service will not normally give way to obvious unreason or naked self-interest. It will try to apply tests of reasonableness and public interest to the proposals of interested groups. But these tests are not always easy to apply: there is no equivalent of the chemist's litmus paper. Where there is doubt and confusion, it may sometimes seem unreasonable not to concede a case pressed with vigour and intelligence.
- The Cabinet will have to approve of major changes of policy. With its overall political responsibility, the claims of national or public interest will not be overlooked, though they will be subject to interpretation. The average Cabinet Minister does not stand outside or above the battle. The Cabinet Minister is both a player and an umpire, and rather wanting everyone (including himself) to win so that all may have prizes. His Cabinet colleagues will also be playing and not necessarily on the same side. Out of this complicated conflict, only a Cabinet which has a collective mind, and knows it, can consistently control the interest group.
- Some major changes of policy will stand as planks in the party's platform, and neither group nor Minister can act freely on these matters, once decided. This may simply change the point at which interest group pressure is applied – before the formation of party policy and while it is open for modification. No party, however, is absolutely the prisoner of any one interest group.

These considerations suggest that interest groups are very far from being dominant forces. Their failures are not infrequent but receive less publicity than their successes.

f) The agreed assumptions of British politics moderate the self-interest of interest groups. The last point dealt with the institutions of government as if they formed a castle or defensive system, threatened by invading interest groups. One of the government's weapons it was suggested, was the assertion of 'public interest'. Now this picture requires modification: although there is often a battle, a sharp opposition of interests and

profound conflict, yet both sides share some common assumptions and aspirations. The interest groups do not like to think of themselves as nakedly self-interested: they too appreciate, and indeed serve, the common weal. If it comes to a battle they fight, most of the time at least, under a Geneva Convention of political warfare; it is not a conflict with no holds barred. Thus they are ready to listen to arguments about the public interest, and they may not often resort to undue pressure except under what they would consider gross provocation.

g) The above is the outlook of interest groups; no doubt it exaggerates their altruism (an altruistic interest group would be an absurdity). But it may not exaggerate their good sense. For it is sensible of them to play the game according to some rules, for fear that the game will otherwise be called off. Most interest groups act with this kind of consideration of enlightened self-interest. The most powerful have the most to lose by the breaking of their established links with the government. The less powerful have less to lose, but then they also lack the means of undue pressure. The tendency for pressure to be in the hands of the group's officials, not the members, strengthens this sense of playing according to the rules. The official is a professional player of the game, with an interest in keeping the game going.

All this is to justify interest groups as necessary and wholesome, or at least difficult to do without, mostly useful and not often actually harmful. This is the case for 'pluralist' democracy, in which power is diffused, and government has to bargain and persuade in order to rule. But there are some grounds for concern: all is not for the best in this pluralist paradise of politics.

2 The case for concern about interest groups

a) Interest groups are self-interested – by definition, despite their claims to the contrary, and modified only a little by the points made above.

b) In this free-for-all conflict between groups and government, some groups have too big a voice and too much power. For example, in resisting the radical reforming zeal of the Minister of Health the British Medical Association spent about £6m; in resisting the same Minister when he transferred his radical energies to another profession, the

National Union of Teachers spent £1m. So no doubt doctors could mount a better campaign then teachers; but neither patients nor parents could compete. The interests of producers are over-represented, because they can be easily organised and have the money. Meanwhile, the interests of consumers, old people, children, all of whom are difficult to organise and comparatively poor, may go unheeded. There is a geographical bias too: the metropolitan wins over the provincial, for example in the arts, and in hospitals. A hospital closure in London rates the national news and Ministerial attention: in Wigan, only the local media and the local Member take notice.

For the civil service it is easier to work for agreement among the interests than to try to define and advocate a public interest. Unappeased private interests make trouble; the public interest is often silent and uncomplaining – unless, exceptionally, it is voiced by a major party. Altogether, the worrying thing about the free-for-all is that it is free-for-some, not for all; and that is always the path of less resistance.

c) The power of the groups is to veto as well as to promote, and is stronger in its negative aspect where its impact goes unnoticed. A notable example is the success of the 'polluters' in suppressing for many years the development of the environment as a political issue.

d) The activities of interest groups go on mostly in private in the corridors and environs of Whitehall. Some of their public activity, as in Parliament, and in the feeding of news and opinion to the press, is not open and avowed; although company contributions to political parties must now be revealed, and Members of Parliament are compelled to disclose their connections with outside bodies. For the most part interest groups do not often operate in full public view, and then only when they are not getting their own way. Thus an innocent observer might conclude that interest groups were underdogs in politics, hastily banding together to tell the government how ill it was treating them. This is not the case, and there is much to be said for Professor Finer's conclusion: 'through this secrecy', he wrote, the lobbies become 'faceless, voiceless, unidentifiable: in brief, anonymous' (1966, p. 145).

e) A further cause for disquiet is that the scope for refusal of co-operation, or sabotage which necessarily exists in a civilised community, may be exploited. This kind of activity is most often seen in industry, where groups like transport workers, dockers or doctors sometimes use their power to damage the whole community by striking or threatening to strike, in order to wrest increases in income or other advantages. But non-co-operation or the withholding of goodwill occurs less visibly among bankers, international financiers and industrialists.

This use of industrial and financial power for private ends is of course natural and legitimate. It may even be sanctified as the freedom of the market or a free system of collective bargaining, the assumption being that freedom is a good in all circumstances. But its results are often damaging to the interests of the community and are therefore of political concern.

The problem here is to balance the 'right' of private property, including the ownership of a professional or working skill, against the 'right' of the community. Each case has to be assessed on its merits, within a framework of political principle. Such questions as these have to be answered:

● Is it proper to regard Parliament (hence the government) as the only judge of community and individual interests, subject to the right of others to offer their views? Or is Parliament only one among the groups whose combined views and interests should determine policy?
● Does the government balance fairly the interests of the community and the interests including the freedom of the individual?

At times there is no doubt that such difficult questions are brushed aside, and the matter is decided by political or industrial clout or force majeure. The public interest is by its nature obscure, difficult to identify and argue for, likely to be overcome by sharply defined private interests, and to emerge at best as the outcome of the conflict of competing private interests.

3 Interest groups, effective government and democracy

These questions seek to assess the operation of

interest groups in the light of theories of representation and consent in democracies. There is another set of criteria, those of effective government. Plainly interest groups may help or hinder government, and there is variation by policy area and time.

An overall judgement might be that the interest groups operate a veto power over much of government activity and have contributed to the immobilisation and lack of direction of modern government. Neither side dominates the other, but a cosy, co-operative partnership has emasculated both sides.

This was the argument of an American political scientist, Samuel Beer, in the early 1980s. Beer concluded that Britain had been reduced by changes in political culture, the collapse of the party system and the development of powerful and clamant interests, to a condition of 'pluralistic stagnation', and the paralysis of public choice (Beer, 1982). The analysis is illuminating, especially in the way the influence of interest groups is related to other changes in the political system. The analysis seemed pertinent in the late 1970s, when the Labour government surrendered to the unions, but turned out to be less dramatically correct under Margaret Thatcher's determined government. But Margaret Thatcher vanquished the unions not the whole universe of interest groups.

The three views of interest groups set out in these Assessments reflect the major lines of thought about interest groups – about what actually goes on and which is to be preferred. The first approves of the groups, and accepts their contribution to a representative system. Democracy emerges from the relatively equal contest of the groups, and government itself is an umpire rather than a dominant force. This view is called pluralist.

The second view is based on serious doubts about the operation of the interest groups, particularly from the point of view of representative democracy. The tendency of this view is to re-emphasise the role of the state as upholder of the public interest – an old-fashioned and neglected view which might be called 'statist'. The third view, the 'corporatist', may be presented in a favourable light as a creative partnership, or as above, as something of a conspiracy against good government.

The problem for democracy is to arrange a basis for the exercise of power with consent. Democracy is not just about resistance to power; the democrat still needs government, as the ultimate guarantor of equity, justice, peace and even prosperity. The NIMBY phenomenon, the private veto of a public interest, not just in a local planning dispute but on the larger scale of economic power, is just as disturbing for the democrat as the abuse of public power. Governments make three kinds of decision, popular, neutral and unpopular. There is no problem with the first, nor much with the second, which is the happy hunting ground of interest groups; but unpopular – and essential – decisions are difficult for a democratic government, which must sometimes defy both popular opinion and the protestations of the interest groups. The politician comes to understand that his profession is indeed a demanding one.

Concept

Interest

Interest is a difficult word despite its frequent and confident usage, as in this chapter. It implies advantage, usually an economic advantage, a gain in income, goods, welfare or comfort, or the defence of earlier gains. The context usually implies competition; the advantage is won at the cost of disadvantage to others, and the pursuit of interest is self-seeking and may be considered selfish. This is a formidable weight of meaning and implied or contextual significance for the term to carry.

The burden of meaning of the term is not limited by consideration of preferences, desires, needs and values; it is a term of sociology, not psychology. This tendency to exclude considerations of personal motivation makes a point: the pursuit of self-interest is the dynamic of society and public life. It is not relevant to note that the local farmer is a kindly and generous parent, patron of the local cricket team and so on; as a farmer he will pursue his economic interests with little regard for others. Sounds convincing?

Perhaps so. Economic life is like that: there are few generals who believe that armies are a waste of money, nor teachers who think education is not worth more generous support by tax-payers. More especially, people organised in their 'groups' are programmed, so to say, to pursue economic self-interest; groups, organisations, corporations are more selfish than individuals. Hence the pursuit of self-interest is a consequence of the presence of interest groups; and, in a circular process, the groups are a consequence of self-interest.

'Public interest' is posed against the selfish ends of the interest groups; but the public interest is difficult to identify, and is likely to be defined politically, according to competing interests and values. The public interest may include competing interests, the interests of the majority if they can be ascertained, also the interests of minorities. Often the public interest will be defined in ways which few people like, for example, the constraint of incomes, the severe limitation of the use of motor cars. At that point it is clear that the identification and maintenance of the public interest is at the heart of the political process.

The policy process

The study of policy-making

What is policy?

Moliere's 'bourgeois gentilhomme' discovered to his surprise and pleasure that he had been speaking prose all his life without knowing it. Readers of this book have been studying 'the policy process' so far without much reference to that term. This chapter is therefore a drawing together of previous material, and an identification of policy as an output of government and policy-development as a central process of government. This is a shift in focus, a re-viewing of government, and a re-description in terms of policy and process.

'Policy' is often treated by politicians, especially during elections as something hard, defined, clear, a little like the curiously named insurance 'policy'. Policy is said to be 'in place', installed, like a piece of kitchen equipment. At election times policy is likely to be a short document conveying a set of positions, aspirations and intentions on a current problem. However, in the process of government, day-to-day policy is often much less well-defined, and the term itself has an extensive meaning.

Defined narrowly, policy is simply a position, a stance – to be offered to, or in favour of something relevant to, a problem or issue, for example, crime, privatisation, subsidies, defence spending. A policy, thus defined, is not a decision, but underlies decision and indicates continuity of decisions. Thus, policy becomes a stance extended over time and related to different situations: it acquires a coherence going beyond the instant reaction of the specific decision. In this extended definition, a fully formulated policy requires a statement of purpose, of aims and objectives, and of strategy, that is ways and means of achieving the objective – in short, answers to the questions what? and where? how? and why?

The fully formulated policy is an ideal. Sometimes a policy is formulated after a series of decisions which indicate a policy; policy is then made retrospectively in reviewing ad hoc decisions. This is policy 'made on the hoof', or 'ad hockery'. It is often a necessary form of policy-making in face of sudden and unforeseen problems, and has the advantage of flexibility. Most individuals, families and small organisations, including schools and colleges, make policy in this way, accumulating choices, and discovering in due course that they do have a policy.

Larger groups, and massive organisations like governments, try to foresee problems and plan ahead, but are still to be found 'making it up as we go along', or 'muddling through'. The privatisation 'policy' of Margaret Thatcher's last government is an example of a tentative predisposition converted by early success into a major economic programme. In war most great battles, though carefully planned by the generals, collapse into scores of barely related encounters led by corporals. But the generals, like the politicians, write their memoirs and recreate order out of chaos and they, not the corporals, have statues erected in their honour.

It follows that government policy is not always clearly defined and there is often no single moment of decision. Hence the pursuit of the question who took or influenced this decision? is often difficult, since it is hard to tell when exactly the decision was made or even whether a decision was made. Policy begins with predispositions and understandings, and moves through choices or decisions to the status of policy, and then to funding and implementation. At that stage a policy becomes a programme. Thus a Minister might say:

1 We are well-disposed towards nursery education.

2 We have a policy for nursery education.
3 We have a programme for nursery education.

It is clear that position 3 is the most likely to deliver some nursery education.

Biological analogies may look attractive (from frog spawn to frogs) but there is a life force and genetic coding driving the frog spawn: in government policy the frog spawn equivalent may not develop, because it lacks the life force.

The discussion so far assumes an open space, or 'tabula rasa', on which a new policy may be developed. In practice there is already policy in place, – or a set or mass of incompatible or competing policies, or a deliberate absence of policy, so the single most important influence on policy is the 'given' situation. This gives rise to 'inertia', resistance to moving or varying the pace and direction of movement, and that is the most common and powerful characteristic of the policy process – when in doubt do not change what we are doing, especially if we are doing nothing!

The analysis of policy-making
The analysis of policy-making is concerned particularly with the following questions.

● The nature of policy – what is policy as discussed above?
● The nature of the process of policy-making, in particular, the question of how policy is made in the different major fields, economic, social, external (foreign).
● The distribution of influence – an answer to the question, Who governs?, approached not from an analysis of the structure and institutions of government, but from a consideration of the output of government.
● What is good government? Or, to be practical, are there grounds for preferring one form of government, one form of policy-making to another? This is the 64 000 ECU or Deutschmark question, and we shall be lucky to wring an answer out of a study of policy-making.

■ DOCUMENT 22.1
Policy-making: an instructive case

Based on Leo Pliatzky, 1982, pp. 4–6
Sir Leo Pliatzky, who retired as Second Permanent Secretary at the Treasury, tells of one of his earliest experiences as a civil servant in the Ministry of Food from 1947. He worked in the Animal Feeding Stuffs Division, and included in his many duties mainly derived from wartime controls the responsibility for National Pigeon Food. This was composed of maple peas and maple beans, imported from Australia and New Zealand and so categorised as 'hard currency imports', to be strictly controlled.

As Ministers, including the young Gaitskell and Harold Wilson, began to think of 'a bonfire of controls' (Wilson's phrase), Pliatzky and his colleagues thought National Pigeon Food might be a candidate for decontrol. Pliatzky wrote:

During the war National Pigeon Food had been allocated, at controlled prices, only for members of the various homing unions, as they were called, who registered their racing pigeons as available to fly missions for the country in the National Pigeon Service.' Whether or not any pigeon had ever been put at physical risk, now, years after the war, these privileged birds remained the only pigeons entitled to this special price-controlled food. It seemed to us that the time had come for them to take their chance in competition with other pigeons.' On the basis of these arguments, the Treasury agreed to abandon National Pigeon Food.

Pliatzky was taken aback by the subsequent storm of protest from the pigeon 'homing unions'. These, Pliatzky was warned, were strong in coal mining areas and the miners were regarded – until the 1980s – as possessed of substantial political clout. A deluge of 50 000 letters of protest arrived, sent on by Members of Parliament, and Pliatzky drafted a standard reply. In time the uproar died down, and the young Pliatzky's first effort at policy-making in the tricky area of Animal Feeding Stuffs was successful. ■

EXERCISE
A policy for pigeons

22.1 What lessons can be drawn from this story?

A number of lessons may be drawn from this story.

● Inertia is a powerful force in the making of policy; most policy is given, not invented but already there, defying change.
● Ministers may deal in the grand sweep of policy, in this case the bonfire of controls, junior civil servants deal in the 'nitty-gritty', the detail, and the implementation.
● Policy change damages some interests, and those who lose are likely to protest; the gain is often to an amorphous and ill-represented

'public interest' (in this case the country's hard currency imports bill).

- Rationality is not enough; some political will is necessary to face down opposition.

Models of the policy process

The policy process
An ideal model of the policy process would look something like the diagram in Figure 1. But this assumes a clear field or tabula rasa, a new problem 'processed' by the system in a logical order, from recognising the problem to implementing a solution. This is what the system aspires to, but not often what it can deliver. In any case, the agenda of government is not always to be simplified into problem and solution – there are too many problems and not enough solutions.

1 *Finding, identification*
Discovering a condition, situation, problem, or opportunity requiring or justifying action. This is more complex than it sounds. Life is full of problems; most of them go undiscovered, and some are deliberately avoided.

2 *Recognition*
The finder has to persuade others that he has found a 'problem', of which they must take notice. This is a crucial stage. Most problems are not 'found' and 'recognised'; and the non-recognition of problems is a feature of politics, a consequence of the political system, and an indication of the distribution of power.

3 *Raising as a public issue*
The development of the problem as an issue requiring processing through the political system. In practice this means complaining and calling for redress. The political market opens: citizens make demands, governments respond, in return for support.

4 *Development towards policy*
At this point the problem/issue enters the realm of government, as a candidate for attention, and for the development of policy options. Access to government, the flow between government and issue or problem area, is crucial here.

5 *Formulation of policy proposals*
The government machine takes over and the new policy is set out and developed for approval, legislation and funding.

6 *Parliamentary stage*
This is the formal stage of legislation of the policy already agreed.

7 *Implementation*
This stage is carried out by departments, local

government, agencies, with little scope for modification of policy.

8 *Monitoring and review*
Ideally the policy once implemented is subject to continuous review and modified as necessary. In practice inertia may take over, either in the form of immobility (thus far, and no further) or moving in the same direction, but with increased funding.

9 *Reformulation of problem*
The process is circular, solutions change the form of the problem.

This 'rational' model of policy-making has to be fitted into the political system; but the fit is awkward. How it might be represented is shown diagramatically in Figure 1.

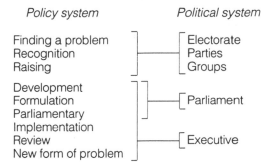

Figure 1 A model of the policy-making process

Characterisations of the policy process in Britain
There are six major characterisations or interpretations of the policy process in Britain. They are not mutually exclusive, and in practice some shifting combination of these interpretations is likely to be near to reality.

1 *Institutional*
It is assumed that what you see is what you get. The great institutions of British parliamentary democracy determine the distribution of power and the making of policy. There are no massive non-constitutional pressures lurking behind the Westminster facade: the Westminster model of responsible government is a working model.

More sceptical versions of the Westminster model can still be accommodated under this head, for example, taking account of the dominant executive, and the influence of the bureaucracy and major interest groups.

2 *Bureaucratic/corporatist*
Policy is developed and to some extent determined within an iron circle of continuing

relations between the departments and the major economic interests, including the financial interests of the 'City'. In the past the major unions have been included in the circle, especially in the 1970s, when, it was argued, the system was based on tri-partite corporatism.

3 *Pluralist*

Power is diffused. No major interest dominates the political and policy systems. Government itself does not dominate, but does more than hold the ring for contending groups. Rather its function is to ensure that the system takes account of minority interests. Government serves a public interest based on principled compromise.

4 *The dominance of major economic interests*

In this interpretation, Westminster institutions are a facade, behind which the power and interests of capitalism are maintained. This may look unlikely since the facade appears to be substantial and active, and the operators of finance capital are not apparent. On the other hand, the evidence of what governments do, and fail to do, clearly indicates the power of the economic system over government. Governments are powerful actors in the market, no less and no more.

5 *An Establishment or ruling class*

This is a version of 4. What governments do is determined to a large extent by the wishes of an 'establishment' – a shadowy network of persons of influence, connected by birth, class and education, occupying positions of strategic power in the major areas of public life, economic, financial, commercial, legal, military, and located in and around London. The establishment is a metropolitan establishment. This is an attractive theory, but elusive and circular in its argument: it hovers on the brink of saying, influence is wielded by influential people in positions of influence.

It may be accepted that persons of influence, indeed power, in their own spheres are connected by common background and way of life and do meet together informally in London clubs and restaurants, at sporting and cultural functions, on the golf course and so on. For example, when defence cuts are threatened, it is said that the generals and admirals have 'dining power'. There is a potential for influence here arising from access and a domination of assumptions and expectations. Who could doubt that an admiral is a wise and disinterested judge of the public interest in matters of naval defence and the nation's need for admirals?

However, on the other side it may be argued that such 'establishment' influence has to contend with the whole weight of government, Ministers, civil service, Parliament, electors. Moreover, the 'establishment' is not a monolithic structure organised for power: it is itself fragmented and weakened by its own conflicting interests. The admirals are opposed by the generals and air marshals, and the makers of military aircraft and tanks, as well as by Treasury officials. The Establishment is also subject to change, reflecting shifts in societal distribution of influence. For example, the Church (of England) has declined in influence and so too have the trade unions and the press. As recently as 1963, Macmillan, about to resign the prime ministership, consulted nine colleagues, eight of them Etonians; but he omitted to consult Iain Macleod, who was Leader of the House and chairman of the party. His successor turned out to be Lord Home, a peer and landowner, educated at Eton and Oxford.

But the last three Conservative Prime Ministers have been grammar school educated. John Major came from a modest South London background, left school at 16, but wisely chose a career in banking. Margaret Thatcher set out to 'de-privilege' some parts of the old establishment and attacked the universities, the BBC, the Church, the civil service. But high finance, the law, farming, land-owning and the armed forces all prospered; honours, including hereditary titles, were given out generously, and the House of Lords was left undisturbed.

If the Labour Party had won the election of 1992, the Labour Cabinet would have marked the arrival of the Celtic Universities – and the House of Lords might have faced reform. But the Labour Party was unable to win enough votes in England, which remains Conservative enough to sustain a governing class for the United Kingdom.

It remains difficult to identify and measure the precise influence on policy of an 'establishment'. There are certainly grounds for assuming that some areas of high policy, notably to do with business, finance, land ownership, the armed forces and the diplomatic service do enjoy protection and privilege – compared for example with social work, or state education. These examples indicate not one establishment but specialised establishments, linked and overlapping circles of power.

6 *A dominant culture*

This is a variation of the establishment interpretation. Policy is determined by a culture of government, a traditional set of prescriptions and assumptions, which limit the freedom of action of policy-makers. Mainly these have a conservative force: the National Health Service or education should not be radically reformed, defence spending should not be reduced, foreigners should be regarded with suspicion, roads should be built....

The problem of cultural explanations of politics were considered in Chapter 2. Such explanations are likely to be valid, but still quite difficult to substantiate. Moreover, the culture does change, and it is the task of policy-makers to bring about change. For example, the 'culture' did not favour a National Health Service in the 1930s; environmental and feminist considerations are more powerful now than say twenty years ago; support for 'strong defence' may well diminish if no new enemies appear or can be invented.

The major policy arenas

Economic policy

Economic policy is at the heart of a government's concerns and endeavours. A government may hope to achieve economic success, prosperity and growth and thus pay for its programmes – and go on to win the next election. But continuous economic success has proved elusive. Britain is part of a complex and unfriendly world economy and full control of the British economy is beyond the grasp of the government. Nevertheless a massive part of government activity is dedicated to protecting and promoting the economy.

There are four interlocking areas of economic policy.

- Macro-economic policy: the steering of the economy as a whole, in the context of the world economy. This includes relations with other countries of the EC, and international networks such as 'G7' and GATT (the seven most industrialised countries, and the countries covered by the 'General Agreement on Tariffs and Trade'). Policy is thus an exercise in international relations, but also in the understanding and application of economic theory, monetarist, Keynesian, or simply pragmatic.
- Micro-economic policy: attention to what is sometimes called the 'supply-side', for example, the encouragement of investment and training in industry, the regulation of working conditions, provision of roads, airports, communications (the 'infrastructure'). Much of this requires government funding, and is open to dispute about the proper extent of government intervention.
- Government programmes and public expendi-

ture of all kinds, including defence, education, health, social security. These are affected by differing ideological preferences, and above all by questions of what can and should be afforded. Considerations of public expenditure have come for good reason to dominate disputes in domestic politics. You can have the policies you can afford, possibly no less, and certainly no more.
- Government income, public finance, fiscal policy: this is the obverse of expenditure, and is a major constraint on all governments. Significant political judgements have to be made about the appropriate total level of taxation (30, 40, 50 or 60 per cent?) and its distribution; about kinds of taxation (direct/indirect, individual/corporate, national/local). It is highly relevant here that in the 1990s, compared with forty years earlier, almost everyone in work pays income tax. Behind judgements on taxation and on expenditure lie questions of political and social values, the distribution and redistribution of good fortune – should government play Robin Hood, Father Christmas, Ebenezer Scrooge, Samuel Smiles, the Good Samaritan....?

The full weight of British government is mobilised to develop and deliver this massive and complex set of policies; and as might be expected, economic policy-making displays the fundamental characteristics of the system:

- executive dominance in the form of Prime Ministerial power and bureaucratic influence
- policy is necessarily transdepartmental, involving many departments, but the Treasury aims to dominate not simply co-ordinate
- the most salient and weighty of the interest groups exert heavy pressure
- party principles are seen to be at stake, so political turbulence is generated
- the brutal facts of economic decline tend to determine outcomes.

Some of these points are illustrated in the chapters on executive government. The system of Ministerial Committees ensures that economic policy is kept in the hands of a small group of senior Ministers in the main economics committees. But there remains a significant element of alternative decision making: the Prime Minister and his own economic advisers and the Prime Minister in close and exclusive consultation with the Chancellor.

The Treasury has a continuing heavy influence, through briefing, persuasion and dissuasion. Enoch Powell believed the Treasury blocked any major change in policy in 1958 (when Powell and the Chancellor resigned). Roy Jenkins wrote that in effect his decision on a pre-election budget would be influenced by the opinion of the senior Treasury officials and advisers. It may be surmised that Norman Lamont's cautious tax-cutting before the 1992 election reflected political tactics modified by Treasury judgements.

However, such interpretations of relative influence tend to underestimate the disagreement and disarray which arise so often in the management of an open and vulnerable economy. Influence is diminished by the fact that many of the actors either do not know or do not agree about what to do (and no discredit in that). This is evident in time of crisis, for example, in 1987–8, when Margaret Thatcher and her Chancellor, Nigel Lawson were in disagreement. Again in the economic crisis of 1974–6, leading up to the intervention of the IMF, and the crisis of September 1992, leading to the withdrawal from the ERM and the devaluation of the pound, economic policy appears to have been in spectacular disarray. In a policy area with a major international dimension, events, shifts in the real world, have a terrifying capacity to destroy settled policy.

Economic policy also reflects movements of ideas among economists and political economists. Such ideas are technical, to do with economic theory but relate to political ideology. In analysing the economic aims of 1976 Burk and Cairncross (K. Burk and A. Cairncross, 1992, pp. 129ff) point to a progression of interpretations of the problems of 1976 by successive heads of the Treasury. These interpretations reflect the shift from Keynesian to monetarist ideas, though there was never a complete conversion.

■ DOCUMENT 22.2
Change in economic opinion 1968–98

Based on K. Burk and A. Cairncross, 1992, pp. 129–132
a) William Armstrong in 1968 was committed to demand management and tax changes, and incomes policy not monetary policy; on the whole, he believed modern economic policy had been a success.
b) Douglas Wass in 1978 was much less confident than Armstrong. He was aware of 'major uncertainties and controversies in fundamental issues', of the rapid growth of

'financial flows within and between countries', and of increased limits in the freedom of governments to influence the rate of exchange. He accepted the usefulness of monetary targets and perhaps of incomes policy.
c) Peter Middleton in 1988, reflecting the views of the government of the time, dismissed the post-war policies of expanding demand and hoping to control inflation by incomes policy. The decisive consequences associated with the 1976 crisis were the establishment of monetary targets, ceilings for public borrowing and cash control of public expenditure and the introduction of a medium-term financial strategy. ■

There are problems about the last analysis – the monetary targets were missed, the strategy was not adhered to and the rise in public expenditure was paralleled in other European countries. Burk and Cairncross conclude that, though 1976 marked the triumph of the market over a government in deficit, the market may be mistaken, takes a short view, changes its mind, and 'neglects many things that matter greatly'. Governments, it is implied, are not powerless in face of the market. Hence in 1998 the head of the Treasury may offer different interpretations of the course of economic policy since the mid-1970s. Indeed, this seems to have happened by 1993.

EXERCISE
Who governs economic policy?

22.2 Does this account of economic policy suggest the economy is in effect ungovernable?

It is evident from these considerations that economic policy is now heavily influenced by international forces, and sovereignty has been lost. This is clearer in the case of economic policy than in most areas of social policy, where governments may still hope to do what they like – but within the limits of finance and the EC. Indeed the idea that governments can do exactly what they like in any sphere of policy is improbable.

Social policy
Social policy covers several major areas of government programmes:

● the social security system, including old age pensions and unemployment 'insurance'
● the massive and expensive social services of health and education

- the economic 'infrastructure', in particular housing, roads and public transport, which have a social service function.

Social policy is departmental territory, and the departmental Ministers come into their own. But there are two good reasons for a Prime Minister not to leave these matters entirely to his Ministers. First, social policy is very expensive, with all the consequences that flow from the continuing heavy demand for money; the diagram shows the way the cake is eaten up.

Second, social provision goes to the heart of political values, raising acute questions of equality, opportunity and the balance between the public and private sector. Both factors are politically sensitive – threatening fierce competition within the government, and shaping the electoral appeal of the party.

There are several features of the making of social policy which illustrate the nature of governing. There are, first, serious limits on the government's freedom of action arising from the 'givens'. Policy in these areas is for the most part on-going, based on established principles, continuing expenditures and long-term commitments. Many elements in policy are beyond the control or influence of governments – demographic factors (people are born, grow old or ill),

decay of the social fabric (houses fall into disrepair), new aspirations (children stay on at school), technical advance (new health procedures), economic recession (unemployment is very costly for governments). Citizens receiving long-established benefits come to regard them as entitlements, or 'rights', not to be denied by a reforming or economical government.

Second, the structure of social policy-making is complex. The delivery of policy is generally in other hands – local government, the National Health Service, the Benefits Agency, and central government must manage its relations with these partly independent or at least 'arm's-length' agencies. Further, the government is thus led into policy arenas in which professionals and interest groups, including the professionals' own groups, are inevitably influential. Each policy arena becomes a separate territory or sector, in which government engages hopefully as a dominant actor, in practice sometimes with the status of partner, respected or resented. Policy analysts then talk of 'policy communities' and of 'micro-climates' of policy. The terms imply relationships and environments which cannot be radically reshaped by central government. Policy has to be negotiated.

Each of the major sectors of social policy has its own characteristics and problems. Thus, the National Health Service faces acute problems of

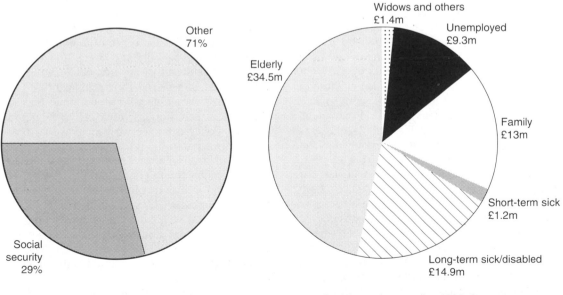

General government expenditure 1991–2

Social security spending 1992–3
£ m at 1992–3 prices

Note: total excludes rent and council tax rebates; discrepancy due to rounding

Figure 2 The financial dimensions of social security

cost, especially with an ageing population and rapid advances in medical techniques. Demand is virtually unrationed, expectations are high, the unions, especially the doctors, are powerful, and the Opposition stands ready to exploit failings, parade the sick child and raise the cry, 'privatisation!'. Few doctors, administrators or politicians are willing to say clearly that if funding is not limitless, then health care must be rationed, and this leads inevitably to pain, disability and premature death for those who cannot afford to pay for private treatment. Who would run a political campaign on such a platform?

Housing policy faces a similar problem. A rational housing policy would attempt a balance between rented public housing, private ownership (through mortgages) and a private rented sector. It may be argued that government intervention has failed in all three areas. The public (council) housing sector initially met housing need, but was expensive, inefficient and not without corruption; since a council tenancy created a permanent right (which could be inherited), the matching of housing to need declined. The sale of council houses in the 1980s recognised that many council tenants could not be moved but were no longer in need, and sold them their freeholds at generous discounts. The problem of real housing need remained.

Meanwhile the rented sector had been sharply reduced by well-intentioned but badly designed government regulation of private landlords. Encouragement of house ownership by tax relief on mortgages succeeded in extending house ownership (to two thirds of households by 1991), but ran into difficulties when the market collapsed in the late 1980s. Governments have spent as much on mortgage tax relief as on subsidies to public housing, thus benefiting the middle classes as much as the poor. This was not exactly the intention of housing policy. But mortgagors are now a massive silent interest group. No politician dare suggest the abolition of the mortgage tax subsidy; its most prominent public opponent is significantly the Duke of Edinburgh, who does not himself have housing problems. The policy-makers have approached the matter gingerly: tax relief has been restricted (to the basic rate of tax, and only one 'relief' on each property) and is likely to be progressively reduced by the effects of inflation. Thus inflation comes to the rescue of the politically prudent policy-maker.

Transport policy is also much influenced by a massive but silent interest group – the owners and drivers of private cars. Their interests are articulated by organisations like the AA and the RAC and more heavily backed by the well-organised road transport interests, who need the government to provide the roads for their heavy lorries to pound along (subject they hope to only loose regulation about axle-weights, speed limits and drivers' hours). Hence a traffic-jam on the M25 or the M6 is a good place to reflect on policy-making.

It is no surprise that the environment lobby has by contrast been much less successful. Inertia has played its part too: the Transport Department has existed historically to deal with roads rather than railways. The engineers spend years planning their roads, and like to see them built, not cancelled. The civil engineering companies are happy to do the building. An expanded and efficient system of public transportation, coupled with restrictions on the private car, is in the interests of everyone in general, but no-one in particular. Once again rational policy-making gets squeezed.

Note that there are brief discussions of education policy in Chapter 7 and in the case at the end of this chapter.

Foreign and defence policy

A large part of foreign policy is now to do with economics; and in matters of immigration and labour, and in many other matters within the scope of the EC, it is to do with social policy. But foreign policy in the traditional sense of international relations, national security and peace and war, remains a salient part of government – though its salience sometimes exceeds its significance.

Foreign policy differs from economic and social policy mainly in its historical and cultural context. Policy is subject to very powerful pressures derived from the sense of national identity, feelings of hostility, distrust or even friendliness towards foreign countries, militaristic passion, or fear of war. Delusions of grandeur smother cool rational appraisals. The grip of the past is strong. The procedural weight of international diplomacy also affects policy. Countries with a respectable past as a great power, seek a role on the international stage, even when nothing worthwhile can be accomplished.

The national sentiment which lies behind foreign policy spreads across the political spectrum, and much of foreign policy is bipartisan. However, there is a strong element of pacifism on the left of British politics, and the

Labour Party has often suffered serious divisions over foreign policy issues – German re-armament in the 1950s, nuclear weapons from the 1950s until the suppression of the issue at the end of the 1980s. Apart from these divisions on the left, the European issue has sharply divided both Conservative and Labour Parties, so that the conduct of foreign policy has become a matter not of diplomacy but party management. Where there is disagreement the issues carry a high emotional charge, so that there are fierce controversies against a background of bi-partisan agreement.

Foreign policy, more than domestic policy, is about reacting to crises – the invasion of the Falklands, a civil war in Yugoslavia, terrorism in the Middle East. Policy is a mixture of high and general principle and immediate fast reaction to half-understood events. A framework is provided by alliances and international organisations; by the high-powered, high prestige Foreign Office and the diplomatic service and by the Armed Services, the most powerful in-house interest groups in the country; and the combined pressures of the corporations and trade unions of the defence industry. This leaves the Foreign Secretary with little space or freedom, except in the very short term, when he is coping with a crisis.

Thus, at the point of decision, the making of foreign policy has much in common with domestic policy – unforeseen problems and crisis-management, the pressure of external factors, the weight of interest groups, an influential bureaucracy, and an unpredictable political dimension. Yet much of this is writ large, national prestige is at stake on an international stage, and foreign secretaries may feel that colleagues concerned with opening or closing hospitals, motorways or grammar schools have an altogether easier time.

GUIDE TO EXERCISES

22.1 See following text.
22.2 Yes, to some extent. Monetarism was meant to be in part a response to ungovernability – if you can't beat it, don't join it. There is little doubt that the economy is now so much subject to international market pressures that it is not fully in the control of any national government. It is like trying to ride a tiger. The crisis of Autumn 1992 confirms this point. Governments have tried intervening and standing aside; neither worked well and it is assumed a selective combination of

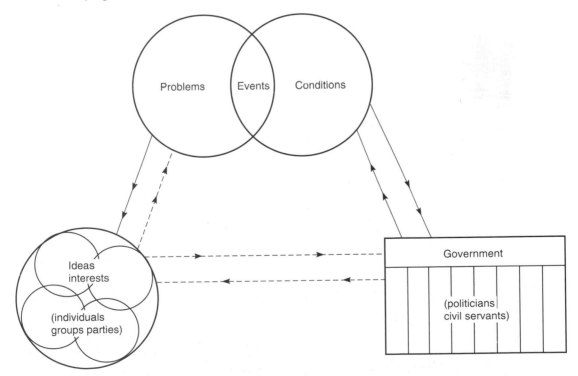

Figure 3 Policy-making: the triangle of forces

intervention and non-intervention may work better.

ASSESSMENT

A brief review of policy-making produces insights and observations, without yielding a satisfactory overall framework of understanding. The stages of policy-making remain a useful model which prompts relevant questions, but in practice policy-making does not often follow such a rational course. Problems and solutions are already with us – we do not send out a search party to look for problems and then another to look for solutions. But at least the model enables us to probe systematically the messy facts of actual policy-making.

The six characterisations of policy-making survive more detailed study: none is confirmed, none eliminated. An eclectic conclusion is justified: all of these interpretations have some validity in some cases, usually in combination. A single interpretation, interesting though that would be, is not justified.

The brief descriptions of the major policy areas confirm broad features of policy-making.

1 There is a triangle of forces – the problems; the pressures for action from ideas, interests, parties; and the institutions of government. The problems are defined for the most part by custom and inertia; but may be thrust forward by urgency and crisis. The prudent policy-maker soon discerns political and financial costs and benefits, and may promote or suppress the problem accordingly. This is the gambit of Nelson's Blind Eye.

The pressures are to do with ideas and climates of opinion, as well as interestgroups. Nothing is as influential in policy-making as an Idea Whose Time Has Come, nothing as inconsequential as an Idea Whose Time Has Passed. The policy-maker has to spot the Time, and move the policy idea on to or beyond the political agenda. But what determines the Time is often obscure; there are sudden, inexplicable shifts in the clock of policy. What was yesterday unthinkable becomes today's favourite move.

The institutions are what they are – characterised by executive dominance and high bureaucratic influences. But specific policy areas develop policy networks or communities, a temporary construction which ties the problem and the pressures into the institutions. Like many temporary constructions, these may last a long time.

2 The development of policy is often rather messy, incoherent, full of muddles and unintended consequences. The politicians cannot master the technical detail, the technicians cannot assess political considerations, values and costs. The development of political values and ideas is particularly haphazard. The work of the supposedly ideological and programmatic parties is often obscure and unhelpful – as the election manifestos show.

One commentator (Maurice Kogan) has compared policy-making to a kaleidoscope, rather than a staircase. In the latter, policy is made a step at a time, steadily in one direction. In the kaleidoscope, many different elements form and reform; often the pattern is little better than muddle, but sometimes, miraculously, elements of different shapes and colours are shaken into a coherent and apparently meaningful pattern.

3 The dominant influences affecting the pattern in the kaleidoscope are those of the forces of adversarial politics engaged in relations of attraction and repulsion with the complexities of policy and the policy process.

An American observer, Douglas Ashford, has written:

'The politics of British policy-making...are about combining the adversarial requirements of British democracy with the necessity to acknowledge shared objectives and long-term problems in the policy process' (1981, p. 297).

4 The gaps in the pattern of policy ideas are partly filled by the special interests, the professionals, or nothing much at all; hence, the persisting influence of farmers and landowners, the military-industrial complex, NIMBY campaigners.

5 Inertia is a powerful force. Nelson's Blind Eye (the new problem you choose not to see) is supplemented by 'Withering on the Vine' (old policies you leave to die).

6 Policy leadership requires a combination of:

● personal authority and stamina to overcome inertia and interests
● political appeal, energy and skills to harness political forces
● policy ideas based on a doctrine of some coherence and substance

- problems amenable in the short term to practicable solutions.

It is not surprising that we do not often get from our governments the policy leadership we undoubtedly need and even deserve. But at least this assessment properly connects policy with politics, and so leads back to questions about Prime Minister and Cabinet, Ministers and civil servants, Parliament and parties. Policy is what politics is about, and policy-making is the essential part of the political process.

Concept

Policy

The nature of policy was discussed at the beginning of this chapter and in Chapter 7. Ideally policy is a fully thought-through and coherent position relating to action (or inaction) in a significant area of concern to the government or other organisation. It should be based on fundamental principles and applied consistently over time, though subject to review. This may sound fine, but it is well to remember that the generals of the 1914–18 war followed a settled policy, and so too the engineers who built the Titanic!

In practice, as we have seen, policy is often not much more than an ad hoc instant reaction to an unforeseen problem, or a series of such reactions, collected over time and presented as a coherent policy. Instant policy, like instant coffee, is sometimes an acceptable substitute for the real thing. But it may also be a shambles – the Grand Old Duke of York or the Charge of the Light Brigade for example, or the extraordinary events of late September 1992, when the government reversed its economic policies but claimed the policy objectives were unchanged. Other ex-amples are to be found under Margaret Thatcher in the 1980s and Harold Wilson in the 1960s and 1970s.

Thus, remembering Macmillan's fear of events, we can re-define policy as good intentions damaged by events.

● CASE STUDY
Policy communities and weather fronts in policy-making; the case of education

Note that there is some discussion of the Department for Education in Chapter 7.
Since the establishment of the School Boards after 1870 and the Local Education Authorities after the Act of 1902, education developed as the most significant local government service. It was initially a partnership between the centre, the local authorities and the churches, and became the classic partnership between central and local government. The partnership was extended by the Education Act of 1944.

Thus education used to look like a good example of a 'policy community', in which a complex set of policies (there is not just one education policy) is developed and applied in a more or less co-operative relationship with an extensive collection of interest groups. The 'community' was dominated by the teachers' unions and the local authorities. A Minister of Education, Sir Edward Boyle said: 'The starting point for educational questions was the education world itself' (E. Boyle and A. Crosland, 1971, p. 90). It seemed to Boyle in the 1960s that education policy came up from the bottom, and could not be imposed from the top. This was the age of a central government partner-ship with local government.

Hence the major re-organisation of secondary schools on comprehensive lines in the 1960s and 1970s was carried through not initially by mandatory legislation but mainly by advice, the pressure of funding for new buildings, and the administrative instrument of the Ministry 'Circular'. This is a memorandum to all local authorities offering advice, guidance, recommendations, which never quite amount to an instruction. Given time and the need for funds and approval for new building, the centre was always going to get most of its way in the end; but a few local authorities resisted, and the iron fist of central command (in the shape of legislation) was used in the end. In these matters of re-organisation the courtesies of partnership were more or less preserved. On the other hand the curriculum still remained a 'no-go area' for central government and was determined by schools, teachers and the examining boards, and even by the preferences of pupils (for the study of subjects more interesting but less useful than chemistry).

Such a tolerant, hands-off approach by government seemed especially appropriate for education because it matters directly to many people (parents as well as professionals); there was much scope for disagreement; educationists and middle-class parents were articulate; and the decentralised structure encouraged interest group activity and local political initiative.

The old policy community
Major groups included:

a) professional bodies, notably the unions or professional associations of teachers

b) the Churches, especially the Church of England and the Roman Catholic Church, and now the Muslims, who can promote their faith by securing financial assistance for the provision of schools, or favourable treatment of religious worship and instruction

c) the local authorities, represented by their officials

d) the local authorities, represented by their associations (County Council Associations, etc.)

e) the institutions themselves in the case of private and independent schools and universities

f) advisory bodies, established by government, but having limited independence, on such matters as teacher training, vocational education

g) groups with ideas or ideals to promote (e.g. the Council for Educational Advance, the Workers' Educational Association, the Classical Association)

h) parents, informally and in local and national organisations, for example, the National Organisation of Parent-Teacher Associations, the Council for the Advancement of State Education

i) thinkers, writers, publicists and other 'public persons' usually belonging to some part of the educational system, but acquiring a standing quite beyond that of a mere spokesman.

This is a formidable collection of pressures, yet the recent history of education suggests that policy making can no longer be explained simply by reference to this 'community' of policy interests.

First, the community necessarily worked in a 'climate' of ideas, which at times seemed to build into strong winds, blowing beyond the control of the thinkers themselves and the policy community. The abolition of the 'eleven-plus' selection examination and the replacement of selective schools by comprehensive schools were part of a policy 'weather front', propelled by, and at the same time sweeping along, the educational progressives and the Labour Party, and winning the support of parents who thought their children might not pass the dreaded eleven-plus.

In the 1980s the weather changed; a profound shift in popular culture transformed schools (by transforming their pupils, and teachers too). The comprehensive principle was sharply challenged, under the influence of a new set of educational thinkers, a government committed to competition as a principle, and with the support of parents who thought their children needed more formal instruction and would pass a selection test.

The rapid expansion of higher education from the 1960s onwards was also the product of a 'weather front' blowing along ideas about education as a key to the economic re-vitalisation of Britain, and pressed forward by influential university vice-chancellors. The Robbins Committee, reporting in 1963, recommended an immediate and rapid expansion of university education. The government, facing an election and anxious to present itself as a 'modernising' government, accepted its recommendations with extraordinary speed. This was a most striking success for the Robbins Committee with its majority of university academics, and for the pressures behind it. Whether it was good policy-making is another matter. The Treasury said university expansion could proceed on the expectation of a four per cent economic growth. This was never achieved, and the financing of a vastly expanded higher education system, desirable though it is, remains a problem.

Second, government was not the passive recipient of pressures from the policy community or the climate of opinion, though the Robbins example shows that its defences could be by-passed. The hand of the central administrators, including the School Inspectorate, was evident in the Act of 1944 as it had been in that of 1902. The Ministry went along with the comprehensive re-organisation of secondary schools; it was a process they controlled through the funding of building programmes. Officials were more sceptical about university expansion, and invented the 'binary divide', with the Polytechnics safely, so they thought, in the public sector, and ready to teach useful subjects to the workers.

Ministers too played an increasing role in education policy. Although they did not invent the comprehensive principle – that came originally from the policy community – their interventions were decisive. It was Ministers, first Labour, then Conservative, who decisively pushed forward and then slowed down comprehensive reorganisation. Here parties and governments made a difference. In 1974 substantial funds were given to a new Manpower

Services Commission to provide training for young people, and funds were retained for direct use by DES in technical education.

In the 1980s Conservative governments applied to education their principled hostility to local government, trade unions, public expenditure and 'liberal' educational ideas. The Education Reform Act of 1988, including the establishment of a National Curriculum and provision for the opting-out of schools from local authority control, was a powerful blow against the old policy community, or important sections of it. The inspectorate was privatised.

In 1992 a White Paper on Education July 1992, subsequently embodied in legislation, proposed to extend the 'opting-out' of schools and establish a central funding agency for the Grant Maintained Schools, establish new 'Educational Associations' to take over 'failing schools', and even abolish the requirement for local councils to have education committees. The White Paper thus carried forward vigorously the reform of the education system, and envisaged the reduction of the role of the Education Authorities towards the residual.

The former cosy partnership with local government was thus destroyed and replaced by central control or hastily contrived forms of 'parent power', hiving-off and privatisation. The pattern of education policy making was now a very long way from Boyle's laissez-faire model; nor was it dominated by the officials.

This account raises the question of a 'proper' balance of influence in policy-making. Clearly the government has a constitutional right to do as it pleases, but a political duty to ensure a measure of consent. The government ought to consult the policy interests, take them along, as far as possible; but a policy community is not entitled to a veto. After all, a policy community is in part simply a network of interests; it is for the government, not the policy community, to represent the public interest (elusive though that may be). ●

● CASE STUDY
Not cancelling Concorde

France and Britain had agreed to build a supersonic passenger aircraft, known as Concorde, in the early 1960s. That decision reflected the new European and technological enthusiasms of Macmillan's government, the aspirations of the responsible minister, and the influence of government technologists and the aircraft industry, unrestrained by commercial considerations. It was characteristically the decision of a British government which had still to discover its economic weakness. In the out-turn the development costs of Concorde grew to £1bn and only 14 were ever built. The development costs had to be written off, so talk of Concorde operating at a profit is misleading. A Channel Tunnel might have made a better investment.

By the time Labour came to power in 1964 the real difficulties of the project were beginning to show up: major technological problems leading to massive cost overruns. Why after all were the great American aircraft makers, dominant in the passenger aircraft market, not rushing to compete? For the British policy makers Concorde became a classic problem about judging when to stop throwing good money after bad, complicated by uneasy relations with France and its by no means anglo-phile President, Charles de Gaulle.

Roy Jenkins inherited the problem as Minister of Aviation in 1964. He believed the original decision was not based on a rigorous cost-benefit study, but the new Government's proposal to cancel the project was 'government by rush of blood to the head'. He eventually secured a reversal of the government's decision, but this was mainly due to the opposition of the French, who were legally in a strong position. Lobbying from the industry and the trade unions helped to keep the project going. Jenkins thought that the aircraft industry was much too political – for the good reason that the government was a major customer. He noted that a good performance by him in the House had far more effect then than it would in the 1980s; and on a difficult mission to Paris in the company of experienced civil servants and government scientists he was aware that he was left to descend the aircraft steps first and so face the waiting press. This was ministerial responsibility in practice; he was the front man.

Concorde continued to trouble governments as costs mounted (estimated at £250m in 1966, £600m one year later and £800m by 1974) and commercial prospects diminished. The project was saved mainly by the terms of the agreement with France and the French patriotic enthusiasm for high technology and public investment.

Tony Benn, as Minister for Technology, took the problem over in 1967. He was an enthusiast for technology and sat for a plane-making constituency. Nevertheless, as he recorded in his Diary, 'Concorde was an almost daily problem because of the escalation of costs, pressure for cancellation, difficulties with the French and so on' (31 December 1967, A. Benn, 1987, p. 515).

He arranged for a trial of the sonic boom over London – which caused quite a shock – and attended the roll-out of the first Concorde at Toulouse. He announced to a cheering crowd that the 'e' would be restored to the British Concord (it had been withdrawn after de Gaulle had vetoed British entry to the Common Market) – 'e' for 'excellence', 'England' and 'Entente Concordiale', he said, while thinking that he could have added 'extravagance' and 'escalation'.

None of this was policy making in the sense of initiation and development, but policy making in the frequent and routine sense of making the best of a bad job, damage-limitation and 'sub-optimisation'.

Negotiations with France continued under the close control of the Attorney-General. In April 1970 Benn went on a test flight in Concorde 002, his excitement intensified by the provision of a parachute – which proved unnecessary. In May, according to Benn, an exasperated senior civil servant 'lost control' in a meeting and urged immediate cancellation. But it was too late, and the French would not allow it.

Under the Conservative government, 1970–4, there was warmer support for the project (it was after all a Conservative project). But there were still the final battles left for Benn to fight as Secretary of State for Industry in the Labour government of 1974, in alliance with the trade unions, the British Aircraft Corporation and the French – and the lawyers.

In a crucial Cabinet of March 1974 Benn claims to have won the argument, mainly against the Chancellor, Denis Healey. Later Barbara Castle conceded that Benn's tenacity had some effect; at the end Benn's colleagues must have been desperate to get the matter off the agenda. In July the Prime Minister, Wilson, and the French President (for this was a matter to be dealt with at the very top) finally agreed to build 14 Concordes – rather less than the 150 originally envisaged.

Tony Benn declared grandly, 'I have saved Concorde!' Most of his other projects were frustrated by the Prime Minister. Healey later wrote that Concorde was 'another disaster for eco-

nomic common-sense' (1989, p. 408). He pointed out that the two ministers mainly concerned represented Bristol and Toulouse, where Concorde was built – an extraordinary coincidence, he thought. No other country has bought it or produced its own. Healey's message is, never trust the scientists, and probably too, for he and Benn were not political allies, never trust Mr Benn!

At least four lessons can be drawn from the Concorde saga:

- projects in advanced technology are certain to be expensive, and very likely much more expensive than the technologists predict
- collaboration with other countries makes control even more difficult
- such projects gain their own momentum, soon pass a point of, so it seems, no return; it is always difficult 'to stop throwing good money after bad' because that means admitting failure and accepting waste
- 'high profile' projects take up a good deal of ministerial and Cabinet time, more than could be rationally justified, and may lead to serious divisions and a general decline of cabinet morale. ●

● CASE STUDY
The Foreign Office resists radical reform

The Foreign and Commonwealth Office is one of the more influential of the 'insider' departmental interest groups. It is set apart as an elite, because it is based on its specially recruited section of the civil service, with its own high skills and sphere of work. To the criticism that it is an elite the Foreign Office can reply, of course, and why not!

This does not stop the criticism. Joe Haines, press secretary and adviser to Harold Wilson, called the Foreign Office 'a state within a state', with its own outlook, and rooted distrust of politicians and the French. Their engagement in overseas representation and separation from the home departments led inevitably to isolation and ignorance.

Haines and other critics, not least Margaret Thatcher, believed the Foreign Office had fought for entry into Europe as an alternative mission for the diplomats, once Britain's diminished status as a 'great power' became clear. David Owen, Labour's Foreign Secretary, 1977–9, was inclined to agree; he thought the Foreign Office operated at times independently of ministers. Like the admirals and generals, the diplomats believed their own views coincided with the national interest and the security of the state.

In fact, Britain's accession to the EEC was more than a Foreign Office conspiracy. But the Foreign Office added substantially to the pressures which made the move to Europe into an unstoppable 'manifest destiny'. The Foreign Office was also influential in preserving delusions about Britain's true role in the post-war world, though ministers, Labour as well as Conservative, were happy enough to accept the world role.

One of the most striking and public demonstrations of the power of the Foreign Office as an interest group operating within Whitehall was its successful resistance to the recommendations of the Review of Overseas Representation (1977) prepared by the Central Policy Review Staff at the request of the government. The critical report, with its radical recommendations was 'seen off' as effectively as the Civil Service had dismissed the Fulton Report a decade earlier.

The Report challenged fundamental assumptions about the work of the Foreign Office – what was it for in the post-war world in which power depended on economic performance? The Report criticised the scale of representation in some countries (for example, a total staff of over 500 in Germany), the comparatively lavish life-style of some diplomats, the lack of specialist expertise and of substantial links with relevant home departments. The Diplomatic Service should be reduced in scale, and re-distributed, and more of its diplomats should spend more time in home postings; preferably the diplomats should be joined with home civil servants in a special external relations section of the Home Civil Service.

The days of the all-purpose diplomat were over.

All of this was set out in bright challenging language, notably in the first chapter (this was a tactical error made by the Fulton Report too – radical recommendations need to be dressed in dull language and hidden). The Foreign Office naturally resisted; indeed their impressive resistance efforts were already established in a special section called 'the Anti-Tank Unit' (the CPRS being the Think Tank). The vigour and quality of the campaign against the Report would excite envy in a professional lobbyist.

Public figures, professors, diplomatic correspondents were recruited to the campaign, and the BBC (whose External Services had been reported on) was ready to exploit its own strategic control of the media. In half-an-hour of the BBC's lunchtime news programme on the day the Report was published three lengthy items torpedoed the report. By half-past-one, it was sunk.

Some parts of the campaign might have made a professional lobbyist blush (though that sounds a bit unlikely). Wild exaggerations of the Report's recommendations were leaked in advance. The Foreign and Commonwealth Office was to be abolished. The Ambassador to France should abandon his eighteenth-century palace and live in a distant Paris suburb, commuting to work in the Metro (why not? you may ask). There were frequent references to the composition of the CPRS team – it was young (average age 38 – the same as the Foreign Secretary, David Owen), it included sociologists, people with left wing beliefs; and a frequent reference to the colour of the eyes of one of the team conveyed that some of the team were...women! For the Foreign Office to be reviewed by a young female sociologist was quite intolerable. The Ambassador in Paris charged that the Report was based on a class-war attitude. This was Whitehall street-warfare at its most vicious.

The House of Lords rang with denunciations. The letter columns of The Times filled with indignation. Professor (later Lord) Beloff wrote in a learned journal of the value of 'a committee of men of weight and distinction.... One can see that busy public servants might well find it profitable to discuss their concerns with an eminent public servant like Lord Plowden...or a highly regarded man of business...and not extend the same tolerance to thrustful youngsters, with no such personal claims on their time and attention' (quoted in Blackstone and Plowden 1990, p. 177). Here was the establishment view encapsulated.

The CPRS Review of Overseas Representation was not totally without effect. Some of its lesser recommendations were taken up, and, as is often the case, the more fundamental points, dismissed so contemptuously, gained some limited acceptance when they were not being proposed by strangers.

The Report had more, and ultimately fatal, consequences for the CPRS itself, since it demonstrated the inevitable conflict between government and advisers. The established civil service and the government would not tolerate review by such a body of the structure and functions of a major department, based on premises about Britain's world role which had not been agreed. Independent advisers cannot take over the responsibilities of government. This constitutional point had been obscured by Foreign Office indignation and resentment. The episode contributed to the decline and eventual fall in 1983 of the CPRS. ●

Supra-national government

Inter-governmental relations

The simplest political structure sets one supreme government over an identifiable people inhabiting a single clearly demarcated territory. Such simplicity is not available except perhaps in a small primitive island community of contented people, ruled in religious as well as economic and social matters by a revered chief of undisputed authority. Medieval Britain could not attain such a simple pattern of government, and if in any remote area it seemed possible, then there were the Romans, the Vikings, the Normans, not to mention the Church and rapacious barons, to complicate the business of government – or perhaps, to politicise government. Nevertheless a comparable simple understanding of government is widely accepted, and even posited as a present desirable reality to counter proposals for devolution or the extension of the European Community.

The beginning of wisdom in these matters is to understand that sovereignty, the supreme authority of a single governor, is not attainable even in the army or a Japanese factory, and certainly not in the government of a large country in the modern world. Government is rather enmeshed in a net of competing and complementary jurisdictions. These may be categorised as:

- sub-national and supra-national (e.g. international organisations, or local governments)
- government, quasi-government and non-government (e.g. government ministries, public corporations, private agencies delivering public services).

The relationship of the Government to such jurisdictions may be:

- inter-governmental (between governments, involving bargaining or negotiation, freely or under the constraints of treaties and other formal agreements, and associated with international relations)
- intra-governmental (within a government structure, either involving the institutionalised sharing of power within a governmental structure, as with local government, decentralisation, devolution and, in other countries, with federalism and forms of provincial government; or commanding within a hierarchical structure).

The political values inherent in these forms and relationships of government are: nationalism and internationalism; centralism; decentralisation; sub-sidiarity; and finally, effectiveness and democracy.

Britain's involvement in these forms and relationships of government is mainly but not exclusively through local government and membership of the European Community.

Collaborative relations between governments

The common form of international relationships is collaboration for economic or security purposes, based on a treaty or agreement freely entered into and proceeding by negotiation. National sovereignty is not infringed, since the agreement itself is freely made, and negotiation is subject to national consent or veto. In practice such organisations cannot survive and prosper under the perpetual threat of veto or resignation – just like the Cabinet or a club or choir committee. Members take on obligations in honour and courtesy, do not walk out at the first disagreement, are caught up in the continuing relationships of the organisation, rules, procedures and understandings.

Thus governments come to yield or share power; but since the concession is made voluntarily, and may be withdrawn, sovereignty is deemed not to have been infringed. A very determined government could withdraw from NATO – President de Gaulle of France demonstrated that this was more or less possible. Withdrawal from the European Community is by the 1990s much more difficult, but no doubt possible. In practice a government is locked into many international agreements and organisations, and freedom of action is constrained.

The major collaborative or treaty organisations to which Britain belongs include the following:

- The North Atlantic Treaty Organisation (NATO). The organisation was established in 1949 as a response to the perceived threat from the USSR and the onset of the Cold War. It was dominated by the USA, the main source of economic and military power. Britain's postwar foreign policy was closely tied to NATO and the 'special relationship' with the USA, and Britain secured thereby nuclear weapons claimed to be independent. In fact Britain's independence was based on voluntary dependence on the USA.

- International Monetary Fund (IMF). The fund was established in 1944 to provide greater stability in the post-war international financial system. There are about 150 members, dominated by the richest, in the past mainly the USA. The IMF acts as an international bank, lending money to countries in serious deficit in trade and with short-term currency problems. Britain has twice sought the support of the IMF, in 1967 and 1976, under Labour governments, and accompanied by Cabinet and party crises. The IMF lays down conditions for support, usually including substantial reductions in public spending.

  In 1976 the Prime Minister and Chancellor may not have been reluctant to accept the IMF discipline – so a kind of free choice was preserved! Under Conservative governments a sufficient discipline has been maintained to avoid submission to the IMF, so the IMF has a silent influence, the influence of the 'law of anticipated reactions'. In the 1990s financial discipline of this kind for Britain passed to the rigours of the Exchange Rate Mechanism of the European Monetary System. Again the appearance of sovereignty was preserved by freely choosing to give up free choice. But in September 1992 the international financial markets took a hand and forced Britain to devalue and leave the ERM – a case of enforced freedom.

- United Nations Organisation (UN or UNO). This organisation was established in 1945 as a development of the wartime alliance of the Western powers and USSR. It was intended to be a stronger and more inclusive version of the League of Nations (1919) to provide for 'collective security' and international peace-keeping. Britain, as one of the victorious allies of 1945, is a permanent member of the Security Council. The most valuable work of the UN is as a forum including Western and Eastern and 'Third World' countries, and as a continuing basis for peace-keeping operations. The members of the UN participate in it as independent countries, and the five permanent members of the Security Council hold an absolute veto over its resolutions. (The Korean War was fought under the UN flag because the USSR was absent from the Council at the time.)

NATO and the IMF have been very powerful. British post-war defence policy, and therefore British foreign policy, has been shaped by its membership of NATO, and subject to strong influence by the USA, cheerfully accepted without any Gaullist concern for national pride. The influence of IMF on economic policy has been less cheerfully accepted in return for support in times of crisis – as in 1976. This kind of collaboration in an interdependent world seemed an appropriate development of the international 'settlements' by diplomacy which were attempted in Vienna in 1815 or Versailles in 1919; and a proper response to the calamitous breakdown of international co-operation between 1919 and 1945.

In that context some of the countries of Western Europe established in the Treaty of Rome, 1957, the European Economic Community. This, with the Coal and Steel Community and the Atomic Energy Community, grew into a unique international organisation, aiming at economic integration and the establishment of a 'common market'. This was more than an agreement to collaborate for specific purposes, like NATO, but less than a federal union, like the USA. Here the constraint on national sovereignty was more marked and more deliberate, and its effect on the government and constitution of Britain were far-reaching.

The European Community

Britain and the European Community

For the original six nations of the EEC the project was a response to the terrible events of the 1930s and 1940s, the history of war between France and Germany and Italy and of the German conquest of France and the 'Benelux' countries. The EEC was also a response to the 'Cold War', the development of a new hostility with the USSR and Eastern Europe and to the economic uncertainties of the post-war world. For some European enthusiasts the EEC offered a project for a united Europe, a response to the vision set out by Churchill in 1945. That political ideal, battered and diminished by brute reality, remains part of the 'mood music' of contemporary European politics.

For Britain, basking in her own hard-earned triumphs in the war of 1939–45, the imperatives of history pointed to the Commonwealth and the USA, rather than Europe. The grand European project was spurned by the Conservative governments of the 1950s, seduced by the broader imperial perspectives, aspiring still to the status of a 'Great Power' and accustomed to liberating Europe, not to leading it. Britain's belated conversion to the European project in the 1960s was motivated partly by economic anxieties, but met little sympathy from President de Gaulle in particular, and the first two applications were humiliatingly vetoed (1963 and 1969).

Britain finally joined the EEC in 1972 (effective 1973), and membership was confirmed in Britain by a referendum in 1975 – one of Harold Wilson's great political achievements, though more to do with the management of the historic divisions of the Labour Party than of Europe. Much of the debate during the referendum campaign concentrated on the economic consequences of not joining and on the issue of sovereignty. The government tried to allay fears about sovereignty in its Report on Wilson's 'Renegotiation' and in its official leaflet.

■ DOCUMENT 23.1
The EEC and the British constitution

a) From *Membership of the European Community Report on Renegotiation, Cmnd 6003, HMSO, 1975*
134 Thus membership of the Community raises for us the problem of reconciling this system of directly applicable law made by the Community with our constitutional principle that Parliament is the sovereign legislator and can make or unmake any law whatsoever. That principle remains unaltered by our membership of the Community: Parliament retains its ultimate right to legislate on any matter.
135 The problem therefore has to be considered from two aspects: first, the general issue of whether the ultimate sovereignty of Parliament has been weakened, and secondly, whether Parliament can play an effective role in the making of any particular new Community law. On the general issue, Parliament by the European Communities Act 1972 authorised the application in this country of directly applicable Community Law and to that extent has delegated its powers. Parliament has however the undoubted power to repeal that Act, on which our ability to fulfil our Treaty obligations still depends. Thus our membership of the Community in the future depends on the continuing assent of Parliament.
136....Parliament, by passing the 1972 Act, in effect remitted to the Government responsibility for safeguarding United Kingdom interests in the Council deliberations which result in directly applicable Community law. United Kingdom Ministers remain directly answerable to Parliament, since the continuance of any Government depends on Parliament's support.

b) *From the official referendum leaflet*, Britain's New Deal in Europe, 1975
Fact No. 2 No important new policy can be decided in Brussels or anywhere else without the consent of a British Minister answerable to a British Government and British Parliament...
Fact No. 3 The British Parliament in Westminster retains the final right to repeal the Act which took us into the Market... ■

EXERCISE

The EEC and the British constitution

23.1 Was it realistic to claim that Parliament could repeal the European Communities Act?

Development of the European Community

The European Community has developed substantially since Britain's accession. Denmark and Ireland joined at the same time as Britain; Greece followed in 1981 and Spain and Portugal in 1986, so making a Community of Twelve comprising 340m people, the largest single trading block in the world. The extension of the Community to the East and the North is projected, though such widening of the Community is seen, by Britain in particular, as a preferred alternative to 'deepening', that is, strengthening its powers.

The scope of the Community was extended in the Single European Act of 1985, which provided for the completion of the Single Market by the end of 1992, some changes in legislative procedure to diminish national vetoes, and a commitment to further co-operation in foreign policy. The main objectives of the Treaty of Rome, as amended by the Single European Act, are indicated in the Document.

■ DOCUMENT 23.2
Objectives and Principles of the European Community as set out in the Treaty of Rome 1957, amended 1985

[Preamble]
The High Contracting Parties
Determined to lay the foundations of an ever closer union among the peoples of Europe,

Resolved to ensure the economic and social progress of their countries by common action to eliminate the barriers which divide Europe,

Affirming as the essential objective of their efforts the constant improvement of the living and working conditions of their peoples,

Recognising that the removal of existing obstacles calls for concerted action in order to guarantee steady expansion, balanced trade and fair competition,

Anxious to strengthen the unity of their economies and to ensure their harmonious development by reducing the differences existing between the various regions and the backwardness of the less favoured regions,

Desiring to contribute, by means of a common commercial policy, to the progressive abolition of restrictions on international trade,
Intending to confirm the solidarity which binds Europe and the overseas countries and desiring to ensure the development of their prosperity, in accordance with the principles of the Charter of the United Nations,

Resolved by thus pooling their resources to preserve and strengthen peace and liberty, and calling upon the other peoples of Europe who share their ideal to join in their efforts,

Have decided to create a European Economic Community...

[Principles – paraphrased in part.]
To establish a common market and approximating economic policies, to promote a harmonious

development of economic activities, abolish obstacles to free movement for persons, services and capital, adopt common custom tariffs, common policies for agriculture and transport, establish a European Social Fund and a European Investment Bank. ■

The Maastricht Treaty (December 1991) projected 'an ever closer union' (deliberately avoiding use of the term 'federal union') by the end of the 1990s. The aspirations of some of the more enthusiastic member states were modified during prolonged negotiations at Maastricht, especially by the resistance of the British. Even so, the Treaty projected radical movement towards a 'deeper' economic and political union. Hence, not surprisingly, ratification and implementation of the Treaty was delayed and uncertain.

■ DOCUMENT 23.3
The main provisions of the Treaty of Maastricht, 1991

The EC is envisaged as one part of a grander and more portentous European Union based on the three pillars of economy, interior/justice and foreign policy/defence. The European Union arises from a new treaty and is thus in origin intergovernmental, but appears to project something like a federal state at the European level, of which we should all be citizens, with its own foreign, and eventually, defence, policy.

The European Community is confirmed in that title (no longer EEC) and is to proceed by stages (subject to the achievement of economic 'convergence', and optional for Britain) to a single currency and a European Central Bank, thus strengthening the European constraints on economic policy already in place through the European Monetary System and its Exchange Rate Mechanism.

The EC gains powers to act in new areas including education, cultural policy, health, immigration, criminal justice, consumer protection and 'trans-European networks' of transport, telecommunications and energy supplies.

Britain specifically excluded itself from participation in the provisions of the 'Social Chapter', for which it was agreed ingeniously, to avoid embarrassing Britain, that the other eleven would opt in. It is evident that the European Community is no longer to be strictly a European economic community.

Majority voting in the Council of Ministers was to be extended, and the powers of the

European Parliament were modestly enhanced. A fund, known as the cohesion fund, was to be established to assist the poorer countries (not Britain) to catch up. ■

The Maastricht agreement included a commitment to 'subsidiarity' as understood by the British (no unnecessary supra-nationality) and avoided mention of federalism; but the agreement nevertheless represented a substantial commitment to progress towards an Economic and Monetary Union, and for some, a European Political Union.

Perhaps it was not surprising that the ratification of the Maastricht Treaty was delayed and almost lost in Denmark and Britain. The near collapse of the ERM in 1992–3 must at least delay the achievement of economic convergence and the institution of a single currency. The difficulties of developing common policies on border controls and intervention in former Yugoslavia indicate that the other pillars of the European Union are weak.

The institutions of the European Community
The European Council
National governments are formally represented in the Council of Ministers and in the summit meetings, now regularised and known as the European Council. This has become the pre-eminent institution of the EC. Insofar as the EC is a treaty organisation, voluntarily entered into, then national governments are a fundamental element in the constitution of the EC. They exercise vetoes, hold up decisions, insist on compromises and when all else fails use opt-outs and opt-ins, as in 1991, to accommodate awkward members. In the

face of national independence, the Community may indeed develop into an à-la-carte or pick-and-mix organisation, and the aspiration to supra-nationality would dissolve.

Britain is not the only awkward member of the Community. In particular, France has defied Community directives in defence of its farmers (over wine in 1975 and lamb in 1980). Every country takes good care of its own national interests, and some of the Euro-enthusiasts are simply counting the benefits they derive from what everyone but the farmers recognises as an insane agricultural policy. But Britain, as a late and not fully converted member, has often demonstrated the capacity of member states to bring the work of the Community to a standstill. Here is the account by Roy Jenkins, then President of the Commission, of the long drawn-out efforts to settle the British Budgetary Question in 1979–80.

■ DOCUMENT 23.4
The bloody British Question
Based on R. Jenkins, 1991, pp. 491–508, especially pp. 505–8. Jenkins' account offers interesting insights into the performance of Margaret Thatcher on the international scene
The British Budgetary Question (re-named by Jenkins in exasperation) arose because Britain, one of the poorer members of the Community, contributed a disproportionate amount to the Community budget; this came about because of the pattern of British trade and the comparatively small size of British agriculture. The problem had been recognised in the early 70s and had not been dealt with by Wilson's 'largely

The structure of the Community

		Executive	Representative	Judicial
Directing	{	National governments		
		European Council		
		Council of Ministers		
Bureaucracy	{	Committee of Permanent Representatives	European Parliament	Court of Justice
		The European Commission		

Figure 1 Community structure

cosmetic' re-negotiation. Margaret Thatcher picked up the problem and it was fought over, long and hard, for a year from May 1979 to May 1980, and was not finally settled until 1984.

Jenkins records frequent, long and acrimonious meetings, always worse when Margaret Thatcher and the heads of government were present. They were not willing, like her colleagues at home, to placate her; rather the reverse – Jenkins feared they would insist on penalties for the trouble she caused them and extra guarantees of good faith. He was right. At a meeting of the European Council in April 1980 Margaret Thatcher rejected a reasonable offer proposed by Germany. (This was the occasion when she told Jenkins: 'Don't try persuading me, you know I always find persuasion very counter-productive'). A month later, on 29 May 1980, the Council of Foreign Ministers tried again. Jenkins spent the morning with the President of the Council of Foreign Ministers, then held a meeting of the Commission. The Council meeting followed and lasted for five hours plus a working dinner, but still with no agreement.

Just before midnight the President of the Council of Foreign Ministers began a series of bi-lateral meetings, which finally produced the basis of a settlement. By then it was 6.30 a.m. The full Council re-assembled at 7.15 a.m., while officials worked on a formula amounting to a promise of good behaviour by the British over the next agricultural price settlement. The Secretary-General of the Commission was able to produce what Jenkins calls 'a few lapidary words of simple but subtle brilliance', which meant different things to different people, served the immediate purpose satisfactorily – and were never heard of thereafter. Even so the French were not certain they could accept, asked for a 15-minute recess, took nearly two hours and finally agreed. It was by then past 10 a.m. on the 30 May.

The two British Ministers then set off for Chequers to sell the agreement to Margaret Thatcher. They were received coldly and endured three-and-a-half-hours of hostile cross-examination, at the end of which it was not clear what the Prime Minister's verdict was to be. In the event she 'left the issue to be settled by the British press'; the press reaction proved favourable and the Cabinet subsequently approved the settlement. (In fact the Foreign Secretary, Lord Carrington, briefed the press to play the episode as a personal triumph for Margaret Thatcher, so she did not then reject her own diplomatic triumph!)

Roy Jenkins concluded that the cost of the episode in lost sympathy far outweighed the financial gain, and 'made the disputes of the next decade more difficult to handle...the eight lost their faith in Tory Europeanism, and Margaret Thatcher became an instinctive Euro-basher'. ∎

EXERCISE
The bloody British Question

23.2 Was Margaret Thatcher being unreasonable?

The Council of Ministers
The Council consists of Ministers representing each member state, varying according to the policy (foreign, financial, agriculture, environment), and meeting frequently (87 times in 1989). The Presidency is held for six months in rotation, a necessary provision, but one which weakens the office. The Council issues regulations which have an immediate and direct effect, and directives which are for implementation by the states; and also resolutions and recommendations.

The Council of Ministers is the centre of power of the community. It combines legislative and executive powers, and acts like a super-Cabinet, except that it has neither the solidarity nor the direct responsibility of a British Cabinet.

Voting has been mostly by unanimity, so each member held a veto; but development is towards voting by qualified majority (the 'big four' have 10 votes each, and a qualified majority is 54 out of 76 – work it out!). The Luxembourg compromise of 1966 specifically allowed a national veto to protect 'vital national interests', mainly then to accommodate the irreconcilable French, but has not been much used. The Council has preferred to battle on to an agreed solution, under the pressure of the ultimate threat of veto, which has disadvantages for both sides.

Committee of Permanent Representatives
The Committee of Permanent Representatives (COREPER) is the bureaucracy of the Council of Ministers; these are highly developed missions, but unlike ordinary embassies since they take part in the government to which they are accredited.

COREPER works closely both with the home

departments and with the Commission, so there arises a network of officials, or what the French call 'engrenage', gears meshing together. Another example of this is the secondment of home civil servants to work in the Commission; for example, a senior MAFF official may be one of four deputy directors-general in the Commission's agricultural directorate.

The Commission

The Commission is the EC executive, in the weaker sense of that term. It is the executant bureaucracy of the EC. It is composed of commissioners (usually men of some political standing) nominated by the member governments, two for the larger states, one each for the rest, with a President chosen by the member states. The Commission is designed to act as a supra-national collectivity, unlike the ministerial bodies. Commissioners are expected to serve the Community, not their own government, and work by majority vote. They have the right to propose policy and to frame legislation, but decision rests with the Ministers. The two Presidents, of the Commission and the Council, are the leading figures of the Community.

The Commissioners have some of the familiar advantages of bureaucrats in relation to Ministers – time and expertise, though not permanence – and the advantages and disadvantages of working in something of a vacuum. They are not directly accountable to the European Parliament, and the Ministers are not there most of the time; so they have space and scope to develop their own policy projects and initiatives. But in the end the Ministers descend on Brussels or assemble in a summit and decide. The Commission is perceived as exercising power, and denounced for it, but the appearance is misleading.

The Commissioners direct the bureaucracy of the EC, about 14 000 officials arranged in a score of Directorates-General. The EC's bureaucracy may be regarded as large or small, according to what you compare it with (a government department or a local authority), what its tasks are (given that it is a headquarters organisation and some of its work is necessarily carried out by national bureaucracies), and whether you are engaged in denouncing the community as a bloated, collection of interfering Eurocrats.... Inevitably much of the work of the EC is to do with the detailed development, drafting and monitoring of highly detailed prescriptions for the content of water or sausages, or the conditions under which olive trees are to be subsidised – all in nine languages. Like all modern governments, the Community is nine tenths bureaucracy and one tenth politics – and the politics is nine tenths secret and one tenth open and potentially democratic.

Economic and Social Committee

Much of the work of the Community goes on in specialist committees, for example, on agriculture, which bring together the relevant Commissioner and Ministers. The Economic and Social Committee is composed of almost 200 representatives of member states drawn from major economic and social interests, employers, workers, consumers and of course farmers. Its work is advisory but not without some influence. The Committee introduces into the work of the Community an element of corporatism, the incorporation of major interests into the process of government, as happened to some extent in Britain in the 1970s, but not thereafter.

The establishment of the Economic and Social Committee appears to acknowledge the role of interest groups. In fact, with or without formal acknowledgement, the interests arrived in Brussels to set about direct lobbying of the Commission. Since EC legislation bears down directly on economic, social and environmental interests, this development was inevitable, and lobbying must be accounted one of the Community's characteristic modes of policy-making.

European Parliament

The Parliament of the European Community meets in Luxembourg and Strasbourg, but many of its committees and groups meet in Brussels (not you might think the most effective way of working). The Parliament has (1992) 518 members, directly elected by some form of proportional representation, except, of course, in Britain. Elections are held every five years and are due in 1994. The larger countries have 81 members (to be increased by 18 for unified Germany and 6 each for France, Italy and Britain). There are about ten substantial party groups, the largest after the 1989 elections the Socialist group (180) and the Conservative group known as the Christian Democratic Group or the European People's Party (121). The Greens have 30 members.

The party groups are significant in the work of the Parliament, but of course they do not function as government and opposition. British MEPs mostly do not enjoy the modest prestige of Members of the House of Commons, and are accorded few special privileges in the House. Nor are they well-known in the country or in their gigantic constituencies, almost eight times the size of a parliamentary constituency; few people know even the name of their MEP.

The functions of the European Parliament are legislative and budgetary, advisory and supervisory, but it lacks entirely the political weight that arises from the parliamentary responsibility of a government. Parliament has little control over Ministers, and its power to dismiss the Commission as a whole (but not individual Commissioners) by a two thirds vote has not been used, and is not much of a threat. The most significant legislation for the Community is in the treaties, which are negotiated by Heads of Government and Ministers. The Parliament and the Commission are thereafter concerned with the secondary legislation known as regulations, decisions and directives. Parliament's role in legislation is not overriding, but amounts to some significant sharing of power with the Commission and the Council of Ministers. The Parliament may propose legislation on its own initiative, and delay and effectively veto draft proposals for regulations and directives.

Under the Single European Act a new 'assent' procedure gives the Parliament special powers in relation to commercial treaties with countries outside the EC and the admission of new members; and under a complex 'co-operation' procedure the Parliament has the right to take a position on a legislative proposal. This constrains the Council of Ministers, but the final power of the Council is preserved. The legislative role of Parliament is further modestly enhanced by the Maastricht Treaty.

Parliament's influence in making the budget is similar to its legislative role. It does not initiate but may propose modifications to 'compulsory' expenditure (mainly agriculture which is a Treaty commitment) and more significant amendments, including additional expenditure, to other items. The Council may reject Parliament's modifications, but has to engage in a 'conciliation' procedure in the non-compulsory budget. At the end of the process Parliament may reject the whole budget by a two thirds majority – and has done so on two occasions (1979 and 1984). The detail of these procedures is tedious to recount and to work to, but gives the flavour of this institution created and sustained by a handful of idealists and an army of legal draftsmen!

The supervisory and advisory role of the Parlia-

ment is carried on informally in the negotiation arising from the legislative role and formally in 18 specialist committees, in Questions to Ministers and in the discussion of reports by Ministers and commissioners, who attend sessions for these purposes.

The powers of the European Parliament are evidently limited by comparison with national legislatures; and indeed the national legislatures would be weakened by any further strengthening of the European Parliament. Nevertheless the European Parliament has enough real power to engage as a player in its own right in the negotiating and bargaining of Council and Commission which characterise the policy-making in the Community. It can make its voice heard.

EXERCISE
Parliamentary democracy in the European Community

23.3 The EC is sometimes described as suffering from a 'democratic deficit'. Why has the EP been kept so tightly constrained?

The European Court of Justice
The European Court affirms and gives effect to the supremacy of Community laws (specific laws, rather than the law in general) in the member states. The Court consists of thirteen justices, persons of high legal standing, chosen by the member states. It sits in Luxembourg and is assisted by a Court of First Instance and, on the French model, six Advocates-General. It should not be confused with the European Court of Human Rights sitting at Strasbourg, which was created by international treaty, the European Convention on Human Rights (there is also a United Nations Charter on Human Rights).

The European Court adjudicates on disputes between member states and between the states and the Community, ruling on the legality of the actions (and inaction) of the states and the institutions of the Community, especially its executive, the Commission. Cases may be brought by the member states or the Commission or occasionally an individual. The Court interprets the basic treaties and the law of the European Community, defining, and thus confirming the law. The ECJ exercises a direct jurisdiction (deciding cases) in relation to EC institutions and the enforcement of EC regulations and directives. The Court exercises an indirect jurisdiction when it rules on a conflict between EC and national law: the ECJ clarifies the law, the national court decides the case.

Thus the Court comes to rule upon the states. It has developed the concept of 'direct effect' of Community law on the citizens of the Community, so national governments, courts and law cannot interpose or mediate. The Court has taken up a position as a superior and constitutional court, basing itself on the necessary primacy of Community law.

The Court is kept busy by the flow of cases; for example, in 1989 it heard 385 cases, including preliminary hearings, and made 253 judgements. Much of the work of the Court is to do with the main concerns of the Community in economic and social conditions related to the construction of the Single Market and commercial competition. The attainment of the objective of free competition opens up working conditions and leads on to social conditions and the environment. Hence Community laws range widely over matters of political and social significance such as employment, social welfare, support to industry and safeguarding of the environment.

These are happy developments for enthusiastic communitarians, but for sceptics, British nationalists and constitutionalists they present a grave threat to parliamentary sovereignty. The Court has supported the invasion of these areas by the Community in accordance with the Treaties and following the logic of economic integration. It may be praised or criticised for following the spirit of the laws rather than keeping to its letter, as an English court would. In the USA the Court would be accused of, or possibly admired for, 'judicial activism'. The European Court is the most effectively integrative and supra-national of the institutions of the Community, but it is pursuing with vigour the objectives accepted by the national politicians in the Treaties.

The European Court of Justice suffers from the disadvantages of all higher courts that its judgements are long-delayed, voluminous and sometimes ambivalent or obscure. For example, the position under European law of the import of toxic waste is not clear either to commercial interests or environmental groups. Only the lawyers can rejoice about the cost and complexity of this new layer of law.

If the detailed impact of the ECJ is open to question, the political and constitutional achievement is more certain. The European Court has filled the gaps left by the politicians. It is a constituent court, making up a European Constitution

as it goes, and it is a political court in that it stands for integration not for states rights, and has so far been judicially active in that cause. This is an unwonted and uncomfortable experience for British governments with their non-judicial tradition of parliamentary sovereignty.

■ DOCUMENT 23.5
The work of the European Court of Justice

a) *Extract from Article 177 of the Treaty of Rome*
The Court of Justice shall have jurisdiction to give preliminary rulings concerning:
a) the interpretation of the Treaty
b) the validity and interpretation of acts of the institutions of the Community
c) the interpretation of the statutes of the bodies established by an act of the Council, where those statutes so provide.

Where...a question is raised before any court or tribunal of a Member State, that court or tribunal may...request the Court of Justice to give a ruling thereon.

Where any such question is raised in a case pending before a court or tribunal of a Member State, against whose decisions there is no judicial remedy under national law, that court or tribunal shall bring the matter before the Court of Justice.

b) *The Factortame case (1990)*
This case confirmed and advertised the supremacy of EC law. The Spanish fishing industry proceeded against the British government, specifically the Merchant Shipping Act of 1988, which regulated quotas for fishing in British waters. The Court upheld the Spanish claim that rights granted under European law could not be constrained by national law, and the British law was adjudged to be non-operative, that is effectively suspended. (The judgement of the ECJ was in fact a ruling requested by and made for the House of Lords, in its legal capacity, so it was the House of Lords which actually did the suspending).

The Court has no power of implementation, but there was no doubt that the principle of parliamentary sovereignty was breached − not by the Court but by the laws it applied. There was uproar in the House of Commons. One Member claimed that the judgement demonstrated that the Bill of Rights had suffered implied repeal; another that the threat to the House was greater than that posed by Guy Fawkes, the in-

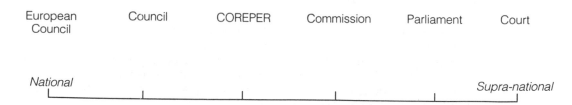

Figure 2 Nationality and supra-nationality in the institutions of the EC

ventor of parliamentary reform by explosion and arson. The judgement and its implication remains.

c) Discrimination between the sexes

In 1982 the Commission brought an action against the United Kingdom for failing to comply with a Council Directive of 1975 'on the approximation of the laws [relating to] equal pay for men and women as regards the elimination of discrimination for work to which equal value is attributed.' The Equal Pay regulations were subsequently amended to improve the position of women.

A Directive of 1979 establishes the principle of equal treatment in the matter of social security. Subsequent proceedings have made clear that this is applicable to the discrimination practised in the State Retirement Pensions scheme whereby women are entitled to a pension at age 60, and men at age 65. This grave injustice will be remedied in due course, but not by giving men a pension at age 60!

d) Sunday Trading (1992)

The Court is not always active and interventionist. Faced with cases on the banning of Sunday trading brought by local authorities against some of the big DIY warehouse stores, the Court has so far taken the view that a shopping ban does not in principle contravene EC law, and has passed the matter back to the House of Lords, or to the government for new legislation. ■

EXERCISE

The European Court of Justice

23.4 Does the Court make the 'democratic deficit' worse?

All of these institutions of the European Community display the inherent ambivalence of an organisation suspended between national interest and supra-national aspiration. This necessary am-

bivalence is a source of tension which is both debilitating and creative. Each institution can be roughly placed on a scale according to its proportions of nationality and supra-nationality (Figure 2).

What kind of polity is the European Community?

The European Community may be judged as a polity or political animal first by what it does, by its impact on the member states; second, by how it works, the institutions and the policy processes.

1 What the EC does

The European Community began as a customs union and has proceeded towards the harmonisation of economic and social policies and the free movement of goods, capital and persons in a single market, and aspiring beyond that to monetary union, a single currency, a European Central Bank and eventually political union in some form. Most of its power to intervene derives from the logic of the creation of a single market: if you will that end, then these are appropriate means.

Nevertheless enthusiasm for development up to and beyond the single market is uneven, and in many areas the Community projects two steps forward, makes one and then retreats half a step, while the Court is called upon to adjudicate between half a step and no step at all. Nevertheless, the Community does wield power over matters of central concern to its member states. Compared to a sovereign nation state the EC is like a tortoise to a hare, but like the tortoise it has so far kept moving forward.

There are many examples. Thus taxation policies remain distinctively national. A minimum rate for VAT was agreed only in 1992, but subject to review after four years, and in return Britain secured a concession on the taxation of whisky (also angostura bitters and black beer brewed in Yorkshire), and retained its special exemptions on food and children's clothes. Income tax remains a national prerogative. Much work has gone into the harmonisation of product

Germany, and perhaps to some of the smaller and poorer countries; but no country is entirely free of doubts based on the most powerful popular political motive force after religion, nationalism.

- The policy-making substance and style of the Community rests in hard bargaining between Ministers, penetrated and mediated to some extent by the Commission. However, between summits, much of the work of the Community is detailed and essentially the stuff of bureaucracy. So there is overall a mix, as in national governments, of ministerial power and bureaucratic influence – streaky like the bacon.
- Policy-making is characteristically by compromise and 'fudge'. There is diminishing scope for direct national veto and a continuing pressure towards unanimous decision, but at the same time a persisting tendency towards obstruction and delay in support of perceived national interests. Hence decisions are often achieved:
  a) by meeting obstruction and delay with patience and the endless extension of time, through the familiar mechanisms of deferment, remission to a committee and the characteristic Community device of stopping the official clock
  b) by ingenious formulae and compromises, as in the Jenkins example, or the Maastricht devices of opting in or out of Community procedures and programmes.
  In these ways delay on an heroic scale and 'sub-optimisation' (settling for less than the best) are normal and seriously debilitating characteristics of Community decision-making.
- The Community is based on constitutional law and judicial review. The European Court has acted as an integrator of this constitutional framework, filling in and tidying up, so that the Community has advanced from a sketchy international organisation depending on treaties and continuing summit negotiations to something like a form of government. This kind of law-based constituent process is unfamiliar in British political culture.
- The community attracts and responds to the pressures of interest groups. Over 700 groups are active in Brussels, about one third concerned with food and agriculture. This is due to the nature of its policy concerns, and its intra-bureaucratic policy style. What the Community does matters to major economic and social interests, and they feel able to protect and promote those interests in Brussels. Thus the EC is to some extent 'corporatist'.

3 A summing-up

The European Community 'may be a new level of government, over a limited range of issues, but it is not yet a fully developed political system' (W. Wallace, 1983, p. 410). This judgement of the early 1980s may seem less appropriate for the 1990s, but it is still difficult to fit the EC into our normal understandings of government. Two questions arise:

- Is the EC a federation or confederation, or something else?
- Does it have the elements of democratic accountability and connection with the people which would be expected of a polity arising from a group of democratic states?

4 Federation, confederation or what?

■ DOCUMENT 23.6
Defining federalism

a) From K. Wheare, 1963
An association of states, which has been formed for certain common purposes, but in which the member states retain a large measure of their original independence (p.1).

By the federal principle I mean the method of dividing powers so that the general and regional governments are each, within a sphere, co-ordinate and independent (p. 10).

What is necessary for the federal principle is not merely that the general government, like the regional governments, should operate directly upon the people, but, further, that each government should be limited to its own sphere and, within that sphere, should be independent of the other (p. 14).

b) From W. Wallace, 1983
The crucial dividing line between an international regime and a confederation...must be drawn between the presence or absence of authority and resources at the centre which effectively limit the behaviour of the member states and which impose obligations on them which are generally accepted (p. 406).

Federalism in the USA is characterised by 'messy compromises and the constant pulling and hauling between the states and the federal government...the workings of federal government disperse and decentralise power, specifications, to ensure that trade is not constrained by national regulations (which may be used as undercover protection of home industries). Other direct or indirect support and subsidy for home industry has been targeted but not eliminated (note Lord Young's difficulties over the alleged hidden 'sweeteners' in the sale of Rover to British Aerospace). The concerns of the EC may often sound trivial – the content of tufted carpet or sausages, the naming of cheeses and so on but this is the necessary detail of the business of international trade. (Imagine the problems a tourist has with currency and customs extended to a major exporting business).

The Community's most notorious achievement is the Common Agricultural Policy which costs about £23bn (1992) a year; the CAP protects and subsidises farmers and supports massive overproduction of food, about one quarter more than is required in the case of dairy products and wine, which are stored at some cost in the celebrated mountains and lakes, and sometimes sold off outside the EC at absurd prices. The CAP takes up about two thirds of the whole EC budget, and costs the average British family about £15–18 per week in extra food prices and taxation. (The price of sugar is doubled and even baked beans cost 16 per cent more.) It is without exaggeration an expensive folly, a crazy tribute to the influence of farmers, and especially to the power of the peasant farmers of France and Germany.

Some explanation for this tenderness towards farmers is set out in Chapter 21; no similar concern is shown for miners or car workers. Perhaps it can be said in mitigation of this agricultural folly that governments do spend huge sums of money on white elephants of various kinds, some with little more plausibility than a butter mountain. The reports of the National Audit Office abound with examples, especially in defence procurement; and public bureaucracies not subject to market discipline do create their own metaphorical mountains and lakes of unwanted goods.

The European Community cannot escape responsibility for the CAP, but this should not hide the overall purposes, achievements and ambitions of the Community. The Community is primarily concerned with economics, the creation of a single market and the progressive harmonisation of large tracts of economic and social life. Thus conditions of employment, welfare provision, pensions, and the politically sensitive subject of immigration all come within the ambit of the Community. Environmental concerns, such as the quality of water or the cleanliness of beaches go beyond the strict requirements of the single market, but are acceptable to Euro-citizens if not governments.

The currencies of member states are already tightly constrained by membership of the Exchange Rate Mechanism of the European Monetary System. In effect member states yielded national control of exchange rates, and indirectly of interest rates and levels of public borrowing. This is a massive derogation of sovereignty; yet Britain joined the ERM in 1989 under John Major as Chancellor and Margaret Thatcher, the Euro-basher. This is a good illustration of the momentum of the Community, which keeps it rolling along, despite the protests of some of its members, who are not supposed to be passengers on a mystery tour! On the other hand, Britain's hasty withdrawal from the ERM in September 1992 demonstrated the realistic limits of rapid supra-national integration.

2 *The institutions and modes of policy-making*
Judged by its institutions and modes of policy-making the Community is an ambivalent polity, mixed and messy.

- The EC is almost a government: it has a central institutional structure with authority to make and implement law over significant areas of policy, backed up by a Court, with a Parliament in the background and a highly visible international negotiating forum in the foreground.
- The Community also has in effect a power to tax its members (to an agreed common proportion of its GDP), and has a budget now approaching £60bn. This is about a quarter of the British budget – not a heavy burden, but a significant sum to spend, given that the EC does not carry the financial responsibilities of national governments.
- There is a persistent strong thrust towards the safeguarding of national interests, and most of the member states, especially the large ones, have shown themselves willing and able to defend their interests. The Gaullist vision of 'L'Europe des patries' lives on, and not just among the more famous 'Euro-sceptics' like Margaret Thatcher.
- There is an equally persistent counter-thrust, unevenly and inconsistently supported, towards a supra-national Community. For historical reasons this appeals particularly to

and...policy-making is thus a combination of log-rolling, coalition-building, unblocking deadlocks, making side-payments to particular interests, living with unavoidable delay and half-completed agreements' (p. 407).

c) From M. Vile, 1961, p. 199

Federalism is a system of government in which central and regional authorities are linked in a mutually interdependent political relationship; in this system a balance is maintained such that neither level of government becomes dominant to the extent that it can dictate the decisions of the other, but each can influence, bargain with, and persuade the other. ■

EXERCISES

Federalism and the European Community

23.5 Is the EC a federation?
23.6 Is federalism as described above (bargaining, interdependence, messy compromises) a desirable form of government?

In the light of this account of the nature of the EC and the discussion of federalism, the question is posed, is the EC properly described as a federation, in that it constitutes a government itself and even a shadowy state? The answer is a qualified negative. Essentially the Community is an international organisation in which the members pursue national interests in competition between themselves and with the Commission, and with organised interest groups. The qualification is that the whole is significantly modified by federal aspirations and some supranational substance, especially arising from the construction of EC law and its interpretation and confirmation by the ECJ.

Both the negative and the qualification were confirmed by the Maastricht summit of December 1991. The Treaty of Maastricht deliberately avoided the word 'federal', and the EC was re-designated as one pillar of a grander European Union. Nevertheless, under the Treaty the power of the EC and its supra-national components, the Commission, the Court and the Parliament, is set to be substantially enhanced. *The Economist* commented: '...there will be scarcely a Minister who does not now spend time ruling jointly with European counterparts, not because he chooses to but because he has to. Call it what you will: by any other name it is federal government' (14 December 1991).

That was the federal qualification. The negative was re-asserted in the reaction to the Treaty, especially following its rejection in a referendum in Denmark. It is not yet clear whether the stronger federal qualification can now override the negative, or the reverse. On past form it is likely that there will be many more late nights and messy compromises and still no clear answer. After all the most successful federal system in history, the USA, was not securely established until after a long and bloody civil war. Better to exhaust members of the Council and Commission in more all-night sittings; better a Europe of exhausted big cats than a Europe once again of civil war.

5 Is the EC a democratic system with accountability and a connection with its people?
This is the problem of what is sometimes called the 'democratic deficit'. It may be argued, as in 1975, that the Community is indirectly but fully democratic through the accountability of Ministers to the elective institutions of each country. This is undeniably true, though in the case of Britain and indeed of some other countries the line of accountability lacks openness and political vigour.

On the other hand, most of the policy-making is done between the Ministers and the Commission. The Court, though significant in the construction of the Community, is concerned with legality, not consent. The Parliament, the one institution which carries a real potential for direct accountability, is comparatively weak. Further, there is an absence of the public drama which arises from political competition, the necessary political theatre which is fed by lively media reporting, and promotes both political leadership and popular interest and participation.

Hence the answer is a streaky one. The characteristic institution of the EC is the European Council and its summit meeting of Heads of Government. Here is political power engaging in a political tug-of-war, the Community defined by the push and pull of the member countries. One recent observer saw the European Council as the true seat of Community power, but representing the political elites not the peoples of Europe.

The crucial issue in this whole debate is the nature and role of the European Parliament. While Parliament remains comparatively weak, as it does, the Community remains an intergovernmental organisation, based on bargaining, rather than a political union.

The impact of the EC on British government and politics

Membership of the EC has radically changed British government and politics; it might even be claimed that a transformation, a constitutional reformation has taken place. The changes have been indicated above and may be summarised as follows:

- Britain freely entered and is now locked into a quasi-federal system. It retains a theoretical right to withdraw but in practice it simply resists the further transfer of power to the Community, and asserts the principle of subsidiarity (see Concepts below) to protect national power against what is seen as the centralising encroachments of federalism.
- Dismay, reluctance and protests cannot do much to change the policy consequences of membership of the EC. Over significant areas policy now has to be developed collaboratively, negotiated and agreed within the framework of the Community. This is a new and uncomfortable experience for British governments accustomed to their winner-takes-all system of absolute power. Policy-making by bargaining and coalition-building is a familiar and acceptable, indeed essentially democratic, process in other countries in which governments are not supported by cast-iron majorities.
- Prime Ministers have seized the promotional opportunities of European summitry. It helps if the Prime Minister is a first-rate negotiator and diplomat – Margaret Thatcher's warrior approach to her fellow Community Heads proved damaging. Thus the job of the British Prime Minister has been changed significantly through membership of the Community.
- Policy areas set in a Community framework now include the substance of macro-economic policy, conditions of employment, regulation of industry and agriculture, commerce and the environment, welfare provision and immigration. The accession of Britain to the Exchange Rate Mechanism brought a significant constraint on economic policy-making, and the freedom of manoeuvre of the Chancellor of the Exchequer; hence the Chancellor's reported pleasure ('singing in the bath') when Britain fell out of the ERM. But, in or out of the ERM, British governments have yielded some freedom in matters both fundamental and politically sensitive (for example, border controls, conditions of employment and even taxation).
- Departments of State and the civil service have had to adjust to a new European dimension in their work. This is true in particular of the Treasury and the Foreign Office, Agriculture, the Home Office (immigration and border controls), Employment (working hours, parental leave), Social Security (qualifying age for pensions), Trade and Industry (completion of the Single Market and trade relations with non-EC countries), Defence (equipment and co-operation), Environment (water quality), Transport (lorry axle weights, air fares).

  The Foreign Office has kept a firm hand on the main work of representation in the EC, and, with the Cabinet Office and under a Cabinet committee, co-ordinates the whole operation. However, the extension of an international dimension into much of what was formerly regarded as 'low politics' (not the sort of thing the Diplomatic Service knew or cared about) has diffused power and may have diminished the pre-eminence of the Foreign Office in the new diplomacy in Western Europe. About two-thirds of the British COREPER staff are home civil servants, not diplomats. Many more civil servants have discovered the pleasures and pain of foreign travel and learning foreign languages. Generally the higher ranks of the civil service have risen to the challenge of the new complexities of making domestic policies in a European context; this is just the kind of thing the British civil service is good at.
- The influence of Parliament has been diminished, and the executive, both Ministers and bureaucracy, has gained some freedom from constraint. National sovereignty has itself been diminished, but in its place Ministers go bargaining in Brussels, and cannot be pursued there by Parliament. International negotiations always lie beyond the reach of legislatures, and under the EC substantial areas of domestic policy are moved beyond Parliament's grasp. Prime Ministers and Ministers report to Parliament on the outcomes of their European negotiations, but inevitably much that is reported is fait accompli, not to be undone except by humiliating the government. The only qualification of this point is that Parliament's role even in non-European matters is not substantial, so there is not much to diminish anyway.

  Apart from major policy Parliament does have the right to scrutinise European Community legislation. The difficulty lies in the sheer bulk of the documentation and the shortage of time and expertise. In 1988 the committee 'dealt with' 800 reports, but considered only 109 of these in 39 debates. The debates are infrequent, late, short, thinly attended, and of little import to the Minister. Thus scrutiny is largely a gesture. The House of Lords does rather better, spends more time on this work, uses specialist sub-committees, calls witnesses, debates the merits of the legislation. The achievement of the Lords is limited, but the comparative vigour of its European scrutiny adds to the claim of a House of Lords renaissance.

• EC law has primacy over national laws, where it is applicable, and the courts in consequence have to engage in the novel function of reviewing the constitutionality (that is, conformity to EC law) of acts of the British Parliament and government. This development of the judicial function may reinforce the concurrent tentative shift of the courts towards a more vigorous review of government – that would be a significant change in the judicial culture.

Party politics in Britain have been seriously disturbed by the European issue. Both major parties have been split in a way which cuts across the old class divisions of British politics. In 1975 Harold Wilson hoped to resolve the divisions in his Cabinet and party by the device of the referendum, but divisions re-opened later, and the European issue in part motivated the SDP breakaway from the Labour Party in 1981. In 1983 the Labour manifesto included a commitment to leave the EC, but by 1992 the party was officially committed to vigorous participation in the Community.

The Conservative Party has also suffered severe divisions, and Margaret Thatcher's fall was in part driven by the dismay of some of her senior colleagues at her hostility to the Community. John Major's policy is summed up in the deliberately ambiguous formula 'at the heart of Europe but fighting for British interests'. This is similar to the Labour position. The Liberal Democrats are the only party to be enthusiastic for Europe, without much qualification. The forward policy set out in the Maastricht agreement poses a severe test for Labour and the Conservatives. Despite the disruptive consequences for the political parties, membership of the EC has not had a sharp impact on popular politics. The concerns of the political elites have not been fully shared with the public, except in the referendum campaign of 1975.

• The cost of membership of the EC is enough to concern opponents of British membership, but not really enough to have a profound effect on Britain's hard-pressed economy. Britain, though relatively poor among the larger states, contributes a disproportionate share of funds to the EC, taking into account what it receives back in benefits. This was the basis of the Bloody British Question recounted in Document 23.4, and further crises in the 1980s. The actual sums involved are not large – something like under 1 per cent of national income and 2 per cent of public expenditure. But how do you assess size and acceptability? Clearly if these sums are measured as schools, hospitals or rail subsidies (or any other favoured services) then they are large, perhaps unacceptably so.

On the other hand it may be contended that Britain does get value from the EC in many other ways, not to be measured in financial terms. The whole business of a very costly diplomatic and defence effort aims to buy international influence and security. However, influence and security have a significant economic and cultural dimension, often neglected in favour of military power. Just as Britain buys at a very modest price substantial influence in world affairs through the operation of the BBC World Service and higher education for overseas students, so Britain buys a place of influence in the affairs of Europe for the costs of membership of the European Community. At least, so it may be argued.

The costs of membership of the EC are political and constitutional as well as financial. For some these costs are much too high. The Assessment at the end of the chapter illustrates the views of Enoch Powell, a passionate and principled opponent of membership of the EC. The benefits of British membership of the EC are still substantial, though they have been obscured by early over-selling, and by the undoubted and uncomfortable constitutional implications. The argument briefly is that in an economically hostile world Britain (and other members) gain from joining together as a trading group, and can survive and even prosper in a world otherwise to be dominated by the USA and Japan. This has yet to be convincingly demonstrated. But the question now is not whether Britain should stay in the Community, but what sort of Community it will be.

GUIDE TO EXERCISES

23.1 It was legally correct and politically possible. However, the scale, complexity and aspirations of the EEC made it more than a simple instrument of intergovernmental co-operation, rather a European institution of government. The practical difficulties and political costs of withdrawal were certain to be high, but not perhaps unacceptably high. Realistic? – just about.

23.2 Jenkins thought so; in any case he believed Margaret Thatcher had a vigorous but muddled mind, so literally unreasonable. The amount of money was insignificant, yet helped to buy substantial influence in European affairs – far more than was bought by Britain's enormous expenditure on defence. But that was lateral thinking, not appreciated by the Prime Minister. It may be further argued that membership of the EC requires reasonable collaboration with other members. But this point shows up the ambivalence of Britain's position in the EC, but not whole-heartedly of it. Margaret Thatcher had a kind of courageous integrity to express in herself the ambivalence of so many of her countrymen, including the two major parties, towards this peculiar continental creation.

23.3 Because a Parliament with substantial power in relation to the Council of Ministers and the Commission would propel the Community firmly towards the form and status of a federal government, indeed a federal state, claiming power in direct competition with the governments of the member states. The European Parliament has a supranational potential; the Council of Ministers and the European Council still sustain national sovereignty. The Commission stands in between, but necessarily leaning towards the Ministers. So, as far as Parliament is concerned, the democratic deficit arises not by oversight, or even by hostility towards parliamentary democracy in general, but as a protection against the extension of federalism and supra-nationalism.

23.4 The Court could be regarded as undemocratic only if its judgements went far beyond what a reasonable interpretation of the law allowed. This does not seem to be so. If the law itself is made democratically then the Court merely applies democratic law. It may still be argued that the laws are not made democratically in a full sense, and the Court's activism in applying that law compounds the sin. Further, for some critics, the less the courts have to do with politics the better, and by implication the more democratic; there being no special virtue and much complexity, cost and obfuscation in the law. This is what might be called the Dickensian view of the law, and there is still much to be said for it!

23.5 Yes, according to these definitions, though the EC is a long way from the US model. An alternative term is 'confederation', which implies the coming-together of sovereign states for specific purposes but without ceding sovereignty. A military alliance like NATO was confederal, though its limited sphere of concern does not justify the description 'confederation'. Insofar as precise categorisation is possible, it may be said that the European Communities began as confederation and have moved towards federation.

23.6 It sounds messy; clear-cut, undivided central power may seem preferable. But the messiness is a consequence of the sharing of power, and may indicate pluralism, tolerance, a reliance on persuasion rather than coercion, participation, representation.... In short, federalism may be a democratic approach to the government of complex societies. On the other hand, it may give power to organised groups and be powerless to act on behalf of the people. Note that federalism often arises in a historical situation in which existing independent states need some degree of unification, and is adopted as a practical necessity rather than an ideal form of government.

ASSESSMENT
The erosion of sovereignty

There is no doubt at all that the absolute sovereignty of Britain and the British Parliament has been eroded by accession to the European Community and threatened at least by talk of devolution to Scotland and Wales. The assurances given in 1975 (quoted in Document 23.1) have not been kept to the letter. It may be argued that the loss of sovereign power does not matter, and was inevitable anyway, but it cannot now be argued that there has been no loss of sovereignty.

Enoch Powell has been one of the foremost defenders of the historic sovereignty of Britain's Parliament. Here is an extract from a speech of February 1977 (reprinted in R. Ritchie (ed), *A Nation or No Nation*, Elliot Right Way Books, 1979, pp. 135–6):

'Parliament is being ground – indeed, has voluntarily offered itself to be ground – between the upper and the nether millstones. The upper millstone is the European Economic Community, to which the Parliament of 1970 ceded overriding power to tax and make laws and policies for the British people – something for which there has not been the remotest precedent since the Middle Ages, and only dubiously then.

The nether millstone is the process – euphemistically called 'devolution' – of setting up within the United Kingdom directly elected bodies or anti-parliaments which purport to represent nations and which, being in principle endowed with the right to make or change the law, cannot logically be subordinated to Parliament itself or denied the power of taxation.'

Concepts

There is more discussion of ideas about the state and sovereign power in this part than in other parts of the book, and the reason should be obvious. The government has not had to worry about its place in the political system: it was as far as it could see the political system. Ireland posed a challenge it has become accustomed to; Scottish and Welsh separatism or nationalism could be contained; but the European Community really did raise awkward questions about the British state. Hence some neglected basic concepts suddenly became important.

Sovereignty

Supreme or absolute power, residing constitutionally in Parliament, though in practice exercised by the executive which it supports. Sovereignty is characteristic of an independent state, but there is some doubt whether national sovereignty survives in its absolute form in an interdependent world.

Federalism

The sharing of sovereign power, so that a group of formerly independent states may join together for certain common purposes, while retaining their separate spheres of authority. The basis is a bargain or treaty (foedus is the Latin for treaty), the arrangement is likely to be imprecise in parts, and sometimes messy and conflictual in practice (see Document 23.6). Federalism is often thought to be un-British, but the old Colonial Office exported federal constitutions to the former colonies, and the Commonwealth includes successful federations, notably Australia and Canada. In debate about the EC federalism is used to denote (and deplore) a European union; so federalism becomes for polemical purposes central supra-national power.

Confederation

A weaker form of a federal union, in which the component parts retain their statehood, more or less undiminished, yet join in a union for limited and specific purposes.

● CASE STUDY
The EC and education

Education offers an example of the extension of EC intervention into a domestic area of policy by:

a) the application of the logic of the single market
b) the active approach of the European Court of Justice.

The Single European Act requires the free movement of workers and the absence of discrimination against other EC nationals on the grounds of nationality. Since such discrimination has been a normal feature of the immigration and employment law of most countries, this represents a radical break with the past, with social as well as economic implications. The Maastricht Treaty strengthens these provisions for free movement, but the Court ran ahead of the treaty-making in applying the objective of the single market and eventual economic union to the conditions of economic competition. These considerations took the Court into matters such as wages, social benefits and training and thus into social policy.

Issues of discrimination in training brought the Court into questions such as: who, not being a national of the country in which the education is sought, is entitled to pursue what kind of course without additional fee (i.e. more than a home student would pay)?. On the first question the Court moved through qualification as worker, family of worker and previous residence towards unlimited entitlement of EC nationals to vocational education on the same terms as home students. On the second question, the definition of vocational courses (which are specifically covered by the Treaty), the Court took the view that university courses were vocational if the students intended to proceed to professional employment. Thus EC nationals acquired an entitlement to many university courses without additional fees.

There remained the question of grants. On this the Court held that grants for tuition and registration fees were due to foreign nationals of the EC if the student was or had been a worker in the country where he sought education, and the work was related to his course. So far the Court has not moved to apply its non-discrimination rules to maintenance grants.

One consequence of these developments in EC law is that a country with a generous provision of education deemed to be vocational may be used (exploited?) by nationals from a less well-provided Member State. The number of students from the Irish Republic attending universities in Britain has already increased substantially.... An alternative approach would be for the Court to rule that discrimination could be avoided, and the 'level playing field' constructed by equal provision of 'vocational' education in all Member States. But that would look more obviously like the making of educational policy by the Court. ●

Sub-central government

The sub-central map of government

Government plainly loses power to supra-national governments; it also shares power with forms of sub-national government. In this context, given that there are four nations in the United Kingdom, it is appropriate to call sub-national 'sub-central'. The sharing of power by the centre with sub-central entities is less threatening to sovereignty than supra-national relationships, but is nevertheless significant.

There are broadly two kinds of political sub-central entity. First, there is local government – a hierarchy of formally designated government authorities associated with territories, and carrying out a range of functions. Second, there is a various collection of bodies 'aside' from government and working indirectly, concerned with specific functions as advisers, agents, implementers, regulators. This category includes what are sometimes called Quangos. The Q is for 'quasi' or 'almost' or 'as if'; and a Quango is a quasi-autonomous non-governmental organisation. There are also NELGOs, non-elected local government organisations. Alternative terms are NGO or even NQGO – Not Quite Governmental Organisation. But since such bodies vary significantly the more awkward term NDPB (Non-Departmental Public Body) is inclusive and accurate but not very informative.

The whole field of government is represented in Figure 1. It is proposed here to deal briefly first with 'aside' or indirect government; second, local government; third, the regions and nations of the United Kingdom. The third section includes Northern Ireland, but there is a further account of the special problem of Northern Ireland in the Case Study at the end of the chapter.

In some ways local government appears to be the most significant part of this collection of governments below or aside from central government. Although that is justified by considerations of size, functions, expenditure, political salience, it is important not to undervalue the increasing significance of the 'aside' bodies in policy implementation, advice and development, that is, in the business of government.

EXERCISE
Government and daily life

24.1 It may be helpful to review daily life for you and your family and check which of your conditions and activities are touched in some way by central, local government and NGOs.

Indirect and aside government: NGOs, NQGOs and NDPBs

■ DOCUMENT 24.1
Examples of NDPBs

Public corporations – BBC; nationalised industries, e.g. British Coal, British Rail.
National Health Service – sui generis, as the Romans say, an enormous organisation, the largest employer in Western Europe, divided into regional and local authorities and including independent hospital 'trusts'.
Executive agencies – distinct from departments, e.g. Training and Education Councils, and agencies established under the 'Next Steps' programme, e.g. Benefits Agency, Employment Service, Passport Office, Vehicle Licensing Centre.
Intermediate bodies – intended to separate the Government (partly at least) from the function, in an 'arm's length' or 'hands off' relationship e.g. Arts Council, the old University Grants

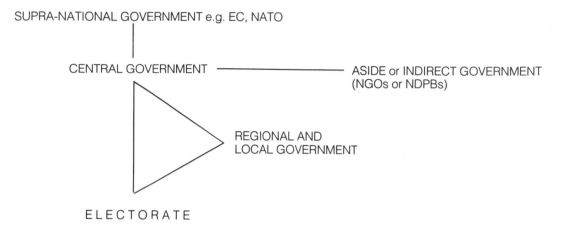

Figure 1 The division of the field of government

Committee. The new education Funding Councils are designed to be tied more closely to government. The Law Society runs the legal aid scheme (civil cases) for the government, a notable and rare example of a trade union running its own industry.

Advisory bodies – e.g. on food and medicines and on building standards, where government needs to tap outside expertise.

Regulatory bodies – e.g. OFTEL, SIB (Securities and Investment Board). These are of increased significance as government retreats from nationalisation into private ownership; regulation is the last hope for the protection of the public interest.

Tribunals – e.g. on industrial injuries, fair rents, racial discrimination.

Private bodies – subject to regulation or informal pressure. ■

This looks a bit of a mess, and phrases like 'arms length' are obscure. The functions of the NGOs are all matters in which government has an interest, needs to get work done or to regulate; there is, difficult though it is to define, an element of public interest. The relation of NGO to government is close or distant according to various factors:

- the interests of the government
- mode of establishment (by government or already in being)
- mode of appointment
- extent of responsibility to Minister and Parliament;
- political salience.

The problems of finding an appropriate relation-

ship between government and non-government bodies concerned with matters of public interest have arisen recently for the privatised public utilities (gas, water, electricity). Complete independence for the monopolistic operation of public utilities is not acceptable, so regulation is necessary in place of public ownership – a new form of the old problem.

The appearance of separation from government may be deceptive. For example, the independence of the BBC and the Arts Council is constrained by government pressure on finance, appointments and tacit threat of radical reform. The Press Complaints Commission works under threat of new legislation on the press. The old nationalised industries were notoriously subjected to ministerial intervention on prices and wages. The new Funding Councils for education are controlled by total funding and a specific mandate. Altogether these NGOs are best characterised as just that – not government or not quite government – rather than as independent or even 'arms length' and 'hands off'. The government's powers of legislation, patronage, finance and the specification of a mission fall short of direct command but not of significant constraint.

Local government

Britain as a unitary and centralised state

Local government is more significant than forms of indirect government because of the scale of its functions and expenditure, and its political basis in elections. While federal governments are based on the sharing of power with a provincial or 'state' sector of government (as in USA or

Germany), British government shares power only with local government, and now with the European Community. However, sharing power does not come easily to the British or at least their governors – hence all the problems of British membership of the EC, and often uneasy relations with local government.

Britain is a unitary state in the sense that sovereign power rests with the centre, the Crown-in-Parliament, in practice the executive. Local government is the creation of the centre, and can be, and often is, reformed, deprived of powers or abolished by the centre. It is hardly able to develop into a significant political sector of its own, with prestigious leaders, as is the case in the state governments of the USA (where state governors contest the Presidency) or in France (where leading national politicians proudly hold office in the localities). Serious politicians in local government in Britain tend to move to Westminster where the power lies.

■ DOCUMENT 24.2
Britain as a unitary and centralised state

From V. Bogdanor, 1979, p. 7
Perhaps the strongest of these 'tacit understandings' [of the British constitution] is the profoundly unitary nature of the United Kingdom, as expressed in the supremacy of Parliament. We find it difficult to think in terms of a separation of powers and also to think in terms of a series of interdependent layers, each with its own rights and responsibilities. Britain is, amongst democracies, the largest of the unitary states, apart from Japan; for other democracies do not seek to manage the affairs of so large a population through a single Parliament. Britain is also an extremely centralised country and probably more centralised in practice than France, traditionally the paradigm of centralised governments. ■

EXERCISE
Britain unitary and centralised

24.2 Is this 'tacit understanding' impervious to change?

We here touch the heart of British political culture. Centralism in Britain is powerful but largely not self-conscious, like British nationalism. By contrast the Americans have had deliberately to create their nationhood, and, at the same time, preserve 'states' rights' in a federal system. Without such a history Britain offers an unpromising constitutional context for vigorous local governments, still less any form of devolved regional government. Significantly in Britain local government has remained the term for a level of government, but it is never used in the plural. Local 'authorities' are not to be regarded as local governments.

The territorial structure of local government
Constitutionally local government is the creation of central government, and central government uses its power to change boundaries, re-construct, remove functions and if it pleases abolish. Until the 1970s local government was a favoured area for Royal Commissions and Committees of Inquiry and for subsequent moderate reform; since then Conservative governments have had their own thoughts about local government, mostly hostile, and radical change has ensued.

Recent radical change has been about constraining the taxing powers and high spending of local authorities, and diminishing the range of their functions. The earlier moderate reform, on which the present system is based, was mainly about areas and functions. The conventional wisdom of the reformers of the 1960s was that size was related to good government; larger authorities would have advantages in efficiency and democratic vigour. Research did not confirm such wisdom, but there was some agreement that single or unitary authorities, embracing town and country, would be better for the many counties which had been divided administratively into county and borough councils (for example, the city of Leicester and the old county of Leicestershire).

The new system of local government established under the Conservative government in 1972 was a compromise. The total number of local authorities at county and district level was reduced (in England, for example, from over 1300 to under 400). New unitary county authorities were established but a second tier of districts was retained within them. Larger 'strategic' authorities were established in London and six 'metropolitan' conurbations of England – an acknowledgement of the size argument – but these were all abolished in 1985, because they had too little to do, still spent too much and were controlled by the Labour Party. The dealings of central government (that is, government) with local government are of course heavily influenced by party political considerations.

The reform differed slightly in Wales and Scotland. In Scotland a system of regions and districts

Table 1 The reorganised system of local government 1972

England conurbations	England other	Wales	Scotland
GLC + Met Counties (6) London Boroughs (32) +Met Districts (36)	Counties (39) Districts (296)	Counties (8) Districts (53)	Regions (9) Islands (3)
	Parishes (c. 8000)	Communities (c. 680)	Communities (c.1300)

Note: GLC (Greater London Council) plus the Inner London Education Authority and Metropolitan Counties abolished 1985. Northern Ireland has 26 District Councils (elected by proportional representation), but some local government functions are carried out at the provincial level under 'direct rule'

was established, and the Strathclyde Region became the largest local authority in the United Kingdom – and Labour controlled.

The Table on its own is not very revealing about the nature of these territorial units. The typical county in England and Wales is between half a million and a million in population with about six or so districts within it. It is best to look at an area you know and consider the territorial pattern.

EXERCISES

The reorganisation of local government

24.3 How do the size of local authorities and the tiers relate to 'natural' local communities? Draw on your knowledge of particular areas.

24.4 Why should very large authorities be better than smaller?

Political dynamics

The formal structure of local government is brought to life by three additional elements.

1 Local authorities organise themselves into associations (for example, of district and county councils, education authorities).

2 Most election candidates and councillors are organised in political parties or sometimes in informal groups. Where a party has a clear majority the business of the council is controlled by the party, more or less on the 'winner-takes-all' principle familiar in national government. Usually Labour tends to hold the cities, especially in its Northern heartlands, and Conservatives used to hold the shires; but the Liberal revival of the 1980s has been sustained in local

government and over one half of shire county councils in England and Wales are 'hung', and so are forced to learn the disciplines of power-sharing so alien to Westminster.

3 The associations and the parties together with professionals and special interests make up networks which are important in the policy process, at least when the government has no firm policy goals, or wishes to proceed in a consultative partnership. This remains a customary mode of policy-making, though now threatened by the government's radical approach to local government.

Political leadership, insofar as there is scope, may be exercised by councillors, but people of high political drive and ambition look to national not local politics (John Major a distinguished example). It was hoped that reforms would improve the quality of local councillors. Whether or not the assumption of inadequate quality was fair, there has been little change in the kind of people serving as local councillors. The problem is to attract candidates at all for time-consuming, demanding and ill-rewarded service in a poorly regarded sphere of politics. Most men and women are too busy to give the time, and local councils draw disproportionately on the elderly and retired, owners of small businesses (sometimes with a special interest), farmers and public sector workers and trade union officials.

A generation ago local government in Britain might have been aptly illustrated by the figure of the ceremonial Mayor, in full regalia, opening some new municipal facility, or presiding at a speech day or a garden show. He would be accompanied by the bewigged and gowned Town

Clerk, the senior official, trained in the law, and especially concerned to draw the boundaries of municipal action by the formula of ultra vires (beyond legal powers). Recently local government in Britain has shed the image of ceremonial pomp, restricted by passive legalism. The new councillor-politicians, backed by their chief executives, look much more business-like; or, taking note of the informal dress favoured by some younger councillors, more politician-like. This is not to say that they are encouraged to behave as a significant part of the British system of government.

The chief actors in British local government are the councillors and the officials – but the true hero is the corporate body of councils and committees. Executive power is vested in the Council, and is exercised through the committees. Committees may be organised by party majorities, and dominated by able and influential individuals. But the structure and the style are 'conciliar', based on the committee, and this central characteristic has been strengthened by recent fragmentation of party majorities. The chairmen of committees cannot be as autocratic as a Minister in central government; and committee members have rights of information and access to officials – they are not like backbench MPs. Within the committee system councillors may take up passive or positive roles.

The role of the official in the council/committee system is crucial and arguably very powerful. It differs significantly from that of the official at the centre.

■ DOCUMENT 24.3
The official in British local government

From G. Jones and J. Stewart, 1983, 20–1
Local government officials, unlike civil servants, serve not just a single Minister, but a committee, including opposition members....

...Local officials are more public figures than remote and anonymous central civil servants. Their views are widely known through their reports publicly presented to committees and at times even speeches to their committees. They are publicly questioned by councillors, not occasionally as when a select committee of the Commons calls civil servants before it, but as part of the normal working of committees. They are frequently identified in the press, appear on local radio and TV, speak at public meetings and are active in the community life of the local areas they serve, and in which, or near to which, they usually live. They are thus closer, more visible and accessible to local citizens than any civil servant. ■

EXERCISE
The accountable bureaucrat

24. 5 These passages suggest that the local official is much less powerful, much more accountable to elected politicians than is the case in central government. Are you convinced?

Table 2 The functions of local government

Counties	Districts
Education	Environmental Health
Libraries	Housing
Personal Social Services	
Youth Employment	
Fire Service	
Planning (strategic)	Planning (local)
Highways	Highways (maintenance of minor)
Public Transport	
Road Safety	
Parking (all)	Parking (off-street)
Consumer Protection	Markets and Fairs
Refuse disposal	Refuse collection
	Parks and Open Spaces
	Cemeteries and crematoria
Police (special authority, see Chapter 25)	

Functions and powers

The territorial pattern, structure and political dynamic of local government have to be related to functions and powers, and then understood in the context of the crucial relationship with central government.

Local government in the 1980s employed about three million people and spent (that is, disbursed) about one quarter of the whole of public expenditure. It is by any standard big business, or big government. The main functions are set out in the Table.

About one half of all local government spending is for education, but much of that is simply the disbursement of central funds on agreed national lines, especially teachers' salaries. About 16 per cent is for law and order, and roughly 10 per cent each on health and personal social services, environmental services and transport. The role of local government in education, housing, and some other services including refuse collection is now challenged by policies of 'contracting-out' and privatisation pursued by Conservative governments in the 1980s and 1990s. Thus serious questions are raised about the proper role of local government and the relationship of centre and locality.

These questions amount to a fundamental challenge to the British mode of governing, the constitution no less, and are of the greatest interest to students and concern to citizens. The underlying question is: do we need local government? One preliminary or limbering-up question is posed in the Exercise.

EXERCISE

Local services and local government

24.6 Is there a Conservative and a Labour way of emptying dustbins?

The central-local relationship

The role of local government in the political system is largely determined by the relationship between the central government and the locality. In British terms this means between the government (there is no other) and local authorities.

The relationship may be located along two complementary scales (see Figure 2).

Deconcentration refers to the dispersal of central government through the country, as in the local Benefits Agency. Devolution implies the passing out of full powers, and in Britain usually refers to the 'national regions' of Scotland, Wales and Northern Ireland. Decentralisation covers partial grants of power, most frequently authority to implement, with some discretion, falling short of the sharing of power, or central government letting go. Significantly it is usual to refer to these relationships as vertical or top-down: the centre is on top!

Historically local government in Britain moved from the agency position towards partnership. As agents of the centre local authorities were told by the legally qualified Chief Clerk what was ultra vires, beyond their powers. Find out what they want to do and tell them to stop! However by the 1970s there had developed in some policy areas a kind of paternalistic partnership between central and local government. The centre, like Queen Victoria, 'advised, encouraged and warned', but held on to the purse strings and the ultimate power of legislation.

The failure of financial control together with the intense politicisation of local and central government in the 1970s and 1980s brought about the Conservative government's radical reform of, or assault on, local government in the 1980s and 1990s. The partnership was dissolved, functions shifted to the centre or the private sector, and a diminished local government was left in something of a black hole (see Figure 3).

a) *A scale of centralisation of power*

b) *The traditional position of local government*

Figure 2 Scales of centralisation

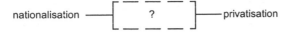

Figure 3 The new position of local government?

The reformed or reformulated central-local relationship was and remains complex, a mix of the formal and constitutional and the informal and political, dominated by funding.

■ DOCUMENT 24.4
Elements in the central-local relationship

Constitutional – the position of local government in the British constitution, its subordination to parliamentary sovereignty and statutes – it can be and do only what Parliament says it can.
Financial – it is dependent on central government directly for about half (or 80 per cent if the new business rate is regarded as central income) of its income, and its independent income from local taxation is now tightly controlled by the centre.
Formal controls by the centre – direction, consents, confirmation, approval.
Regulation, inspection, audit including the Local Government Audit Commission.
Informal – advisory, consultative, guidance.
Political – influence and bargaining in the networks of parties and local authority associations.
Bureaucratic or technocratic – the capabilities of local professionals and politicians to solve problems. ■

This framework of central-local relations is clearly weighted towards central power. There is some political scope for local government: it can argue back (civil servants do not like to behave unreasonably), exploit its political resources (voters, parties and some sympathetic Members of Parliament and Peers), apply its superior expertise (knowledge of the locality), and 'sit on its hands' (non-compliance and confrontation). This amounts to a modest but exploitable negotiating position, but a determined central government can refuse to negotiate (which must mean that local government is in a seriously flawed negotiating position).

Conservative governments since 1979 have radically altered the central-local relationship in a series of laws (a new one on average every two years) and administrative changes.
● The level of grant to local government (in rela-

tion to the services provided) was sharply reduced, with levels of expenditure determined in Whitehall, and penalties for overspending.
● Local taxation was controlled by the 'capping' of rates, as determined by targets set by the government. The replacement of the property tax (rates) by the Community Charge (poll-tax) was also intended to curb local authority spending (see Case). Its successor, the Council Tax, is subject to 'capping'. At the same time the local business rate was converted to a National Non-Domestic Rate, set, collected and distributed by national government.
● The GLC and the Metropolitan Counties were abolished.
● The Local Government Audit Commission was established to investigate and report on the 'value for money' of local government.
● The functions of local government were reduced by contracting-out or privatisation or transfer to non-elected bodies (e.g. in housing and urban development), by the sale of council houses (the basis of some Town Hall political machines), and in the case of local government's most expensive and prestigious activity, education, by a mixture of centralisation and opting-out. In 1993 the government relieved county councils of the statutory requirement to have an education committee.

These changes in local government amounted to the most radical reform of British government since 1945 (though concurrent changes in the civil service compete for the title). The old partnership between centre and locality was dissolved and the values and administrative forms implied in the scale of decentralisation were scrapped. Under the old partnership local government raised between 40 and 60 per cent of its own revenue; under the new system local government raises less than 20 per cent, and even that is controlled. Such radical reform was inevitably controversial and needs to be assessed carefully: the controversy is in fact illuminating for the understanding of democratic government in a complex society.

Local government radically reformed
The reformation of local government in the 1980s and 1990s raises questions about its justification and achievement, and the new place of local government in the British system of government.

First, local government remains a major factor in government. It has lost powers and functions, but only after decades of expansion (for example,

Table 3 Central government financing of local government

Estimated outturn in £ billions 1992–3

	NNDR	RSG	Specific grants	CCG	Trans	Total
England	12.3	16.7	4.2	0.2	1.0	34.4
Scotland	1.2	3.5	0.3	0.02	0.1	5.12
Wales	0.5	1.6	0.2	0.03	0.04	2.4
SUB-TOTAL						42.0
Other current grants						10.8
Capital						6.2
TOTAL						59.0

Notes:
NNDR   National non-domestic rate (formerly the business rate)
RSG   Revenue support grant (formerly Rate Support Grant)
CCG   Community Charge Grant
Trans   Transitional relief to soften impact of introduction of Community Charge

Source: H M Treasury

total expenditure adjusted for inflation in 1980 was over six times as large as in 1900). The sale of council houses has removed over one million from the councils but left about five million in the stock. The opting-out of schools had by 1993 affected only small numbers, though the intention of the government is to replace the local authorities as the main providers of education. The Reformation is as yet incomplete.

Second, diminishing local government is not a new theme for central governments. The post-war Labour government chose to establish the National Health Service separate from local government, and removed the utilities (gas and electricity) from local government by nationalisation. The Labour Party first sought to restrain local government expenditure in the 1970s – 'the party's over', declared the Minister, with more meaning than he intended. But Labour still saw local government as a place where it could exercise power. The Conservatives, more confident of holding central power, conscious of the open challenge of Labour's local political leaders, and fortified by their new ideas on privatisation, took a far more radical line towards local government.

Third, the Conservative assault on local government was not unconstitutional, but there were grounds for some concern about constitutional courtesies and the loss of the essential political pluralism provided by local government. The Conservatives showed impatience and even some recklessness in pushing through their reforms; there was little consultation, rapid and ill-consid-

ered changes of mind, a bewildering rush of financial schemes, and some legislation which was retro-active and appeared to be targeted on specific authorities (all Labour-controlled). This was not unconstitutional, it was not contrary to the rule of law strictly understood, but it was a little more than discourteous: it was bad government by the simple but meaningful test, 'do as you would be done by' (good pragmatic morality in most situations).

The government's general hostility to local government was of more constitutional significance, especially because it was deliberate and to some extent principled. In almost every other modern constitution there is an acceptance in principle that democratic government requires a local level of political significance, not simply for administrative convenience but to diffuse power, to introduce a pluralistic element of competition and challenge. In the past this has been a Conservative principle too, especially honoured in the countryside, and influential in the House of Lords, which did indeed show some concern about the government's rough treatment of local government in the 1980s.

Fourth, this was not a one-sided struggle. Local government was first politicised in the big cities by what may be called the New Urban Left, known to the Tory tabloids, not without some justification, as the 'loony Left' – typically young left-wing militants, usually engaged full-time in politics, and fighting for 'jobs and services' with a zealous concern for the problems of the 'inner city' under-class but less than a Conservative accountant's concern for cost. They found a constituency among the poor, especially among ethnic minority groups suffering the further oppression of racial discrimination. Since few of the poor paid rates (directly at least) or taxes, there was an attractive political opportunity to spend other people's money and win gratitude and votes. The high-spending Labour councils of the 1980s were rarely in trouble at the polls, despite massive increases in rates.

In the prevailing Thatcherist perspective of the 1980s such indulgence, extravagance and irresponsibility were intolerable examples of political corruption and the despised 'dependency culture'. Nicholas Ridley instances absurdly low council house rents and cites a council distributing a Christmas hamper to all of its tenants. This was local politics in the style of the old corrupt bosses of Tammany Hall in New York or Mayor Daley's Chicago, with the public sector unions providing the equivalent of the political machine. Like the old machines of the USA, there was a touch of political corruption about the behaviour of some city councils; but 'profligate' expenditure was mostly on behalf of the deserving poor, and in any case, was insignificant by comparison with central government spending on, say, Covent Garden opera or military bands, or technological marvels for the army.

Thus a Thatcherist central government confronted local governments, which were assumed in the heat of battle to be composed entirely of 'loony Left' councils. Those who deplored the 'dependency culture' and those who proudly served it met in unequal battle. At least it seemed unequal, but the struggle over the Poll-Tax was long and bloody, and when it ended both the tax and the Prime Minister who pressed for it had fallen.

The case for and against local government
Local government ought not to have to justify itself. Historically, some form of local government normally exists before a central government is imposed on, or acquires dominion over, a large and diverse territory. This is the case in Britain where local government in the form of Justices of the Peace, Poor Law Boards, Turnpike Trusts, Sanitary Commissioners and the like developed alongside the central state. As late as the nineteenth century governments managed foreign affairs while various local bodies got on with the serious business of domestic government.

The medieval Justices of the Peace or magistrates of provincial Britain were once characterised as exercising 'self-government at the King's command'. This remained the constitutional basis of local government, though the delicate balance implied has shifted away from local self-government as modern democracy developed. Writing in the mid-1960s Professor Birch drew a contrast between France, Britain and the USA in the status of local government.

'France has a system of local administration.... The United States, on the other hand, has a system of genuine local self-government.... British local government...has the appearance and trappings of a system of local self-government but not much of the reality' (1967, pp. 235–6).

Much of the work of local governing can be done by local field offices of the central ministries (as in the case for example of social security payments in Britain). However, a local political system with some autonomy offers central government some advantages over a system of local administration by the central ministries.

■ DOCUMENT 24.5
The case for local government

The gains

- The efficiency of delivery of local services by local bodies (information, sensitivity and responsiveness, short lines of communication).
- The lightening of the tasks and workload of central government and a moderation of overloading of both politicians and administrators at the centre.
- The sharing and lessening of the responsibilities of central government, so that the centre does not take the blame for everything that goes wrong, however trivial, in the remotest village. (The centre may still hope to take the credit for what goes right!)
- The enhancement of democratic values arising from gains in participation and consent and from the responsiveness of a plural structure, and the potential improvement in support and legitimacy for government as a whole. ■

Of course a local government system imposes some costs on the central government. The gains in efficiency may be offset by loss of central control; the gains in democratic values may create opposition and obstruction. The scope and visibility of local services create political risks (pot-holed roads or ill-equipped schools cost votes), while the scale of local spending threatens the government's control of public expenditure (not as much as central spending, but local government is an easier target). So central governments are often at the least ambivalent and sometimes hostile towards local government. There is, it must be conceded, a case at least for the government's lack of full confidence in local government.

■ DOCUMENT 24.6
The case against local government

- The claim to be democratic is not well realised in practice: electors are ill-informed and apathetic, elections are dominated by national politics, and turn-out is low, ratepayers have been only a bare majority of the electorate, and councillors, so it is asserted, are unrepresentative, unskilled and partisan (unlike MPs?).
- The claim to be efficient is not well realised in practice: the professionals and the public sector unions dominate, the latter often in a close relationship with the Labour Party, staff numbers are excessive, productivity is low, councillors do not have the capacity or the power to intervene in management. The success of contracting out and privatisation has demonstrated the broad truth of these charges – at least, so it is argued.
- The ideals of democracy and effectiveness can be achieved better in other ways, notably by privatisation and commercialisation, which give the citizen the rights of the customer in the market-place.

If some part of this case against local government is accepted, then the defence of local government rests on the arguments:

- that local government must be judged by what it can do on average or even at its best, not its worst
- that inefficiency is a characteristic of all large organisations (central government being a notable example according to the reports of the National Audit Office)
- that a mass democracy is likewise necessarily imperfect
- that the power of choice given through the market is illusory. ■

It does look as if the case against local government is based on the worst not the best of local

government, so the question is where does the average lie?

Two further considerations arise: the problem of redistribution or equalisation and the problem of relating the spending power to taxation.

1 *Redistribution*
An important function of government is to redistribute resources to provide a greater degree of equality than exists naturally. Those who live in comparatively wealthy areas may not be convinced that this is a proper objective of governments, while those in poorer areas may readily agree. In any case there is a sound (attractive anyway) moral argument that services, comforts and life-chances should not differ widely within the territory of one government, even if absolute equality is neither desirable nor, quite certainly, practicable.

Now local government provides a mechanism for redistribution, but obviously the essential choices have to be made at the centre, overriding local autonomy. Redistribution conflicts with local autonomy: you can have one or the other, but not both.

EXERCISE
Redistribution and local autonomy

24.7 Can the principles of equality and local autonomy be reconciled?

2 *Taxation and the power to spend*
One principle in the development of democracy, in early Parliament and in the American Revolution, was: 'No taxation (i.e. tax raising by the government) without representation'. This was achieved, but the link between taxation and representation now arises in a reversed form – no representation without tax-paying. Does entitlement to take part in local government, to vote and receive its services, depend on the paying of local taxes? – this was the issue of principle behind the Poll-Tax (see Case Study). But the principle was conceded in national government with the ending of a property qualification for the vote: membership in the political community was free. The intention of the Poll-Tax was not of course to take away the vote but ensure that voters paid taxes. It was in a way a reversion to a property qualification for the vote.

This concern that local voters should pay a local tax highlighted the question who should spend tax-payers' money? The question is at the heart of central-local relations, and indeed at the heart of the power of modern government which derives its immense capacities from the great engine of income tax. In central-local relations the question is raised, should tax payers through their representatives in Parliament control the spending of tax-derived funds passed to local government? One version of this is: should the man who pays the piper call the tune?

EXERCISE
Paying the piper, calling the tune

24.8 Is it generally true and desirable in the relations of central and local government that 'he who pays the piper calls the tune'?

One response to the problem of local government finance is to establish a more substantial source of local revenue, a local income tax. The case was made by the Layfield Committee on Local Government Finance in 1976 (see Assessments). The Treasury objects (of course), there are evident practical difficulties (not insurmountable with computerised administration), and the tax payers might storm County Hall (an end to political apathy at least); but those who were too poor to pay tax would still have a free ride. It is all very difficult, and this may help to explain the Poll-Tax fiasco.

A fault line in the British polity?
There is a fault line in British government running between the centre and the locality, a gap in institutions and in the informal linkages provided in other countries by political elites, the parties and the media. The gap is not total; a number of Members of Parliament have some experience of local government service. Most MPs deal with constituency problems in the field of local government; the local authorities through their associations take part in policy committees and informal communities which bridge the gap. But, notably, only one or two local politicians are prominent in national politics in Britain.

Thus the two major arenas of government and politics are not properly joined together in mutual tolerance and respect, accepting interdependence and engaging in more or less friendly collaboration. The condition is fundamental in the British constitution, political culture and administrative practice. This gap, and the assumption which underlies it, has been called the 'dual polity'. Some aspects of the dual polity are explored in the document.

■ DOCUMENT 24.7
The dual polity

a) From J. Bulpitt, 1983, p. 3
First, over time, territorial politics in the United Kingdom has been characterised by a structural dichotomy between Centre and periphery...the basic division has been between the court and the country.... Secondly, the Centre or court sought increasingly to operate a distinction between 'High Politics' and 'Low Politics'...a Dual Polity operated in territorial terms: both Centre and periphery achieved a relative autonomy from one another, the degree of interpenetration between national and local politics was low.

b) From N. Johnson, 1977, p. 128
...the crucial characteristic of British local government is not so much its dependence on the centre in relation to its executive functions, but rather its political weakness and insignificance.... The most persuasive explanation of this peculiarity in the structure of British politics lies in the dominance over a very long period of national political elites and their relatively sharp separation from local politics understood as the maintenance of local positions of political influence.

c) From D. Ashford, 1981, pp. 147–8
The concentration of policy-making powers in Westminster and Whitehall has severely limited the capacity of the British political system to deal with localised policy conflicts and choices. Nearly every other modern democratic state has well-defined organisational links to lower-level governments. What differentiates Britain from France, which also has a unitary system, is how easily national policymakers can act without careful consultation with local government and how easily national objectives are imposed on this vast subnational structure. ■

EXERCISE
The dual polity

24.9 How does the dual polity come to be characteristic of Britain but not of other countries?

In the 1980s and 1990s central government intervened in local politics, because it wished to control public expenditure – 'low' politics is too expensive after all to be left to the locals. But local government was not in a position to respond, to negotiate, to bargain. When tested in this way the constitution crumbled, for there was indeed nothing of substance there.

The nations and the regions

The United Kingdom is dominated by the English, and governed from London, in the remote South-Eastern corner of Britain. The Scots and the Welsh have sometimes shown signs of discontent with this arrangement. Scotland has been part of the Union (the United Kingdom) since 1707, but has retained separate systems of law, religion and education. There is a Secretary of State for Scotland in the Cabinet, and a powerful separate (but not really independent) administration, the Scottish Office. This is largely based in Edinburgh and most of the domestic ministries do their work in Scotland through or under it. Wales as a nation has had a thinner time, being governed as part of 'England and Wales' since the sixteenth century. In most important ways it is assimilated, but since 1964 it has, like Scotland, acquired its own Secretary of State and Welsh Office, with powers falling short of autonomy. The existence of a Welsh language and an historic culture has nourished national sentiment, which is perhaps the most intense centrifugal force in British politics.

Both countries have for long had nationalist movements either as separate parties (Scottish National Party and Plaid Cymru), or as groups or tendencies within the United Kingdom parties. In the late 1960s, partly because of the economic failures of British governments, these nationalist parties began to make an impact on parliamentary politics. The government hastily appointed a Commission on the Constitution which after four years of inquiry recommended various systems of 'devolution' of power to Welsh and Scottish Assemblies. Separatism and federalism were rejected: it was assumed that the measures of 'devolution' proposed need not much disturb the unity of the United Kingdom. The government's proposals (1975) were, briefly, to establish a legislative assembly for Scotland, headed by a Scottish Executive, and an administrative assembly for Wales. Both assemblies were to have powers in the fields of local government, planning and social services, and would enjoy block grants, voted by Parliament, which retained supreme powers.

The proposals were rightly regarded as an awkward attempt to devolve power to Scotland and Wales without losing control at the centre. Opponents of devolution forced the government to concede referendums, with a 40 per cent minimum vote required for ratification of the devolution Bills. Both assemblies were voted down, and this curious episode in British constitutional history closed.

Yet the issue would not go away. The voting against the devolution Acts was decisive in Wales but ambivalent (strictly, tri-valent) in Scotland, where the voters divided one third in favour (in fact a small majority), one third against, and one third not voting. Support for the Scottish National Party and for separation fluctuated, but support for a Scottish legislative assembly within the United Kingdom was steady and substantial. Both Labour and the Liberal Democrats were committed to such a development in the election of 1992, and the legitimacy of Conservative government in Scotland looked vulnerable when they held only 11 seats and 26 per cent of the vote.

The case for devolution to Scotland is strong, but there are severe practical difficulties. Complete independence is more logical but that too is not easy. The difficulty about devolution is to concede substantial power without fatally weakening the Union itself. For example:

- How can a Scottish Assembly be related to the Westminster Parliament?
- Should Scottish MPs continue to vote on English matters, and English MPs on Scottish matters?
- Where should all those Scottish and Welsh politicians prominent in the Labour and Liberal Democrat parties choose to serve?
- What about taxation and finance, and the control of resources, such as oil?
- Should the UK government continue to redistribute UK revenues, to give Scotland more than its proportionate share? Scotland has done quite well out of this in the past.

Apart from these structural problems of the constitution, Scotland raises underlying constitutional issues about centralisation, 'overload', participation and 'powerlessness' – which have yet to be answered. The immediate, pragmatic response of the British people, including the Scots and the Welsh, was that the performance of governments, especially in economic affairs, mattered far more than constitutional reform. The British people have inherited, along with a distinguished constitutional history, a marked complacency and conservatism in constitutional matters.

The third of the nations of the United Kingdom, Northern Ireland, has provided the British people with a more disturbing constitutional problem. When virtual independence was conceded to southern Ireland in 1922, Protestant Ulster (the six Northern counties) was granted a unique status of autonomy within the United Kingdom. Northern Ireland had its own Parliament in Belfast (Stormont), a government of its own (with Prime Minister, Cabinet and civil service) and almost complete power in domestic matters. The province sent twelve (now seventeen) Members to the Westminster Parliament. Thus was established a model for a provincial system.

However, Ulster did not seek separation from the Union, which was its protection against any move to unification by the nationalist and Catholic South (Eire as it had become). Ulster expected to be treated as an integral part of the United Kingdom in respect of economic and social policies. The situation was changed by the critical events of the 1960s and 1970s. The movement of Ulster Catholics for civil rights, and of Irish nationalists for unification, led to political breakdown, and finally the suspension in 1972 of the Northern Ireland Constitution and direct rule from Westminster.

The response of the Protestant majority in Ulster is ambivalent. What is at stake for them is their own dominance in Ulster. This is best served by the Westminster connection, though within that they would prefer their old provincial autonomy. They are, unusually, nationalists who do not seek independence. They are the most consistent supporters of the Union of the United Kingdom.

The British government is caught in a historical trap. It bears some historical responsibility for the present form of the problem, since it was responsible for the partition and the emergence of Northern Ireland as a province of the United Kingdom, and it tolerated the long dominance of the Protestant majority in Northern Ireland. But the British government cannot be held responsible for the stance of the two communities, confronting each other in armed hostility based on the potent and destructive drives of religion and nationalism (see Case Study). So Britain acts perforce as the peace maker in a civil war, in which both sides can claim a majority status (the Protestant Union in Northern Ireland, the Catholic Republican Nationalists in Ireland).

The problem has no solution short of amicable power-sharing. The British government has kept the peace as far as it could, reduced discrimination (not as forcefully as some would wish), upheld the rule of law (insofar as civil war and the nature of the security forces allow), encouraged power-sharing (in the abortive Northern Ireland Assembly of 1974) and insisted on talking with the government of Ireland (in the Anglo-Irish Agreement of 1985, concluded in defiance of Unionist opinion).

Since the 1960s British governments have come to recognise that Britain is a multi-national state known as the United Kingdom. The recognition (no more) gains significance in the fresh perspective of European developments, in which the salience of the nation state is diminished, while comparatively small states like Belgium and Luxembourg gain in status, and the interests of regions are also recognised.

In Britain, apart from the 'national regions' (not a term much favoured in Edinburgh and Cardiff), regional politics is weak. There is a shadowy regional structure of administration. This was of most significance during the War and in face of the threat of invasion; and in the 1960s when regional planning was in fashion and Regional Planning Boards and Councils were established. But the retreat from planning and the push to privatisation has much diminished this shadowy regional state apparatus. The utilities have gone and only Regional Health Authorities remain, together with regional offices of departments such as transport with significant territorial functions.

Some English regions, notably the North, look with envy at the Scottish and Welsh Offices, both vigorous examples of decentralised administration, backed by Cabinet Ministers. But what is a region? There is really no political basis for regional politics, no elected governments, and very little sense of identity, except at the level of folktales and sentiment – Cockneys, Geordies, Tykes and so on. Sport, particularly football, is a source of vigorous territorial loyalty, but is not related to the English regions (indeed, local football heroes now go off to play for foreign teams).

It seems that as in other cases, devolution, the reform of local government, or indeed the reform of the House of Lords or the ballot system, the British people are interested in the results rather than the form of government, and have a remarkable trust in their institutions. They are deeply conservative in constitutional matters, and it is clear that if they had been fully consulted before British accession to the European Community, they would never have agreed – because they distrust change and foreigners. Enoch Powell speaks for them on the erosion of sovereignty (see Assessment in Chapter 23).

GUIDE TO EXERCISES

24.1 Peace and prosperity (if you have them) and the overall quality of public services are mainly the responsibility of central government. Then there are the stability and comfort of your house, the safety of furniture and food, the quality of clothes, schools, television, the efficiency of the police or the railways, the reliability of a travel agent and so on. In the nineteenth century you might have marvelled at the growth of municipal services and in the mid-twentieth century, at the rapid expansion of central government services; by the year 2000 you may wonder at the decline of direct state services and the rise of regulation by the state, and the overall impact of the EC.

24.2 The constitution is without doubt unitary, but it is possible that over time the weakening of the unity of government by the EC, and by pressure for, and some concessions to, devolution will be evident, and new 'tacit understandings' arise. But this is a matter for decades, not years.

24.3 Some attempt is made to arrange a conformity to 'natural' communities, but such natural communities hardly exist except at a village or neighbourhood level.

24.4 'Better' in what way? It was argued that there were economies of scale (as in a school for example) and the larger authority could sustain specialist staff and services, and attract staff and councillors of higher calibre. But there are also diseconomies of scale (as in very large schools), and quality of personnel does not seem to be closely related to size.

24.5 The case is persuasive, but the position may sometimes be that the official in local government is not only more responsive to councillors and the locality, but also has considerable standing in his own right. The official always has the advantage of his full-time, permanent professional expertise, and his own network of bureaucratic and political relations. He is allowed more freedom than a civil servant to make his own case and to deal with opposition politicians. He has some standing in relation to the officials of central government, since he is in a separate career service. Unlike his counterparts in France

and USA for example he is not plainly subordinated to other prestigious and politically significant local figures like prefects or elected mayors.

24.6 If it is run as a council service, then one party may claim that they would do the job more efficiently (usually meaning more cheaply) but roughly in the same way. But the answer of radical conservatism in the 1980s was Yes! – and similarly for many other services: the service should be organised as a business, either 'contracted-out' or wholly in private hands, run for profit and freed from the constraints of the public sector unions. Applying the same strategy to schools is more difficult (why?). The Conservative's radical strategy raises the question, what will be left of local government? The radical answer is, not very much, but so what?

24.7 With difficulty! But it is not impossible. The central government's judgement about equalisation removes choice from the locality, but it is conceivable that there would be general agreement on some redistribution. Further the implementation of the policy, including some choice in detail, can still be left to the locality. In practice central governments pursuing redistributive policies are more concerned with the outrage of rich areas than with delicate considerations of local autonomy; so redistributive policies exercised through local government will never be pressed far. Still the contradiction remains; local autonomy means the rich stay rich; equalisation always requires strong interventionist central government to make the hard decisions and collect the taxes.

24.8 True generally – central government has been reluctant to give money to local government 'without strings'. But the complex grant arrangements showed genuine efforts to leave some autonomy with the local governments – hence their complexity. This was partly from a genuine commitment to local democracy, partly from a wish to avoid the constitutional absurdity and the burden of taking over entirely the work of what are intended to be other jurisdictions.

Desirable? The value of local autonomy has to be balanced against the risk of giving local governments a 'blank cheque';

there is in the financing of local government by grants an element of irresponsibility (both in the narrow and the general meaning of that term). Further, the tax payers, central and local, have rights in the matter under the original principle of no taxation without representation.

24.9 The answer has to do with the whole constitutional standing (or lack of standing) of local government, the absence of political rewards for local politicians, and elements of political culture, metropolitan dominance, the concentration of government on foreign and imperial affairs. The institutions reflect the dual polity, and the parties conform to it. By contrast, the two polities are joined in France by the 'dual mandate' (politicians holding both national and local elected office), in the USA and in Germany by the federal system.

ASSESSMENTS

1 A centralised system?

The British constitution is unitary: sovereign power rests in Parliament and has not been challenged by any other substantial centre of government, at least until Britain joined the European Community. The unitary constitution supports a centralised system of government based on a powerful executive, disciplined national political parties, a unified and entrenched bureaucracy, the central command of taxation and most economic controls (with a proviso about joining the EC), and a dominant metropolitan political culture.

However there are some elements of diversity and pluralism in the polity. The centre cannot work like a signal box, with all the levers connected to mandatory red and green lights. There are elements of disconnection, disaggregation and dispersal. The centre cannot do very much on its own; it is dependent on other bodies to do its work for it. Dependence diminishes coherence and power; countervailing power grows in the interstices of the networks of government. Interdependence replaces absolute central power.

Government is, in the accurate if inelegant words of the Layfield Report, not 'a cohesive or comprehensive totality', nor 'a manageable system related to the present day needs of the community', but 'an agglomerate of innumerable accretions that have compounded over the centuries' (Layfield Report, 1976, App. 2, pp.

281–2). In brief, government is much messier than the governors like to think, and there is a good deal of retrospective tidying-up, rationalisation, self-deception and hypocrisy.

Insofar as this interpretation is valid then the power of the centre is shared not just with local governments but with all the organisations referred to in this chapter, including regional and supranational bodies, and the policy communities arising from them, and the professional and technical cadres and interest groups. Thus centralisation may be too simple a notion to encompass the complexities of the business of government.

The absolute power of central command obtains in conditions of last resort, or 'when the chips are down'. But the power of last resort may act as a deterrent without being used, so last resort power is a continuing factor. There is a parallel with nuclear weapons, except that nuclear weapons destroy the user. The centre is not destroyed or even much damaged by using its weapons of last resort. The abolition of the GLC was a potent demonstration of the capacity of the centre to exercise its absolute power.

2 A democratic deficit?

The European Community, it is argued, suffers from a 'democratic deficit': in particular the powers of the European Parliament have lagged behind the development of the Community and its policy making institutions. The argument may also be applied to sub-central government in Britain. A quarter of a century ago the Commission on the Constitution concluded that there was a case for devolution of power to Scotland and Wales. In a forceful Minority Report it was argued that the British people suffered a condition of 'powerlessness'; 'government appears to be, and is, remote from the people...everywhere there is a growing "we-they" syndrome...and people are increasingly alienated from the political process' (Report, II, xii–xiii). The Minority Report went on to recommend a complete system of regional government for England as well as Scotland and Wales. The argument for English regions was not accepted by the government, and has little resonance for the governing class of the South-East of England.

The Layfield Report on Local Government Finance was established after the Committee to reform the structure of local government had reported – an absurd illogicality. This was the age, now past, when governments asked

Commissions and Committees to consider reform and make proposals, which were then ignored. Layfield had the great merit of posing to government the fundamental choice between central and local responsibility, and arguing that a serious system of local government required a serious source of local revenue, local income tax. This for Layfield was the crux of the argument about local democracy.

From Committee on Local Government Finance, Report, Cmnd 6453, HMSO, 1976
'58 We have suggested that the main responsibility for local expenditure and taxation should be placed either upon the government or upon local authorities....
59 First, introducing LIT (local income tax) is a necessary condition of greater local responsibility....
61 The second main issue is the implications for economic management....
63 The third, and perhaps the most important, issue is whether all important governmental decisions affecting people's lives and livelihood should be taken in one place on the basis of national policies; or whether many of the decisions could not as well, or better, be taken in different places, by people of diverse experience, associations, background and political persuasion....
66 Much turns on the value which is placed on local democracy itself....
67 The choice we have posed is a difficult one. There is a strongly held view amongst us that the only way to sustain a vital local democracy is to enlarge the share of local taxation in total local revenue and thereby make councillors more directly accountable to local electorates for their expenditure and taxation decisions.'

Layfield's argument has not so far impressed governments.

Dis-inventing or reinventing government

It is beginning to be apparent that a radical reform of the nature of British government is in train. This began as a Conservative assault on the public sector, and in particular the bureaucracy and the trade unions; but that gave political momentum to the more systematic thinking of the radical right.

The broad aim is to substitute for the large monopolistic public sector of the post-war welfare state an altogether leaner system based on diversity, competition, entrepreneurship, and modern business and managerial practice (the accountants and the management consultants take over). The impact of this reformist drive is evident in sub-central government in the introduction of 'market' disciplines, privatisation, contracting-out, introduction of competition and bidding, separation of purchasing and providing functions, redefining clients as customers. The tendency of these reforms is to change the role of local government from all-purpose provider to purchaser and enabler, possibly co-ordinator and, if it cannot be avoided, advocate. These are still significant functions, but not on the scale of local government of the 1960s.

The progress of reform is uneven: there is an impression of a government raiding the territory, rather than conquering, occupying and re-ordering it. There are new institutional forms and practices, including Executive Agencies, Housing Action Trusts, Education Associations, 'opted-out' schools, privatised services, and the performance standards of the Citizen's Charter. But much of the old welfare state and local government remains. Some of the Government's changes, notably in education, seem to be centralising. New central bureaucracies are developing and government-appointed quangos flourish. The parents and patients who should be enjoying the empowerment of citizens may not find in practice that there is much real choice for them in underfunded schools and hospitals. Still, the Conservative governments of the 1980s and 1990s have carried through more substantial and radical reform of government than ever was achieved by the Labour Party and the Commissions and Committees in the previous two decades.

Such radical reform creates some constitutional problems. It is not clear what the eventual role of local government and the civil service will be, and how the responsibility of Ministers to Parliament can be maintained. Here the empowerment of the citizen as customer, or as citizen with rights under the Citizen's Charter, may have to bear a substantial weight of constitutional oversight.

Membership of the EC also raises problems for new forms of entrepreneurial government, for it looks as if the EC deals naturally with member governments, and operates through bureaucracy and regulation. It may well turn out that the liberating thrust of the reform of government towards privatisation, de-centralisation, and enterprise (if that is con-ceded) is not compatible with membership of the European Community.

Concepts

Subsidiarity

The term is newly fashionable but the principle is of long standing. It conveys the preference that government functions should be carried out at the lowest level practicable, that is as near to the people as possible. The implication is that good government should be de-centralised, unless there are demonstrable benefits in moving the function to the centre, or a 'higher' level. The term has been used in the debate over the EC and in the Maastricht Treaty to affirm that power should rest with national governments where there is no necessity or advantage in passing it to Brussels. In this limited form the British government strongly favours subsidiarity.

It may be argued contrary to the subsidiarity principle that good government requires moving power to the highest level possible, world government being the ultimate goal. This looks plausible only in relation to matters which can be managed at those levels and not lower, for example, world trade, Third World poverty and some environmental conditions.

Nationalism

Nationalism arises from the identification of a people with a territory, especially when the sense of identity is strengthened by religion, language, history and culture. It is especially forceful when invigorated by hostility towards a nation or country or government regarded as the historic oppressor or occupier of the homeland. Nationalist movements may be directed towards the ejection of the occupying oppressor (Wales, Ireland) and the achievement of an independent nation state (Scotland), the unification of territories (nineteenth century Germany and Italy), or the recovery of lost territory (Germany in the 1930s), or 'ethnic cleansing' (Germany in the 1930s, Serbia in 1992–3).

Altogether nationalism can be a powerful and destructive force, exploited by political leaders playing on popular sentiment; excessive zeal and mass hysteria are never far away. The English, having been top nation in the nineteenth century, and enjoying for so long an easy dominion over the homeland and much of the rest of the world, have their own peculiar form of nationalism, mainly an unwarranted self-confidence and conceit, punctuated by bouts of jingoism when aroused. We all might be better off without nationalism, but we are what we are.

● CASE STUDY
Northern Ireland

The conflict, like most of the conflicts around the world, is a conflict of communities, defined and set in mutual hostility by nationalist and religious loyalties, rooted in history and continuously reinforced by contemporary conflicts over discrimination, security operations and justice. The historical struggle between two hostile communities is continuously reinvented on the streets of Belfast and in the villages of the Ulster countryside. The victims of the conflict are subjected to a strong socialisation, the leaders and activists of violence are for the most part professionals.

The ancient cause of dispute lies in the history of Ireland as a kind of British colony, the 'plantation' of Ulster mainly by Scottish Presbyterians in the seventeenth century, some brutal and bloody military episodes of the 1640s and 1650s and 1690 (still ritually remembered) and the famine of the 1840s. The modern form of the problem was created by Lloyd George (after the failure to create 'Home Rule' for the whole of Ireland) by the establishment in 1922 of the province of Northern Ireland, based roughly on the largest area which could be dominated by the Protestants . Thus the Protestants were in a majority of two to one in the North and a minority of one to three in the whole of Ireland. This is a structure the Protestant Unionists will not change and the Catholic Republicans of the South will not accept.

The conflict thus drawn from Irish history is sustained by fierce communal loyalties based on a strong sense of national identity bound up with continuing and intense 'religiosity' – two thirds of Protestants think of themselves as British, two thirds of Catholics think of themselves as Irish. The hostility of the two 'communities' is reinforced by the experience of past discrimination by the Unionist majority against Catholics in employment and government services, bitter hostility to the security forces, including the British army, the continuing influence of Catholicism in the government of the Irish Republic, and the maintenance of its claim to govern the whole island of Ireland.

The solution to the conflict in Northern Ireland must lie in power–sharing (which has failed so far) and in a fundamental change in communal loyalties (which in the short term is unlikely). Unlike the economic and distributional problems which dominate the rest of British politics, the problem of Northern Ireland is not amenable to bargaining and compromise. There is no solution, but there may be alleviation. ●

● CASE STUDY
The Poll-Tax

The Community Charge or Poll-Tax was the Conservative government's solution to the problem of local government finance. It was introduced in 1990, proved unworkable and unpopular, played a significant part in bringing down Margaret Thatcher and was immediately repealed by her successor. Thus the Poll-Tax provides an interesting study of a policy which proved disastrous – how did it come to be adopted? The story is instructive.

[There are good accounts of the political side in H. Young, 1991, N. Ridley, 1991 and A. Watkins, 1991.]

1 *The problem.* There is no doubt that the finance of local government is a severe problem. Local government now disburses over one quarter of all public expenditure, and much of this (in the 1970s about three fifths, now nearer four fifths, counting the Business Rate as central) comes direct from central government. The main independent source of local revenue was the property tax known as the rates, which was plainly inadequate.

If local government is to be truly democratic and responsible it needs a substantial source of revenue of its own, for which it is accountable to its electorate. There were grounds for concern either that local government did not have enough funds for independent activities, or – and this worried the Conservatives – that local government was able to spend irresponsibly, since its main funding was from central government, with additional funding from the rates, which were not paid at all, or not paid directly, by many of its poorer clients.

The Conservatives claimed with some justification that local governments were able in effect to sign cheques from someone else's cheque book, and some Labour councils were spending extravagantly for the benefit of clients who voted but did not pay rates. At its worst the system was corrupt – votes were being bought with tax-payers' money; at its best local government was over-de-

pendent on central government. The problem had been long recognised, and the frequent revaluation of property for rating had on six occasions since 1945 led to calls for reform. Although property was related to income and ability to pay, awkward anomalies arose under rating, for example, the much quoted widow in the large, heavily rated house, living next door to a similar house with four earners. It was accepted that the rate was an unsatisfactory and unpopular tax. This helps to explain how the government came to impose the Poll-Tax: it had some good reason on its side.

2 *The solution.* The difficulty was to find an alternative. Other countries used sales and local income taxes as well a property tax. The Layfield Committee on local government finance (1976) had recommended that a local income tax was a necessary condition for greater local responsibility. A sales tax was rejected on the grounds that it was difficult to collect and could lead to the migration of shoppers to cheaper areas. Income tax was easier to collect, but was guarded jealously by central government as its main source of funding.

A third possibility, a Poll-Tax, a single charge levied on each adult resident, with a few socially justified exceptions, had the merits of simplicity and improved accountability: it made the necessary link between voter, charge and service. This was, and remains, its greatest advantage. The disadvantage, which should have been equally plain, was that the tax was not related to ability to pay. It was also a very obvious tax, and not so easy to collect. It might work if it was fairly small, but then was it worth the trouble?

In all these cases there are problems about relating revenue to local needs, equalising as far as possible the richer and poorer areas. The demand for equality, so that local services are of roughly similar standard throughout the country, is strong in the poorer areas, and is generally accepted (not that it is well understood) as a proper objective of a modern government. Given the large contribution to local government made by the central government, equalisation has to be achieved, under any local tax system, by complex calculations about the distribution of central funds (the Revenue Support Grant). Again the government was often blamed for this, but local choice, though simpler, would have been resented in the poorer areas.

3 *The policy process.* This account of the problem and the possible solutions goes a long way to explain the process of policy making. There are good reasons for doing something about the problem, and equally good reasons for doing nothing. The lesson is that many problems faced by governments are more or less insoluble.

- The initial pledge. The Conservative party pledged in the election of October 1974 to replace the rates 'by taxes more broadly based and related to people's ability to pay'. The idea may well have come from the Leader, Edward Heath, but the Environment spokesman, Margaret Thatcher, was committed to the policy, and with increasing conviction as the tales spread of high spending Labour councils, controlled by what the tabloid papers called the 'loony left'. The Conservative 'grassroots' also favoured reform of the rates, for old and new reasons, and the Conference of 1987 made a decisive call for immediate implementation of the Poll-Tax.

- Ministerial action and inaction. A succession of Environment Ministers picked up the problem. Heseltine introduced 'rate-capping', a gross intervention by central government in the affairs of independent local government, but one deemed to be justified by the profligacy of local government. Having considered the options for reform of the rates, Heseltine, wisely it now seems, decided to do nothing, or, if you like, did not decide to do anything. Heseltine was shortly succeeded by Patrick Jenkin, and then by Kenneth Baker. The Prime Minister, Margaret Thatcher, continued to press for action, and characteristically put together a kind of task-force including advisers as well as officials. Baker was willing to run with it, for Ministers do the Prime Minister's bidding; but he devised a slow transition to the new system, which would have taken ten years in all. A Minister with doubts about the wisdom of the Prime Minister does her bidding very slowly.

- The final push: Nicholas Ridley. In 1986 Nicholas Ridley was appointed Secretary of State for the Environment. Ridley was a Thatcherite, on the right of the party and personally loyal to Margaret Thatcher, with a no-nonsense approach to policy making. Under him there was a clear pledge in the election manifesto of 1987, and the legislation followed in 1987–8. Ridley moved on in 1989 and the implementation of the tax was left to Christopher Patten. This constant and characteristic moving on of Ministers can have done little for the steady development of the policy, but had the advantage that several senior Ministers were implicated in the policy, and so had unclean hands.

- Factors in the final push. The Poll-Tax was pushed forward by the revaluation in Scotland, and by the call of the Conference of 1987 for immediate action. The revaluation had the effect of raising rates bills in many areas (or appeared to have that effect). The real problem was that in Scotland as in England and Wales local government expenditure was rising sharply in face of heavy demand for services and decreasing central grants, and was urged on by some extravagant, mostly Labour, councils. Many councils, both Labour and Conservative, were overspending according to the government's standards by 30 per cent or more; not all of this was defiant protest.

- Opposition. There was opposition to the Poll-Tax. The Chancellor, Nigel Lawson, and the Treasury objected. Lawson put a paper to Cabinet in 1985 arguing that the Tax was 'completely unworkable and politically catastrophic' (H. Young, 1991, p. 536); it had little impact. The weight of professional and academic opinion was opposed to the new Tax. Conservative backbenchers raised one of their most serious rebellions; in April 1988 Michael Mates' amendment to introduce into the tax some relationship to ability to pay was supported by 37 Conservatives with 11 further abstentions – and Mates was then removed on the instruction of the Whips from all elective office in the party. There was more disturbing opposition to the tax when it was introduced – serious riots in London, in the streets and in council chambers; Robin Hood reappeared in Nottingham and 18 Conservative councillors in West Oxfordshire resigned.

- The consequences of the Poll-Tax. The Poll-Tax was introduced in 1990, with wide variations in the charge, and many above £300 p.a. The legislation was repealed in 1991 and the Tax was replaced in 1993. By then the government had spent perhaps £8.5bn to moderate its impact, and large sums remained uncollected. A culture of non-payment had developed. The more dramatic costs were political. Margaret Thatcher fell because of policy disagreements, especially over Europe, and personal tensions, between her and her colleagues, but mainly because her government was very unpopular. That unpopularity was caused above all by the Poll-Tax. All the candidates for the succession were pledged to reform the tax.

4 *Conclusions.*The Poll-Tax project failed because the tax was very unpopular. Even more than the rates, it was a visible, lumpy tax; worse, it was not based on the accepted principle of progressive taxation. The duke paid the same as the dustman, and it was not enough to say, as Ridley did, that the duke was already paying a far heavier weight of income and other taxes.

The tax might have been saved if it had not been set so high -- at least twice as high as its advocates had expected. Ridley was aware of this, and tried and failed to get a higher central grant from the then Chief Secretary, John Major. Local governments needed to spend more in order to sustain their services; but it does seem that they took the opportunity to spend more and so inflate the Poll-Tax – for which the central government would take the blame. But it should be said that even very small increases in local expenditure had to be taken wholly from the proceeds of Poll-Tax, so the tax consequences of extra spending shot up alarmingly. (This is what is known as gearing).

Soon the Poll-Tax had acquired an aura of injustice and failure. Even its name seemed to signal injustice: the government insisted in vain on the official 'Community Charge' (previously the Residents' or Services Charge). Then the government invented various schemes to moderate the tax. Most were expensive, and looked to be unfair or at best a desperate tinkering with a policy now admitted to have failed.

The account above relates how the policy came to be adopted and driven through. The Poll-Tax was one more example of the force of momentum in policy development. Hugo Young wrote of it:

'All policies pass some point of no return.... They acquire a kind of self-propelling energy which sweeps from the path all fundamental objections, drowns out all cautionary noises.... the more hazardous the policy, the sooner this tends to happen, as Ministers rush to erect the soundest defences around something they know will be controversial' (1991, p. 534).

Young adds that the decisive moment in the Thatcher government 'usually coincided with the leader's own conversion or commitment'. In this case the decision was effectively taken at Chequers, in an informal meeting with relevant Ministers and others. Margaret Thatcher had constructed and mobilised a task force. Doubters prudently 'kept their heads down', reluctant in any case to defend the rates.

The Poll-Tax had a temporarily damaging effect on the Conservative Party, but it was not as profoundly disturbing as the European issues, or the earlier tensions for an imperialist party arising from decolonisation. The only problem was unpopularity just before an election. The party moved in to change the leader and the policy. By April 1992, under a new Leader, John Major, the Conservatives were re-elected to a fourth term in office, with a secure majority. The Conservatives' capacity for adaptation and survival was plainly demonstrated. Still the Poll-Tax saga shows that governments cannot avoid confronting insoluble problems. Denis Healey's famous advice, 'if you're in a hole stop digging', turns out to be little more than a plea for masterly inactivity. Unfortunately governments live in holes, and are expected to keep digging. ●

Government, the courts and the citizen

The limits of judicial review in Britain

The law, and its instrument, the courts, do not figure prominently in political discourse in Britain. This is unusual; in most other European countries, the study of government and the law are inseparable, and an understanding of American politics is incomplete without an account of the courts, and, in particular, the Supreme Court. The comparative insignificance of the courts in the study of British government is not due simply to the ignorance and misunderstanding of political scientists, but reflects the realities of politics.

There are good reasons for the weak position of the courts in politics in Britain.

- There is no formal constitution, and no constitutional or 'supreme' court, indeed no scope for a court to make judgements about constitutionality.
- The doctrine and practice of parliamentary sovereignty gives to Parliament the authority in effect to say what the constitution is, to lay down what is constitutional, and to change the constitution as it thinks fit. Parliament carries out this function for the most part by masterly inactivity. It rarely mentions the constitution; constitutionality is defined by what it does, unconstitutionality by what it does not do.

  Parliamentary sovereignty excludes judicial review of legislation, and the doctrine of ministerial responsibility (to Parliament) excludes review of acts arising from policy or (within limits) ministerial discretion.
- The doctrine of the 'rule of law' (see Concepts) is too vague to strengthen the position of the courts, and comforting enough to persuade us that we need not be concerned for the further protection of the law.

It follows from this weakness of the constitutional structure that there is little scope in Britain for 'judicial review', that is the review by the courts of the actions of government, both the executive and the legislature.

The limits on judicial review in Britain are not much extended by the element of constitutionalism in British political culture. This ascribes considerable status and prestige to lawyers, courts and judges (dented by recent cases of spectacular miscarriage of justice but largely untouched by reform), and judges are called on as impartial and wise 'elders' to preside over various commissions and inquiries. However, Parliament remains the pre-eminent institution. In mass political culture there seems to be a broad commitment to an ill-defined constitutional morality (Magna Carta and All That), but no precise understanding of constitutional relationships. There is no enthusiasm for resorting to the courts (unlike USA); and some hostility, especially on the Left, towards judicial intervention in politics. Altogether there is not much scope for judicial review arising out of the constitution or a constitutional culture.

The British state is centralised in structure. There is not a hint of federalism, and local government is purely the creation of Parliament. So there is little ground for judicial intervention in jurisdictional disputes, though some cases have arisen in the relation of central and local government. It should be noted, further, that the legal systems in Scotland and Northern Ireland differ from that in England and Wales, but the British Parliament retains its supremacy. Even in the schemes for devolved assemblies in Scotland and Wales proposed in the 1970s, parliamentary sovereignty was retained.

The classic model of judicial review is the USA. The US Constitution, Article III, has been interpreted to empower the Supreme Court to review the acts of the other two 'branches' of government. From time to time the Supreme Court has used this power in notable decisions relating, for example, to racial discrimination, religion in public life, abortion, the drawing of congressional district boundaries, and a series of welfare and regulatory laws under the 'New Deal' programmes of the 1930s. The Court then earned itself the title, 'a third House, unknown to the constitution', but since the 1930s the Court has been less 'activist', confining itself more often to strict construction (interpretation) of the constitution.

Most of the work of the US Supreme Court lies in practice not in judging what is constitutional but in settling jurisdictional disputes arising within the federal system between the states and the federal (Washington) government, and in interpreting the meaning of statutes. However, the US Supreme Court is clearly a Supreme Court, able to engage in judicial review in the broadest sense of pronouncing on the constitutionality of the acts of government. There is no question that the Court is part of the political process; by its mode of appointment and its remit it is a political court, and none the worse for that, Americans might say.

By contrast the process of judicial review in Britain is limited; the term refers not to the broad sweep of American constitutional review, but to the narrower procedures of the review of government administration as distinct from policy. This weakness of judicial review in Britain may be regarded as a constitutional anomaly or defect, for the American democratic ideal of separate but mutually checking and balancing powers is not achieved. The liberal constitutionalists of the eighteenth century who drew up the US Constitution were concerned to preclude or moderate despotism. The US Constitution goes some way to achieving separation of powers, though at some cost in effective power of government. In Britain the executive and legislature are virtually fused, the judiciary is formally separate, but there is only weak review of either by the judiciary. Effective power to govern is achieved at the expense of checks and balances. By American standards the British parliamentary system is decidedly unbalanced.

EXERCISE
An unbalanced constitution

25.1 Does it worry you that the law is comparatively weak in the British system of government?

■ DOCUMENT 25.1
The limits of the law
Duport Steels Ltd v Sirs 1980, [1980] IWLR 142 House of Lords

The case involved the legal immunities of trade unions in conducting strikes. This was a matter of public controversy. The Appeal Court had decided in effect against the union. This reflected the wishes of government and probably the trend of public opinion, but of course the question was whether it reflected Britain's (perhaps old-fashioned and out-dated) labour laws. Lord Scarman in his judgement asserted the necessary subordination of the courts to Parliament where statute law applied. This is a cogent statement of a fundamental principle of the British Constitution.

The immunities of trade unions were substantially reduced by Parliament during the 1980s; Lord Scarman declared that they should not be reduced by the courts acting as law-makers:

'My basic criticism of all three judgements in the Court of Appeal is that in their desire to do justice the court failed to do justice according to law. When one is considering law in the hands of the judges, law means the body of rules and guidelines within which society requires its judges to administer justice. Legal systems differ in the width of the discretionary power granted to judges: but in developed societies limits are invariably set, beyond which the judges may not go. Justice in such societies is not left to the unguided, even if experienced, sage sitting under the spreading oak tree.

In our society the judges have in some aspects of their work a discretionary power to do justice so wide that they may be regarded as law-makers....

But in the field of statute law the judge must be obedient to the will of Parliament as expressed in its enactments. In this field Parliament makes, and un-makes, the law: the judge's duty is to interpret and to apply the law, not to change it to meet the judge's idea of what justice requires. Interpretation does, of course, imply in the interpreter a power of choice where differing constructions are possible. But our law requires the judge to choose the construction which in his judgement best meets the legislative purpose of the enactment. If the result be unjust but inevitable, the judge may say so and invite Parliament to reconsider its provision. But he must not deny the statute....'

Within these limits, which cannot be said in a free society possessing elective legislative institutions to be narrow or constrained, judges, as the remarkable judicial career of Lord Denning himself shows, have a genuine creative role. ■

Lord Scarman's exposition indicates the nature of the judicial function. The judge considers and identifies the facts of the case, and relates them to:

- the past, the law and precedent
- the future, the consequences – some understanding here of right and justice
- the present, the procedures of the court and the proper role of the judge.

There is much scope for creativity in these functions – the facts, precedents, the meaning of words, the intentions of Parliament, the consequences of particular decisions are open to endless dispute. The law, it has been said, is like a piano – it needs a score and a player to make music; and the judge is the player, not the composer.

The institutional structure

Separation of powers
The judiciary stands apart from executive and legislature, and is formally non-political. But, of course, the complete separation of the judiciary is impossible, even if independence from government is largely secured. Three government Ministers have responsibilities for matters connected with the judiciary.

1 The Lord Chancellor, a member of the House of Lords and of the Cabinet and usually a lawyer-politician, is responsible for the running of the courts and appoints all judges.
2 The Attorney-General and the Solicitor-General for England and Wales again are lawyer-politicians, sitting in the House of Commons. They advise the government and departments, appear in Court on behalf of the Crown; and the Attorney-General supervises the work of the Director of Public Prosecutions.
3 The Home Secretary is responsible for the maintenance of law and order, and for the work of the police forces (and has a direct responsibility for the Metropolitan Police) and the prisons, and takes charge of legislation related to criminal justice.

An incomplete separation of powers?

25.2 Is it satisfactory that the judicial system should be in the hands of 'lawyer-politicians'?

Thus government and the judiciary are not absolutely separated, but judges enjoy high standing, and are drawn from the small (6–7000) largely autonomous profession of barristers, the senior branch of the divided profession of law. Judges are appointed for life, and are not beholden to the government. It may be contended that judges are upper middle class in origin and education, and conservative and narrow in outlook. But, even more than in the US Supreme Court, they are subservient to the law rather than the government. Hence it is not usually convincing, as it may be in USA, to describe a judge as 'conservative', 'liberal' or 'activist'.

The structure of the courts
The legal system described here is that of England and Wales; Scotland has its own legal system and Northern Ireland is different again. The general analysis still applies.

The lower courts include:

- Magistrates' Courts – several hundred local courts, in which mostly lay magistrates (Justices of the Peace) deal with petty crime
- County Courts – over one hundred, in which judges and 'Recorders', part-time, judges deal with civil cases
- Crown Courts – almost one hundred centres, in which judges and 'Recorders' deal with criminal cases.

The higher courts include:

- The High Court with three divisions: Chancery (finance, tax, wills); Family; and Queen's Bench (civil law) all with judges of the High Court under respectively the Vice-Chancellor, the President and the Lord Chief Justice (the highest judicial office)
- The Court of Appeal with Criminal and Civil Divisions, the latter presided over by the Master of the Rolls (the second highest judicial office)
- The House of Lords – not the House of Lords really, but specially appointed Lords of Appeal, presided over (but not often in person) by the Lord Chancellor

- The Judicial Committee of the Privy Council is a group of Law Lords acting as a Court of Appeal from some members of the Commonwealth – not often called upon now.

The profession of law

The legal profession no doubt enjoys the cautious respect of the people (at least the non-criminal section), but has many critics.

■ DOCUMENT 25.2
The lawyers denounced

a) From Noel Annan, 1990, p. 175
Lawyers are the most self-intoxicated and oblivious to the public needs of any profession in England.

b) From A. Sampson, 1983, p. 169
The law is the most extreme British example of a closed and self-regulating community, with all its strengths and weaknesses...they enjoy the most restrictive monopoly of all, protected by one of the oldest trade unions.

c) From J. Paxman, 1991, p. 108
It is a deeply conservative trade which has resolutely resisted most attempts to bring it into the twentieth century, to make it more efficient, or to make access to the law more available to the ordinary citizen ■

EXERCISE
The lawyers denounced

25.3 Do these criticisms look wildly extravagant?

The profession is still small by US standards, proportionately about half the size of the American profession, which suggests the basic problem, that you cannot have the benefits of law without lawyers, and all that implies about cost, mystification, delay and the true professional's concern for personal performance and self-esteem as against public service.

The profession is divided between solicitors (now about 70 000) and barristers (6–7000). Only barristers have the right to speak in the higher courts (a hardly defensible but jealously guarded privilege), and full-time judges are still drawn exclusively from among barristers. The bar is also the training ground for many Members of Parliament and Ministers (there are 53 barristers in the House of Commons, mostly Conservative) and this reinforces the characteristic style of British politics, adversarial debate, defending innocent and guilty with equal vehemence, concerned for victory not for truth.

The nature of the profession of barrister is of particular significance since judges are drawn from it, by secret processes within the Lord Chancellor's Department. That Department also controls conferment of the title of Queen's Counsel or QC (known in the trade as 'taking silk') upon senior and distinguished barristers, and a qualification in practice for promotion to the bench of judges.

Barristers reflect the well-known characteristics of the male half of the English upper middle class. Its leading members, the QCs, are typically public school and Oxbridge educated. Of the QCs appointed in the 1980s about two thirds were from public schools (and hence mostly it may be assumed from affluent and aspirant families) and the same proportion attended Oxford or Cambridge (J. Paxman, 1991, p. 109). It is contended that a narrow social background, unrepresentative of the mass of the people, and unfamiliar with ordinary lives, is damaging to the practice of the profession. This is a familiar argument in England, applicable to the civil service, Conservative Cabinets, the army and indeed almost any substantial organisation, public or private (with the exception of the police) where there is money to be made, and prestige and power to be acquired.

The argument is plausible enough.

- Direct experience is a good source of sympathy and understanding, and applies in most areas of life. Only the teacher fully understands the problems of teaching, only a student knows what it is really like to be a student, only the poor...and so on.
- Relevant experience is broadly shaped by the forces we call social class, and class background shapes and limits our understanding of life and people.

Evidence for the broad thesis is not difficult to find, especially where the class background is reinforced by a narrow or enclosed work situation – for example, the Old Etonian judge, concerned for the morals of maidservants or the virtues of Old Etonian bank-robbers, or the poorly educated trade union shop steward who sees the new productivity programme as a move in the class war. Such examples may be caricatures, but not inventions.

There is truth here but it is difficult to make out a more precise case. There are counter-arguments.

- Most people are subject to a range of influences; by the time they reach their 40s or 50s their experience of adult, and especially professional, life is more significant than education.
- An able and well-trained professional, whether in the law, the civil service or a trade union, ought, as part of professional expertise, to be able to transcend the limitations of background. This may reasonably be expected in all kinds of activities. For example, it is well-known that some of the best coaches are not themselves the best athletes; and many (but not all) women trust male gynaecologists and even male midwives.
- The limitations of background can be directly resisted. A judge may, indeed, should, strive to understand the point of view of the poor, the unemployed, the ill-educated, even the maid-servant reading about Lady Chatterley.

The problem in the case of the law is that the socialisation and training derived from professional life may fail to broaden experience and counteract the limitations of early background. The wigs and fancy dress emphasise the apartness of the profession and the claim to special status protects the profession from any form of accountability or even criticism as undermining the rule of law. The huge costs of the law round off the argument: the law is a service for the rich. This is a serious argument which affects the reception of any plea for the extension of law into the area of government. If more law means more lawyers – as it must – then the case for more law loses some of its appeal, and the claim that more law means more democracy looks especially weak.

The argument that the judiciary suffers from a fundamental bias has been forcefully put by a distinguished Professor of Public Law, John Griffith. Professor Griffith's thesis is persuasive in general, but it has not yet been demonstrated that there is an extensive and consistent bias in the decisions of the judges. We know that there have been grave miscarriages of justice, and there is some evidence that judges lose some of their sharpness and even their capacity for staying awake after what is a normal retiring age in other professions. But there is no consistent evidence of persistent bias, for example, in favour of property or the government or against particular classes of appellant. Indeed, in many cases on appeal the judges are divided, and sometimes criticise each other quite strongly. We know, too, that judges sometimes make policy by their decisions, but this is a consequence of the nature and role of law in society.

The 'insufficient evidence' argument against the Griffith thesis is valid though it does not preclude the truth of the proposition. However, in the case of the judges the evidence of systematic bias is not totally convincing. Rather the tendency of British judges is to interpret the law narrowly, and as far as possible to leave to Parliament the policy questions. If there is a bias it is towards the law as it stands, interpreted conservatively; the judges are in favour of order based on law, and do not see the courts as the engines of change. But to concede this, is to concede some part of the thrust of Griffith's argument.

Reform of the judicial structure

Reform of the profession of the law is a slow process, resisted by a privileged and conservative profession, claiming that most of its privileges are 'in the public interest'. Reform is most likely to be initiated by a reforming Lord Chancellor, Lord Mackay and new senior judicial appointments – in effect, reform from within. The adoption of a Bill of Rights (not favoured by the Conservative Party) would change the work of the judiciary, and thus change their behaviour. The growing impact of European law, now unavoidable, has a similar effect. In 1992 the Labour Party proposed a Department of Legal Administration and a Courts Inspectorate; the Liberal Democrats proposed a Ministry of Justice ('separating responsibility for civil liberties and justice from that for order and security') and a Judicial Services Commission to appoint judges.

The Conservative government has moved one step towards reform by making the Lord Chancellor's Department answerable to the House of Commons through a Minister, and through the Home Office Select Committee. Lord Mackay has initiated some reforms, and a Royal Commission on Criminal Justice has been established. But the Thatcher government's approach to the legal profession showed none of the determination, not to say deep hostility, of its assault on the public professions (teachers, civil servants, even doctors), and the achievements of reform have been slight (notably the solicitors' conveyancing monopoly, a legal racket for sure, remains virtually undisturbed).

Altogether the judicial structure has moved on to the political agenda under the impact of European law, the pressure for constitutional reform, grave miscarriages of justice, the Citizen's Charter initiatives, and the high cost and inaccessibility of the law to most people. The Lord Chancellor and the senior judges who direct the system are no longer either remote or respected without question.

The principles and practice of judicial review

Judicial review

The scope for judicial review of acts of government is limited and judges draw back from questions of policy, which challenge the sovereignty of Parliament. Legislation is drafted in some detail and the courts have preferred to confine themselves to questions of legality based on the strict interpretation of statutes. Nevertheless, there is scope for judicial review of the acts of government even under its statutory authority: the statute itself and the policy implied cannot be called in question, but administrative acts may be reviewed by the courts if a complaint is put forward.

Britain has no separate code of administrative law or practice, but in the last 50 years the courts have developed what amount to principles of administrative law. The 'Wednesbury' case (1948) has become a classic source for a doctrine of reasonableness. The case concerned the opening of cinemas on Sundays. The Corporation had imposed a condition that no children under 15 should be admitted. The condition was declared acceptable on the grounds, not that the Corporation thought it reasonable nor that the court thought it reasonable, but that the Corporation had come to a decision which was not 'so unreasonable that no reasonable authority could ever have come to it'. An example of unreasonableness offered by a judge was the dismissal of a teacher because she had red hair.

EXERCISE

The Wednesbury rule

25.4 Does the Wednesbury rule appear to be satisfactory?

The grounds for judicial review have now been developed beyond the Wednesbury rule of reasonableness. In the GCHQ case (1985) Lord Diplock summarised the grounds for review as follows:

1 the decision-maker must be qualified, 'empowered by public law to make decisions'
2 the decision must be legal, based on a correct understanding of the law that regulates his decision-making

3 the decision must be rational – the Wednesbury rule
4 the decision must be procedurally proper, observing express procedural rules; also, observing basic rules of natural justice (a right to be heard by an impartial judge), and procedurally fair.

Thus the three crucial tests are:

1 illegality
2 irrationality
3 procedural propriety including contravening the rules of national justice.

There is a fourth ground, proportionality, favoured by Lord Diplock, and the European Courts of Justice and Human Rights, but not yet accepted in Britain.

Armed with this guidance the courts proceed to engage in the judicial review of government administration. The number of cases of judicial review increased markedly in the 1980s from under 400 in 1981 to over 2000 in 1990.

Consider these cases.

■ DOCUMENT 25.3
Cases in the judicial review of administration

a) Padfield v Minister for Agriculture and Fisheries 1968, House of Lords AC 997
Lord Reid stated:
'The question at issue in this appeal is the nature and extent of the Minister's duty under...the Act of 1958 in deciding whether to refer to the committee of investigation a complaint as to the operation of any scheme made by persons adversely affected by the scheme. The respondent [the Minister] contends that his only duty is to consider a complaint fairly and that he is given an unfettered discretion with regard to every complaint either to refer it or not to refer it to the committee as he may think fit....

I do not think that is right. Parliament must have conferred the discretion with the intention that it should be used to promote the policy and objects of the Act; the policy and objects of the Act must be determined by construing the Act as a whole and construction is always a matter of law for the court. In a matter of this kind it is not possible to draw a hard and fast line, but if the Minister, by reason of his having misconstrued the Act or for any other reason, so uses his discretion so as to thwart or run counter to the policy and objects of the Act, then our law would be very defective if persons aggrieved were not entitled to the protection of the court. So it is first necessary to construe the Act....'

[Thus the Minister's discretion was not unfettered: it was discretion to serve the purposes of the Act. So the Minister was told to submit the complaint to the committee of investigation. He did so and then rejected its advice – as was his right.]

b) Laker Airways (Laker Airways v Department of Trade 1977, Court of Appeal QB 643)
Laker was granted permission by the Civil Aviation Authority to fly a cut-price service (Skytrain) between London and New York. The Secretary of State subsequently issued 'guidance' to CAA, in effect confirming the monopoly right of the nationalised British Airways on long-haul routes. The court ruled that the Secretary of State's guidance was invalid (ultra vires); the Civil Aviation Act of 1971 permitted 'guidance' but only within the objectives of the Act which included the avoidance of a BA monopoly on long distance routes.
[In effect the Labour government was trying to vary the policy of its predecessor without changing the legislation. It did not work.]

c) Leicester Rugby Football Club (Wheeler v Leicester City Council, 1985, House of Lords AC 1054)
In this case the courts considered whether the City Council could ban the RFC from using its recreation ground for 12 months because three of their players were joining a RFU tour to South Africa. The lower courts held that the Council's action was not unreasonable in the Wednesbury sense. The Appeal Court held that the Council had acted unreasonably, and in particular, the procedures adopted had been unreasonable. One judge said that the Council's action constituted a punishment, but the Club had done no wrong in law, and could not be punished.

d) The Home Office and television licences (Congreve v Home Office 1976, Court of Appeal IQB 629)
The cost of a television licence was raised. Some 20 000 licence holders chose to renew their licences one month early (before the increase came into force) since there was a sav-

ing. The Home Office threatened to revoke such licences if an extra fee were not paid. The Court of Appeal ruled finally against the Home Office; revocation was an improper use of the discretionary power available to him under the relevant legislation.

e) Lee v Department of Education and Science 1967, Court of Appeal 66LGR 21
The governors of Enfield Grammar School submitted that they had insufficient time [four days] to make representations about changing the selective character of the school. [The judge wished] 'to show and to stress that at no time have the courts been concerned with the merits of this educational controversy. The duty of the courts – and it is one which they will never shirk – is to be vigilant to ensure that the government of this country, whether it be local or national, is conducted in accordance with the will of Parliament.... So long...as the rule of law is observed, the courts take no part in controversies of that nature, leaving them to be resolved through discussion, persuasion and the ballot box.... [The plaintiffs claim] that the time allowed so far by the Secretary of State for representations has been far too short.... [In] my judgement the time so far allowed by the Secretary of State is wholly unreasonable, in the circumstances of the case, and amounts to a denial to the persons named in section 17(5) of the rights conferred upon them by that subsection...' ∎

EXERCISES
The ground of judicial review

25.5 Which of the three grounds are used in each of these cases?
25.6 Do the judges find ample scope for intervention in these rules?

The courts and the executive
There is one area, national security on which the courts are reluctant to intrude. This is an area of 'executive privilege' where the judgement of the executive is deemed to lie beyond challenge. Some cases were considered in Chapter 20, in the discussion of secrecy and the reporting of the civil war in Northern Ireland. It is raised again in questions of freedom of speech (see below). The classic recent case is again GCHQ; and the pre-eminence of the governments assessment of national security was confirmed.

■ DOCUMENT 25.4
The GCHQ case

a) Council of civil service unions v Minister for the Civil Service 1985, AC 374, House of Lords
Lord Diplock:
'The reason why the Minister for the Civil Service decided on 22 December 1983 to withdraw this benefit [the right to belong to a trade union) was in the interests of national security. National security is the responsibility of the executive government; what action is needed to protect its interests is, as the cases cited by my learned friend, Lord Roskill, establish and common sense itself dictates, a matter upon which those upon whom the responsibility rests, and not the courts of justice, must have the last word. It is par excellence a non-justiciable question. The judicial process is totally inept to deal with the sort of problem which it involves.

The executive government likewise decided, and this would appear to be a collective decision of Cabinet Ministers involved, that the interests of national security required that no notice should be given of the decision before administrative action had been taken to give effect to it.

There was ample evidence to which reference is made by others of your Lordships that this was indeed a real risk; so the crucial point of law in this case is whether procedural propriety must give way to national security when there is conflict between (1) on the one hand, the prima facie rule of "procedural propriety" in public law, and (2) on the other hand, action that is needed to be taken in the interests of national security, for which the executive government bears the responsibility and alone has access to sources of information that qualify it to judge what the necessary action is. To that there can, in my opinion, be only one sensible answer. That answer is "Yes"' ■

Apart from the issue of national security, the government's claim to the confidentiality of Cabinet proceedings was tested in the courts in relation to the publication of the Crossman Diaries (Attorney General *v* Jonathan Cape Ltd 1976). The government's claim was upheld, though in this case because of the lapse of time, about ten years, the government held that confidentiality was no longer justified.

Jurisdictional disputes
In the USA a major function of the courts is to ad-
judicate or referee disputes between the two elements in the federal system, the states and the federal government. Each has entrenched rights under the constitution, and neither can claim sovereign power. Supremacy rests in the constitution, or in the Supreme Court which interprets it, or, more problematically in the people. Britain is – happily, some would say – free of such jurisdictional uncertainties and disputes. Local government is entirely the creature of central government, and the only scope for dispute lies in the grounds of illegality, irrationality and improper procedure.

In the last two decades the relations of central and local government have been tense, and conflicts have arisen (see Chapter 24). When these came before the courts it was not open to the courts to declare that the central government was acting unconstitutionally, nor even that there should be a presumption in favour of the existence and vitality of local government. There can be no such presumption in law. Instead disputes between centre and local government were settled according to the standard grounds for review.

■ DOCUMENT 25.5
The Tameside case

Secretary of State for Education v Tameside Metropolitan Borough Council 1976–7, 3 WLR 641. Appeal Court
Under the Education Act of 1944 the Secretary of State was empowered to issue directions to an education authority which in his view [the Act says, 'if he is satisfied'] was proposing to act 'unreasonably'. In this case the Secretary of State directed Tameside to continue with its scheme of reorganisation of secondary schools [as non-selective schools], as proposed by the former Labour council, while the newly elected Conservative council proposed to continue with existing selective grammar schools. The House of Lords held that 'unreasonable' was not the same as 'wrong in the eyes of the Secretary of State'. There was no evidence to support unreasonableness. Thus, some administrative disruption was unavoidable following an election and a change of controlling majority on the council; but the selection process was acceptable; the co-operation of teachers could be assumed. The Court concluded that the Council had not acted unreasonably, so the Secretary of State had 'misdirected himself' – an interesting phrase, allowing the court to suggest a

wrong process of decision making, rather than a wrong Minister. ■

EXERCISES
The Tameside case

25.7 Was the Court showing its bias against the Labour government's policy of reorganisation of schools on comprehensive lines?

25.8 Was the Court right to take note that the new Council had fought the election on a platform of maintaining some selective schools?

In cases of judicial review the courts do not put forward their own views, nor assess the policies of government, nor challenge statute law; but within the grounds of judicial review they have proposed for themselves, they may exercise significant influence on the activity of government. Elected governments could be left to judge for themselves the reasonableness of their actions and the propriety of their procedures. In fact the courts have successfully claimed to make or review those judgements. This constitutes a significant limitation on the freedom to act of duly elected governments – for better or for worse. Given the substantial powers of British governments there is a good case for preferring such limitations on governments.

Police accountability

In happier days (an indefinite time in the past) the policeman was the village bobby, helping old ladies across the street, and effortlessly frustrating a robbery at the local bank. By the 1990s our picture of the police had been transformed by rapidly rising crime (despite much increased expenditure on the police), and disturbing evidence of improper conduct, indiscipline and corruption not to mention incompetence, in police forces, and ugly pictures of police in riot gear dealing violently with violence.

Of course the old idealised picture was inaccurate, and the new stereotype no doubt reflects some selective exaggeration of recent experience. Even so, it is evident that there is something of a crisis in police affairs; the police have responded inadequately to formidable new challenges, including urban decay, immigration, drugs, a massive increase in crime, terrorism and some specially difficult problems in public order – violent picketing, and unruly political protest. In the light of this menacing catalogue of social change, it is not perhaps surprising that a force of village bobbies has been tested almost to destruction.

The failures of the police are evident and disturbing, but the police are necessarily more than just another failing and inadequate public service. Their failings are the more serious, because the police exercise a substantial part of the coercive power of the state. The police are not simply part of the welfare state or a nationalised industry; they keep the peace and wield substantial powers over the citizen, including the power of arrest. Hence the 'police crisis' has raised the question of police accountability, and the place of the police in the structure of government has become a political issue.

The police do not fit well into the structure of government, partly for historical reasons – the constable was an officer of the law, rather than of government, and developed within the shadowy structure of early government, among parishes, boroughs, and shires, along with the ancient office of Justice of the Peace. The police constable still, in theory, carries out his duties as a peace officer by virtue of his personal office rather than as an employee – in this the constable resembles a Justice of the Peace.

This locally based, devolved power was accepted by central government, which occasionally called out the troops (some of whom were local militia) in times of trouble (Peterloo, the Chartists, the General Strike) but held back from instituting a national police force. Peel's establishment in 1839 of the Metropolitan Police (the Peelers or Bobbies), under a responsibility to the Home Office, marks a pragmatic attempt to improve policing where it seemed (to people living in the capital) to matter most, without tackling the formidable problems inherent in any kind of national system. The story sketched here is an interesting indication of how government was not invented but grew, and improvisation and 'adhockery' preceded systematic planning – with remarkable success, it must be said. Contemporary forms of government have to be seen in this third dimension of history with its geological sub-stratum of structures and assumptions.

The place of the police in government is now based on the Police Acts of 1964 (1967 in Scotland), and 1976, the Police and Criminal Evidence Act 1984, and the Public Order Act of 1986. The police service is a peculiar (sui generis) combination of local and central government, and the common law.

- Police authorities (41 in England and Wales, 8 in Scotland) are based on local authorities (counties or amalgamated counties). Two thirds of members are councillors but one third are drawn from the nominated Justices of the Peace.
- The Home Secretary has substantial powers in funding and certain supervisory powers, and is advised by H M Inspectors of Police.
- The Chief Constable heads the local police force, and directs its operations. The Chief Constable wields substantial power and his accountability to the authority and even to the Home Secretary is in practice limited. He is not in the position of an employee of either local or central government. It would not be true to say the Chief Constable is 'a law unto himself' but in practice accountability can be thin. Here is some indication of the complex mix of authority and accountability of the Chief Constable.

EXERCISE
The powers of the Chief Constable

25.9 Does the Chief Constable appear from this analysis to be 'a law unto himself'?

The power of the Chief Constable in relation to Police Authorities and the Home Secretary is the main, political or structural, part of the general problem of the accountability of the police. Police accountability can be summed up in the following document.

■ DOCUMENT 25.7
Police accountability

1 Structural or political – the relationship of the Chief Constable to Police Authorities and Home Secretary (Document 25.6).
2 Judicial – the police constable is not an employee, and can be sued. Similarly a Chief Constable is answerable to the courts for an illegal decision or action.
3 Administrative – there is a Police Complaints Authority, with an independent chairman. The police investigate complaints themselves, but the PCA monitors the outcome or in the more serious cases, supervises the investigation.
4 Parliamentary – Questions may be asked in the indirect form of asking whether the Home Secretary intends to inquire, call for a report etc. In most cases the Home Secretary draws back from involvement in operational matters.
5 The Parliamentary Commissioner for Administration (Ombudsman) does not investigate complaints against the police. ■

There is no easy solution to the problem of the ac-

■ DOCUMENT 25.6
The position of the Chief Constable

	Police Authority	Home Secretary	Chief Constable
Appointment of Chief Constable	Yes	approve	–
Compel retirement	Yes	approve	–
Direction and control of police	No	No	Yes
Budget, expenditure	Yes	Yes, overall funding	–
Other appointments	No	No	Yes
Discipline	No	No	Yes
Calling for Reports	Yes, though limited in practice	Yes	–
General policy	No	Yes – issues instructions, guidelines, requires reports	Yes

■

countability of the police in a democracy. It may be contended that the police should properly be independent, like judges for political reasons, or doctors of medicine, on technical or professional grounds. This argument is not totally convincing (even for judges and doctors). On the other hand, control by elected politicians raises dangers of a political police, or even a 'police state', or corruption, or most likely, the simple distortions of the party system based on the 'winner-takes-all' ballot. The possibilities of corruption exist under independence or democratic control, and are high where one party rules an authority continuously. Hence it may be that the present hybrid system of mixed control, and semi-independence meets some of the difficulties. But there remains scope for improving the complaints procedure, and the liaison and communication between the police and the community. Much has been done in this connection since Lord Scarman reported on the Brixton riots of 1981.

EXERCISE
The democratic control of the police

25.10 Is a Police Authority entitled to withhold funds for police equipment it disapproves of – e.g. horses or CS gas?

The historical development of the police force from the medieval office of constable, and a desire (based on good intentions but muddled thinking) to avoid a single police force, have left Britain one of the few modern states without a national police force. Most countries (e.g. USA, France) have both a national force and local forces. Britain has edged toward a national police force through the co-ordination of the local forces by the Association of Chief Police Officers, and by the Home Office. In the Miners' Strike of 1984–5 there was well-organised co-operation through a 'National Reporting Centre', and there is a national computer system. Further, a Crown Prosecuting Service has taken over the work of deciding upon and pursuing prosecutions.

This creeping nationalisation is a typically British response to a complex problem – better to tinker and tack, rather than make any radical reform based on a rethinking of fundamentals. It may well be that a national police force, made politically accountable through a Minister to Parliament, would be a genuinely democratic alternative to the present system of over-mighty Chief Constables.

Rights, civil liberties and the citizen

Right
'Right' is a difficult word, like community, but with a stronger emotional charge. It has a long history in the struggle for freedom, especially those freedoms of the citizen in organised or civil society which are known as civil liberties. These include notably freedom of expression (including public assembly and meetings), freedom of religion and freedom from arbitrary arrest. These are the freedoms we associate readily with the Western democratic ideal, in contrast to the practices of former communist states, or Latin American 'dictatorships'. Such freedoms are regarded as so fundamental that they are promoted as 'rights' – from the Bill of Rights through the Declaration of Rights of Man of 1789 to the Bill of Rights of the Charter 88 campaign in contemporary Britain.

A 'right' is a claim to a condition or kind of treatment (freedom or privilege) which cannot be denied. It may be justified as divine or natural in origin, but more rationally as a claim which is essential to life itself, or more specifically, civilised life in a democracy. The argument is circular – tending to define rights by notions of democracy, and democracy by assertions of right; in the end the ground of a right might be simply the existence of a strong preference. However, some implied justification of this kind is necessary, if only to head off competing rights (e. g. of property or religion). But thereafter a right should be established without question or challenge as an entitlement for which the only qualification is 'citizenship'. This begs the question of the rights of minors (children) and non-citizens, notably immigrants and unborn babies, prisoners of war.

Historically, rights have been asserted in broad terms rather than defined. The historical inheritance of a rhetoric of rights, and the modern endeavour to define and establish them in a Bill of Rights are treated in the Assessment. Here we consider three of the legally based 'freedoms' which figure in most statements of rights – freedom of the person, speech and protest.

Freedom of the person
This includes freedom from arbitrary arrest and unlawful detention. This is based on the legal remedy of Habeas Corpus, established since the late seventeenth century. In practice the citizen's protection from arrest and detention without charge is established by statute, though difficul-

ties arise for mental health patients and prisoners. The practice of internment in Northern Ireland (now abandoned) was possible only by the suspension of Habeas Corpus (which trans-gresses the Bill of Rights 1688).

While 'law-abiding' citizens may feel safe in their rights as free-born Englishmen, the law needs to protect those upon whom fall the suspicions of the police – both the innocent and the guilty. The rights of police and suspect are covered by Judges' Rules, the Police and Criminal Evidence Act 1984 and other laws (e.g. the Bail Act of 1976) and administrative rules. A series of miscarriages of justice notably in cases involving Irish 'terrorist' offences has raised grave questions about the conduct of the police, the capacity of police officers to observe the proper codes and limitations on the treatment of suspects, the attitude of the police to the Irish and ethnic minorities, and the accountability of the police (see above).

It is apparent that the police have not adequately met the professional challenges arising from major social and political change – the extension of the continuing civil war in Northern Ireland to the mainland of Britain, immigration, unemployment and urban decay, together with a collapse of the culture of deference. The formerly idealised 'British Bobby', PC Dixon of Dock Green, friendly but authoritative and absolutely incorrupt, has passed away, along with the unstressed society which gave rise to the culture of the Ealing comedy films.

Freedom of Speech

The freedom of speech which counts is the freedom to speak in public (see also Chapter 20). What you say within the circle of family and friends is between you all; what you say on the soap-box at Hyde Park Corner matters more, and when it comes to publication for a sizeable number of readers and listeners, then your freedom is restricted. Such restrictions are justified, and for the most part justifiable, 'in the public interest'. But, as Chapter 20 on the Media showed, the balancing of individual freedom against the claims of public interest is a sensitive and difficult matter, and the government is always inclined to overestimate the interests of the state (of which it is the embodiment), especially in secrecy, and ought not to be allowed to act as judge in its own case.

Free speech is not of course guaranteed in a constitution or Bill of Rights, and its protection depends on the law and the courts' interpretation of the law. Freedom is defined negatively: you are free to do what so far has not been prohibited. However, the courts have to work within a formidable collection of legal restrictions on free speech. In addition to the Official Secrets Act and considerations of national security, there are legal restrictions on defamation, blasphemy, obscenity, and the incitement to racial hatred. There is also a range of restrictions on meetings and demonstrations as well as speech, relating to the preservation of public order – riot, affray, rout, unlawful assembly, creating a public nuisance, obstructing a police officer. (Hyde Park is a local exception, not a symbol of freedom). The media are also restrained by their own rules, codes of practice and complaints procedures.

There are further restrictions arising under the law of confidentiality. When the court allowed the publication of the Crossman Diaries (including much material based on Cabinet meetings) the law of confidentiality was reinforced. The law of contempt (of court) imposes further restraint on the reporting of cases pending or ongoing in the courts (sub judice), in order to avoid 'trial by newspaper or television'. This leads to the initiation of legal proceedings in order to avoid media reporting (the issue of gagging writs as practised by Robert Maxwell to forestall investigation of his business practices). The law of contempt also bears heavily on the media when they refuse to name the sources of their information.

Altogether the freedom of public speech is much restricted, and a government inclined to secretiveness and with easy access to the courts can find support in the law, and no bar in a constitutional affirmation of a right to free speech. In one area, privacy, there are few legal restrictions. There is no law against taking a photograph by a giant telephoto lens of a bathing princess (but there are laws about trespass, obstruction, monitoring of telephone conversations). The media believe they labour under enough restrictions already. The true upholder of the principle of freedom of speech must argue that the freedom cannot be limited to those things which are acceptable in the politest society. The US Supreme Court specifically extended the right of free speech to the right to burn the national flag in public. The insulting of the national flag is a much more serious matter than the embarrassment of a princess.

Contempt of Court

■ DOCUMENT 25.8
The Thalidomide case

*Attorney General v Times Newspapers Ltd 1974
Act 273, House of Lords*
The drug, thalidomide, manufactured by the
Distillers Company, caused women who took it
in early pregnancy to give birth to deformed
babies. The drug was withdrawn in 1961. Some
ten years later *The Sunday Times* proposed to
publish a second article criticising the Distillers
Company's scheme of compensation to
families suffering the effects of the drug. The
Attorney General sought an injunction to
prevent publication on grounds of contempt of
court. He won in the Divisional Court, lost in the
Court of Appeal and won again in the House of
Lords.

Lord Simon's judgement included the
following passage:

'The public interest in freedom of discussion
(of which the freedom of the press is one aspect) stems from the requirement that members
of a democratic society should be sufficiently informed that they may influence intelligently the
decisions which may affect themselves. The
public thus has a permanent interest in the
general administration of justice and the general
course of the law. This is recognised by justice
being openly administered and its proceedings
freely reported, by public debate on the law and
on its incidence. But, as regards particular
litigation, society, through its political and legal
institutions, has established the relevant law as
a continuing code, and has further established
special institutions (courts of law) to make the
relevant decisions on the basis of such law. The
public at large has delegated its decision-
making in this sphere to its microcosm, the jury
or judge...the paramount public interest...is that
the legal proceedings should progress without
interference...once the proceedings are concluded...the public interest in freedom of
discussion becomes paramount.' ■

EXERCISE
The Law of Contempt

25.11 Does this restriction of freedom of speech
appear reasonable?

Obscenity

■ DOCUMENT 25.9
The law of obscenity

*Last Exit to Brooklyn: R v Calder and Boyars Ltd
1968–9, [1969] 1QB 151 Court of Appeal*
The publishers appealed against their conviction under the Obscene Publications Act 1959.
Their appeal was allowed on the grounds that
the jury had been wrongly directed by the trial
judge.

Lord Justice Salmon's judgement included
the following passages:

'The test of obscenity is now laid down in
Section 1 of the Act of 1959 which, insofar as it
is material, reads as follows:
"(1) For the purposes of this Act an article
shall be deemed to be obscene if its effect...is,
if taken as a whole, such as to tend to deprave
and corrupt persons who are likely, having regard to all relevant circumstances, to read ...it."
[The judge emphasised the words "taken as a
whole".]
...Those other vital words "tend to deprave
and corrupt" really mean just what they say.
You have heard several efforts to define them.
"Tend" obviously means "have a tendency to"
or "be inclined to". "Deprave" is defined in some
dictionaries, as you heard, as "to make morally
bad; to pervert or corrupt morally".... The essence of the matter, you may think, is moral
corruption.
The appellants contend that this direction as
to the meaning of obscenity does not go far
enough; the learned judge should have gone
on, so they say, to explain that the essence of
moral corruption is to make a person behave
badly or worse than he otherwise would have
done, or to blur his perception of the difference
between good and bad. This court cannot accept that contention.... When, as here, a statute
lays down the definition of a word or phrase in
plain English it is rarely necessary and often
unwise for the judge to attempt to improve on or
redefine the definition.'
The judge went on to criticise the direction
given to the jury:
'In the view of this court, the proper direction
on a defence under Section 4 in a case such as
the present is that the jury must consider on the
one hand the number of readers they believe
would tend to be depraved and corrupted by
the book, the strength of the tendency to
deprave and corrupt, and the nature of the

depravity or corruption; on the other hand, they should assess the strength of the literary, sociological or ethical merit which they consider the book to possess. They should then weigh up all these factors and decide whether on balance the publication is proved to be justified as being for the public good....

The jury must set the standards of what is acceptable, of what is for the public good in the age in which we live.' ■

EXERCISE
Depravity and corruption

25.12 Note that the judge does after all spend time exploring the meaning of 'deprave and corrupt'. Is this formulation sufficient for a jury to come to a proper assessment about a book or other publication?

Public order and the right of peaceful protest

■ DOCUMENT 25.10
Public order

Extract from the Public Order Act 1986
12 Imposing conditions on public processions
(1) If the senior police officer, having regard to the time or place at which and the circumstances in which any public procession is being held or is intended to be held and to its route or proposed route, reasonably believes that:
   a) it may result in serious public disorder, serious damage to property or serious disruption to the life of the community, or
   b) the purpose of the persons organising it is the intimidation of others with a view to compelling them not to do an act they have a right to do or to do an act they have a right not to do, he may give directions imposing on the persons organising or taking part in the procession such conditions as appear to him necessary to prevent such disorder, damage, disruption or intimidation, including conditions as to the route of the procession or prohibiting it from entering any public place specified in the directions. ■

EXERCISE
Public processions

25.13 Does this clause infringe a right to peaceful protest by means of a public procession?

The redress of grievances – administrative justice

Modern governments intervene extensively in the life of the citizen. There is a large area of life in which the citizen is the client or receptor of the state's administration, taxed, regulated or provided for and looked after. In some cases, for example, welfare provision, the citizen is a willing receptor; in other cases, notably taxation, he or she resists. In these relationships the citizen does not enjoy the freedom of the customer to take his taxes and seek his benefits elsewhere. What remedies are open to the aggrieved citizen in face of a monopolistic and sometimes coercive state?

Remedies for the aggrieved citizen
1 The existing political system, which offers routes for the redress of grievances through Parliament, and the work of the MP in the constituency, to some extent through local government, and in the long term, through parties and elections.
2 The judicial system, which in some cases may offer costly and uncertain remedy.
3 Administrative tribunals, specially established to deal with grievances in matters such as welfare benefits, immigration, and procedures for inquiry and appeal in planning.
4 The special institution known as the Ombudsman, or Parliamentary Commissioner for Administration; and other Commissioners for local government and the Health Service.
5 A return to the market – government to intervene less; where possible, the citizen to become a customer in a competitive market, with all the rights of a customer, reinforced by regulation and by the 'Citizen's Charter'.

The role of the political system and the courts has been discussed above. The special procedures for redress of grievance or administrative justice (3,4 and 5) are now discussed.

Administrative tribunals
Over the last fifty years a number of special tribunals have been established to resolve disputes between citizen and state in matters such as welfare benefits, immigration, taxation; between individual and semi-independent corporations (for example, the producer boards in agriculture);

and between individuals, where the state carries some responsibility (notably between landlord and tenant in relation to the Rent Acts, and employers and workers in relation to employment law).

In some of these cases the state, or its servants, exercise powers verging on the arbitrary. Concern about the growing power of the 'bureaucracy' grew particularly at the time of the Crichel Down case (1954). The decision in that and similar cases infringed the rights of property. The report and recommendations of a Committee on Administrative Tribunals and Inquiries, presided over by Lord Franks (1957), led to the Tribunals and Inquiries Act 1958 (amended and consolidated 1971) and a standing Council on Tribunals (in Scotland a Committee). Ironically the Franks proposals have proved of most relevance and benefit not to the propertied classes but to the beneficiaries of the welfare state.

Franks rejected the argument that most disputes should be referred to the ordinary courts, which alone had the independence and proper procedures to dispense justice. Nevertheless, tribunals were not a branch of administration; they should be concerned to adjudicate rather than administer, seeking fairness and impartiality, under legally qualified chairmen. But, unlike the courts, the tribunals are intended to be quick, cheap, and informal, relying on expertise and commonsense, rather than case law.

On this basis, hundreds of cases are resolved each year in a variety of fields, and with no less satisfaction than before a court of law. The system is not without problems – for example, closed hearings, the reluctance to give reasons for decisions, the absence of case law and precedent, the non-availability of appeals, and the question of representation of parties, and legal aid. Some of these problems could be resolved by the use of the courts; that is, if you want a better system, there is a Rolls Royce system available, as long as you do not mind paying. Most aggrieved citizens settle happily for the homelier virtues of the Tribunal. In some small scale planning appeals there is a deliberate use of a 'seminar' method, which encourages applicants and neighbours to set out their claims and objections in a more or less friendly fashion.

Tribunals are often bracketed with Inquiries, but they are really quite different. A Tribunal typically adjudicates on an administrative decision or application, within the limits of an established policy. It works rather as an informal court, making a final decision, not usually open to appeal, and separate from the Minister. An Inquiry, frequent in the field of planning, is an open public inquiry to discover facts and make recommendations to the Minister, who may or may not accept them. In some cases, for example, the siting of a nuclear power station, or an airport, the issues are of major public interest and there is no question that the final choice is for the Minister not the Inquiry.

EXERCISE
Administrative justice

25.14 The Education Act of 1988 confers on parents some freedom of choice of school for their children: it allows them to state a preference, but given that places in favoured schools are limited, parents may be denied their preference. They have a right of appeal. Find out what arrangements are made by the local education authority for adjudicating appeals, and assess whether they are fair and impartial. (For example, who adjudicates the appeal, how easy is it for an appellant to present a case, what arguments are used).

Ombudsmen
This is the Swedish term now accepted to cover the Parliamentary Commissioners for Administration (1967) and similar officers (though not related to Parliament) for Northern Ireland (1969), the Health Services (1972–3) and Local Government (1974).

The Commissioners are by the terms of appointment independent of government, though their staff are civil servants on secondment. In fact the remit of the Commissioners is tightly drawn and there is, properly, no scope here for a radical campaign on behalf of the oppressed people; this is very much judicial rather than political territory. The concern of the Commissioners is with maladministration, that is with procedures, not the nature, quality or reasonableness of a decision – the manner not the matter (compare judicial review). Once again, it is for the government and Parliament to lay down a policy and that is not open to challenge, except as indicated under judicial review. The Ombudsman's review is more restricted than that which the judges have allowed themselves; on the other hand, the Ombudsman proceeds by investigation, with access to the department and the relevant papers, and his ability to comment, even when short of a verdict of maladministration, may be helpful to the complainant, and have some influence on the conduct of administration.

'Maladministration' is not further defined in the Act. The Labour Party's election manifesto of 1964 used the phrase 'any misuse of Government power as it affects the citizen'. But the word 'misuse' is too wide to be a definition at all. The Act uses the word 'maladministration', and a Minister, not intending to be helpful, mentioned 'bias, neglect, inattention, delay, incompetence, ineptitude, perversity, turpitude, arbitrariness' as examples of what might constitute 'maladministration'.

The Act goes on quite specifically to exempt from the Commissioner's purview 'the merits of a decision taken without maladministration by a government department...in the exercise of a discretion vested in that department'. This is a restrictive definition, for it confines the Commissioner's powers to impropriety in procedure, thus excluding a decision which may be correctly arrived at but mistaken or unfair or unjust, especially having regard to its consequences. But such a broad remit would give the Commissioner a crusading or marauding role, which would cut across the function of the Minister and Parliament. That is the traditional argument, even when Minister and Parliament take little interest in the matter.

The Commissioners work by investigation, not by an adversarial hearing, and have access to relevant persons and papers in the departments. The Commissioners have done useful work but their impact has not been substantial. The number of cases dealt with is not high. The PCA takes cases only through a Member of Parliament (though he will refer a complaint sent directly to him). Many complaints are rejected because they are not about maladministration but the unfairness of a decision properly arrived at (like the batsman given out lbw, we think the decision is wrong, but the umpire was fully entitled to take the decision, as a glance at the next day's newspapers will confirm). There are other grounds of exclusion: the Commissioners will not take up public service personnel matters, nor other matters where there is already a right to appeal to a tribunal, nor contractual or commercial matters. The indirect access to the PCA does restrict the publicity of the office and the possibility of taking the initiative; and, of course, the Parliamentary Commission is restricted to matters coming within the responsibility of Ministers in Parliament.

Most complaints have been about taxation, a reminder that taxation is still perceived (correctly for most of us) as the most repressive of government's dealings with the people. In local government grievances about taxation are comparatively heavy but exceeded by complaints about housing and planning. The area of civil liberties is not of major public concern.

For the PCA two cases stand out in the record as significant. In the Barlow Clowes case (1988–90) investors lost money when the company collapsed and the PCA after investigation concluded that the Department of Trade and Industry had been lax in its regulation and licensing of the company. The government, while not accepting all of the criticisms made and denying responsibility, agreed to pay compensation of about £150m to investors, in accordance with the PCA's recommendations. The government was a little ungracious in its response; on the other hand, the taxpayers may reasonably complain if their money is used to compensate people who invested unwisely in a risky market, promising dubiously high returns.

In the Sachsenhausen Case (1967) the Foreign Office was criticised for excluding some claimants from compensation for wartime internment in Germany. The case is chiefly notable because it led the Foreign Secretary, George Brown, in effect to warn off the PCA from attacking civil servants by name. This was an attack on both Commissioners and Select Committee. Since then the rights of the Select Committees to patrol the border between administration and policy (with occasional cross-border raids) have come to be accepted, at least to the extent that Ministers, while rejecting the incursions in principle, do not always reject them so huffily as George Brown did.

Ministerial responsibility is regularly cited as a justification for Ministers to escape any critical review of their acts, except in Parliament, where they are protected by a secure party majority; and for civil servants to remain anonymous and irresponsible in the parliamentary sense. As a constitutional principle in a democracy, ministerial responsibility is quite inadequate (see Chapter 9). In the case of the Parliamentary Commissioner, again, the constitutional difficulties arising from ministerial responsibility seem to have been exaggerated. First, civil servants may properly be answerable in private to the

Parliamentary Commissioner, as they are already to the Comptroller and Auditor-General. These officials are not constantly at the administrator's elbow, and their occasional scrutiny is likely to be much less restrictive than the continuing oversight that a civil servant must expect from his departmental superiors. Second, the existing limited answerability to the Parliamentary Select Committees is already accepted and has not led to disaster. The Minister's responsibility for policy has been largely protected (indeed, too easily and too well protected) and civil servants have been questioned about 'administration'. Third, the House of Commons may be expected to behave with restraint. It would indeed, be unfair to individuals and damaging to the morale of the public service for Members to pillory by angry speeches some comparatively humble civil servant who had made a mistake. The anonymity of civil servants below the highest rank should be preserved, but this must not be allowed to annul the public responsibility of the public service. Thus it should be possible to reconcile the doctrine of ministerial responsibility with an enlargement of the work of the Parliamentary Commissioner for Administration.

The work of the various Commissioners is not well known and has had little impact on the public consciousness of entitlement to fair-dealing from the state. The PCA has dealt with about 700 complaints each year, the Local Commissioners up to 10 000; of these only a few, up to a quarter, are investigated. The PCA may pursue a hundred cases each year and find a complaint justified in perhaps 50 of them and comment on many of the rest. Such a scale of operation is insignificant for the public in terms of justice done, but of some significance for the administrators concerned, in terms of pressure to do better.

The PCA has been comparatively successful in securing compliance with his recommendations, or at least some review and remedy. The fact that he reports to a special House of Commons Select Committee ensures some force for his reports. Yet there are failures too. In the Congreve case (about television licences) described above the PCA criticised the Home Office for lack of foresight and inefficiency, but not for maladministration. Only resort to the courts provided a remedy and reversal of policy. The Local Government Commissioners have had more difficulty in face of confident, not to say obstinate, authorities. There is probably a mild general effect for all Commissioners of raising the standard of administrative

practice.

Legal enforcement of decisions is not available except in Northern Ireland, and has the disadvantage of bringing in the costs, delays and formalities of the law and discouraging informal approaches. For example, a Commissioner may secure a satisfactory remedy by telephoning a local authority Chief Executive: this is not the sort of thing a judge could do.

Citizen's Charters
The courts, tribunals and the ombudsman deal with grievances and complaints. The Citizen's Charter initiative associated with John Major's government, is intended to make a more positive contribution to the standards of public service. The Conservative manifesto for the 1992 election proclaimed: 'The Citizen's Charter is the most far-reaching programme ever devised to improve quality in public services. It addresses the needs of those who use public services, extends people's rights, requires services to set clear standards – and to tell the public how far those standards are met.' These are the main objectives of the Charter – information about standards, leading not to an enforceable right but the pressure of explicit expectation. In the new government a Cabinet Minister was made responsible for the initiative.

One of the strengths of the Charter initiative, not always appreciated by its detractors, is that it does not stand alone. It is part of a much broader and various commitment to the standards of public service. For example the Audit Commission is to publish comparative material on the performance of local government and the Health Service. The powers of the local government ombudsman are to be 'reviewed' (though a review is a cost-free promise for a politician). Competitive tendering, inspection, regulation and performance monitoring will be extended. The idea of a new Lay Adjudicator for disputes is floated; government will be more open, Parliament will be reformed.... It is evident that such generous and wide-ranging promises belong to the rhetorical territory of the election manifesto; but it is fair to note that the Conservative government has good intentions, and the Charter itself is set in a formidable context of modernisation of government.

Charters have been published for hospitals, schools, council estates and other public services. The Charters reflect the Conservative preference for markets and the conviction that the public services, lacking the discipline of the market, do not serve the public well. The Charter's emphasis on publicly declared standards of performance is intended to provide a substitute discipline. Sceptics may say that the faith in markets is naive, given that so many markets are not truly competitive and may indeed be rigged against the customer; and that the public services are grossly underfunded, frequently maligned by Ministers and do work which cannot realistically or beneficially be measured by performance targets and the like (tables of school examination results, for example).

Some Charter proposals may seem to add insult to injury – for example, expecting 40 year old rolling stock on the under-funded railways to run on time, or grossly under-paid teachers to work miracles in decaying inner city schools. There is ground for scepticism about Conservative attitudes to public services which Ministers do not like and try not to use. Alternative or complementary approaches to the maintenance of high standards – including funding, and the remuneration, motivation and training of staff – are neglected. The Charter is intended to be a cheap but politically attractive policy.

For all these reasons the importance and potential value of the Charter initiative is likely to be under-valued on the Left. It is after all undeniable that the citizen as customer of the public services has often had a poor deal; and the big public sector trade unions have not always taken service of the public as their prime objective. The 'incestuous relationship' (Professor Kavanagh's phrase) of these unions with the Labour Party did not help, and the Labour Party must bear some responsibility for the decline of the public service ideal. Altogether, neither of the main political parties has done well by the public services; and in that perspective the Citizen's Charter may be the beginnings of a valuable movement.

EXERCISE
The Citizen's Charter

25.15 The Citizen's Charter is a recent innovation, and still under development. Find out what progress has been made with the Charters, and what difference has been made to the delivery of public services, the privatised utilities and British Rail. Assess the value to the citizen-customer of the Charter.

The regulated market

It has come to be accepted in Britain, and indeed much of Europe, including the former communist countries, that the market offers a mechanism superior to the state for the production and distribution of goods. The market creates prosperity and the people are transformed from aggrieved citizens to satisfied customers. This is the Sainsbury's or Marks and Spencer view of politics, the politics of the happy shopper in the supermarket.

Unfortunately for us all, the triumph of the market does not lead swiftly to universal contentment. Some markets are neither competitive nor efficient, and the customer/consumer gets a poor deal; a shopper soon discovers, for example, that despite apparently massive discounts, prices are often remarkably similar from shop to shop. Competitive tendering turns out to be not competitive at all – and so on. More seriously, many goods we need (schools, hospitals, roads, legal services) are beyond the capacity of most people to buy.

At this point the advocate of the free market has three strategies. First, the market must be 'regulated' in the 'public interest', specifically and narrowly, to avoid gross abuse of market power.

Hence, there is a growing collection of regulatory and consultative bodies, for example, OFT (the Office of Fair Trading), OFGAS, OFWAT, OFSTED (the new name for the Schools Inspectorate). In principle these are not new; for example, there are long established consumer consultative bodies for the nationalised industries; and a public corporation like the BBC may be said to be regulated in the public interest by its Board of Governors. The Monopolies and Mergers Commission is a new form for an established function. In some cases departments of government act as regulators – for example, the Department of Trade and Industry. Some important areas of the market economy, notably the financial services industry, and legal services, have been left to forms of 'self-regulation', for reasons which are understandable, even plausible, but not convincing.

There is little doubt that some of the new regulatory bodies have set about their tasks with creditable vigour. This statement by the Chairman of recently privatised British Telecommunications reflects the distress of the regulated, or over-regulated, as they would complain.

■ DOCUMENT 25.11
A complaint about regulation

From AGM address by the Chairman of British

Telecommunications, 30 July 1992
We believe [in]...the need for the regulator to stick to preserving the overall public interest, leaving management to decide how the business is to be run, free from regulatory interference. Regrettably, the trend in regulation in the UK...appears to be towards greater intervention in management, without a clearly expressed vision or set of long-term objectives.

Regulators can be tempted to embark on a course of social engineering, or to tinker with operational matters in response to short-term political or media pressures. Paradoxically, there is a real danger that regulated privatised businesses may be subject to more state interference than they were as nationalised industries.

It is also unclear how the regulators themselves are to be held accountable. The regulated industries have little right of appeal and, in practice, no effective recourse to judicial review. In our case, our only course, if we fail to agree with Oftel even on minor issues, is to allow the matter to be referred to the Monopolies and Mergers Commission.... ■

EXERCISES
Regulation

25.16 Does it appear that regulation is effective?
25.17 Is there a simple distinction between the public interest and running the business?
25.18 Who is to regulate the regulators?

The second strategy for coping with the imperfect market, is to introduce simulated market conditions into areas where there is no naturally occurring market. Hence, schools are encouraged to leave the organised system ('opting-out') and bid for pupils; universities are compelled to bid for funds in a mock-market. The Health Service is divided into purchasers and suppliers of services, and the family doctor with his own budget, exercises a commercial choice about where to refer his patients. Some of the consequences of the introduction of markets may be wholly good. For example, market pressures are likely to reduce the excessive concentration of major hospitals in London, an objective which years of bureaucratic endeavour had failed to achieve. Other consequences may be less good.

The third strategy is the most direct – privatisation. This has been carried through in several of the former nationalised industries and public utilities, with consequences still to be assessed. Public

subsidy has ended and industries can no longer thrive on a 'cost-plus' basis; but many of them are still monopolies. The powers of individual shareholders are negligible. The most obvious consequence of privatisation is a massive increase in the remuneration of senior management! The Next Steps initiative for the civil service, involving the 'hiving-off' of government operations (except the higher policy-making) into semi-independent agencies, is part of this strategy. One consequence for citizens is that they may have to pay economic fees for services such as driving tests and the issue of passports, and service may reflect price difference. (For example, charging a higher fee for driving tests on Saturdays is good commercial practice, but bad public service?)

Developments on those lines under the heads of regulation, markets and privatisation are central to the government and public administration of the 1990s. Such strategies, compared with judicial and quasi-judicial procedures, offer a different and conceivably more powerful approach to the redress of the citizen's grievances. These considerations take us back to the mainland of British government and the whole structure of politics directed towards the creation and management of a civilised state, oriented towards the welfare of its citizens. However, there will still remain areas where the citizen is, so to speak, alone with his grievance, and at that point it is necessary to devise a range of accessible and effective procedures for individual redress.

GUIDE TO EXERCISES

25.1 Britain does seem to be unusual in this respect, and the general argument for 'balance' and checking looks sound. But it may be argued that government is for elected bodies; and law and the lawyers are notoriously complex, costly and so on – see next section of text. The major question needs to be reviewed in the light of the whole chapter.

25.2 There is a delicate balance to be achieved. There should not be 'political' interference with judges and the courts; on the other hand the judicial system ought not to be above the state (though some judges claim such independence). Lord Hailsham thought it essential that the Lord Chancellor as a Minister must command the respect of lawyers, as a judge capable of presiding over the highest Court of Appeal. Why does not a similar argument apply to Ministers of Health or Education? or perhaps it should?

25.3 No! Even Lord Hailsham, who as Lord Chancellor 1979–1987, according to Hugo Young, 'personified a conservatism towards the law which Dickens would have found difficult to caricature' (1991, p. 611), thought the profession was conservative. Most professions are, of course. There is much evidence of complacency and self-satisfaction among lawyers, especially in the way the historic prestige and constitutional value of the law is exploited to resist accountability and reform. On the other hand, there has been a series of inquiries and reports on most aspects of the law, and there are some signs of a more vigorous approach to reform in the 1990s, even a proposal to abandon the wearing of wigs.

25.4 Satisfactory in the review of administrative action by the courts? It is circular in that it tries to define 'unreasonable' by reference to 'reasonable', but it does push the concept of unreasonableness to the point of meaning gross irrationality, as in the example of the teacher with red hair. However, 'reasonable' and 'unreasonable' remain rather soft words used in everyday conversation to mean not much more than 'sensible', 'silly', or to express a vague preference. So the Wednesbury rule still leaves much discretion to the judge.

25.5 a) illegality – not serving the purposes of the Act, b) illegality – ultra vires, c) irrationality, d) illegality, e) illegality and irrationality. Note that a consideration of procedure tends to be incorporated in the judgement of legality and irrationality.

25.6 Yes; a judge inclined to intervene, perhaps because he perceives injustice or just because he is an interventionist by nature or principle, has ample scope for intervention.

25.7 No. The Court was making a judgement about the Minister's 'satisfaction with' the reasonableness of the Council's action, this being the test laid down in the Education Act. Strictly interpreted the question should have been, was the Minister satisfied? – a matter on which the Minister was the best and only judge. But the judges, seeking to get a grip on the case, expanded the question to, should the Minister have been satisfied? If there was a bias, it was towards the right of the court to review the acts of the Minister, even when warned off by the drafting of the legislation.

The court did not explicitly concern itself with upholding the rights of local government against a tyrannical central government; nor did it matter that the judges were all from public schools and Oxbridge! The ground of the judgement was a test of procedure as prescribed in the Act, but with judicial review added.

25.8 It seems reasonable, but note that in the Fares Fair (see case at end of chapter) the court treated the GLCs mandate as irrelevant. But in a test of reasonableness the imputed views of the electors do seem highly relevant.

25.9 His power lies in operational control and the day-to-day management of the police force. In the short term he is very powerful, for operational matters cover significant policy choices about the priorities of police work. In the medium to long term the Home Office, with its command of funds and general political weight, carries substantial influence. The police authorities most anxious to control Chief Constables have been Labour authorities; they might have had more influence if they had ever had the support of a Labour Home Secretary, and if too they had moderated their evident principled (or ideological, if you do not like it) hostility to the police.

25.10 This actually happened and the Home Secretary threatened to intervene on behalf of the police. Equipment is an operational matter (though it must involve funding) and so within the responsibility of the Chief Constable. The police may claim that they have an overriding goal of keeping the peace, and even, in strikes, of protecting the right to work, as well as the right to strike and to picket peacefully. The Police Committee may reasonably argue that some kinds of equipment related to new forms of policing on which they had legitimate views. The problem raises the issue whether political control of the police threatens the peace-keeping functions of the police, or whether an unaccountable police force threatens a wholesome democratic process. The problem is difficult to solve in general terms, and it may be wise to attempt a resolution of a particular case. This case is in fact about the policing of strikes, and is best solved by negotiations between the government and the trade unions, or by legislation. However, that takes time, and meanwhile the police at the factory gate have to respond to violent/peaceful picketing.

25.11 Not entirely. The case raised serious issues of public concern. While it is reasonable to believe that a jury might be influenced by media reporting, it should be possible for professional judges to remain unaffected, since they are looking at the facts and the law.

25.12 It has the advantage of focusing on the effect of obscenity, the harm it may do, which is easier to argue about than an inherent quality of obscenity. But the assessment is still difficult; that is why the judge has to go to some lengths to indicate the kind of guidance a jury ought to receive. But would they be any wiser in the end? Consider whether *The Sun* or the *News of the World* or *Sunday Sport* have a tendency to deprave and cor-rupt....

25.13 No, if 'peaceful' is taken literally; however it is in the nature of public processions for the purpose of protest that they fall easily into rowdiness and mild disorder. For example, would traffic hold-ups amount to serious disruption of the life of the community? Rules of this kind will always work easily for the well-behaved (who hardly need rules anyway); good law has to work well for the awkward cases. In such cases it does look as if the senior police officer has a wide discretion to do as he thinks fit – and justify himself (or herself) afterwards. That brings us back to the question of police accountability.

25.14 This you must do for yourself; preferably you should talk with appellants, success-ful and unsuccessful as well as the local authority.

25.15 Again, this is for you to do. It should be easy to note the publication of charters,

much more difficult to assess their effect at least in the short term. (Charters for Further Education and for Higher Educa-tion were published in 1993.)

25.16 Evidently effective enough to cause the chairman some anxiety.

25.17 There must be a substantial middle area where the two overlap; after all, the regulator is concerned with the standards and costs of service, which are central to the tasks of 'running the business'. This is a new and lesser form of the old dilemma about ministerial interference in the former nationalised industries.

25.18 It is well to remember that BT wields the power of a massive commercial near-monopoly, and is not without political influence too. Still the complaint is just, and the answer is that apart from the MMC, mentioned by the chairman, only the government has the power to regulate the regulators.

ASSESSMENTS

1 Law and politics

The judges and the courts are in politics; pretending they are not leads to misunder-standings. They are not at the centre of politics, nor are they essentially policy-makers, still less party politicians. But they do have a significant influence on government; their decisions may have a specific effect on an administrative act or occasionally a policy decision, and may well have a more fundamen-tal long-term effect on the general trend of policy.

The influence of the courts arises first in the interstices of law, the gaps in the netting; for though the courts must accept the supremacy of Parliament's statute law, there is inevitably scope for interpretation in the elusiveness of the meaning of words and the intentions of Parliament. Second, the courts have exploited the broad perspectives of common law over which they claim special powers of understanding, in order to develop and affirm the rules of ultra vires and natural justice. When Parliament has conferred on a Minister the power 'to act as he sees fit', the courts have stepped in to review the Minister's apparently unfettered discretion.

This position can be justified. The supremacy of Parliament means in practice the supremacy of the executive; in a fused system there is very little check or balance between executive and legislature. Moreover, in a centralised system there is very little challenge from a substantial level of local or regional government. The case for a checking or reviewing function for the courts arises first because there is no obvious alternative, and second because the courts can claim some special virtue. It is a case accepted in most modern democracies.

There is ground, too, for reservations. The legitimacy of the judges' constitutional role is open to question: they have elbowed their way in. More seriously the suitability of judges and courts for a constitutional function may be disputed. Leaving aside the grosser trespasses of the judiciary (as in the Fare's Fair case set out below), it may be argued, along with Professor Griffith, that the judges are the wrong people and the courts the wrong procedural arena for the function of constitutional review. The judges have an unfortunate and inevitable tendency to make a very expensive meal out of any issue put to them.

There is also the fact that adjudication is a very different kind of process from policy making. This is not necessarily a problem and may even be a virtue. However, politicians and administrators, battling to hammer out policy, conciliate interests or serve their public objectives, may be dismayed to observe a learned judge picking over the precise meaning of words, and sometimes setting months of government work at nought. This is a price to be paid for letting the judges into the game of politics.

Subject to these reservations, there remains a case for the judicial function in the sphere of government. At the very least it must be conceded that the function is essential, there is nobody else to do it. But it is necessary to understand that judges wield political power: in this case, to understand may be to forgive.

The point has been convincingly put by Peter Cane in relation to the judicial review of administrative decisions (P. Cane, 1986, p. 15):

'...in controlling administrative activity, the courts are asserting and exercising, in their own right and in their own name, a power to limit and define the powers of other governmental agencies. Parliament allocates decision-making powers to governmental agencies by virtue of its unlimited legislative power. The courts, by virtue of their inherent (i.e. self-conferred) common law power of judicial review of administrative action,

decide the exact legal limits of those allocations of power. In so doing they can not only castigate governmental agencies for abuses or excesses of power, but, equally importantly, they can legitimise controversial exercises of power by holding them to have been lawful. The courts, in short, perform an indirect power-allocation function...the courts are not detached umpires in the governmental process...they play an integral part in deciding how it will operate.'

The judges and the courts are in politics; it may reasonably be argued that this is to the advantage of good government.

2 The judges as a conservative political force
This is the thesis cogently argued by Professor J. A. G. Griffith (The Politics of the Judiciary, 1991). The general thesis is persuasive, but some doubts are indicated above. The argument that an upper middle class background leads to a characteristic socially conservative outlook is familiar in relation to the civil service as well as judges. It clearly has some validity, but is excessively deterministic; life is more complex than that. Further the judicial function in English law is interpreted very restrictively and most judgements are tightly argued and adhere very closely to law and precedent and a meticulous consideration of the facts. The record of judgements is perhaps less consistent than Professor Griffith's thesis requires, as the small sample mentioned in this book attests. Nevertheless, recent appointments to the higher judiciary have been hailed as 'liberal'; and this in itself suggests that there was scope for change in a liberal direction. Thus Professor Griffith may have hit a vulnerable target.

Here is part of Professor Griffith's summing-up (1991, pp. 325–329):

'...it is demonstrable that on every major social issue which has come before the courts during the last thirty years – concerning industrial relations, political protest, race relations, governmental secrecy, police powers, moral behaviour – the judges have supported the conventional, established and settled interests. And they have reacted strongly against challenges to those interests. This conservatism does not necessarily follow the day-to-day political policies currently associated with the party of that name. But it is a political philosophy nonetheless....

During the same period the courts failed to develop a coherent doctrine of judicial review.... Each of the three possible bases of judicial review – illegality, irrationality, procedural impropriety – is sufficiently imprecise to enable judges to jump with the cat in any direction they choose....

The judges define the public interest, inevitably, from the viewpoint of their own class.

In the societies of our world today judges do not stand out as protectors of liberty, of the rights of man, of the unprivileged, nor have they insisted that holders of great economic power, private or public, should use it with moderation....'

3 A Bill of Rights for Britain?

It is evident that the role of judges in government in Britain is quite limited because of the nature of a constitution based on parliamentary sovereignty. This is a cause of concern to those who regard the British constitution as unbalanced by the dominance of the executive. The problem can be met in several ways – by reform of Parliament, the electoral system and the executive itself. But some reformers see virtue in the checks and balances of constitutions based on separate and countervailing powers and look to the courts as well as the legislature for countervailing power. In particular the courts are seen as essential upholders of the rights of citizens against a powerful and oppressive government.

This is the basis for the call for a Bill of Rights for Britain – a general argument about executive dominance and a particular argument about the necessary protection of citizen rights. The rights at issue are the traditional civil rights (life, liberty, the equal protection of the law, freedom from discrimination etc.) and the more controversial rights such as privacy, property, right to work, right to strike. In a Britain without a Bill of Rights these rights depend on the common and statute law as it is interpreted in the courts. The record used to be regarded as creditable; Britain did not need the constitutional props to liberty of lesser nations.

However, in the last twenty years such satisfaction has diminished, perhaps with good reason as some of the evidence in this book may attest (see the Case Studies in this chapter and in Chapter 20). There are grounds for concern about the rights and liberties of the citizen in such matters as the press and broadcasting, the security services, the police, measures for the prevention of terrorism especially in Northern Ireland, immigration. The case for a Bill of Rights is that the dominant executive is too often tempted to infringe citizen rights not specially protected, and the courts are powerless or unwilling to intervene. The case is often overstated but by no means negligible.

A Bill of Rights is not without problems.

a) There is a conceptual difficulty about the term 'right' as indicated above. A right begins as a claim, and its special status as a right has to be justified.

b) There is no consensus about the precise content of a Bill of Rights. There is a fair measure of agreement about the broad area of rights understood as civil liberties, but some rights are controversial. For example, the right to work (i.e. employment) may be beyond the power of governments to provide; the right to strike conflicts with the right not to strike (or to work); the right to life of the unborn child conflicts with the mother's 'right to choose'; the right to privacy conflicts with the right to free speech; the right to free speech conflicts with the right not to endure defamation, blasphemy.

c) There is a further difficulty about the drafting of a Bill of Rights. If it is in broad and general terms its value may be slight, and much would be left to the courts. If it is in precise terms, then the drafters will have a hard time, unforeseen problems may arise and amendment or tortuous interpretation will become necessary. (Consider the problem in America of applying the terms of the US Constitution to the question of abortion).

d) However good the drafting the courts will have to interpret and apply a Bill of Rights in their adjudication of cases. The Griffith argument is relevant here: are you satisfied that questions of rights should be placed in the hands of the judiciary and the courts? Griffith argues that the judges are too conservative to be trusted with our civil liberties. In any case most citizens with good reason believe the courts to be inhospitable and expensive institutions. Supporters of a Bill of Rights respond that the protection of civil rights is already in the hands of the judges, insofar as it is not in the hands of the executive; and that reform of the courts, the procedures and even the judiciary is not ruled out.

e) There is at present no way of 'entrenching' a Bill of Rights. A Parliament, being supreme, cannot bind its successor; so a Bill of Rights, enacted as a statute (there is no other way) could be amended in part or repealed by another Parliament. There are several ways around this problem; for example, a bill contravening and thus overruling the Bill of Rights must state that this is so (as in Canada); or special conditions could be set, say, a two-thirds majority, for a bill contravening Rights.

That device offends against the 'rule' about binding a successor, but in fact Parliament does many things including joining the EEC and reforming the structure of local government which are quite difficult for succeeding Parliaments to undo. Moreover, Parliament has in the past, in the Parliament Acts relating to the powers of the House of Lords, made fundamental changes to the legislative procedure; so it can be argued that there is a precedent, hence no breach in the convention that in constitutional matters nothing should be done for the first time. An alternative approach to the entrenchment of a Bill of Rights is to establish a constitutional council or court (France could offer a model), or make use of a reformed second chamber for the purpose.

f) This leaves the problem of composing a Bill of Rights. The great historical examples, Magna Carta, the Bill of Rights (1688), are for the most part no longer pertinent. The American Bill of Rights (the first ten amendments to the Constitution of 1787) and the Declaration of the Rights of Man and the Citizen (France, 1789) are surprisingly modern and relevant, and the former is still effective. The usual model for a Bill of Rights for the United Kingdom is the European Convention of Human Rights. This was drawn up in 1950 and ratified by Britain in 1951, but it has not been incorporated in law; British citizens with sufficient time and money may appeal to the court in Strasbourg, and the government may choose to take some notice of the judgement of the court. The British government has been found in breach of the Convention on many occasions, and has generally taken steps to comply. A simple procedure would be for the Convention to be incorporated into British law.

The European Convention on Human Rights includes the following provisions:

- the right to life is protected by law
- torture and slavery are unlawful
- everyone has the right to liberty and security of person, and the powers of arrest are circumscribed
- there is a right to a fair and public hearing and rights of accused are safeguarded
- everyone has the right to respect for his private and family life, his home and his correspondence
- everyone has rights to freedom of thought, conscience and religion, freedom of expression, peaceful assembly and association
- men and women of marriageable age have the right to marry
- there is a right to the peaceful enjoyment of possessions
- rights must be protected by an effective remedy, even against a person acting in an official capacity
- right to education, including that the State shall respect the right of parents to ensure such education and teaching in conformity with their own religious and philosophical convictions.

This summary of the European Convention indicates the problems of stating rights in ways which are meaningful and justiciable; but these problems exist in the present ill-defined situation. Unless almost every other country is wrong (a possibility that the English are always ready to entertain) then the British constitution does look rather unsuited to the modern age, and indeed hardly good enough for our ancestors, who fought the Stuart monarchy and proclaimed the Petition of Right and then, after two revolutions, the Bill of Rights.

Concepts

Law

Law is usually considered in the Anglo-American legal tradition as rules, regulations, the heavy and all-embracing national version of what we all meet on a smaller scale in our daily lives. Such rules amount to commands laid down by an authority and implemented by someone with a power of enforcement (for example, the rules of football).

This so-called positive view of law has nothing

to do with justice, morality or fair play. By contrast the Natural Law school (common in continental Europe) conceives of law as connected in some way with notions of morality. Many other countries have two words for law, as in the French 'loi' and 'droit', the latter referring to something more general than specific enactments of law. 'Droit' must be translated as 'equity' or 'right'.

The British narrow, positive definition of law raises constitutional problems when we are dealing with custom and convention, which figure largely in Britain's constitutionless state, or the rights of the aggrieved citizen. There is a tendency to play safe and say what is not law does not matter; and considerations of justice are irrelevant.

Separation of powers

A significant element in the liberal constitutionalism of the eighteenth century (Locke, Montesquieu). The three powers (or functions) executive, legislative and judicial, should be based in separate institutions as a protection against arbitrary government. The US Constitution achieves rather more separation than in Britain, where legislature and executive are fused. However, the judiciary is more or less separated from government, an essential condition of the 'rule of law'.

Rule of law

At its simplest the rule of law means that government is by law; citizens are entitled to the protection of the law and governments must act within the law. Historically the term reflects the struggle against the Crown and implies the freedom from arbitrary government. By extension it can carry equality before the law, and the principles of 'natural justice'. This term is 'heavy' or resonant, despite of, or even because of its imprecision.

Justice

Justice is the morality that is implied by law. This may be interpreted procedurally as what is sometimes called 'natural justice'; and the courts are strongly disposed to see that as a right. Substantive justice goes far beyond that to considerations of fairness and even equality. In that sense, interpretations of justice are at the heart of politics and derive from our systems or sense of values, or ideology. The courts do not dispense justice in that sense; but for better or for worse a reading of the decisions of the courts does reveal implicit values and assumptions about what may reasonably be called justice. That understanding is at the centre of Professor Griffith's concern about the politics,

that is, the political values, of the judiciary.

Two other concepts, the rule of law and the separation of powers, are relevant here. Notice that both imply the necessity of law in a civilised polity. Indeed, a civilised polity (to beg a question or two) requires both law and politics, and hence those villains and heroes, lawyers and politicians.

● CASE STUDY
Fares Fair

From Bromley v GLC 1981–3, 1 AC 768, House of Lords
This case has gained notoriety since it offered some evidence for the thesis that judges may exceed their powers, lack wisdom and display political prejudice. For those who wish to argue that the courts cannot be trusted with political power, for example, as guardians of a Bill of Rights, here is the evidence. But even the Law Lords should not be condemned for one bad case.

The GLC (Greater London Council) had won an election on a programme featuring reduced fares on London Transport (the Fares Fair policy), and directed London Transport to reduce its fares by 25 per cent, the balance to be made up by a grant for which a supplementary rate would be levied. One of the London boroughs, Bromley, objected to this large and indiscriminate subsidy by its rate payers, lost its case in the Queen's Bench Division, but won in the Appeal Court and again in the House of Lords.

The decisions of these courts were based on interpretation of the Transport (London) Act of 1969. The judges seemed to put an undue emphasis on the accounting sections of the Act, rather than the policy sections, and made much of the stipulation of the Act that transport facilities should be 'economic'. This was interpreted to mean breaking even, not providing transport as a subsidised social service. The judges also held up the idea of the 'fiduciary duty' (handling rate-payers' money with due care) a judge-made concept not explicitly recognised by Parliament. The individual judgements, though complex and clever, are not consistent or clear; they neglect Parliament's intentions and the widely accepted place of subsidy in modern urban transport and indulge in literally injudicious remarks about the politics of the GLC, the inexperience of its leaders, and the non-legal status of the electoral mandate.

The Council, under its radical leader, Ken Livingstone, was unpopular in Conservative circles and among rate payers who did not use public transport. Within a few years the government abolished the GLC, thus leaving the capital without an integrated government or an integrated transport system. But these matters should not have concerned the courts. The GLC was a fully legitimate elected body, and, as *The Economist* said at the time, even the most careful reading of the London Transport Act suggested the GLC was acting within the spirit of the Act.

This view of the Fares Fair case was confirmed when the GLC took legal advice, and proposed a not dissimilar scheme, which was accepted by the court. This later decision, Professor Griffith wrote, 'bears the marks of a rescue operation, seeking to save some sanity for transport policy in London and for the right of statutory authorities to exercise statutory powers within the statutory terms given to them' (J. Griffith, 1991, pp. 135–6). The case provides grounds for Professor Griffith's views, but there are other equally disturbing cases to be found in his book. ●

Conclusion

An alternative conclusion

It is not easy for a book like this to come to a conclusion – it simply comes to a stop! Along the way there are many suggested conclusions, or propositions, which must be judged in the light of the evidence and arguments presented, and by your own understandings and values. Here as an alternative conclusion are some thoughts on the governance of Britain, written in the Autumn of 1993, when Britain appeared to be facing both economic and political crises (not the first in Britain's long island history).

There are many images and scenes which could be taken to represent some part of the many-faceted truth about the governance of Britain in the late twentieth century.

Images of British governance
Some examples are given below:

- a field of yellow oil-seed rape (not regarded by everyone as an adornment of the English countryside), and grown as a 'cash crop' to earn subsidies from the EC
- a block of high-rise flats built in the 1960s and under demolition in the 1980s because of construction faults and the resistance of the residents
- the M25, London's orbital motorway, often overloaded with traffic, and a monument to the Catch-22 of contemporary transport planning, that a road built to accommodate traffic generates more traffic than it can bear
- any scene of military pomp and show, the trooping of the Colour, or the Falklands victory parade, or the scenes of jubilation in May 1945 at the end of the war in Europe; for it is in such scenes that the British, or the English at least, seem to know best who they are

- a US nuclear submarine moving down the Clyde from its base, demonstrating the successful prosecution of the cold war by the Atlantic alliance, a great triumph of post-war foreign policy, or alternatively, the uncritical subordination of British interests to US anti-communist obsessions
- a new 'high-tech' hospital or a new university of the 1960s, signifying the post-war welfare state at its most munificent, before economic weakness diminished both the substance and the underpinning morality of the welfare state
- beggars in a city street, demonstrating the decline both of the economy and the welfare state
- the Berlaymont building in Brussels, headquarters of the EC, or an exchange dealing room in a London bank, both places where major decisions affecting the government of Britain are taken by powers partly or wholly outside the control of the British government.

Scenes from British political life
- September 1979. James Callaghan, the Prime Minister, teases the TUC conference, the political parties and the people of Britain about the date of the general election. Callaghan sang an old music hall song, 'There was I, waiting at the church....' Most Prime Ministers seem to enjoy this teasing demonstration of their personal power, but they forget that the election belongs to the people, not to them.
- May 1990. Following negotiations in Brussels lasting all night over the British contribution to the EC budget, the two British Ministers flew back to see Margaret Thatcher at Chequers. (This is the episode recounted by Roy Jenkins in Chapter 23, Document 23.4, The Bloody British Question.) One of the Ministers, Ian

Gilmour (in *Dancing with Dogma*, 1992) describes their frosty reception. The Prime Minister complained that they had not achieved all their objectives (Gilmour thought that was true of every successful negotiation); and she fastened on irrelevant detail, though the proceedings were partly salvaged by a Treasury official, who skilfully re-directed Margaret Thatcher's attention ('The Treasury lady turned out to be far more effective at controlling the Prime Minister than two rather jaded Cabinet Ministers.... What a pity [she] was not in charge of the economy'). Lord Carrington then briefed the press to the effect that the settlement represented a triumph for Margaret Thatcher's great diplomatic skills. She soon accepted that this must be the case.

The episode displays Margaret Thatcher's strong distrust of the Foreign Office, which was for her always guilty of quite liking foreigners and employing the non-confrontational methods of diplomacy. Gilmour comments on this episode: 'Not for the last time during her term of office, foreign policy was a tool of party or personal politics. However badly things were going in Britain, Margaret Thatcher could at least win some kudos and popularity as the defender of the British people against the foreigner'. This comment applies to other Prime Ministers too. The patrician, 'laid-back' and politically very 'wet' Sir Ian Gilmour was sacked by the Prime Minister the following year. The rebellious Minister can only take his revenge in his memoirs.

- June 1992. In a corridor of the Palace of Westminster a Conservative Member of Parliament of the 1992 intake walks. He is pleased with himself, especially as he has recently demonstrated his independence of mind by putting his name to a Commons motion calling for a 'fresh start' to the Maastricht negotiations after the Danish referendum. A prowling Tory Whip stops him abruptly in his tracks, spits out 'You s**t!', and stalks off. (Based on a report by David Wastell and Toby Helm in *The Sunday Telegraph*, 12 July 1992.)

None of these images or scenes encapsulates the whole truth, but each presents a small part of reality – government does this sort of thing, government goes on like this. But government is diverse and elusive, not a thing, or entity or event, but a multiple collection of loosely connected activities.

Further we need to bear in mind in the study of politics that the present is unlikely to be fully represented in to-day's headlines, and the future is often either more or less than a tracking forward of current novelties. Spontaneity and sincerity are unusual in politics. What we see and hear is mostly what has been deliberately selected for us to see and hear; what we understand is for the most part what we choose to understand.

Historical perspective – the end of British government?

In the 1990s British government goes on in a historical context radically different from the early post-war years. Politics has been 'globalised'. In 1939 Europe seemed to be the centre of the world. The war, more truly a 'World War' than the war of 1914–18, showed that this was no longer the case. The cold war stabilised a half-world of two superpowers facing one another across Europe. The end of the cold war broke that pattern into a fragmented world, no longer centred on Europe. At the same time the economy was globalised by the flow of capital through an electronic market, and electronic technology brought world events instantly into every home.

These massive historical changes transformed the nature of British politics. First economic policy, or macro-economic policy, ran beyond the capabilities of government, and became entangled in foreign policy, in particular relations with USA and the construction of the European Community. Second, the relative failure of economic policy undermined the consensus (insofar as it existed) in the 'Managed Economy Welfare State'. Third, in this new and complex world, the old drives of British foreign policy, nationalism and imperialism, looked to be largely irrelevant (except for a brief moment of remembered glory in the Falklands), but no new purpose has yet been established. Thus every major area of national policy required to be re-thought. But British government, like most old-established institutions, is characterised by inertia, and does not enjoy a lively capacity for radical re-appraisal of itself and its objectives.

Propositions about British government

- The forces that bear down on government are far greater than the force of government itself; hence government is for the most part not about directing a strategy and imposing a pattern, but about sub-optimisation and the constant adjustment to outside pressures and

constraints. Such constraints include those arising from cultural assumptions and elite interests. This perception is obvious enough, yet
governments habitually present themselves as
masters not victims of external constraint.

- British government is highly politicised, partisan and adversarial. The terms of debate are set
by the competition and confrontation of parties. The majoritarian 'winner-takes-all' system
('government by dogmatic minority') creates a
bastard form of parliamentarism, which effectively transfers the sovereignty of parliament to
the executive.

No other large organisation conducts its affairs in this confrontational way, in which government is never wrong, and the opposition is
composed of fools and knaves. In this process
some issues are fully debated, some are man-
gled, and some, like the European question,
are neglected.

The media thrive on and encourage this confrontation, politicians thrive on the media; it is
an unhealthy relationship.

- Government is dominated by the executive,
subject to only mild concern about parliamentary trouble-making and public embarrassment, more serious anxieties about four-yearly
electoral contests and a dread of losing the
confidence of the international financial markets.
- Government is sustained, but also shaped to
some extent, by a political culture dominated
by southern England, and characterised by
conservatism, residual imperialism, and no
strong sense of the public interest.
- Behind the adversarial facade much of government is conducted by the bureaucracy in negotiation with interest groups, largely in secret.
- Nevertheless, the accepted popular model of
governance is still that of the heroic leader,
wise and fearless, constantly engaged in taking
firm decisions on clearly-defined policies, and
bringing about rapid improvement in the condition of the people and the standing of the
country. This Churchillian or 'star' model of
government is reflected in contemporary management theory, and so has the unfortunate effect of ruining industry as well as politics.

Reform

In the diffuse light of these broad reflections it
may seem irrelevant to talk about reform. In face
of the major historical re-direction which seems to
be required, British government seems above all

to need fresh thinking among politicians and the
political elite, and a reformation or regeneration
of political culture. At the time of writing, it seems
unlikely that Britain is preparing to catch up with
history, and there is much talk of 'anti-politics', or
loss of confidence among many people, not only
the economically excluded.

Perhaps this is to over-dramatise a particular
moment in Britain's long and not unsuccessful
history. In any case radical reformers would argue
that new responses to whatever historic crisis is
upon us will only arise from institutional and political reform. New thinking requires new institutions.

There are several strands to thinking about reform. Most of the proposals for constitutional reform are promoted by Charter 88 as a package
amounting to a new constitutional settlement, the
first since 1688–9. In practice proposals for constitutional reform are related but not inter-depend-
ent.

- Reform of the electoral system to achieve more
proportional representation. This is the most
fundamental proposal since it would create a
multiple party system with coalition government as a norm, and make further reform certain. The adoption of any form of proportional
representation for parliamentary elections
would itself constitute or bring about a new
constitutional settlement (see Chapters 15 and
17).
- Reform of the House of Lords. This goes along
with proportional representation since the
Lords can hardly survive any rational appraisal
of parliamentary representation (see Chapter
12).
- Devolution and the reform of local government.
Advocated on general grounds of decentralisation (more democratic, more efficient), relief of
central government 'overload', and satisfaction
of national sentiment (in Scotland and Wales)
(see Chapter 24).
- Open government and freedom of information.
Freedom of information confers on the citizen
a right to information by and about government, excluding only matters of personal and
commercial confidentiality and national security. Open government falls short of the conferment of rights, but includes a commitment to
making public as much information as is reasonable and practicable, government remaining the judge of what is reasonable and
practicable.

Apart from public access to information

there is a strong case for much higher levels of honesty and candour, a greater readiness to be exposed to embarrassment and even to admit to error – you must be joking! as they say (see Chapter 20).

- A Bill of Rights. This involves the establishment and entrenchment of citizen rights, including freedom of expression, freedom of information, freedom from discrimination on ground of gender, age or ethnic origin. A Bill of Rights is a radical proposal because it raises the question of the constitution and the possibility, even the necessity, of a constitutional court (see Chapter 25).
- The market and privatisation. This amounts to the reform of government by the reduction or 'disinvention' of government. It is accompanied in conservative thinking by Citizen's Charter proposals for the monitoring of the performance of public services (see Chapters 16 and 25).
- A new or revitalised public philosophy concerned with the public interest. This has yet to be addressed by non-Conservative politicians; for the Conservatives have done most of the new political thinking recently. A new public

philosophy begins with the revival, updating and re-statement of the political values once expressed in the post-war Keynesian welfare state.
- The whole European project hovers over any programme of reform, as a necessary underpinning, a contradiction or a parallel development.

The virtues of an unreformed British government.

British government is an unusual example in a hostile world of a successful democracy, successful, that is, in the longer perspectives of history. It has had the good fortune as an island to avoid the military catastrophes which have damaged or undermined political development on the mainland of Europe, and has avoided the sharp breaks and consequent uncertainties of revolutionary change. Britain has always contrived to adjust to popular pressures just in time; it is a deeply conservative democracy, but a democracy nevertheless.

There is no doubt more to be said, but as the first edition of this book said (1970, p. 470) 'this book is quite long enough already'.

Further reading

A select list of books for further reading.

General

Birch, A., *The British System of Government*, HarperCollins, 1993

Dearlove, J. and Saunders, P., *Introduction to British Politics*, 2nd Edn., Polity Press, 1991

Dunleavy, P. et al, *Developments in British Politics*, *4*, Macmillan, 1993

The Executive

Bruce-Gardyne, J., *Ministers and Mandarins*, Sidgwick and Jackson, 1986

Donoughue, B., *Prime Minister*, Cape, 1987

Drewry, G. and Butcher, T., *The Civil Service Today*, 2nd Edn., Basil Blackwell, 1991

Fry, G., *The Changing Civil Service*, Allen and Unwin, 1985

Hennessy, P., *Cabinet*, Basil Blackwell, 1986

Hennessy, P., *Whitehall*, Secker and Warburg, 1989

James, S., *Cabinet Government*, Routledge, 1992

Lawson, N., *The View from No. 11*, Bantam, 1992

Madgwick, P., *British Government; The Central Executive Territory*, Philip Allan, 1991

Parliament

Adonis, A., *Parliament To-day*, 2nd. Edn., Manchester University Press, 1993

Griffith, J. and Ryle, M., *Parliament*, Sweet and Maxwell, 1989

Norton, P., *Does Parliament Matter?*, Philip Allan, 1993

Parties

Ball, A., *British Political Parties*, Macmillan, 1987

Ingle, S., *The British Party System*, 2nd. Edn., Basil Blackwell, 1989

Kavanagh, D. and Seldon, A. (ed.), *The Thatcher Effect*, Clarendon Press, Oxford, 1989

Marquand, D., *The Progressive Dilemma*, Heinemann, 1991

Seldon, A., *UK Political Parties since 1945*, Philip Allan, 1990

Elections

Butler, D. and Kavanagh, D., *The British General Election of 1992*, Macmillan, 1992 (and similar studies for all elections since 1945)

Denver, D., *Elections and Voting Behaviour in Britain*, Philip Allan, 1989

Heath, A., Jowell, R. and Curtice, J., *How Britain Votes*, Pergamon, 1985

Heath, A., Jowell, R. and Curtice, J., *Understanding Political Change*, Pergamon, 1991

King, A. et al, *Britain at the Polls*, 1992, Chatham House, 1993

Media

Harris, R., *Good and Faithful Servant*, Faber, 1990

Miller, W., *Media and Voters*, Clarendon Press, Oxford, 1991

Negrine, R., *Politics and the Mass Media in Britain*, Routledge, 1989

Seymour-Ure, C., *The British Press and Broadcasting since 1945*, Basil Blackwell, 1991

Policy making and interest groups

Grant, Wyn, *Pressure Groups, Politics and Democracy in Britain*, Philip Allan, 1989

Jordan, A. and Richardson, J., *British Politics and the Policy Process*, Allen and Unwin, 1987

Savage, S. and Robins, L. (ed.), *Public Policy under Thatcher*, Macmillan, 1990

Inter-governmental relations

Birch, A., *Political Integration and Disintegration in the British Isles*, Allen and Unwin, 1971

Bogdanor, V., *Devolution*, Oxford University Press, 1979

George, S., *Politics and Policy in the European Community*, Oxford University Press, 1991

Kingdom, J., *Local Government and Politics in Britain*, Philip Allan, 1991

Lodge, J. (ed.), *The EC and the Challenge of the Future*, Pinter, 1989

Stewart, J. and Stoker, G., *The Future of Local Government*, Macmillan, 1989

Constitution

Brazier, R., *Constitutional Practice*, Clarendon Press, Oxford, 1988

Graham, C. and Prosser, T. (eds.), *Waiving the Rules: the Constitution under Thatcherism*, Open University Press, 1988

Holme, R., and Elliott, M., (eds.) *1688–1988 Time for a New Constitution*, Macmillan, 1988

Johnson, N., *In Search of the Constitution*, Methuen, 1980

Jowell, J. and Oliver, D., *The Changing Constitution*, Clarendon Press, Oxford, 1989

Mount, F., *The British Constitution Now*, Heinemann, 1992

Reiner, R., *The Politics of the Police*, Wheatsheaf, 1985

In addition there are a number of biographies and autobiographical works, not all reliable as historical documents.

The following may be recommended:

Pimlott, B., *Harold Wilson*, Harper Collins, 1992
Young, H., *One of Us*, Macmillan, 1991
Clark, A., *Diaries*, Weidenfeld and Nicolson, 1993

The following periodicals are particularly useful:

Parliamentary Affairs (Oxford University Press)
Politics Review (Philip Allan)
Talking Politics (Politics Asociation)

References in the text

Books referred to in the text.
(Books and other sources presented as extracts in Documents, Tables and Figures are listed under Sources and Acknowledgements).

Adonis, A., 1990, *Parliament Today*, Manchester University Press

Annan, N., 1990, *Our Age*, HarperCollins/Fontana

Ashford, D., 1981, *Politics and Policy in Britain*, Blackwell

Barnett, J., 1982, *Inside the Treasury*, Andre Deutsch

Benn, T., 1987-1992, *Diaries*, 5 Vols., 1963-90, Hutchinson

Birch, A.H., 1967, *Representative and Responsible Government*, Allen and Unwin

Blackstone, T., and Plowden, W., 1990, *Inside the Think Tank*, Heinemann

Boyle, E., and Crosland, A., 1971, *The Politics of Education*, Penguin

Bruce Gardyne, J., 1986, *Ministers and Mandarins: Inside the Whitehall Village*, Sidgwick and Jackson

Burk, K. and Cairncross, A., 1992, *Goodbye Great Britain*, Yale University Press

Butler, D., and Stokes, D., 1975, *Political Change in Britain*, Macmillan

Cabinet Office, 1992, *Questions of Procedure*

Callaghan, J., 1987, *Time and Chance*, Collins/Fontana

Cane, P., 1986, *An Introduction to Administrative Law*, Clarendon Press, Oxford

Castle, B., 1980, 1984, *The Castle Diaries*, 1974–76 and 1964–70, Weidenfeld and Nicolson (also pbk. 1964–76, 1990, Macmillan)

Chapman, R., and Dunsire, A., 1971, *Style in Administration*, Allen and Unwin

Clarke, Sir R., 1971, *New Trends in Government*, HMSO 1972

Cosgrave, P., 1989, *The Lives of Enoch Powell*, Bodley Head

Crewe, I., 1984, The Electorate: partisan dealignment ten years on, in H. Berrington (ed.), *Change in British Politics*, Frank Cass

Crosland, A., 1956, *The Future of Socialism*, Jonathan Cape

Crosland, S., 1982, *Tony Crosland*, Jonathan Cape

Crossman, R., 1963, *Introduction to Bagehot: The English Constitution*, Fontana

Crowther-Hunt, Lord, and Kellner, P., 1980, *The Civil Servants*, Macdonald

Donoughue, B., 1987, *Prime Minister*, Jonathan Cape

Dunleavy, P., and Rhodes, R.A.W., 1990, Core Executive Studies in Britain, *Public Administration*, 68, Spring, pp.3-28

Edelman, M., 1966, *The Mirror, A Political History*, Hamish Hamilton

Finer, S., 1966, *Anonymous Empire*, Pall Mall

Franks, Sir Oliver, 1947, *The Experiences of a University Teacher in the Civil Service*, Oxford University Press

Geldof, B., 1986, *Is that it?*, Penguin

Gilmour, I., 1978, *Inside Right: A Study of Conservatism*, Quartet Books

Griffith, J.A.G., 1975, *Parliamentary Scrutiny of Government Bills*, Allen and Unwin

Griffith, J.A.G., and Ryle, M., 1989, *Parliament*, Sweet and Maxwell

Griffith, J.A.G., 1991, *The Politics of the Judiciary*, Harper Collins/Fontana

Harris, K., 1987, *David Owen Personally Speaking*, Weidenfeld and Nicolson

Harris, K., 1988, *Thatcher*, Weidenfeld and Nicolson

Harris, R., 1990, *Good and Faithful Servant*, Faber and Faber

Headey, B., 1974, *British Cabinet Ministers*, Allen and Unwin

Healey, D., 1989, *The Time of My Life*, Michael Joseph

Heath, A., Jowell, R., and Curtice, J., 1991, *Understanding Political Change*, Pergamon

Heclo, H. and Wildavsky, A., 1974, *The Private Government of Public Money*, Macmillan

Heseltine, M., 1987, *Where There's a Will*, Hutchinson

Ingham, B., 1991, *Kill the Messenger*, Fontana

James, R.R., 1971, *Memoirs of a Conservative*, Weidenfeld and Nicolson

Jenkins, P., 1987, *Mrs Thatcher's Revolution*, Jonathan Cape

Jones, A., 1973, *The New Inflation*, Penguin

King, A., (ed.) 1969, *The British Prime Minister*, Macmillan

King, A., (ed.) 1985, *The British Prime Minister*, Macmillan

Layfield Report, 1976, *Committee on Local Government Finance*, Cmnd 6453, HMSO

Mackintosh, J.P., 1977, *The British Cabinet*, Stevens

Macmillan, H., 1971, *Memoirs*, Macmillan

Madgwick, P.J., 1984, *Introduction to British Politics*, 3rd edn., Hutchinson

McKenzie, R., 1955, *British Political Parties*, Heinemann

Martin, Kingsley, 1953, *Harold Laski*, Gollancz

Michels, R., 1968, *Political Parties*, Collier Macmillan

Miller, C., 1987, *Lobbying Government*, Blackwell

Morgan, K., (ed.), 1984, *Illustrated History of Britain*, Oxford University Press

Northcote-Trevelyan Report, 1854 (Appendix B of Fulton Report, Vol. I, 1968)

Paxman, J., 1991, *Friends in High Places*, Penguin

Pliatzky, L., 1989, *The Treasury under Mrs Thatcher*, Blackwell

'Plowden Report': *The Control of Public Expenditure*, Cmnd 1432, HMSO

Ponting, C., 1986, *Whitehall: Tragedy and Farce*, Sphere

Ponting, C., 1989, *Breach of Promise: Labour in Power 1964-79*, Hamish Hamilton

Pym, F., 1984, *The Politics of Consent*, Hamish Hamilton

Ridley, N., 1991, *My Style of Government*, Hutchinson

Ritchie, R., (ed.), 1979, *A Nation or No Nation*, Elliot Right Way Books

Sampson, A., 1983, *Anatomy of Britain Today*, Hodder and Stoughton

Sellar, W.W. and Yeatman, R.J., 1960, *1066 and All That*, Magnum

Seymour-Ure, C., 1974, *The Political Impact of Mass Media*, Constable

Trenaman, J. and McQuail, D., 1961, *Television and the Political Image*, Methuen

Vile, M., 1961, *The Structure of American Federalism*, Oxford University Press

Wallace, H., et al, 1983, *Policy-making in the European Community*, Wiley

Watkins, A., 1991, *A Conservative Coup*, Duckworth

Wheare, K., 1963, *Federal Government,* Oxford University Press

Whitelaw, W., 1989, *The Whitelaw Memoirs*, Aurum Press

Williams, F., 1961, *A Prime Minister Remembers*, Heinemann

Wilson, H., 1976, *The Governance of Britain,* Weidenfeld and Nicolson and Michael Joseph

Wilson, H., 1979, *Final Term – the Labour Government*, 1974–1976, Weidenfeld and Nicolson and Michael Joseph

Young, H., 1989, 1991, *One of Us*, Macmillan

Sources and acknowledgements

Sources of extracts presented in documents, tables and figures. The list includes extracts of any length, and some material based on or derived from other works.

Thanks are due to the following publishers and authors for permission kindly granted to reproduce extracts from copyright works.

Chapter 2

Phoenix House: A. Maude and E. Powell, *Biography of a Nation*, 1953

Clarendon Press, Oxford: G. N. Clark, *The Later Stuarts*, 1660-1714, 1934

Macmillan Press Ltd: D. Butler and D. Stokes, *Political Change in Britain*, 1977

Longman Group: map from R. J. Johnston, C. J. Pattie and J. G. Allsop, *A Nation Dividing*, 1988

William Heinemann Ltd: R. S. Churchill, *Winston S. Churchill, Vol. 1*, 1966

William Heinemann Ltd: M. Gilbert, *Never Despair, Winston S. Churchill, Vol. viii*, 1988

Oxford University Press: H. C. G. Matthew, The Liberal Age, in K. O. Morgan, *The Oxford Illustrated History of Britain*, 1984

Pergamon Press Ltd: A. Heath et al, *How Britain Votes*, 1983

Little, Brown: G. Almond and S. Verba, *The Civic Culture*, 1965

Chapter 3

William Heinemann Ltd: C. Leys, *Politics in Britain*, 1985

Fontana (HarperCollins Publishers Ltd): W. Bagehot, *The English Constitution* (1867), 1963

Cambridge University Press: W. I. Jennings, *The British Constitution*, 1947

Oxford University Press: R. Miliband, *Capitalist Democracy in Britain*, 1984

Chapter 4

The Observer : article by Simon Hoggart in *The Observer*, 2 January 1983

Weidenfeld and Nicolson: H. Wilson, *The Governance of Britain*, 1976

Collins: D. Hurd, *An End to Promises*, 1979 (reprinted by kind permission of Peters Fraser and Dunlop Group Ltd)

BBC: Interview with Mr Wilson by Dr Norman Hunt in *Whitehall and Beyond*, 1964

Jonathan Cape: B. Donoughue, *Prime Minister*, 1987

Royal Institute of Public Administration: D. Willetts, The Role of the Prime Minister's Policy Unit, *Public Administration, 65*, Winter 1987

Hutchinson: J. E. Wrench, *Geoffrey Dawson and Our Times*, 1955

Macmillan Press Ltd: Interview between Mr Wilson and Dr N. Hunt, *The Listener*, 6 April 1967, reprinted in A. King, *The British Prime Minister*, 1969

Macmillan Press Ltd: H. Heclo and A. Wildavsky, *The Private Government of Public Money*, 1974

Cassell: W. S. Churchill, *The Gathering Storm*, 1948

William Heinemann Ltd: C. R. Attlee, *As it Happened*, 1954

Chapter 5

Macmillan Press Ltd: H. Young, *One of Us*, 1989

Bloomsbury: P. Walker, *Staying Power*, 1991

Cabinet Office: *Questions of Procedure for Ministers*,

1992, Oxford University Press: Thomas Jones, *Diary with Letters* 1931–1950, 1954

Weidenfeld and Nicolson: Kenneth Harris, *Thatcher*, 1988

Hutchinson: Lord Vansittart, *The Mist Procession*, 1958

Macmillan Press Ltd: H. Macmillan, *Memoirs*, 1971

Jonathan Cape: J. Haines, *The Politics of Power*, 1977

William Heinemann Ltd: Lord Hill of Luton, *Both Sides of the Hill*, 1964

Arrow Books: F. Williams, *A Pattern of Rulers*, 1965

Penguin Books Ltd (Michael Joseph) and W. W. Norton: Denis Healey, *The Time of my Life*, 1984

The Observer : Interview with Mr Harold Wilson by Kenneth Harris in *The Observer Magazine*, 24 October 1965

Jonathan Cape: P. Jenkins, *Mrs Thatcher's Revolution*, 1987

Cabinet Office: *Questions of Procedure for Ministers*, 1992

Hodder and Stoughton: Lady G. Cecil, *Life of Robert, Marquis of Salisbury, Vol. II*, 1921

Her Majesty's Stationery Office: *H. C. Deb., Vol. 487*, 24 April 1951, col 230

Hutchinson: T. Benn, *Diaries*, 1988, 1989, 1990

Routledge and Kegan Paul: D. Wass, *Government and the Governed*, 1984

HarperCollins Publishers Ltd: J. Callaghan, *Time and Chance*, 1987

Chapter 6

Hutchinson: Lord Simon, *Retrospect*, 1952

Macmillan Press Ltd: Letter quoted in K. Feiling, *The Life of Neville Chamberlain*, 1947

Rupert Hart-Davis: G. M. Young, *Stanley Baldwin*, 1952

The Observer. Interview with Harold Wilson by Kenneth Harris in The *Observer Magazine*, 24 October 1965

Weidenfeld and Nicolson: R. R. James, *Memoirs of a Conservative*, 1967

The Observer. article by Simon Hoggart, 2 January 1983

Weidenfeld and Nicolson: K. Harris, *Thatcher*, 1988

Jonathan Cape: Bernard Donoughue, *Prime Minister*, 1987

Rupert Hart-Davis: G. M. Young, *Stanley Baldwin*, 1952

Charles Knight: Peter Jenkins, *The Battle of Downing Street*, 1970

Oxford University Press: D. Kavanagh, *Thatcherism and British Politics*, 1990

Basil Blackwell Ltd: G. W. Jones, 'The United Kingdom', in W. Plowden (ed.), *Advising the Rulers*, 1987

Cambridge University Press: W. I. Jennings, *The British Constitution*, 1941

Basil Blackwell Ltd: Lord Hunt of Tamworth quoted in W. Plowden, *Advising the Rulers*, 1987

Weidenfeld and Nicolson: John P. Mackintosh (ed.), *Prime Ministers*, 1978

Oxford University Press: Lord Morrison, *Government and Parliament*, 1960

Hodder and Stoughton: Sir J. Reith, *Into the Wind*, 1949

Cassell and Co., Ltd: Earl of Oxford and Asquith, *Memories and Reflections*, 1928

Weidenfeld and Nicolson and Michael Joseph: Harold Wilson, *The Governance of Britain*, 1976

Macmillan Press Ltd: A. King (ed.), *The British Prime Minister*, 1985

Hutchinson: N. Ridley, *My Style of Government*, 1991

Chapter 7

BBC: H. Young and A. Sloman, *The Thatcher Phenomenon*, 1986

Jonathan Cape: Sir James Grigg, *Prejudice and Judgement*, 1948

Hamish Hamilton and Jonathan Cape: R. H S Crossman, *Diaries of a Cabinet Minister, Vol. I*, 1975

Weidenfeld and Nicolson: Nicholas Henderson, *The Private Office*, 1984

Jonathan Cape: R. H. S Crossman, *Inside View*, 1972

Oxford University Press: D. Owen, *Face the Future*, 1981 (reprinted by kind permission of Deborah Owen)

Weidenfeld and Nicolson: K. Harris, *Personally speaking to David Owen*, 1987

Hutchinson/Arrow: M. Heseltine, *Where there's a Will*, 1990 (reprinted by kind permission of the Peters Fraser Dunlop Group Ltd)

Penguin Books Ltd: Shirley Williams, *Politics is for People*, 1981

Allen and Unwin: Sir Edward Bridges, *Portrait of a Profession*, Cambridge University Press, 1950 reprinted in R. A. Chapman and A. Dunsire, *Style in Administration*, 1971

Sidgwick and Jackson: J. Bruce-Gardyne, *Ministers and Mandarins*, 1986

Sphere Books: C. Ponting, *Whitehall, Tragedy and Farce*, 1986

Chapter 8

Basil Blackwell Ltd: L. Pliatzky, *Getting and Spending*, 1982

Jonathan Cape: B. Donoughue, *Prime Minister*, 1987

Sphere Books: C. Ponting, *Whitehall, Tragedy and Farce*, 1986

Penguin Books Ltd (Michael Joseph) and W. W. Norton: D. Healey, *The Time of My Life*, 1989

Basil Blackwell Ltd: Leo Pliatzky, *The Treasury under Mrs Thatcher*, 1989

Macmillan Press Ltd: H. Heclo and A. Wildavsky, *The Private Government of Public Money*, 1974

Sidgwick and Jackson: J. Bruce-Gardyne, *Ministers and Mandarins*, 1986

Basil Blackwell Ltd: Leo Pliatzky, *Getting and Spending*, 1982

Chapter 9

Macmillan Press Ltd: R. Rose, *The Problem of Party Government*, 1974

Clarendon Press, Oxford: R. Rose, *Ministers and Ministries: A Functional Analysis*, 1987

Allen and Unwin: B. Headey, *British Cabinet Ministers*, 1974

Macmillan Press Ltd: K. Feiling, *The Life of Neville Chamberlain*, 1947

Hamish Hamilton and Cape: R. H. S. Crossman, *Diaries of a Cabinet Minister, Vol.3*, 1977

Frederick Muller: Hugh Dalton, *Memoirs*, 1957, 1962

Andre Deutsch: Lord Strang, *Home and Abroad*, 1956

Macmillan Press Ltd: H. Macmillan, *Memoirs*, 1971

Royal Institute of Public Administration: Sir Edward Boyle, Who are the Policy-makers?, *Public Administration*, Autumn 1965

Macmillan Press Ltd: M. Kogan in A. Gold (ed.), *Edward Boyle: His Life by his Friends*, 1991

Weidenfeld and Nicolson: K. Harris, *Personally Speaking to David Owen*, 1987

Chapter 10

Cambridge University Press: Sir Edward Bridges, *Portrait of a Profession*, 1953

HMSO: Report of a Committee on the Civil service, Cmnd 3638, 1968 (*The Fulton Report*)

Jonathan Cape: Sir James Grigg, *Prejudice and Judgement*, 1948

Collins: D. Hurd, *An End to Promises*, 1979 (reprinted by kind permission of the Peters Fraser and Dunlop Group Ltd)

Oxford University Press: W. Plowden in *Parliamentary Affairs*, 38,4, Winter 1985, pp 393–414

Oxford University Press: Sir John Hoskyns in *Parliamentary Affairs*, 36,2, Spring 1983, pp 137–43

The Times: report of a statement by Lord Armstrong, 15 November 1976

The Listener: interview by David Jessel with Sir Antony Part, 11 December 1980

Sunday Times: article by Barbara Castle, 10 June 1973

HMSO: Report to the Prime Minister by the Efficiency Unit, *The Next Steps*, 1988

Hutchinson/Arrow: M. Heseltine, *Where there's a Will*, 1990 (reprinted by kind permission of the Peters Fraser and Dunlop Group Ltd)

Macmillan Press Ltd: R. Jenkins, *A Life at the Centre*, 1991

Chapter 11

Frederick Muller: Hugh Dalton, *Call Back Yesterday*, 1953

HMSO: *H. C. Deb., Vol. 393*, 28 Oct 1943, cols 460–1

Harper Collins/ Fontana: W. Bagehot, *The English Constitution* (1867), 1963

HMSO: *H. C. Deb. , Vol. 738*, 14 Dec 1966, cols 479–80

Chapter 12

Oxford University Press: Lord Morrison, *Government and Parliament*, 1964

Weidenfeld and Nicolson: Edward Pearce, *The Quiet Rise of John Major*, 1991

The Times: article by Lord (Max) Beloff, 1 November 1982

Chapter 13

Basil Blackwell Ltd: L. Pliatzky, *The Treasury under Mrs Thatcher*, 1989

HMSO: Defence Committee, *Minutes of Evidence*, H. C. 169, 1985–6
Agriculture Committee, *Minutes of Evidence*, H. C. 108-11, 1988–9
Defence Committee, *Report*, H. C. 68, 1988–9

Weidenfeld and Nicolson: N. Nicolson, *People and Parliament*, 1958

Chapter 14

Pergamon Press Ltd, Oxford: A. Heath et al, *How Britain Votes*, 1985

Weidenfeld/Michael Joseph: H. Wilson, *Final Term: the Labour Government 1974–1976*, 1979

Chapter 15

Edward Dent: Edmund Burke, *Speeches and Letters on American Affairs*, 1908

Chapter 16

Penguin Books Ltd: D. Willetts, *Modern Conservatism*, 1992

Pergamon Press Ltd, Oxford: A. Heath et al, *How Britain Votes*, 1985

Penguin Books Ltd: Q. Hogg, *The Case for Conservatism*, 1947

Penguin Books Ltd: T. Raison, *Why Conservative?* 1964

The Times: Speeches by J. Nott and K. Joseph, 17 September 1993

Sunday Telegraph: article by Peregrine Worsthorne, 15 May 1988

Hutchinson/Arrow: Michael Heseltine, *Where There's a Will*, 1987 (reprinted by kind permission of the Peters Fraser and Dunlop Group Ltd)

Allen and Unwin: R H. Tawney, *Equality*, 4th ed 1952

Jonathan Cape: A. Crosland, *The Future of Socialism*, 1956

Chapter 17

The Times: Leading article, 22 April 1965

Chapter 18

MORI/*Sunday Times*: *Voting by class 1983 and 1992*

BBC/Gallup: Ivor Crewe, The votes of a new and old working class, *The Guardian*, 13 June 1983

Pergamon Press Ltd, Oxford: A. Heath et al, *Understanding Political change*, 1991

MORI: John Curtice, Floating voters changing their mind, *The Guardian*, 13 April 1992

NOP: Regional patterns of voting 1992, *Independent on Sunday*, 12 April 1992

Methuen: J. Trenaman and D. McQuail, *Television and the Political Image*

Chapter 19

Audit Bureau of Circulations: *National Newspaper Circulation* 1992

National Union of Teachers: *Report of a Conference on Popular Culture and Personal Responsibility*, 1960

Arrow Books: Francis Williams, *Dangerous Estate*, 1959

Macmillan Press Ltd: A. Hetherington, *News, Newspapers and Television*, 1985

The Guardian: Article by Robin Morgan, 15 July 1991

Weidenfeld and Nicolson and Hodder and Stoughton: Harold Evans, *Good Times, Bad Times*, 1984

The Guardian: article by Dave Hill, 9 March 1972

HMSO: Sir John Reith's *Memorandum and Evidence to the Broadcasting Committee*, 1949, (Report Cmnd 8116, 364)

Chapter 20

HarperCollins Publishers Ltd: Bernard Ingham, *Kill the Messenger*, 1991

Methuen: J. Curran et al, (ed.), *Impacts and Influences*, 1987

Constable: C. Seymour-Ure, *The Political Impact of Mass Media*, 1974

The Guardian: Report of Mr Justice Scott's judgement in the Spycatcher case, 22 December 1987

Macmillan Press Ltd: D. Butler and D. Stokes, *Political change in Britain* 1974

Clarendon Press, Oxford: W. Miller et al, *Media and Voters*, 1991

The Listener: article by J. Naughton, 5 Oct 1983

Chapter 21

Basil Blackwell Ltd: Charles Miller, *Lobbying Government*, 1987

Penguin Books Ltd: Bob Geldof, *Is that it?*, 1986

Hodder and Stoughton: Brian Sedgemore, *The Secret Constitution*, 1980

Macmillan Press Ltd: Anthony King, *British Members of Parliament, a self-portrait*, 1974

The Guardian: article by Simon Hoggart, 31 October 1978

HMSO: *H. C. Debates, Vol. 440*, 15 July 1947, cols 284–5

Chapter 22

Basil Blackwell Ltd: Leo Pliatzky, *Getting and spending*, 1982

Yale University Press: K. Burk and A. Cairncross, *Goodbye Great Britain*, 1992

Chapter 23

HMSO: Cmnd 6003, *Report on Renegotiation*, Cmnd 6003, 1975

Macmillan Press Ltd: Roy Jenkins, *A Life at the Centre*, 1991

Oxford University Press: K. C. Wheare, *Federal Government*, 1963

Wiley: W. Wallace in H. Wallace et al, *Policymaking in the European Community*, 1983

Oxford University Press: M. Vile, *The Structure of American Federalism*, 1961

Elliot Right Wing Books: R. Ritchie (ed.), *A Nation or No Nation*, 1979

Chapter 24

Oxford University Press: Vernon Bogdanor, *Devolution*, 1979

Allen and Unwin: G. Jones and J. Stewart, *The Case for Local Government*, 1983

Manchester University Press: J. Bulpitt, *Territory and Power in the United Kingdom*, 1983

Methuen: Nevil Johnson, *In Search of the Constitution*, 1977

Basil Blackwell Ltd: D. Ashford, *Policy and Politics*, 1981

HMSO: *Report of the Committee on Local Government Finance*, (Layfield Committee), Cmnd 6453, 1976

Macmillan Press Ltd: Hugo Young, *One of Us*, 1991

Chapter 25

Clarendon Press, Oxford: P. Cane, *An Introduction to Administrative Law*, 1986

HarperCollins/Fontana: J.A.G. Griffith, *The Politics of the Judiciary*, 4th Edn., 1991

Every effort has been made to trace the owners of copyright material for which permission to reproduce is required. The author apologises for any omissions, and would be grateful to know of them, so that acknowledgements may be made in future editions.

Index